POLITICAL PROFILES

☆ ☆ ☆

The Johnson Years

POLITICAL PROFILES

The Johnson Years

EDITOR:

Nelson Lichtenstein, Ph.D., University of California, Berkeley

ASSOCIATE EDITORS

Eleanora W. Schoenebaum, Ph.D., Columbia University
Michael L. Levine, Ph.D., Rutgers University

Facts On File, Inc.
119 West 57th Street, New York, N.Y 10019

POLITICAL PROFILES
The Johnson Years

 Published by Facts on File, Inc., 119 West 57th Street, New York, N.Y. 10019.

Library of Congress Catalog Card No. 76-20898
ISBN 0-87196-451-1
9 8 7 6 5 4 3 2 1

PRINTED IN THE UNITED STATES OF AMERICA

Contents

Preface

The Johnson Years is one volume in the *Political Profiles* reference series. This volume contains the biographies of 568 individuals who played an important role in American politics in the mid and late 1960s. When complete the entire *Political Profiles* series will consist of six volumes including biographies of more than 2,500 men and women who dominated American politics in the years since the end of World War II. Each volume in the series covers the period of a single presidential administration and profiles the several hundred figures who were most influential in shaping public life during that period.

Each entry is a detailed account of an individual's career, including his social and political background, his major accomplishments and activities, and an assessment of his impact on politics, international affairs, social thought or political ideology. Individuals with long public careers, like Walter Reuther, Barry Goldwater and Clark Clifford, appear in two or more volumes in the series. In such cases, each volume's profile briefly summarizes the individual's entire career but focuses on his activity during the years of the presidential administration covered by that volume. For example, John Connally's profile in *The Kennedy Years* records his role as Secretary of the Navy and his early record as governor of Texas. His entry in *The Johnson Years* focuses on his governorship, his recurring feuds with Texas liberals and the Mexican-American community and his close relationship with the President. Connally's longest entry, in the volume covering the Nixon Administration, provides a full account of his tenure as Secretary of the Treasury, White House adviser and influential figure in the business community and the Republican Party.

This unique organizational structure enables the *Political Profiles* series to be continuously updated and provides a richness of personal detail, political context and historical perspective unavailable in any other biographical reference work. Readers can trace the career of an important figure systematically through several volumes or can compare the interaction of many individuals using just a single volume.

Each profile begins with the name of the individual, his or her date and place of birth, and the date and place of death. The headnote continues with the name of the most important office or offices he or she held, or the activity or occupation for which the subject was most noted during the period covered by the volume. In the case of those holding important political office the years—and where relevant, the months—at which they began and ended service are also given. Thus, Robert McNamara is listed in this volume as "Secretary of Defense, January 1961-February 1968." Norman Mailer, however, is recorded simply as "Novelist, journalist."

The body of the profile then follows, its length roughly commensurate with the significance of the individual during the years covered by the volume. If the figure has another profile in a preceding or succeeding volume this is indicated by a bracketed notation in the text. The notation [*q.v.*] (i.e. *quod vide*) follows the name of another individual whose profile appears in the same volume. We have not given this notation following the names of presidents to avoid unnecessary repetition. Each profile ends with the initials of its author. Many also include brief suggestions referring the reader to the most readily available books or articles where additional information on the subject can be found.

One of the most critical tasks in the preparation of a biographical reference work is the selection of those to be included. Although a substantial portion, probably a majority, are self-evident, many other individuals should be included who are significant and interesting but who are not of immediate and obvious importance. In choosing, we were guided by two questions: Did the individual under consideration have an important, measurable impact on American politics as defined in its commonly accepted and broadest sense? And second, even if the potential subject was not of lasting political importance, did he or she achieve such fame or notoriety that, for a moment, that person captured the political attention of the nation? We have included, therefore, not only elected and appointed officeholders but also influential journalists and intellectuals, business and labor leaders, civil rights and anti-war activists, leaders of left and right-wing movements and cultural and social trendsetters.

In some cases our selections were made ex officio: the president and vice president, all Supreme Court justices and cabinet officers and almost all congressional committee chairmen are included in each volume of the series. Beyond these categories, we were more selective. Because of the importance of the executive branch in the postwar era we have included the president's influential aides and advisers. *The Johnson Years* also includes biographies of the most important figures from the Central Intelligence Agency, the Federal Bureau of Investigation, the military services and the Departments of Defense, State and Treasury. The importance of many of these individuals has only recently become apparent with the publication of the *Pentagon Papers* and congressional probes of intelligence activities.

Because of the traditional and prominent role in national politics played by almost every member of the U.S. Senate, we have included profiles of nearly the entire membership of that chamber. Given the larger membership and shorter terms in the House of Representatives, individual congressmen tend to hold less influence and are often more parochial in their interests than senators. Therefore, we have been more selective in choosing representatives to be profiled. The volume contains biographies of governors, mayors and local figures who had an impact on national politics or who represented important political forces in their area. We have also included about a score each of the most important business and labor leaders. Because of the importance of the civil rights movement in the mid-1960s some 45 prominent black political leaders are included in *The Johnson Years*. The dramatic rise of the anti-war movement and the student-based New Left is also chronicled in this volume through the inclusion of several of the most important radical activists of the late 1960s.

Some of the more difficult selections we had to make involved choosing among those intellectuals whose influence was widespread but hard to measure. We chose, among others, Irving Howe, Robert Lowell, William F. Buckley, Herbert Marcuse and John Kenneth Galbraith because of their roles as creative spokesmen for a particular intellectual trend or ideology. Left out of our list were many academic figures whose influence, though great within their disciplines, failed to touch a responsive chord in the larger body politic. Finally we chose a number of individuals who enjoyed a brief moment of national political recognition. Among these were Father James E. Groppi, a Milwaukee civil rights leader, and Sirhan Bishira Sirhan, convicted assassin of Robert F. Kennedy.

One final point should be made about our selection process. We have sought to include those persons who collectively dominated the visible surface of public affairs in the years when Lyndon Johnson was president. The list of those included in our volume contains no quotas. No attempt was made to provide an even geographical, political or ethnic balance. There are few women and no American Indians. On the other hand a large proportion of those profiled are white males, many educated in the Ivy League and living in Washington, D.C., New York and several other cities. Of course, *The Johnson Years* does not purport to be a collective biography of the American political and economic elite. For example, while three members of the politically active Rockefeller family are included, there are no representatives of the Mellon or DuPont dynasties.

Naturally, the selection of individuals included in each volume of the series is governed by the changing nature of national politics under each president. *The Truman Years,* for example, will have a larger number of trade union figures than does the present collection. The volume covering the Nixon Administration will contain more radicals, more women and minority group representatives than *The Eisenhower Years.*

Almost all of the profiles in this volume were written by trained historians, either advanced graduate students or Ph.Ds. Edward W. Knappman, the executive editor of Facts On File, conceived the *Political Profiles* series, worked closely with the editors in its completion and reviewed all entries included in the volume. Judith Buncher, Howard Langer and Allen Schechter provided valuable assistance on many of the profiles. Martin Goldberg took on the arduous task of compiling the index. A distinguished editorial board of historians, social scientists and journalists assisted us in the selection of those to be profiled and reviewed many of the entries. In all cases, however, responsibility for the selection of subjects and for their content rests solely with Mr. Knappman and the editors.

The Johnson Years contains several useful appendixes. It has a complete chronology, the membership role of the entire 88th, 89th and 90th Congresses, a list of the Johnson cabinet and the Supreme Court justices, the membership of the most important regulatory agencies and a list of the state governors. The volume also contains an extensive bibliography covering Johnson era politics.

We thought it useful to include a career index among the appendixes for the convenience of those seeking information about related groups of individuals. Of course, the volume also contains an extensive combined name and subject index.

New York City

Nelson Lichtenstein

The Johnson Years: An Introduction

Although the Johnson years ended in division and strife, they began in consensus. The shared grief and stunned disbelief following Kennedy's assassination dampened political conflict and fused, if only briefly, a sense of national unity. Reacting coolly to the crisis, Lyndon Johnson took over the reins of government with smoothness and finesse. Liberals had grave misgivings about Johnson's conservative record as Senate majority leader in the 1950s, but he quickly adopted Kennedy's unfinished legislative program as his own, urging passage of the late President's $11 billion tax cut to stimulate the economy and taking special care to press for congressional passage of the long stalled civil rights bill as a memorial to Kennedy. Johnson also emphasized the continuity of his Administration with that of his predecessor by asking all of Kennedy's former advisers and cabinet officers to remain at their posts. A remarkable number did. Dean Rusk, Robert McNamara, McGeorge Bundy, Walt W. Rostow and Maxwell Taylor became key figures on the Johnson foreign policymaking team, while Richard Goodwin, Lawrence O'Brien, R. Sargent Shriver, Nicholas Katzenbach, Orville Freeman and Stewart Udall continued to serve the new President in important posts affecting domestic policy.

Although the new President inherited a Congress that had repeatedly frustrated Kennedy, Johnson skillfully bent the legislature to his will. Since his early days in the faction-ridden Texas Democratic Party, Johnson had learned to win and keep power by gathering the crucial elements of each group, satisfying their interests and catering to their influence, doing whatever was necessary to establish a broad coalition behind his personal leadership. As Senate majority leader, and now as President, Johnson applied this strategy in an adroit and sophisticated fashion. "This ponderous, protean Texan . . . knows more about the sources of power in the political world of Washington than any President in this century," reported journalists Rowland Evans and Robert Novak. "He can be gentle and solicitous as a nurse, but as ruthless and deceptive as a riverboat gambler." Soon Johnson established close working relationships with Republicans like Sen. Everett M. Dirksen (R, Ill.) and Rep. William McCulloch (R, Ohio), with Southern conservatives like Sen. Harry Byrd (D, Va.) and Rep. Wilbur Mills (D, Ark.) and with businessmen like Donald Cook, Henry Ford and Frederick Kappel. He called black leaders like Whitney Young and Roy Wilkins to the White House frequently, kept in touch with the left wing of the Democratic Party through Joseph Rauh and Walter Reuther and attempted to maintain cordial relations with the intellectual community by appointing first Eric Goldman and then John C. Roche as White House "intellectuals in residence."

The political consensus that Johnson sought as a broad base for his leadership was greatly expanded in the mid-1960s by conservative Sen. Barry Goldwater's (R, Ariz.) capture of the Republican presidential nomination in 1964. During the early 1960s an ideological conservative movement had emerged in the South and West. Hostile to the moderate Eastern Republicans who had dominated the Party since 1940, these conservatives rejected compromise with either welfare liberalism at home or the Communist nations abroad. Orchestrated by political strategist F. Clifton White, the movement organized early, worked hard and succeeded in defeating the Eastern wing, then led by such national figures as Govs. William Scranton and Nelson Rockefeller and former Ambassador to South Vietnam Henry Cabot Lodge.

Once his nomination was assured in early June, Goldwater virtually destroyed the possibility of a broadly-based Republican campaign against Johnson by voting on June 10 with Southern conservatives against cloture on the 1964 civil rights bill and then by selecting an obscure and conservative representative, William E. Miller (R, N.Y.), as his running mate. Goldwater's militant conservatism and his opposition to such popular and well-established social programs as Social Security and the Tennessee Valley Authority broadened Johnson's electoral coalition as it narrowed his own constituency. Especially damaging were Goldwater's proposals to employ low-yield atomic weapons to defoliate Vietnamese jungles and to give Army field commanders more control over the use of tactical nuclear weapons. Such statements enabled Johnson to present himself as the "peace candidate" despite the retaliatory bombing of North Vietnam that followed the Tonkin Gulf incident in early August. Furthermore Goldwater did little to dispel the widespread fear that he was in some sense a captive of the more extreme conservative groups such as the John Birch Society, which linked all of the nation's ills to internal domestic conspiracies. As a consequence many liberal Republicans—including Sen. Jacob Javits (N.Y.), Sen. Thomas Kuchel (Calif.), Rep. John Lindsay (N.Y.) and Michigan Gov. George Romney—refused to support the Arizona Senator, while top Party leaders such as former President Dwight D. Eisenhower and Sen. Hugh Scott (Pa.) gave him lukewarm backing at best. Only among Party regulars like Richard Nixon and Sen. Bourke Hickenlooper (Iowa) was his support firm, and only in the Deep South and in some areas of the Southwest did Goldwater win traditionally Democratic votes.

The 1964 election returns vindicated fully Lyndon Johnson's strategy of consensus politics. Johnson captured all but six states and took 61% of the popular vote. His party won an immense electoral victory, scoring a 37-seat net gain in the House and trading a number of conservative Democratic seats in the South for liberal seats in the North. Democratic Party margins were overwhelming, both in the House (295-140) and in the Senate (68-32). For the first time since 1936, liberal Democrats held clear majorities in each chamber. As a result the conservative coalition of Southern Democrats and Republicans was reduced to a defensive minority. The coalition was victorious on only 25% of all House roll call votes in 1965 compared with 67% in 1963 and 74% in 1961. Liberal Democratic strength in the House was further enhanced by approval in early 1965 of a revision of House rules that gave Speaker John McCormack (D, Mass.) authority to bring to the floor legislation blocked by the conservative Rules Committee. The liberal Democratic majorities enabled the President to pass a phenomenal 69% of his legislative proposals during the 89th Congress.

Two major pieces of legislation that had been unsuccessfully pushed by

President Kennedy were passed in the first half of 1965: medicare, which established a compulsory hospital insurance program for the aged under Social Security, a plan that had been sought by liberals for 20 years; and the Elementary and Secondary Education Act, which authorized the first general program of federal school aid in the nation's history. The explosive issue of assistance to parochial schools, upon which Kennedy's education program had foundered, was circumvented by providing funds to public and private schools on the basis of the number of students from poor families. Other new education programs included a Teacher Corps to improve classes in impoverished schools (although funds were not appropriated until 1966), scholarship and loan programs for undergraduates and construction and library funds for colleges. Altogether, Congress appropriated over $2 billion for education in 1965. The vast array of additional domestic measures adopted in 1965 included the most far-reaching housing program since 1949, an aid bill for depressed areas, a law liberalizing immigration and legislation to expand national parks and wilderness areas.

Johnson's most ambitious and innovative program, pushed through Congress in 1964 and 1965, was a "War on Poverty," designed, in the words of the Economic Opportunity Act of 1964, "to eliminate the paradox of poverty in the nation by opening to everyone the opportunity to live in decency and dignity." The Administration's decision to launch the program came as a result of a fortuitous convergence of political will and economic possibility. For several years economists, social scientists, union leaders and liberal office holders had been perplexed by the continued existence of poverty in the midst of the general postwar American prosperity. Sen. Paul Douglas (D, Ill.) had long crusaded for federal aid to depressed regions like Applachia and to urban areas of chronically high unemployment. In 1962 socialist Michael Harrington won wide recognition for the problem with the publication of his influential *The Other America.* Meanwhile, the growing civil rights movement made many aware not only of the legal discrimination practiced against American blacks, but also of their economic deprivations. Civil rights leaders like Bayard Rustin, A. Phillip Randolph and Whitney Young emphasized that for American blacks the average rate of unemployment was double that of whites; even for those with jobs, they noted, the pay was often below the official poverty line.

At the same time that the problem of poverty was reborn as a political issue, the money to do something about it became available. Under the Keynesian fiscal policies begun during the Kennedy Administration, the Gross National Product increased dramatically between 1961 and 1967, rising from about $503 billion to about $807 billion. This stable growth offered Johnson and his economic advisers a four to five billion dollar "fiscal dividend" each year that had to be spent to continue stimulation of the economy. A federal attack on poverty would pump this fiscal dividend back into the economy and help advance Johnson's reform program. Like his mentor and hero, Franklin D. Roosevelt, Johnson thought new and innovative programs demanded new governmental agencies free of bureaucratic inertia and tradition. Therefore, over the objections of HEW Secretary Anthony Celebrezze and Labor Secretary W. Willard Wirtz, he insisted on creation of an independent Office of Economic Opportunity to plan and administer the War on Poverty. In February 1964 he chose Peace Corps Director R. Sargent Shriver to head the agency. Shriver, an open-minded and enthusiastic liberal, called upon an imaginative group of social planners and administrators including Daniel P. Moynihan, Adam Yarmolinsky, Frank Mankiewicz and Jack Conway to help organize the program. During the summer of 1964 Congress passed the Economic Opportunity Act, authorizing just under $1 billion for the first year's antipoverty activities.

The primary function of the OEO was not to raise the income of the poor directly by providing them with jobs and money. Rather, it had the more difficult task of breaking the poverty cycle within low income families by equipping the poor with a higher level of economically usable skills. Much effort was directed at job training and counseling through the Job Corps and the Neighborhood Youth Corps for young people and the Work-Experience Program for unemployed heads of families. Educational programs included Project Head Start, designed to prepare economically deprived preschool children for elementary school, and Upward Bound, whose purpose was to encourage low-income high school students to go to college. The most controversial activity of the OEO involved encouragement of participation by the poor themselves in the administration of local community action programs that often challenged municipal elected officials and local power structures.

The broad consensus that Johnson built in 1964 and 1965 collapsed during the final three years of his Administration. Changes in the ideology and tactics of the civil rights movement from 1965 to 1968 suggest that the reversal of the President's political fortunes resulted in large measure from the raised expectations aroused among blacks by his early successes on behalf of civil rights. In 1965 the movement reached the height of its power and prestige. Nonviolent and integrated, the civil rights cause won wide acceptance throughout the North and West. Even conservative Sen. Dirksen declared civil rights "an idea whose time has come." Johnson considered the black community a part of his national coalition, and he frequently conferred with such leaders as Roy Wilkins and Clarence Mitchell of the NAACP, Whitney Young of the Urban League and Bayard Rustin, A. Philip Randolph and Martin Luther King. With the enactment of the Voting Rights Act of 1965, the movement achieved the virtual elimination of de jure segregation and discrimination.

This triumph, however, marked the end of one phase of the movement's history and the beginning of a more radical period. The advances made in the South hardly affected economic problems such as unemployment, low wages, crime and poor housing which afflicted black ghettos throughout the country. These ills proved far less amenable to government remedy than the legalized racism of the South. The War on Poverty, which was directed at such problems, began with high hopes. Officials in the OEO were convinced that poverty could be eliminated by 1976. However, it soon became clear that this goal could not be achieved or even approached. Anticipated funding for the program dissipated when Vietnam war spending began increasing dramatically in 1965. Late in the year the Administration reduced OEO's share of the planned fiscal 1967 budget from $4 billion to $1.75 billion. In November 1967 economist Ben Seligman asserted that "the government program for warring on poverty has reached no more than about 6% of the poor." Money was not the only difficulty. Community action projects often became mixed in triangular power and policy disputes among local officeholders, poverty officials and the poor themselves. Furthermore, it appeared that the poverty cycle perpetuated in the ghetto environment was far more resistant to OEO's programs than had been expected. From its inception the Job Corps had a high dropout rate, and studies of Project Head Start made in 1967 raised serious questions about the program's lasting effects.

The initial achievements of the civil rights movement and of the Johnson Administration served to make blacks more aware of the unsolved problems that remained, and the voices of angry militants won a wider audience in the ghettoes. Malcolm X, who scoffed at integration as irrelevant to the needs of most blacks, gained a wide following outside of the Black Muslims. The black nationalist poet and playwright Leroi Jones became as popular as the well-known black author James Baldwin. Both Malcolm and Jones, by their contemptuous disdain for white society, helped undermine a fundamental and necessary assumption of the integration movement: the basic decency of America's people, institutions and values. In 1965 and 1966 a number of the movement's integrationist leaders were replaced by militants. Floyd McKissick replaced James Farmer as head of the Congress of Racial Equality in late 1965, while Stokely Carmichael and H. Rap Brown became leading personalities in the Student Nonviolent Coordinating Committee (SNCC), supplanting John Lewis, James Forman and Robert Parris Moses. In California, meanwhile, Huey Newton, Eldridge Cleaver and Bobby Seale organized the Black Panther Party, whose armed, leather-jacketed members patrolled the Oakland ghetto.

National awareness of a growing split in the civil rights movement came in June 1966 when Carmichael first used the slogan "black power" on a Mississippi civil rights march. Established civil rights leaders like Wilkins, Young and King repudiated the term; nevertheless, it immediately captured the imagination of many blacks both in the North and South. The meaning of the phrase was not well-defined, but it clearly represented a renunciation of liberalism, a rejection of the established political system as a vehicle for progress, a call for black pride and an pronouncement that whites would henceforth be excluded from institutions that blacks thought they should control. For some it meant a complete separation from white society.

Increasingly frequent outbreaks of racial violence were another facet of growing black frustration. A riot in the Watts section of Los Angeles in August 1965 was followed by disturbances in scores of towns and cities during the next two summers. The succession of riots climaxed in July 1967 in Newark and subsequently Detroit, where 43 were killed and 5,000 left homeless. Some militant black leaders hailed the violence as a legitimate, insurrectionary response to oppression, and H. Rap Brown, chairman of SNCC, toured ghettos in 1967 urging blacks to arm themselves.

Despite increasing disaffection in the ghetto, blacks had no realistic alternative but to vote for liberal Democrats, and by and large they continued to do so. The great political danger for Johnson lay in a white backlash. Many, perhaps most, whites in the North and West had supported the drive against legalized discrimination in the South. But when the civil rights movement and the Johnson Administration began to move against the economic and social problems of the ghetto, their attitude towards the struggle for social equality changed. Ethnic whites who had struggled to reach a marginal position in the middle class were in the vanguard of the backlash. They feared that black gains would be made at their expense, jeopardizing their hard earned, tenuously maintained advances. Demonstrations and riots represented the perceived threat to their status in its most direct and menacing form. When Martin Luther King led rallies and marches in Chicago against segregated housing during the summer of 1966, the demonstrators were attacked by thousands of whites. To many it appeared that the government was allied with the black assault, helping through the antipoverty program and other domestic social welfare measures those who refused to help themselves while ignoring the interests of hard-working and law-abiding citizens.

The political effects of white backlash became apparent between 1966 and 1968. In the 1966 congressional elections the Republicans gained 47 House seats, achieving their largest membership in the lower chamber since 1956. In 1967 the conservative coalition was victorious 63% of the time, and Johnson suffered a number of major domestic defeats, including drastic cutbacks in funds for such social welfare programs as Model Cities, rent supplements and the Teacher Corps. Congress became increasingly disposed to punish criminals rather than attack the allegedly economic and social roots of crime. In August 1967 the Senate, over liberal objections, assigned the task of probing the causes of urban rioting to conservative Sen. John McClellan's (D, Ark.) Permanent Investigations Subcommittee. McClellan directed the investigation towards finding the agitators who, he believed, had provoked the disturbances. After failing to pass an open housing bill in 1966 and 1967, Congress finally adopted the measure in April 1968, but only during the emotional aftermath of Martin Luther King's assassination and after adding anti-riot clauses providing federal penalties for persons crossing state lines with intent to incite or participate in civil disturbances. Another signal of the shift in congressional sentiment was the passage of the Omnibus Crime Control and Safe Streets Act, adopted in June 1968, which attempted to reverse *Miranda v. Arizona* (1966) and other Supreme Court rulings that had expanded the rights of criminal suspects.

Backlash was also apparent in local and state politics. Mayors Sam Yorty of Los Angeles and John Shelley of San Francisco jointly denounced the antipoverty program for "fostering class struggle." Boston City Councilwoman Louise Day Hicks mobilized Irish and Italian voters against integration of the city schools, and in California conservative Republicans Ronald Reagan and Max Rafferty used the issue of black radicalism and unrest to win state office. In New York City the traditionally liberal Jewish population opposed the black demand for community control of the schools when it appeared to threaten the hard-won job security of teachers.

While Johnson's consensus was shaken by domestic issues, it was his conduct of foreign policy in Southeast Asia that ultimately led to its collapse. Johnson's inflexible attitude regarding the defense of what he perceived were the nation's interests abroad was evident early in his Administration. During January 1964, when Panamanians rioted against United States control of the Canal Zone, Johnson declared that there would be no negotiations on the Canal treaty until law and order was restored. In April 1965 a revolution erupted in the Dominican Republic against that nation's military dictatorship. Late in the month Johnson dispatched several hundred Marines to the island, ostensibly to protect American citizens. Soon afterwards he sent thousands of additional troops, contending that Communists had taken over the revolution. Johnson's claims regarding the political power of Dominican Communists were seriously questioned, and many liberals condemned U.S. intervention. But the American military presence quickly subdued the civil strife, and the United States was subsequently able to guide political events in the Dominican Republic. Therefore domestic debate over the matter soon died.

The seemingly endless Vietnam war proved to be an entirely different matter. Johnson was a firm believer in the "domino theory" of Communist expansion. Shortly after assuming office he told Ambassador to South Vietnam Henry Cabot Lodge, "I am not going to lose Vietnam. I am not going to be the President who saw Southeast Asia go the way of China." Like his chief foreign policy advisers, Dean Rusk, McGeorge Bundy, Robert McNamara and W. W. Rostow, Johnson's political consciousness had formed in the late 1930s, when the spread of fascism in Europe and the appeasement policy of the Western democracies had helped lead to World War II. Johnson, Rusk and Bundy argued that Vietnam was analogous to Czechoslovakia on the eve of Munich; they warned that if the U.S. did not make a strong stand in Vietnam, the nation would, in effect, be inviting Communist aggression in the rest of Southeast Asia and throughout the world. Therefore, when the military situation deteriorated in 1964 and 1965, American strategists made the decision to escalate the war, first by inaugurating a bombing campaign against the North in February 1965 and then by dispatching ground troops in the spring and summer.

For the next two-and-a-half years there was an ongoing policy conflict within the Administration over the pace of escalation, especially as it concerned the sensitive air war over North Vietnam. Military figures like Earl G. Wheeler, chairman of the Joint Chiefs of Staff, William C. Westmoreland, U.S. Commandant in Vietnam, and Curtis LeMay, Air Force Chief of Staff, wanted a full-scale bombing campaign against the North that would have included the heavily industrialized population centers of Hanoi and Haiphong. Backed by Bundy and McNamara, Johnson chose a policy of graduated increases in bombing. He selected this course for two reasons. First, Johnson and most of his civilian advisers feared that a major escalation would precipitate direct Chinese or Russian intervention in the war. Second, they hoped that the relatively slow increase in the pressure on the North might force Hanoi to negotiate in order to prevent the terrible damage that large-scale bombing would inflict. In accordance with this strategy Johnson punctuated the bombing campaign with peace overtures followed by further escalation and extension of the bombing. But by 1968 Johnson had given the military most of what it had originally wanted. Ground troop levels stood at over half-a-million men, while few targets, except those in the immediate Hanoi-Haiphong area, were off-limits to U.S. bombers.

The deeper America's involvement in the Vietnam conflict, the more the nation's international prestige was staked on its outcome. The initial goal of preserving South Vietnamese independence was soon replaced by the larger purpose of preserving America's credibility as a great power throughout the world. "To leave Vietnam to its fate," announced Lyndon Johnson in an April 1965 speech, "would shake the confidence of all [free] people in the value of an American commitment and in the value of America's word." A year later, when it was apparent that the U.S. faced a stalemate in the war, Assistant Secretary of Defense John McNaughton succinctly phrased the prevailing view within the Administration. "The present U.S. objective in Vietnam," he told his chief, Robert McNamara, "is to avoid humiliation. The reasons why we went into Vietnam to the present depth are varied; but they are now largely academic." In the absence of a realistic possibility of imminent victory, the Vietnam war became an open-ended U.S. commitment to save its own reputation.

The closest analogy to Vietnam in recent American history was the Korean war. But that conflict had been sparked by a clear-cut invasion into South Korea by Communist North Korea. Furthermore, there had been little pro-Communist sentiment in South Korea. In Vietnam the North aided the Communist National Liberation Front (NLF), but the NLF had significant popular backing in South Vietnam and was conducting a guerrilla war difficult to combat by conventional military methods. In addition, there had been a relaxation of Cold War tensions since the early 1950s, and many liberals began to argue, after the Sino-Soviet split, that world Communism was becoming polycentric and no longer represented a monolithic threat to the West. Even in the case of the Korean stalemate, the indecisiveness of the conflict had caused considerable restlessness at home. In the politically and morally more ambiguous situation in Vietnam, the failure of American forces to achieve victory produced mounting anti-war sentiment. In Congress Sens. Wayne Morse (D, Ore.) and Ernest Gruening (D, Alaska), the only opponents of the Tonkin Gulf Resolution in 1964, were joined in their opposition to the war during the next three years by a slowly growing number of congressmen. One of the most articulate critics of U.S. policy was Sen. J. William Fulbright (D, Ark.), chairman of the upper chamber's Foreign Relations Committee. In the spring of 1965 he questioned the Administration's contention that the war was a result of Chinese aggression, suggesting that the enemy represented a Vietnamese nationalist movement. His Committee's televised hearings on the war in January and February 1966 gave such respected Establishment figures as retired Gen. James J. Gavin and former Ambassador George F. Kennan an opportunity to present their reservations about the war before a national audience. Other early congressional critics included Sens. Frank Church (D, Idaho), Vance Hartke (D, Ind.), George McGovern (D, S.D.), Eugene McCarthy (D, Minn.) and Stephen Young (D, Ohio). Most of them questioned the validity of the domino theory and the ability of the U.S. to suppress guerrilla warfare without unacceptable losses. In January 1966 15 Democratic senators signed a letter to the President urging the continuation of a bombing halt declared the previous month. In March 78 Democratic representatives expressed their support for American troops in Vietnam but stressed that they favored a limited rather than an open-ended commitment.

Meanwhile, public opposition to the war increased. Nationwide demonstrations were held in October 1965 in about 40 U.S. cities, and the following month a Washington rally drew a crowd estimated at up to 35,000 people. A Harris Poll released in February 1966 showed approval for Johnson's Vietnam policies down to 49%, and by the summer of 1967 the approval rating was below 35%. Anti-war demonstrations grew steadily larger. In April 1967 Martin Luther King, who had recently announced his opposition to America's involvement in Vietnam, led a march of over 100,000 war protesters in New York City. A November 1967 Washington rally, culminating in a march to the Pentagon, drew between 50,000 and 150,000 persons.

Johnson's relations with key opinion making groups became strained over the war. A White House Festival of the Arts in June 1965 brought to public attention the intensity of anti-war sentiment among many intellectuals when poet Robert Lowell declined to attend and social critic Dwight MacDonald circulated an anti-war petition among the participants. Subsequently intellectuals became one of the most strongly anti-war segments of American society, and by 1968 most prominent intellectuals outside of government were critics of Administration policy. The media was a continuing source of embarrassment to the Administration because newspaper, television and radio reports from the early days of the Vietnam conflict often conflicted with official versions of events. There were frequent reports of civilian casualties and the torture of prisoners by South Vietnamese soldiers. The Administration's optimistic military reports often were not taken at face value as they generally had been in previous American wars. In 1966 media reference to an Administration "credibility gap" multiplied. Journalists resented Johnson's efforts to influence reporting on Vietnam, and the President felt that the media bore an animus towards him.

Some segments of the anti-war movement, particularly on college campuses, became seriously disaffected from American society and moved towards political radicalism and more militant forms of activism. Beginning in 1966 Students for a Democratic Society, a major vehicle for the campus left, denounced the war as a manifestation of an imperialistic American foreign policy and adopted a neo-Marxist philosophical perspective. Draft card burnings by students became a much-publicized activity in 1966, and student demonstrations against the war were sometimes accompanied by violence. In 1967 efforts were made to obstruct the work of draft boards. During the same year a youth counter-culture movement emerged on the campuses as an outgrowth of anti-war sentiment. This movement was not characterized by political activism but, rather, by a rejection of many fundamental social values. Competition, upward economic mobility and technological progress were rejected in favor of communalism, material simplicity and self-discovery, often through drugs.

Many of the same marginally middle class whites who felt threatened by the demands of blacks were also frightened by the opposition to the war. Blacks were perceived as a threat to their middle class status from below, while the reaction against the Vietnam conflict was seen as a denial of the worth of that status, for they interpreted anti-war sentiment and the counterculture as an elitist denial of the traditional values of the American social mainstream that they had fought to enter. These "middle Americans," as they came to be known, deeply resented the fact that intellectuals and students, privileged members of society who commanded great respect, seemingly repudiated patriotism, often violated the law and in some cases renounced their material privileges. Within the framework of this socially conservative populist perspective, the media, an unelected elite challenging a democratically elected government, emerged as a leading scapegoat.

However, President Johnson did not benefit significantly from this phenomenon. Not only did reaction against anti-war sentiment overlap significantly with backlash against Administration efforts on behalf of blacks, but many of the persons who were part of the reaction blamed the President for not escalating the war rapidly enough. The coalescing of opinion on the war on both the left and right of the President was indicated by a Gallup Poll released in October 1967. It reported that 48% thought the U.S. should reduce the scale of fighting in Vietnam or get out, 37% felt the war should be escalated and only 28% approved the President's handling of the conflict.

Public opinion polls did not constitute the limits of Johnson's Vietnam-related problems. As a result of the 1964 tax act, an already modestly expanding economy enjoyed a great surge of growth under Johnson. Spending on the Vietnam war added to the impetus, and the Gross National Product increased by more than 7% per annum. But as the war expanded inflationary pressures increased. The rate of inflation, stable at about 1% for the first half of the decade, began to step up noticeably at the end of 1965 and reached 5% in 1968. As a countermeasure Johnson began limiting the expansion of the antipoverty program as early as 1965. Secretary of Labor W. Willard Wirtz and the Council of Economic Advisers tried to hold down wage and price increases by "jawboning" labor and management. Their appeal failed. While AFL-CIO President George Meany supported the war, he insisted that wage increases keep pace with or exceed the rise in the cost of living. Beginning in 1965 organized labor negotiated a number of major contracts that exceeded the Council of Economic Advisers' 3.2% wage guideposts.

To stem inflation Johnson asked Congress for a 10% tax surcharge in August 1967. As Johnson feared, congressional conservatives, led by Rep. Wilbur Mills (D, Ark.), chairman of the House Ways and Means Committee, demanded substantial cuts in domestic social programs before they would support the tax surcharge. After several months of impasse Johnson reluctantly agreed to $6 billion in non-defense reductions, and the tax surcharge finally went into effect at the end of 1968. Partly as a result of the delay, the federal budget deficit grew from $8.7 billion in fiscal 1967 to $25.2 billion in fiscal 1968. The deficit added to inflationary pressures, and the 5% Consumer Price Index increase of 1968 was exceeded in subsequent years.

Surprisingly, Johnson's hard-line stand against Communism in Vietnam did not result in an escalation of Cold War tensions with the Soviet Union. Despite extensive Soviet military assistance to North Vietnam, Johnson attempted, with partial success, to continue the gradual thaw in U.S.-USSR relations that had begun in the late 1950s. A U.S.-Soviet consular treaty, signed in 1964, was delayed in the Senate in 1965 and 1966 by the Administration because of the conflict in Vietnam. But in 1967 the treaty was ratified by a narrow margin over the opposition of hawkish senators, who opposed approval while the war continued. During the June 1967 Middle East War, Johnson and Soviet Premier Aleksei Kosygin agreed to avoid belligerency, and later in the month they conferred in a cordial, if not particularly productive, summit meeting in Glassboro, N.J. The most important result of U.S.-Soviet cooperation during the Johnson years was the signing of an 18-nation nuclear non-proliferation treaty early in 1968. Designed to check the spread of nuclear weapons, the treaty became possible only after the U.S. and the Soviet Union were able to agree on international inspection and on a controls system. But efforts by the President in 1966 and 1967 to remove barriers to East-West trade were thwarted by congressmen who opposed expanded trade with the Communist bloc until the war ended.

Events in early 1968 forced Johnson to reassess both his Vietnam policy and his political future. The NLF's spectacular Tet offensive of February 1968 was a severe blow to the Administration's already battered credibility. When Gen. Westmoreland asked for over 200,000 additional troops, Johnson sought the judgment of his advisers. McNamara, no longer confident of the success of the policy of escalation, had just resigned as Secretary of Defense. His successor, Clark Clifford, was named to head a task force to study Westmoreland's request. Although previously a firm hawk on the war, Clifford concluded that the conflict had to be wound down. He saw the alternative as endless escalation of the conflict with no promise of victory and a steady expansion of the anti-war opposition.

Meanwhile, in the March 13 New Hampshire primary, Sen. Eugene McCarthy, a peace candidate for president aided by a legion of young campaign volunteers, ran a surprisingly strong race against Johnson. Three days later Sen. Robert Kennedy (D, N.Y.) announced his candidacy for the Democratic nomination on an anti-war platform. After relieving Westmoreland of his command on March 22, the President convened a Senior Advisory Group on Vietnam, a majority of which concluded on March 26 that further escalation of the war would be politically and financially untenable. The power recommended de-escalation of the war and negotiations with North Vietnam. On March 31 Johnson appeared on television to announce a unilateral halt to the air and naval bombardment of most of North Vietnam, to call for the immediate start of negotiations and to reveal that he would not run for another term as president.

Johnson's abandonment of his renomination effort left the Democratic race to McCarthy, Kennedy and Vice President Hubert Humphrey. The former two senators, both anti-war candidates who essentially backed

Johnson's domestic programs, each sought to upset Humphrey, a supporter of the President's policies both at home and abroad. McCarthy and Kennedy, both favoring a complete bombing halt and NLF participation in the South Vietnamese political process, competed in the primaries while Humphrey accumulated delegates in the nonprimary states. Kennedy, with a greater appeal among blacks and other minorities, defeated the Minnesota senator in the crucial California primary in early June. But he was mortally wounded on the night of his victory. His death, following by two months the assassination of Martin Luther King, shocked the nation and shattered the possibility that the Democratic Party might choose an anti-war candidate. Humphrey won the nomination under extremely unfavorable circumstances as the badly divided Party was split further by violent confrontations between anti-war demonstrators and Chicago police near the site of its Convention.

The anti-war constituency was without a representative in the election, but two candidates attempted to speak for the frustrated and frightened Americans to Johnson's right. George Wallace, former Alabama governor famous for his resistance to integration in the early 1960s, ran as a third party candidate. He attacked "minority appeasement," denounced riots and violent anti-war protests and promised to "keep the peace if I had to keep 30,000 troops standing on the streets . . . with two-foot-long bayonets." Because of his third party status and the stridency of his appeal, Wallace's constituency was too narrow to permit him to play anything but a spoiler's role.

The Republicans once again selected former Vice President Richard M. Nixon as their candidate. Nixon, like Wallace, appealed to those who felt trapped by menacing forces from above and below. Calling for "order in America," he proposed to speak for "the great majority of Americans, the forgotten Americans, the non-shouters, the non-demonstrators . . . [who] work and save and pay their taxes . . . ." Government social welfare programs, Nixon said, had produced an "ugly harvest of frustrations, violence and failure." He attempted to broaden his appeal by calling for "new programs" to give everyone an "equal chance" while securing his base by promising to promote small entrepreneurship rather than continuing "government programs which perpetuate dependency." By suggesting, without providing any specifics, that he had a better chance to secure peace than Humphrey because of the Vice President's long association with Johnson's Vietnam policy, Nixon was able to profit from the almost universal disenchantment with the war while offending few voters with strong opinions about the war.

Humphrey, asserting that "anyone who tells the country, as Mr. Nixon has, that poverty and crime have little relationship, is fooling you and himself," attempted to reconstitute the Democratic alliance of organized labor, ethnic whites, blacks and intellectuals. But his last-minute attempts to move away from the Administration's Vietnam views did not mollify the anti-war faction of the Party, and he lost to Nixon although almost equalling the Republican candidate's popular vote.

The precise meaning of the election for future Vietnam policy was not clear. But it was apparent from the year's events that unless the next president could find some way to extricate the United States from military involvement in Southeast Asia, his political future would be bleak. For domestic policy the significance of the election was less ambiguous. Johnson's unprecedented effort to attack the problems of the ghettos, whose apparent effect had been the creation of frustration and violence rather than achievement of its goal, had been rejected by the victor and the voters. Having responded to a wave of hostility towards the demands of the poor, Nixon was primarily committed to seeking an end to social disruption rather than to searching for ways to meet those demands.

The broad consensus built by Johnson in 1964 was in shambles. The President had established his remarkable political base in large measure by offering the hope that his programs could solve or at least ameliorate many of the nation's problems. The failure of his Administration to achieve either its major domestic or foreign policy goals had undermined this key element of Johnson's political success, thereby ending his political career and shattering, at least for a time, his party's New Deal coalition.

POLITICAL PROFILES
The Johnson Years

ABEL, I(ORWITH) W(ILBUR)

b. Aug. 11, 1908; Magnolia, Ohio. President, United Steelworkers of America, 1965- .

Born the son of an Ohio blacksmith, Abel began work in the steel mills at age 17 and later helped start the first Steelworkers Organizing Committee (later renamed United Steelworkers of America) local at Canton Timkin Roller Bearing in 1936. The next year he was appointed a union staff representative and in 1942 was elected District Director for the Canton, Ohio area. When David J. McDonald [*q.v.*] succeeded Philip Murray as President of the United Steelworkers of America (USW) in 1952, Abel stepped into McDonald's old post as the union's secretary-treasurer. During the next 12 years Abel loyally served McDonald as USW second in command.

In the early 1960s Abel and other steelworkers grew increasingly critical of McDonald's leadership. Collective bargaining contracts negotiated by McDonald ignored many important local issues. By late 1964 he had failed to win an across-the-board wage increase in more than three years. USW district directors were also critical of McDonald's centralization of union power and his use of a small labor-management "Human Relations Committee" to secretly negotiate new contract settlements without the participation of the full USW executive board.

In December 1964 Abel announced his candidacy for the USW presidency. Running with district directors Walter J. Burke and Joseph Moloney (candidates for secretary-treasurer and vice-president respectively), Abel charged McDonald with "tuxedo trade unionism" because of his friendly relationships with some steel industry leaders. Abel promised "hard-nosed, arms-length bargaining" and a renewed rank-and-file role in union policymaking. His insurgent campaign was supported by about half the USW district directors, including Joseph Germano, powerful head of the Chicago area's District 31, the largest in the union. Abel also won strong support from many black USW members and from another important but underrepresented "minority" in the union, the Canadian steelworkers. A hard fought two-month campaign culminated in union-wide balloting on Feb. 9, 1965. In perhaps the most important ouster of an incumbent union president since the early postwar years, Abel defeated McDonald by some 8,000 votes out of 606,000 cast. Following Abel's succession to the union presidency on June 1, 1965, he negotiated without a strike a new contract with the steel industry providing for a 40-cent-an-hour increase over three years.

During the first half of 1967, Abel helped negotiate the merger into the USW of the 40,000-member Mine, Mill and Smelter Workers Union, which had been expelled from the Congress of Industrial Organizations in 1949 on charges of Communist domination. With 80% of all non-ferrous metal miners now in one union for the first time, the USW struck Western copper mines July 15, 1967 in what turned out to be a protracted nine-month conflict, resolved only after federal intervention in the spring of 1968. The strike generated widespread support for the USW within the labor movement and helped Abel pass the union's first dues increase in 12 years at a special convention in March 1968.

During McDonald's presidency the USW had become somewhat aloof from other unions in the AFL-CIO. Abel sought to end this self-imposed isolation and move the union in a liberal direction, "into the mainstream of American labor." He spoke at the Americans for Democratic Action (ADA) convention in April 1965 and invited liberal union presidents A. Philip Randolph [*q.v.*] and Walter Reuther [*q.v.*] to address the USW convention in September 1966. Abel also introduced a strong civil rights resolution at the convention and the next year served on the National Commission on Civil Disorders chaired by Illinois Governor Otto Kerner [*q.v.*].

In the acrimonious dispute between Reuther and AFL-CIO President George Meany [*q.v.*] over foreign policy issues, Abel sided with Meany. With Meany's approval President Johnson appointed Abel a member of the United States delegation to the United Nations in September 1967. Abel supported the President's conduct of the war in Vietnam and resigned from the ADA national board in February 1968 after the liberal political organization endorsed Sen. Eugene McCarthy (D, Minn.) [*q.v.*] for President. Four days after Johnson's decision not to run for reelection on March 31, Abel endorsed Vice President Hubert Humphrey [*q.v.*] for the Democratic presidential nomination. In California Abel ordered local steelworker officials not to support Sen. Robert F. Kennedy (D, N.Y.) [*q.v.*] in the May primary. During the fall, sustained USW support for Humphrey helped the Vice President carry Pennsylvania in the general election. Thereafter Abel remained an important labor spokesman in Democratic Party councils. At the 1972 National Party Convention, Abel seconded the nomination of Sen. Henry Jackson (D, Wash.) [*q.v.*] to be the Democratic presidential candidate.

In 1968 and 1971 Abel signed collective bargaining agreements in basic steel without a strike. However, the settlements were preceded by massive company stockpiling and followed by widespread layoffs. To end this boom and bust cycle, Abel signed in March 1973 an Experimental Negotiating Agreement, which provided for binding arbitration of unresolved national contract issues, thus precluding industry-wide strikes for the life of the four-year agreement. [See NIXON Volume]

[NNL]

For further information:
John Herling, *Right to Challenge: People and Power in the Steelworkers Union* (New York, 1972).

ABERNATHY, RALPH D(AVID)

b. March 11, 1926; Linden, Ala.
Secretary-Treasurer, Southern Christian Leadership Conference, 1957-65; Vice President, 1965-68; President, 1968- .

Abernathy grew up in Marengo County, in the heart of Alabama's Black Belt, where his parents owned a 500-acre farm. He was ordained a Baptist minister in 1948, received a B.S. from Alabama State College in 1950 and an M.A. from Atlanta University in 1951. In that year Abernathy was named pastor of the First Baptist Church in Montgomery, Ala., and he developed a close friendship with Martin Luther King [*q.v.*] after King became pastor at the city's Dexter Avenue Baptist Church in 1954. The two ministers helped organize the historic Montgomery bus boycott. When King was chosen to lead the protest in December 1955, Abernathy emerged as his chief adviser and aide. In 1957 King was elected president and Abernathy secretary-treasurer of the Southern Christian Leadership Conference (SCLC), an organization they helped establish to further nonviolent direct action in the South. As King's top aide in the SCLC, Abernathy shared King's commitment to nonviolence. The two were constant companions, preaching, marching and going to jail together. [See EISENHOWER, KENNEDY Volumes]

Beginning in March 1964 the SCLC supported a desegregation effort by the black community in St. Augustine, Fla. Abernathy was arrested on June 11 with King and 16 other protesters when the group demanded service at a segregated motel restaurant in the city. Abernathy accompanied King on a speaking tour of Europe in the fall of 1964 and returned with him in December when King was awarded the Nobel Peace Prize in Oslo, Norway.

On their return home SCLC launched a campaign focused on Selma, Ala., to secure voting rights for blacks. Abernathy joined many of the almost daily marches in Selma in January and February 1965 and was arrested with King on Feb. 1 when they led a march to the county courthouse. He helped organize and was a participant in the famous march from Selma to Montgomery which began on March 21.

In June 1967 the Supreme Court upheld the contempt of court convictions of King, Abernathy and six other ministers resulting from the 1963 Birmingham demonstrations. While serving their five-day prison terms beginning on Oct. 30, King discussed with Abernathy and other aides a plan to bring an interracial coalition of the poor to Washington to pressure the federal government into enacting far-reaching antipoverty legislation. Abernathy helped plan this Poor People's Campaign over the next few months. In the meantime King gave his support to a strike by the virtually all-black sanitationmen's union in Memphis in March 1968. On April 4 King and Abernathy were in Memphis planning a march with other SCLC officials when King was shot in the head by a sniper while standing on the balcony of his motel room.

The day after King's assassination Abernathy was named his successor as president of the SCLC. He announced that the organization's first task would be to carry out the march King had planned in support of the Memphis sanitationmen. A giant march was held on April 8, and the strike was settled eight days later.

Promising that the SCLC would be "more militant than ever" while continuing to use nonviolent methods, Abernathy also went forward with the Poor People's Campaign planned by King. For three days beginning April 29, Abernathy led an interracial "delegation of 100" in conferences with congressional leaders and cabinet members in Washington to present the grievances and demands of the poor. The first group of nine caravans of poor people arrived in Washington on May 13 and began setting up an encampment called "Resurrection City" in Potomac Park near the Lincoln Memorial. Over the next month groups of poor persons attended sessions of Congress and committee hearings and demonstrated outside the headquarters of various government departments and agencies.

The campaign showed signs of insufficient organization and disunity among staff leaders, and Resurrection City, which held 2,500 people at its peak, was plagued by inadequate facilities and some incidents of violence and crime. A Solidarity Day march on June 19 brought 50,000 supporters of the campaign to Washington. On June 23 the Interior Department refused to extend the permit for Resurrection City, and the next day the Washington police closed the encampment. Abernathy was arrested the same day while leading a demonstration on the Capitol grounds, and he remained in jail until July 13.

The Poor People's Campaign did secure an expanded food distribution program, changes in welfare eligibility requirements and new provisions for participation of the poor in local operations of several government agencies. But the campaign, as Abernathy admitted, had failed in its major goal of getting Congress "to move meaningfully against the problem of poverty" by adopting legislation for jobs, low income housing and a guaranteed annual income for the unemployed. Abernathy announced the end of the Washington phase of the campaign on July 16. In August he opened a new phase, leading demonstrations by poor people at the Republican National Convention in Miami Beach and the Democratic National Convention in Chicago.

Abernathy and the SCLC continued to emphasize the problems of poverty and unemployment over the next several years. He was also active in the anti-war movement, speaking at numerous peace rallies and marches. Abernathy was critical of the Nixon Administration for its Supreme Court nominations and for its opposition to busing as a means to achieve school desegregation. [See NIXON Volume]

[CAB]

ABRAMS, CREIGHTON W(ILLIAMS)
b. Sept. 15, 1914; Springfield, Mass.
d. Sept. 4, 1974; Washington, D.C.
Commander, U.S. Military Assistance Command, South Vietnam, June 1968-June 1972.

During World War II Creighton Abrams distinguished himself as a tank commander, whom Gen. George Patton considered the best in the U.S. Third Army. He served with the Army Chief of Staff in Korea in 1953 and 1954. While assigned to the Pentagon in the early 1960s, Abrams directed the federal troops that were put on alert in the South to prevent racial violence. In 1965 he was named a major general.

President Johnson appointed Abrams deputy commander of the U.S. Military Assistance Command in South Vietnam in April 1967. One month later Abrams and presidential assistant Robert W. Komer [*q.v.*] assumed responsibility for the South Vietnamese rural pacification program. By that time the program—originally designed to provide protection from Communist attack and give economic, social and medical aid to the countryside—almost exclusively stressed local security. Under the plan large numbers of rural Vietnamese were moved to safe military areas. Critics estimated that the program resulted in the dislocation of over two million people.

In June 1968 Abrams succeeded William Westmoreland [*q.v.*] as commander of the half-million American troops stationed in South Vietnam. Abrams's handling of the war was dictated in large measure by Johnson's March 1968 decision to de-escalate the conflict, turn most of the fighting over to the South Vietnamese and begin negotiations. Peace talks began in May 1968. With its renunciation of a goal of military victory, the Administration was no longer willing to accept high casualties. Abrams, therefore, had to abandon Westmoreland's use of large-scale, "search-and-destroy" missions and massive firepower. Instead, he based his strategy on the use of night patrols, ambushes and B-52 attacks.

The President often consulted Abrams about the impact of peace negotiations on the military effort. In the fall of 1968 Abrams supported the Johnson decision to halt bombing North Vietnam as a prelude to substantive talks. During October he also negotiated the grants of weapons necessary to get the South Vietnamese to accept a halt and enter the peace talks.

During the Nixon Administration Abrams oversaw the withdrawal of U.S. troops from Vietnam. He was named Army Chief of Staff in June 1972. In this position he worked to increase military efficiency and update the training of reserve forces. Abrams died in September 1974 of complications resulting from lung cancer surgery. [See NIXON Volume]

[JLW]

ACHESON, DEAN G(OODERHAM)
b. April 11, 1893; Middletown, Conn.
d. Oct. 12, 1971; Silver Spring, Md.
Foreign policy adviser.

After graduating from Harvard Law School in 1918, Acheson served as private secretary to Supreme Court Justice Louis Brandeis and then entered private law practice with the Washington firm of Covington and Burling. With the exception of a few months spent as undersecretary of the treasury in 1933, Acheson remained out of government until he was appointed assistant secretary of state in 1941. Four years later he became undersecretary of state. At this post Acheson helped plan the United Nations and formulate the Truman Doctrine for aid to Greece and Turkey and the Marshall Plan for the economic recovery of Europe. [See TRUMAN Volume]

Acheson left the State Department to return to his law practice in 1947 but was recalled to become Secretary of State in 1949. As Secretary he implemented the containment policy toward the Soviet Union which shaped the early American response to the Cold War. Acheson returned to his law practice at the end of the Truman Administration. Despite his advocacy of a strong Cold War posture, he was attacked by conservative Republicans for "losing" China, pursuing a "no-win" policy in Korea and "coddling" Communists in government.

Acheson served as a foreign policy adviser to President Kennedy during the 1961 Berlin and 1962 Cuban missile crises. In both these situations he took a hard-line stand that reflected his postwar philosophy. Acheson recommended the buildup of both nuclear and conventional forces in preparation for what he assumed would be a Soviet-American armed confrontation over Berlin and advocated the use of low-level bombing strikes against the Soviet missile installations discovered in Cuba. [See EISENHOWER, KENNEDY Volume]

In March 1968, following the request of high military officials for over 200,000 additional ground troops for Vietnam, President Johnson asked Acheson to assess the Administration's war policy. Not trusting the briefings given by the Joint Chiefs of Staff, Acheson conducted his own investigation of the situation. Despite his earlier support of the war, Acheson concluded that he could no longer back the policy of seeking military victory. He believed that such a goal was impossible without the application of the nation's total resources and was not consistent with American interests. Acheson recommended that America get out of Vietnam as soon as possible because the public no longer supported the war. He reiterated his position at a meeting of the Senior Advisory Group on Vietnam on March 25 and 26. Acheson's recommendation was one of the factors contributing to Johnson's announcement of de-escalation on March 31, 1968.

Acheson died of a heart attack on Oct. 12, 1971.

[EWS]

ACKLEY, (HUGH) GARDNER

b. June 30, 1915; Indianapolis, Ind. Chairman, President's Council of Economic Advisers, November 1964-January 1968; Ambassador to Italy, January 1968-August 1969.

Gardner Ackley earned his Ph.D in economics from the University of Michigan in 1940. A supporter of the New Deal, he worked for the Office of Price Administration during World War II and served for a year with the Office of Strategic Services. After the war Ackley taught economics at the University of Michigan, becoming a full professor in 1952.

In July 1962 President Kennedy appointed Ackley to the President's Council of Economic Advisers (CEA). Like his colleague, CEA chairman Walter Heller [*q.v.*], Ackley was an enthusiastic proponent of the Keynesian "new economics," which held that the federal government could promote economic growth and maintain price stability through an activist fiscal policy. He played a key role in the formulation of the Administration's wage-price guidelines, which were intended to keep wage increases below 3.2% a year and curb price increases as well. Ackley also supported the massive tax cut proposed by Kennedy and signed by President Johnson in February 1964. In November, upon the outgoing Heller's recommendation, Johnson named Ackley chairman of the CEA.

Ackley's three-year tenure as chairman coincided with a period of economic boom and large budget deficits incurred to finance the Vietnam war. He devoted most of his energy to fighting inflation, chiefly by exhorting business and labor to remain within the wage-price guideposts and by denouncing conspicuous violators of the standards.

The Administration had mixed success in its anti-inflation campaign. When aluminum producers raised their price to 25 cents a pound in the fall of 1965, Ackley denounced the move as "inflationary." He argued that the latest rise brought the total price increase to 11% in 25 months, an unjustified rate since the industry's productivity was "substantially above the average for the economy." The Administration's response went beyond exhortation when Ackley and Secretary of Defense Robert McNamara [*q.v.*] announced on Nov. 6 their intention to release 200,000 tons from the government's stockpile to force down the price of aluminum. On Nov. 10 the producers rescinded their increase.

In January 1966 Bethlehem Steel also reduced a price increase of $5 a ton on structural steel products to $2.75 after Ackley and President Johnson attacked the original figure. In July the American Metal Corporation and the Molybdenum Corporation of America withdrew a 5% increase in the price of molybdenum in response to Administration pressure. Ackley called the rollback "an act of industrial statesmanship." In December 1967 Ackley privately warned General Motors (GM) chairman James Roche [*q.v.*] that the $61-increase in automobile prices planned by GM might provoke the Administration into a public confrontation. "I believe I shook him up a little," Ackley wrote in a memo to Johnson. GM lowered the increase to $23.

Yet, as Ackley admitted in August 1966, the Administration's wage-price program had suffered some "stunning defeats." In August 1966, August 1967 and December 1967, the major steel producers put into effect substantial price increases despite Administration opposition. Ackley criticized the "inflationary" wage settlements that concluded the January 1966 strike of the Transport Workers Union in New York City and averted an American Airlines strike in October of the same year, but his admonitions proved futile in these instances.

Ackley contributed to the confusion surrounding the economic cost of the Vietnam war. In the fall of 1965 he projected the maximum possible increase in the cost of the conflict at $3 to $5 billion, while Sen. John Stennis (D, Miss.) [*q.v.*] and Rep. Mendel Rivers (D, S.C.) [*q.v.*], chairmen of the Senate and House Armed Services Committees, were predicting $10 billion as a more likely figure. After consulting with Secretary of Defense McNamara, Ackley, in a speech before the American Statistical Association, dismissed the $10 billion estimate as unrealistic. In 1972, however, he said that the speech was "a major mistake. Stennis knew more about what the generals were thinking than we knew about what LBJ was thinking."

Ackley played a vital role in persuading President Johnson to seek a tax increase in 1967 to curb inflation. In testimony before the House Ways and Means Committee in August, Ackley said that the increase was necessary to stem a "hectic" expansion in the Gross National Product. Congress delayed passing the proposed 10% surtax until May 1968, however, when the Administration agreed to compensating budget cuts.

In January 1968 Johnson appointed Ackley ambassador to Italy. (Ackley had spent a number of years in Italy studying the Italian economy.) Ackley remained at the post until August 1969, when he resigned and returned to the University of Michigan as a professor of economics. [See NIXON Volume]

[TO]

ADDONIZIO, HUGH J(OSEPH)

b. Jan. 31, 1914; Newark, N.J.
Mayor, Newark, N.J., 1962-70.

The son of Italian immigrants, Addonizio attended Fordham University on an athletic scholarship and upon graduation in 1939 returned to Newark to join his father's clothing business. In 1948 Addonizio was elected to Congress. Strong support from black and Italian voters enabled him to become the first Democrat in half a century repeatedly to win reelection. He resigned from Congress in 1962 and defeated Newark's incumbent Mayor Leo P. Carlin.

Elected as a reformer, the Mayor supported Lyndon Johnson's Great Society programs and during the mid-1960s was praised for keeping Newark "cool" while racial violence beset other large cities. That calm was shattered July 12, 1967 when violence broke out in the predominantly black central ward in response to the arrest of a black taxi driver and subsequent rumors that Newark police had beaten him to death. "Police brutality" was the immediate issue. But black leaders charged the next day that Addonizio's refusal to appoint a black secretary to the school board and the city's selection of a central ward site for the proposed New Jersey College of Medicine and Dentistry, construction of which threatened to destroy black neighborhoods, increased tensions in Newark's black community. On July 14 Addonizio charged that the disorders "might be controlled by people from outside," but two days later U.S. Attorney General Ramsey Clark [*q.v.*] stated there was "little evidence of intercity activity to deliberately activate" the Newark violence. The riots lasted from

July 12 to July 17 and resulted in 26 deaths, 1,500 reported injuries, 1,397 arrests and $10 million in property damage. The Governor's Select Commission on Civil Disorder in New Jersey issued a report Feb. 10, 1968 charging Addonizio with an inability to recognize black bitterness and with indecisiveness. The Commission's recommendations included a grand jury investigation into charges of corruption in Newark's city government.

The grand jury indicted Addonizio and nine current or former municipal administrators on Dec. 18, 1969. On June 2, 1970 Addonizio's trial on 66 counts of conspiracy to extort over $250,000 from a Newark engineering firm began. Despite the trial Addonizio ran for reelection against Kenneth Gibson, a black engineer who had been nominated by a black and Puerto Rican convention in 1969. After a bitterly contested campaign centering on the issues of race and corruption, Gibson defeated Addonizio in the June 16 election. On July 22 Addonizio was found guilty of 64 counts of conspiracy to commit extortion. In September 1970 he was sentenced to 10 years in prison and fined $25,000. [See NIXON Volume]

[DKR]

AGNEW, SPIRO T(HEODORE)
b. Nov. 9, 1918; Baltimore, Md.
Governor, Md., 1967-69.

The beneficiary of liberal support while running for governor of Maryland, Agnew eventually became known as a vigorous supporter of "law and order." He was forced to resign the vice presidency of the United States in 1973 because of crimes committed during and after his governorship. Agnew, the son of a Greek immigrant, attended Baltimore public schools and then entered Johns Hopkins University to study chemistry. Because of a lack of money he transferred to Baltimore Law School, attending classes at night and working during the day. Following service in France and Germany during World War II, he returned to his law studies, earning his degree in 1947. Agnew began to practice law in suburban Maryland but was not successful and was forced to take jobs as an insurance claims adjuster and personnel manager for a supermarket chain.

Originally a Democrat, Agnew became active in Republican politics and local civic affairs on the advice of a law partner who assured him that his political prospects would be better in Maryland's small Republican Party than in the overcrowded Democratic field. In 1957 he was appointed to the Baltimore county zoning board of appeals, but the Democratic majority on the Board blocked his reappointment in 1960. Agnew, charging that the board members were trying to get rid of a man they could not control, used the incident to generate publicity and establish his reputation as a man of integrity.

In 1962 Agnew was elected county executive of Baltimore County on a reform platform. During his tenure teachers' salaries were raised, new schools were built and the county's water supply and sewer systems were improved. Although he had campaigned against racial bias in public places and sponsored a bill requiring equal accommodations in the county. Agnew changed his civil rights position while executive. Angered at their use of civil disobedience and demands for immediate change, he insisted that blacks work through government channels for gradual integration.

Agnew successfully ran for governor of Maryland in 1966. His victory was, in part, the product of dissension within the Democratic Party. Because of bitter infighting the two principal Democratic candidates split the liberal-moderate vote in the primary and the Party's nomination went to George P. Mahoney, a wealthy contractor who campaigned on the segregationist slogan, "A Man's Home is His Castle—Protect It." Against the ultraconservative Mahoney Agnew attracted the support of blacks and liberals who viewed the Republican as the last line of defense against racism in the statehouse.

In addition, Agnew had secretly negotiated a deal with the chairman of the liberal Montgomery County Democratic organization that resulted in the founding of a Democrats for Agnew Committee in the state's wealthiest county. Under the agreement Agnew allowed the Democrats to review all his position papers, promised not to campaign for local Republicans, assumed the financing of the organization and promised local patronage appointments to supporting Democrats. Agnew carried the county, but the patronage agreement was not carried out because the Democrats found it politically compromising.

During his first year in office, Agnew pushed several reform measures through the legislature: a budget making possible increased aid to antipoverty programs and local governments; an open housing law applicable to all but privately owned individual dwellings; repeal of the state law banning racial intermarriage; a graduated state sales tax; a liberalized abortion law and the country's toughest state water pollution law.

By the spring of 1968, however, Agnew had reversed many of his liberal stands. He cut the state budget, particularly spending for health and welfare, and obtained new police powers, including the right to call out the militia in anticipation of an emergency. Agnew was increasingly angered by the tactics of the civil rights movement. Following 1967 riots in Baltimore he scored militant blacks as "Hanoi-visiting, caterwauling, riot-inciting, burn-America-down types." The next year he denounced the 1968 Poor People's March on Washington.

Agnew's shift to the right surprised many political observers. But others believed that Agnew had always been a conservative and had only looked liberal in contrast to Mahoney. Some attributed Agnew's shift to political pragmatism and a desire to take advantage of the conservative mood generated in part by the racial disturbances of 1967 and 1968. Still others attributed his swing to the right to his disillusionment with such Republican moderates as Michigan Gov. George Romney [*q.v.*] and New York Gov. Nelson Rockefeller [*q.v.*], who seemed incapable of or unwilling to lead the nation.

An early backer of Rockefeller for the Republican presidential nomination in 1968, Agnew threw his support behind Richard M. Nixon [*q.v.*] when Rockefeller announced his withdrawal from the presidential race. Agnew placed Nixon's name in nomination at the Republican convention in August 1968, and the next day he became the Party's vice presidential candidate. Nixon's choice of Agnew was generally attributed to his perception of the Governor as a Party "centrist." In Agnew's words, "I was the least offensive to all Republicans." In addition, Nixon hoped that Agnew's Greek background would appeal to many normally Democratic ethnic voters.

During the campaign Agnew became a blunt champion of "law and order." On a number of occasions his spontaneous remarks also made him the subject of ridicule. He lashed out against black militants and anti-war protesters, branded Democratic presidential candidate Sen. Hubert Humphrey (D, Minn.) [*q.v.*] "squishy soft on Communism," called Polish-Americans "Polacks" and referred to a Japanese-American reporter as "the fat Jap." In the November balloting the Republican ticket received 43.48% of the popular vote; the Democratic ticket 42.97%. The Nixon-Agnew team won 302 out of 538 electoral votes.

During his term in office Agnew became Nixon's "hard-line" spokesman, attacking opponents of the Vietnam war, reporters and intellectuals. He also voiced the Administration's belief that American values were threatened by the social turbulence and "permissiveness" of the period. Reelected with Nixon in 1972 Agnew resigned his office on Oct. 10, 1973 following revelations that a Baltimore grand jury had uncovered massive evidence of personal corruption while he was governor and vice president. According to the report made public at his trial, Agnew, shortly after becoming governor in 1967, accepted payments from engineering firms in turn for state contracts. The document also detailed an arrangement by which the presidents of two engineering firms made direct cash payments to Agnew while he was governor and vice president. According to the grand jury, these payments totaled about $100,000. Agnew pleaded *nolo contendere* to a lesser plea of income tax evasion at his

Oct. 10 trial. He was fined $10,000 and placed on three years unsupervised probation. [See NIXON Volume]

[EWS]

For further information:

Richard M. Cohen and Jules Witcover, *A Heartbeat Away: The Investigation and Resignation of Vice President Spiro T. Agnew* (New York, 1974).

Jules Witcover, *White Knight: The Rise of Spiro Agnew* (New York, 1972).

AIKEN, GEORGE D(AVID)

b. Aug. 30, 1892; Dummerston, Vt.
Republican Senator, Vt., 1941-75.

Aiken owned a Vermont nursery business for many years and became one of the nation's leading experts in the commercial cultivation of wild flowers. In 1930 he was elected to the Vermont House of Representatives. He became speaker of the House in 1933 and two years later was elected lieutenant governor. Aiken was governor of Vermont from 1937 to 1941. He was elected to the U.S. Senate in 1940 and over the next 34 years had little difficulty winning reelection. [See TRUMAN, EISENHOWER, KENNEDY Volumes]

Aiken was generally associated with the moderate wing of the Republican Party, though his voting record was difficult to categorize. In the early 1960s he voted for the Kennedy Administration's minimum wage and school aid bills. He opposed medicare in 1962 but three years later voted for the Johnson Administration's health care measure. In the mid-1960s Aiken's voting pattern remained unpredictable. The liberal Americans for Democratic Action gave him a 35% rating in 1965 and a 66% rating in 1966.

During the 1960s Aiken served on the Senate Foreign Relations and Joint Atomic Energy Committees. As the ranking Republican on the Senate Agriculture and Forestry Committee, his advocacy of the food stamp program was significant. This program, he argued, had greatly improved the health of many Americans who were "unable to get enough of the right kind of food to live decently." In 1964 Aiken helped win approval of an Administration-sponsored bill placing the food stamp program on a permanent footing. Long an advocate of federal aid to rural communities, Aiken sponsored legislation authorizing $55 million for the development of rural water-supply and waste-disposal systems in 1965. This measure was initially opposed by the Bureau of the Budget, but in August 1965 President Johnson endorsed the Aiken bill, which then passed both houses and was signed into law.

In August 1964 Aiken, "with misgivings," voted for the Gulf of Tonkin Resolution giving the President broad authority to use military force in Southeast Asia. However, in April 1965 Aiken denounced U.S. bombing of North Vietnam, arguing that it would stiffen rather than weaken the North's will to resist. In November of that year Aiken and four other senators conducted a "fact-finding" tour of South Vietnam and returned with a pessimistic appraisal of the situation. Aiken believed that the presence of U.S. troops in South Vietnam had prevented the North from overrunning the country, but he thought that in the long run the Administration should seek a "political" rather than a military solution to the Vietnamese conflict. In a widely publicized speech delivered to the Senate on Oct. 19, 1966, Aiken proposed that the U.S. declare that "we have 'won' [the war] in the sense that our Armed Forces are in control of the field and no potential enemy is in a position to establish its authority in South Vietnam." Such a declaration, said Aiken, should be accompanied by gradual redeployment of U.S. military forces around strategic centers and the substitution of intensive reconnaissance for bombing.

Despite his opposition to an escalation of the war, Aiken continued to vote for bills to fund the military effort. To do otherwise, he believed, would be to disarm our troops in the field. In May 1967 Aiken declared that the Administration "cannot achieve an honorable peace in Vietnam" and called for the Republican Party to develop an alternative to President Johnson's policies. Because most Republicans supported the Administration, little came of Aiken's appeal.

Despite his outspoken stand on Vietnam,

Aiken remained an immensely popular figure in Vermont. In 1968 he won overwhelming victories in both the Republican and Democratic primaries and was unchallenged in the general election.

Aiken urged the U.S. to begin pulling its troops out of Vietnam in May 1969; a year later he voted for the Cooper-Church Amendment barring the President from sending funds to maintain U.S. troops in Cambodia. [See NIXON Volume]

When Aiken retired from the Senate in 1975, he was 82 and the chamber's oldest member.

[JLW]

ALBERT, CARL (BERT)

b. May 10, 1908; McAlester, Okla.
Democratic Representative, Okla., 1947-77; House Majority Leader, 1962-71.

Albert was the son of a poor cotton farmer and coal miner. He graduated Phi Beta Kappa from the University of Oklahoma in 1931 and received a Rhodes Scholarship to study at Oxford University, where he earned two law degrees. In 1946, after practicing law and serving in the Army, Albert won a seat in the U.S. House of Representatives from Oklahoma's impoverished third district.

In Congress Albert consistently backed both liberal welfare measures and legislation favored by the oil industry, which was a major interest in his state. Albert uniformly supported the House leadership. From his earliest days as a representative, the congressman later recalled, he carefully observed the operations of the House to familiarize himself with its procedures and with the voting patterns of its members.

Impressed by Albert's loyalty and diligence, Speaker Sam Rayburn (D, Tex.) and Majority Leader John W. McCormack (D, Mass.) [*q.v.*] tapped him to serve as majority whip in 1955. As whip his function was rounding up votes for positions favored by the House Democratic leadership. In January 1962, following the death of Rayburn, McCormack was elevated to the speakership and Albert was chosen majority leader. His responsibilities in that post included devising Democratic floor strategy and speaking on behalf of Administration programs. [See EISENHOWER, KENNEDY Volumes]

As majority whip and later as majority leader, Albert shunned publicity and employed quiet, behind-the-scenes persuasion in his efforts to secure the passage of legislation. His critics believed that more forceful methods would produce greater results, but Albert felt that the representatives, and particularly the powerful committee chairmen, could not be compelled to act as he wished and that the excessive use of pressure would create antagonism towards the Democratic leadership. However, during the Johnson Administration he sometimes used power rather than persuasion when important bills faced serious obstacles in the House. In 1964 President Johnson was pressing intensively for the passage of his antipoverty program but found strong resistance in the lower chamber. Albert spoke to the committee chairmen who handled public works bills and suggested the possibility of blocking pending projects in the districts of those representatives opposed to the program. This step, observers believed, helped to secure the votes needed to pass the antipoverty bill in August 1964.

Albert was one of the leading legislative defenders of President Johnson's domestic programs. In October 1965 he praised the first session of the 89th Congress, which had adopted more Administration bills than were usually passed in two sessions, as "the most significant in all our history." During March 1966, in reply to attacks on Great Society programs, Albert said that Republicans "have been blind for 35 years . . . blind in their opposition to progressive legislation; blind in their concern for human beings. . . ."

Believing that Congress should play a secondary role to the chief executive in the shaping of foreign policy, Albert was a strong supporter of Administration foreign policy. In January 1965 he opposed a House amendment to cut off aid to Egypt, asserting, "The issue here is whether a matter of major foreign policy should be determined by legislative action . . . without the advice, the information and the help of the President in his handling of this delicate international matter." He backed President Johnson's Vietnam policies, and many observers felt that Albert, as chairman of the 1968 Democratic National Convention in Chicago, ruled arbitrarily against the motions of delegates supporting the anti-war presidential candidacies of Sens. Eugene J. McCarthy (D, Minn.) [*q.v.*] and George S. McGovern (D, S.D.) [*q.v.*].

During the Nixon presidency Albert continued to back Administration policies in Indochina but opposed the Republican President's domestic programs. In the early 1970s he backed such congressional reforms as the recorded teller vote, the wider dispersion of House chairmanships and disclosure of campaign contributions. In 1971 Albert succeeded McCormack as Speaker of the House. He subsequently came under attack from liberal Democrats for not articulating coherent policy alternatives to the programs of the Republican Administration. [See NIXON Volume]

[MLL]

ALEXANDER, CLIFFORD L.

b. Sept. 21, 1933; New York, N.Y.
Chairman, Equal Employment Opportunities Commission, June 1967-April 1969.

After graduating from Harvard in 1955 and from Yale Law School in 1958, Alexander served as assistant district attorney for New York County. He then entered private law practice in New York City. Alexander served in several antipoverty programs, including Haryou, Inc., where he was executive and program director from 1962 to 1963. At the request of McGeorge Bundy [*q.v.*], Alexander joined the staff of the National Security Council in 1963. From 1964 to 1967 he successively held posts as deputy special assistant, associate special counsel and deputy special counsel to the President, serving as an adviser to Johnson on various domestic problems, including civil rights.

On June 27, 1967 Alexander was named chairman of the Equal Employment Opportunities Commission (EEOC), the agency established by the 1964 Civil Rights Act to help end job discrimination by unions and industry. With Senate confirmation of his appointment on Aug. 2, Alexander became the first black to head the Commission. Because the agency lacked the power to force industries to end discrimination and could use only conciliation to settle disputes, Alexander relied on publicity and pressure to prompt businesses to hire minorities. In two October 1967 studies, for example, the Commission reported the existence of widespread discrimination against blacks in the nation's drug industry and in white-collar jobs. During January 1968 Alexander held four days of hearings documenting discrimination in New York City's white-collar occupations, particularly in the financial and communications industries. At the conclusion of the investigation, he charged: "If future intentions were gauged by the past standard of performance, it would mean that Negroes and Puerto Ricans would probably be waiting until the year 2164 for a democracy to say what he or she shall have."

Alexander's efforts led to criticism from business and congressional leaders. In March 1969 Sen. Everett M. Dirksen (R, Ill.) [*q.v.*] threatened to "get somebody fired" if the Commission did not stop "punitive harassment" of businessmen. On April 9 Alexander resigned as chairman of the EEOC because of what he termed "a crippling lack of [Nixon] Administration support." However, he remained a member of the Commission. Two weeks later Jerris Leonard, head of the Justice Department civil rights division, charged that the Commission had been ineffective under Alexander, and without naming him directly, called for his resignation as a member of the agency. Alexander remained on the panel until Aug. 8, when he resigned to become a partner in the Washington, D.C. law firm of Arnold & Porter. In September 1974 he made an unsuccessful attempt to win the Democratic mayoral nomination in Washington.

[CAB]

ALI, MUHAMMAD

b. Jan. 17, 1942; Louisville, Ky.
Professional boxer.

Muhammad Ali was born Cassius Marcellus Clay, Jr., in Louisville, Ky. Encouraged at the age of 12 to take up boxing, Clay fought successfully for six years as an amateur. In 1960 he won an Olympic gold medal in the light heavyweight division and turned professional shortly thereafter. From the outset of his career Clay aroused and encouraged controversy by his bragging predictions of victory—often delivered in doggerel—and skillful bantering with sports writers.

The day after his stunning seventh round victory over heavyweight champion Sonny Liston in February 1964, Clay announced that he had become a Black Muslim and had dropped his "slave name" of Clay for the name Muhammad Ali. The next month the World Boxing Association (WBA) refused to recognize Ali as the heavyweight champion, ostensibly because of his zealous promotional efforts before the Liston fight. The WBA action, however, did not deter a Liston-Ali rematch in May 1965, which Ali won with a knockout in the first round.

During the next two years Ali defended his heavyweight crown eight times, scoring easy victories in each and building a reputation as one of the greatest heavyweight boxers in history. On April 28, 1967 in Houston, Tex., Ali refused induction into the Army on the grounds that he was a full-time Black Muslim minister and, therefore, exempt from the draft. His feelings about the war in Vietnam were already widely known and quoted: "We [Muslims] don't go to wars unless they are declared by Allah himself. I don't have no personal quarrel with those Viet Congs." The same day that he refused induction, Ali was stripped of his world heavyweight title by both the WBA and the New York Boxing Commission, whose chairman declared that Ali's "refusal to enter the service is regarded by the Commission to be detrimental to the best interests of boxing." After being denied conscientious objector status, Ali was convicted by a federal jury in Houston, Tex., on June 20, 1967 of violating the Selective Service laws. He was given the maximum penalty of five years in jail and a $10,000 fine.

Following the verdict Ali's career went into a three-and-one-half year hiatus pending legal appeals. During this period Ali's militant stand against both the draft and the Vietnam war provoked considerable animosity throughout the country. Conservative columnist William F. Buckley, Jr. [*q.v.*], called for "someone to succeed in knocking sense into Clay's head before he's done damaging the sport." Many sports reporters also joined in condemning Ali's action.

As a result of increased public interest and intensive negotiations with officials, Ali returned to boxing in 1970. On Oct. 26 he defeated Jerry Quarry in Atlanta in his first fight since 1967. Two months later Ali stopped Argentine heavyweight Oscar Bonavena, but in March 1971, in what was billed as the "Fight of the Century," he suffered his first ring defeat when he was outpointed by WBA heavyweight champion Joe Frazier in a fight that went 15 rounds in Madison Square Garden and earned $2.5 million for Ali.

On June 28, 1971 a unanimous U.S. Supreme Court voted to reverse Ali's draft conviction and prison sentence. The Court ruled that the Selective Service had refused to grant Ali conscientious objector status due to advice from the Justice Department that "was simply wrong as a matter of law."

Ali regained his world heavyweight boxing title on Oct. 30, 1974 with an eighth round knockout of George Foreman in Kinshasa, Zaire.

[FHM]

Muhammad Ali, *The Greatest* (New York, 1975).

ALINSKY, SAUL D(AVID)

b. Jan. 30, 1909; Chicago, Ill.
d. June 12, 1972; Chicago, Ill.
Social activist, 1938-72.

Born in a Chicago slum tenement, Alinsky studied sociology at the University of Chicago, where he was awarded a graduate fellowship. After working briefly as a criminologist, Alinsky worked with John L. Lewis during the Congress of Industrial Organization's formative years. An admirer and biographer of Lewis, Alinsky was nevertheless convinced that his own role lay outside the labor movement. In 1938 he moved into "Back of the Yards," an Irish neighborhood behind the Chicago stockyards. There he formed the Back of the Yards Council and employed direct action tactics such as picketing and rent strikes to win concessions from meat packing companies, landlords and the local political machine. With the backing of philanthropist Marshall Field III, Alinsky founded the Industrial Areas Foundation in 1940. During the next two decades his foundation "contracted" to build community organizations in poor communities across the country. In the 1950s Alinsky received a contract from the Bishop of Milan, later Pope Paul VI, to organize anti-Communist labor unions in Italy.

Alinsky made his first attempt to organize a Chicago black ghetto in 1960, out of which grew The Woodlawn Organization (TWO) on Chicago's South Side. Organized in opposition to urban renewal plans, TWO developed into a multi-issue organization that Charles Silberman, author of *Crisis in Black and White*, described in 1964 as "the most significant social experiment going on among Negroes today."

In 1965 the Rochester Council of Churches invited Alinsky to organize Rochester's black community. He created Freedom, Integration, God, Honor—Today (FIGHT), an organization that won some concessions from corporations in the hiring and training of blacks and formal recognition as the voice of Rochester's black poor. During FIGHT's struggle with Eastman Kodak over the corporation's job training program, Alinsky first sought to use stock proxies as a source of leverage against the company. In March 1967 FIGHT bought 10 shares of Kodak stock and sent out letters to 700 clergymen and civil rights organizations requesting that they persuade other shareholders to withhold their proxies at the April 25 stockholders meeting. Alinsky told Marion Sanders, who interviewed him for *Harper's Magazine*, that the proxies "turned out to be our major weapon in getting Kodak to deal with FIGHT."

Believing that social change would come from only a well organized majority, Alinsky turned his attention to organizing the middle class, which he thought included almost 80% of America's population. In August 1968 he announced the establishment of the Mid-America Institute to train representatives of the middle class to organize in their own communities. The same year Alinsky launched an anti-pollution drive in Chicago. Alinsky outlined his strategy for middle class organizing in *Rules for Radicals*, published in 1971. Until his death in 1972 Alinsky continued to train organizers at his institute.

[DKR]

ALIOTO, JOSEPH (LAWRENCE)

b. Feb. 12, 1916; San Francisco, Calif.
Mayor, San Francisco, Calif., 1968-76.

Alioto's Sicilian immigrant father was the founder of the prosperous International Fish Company in San Francisco. After taking a B.A. at St. Mary's College and a law degree at the Catholic University of America, Alioto worked in Washington during the war for the Justice Department's Antitrust Division and later for the Board of Economic Warfare. He returned to San Francisco after the war and opened what was to become one of the nation's largest law firms specializing in antitrust cases. Alioto counted movie magnates Samuel Goldwyn and Walt Disney among his clients and won victories against the price fixing of electrical equipment, children's books and chemicals. He was also a successful businessman, sat on the San Francisco Board of Education, helped direct the city's urban renewal program, advised the governments of Hawaii and Puerto Rico and helped develop the federal Food for Peace program.

Although an active Democrat Alioto showed little interest in public office until 1967, when State Sen. Eugene McAteer, the Democratic favorite to win San Francisco's mayoral contest, died two months before the election. The incumbent Democrat, John L. Shelley, encouraged Alioto to replace McAteer in competition with 17 other candidates. With the backing of San Francisco labor and the "downtown" business interests, Alioto campaigned as a moderate Democrat, voicing support for President Johnson's Vietnam policy and promising both strict law enforcement and new social programs. He won a landslide victory, getting 15,000 more votes than his closest opponent and running extremely well among minority groups and working-class people.

Alioto took office during a strike against San Francisco's two major newspapers. He appointed a mediator, and in late February he was able to announce an end to the 52-day walkout. His most notable efforts, however, were devoted to answering the needs of the city's minorities. He increased the number of minority group members employed by the city's civil service and encouraged and sometimes pressured unions and businesses to hire more blacks, Chicanos and other minorities. In order to forestall the summer violence that had engulfed other cities, Alioto, like New York Mayor John Lindsay [*q.v.*], took well-publicized walks through the ghettos, tried to expand summertime employment for minority teenagers and initiated a summer program of sports, entertainment and cultural activities. He soon became a national figure, recognized as one of the most persuasive spokesmen for the needs of the cities. Many of his prescriptions for urban ills were consistent with President Johnson's Great Society programs, but he also advocated augmenting the authority of urban governments so that they could deal more effectively with their special problems. Recognizing that the migration of middle and working-class groups to the suburbs was largely responsible for urban decay, he recommended taxing suburbanites who worked in the city and reducing real estate taxes for urban homeowners. Alioto was portrayed so favorably in the press during his first seven months in office that he was considered a possible Democratic vice-presidential candidate and was chosen to deliver the nominating speech for Hubert H. Humphrey [*q.v.*] at the Democratic National Convention in August.

When black militants and other radicals disrupted the San Francisco State College campus in the autumn of 1968 because of the dismissal of a black instructor, Alioto collaborated with the school's acting president, Dr. S. I. Hayakawa, to keep order on the campus. He also sought the cooperation of community leaders to settle the crisis. Although Alioto's actions cost him some support on the left, he and Hayakawa proved that relatively liberal Democrats could be as "tough" with dissidents as conservatives such as California Gov. Ronald Reagan [*q.v.*] without resorting to their extremes of rhetoric. Some observers have suggested that Alioto's conduct may have blunted the appeal of extreme right-wingers to the California electorate.

Alioto was considered a strong contender for the Democratic gubernatorial nomination in 1970, but allegations appearing in a 1969 *Look* magazine article that he had ties to the Mafia led him to announce in January 1970 that he would not seek the nomination. Two subsequent indictments, one on charges of interstate racketeering and the other on charges of fee-splitting, further damaged his reputation. He won his 1971 reelection bid by almost 30,000 votes and survived the indictments, but he failed in his efforts to win the gubernatorial nomination in 1974. Unable to run for a third mayoral term because of a state law, Alioto stepped down as mayor in January 1976. [See NIXON Volume]

[JCH]

ALLEN, IVAN, JR.

b. March 15, 1911; Atlanta, Ga.
Mayor, Atlanta, Ga., 1961-69.

Upon graduating from the Georgia Institute of Technology in 1933, Allen entered his father's successful office supply company in Atlanta. His aggressive entrepreneurial efforts increased the profits of the firm and enabled him to accumulate a large fortune. He played an active role in the affairs of the business community, culminating in his election to the presidency of the city's Chamber of Commerce in 1960.

Allen was also active politically. He served as executive secretary to liberal Georgia Gov. Ellis Arnall immediately following World War II, and in 1954 he briefly entered the race for governor but withdrew when he failed to attract sufficient support. In a series of speeches associated with this abortive effort, Allen stated the conventional Southern view of segregation, defending it as a fundamental part of the region's way of life.

Allen's position on segregation changed during the next decade. He belonged to a dynamic, powerful and politically active local business community that was more interested in promoting the economic growth of Atlanta than in defending traditional Southern social mores. He ran, with black support, in the 1961 Democratic mayoral primary against arch-segregationist Lester Maddox [*q.v.*] and became Atlanta's mayor later that year.

Allen used his influence to integrate many of the city's public facilities, particularly after black and white college students staged anti-segregation sit-ins in restaurants and hotels during the spring of 1963. In July of that year Allen, testifying before the Senate Commerce Committee, became the only major Southern white politician to back the Kennedy Administration's bill for the desegregation of public accomodations. The Atlanta Mayor declared, "I am firmly convinced that the Supreme Court insists that the same fundamental rights must be held by every American citizen." [See KENNEDY Volume]

Allen was reelected in 1965 with 70% of the vote, but substantial tension between the city administration and the black community developed during his second term. The problems of the high rate of black unemployment and of segregated housing proved to be less tractable than those associated with the integration of public facilities. According to a National Opinion Research Center survey of 1966, only 3.8% of Atlanta's whites lived in integrated neighborhoods. An Equal Employment Opportunity Commission study made the following year indicated the unemployment rate in the city's black ghettoes was 15.5% in comparison to the overall city figure of 2.6%.

In Atlanta, as in Northern cities, the persistence of these conditions, despite the gains of the civil rights movement, produced growing discontent. The shooting of blacks by Atlanta policemen sparked riots in 1966 and 1967. Allen gained national prominence in September 1966 by entering the violence-stricken areas and appealing to the rioters to disperse. Denouncing black militant opponents of nonviolence as vehemently as he had condemned segregationists in previous years, he charged that Stokely Carmichael [*q.v.*] and other leaders of the Student Nonviolent Coordinating Committee were responsible for inciting the disturbances and declared that "if Stokely Carmichael is looking for a battleground . . . he'll be met in whatever situation he creates."

But Allen had not abandoned his racial liberalism. He agreed with the conclusions of the 1968 report of President Johnson's National Advisory Commission on Civil Disorders, which cited poverty as the principal cause of black riots. In March of that year he asserted, "We are responsible for the condition the Negro is in today." Allen supported the report's recommendation of massive federal programs to eliminate urban slums. A month later he reaffirmed his sympathy for the civil rights movement, stating that the assassination of Martin Luther King [*q.v.*] "takes from Atlanta one of its greatest citizens."

In the summer of 1969 Allen gave his backing to President Nixon's proposals for sharing federal revenues with local governments, but the Mayor said he did not think the amount of aid being offered was sufficient to cope with urban problems. Earlier in the year Allen had announced that, for personal reasons, he would not seek reelection in 1969.

[MLL]

For further information:

Reese Cleghorn, "Allen of Atlanta Collides with Black Power and White Racism." *The New York Times Magazine* (Oct. 16, 1966), p. 33+.

ALLEN, JAMES E(DWARD), JR.
b. April 25, 1911; Elkins, W. Va.
d. Oct. 16, 1971; Peace Springs, Ariz.
Commissioner of Education, N.Y., 1955-69.

After receiving his B.A. from Elkins College in 1932, James E. Allen, Jr., worked for six years in the West Virginia State Department of Education. He left to study educational administration at Harvard, where he earned a Ph.D. in 1945. Two years later he joined the New York State Department of Education. In 1955 Allen became commissioner of education, an office with broad powers in the administration and planning of the state's numerous local school systems and universities.

Allen established a liberal record in the civil rights field. He opposed the existence of de facto segregation through maintenance of district boundaries that systematically partitioned black and white student populations. In the summer of 1963 Allen directed all New York school systems with districts having black enrollments of more than 50% to submit plans designed to reduce such racial imbalances. Most local boards and administrators immediately complied with the Commissioner's ruling. [See KENNEDY Volume]

Allen's enforcement of the Supreme Court's call for equal access to education made him a controversial leader in school administration. He ordered school boards that attempted to maintain segregated facilities over the period to draw up new school district boundaries. He then evaluated the newly demarcated school districts' racial balance. After a prolonged disagreement with the Mount Vernon board, Allen issued a June 1968 plan for that city's system. Allen's order required the busing of all pupils, including those in elementary schools, by age instead of by neighborhood. The Mount Vernon board successfully reversed Allen's plan in the state appeals court in July 1969.

In 1968 Allen became embroiled in the struggle over decentralization of New York City's million-student school system. Beginning in September 1966 black parents and community leaders had demanded greater control over the operation of their neighborhood schools. In response, a special task force set up by the mayor and chaired by Ford Foundation President McGeorge Bundy [*q.v.*] proposed a local governing board committee scheme, establishing community school boards representative of each neighborhood's population. Allen endorsed the Bundy plan.

A quarrel between the Ocean Hill-Brownsville board and the United Federation of Teachers (UFT) over the transfer of personnel began in March 1968. It resulted in two citywide UFT strikes in September. At the request of the city board, Allen entered into the negotiations among the UFT, city officials and black community leaders. Two months and one more UFT walkout later, Allen obtained a settlement that placed the Ocean Hill board in a state of indefinite suspension while restricting the neighborhood panel's authority to reassign teachers and principals.

In February 1969 President Richard M. Nixon bewildered many of his conservative followers by appointing Allen U.S. Commissioner of Education. By strictly enforcing federal guidelines for school desegregation, Allen earned the displeasure of the President, and Nixon fired him in June 1970. Allen and his wife died in a plane crash in October 1971. [See NIXON Volume]

[JLB]

ALLOTT, GORDON (LLEWELLYN)
b. Jan. 2, 1907; Pueblo, Colo.
Republican Senator, Colo., 1955-73.

A native in a state of transients, Gordon Allott received his law degree from the University of Colorado in 1929 and five years later entered politics as chairman of the Colorado State Young Republican League. During World War II Allott saw action with the Army Air Force in the South Pacific. He won election as lieutenant governor of Colorado in 1950 and upset a popular Democrat for the U.S. Senate four years later. In a successful campaign for reelection in 1960, Allott captured 53.5% of the vote. Allott voted against most of the Kennedy Administration's domestic programs and led the Senate opposition to the President's wilderness preservation legislation. [See EISENHOWER, KENNEDY Volumes]

With the exception of civil rights legislation, Allott voted as a conservative Republican through the Johnson years. He supported cloture to end the Southern Democrats' filibuster against the 1964 civil rights bill in June and spoke out in favor of the measure's controversial provision granting federal agencies the right to cut off funds to states or localities guilty of discriminatory practices. Allott remarked in June that the bill "represents nothing if we continue to use the taxes of this country for the benefit of one group." He supported the 1965 Voting Rights Act and the 1968 open housing law, although he voted for an amendment to the 1968 bill that would have limited its jurisdiction to apartments and condominiums.

Allott opposed much of the rest of the President's domestic legislative program. In January 1965 he condemned the aid to Appalachia bill, declaring that if it were enacted, "federal funds will gush forth without restraint of reason." He voted against medicare in July 1965 and the effort to repeal Section 14(b) of the Taft-Hartley Act in October. He led an unsuccessful move to reduce appropriations for the Administration's Model Cities program in September 1967, but he succeeded in cutting 4% from the Model Cities appropriation in July 1968. The liberal Americans for Democratic Action (ADA) gave Allott a 42% rating on selected issues during the 1964 session dominated by the civil rights debate, but Allott's ADA rating fell to 15% or less in each of the next four years. The ADA's conservative counterpart, the Americans for Constitutional Action, gave Allott an 86% rating in 1968.

Allott supported appropriations for American intervention in Vietnam in 1965 and 1966. During his successful campaign for reelection in 1966, he clearly identified his candidacy with the war's more "hawkish" proponents. "Our aim must be directed more by our military leaders than civilians," Allott declared in opposition to "another Korean stalemate." In September 1967, however, Allott joined nine other Senators in endorsing a proposal by Senate Majority Leader Mike Mansfield (D, Mont.) [*q.v.*] that called for the U. S. to seek a negotiated settlement in Vietnam through the United Nations.

Allott worked against the appointment of Associate Justice Abe Fortas [*q.v.*] as Chief Justice in 1968. In June he joined 18 other Republican Senators in opposition to the Fortas nomination despite its endorsement by Senate Minority Leader Everett M. Dirksen (R, Ill.) [*q.v.*]. Allott argued in September that the help Fortas gave the Administration in drafting legislation to provide Secret Service protection for presidential candidates indicated his inability to separate his judicial responsibilities from the executive branch. Allott questioned the unusual decision of Chief Justice Earl Warren to step down only upon the selection of a successor. Led by Sen. Robert P. Griffin (R, Mich.) [*q.v.*], the anti-Fortas forces succeeded in blocking the appointment. In December Warren agreed to retire after the inauguration of Richard M. Nixon.

Allott won the chairmanship of the Senate Republican Conference (Policy) Committee in January 1969, becoming an official member of the Party's Senate power structure. Despite appeals to his constituents based upon his seniority and prestige, Allott lost his campaign for reelection in 1972 to Floyd Haskell, a former Republican turned Democrat, who opposed the Vietnam war. [See NIXON Volume]

[JLB]

ANDERSON, CLINTON P(RESBA)

b. Oct. 23, 1895; Centerville, S.D.
d. Nov. 11, 1975; Albuquerque, N.M.
Democratic Senator, N.M., 1949-73.
Chairman, Aeronautical and Space Sciences Committee, 1963-73.

A native of South Dakota, Anderson went to Dakota Wesleyan and the University of Michigan. He was rejected for service in World War I because he was suffering from tuberculosis. At the age of 22 he settled in New Mexico, where the climate helped him recuperate. Between 1918 and 1922 Anderson worked as a reporter for the *Albuquerque Journal* and helped uncover evidence relating to the Teapot Dome scandal. In 1922 he entered the insurance business and three years later became the owner of his own agency.

In 1933 the governor of New Mexico appointed Anderson to the post of state treasurer following the death of the incumbent. He later served as an administrator of New Deal relief and unemployment compensation programs in New Mexico, serving as head of the New Mexican Relief Administration during 1935, state representative of the Federal Emergency Relief Administration from 1935 to 1936 and chairman and executive director of the Unemployment Compensation Commission of New Mexico from 1936 to 1938. Anderson won election to Congress in 1940 and served three terms. Early in 1945 he headed a congressional probe concerning food shortages; his report so impressed President Harry S Truman that he appointed Anderson Secretary of Agriculture in the spring of 1945. Anderson held the post for three years. He won election to the Senate in 1948 and served for the next 23 years. [See TRUMAN, EISENHOWER Volumes]

During the 1960s Anderson's influence was based on his seniority, his important committee chairmanships and close ties to both the Kennedy and Johnson Administrations. Anderson was particularly close to President Johnson, with whom he established friendly relations when Johnson was serving in the Senate. Anderson was widely regarded as one of the more liberal members of a group of senators who wielded significant power. This liberal reputation was based on his support for the domestic legislation of the two Democratic Administrations, his efforts to gain the passage of civil rights and social welfare bills by changing Rule 22 to allow the Senate to end filibusters with less than a two-thirds majority and his sponsorship of medicare legislation. [See KENNEDY Volume]

Between 1961 and 1964 Anderson, a ranking member of the Senate Finance Committee, and Rep. Cecil R. King (D, Calif.) sponsored legislation to raise Social Security taxes to provide hospital care for the elderly. Their bill won the support of both the Kennedy and Johnson Administrations but was defeated because of the stiff opposition of the American Medical Association and Rep. Wilbur Mills (D, Ark.) [*q. v.*], the conservative chairman of the House Ways and Means Committee. Following the sweeping congressional victory of the Democrats in 1964, Rep. Mills abandoned his opposition, and a version of the King-Anderson bill became law in the summer of 1965.

Anderson became chairman of the Senate Aeronautical and Space Sciences Committee in January 1963 and held the post for nine years. He was an enthusiastic supporter of the space program and generously supported National Aeronautics and Space Administration (NASA) requests for increased funds. In 1967 Anderson chaired a Senate panel probing the causes of a Jan. 27 launchpad fire that had killed three astronauts during a ground-flight simulation test. On May 12 Anderson stated that complacent management and "admitted overconfidence by NASA and North American [Corp.] based on past successes, proved fatal."

Anderson maintained a long-standing interest in atomic energy. From 1959 to 1961 he chaired the Joint Congressional Committee on Atomic Energy and remained an influential member of that Committee throughout the decade. In 1966 Anderson prevailed upon President Johnson to extend the tour of duty of Vice Admiral Hyman G. Rickover [*q.v.*] when the Navy attempted to force the controversial developer of the atomic submarine into retirement.

Anderson supported the Administration's Vietnam war policy, favored large-scale military appropriations and opposed rigorous gun-control legislation. As a result of such stands, the liberal Americans for Democratic Action, which had accorded Anderson a 80% rating in 1961, gave him only 21% in 1968.

In ill health, Anderson retired from the Senate in 1972. He died three years later at the age of 80.

[JLW]

ANDERSON, JACK(SON) NORTHMAN

b. Oct. 19, 1922; Long Beach, Calif.
Syndicated columnist.

Jack Anderson described himself as the son of "strait-laced, honest, salt-of-the-earth Mormons." He grew up in Salt Lake City, Utah, worked on the church-owned *Deseret News* and briefly attended the University of Utah before serving as a civilian war correspondent during World War II. Drafted into the Army in 1945, Anderson was discharged in 1947 and the same year obtained a job on the Washington staff of the widely syndicated muckraking columnist Drew Pearson [*q.v.*]. Rarely credited for his contributions to the *Washington Merry-Go-Round* during the 1950s and early 1960s, Anderson was finally granted an equal byline with Pearson in 1965.

In June 1965 two employes of the powerful Sen. Thomas Dodd (D, Conn.) [*q.v.*] turned over to Anderson nearly 6,000 documents that indicated the Senator had used his political influence to promote the private interests of Chicago public relations man Julius Klein. The documents also revealed that Dodd had converted tax-free campaign contributions to his personal use. Anderson subsequently wrote 98 of over 100 columns concerning the Dodd affair that appeared under the Pearson-Anderson byline during the next few years. Dodd filed a 14-count, $5 million libel and conspiracy suit against Pearson and Anderson. The charges leveled against the Connecticut Senator were so serious that on June 20, 1966 the Senate Select Committee on Standards and Conduct opened hearings on Dodd's misconduct. The Committee's lengthy investigation resulted in Dodd's formal censure on June 23, 1967 by a vote of 92-5. In 1970 Dodd was unseated by Republican Sen. Lowell Weicker.

Anderson also collaborated with Pearson on the best-selling 1968 book, *The Case Against Congress*, an indictment of corruption in Washington that concentrated on abuses of power and privilege as well as the foibles of individual congressmen. After Pearson's death in September 1969, Anderson took over the column, which by then was syndicated in 650 papers. The differences in journalistic approach between Pearson and Anderson were immediately evident. While Pearson had often reported mere personal gossip concerning public figures, Anderson sought to direct the column toward matters of greater substance. After Anderson took over *Washington Merry-Go-Round*, he instructed his assistants to keep their distance from politicians and avoid White House functions or social meetings with informants.

In 1972 Anderson was responsible for two journalistic "scoops," the publication of secret papers showing that President Nixon wanted the U.S. to "tilt" toward Pakistan in the India-Pakistan war over Bangladesh and a report by Anderson that the Justice Department had settled an antitrust suit in favor of International Telephone and Telegraph Corporation (ITT) at about the same time the Corporation had pledged $400,000 to the forthcoming Republican National Convention in San Diego. Subsequently, Anderson was active, through his columns, in probing the events surrounding the Watergate affair. [See NIXON Volume]

[FHM]

For further information:
Drew Pearson and Jack Anderson, *The Case Against Congress* (New York, 1968).

ANDERSON, ROBERT B(ERNARD)

b. June 4, 1910; Burleson, Tex.
Businessman, presidential adviser.

Anderson grew up on a farm in Texas and taught high school after graduating from college in 1927. In 1932 he was elected to the state legislature on the same day he graduated from the University of Texas Law School. After serving as the state tax commissioner and chairman of the Texas Unemployment Commission, Anderson became general attorney for the W. T. Waggoner estate, a huge conglomerate whose operations included livestock raising, oil refining and the handling of stock and bond investments. He frequently appeared before Congress as a lobbyist for oil interests.

The conservative Anderson held several

high positions in the Eisenhower Administration: Secretary of the Navy from 1953 to 1954, deputy secretary of defense from 1954 to 1955 and Secretary of the Treasury from 1957 to 1961. During the Kennedy years he was a partner in the investment house of Loeb, Rhoades & Co., a director of several corporations and a member of a prestigious panel named by President Kennedy to study the U.S. foreign aid program. [See EISENHOWER Volume]

Anderson was one of the first people called by President Johnson in the aftermath of President Kennedy's assassination. Summoned immediately to Washington he spent four hours with Johnson on Nov. 24, 1963 discussing economic policy. Anderson argued strongly that Johnson should pursue a conservative fiscal course by cutting the budget and abandoning the $11 billion tax cut pushed by Kennedy. Johnson chose to make spending cuts while maintaining the Administration's commitment to the tax cut, which he signed in February 1964. He continued to rely on Anderson for advice. According to *Newsweek* magazine, "President Johnson frequently telephones Anderson in his handsome, 27th-floor offices at No. 1 Rockefeller Center or has him down to the White House for visits which rarely show up on the official callers list.

Anderson also often served Johnson as a diplomatic troubleshooter. Two of Anderson's foreign trips were to see French Foreign Minister Maurice Couve de Murville and Egyptian President Gamal Nasser. His most important assignment began with his appointment in April 1964 as special ambassador for the negotiations over the Panama Canal. After two-and-one-half years of negotiations, an agreement on the texts of new treaties governing the Canal was reached in June 1967. Under the three proposed treaties the U.S. would surrender sovereignty over the Panama Canal Zone, and Panama's sovereignty over the zone would be "effectively" recognized. The existing canal would become the property of a U.S.-Panamanian authority. In 1970, however, a new Panamanian government rejected the three proposed treaties on the ground that the U.S. was granted a majority on the joint governing board. After his involvement with the Canal question, Anderson devoted himself to his diverse business interests, including directorships in numerous corporations and the chairmanship of Robert B. Anderson & Co. Ltd.

[TO]

ARENDS, LESLIE C(ORNELIUS)

b. Sept. 27, 1895; Melvin, Ill.
Republican Representative, Ill., 1935-74.

Arends represented a prosperous farming district south of Chicago. He became House Republican whip in 1943. His primary function as whip was to round up Republican votes on key bills for which a Party position had been determined by the Republican Policy Committee.

During the Kennedy years the conservative Arends generally opposed the Administration's domestic legislation. As the ranking Republican member of the House Armed Services Committee, he consistently voted for increased military appropriations. He generally sided with the Joints Chiefs of Staff in its disputes with Secretary of Defense Robert S. McNamara [*q.v.*] [See KENNEDY Volume]

Arends voted against the Johnson Administration's medicare, school aid and poverty program bills. He supported the 1964 Civil Rights Act, however, and the Administration's Vietnam war policy.

In January 1965 Rep. Gerald R. Ford (R, Mich.) [*q.v.*] replaced Rep. Charles Halleck (R, Ind.) [*q.v.*] as House minority leader. Arends had supported Halleck, and Ford demanded that Arends be replaced as whip. House Republicans, however, voted 70 to 59 to retain him.

Arends was a consistent supporter of President Richard M. Nixon. When Rep. Ford became Vice President in 1974, Arends made a nominal bid to become House minority leader. He was then nearly 80 years old, and Republicans chose John J. Rhodes (R, Ariz.) [*q.v.*] instead. Arends retired that year and was replaced by a Democrat. [See NIXON Volume]

[JLW]

ASHBROOK, JOHN M(ILAN)

b. Sept. 21, 1928; Johnstown, Ohio.
Republican Representative, Ohio, 1961- .

John M. Ashbrook was the son of a conservative, anti-New Deal Democratic representative from Ohio. He received his A.B. from Harvard in 1952 and returned to Ohio. He graduated from Ohio State Law School, ran his family's central Ohio county weekly and remained a conservative in his father's mold.

Unlike his father Ashbrook became a Republican. He participated in the Ohio and National Young Republican Clubs during the 1950s. In 1956 he defeated an incumbent Democrat for the state House of Representatives and won reelection two years later. Ashbrook again defeated an incumbent Democrat, Rep. Robert W. Levering, for the U.S. House in 1960. Reelected in 1962 Ashbrook became a member of the House Un-American Activities Committee (HUAC) the following January. Young and aggressive, he practiced the new, more strident anti-Communist conservatism common in the Southern and Western wings of the Republican Party during the 1960s. Right-wing journalist William F. Buckley, Jr. [*q.v.*], a close associate, described Ashbrook as "by all odds the most exciting young man in the Republican Party" in the mid-1960s.

Ashbrook joined early in the effort to nominate conservative Sen. Barry M. Goldwater (R, Ariz.) [*q.v.*] for president. In conjunction with political consultant F. Clifton White [*q.v.*] and William Rusher, editor of Buckley's *National Review*, he formed the nucleus of what would be the Draft Goldwater for President Committee in September 1961. Ironically, Goldwater's subsequent nomination in July 1964 almost cost Ashbrook his House seat. In November he narrowly edged Levering, 51.5% to 48.5%, while Goldwater lost his district 57.5% to 42.5%. Ashbrook trailed the less conservative senatorial candidate, Robert A. Taft, Jr. [*q.v.*], by just under 13,000 votes.

Despite Goldwater's national debacle Ashbrook continued to participate in far-right causes. He served on the steering committee of the Committee of One Million Against the Admission of Red China to the United Nations. Between 1966 and 1971 he chaired the American Conservative Union (ACU), a political education association established by conservatives following their January 1965 loss of the Republican National Committee chairmanship. Ashbrook allied ACU activities with those of the Buckley-sponsored Young Americans for Freedom. Together the two rightist factions fought for control of the National Young Republican Federation. Ashbrook was one of the earliest elected officials to oppose the Administration's policy towards Rhodesia. In 1966 he and Rusher visited Rhodesia and then defended the African nation's white minority government, which had declared itself independent of the United Kingdom. Conservative millionaire H. L. Hunt [*q.v.*], who sponsored the trip, reprinted Ashbrook's Rhodesian statement—entitled "Give Rhodesia a Fair Break" —in his newsletter *Life Lines*.

In the House Ashbrook consistently opposed the Johnson Administration's social welfare legislation. A member of the Education and Labor Committee, he boycotted a subcommittee's vote on the first elementary-secondary education bill in February 1965. He voted against operating funds for the War on Poverty in 1966 and 1967. In 1968 the conservative Americans for Constitutional Action gave Ashbrook a 100% rating on selected issues. Its liberal counterpart, Americans for Democratic Action, marked Ashbrook "zero."

Ashbrook stood apart from the Ohio Republican organization. His independence almost cost him his seat in 1966 and denied him a role at the 1968 Republican National Convention. In December 1964 the Republican state legislature, unsympathetic to Ashbrook's interests, redrew his district and forced him into a 1966 reelection contest with another incumbent, Rep. Robert Secrest (D, Ohio). Although the President and other high Democratic officials campaigned on Secrest's behalf, Ashbrook won 55% to 45%. Again, however, he ran behind the state Republican ticket, in this case by 13,000 votes. In Ohio's May 1968 presidential primary, Ashbrook opposed Republican Gov. James A. Rhodes [*q.v.*], who wanted an uncommitted slate pledged to him. Ashbrook won in his own district. Like most other conservatives, he actively supported former Vice President Richard M. Nixon for president. At the August National Convention Ashbrook unsuccessfully tried to persuade Rhodes into releasing the large Ohio delegation in Nixon's favor. "The boat's moving out," he pleaded, "and we're still on the shore." Rhodes, however, ignored Ashbrook's counsel and refused to climb onto the Nixon bandwagon.

Once President, Nixon quickly disillusioned Ashbrook. The Congressman castigated Nixon's welfare reform bill and new China policy. Ashbrook ran against Nixon for the 1972 presidential nomination but failed to win over 10% of the vote in any primary or to capture a single delegate. [See NIXON Volume]

[JLB]

ASHLEY, THOMAS L(UDLOW)

b. Jan. 11, 1923; Toledo, Ohio.
Democratic Representative, Ohio, 1955- .

Born to an old, rich and Republican Toledo family, Thomas L. Ashley earned his B.A. at Yale in 1948 and his LL.D. at Ohio State in 1951. Ashley worked briefly for Radio Free Europe. Running on the Democratic ticket, he won a narrow victory in a 1954 race for the U.S. House. Reelected without difficulty through the 1960s, he served on the Banking and Currency Committee and became a specialist in housing legislation. He secured federal funds for the rebuilding of downtown Toledo. In 1959 and 1961 Ashley was one of only two House members to vote against resolutions reiterating Congress's opposition to the admission of mainland China into the United Nations.

During the Johnson years Ashley voted for all major Great Society legislation and maintained a solid liberal record. In 1968, for example, the liberal Americans for Democratic Action gave the Toledo Democrat a 100% rating on selected issues. But Ashley did not join those House liberals who criticized Johnson's Vietnam policies.

As a member of the Banking and Currency panel, Ashley initiated legislation favorable to banking interests. In 1965 Congress sought to revise the vaguely phrased Bank Merger Act of 1960, which the Justice Department had interpreted as requiring bank regulatory agencies to obtain the Attorney General's approval for bank mergers. The measure also sought to place mergers outside the authority of existing antitrust regulations. In a 1963 test case by the Justice Department, the Supreme Court had ruled that bank merger activity still fell under the guidelines set by the Sherman and Clayton Acts. In September 1965 Ashley proposed a House version of a bill authored by Sen. A. Willis Robertson (D, Va.) [*q.v.*] that effectively removed banks from the Sherman and Clayton laws. It compelled the Justice Department to follow what Ashley and others considered the more flexible anti-concentration guidelines established in the 1960 statute. The following month Ashley invoked a rarely-used rule and called a special Banking and Currency Committee meeting in the absence and without the foreknowledge, of Chairman Wright Patman (D, Tex.) [*q.v.*]. As planned the Ashley bill—which Patman opposed—received Committee approval. The full House delayed a vote until January 1966, and Patman persuaded Ashley to accept a mild rewording of his bill. The final measure, an amendment to the 1960 merger act, became law in February 1966 and closely resembled the original Ashley proposal.

Bank lobbyists considered the clarification of the 1960 merger statute to be a victory, a curb on Justice Department suits against ambitious bank mergers. The executive director of the Ohio Bankers Association endorsed Ashley for reelection and, in a letter to Ohio bankers, called the Toledo Democrat one of seven House members who has "shown an understanding of banking matters and a willingness to help develop sound laws on these subjects." Two Supreme Court decisions, however, later neutralized Ashley's labors. In separate 1967 and 1968 anti-merger orders, the high court upheld the Justice Department's contention that the 1966 amendment, like its parent statute, had been too imprecisely worded to remove banks from previous antitrust legislation.

Ashley chaired the Banking and Currency Committee's International Trade Subcommittee and, with three other panel members, challenged a late 1966 Republican and Southern Democratic attack upon the U.S. Export-Import Bank (Eximbank), which planned to participate in the financing of the Italian Fiat automobile company's proposed plant in the Soviet Union. Drawing upon CIA estimates of the facility's impact on the Soviet economy, a special four-member panel chaired by Ashley endorsed the loan in March 1967. Senate foes of Eximbank enacted a ban on support for the Fiat project, but in November the full House Banking and Currency Committee forced through a presidential waiver with the ban, thus effectively defeating the loan adversaries.

Ashley remained in the House during the Nixon years and helped draft the 1970 Omnibus Housing Act. His work was rewarded by the government's decision to build a new "model cities" town near Toledo. [See NIXON Volume]

[JLB]

ASHMORE, HARRY S(COTT)
b. July 27, 1916; Greenville, S.C.
Director, Center for the Study of Democratic Institutions, 1959- .

The son of a Greenville merchant whose grandfathers served in the Confederate Army, Ashmore began his career in journalism covering the local courthouse for the Greenville *Piedmont*. In the late 1930s he toured the poverty areas above the Mason-Dixon line to do a series on Northern "tobacco roads." In 1941 Ashmore studied journalism at Harvard as a Nieman fellow. Following wartime service he was named associate editor of the Charlotte (N.C.) *News*, where he wrote editorials that advocated two-party Southern politics, racial and religious tolerance and the enfranchisement of Negroes. In 1948 Ashmore became executive editor of the *Arkansas Gazette* in Little Rock. He took a leave of absence in 1955 and 1956 to serve on Adlai Stevenson's presidential campaign.

Under Ashmore's direction the *Gazette* supported the two successful gubernatorial campaigns of Orval E. Faubus in the 1950s. But in 1957 Gov. Faubus ordered National Guardsmen to Little Rock to prevent nine Negroes from integrating Central High School. The *Gazette* editorially denounced the Governor and endorsed President Eisenhower's dispatch of federal troops to Little Rock to enforce implementation of the court order desegregating the school. Ashmore won national recognition for the support he gave to school integration in Little Rock, and the next year he won a Pulitzer Prize for the "forcefulness, dispassionate analysis and clarity" of his *Gazette* editorials. [See EISENHOWER Volume]

In September 1959 Ashmore resigned as the *Gazette*'s executive editor to become a director of the newly founded Center for the Study of Democratic Institutions. The Center, headed by educator Robert Hutchins [*q.v.*], was supported by the Fund for the Republic, which in turn had been created by the Ford Foundation. The Center assembled representatives of academia, government, the press, business and labor to examine "the major institutions of the 20th century in the light of their impact on the possibilities for the continued existence of democracy." At the Center Ashmore concentrated his attention on race relations and the press, defending the growing militancy of the civil rights movement in the mid-1960s and arguing that the quality of the news media, especially television, would be enhanced if a national nongovernmental commission were established to annually review its quality and make recommendations for improvement.

Traveling on behalf of the Center and with the authorization of the State Department, Ashmore visited North Vietnam in early January 1967. He was accompanied on the trip by *Miami News* editor William C. Baggs. Ashmore stayed in Hanoi for nine days and had a rare two-hour talk with President Ho Chi Minh. He reported on his return to the U.S. that damage inflicted by American bombing was "offset by the unifying influence" it had on the North Vietnamese people.

Upon his return from Hanoi Ashmore reported to the State Department that Ho's conditions for the start of peace talks were the cessation of American raids on North Vietnam and a halt to the buildup of American forces in South Vietnam. With Assistant Secretary of State William P. Bundy [*q.v.*], Ashmore and Baggs drafted a note to Ho shortly after their return from Vietnam. According to Ashmore the letter modified previous U.S. conditions for "reciprocal restraint" on the part of Hanoi in exchange for a halt to the bombing of the North. The note also indicated that the U.S. would respect the Geneva Accords as the basis for the peace talks. The Ashmore-Baggs note was sent to Hanoi on Feb. 5, 1967.

In September 1967 Ashmore published an article in *Center Magazine* charging that President Johnson had "effectively and brutally canceled" the Ashmore-Bundy peace initiative of January-February. According to Ashmore's article, "The Public Relations of Peace," Johnson had sent another note to Ho, dated Feb. 2, but received by Hanoi on Feb. 10, that nullified the effect of the Ashmore letter by insisting that any proposal for a de-escalation of the war go into effect at the end of the scheduled Tet truce on Feb. 12.

In the ensuing controversy over the peace initiative, Bundy denied that Johnson's letter had contradicted the Ashmore note. Bundy said, "Mr. Ashmore yields to an understandable feeling that his own channel was the center of the stage. It was not; it was a very, very small part of the total picture." On Sept. 18, 1967 Ashmore reiterated his view that the two letters were "inconsistent in tone and content. . . . The tone of ours is quite conciliatory. The tone of the President's is quite harsh." Sen. J. William Fulbright (D, Ark.) [*q.v.*] noted the next day that the incident indicated that the U.S. could have entered into peace talks with North Vietnam if it had been willing to consider "anything short of surrender" by Hanoi. Ashmore and Baggs collaborated on a 1968 book, *Mission to Hanoi*, which recounted their negotiations with Ho and the subsequent frustrations their peace efforts encountered in Washington.

In 1974 a severe financial crisis compelled the Center to eliminate its program of grants that enabled distinguished scholars to devote full-time to discussion and writing. In the midst of this crisis, Ashmore resigned.

[TJC]

ASPINALL, WAYNE N(ORVIEL)

b. April 3, 1896; Middleburg, Ohio.
Democratic Representative, Colo., 1949-73; Chairman, Interior and Insular Affairs Committee, 1959-73.

Aspinall, the son of a fruit grower, was raised in Palisade, Colo. He studied at the University of Denver, where he received an LL.B. in 1925. After several years as a teacher and school administrator, Aspinall entered Colorado politics in 1930 and served in the state legislature until 1948. In that year he was elected to the House of Representatives from a large rural district in western Colorado. Assigned to the Public Lands Committee (later called the Interior and Insular Affairs Committee), Aspinall soon became an important figure in natural resources policy. He was a strong advocate of land reclamation projects and also favored a "multiple use" approach to resources development, combining recreation and commercial exploitation. This policy was supported by the powerful timber and mining interests in Aspinall's district, which gave him strong financial support.

Aspinall became chairman of the Interior and Insular Affairs Committee in 1959 and subsequently played a key role in all natural resources legislation. A strong opponent of what he called "conservation extremists," he helped delay and then weaken a wilderness preservation bill during the early 1960s. Observers also linked Aspinall to delays in the funding and construction or an irrigation project for Navaho Indian lands in New Mexico. [See KENNEDY Volume]

The most important piece of natural resources legislation to gain Aspinall's attention during the mid-1960s was the Central

Arizona Project (CAP), a $1.3 billion construction plan for facilities to divert Colorado River water to cities and farmlands in Arizona. Negotiations over CAP extended from 1963 to 1968, when Congress authorized the plan. Aspinall's main concern was to ensure that CAP would not deplete the supply of Colorado River water that the state of Colorado claimed. Therefore he worked for the addition of five irrigation projects to the CAP bill, all of which benefited his own Colorado district. Although three of the projects had previously received unfavorable reports from the Budget Bureau, the bill's sponsors accepted Aspinall's conditions in order to gain his support. The additional cost was $392 million.

Aspinall was less successful in other water-use conflicts of the mid-1960s. Vigorous opposition from Sen. Henry Jackson (D, Wash.) [*q.v.*] quashed an Aspinall proposal to study the feasibility of augmenting the Colorado River flow by tapping the river basins of the Pacific Northwest. Aspinall also failed to put through legislation for the construction of two dams and a hydroelectric power station in the Grand Canyon section of the Colorado River. A massive lobbying campaign by the Sierra Club, a conservationist group, frustrated this plan in 1967.

Aspinall was a strong advocate of defense spending and the Vietnam war. These positions, as well as his stance on natural resources, helped him survive in conservative western Colorado. The liberal Americans for Democratic Action gave Aspinall a "correct" rating of 57% for the mid-1960s. Redistricting in 1964 and 1966, however, increased the liberal and pro-conservation elements in Aspinall's constituency. Aspinall was defeated in the 1972 Democratic primary by Alan Merson, a University of Denver law professor strongly supported by environmental and anti-war groups. [See NIXON Volume]

[SLG]

For further information:
Richard L. Berkman and W. Kip Viscusi, *Damming the West* (New York, 1973).

BAEZ, JOAN

b. Jan. 9, 1941; New York, N.Y.
Folksinger, pacifist.

In 1958 Baez began singing folksongs in the Boston area, then the center of a folk music revival. After successful appearances at the 1959 and 1960 Newport Folk Festivals, she signed a recording contract with Vanguard Records. Her first albums consisted mostly of traditional English and American ballads and Afro-American spirituals, but she later began to perform contemporary songs and songs of her own composition as well. Baez rapidly became one of the country's most popular folksingers, helping to broaden the interest in folk music and serving in manner and dress as a model for many young women.

Baez was outspoken on social issues and became increasingly involved in political activity throughout the 1960s. She was an active supporter of the civil rights movement and took part in a number of demonstrations, including the Aug. 28, 1963 March on Washington, where she sang from the podium. Baez sang *We Shall Overcome* to a Dec. 2, 1964 rally of several thousand Free Speech Movement supporters at the University of California, Berkeley just before they occupied Sproul Hall, in a demonstration that first brought national attention to the growing student movement. She also sang at the first major national demonstration against the war in Vietnam, held in Washington, D.C., on April 17, 1965.

Baez was a pacifist and in 1965 founded the Institute for the Study of Nonviolence in Palo Alto, Calif. She advocated the use of non-violent tactics to oppose the war in Vietnam and was one of 350 people who announced in an April 14, 1966 advertisement in the *Washington Post* that they would protest the war by refusing to pay their federal income tax. Among the many anti-war activities Baez participated in were the "Stop-the-Draft-Week" protests in Oakland, Calif., in October 1967. On Oct. 16 Baez, her mother and her sister, folksinger Mimi Farina, were among 125 picketers arrested at the Oakland Draft Induction Center. The arrested demonstrators received 10-day prison sentences. At the same center, Baez was again arrested on Dec. 19 and received a 45-day sentence, which she began serving the next day. Baez was also a strong supporter of the United Farm Workers in their effort to unionize California agricultural workers.

Throughout much of her early career, Baez was closely associated with singer-songwriter Bob Dylan. In the fall of 1963, when Dylan was still largely unknown, Baez introduced him as a guest artist at many of her concerts, and their close friendship continued for several years. In 1968 Baez married David Harris, a leader of the Resistance, a draft resistance group. Harris himself was later jailed for failing to report for induction into the Army.

In 1967 and 1968 Baez made many speeches and television appearances urging resistance to the U.S. role in Vietnam, and she continued to be a vocal opponent of the war until its end. As one of a group of four Americans visiting North Vietnam in December 1972, she met with U.S. prisoners of war and was one of the few Americans other than the prisoners to be in Hanoi during the Christmas bombing raids.

[JBF]

For further information:
Joan Baez, *Daybreak* (New York, 1968).

BAILEY, JOHN M(ORAN)

b. Nov. 23, 1904; Hartford, Conn.
d. Apr. 10, 1975; Hartford, Conn.
Chairman, Connecticut Democratic State Committee, 1946-75; Chairman, Democratic National Committee, 1961-68.

Politics became John Bailey's life work three years after he received his law degree from Harvard. In 1932 Bailey became a member of the Connecticut State Democratic Committee and in 1946 assumed the chairmanship. Allying himself with former Rep. Abraham A. Ribicoff (D, Conn.) [*q.v.*], Bailey created a powerful Democratic organization, which by 1963 held both of the state's U.S. senate seats and the governor's post. In national politics Bailey supported John F. Kennedy for the Democratic vice presidential nomination in 1956 and for the presidential nomination four years later. At the 1960 Democratic Convention Kennedy managers charged Bailey with responsibility for rounding up delegate support in New England. He proved successful. Every delegate in the entire six state region cast a vote for Kennedy, who won on the first ballot. As a reward for his labors, Kennedy named Bailey chairman of the Democratic National Committee (DNC) in January 1961. More of a campaign strategist than an orator or ideologue, Bailey began detailed preparations for Kennedy's reelection in early November 1963. [See KENNEDY Volume]

After Kennedy's assassination Bailey continued as national committee chairman, although President Johnson gave him only a minor part in the 1964 campaign. Bailey described his role at DNC as a "housekeeping job," overseeing the Party's voter registration drive and aiding Democratic congressional candidates. On Sept. 11, 1964 Bailey signed, with his Republican counterpart Dean Burch [*q.v.*], an agreement drafted by the Fair Campaign Practices Committee. The code called for both parties to concentrate on the "real issues" during the campaign, refrain from the defamation of opponents and eschew appeals to racial or religious prejudice. Soon after, however, Burch accused the Democrats of violating the code. He criticized a Democratic television commercial that depicted a little girl picking a daisy as a nuclear bomb exploded in the background, supposedly indicative of the nuclear arms policy of the Republican presidential candidate, Sen. Barry M. Goldwater (R, Ariz.) [*q.v.*]. Bailey dismissed Burch's accusations by saying that "any image of Mr. Goldwater has been created by Mr. Goldwater himself," but the Democrats withdrew the commercial immediately after Burch's protest. Johnson won the election with 61% of the vote, while the Democrats increased their senatorial advantage by two and gained 38 seats in the House.

President Johnson displayed little interest in the functions of the DNC following the Party's 1964 triumph and, in 1966, severely cut the Committee's operations budget and eliminated its voter registration program. In the November 1966 elections the Democratic Party lost three Senate seats, 47 House districts and eight governorships to the Republicans. Despite the Party's poor showing, Johnson ignored demands by some state Democratic officials to remove Bailey and instead reaffirmed his faith in the DNC chief in January 1967. The National Committee revived its registration program and sought to improve relations with state leaders.

In defense of the President Bailey spoke out against critics of the Vietnam war in 1967. When Michigan Governor and Republican presidential hopeful George W. Romney [*q.v.*] complained in September 1967 of having been "brainwashed" during a Vietnam tour, Bailey accused the Governor of having "insulted the integrity" of Gen. William Westmoreland [*q.v.*] and Ambassador Henry Cabot Lodge [*q.v.*], both of whom had briefed Romney. Bailey charged Republicans the next month with playing "an opportunist game" on Vietnam. In January 1968 the Party Chairman expressed his certainty that the President and Vice President would win renomination.

When Johnson unexpectedly withdrew from the race on March 31, Bailey found himself without a candidate. He appeared representative of the "old politics" to the Party's anti-war forces supporting the candidacies of Sens. Eugene J. McCarthy (D, Minn.) [*q.v.*] and Robert F. Kennedy (D, N.Y.) [*q.v.*]. In his own state, where he had remained chairman, Bailey confronted a well organized McCarthy-for-President movement. As state chairman he wanted an unpledged delegation to the National Convention despite a 44% write-in vote for McCarthy in the primary. The McCarthy forces demanded 10 seats on the state's 44-member delegation, threatening to oppose Ribicoff for the Democratic senatorial nomination if Bailey denied them. On June 26, however, Joseph Duffey, chairman of the state McCarthy committee, accepted Bailey's offer of nine delegates under orders from the candidate himself.

Bailey retired as national chairman immediately after the August 1968 Democratic National Convention and returned to Connecticut as state leader. Duffey defeated Bailey's choice for the U.S. Senate in the August 1970 Democratic primary, but the Republicans defeated both Duffey and Rep. Emilio Q. Daddario (D, Conn.), Bailey's candidate for governor, in the November general election. Bailey reasserted his influence four years later when he skillfully organized the landslide election of Ella Grasso as the first woman governor of the state. Just six months after the election, John Bailey died in Hartford.

[JLB]

BAKER, BOBBY (ROBERT GENE)
b. 1928; Pickens, S.C.
Secretary to the Senate Majority, January 1955-October 1963.

Bobby Baker came to Washington, D.C. in 1943 at the age of 15 to be a Senate page. He held a succession of minor positions over the decade, accumulating a valuable fund of knowledge about the Senate and impressing senators with his energy and ability. Simultaneously he earned a college degree from George Washington University and then attended night law classes at American University. Sen. Lyndon Johnson (D, Tex.) [*q.v.*] and Sen. Robert Kerr (D, Okla.) [*q.v.*] became Baker's most powerful patrons. Appointed assistant secretary to the Democratic minority in 1953, Baker, dubbed "Lyndon Junior" by Sen. Alan Bible (D, Nev.) [*q.v.*], became secretary to the majority in 1955 when Johnson became Senate majority leader.

With a sophisticated understanding of the traditions and procedures of the Senate and a shrewd knowledge of individual senators, Baker helped Johnson run the upper house. "Bobby Baker is my strong right arm," Johnson said in 1960. "He is the last person I see at night and the first person I see in the morning." It was Baker's task to round up senators to back measures favored by the leadership; the precision of his preliminary "head counts" was celebrated. Baker's ability to perform numerous favors for senators and others won him power and prestige in the Capitol, and his position as secretary-treasurer of the Senate Democratic Campaign Committee enhanced his influence. Some liberal Democrats outside the Senate establishment resented Baker's power; Sen. Joseph Clark (D, Pa.) [*q.v.*] identified him as "a protagonist of the conservative coalition." The new Senate majority leader, Mike Mansfield (D, Mont.) [*q.v.*], kept Baker as majority secretary after 1961, but Baker worked more closely with his wealthy conservative sponsor, Kerr, than with his ostensible superior, Mansfield. [See KENNEDY Volume]

Baker also used his political connections to enrich himself; his net worth in 1963 was $1.7 million, although his annual salary was only $19,600. His financial machinations led to his political downfall in the fall of 1963, when a disgruntled business associate sued him, charging that Baker had "conspired maliciously" against his business. Amid accusations of "influence peddling" and rumors about his diverse sources of income, Baker was forced to resign as secretary to the majority in October.

During 1964 and 1965 the Senate Rules and Administration Committee carried out an intermittent investigation to uncover Baker's complex network of money-making ventures. His most lucrative investment was his interest in the Serv-U Corporation, a vending company dependent upon Baker's contacts for its business. Its chief customer was the aerospace industry, which relied heavily on federal contracts. Sen. Kerr was chairman of the Senate Aeronautical and Space Sciences Committee, and the head of the National Aeronautics and Space Administration (NASA), James Webb [*q.v.*], was a former employe of Kerr's oil firm. Baker estimated his 28% interest in Serv-U to be worth $1 million.

In the case of the Mortgage Guarantee Insurance Corporation (MGIC), Baker's inside information and associations enabled him to earn handsome profits. Learning from his banking contacts that MGIC stock was about to soar in value, Baker bought $9,700 worth of stock from MGIC's president, Max Karl, in 1959. Subsequent stock splits and a favorable tax ruling from the Internal Revenue Service pushed the value of the shares to $145,000 by 1964. Karl admitted that there was "some question of the legality" of the sale of the stock before it was registered with the Securities and Exchange Commission, but he said that he had wanted "prominent stockholders" for MGIC and that Baker "knew a lot of people." Baker also made substantial sums by tipping off friends to MGIC and other opportunities in exchange for a share of the profits.

Baker traded on his official position and his access to political decision makers in a host of other ventures. Baker's political contacts figured prominently in the financing and patronage of the Carousel Motel in Maryland, of which he was a part owner. He joined Sen. George Smathers (D, Fla.) [*q.v.*] in a Florida real estate project and invested in an Oklahoma bank recommended by Sen. Kerr with funds borrowed from Kerr's own bank. Baker received fees for helping banks to gain charters, ocean freight forwarders to pass a licensing bill and a Haitian slaughterhouse to obtain a license to export meat to the United States and Puerto Rico. He usually received compensation for his services in the form of legal fees paid to his Washington law firm, Tucker & Baker. Baker himself was never admitted to the District of Columbia bar.

The Rules Committee revelations made the Bobby Baker case an issue during the 1964 presidential campaign. A Baker associate, insurance man Don Reynolds, testified that for the privilege of selling life insurance to Lyndon Johnson, he had been compelled by Johnson's aide, Walter Jenkins [*q.v.*], to buy advertising time on Johnson's Texas television station and give Johnson a hi-fi set. Throughout the scandal Johnson tried to dissociate himself from Baker, refusing to comment on the case except to call his former aide "no protege of anyone." Republican presidential candidate Sen. Barry Goldwater (R, Ariz.) [*q.v.*] repeatedly claimed the scandal was symptomatic of the ethics of Johnson's Washington. Goldwater maintained that Bobby Baker was the issue that hurt Johnson "more than anything else."

Partisan politics also marked the Senate's Baker investigation. While the Rules Committee's Democratic majority endeavored to narrow the scope of the probe, the Republican minority sought to widen it. Committee Republicans accused the Democrats of conducting a "whitewash" and of sidestepping matters such as Baker's alleged use of "party girls" for political and business purposes. Several important revelations came not from the Rules Committee but from Sen. John Williams's (R, Del.) [*q.v.*] independent investigation. In May 1964 Williams proposed that the Committee's inquiry be expanded to include senators as well as Senate employes and to probe improper campaign contributions. The Senate rejected the resolution, 42-33, after a bitter partisan debate.

The Rules Committee's report, issued in July 1964, found Baker "guilty of many gross improprieties." His business activities were "certainly in conflict with his official duties," the report said, but not in technical violation of conflict-of-interest statutes. The Committee's three Republicans issued a dissenting report charging that "the full story has not been disclosed concerning Bobby Baker . . . because the majority prevented the investigation from proceeding." The report recommended amending Senate rules to require disclosure of financial interests by senators and Senate employees, but the full Senate turned aside the proposal. The Senate did approve, by a 61-19 vote, the creation of a six-member bipartisan committee to investigate future "allegations of improper conduct" by senators and Senate employes. In February 1967 the Senate again rejected an internal reform package—the so-called "Bobby Baker amendments" sponsored by Sen. Clark. Besides financial disclosure, the reforms would have restricted outside income for senators and receipt of gifts from lobbyists.

The Baker investigation did not end with the filing of the Rules Committee report in July 1964. In September Sen. Williams charged that Baker and builder Matthew McCloskey had conspired to make an illegal $25,000 contribution to the 1960 Democratic campaign in order to secure for McCloskey's construction firm the contract to build the District of Columbia stadium. Williams's source was Don Reynolds, who claimed that the $25,000 was passed on through his insurance company as an overpayment by McCloskey on a performance bond for the stadium project.

The Rules Committee resumed hearings on the Baker matter after the November election. Baker appeared and, as he had done in February, refused to testify. McCloskey said that the $25,000 overpayment was an honest "goof." An FBI report discredited Reynolds's credibility. The Committee—with the Republican minority objecting to the majority's "continuing effort to discredit witnesses"—found McCloskey had not been proven guilty of any wrongdoing but termed Baker's involvement "impropriety on his part as a public servant.

In January 1967 a U.S. District Court convicted Baker of income tax evasion, theft and conspiracy to defraud the government. Baker was found guilty of, among other offenses, misappropriating $100,000 in campaign contributions he had solicited from savings and loan company executives anxious to defeat a tax proposal before the Senate Finance Committee. Baker started serving a one-to-three-year sentence in January 1971 and was paroled in June 1972.

[TO]

BAKER, HOWARD (HENRY), JR.

b. Nov. 15, 1925; Huntsville, Tenn.
Republican Senator, Tenn., 1967- .

Born into a politically active family, Baker was raised in the traditionally Republican eastern mountain enclave in Democratic-dominated Tennessee. Baker's father represented the state's second congressional district from 1951 until his death in 1964. The younger Baker received an LL.B. degree from the University of Tennessee in 1949 and became an affluent criminal and corporate lawyer.

Baker's father-in-law, Senate Minority Leader Everett M. Dirksen (R, Ill.) [*q.v.*], urged him to run for his father's congressional seat in 1964. Instead, Baker decided to seek the last two years of the term of Sen. Estes Kefauver (D, Tenn.), who had died the previous year. He campaigned on a conservative platform, advocating a limited federal role in local education and in the enforcement of civil rights laws. However, Baker avoided identification with Republican presidential candidate Sen. Barry M. Goldwater (R, Ariz.) [*q.v.*]. Baker lost the race to liberal Democrat Ross Bass by 50,000 votes but received more votes than any other Republican in the history of Tennessee.

In 1966 Baker ran for a full Senate term against Gov. Frank Clement [*q.v.*]. Baker adopted more moderate positions than he had in 1964 and sought to improve upon the 2% support among blacks that he had received in his first race. Receiving from 15% to 20% of the black vote, Baker won the election by almost 100,000 votes and became the state's first popularly elected Republican senator.

During his first two years in the Senate, Baker compiled a fairly conservative record. According to *Congressional Quarterly*, he voted with the upper chamber's conservative coalition on 70% and 76% of key roll-call votes in 1967 and 1968. In 1967 he opposed a liberal effort to facilitate the invoking of cloture against filibusters. During the fall of the same year, Baker supported the conservative coalition in its effort to grant governors veto power over federal grants-in-aid to states and localities. A consistent supporter of military expenditures, he backed the Sentinel anti-ballistic missile system in the fall of 1968.

On some major issues Baker deviated from a conservative voting pattern. In June 1967 he backed an amendment offered by Sen. Edward M. Kennedy (D, Mass.) [*q.v.*] to establish a maximum 10% population variation between the largest and smallest congressional districts beginning in 1968. The proposal was made during Senate debate over compliance with the Supreme Court's historic "one-man, one-vote" decision. Baker circulated among Republicans a statistical study indicating that equal-population districting would assist their Party in the 1968 elections. He was also credited with helping to convince his father-in-law in 1968 to abandon his opposition to open housing proposals and support a compromise bill that exempted certain privately owned homes.

After Dirksen died in 1969 Baker sought to replace him as minority leader but lost by five votes in the Republican caucus to Sen. Hugh Scott (R, Pa.) [*q.v.*]. Scott defeated Baker again in 1971. In 1972 Baker won reelection with 62% of the vote. The following year he gained national attention as the ranking Republican on the Senate Select Committee on Presidential Campaign Activities, popularly known as the Watergate Committee. [See NIXON Volume]

[MLL]

BAKER, (JOHN) WILSON

b. Jan. 31, 1915; Shallote, N.C.
d. Sept. 11, 1975; Selma, Ala.
Director of Public Safety, Selma, Ala., 1963-66; Sheriff, Dallas County, Ala., 1967-75.

During the 1950s Baker served as a captain in the Selma, Ala., police force. In 1958 he left the city to teach an extension course in law enforcement at the University of Alabama. Baker returned to Selma in 1963 to take charge of its police force as director of public safety.

From January through March 1965 Rev. Martin Luther King's [*q.v.*] Southern Christian Leadership Conference (SCLC) sponsored a series of demonstrations in Selma, culminating in a march from that city to Montgomery, to protest discrimination in the registration of voters and demand federal action to end it. Blacks constituted a majority of the population of Dallas County, of which Selma was the seat, but only 300 were registered to vote.

Selma's city administration and business leaders favored a conciliatory approach to the demonstrators. Although Baker asserted that he was a segregationist, he regarded himself as a professional police officer and attempted to negotiate with protest leaders and to use a minimum of force against illegal demonstrations. The Rev. Hosea L. Williams [*q.v.*], a SCLC leader, praised Baker for his restraining influence upon white "haters." As a result of his methods, Baker clashed with Dallas County Sheriff James G. (Jim) Clark [*q.v.*], a militant segregationist who employed what the protesters and many other observers regarded as unnecessary and brutal violence to break up demonstrations.

In April 1965 Baker joined other city officials and local business leaders in sponsoring newspaper advertisements urging acceptance of the Civil Rights Act of 1964 and of equal voting rights for Negroes. Baker commented, "This is what we must do under the law, like it or not."

Baker challenged Clark in the May 1966 primary for the Democratic nomination for sheriff. Baker stressed his commitment to fair and efficient law enforcement, while the incumbent emphasized his belief that the civil rights movement was a Communist-inspired uprising. Thousands of blacks had been registered since the beginning of SCLC's activities in Dallas County, and civil rights leaders regarded the primary as an important test of their voting strength. Baker defeated Clark with the support of almost all of the new voters. Clark ran a write-in campaign in the general election and was again defeated by Baker. Assuming office in January 1967, the new sheriff announced that he would appoint a black deputy.

Baker was reelected sheriff twice and died on Sept. 11, 1975, while still holding that post.

[MLL]

BALDWIN, JAMES A(RTHUR)
b. Aug. 2, 1924; New York, N.Y.
Author.

The son of an indigent minister, Baldwin described his Harlem childhood as a "bleak fantasy." During his adolescence Baldwin tried preaching but gave up at age 17 and left home shortly thereafter. Unable to sell his first two books, Baldwin at age 24 left for France, where in 1953 he finished *Go Tell It On the Mountain*, his highly praised novel of religious experience in Harlem. His most widely acclaimed work of the 1950s was *Notes of a Native Son*, a collection of personal essays that probed what one reviewer called "the peculiar dilemma of Northern Negro intellectuals who can claim neither Western nor African heritage as their own." During the early 1960s Baldwin was probably the most widely read and discussed black writer in America. In *The Crisis of the Negro Intellectual,* Harold Cruse characterized Baldwin as "the chief spokesman for the Negro among the intellectual class" during the early years of the decade. In May 1963 Baldwin arranged a meeting between President Kennedy and a dozen black leaders and artists.

In *The Fire Next Time*, two essays published in 1963, Baldwin argued that black people in America "are very well placed indeed to precipitate chaos and ring down the curtain on the American dream." He went on to predict that "if we do not dare everything, the fulfillment of that prophecy, recreated from the Bible in song by a slave, is upon us: 'God gave Noah the rainbow sign, no more water, the fire next time.' " Read in light of the 1965 Watts riot and later violence in black ghettos across the nation, *The Fire Next Time* came to be regarded as a prophetic and insightful study of American race relations. In his history of the civil rights movement, Thomas Brooks wrote that no one else predicted the events "with such verve and before such a wide audience." [See KENNEDY Volume]

Baldwin returned from Europe in March 1965 to participate in the march from Selma to Montgomery, Ala., led by Martin Luther King, [*q.v.*]. Although Baldwin lived abroad and devoted most of his energies to creative writing, he continued to take an active interest in the course of the black movement in America. In February 1967 he resigned from the advisory board of *Liberator*, a black nationalist monthly he had been associated with since 1961, in protest against the magazine's publication of allegedly anti-Semitic articles. Baldwin also contributed the introductory essay to *If They Come In The Morning*, a collection of essays that assessed the significance of the trial of Angela Davis's trial, which was published in 1971.

[DKR]

For further information:
James Baldwin, *Going to Meet the Man* (New York, 1965).

BALL, GEORGE W(ILDMAN)
b. Dec. 21, 1909; Des Moines, Iowa. Undersecretary of State, November 1961-September 1966.

A specialist on European trade policy, Ball eventually achieved his greatest prominence as the only high-ranking presidential adviser to consistently oppose the Vietnam war during the Johnson Administration. Following his graduation from Northwestern University Law School in 1933, Ball worked in several New Deal agencies before returning to Illinois to practice law. Ball reentered government service in 1942 in the Office of Lend-Lease Administration and in 1944 was appointed director of the U.S. Strategic Bombing Survey, a civilian group established to assess the effect of the air offensive against Germany. After the war Ball resumed private law practice and became a specialist on international trade. Ball was appointed undersecretary of state for economic affairs in January 1961; in November of that year he became undersecretary of state.

During the Kennedy Administration Ball was concerned primarily with the formulation of U.S. trade policy and with international problems in such areas as the Congo and Cuba, but he also became involved in the growing war in Vietnam. In 1961, when the Administration was discussing policy options in Vietnam, Ball cautioned against the introduction of U.S. combat forces because he felt such a course would mire the U.S. in a war it oculd not win. [See KENNEDY Volume]

Ball's opposition to American involvement in the war continued during the Johnson Administration. Following the spring 1965 decision to increase troop commitments and launch regular bombing attacks upon North Vietnam, Ball wrote a memorandum in July entitled "Cutting our Losses in South Vietnam," which argued for de-escalation and political compromise. Ball viewed South Vietnam as a "lost cause" because of the lack of popular support for the Saigon regime and the deep commitment of the Communists. He cautioned that continued troop increases would not assure victory.

Ball recommended that the Administration hold forces at current levels while arranging a conference to negotiate a withdrawal. He recognized that America would lose face before its Asian allies, but he felt that the loss would be of short duration and that the U.S. would emerge as a "wiser and more mature nation." If this step were not taken, "humiliation would be more likely than the achievement of our objectives—even after we paid terrible costs."

In January 1966 Ball again wrote a memorandum to Johnson opposing the bombing of North Vietnam because that policy contained "a life and dynamism of its own" and could result in retaliation by Hanoi or involve the U.S. in a war with China. Drawing on his wartime experience he also argued that massive air strikes would strengthen, not weaken, North Vietnamese resolve.

Convinced that he could not change American policy, Ball left office in September 1966 to return to his law firm and to investment banking. In March 1968 Ball served as a member of the Senior Advisory Group on Vietnam. This gathering of "elder statesmen" had been called by President Johnson to advise him on the military's request for over 200,000 additional troops. In their high level meetings Ball continued to press for de-escalation. A majority of Johnson's advisers, fearing the domestic social and political consequences of still another troop increase, now supported the point of view advanced for so long by Ball. On March 31 Johnson announced a policy of gradual de-escalation and a curtailment of the bombing.

A quiet man who remained personally loyal to Johnson and Secretary of State Dean Rusk [*q.v.*], Ball's determined opposition to the war only became widely known after the publication of the *Pentagon Papers* in 1971.

[EWS]

For further information:
David Halberstam, *The Best and the Brightest* (New York, 1972).
U.S. Department of Defense, *The Pentagon Papers*, Senator Gravel Edition (Boston, 1971), Vols. II and IV.

BARR, JOSEPH W(ALKER)
b. Jan. 17, 1918; Vincennes, Ind.
Chairman, Federal Deposit Insurance Corporation, January 1964-April 1965; Undersecretary of the Treasury, April 1965-December 1968; Secretary of the Treasury, December 1968-January 1969.

The son of an Indiana businessman, Joseph Barr received his B.A. from De Pauw University and his M.A. degree in economics from Harvard University. During World War II he commanded a submarine chaser in the Mediterranean. He returned to Indiana after the war to help manage his family's businesses, which included grain elevators, farm equipment financing, real estate and theater operations. Elected to the House of Representatives in 1958 as a Democrat from a traditionally Republican district, Barr served on the Banking and Currency Committee, where he concentrated on the balance-of-payments problem and helped write legislation creating the Inter-American Bank and the International Development Association. After being defeated for reelection in 1960, he was named an assistant to Undersecretary of the Treasury Henry Fowler [*q.v.*]. For the next three years Barr concentrated on recommending Treasury Department proposals to Congress.

In January 1964 President Johnson appointed Barr chairman of the Federal Deposit Insurance Corporation (FDIC). The main tasks of the FDIC were to insure bank depositors against bank failures and to regulate those banks outside the purview of the Federal Reserve System and the Comptroller of the Currency, about one-seventh of all U.S. banks. Along with other banking regulatory officials, Barr came into conflict with controversial Comptroller James J. Saxon [*q.v.*]. Barr objected to Saxon's policy of liberally granting bank charters, and his office engaged in bitter disputes with Saxon's over various technical matters. In March 1965 Barr told Congress that 13 banks had failed since 1963, as compared with an average of only one or two a year over the previous 20 years. He dismissed fears of a rash of bank failures, however, stating that the assets of the failed banks amounted to only $113 million, a fraction of the $366 billion in total assets of all insured banks.

In April 1965 Barr became undersecretary of the treasury at the request of Fowler, who had just become Secretary of the Treasury. In addition to his administrative duties, Barr took chief responsibility for congressional relations, working to win approval for a broad range of Administration proposals. He was a strong defender of the college-student loan program and a truth-in-lending proposal long held up by the Senate. The latter bill, requiring lenders to state clearly the interest and finance charges on consumer loans, was finally passed in July 1967.

Barr appeared before congressional committees on several occasions to promote the Administration's campaign-finance reform plan, which involved federal subsidies for presidential and senate campaigns and income tax credits for campaign contributions. The plan failed to pass during the Johnson Administration. In March 1968 he called for approval of the Administration's tax surcharge and implementation of budget cuts, both designed to curb inflation.

Following Fowler's retirement in December 1968, Barr served as Secretary of the Treasury for the final month of the Johnson Administration. After leaving the Treasury he became president of the American Security and Trust Company in Washington, D.C.

[TO]

BARTLETT, E(DWARD) L(EWIS)
b. April 20, 1904; Seattle, Wash.
d. Dec. 11, 1968; Washington, D.C.
Democratic Senator, Alaska, 1960-68.

E.L. "Bob" Bartlett was Alaska's non-voting delegate in Congress from 1945 to 1959. There he lobbied effectively for Alaskan statehood, finally granted in 1959. That year he was elected to the Senate along with Ernest Gruening (D, Alaska) [*q.v.*]. During the Kennedy years Bartlett compiled a liberal record and was one of a small bloc of liberals in the Senate to oppose creation of the privately owned Communications Satellite Corporation [See KENNEDY Volume]

Bartlett maintained his liberal record during the Johnson years, voting for school aid, civil rights, medicare and antipoverty legislation. Shipping and fishing were important Alaskan industries, and Bartlett, as a member, and, after 1967, as chairman of the Merchant Marine and Fisheries Subcommittee of the Senate Commerce Committee, played an important role in shaping maritime legislation. In 1966 he won enactment of a bill providing federal aid for research and experimentation in the production of fish protein concentrate. He also won approval of a Coast Guard bill passed in June 1967, which appropriated $58 million more than the Administration requested for the construction of five high-endurance Coast Guard cutters. The Administration had asked for funds for only one such vessel.

As subcommittee chairman, Bartlett clashed with the Administration in shaping legislation to help the foundering U.S. merchant marine. In the fall of 1968 President Johnson pocket-vetoed a bill sponsored by Bartlett creating an independent federal maritime administration within the executive branch. Earlier that year Transportation Secretary Alan S. Boyd [*q.v.*] had proposed a scaling down of federal subsidies to the shipping and shipbuilding industries so that they would, in time, become competitive in world markets. Boyd admitted that this proposal violated previous agreements worked out with Bartlett, Commerce Committee Chairman Warren Magnuson (D, Wash.) [*q.v.*] and other congressional leaders who favored substantial aid to American maritime industries. As a result of this conflict, no significant legislative program for the maritime industry was passed during the Johnson Administration.

Bartlett, who voted for the Tonkin Gulf Resolution of August 1964, soon earned a reputation as a critic of escalation in Vietnam. He was among 15 senators who sent a letter to President Johnson on Jan. 27, 1966 calling on him to continue the pause in the bombing of North Vietnam. In May 1968, however, Bartlett joined 16 Senate critics of the war who warned Hanoi that "they remained steadfastly opposed to any unilateral withdrawal of American troops from South Vietnam." Bartlett died in December 1968.

[JLW]

BATTLE, LUCIUS D(URHAM)

b. June 1, 1918; Dawson, Ga.
Assistant Secretary of State for Educational and Cultural Affairs, June 1962-July 1964; Ambassador to the United Arab Republic, July 1964-January 1967; Assistant Secretary of State for Near Eastern and South Asian Affairs, January 1967-September 1968.

Lucius Battle received his B.A. from the University of Florida in 1936 and, following wartime naval service in the Pacific, returned to Florida to earn a law degree in 1946. That year he also joined the State Department. From 1949 until 1953 Battle served as a special assistant to Secretary of State Dean Acheson [*q.v.*]. He was then appointed first secretary of the American embassy in Copenhagen, his only diplomatic post before assignment by the Johnson Administration. In 1956 Battle resigned from the foreign service to become vice president of Colonial Williamsburg. He rejoined the Department in 1961 as special assistant to Secretary of State Dean Rusk [*q.v.*]. In 1962 he became assistant secretary of state for educational and cultural affairs. By the time he was appointed ambassador to the United Arab Republic (UAR) in July 1964, he had acquired a reputation as a tough, effective administrator with little diplomatic experience.

Battle arrived at his post during a period of tension between the two countries. In part, the friction resulted from America's African and Middle Eastern policy and a refusal to grant Egypt long-term agricultural aid. Egypt's close contacts with the Soviet block strained relations still further. In addition, President Gamal Abdel Nasser had an instinctive personal dislike for President Johnson that prevented close communications between the two leaders.

Relations between the U.S. and the UAR became increasingly tense during November and December 1964, after mobs attacked the American embassy and Cairo shot down a U.S. oil company plane belonging to a close friend of Johnson. Misunderstandings caused the situation to deteriorate still further. Shortly after the plane crash Nasser received an incorrect report that Ambassador Battle had rejected an Egyptian request for more wheat. The account prompted Nasser to deliver a general attack on U.S. foreign policy on Dec. 23. During his speech he personally insulted both Battle and Johnson. In reaction, the U.S. held up wheat shipments until June 1965. Battle eventually negotiated an agreement for the sale of $55 million worth of surplus U.S. agricultural products in January 1966.

Tensions between the two countries continued during 1965 and 1966 because of Washington's seemingly inconsistent policy toward Egypt. During these years Egypt attempted to improve relations and ensure future American aid by underplaying its role in Middle Eastern affairs and concentrating on national economic development. Although these actions had been recommended by the U.S., neither Battle nor the State Department gave any indication of approval. Instead, the embassy continued to focus on Egypt's position in foreign affairs. The Ambassador's attitude convinced Nasser to reassert Egypt's leadership in the Arab world, particularly in the struggle against Israel. Consequently, U.S.-UAR relations deteriorated further.

In January 1967 Battle was appointed assistant secretary of state for Near Eastern and South Asian affairs. He resigned the post in September 1968 to become vice president of the Communications Satellite Corporation. Battle became president of the Middle East Institute in 1973.

[EWS]

For further information:

Miles Copeland, *The Game of Nations: The Amorality of Power Politics* (New York, 1969).

Mohamed Hassanein Heikal, *The Cairo Documents* (New York, 1973).

BAYH, BIRCH E(VANS)

b. Jan. 22, 1928; Terre Haute Ind.
Democratic Senator, Ind. 1963- .

After graduating from Purdue University's School of Agriculture, Birch Bayh settled on a 340-acre farm outside Terre Haute in 1951. He won election as a Democrat to the largely Republican Indiana House of Representatives in 1954. Following the elections of 1958, a new Democratic majority in the State legislature chose the 30-year-old Bayh speaker of the House for the 1959-1960 session. Simultaneously, Bayh studied law at the Indiana University School of Law, receiving his degree in 1960. In 1962 Bayh was elected to the Senate in a spectacular upset victory over the conservative Republican incumbent, Sen. Homer E. Capehart. [See KENNEDY Volume]

As chairman of the Judiciary Committee's obscure Subcommittee on Constitutional Amendments, Bayh became responsible for removing constitutional flaws in the procedure for presidential succession suddenly made apparent by the death of President Kennedy. In conjunction with Rep. Emanuel Celler (D, N.Y.) [*q.v.*], chairman of the House Judiciary Committee, Bayh introduced a constitutional amendment in January 1965 outlining the steps to be taken by the vice president, the cabinet and Congress in case of presidential disability. The amendment also provided for the filling of a vice presidential vacancy by presidential appointment subject to congressional approval. The amendment passed both houses of Congress in the summer of 1965 and finally became the 25th Amendment after it was ratified by the 38th state legislature in February 1967.

Along with Sen. Sam Ervin (D, N.C.) [*q.v.*], Bayh led the fight against a constitutional amendment proposed by Sen. Everett M. Dirksen (R, Ill) [*q.v.*] that would have nullified the Supreme Court's decision barring prayer and Bible reading in public schools. In the Senate the proposed amendment fell short of the required two-thirds majority by nine votes in September 1966. As a substitute for the Dirksen amendment, Bayh offered a resolution stating it was "the sense of Congress" to encourage, but not require, "voluntary silent prayer and meditation" in public schools. The Senate rejected Bayh's proposal by a 52-33 vote.

In the latter years of the Johnson Administration, Bayh also promoted a constitutional amendment to abolish the electoral college and institute direct, popular election of the president, but the reform was never enacted.

Bayh supported the major civil rights and social welfare proposals of the Johnson Administration. His overall voting record was that of a moderate liberal; *Congressional Quarterly* reported in 1964 that Bayh voted against measures favored by the conservative coalition of Republicans and Southern Democrats 65% of the time. In 1968 Bayh voted against the coalition 52% of the time and in favor of AFL-CIO positions on 91% of his votes. Reelected in that year, Bayh was often in the forefront of constitutional and judicial action in Congress during the Nixon Administration. He helped to enact the 26th Amendment extending the franchise to 18-year-olds and led the Senate fight against the confirmation of Clement Haynsworth and G. Harrold Carswell, Nixon's nominees to the Supreme Court in 1969 and 1970. [See NIXON Volume]

[TO]

BEIRNE, JOSEPH A(NTHONY)

b. Feb. 16, 1911; Jersey City, N.J.
d. Sept. 2, 1974; Washington, D.C.
President, Communications Workers of America, 1947-74.

Beirne began working for Western Electric in 1928 and became an important leader of its employes association during the 1930s. Initially resisting Congress of Industrial Organization (CIO) efforts to organize telephone workers, Beirne was elected president of the independent National Federation of Telephone Workers in 1943. He negotiated the first national contract with the American Telephone and Telegraph Company (AT&T) in 1946. Following the first nationwide strike the next year, he became president of the reorganized Communications Workers of America (CWA), which affiliated with the CIO in 1949. Beirne became a CIO vice president and, after the AFL-CIO merger in 1955, a vice president of that organization. [See TRUMAN Volume]

In 1957 Beirne helped expel the International Brotherhood of Teamsters from the labor federation, and during the early 1960s he thwarted Teamster efforts to raid the CWA. A strong Kennedy supporter, Beirne in 1960 proposed a broad AFL-CIO training program for Latin American unionists similar to one already operated by the CWA. President Kennedy backed the plan as a means of countering the influence of Cuban leader Fidel Castro in the region. The American Institute for Free Labor Development (AIFLD) was established in 1961 under government, AFL-CIO and private corporate sponsorship. [See KENNEDY Volume]

In 1967 it was revealed that the AFL-CIO had accepted CIA funds for anti-Communist activities abroad. Beirne, who served as secretary-treasurer of the AIFLD, denied that it had received CIA money and maintained that it drew its government funding from the Agency for International Development. In February 1967 the *New York Times* reported that the CWA was the recipient, through Cornell University's School of Industrial and Labor Relations, of funds from foundations that had been identified in 1964 congressional hearings as CIA conduits. Beirne said he was unaware that the funds had any connection with the CIA.

As president of the 440,000-member CWA, Beirne was a prominent figure in organized labor. Within his union, however, many considered him insufficiently aggressive toward AT&T. "A strike against the Bell System is like throwing pebbles at the Queen Mary," Beirne once remarked, noting that automation had reduced the system's vulnerability to work stoppages. In 1968 contract talks with AT&T, the CWA sought large wage increases well beyond the Johnson Administration's anti-inflation guideposts. Beirne maintained that increased efficiency and automation would keep overall wage costs down. Reluctant to call a strike Beirne finally did so because of strong rank-and-file pressure. On April 18 the CWA rejected the company's fourth and final offer and began the first nationwide telephone strike in 21 years. Although union members overwhelmingly supported the action, there was little disruption of phone service. Many women employees did not belong to the CWA, and supervisory personnel filled in for strikers. Direct dial communications were, for the most part, unaffected. Despite the phone company's success in maintaining services during the walkout, the Bell System agreed to a three-year 19% pay raise for CWA members on May 9, 1968.

An active Democrat, Beirne was one of several labor leaders who resigned in February 1968 from Americans for Democratic Action when the organization endorsed anti-war presidential aspirant Sen. Eugene McCarthy (D, Minn.) [*q.v.*]. During the 1972 presidential campaign, however, Beirne defied AFL-CIO President George Meany's [*q.v.*] policy of neutrality to become secretary-treasurer of a national labor committee for Democratic candidate George McGovern [*q.v.*]. He remained president of the CWA until his death in 1974. [See NIXON Volume]

[MDB]

BELL, DAVID E(LLIOTT)

b. Jan. 20, 1919; Jamestown, N.D.
Administrator, Agency for International Development, January 1963-July 1966.

Brought up in Palo Alto, Calif., Bell received an M.A. in economics from Harvard. He joined the Bureau of the Budget briefly in 1942 and returned in 1945 following service in the Marine Corps. Between 1947 and 1953 Bell alternated between the Budget Bureau and the White House, specializing in drafting presidential budget messages and speeches on economic affairs. After helping with Adlai Stevenson's [*q.v.*] presidential campaign, Bell returned to Harvard and from 1954 to 1957, as a member of a Harvard-Ford Foundation team, assisted the government of Pakistan in formulating fiscal policies. He became a recognized authority on the economic problems of underdeveloped countries. [See TRUMAN Volume]

Bell was named Kennedy's director of the Bureau of the Budget soon after the 1960 election. Known as an adherent of the "new economics," he favored deficit spending when recession and high unemployment were the nation's major economic problems. While still working on Kennedy's controversial tax cut proposal in November 1962, Bell was appointed administrator of the Agency for International Development (AID). He assumed his new duties at the beginning of 1963. [See KENNEDY Volume]

Kennedy created AID in 1961 to coordinate and rationalize the allocation of money authorized for foreign aid. AID was intended to further a Kennedy foreign aid program that emphasized development rather than short-term assistance. As Bell stressed in 1965, "development assistance leads to permanent progress. . .and the earliest possible termination of economic assistance." AID was organized on a worldwide regional basis with missions attached to U.S. embassies. It paralleled the State Department in the economic field.

In early 1964 the Johnson Administration inherited much of the congressional and public criticism of the Kennedy foreign aid program. Undersecretary of State George W. Ball [*q.v.*], head of a panel studying the program, recommended that AID be abolished and its centralizing function be transferred to the State Department. Many critics charged that, because of AID red-tape, large amounts of foreign aid money were not spent within the fiscal year for which they were appropriated. The slowness was unavoidable, however, since development projects, unlike outright grants, had to pass through a number of legal channels. Johnson decided to retain AID, but as an economy measure he instructed Bell to reduce by 1,200 the number of AID employes by the end of fiscal 1965.

Most of Johnson's reductions were made in economic assistance—funds for military projects were only slightly affected. The 1965 aid request of $3.38 billion was the smallest in the history of the program. In the years Bell served under Johnson, development assistance in loans and grants approached $1 billion in the annual foreign aid appropriation. The Alliance for Progress, a separate funding category, usually received about $500 million. Supporting assistance, which in 1960 amounted to approximately $1 billion, was cut to $369 million in fiscal 1966.

Bell concentrated development spending in those countries that showed the ability to benefit from development loans and a willingness to cooperate politically with the U.S. Most of these nations—Brazil, Chile, Turkey, Nigeria, India, Pakistan—were large and politically sensitive. At the same time 14 nations no longer received supporting assistance grants because their economies were thought to be strong enough to dispense with such aid. Bell also encouraged participation from private sources and the governments of other developed countries. Other nations stepped up their aid programs and multilateral projects became more common. By emphasizing development Bell was also able to answer critics who charged that foreign aid contributed to the gold drain and the balance-of-payments problem. Speaking before the Senate Banking and Currency Subcommittee on International Finance in March 1965, Bell noted that "80% of the AID's expenditures last year represented not dollars going abroad, but steel, machinery, fertilizer and other goods and services purchased in the United States." Cutting AID appropriations "would primarily reduce U.S. exports, and would have only a very small effect on the balance-of-payments."

In January 1966 Johnson requested an additional $415 million for AID for the current fiscal year. Most of this money was asked as a part of a supplemental request for $13 billion to meet Vietnam costs. During the previous year AID had spent funds in Vietnam that had been earmarked for other areas. Vietnam not only received more military aid—now computed as part of the Defense Department budget—than any other nation, but in fiscal 1967 it became the largest recipient of AID assistance. Much of the aid was in the form of short-term grants, which Bell had tried to eliminate from the foreign aid program. At the same time AID concentrated on development in Vietnam, attempting to build a modern economy in the midst of war. AID saw itself in a race with time, believing that the South Vietnamese would have the strength and will to defeat the Communists as soon as they possessed a functioning economy. More than in the past, therefore, AID assumed tasks of a military and political nature, and Bell frequently participated in Vietnam policymaking sessions. He decided to resign, however, in July 1966 to become the Ford Foundation vice president, in charge of its overseas programs. Bell was succeeded by AID deputy administrator William S. Gaud.

[JCH]

BELLMON, HENRY

b. Sept. 3, 1921; Tonkawa, Okla.
Governor, Okla., 1962-66.

A farmer from the dry wheatfields of north central Oklahoma, Bellmon was elected to one two-year term in Oklahoma's House of Representatives in 1946. In 1960 he became the state Republican Party's chairman and in that post built a vigorous Party organization. In 1962 Bellmon, a comparatively unknown political figure, launched a gubernatorial campaign in which he stoutly opposed an increase in the state sales tax. His Democratic opponent, W.P. Atkinson, was hampered by his advocacy of a one-cent sales tax increase and the disarray of his Party following a bitterly divisive primary campaign. Bellmon campaigned as the common man's candidate, and his decisive victory margin of 76,000 votes demonstrated the effectiveness of his appeal. He was elected the state's first Republican governor since Oklahoma's admission to the union in 1907.

Bellmon's victory on a "no new taxes" platform precipitated a major crisis in the state's public educational system. Oklahoma had had no general statewide tax increase since 1937, and its school system, struggling against rising postwar enrollments and increased operating costs, had by 1963 reached "a critical plane" according to the National Education Association (NEA). Although Oklahoma ranked 37th in the nation in teacher's pay, Bellmon vetoed a proposed 1963 raise in salaries and campaigned vigorously against a sales tax increase scheduled to be put before the state's voters in April 1965.

In November 1964 Oklahoma teachers took a "professional holiday" to stress their dissatisfaction with state educational funding, and in May 1965, after the defeat of the sales tax referendum, the NEA declared sanctions against the state for a school system that it termed "subminimal . . . in almost every area." Sanctions, in lieu of a strike, consisted of a warning to teachers in other states not to accept public-school jobs in Oklahoma and a "censure, through public notice, that Oklahoma, despite ample resources, maintains a subminimal pub-education program." Bellmon denounced sanctions as "disgusting, disgraceful and distasteful" and was chiefly concerned with the "black eye" that those sanctions gave to a state seeking to attract new industry and investment capital. In September 1965 the NEA lifted its sanctions, although it warned that it would continue to keep a watchful eye on the situation.

In December 1965 Bellmon announced "Operation Giant Stride," a plan to upgrade state social services, raise teachers' salaries by $800 over two years, raise the minimum wage for public employees, add to the highway program and strengthen the state's public and mental health services. The plan, which Bellmon argued would not "strangle" Oklahoma's growth by raising taxes, died in a committee of the Democratic-controlled legislature.

Bellmon's fiscal conservatism and pro-industry attitude was reflected in his opposition to pollution-control expenditures in the mid 1960s. At a two-day national water conference in Washington D.C. in December 1965, Bellmon expressed the view that the nation's waterways should be recognized in part to be repositories of waste, a policy that the Johnson Administration had repudiated. "The objective of any pollution abatement program must be the attainment and preservation of usable water—not the elimination of waste discharges," Bellmon said. "Assimilation of waste is unavoidably one of the multipurpose uses that water must serve and this must be recognized by all."

Bellmon was defeated in his bid for reelection to a second term in the Republican Party's 1966 gubernatorial primary. In August 1967 Bellmon was named chairman of the Nixon for President Committee. The next month Bellmon asserted that Gov. George Romney's [*q.v.*] announcement that he had been "brainwashed" regarding the situation in Vietnam "shows weakness" that would be "very damaging" to the party in a presidential campaign. Bellmon also held that "the mere fact that there's been a riot" in Detroit demonstrated Romney's potential weakness on domestic issues. In November 1968 Bellmon ran for the Senate and defeated three-term liberal incumbent Senator A. S. Mike Monroney (D., Okla.) [*q.v.*]

A consistent supporter of Nixon Administration programs, Bellmon was reelected to a second Senate term in 1974. [See NIXON Volume]

[TJC]

BENNETT, JOHN C(OLEMAN)

b. July 22, 1902; Kingston, Canada
Protestant Theologian; President, Union Theological Seminary, 1964-70.

Bennett, a leading representative of liberal Protestant theology in the U.S., was educated at Oxford University and New York's Union Theological Seminary, where he graduated in 1929. After teaching at the Auburn Theological Seminary in New York and the Pacific School of Religion in Berkeley, Calif., he returned to Union Theological Seminary in 1943 as professor of Christian theology and ethics.

Bennett became known in the 1940s as one of the originators of Christian realism, a theological school that argued that religious leaders should involve themselves in the political and social issues of their age. His immediate concern was the fight against fascism, but he later devoted himself to broader problems of peace and international order. In 1946 Bennett helped create the World Council of Churches, which sought to stimulate discussion on such matters as interfaith contacts and the role of religion in social change. Much of this discussion was carried on in *Christianity in Crisis*, a journal that Bennett helped establish in 1941 as an organ of Christian realist opinion. In this and other efforts he cooperated with Reinhold Niebuhr, the eminent liberal theologian who became Bennett's mentor at Union Theological Seminary.

Bennett was appointed dean of Union Theological Seminary in 1955 and nine years later became the school's president. He remained involved during the 1960s in both theological and political debate. A strong advocate of closer Catholic-Protestant contact, Bennett condemned Protestant leaders who opposed John F. Kennedy in the 1960 presidential campaign because of the candidate's Catholicism. "The implication that no Roman Catholic should ever be President," Bennett stated, "is an affront to 40 million of our fellow citizens." He also spoke out on foreign policy issues, criticizing the Cold War concept of monolithic Communism as an outmoded "obsession" of U.S. policymakers.

Bennett opposed the Vietnam war from its inception and joined with other religious leaders in numerous statements urging an end to American involvement. In 1965 he helped form Clergy and Laymen Concerned About Vietnam, a national anti-war group. Bennett repeatedly accused the Johnson Administration of ignoring the Vietnamese people in a preoccupation with "Communist aggression" and outdated concepts; he urged U.S. leaders to entrust the political fate of Vietnam to an international body, either the United Nations or a revived Geneva conference. Bennett was one of three religious leaders invited to testify on the Vietnam war before the Senate Foreign Relations Committee in March 1970. Two months later he was arrested outside the White House with Dr. Benjamin Spock [*q.v.*] and other demonstrators protesting the U.S. invasion of Cambodia.

Bennett retired as president of Union Theological Seminary in 1970. He returned to California during the early 1970s as a professor at the Pacific School of Religion. Though less closely associated than before with *Christianity in Crisis*, he maintained his interest in political and social issues. In numerous articles and lectures he urged the development of a "new conception" of Christianity based on the example of activists like Martin Luther King [*q.v.*], who "show in their lives the cost of human struggles for justice and peace."

[SLG]

For further information:
David H. Smith, *The Achievement of John C. Bennett* (New York, 1970).

BENNETT, WALLACE F(OSTER)

b. Nov. 13, 1898; Salt Lake City, Utah.
Republican Senator, Utah, 1951-75.

The son of Mormon pioneers, Wallace Bennett entered his family's plate and glass manufacturing business after graduating from the University of Utah. Beginning as a clerk he advanced through all phases of the business, taking over general management in 1932. Bennett's business interests also came to include a Ford dealership, a jewelry company, an investment concern and a bank. After serving as president of the National Association of Manufacturers (NAM) for 1949, Bennett was elected to the Senate as a Republican from Utah in 1950.

In the Senate Bennett espoused the same free enterprise views he had promoted for the NAM, opposing government restrictions on business and firmly defending "right-to-work" laws that allowed states to ban the compulsory union shop. He became an influential proponent of pro-business thinking on the Finance Committee and the Banking and Currency Committee, and Republican senators often looked to Bennett for conservative guidance on economic questions. [See TRUMAN, EISENHOWER, KENNEDY Volumes]

Bennett consistently opposed the social welfare programs of the Kennedy and Johnson Administrations. He voted against medicare in September 1964, against federal aid to education in April 1965 and against model cities and a minimum wage increase in August 1966. In a minority report on a 1965 housing bill, Bennett denounced "new and enlarged urban programs, bulging with money, designed to step up the pace of creeping federalism." In July 1968 Bennett argued that the answer to poverty lay in the involvement of business, rather than the federal government, in black ghettos.

Nevertheless, Bennett's overall voting record during the Johnson Administration showed a gradual movement toward the Republican center. *Congressional Quarterly* reported that Bennett voted with the Senate's conservative coalition 92% of the time in 1961 and 94% in 1964 but on only 57% of key votes in 1966 and 67% in 1968. He supported the presidential candidacy of fellow-Mormon Gov. George Romney [*q.v.*] of Michigan in 1964 and 1968, although it was more Romney's religious than his political affiliation that attracted Bennett. Bennett voted for the Civil Rights Act of 1964, the Voting Rights Act of 1965 and the open housing Civil Rights Act of 1968, but he favored an amendment to the latter exempting single-family homes from anti-discrimination coverage. He also was a strong supporter of the Vietnam war and high military spending.

Bennett was one of the few Western senators to approve the Administration-backed Coinage Act of 1965, which eliminated silver from nickels and dimes. In 1967 he finally relaxed his opposition to a truth-in-lending law to require merchants to furnish borrowers with full information about finance charges and interest rates. Maintaining that he had always favored full disclosure and opposed only the application of a single formula to many different types of credit, Bennett in July agreed to support a compromise version that exempted revolving charge accounts from the annual disclosure requirement. The compromise bill also exempted retail credit contracts when the finance charge was less than $10.

Bennett was one of five senators on the Finance Committee to vote against the Administration's $11 billion tax cut in January 1964. Bennett preferred repeal of many excise taxes and a lowering of capital gains taxes. In 1965 he pushed through a depletion allowance of 10%-22% for beryllium, rich deposits of which were located in Utah. Bennett backed the Administration's tax increase when combined with a spending ceiling in 1968.

In October 1965 Bennett was chosen vice chairman of the Senate Select Committee on Standards and Conduct, the panel charged with investigating the ethics controversy revolving around Sen. Thomas Dodd (D, Conn.) [*q.v.*]. In April 1967 Bennett presented the Committee's report recommending censure of Dodd for channeling campaign funds to his personal use. In February, however, Bennett had objected to Sen. Joseph Clark's (D, Pa.) [*q.v.*] "Bobby Baker amendment" to require senators to disclose all their assets and income. Bennett said that such a requirement came "perilously close to infringing upon the private affairs of a senator."

After defeating the Utah state coordinator for the John Birch Society in the Republican primary in September 1968, Bennett won reelection over his Democratic opponent in November with 54% of the vote. During the Nixon years he acted as the Administration's spokesman on finance in the Senate. [See NIXON Volume]

[TO]

BERRIGAN, DANIEL

b. May 9, 1921; Virginia, Minn.
Anti-war activist.

One of six children, Daniel Berrigan moved with his family to Syracuse, N.Y., after his father was fired from his job on a railroad in Minnesota for his activity in the Socialist Party. In Syracuse the elder Berrigan helped organize a local of the United Electrical Workers' Union and was a founder of the Syracuse Catholic Interracial Council. At the age of 18 Daniel Berrigan applied for admission to the Society of Jesus. After his novitiate he studied philosophy and theology at Woodstock College in Maryland and West College in Massachusetts. He was ordained in 1952.

In 1953 and 1954 Berrigan served as an

auxiliary military chaplain in Germany. While in Europe he came into contact with a group of French worker-priests. After returning to the U.S. in 1954, he taught French and theology at the Jesuits' Brooklyn Preparatory School. Berrigan also led a chapter of the Young Christian Workers in work among Puerto Ricans living on Manhattan's Lower East Side. From 1957 to 1963 he was a professor of New Testament studies at Le Moyne College in Syracuse, where he drew around him a dedicated group of young followers committed to pacifism and civil rights—one of whom was David Miller, later the first convicted draft-card burner.

Beginning in 1964 Berrigan fasted, picketed, sat-in and spoke against the Vietnam war. In the summer of 1965 he helped form the interdenominational Clergy and Laymen Concerned about Vietnam. As a result of his anti-war activity his superiors decided to send him to South America, apparently under pressure from the Archdiocese of New York, which was headed by the hawkish Francis Cardinal Spellman [*q.v.*]. Protests from liberal Catholics forced his recall after three months, and Berrigan resumed his organization of anti-war work.

In October 1967 Daniel Berrigan's brother, Father Philip Berrigan, a Josephite priest in a black parish in Baltimore, entered the Baltimore Customs House and poured blood on the Selective Service files. While awaiting sentencing for this action, he persuaded Daniel to join him in a second protest. On May 17, 1968 the two priests and seven other Catholics walked into the draft board office in Catonsville, Md. and set fire to the draft records with homemade napalm. The Catonsville Nine, as they came to be known, had selected the Catonsville draft board because it was housed in a Knights of Columbus hall and therefore symbolized, in their view, the collusion of the Church and those directing the war. The Nine were tried in October 1968 for conspiracy and destruction of government property. Daniel Berrigan and the others were found guilty, and he was sentenced to three years in prison. In April 1969, when he was to have begun serving his sentence, he went underground, later explaining that he had refused to accept the legal consequences of his lawbreaking because "there is no machinery of recourse with our law about this war." In August 1970 FBI agents apprehended him on an island off the Rhode Island coast, and he was sent to federal prison in Danbury, Conn., where he served 18 months. In 1972 he was named as an unindicted co-conspirator in connection with the federal government's unsuccessful prosecution of Philip Berrigan on charges of conspiracy to kidnap Henry Kissinger. [See NIXON Volume]

[TLH]

BEVEL, JAMES L(UTHER)

b. Oct. 19, 1936; Itta Bena, Miss.
Organizer and Project Coordinator for Southern Christian Leadership Conference, 1963- .

Bevel became a Baptist minister in 1959 and shortly afterwards became active in the civil rights movement. While studying at the American Baptist Theological Seminary in Nashville, Bevel worked as an organizer for the Student Nonviolent Coordinating Committee (SNCC). In 1962 SNCC members joined with Martin Luther King's [*q.v.*] Southern Christian Leadership Conference (SCLC) to protest the trial of freedom riders in Albany, Ga. This was Bevel's first close contact with the SCLC; one year later, he joined King's organization as Alabama project coordinator.

Bevel was closely associated with King during the most important civil rights struggles of the mid-1960s. In April and May 1963 he helped organize the SCLC campaign to end segregation in Birmingham, Ala. Bevel also directed the statewide drive to register black voters in the spring and summer of 1965. Many of the marches that he led were broken up by police, and Bevel himself suffered cranial injuries at the hands of Selma police in March 1965. Bevel aided King at this time not only as an organizer but also as a contact man with SNCC and other civil rights groups that increasingly objected to the nonviolent strategy of SCLC.

When King decided in 1966 to expand civil rights activity in Northern cities, Bevel was chosen head of the SCLC Chicago program. His main task was to coordinate the activities of 100 neighborhood improvement and community action organizations in the city's large west side ghetto. Bevel soon came to believe that the ghetto's condition resulted from "internal colonialism," which he defined as the efforts of businessmen and city officials to take money from blacks without reinvesting it in the black community. Attempting to reverse this pattern, he formed an association of welfare recipients in Chicago and directed a boycott of four local dairy companies that had refused to hire black workers. Bevel also helped organize several marches into all-white ethnic neighborhoods in May 1966, dramatizing black demands for an end to housing discrimination. The practical effects of the SCLC Chicago campaign were not great, but it did publicize the problems of black communities in the North.

In addition to his civil rights activities, Bevel became a strong opponent of the Vietnam war during the mid-1960s. As early as 1965 he urged the formation of an "international peace army" in which civil rights groups would share tactics and organizers with the anti-war movement. Bevel attacked American involvement in Vietnam as a "war of oppression against a foreign colored people," paralleling the oppression of blacks in the U.S. According to sources in SCLC, Bevel persuaded King in early 1967 to come out openly in support of the anti-war movement. This stand drew the criticism of several black leaders, including Roy Wilkins [*q.v.*] and Whitney Young [*q.v.*], who wanted to keep civil rights separate from issues of foreign policy. But Bevel continued working to bring the two together. In January 1967 he became head of the Spring Mobilization Committee to End the War in Vietnam, and he helped organize the large anti-war demonstrations of April 15 in New York and San Francisco. In New York 125,000 participated, including King himself.

Bevel took a leave of absence from the SCLC in 1967 to devote himself to further anti-war activities. By the time of King's assassination in April 1968, however, Bevel had returned to the civil rights movement. He was present in Memphis when King died, and he led the march King had planned in support of the city's striking sanitation workers. One month later Bevel was a leader of the SCLC Poor People's Campaign in Washington, a series of demonstrations to demand greater government attention to poverty problems. He subsequently coordinated SCLC activities in Philadelphia and worked as an aide for Ralph Abernathy [*q.v.*], King's successor as head of the SCLC.

[SLG]

For further information:
James Baldwin, *Nobody Knows My Name* (New York, 1961).
———, *The Fire Next Time* (New York, 1963).

BIBLE, ALAN D.

b. Nov. 20, 1909; Lovelock, Nev.
Democratic Senator, Nev., 1954-75;
Chairman, District of Columbia Committee, 1957-68.

Attorney General of Nevada from 1942 to 1950, Alan Bible was elected to the Senate in 1954 to fill the seat vacated by the death of Sen. Patrick McCarran (D, Nev.), a former law partner. During the campaign Bible promised to continue McCarran's efforts for higher wool, lead and zinc tariffs. Throughout the Eisenhower and Kennedy Administrations he voted as a moderate Democrat and established himself as a very effective but "low profile" senator. Bible's committee assignments attested to his broad range of influence: he sat on the Committees on Appropriations, Interior and Insular Affairs, Select Small Business, Special Committee on Aging and the Democratic Steering Committee and was chairman of the District of Columbia Committee. [See EISENHOWER Volume]

Bible had a mixed record of support for the liberal measures of the Johnson era. He voted against imposing cloture during Southern Democratic attempts to filibuster the Civil Rights Act of 1964 and the Voting Rights Act of 1965, but he favored those bills after cloture had been imposed. Bible's vote against cloture was explained by his belief that the filibuster was the ultimate protection for the small states against the large. He voted in favor of medicare and the Economic Opportunity Act of 1964 but was one of only two Northern Democrats to vote against creation of the Department of Housing and Urban Development in August 1965. Representing the "Silver State," Bible was one of nine senators to vote against the Administration-backed Silver Coinage Act of 1965, which eliminated silver from all dimes and quarters. During the 89th Congress, according to *Congressional Quarterly*, Bible supported Administration measures 65% of the time.

Bible took an active interest in policy on land management, parks and recreation. He was appointed in September 1964 to the Public Land Law Review Commission to study public land laws and administrative policies. As chairman of the District of Columbia Committee, Bible successfully managed a home rule bill through the Senate in July 1965, but the House passed an entirely different measure and the bill died in conference. Bible gave up his chairmanship of the District Committee in 1968 and in 1969 was appointed chairman of the Select Committee on Small Business. [See NIXON Volume]

[TO]

BIEMILLER, ANDREW J(OHN)

b. July 23, 1906; Sandusky, Ohio.
Director, Department of Legislation, AFL-CIO, 1956.

A former union organizer, Wisconsin state legislator and congressman, Andrew J. Biemiller helped pave the way for the merger of the American Federation of Labor with the Congress of Industrial Organizations in 1955. He subsequently was named head of the AFL-CIO department of legislation and became one of Washington's most influential lobbyists. [See EISENHOWER, KENNEDY Volumes]

The AFL-CIO's basic political agenda was determined by its National Legislative Council under the chairmanship of Federation President George Meany [*q.v.*]. Biemiller's department, manned by five or six full-time lobbyists and several representatives of the major international unions, was charged with responsibility for carrying out the daily AFL-CIO lobbying effort on Capitol Hill. Biemiller's staff also maintained close relations with both the Kennedy and Johnson Administrations. "We were in agreement with the White House on almost every piece of legislation," Biemiller later stated. "At least once a week I would compare notes with Larry O'Brien [*q.v.*], when he was in charge of congressional relations and then with [Harold] Barefoot Sanders who succeeded him. Occasionally, we would sit in on the White House legislative meetings and vote-counting operations."

During the Kennedy years Biemiller became a familiar figure on Capitol Hill, lobbying on behalf of the Administration's manpower training, education and foreign aid bills. Biemiller's office also played an important role in winning enactment of the Johnson Administration's civil rights, school aid and antipoverty legislation. Biemiller and Nelson Cruikshank of the AFL-CIO department of social security successfully countered American Medical Association opposition to the medicare bill that was enacted in the summer of 1965.

From time to time relations between the AFL-CIO and the Johnson White House were strained. Biemiller's office was critical of the Administration for its failure to exert its full authority to win repeal of Section 14b of the Taft-Hartley Act, which permitted states to pass right-to-work laws banning the union shop. The AFL-CIO was also critical of the Administration for its failure to maintain firm control over prices in exchange for labor's wage restraint in the mid-1960s. However, Biemiller and Meany steadfastly supported the Vietnam war policy of the Administration.

Biemiller worked actively in Vice President Hubert H. Humphrey's 1968 presidential campaign. During the Nixon years the AFL-CIO frequently found itself in an adversary position toward the Administration. Biemiller played an important role in blocking the appointment of conservative Southern judges Clement R. Haynsworth and G. Harrold Carswell to the U.S. Supreme Court. [See NIXON Volume]

[JLW]

BLACK, EUGENE R(OBERT)
b. May 1, 1898; Atlanta, Ga.
Presidential Adviser on Southeast Asian Economic Affairs, April 1965-January 1969.

Black, the son of a lawyer and banker, grew up in Atlanta. After graduating from the University of Georgia in 1918 and serving briefly in the Navy during World War I, he began a successful career as an investment banker, first in Atlanta and later in New York. By 1933 he was vice president of the Chase National Bank of New York. Widely respected in the financial community for his judgment and international contacts, Black was appointed executive director of the World Bank by President Harry Truman in 1947. Three years later he became president of the internationally funded bank, which made loans to developing countries on a commercial basis. Black remained with the World Bank until 1963, administering it according to conservative, low-risk policies. [See EISENHOWER Volume]

Black's contacts and experience made him an important link between the financial community in New York and the federal government in Washington. This was especially true during the 1960s. In 1963 Black served on a committee of businessmen and public figures formed to study the U.S. foreign aid program; he endorsed the committee's report, which criticized the program and recommended cuts in foreign aid levels. In September 1964 President Lyndon Johnson appointed Black to a foreign policy advisory panel, and in March 1965 Black joined a committee working on proposals for improvement of the foreign aid program. [See KENNEDY Volume]

Black moved from an advisory position to a more active foreign policy role in April 1965, when President Johnson put him in charge of the Administration's economic program in Southeast Asia. Johnson, hoping to deflate criticism of increasing American involvement in Vietnam, promised in an April 7 speech that the U.S. would sponsor a massive development and reconstruction effort in the area. He immediately chose Black as his agent to convince congressional skeptics that the program would be soundly managed. Black's main task was to arrange the creation of a multinational Asian Development Bank (ADB), which would provide investment funds and planning research staffs for Southeast Asian countries. Black enlisted the support of United Nations Secretary General U Thant, argued for the ADB before the House Banking and Currency Committee and represented the U.S. in negotiations over the bank's funding and charter. When the ADB was formally established in December 1965, Congress approved the requested $200 million appropriation with little resistance.

In addition to the ADB, Black helped organize other U.S. aid projects in Southeast Asia, including a Mekong River Redevelopment Commission. Such programs faded, however, as the U.S. military effort in Vietnam grew. By the late 1960s Black's direct involvement in foreign policy had largely ended. In January 1969 President Johnson awarded him the Medal of Freedom, America's highest civilian honor.

Black did not break his ties with the business community because of his government activities during the 1960s. He remained associated with the Chase Manhattan Bank, which appointed him to its board of directors in 1963, and also served on the boards of the New York Times Company, International Telephone and Telegraph and several other large corporations. In 1969 he became president of the Overseas Development Council, a social and economic research organization funded by U.S. businesses and foundations. Black went into semi-retirement in 1970, resigning from most of his corporate positions.

[SLG]

For further information:
Rowland Evans and Robert D. Novak, *Lyndon B. Johnson: The Exercise of Power* (New York, 1966).

BLACK, HUGO L(AFAYETTE)
b. Feb. 27, 1886; Harlan, Ala.
d. Sept. 25, 1971; Bethesda, Md.
Associate Justice, U.S. Supreme Court, 1937-71.

Hugo Black, born in rural Alabama, graduated from the University of Alabama Law School in 1906 and then practiced law in Birmingham. Elected to the U.S. Senate in 1926 and again in 1932, he was an ardent supporter of the New Deal. He was appointed to the Supreme Court by President Franklin Roosevelt in August 1937. Justice Black took a broad view of government power in the economic sphere and voted to sustain New Deal regulatory legislation and to extend federal antitrust laws.

His judicial reputation, however, was based primarily on his insistence that the Court should protect the individual liberties guaranteed by the Bill of Rights against government intrusion. Black argued that the 14th Amendment made those guarantees fully applicable to the states as well as to the federal government, and he became the leading judicial advocate of the incorporation of the Bill of Rights into the 14th Amendment. He also contended that the provisions of the Bill of Rights were absolutes that could not be infringed upon by government. Viewing the First Amendment as the core of individual liberty, Black insisted that it barred the government from placing "legal restrictions of any kind upon the subjects people could investigate, discuss and deny." [See TRUMAN, EISENHOWER, KENNEDY Volumes]

Justice Black initially set forth many of these views in dissent, but during the 1960s the ends he advocated were often adopted by the Court. Although a majority never subscribed to Black's position on "total incorporation" of the Bill of Rights, the Warren Court, on a case-by-case basis, gradually incorporated the major provisions of the Fourth, Fifth, Sixth and Eighth Amendments into the 14th. At the same time the Court liberalized its interpretation of the criminal rights guarantees in the Fifth and Sixth Amendments, thus adopting positions close to those advocated by Black.

The Court again adopted a point of view held earlier by Black when it asserted in March 1962 that federal courts could try state legislative apportionment cases. In February 1964 Black wrote a majority opinion extending this ruling to congressional districting. The ruling held that such districts should be as equal in population as possible so that each person's vote in a congressional election would have equal worth.

Black's arguments for an absolutist approach to the First Amendment also helped move the Court to increasingly liberal positions on free speech, free press and obscenity issues. During the 1950s Black had dissented in cases in which the majority upheld various subversive activities laws as necessary government regulations of speech and other liberties. By the mid-1960s the trend of Court decisions had changed. Black voted with the majority in June 1964 to nullify a federal law denying passports to members of the Communist Party. He also joined majorities that overturned a federal law making it a crime for a Communist Party member to serve as a labor union official in June 1965 and voided a set of New York State teacher-loyalty laws in January 1967.

Black believed that even libelous and obscene utterances were protected by the First Amendment. Consequently, he opposed all government censorship of allegedly obscene materials and urged the Court to protect even malicious criticism of public officials. The Warren Court never fully adopted these views, but it increasingly narrowed the definition of obscenity and raised the level of procedural safeguards in censorship systems throughout the 1960s. In a series of cases beginning in March 1964, the Court also expanded freedom of the press by ruling that a public official could not recover damages for a defamatory falsehood relating to his official conduct unless he could prove the statement was made with "actual malice."

In his last years on the Court, Black sometimes took "conservative" positions that surprised many observers. He dissented in June 1965 when the majority voided a Connecticut anti-contraceptive law as an invasion of the right to privacy. He said he could find no "right of privacy" in the

Constitution. Black's literal approach also led him to take a narrow view of the Fourth Amendment's ban on unreasonable searches and seizures. Dissenting in a June 1967 case where the majority invalidated a conviction based on electronic eavesdropping, Black argued that the language of the Fourth Amendment could not be extended to protect individuals from electronic bugging.

Black was a consistent supporter of the Warren Court's decisions against racial segregation and discrimination. In a sharply worded majority opinion in June 1964, Black held that the closing of public schools to avoid desegregation in Prince Edward County, Va., was unconstitutional. He voted to sustain the 1964 Civil Rights Act and joined the majority in June 1968 in upholding an 1866 federal law barring race discrimination in the sale and rental of housing and property.

Given this record Black startled legal commentators with several opinions in other civil rights cases of the mid-1960s. In March 1966 he dissented from a decision that voided a Virginia poll tax applicable to state elections on the ground that it was a violation of the 14th Amendment's equal protection clause. Black accused the majority of writing its own notions of good government policy into the Constitution under the guise of equal protection. Although he had voted in 1961 and 1963 to void the convictions of nonviolent civil rights demonstrators, Black dissented in June 1964 when the Court overturned the trespass convictions of protesters who sat-in at a Baltimore restaurant. He dissented when the Court voided similar convictions growing out of nonviolent civil rights demonstrations in cases decided in December 1964, January 1965 and February 1966. Black finally spoke for a five-man majority in November 1966 to sustain the trespass convictions of demonstrators who had gathered outside a Florida jail to protest the arrest of fellow demonstrators.

The Justice rejected the argument that these demonstrations were a form of free speech and assembly protected by the First Amendment. As he explained in one dissent, he believed that the First Amendment protected expression in any manner in which it could be "legitimately and validly communicated." But it did not give people a "constitutional right to go wherever they want, whenever they please, without regard to the rights of private or public property or to state law." While some observers felt these votes signaled a shift toward conservatism on Black's part, others, including the Justice himself, held that his opinions were consistent with earlier statements that government could regulate the place, though not the content, of speech.

In his remaining years on the Court, Black dissented in cases reversing the Warren Court's expansion of the rights of criminal suspects. After 34 years on the Supreme Court, Black resigned on Sept. 17, 1971 because of poor health. He died a week later at the age of 85.

Virtually all legal scholars ranked Black as one of the greatest and most influential justices in the Court's history. Summarizing the views of many other analysts, John P. Frank said that "no other single individual has more sharply put his own personal imprint upon the law as declared by the Supreme Court from 1937 to the present day than Justice Black." Beginning in "lonely and persistent dissent," Professor Norman Dorsen noted, "Justice Black again and again marshalled arguments to convince the Court of his views on the First Amendment, reapportionment, due process and other issues. At the end, much of what he professed was accepted, and his profound contribution to constitutional law was assured." [See NIXON Volume]

[CAB]

BLAKE, EUGENE CARSON

b. Nov. 7, 1906; St. Louis, Mo.
Clergyman; Secretary General, World Council of Churches, 1966-72.

Educated at Princeton and Edinburgh University, Eugene Carson Blake took over his first pastorate in 1932 in New York City. In 1951 he was elected to the first of a series of terms as the stated clerk of the General Assembly of the Presbyterian Church in the U.S.A., which became the

United Presbyterian Church after a 1958 merger with another Presbyterian group. He served as a U.S. delegate to the World Council of Churches and between 1954 and 1957 was the elected president of the National Council of Churches of Christ in the U.S.A., an organization of Protestant and Orthodox churches that took positions on social issues and furthered interdenominational cooperation.

Blake's official posts made him the most influential spokesman of liberal American Protestantism. During the 1950s he publicly attacked McCarthyism for its infringement of human and civil rights and for an "anti-intellectualism . . . which tends to blur all distinctions except that of white and black." Speaking for the World and National Councils of Churches, he advocated a world peace program, specifically backing the United Nations, armaments regulation and reduction, and economic and technical assistance to the underdeveloped world. In the early 1960s Blake sought interdenominational cooperation in support of the civil rights struggle and initiated plans for the merger of some of the leading Protestant denominations. [See EISENHOWER, KENNEDY Volumes]

Blake tended to stress the fundamental beliefs shared by all religions rather than theological differences, partly because he believed that in the modern world all religion was threatened by atheistic communism and humanistic secularism. In addition, his social activism subordinated the particulars of theology to the Christian responsibility to work for the "transformation of society."

In the mid-1960s Blake continued to enlist widespread clerical support for the civil rights movement. He was named chairman of the National Council of Churches' Emergency Commission on Religion and Race in 1964 and the following year served on a National Advisory Council for the Administration's antipoverty program.

Exchanging the chief executive post in the Presbyterian Church for the secretary-generalship of the World Council of Churches in 1966, Blake now represented a global constituency and could speak with greater authority on international issues, including the war in Vietnam. Having founded the National Emergency Committee of Clergy Concerned About Vietnam in January 1966, he at first supported President Johnson's "policy of restraint," but by the end of the year, he admitted that there was some "suspicion" about the sincerity of U.S. peace initiatives. In April 1967 he asserted that U.S. activity in Vietnam constituted the "greatest danger to human survival with the. . .exception of [Communist China]." In addition, he contended that the war was "our excuse not. . .to win the war against poverty in our cities, not to establish racial justice in our nation."

Blake's dream for the unification of the Protestant denominations in the U.S. seemed close to realization when in May 1966 the Consultation on Church Union, which he had founded in 1962, issued a timetable leading to the merger of eight leading Protestant denominations before the end of the century.

Blake was replaced as secretary general of the World Council of Churches in 1972 by a black Methodist minister from Dominica, a choice that indicated the Council's commitment to the underdeveloped countries. But many of Blake's efforts toward inter-denominational unity went unfulfilled. Despite joint ventures with Rome in peace and relief work and Catholic attendance at World Council meetings, doctrinal differences prevented the Catholics from joining his organization.

Blake's opposition to the war in Vietnam increased the already intense hostility felt toward him by conservative American Protestants. Orthodox Presbyterians, in particular, objected to the centralized control exercised by Blake and the church hierarchy and their modification of traditional teachings on predestination, the ordination of women and the literal interpretation of the Bible. In 1973 a number of churches seceded to form the Southern-based Continuing Presbyterian Church. In the same year the Constitution on Church Union decided to indefinitely postpone plans for an American Protestant merger due to the difficulty in reconciling doctrinal differences. [See NIXON Volume]

[JCH]

BLATNIK, JOHN A(NTON)
b. Aug. 17, 1911; Chisolm, Minn.
Democratic Representative, Minn.
1947-75.

Elected to Congress from the depressed northern mining district of Minnesota, Blatnik gained a reputation during the 1950s as a strong supporter of clean water legislation and as a proponent of many large-scale public works projects, among them the St. Lawrence Seaway.

A liberal on social issues, he supported all civil rights legislation, including the Civil Rights Act of 1964 and the Voting Rights Act of 1965. Blatnik also backed medicare, the model cities program, aid to mass transit, anti-poverty programs and comprehensive child care facilities for the working poor. In 1968 the liberal Americans for Democratic Action gave him a 75% rating and the Committee on Political Education, the political arm of the AFL-CIO, credited Blatnik with a 100% correct record on selected issues.

Although a prime force behind the development of federal water pollution control in the 1950s, Blatnik ceased to be a vigorous proponent of clean water legislation during the 1960s. Consequently, many of the pollution measures pushed through the Senate were dismembered by the pro-industry House Public Works Committee, where Blatnik had once skillfully supported reform. The reasons for this change were not clear, but critics suggested that it was the result of the federal Water Quality Control Administration's attempt to stop the Reserve Mining Company, the largest employer in Blatnik's district, from dumping industrial wastes into Lake Superior.

In late 1965, when a biologist at the National Water Quality Laboratory in Duluth reported that pollutants from the Reserve Mining Company were being spilled into Lake Superior, his superiors directed the scientist to stop research on the project. Although the reasons behind his order were never precisely determined, David Zwick, in his history of pollution legislation, *Water Wasteland*, implied that it was a result of fear that Blatnik, as chairman of the powerful House Public Works Committee's Rivers and Harbors Subcommittee, would vote to cut off funds to the laboratory. According to Zwick, a man friendly to Blatnik and Reserve Mining was named assistant director of the Duluth laboratory in 1967. The issue of Reserve Mining's pollution continued into the 1970s. In March 1975, after a series of court fights, the U.S. Court of Appeals ordered Reserve Mining to plan to end water pollution "within a reasonable time." Blatnik retired in 1975 and was replaced by his long-time assistant James Oberstar. [See NIXON Volume]

[EWS]

BLISS, RAY C(HARLES)
b. Dec. 16, 1907; Akron, Ohio.
Chairman, Ohio Republican State Central Committee, February 1949-March 1965; Chairman, Republican National Committee, April 1965-February 1969.

The son of German immigrants, Ray C. Bliss received his B.A. from the University of Akron in 1935. While establishing a lucrative insurance and real estate agency, Bliss filled various posts within the Akron Republican organization and in 1942 became chairman of the Summit County Republican Central Committee.

In February 1949 state Republican leaders, disheartened by their Party's poor showing in the 1948 election, elected Bliss chairman of the State Central Committee. Bliss asked for and received a salary and staff commensurate with making his position a full-time job. Avoiding the spotlight, Bliss assumed the role of a "nuts and bolts" Party leader, reorganizing state and local party machinery. Except for two years—1958 and 1964—and the repeated election of one Democrat—Sen. Frank J. Lausche (D, Ohio) [*q.v.*]—Bliss enjoyed striking success as party chairman. Political observers credited Bliss with putting Ohio in the Republican column in the 1960 presidential contest and with the Ohio GOP's impressive showing in 1962. National Party leaders considered Bliss for the chairmanship of the Republican National Committee (RNC) in 1961 and 1964.

The Republican's disastrous showing in 1964 set the stage for Bliss's elevation to RNC chairman in 1965. In the battle for the Party's 1964 presidential nomination, Bliss had feared the impact of conservative Sen. Barry M. Goldwater's (R, Ariz.) [*q.v.*] candidacy on the state ticket. But Gov. James A. Rhodes [*q.v.*], whom Bliss had unenthusiastically supported for the 1962 gubernatorial nomination, disregarded Bliss's counsel in July 1964 and released the Ohio delegation to the Republican National Convention in favor of Goldwater. The Ohio chairman's instincts proved correct in November. Goldwater lost the Buckeye State by one million votes and carried the Party's highly favored senatorial nominee and four incumbent representatives down to defeat with him. Soon after the election liberal-moderate leaders, led by Gov. Robert E. Smylie (R, Ida.) [*q.v.*], demanded the resignation of RNC Chairman Dean Burch [*q.v.*], a Goldwater appointee, as retribution for the Senator's poor showing in the November election. Following discussions initiated by former Vice President Richard M. Nixon [*q.v.*], Goldwater acquiesced to the pressure of moderate Republicans and announced the designation of Bliss, the leading candidate for the position, as Burch's successor in January 1965.

Taking office in April 1965 Bliss inaugurated a series of reforms designed to revitalize a party badly divided by internal factionalism. Under his direction the RNC sponsored workshops for state and local chairmen and 20,000 party volunteers. Retired Army General Lucius D. Clay became finance chairman at Bliss's request, and the RNC raised $4 million in 1965 and a record $6 million in 1966. Author of a 1961 RNC study that had urged a greater Party effort in the larger metropolitan areas, Bliss encouraged liberal Republican candidacies in urban areas. In November 1965 Republicans won elections for mayor of New York and district attorney in Philadelphia.

More basic to the GOP's dilemma was an intense factionalism, which, if uncontrolled, threatened the Party's very existence. In part because of his personality, Bliss quickly emerged as an excellent choice for RNC chairman. A nervous man given to chain-smoking, Bliss disliked partisan speech-making and frequent press conferences. Instead, he fostered the creation of the Republican Coordinating Committee made up of an ideologically broad spectrum of former presidential candidates, governors and congressmen. Between 1965 and 1966, the Coordinating Committee issued 18 position papers couched in language bland enough to please Republicans of all persuasions. Anxious over the possibility of another heated campaign for the presidential nomination in 1968, Bliss maintained an early neutrality and forbade the RNC to pay for the airplane used by Nixon in his extensive 1966 election tours.

The 1966 elections signaled a Republican revival. The GOP gained three Senate seats, 47 House seats and eight governorships. The Party won control of 15 state legislatures—a gain of nine—a sign that the GOP's success had come "from the bottom up," as Bliss remarked. Paying far greater attention to the urban electorate, Republicans generally improved upon their 1964 tallies in Baltimore, Detroit, Boston, Chicago and Los Angeles.

The August 1968 Republican National Convention marked the high point of Bliss's tenure as RNC chief. The Convention proved an efficent operation, and following Nixon's nomination, Bliss won reelection as chairman. However, the Ohio politician played a minor role in Nixon's campaign and instead concentrated his efforts on state contests. Although the GOP failed to capture either house of Congress, the Party won five more governorships.

Preferring a loyal spokesman over a Party technician, and mindful of Bliss's refusal to provide him with a plane in the 1966 campaign, President Nixon removed Bliss as national chairman in February 1969. Bliss declined Nixon's offer of a diplomatic post and retired to Akron to sell insurance while remaining a RNC member from Ohio. [See NIXON Volume]

[JLB]

For further information:
Stephen Hess and David S. Broder, *The Republican Establishment* (New York, 1967).

BOGGS, (THOMAS) HALE
b. Feb. 15, 1914; Long Beach, Miss.
d. Oct. 16, 1972; Alaska.
Democratic Representative, La., 1941-43, 1947-72; Chairman, Joint Economic Subcommittee on Foreign Economic Policy, 1957-72.

After receiving his law degree from Tulane in 1937, Boggs began his political career in 1939 as a member of the People's League, a business and professional men's organization antagonistic to the Long political machine. First elected to Congress in 1940 as a "reform" candidate, Boggs was defeated in 1942 but returned in 1946. Boggs became one of Speaker Sam Rayburn's (D, Tex.) proteges and received a seat on the powerful House Ways and Means Committee in 1949. He was made chairman of the Ways and Means Subcommittee on Foreign Trade Policy in 1955 and the Joint Economic Committee's Foreign Economic Policy Subcommittee in 1957. Boggs strongly supported attempts by the Eisenhower and Kennedy Administrations to increase the chief executive's authority to lower tariffs. He called the Trade Expansion Act of 1962, which gave the President unprecedented tariff reduction authority, "one of the most significant events of the century." [See EISENHOWER, KENNEDY Volumes]

Boggs voted against the 1964 Civil Rights Act but received a standing ovation on the House floor on July 9, 1965 when he announced his support for the voting rights bill. Boggs again broke with most of his Southern colleagues when he supported the 1968 Civil Rights Act, including its controversial open housing provision. As a result of his support for civil rights and antipoverty legislation, Boggs defeated his Republican opponent by only a small margin in November 1968.

As part of congressional evaluation of America's long range trade position, Boggs's Joint Economic Subcommittee on Foreign Economic Policy held hearings in July 1967 on the effects of the Kennedy Round of tariff negotiations. The subcommittee's report, which generally reflected Boggs's liberal trade stance, advocated new negotiating powers for the President, aid for industries injured by imports, an attack on tariff trade barriers and trade preferences for less developed countries.

The retirement of House Speaker John McCormack (D, Mass.) [*q.v.*] in 1971 and the subsequent elevation of Majority Leader Carl Albert (D, Okla) [*q.v.*] placed Boggs in line for the position of majority leader. Boggs was challenged by a group of reform-minded Democrats who supported Rep. Morris Udall (D, Ariz.) [*q.v.*]. According to *The Almanac of American Politics*, Boggs used his position on the Ways and Means Committee to promise wavering congressmen desirable committee posts. Boggs won an easy second ballot victory in January 1971, and the Ways and Means Committee rewarded many liberals with choice committee assignments. Before his October 1972 death in an Alaskan plane crash, Boggs was widely regarded as Carl Albert's probable successor when the new speaker chose to retire. [See NIXON Volume.]

[DKR]

For further information:
Stephen Hess and David S. Broder, *The Republican Establishment* (New York, 1967).

BOHLEN, CHARLES E(USTIS)
b. Aug. 30, 1904; Clayton, N.Y.
d. Jan. 1, 1974; Washington, D.C.
Ambassador to France, August 1962-December 1967; Deputy Undersecretary of State for Political Affairs, December 1967-January 1969.

The son of a wealthy sportsman, Charles Bohlen joined the foreign service in 1929, specializing in Soviet affairs. Bohlen was a member of the first U.S. embassy to the Soviet Union from 1934 to 1940 and served as Russian translator at the Teheran conference of 1943 and the Yalta and Potsdam conferences of 1945. Despite objections from Sen. Joseph McCarthy (R, Wisc.), who linked him with the "Truman-Acheson policies of appeasement," Bohlen was appointed ambassador to Moscow in 1953. In

1957 Secretary of State John Foster Dulles sent Bohlen to the Phillipines amid rumors that the Ambassador was being "exiled" because he disagreed with Dulles's Russian policies. In 1960 he was made special assistant for Soviet affairs in the State Department. [See TRUMAN, EISENHOWER Volumes]

During the Kennedy Administration the new President asked Bohlen's advice on a wide range of foreign policy issues including Laos, Cuba and Berlin. However, Bohlen rarely became involved in any one area of policymaking for a long period of time. In August 1962 Kennedy appointed him ambassador to France. There, according to his autobiography, Bohlen was able to accomplish little in terms of improving Franco-American ties because of President Charles De Gaulle's desire to pursue an independent foreign policy. [See KENNEDY Volume]

During the Johnson years Bohlen remained at his post in France. Despite continued stress he was able to maintain good relations between the U.S. and France by convincing President Lyndon B. Johnson to avoid an open conflict with De Gaulle no matter what the provocation. Thus, when France announced her intention to pull out of the North Atlantic Treaty Organization in 1966 and demanded the removal of American troops by April 1967, Bohlen advised Johnson to meet the conditions without delay.

In 1966 Johnson asked Bohlen to return as ambassador to Moscow. Bohlen refused the appointment because, in his opinion, the tediousness of dealing with the Russians and the boredom Americans faced in that capital made a second term undesirable.

In December 1967 Bohlen was appointed deputy undersecretary of state for political affairs. In this post he was responsible for briefing other government departments on international developments and coordinating policy between these agencies. Never on close terms with Johnson, Bohlen opposed the continued bombing of North Vietnam on the grounds that it forced the Kremlin to increase its aid to North Vietnam and because the unpopular bombing policy turned Western European public opinion against the U.S.

During the Russian invasion of Czechoslovokia in August 1968, Johnson asked Bohlen's advice on possible American action. Bohlen counselled the President to adopt a low-key policy since any threat of active American intervention would lead the U.S. into a confrontation with the USSR in which the President would be faced with the necessity either to back down or escalate the crisis.

Bohlen retired from the State Department in January 1969. He died on Jan. 1, 1974.

[EWS]

For further information:
Charles Bohlen, *Witness to History, 1929-1969* (New York, 1973).

BOLLING, RICHARD W(ALKER)

b. May 17, 1916; New York, N.Y.
Democratic Representative, Mo., 1949- .

Born in New York City, Richard Bolling spent much of his boyhood in Huntsville, Ala. Following college and four years of military service overseas, Bolling became midwestern director of Americans for Democratic Action in 1947. He ran for the House of Representatives in 1948 on a platform advocating repeal of the Taft-Hartley Act and was elected from Missouri's fifth (Kansas City) district over a Republican incumbent. Serving on the Joint Economic and the Rules Committees, Bolling, although a liberal with an urban constituency, became a protege of Speaker Sam Rayburn (D, Tex.) during the later years of the Eisenhower Administration. Bolling was a leader of the successful effort in January 1961 to dilute the power of the conservative majority on the Rules Committee by expanding the body from 12 to 15 members. [See KENNEDY Volume]

A supporter of the antipoverty and civil rights legislation of the Johnson Administration, Bolling played a key role in House passage of the Civil Rights Act of 1966. Title IV of this bill, as proposed by the Administration, would have banned discrimination in the sale or rental of all housing;

the vote on a compromise amendment introduced by Charles Mathias (R, Md.) [*q.v.*] to permit discrimination in the sale of individual homes (60% of the nation's housing) ended in a 179-179 tie. Bolling, temporarily presiding over the House, broke the tie and voted for the amendment on the grounds that only such a compromise version could pass.

Following the failure of the House to pass much of Johnson's legislative program in 1967, Bolling called upon Speaker John McCormack (D, Mass.) [*q.v.*] to resign. He asserted on Oct. 27 that the Speaker failed to provide effective leadership and lacked "the skill to anticipate trouble." Author of two critical studies of the House, *House Out of Order* (1964) and *Power in the House* (1968), Bolling was the leading congressional advocate of internal House reform. Among his recommendations were full financial disclosure by members, limitations on conflicts of interest and a weakening of the seniority system along with a strengthening of the role of the speaker and the party caucus. Bolling backed the Johnson and Nixon Administrations on the Vietnam war, sponsoring a successful motion to kill an amendment in August 1972 that mandated a halt to U.S. military activity by October 1. [See NIXON Volume]

[TO]

BOLTON, FRANCES P(AYNE) (BINGHAM)

b. March 29, 1885; Cleveland, Ohio.
d. March 9, 1977; Lyndhurst, Ohio.
Republican Representative, Ohio, 1940-69.

A descendent of one of Cleveland's oldest and wealthiest families, Frances Bingham married Chester C. Bolton, a steel executive, in 1907. She then devoted her time and a great deal of her money to a variety of progressive causes, including black self-help programs and the Tuskegee Institute. With a special interest in nursing, Bolton helped persuade the government to establish the Army School of Nursing during World War I. She participated in her husband's usually successful Republican campaigns for the House beginning in 1928.

Upon her husband's death Bolton succeeded to his suburban Cleveland seat in a special 1940 election and served consecutively for nearly 30 years. As a congresswoman during World War II, she called for the desegregation, both by race and sex, of military nursing units. In 1949 she argued for the inclusion of women in the Selective Service System. Appointed to the House Foreign Affairs Committee, Bolton strongly advocated American entry into the United Nations and independence for colonial Africa. She also led efforts that resulted in the restructuring of committee procedure. [See TRUMAN, Volume]

During the Johnson years Bolton was the ranking Republican member of the Foreign Affairs Committee. In her committee assignment she criticized America's foreign aid and Vietnam policies but consistently supported the Administration on crucial votes. An energetic campaigner, Bolton won reelection in 1964 at age 79, leading the Party's presidential ticket in her district by 27% of the vote. She handily won another term in 1966. In the drafting of civil rights legislation, she worked to include bans against sex discrimination.

Despite a longtime philanthropic connection with American blacks and a large Negro population in her district, her minority rights voting record during the 1960s was uneven. She voted for the 1964 and 1965 civil rights acts but against the 1968 housing law. In July 1968, however, she voted with a minority of House Republicans in favor of the Housing and Urban Development Act, which provided funding of housing units for the disadvantaged.

Blacks and blue-collar Democrats abandoned Bolton in 1968 and combined with opponents of the Vietnam war to deny her reelection. Rep. Charles A. Vanik (D, Ohio) [*q.v.*], an anti-war liberal of Czech heritage, ran against Bolton following a reapportionment of her Cleveland district by the Ohio legislature. With Bolton's age the silent issue of the campaign, Vanik defeated the veteran Representative with 55% of the vote.

[JLB]

BOND, (HORACE) JULIAN
b. Jan. 14, 1940; Nashville, Tenn.
Communications Director, Student Nonviolent Coordinating Committee, 1961-66; Member, Georgia House of Representatives, 1966- .

Bond grew up on the campuses of Fort Valley State College in central Georgia and Lincoln University in Pennsylvania where his father, historian Horace Mann Bond, served as president. He enrolled in Atlanta's black Morehouse College in 1957, and when the sit-in movement began in February 1960, Bond co-founded the Committee on Appeal for Human Rights (COHAR), which organized a series of student sit-ins in Atlanta. Bond was arrested in the first sit-in at the City Hall cafeteria in March, but he soon left sit-in campaigns to do communications and publicity work for COHAR and to report for the Atlanta *Inquirer*, a newspaper Bond and other students founded in 1960. COHAR coalesced with other student groups in April 1960 to form the Student Nonviolent Coordinating Committee (SNCC), and in the spring of 1961 Bond became communications director for SNCC. Working mainly at SNCC's Atlanta headquarters, Bond edited its newspaper, *The Student Voice*, prepared radio tapes and news releases for the press and supervised publicity for SNCC voter registration and civil rights drives.

Early in 1965 Bond entered the Democratic primary for the Georgia House of Representatives in the 136th district, a new and predominantly black Atlanta district created as the result of a court-ordered reapportionment of the state legislature. Bond swept both the May primary and the general election in November. On Jan. 6, 1966, four days before Bond was to be sworn in as a House member, SNCC issued a policy statement condemning the Vietnam war and expressing support for men who resisted the draft. Bond endorsed the statement the same day. On the grounds that the statement was "un-American," the Georgia House voted 184-12 on Jan. 10 not to seat him. Bond immediately filed suit in federal court to challenge his exclusion, but a three-judge court ruled 2-1 on Jan. 31 that the House's action was constitutional. While this decision was on appeal to the Supreme Court, Bond ran unopposed in a Feb. 23 special election in his district but was again denied his seat by the House Rules Committee on May 23.

Bond ran a third time for the House seat in a September Democratic primary and this time won in a very close race. On Sept. 8, just before the primary, he resigned from SNCC for "personal reasons." In later years Bond said economic necessity, the desire to start a new career and SNCC's growing emphasis on the North rather than the South contributed to this decision. According to Roger M. Williams, who wrote a biography of the Bond family, Julian also felt that SNCC was no longer doing enough constructive and concrete work under its new chairman, Stokely Carmichael [*q.v.*]. Carmichael's presence in Atlanta during riots on Sept. 6 and 7 and his arrest on Sept. 8 on a charge of inciting to riot may also have forced Bond to disassociate himself from SNCC in order to win the primary. Bond won the November general election, and on Dec. 5, 1966 the Supreme Court ruled unanimously that the Georgia House had violated Bond's First Amendment right to free expression in expelling him for his anti-war statements. On Jan. 9, 1967 Bond was finally sworn in as a member of the Georgia House of Representatives. During the year-long fight for his seat, Bond became a national political figure. He spoke at numerous anti-war rallies and in June 1966 was elected cochairman of the National Conference for New Politics.

Bond was cochairman of an insurgent delegation called the Georgia Loyal National Democrats at the Democratic National Convention in Chicago in August 1968. Before the Credentials Committee Bond argued that Georgia's regular delegation, led by Gov. Lester Maddox [*q.v.*], should not be seated because blacks were excluded from any real participation in the regular Democratic Party in the state. A majority on the Credentials Committee recommended a compromise in which Georgia's votes would be split between the regular and insurgent groups. After a floor fight in which Bond's delegation came very close to unseating the regular delegation entirely, the compromise was accepted by the Convention on Aug. 27.

At the Convention Bond delivered one of two seconding speeches for anti-war presidential candidate Sen. Eugene McCarthy (D, Minn.) [*q.v.*], and on Aug. 29 Bond's own name was placed in nomination for the vice presidency. His nomination, Bond later explained, was "a diversionary effort" to extend the Convention and give those who opposed the Vietnam war and the tactics used by Chicago police against anti-war demonstrators a chance to speak in protest. Bond received 48½ votes for the nomination before withdrawing his name during the course of the balloting. Bond continued to serve in the Georgia House of Representatives after 1968 and maintained an extensive speaking schedule as the national spokesman for a liberal political coalition of the black and white poor.

[CAB]

For further information:
Roger M. Williams, *The Bonds: An American Family* (New York, 1971).

BOOTH, PAUL
b. June 7, 1943; Washington, D.C.
National Secretary, Students for a Democratic Society, September 1965-June 1966.

Booth was the son of a professional, politically involved couple. His father was chief of the Unemployment Security Bureau's Division of Program and Legislation and later a professor of social work at the University of Michigan. His mother was a psychiatric social worker in Washington, D.C., where Booth grew up. Both his parents were active in the the Americans for Democratic Action. In 1962, while a freshman at Swarthmore College, Booth was a delegate to the founding convention of the Students for a Democratic Society (SDS) in Port Huron, Mich., and was elected vice president of the organization.

In the fall of 1964 Booth started the Peace Research and Education Project (PREP) in Ann Arbor, Mich., an SDS-sponsored study of the problems involved in converting the economy from reliance on military spending. With the escalation of the Vietnam war in 1965, however, the whole notion of "peace research" seemed pointless to Booth, and PREP was dropped. In the summer of that year, he moved to Oakland, Calif., where he worked as an organizer for an SDS Economic Research and Action Project (ERAP) in the inner-city area.

In the fall of 1965 SDS national leaders summoned Booth to Chicago to become national secretary and bring "order and politics" to the chaotic and directionless national office. During his one-year term SDS was the focus of national publicity. It had an unprecedented growth in membership and became "the largest, most influential, most intellectual and most idealistic of the New Left organizations," according to the *New York Herald Tribune*.

In October 1965 the syndicated columnists Rowland Evans and Robert Novak [*q.v.*] accused SDS of drawing up a "master plan" to "sabotage the war effort" by organizing systematic draft evasion. Sen. John Stennis (D, Miss.) [*q.v.*] called on the government to "jerk this movement up by the roots and grind it to bits." The chorus of denunciation was joined by a number of other senators, and Attorney General Nicholas Katzenbach [*q.v.*] threatened an official investigation. At this time SDS had no draft program beyond providing counseling for conscientious objectors, and Booth feared a "draft-dodging" image would hurt the organization. With SDS President Carl Oglesby [*q.v.*] he flew to Washington, D.C., to give a press conference at which he declared: "We are fully prepared to volunteer for service to our country and to democracy. We volunteer to go into Watts . . . to help the Peace Corps . . . to serve in hospitals and schools in the slums, in the Job Corps and VISTA . . . let us see what happens if service to democracy is made grounds for exemption to the military draft." The tone of the statement and the organization's slogan, "Build, Not Burn," disarmed many critics, but it provoked a strong reaction against Booth among many of the SDS rank and file who believed that the statement was excessively moderate and apologetic and did not attack the draft itself.

During Booth's term SDS formally severed its ties with its parent organization, the League for Industrial Democracy, and began to pursue an independent course. By April 1966 it claimed 5,000 members in 175 to 200 chapters. Most of these new recruits were young anti-war activists hostile to what they regarded as the "elitism" of the SDS "old guard." As a result, Booth found himself increasingly isolated by the end of his term. By that time he was involved independently with the National Conference for New Politics (NCNP), a coalition of anti-war and civil rights spokesmen organized to raise funds and manpower for the campaigns of Democratic insurgents in the primary elections of 1966. SDS did not endorse the NCNP, and at one point Booth was censured for giving the public impression that it did.

Booth subsequently took a job as an aide with the Packing House Workers Union in Chicago. In August 1968 he participated in the abortive efforts of the New Party to convince Sen. Eugene McCarthy (D, Minn.) [*q.v.*] to run for President as an independent candidate in the fall elections.

[TLH]

For further information:
Kirkpatrick Sale, *SDS* (New York, 1973).

BOUTIN, BERNARD L(OUIS)

b. July 2, 1923; Belmont, N.H.
Deputy Director, Office of Economic Opportunity, 1965-66; Director, Small Business Administration, 1966-67.

The son of a real estate and insurance company owner, Boutin grew up in Belmont, N.H. He graduated in 1945 from St. Michael's College in Vermont and returned to New Hampshire to work in his father's business. In 1955 Boutin became active in New Hampshire politics as a Democrat; he served as mayor of Laconia, N.H., until 1959, and as Democratic national committeeman from New Hampshire until 1960. He was also coordinator of the 1960 Democratic presidential campaign in New Hampshire.

In 1961 President Kennedy appointed Boutin director of the General Services Administration, where he supervised the use and operation of government property. He served in this position until 1964, gaining praise from observers as a "hard-nosed, first-rate administrator." After a brief period as vice president of the National Association of Home Builders, Boutin returned to the federal government in 1965 as deputy director of the Office of Economic Opportunity (OEO). There he utilized his administrative experience to establish standards and distribute funds for a wide variety of community action programs sponsored by the OEO.

In May 1966 Boutin left the OEO to become director of the Small Business Administration (SBA). He took control of the SBA at a time when the agency had been without a director for one and a half years; some of its programs had been suspended, and speculation had grown that the SBA would be absorbed by the Department of Commerce. Boutin brought the agency back to life and restored its programs, including federally guaranteed loans to small businessmen. It was later revealed, however, that more than $1 million in SBA loans had been granted to a Mafia-connected leasing company in New York and that the loans had continued for a time even after the firm's background had become known. A memo, written for Boutin in January 1967, urged that the incident not be made public.

Boutin left the SBA in July 1967, returning to New Hampshire to serve as consultant to an electronics firm. In 1968 he managed President Johnson's write-in campaign in the New Hampshire Democratic primary; Johnson's relatively poor showing against anti-war candidate Sen. Eugene McCarthy (D, Minn.) [*q.v.*] destroyed Boutin's own hopes of running for governor in 1970. After serving briefly on the state board of education, Boutin was chosen in 1969 to be president of St. Michael's College, his alma mater.

[SLG]

BOWLES, CHESTER

b. April 5, 1901; Springfield, Mass.
Ambassador to India, May 1963-April 1969.

Chester Bowles was born into a well-to-do Yankee family. After graduating from Yale University in 1924, he went into the advertising business. During World War II he held a succession of administrative positions in Connecticut's rationing program before being appointed director of the federal Office of Price Administration in 1943. In 1948 Bowles was elected governor of Connecticut. When he lost his reelection bid in 1950, President Truman named him ambassador to India, where he served until 1953. From 1958 until 1960 Bowles served in the House of Representatives. In November 1959 he became the first nationally prominent liberal to endorse John F. Kennedy for president and served as the candidate's chief foreign policy adviser during the campaign. [See TRUMAN, EISENHOWER Volumes]

Although mentioned as a possible candidate for Secretary of State, Bowles was passed over because his liberal views angered many prominent politicians. Instead, he was named undersecretary of state in January 1961. While at the post he urged the President to reorient American policy to support the growing nationalist movements in the undeveloped nations. Bowles's views made enemies within the State Department and Congress while his frequent clashes with Robert F. Kennedy [*q.v.*] lost him the support of the President. In November 1961 he was ousted from his State Department position.

During the next year Bowles served as the President's special representative and adviser on Asian, African and Latin American affairs but had little influence within the Administration. Frustrated by his inability to reshape the foreign aid program or head off what he believed would be a major military involvement in Vietnam, he submitted his resignation in December 1962. Kennedy suggested that instead of leaving the Administration, Bowles return to his former post as ambassador to India. Bowles accepted the offer with some reluctance. He was designated ambassador in April 1963. [See KENNEDY Volume]

When Bowles arrived in India relations between the two countries were close because of India's general sympathy for the U.S., America's continued economic aid and its military assistance during the 1962 border war with China. However, despite Bowles's close personal friendship with Indian leaders, relations between the two nations declined during the remainder of the decade. The Ambassador attributed this to President Johnson's inconsistent policies toward India, his use of aid as a weapon against nations opposing U.S. policy in Vietnam and his failure to recognize the importance of India in Asia.

During his tour one of Bowles's primary concerns was to increase long-term economic aid to India. In the spring of 1965 he submitted a detailed proposal for increased U.S. and World Bank assistance to enable India to achieve self-sustained growth within a decade. Although the Administration received the initial report favorably, the plan was never put into effect. Instead, when full-scale war broke out between India and Pakistan in September 1965, the U.S. stopped all aid to both belligerents.

When India's monsoons failed in 1965 and 1966, Bowles urged emergency aid to that country. Despite initial assurances from Johnson that wheat shipments would be forthcoming, the President granted the grain only grudgingly, releasing the shipments just days before the wheat was needed. Bowles attributed this conduct to Johnson's anger over the Indian government's opposition to the Vietnam war and the President's belief that the grain could be used to compel support for U.S. policy. Only Bowles's continual prodding and support from lower levels of the Administration kept the grain flowing. Indians found U.S. policy confusing and irresponsible; one official termed it "something approaching sadism."

Bowles's second major concern while in India was the reorientation of America's Asian policy from a focus on Pakistan to one stressing the importance of India. During the postwar period the U.S. had funneled large amounts of economic and military aid to Pakistan in the belief that its strategic position near the Soviet and Chinese borders made its stability vital for the prevention of Communist expansion in Asia. Bowles believed that this emphasis was inappropriate because that country did not share the American democratic philosophy and because Pakistan had consistently used military aid not to protect itself from China but to attack India. Pointing out that India's large population and democratic tradition made it the keystone of a stable, democratic Asia, the Ambassador recommended that the U.S. cut off large-scale military aid to Pakistan and begin supplying such assistance to India.

During his six-year tenure Bowles had little success in reorienting American policy. A strong pro-Pakistan lobby in the U.S. prevented the passage of military aid measures for India. When war broke out between the two Asian countries in September 1965, Bowles again saw India attacked with U.S.-supplied weapons. The U.S. did cut off aid to Pakistan during the conflict but also stopped assistance to India. Despite Bowles's continued pleas, military aid was restored to Pakistan in 1967.

In January 1968 Johnson sent Bowles to Phnom Penh to discuss ways of curbing Communist use of Cambodian territory, which would eliminate the prospect of U.S. "hot pursuit" into Cambodia to attack Communist installations. On Jan. 12 the U.S. and Cambodia agreed to strengthen the three-nation International Control Commission to police the Cambodian-South Vietnamese border. The U.S. also assured Cambodia that incursions were not American policy and promised to inform Phnom Penh of border violations rather than stage attacks. However, Bowles emphasized that the U.S. had the right of self-defense and would pursue Communist troops launching attacks from Cambodia if no other action were taken against them. Despite the January agreement the issue of "hot pursuit" was never resolved. The U.S. continued making secret raids into Cambodia and in May 1970 staged a full-scale invasion of that country.

In April 1969 Bowles was replaced as Ambassador to India. Two years later he published his memoirs describing his public life and outlining his ideas on foreign policy.

[EWS]

For further information:
Chester Bowles, *Promises to Keep: My Years in Public Life, 1941-1969* (New York, 1971).

BOYD, ALAN S(TEPHENSON)

b. July 10, 1922; Jacksonville, Fla. Member, Civil Aeronautics Board, November 1959-May 1965; Chairman, Civil Aeronautics Board, February 1961-May 1965; Undersecretary of Commerce for Transportation, June 1965-January 1967; Secretary of Transportation, January 1967-January 1969.

After service in the Army Troop Transport Command in World War II, Boyd earned a law degree from the University of Virginia in 1948. He returned to his native state to practice law and to serve on state commissions dealing with transportation development and regulation. In May 1959 President Dwight D. Eisenhower appointed Boyd to an unexpired term on the Civil Aeronautics Board (CAB). During the Kennedy Administration Boyd, a Democrat, chaired the Board. As CAB head Boyd aided the commercial airline industry's recovery from a period of disappointing profits. Boyd sought to standardize airline industry fare reductions, and under his chairmanship the CAB authorized subsidies to financially troubled lines for their less profitable runs between small cities. Boyd left the CAB to become undersecretary of commerce for transportation in June 1965. [See KENNEDY Volume]

Two positions taken by Boyd while at Commerce resulted in verbal confrontations with organized labor. Nine days after Boyd assumed his new post, Commerce Secretary John T. Connor [*q.v.*] selected him to chair a special interagency task force to study the nation's maritime industry. A preliminary report by the Boyd group, issued in September 1965, called for a reduction of the government's merchant fleet subsidy program and fewer legal restrictions on the industry's operation. The task force's tentative conclusions provoked strong denunciations by the industry's labor leadership, including Joseph Curran [*q.v.*] of the National Maritime Union. Speaking for the White House, Vice President Hubert Humphrey [*q.v.*] disavowed the suggestions of the Boyd committee. He told the International Brotherhood of Boilermakers in November 1965 that "this administration has not determined the long-range merchant marine policy." Amid the threat of a nationwide rail strike in September 1965, Boyd angered the railway brotherhoods when he criticized "featherbedding" by railroad firemen, calling for greater flexibility by rail union officials in the reassignment of workers removed from jobs due to modernization.

Boyd and other Administration representatives began a campaign in January 1966 to establish a cabinet-level Department of Transportation (DOT). The Johnson Administration sought to unify under one authority 35 government transportation agencies, ranging from the Coast Guard to the airline, rail and federal highway commissions. The new department would also direct governmental policy on automotive safety, an issue of growing public concern after the recent publication of Ralph Nader's [*q.v.*] book, *Unsafe at Any Speed.* Boyd served on the five-member interagency committee that first recommended a Transportation Department to the President in September 1965, and Johnson endorsed the proposal in his 1966 State of the Union Message. Although presidential counsel Joseph A. Califano [*q.v.*] directed the congressional lobbying effort, Boyd was the most frequent witness before committees scrutinizing the Administration's bill.

By the time Congress passed the DOT bill in October 1966, the new Department's Secretary possessed much less authority than the law's original authors had intended to grant him. AFL-CIO representatives successfully argued against transfer of the Maritime Administration to DOT, a union accomplishment some observers described as a major defeat for the Administration. Despite the efforts of Boyd and Califano, regulatory agencies placed under the new department retained more autonomy than the White House had originally wished. Congress also curbed the Secretary's control over transportation expenditures. The *Washington Post's* Richard Harwood wrote that legislative leaders had so weakened the measure that the Secretary of Transportation had "authority to assign office space and little else."

Johnson named Boyd to serve as the nation's first Secretary of Transportation in November 1966, and the Senate confirmed his nomination two months later. Although 12th in cabinet seniority, Boyd led a department fourth in personnel and fifth in annual expenditures. Involved in a wide range of transportation issues, Boyd directed staff projects on airport modernization and air traffic control requirements. In June 1967 he defended appropriations for Lady Bird Johnson's [*q.v.*] Highway Beautification Program before a Senate committee. As called for in the Highway Safety Act of 1966, Boyd issued state auto safety standards for driver education and alcoholism.

During its fight with Congress over the 1967 budget, the Administration utilized Boyd's control over interstate highway funds to put muscle behind Johnson's tax surcharge. Boyd announced in February 1967 that $175 million of federal highway funds had been impounded by the President since November 1966 as an anti-inflation move. In October 1967 Boyd sent telegrams to all state governors warning that the budget issue between the Administration and Congress "may have a profound effect on highway construction expenditures." The possibility existed, Boyd explained, that federal highway funds would have to be reduced from $4.4 billion to $2.2 billion in fiscal 1969.

DOT proved unable to revitalize passenger rail service. Congress declined to appropriate the full amount authorized in the High-Speed Ground Transportation Act of 1965, a measure designed to subsidize passenger railroad research and development costs. With the limited funds available in 1967, Boyd reported delays in the test runs of new models.

Boyd also devoted attention to the maritime industry and again antagonized ship industry labor officials. In May 1968, he proposed to restructure and reduce the government's subsidy programs as part of a comprehensive maritime proposal. As in 1965 the Maritime Committee of the AFL-CIO condemned Boyd's suggestion, with Curran calling it "inadequate, unimaginative and unsatisfactory." Again the Administration dropped Boyd's plan and postponed further action to salvage the country's declining merchant fleet industry.

With President-elect Nixon's nomination of John A. Volpe [*q.v.*] as DOT secretary, Boyd returned to private life in January 1969 and became president of the Illinois Central Railroad. Conflict-of-interest charges arose when Scripps-Howard newspapers reported on Jan. 24, 1969 that DOT had granted Illinois Central $25.2 million for commuter car expenditures late in December 1968. At Boyd's request, DOT investigated the payment transfer and cleared the former Secretary of any wrongdoing.

[JLB]

BOYLE, TONY (WILLIAM) (ANTHONY)

b. Dec. 1, 1904; Bald Butte, Mont.
President, United Mine Workers, 1963-72.

The son of a miner, Boyle began working in the mines after he finished high school. He rose quickly through the United Mine Workers (UMW) ranks and in 1940 became president of the union's District 27, covering Montana and other Western states. Boyle served as a regional director of the Congress of Industrial Organizations for two years and also represented the UMW on several government boards during World War II.

In 1948 Boyle moved to UMW headquarters in Washington, D.C. to become UMW President John L. Lewis's administrative assistant. Over the next decade Boyle won increasing power as the day-to-day administrator of the UMW. His power grew further when Lewis retired in 1960 and Thomas Kennedy became president. Boyle took over the presidential office upon Kennedy's death in January 1963.

Heir to a highly centralized union structure, Boyle faced both growing rank-and-file pressure for democratization of the UMW and charges of collusion with large coal operators. Post-war automation had been rapid, and the union's membership declined by more than 200,000 between 1950 and 1970. Although the UMW won substantial wage increases during the 1960s, unauthorized wildcat strikes increased dramatically, and Boyle was challenged for the presidency in 1964. Dissatisfaction with the central leadership's tight grip on union affairs stemmed from the UMW's failure to win improved mine safety standards or guarantees of stable employment.

In August 1967 the Supreme Court found the UMW guilty of violating the Sherman Antitrust Act because it had made large loans to the Western Kentucky Coal Company, enabling the company to monopolize Tennessee Valley Authority coal contracts. The collaboration issue mushroomed again when an explosion at a Consolidation Coal Company mine killed 78 miners in November 1968. Three weeks earlier the UMW and the Company had been fined $7 million for conspiring with other large companies since 1950 to monopolize production. Following the accident Boyle praised Consolidation's safety record and stated, "As long as we mine coal, there is always this inherent danger." Boyle also said the UMW "will not abridge the rights of mine operators in running the mines. We follow the judgments of the coal operators, right or wrong."

Boyle's defense of the coal companies was unpopular among rank-and-file miners. Soon after the Consolidation explosion an organized militant challenge to Boyle's leadership emerged. In December 1968 West Virginia miners formed the Black Lung Association. Led by Arnold Miller, the group demanded state workmen's compensation for miners suffering from pneumoconiosis, or black lung, a disease caused by the accumulation of coal dust particles. Joseph A. Yablonski, a member of the union's executive board, announced his candidacy for UMW president in May 1969. After a sometimes violent campaign Boyle won what Yablonski charged was a fraudulent election in early December 1969. On Dec. 31, 1969 Yablonski and his wife and daughter were murdered in their Pennsylvania home. In 1972 the Department of Labor invalidated the 1969 election. In a subsequent election Boyle was defeated for UMW president by Arnold Miller. Boyle was convicted in 1973 for making illegal use of union funds. He subsequently tried to commit suicide with an overdose of drugs. Later that year he was convicted of conspiring to kill Yablonski and was sentenced to three life prison terms. [See NIXON Volume]

[MDB]

For further information:
Stuart Brown, *A Man Named Tony* (New York, 1976).
Brit Hume, *Death in the Mines* (New York, 1971).

BRADEMAS, JOHN

b. March 2, 1927; Mishawaka, Ind.
Democratic Representative, Ind.
1959- .

During the Johnson years John Brademas earned a reputation as one of the leading advocates of federal aid to education. A 1949 magna cum laude graduate of Harvard University, Brademas later earned a doctorate from Oxford University. He then taught political science at St. Mary's College in Notre Dame, Ind. At the same time he gained practical political experience as an assistant in charge of research for Adlai Stevenson's 1956 presidential campaign.

First elected to Congress in 1958, Brademas represented the northern Indiana district that included the cities of Elkhart and South Bend. During the Kennedy and Johnson years, the liberal Americans for Democratic Action rated Brandemas's "correct" voting record at 80% to 95%. Brademas sat on the House Labor and Education Committee, and despite his relatively low seniority, became an influential spokesman on educational affairs. His opinions on school legislation were particularly well-regarded by the liberal Democratic Study Group.

Brademas played an active role in winning approval of the 1965 Elementary and Secondary Education Act and two years later served as the successful floor manager of the bill amending the original legislation. In 1967 Brademas won approval of a bill authorizing federal assistance for international studies programs in American colleges and universities and for legislation extending the teacher corps for three years. Brademas also won the praise of environmental groups for his support of legislation protecting estuaries and imposing water pollution controls.

Unlike a number of House liberals, Brademas was not an outspoken opponent of the Vietnam war during the 1960s. Beginning around 1970 he began voting for anti-war legislation while insisting that withdrawal of American troops from Vietnam be contingent on release of U.S. prisoners of war.

In 1971 Brademas sponsored comprehensive child-care legislation as part of a bill extending the Economic Opportunity Act. This major bill, passed by both houses, was vetoed by President Nixon. [See NIXON Volume]

[JLW]

BREATHITT, EDWARD T(HOMPSON) (NED)

b. Nov. 26, 1924; Hopkinsville, Ky.
Governor, Ky., 1963-67.

A lawyer from an old Kentucky family whose tradition of public service predated the Civil War, Breathitt served three terms in the state House of Representatives from 1952 to 1958. As state personnel commissioner from 1959 to 1960, he instituted a merit system for state civil service employes. He was appointed state public service commissioner in 1960 by Gov. Bert T. Combs.

In 1963 Gov. Combs, unable to succeed himself, endorsed Breathitt as his successor. In a Democratic primary termed by the *Washington Post* "probably the bitterest campaign in Kentucky history," Breathitt was challenged by A. B. (Happy) Chandler, a former Kentucky governor,

U.S. senator and commissioner of baseball. The foremost issues were a recently enacted 3% sales tax (which Chandler denounced and Breathitt supported) and Chandler's age, then 65. Breathitt defeated Chandler by a landslide in the Democratic primary. He faced the young, ardent pro-Goldwater lawyer, Louie B. Nunn, in the general election. During the campaign—the first in recent years in which the race issue had figured prominently in Kentucky politics—Breathitt was attacked for his supposed links to Northern civil rights organizations and his presumed support of the Kennedy Administration's policies on racial integration. With a record 870,000 votes cast on Nov. 5, Breathitt narrowly defeated Nunn by 15,000 votes.

Shortly after taking office Breathitt confronted the problem of civil rights. Civil rights leaders argued that because of the closeness of the election Breathitt found it expedient to procrastinate on a state public accommodations bill outlawing segregation in public places. To bring pressure upon the Governor and state legislature, 10,000 persons, led by Martin Luther King [*q.v.*], marched on Frankfort in March 1964. A compromise resolution was passed on March 19 favoring voluntary integration of public facilities. Kentucky political observers doubted whether the Governor could have secured passage of the original measure under any circumstances.

At the 1964 Democratic National Convention, Breathitt seconded the nomination of Lyndon B. Johnson. During the October 1964 Southern Governors Conference, he was among a minority of three who quashed George Wallace's [*q.v.*] constitutional amendment to give the states and state courts sole jurisdiction over their public schools. Conference backing required unanimity.

In 1966 Breathitt proposed a state civil rights bill broader in scope than the 1964 federal Civil Rights Act. The employment section of the bill brought 90% of Kentucky labor under a provision that barred racial discrimination in employment. The federal law covered only 60% of the state labor force. The public accommodations section of the Kentucky measure applied to such businesses as bowling alleys and coin-operated laundries not covered under the federal measure. In signing the bill into law on Jan. 27, 1966, Breathitt said it was "a moral commitment kept after a hundred years of hope deferred—a promissory note long overdue."

On Jan. 27, 1966 the Kentucky legislature overwhelmingly adopted a tough new law designed to end strip mining abuses. Enactment of this sweeping measure, which coal operators said would put them out of business, was a major victory for Breathitt over the state's powerful coal industry. In 1967 Breathitt headed the President's Advisory Commission on Rural Poverty. The panel's report, released Dec. 9, asserted that "rural poverty is so widespread, so acute, as to be a national disgrace, and its consequences have swept into our cities violently."

Constitutionally unable to seek reelection in 1966, Breathitt became vice president in charge of public affairs of the Southern Railway System.

[TJC]

BRENNAN, WILLIAM J(OSEPH), JR.

b. April 25, 1906; Newark, N.J.
Associate Justice, U.S. Supreme Court, 1956-

The son of Irish immigrants, Brennan received a B.S. from the Wharton School of Finance in 1928 and graduated from Harvard Law School in 1931. He then joined a law firm in his home town of Newark, N.J., where he specialized in labor law. He was appointed to the state Superior Court in 1949, to the Appellate Division of the Superior Court in 1950 and to the state Supreme Court in 1952. President Eisenhower named Brennan to the U.S. Supreme Court in September 1956, and he began serving under a recess appointment that October. The Senate confirmed the appointment in March 1957.

In his early years on the bench, Brennan often played the role of a bridge-builder between the Court's liberal and conservative wings, writing narrowly based opinions to gather a majority. When a solid liberal majority developed in the early 1960s, Brennan became more activist and creative in his opinions and a leader in expanding individual rights and protecting them from government intrusion. Aligned with the Court's liberals, Brennan became known for his special dedication to First Amendment freedoms and to procedural fairness. In March 1962 he wrote the majority opinion in *Baker v. Carr*, holding that federal courts could decide cases involving legislative apportionment. [See EISENHOWER, KENNEDY Volumes]

Brennan wrote some of his most important First Amendment opinions in the Johnson years. Speaking for a unanimous Court in March 1964, Brennan expanded the freedom of the press in *New York Times v. Sullivan*, holding that a public official could not recover damages for a defamatory falsehood relating to his official conduct unless he proved the statement was made with "actual malice." Later that year Brennan extended this ruling to cover cases of criminal as well as civil libel, and in a February 1966 decision he gave a broad definition to the term public official. In *Time Inc. v. Hill*, decided in January 1967, Brennan applied the same principle to invasion of privacy suits against the press by newsworthy persons. Brennan found in the 1965 case *Dombrowski v. Pfister* an exception to the general rule that federal courts will not intervene to enjoin threatened state court criminal proceedings. Federal courts could act, he held, when a defendant's First Amendment rights were endangered by the fact of state prosecutions.

Throughout the Warren Court years Brennan wrote the leading opinions in the difficult and divisive area of obscenity law. In the 1957 *Roth* decision Brennan held obscenity was not protected by the First Amendment and declared the test of obscenity was "whether, to the average person, applying contemporary community standards, the dominant theme of the material taken as a whole appeals to the prurient interest." The first major reexamination of the definition of obscenity came in June 1964 in *Jacobellis v. Ohio* with Brennan's opinion reaffirming the *Roth* test. He gave greater emphasis, however, to the notion that obscene material was utterly without redeeming social importance and said the community standards of the *Roth* test were national, not local, standards. In three March 1966 cases Brennan constructed a narrower test of obscenity and held that to be judged obscene a work had to meet each of three criteria: its dominant theme must appeal to the prurient interest, it must be patently offensive and utterly without redeeming social value.

In one of these cases, *Ginzburg v. U.S.*, Brennan also ruled that "titillating" advertising and pandering in the sale and publicity of a work could be used to determine obscenity. This finding of offense in the conduct of the seller, even though the work itself might not be obscene, has been considered an anomaly for Brennan who was usually careful to guard against the suppression of any non-obscene materials. In a June 1964 case Brennan's plurality opinion reversed a judgment of obscenity by Kansas courts because the books involved had been seized in a manner that endangered non-obscene literature. Brennan overturned Maryland's film censorhip system in March 1965 because it provided inadequate safeguards against the suppression of films protected by the First Amendment, and he set out strict procedural guidelines for film censorship systems.

Brennan's majority opinion in the 1966 case *Katzenbach v. Morgan* upheld a section of the 1965 Voting Rights Act designed to guarantee the right to vote to non-English speaking Puerto Ricans. Brennan sustained the law holding that section five of the Fourteenth Amendment gave Congress independent authority to decide if certain conduct violated the Amendment's equal protection clause. This new and broader interpretation of section five has been judged to hold the potential for a vast expansion of federal power.

Brennan also contributed to the Warren Court's criminal decisions. His majority opinion in a June 1964 case held the Fifth Amendment's privilege against self-incrimination applicable to the states. In a June 1966 decision Brennan rejected a claim that a blood test to determine if a defendant was driving while drunk, conducted over the defendant's protest, violated his Fourth and Fifth Amendment rights. Writing for an eight-man majority in May 1967, Brennan overruled a 1921 Court decision and extended the right of police to use evidence seized in lawful searches of suspects' homes.

Over the next several years Brennan wrote important opinions on the rights of welfare recipients, and he dissented from the Burger Court's decisions cutting back on the 1966 *Miranda* ruling. The difficulties of formulating a clear and manageable definition of obscenity led Brennan to a sharp reversal of his position in 1973. Dissenting in two cases where the majority modified his *Roth* standards, Brennan wrote that except to protect juveniles and to prevent the obstrusive exposure to unconsenting adults, the First Amendment prohibited all attempts to suppress materials on the basis of their alleged obscenity. Considered one of the Court's more eminent justices by legal scholars, Brennan became the senior member of the Court following the retirement of Justice William O. Douglas [*q.v.*] in 1975. [See NIXON Volume]

[CAB]

For further information:

Stephen J. Friedman, ed. *An Affair with Freedom: William J. Brennan, Jr.* (New York, 1967).

Stephen J. Friedman, "William J. Brennan, Jr.," in Leon Friedman and Fred L. Israel, eds. *The Justices of the United States Supreme Court, 1789–1969* (New York, 1969), Vol. IV.

"William J. Brennan, Jr.," *Rutgers-Camden Law Journal* (Fall 1972), Vol. IV.

BREWSTER, DANIEL B(AUGH)

b. Nov. 23, 1923; Greenspring Valley, Md.

Democratic Senator, Md., 1963-69.

A millionaire's son born in the horse country of Maryland, Brewster served four terms in the Maryland House of Delegates and two terms in the U.S. House of Representatives before being elected to the Senate in 1962. Supported by the Baltimore County Democratic organization, the most powerful faction in state politics outside the Baltimore city organization, Brewster won each of his campaigns effortlessly.

While in the House Brewster established a liberal voting record, supporting civil rights legislation, increases in minimum wage protection and aid for housing and education. During the Kennedy years the liberal Americans for Democratic Action gave him an average rating of 87%.

The Senator continued to support many domestic social welfare proposals during the Johnson era, voting in favor of aid to education, mass transit, model cities and Appalachia, civil rights measures and the antipoverty program. In 1966 Brewster drafted a bill to establish a bipartisan Commission on Political Activity of Government Personnel to review the Hatch Act of 1939. That act limited the participation of government workers in national and local politics. When Johnson signed the bill in the autumn of 1966, he appointed Brewster one of the Commission members. The Commission report, issued at the end of 1967, recommended an easing of restrictions on political activities of most federal employes but urged a strengthening of provisions intended to protect public workers from coercion by their superiors.

During the 1964 presidential campaign Brewster served as a stand-in candidate for Lyndon Johnson in the Maryland Democratic primary. Calling the primary a "ridiculous" exercise and an invitation to "irresponsible voting," Brewster ran a lackluster race against Alabama Gov. George Wallace [*q.v.*]. Pitted against the flamboyant Wallace, Brewster received only 53% of the vote; Wallace polled a surprising 43%. Analyzing the reasons for Brewster's failure, the *New York Times* attributed the poor showing to a conservative backlash against the tactics used by civil rights demonstrators.

Following his unsuccessful bid for reelection in 1968, Brewster became the subject of several investigations involving charges of impropriety in the introduction of immigration bills. He was also charged with violating federal bribery laws while a senator. In September 1969 the Senate Select Committee on Standards and Conduct began a preliminary investigation into allegations that a number of senators, including Brewster, received gifts or campaign funds in return for sponsoring private immigration bills to help illegal Chinese immigrants escape deportation. Brewster denied the charges, and no action was taken on the matter.

Three months later, in December 1969, Brewster was indicted on 10 counts of having violated federal bribery laws by accepting payments "in return for being influenced" to vote against an increase in third-class bulk mail rates while he was a member of the Senate Post Office and Civil Service Committee. In 1972 Brewster was convicted on a lesser charge of accepting an unlawful gratuity—a charge that in effect he had taken money without corrupt intent. He was sentenced to two-to-six years in jail and fined $30,000 in 1973. A retrial was ordered on appeal, but in 1975 he pleaded no contest to the charge and was fined $10,000.

[EWS]

BRIDGES, HARRY (ALFRED) (RENTON)

b. July 28, 1901; Melbourne, Australia. President, International Longshoremen's and Warehousemen's Union 1937- .

Bridges spent five years at sea before he began working on the San Francisco docks in 1922. Close to the Communists in the early 1930s, Bridges emerged in 1934 as the most important leader of the San Francisco longshoremen's work stoppage and the citywide general strike that immediately followed. As a consequence of his strike leadership, Bridges played a key role in the organization of Pacific Coast longshoremen and in 1937 was elected president of the CIO-affiliated International Longshoremen's and Warehousemen's Union (ILWU). During the 1930s and 1940s, his 60,000-member union was an important base of Communist strength within the CIO.

For more than a decade and a half after 1939, the Justice Department tried to deport Bridges on the grounds that he was or had been a Comnunist. These efforts failed, and by the late 1950s Bridges had reached a working accommodation with both the government and with the once bitterly hostile Pacific Maritime Association (PMA).

In 1960 Bridges signed a five-and-one-half-year collective bargaining contract with the PMA that had a far-reaching impact on the nature of longshore work and the future of the ILWU. Known as the Mechanization and Modernization Agreement (M & M), the new contract traded long-standing ILWU work rules and production standards for a guaranteed 35-hour week and a $29 million pension fund. The new contract was widely hailed in business and academic circles as an important step toward an increase in labor productivity and job security. [See TRUMAN, EISENHOWER, KENNEDY Volumes]

During the mid-1960s the M & M Agreement created a number of problems for the ILWU and its leader. When the contract was signed in 1960, the PMA and the ILWU expected the 14,000-man Pacific Coast longshore work force to shrink. Both the union and employers therefore agreed to the continuation of a category of semi-casual workers known as B-men, who did longshore work, usually the least desirable, but who were not beneficiaries of the new contract. In June 1963 most of these B-men were admitted to full standing in the union, but a predominantly black group of some 80 were expelled. The excluded longshoremen were dissidents and radicals, opponents of M & M. They sued both the ILWU and the PMA and enlisted the aid of a group of prominent writers, intellectuals and civil rights leaders in their defense.

In August 1965 Bridges countersued some 15 B-men supporters, including writers Paul Jacobs, Harvey Swados, Herbert Gold and Nat Hentoff. Bridges claimed that they had falsely accused him of being an autocratic labor leader practicing racial bias. Both suits proved inconclusive. However, according to biographer Charles Larrowe, the public dispute over the B-men, coupled with the M & M agreement itself, did much to tarnish Bridges's reputation as a "labor radical" in the mid-1960s.

The M & M Agreement was renewed for another five years in 1966. Because of the introduction of more efficient containerized cargo handling procedures, the ILWU became involved in a series of disputes with the Teamsters Union in the late 1960s. Both unions claimed jurisdiction over the loading of the truck-length containers, and a number of local jurisdictional strikes began in early 1969. These culminated in a half-year-long ILWU strike in 1971-1972.

Although the ILWU took strong stands against the war in Vietnam and in favor of the farm workers' organizing drive, Bridges developed close ties to moderate and conservative Democratic Party figures in the mid-1960s. He backed the San Francisco mayoral candidacies of Jack Shelley in 1963 and Joseph Alioto [*q.v.*] in 1967. Most observers thought Alioto's appointment of Bridges to the powerful San Francisco Port Commission in 1970 marked "official" recognition of the union leader's place in the Bay Area establishment. [See NIXON Volume]

[NNL]

For further information:

Charles P. Larrowe, *Harry Bridges, the Rise and Fall of Radical Labor in the United States* (New York, 1972).

Stanley Weir, "The Retreat of Harry Bridges," in Burton Hall, ed., *Autocracy and Insurgency in Organized Labor* (New Brunswick, 1972).

BROOKE, EDWARD W(ILLIAM)

b. Oct. 26, 1919; Washington, D.C.
Republican Senator, Mass., 1967- .

Brooke, whose father was a lawyer in the Veterans Administration, grew up in a prosperous black family. He received a bachelor of science degree from Howard University in 1941. After serving in the Army during World War II, Brooke entered Boston University Law School, earning LL.B. and LL.M. degrees in 1948 and 1949. In 1950 Brooke ran for a seat from Roxbury in the Massachusetts legislature by entering both the Democratic and Republican primaries. He won the latter contest and thereafter remained a Republican. Brooke lost the election and was defeated again in a 1952 bid for the state legislature.

For the next eight years Brooke practiced law. In 1960 he ran as the Republican candidate for Massachusetts secretary of state. He lost by about 12,000 votes, but his total vote of approximately 1.1 million impressed political observers in a state that was both strongly Democratic and 98% white.

In 1962 Brooke was elected state attorney general. He was reelected in 1964 with a plurality of almost 800,000 votes, one of the largest margins of victory of any Republican in the country that year. As attorney general Brooke gained prominence for his investigations of government corruption. A number of high-ranking politicians, including a former governor and two speakers of the house, were indicted. He also pressed for bills to reduce air pollution and protect borrowers against excessively high interest rates.

Brooke was identified with the liberal wing of the Republican Party. At its 1964 National Convention in San Francisco, Brooke gave the seconding speech for William Scranton [*q.v.*]. He declined to endorse conservative Sen. Barry M. Goldwater (R, Ariz.) [*q.v.*], the Convention's nominee.

Brooke declared his candidacy for the U.S. Senate in December 1965 immediately after incumbent Republican Sen. Leverett Saltonstall [*q.v.*] announced his plans to retire. In November 1966 he defeated former Gov. Endicott Peabody by more than 400,000 votes to become the first black since Reconstruction to win a Senate seat and the first black in history to be elected to that body by popular vote.

Brooke's electoral victories in the face of the handicaps of party and race were widely attributed to his success in presenting himself to the voters on the basis of his personal merits. His appearance and style were impeccably middle class; Stephen Hess and David S. Broder wrote in *The Republican Establishment*, "He is really not a Negro politician at all, but a Negro in politics." Brooke supported civil rights legislation but did not attempt to play a leadership role in the area of civil rights. During his senatorial campaign he denounced both Stokely Carmichael [*q.v.*] and Lester Maddox [*q.v.*]. Some liberals criticized him for being less outspoken than Peabody on behalf of antidiscrimination laws.

Before entering the Senate Brooke was mildly critical of the Johnson Administration's Vietnam policies and favored a cessation of the bombing of North Vietnam. In January 1967 he visited Southeast Asia. While in Cambodia he vainly attempted to contact the North Vietnamese in an effort to ascertain the possibilities of a negotiated settlement to the war. Upon his return Brooke reversed his earlier view and stated, "It does not appear that suspension of the bombing in the North would, by itself, produce fruitful negotiations. . . ." Brooke's change of opinion was widely reported as a significant setback for anti-war forces in Congress.

Brooke was known as a cautious senator who deliberated carefully before reaching conclusions. He strongly opposed illegal and violent political protest, but he generally supported liberal reform programs. According to *Congressional Quarterly*, he was the third leading Republican senatorial opponent of the conservative coalition in 1967 and 1968.

One of Brooke's major interests was low and middle-income housing. In August 1967 he said it might be necessary to establish a new low and moderate-income housing division within the Department of Housing and Urban Development (HUD). Brooke complained that in the previous six years the Federal Housing Administration (FHA) had written insurance for only 40,000 low-income housing units, a figure he called "pitifully inadequate." Early in 1968 he introduced a bill to create the new division. The measure was not adopted, but a housing bill passed in 1968 required the FHA to expand its insurance program for low-income housing.

Like most Republican congressmen Brooke favored the promotion of home ownership as a means of improving living standards and fostering individual responsibility. In November 1967 Brooke joined his Republican colleagues on the Banking and Currency Committee's Housing and Urban Affairs Subcommittee in praising a bill designed to aid low-income families in purchasing homes. They asserted that "the responsibility and self-sufficiency that is inherent in home ownership can be expected to make a marked contribution toward bettering a family's living standards and environment."

In July 1967 President Johnson appointed Brooke to the 11-member Special Advisory Commission on Civil Disorders, also known as the Kerner Commission. Its function was to investigate the causes of the black urban riots that erupted during the summer of that year. The Commission released its findings on Feb. 29, 1968. It found no evidence of a conspiracy or of an organization behind the disturbances and blamed them on what it called "white racism."

Brooke endorsed the Republican presidential candidacy of Richard M. Nixon in 1968 but subsequently disagreed with the new Administration on a number of important issues. He opposed the President's nominations of Clement F. Haynsworth and G. Harrold Carswell for the Supreme Court in 1969 and 1970. During the early 1970s he consistently supported anti-war proposals, including the McGovern-Hatfield and Cooper-Church amendments. In 1972 he was reelected with 65% of the vote. [See NIXON Volume]

[MLL]

BROWER, DAVID (ROSS)

b. July 1, 1912; Berkeley, Calif.
Executive Director, Sierra Club, 1952-69.

Brower was first exposed to the wilderness on family camping trips to the Sierra Nevada Mountains. Intensely interested in nature, he discovered the butterfly *Anthocaris sara reakirtii broweri* at the age of 15. While working at Yosemite National Park in the 1930s, Brower gained a reputation as a pioneer rock climber. Between 1941 and 1952 he was an editor at the University of California Press, except for two years as an Army climbing instructor during the war. A member of the Sierra Club since 1933, Brower became the San Francisco-based organization's executive director in 1952.

Since the death of its founder, John Muir, in 1914, the Sierra Club had been neither active nor effective in advancing the cause of conservation. Brower transformed the Club into a successful political pressure group while furthering its traditional role as a proponent of wilderness values to the American public. The Club's lavish photo books, produced under Brower's direction in the 1960s, brought an appreciation of the wilderness to large numbers of Americans and won sympathy for the organization's lobbying efforts on behalf of conservation legislation. During Brower's tenure the Sierra Club also became a national organization, increasing its membership from 7,000 to 70,000 and the annual budget from $75,000 to $3 million. It was easily the most powerful conservationist group in the country. [See KENNEDY Volume]

The Sierra Club's influence was at its peak during the late 1960s, aided by the Johnson Administration's own commitment to highway beautification, recreation and anti-pollution measures as integral elements in the Great Society program. In 1964 the Club claimed some of the credit for the creation of the Land and Water Conservation Fund and the establishment of Canyonlands National Park, the first national park created since 1956. It also helped push through Congress the Wilderness Act of 1964, which established a National Wilderness Preservation System. The Club's lobbying efforts culminated in 1968 when Congress established the North Cascades and Redwood National Parks. Congress also set up a wild-and-scenic rivers system and a national trails system. It was indicative of the Club's influence in the 1960s that the Kennedy and Johnson Administrations added 2.4 million acres to the National Park Service lands. Only 30,000 acres had been added in the 1950s. In addition, the Club was responsible for blocking billions of dollars worth of construction projects that it considered a threat to the natural environment.

With Brower taking aggressive leadership the Sierra Club won its biggest victory in 1966 and 1967 by preventing the construction of two large hydroelectric dams on the stretch of the Colorado River that runs through the Grand Canyon. The victory was remarkable because the dams' proponents included the Interior Department's Bureau of Reclamation, the Colorado River Association, private power companies and the entire congressional delegation of the seven states located in the Colorado Basin. Interior Secretary Stewart Udall [*q.v.*] first proposed the two dams in 1963 as part of an Administration's Southwest Water Plan. The legislation moved slowly in order to work out compromises among the various interests involved, including the seven states. Brower soon undertook a vast publicity and lobbying effort to stop the plan. In 1964 the Sierra Club published *Time and the River Flowing*, a photo book on the Grand Canyon, and distributed copies of the $25 volume to every member of Congress. In the following year Brower testified for the first time in congressional hearings against the legislation. His remarks, reproduced as a pamphlet "Dams in the Grand Canyon—A Necessary Evil?," and a Sierra Club *Bulletin* editorial were widely distributed, sparking a massive letter-writing campaign.

In early 1966, when agreement on Colorado River legislation that would include the two dams seemed imminent, Brower stepped up the Sierra Club's campaign. On June 9, 1966 he attacked the dams in full-page ads in the *New York Times* and the *Washington Post*. The Internal Revenue Service (IRS) acted immediately to remove the Club's tax-exempt status on the basis of its lobbying activity. The Club charged that the IRS action was politically motivated and appealed the decision. Meanwhile, the ads generated what Sen. Thomas Kuchel (R, Calif.) [*q.v.*] called "one of the largest letter-writing campaigns . . . in my tenure in the Senate."

The Brower strategy was successful. The Administration withdrew its support of one of the dams in 1966 and of the second in 1967. The Colorado River bill was passed in 1968 but without authorization for the Grand Canyon dams. Rep. Morris Udall (D, Ariz.) [*q.v.*], a key supporter of the bill, said, in discussing the conservationists' campaign, that he could not think of "any group in this country that has had more power in the last eight years."

Despite the Sierra Club's victories Brower's campaigns were considered financially irresponsible by many in the Club. In addition, his tendency to make decisions unilaterally brought criticism from the Club's board of directors. Richard Leonard, a former president of the Club and one of Brower's closest friends, said that Brower "believes that if he bankrupts the Sierra Club it is in a glorious cause." Brower also wanted to expand the Club's book series, although his colleagues pointed out that the Club could not afford to increase production of books that had not been financially successful. Some critics described Brower as rigid and argued that he had unnecessarily alienated many potential allies in business and government. In 1969 the board of directors forced his resignation. Brower then founded the John Muir Institute for Environmental Studies and Friends of the Earth. The former was a research and educational organization, while the latter was devoted to lobbying on conservation issues and campaigning for political candidates. Brower headed both organizations. [See NIXON Volume]

[JCH]

For further information:
John McPhee, *Encounters with the Archdruid: Narratives about a Conservationist and Three of His Natural Enemies* (New York, 1971).

BROWN, EDMUND G(ERALD), SR.
b. April 21, 1905; San Francisco, Calif.
Governor, Calif., 1959-67.

"Pat" Brown attended San Francisco public and parochial schools and took evening courses at the San Francisco Law School. Originally a Republican, he became a Democrat in 1939 and advanced his career in San Francisco through one of California's few solid party organizations. Brown was the city's district attorney in 1943 and was elected attorney general of California in 1950 and 1954. He was the only Democrat to hold statewide office in the early 1950s. In 1958 Brown broke the Republican stranglehold on the state by winning the governorship and carrying with him the first Democratic majorities in both houses of the legislature since 1889. [See EISENHOWER Volume]

Brown's governorship coincided with a period of tremendous growth, during which California became the nation's most populous and wealthiest state. He claimed credit for passage of legislation that both answered the needs of a greatly increased population and realized liberal principles. Brown's administration expanded the freeway system, the public schools and jobless benefits and enacted consumer protection and fair employment practices legislation. Most importantly, it passed a $1.7 billion water plan, which provided water for populous but arid Southern California, and a "master plan" offering some form of college education to all California high school graduates. Brown's record of "responsible liberalism" won him a dramatic reelection victory in 1962 over former Vice President Richard Nixon [*q.v.*]. Nonetheless, in a state known for its fluid political loyalties, Brown could not always exercise control over his own party. The Kennedy Administration looked to Democratic Assembly Speaker Jesse Unruh [*q.v.*] as its chief political liaison in the state, and Brown depended on an often uncooperative Unruh for the success of his legislative program. In addition, the Governor often faced criticism from both the left and right of his party as well as from hostile conservative Republicans. [See KENNEDY Volume]

Brown's second term saw a drastic deterioration in both his popularity and in Democratic unity as well as a marked decline in the success of his legislative program. The Governor's feud with Unruh, the most powerful state legislator in the country, continued. Unruh frequently pushed his own bills through the legislature without Brown's support. In his battles with Unruh the Governor enlisted the backing of the labor unions and the liberal California Democratic Council (CDC), an independent group that sought to influence party policy. The conflict came into full view in 1964 when incumbent Sen. Clair Engle (D, Calif.) became so seriously ill that it was doubtful he could stand for reelection in November. The CDC, therefore, early in the year chose State Controller Alan Cranston to run for Engle's Senate seat. Brown endorsed the nomination. Unruh refused to back Cranston and offered tacit encouragement to the senatorial candidacy of President Kennedy's former press secretary, Pierre Salinger [*q.v.*]. Salinger's defeat of Cranston in the June primary damaged Brown's prestige. After Engle's death in July the Governor was pressured into appointing Salinger to fill out the remainder of Engle's term.

The mid-1960s in California were characterized by a political trend to the right. Unruh early sensed this shift, but Brown remained publicly committed to liberal positions that undermined his popularity. He backed a 1963 fair housing law, and, when Californians voted to repeal the act by a 2-1 margin in 1964, Brown bluntly criticized the voters for their "bigotry." Brown's difficulties with conservatives increased in August 1965 when riots broke out in Watts, Los Angeles's black ghetto. Brown interrupted a vacation in Greece to return to Los Angeles. Following a restoration of order in Watts, he appointed an eight-member commission, headed by former Central Intelligence Agency Director John McCone [*q.v.*], to investigate the causes of the riots and to recommend means to prevent their recurrence. Immediately, the conservative Democratic mayor of Los Angeles, Sam Yorty [*q.v.*], attacked one of the Governor's appointments to the commission. Yorty and other conservatives blamed Brown's social welfare programs for raising poor people's expectations unrealistically, thereby making the riots possible.

By the election year of 1966, Californians, who were angered by the Watts riots, the student disturbances at the University of California's Berkeley campus and a rising crime rate, apparently had concluded that the "soft" liberal policies of the Brown Administration were responsible for the state's problems. The extent of Brown's difficulties were evident when he defeated Mayor Yorty in the June Democratic gubernatorial primary by only 375,000 votes out of more than 2.3 million cast. Meanwhile, his approval of President Johnson's Vietnam policy and his unwillingness to strongly support the National Farm Workers' organizing efforts in California hurt his credibility among CDC liberals. His liberal standing was further damaged at the Democratic state convention in August when he unsuccessfully opposed adoption of a platform plank unreservedly supporting fair housing legislation.

Brown's Republican opponent in the general election was former movie star Ronald Reagan [*q.v.*]. The Governor's supporters were pleased with Reagan's primary victory over a moderate opponent, thinking that Brown could easily defeat an "ultraconservative" who lacked previous government experience. Yet anti-Brown feeling was so great that his chances of victory against any opponent were considered slim. Surrounded by angry liberals and radicals on his left and by a tough-talking Reagan on his right, the Governor appeared indecisive. The Reagan campaign's portrayal of Brown as bumbling and weak was aided by the articulate speech and glamor of the Republican candidate. Reagan's attacks on professional politicians and the wastefulness of big government clearly appealed to the California electorate. Brown lost his reelection bid by almost a million votes out of approximately 5.4 million.

In March 1967 President Johnson appointed Brown head of a newly created National Commission on Reform of Criminal Laws. Brown remained a vociferous critic of his successor in the California governorship, publishing two books, *Reagan and Reality: The Two Californias* (New York, 1970) and *Reagan: The Political Chameleon* (New York, 1976).

[JCH]

BROWN, HAROLD

b. Sept. 19, 1927; New York, N.Y.
Director of Defense Reseach and Engineering for the Department of Defense, May 1961-September 1965; Secretary of the Air Force, September 1965-January 1969.

A nuclear physicist interested in atomic weapons development, Harold Brown was director of the University of California's

Livermore Laboratory before joining the Defense Department as director of defense research and engineering in May 1961. He had also acted as a Pentagon scientific consultant and technical adviser to the Conferences for the Cessation of Nuclear Tests in 1958 and 1959.

As research director, Brown aided Secretary of Defense Robert S. McNamara [*q.v.*] in the Secretary's attempts to find alternatives to the use of nuclear force. He developed the technical compromises necessary for military acceptance of the proposed multiservice bomber/fighter, the TFX. Brown, testifying before a House Approporations Subcommittee in May 1963, advocated the use of chemical warfare as an intermediate step between conventional and nuclear weapons. Several months later, in August 1963, he supported McNamara in asking Congress to ratify the nuclear test ban treaty. [See KENNEDY Volume]

Brown became Secretary of the Air Force in September 1965. During his first two years in office, he acted as spokesman for Administration opposition to the expansion of bombing campaigns against North Vietnam. In a televised interview on May 22, 1966, and later in a speech on Dec. 8, 1966, Brown conceded that bombing had reduced but not cut off infiltration from the north. However, he cautioned that Johnson did not want to widen raids to include Hanoi and Haiphong for fear of involving Communist China in a nuclear war.

Brown was one of Johnson's advisers who counseled de-escalation of the war following the military request for further massive troop build-ups in February 1968. At the instruction of Secretary of Defense Clark Clifford [*q.v.*], Brown and his staff, led by Townsend Hoopes [*q.v.*], developed three alternative strategies to the military proposal: (1) intensive bombing of the North, including attacks on Haiphong; (2) a greater effort against supply trails in the southern portions of North Vietnam; and (3) a campaign designed to substitute tactical airpower for a large portion of the search-and-destroy missions conducted by various ground troops in the South. Brown, believing that military victory was impossible at any price consistent with U.S. interests, supported the third position as that most likely to provide a strong negotiating posture. President Johnson, however, adopted the second proposal at the end of March.

In 1969 Brown resigned as Secretary of the Air Force to become president of the California Institute of Technology. He was named Secretary of Defense in 1977.

[EWS]

BROWN, H(UBERT) RAP (GEROID)

b. Oct. 4, 1943; Baton Rouge, La.
Chairman, Student Nonviolent Coordinating Committee, May 1967-June 1968.

Brown grew up in Baton Rouge and enrolled at Southern University there in 1960. He spent the summers of 1962 and 1963 in Washington, D.C., where he joined demonstrations organized by the Nonviolent Action Group (NAG), an affiliate of the Student Nonviolent Coordinating Committee (SNCC). Brown quit school in 1964 and moved to Washington, where he became chairman of NAG in the fall of 1964 and a neighborhood worker in a local antipoverty program during 1965. He began working as a SNCC organizer in Greene County, Ala., in 1966 and was named SNCC's state project director in Alabama late that year. In 1967 Brown was elected chairman of SNCC, replacing Stokely Carmichael [*q.v.*].

The militant Carmichael told reporters at the time of Brown's election that "people will be happy to have me back when they hear him." As SNCC chairman Brown quickly captured media attention for his statements in support of black power, his condemnation of American society and government and his advocacy of violence and revolution. He repeatedly accused white America of conspiring "to commit genocide against black people" and counseled blacks to "get yourself some guns." Brown called President Johnson a "wild, mad dog, an outlaw from Texas" who sent "honky, cracker federal troops into Negro communities to kill black people." He applauded ghetto riots and called on blacks to celebrate Aug. 18, the day the 1965 Watts riot had begun, as their "day of independence." He warned that the riots were only "dress rehearsals for revolution" and predicted that "the rebellions will continue and escalate." Violence "is necessary," Brown asserted. "It is as American as cherry pie."

Brown became controversial not only for his public statements but also for the role he allegedly played in instigating riots in 1967. Rioting erupted in Dayton, Ohio, in June and in East St. Louis, Ill., in September shortly after speeches by Brown in each city. In a widely publicized incident Brown addressed a rally of blacks in Cambridge, Md., on July 24, reportedly telling his audience that they should get their guns and that they "should've burned . . . down long ago" a 50-year-old all-black elementary school in the city. Later that night a fire broke out in the school and quickly spread throughout the black business district, destroying nearly 20 buildings.

Brown was arrested in Washington on July 26 by federal officials and taken to Alexandria, Va., where he was rearrested by state authorities on a fugitive warrant, charged by Maryland with arson and inciting to riot. Released on bond on July 27, Brown was again arrested in New York City on Aug. 19 on a warrant issued by a federal court in New Orleans and charged with violating the Federal Firearms Act by carrying a gun across state lines while under indictment. He was also arrested in February 1968 for violating travel restrictions imposed on him by a federal judge while he was out on bond. From the time of his July 1967 arrest on, Brown spent various periods of time in jail while raising bail ranging from $10,000 to $100,000 on different charges.

Brown, who repeatedly insisted that the charges against him were trumped-up, was often singled out by proponents of a federal anti-riot bill as one of their major targets. The 1968 Civil Rights Act included a section making it a crime to cross state lines with intent to incite a riot, and the controversial provision was popularly known as the "Rap Brown amendment." In May 1968 Brown was convicted of violating the federal firearms law and given the maximum sentence of five years and a $2,000 fine, but he was released on bond pending appeal.

From February to July 1968, while SNCC and the Black Panther Party were allied with each other, Brown served as the Black Panthers' minister of justice. He was replaced as SNCC chairman in June 1968 but then reelected to the post in July 1969 at a meeting where SNCC also changed its name to the Student National Coordinating Committee. Brown's trial on the Maryland charges was scheduled for March 16, 1970 but was twice postponed when Brown failed to appear in court. Brown disappeared in March 1970, and in May he was placed on the FBI's ten-most-wanted list. He was not seen until October 1971, when he was shot and captured by police in New York City. The police charged that Brown had participated in the armed robbery of a Manhattan bar and was shot while trying to make a getaway. In March 1973 Brown was found guilty of armed robbery in New York and was sentenced to a term of 5 to 15 years. Maryland dropped its riot and arson charges against Brown in November when he pleaded guilty to a lesser charge of failing to appear for trial in 1970.

[CAB]

For further information:
H. Rap Brown, *Die Nigger Die!* (New York, 1969).

BRUCE, DAVID K(IRKPATRICK) E(STE)

b. Feb. 12, 1898; Baltimore, Md.
Ambassador to Great Britain, February 1961-February 1969.

Born into a politically prominent Baltimore family, Bruce successfully employed his talents in law, politics, the diplomatic service and business. Associated with the Bankers Trust Company and Harriman and Co., he was at one time the director of 25 corporations. Between 1926 and 1945 he was married to Ailsa Mellon, the daughter of Andrew Mellon and reputedly the richest woman in the United States.

After working in the Office of Strategic Services in the European theater during World War II, Bruce became one of the leading diplomats in Europe. He was the only U.S. diplomat to hold the three most important ambassadorships in Europe: he served as ambassador to France from 1949 to 1952, as ambassador to Germany from 1957 to 1959 and as ambassador to Great Britain during the 1960s. Bruce's considerable personal wealth met one of the prerequisites for the post. But he was, in addition, greatly respected for his diplomatic skills; for a time in December 1960 Kennedy had considered him for Secretary of State. [See TRUMAN, EISENHOWER, KENNEDY Volumes]

After Kennedy's assassination Bruce remained at his post at President Johnson's request. He not only represented Washington's views in London but spoke out on European affairs as well. A proponent of European integration, he attacked French President Charles deGaulle in May 1966 as "ideologically reckless" for his repudiation of an integrated North Atlantic command structure and his demand for the withdrawal of American troops from France.

Bruce faced his most delicate task in communicating Washington's views to British Prime Minister Harold Wilson during Wilson's February 1967 talks with Soviet Premier Alexei Kosygin in London. Wilson and Kosygin hoped to use their influence in Washington and Hanoi to extend the Tet ceasefire and to arrange negotiations aimed at ending the war in Vietnam. Acting on instructions from Washington Bruce and U.S. envoy Charles Cooper indicated that the U.S. would stop the bombing of North Vietnam as a sign of good faith with the understanding that Hanoi would then give private assurances that infiltration of the South would cease. The U.S. in turn would stop augmenting its troop strength in Vietnam. Wilson and Kosygin were ready to act on this proposal, but presidential adviser Walt W. Rostow [*q.v.*] phoned Bruce indicating that the U.S. had suddenly changed its position. Taking a more "hawkish" line the Johnson Administration stated it would not stop the bombing until Hanoi promised to stop infiltration. The new White House policy effectively killed what was, at least to Harold Wilson, one of the most promising peace initiatives taken during the Johnson Administration. In addition, Wilson was angry with Washington, because he, Bruce and Kosygin had been put in an embarrassing position.

In July 1968 in London Bruce signed the nuclear non-proliferation treaty for the U.S. He remained at his post until February 1969, having served the longest term of any U.S. ambassador to Great Britain. After his retirement Bruce agreed to consult with the State Department on a part-time basis. In 1970 he returned to full-time responsibilities as the U.S. representative at the Vietnam peace talks in Paris, and in 1972 he went to Peking as liaison officer to the People's Republic of China. [See NIXON Volume]

[JCH]

BUCKLEY, WILLIAM F(RANK), JR.
b. Nov. 24, 1925; New York, N.Y.
Editor-in-chief, *National Review*, 1955- .

Born to a wealthy Roman Catholic family, William F. Buckley, Jr., attended private schools in Great Britain and served in the Navy during World War II. A year after his 1950 graduation from Yale, Buckley wrote *God and Man at Yale*, a best-selling condemnation of what he regarded as his alma mater's political and irreligious liberalism. In *McCarthy and His Enemies* (1954), he championed the anti-Communist activities of Sen. Joseph R. McCarthy (R, Wisc.).

By the mid-1960s Buckley had emerged as the intellectual leader of a new, postwar conservatism linking militant opposition to Communism abroad with antagonism toward political liberalism at home. To provide a forum for conservative opinion, Buckley founded the bi-weekly *National Review* in 1955. Edited by Buckley and partially subsidized by his family, the *Review* became the rightist counterpart to the left-leaning *New Republic* and *Nation*. In the *Review*, a widely syndicated newspaper column begun in 1962, and in frequent debates and on lecture tours, Buckley argued against a host of programs and policies supported by liberals, including Social Security, U.S. membership in the United Nations and the federal judiciary's school desegregation orders. A vigorous critic of the Soviet Union, Buckley compared it to Nazi Germany and said he agreed with the proposition "Better the chance of being dead than the certainty of being Red." [See EISENHOWER, KENNEDY Volumes]

Buckley supported conservative Sen. Barry M. Goldwater (R, Ariz.) [*q.v.*] for president in 1964 but did not play a role in his campaign. In his columns Buckley strove to differentiate Goldwater's candidacy from the extreme, right-wing John Birch Society, which he deemed a threat to a genuine conservative political movement in America. At the same time, however, members of the Goldwater staff rejected Buckley's offer of assistance.

In 1965 Buckley championed conservative politics in the New York City mayoralty campaign. Running as the candidate of the Conservative Party, established with his assistance in 1962, Buckley hoped to frustrate the political ambitions of Rep. John V. Lindsay (R, N.Y.) [*q.v.*], the Republican-Liberal Party mayoral candidate who had refused to endorse Goldwater in 1964. Defending an ideological party system, Buckley declared in August that "a party thrives on its distinctiveness." Lindsay's voting record and political pronouncements, Buckley charged, "put him left of center of the Democratic Party." Declining to campaign in the traditional New York fashion—in the streets, eating blintzes and pizza—Buckley instead offered lengthy position papers and denunciations of Lindsay's grammar and the predominant social welfare philosophy of the nation's largest city. He criticized the city's budgetary policies and voting-bloc politics. Among other proposals Buckley offered tax relief for minority business enterprises, legalization of gambling, access to drugs by addicts with a doctor's prescription, compulsory work for able-bodied welfare recipients and an elevated bicycle expressway along First Avenue. Buckley did not anticipate victory. When asked if he wanted to be mayor, he replied in August, "I have never considered it." Although he failed to accomplish his principal objective, that of denying Lindsay's election, he succeeded in a secondary purpose of his campaign. With 13.4% of the vote, he exceeded Lindsay's tally on the Liberal Party line. He drew most of his support from Republican districts outside Manhattan.

Becoming something of a celebrity Buckley pursued his conservative crusade nationwide. Beginning in 1966 he hosted *Firing Line*, a syndicated television interview program in which he debated, with acumen and sarcasm, liberals and radicals. An early critic of both the civil rights and anti-war movements, Buckley attacked their militance and emphasis upon civil disobedience as subversive to an orderly and rational society. Still protesting his college's "liberal bias," Buckley ran for a seat on the board of the Yale Corporation in 1967. Former Deputy Defense Secretary Cyrus Vance [*q.v.*], a liberal Democrat, defeated him.

In 1968 Buckley supported former Vice President Richard M. Nixon [*q.v.*] for president and managed his brother's campaign for the U.S. Senate. Running on the Conservative Party line, James L. Buckley lost to Sen. Jacob K. Javits (R-Lib, N.Y.) [*q.v.*] in November, but an impressive display of voter support (16.7%) set the stage for James Buckley's successful senatorial campaign two years later. William F. Buckley held two largely honorific appointments in the Nixon Administration. In 1972 he declared a "suspension of support" for Nixon because he differed with the President's policy of detente with the People's Republic of China and the Soviet Union and his planned budget deficit. [See NIXON Volume]

[JLB]

For further information:

William F. Buckley, Jr., *The Unmaking of a Mayor* (New York, 1966).

———, *The Jeweler's Eye* (New York, 1968).

Charles Lam Markmann, *The Buckleys* (New York, 1973).

George Nash, *The Conservative Intellectual Movement in America: Since 1945* (New York, 1976).

BUNCHE, RALPH J(OHNSON)
b. Aug. 7, 1904; Detroit, Mich.
d. Dec. 9, 1971; New York, N.Y.
U.N. Undersecretary for Special Political Affairs, 1957-71.

The son of a barber, Ralph Bunche was orphaned at 13 and raised in Los Angeles by his maternal grandmother. He graduated Phi Beta Kappa from the University of California at Los Angeles and in 1934 received a Ph.D. in government and international relations from Harvard. From 1938 to 1940 Bunche served as Gunnar Myrdal's chief aide and gathered materials for *An American Dilemma*, Myrdal's highly regarded study of race relations in America. During World War II Bunche entered the State Department, serving in the division of dependent area affairs, which dealt with colonial problems. While in the government Bunche helped to plan the United Nations and in 1947 left the State Department to join the secretariat of the new world body.

In 1948 and 1949 Bunche helped mediate the Arab-Israeli war after Count Folke Bernadotte of Sweden was assassinated in Jerusalem. For his efforts Bunche was the first black man ever awarded the Nobel Peace Prize. Bunche served Secretary General Dag Hammarskjold and his successor U Thant as a principal U.N. troubleshooter. He supervised the U.N.'s peacekeeping force at Suez in 1956 and was promoted to U.N. undersecretary for special political affairs. In 1960 Bunche directed the U.N.'s peacekeeping force in the Congo, returning in January 1963 to oversee the U.N.'s capture of Elisabethville, Katanga and the reunification of the Congo. In March 1964 he assumed control of the U.N. peacekeeping force on Cyprus. [See EISENHOWER, KENNEDY Volume]

Dr. Bunche often lent his international prestige to the American civil rights movement. An early supporter of the Rev. Martin Luther King [*q.v.*], Bunche, who first walked a picket line for the NAACP in 1937, spoke at the 1963 March on Washington and joined King on the Selma-Montgomery march in March 1965. However, Bunche opposed King's attempt to link the civil rights movement with those who opposed the growing war in Vietnam. In October 1965 Bunche suggested that King should "positively and publicly give up one role or the other, that of civil rights leader or that of international conciliator." Bunche's opposition to King's position received greater publicity when he announced at an April 10, 1967 news conference that "the two movements have little in common" and that he had convinced the NAACP board of directors to adopt language characterizing King's position as "a serious tactical mistake." King immediately denied advocating a merger of the movements and challenged the NAACP to assume a "forthright stand on the rightness or wrongness of the Vietnam war." On April 13 Bunche announced that King's statement "takes care of the issue to which my statement had been directed."

Declining health, "frustrations" with U.N. peacekeeping operations and "the calamitous war in Vietnam" led Bunche to consider retirement in January 1967, but U Thant persuaded him to remain. Responding to the increasing number of plane hijackings throughout the world, Bunche met with the president of the International Airlines Pilots Associations in February 1970 and discussed strategies to block attacks on civil aircraft. Bunche died on Dec. 9, 1971 after several years of poor health.

[DKR]

BUNDY, McGEORGE
b. March 30, 1919; Boston, Mass.
Special Assistant to the President for National Security Affairs, January 1961-February 1966.

McGeorge Bundy, a close adviser to Presidents Kennedy and Johnson, was born into a family that had included a Revolutionary War general, a prominent poet and a president of Harvard. His father, Harvey Bundy, had served in the State and War Departments under Henry L. Stimson. Stimson proved a great influence on the younger Bundy, instilling in him the importance of disinterested public service. The statesman's philosophy of military preparedness and his willingness to use force in foreign affairs also affected Bundy's thought.

Bundy graduated first in his class at Yale in 1940 and the next year became a junior fellow at Harvard. Following service in the Army during World War II, Bundy helped Stimson write his autobiography. In 1948 he went to work for the agency responsible for implementing the Marshall Plan but left government to join Thomas Dewey's presidential campaign. After Dewey's defeat Bundy became a political analyst for the prestigious Council on Foreign Relations.

In 1949 Bundy returned to Harvard as a lecturer in government. A superb teacher, Bundy quickly rose to full professor, and at age 34, he was appointed dean of arts and sciences, the second-ranking position at Harvard.

Although a nominal Republican, Bundy campaigned for John F. Kennedy in 1960. Following the election he was appointed the President's special assistant for national security affairs. During the Kennedy years Bundy was one of the President's closest advisers, counseling him on all important foreign policy decisions, including those on Berlin, Cuba and Vietnam. [See KENNEDY Volume]

Unlike many of Kennedy's close associates, Bundy did not leave government following the assassination. Instead, asserting that he served the presidency, not the president, he remained at the White House as an adviser to Johnson. Despite initially cool relations between the two men, Bundy eventually became one of Johnson's closest foreign policy consultants. Bundy considered himself a pragmatist and was, therefore, anxious to base American policy on reactions to specific situations rather than on what he believed were long-term commitments prompted by ideological abstractions. Consequently, much of his counsel was directed at advising the President of all possible policy options and in keeping choices open until a major decision was unavoidable.

Bundy frequently served as Johnson's personal representative on important fact-finding and troubleshooting missions. In May 1965 Johnson sent him to the Dominican Republic to find a solution to the crisis precipitated by a civil war between leftists and a rightist military junta. After the April landing of American troops to prevent what the President thought would be a Communist takeover, the U.S. ambassador and the military had supported the junta. This policy threatened to continue the conflict and increase American involvement. Bundy forced the American military into genuine neutrality and initiated negotiations on the formation of a coalition government. At the last minute his plan collapsed because the junta refused to participate. However, Ellsworth Bunker [*q.v.*] successfully worked out similar arrangements in August.

As the Johnson Administration became increasingly absorbed by Vietnam, Bundy became an important force in policy formation. During early 1964 he was on the periphery of decision-making, helping to direct the targeting of South Vietnamese torpedo-boat raids against the North. These missions, known as 34A operations, were theoretically independent efforts by the South Vietnamese, but they were in fact planned and initiated by the U.S. military command and high-level officials in Washington.

Bundy's role in the Administration's reappraisal of U.S. policy during late 1964 is a matter of historical controversy. The reassessment was carried out in November by the National Security Council Working Group under the leadership of Bundy's brother William [*q.v.*]. The Group recommended an extensive air campaign against the North, with the intensity of raids varying with the rate of Communist troop infiltration and military action in the South. Journalists such as David Halberstam have suggested that McGeorge Bundy did not take a stand on bombing during the debate. However, Ralph Stavins has maintained the McGeorge Bundy was an early proponent of increased bombing but was told to mute his advocacy until after the presidential election.

By January 1965 Bundy had become convinced that the President would have to make a decision on further U.S. action within the near future. In his opinion both the military effort and the political situation in Saigon had deteriorated to such an extent that a major American commitment was necessary if South Vietnam were to remain a viable nation. The decision was, to Bundy, a litmus test of America's readiness to save the rest of Southeast Asia. He believed a formidable effort was important to maintain the world's trust in American willingness to prevent the spread of world Communism.

Following a trip to Vietnam in early February, Bundy recommended that the U.S. adopt the plan suggested by the Working Group. According to Lyndon Johnson, Bundy opposed any attempt to negotiate a withdrawal on the grounds that it would mean "surrender on the installment plan." President Johnson approved the plan in February, and the bombing raids, called Operation Rolling Thunder, began in March. During the remainder of his stay at the White House, Bundy reviewed targets for the raids and became a leading spokesman for the Administration's policy in Vietnam.

Bundy was unable to accommodate himself to Lyndon Johnson's style of dealing with advisers and therefore resigned in December 1965. Over the next two years he did not dissociate himself from American Vietnam policy, but in early 1967 he wrote a private letter to Johnson opposing further escalation of the war as counterproductive. During a symposium held at DePauw University in October 1968, Bundy, whose counsel had contributed to large-scale involvement in Vietnam, called for lowering the cost of the conflict and systematic reduction of the number of American troops there.

Following his resignation from the White House staff, Bundy became president of the Ford Foundation. He pledged that the Foundation's first priority would be to eliminate racial discrimination. During his tenure Ford authorized grants, totaling several million dollars, to train black leaders in the fields of education, social service and politics. Among the most controversial of its grants was a large 1967 contribution to the Congress of Racial Equality. It was designed to increase black voter registration in Cleveland shortly before the election in which Carl Stokes [*q.v.*] was elected as the first black mayor of a major city.

Bundy's other top priorities were the fiscal problems facing the nation's colleges and universities, which Bundy believed were caused, in part, by their conservative investment policies. To promote more aggressive investment of endowment portfolios, the Foundation tied grants to the individual institution's income. The effort proved unsuccessful, especially after the stock market decline began in 1969.

During 1967 Bundy served as chairman of an advisory panel on decentralization of New York City schools. The Bundy panel compiled a report that recommended the reorganization of the system into 30 to 60 largely autonomous school districts with authority over all regular schooling in their areas and the power to hire and fire personnel. The districts were to be governed by boards, partly elected by parents and partly selected by the mayor, and were to be under the general supervision of a small central educational agency. Although the Bundy plan was rejected by the state legislature, the Ford Foundation helped begin decentralization by providing planning grants to three small experimental projects, including the controversial Ocean Hill-Brownsville district in Brooklyn. The attempt to implement school decentralization engendered an enormous controversy, led to a series of citywide strikes by the United Federation of Teachers and increased the polarization between New York's Jewish community and its black and Puerto Rican residents.

Bundy remained at the Foundation into the 1970s. During that period Ford made dramatic cuts in grants to meet a much lower level of investment income. In 1973 Bundy testified for the defense at the trial of Daniel Ellsberg. [See NIXON Volume]

[EWS]

For further information:

Ralph Stavins, et al., *Washington Plans an Aggressive War* (New York, 1971).

U.S. Department of Defense, *The Pentagon Papers*, Senator Gravel Edition (Boston, 1971), Vols. III and IV.

BUNDY, WILLIAM P(UTNAM)
b. Sept. 24, 1917; Washington, D.C.
Assistant Secretary of Defense for International Security Affairs, October 1963-February 1964; Assistant Secretary of State for Far Eastern Affairs, February 1964-March 1969.

William Bundy, one of the prime architects of the Johnson Administration's policy in Southeast Asia, was born into a socially and politically prominent New England family. A brilliant student, he was educated at Groton and Yale, graduating from the latter in 1939. After serving in the Army during the war, Bundy received his law degree from Harvard in 1947 and entered the prestigious Washington law firm of Covington and Burling. Three years later he joined the Central Intelligence Agency, where he was put in charge of overall evaluation of international intelligence.

In 1960 Bundy became staff director of the President's Commission on National Goals, which had been founded to formulate broad, long-term objectives and programs. President John F. Kennedy appointed Bundy deputy assistant secretary of defense in charge of international security affairs in January 1961. At this post he was responsible for coordinating military aid programs throughout the world. [See KENNEDY Volume]

Although his role in Vietnam policymaking was less well-known than that of his brother McGeorge, William Bundy was an important figure in America's growing involvement in the war. In the fall of 1961 he was one of the officials who analyzed South Vietnam's request for a bilateral defense treaty and increased American military aid. Bundy recommended "an early, hard-hitting operation" to arrest Communist expansion. However, President Kennedy decided to send only support troops and equipment in November 1961.

Bundy carried his hawkish views to the State Department when he became assistant secretary of state for Far Eastern affairs in February 1964. As the political and military situation in Vietnam deteriorated in the fall of 1964, President Johnson ordered the National Security Council Working Group, led by Bundy and John McNaughton [*q.v.*], to review operations and make recommendations on the future course of the war. The panel was asked to determine the pace of future bombing in North Vietnam, which until then had been carried out only in retaliation for specific attacks on American bases. The committee was also told to investigate the need for increased American ground forces and to analyze the relationship between U.S. military strategy and its overall political goals.

In its report, completed at the end of November, the Group recommended aerial attacks on the North, their intensity to vary with the level of Communist infiltration and the pace of the war in the South. The panel based its recommendation on the belief that an American defeat in Vietnam would make the defense of the rest of Southeast Asia extremely difficult. Bundy did not support the domino theory, which held that if Vietnam fell the rest of Southeast Asia would shortly become Communist. However, he calculated that a Communist takeover would be probable by the end of a decade.

The panel did not believe that the use of air power would settle the war but rather saw the bombing strikes as a means of upholding and improving South Vietnamese morale. In Bundy's estimation the prospect was "for a prolonged period without major strikes or escalation, but without any give by Hanoi." He rejected a negotiated settlement at this time because he believed it would neither lead to a stable peace nor help South Vietnamese morale.

Johnson adopted the committee's proposals in February 1965. These recommendations determined the course of the war until July 1965, when the Administration committed extensive ground forces to the conflict. In the months that followed the decision to launch what was known as Operation Rolling Thunder, Bundy was one of the officials responsible for choosing targets for the bombing campaign.

Despite his support of bombing Bundy was reluctant to back the large-scale introduction of American troops, fearing that the U.S. would have the same experience as the French in Indochina. However, once the decision was made he supported the position and eventually became a leading defender of the Administration's policy.

During the years that followed the introduction of systematic bombing raids, Bundy helped formulate the conditions under which the U.S. would halt the attacks and begin peace negotiations. In May 1966 he submitted a memorandum to Secretary of State Dean Rusk [*q.v.*] that served as a guideline for U.S. policy until 1969. In this paper bombing was seen as a means of driving North Vietnam to the negotiating table. The U.S. would stop bombing only if North Vietnam agreed to limit infiltration and end Communist action in the South. A halt in return for an agreement to negotiate was considered unacceptable.

In the spring of 1967 Bundy opposed the continued escalation of the conflict, and particularly the proposed mining of Haiphong harbor, on the grounds that such action would not change Hanoi's position but would have an adverse effect on relations with U.S. allies. Further buildups, he believed, would also convince the South Vietnamese that the U.S. could win the war without their all out support. Despite the lack of progress in the war, he argued against negotiations as useless and, instead, favored "sticking it out if necessary."

Bundy left the government in March 1969 to become a visiting professor at the Massachusetts Institute of Technology's Center for International Studies. In 1972 he became editor of *Foreign Affairs*.

[EWS]

For further information:
U.S. Department of Defense, *The Pentagon Papers*, Senator Gravel edition (Boston, 1971), Vols. III and IV.

BUNKER, ELLSWORTH

b. May 11, 1894; Yonkers, N.Y.
Ambassador to the Organization of American States, January 1964-October 1966; Ambassador-at-Large, October 1966-April 1967; Ambassador to South Vietnam, April 1967-March 1973.

The son of a wealthy sugar manufacturer, Bunker joined his father's firm, the National Sugar Refining Company, following his graduation from Yale in 1916; he rose to become chairman of the board in 1948. Three years later Bunker left private industry to become ambassador to Argentina. From 1952 to 1953 he served as ambassador to Italy and from 1956 to 1961 was ambassador to India. In 1962 and 1963 Bunker mediated disputes between the Dutch and Indonesians over West Irian and between the Saudi Arabians and Egyptians over Yemen. [See EISENHOWER Volume]

Shortly after President Johnson appointed Bunker ambassador to the Organization of American States (OAS) in January 1964, the diplomat was assigned to help reestablish U.S.-Panamanian diplomatic relations, severed following an incident in which American troops fired on Panamanian rioters. By April Bunker had succeeded in reaching an agreement with Panama to resume diplomatic ties and discuss problems between the two countries.

In 1965 Bunker undertook a year-long mission in the Dominican Republic, then torn by a civil war between leftists and the military. Fearing that the war would result in a takeover by Castro-allied leftists, President Johnson had ordered troops to that Caribbean country in April 1965. In May he sent a negotiating team headed by McGeorge Bundy [*q.v.*] to try to persuade the factions to establish a coalition government, but the mission failed. Bunker arrived in Santo Domingo in June as a member of a three-man OAS peace mission. By winning the personal trust of leaders on both sides during the course of three months of patient negotiation, Bunker was able to find a provisional president agreeable to all and to arrange terms for the surrender of rebel arms. Bunker also helped stabilize the provisional regime by convincing rightist plotters that Washington would not support a new coup. At the same time he demanded and received from the Johnson Administration assurances that no matter what its reservations about the new government, it would not support a military takeover. For his condust in this affair, Walter Lippmann called Bunker "America's most accomplished diplomat."

In April 1967 President Johnson named

Bunker ambassador to South Vietnam, an appointment applauded by both "hawks" and "doves" in Congress and the press. Bunker's reputation as a disinterested mediator was severely damaged by his stay in Vietnam. While there he became, in the words of David Halberstam, "one of the three most resilient hawks in the Johnson Administration." Bunker opposed bombing halts in the winter of 1967, which were designed to bring North Vietnam to the negotiating table, and he asserted that progress was being made in the conduct of the war even after the disastrous Tet offensive of January 1968. Bunker was a strong supporter of the regime of President Nguyen Van Thieu and ignored many of its repressive policies. Because of his great reputation as a diplomat, this support carried great weight within the Johnson Administration.

Bunker remained at his post during the early 1970s and employed his skills as a diplomat to coordinate U.S.-South Vietnamese bargaining strategy during the Paris peace talks. He was replaced by Graham Martin [*q.v.*] in March 1973 and returned to Washington to assume the position of ambassador-at-large. [See NIXON Volume]

[EWS]

BURCH, DEAN

b. Dec. 20, 1927; Enid, Okla.
Chairman, Republican National Committee, July 1964-April 1965.

Less than two years after graduating from the University of Arizona Law School, Dean Burch joined the Washington staff of Sen. Barry M. Goldwater (R, Ariz.) [*q.v.*]. As Goldwater's administrative assistant from 1955 to 1959, he earned the conservative leader's trust, and when Goldwater decided to run for president in 1963, Burch quit his Phoenix law practice to serve on the candidate's presidential campaign staff. Burch scheduled Goldwater's public appearances during the preconvention races.

On the day following his nomination, Goldwater surprised Republican officials by naming Burch, at age 36, chairman of the Republican National Committee (RNC). Observers had expected the presidential nominee to select a veteran Party leader, like Ohio Republican Chairman Ray C. Bliss [*q.v.*], who had not been identified with the Goldwater entourage and whose designation might reconcile moderate and liberal Republicans to the conservative Senator's first-ballot victory. Although well-regarded by reporters covering Goldwater in the primaries, Burch had remained an anonymous, if competent aide. Until 1964 he had never served in a national campaign and knew little about the RNC. Senior adviser Richard Kleindienst counseled against Burch's appointment and proposed Bliss. However, Goldwater, bitter over the persistence of the moderate-liberal opposition to his candidacy, vetoed the Ohioan. Not only would Burch be loyal, Goldwater reasoned, but his position as RNC chairman would keep the Party's national organization in conservative hands even if the Republicans lost in November.

Entrusting Burch with the RNC post, Goldwater ran his campaign through the National Committee. Burch and Alabama Republican Chairman John Grenier made most of the Goldwater campaign's strategic decisions. Other preconvention advisers either traveled with the candidate or suffered demotions; Kleindienst and Paul Fannin ran for office in Arizona. Unprepared for his leadership role Burch proved a poor campaign director. According to long-time Goldwater aide Stephen Shadegg, Burch and Grenier failed to plan adequately, making the campaign "an impromptu effort." Because the RNC would not buy television time in advance of contributions to pay for it, other advertisers bought out most of the limited number of choice TV spots available. In his campaign appearances Goldwater devoted 17% of his time to four states, three of which Burch and others had privately conceded to the Democrats.

Burch also failed in his most basic task, that of actually running the RNC organization. Like Goldwater, Burch had become deeply embittered by the liberal-moderate wing and anyone identified with it. He removed anti-Goldwater Republicans from the RNC Executive Committee and replaced them with loyalists from the Deep South and Arizona. Suspicious and petty over matters like coffee breaks and mimeograph privileges, Burch and his aides reportedly sapped morale among RNC permanent employees. More substantively, the Goldwater managers ignored detailed RNC reports and public opinion surveys.

From his post at the Committee, however, Burch delivered effective partisan attacks on the Democrats. In August 1964 Burch questioned President Johnson's public statement concerning his personal wealth. He added that "it is peculiar that the bulk of [Johnson's] fortune was made in areas subject to federal control." In September Burch heatedly castigated a controversial anti-Goldwater advertisement that implied that the Senator would be reckless with nuclear weapons. The Democrats quickly withdrew the offensive commercial.

Under Burch's direction the RNC identified voters likely to back Goldwater in November, recruited volunteers and set up an extensive house-to-house and telephone canvassing effort. Surveys indicate that 3.9 million GOP workers reached 12.2 million homes by Oct. 15, roughly outdoing the Democrats's 2.5 million volunteer force by four million households. As a result, Goldwater's actual November tally ran ahead of election-eve opinion poll estimates.

Following Goldwater's defeat GOP moderates demanded Burch's removal, while his determination to keep his office promised another intraparty battle. Initially he possessed Goldwater's firm support, but former Vice President Richard Nixon [*q.v.*] and several influential, Midwestern RNC members favored the non-ideological Ray Bliss [*q.v.*] as his replacement. With a committee majority ready to elect Bliss, Nixon persuaded Goldwater to abandon Burch, who then withdrew from the January voting. Bliss won election as RNC chairman in January 1965 and assumed office in April.

Burch returned to Phoenix to practice law. In 1968 he successfully directed Goldwater's reelection to the Senate. President Nixon designated Burch chairman of the Federal Communications Commission in September 1969. He resigned in February 1974 to aid in the President's defense during the Watergate crisis. Burch stayed on in the Ford Administration until December 1975. [See NIXON Volume]

[JLB]

For further information:

David Brody and Stephen Hess, *The Republican Establishment* (New York, 1967).

Karl A. Lamb, "Under One Roof: Barry Goldwater's Campaign Staff," in Bernard Cosman and Robert J. Huckshorn, eds., *Republican Politics* (New York, 1968), pp. 9-45.

Stephen Shadegg, *What Happened to Goldwater?* (New York, 1965).

BURDICK, QUENTIN N(ORTHRUP)

b. June 19, 1908; Munich, N.D.
Democratic Senator, N.D., 1960- .

The son of a pioneer family, Burdick graduated from the University of Minnesota Law School in 1932. While practicing in his father's law firm, he became active in the Nonpartisan League, which had been formed to aid small farmers. Burdick was elected to the U.S. House of Representatives in 1958 as the first Democratic congressman in North Dakota's history. After the death of Sen. William Langer (R, N.D.) in 1959, he won a special election to the Senate. According to *Congressional Quarterly*, Burdick supported Kennedy Administration legislation on more than 65% of key roll-call votes and backed such Administration measures as the Area Redevelopment Act and civil rights and public works bills. [See KENNEDY Volume]

During the Johnson Administration Burdick supported Administration legislation on over 60% of key roll-call votes. In the 1964 Senate election he defeated businessman Thomas S. Kleppe with 58% of the vote, equaling President Johnson's total in the state. Burdick served on the Interior and Insular Affairs Committee and, in 1965, won the $300 million Garrison Dam and Diversion Project for his state.

On Jan. 27, 1966 Burdick was one of 15 senators who sent a letter to President Johnson calling for the continued suspension of air strikes against North Vietnam.

He was also among a group of Senate critics of the war who issued a statement on May 17, 1967 warning Hanoi that dissent on the war was a minority view in the U.S. and that, while the group would still press for a negotiated peace, they steadfastly opposed any unilateral withdrawal of U.S. troops from South Vietnam.

Regarded as a liberal Democrat and a champion of the interests of the small farmer, Burdick was reelected to the Senate in 1964 and 1970.

[FHM]

BURNS, JOHN A(NTHONY)

b. March 30, 1909; Fort Assinneboine, Mont.
d. April 5, 1975; Kaiwi, Oahu, Hawaii.
Governor, Hawaii, 1963-75.

After spending his youth in Hawaii and Kansas, Burns served as a captain on the Honolulu police force during World War II. Following the war he began to reorganize the territory's Democratic Party with the substantial support of the islands, large Nisei population and the International Longshoremen's and Warehousemen's Union (ILWU), which fostered multiracial unionism and opposed Hawaii's oligarchic economic system. Burns won election as territorial delegate to the U.S. Congress on this third try in November 1956, and once in Washington, fought for Hawaii's application for statehood. He lost the July 1959 gubernatorial election to the incumbent territorial governor, Republican William F. Quinn, but in a November 1962 rematch, Burns, recognized as the architect of Hawaiian statehood, easily defeated Quinn. [See KENNEDY Volume]

Hawaii experienced an economic boom during Burns's first term. A practitioner of "consensus" politics, Burns modeled himself on his close friend and congressional adviser, Lyndon B. Johnson, who sent Burns on diplomatic missions to Korea and Africa in the mid-1960s. Burns helped his proteges, many of them Japanese-Americans, win elective office and contributed to reducing the state Republican Party to one of the weakest in the nation. Yet, despite Burns's close relations with business, labor and Hawaii's ethnic minorities, opposition to increased taxes and government expenditures made his 1966 reelection victory difficult.

During his second term divisions arose within Democratic ranks. Critics charged that, while Burns encouraged the islands' economic expansion, he ignored pressures on the environment and gave greater attention to tourism than to the living needs of the people of Hawaii. Burns, whose optimistic vision of Hawaii included the eventual absorption of the Marianas, the Caroline and Marshall Islands, Guam and American Samoa into the state, argued that there should be no limit on economic development, confident that the people of Hawaii could cope with the problems of prosperity.

Despite a serious primary challenge from his lieutenant-governor, Thomas P. Gill, Burns was reelected again in 1970. However, after learning that he was suffering from cancer, he decided not to run in 1974. In the November election his chosen successor, Lieutenant Governor George Ariyoshi, was elected the nation's first nonwhite governor. Burns died on April 5, 1975. [See NIXON Volume]

[JCH]

For further information see:
Tom Coffman, *Catch A Wave: A Case Study of Hawaii's New Politics* (Honolulu, 1973)

BURTON, PHILIP

b. June 1, 1926; Cincinnati, Ohio.
Democratic Representative, Calif., 1964- .

Burton's father, a Cincinnati physician, moved his family to California in 1939. Burton served in World War II and in Korea, took a law degree in 1952 and soon became deeply involved in California's freewheeling Democratic Party. Burton was elected to the California Assembly from a San Francisco district in 1956. In 1960 he was one of the few elected California officials to support student demonstrations against the

House Un-American Activities Committee when it held hearings in northern California.

Burton was elected to the House of Representatives in 1964 from San Francisco's ethnically heterogeneous and liberal eastern district. His equally liberal brother John filled his vacated Assembly seat, and together the Burton brothers won great influence among Bay Area liberals. In the late 1960s their faction in Northern California's Democratic Party rivaled San Francisco Mayor Joseph Alioto's [*q.v.*] for leadership in the Party.

In the House Burton was among the earliest critics of American involvement in Vietnam, and he belonged to the handful of representatives who consistently dissented from Johnson Administration policies there. In 1965 and 1966 he voted against Vietnam appropriation bills in the House and at the tumultuous 1968 Democratic Convention Burton presented the minority platform position on Vietnam. Known as the McGovern-McCarthy-Kennedy plank, it called for an unconditional end to the bombing of North Vietnam.

Supported by Bay Area labor unions as well as peace groups, Burton was also an active backer of labor and welfare legislation. Assigned to the House Education and Labor Committee, Burton introduced an amendment in 1966 to that year's minimum-wage bill to extend minimum-wage and overtime protection to 700,000 federal employes.

Burton often went further than fellow liberals on civil rights and civil liberties issues. In January 1966 he led 23 representatives who protested the Georgia state legislature's refusal to seat civil rights leader Julian Bond [*q.v.*] because of his anti-war views. Burton also favored the dissolution of the House Un-American Activities Committee. Unlike many congressional liberals he opposed the Committee's investigation of the Ku Klux Klan. "No committee of Congress," Burton said in April 1965, "has the authority to determine whether or not any organization, including the Klan, will be proved to be un-American."

Burton, who continued to sponsor important labor and welfare legislation, was elected chairman of the liberal Democratic Study Group in 1971 and was a leader in the movement for congressional reform. Known in the House for his effectiveness behind the scenes, he helped to abolish the House Un-American Activities Committee's successor, the House Internal Security Committee, by persuading all its Democratic members but the chairman to resign. In 1974 he became chairman of the powerful House Democratic Caucus. [See NIXON Volume]

[MDB]

BYRD, HARRY F(LOOD), SR.

b. June 10, 1887; Martinsburg, W. Va.
d. Oct. 20, 1966; Winchester, Va.
Democratic Senator, Va., 1933-65;
Chairman, Finance Committee, 1955-65.

After establishing himself as a successful apple grower in Virginia's Shenandoah Valley, Byrd won a seat in the state Senate and in 1925 was elected governor of the state. During his four-year term Byrd skillfully employed patronage to establish himself as the leader of a powerful Democratic political machine. For almost forty years Byrd's rurally-oriented organization based on county courthouses maintained nearly unquestioned control of Virginia's politics.

In 1933 Byrd was elected to the U.S. Senate, where he remained for over thirty years. Applying his principles at the national level, he opposed New Deal welfare spending programs and called for balanced budgets. By the late 1940s Byrd was a leader of the Southern Democrat-Republican conservative coalition in Congress. His seniority enabled him to obtain the chairmanship of the Senate Finance Committee in 1955. Other continually reelected candidates of his Virginia machine, such as Sen. A. Willis Robertson [*q.v.*] and Rep. Howard W. Smith [*q.v.*], had also accumulated seniority, and with them Byrd was able to play an effective role in obstructing liberal legislation. [See TRUMAN, EISENHOWER Volumes]

Beginning in 1952 Byrd tacitly endorsed Republican presidential candidates by declining to back the Democratic nominees, whom he regarded as dangerously liberal. Largely as a result of this policy, Adlai Stevenson [*q.v.*] lost the state in 1952 and 1956, and Sen. John F. Kennedy (D, Mass.) likewise failed to carry Virginia in 1960. In Congress Byrd was a potent enemy of Kennedy's New Frontier measures. As chairman of the Senate Finance Committee, he helped kill the Administration's 1962 bill for expanding unemployment compensation benefits and played a major role in preventing the passage of President Kennedy's medicare bill during the same year. In 1963 Byrd held up in his Committee a "New Economics" tax bill, designed to stimulate the economy through a reduction in taxes and a series of planned budget deficits. [See KENNEDY Volume]

President Johnson gave the Kennedy tax bill high priority in the early months of his Administration. The deficits which the measure would create were anathema to Byrd. But by announcing, in his State of the Union message of Jan. 8, 1964, that the budget for fiscal 1965 would be kept below $100 billion, Johnson convinced Byrd to let the Finance Committee vote on the tax cut bill, although the Senator was still against it. On Jan. 23 the Committee voted, 12-5, with Byrd in opposition, to approve the measure. The Senate adopted it two weeks later.

Byrd continued to be a staunch opponent of liberal presidential programs. In May 1964 he asserted that federal spending could be cut by $6.5 billion through the curtailing of such Johnson measures as the mass transit, air pollution, public works, aid-to-education and housing programs. Byrd also opposed the civil rights bill of 1964 and the voting rights and medicare bills of the following year.

However, Byrd proved a less effective opponent of welfare legislation during the Johnson Administration than he had been in former years. Johnson was a skillful manager of Congress and maintained the large network of friends which he had built during his years on Capitol Hill. Furthermore, his power increased as a result of the overwhelming Democratic victory in the 1964 elections. Therefore, the President succeeded in passing a large majority of the Great Society programs he proposed in 1964 and 1965. During the latter year, for example, he pressured Byrd into granting prompt hearings for the medicare bill, and the Senator was thus unable to block the measure through stalling tactics, as he had done in the early 1960s.

As Byrd's power in Congress ebbed, his control over his state's politics also eroded. In the late 1950s a moderate group had coalesced within Byrd's machine in reaction to the Senator's intransigent opposition to court-ordered school desegregation. That group grew in ensuing years as the moderate electorate in urban areas expanded and the size of the black vote increased. In 1964 the Virginia Democratic convention, in defiance of Byrd, endorsed President Johnson for reelection. Not only were the state's voters moving toward the political center, but many of Byrd's political lieutenants feared that continued failure to endorse Democratic national tickets would eventually reduce the Party's strength in state and local elections.

Illness ended Byrd's career before he suffered any further setbacks. He resigned from the Senate because of poor health in November 1965 and died of a brain tumor on Oct. 20, 1966.

[MLL]

For further information:
J. Harvie Wilkinson III, *Harry Byrd and the Changing Face of Virginia Politics, 1945-1966* (Charlottesville, 1968)

BYRD, HARRY F(LOOD), JR.

b. Dec. 20, 1914; Winchester, Va.
Democratic Senator, Va., 1965- .

Harry F. Byrd, Jr., was the son of U.S. Senator Harry F. Byrd (D, Va.) [*q.v.*], whose organization dominated Virginia's politics from the late 1920s to the mid-1960s. The younger Byrd won election to the state Senate in 1948 and served in that body until November 1965, when Gov. Albertis S. Harrison appointed him to fill the U.S. Senate seat of his father, who had just retired because of illness. One year later he won election to his father's seat.

"Little Harry," as he was known in Virginia, proved as staunchly conservative as the senior Byrd. Throughout his political career he opposed civil rights measures and large government expenditures, especially for social welfare programs. As a state senator he favored reductions in taxes and unyielding resistance to school integration. In the U.S. Senate he strongly opposed President Johnson's Great Society programs. According to the *Congressional Quarterly*, Byrd voted against Johnson Administration bills more often than any other Democratic senator in 1966, 1967 and 1968.

In October 1966 he offered an amendment to an antipoverty bill that would have banned aid to subversives and inciters of riots. Congress ultimately adopted a proviso that barred funds to anyone convicted of inciting riots. The following year he unsuccessfully proposed that the ceiling on the federal debt be lowered from $358 billion to $348 billion. In September 1968 he declared his opposition to President Johnson's nomination of Supreme Court Associate Justice Abe Fortas [*q.v.*] to be Chief Justice, asserting that the Court had contributed to "the current permissiveness pervading the land."

Byrd ardently supported the war effort in Vietnam. In 1966 he offered an amendment to a foreign aid bill that denounced West Germany for indirectly aiding North Vietnam through economic assistance to Communist China. The Senate adopted the amendment, but it was dropped in a House-Senate conference. The following year he proposed an amendment to an Export-Import Bank bill to bar the Bank from extending credits to any country trading with North Vietnam. The House revised the amendment so that it would apply only to Communist nations. During the same year the Senate adopted a Byrd resolution that advocated that the United Nations impose economic sanctions upon North Vietnam similar to those which the world body had applied to Rhodesia.

Primarily because of the growing number of moderate urban and black voters in the 1960s, the Byrd organization's control over Virginia politics declined. Furthermore, the younger Byrd did not exercise the strong leadership that had characterized the political work of his father, who was inactive after his retirement from the Senate and who died in October 1966. During the summer of 1966 the younger Byrd narrowly won the Democratic primary with 50.9% of the vote, while U.S. Senator A. Willis Robertson [*q.v.*] and U.S. Rep. Howard W. Smith [*q.v.*], both conservative stalwarts, lost. After a liberal won the 1969 Democratic gubernatorial primary, Byrd decided to abandon the Party and run for reelection as an independent. Effectively exploiting opposition to school busing, he won election to a full term in 1970 with 54% of the vote. [See NIXON Volume]

[MLL]

For further information:
J. Harvie Wilkinson III, *Harry Byrd and the Changing Face of Virginia Politics, 1945-1966* (Charlottesville, 1968).

BYRD, ROBERT C(ARLYLE)

b. Nov. 20, 1917; North Wilkesboro, N.C.
Democratic Senator, W. Va., 1959;
Secretary, Senate Democratic Caucus, 1967-71.

Orphaned at an early age, Robert C. Byrd grew up on a West Virginia dirt farm. He attended two state colleges and after eight years of night classes earned a law degree from American University in 1963. During World War II Byrd worked as a shipyard welder and briefly belonged to the Ku Klux Klan. In 1946 he won election to the West Virginia legislature and six years later became a member of the U.S. House of Representatives from Charleston. Twice reelected Byrd defeated incumbent Sen. Chapman Rivercomb (R, W. Va.) in 1958 with 59.2% of the vote and quickly emerged as the most powerful Democrat in the state. Although he usually voted with the Senate Democratic leadership, in 1963 Byrd opposed the Kennedy Administration's nuclear test ban treaty and civil rights bill. [See EISENHOWER, KENNEDY Volumes]

Byrd joined the Southern Democrats' filibuster against the 1964 civil rights bill and on June 9 gave the longest speech in opposition, lasting 14 hours and 13 minutes. He also opposed the 1965 Voting Rights Act. In September 1964 he joined a group of Southern Democrats and Republicans who sought to overturn the Supreme Court's recent ruling requiring the reapportionment of state legislatures. Byrd endorsed Johnson in 1964 and won reelection in his own state with 67.7% of the vote.

Between 1961 and 1969 Byrd chaired the Appropriations Subcommittee on the District of Columbia. A self-proclaimed foe of welfare recipients "trying to get a free ride," Byrd frequently attacked the Aid-to-Dependent Children program and oversaw the creation of welfare inspectors for the district. However, he also approved appropriations for the hiring of additional teachers and social workers and construction of the city's first public pools in 30 years.

Although he did not oppose passage of the relatively mild Coal Mine Safety Act of 1966, Byrd declined, like most members of his state's congressional delegation, to take an active role in mine safety legislation. Coal mining was West Virginia's largest single employer. Indeed, the top leadership of the United Mine Workers in 1966 praised the coal operators' efforts to improve job safety. In his 1964 reelection campaign Byrd enjoyed overwhelming support from rank-and-file miners, although his finance chairman was an executive vice president of Consolidated Coal, the state's largest coal producer. Not until the Huntington, W. Va., Mountaineer Mine No. 9 disaster of November 1968 did Congress consider major legislation to alleviate hazardous working conditions for miners.

According to *Congressional Quarterly*, Byrd voted with the Administration on 57% of the tallies for which Johnson announced a position during the historic 1965 session of the 89th Congress. In February he supported the Appalachia Regional Development Act, an antipoverty aid measure that affected all of West Virginia. He voted for medicare in July but against the Senate leadership's efforts to repeal Section 14(b), the "open shop" provision, of the Taft-Hartley Act.

During the 90th Congress Byrd voted with the majority of Southern Democrats on 60% of the roll call votes. (In contrast he voted with the Northern Democrats 31% of the time.) He opposed the consular treaty with the Soviet Union in March 1967 and voted against the confirmation of Thurgood Marshall [*q.v.*], a black, as an associate justice of the Supreme Court in August of the same year. However, he successfully sponsored an amendment in April 1967 that made persons eligible for reduced Social Security benefits at age 60.

Byrd denounced riots in northern cities and, in perhaps his most quoted statement of the Johnson years, declared in July 1967 that "brutal force" should be used to quell urban disturbances and that looters should be "shot on the spot." A Byrd amendment to the Crime Control Bill in May 1968 denied federal employment for five years to anyone convicted of inciting a riot. After heavy rains in June 1968 turned "Resurrection City," the camp of thousands of poor brought to Washington to lobby for antipoverty legislation, into a quagmire, Byrd termed the temporary community a "festering sore which must be excised."

In his first decade in the Senate, Byrd established a reputation for tireless dedication to his Senate duties. He voted on 92% of all Senate roll calls during the 89th Congress and on 93% of the tallies during the 90th Congress. In January 1967 he defeated Sen. Joseph Clark (D, Pa.) [*q.v.*], a liberal, by a vote of 35 to 28 for the post of secretary of the Party Conference, the Democrats' third-ranking position in the Senate. Chosen again unanimously two years later, Byrd assumed many of the responsibilities assigned to Majority Whip Edward M. Kennedy (D, Mass.) [*q.v.*] and in 1971, following his reelection in West Virginia, unseated Kennedy for the Senate Democrats' second-ranking leadership position. [See NIXON Volume]

[JLB]

For further information:

In 1977 Byrd became majority leader.

BYRNES, JOHN W(ILLIAM)
b. June 12, 1913; Green Bay, Wisc.
Republican Representative, Wisc., 1945-73.

A graduate of the University of Wisconsin Law School, John Byrnes was appointed Wisconsin's special deputy commissioner for banking in 1938. Elected to the state Senate in 1940, he was named majority floor leader in 1943. He won election to the House as a Republican in 1944 and in 1947 gained a position on the Ways and Means Committee, where he built a reputation as a fiscal conservative. In 1959 Byrnes became chairman of the House Republican Policy Committee after helping Rep. Charles A. Halleck (R, Ind.) [*q.v.*] depose Rep. Joseph W. Martin (R, Mass.) as House minority leader.

During the Kennedy Administration Byrnes was the leading House Republican spokesman on economic policy and, according to the *New York Times*, "second only to Mr. Halleck as a power among House Republicans." Byrnes frequently led Republican efforts to reduce or eliminate Kennedy Administration social welfare expenditures and was a vocal opponent of Kennedy's proposed $11 billion tax cut in 1963. [See EISENHOWER, KENNEDY Volumes]

Byrnes remained in the vanguard of House Republican conservatism throughout the Johnson years. His voting record, as evaluated by the conservative Americans for Constitutional Action, ranged from 78% in favor of conservative positions in 1964 to 93% in 1967. He voted in favor of the Civil Rights Act of 1964 and the Voting Rights Act of 1965 but consistently opposed Great Society antipoverty programs.

Byrnes lost some influence when the Republican caucus that unseated Halleck as minority leader in January 1965 also adopted a rule barring a Party leadership post to any ranking Republican on a legislative committee. Byrnes elected to drop his post as chairman of the Republican Policy Committee and continue as senior Republican on the Ways and Means Committee.

In 1965 Byrnes spearheaded Republican opposition to the Johnson Administration's proposed program of financing medical care for the aged through the Social Security system (medicare). The Byrnes Plan, put forth as a substitute by the House Republican leadership, was similar to medicare in certain respects but would have provided that health insurance for the aged be voluntary and be financed by individual contributions combined with subsidies from federal general revenues. The House rejected Byrnes's substitute, 236-191, in April and then passed the Administration plan, 313-115. The final bill, however, incorporated an important element of the Byrnes Plan, whereby a person over 65 could purchase supplementary insurance covering doctors' bills as well as hospital costs. With his senior position on the Ways and Means Committee, Byrnes exerted greater influence on tax policy than any other House Republican. Although frequently in opposition to tax measures proposed by the Johnson Administration, the pragmatic Byrnes developed an effective working relationship with the Committee's chairman, Rep. Wilbur D. Mills (D, Ark.) [*q.v.*]. Byrnes and Mills usually worked together to round up a consensus behind compromise measures.

Among Administration initiatives opposed by Byrnes was the "interest equalization tax" in March 1964. The tax was levied on foreign securities sold in the United States and was intended to ease the balance of payments deficit by making it more expensive for foreigners to borrow in the U.S. Byrnes called it an "ill-advised and dangerous expedient that would not eliminate the balance of payments deficit," which he blamed on non-income-producing government expenditures abroad. The tax measure passed the House over Republican opposition, 238-142.

Byrnes and the Committee's Republicans often opposed various excise and luxury taxes favored by the Administration. His most telling moment of resistance, however, came when President Johnson requested a 10% income tax surcharge in 1967. Byrnes joined Mills in holding up the tax increase for over a year until Johnson agreed to substantial budget cuts. Byrnes voted for the increase in June 1968 after it had been coupled with $6 billion in spending cuts.

Byrnes remained a key House Republican until his retirement in January 1973. [See NIXON Volume]

[TO]

CALIFANO, JOSEPH (ANTHONY)

b. May 15, 1931; New York, N.Y.
White House Special Assistant, July 1965-January 1969.

Califano graduated from Holy Cross in 1952, took his law degree from Harvard Law School in 1955 and the same year joined the Navy, where he served as a legal officer in the Defense Department. Bored with "splitting stocks for Tom Dewey's law firm"—Dewey, Ballantine, Bushby, Palmer and Wood—Califano joined the Defense Department in 1961. By 1965 he was special assistant to Secretary of Defense Robert S. McNamara [*q.v.*] and had gained the attention of President Johnson and Bill Moyers [*q.v.*], who admired Califano's sharp analytical ability and his talent for devising clear proposals for solving governmental problems.

Califano was named a White House special assistant in July 1965. The only important Johnson aide drawn from another part of the executive branch, Califano's shift from Defense indicated that President Johnson was determined to employ McNamara's "systems-analysis" methods—in which Califano was an expert—to the conduct of domestic affairs. In August 1965 Johnson initiated a Planning-Programming-Budgeting System, which involved the utilization of computers and sophisticated statistical and mathematical techniques for evaluation of domestic problems.

In addition to initiating the systems analysis approach at the White House, Califano assumed the role of coordinator of Johnson's legislative program from Moyers, who in July 1965 had been named White House press secretary.

On Jan. 12, 1966 Johnson announced his intention to create a Department of Transportation. The President put Califano in charge of the legislation and told the Cabinet the next day, "When Joe speaks, that's my voice you hear." The bill was an enormously complex piece of legislation involving some 30 autonomous and semi-autonomous agencies, including the Civil Aeronautics Board and the Interstate Commerce Commission. Its progress was slow because many members of Congress regarded many of the affected government activities, such as highways, dams and waterways, as valuable "pork-barrel" projects. After passage of the Department of Transportation bill in October 1966, Califano's power and prestige within the White House increased. Upon the resignation of Moyers in December 1966, he assumed the role of domestic chief of staff.

Unlike Walter Jenkins [*q.v.*] or Moyers, Califano was never an "alter ego" to Johnson, nor did he attract significant public attention. Describing himself as "the President's instrument," he was described by Secretary McNamara as "the man who, next to the President, has contributed more than any other individual in our country to the conception, formulation and implementation of the program for the Great Society."

After Moyers's departure Califano continued to expand the "task-force system" initiated by Moyers and Richard Goodwin [*q.v.*]. He exercised White House control over the Department of Labor, various welfare programs within the Department of Health, Education and Welfare, the poverty program, the Agency for International Development program and all aspects of foreign trade. Concerned with the legislative proposals of these agencies and with many of their day-to-day activities, Califano's role went well beyond guiding the Administration's legislative program through Congress. In the Model Cities program, for example, Johnson told Califano he wanted a big, innovative housing program but that the response from housing officials had not been imaginative enough. Califano then helped to organize a task force to advocate the Model Cities plan, meanwhile overcoming resistance from housing officials who insisted the program was too large and controversial to undertake in the first year of the new Department of Housing and Urban Development. A modified version of the Model Cities program, allocating $11 million for the project, was passed by Congress in 1966.

Throughout his White House career Califano concentrated on domestic affairs and made a conscious decision to avoid the issue of Vietnam. Although he had both the position and the expertise to become an authority on the war, Califano preferred to remain silent in order not to place himself in conflict with national security affairs adviser McGeorge Bundy [*q.v.*]. As the Vietnam war expanded Johnson began to devote less time to domestic matters until, by 1968, Califano had taken over almost complete supervision of domestic affairs.

In 1969 Califano joined the law firm of Arnold and Porte. From 1970 through 1972 he served as general counsel to the Democratic National Committee. In 1977 he became Secretary of Health, Education and Welfare. [See CARTER Volume]

[FHM]

CANNON, HOWARD W(ALTER)

b. Jan. 26, 1912; St. George, Utah.
Democratic Senator, Nev., 1959- .

Shortly after receiving a law degree from the University of Arizona in 1937, Cannon opened a legal practice in his native state. He served as an Air Force fighter pilot during World War II, receiving a number of decorations. Soon after the war he became a partner in a Las Vegas law firm. Cannon was the elected city attorney in Las Vegas from 1949 to 1957.

In 1958, following his victory in the Democratic senatorial primary, he opposed incumbent Republican George W. Malone. Malone's links were with the old mining interests of the northern and western areas of the state, interests that had long dominated Nevada's economy. Cannon's ties were to new, expanding and politically more liberal industrial interests of the state's southern region. Aided by his war record, support from organized labor and a national Democratic trend, Cannon attacked the conservatism of his opponent and defeated Malone with more than 56% of the vote. In the early 1960s Cannon established himself as a moderately liberal Democrat. According to *Congressional Quarterly*, he backed the Kennedy Administration on 71% of the domestic roll call votes in the 87th Congress. [See KENNEDY Volume]

After he won reelection in 1964 by a bare 48 votes, Cannon's support of the Administration on domestic legislation dropped during the Johnson presidency, declining to 60% and 58% in the 89th and 90th Congresses. He did, however, vote for most of the Administration's major civil rights bills and Great Society programs. Cannon also defended President Johnson's Vietnam war policies. In the summer of 1967, when such prominent Senate Democrats as majority leader Mike Mansfield (D, Mont.) [*q.v.*] and Foreign Relations Committee Chairman J. William Fulbright (D, Ark.) [*q.v.*] condemned the bombing of North Vietnam near the Chinese border, Cannon asserted the military necessity of this strategy. His major legislative interests, stemming from his service in the Air Force, were aviation and the space program. He was, by preference, a member of both the Armed Services and the Aeronautics and Space Committees of the Senate. During the Johnson years he was also a general in the Air Force Reserve, a Senate adviser to the United Nations Committee on Peaceful Uses of Outer Space and a member of the Board of Governors of the National Rocket Club.

Reelected in 1970, Cannon spoke out strongly for both the supersonic jet transport and the space shuttle program. He first received national attention during the fall of 1973 when, as the chairman of the Senate Rules and Administration Committee, he led that panel's consideration of President Richard M. Nixon's nomination of Rep. Gerald R. Ford (R, Mich.) [*q.v.*] for vice president. The following fall, in the same capacity, he directed the investigation of President Ford's choice of Nelson Rockefeller [*q.v.*] for the vice presidency. [See NIXON Volume]

[MLL]

CAREY, HUGH L(EO)

b. April 11, 1919; New York, N.Y.
Democratic Representative, New York, 1961-75.

After winning a Bronze Star as an infantry officer during World War II, Hugh Carey entered St. John's Law School, receiving his degree in 1951. He then began work for his family's oil company, the Peerless Oil and Chemical Corporation. In 1960 Carey, a political unknown, ran for Congress in Brooklyn's twelfth district, which had been gerrymandered in favor of the borough's only Republican congressman. Attaching himself to the campaign of John F. Kennedy and endorsing aid to education and medical care for the aged, Carey defeated the incumbent Republican, Rep. Francis E. Dorn, by a narrow margin. He won reelection in 1962 by only 383 votes, although subsequent victories came more easily.

Carey was a faithful supporter of the liberal civil rights and social welfare programs of the Kennedy-Johnson Administrations. Assigned to the Education and Labor Committee in 1962, he was a principal author and sponsor of the Elementary and Secondary Education Act of 1965, which authorized federal aid to education. Carey was a champion of aid to private as well as public schools; the 1965 law included some forms of assistance to parochial school students, but not to the schools themselves. Carey was also a strong advocate of the Administration's antipoverty program and special aid for the handicapped.

Along with the other members of the Brooklyn congressional delegation, Carey labored to persuade the Johnson Administration to sell the Brooklyn Navy Yard to New York City for development as an industrial park. The sale was finally consummated on Jan. 24, 1969. Carey was criticized by columnists Drew Pearson and Jack Anderson [*q.v.*] for using his influence as chairman of the Interior Committee's Subcommittee on Territories. They charged that Carey called the Department of the Interior to obtain permission for the Commonwealth Oil Refining Company, founded and controlled by his brother Edward, to export 14,000 barrels a day to the United States mainland from its Puerto Rican refinery. Rep. Carey denied making the calls.

Carey ran for president of the New York City Council in the 1969 Democratic primary on a ticket headed by former Mayor Robert F. Wagner [*q.v.*] but lost in a very close race. He remained in Congress, moving to the Ways and Means Committee in 1970, until his election as governor of New York in 1974. [See NIXON Volume]

[TO]

For further information:
Patrick Anderson, *The President's Men* (New York, 1968).
Eric F. Goldman, *The Tragedy of Lyndon Johnson* (New York, 1969).

CARLSON, FRANK

b. Jan. 23, 1893; Concordia, Kan.
Republican Senator, Kan., 1951-69.

The son of Swedish immigrants, Frank Carlson grew a special hybrid "streamlined" wheat that he had developed on his north-central Kansas farm. He won the first of two terms in the state House of Representatives in 1928. In 1934 later he won election to the U.S. House. Reelected five times, Carlson supported the Roosevelt Administration's farm-price support system but criticized most other aspects of the New Deal. By the late 1940s he had clearly identified himself with the older Kansas Progressivism of William Allen White and Sen. Arthur Capper. In 1946 Kansas voters elected Carlson governor; he won reelection two years later.

Carlson became a U.S. senator in 1951 and was returned to the upper house in 1956 and 1962. Identified at the time of his first Senate election with the Party's liberal "Eastern" wing, Carlson was an early participant in the 1952 presidential nomination campaign of Gen. Dwight D. Eisenhower. Once President, Eisenhower received Carlson's loyal support. The Kansan served on the 1954 panel that urged the censure of controversial Sen. Joseph R. McCarthy (R, Wisc.) in 1954. During the Kennedy years Carlson opposed much of the New Frontier social welfare legislation but endorsed the

President's foreign aid policy. In September 1963 he voted for the nuclear test ban treaty. [See EISENHOWER Volume]

Carlson's record in the Johnson years was mixed. He opposed medicare and favored reductions in annual War on Poverty appropriations, but he endorsed the President's "demonstration cities" program in August 1966. Under pressure from Minority Leader Everett M. Dirksen (R, Ill.) [*q.v.*], Carlson twice voted to invoke cloture and cut off debate (an unusual step for a small-state senator) to aid enactment of the 1964 and 1968 civil rights bills.

A member of the Senate Foreign Relations Committee, Carlson was skeptical of Johnson's Vietnam policy. At the August 1964 hearings following the Gulf of Tonkin incident, he commented that the Administration's growing participation in the Vietnam war "involves us in a situation from which it is most difficult to extricate ourselves." While Carlson voted for the Gulf of Tonkin Resolution and never joined the ranks of the Senate's Vietnam war critics, he occasionally called for peace negotiations. In a March 1968 debate following the North Vietnamese Tet offensive, Carlson asked if the U.S. had not "reach[ed] a saturation point" at which "we have lost the support of the civilian population."

Carlson did not seek another term in 1968. The Kansas delegation to the Republican National Convention in August chose him as its presidential "favorite son." He promised to release these 20 votes to Richard M. Nixon [*q.v.*] if the former Vice President needed them. Nixon never did.

[JLB]

CARMICHAEL, STOKELY

b. June 29, 1941; Port-of-Spain, Trinidad.
Chairman, Student Nonviolent Coordinating Committee, May 1966-May 1967; Prime Minister, Black Panther Party, February 1968-July 1969.

Carmichael grew up in Trinidad and New York City and then enrolled at Howard University in Washington, D.C., in 1960. There he joined an affiliate of the Student Nonviolent Coordinating Committee (SNCC) known as the Nonviolent Action Group (NAG), which organized sit-ins and demonstrations to desegregate public facilities in the Washington area. Carmichael also participated in the 1961 Freedom Rides, and following his graduation from Howard in 1964, he became a full time worker for SNCC. During the 1964 Mississippi Freedom Summer, he served as project director in the state's second congressional district. Carmichael also became director in 1965 of a SNCC voter registration project in Lowndes County, Ala., where he organized the Lowndes County Freedom Organization, an independent political party with a black panther as its emblem. Carmichael's work in Alabama made him a symbol of the greater militance and emphasis on blackness that many SNCC members were advocating by 1965, and he was elected SNCC chairman in May 1966.

Little known outside of SNCC at the time of his election, Carmichael soon became a much-publicized and highly controversial figure. He first attracted nationwide attention on a June 1966 protest march in Mississippi. The march was begun by James Meredith [*q.v.*] but continued by other civil rights leaders after Meredith was shot from ambush. When the march reached Greenwood, Miss., Carmichael raised the cry of "Black Power." The phrase, voiced repeatedly on the rest of the march, quickly captured national attention and generated great debate over its meaning. No one definition of black power was ever established. Depending upon the speaker, it could mean pride in blackness and in black history and culture, more political officeholding by blacks, greater black control of economic institutions, black nationalism and separatism or violence and revolution by blacks. At the outset black power was frequently alleged to be "racism in reverse" or black "extremism." It was often identified with black militants in the civil rights movement who were turning away from interracial cooperation, integration and nonviolence.

A prominent advocate of black power,

Carmichael gave his most complete statement of its meaning in *Black Power: The Politics of Liberation in America*, written with Charles V. Hamilton and published in November 1967. Black power, the authors wrote, meant first that blacks would redefine themselves, developing a positive self-image based on a "recognition of the virtues in themselves as black people." Black power also meant a rejection of the traditional civil rights goal of integration on the grounds that that goal was based on the erroneous notion that there was nothing of value in the black community and because it required acceptance of the white middle class values and institutions which were actually the mainstays of racism. Within the framework of black power, blacks would "reject the racist institutions and values" of American society, "define their own goals" and establish independent organizations to serve as "power bases . . . from which black people can press to change local or nationwide patterns of oppression." This organized black power would result in control of community institutions by blacks where they were in the majority and "full participation" by blacks in "the decision-making processes" affecting their lives.

Aside from his advocacy of black power, Carmichael generated controversy for frequently denouncing the Democratic Party as the "most treacherous enemy the Negro people have," for opposing the Vietnam war and for encouraging black men to resist the draft. Carmichael was also considered by some a professional agitator and an instigator of ghetto riots. He was in Atlanta in September 1966 when riots broke out there and was arrested on charges of inciting to riot. He spoke at a symposium in Nashville in April 1967, and riots erupted less than an hour after he left the city. He was again in Atlanta during disorders in June 1967 and in Washington during April 1968 riots there. Whether Carmichael's presence encouraged the riots remained debatable, but Carmichael and his successor as SNCC chairman, H. Rap Brown [*q.v.*], were the two figures most often cited as targets of anti-riot bills by congressmen who favored such legislation in the late 1960s.

Carmichael did not seek reelection as SNCC chairman in May 1967, and from July to December he traveled extensively in Europe and Africa and made trips to North Vietnam and to Cuba. During his travels Carmichael adopted a revolutionary position that went beyond the program outlined in his book on black power. At a conference of the Organization of Latin American Solidarity held in August 1967 in Havana, for example, Carmichael said that American blacks were fighting to change the "imperialist, capitalist and racialist structure" of the U.S. "We have no other alternative," he proclaimed, "but to take up arms and struggle for our total liberation and total revolution in the United States." Carmichael also advocated guerrilla warfare and armed struggle at various times after his return to the U.S., further inflaming the controversy which surrounded him.

In January 1968 Carmichael helped establish the Black United Front to organize Washington's blacks, and he began working as a community organizer in that city. When SNCC established an alliance in February 1968 with the Black Panther Party founded by Huey P. Newton [*q.v.*] and Bobby Seale [*q.v.*], Carmichael was named prime minister of the Party. The alliance was broken in July, but Carmichael stayed on as the Black Panther prime minister and was expelled from SNCC shortly afterwards. He resigned from the Black Panther Party in July 1969, denouncing it for its "dogmatic" party line and its willingness to ally itself with white radicals. Late in 1968 Carmichael left the U.S. and began living in self-imposed exile in Guinea.

[CAB]

For further information:

Thomas R. Brooks, *Walls Come Tumbling Down: A History of the Civil Rights Movement 1940-1970* (Englewood Cliffs, 1974).

Stokely Carmichael and Charles V. Hamilton, *Black Power: The Politics of Liberation in America* (New York, 1967).

Ben W. Gilbert, et al, *Ten Blocks from the White House: Anatomy of the Washington Riots of 1968* (New York, 1968).

David L. Lewis, *King: A Critical Biography* (New York, 1970).

CARPENTER, ELIZABETH S(UTHERLAND)

b. Sept. 1, 1920; Salado, Tex.
Staff Director and Press Secretary to Mrs. Lyndon B. Johnson, 1963-68.

Elizabeth Carpenter described herself as "a political animal by nature, a Southerner by birth and a P. T. Barnum by instinct." The daughter of a building contractor, she was born Elizabeth Sutherland in Salado, Tex. After her graduation from the University of Texas School of Journalism in 1942, she moved to Washington, D.C., where she became a close friend of Sen. Lyndon B. Johnson and his wife Lady Bird [*q.v.*]. In 1944 she married newspaperman Les Carpenter. Three years later she and her husband started the Carpenter News Bureau in Washington.

After Lyndon Johnson secured the Democratic vice presidential nomination in 1960, Elizabeth Carpenter served as an executive assistant to Johnson and as press aide to Lady Bird Johnson. According to historian Eric Goldman [*q.v.*], she was "the most independent and outspoken member of the whole Johnson group" during his vice presidency.

Aboard Air Force One in the immediate aftermath of John Kennedy's assassination in Dallas on Nov. 22, 1963, Carpenter wrote Johnson's first presidential message, which he delivered at Andrews Air Force Base in Washington the same day: "This is a sad time for all people. We have suffered a loss that cannot be weighed. I will do my best. That is all I can do. I ask for your help—and God's."

In December 1963 Carpenter was appointed Mrs. Johnson's press secretary. The first professional newswoman ever to become press secretary to a First Lady, she immediately took over all news functions concerning Mrs. Johnson from presidential Press Secretary Pierre Salinger [*q.v.*]. In 1964 she was instrumental in planning Mrs. Johnson's whistle-stop Southern campaign tour three months after the signing of the Civil Rights Act in July. Between Oct. 6 and Oct. 9 the tour covered 1,682 miles, eight states and 47 stops and garnered considerable publicity. In her book *Ruffles and Flourishes*, Carpenter later wrote: "Our star attraction [on the tour] was a Southern-bred First Lady. We were supposed to blow kisses and spread love through eight states and make them . . . forget about Barry Goldwater and vote for 'that nigger-lover in the White House.' " Mrs. Johnson's tour was widely credited with helping the President to carry four Southern states in the November election.

Carpenter did an effective job, through frequent news briefings, of projecting Mrs. Johnson in the way she wished to appear—as a First Lady with a specific set of interests, including beautification and conservation, that were ancillary but similar to those of the President's.

Following the departure from the White House in 1969, Carpenter published *Ruffles and Flourishes*, a memoir of her years in Johnson White House that was subtitled "the warm and tender story of a simple girl who found adventure in the White House."

[FHM]

CASE, CLIFFORD P(HILIP)

b. April 16, 1904; Franklin Park, N.J.
Republican Senator, N.J., 1955- .

Case, whose father was a Dutch Reformed minister in Poughkeepsie, N.Y., studied at Rutgers University and Columbia University Law School and joined a Wall Street law firm in 1928. A Republican, he entered local New Jersey politics in 1937 and seven years later was elected Union County's U.S. Representative. Case left the House in August 1953 to become president of the liberal Fund for the Republic, but he resigned the following March to run for the U.S. Senate. Stressing his opposition to the investigative methods of Sen. Joseph R. McCarthy (R, Wisc.) during the campaign, he narrowly defeated his liberal Democratic opponent in the November 1954 election. In the Senate Case was one of the most progressive members of the chamber. His electoral candidacies frequently won the endorsement of the liberal Americans for Democratic Action (ADA) and organized labor. [See EISENHOWER, KENNEDY Volumes]

Case was a consistent critic of the growth of ultraright influence in the Republican Party in the early 1960s. In April 1963 he announed his support of New York Gov. Nelson Rockefeller's [*q.v.*] presidential aspirations in the hope of preventing the nomination of conservative Sen. Barry Goldwater (R, Ariz.) [*q.v.*] as the 1964 Republican candidate. At the Republican National Convention in July 1964, Case joined the forces behind Pennsylvania Gov. William Scranton [*q.v.*] and fought to liberalize the Party's platform. With the nomination of Goldwater and the adoption of a conservative platform, Case declared that he could not give his support to the national ticket.

While Republican liberals in other parts of the country often suffered political reprisals for their lack of loyalty to the Party, Case's influence in New Jersey was not affected. His liberalism and pro-labor record were assets in the nation's most thoroughly urbanized state. The financial backing of some of the wealthiest members of the Eastern Republican Establishment helped make Case independent of New Jersey's weak Republican Party organization. After the failure of a conservative challenge to Case in the 1960 primary, his hold on the Senate seat was never again seriously contested.

The ADA gave Case a rating of 100% in both 1967 and 1968, and he scored nearly as high in other years. In 1965 and 1966 he was one of only three Republicans to oppose Sen. Everett Dirksen's (R, Ill.) [*q.v.*] efforts to overturn the Supreme Court's reapportionment ruling of "one man, one vote" through the adoption of a constitutional amendment.

Beginning in 1957 Case annually offered a bill to require members of every branch of government to publicly disclose their financial holdings and transactions and all their oral and written communications to regulatory agencies. The Bobby Baker [*q.v.*] scandal gave Case the opportunity to intensify his drive for higher standards of congressional ethics. In March 1964 he attacked the Senate Rules Committee for its "perpetuation of the double standard which Congress has long practiced, one standard for all others, another for its members." Case wanted the Committee to question all senators on their business and financial dealings with Baker. After a resolution offered by Sen. John J. Williams (R, Del.) [*q.v.*] to extend the Baker probe was tabled, an angry exchange took place between Case and Senate Majority Leader Mike Mansfield (D, Mont.) [*q.v.*]. Case tried unsuccessfully to get the floor as Mansfield attacked "the sly innuendo, the intemperate inference . . . in which some have indulged." Some observers believed that the highly partisan nature of the proceedings threatened to destroy a bipartisan effort to enact significant civil rights legislation in 1964.

Long a proponent of a relaxation of Cold War tensions, Case became deeply involved with foreign affairs when he joined the Senate Foreign Relations Committee in 1965. In September 1966 he was confirmed as a U.S. representative to the 21st session of the United Nations General Assembly. In June 1967 he visited Vietnam. In his first two years on the Foreign Relations Committee, Case often voted with the conservative members in support of foreign military aid. By 1967, however, he had become highly critical of U.S. military intervention in Vietnam. In a Senate speech delivered during the fall of 1967, he emphasized President Johnson's lack of honesty in informing the Congress and the American people about the situation in Vietnam. Case was also disturbed that Johnson's Indochina policies affected the constitutional relationship between the legislative and executive branches.

Although Case supported Richard M. Nixon [*q.v.*] in the 1968 presidential campaign, he became a critic of Nixon's Vietnam policy and opposed the President's first two Supreme Court nominees. Case easily won reelection in 1972. [See NIXON Volume]

[JCH]

For further information:

Neal R. Peirce, *The Megastates of America* (New York, 1972).

CATER, DOUGLASS
b. Aug. 24, 1923; Montgomery, Ala.
White House Special Assistant, May 1964-October 1968.

Cater served in the Office of Strategic Services during World War II. He graduated from Harvard in 1947, took his M.A. from that university the next year and became Washington editor of the *Reporter* magazine in 1950. Cater met Sen. Lyndon B. Johnson (D, Tex.) in 1952 and later wrote stories sympathetic to Johnson, describing the Senator as a "politician's politician" and a "pragmatic centrist." At the beginning of the Kennedy Administration, Secretary of State Dean Rusk [*q.v.*] planned to make Cater assistant secretary of state for public affairs—the press relations post—but White House Press Secretary Pierre Salinger [*q.v.*] moved Roger W. Tubby into the job.

While national affairs editor of the *Reporter*, Cater wrote the 1964 book *Power in Washington*, which offered a closely reasoned and critical analysis of leadership problems within the Kennedy Administration. Referring to Kennedy's inability to gain congressional passage of his legislative program, Cater characterized the Administration as one of "courageous expectations and cautious operations."

On May 8, 1964 Johnson named Cater a White House special assistant. At first his exact duties were not clearly defined; Johnson only advised him to "think ahead," and it was widely believed that Cater would become strictly a speechwriter and "idea" man. He began his White House career by ghostwriting Johnson's 1964 book *My Hope for America*.

During the 1964 presidential campaign Cater wrote speeches that focused on U.S. educational problems. As a result, Johnson began to think of Cater as his expert on education. Named chief White House liaison with the 1964 Task Force on Health and Education, Cater worked closely with Task Force Chairman John Gardner [*q.v.*] and U.S. Commissioner of Education Francis Keppel [*q.v.*] to turn Task Force recommendations into the $1.3 billion 1965 education bill. Cater played a major role in shaping some 40 health and education bills that were passed by Congress in 1965 and 1966, including such measures as medicare, elementary and secondary education and the heart, cancer and stroke bill.

Cater sought ideas on health and education from both the government bureaucracy and from the academic community. In addition he was the central point of access to the White House for the educational community. He was also a point of access to the President for congressional and executive officials in the educational policy process. Cater saw his role in government as that of increasing Johnson's interest in educational policy, "It is a nebulous role—not at all systematic. . . . I know the President's ideas and try to see to it that they are always considered. . . . I keep things moving."

In the winter of 1965-1966, Cater was a major force in drafting the international educational and health bill, which President Johnson sent to Congress on Feb. 2, 1966. Cater hoped the legislation would demonstrate Johnson's concern for worldwide health and education problems. As a collection of 40 measures designed to aid international health and education, the bill was to have cost $524 million in its first year but remained unfunded because of budget cuts due to the Vietnam war.

Described as "a unique combination of journalist, intellectual, academic, bureaucrat, political scientist and presidential confidant," Cater was one of the few specialists in an Administration where aides and special assistants dealt with many governmental areas. On Oct. 3, 1968 Cater resigned as White House special assistant to join Vice President Hubert H. Humphrey's [*q.v.*] campaign staff.

[FHM]

For further information:
Patrick Anderson, *The President's Men* (New York, 1968).
Douglass Cater, *Power in Washington* (New York, 1964).
Roland Evans and Robert Novak, *Lyndon B. Johnson: The Exercise of Power* (New York, 1966).
Norman C. Thomas, *Education in National Politics* (New York, 1975).

CAVANAGH, JEROME P(ATRICK)
b. June 16, 1928; Detroit, Mich.
Mayor, Detroit, Mich., 1962-70.

The son of a boilermaker, Cavanagh received his law degree from the University of Detroit and joined the Detroit firm of Sullivan, Romanoff, Cavanagh and Nelson in 1955. Cavanagh entered Detroit's nonpartisan mayoral race in 1961 against incumbent Louis Miriani, who was supported by almost the entire city power structure: the United Auto Workers, big business and both Detroit newspapers. A political unknown, Cavanagh was backed by city employes and the Trade Union Leadership Council, a predominantly black trade union caucus that mobilized the minority community against what it considered racism in the Detroit police department. During the campaign Cavanagh attacked corruption in municipal government and called for an income tax on city residents and commuters to offset a large municipal debt. He decisively defeated Miriani on Nov. 7 in what B. J. Widick called the "biggest upset in Michigan politics in 32 years." Cavanagh carried black precincts by margins of up to five to one and ran ahead of the incumbent mayor in some white neighborhoods.

During his first term in office, Cavanagh appointed a police commissioner sympathetic to the black community, enacted a 1% city income tax, reduced property taxes and erased a multi-million dollar budget deficit. Many observers thought Cavanagh's reform administration a key to urban reconstruction in the early 1960s. Three hundred and sixty million dollars in federal assistance poured into the city during his tenure in office. Both Henry Ford [*q.v.*] and Walter Reuther [*q.v.*] applauded his efforts, and the Mayor won the support of Detroit's two major newspapers. A 1965 *Fortune* magazine survey of Detroit thought prospects for the city encouraging, in part because "All the diverse elements that make up Detroit's power structure, once divided and pitted against itself, are being welded together in a remarkable synthesis." Cavanagh was reelected mayor in 1965 by a 150,000-vote plurality and the next year was elected president of both the U.S. Conference of Mayors and the National League of Cities. In March 1966 Cavanagh announced his candidacy for the U.S. Senate but lost the Democratic primary election to former Michigan Gov. G. Mennen Williams.

Detroit's apparent progress was shattered in the summer of 1967 when a major riot erupted that left 41 persons dead and caused up to half a billion dollars worth of property damage. Disturbances began shortly before 4:00 a.m. July 23, when police raided an after-hours drinking club in the black ghetto and arrested 74 people. A crowd pelted police with stones and bricks and soon began looting nearby stores.

Almost immediately law enforcement became a major issue. When the violence began Cavanagh, seeking to avoid an incident that might lead to a charge of police brutality, instructed police to avoid confrontations with the crowds. An initial force of 600 national guardsmen, 200 state troopers and 600 Detroit policemen failed to contain the violence. That evening Gov. George Romney [*q.v.*] described the situation as "out of control" and declared a state of public emergency. On the morning of July 24 Romney requested federal troops. President Johnson sent former Deputy Defense Secretary Cyrus Vance [*q.v.*] to Detroit as his personal representative, and that evening Vance placed 1,800 federal troops on stand-by alert. Cavanagh, who yielded responsibility for city law enforcement to Romney and Vance under the emergency declaration, stated at a July 24 news conference that the troops were needed immediately. Federal troops moved into the city's east side shortly after 2 a.m. July 25 and remained in the city until July 30. On the same day the city's black newspaper attacked Cavanagh for failing to use sufficient force at the onset of the violence. Gov. Romney, the leading Republican presidential contender at the time, charged at a July 31 news conference that Administration "quibbling" unnecessarily delayed the arrival of federal troops.

Cavanagh began plans for reconstruction of the city even before the riot ended. On July 25 he met with 15 black leaders to discuss the causes of the violence and plan "ways to pick up the pieces again." Romney and Cavanagh telegraphed the President July 27 asking that Detroit be declared a disaster area, thus making the city eligible for emergency federal aid. Cavanagh met with 150 community leaders the same day and on Aug. 3 joined with Romney in appointing a "blue ribbon" 37-member New Detroit Committee headed by department store owner Joseph L. Hudson, Jr. Backed by leaders of Detroit industry, labor and government, the Committee was to organize support for a rapid rebuilding of the city.

Continuing racial polarization, a decline in federal and state funds and the onset of the recession of 1969-70 stalemated the ambitious plans of the New Detroit Committee and virtually ended Cavanagh's political career. Detroit political writer William Serrin reported in October 1968 that fifteen months after the riot "the city has been unable to effect even the beginnings of meaningful reconstruction . . . .Cavanagh himself, bitter over his defeat in the Democratic senatorial primary in 1966, and still dazed by the 1967 riot, appears sullen and defensive, unwilling to grasp the levers of government." Cavanagh declined to seek reelection in 1969, and Detroit voters elected conservative Wayne County Sheriff Roman Gribbs as their next mayor. Cavanagh resumed his law practice in Detroit when his term ended.

[DKR]

For further information:
B. J. Widick, *Detroit: City of Race and Class Violence* (Chicago, 1972).

CELEBREZZE, ANTHONY J(OSEPH)
b. Sept. 4, 1910; Anzi, Italy.
Secretary of Health, Education, and Welfare, 1962-65; Court of Appeals Judge, 1965- .

Anthony J. Celebrezze grew up in the slums of Cleveland and worked his way through Ohio Northern Law School laying track for the New York Central Railroad. After three years in the Ohio Senate, Celebrezze ran successfully for mayor of Cleveland in 1953. He proved highly popular with Cleveland voters, winning reelection five times by substantial majorities. As mayor he sponsored a $140 million urban renewal project and earned a reputation as an efficient city administrator. Kennedy appointed Celebrezze Secretary of Health, Education and Welfare (HEW) in July 1962. Celebrezze sought both to reorganize his massive department while lobbying for the Administration's civil rights, aid-to-education and medicare bills. [See KENNEDY Volume]

Early in the Johnson presidency Celebrezze became involved in a dispute with other cabinet heads over the President's War on Poverty program. Celebrezze and Labor Secretary W. Willard Wirtz [*q.v.*] objected to the creation of a separate antipoverty agency headed by Peace Corps Director R. Sargent Shriver [*q.v.*]. In arguments before the President in March 1964, both Secretaries insisted that their departments could and should absorb the functions of the Office of Economic Opportunity (OEO). But Johnson insisted on an independent agency for his poverty program. "The best way to kill a new idea is to put it in an old-line agency," the President commented during the administrative debate. Celebrezze acquiesced in Johnson's decision and defended the OEO before congressional critics. To Republican House members critical of Shriver's elevation to "poverty czar," Celebrezze asserted in March 1964 that he found "no conflict whatsoever" between Shriver's agency and his own. "I have absolutely no fear," he added, that "the powers of any department are going to be usurped" by the OEO.

During Celebrezze's tenure as HEW Secretary, Congress passed perhaps the most important body of social legislation since the New Deal. In June 1964 Congress finally approved the Kennedy-Johnson civil rights proposals that gave the HEW Secretary broad powers to restrict funds from any federal program to states or institutions found violating desegregation guidelines. Congress also enacted the Administration's medicare program in July 1965. Although Celebrezze testified for the measure, Assistant HEW Secretary Wilbur J. Cohen [*q.v.*] wrote the final bill and conducted the Administration's lobbying effort with House Ways and Means Committee Chairman Wilbur Mills (D, Ark.) [*q.v.*].

The HEW chief proved more active in the Administration's campaign for a comprehensive aid-to-education bill in the spring of 1965. Although Republican losses in the 1964 election had strengthened liberal ranks, the White House still needed to overcome traditional opposition to federal aid to private and parochial schools. In congressional hearings held in January 1965, Celebrezze gave a variety of arguments in defense of assistance to parochial education. To the most pronounced defenders of the separation of church and state, he pointed out that governments subsidized subways that people used to ride to church and funded libraries that private school children utilized to check out books for class.

Before the bill went to Congress, Celebrezze and other Administration figures won the approval of most Catholic and public school representatives for the measure. Drafted by a presidential task force chaired by John W. Gardner [*q.v.*], then president of the Carnegie Corporation, the bill provided sufficient aid to private institutions to prevent their leaders' outright opposition, while not granting a sum large enough to provoke protests from public school spokesmen. The final bill, revised by Sen. Wayne Morse (D, Ore.) [*q.v.*] and Cohen, overcame the greatest obstacles to passage by providing the most assistance to school systems in poverty-stricken areas. Congress approved the Elementary and Secondary Education Act in April 1965.

Johnson offered Celebrezze an appointment to the U.S. Sixth Circuit Court of Appeals in July 1965. Celebrezze, who had originally wanted a judgeship when Kennedy asked him to head HEW, immediately accepted the President's offer. Johnson named Gardner to succeed Celebrezze as head of HEW.

[JLB]

For further information:
Rufus E. Miles, Jr., *The Department of HEW* (New York, 1974).

CELLER, EMANUEL

b. May 6, 1888; Brooklyn, N.Y.
Democratic Representative, N.Y., 1923-73; Chairman, Judiciary Committee, 1949-53, 1955-73

After graduating from Columbia College and Law School, Celler practiced law in New York from 1912 to 1922. In the latter year he won election to Congress from Brooklyn's 10th congressional district, beginning a fifty-year career in the House. A liberal Democrat, Celler consistently supported the domestic legislation of Democratic presidents from Roosevelt to Johnson. As chairman of the House Judiciary Committee, Celler developed a special expertise in the fields of antitrust and civil rights. In 1949 he established a new Judiciary subcommittee to focus on antitrust violations and monopolies. As the subcommittee's head Celler conducted widely publicized investigations during the 1950s into such areas as the steel industry, monopoly practices in baseball and Justice Department consent decrees. He coauthored the Celler-Kefauver Anti-Merger Act of 1950 and was the main architect of both the 1957 and 1960 Civil Rights Acts. [See TRUMAN, EISENHOWER Volumes]

Celler's initiative in antitrust began to wane in the 1960s; from 1963 to 1970 his Antitrust Subcommittee averaged only five hearings or reports per Congress compared with an average of fourteen from 1955 to 1962. But Celler's role in civil rights expanded. He sponsored the 24th Amendment, ratified in 1964, which abolished the poll tax in federal elections, and he was a principal author of the 1964 Civil Rights Act. [See KENNEDY Volume]

In 1964 Celler helped thwart efforts to adopt a constitutional amendment allowing prayer in public schools. An opponent of all such proposals, Celler held hearings on various prayer bills in the spring and brought in as witnesses constitutional lawyers who testified against the legislation.

Celler achieved a series of legislative victories in 1965. With Sen. Edward Kennedy (D, Mass.) [*q.v.*], he won passage of the Immigration and Naturalization Act, which ended the national origins quota system. He helped secure approval for a law to prohibit gerrymandering of congressional districts, a measure he had favored for fifteen years. He sponsored a constitutional amendment providing for the execution of the president's duties in the event of presidential disability and for filling a vice presidential vacancy. Adopted by Congress in July 1965, this act was ratified as the 25th Amendment in 1967. Celler also managed the Voting Rights Act of 1965; after introducing the Johnson bill in March, he led the Judiciary Committee hearings on the proposal and secured House passage on Aug. 3.

Celler became embroiled in the controversy surrounding Rep. Adam Clayton Powell's (D, N.Y.) [*q.v.*] expulsion from the House in 1967. The House voted on Jan. 10 not to seat Powell until a special committee completed an investigation of his fitness to serve in Congress. Celler was named chairman of the nine-member special committee, and on Feb. 23, 1967 the committee reported that Powell had, among other things, misused congressional funds, improperly kept his wife on his payroll and treated the special committee with contempt. The report recommended that Powell be seated in the House but that he be censured for "gross misconduct," stripped of his seniority and fined $40,000. In a surprise development on March 1, the House rejected the committee's recommendations and instead voted 307-116 to exclude Powell from the 90th Congress. Celler opposed Powell's expulsion, arguing that the Harlem Congressman met the constitutional requirements for House membership and that his wrongdoings did not merit so extreme a measure. After the House vote Celler declared that racism had been a factor in the move to unseat Powell and that his exclusion had set a bad precedent for the future.

During the same session of Congress, Celler introduced an Administration-backed crime control bill authorizing federal funds to aid local law enforcement agencies. On the House floor the bill was amended to reduce federal control over the program. Celler unsuccessfully opposed the change, and he also failed to block House action on an anti-riot bill making it a crime to cross state lines with intent to incite a riot.

The Senate took no action on either bill in 1967, but in May 1968 it adopted the Omnibus Crime Control Act. The measure included a federal grant program similar to that passed by the House, a provision authorizing court-supervised wiretapping and a relatively weak gun control section. Celler disliked the wiretap provision and wanted a stronger gun control measure, but the House passed the entire act on June 6. Celler labeled the law "a cruel hoax," destructive of constitutional liberties. On June 10 he introduced a much stronger Administration bill for gun control that would ban mail-order sales of rifles and ammunition and require the licensing and registration of guns. His Judiciary Committee reported the bill favorably, but to secure passage of the mail-order ban, Celler was forced by House Rules Committee Chairman William Colmer (D, Miss.) [*q.v.*] to drop the licensing and registration section. Congress passed the bill, without any registration requirement, in October 1968.

Celler also played a key role in the passage of the Administration's Civil Rights Act of 1968, which barred racial discrimination in the sale and rental of approximately 80% of all housing and supplied protection for civil rights workers. After committee hearings Celler pushed the bill through the House in August 1967. Senate approval followed in March 1968, but the Senate tacked onto the act an anti-riot provision of the sort Celler opposed. Celler nevertheless pressed for quick House action accepting the Senate version of the bill to insure that the open housing section, the core of the measure, would become law. The House finally adopted the Senate's bill on April 10, and it was signed into law the next day.

Celler's long legislative career was marred in its last years by charges of potential conflicts of interest, especially in the corporate and antitrust field, resulting from his long-standing connection with a New York City law firm. Celler was also scored for the way he ran the Judiciary Committee. A 1975 report by the Ralph Nader Congress Project, *The Judiciary Committees*, called Celler "a willful potentate" who "ran his committee as his personal fiefdom." Celler frequently bottled up controversial bills, such as abortion reform and proposals for amnesty for Vietnam war resisters, by refusing to refer them to a subcommittee or to hold hearings. He was also criticized for failing to seek larger appropriations and a larger staff to handle the Committee's workload. In the 92nd Congress over 5,000 bills and resolutions were referred to his Judiciary Committee to be handled by a 36-member staff, while the Senate Judiciary Committee, with far fewer bills to consider, had a staff of 204.

During the Nixon Administration Celler fought an effort to impeach Supreme Court Justice William O. Douglas [*q.v.*] and in June 1970 secured an extension of the 1965 Voting Rights Act. In his final years in the House, Celler led hearings on six major conglomerates and opposed both the Equal Rights Amendment and an amendment to prohibit busing for school desegregation. In June 1972 Celler was defeated in the Democratic primary in his district by Elizabeth Holtzman, a 31-year-old attorney, who charged that Celler had lost touch with his constituency. Celler, who had amassed enormous power in the House, did not have an office in his district at the time of his defeat. [See NIXON Volume]

[CAB]

CHAFEE, JOHN H(UBBARD)

b. Oct. 22, 1922; Providence, R.I.
Governor, R.I., 1963-69.

During World War II John H. Chafee left his studies at Yale for active duty with the Marines in the South Pacific. Returning to Yale at the war's end, he earned a B.A. there in 1947 and a law degree at Harvard in 1950. He reentered the Marine Corps to fight in the Korean conflict. Chafee won the first of three terms to the state General Assembly in 1956; he served as Assembly minority leader from 1959 to 1962.

Rhode Islanders first elected Chafee governor in 1962. As a Yankee Republican in a state overwhelmingly Democratic and "ethnic" and as an Episcopalian in the state with the highest proportion of Roman Catholics (61%), Chafee entered the gubernatorial contest with obvious disadvantages. To overcome his narrow ethnic and political base, he ran a highly personalized campaign. One supporter claimed that Chafee shook hands with about one out of every eight Rhode Islanders, or about 130,000 people. He attacked incumbent Democratic Gov. John A. Notte, Jr., for advocating a personal income tax and promised to revive the stagnant state economy. In November Chafee defeated Notte by just under 400 votes out of about 325,000 cast. In his first term Chafee persuaded the Democratic legislature to approve his medical care for the elderly plan and to expand the state parks system. At his initiative the legislature raised the state sales tax by a half a percentage point.

In his second gubernatorial campaign Chafee ignored the Republican presidential nominee, Sen. Barry Goldwater (R, Ariz.) [*q.v.*], who ultimately polled only 19% of the vote in Rhode Island. Instead, his managers urged voters to "Vote Chafee First." As a result, Chafee captured 61% of the vote, while Johnson and Sen. John O. Pastore (D, R.I.) [*q.v.*] demolished their opponents. Two years later Chafee won again, carrying every town and helping to elect a GOP lieutenant governor and attorney general for the first time since 1938.

Chafee participated in 1968 Republican presidential politics. An attractive voter-getter in a Democratic area, Chafee himself sought consideration for the Republican vice-presidential nomination; but Rhode Island's small population and his identification with liberal Republicanism hurt his prospects. Beginning in November 1966 he and other liberal and moderate Republican governors began working for the presidential nomination of Michigan Gov. George W. Romney [*q.v.*]. When Romney withdrew from the race in February 1968, Chafee came out for New York Gov. Nelson Rockefeller [*q.v.*]. At the Republican National Convention, the liberals saw the nomination go to former Vice President Richard M. Nixon [*q.v.*]. Chafee was dissatisfied with Nixon's choice for vice president, Gov. Spiro Agnew [*q.v.*], and joined in a last-minute attempt to nominate Romney for the post. However, the effort failed.

In November 1968 Chafee lost his bid for reelection, in large measure because of his call for a state income tax. President Nixon appointed Chafee Secretary of the Navy in 1969. He held that office until 1972, when he lost a hard-fought senatorial campaign against incumbent Sen. Claiborne Pell (D, R.I.) [*q.v.*]. In February 1976 Chafee won election to the Senate seat vacated by retiring Sen. John Pastore (D, R.I.). [See NIXON Volume]

[JLB]

CHANCELLOR, JOHN W(ILLIAM)

b. July 14, 1927; Chicago, Ill.
Director, Voice of America, September 1965-May 1967.

John Chancellor left high school in 1942 at the age of 15 and took a series of jobs in and around Chicago before entering the U.S. Army in 1945. After his discharge Chancellor briefly attended the University of Illinois; in 1948 he joined the Chicago *Sun-Times*, where he rose from copy boy to feature writer. In 1950 he joined the staff of WNBQ, the National Broadcasting Company station in Chicago, as a broadcast reporter and covered the 1956 political conventions as a television reporter.

NBC News assigned Chancellor to its Vienna bureau in 1958 in the first of many overseas assignments that eventually took him to London, Rome, Paris, Brussels and Moscow before he returned to the U.S. in July 1961 to become the host of NBC's popular *Today* program. Chancellor covered the 1964 Republican National Convention in San Francisco as a floor correspondent and was arrested by police while broadcasting "live" during an altercation stemming from an attempt by Goldwater forces to restrict the movements of television newsmen.

On July 28, 1965 President Johnson appointed Chancellor to replace Henry Loomis as director of the Voice of America (VOA). As the radio news division of the United States Information Agency (USIA), the VOA broadcast in 38 languages and employed 2,500 people both in the U.S. and abroad. Chancellor took over VOA in September 1965 amid charges by veteran staff members that the organization's news credibility was being sacrificed to favor Johnson Administration policy, especially in Vietnam. The first working newsman ever named to the post, Chancellor took pains to insure that the VOA accurately reported the news, including civil rights issues and the conflicts of opinion within the U.S. over Johnson's Vietnam policy. During his tenure Chancellor introduced a number of new programming techniques to give VOA broadcasts a crisper, less propagandistic style.

Chancellor resigned his post as VOA director in May 1967 to return to active broadcasting. He covered the 1968 political conventions for NBC News. In August 1971 Chancellor was named anchorman of the *NBC Nightly News.*

[FHM]

For further information:
Erik Barnouw, *The Image Empire* (New York, 1970).

CHANDLER, OTIS

b. Nov. 23, 1927; Los Angeles, Calif.
Publisher, *Los Angeles Times*, 1960- .

Chandler was born into the publishing world as the son of Norman Chandler, owner of the Times Mirror publishing company and publisher of the *Los Angeles Times*. Educated at Stanford University, the younger Chandler spent two years in the Air Force before going to work for the family firm in 1953. He served an apprenticeship of several years in various departments of the *Times* and the Los Angeles *Mirror-News*, a Chandler paper that later ceased publication. In 1960 he became publisher of the *Times* when his father left the newspaper to concentrate on expanding the Times Mirror publishing network.

Otis Chandler immediately sought to improve his newspaper's style and image. Under Norman Chandler the *Times*, though the circulation leader on the West Coast, was consistently provincial as well as conservative; its national and international staffs were small, and its pro-Republican editorial policy was allowed to affect news coverage. Otis maintained the paper's conservative political stance but doubled its staff budget and laid down guidelines to improve the objectivity of its news reporting. *Times* bureaus were opened in major U.S. and foreign cities, and large salaries were offered to attract nationally known journalists from other newspapers. Chandler also joined with the Washington *Post* to form the Times-Post News Service, and added several sections to the Sunday *Times*. The *Times* won a Pulitzer Prize in 1966 for its coverage of the Watts riots in Los Angeles; Chandler himself received a Columbia University Journalism Award in 1967 for his role in improving the paper. The *Times* daily circulation increased from 537,000 in 1960 to 850,000 in 1967, making it the fourth largest daily in the U.S.

Chandler's innovations affected not only the content of the *Times* but also its production. At his urging computers were installed to handle most of the paper's technical operations; the *Times* accordingly became the first U.S. newspaper with an automated typesetting room. This was possible because *Times* employees had no union until 1967, giving Chandler unlimited freedom to increase productivity during his first years with the paper. Workers were kept satisfied by relatively high wages, liberal fringe benefits and the company's willingness to retrain anyone whose job was eliminated by automation. The improvements Chandler introduced helped keep the *Times* one of the most profitable newspapers in the U.S.

The *Times* continued in its conservative editorial tradition, supporting Sen. Barry Goldwater (R, Ariz.) [*q.v.*] for president in 1964 and Richard Nixon [*q.v.*] in 1968; it also backed Ronald Reagan [*q.v.*] for governor of California in 1966. Chandler remained publisher of the newspaper during the early 1970s, maintaining its combination of political conservatism and modern reportorial practices. His paper supported the reelection of President Nixon in 1972.

[SLG]

CHAVEZ, CESAR

b. March 31, 1927; Yuma, Ariz.
President, United Farm Workers Organizing Committee, 1966- .

The son of a small farmer and migrant laborer, Chavez left school in the seventh grade to become a full-time field worker in California. After taking part in several unsuccessful strikes of farm workers, he began to consider ways of organizing Mexican-Americans in California. In 1952 he joined the new San Jose branch of the Community Service Organization (CSO), which fostered grass-roots efforts to meet the problems of poor people. As a CSO worker Chavez organized voter registration drives among Mexican-Americans and set up services to provide information on such matters as immigration laws and welfare regulations. He left the CSO in 1962, when the Organization turned down his proposal to create a union of farm workers.

With their meager savings Chavez and his wife Helen immediately established the National Farm Workers Association (NFWA). There followed several years of painstaking organizational work in the fields and migrant worker camps of southern and central California. By 1965 the NFWA had a membership of 1,700 families, but Chavez still considered it too weak for a confrontation with employers. His hand was forced on Sept. 8, 1965, when 800 Filipino grape pickers in Delano struck for higher wages. The striking workers belonged to a separate organization, the Agricultural Workers Organizing Committee (AWOC), affiliated with the AFL-CIO. Chavez called a sympathy strike, which developed into an extended fight to win recognition from grape growers and other employers in California agriculture.

Under Chavez the farm workers' strike had elements of both a labor struggle and a civil rights movement with strong religious overtones. To dramatize union demands for recognition, Chavez led 60 union members in a 300-mile march from Delano to Sacramento in 1966; the march ended with a demonstration of over 10,000 people in the state capital. Chavez himself fasted for 25 days in 1968, hoping to emphasize the nonviolent character of the movement. These and more traditional tactics—including picket lines and organizing work—increased the membership of the farm workers' union to 17,000 in the late 1960s. Chavez decided to affiliate with the AFL-CIO in July 1966, merging the NFWA with the AWOC to form the United Farm Workers Organizing Committee (UFWOC).

The drama of the strike and Chavez's personal magnetism brought together a broad coalition of national support, ranging from civil rights and church groups to traditional labor leaders. Sen. Robert F. Kennedy [*q.v.*] and Walter Reuther [*q.v.*], leader of the United Auto Workers Union, appeared at farm workers' rallies; the UAW also contributed to the UFWOC strike fund. The farm workers' struggle soon became a defining issue in both California and national politics. Democratic Gov. Edmund G. Brown's, Sr. [*q.v.*], sympathy for the growers cost him much liberal support in his state, while the farm workers' enthusiastic endorsement of Sen. Kennedy helped increase his national standing.

Gradually, publicity and labor unrest began to tell on the California growers. The first employers to acknowledge union demands were the growers of wine grapes, who marketed their own brands and were highly vulnerable to a boycott. Between April and September 1966 the major wine manufacturers of California signed contracts with the UFWOC recognizing the union as the sole bargaining agent of the grape pickers.

The growers of table grapes, who employed more workers and did not depend on brand names, continued to hold out against the union. Chavez responded by calling for a national boycott of table grapes, taking advantage of the fact that farm workers were not covered by the National Labor Relations Act. UFWOC organizers, led by union vice president Dolores Huerta, mobilized support in the North and East, where the boycott became an important liberal cause. After table grape sales had dropped by 20%, the major growers agreed in July 1970 to sign contracts with the UFWOC. Like the 1966 contracts, these provided for a minimum wage ($1.80 per hour), union hiring halls for grape pickers and fringe benefits including a health and social service fund.

A growing problem for Chavez was the relationship between the UFWOC and the Teamsters Union, which also attempted to organize agricultural workers in California. An inter-union agreement for the grape industry was reached in 1967, assigning field workers to the UFWOC and processing workers to the Teamsters. The conflict reappeared in 1970, however, when both unions turned their attention to the lettuce workers. A full-scale organizing war developed. According to most observers, the violence was generally directed by the Teamsters against the UFWOC. Employers generally favored the Teamsters, who did not insist on union hiring halls and accepted the importation of docile migrant labor from Mexico. The UFWOC suffered a serious setback in 1973, when the Teamsters began to take over expiring union contracts in the grape industry. Chavez imposed a boycott on lettuce and certain brands of wine, but this was less effective than the earlier grape boycott.

The position of the UFWOC improved again after August 1975 with passage of a California farm labor law. The law, sponsored by Gov. Edmund G. Brown, Jr., and supported by Chavez, created a state board which farm workers could petition for elections to determine which union would represent them. By the end of the year, most of the elections held under the law had been won by the UFWOC. This brought the transfer of a number of Teamsters contracts back to the UFWOC. The new law also left Chavez's most important weapon intact by permitting boycotts against growers who refused to negotiate with a union chosen by their workers.

[SLG]

For further information:

Peter Matthiessen, *Sal Si Puedes: Cesar Chavez and the New American Revolution* (New York, 1969).

Ronald Taylor, *Chavez and the Farm Workers* (Boston, 1975).

CHOMSKY, NOAM A(VRAM)
b. Dec. 7, 1928; Philadelphia, Pa.
Linguist, social critic.

Chomsky, the son of an immigrant Jewish scholar and teacher, grew up in Philadelphia. He was educated in linguistics at the University of Pennsylvania, receiving an M.A. in 1951 and a Ph.D. in 1955. A committed Zionist, Chomsky considered settling in Israel during the late 1940s; but his academic mentor, Professor Zellig Harris, persuaded him to continue his linguistic studies in the U.S.

Chomsky became assistant professor of linguistics at the Massachusetts Institute of Technology (MIT) in 1955. His first book, *Syntactic Structures*, was published in 1957. A revision of his doctoral dissertation, Chomsky's book developed the concept of generative or transformational grammar. Language, according to Chomsky, is a basic human capacity; grammar, in his view, is the surface product of deeper, universal conceptual structures existing in the mind, which can use rules of logic and syntax to generate new thoughts and expressions. Chomsky's thesis challenged the dominant behaviorist school of linguistics, which viewed language entirely as a response to external stimuli. Arguing against this attitude Chomsky pointed out that children are able not only to repeat what they are taught but also to use words and grammatical rules in sentences they have never heard before.

As the founder of a major new school of linguistics, Chomsky gained wide attention in academic circles. He reached the rank of professor at MIT in 1961 and was named Ferrari P. Ward Professor of Foreign Literatures and Linguistics five years later. At this time he also carried his conflict with the behaviorists into broader areas of philosophy and psychology. In his book *Cartesian Linguistics*, published in 1966, Chomsky traced his view of man's creative capacity back to the rationalist philosophers of the 17th century. He expanded on his faith in free individual development as an alternative to what he considered the behaviorist system of social control and manipulation.

Always a close observer of current events, Chomsky was drawn increasingly to political activism during the mid-1960s. He opposed the Vietnam war from its inception and soon broadened his criticism to include most aspects of U.S. foreign policy. In numerous articles in the *New York Review of Books* and other journals he attacked American diplomacy as the product of a bankrupt ruling class attempting to preserve itself by forcefully maintaining the economic and political status quo. His most influential essay, "The Responsibility of Intellectuals," appeared in 1966. Here Chomsky criticized such liberal intellectuals as Walt W. Rostow [*q.v.*] and Arthur Schlesinger, Jr. [*q.v.*], for developing an elaborate justification of American foreign policy in the service of government and industry. Chomsky argued that the proper place for authentic intellectuals was outside the power structure and that their proper function was one of criticism and dissent. This essay and other political writings by Chomsky were collected in *American Power and the New Mandarins*, published in 1969.

Chomsky's strong opposition to the war in Vietnam and his support of the protest movement made him a major influence within the American New Left. He was a participant and frequent speaker at many demonstrations during the mid and late 1960s, including the 1967 March on the Pentagon. He also served on the steering committee of Resistance, a national anti-war group. Chomsky praised the anarchist element in the youth rebellion of the 1960s but favored libertarian socialism as the best path to "a society in which freely constituted social bonds replace the fetters of autocratic institutions." In 1969 Chomsky was appointed to an MIT panel reviewing the University's support of two laboratories involved in defense-related research. The panel urged MIT to recommend a stronger civilian orientation for both laboratories.

Chomsky remained an important academic and protest figure during the early 1970s. He moved away from his originally strong support of Israel in the aftermath of the 1967 Middle East war, urging first a binational state in Palestine and later a separate state for Palestinian Arabs.

Chomsky resumed his long-standing conflict with behaviorism in *For Reasons of State*, a collection of essays published in 1973.

[SLG]

For further information:
John Lyons, *Noam Chomsky* (New York, 1970).

CHRISTIAN, GEORGE (EASTLAND)

b. Jan. 1, 1927; Austin, Tex.
Special Assistant to the President, May 1966-December 1966; White House Press Secretary, January 1967-January 1969.

After service with the Marine Corps during and after World War II, Christian graduated from the University of Texas in 1949 and the same year joined the Texas-based International News Service as a correspondent. In 1956 he became assistant to Price Daniel, then U.S. senator, later governor of Texas, Christian also served as an assistant to Daniel's gubernatorial successor, John Connally [*q.v.*].

A longtime acquaintance of Lyndon Johnson, Christian joined the President's staff in May 1966 as an administrative assistant to White House Press Secretary Bill Moyers [*q.v.*]. Originally, Johnson had intended to make Robert Fleming—hired away from ABC-TV's Washington bureau—press secretary and thus free Moyers for more important administrative duties. Partly because of his resentment over the media's coverage of the Vietnam war, Johnson abruptly changed his plan. He installed Christian as press secretary in January 1967 and made Fleming Christian's assistant in charge of television relations.

Described by Stewart Alsop in his 1968 book *The Center* as a "self-effacing fellow, who follows orders—which may be the only kind of press secretary who can survive with Lyndon Johnson," Christian exerted no influence over policy decisions during the Johnson Administration. Rather, his appointment was representative of the rapid turnover within Johnson's immediate staff and especially in the press relations area. By 1967 many reporters had begun to question Johnson's handling of Vietnam. When Moyers received a favorable press after leaving the White House because of his well-known "private" opposition to the war within the Administration, Johnson himself praised Christian to reporters, insisting that press relations had in fact improved since Moyers's departure. However, relations between the White House and the media remained cool.

Christian left the White House after the inauguration of Richard M. Nixon and founded the public relations concern of Christian, Miller and Honts, Inc.

[FHM]

CHURCH, FRANK (FORRESTER)

b. July 25, 1924; Boise, Ida.
Democratic Senator, Ida. 1957- .

Frank Church, a 1950 graduate of the Stanford University Law School, practiced law in his native city of Boise until elected to the Senate in 1956. Church was then only 32. During the Kennedy years Church compiled a liberal record, voting for the Administration's civil rights, school aid, minimum wage and medicare bills. The liberal Americans for Democratic Action gave Church uniformly high ratings during this period. [See EISENHOWER, KENNEDY Volumes]

Church was a member of the Senate Foreign Relations and Interior and Insular Affairs Committees; he also served on the special Senate Committee on Aging. His name was frequently linked with conservation issues, and in 1962 Church served as floor manager for a bill designed to protect several million acres of wilderness from commercial and highway development. A similar measure became law in 1964. In 1967 Church introduced legislation, passed a year later, that established a National Wild and Scenic Rivers System to protect eight designated rivers from pollution and commercial exploitation. Although conservationists generally praised his work in the Senate, they pointed out that over the years Church had vacillated on the question of whether the Snake River-Hells Canyon area in Idaho should be developed for hydroelectric power—a measure that conservationists had vigorously opposed.

Church could be counted on by organized labor and the Johnson Administration to support major social welfare legislation. Unlike most liberals, however, he voted against gun control legislation in 1968.

As a member of the Senate Foreign Relations Committee, Church generally advocated reduced foreign aid expenditures. He called for a phasing out of aid to prosperous Western European nations and Japan. He also urged an end to military assistance to nations like India, Pakistan, Greece and Turkey that seemed likely to engage in future hostilities.

Church was critical of U.S. military involvement in South Vietnam and in 1963 opposed aiding the regime of Ngo Dinh Diem. In June 1965 he called for direct negotiations with the National Liberation Front, free elections in South Vietnam and a scaling down of the U.S. war effort. Nevertheless, during 1965 and 1966 he voted for the supplemental arms appropriations bills necessary for sustaining the war effort. In May 1967 Church drafted a letter signed by 16 anti-war senators warning the North Vietnamese that "our objective is the settlement of the war at the conference table, not the repudiation of American commitments already made to South Vietnam or the unilateral withdrawal of American forces from that embattled country." In 1969 Church coauthored a bill to prohibit the use of U.S. ground combat troops in Laos and Thailand.

Conservatives in Idaho were bitterly opposed to Church's anti-war stand and his liberal voting record. In 1967 they began a movement to have him recalled, but Church gained a good deal of popular sympathy as a result of this challenge, and he swept to an overwhelming victory in the 1968 elections.

In 1970 Church and Sen. John Sherman Cooper (R, Ky.) [*q.v.*] sponsored an amendment passed by the Senate, but rejected by the House, to prohibit the President from sending U.S. combat troops into Cambodia without consent of Congress. [See NIXON Volume]

[JLW]

CLARK, JIM (JAMES) (GARDNER),

b. 1921; Elba, Ala.
Sheriff, Dallas County, Ala., 1955-67.

A political protege of Alabama Gov. Jim Folsom, Clark was the state's assistant revenue commissioner in Folsom's administration. He became sheriff of Dallas County in 1955. Clark gained national prominence during the first three months of 1965, when Rev. Martin Luther King's [*q.v.*] Southern Christian Leadership Conference (SCLC) sponsored a series of demonstrations in Selma, Ala. These actions culminated in a march from Selma to Montgomery to protest racial discrimination in the registration of voters and to demand federal action to end this practice. Blacks constituted a majority of the population of Dallas County, of which Selma was the seat, but only 300 were registered to vote.

Wilson Baker [*q.v.*], Selma's director of public safety, followed a conciliatory policy towards the demonstrators. Clark, a militant segregationist who denounced civil rights leaders as "the lowest form of humanity," dealt with the protestors in a harsher fashion. Responding to charges of Clark's brutality by protest leaders, a federal district judge on Jan. 23 enjoined the sheriff from employing intimidation and harassment. On Feb. 10 Clark and his posse led black children and teenagers, who had been peacefully demonstrating at the Selma courthouse, on a forced march into the Dallas County countryside. Clubs and electric cattle prods were used by the sheriff's men. That night King said, "Selma will never get right . . . until we get rid of Jim Clark." Later in the year Clark was fined $1,500 for violating the January injunction. On March 7 state troopers and Clark's men lined up near the Edmund Pettis bridge and used teargas, nightsticks and whips to block an attempted march from Selma to Montgomery. These incidents produced a national outcry that spurred Congress's passage of the Voting Rights Act of 1965.

Baker challenged Clark in the May 1966 primary for the Democratic nomination for sheriff. Baker stressed his commitment to fair and efficient law enforcement while the incumbent emphasized his belief that the civil rights movement was a Communist-inspired uprising. Thousands of blacks had been registered since the beginning of SCLC's activities in Dallas County, and civil rights leaders regarded the primary as an important test of the strength of the new voters. Baker, who received almost all of the black votes, defeated Clark. Clark ran a write-in campaign in the general election but was again defeated by Baker, 7,249 to 6,742.

After his defeat Clark served as a speaker for the John Birch Society and other right-wing organizations.

[MLL]

CLARK, JOSEPH S(ILL), JR.

b. Oct. 21, 1901; Philadelphia, Pa.
Democratic Senator, Pa., 1957-69.

Clark was born into a patrician Chestnut Hill family. He attended Harvard and the University of Pennsylvania Law School. Rejecting his family's Republicanism Clark became a New Deal Democrat and served as deputy attorney general of Pennsylvania in 1934 and 1935. Following military service in World War II, he became a leader of the liberal Americans for Democratic Action (ADA) and entered Philadelphia politics as a reform Democrat. He broke the power of the Republican organization in the city by winning elections for city controller in 1949 and mayor in 1951. Clark's progressive record won him a second term in 1955, but he left office the following year to wage a successful campaign for the U.S. Senate.

Clark was a Senate maverick. He demanded open conduct of Senate business and was a severe critic of the methods of Senate Majority Leader Lyndon B. Johnson. His independence reduced his influence, but Clark served as one of the most persistent congressional spokesmen for the ideas of the ADA and the Democratic Party's liberal wing. Not surprisingly, he often earned 100% ADA ratings for his congressional voting record. Clark introduced civil rights and antipoverty legislation, laying special emphasis on the needs of the cities. He was best known for his largely unsuccessful efforts to reform the Senate, recommending changes in the seniority and committee systems, abolition of the filibuster and measures to increase Senate efficiency. [See EISENHOWER, KENNEDY Volumes]

As an enemy of the Senate "Establishment," Clark consistently supported Sen. Clifford Case's (R, N.J.) [*q.v.*] efforts to set standards of congressional ethics. Although Clark joined other Democratic members of the Rules and Administration Committee in refusing to widen the 1964-1965 investigation into Bobby Baker's [*q.v.*] financial and political manipulations, he took advantage of the impetus provided by the case to support ethics legislation. In July 1964 he and Case unsuccessfully introduced a measure that would have required senators to disclose assets of $5,000 or more, provide data on their income and outside business associations and list gifts worth more than $100. The Senate finally passed a code of conduct in 1968, but the measure was not as strong as Clark wanted.

Clark persisted in his efforts to increase congressional efficiency. He met with some success in March 1965 when Congress agreed to create a 12-member bipartisan committee to study the organization and operation of Congress in order to eliminate time consuming minor functions. However, his proposal to include "rules, parliamentary procedure, practices and/or precedents" as part of the new committee's focus was defeated. In 1966 Clark cosponsored a resolution to increase House terms to four years and another to reduce Senate terms from six to four years, but both measures were unsuccessful.

A member of the Senate Labor and Public Welfare Committee, Clark often sponsored Administration civil rights and antipoverty legislation. He believed, however, that Administration funding requests for the War on Poverty were inadequate, charging in December 1966 that the President and Congress "starved" the program to fund the Vietnam war. In August 1966 he made a symbolic effort to postpone action on defense appropriations until consideration was given to the "demonstration cities" program. The Senate defeated his proposal by an 84-5 margin.

Clark became a member of the Senate Foreign Relations Committee in 1965. His views on foreign policy often conflicted with those of the Administration. In June 1965 Senate debate on United Nations charter revision in which heavy criticism was directed against the U.N., Clark recommended creation of an international disarmament organization without vetoes and with a permanent world peace force and world tribunal in place of the U.N. The suggestion was not well received by his Senate colleagues. Clark was also in favor of establishing friendlier relations with Communist China. In November 1965 and again in May 1966, he and Sen. Robert F. Kennedy (D, N.Y.) [*q.v.*] urged the Johnson Administration to invite China to participate in the Geneva disarmament talks.

Clark was a major critic of the Administration's Vietnam policies. As early as April 1965 Clark claimed that his mail indicated overwhelming disapproval of the President's air attacks on North Vietnam. In March 1967 he attempted to add an amendment to a Vietnam war funds authorization that would have prevented use of the funds "to carry out military operations in or over North Vietnam or to increase the number of United States military personnel in South Vietnam above 500,000." Sen. Mike Mansfield (D, Mont.) [*q.v.*], the majority leader, was able to replace Clark's proposal with a less restrictive one. Believing that North Vietnam was exploiting congressional criticism of Administration war policy for propaganda purposes, Clark and other anti-war Senators warned Hanoi in May 1967 that they did not favor unilateral withdrawal of U.S. troops from Vietnam.

In April 1968 Clark was renominated by a narrow margin in the Democratic primary. His poor showing indicated that his stature, never very high among Pennsylvania Democrats and labor leaders, had deteriorated because of his sharp disagreements with the Administration. An appealing young moderate, Rep. Richard Schweiker (R, Pa.), defeated Clark in November, although the Democratic presidential candidate, Vice President Hubert Humphrey [*q.v.*], won Pennsylvania with 48% of the vote.

Between 1969 and 1971 Clark was president of the World Federalists, U.S.A. After 1969 he served as chairman of the Coalition on National Priorities and Military Policy. He remained active in Democratic politics.

[JCH]

CLARK, KENNETH B(ANCROFT)

b. July 24, 1914, Canal Zone.
Educator, psychologist.

Clark was born in the Panama Canal Zone, where his father was a passenger agent for the United Fruit Company. When he was five years old, his parents separated and his mother took him and his sister to live in Harlem. He attended New York City public schools, received a B.A. from Howard University in 1935 and earned a doctorate in experimental psychology from Columbia in 1940. From 1939 to 1941 he worked under Gunnar Myrdal on the Swedish sociologist's famous study of the Negro in America. Clark became an instructor in psychology at City College in 1942 and 18 years later was granted tenure, making him the first black to receive a permanent teaching appointment in the city university system. In February 1966 he became the first black member of the New York State Board of Regents.

Clark specialized in childhood personality disorders and was particularly interested in those related to racial discrimination and the problems of ghetto life. He published a report in 1950 suggesting that racial discrimination adversely affected the emotional development of white as well as black children. This report was cited by the U.S. Supreme Court in its 1954 decision ordering school desegregation. Following that decision Clark pointed out that, although New York City had not deliberately created a segregated school system, such a system had in fact emerged as a result of the city's segregated housing patterns. Throughout the 1950s Clark worked with a variety of groups which urged the city's Board of Education to begin to integrate its schools, but the Board was reluctant to act.

During the 1960s Clark remained a strong advocate of integration but expressed doubt that the goal could be achieved in the foreseeable future. Unlike many civil rights leaders in the early 1960s, Clark opposed forced long-distance busing to achieve integration. Middle class parents, he said, would not permit their children to attend schools in the ghetto. According to Clark, poor blacks therefore should not wait passively for the arrival of integration. They would not receive help from the New York Ciry Board of Education, an over-grown bureaucracy incapable of effecting real change in the quality of education. If blacks and Puerto Ricans wanted better schools, he said, they would have to assume for themselves the responsibility of school management.

Clark also urged blacks to develop a broad range of community service organizations to help compensate for feelings of powerlessness in the ghetto. In June 1962 he helped organize Harlem Youth Activities Unlimited (HARYOU), a group that sponsored retraining and work programs for unemployed youths, dropouts and delinquents. This group became a prototype for antipoverty organizations funded by the Johnson Administration under legislation passed in 1964 and 1965. Many ghetto residents picketed the Board of Education in support of the Clark plan. To qualify for increased federal funding, HARYOU in June 1964 merged with Associated Community Teams (ACT), another Harlem antipoverty group associated with Rep. Adam Clayton Powell, Jr. (D, N.Y.) [*q.v.*]. When former Powell aide Livingston Wingate [*q.v.*] was elected director of HARYOU-ACT, Clark resigned from the board, charging that Wingate intended to use the agency to advance Powell's political influence. To Clark's regret, HARYOU-ACT, plagued by internal dissension and fiscal mismanagement, failed to become a force in Harlem life.

As an eloquent spokesman for school decentralization, Clark was invited by a community parent group in October 1966 to draw up plans for the management of experimental Intermediate School 201 and three nearby primary schools in Harlem. He proposed that these schools be run by a group of parents and university educators rather than the city's Central Board of Education. The plan won the enthusiastic endorsement of Mayor John Lindsay [*q.v.*], State Commissioner of Education James E. Allen [*q.v.*] and most civil rights groups. It was denounced by Albert Shanker, [*q.v.*] head of the United Federation of Teachers (UFT), who charged that establishment of autonomous neighborhood school boards would lead to the abrogation of teachers' rights and protection against punitive transfers. The Clark plan was rejected by the Board of Education on the grounds that it could not delegate authority to any outside agency. A HARYOU report released in February 1964 documented the "massive deterioration" of Harlem schools and pointed out that student performance in the ghetto actually decreased with length of schooling. Late in 1966, however, the Ford Foundation proposed that teachers be given representation on neighborhood boards. The proposal won the tentative approval of the UFT and became the basis for the establishment of local boards in Harlem, the Lower East Side and the Ocean Hill-Brownsville section in Brooklyn.

In April 1968 the Ocean Hill-Brownsville board announced the dismissal of 13 teachers, five assistant principals and one principal from district schools. Three hundred teachers in the district walked off their jobs in protest, and in the fall the UFT called a series of city-wide strikes that lasted nearly two and a half months. Clark was sympathetic to the Ocean Hill-Brownsville board and attempted to bring about a settlement through the offices of State Education Commissioner Allen. As the strike wore on, however, Allen was forced to suspend the board and replace it with a special three-man state supervisory committee.

By the early 1970s Clark had become thoroughly disillusioned with the decentralization experiments in Brooklyn, Harlem and the Lower East Side. Local boards, torn by internal dissension and excessively concerned with politics, had failed, he said, to improve the quality of education in the ghetto. [JLW]

CLARK, (WILLIAM) RAMSEY
b. Dec. 18, 1927; Dallas, Tex.
U.S. Assistant Attorney General, 1961-65; U.S. Deputy Attorney General, 1965-66; U.S. Acting Attorney General, 1966-67; U.S. Attorney General, 1967-69.

Son of former U.S. Attorney General and Supreme Court Justice Tom C. Clark [*q.v.*], Ramsey Clark received a B.A. from the University of Texas in 1949 and an M.A. in history as well as a law degree from the University of Chicago in 1950. He then practiced law in Dallas until he was named U.S. assistant attorney general in charge of the Lands Division in February 1961. In that post Clark cut in half a backlog of 32,000 pending cases and at the same time introduced economy measures that reduced the division's staff and budget needs. He also headed federal civilian forces at the University of Mississippi following court-ordered integration there in the fall of 1962 and traveled to several Southern cities in 1963 to oversee school desegregation.

On Feb. 13, 1965 Clark was appointed deputy attorney general, the second highest position in the Justice Department. He helped draft the 1965 Voting Rights Act and was the coordinator of federal forces sent to Alabama in March 1965 to protect the civil rights march from Selma to Montgomery led by Martin Luther King [*q.v.*]. Following riots in the Watts section of Los Angeles in August 1965, Clark headed a presidential task force charged with working out programs to help rehabilitate the area and to develop means to eliminate the cause of the rioting.

Tall, gangling and soft-spoken, Ramsey Clark became Acting Attorney General on Oct. 3, 1966 with the departure of Nicholas Katzenbach [*q.v.*]. He was named Attorney General on Feb. 28, 1967 and, with his father administering the oath of office, was sworn in on March 10. Justice Clark shortly thereafter retired from the Supreme Court to avoid suspicion of any conflict of interest.

As Attorney General, Clark helped draft the Administration's civil rights proposals and secure passage of the 1968 Civil Rights Act. He stepped up enforcement of fair employment and school desegregation laws and in April 1968 filed the first desegregation suit brought by the Justice Department against a Northern school district.

When Martin Luther King was assassinated in Memphis, Tenn., on April 4, 1968, Clark immediately went to the scene and then carefully followed the investigation of King's murder. Some years later a program of FBI harassment of King was uncovered, and questions were raised about the FBI's investigation of his death. Although Clark then said he "had confidence at the time that we were doing everything that could be done to determine the facts" in King's assassination, he felt the new revelations required the establishment of a national commission to study all government activities with regard to King. In the spring and summer of 1968, Clark resisted pressures to try to prevent a planned Poor People's Campaign in Washington, and instead he and other Justice Department officials negotiated with Rev. Ralph Abernathy [*q.v.*] and other campaign leaders to arrange for the arrival and encampment of the protesters.

To combat organized crime Clark initiated special "strike forces:" teams of attorneys and investigators from key federal agencies who cooperated closely with local law enforcement agencies to investigate, indict and prosecute organized crime figures in a single locale. Clark also centralized the federal anti-narcotics program in 1968 by merging several existing government operations into a new Bureau of Narcotics and Dangerous Drugs. He repeatedly called for improving local police forces by means of more education and training and higher salaries for policemen. He oversaw the administration of a program of federal grants established in June 1968 to upgrade local police, courts and jails. Clark also supported greater emphasis on rehabilitation in the federal prison system, opposed the death penalty and spoke in favor of controversial Supreme Court decisions expanding the rights of criminal suspects. He was a strong proponent of gun-control legislation and worked for passage of stricter federal laws in the summer of 1968 following the assassinations of King and Robert F. Kennedy [*q.v.*].

Clark generally opposed the use of wiretaps and electronic surveillance on the grounds that they were an invasion of privacy, probably unconstitutional and largely unnnecessary and ineffective in fighting crime. When instances of electronic eavesdropping by the FBI were revealed in 1967, Clark instituted a review of all government cases where illegal eavesdropping might have tainted the evidence and then notified the appropriate court when such a case was discovered. In June he issued controversial guidelines sharply restricting the use of wiretaps and secret listening devices by federal agencies. He refused to permit the federal strike force to use electronic surveillance. These restrictions remained despite passage of the 1968 Omnibus Crime Control Act, which greatly broadened the Attorney General's authority in this area. J. Edgar Hoover [*q.v.*] reportedly considered Clark a "jellyfish" and the worst Attorney General he had served under as head of the FBI. He refused to permit Bureau agents to participate in the new strike forces set up by Clark.

In testimony before a 1975 Senate Select Committee on Intelligence Activities, Clark stated that he "had authorized electronic surveillance on a good many embassies in the national security field." He denied knowledge of the FBI's COINTELPRO campaign to disrupt left and right-wing political organizations. He did admit, however, that he had known that the Bureau had undertaken some disruptive activities that went beyond the investigation or prevention of crime.

Late in 1967, following a wave of riots in the nation's cities, Clark established an Interdivisional Information Unit within the Department of Justice. The purpose of this group was to pool information from various sources on the activities of black militants who were thought to be inciting riots. Clark spoke out against Mayor Richard J. Daley's [*q.v.*] April 1968 order to the Chicago police to "shoot to kill" arsonists and shoot to maim or cripple looters in future riots. Clark thought such a policy would aggravate the riot control problem; he advocated instead overwhelming police manpower coupled with restraint and the minimal use of gunfire. Clark also opposed an anti-riot bill passed as a rider to the 1968 Civil Rights Act.

Along with Selective Service Administrator Lewis B. Hershey [*q.v.*], Clark issued a statement in December 1967 outlining the Administration's policy on anti-draft protests. While lawful protest activities would not subject registrants to any special administrative action by the Selective Service, the statement said that any violations of the draft law itself could result in early induction of registrants or legal action against the protesters. These guidelines met much criticism, as did Clark's authorization of the prosecution of Dr. Benjamin Spock [*q.v.*] and four others who were indicted in January 1968 for conspiracy to counsel, aid and abet young men to evade the draft. Clark later said that while he had "doubts about the Spock case," especially in its use of conspiracy charges, he felt his duty as Attorney General was to prosecute Spock and other Selective Service cases when the evidence showed a violation of the law.

Prior to the August 1968 Democratic National Convention in Chicago, Clark unsuccessfully tried to convince Mayor Daley to meet with leaders of the groups planning demonstrations during the Convention and to allow the protesters some peaceful means of expressing their dissent. He also unsuccessfully opposed Daley's request that federal troops be stationed near the city on stand-by duty. Following clashes between police and protesters at the Convention, Clark rejected all demands that he prosecute the demonstration leaders under the 1968 anti-riot law. Instead he instructed the U.S. attorney in Chicago to begin a federal grand jury investigation of police actions during the Convention and possible police violations of the protesters' civil rights.

Clark's liberalism became a center of controversy during the 1968 presidential campaign when Republican candidate Richard M. Nixon [*q.v.*] emphasized that he would begin "to restore order and respect for law in this country" by appointing "a new Attorney General." After leaving office in

January 1969, Clark joined a New York City law firm and soon became an outspoken opponent of the Vietnam war. He offered to testify for the defense in January 1970 at the trial of the "Chicago Seven," who were charged with conspiracy to incite a riot at the 1968 Democratic Convention, but the judge in the case refused to let him take the stand. He defended the Rev. Philip F. Berrigan and five others indicted in January 1971 on charges of conspiring to kidnap Secretary of State Henry Kissinger [*q.v.*] and to blow up the heating systems of federal buildings in Washington. In 1975 Clark also defended several inmates facing criminal charges stemming from the Attica prison uprising of September 1971. Clark made a highly controversial trip to Hanoi in the summer of 1972 on behalf of the International Commission of Inquiry to investigate charges of American bombing of nonmilitary targets in North Vietnam. Running an unorthodox campaign in which he refused all contributions over $100, Clark won the New York Democratic primary for the U.S. Senate nomination in September 1974 but lost the November election. [See NIXON Volume]

[CAB]

For further information:
Ramsey Clark, *Crime in America: Observations on its Nature, Causes, Prevention and Control* (New York, 1970).
Richard Harris, *Justice: The Crisis of Law, Order and Freedom in America* (New York, 1970).

CLARK, TOM C(AMPBELL)

b. Sept. 23, 1899; Dallas, Tex.
d. June 13, 1977; New York, N.Y.
Associate Justice, U.S. Supreme Court, 1949-67.

Clark received his B.A. and his law degree from the University of Texas, spent several years in private practice and then served as civil district attorney in Dallas County, Tex., from 1927 to 1932. Known as a protege of Sen. Tom Connally (D, Tex.) and Rep. Sam Rayburn (D, Tex.), Clark joined the Justice Department in 1937. Over the next six years he helped coordinate the wartime relocation of Japanese-Americans and handled cases on war claims, antitrust and war frauds. Named an assistant attorney general in 1943, Clark cooperated closely with a Senate committee headed by Harry S Truman (D, Mo.) investigating the wartime mobilization effort. He supported Truman's nomination as the Democratic vice presidential candidate in 1944. Appointed Attorney General by Truman in May 1945, Clark became one of the President's closest advisers on domestic issues. He instituted 160 antitrust cases, gave Justice Department support to the expansion of civil rights in Supreme Court cases and played a major role in the development of Truman's domestic anti-Communist program. Truman nominated Clark as a Supreme Court justice in 1949. Although the appointment aroused controversy, it was confirmed by the Senate.

At the outset Clark did not show much independence on the Court. He usually took a conservative position, voting to uphold government regulatory authority and to sustain loyalty-security programs against constitutional challenges. In the 1950s, however, Clark displayed increasing independence and innovation in his decisions. Although he remained a conservative in the loyalty-security field throughout the Warren Court years, Clark supported Court rulings against segregation and was regarded as a "swing" vote between the Court's liberal and conservative blocs on other issues. While he often voted against expansion of defendants' rights, for example, Clark wrote the majority opinion in *Mapp v. Ohio* (1961), one of the Court's most significant criminal justice decisions. With his strong background in antitrust, Clark became the Court's expert in this area. [See TRUMAN, EISENHOWER, KENNEDY Volumes]

Clark continued to support the government's position in loyalty-security matters during the Johnson years, but by then he was usually in the minority. In 1964 Clark dissented in a series of cases in which the Court invalidated state loyalty laws in New York and Washington and a federal law canceling the citizenship of naturalized Americans who returned to their native land for a period of three years or more.

Clark objected when the Court in 1964 nullified a provision in the 1950 Internal Security Act denying passports to members of the Communist Party. He also dissented in 1965 when the Court voided a clause in the Landrum-Griffin Act barring Communist Party members from serving as labor union officials.

Loyalty-security had become a less contentious issue by the mid-1960s, however, and much more controversy was aroused by Court rulings in areas such as reapportionment and criminal rights. Although Clark had concurred in the Court's 1962 decision in *Baker v. Carr*, ruling that federal courts could rule on legislative apportionment, he rejected the "one-man, one-vote" standard established by the majority in two 1964 cases. Clark argued that while the Constitution required "rational" apportionment, it did not mandate exact "one man, one vote" districting.

In criminal justice cases Clark often dissented from the liberal majority's expansion of defendants' rights. He was in the minority, for example, when the Court held in 1964 that the Fifth Amendment's privilege against self-incrimination applied in state as well as federal court proceedings. Clark also dissented in the landmark case of *Miranda v. Arizona* (1966), in which a five-man majority defined the constitutional limitations on the power of police to question criminal suspects and set out specific rules for police interrogations. Clark did not always place society's claims above those of a defendant, however. He wrote the opinion of the Court in a 1967 case that held that the use of electronic devices to record conversations was a search within the meaning of the Fourth Amendment. As a result, Clark overturned a state bribery conviction based on electronic eavesdropping that did not meet the constitutional standards for a legal search. Clark was also sensitive to the possibility of publicity infringing on a defendant's right to a fair trial. He wrote the majority opinion in a 1965 decision overturning the state conviction of Texas financier Billie Sol Estes [*q.v.*] on swindling charges. Estes's trial had been televised, and Clark ruled that the televising of criminal trials could have a prejudicial effect on the judge, jurors and witnesses. Similarly, Clark was the author of a 1966 decision reversing a defendant's murder conviction because of the "massive pretrial publicity" and the "carnival atmosphere," that had reigned during the trial. Clark also joined the majority in a 1967 decision extending to children in juvenile court proceedings the procedural guarantees, such as right to counsel, afforded adults by the Constitution.

In two 1964 cases Clark delivered the opinion for a unanimous Court upholding the public accommodations section of the 1964 Civil Rights Act. He also voted in 1966 to reinstate the federal conspiracy charges against 14 men alleged to have murdered three civil rights workers in Mississippi in 1964 after District Court Judge W. Harold Cox [*q.v.*] had dismissed the charges. In his opinion in that case, Clark urged Congress to adopt broader laws against racial violence. In 1967 he voted to invalidate anti-miscegenation statutes.

Although Clark usually approved the Court's efforts to expand civil rights, he did not always condone the activities of civil rights demonstrators. In a five-to-four decision in 1964, Clark wrote the majority opinion holding that the public accommodations section of the 1964 Civil Rights Act barred state prosecution of demonstrators who had previously tried by peaceful means to desegregate the business places covered by the new law. However, this proved to be an exceptional decision for Clark. In 1966 he voted against reversing the breach-of-the-peace convictions of five blacks who had tried to integrate a public library in Louisiana. He voted to sustain the trespass convictions of demonstrators who had protested outside a county jail in Florida against the arrest of other civil rights demonstrators. Clark was also part of a five-member majority that in 1967 upheld the contempt-of-court convictions of Martin Luther King [*q.v.*] and seven other black leaders who had led protest marches during the 1963 Birmingham demonstrations in defiance of a temporary restraining order.

In February 1967 President Johnson appointed Clark's son Ramsey [*q.v.*] Attorney General. Justice Clark announced that he would retire from the Court at the end of that term to avoid any suspicion of conflict of interest. After he retired in June 1967, legal scholars, assessing Clark's 18 years on the bench, generally portrayed him as a highly productive member of the Court and an able legal craftsman who had written some of its most important opinions. The major criticism leveled against Clark was that he had unduly emphasized the needs of government and society over the rights of defendants and of the individual, particularly in the loyalty-security field. Historian Richard Kirkendall wrote that Clark had "brought the fears of the Cold War to the Supreme Court and helped to translate them into the law of the land."

Clark remained active in the law following his retirement from the Supreme Court. He sat as a judge on the lower federal courts, served as head of an advisory committee of the National Commission on Reform of Federal Criminal Laws and from 1968 to 1970 was the director of the Federal Judicial Center, a research and training agency of the federal judiciary. Clark also headed an American Bar Association Committee that recommended in 1970 reform of disciplinary procedures for lawyers involved in misconduct.

[CAB]

For further information:
Richard Kirkendall, "Tom C. Clark," in Leon Friedman and Fred L. Israel, eds., *The Justices of the United States Supreme Court, 1789-1969* (New York, 1969), Vol. IV.

CLEAVER, L(EROY) ELDRIDGE
b. 1935; Wabbaseka, Ark.
Black Panther Party Leader, 1961-71.

The son of a dining car waiter, Cleaver was born in a small town near Little Rock, Ark. He grew up in Phoenix, Ariz., and in the Watts section of Los Angeles, where his parents separated. Cleaver spent much of the early 1950s in state reformatories and prisons for marijuana-related crimes. In 1957 he began a 2-14 year prison term for assault with intent to murder. The next year Cleaver joined the Black Muslims and became a leader among Muslim prisoners campaigning for religious freedom. When Muslim founder Elijah Muhammad [*q.v.*] and his charismatic spokesman Malcom X [*q.v.*] split in March 1964, Cleaver sided with Malcolm and renounced Muhammad's racial demonology. Expressing his ideological debt to Malcolm X, Cleaver later wrote: "I have, so to speak, washed my hands in the blood of the martyr, Malcolm X, whose retreat from the precipice of madness created new room for others to turn around in, and I am now caught up in that tiny space, attempting a maneuver of my own."

In mid-1965 Cleaver wrote to Beverly Axelrod, a prominent San Francisco attorney specializing in civil liberties cases, to request that she plead his case for parole. Axelrod took his case and also showed Cleaver's manuscripts to the editor of *Ramparts* magazine, which began publishing autobiographical essays and critical pieces by Cleaver in June 1966. In February 1968 these articles were published in a book entitled *Soul On Ice,* which won immediate critical acclaim. A review published in the *New Republic* placed the book "at the exact resonant center of the new Negro writing." Critic Maxwell Geismar described it as having a "true moral affinity with the *Autobiography of Malcolm X.*" *Soul On Ice* became an immediate best-seller and established Cleaver as a leading literary spokesman for black militancy in the late 1960s.

Supported by prominent literary figures such as Norman Mailer [*q.v.*] and with the promise of a job at *Ramparts*, Cleaver was paroled in December 1966. In February 1967 he first met Huey P. Newton [*q.v.*] and Bobby Seale [*q.v.*], the cofounders of the Black Panther Party. A short time later Cleaver joined the Party as its minister of information.

On April 6, 1968 a 90-minute gun battle took place between the Panthers and the Oakland police in which Panther Treasurer Bobby Hutton was killed and four others, including Cleaver, were wounded. Cleaver's parole was immediately rescinded, and he remained in jail until June 12, when Superior Court Judge Raymond J. Sherwin ordered him freed on $50,000 bail. The state successfully appealed Judge Sherwin's decision to the District Court of

Appeals, which ruled that Sherwin had acted beyond his authority in ordering Cleaver's release. Cleaver exhausted his last legal remedy Nov. 26 when U.S. Supreme Court Justice Thurgood Marshall [*q.v.*] denied his request for a stay to prohibit state officials from taking him into custody.

Throughout this appeal process Cleaver maintained his militant posture. The radical Peace and Freedom Party chose Cleaver as its presidential candidate in August 1968, and Cleaver campaigned on a program calling for an alliance of black and white radicals. In the fall he became embroiled in a dispute with California Gov. Ronald Reagan (R) [*q.v.*] and the State Board of Regents over a series of lectures he was slated to deliver at the University of Califormia, Berkeley. Gov. Reagan denounced Cleaver Sept. 17 as an advocate of "racism and violence" and sought to prevent him from lecturing at Berkeley. Three days later the Regents voted to limit Cleaver to one guest lecture and censured the faculty Board of Educational Development for having "abused a trust" in approving Cleaver's lecture series.

Over 2,000 students met Sept. 24 and demanded that the Regents rescind their restrictions on Cleaver's appearances. On Oct. 3 the faculty voted to repudiate the Regent's action, and four days later Berkeley Chancellor Roger W. Heyns announced that a lecture hall would be made available to Cleaver but that no course credit would be given to those attending the series. After Cleaver's first lecture Gov. Reagan submitted a resolution to the Regents barring university facilities for "a program of instruction . . . in which Mr. Cleaver appears more than once as a lecturer." Although Reagan's resolution was rejected by the Regents on Oct. 18, student demonstrations and sit-ins in support of course-credit status for Cleaver's lecture series took place Oct. 23 and 24 and resulted in about 200 arrests.

Having exhausted all legal appeals, Cleaver fled the country on Nov. 28, 1968. He lived in Cuba until July 1969 and then moved to Algiers where he founded the first international section of the Black Panther Party in September 1970. Cleaver was expelled from the Party in February 1971, after he attacked the national leadership's lack of militance.

By the mid 1970s Cleaver had moderated his political views considerably. He returned to the United States in November 1975 and voluntarily surrendered to federal authorities.

[DKR]

For further information:
Eldridge Cleaver, *Soul on Ice* (New York, 1968).
———, *Post-Prison Writings and Speeches*, ed. Robert Sheer (New York, 1969).

CLEMENT, FRANK G(OAD)

b. June 2, 1920; Dickson, Tenn.
d. Nov. 4, 1969; Nashville, Tenn.
Governor, Tenn., 1953-59, 1963-67.

Clement received a law degree from Vanderbilt University in 1942. Four years later he was appointed general counsel of Tennessee's Railroad and Public Utilities Commission, where he earned a reputation as the "people's champion" in rate case fights. The recognition he received in that post helped him to win a two-year term as governor in 1952. Clement employed a Bible-quoting, evangelical campaign style that was popular in rural Tennessee. He once declared, "If you can't mix your politics and your religion, then something is wrong with your politics."

Although his electioneering style was old-fashioned, Clement was, in the 1950s, relatively liberal in the context of Tennessee's traditionally conservative politics. He successfully pressed the legislature to pass greatly increased appropriations for education and mental health and opposed the intrusion of private enterprise into the operations of the Tennessee Valley Authority. A racial moderate, he neither endorsed nor criticized the Supreme Court's 1954 school desegregation decision, and in 1956 he sent the National Guard to Clinton to protect Negro children from white opponents of integration. Clement was expected to have a bright political future, and he received some consideration for the Democratic vice presidential slot in 1956. But his keynote address at his party's presidential nominating convention of that year was derided by some as excessively folksy and sentimental, and Clement was never again seriously considered for national leadership. [See EISENHOWER Volume]

After a compulsory retirement from the Tennessee governorship, Clement was reelected in 1962 despite his opponents' efforts to attack him for personal and business associations with Billie Sol Estes [*q.v.*], a Texas financier then under indictment for conspiracy and fraud. But the expansion of Tennessee's black electorate and the increasing strength of the state's Republican Party in the 1960s accounted, in large measure, for the thwarting of his two bids to enter the United States Senate. In 1964, seeking to complete the unexpired term of the late Sen. Estes Kefauver, he challenged Rep. Ross Bass (D, Tenn.) in the Democratic primary. Although a racial moderate by the standatds of the previous decade, during the campaign Clement criticized Bass for voting in favor of the Johnson Administration's 1964 public accommodations bill. As a result, Bass won Negro precincts in such cities as Nashville and Memphis by ratios of 12 to 1. In addition, Clement's popularity among many voters had declined because of his support for a 3% sales tax on TVA electricity. Bass defeated Clement by almost 100,000 votes out of about 800,000 cast.

After this defeat Clement wooed black voters by appointing Negroes to important posts and sending out recruiting agents to locate qualified blacks for state jobs. He also enhanced his reputation with liberal voters by urging the legislature to abolish capital punishment and by pardoning all five men on death row in 1965 after the lower house had failed by one vote to repeal the death penalty.

In 1966 Clement won a rematch with Bass for the Democratic senatorial nomination. In the general election he faced Republican Howard W. Baker, Jr. [*q.v.*], whom Bass had defeated two years earlier. For almost a century after the Civil War, the strength of Tennessee's Republican Party had been concentrated almost exclusively in the antisecessionist, eastern third of the state. But since Dwight D. Eisenhower's landslide presidential victory in 1952, the Party had been gradually expanding its following in other areas of the state. Baker, a moderate, extended these gains. He competed with Clement for black voters, almost all of whom had been driven to the Democrats by the 1964 Goldwater campaign. Furthermore, Clement's revivalist campaign oratory was losing its appeal as the state became increasingly urbanized. He received only 40% of the ballots, while Baker polled 56% of the vote to become the first popularly elected Republican senator from Tennessee. Clement left office in January 1967. On Nov. 4, 1969, at the age of 49, he was killed in a traffic accident in Nashville.

[MLL]

CLIFFORD, CLARK (McADAMS)

b. Dec. 25, 1906; Fort Scott, Kan.
Secretary of Defense, January 1968-January 1969.

Clifford was born in Kansas and raised in St. Louis, where he attended local schools. He won a law degree from Washington University in 1928, entered a prominent St. Louis law firm and soon established himself as one of the city's leading attorneys. In 1944 he was commissioned a lieutenant in the Naval Reserve. A year later he became assistant to President Harry S Truman's naval aide, James K. Vardaman, and in June 1946 Clifford was appointed a special counsel to the President.

As a close adviser to Truman, Clifford drew up the foreign policy memorandum that became the basis of the Administration's increasingly tough policy toward the Soviet Union. He also drafted the 1947 National Security Act and position papers for the Truman Doctrine to aid Greece and Turkey. In the domestic political arena Clifford plotted the strategy that aided Truman's election in 1948, convincing the President to appeal to the electorate as a militant pro-labor liberal. In 1950 Clifford resigned his position as special counsel to the President to become a senior partner in a Washington, D.C., law firm. Clifford became a millionaire, advising major American corporations on their tax and legal problems. [See TRUMAN Volume]

When John F. Kennedy won the Democratic presidential nomination, Clifford, a supporter of Sen. Stuart Symington (D, Mo.) [*q.v.*], joined the Kennedy staff as an adviser. In May 1961 Kennedy named Clifford to the Foreign Intelligence Advisory Board to oversee the activities of the agencies that had mishandled the Bay of Pigs invasion. He became chairman of the panel in April 1963. [See KENNEDY Volume]

In November 1963 President Johnson called upon Clifford, an old and respected friend, to help organize and recruit a new White House staff. Clifford might well have attained a high-ranking position in the Administration—he was offered the attorney generalship in 1967—but he preferred to maintain his prosperous legal practice. Nevertheless, Clifford soon became a member of President Johnson's inner circle of trusted advisers. In 1964 he helped the President deal with two embarrassing scandals, the first resulting from the business activities of former Senate majority secretary Bobby Baker [*q.v.*] and the second from the arrest on morals charges of White House aide Walter Jenkins [*q.v.*].

In the fall of 1965 Clifford visited Southeast Asia as chairman of the Foreign Intelligence Advisory Board. During the trip, he later recalled, "the optimism of our military and Vietnamese officials on the conduct of the war . . . confirmed my belief in the correctness of our policy." Clifford opposed the 37-day halt in the bombing of North Vietnam beginning at Christmas 1965 because he felt that it "could be construed by Hanoi as a sign of weakness on our part." In Washington Clifford's position on the bombing question earned him a reputation as a "hawk." As an adviser to President Johnson at the 1966 Manila Conference, he remained convinced that the U.S. was winning the war and that its Vietnam policy was sound.

In a July 1969 article for *Foreign Affairs*, Clifford suggested that his doubts about Vietnam began to take shape during the late summer of 1967, when he and Gen. Maxwell Taylor [*q.v.*] toured Southeast Asia at the request of the President. The purpose of this trip was to determine why America's Asian allies, New Zealand, Australia and the Philippines, had sent only token detachments to assist U.S. troops in Vietnam. Clifford discovered that these nations were less troubled by Communist aggression in Vietnam than the U.S. was, despite the fact that they were seemingly more vulnerable. "I returned home," wrote Clifford, "puzzled, troubled, concerned. Was it possible that our assessment of the danger to the stability of Southeast Asia and the Western Pacific was exaggerated? Was it possible that those nations which were neighbors of Vietnam had a clearer perception of the tides of world events in 1967 than we?"

Clifford's doubts were not widely publicized, and when he was named Secretary of Defense in January 1968 it was generally believed, even by the President, that Clifford would advocate an even more aggressive U.S. military posture in Vietnam than his predecessor, Robert S. McNamara [*q.v.*].

Clifford was confirmed by the Senate Jan. 30, 1968 and sworn in March 1. He assumed office during a critical moment in the war. On Jan. 31, 1968 Communist guerrillas and their North Vietnamese allies launched the Tet offensive, a massive attack on South Vietnam's cities and military installations. Before being driven back the Communists had overrun the ancient city of Hue, the cultural capital of South Vietnam, and had even penetrated the American Embassy at Saigon. Some military experts thought the Tet offensive the last desperate effort of a beaten enemy; to many others, however, Tet suggested that the U.S. and their South Vietnamese allies had made little progress in limiting the ability of the Communists to wage war.

On Feb. 28, 1968, two days before Clifford assumed office, he was named chairman of the President's Ad Hoc Task Force on Vietnam. The ostensible purpose of the group was to determine how best to raise the over 200,000 additional troops for Vietnam that had been requested by the Joint Chiefs of Staff and Gen. William C. Westmoreland [*q.v.*]. In fact, at Clifford's request, the Task Force debated the need for these troops and the nature of the entire U.S. role in Vietnam. Among other members of the Task Force, Gen. Earle Wheeler [*q.v.*], chairman of the Joint Chiefs of Staff; Walt Rostow [*q.v.*], special president assistant; and Gen. Maxwell Taylor favored the troop request. Deputy Undersecretary of Defense Paul Nitze [*q.v.*], Undersecretary of State Nicholas Katzenbach [*q.v.*] and Paul Warnke [*q.v.*] of the Defense Department stood opposed. Clifford remained neutral, attempting to use the debate to develop his own position. "After days of analysis," he later wrote, "I could not find out when the war was going to end; I could not find out whether the new requests for men and equipment were going to be enough, or whether it would take more and, if more, when and how much; I could not find out how soon the South Vietnamese forces would be ready to take over. All I had was the statement, given with too little self-assurance to be comforting, that if we persisted for an indeterminate length of time, the enemy would not choose to go on."

The Task Force eventually recommended immediate deployment of 23,000 additional troops in Vietnam, approval of reserve call-ups, larger draft calls and lengthened tours of duty to provide additional men. In transmitting these recommendations to the President, Clifford made known his serious reservations about the entire U.S. Vietnam policy.

According to Undersecretary of the Air Force Townsend Hoopes [*q.v.*] in his study *The Limits of Intervention*, the President was troubled by Clifford's new skepticism and "the warm, long-standing friendship between the two men suddenly grew formal and cool." Clifford held to his position and at a March 13 cabinet meeting presented a pessimistic picture of the American military situation in Vietnam.

On March 28 Clifford met with Secretary of State Dean Rusk [*q.v.*], Walt Rostow, Assistant Secretary of State William Bundy [*q.v.*] and Harry McPherson [*q.v.*], a White House speech writer, to discuss a draft of a scheduled presidential address on Vietnam. McPherson presented a speech that called for a modest 15,000-man troop increase and made a pro-forma appeal to the North Vietnamese to negotiate. The draft made no mention of a bombing halt, which the North Vietnamese had declared a prerequisite for peace talks. Townsend Hoopes called the speech "defiant, bellicose. . . ."

After reading the draft Clifford declared: "The President cannot give that speech! What seems not to be understood is that major elements of the national constituency—the business community, the press, the churches, professional groups, college presidents, students and most of the intellectual community have turned against this war. What the President needs is not a war speech, but a peace speech." Clifford spoke for several hours and proposed that an alternative draft be presented to the President that would include the suggestion that the U.S. stop all bombing north of the 20th parallel, with a promise of total cessation of the bombing if Hanoi refrained from attacking the South Vietnamese cities. McPherson thought Clifford "brilliant" in convincing Rusk and Rostow to reverse their long-standing positions on the war.

President Johnson accepted the peace draft and delivered it over nationwide television on March 31, 1968. His address included the stunning announcement that he would not seek another term as president. However, the speech did not end debate on Vietnam within the Administration. Clifford aligned himself with W. Averell Harriman [*q.v.*] and Cyrus T. Vance [*q.v.*], U.S. representatives to the Paris peace talks, who urged the President to order a total bombing halt to speed the negotiations with North Vietnam. Rusk, Gen. Westmoreland and Gen. Taylor argued that the bombing remained a military necessity. In October President Johnson yielded to the Clifford position and ordered a complete end to the bombing of the North.

Clifford left office in January 1969 and returned to his legal practice. In July of that year he urged unilateral withdrawal of American troops from South Vietnam.

[JLW]

For further information:
Townsend Hoopes, *The Limits of Intervention* (New York, 1969).

COFFIN, WILLIAM SLOANE, JR.
b. June 1, 1924; New York, N.Y.
Chaplain, Yale University, 1958-76.

Coffin came from an upper class family. His father was vice-president of the family furniture business, W. & J. Sloane, Inc., and his uncle, the Rev. Henry Sloane Coffin, was president of the Union Theological Seminary and a fellow of the Yale Corporation. After attending Phillips Exeter Academy Coffin entered Yale, but his studies were interrupted by four years of service as an officer in the Army. He returned to Yale in 1947 and later spent a year at the Union Theological Seminary. There Coffin became a follower of the theologian Reinhold Neibuhr, whose doctrine of "Christian realism" justified and encouraged political activism. From 1950 to 1953 he worked overseas for the Central Intelligence Agency, specializing in Russian affairs. After completing theological studies at Yale, Coffin was ordained a Presbyterian minister in 1956. He served as chaplain at Phillips Andover Academy and Williams College before being appointed Yale University chaplain in 1958.

Coffin took part in a May 1961 Freedom Ride to Montgomery, Ala., where he was arrested for breaching the peace in an effort to desegregate a bus terminal lunch counter. Two years later he was arrested in an effort to end segregation at a Baltimore amusement park, and in 1964 he was again arrested in St. Augustine, Fla., during a similar demonstration. In addition to his civil rights activities, Coffin served as a training adviser to the Peace Corps during the early 1960s.

Beginning in 1965 Coffin was strongly critical of American conduct in Vietnam. He argued that "the war is being waged with unbelievable cruelty and in a fashion so out of character with American instincts of decency that it is seriously undermining them. The strains of war have cut the funds that might otherwise be applied to antipoverty efforts at home and abroad—which is the intelligent way to fight Communism." After first restricting his protests to letters and petitions, Coffin became acting executive secretary of the National Emergency Committee of Clergy Concerned about Vietnam in January 1966.

By the fall of 1967 Coffin was counseling active resistance to the war and was one of the original signers of the September 1967 statement, "A Call to Resist Illegitimate Authority," which supported draft resistance and the refusal of servicemen to obey orders to participate in the war. On Oct. 16 Coffin was the main speaker at ceremonies at the Arlington Street Church in Boston, sponsored by New England Resistance, during which draft-eligible men burned or handed in draft cards. Four days later Coffin was part of a delegation that turned over these and other draft cards to Justice Department officials in Washington. On the steps of the Justice Department he stated: "In our view it is not wild-eyed idealism but clear-eyed revulsion which brings us here," and concluded, "we hereby publicly counsel . . . refusal to serve in the armed services as long as the war in Vietnam continues. . . ."

For these and other acts Coffin, Benjamin Spock [*q.v.*], Marcus Raskin, co-director of the Institute of Policy Studies, writer Mitchell Goodman and Harvard graduate student Michael Ferber were indicted on Jan. 5, 1968 for conspiring to "counsel, aid and abet" young men to "refuse and evade service in the armed services. . . ." After a widely publicized trial all but Raskin were convicted on one conspiracy count, and on July 11, 1968 they were sentenced to fines and two-year prison terms. The convictions were overturned a year later, when the First U.S. District Court of Appeals ruled that the trial judge, Francis J. W. Ford, had made prejudicial errors in his charge to the jury. Coffin and Goodman were ordered retried, while charges against Spock and Ferber were dismissed. On April 22, 1970 the charges against the two remaining defendants were dismissed at the request of the Justice Department. Coffin announced his resignation as Yale University Chaplain in February 1975, effective the next year.

[JBF]

For further information:
Jessica Mitford, *The Trial of Dr. Spock* (New York, 1969).

COHEN, WILBUR J(OSEPH)
b. June 10, 1913; Milwaukee, Wisc.
Assistant Secretary, Department of Health, Education and Welfare, April 1961-April 1965; Undersecretary, Department of Health, Education and Welfare, April 1965-February 1968; Secretary, Department of Health, Education and Welfare, March 1968-January 1969.

After graduating from the University of Wisconsin in 1934, Wilbur Cohen went to Washington as an assistant to his former economics professor, Edwin Witte, the executive director of President Franklin D. Roosevelt's cabinet committee on economic security. Cohen helped draft the 1935 Social Security Act and served for many years thereafter as technical adviser to the Social Security Board. From 1953 to 1956 he was director of the Bureau of Research and Statistics of the Social Security Administration. Cohen was professor of public welfare at the University of Michigan from 1956 to 1961. In January 1961 President Kennedy named Cohen assistant secretary in the Department of Health, Education and Welfare (HEW) and charged him with responsibility for winning congressional approval of HEW legislation.

Cohen formulated and guided through Congress more legislation than any other department official in 1960s. He was active in facilitating passage of some 65 bills relating to education, child welfare, social security, consumer protection, civil rights, mental health and water resources planning. During the Kennedy years, however, he failed to win enactment of two of the measures most prized by the President: the medicare bill linking medical care for the aged to the social security system and the Administration's education bill authorizing federal aid to elementary and secondary schools. [See KENNEDY Volume]

The passage of both bills became feasible following the November 1964 elections, in which the Democrats increased their majorities in the House and Senate. Cohen played a key role in the passage of the medicare bill, mobilizing the strength of organized labor to counteract the opposition of the American Medical Association. He also served as liaison between the White House and Rep. Wilbur D. Mills (D, Ark.) [*q.v.*], who as chairman of the House Ways and Means Committee formulated the bill which became law in the spring of 1965.

Cohen and Commissioner of Education Francis Keppel [*q.v.*] and White House aide Douglass Cater [*q.v.*] played a significant part in working out the compromise between public, private and parochial school groups that expedited passage in the fall of 1965 of the Elementary and Secondary Education Act. Under the compromise, the National Education Association, representing a million public school teachers, agreed to permit some form of public assistance to sectarian schools, while the National Catholic Welfare Conference settled for substantial but less than equal participation of parochial schools in the various aid programs.

Cohen was promoted to HEW undersecretary in April 1965 and three years later succeeded John Gardner [*q.v.*] as head of the Department. With the approval of President Johnson, Cohen issued a sweeping order reorganizing the public health divisions of his agency in March 1968. Along with Gardner, Cohen had come to believe that the commissioned officer corps of the Public Health Service (PHS) could not be expected to adopt innovations necessary for effective administration of federally financed health programs. Under Cohen's order a new assistant HEW secretary for health and scientific affairs assumed authority over many of the functions of the PHS. Cohen also brought the National Institutes of Health, the National Institute of Mental Health and the National Library of Medicine under control of a new agency called the Health Services and Mental Health Administration.

As HEW Secretary, Cohen was particularly concerned with problems relating to welfare and relief. He argued that improved job and educational opportunities coupled with substantial increases in Social Security payments to the elderly would substantially reduce the numbers on local relief rolls. He doubted, however, that Congress would pass a negative income tax or family allowance bill and did not propose one.

Cohen left Washington in January 1969 to become dean of the University of Michigan School of Education.

[JLW]

COLBY, WILLIAM E(GAN)

b. Jan. 4, 1920; St. Paul, Minn.
Central Intelligence Agency Official.

The son of a career Army officer, Colby was raised in a series of military posts in the U.S. and China. Following his graduation from Princeton in 1940, he enrolled in Columbia Law School but left a year later to enter the Army. During the war Colby became a member of the Office of Strategic Services and served on missions in France and Norway. In 1947 he received his law degree from Columbia. Colby practiced law in New York for two years before joining the staff of the National Labor Relations Board.

When the Korean War broke out in 1950, Colby joined the Central Intelligence Agency (CIA). Under cover of diplomatic title he served the Agency as an embassy attache in Stockholm from 1951 to 1953 and as first secretary and special assistant to the ambassador to Italy from 1953 to 1958. In this later assignment Colby worked with Italian political parties to block the expansion of the Italian Communist movement.

Colby was named first secretary of the American embassy in South Vietnam in 1959. As CIA station chief in Saigon, he helped develop the strategic hamlet program and directed the organization of Montagnard tribesmen to aid U.S. special forces.

In 1962 Colby was appointed head of the Far East division of the clandestine services, where he presided over the CIA's expanding programs throughout Southeast Asia. Using a private army of more than 30,000 tribal warriors, the Agency launched a secret war against the Communists in Laos. It also organized commando-type raids into China and North Korea and conducted bombing operations with its own airline, Air America. Because the effort was not costly and American casualties were low, the operation was not widely known until the end of the decade.

As the U.S. became increasingly involved in South Vietnam, CIA activities in that area grew. In 1964 Colby oversaw the establishment of the Vietnam Counter Terror program. The operation, carried on solely by U.S.-organized CIA teams, used intimidation, kidnapping and assassination against the Communist leadership. According to former CIA official Victor Marchetti, Colby also supervised the establishment of Provincial Interrogation Centers where Vietnamese nationals tortured suspected Communists. In 1967 the CIA began still another program, called Operation Phoenix, to coordinate American and Vietnamese attacks on the Communist infrastructure. Under the program 20,587 suspected Communists were killed in its first two and a half years.

Colby was sent to Saigon in April 1968 to assist Robert Komer [*q.v.*], director of Civil Operations and Rural Development Support (CORDS). This program was designed to "win the hearts and minds of the people" through the development of health and social services and the introduction of various economic programs to raise living standards. However, it was eventually coupled with Operation Phoenix and was generally accounted a failure. Colby became director of CORDS in November 1968 when Komer was made ambassador to Turkey.

In June 1971 Colby resigned his post and returned to Washington because of the serious illness of a daughter. He became director-controller of the CIA in January 1972 and was promoted to deputy director for operations in March 1973. At that post he was responsible for organizing the Agency's covert actions and secret political operations. In August 1973 the Senate approved his nomination as Director of Central Intelligence. A series of major congressional investigations of the Agency began late the next year. In November 1975 President Ford announced that Colby would be replaced by George Bush. [See NIXON Volume]

[EWS]

COLEMAN, JAMES S(AMUEL)
b. May 12, 1926; Bedford, Ind.
Sociologist.

A chemical engineer for the Eastman Kodak Company, Coleman began studying sociology as a pastime. He entered Columbia University in 1953 and two years later won a doctorate in his new field. He joined the faculty of Johns Hopkins in 1959.

A provision of the 1964 Civil Rights Act mandated that the U.S. Commissioner of Education undertake a study of the educational opportunities for minority-group school children. In the fall of 1965 Coleman began such a study and in July 1966 *Equality of Educational Opportunity*, the so-called Coleman report, appeared. The report, based on a study of 4,000 schools, indicated that de facto segregation was widespread throughout the U.S. It also concluded that the quality of education for blacks was inferior to that provided to whites. Few blacks, relative to their numbers, attended college; twice as many blacks as whites dropped out of school; and with each succeeding grade, blacks fell further behind their white counterparts in reading ability.

The report indicated that black schools were overcrowded and run-down compared to white schools. However, Coleman attributed the backwardness of black children less to these factors than to the social and educational deficiencies of their environment and their teachers. He doubted that even a great infusion of money into ghetto schools would significantly improve the performance of such students. Coleman proposed instead that the social handicaps afflicting black children might be compensated for if they were sent to middle-class white schools. White pupils, he argued, would suffer no appreciable educational loss from association with ghetto children.

His report was bitterly attacked by black leaders, who were coming to believe that efforts to upgrade the quality of ghetto schools should take precedence over attempts to integrate them. The national director of CORE, Floyd McKissick [*q.v.*], condemned the report, saying it suggested, "Mix Negroes with Negroes and you get stupidity." A number of Coleman's fellow sociologists suggested that the report had been hastily compiled and was filled with statistical errors. Nevertheless, others supported it and a 1969 report by the New York State Department of Education tended to uphold Coleman's findings.

Coleman helped draft President Richard M. Nixon's 1970 message announcing a planned $1.5 billion appropriation to aid school desegregation in the North and the South. In the mid-1970s Coleman expressed pessimism about the progress of school integration. Court-ordered busing to achieve integration, he argued, had accelerated the migration of whites to the suburbs. He thought the prospect of improved educational opportunities for black children was declining. [See NIXON Volume]

[JLW]

COLLINS, JOHN F(REDERICK)
b. July 20, 1919; Boston, Mass.
Mayor Boston, Mass., 1960-68.

Born in the Roxbury section of Boston, John F. Collins received his law degree from Suffolk University in 1941. After duty in the Counter Intelligence Corps during World War II, he practiced law and served as a Democrat in the state House of Representatives. Ten days before a November 1955 contest for the Boston City Council, Collins contracted bulbar poliomyelitis. Despite the illness he won election to the council; the disease, however, confined him to a wheelchair for the next 15 years of an active political career. In November 1959 Collins ran as an independent and upset a heavily favored organization Democrat in the Boston mayoralty race.

Collins worked with considerable success to improve the city's financial condition. He cut the city budget and civil service lists and reorganized executive departments. Between 1960 and 1963 his administration reduced property taxes four times. The mayor won reelection easily in November 1963. [See KENNEDY Volume]

As a master builder Collins left a visible mark on his native city. The Mayor devised the "Prudential Law," passed by the legislature in January 1962 and subsequently copied by many other urban localities. It granted tax relief to the area's larger corporations for the construction of immense, multi-purpose headquarters in areas facing economic stagnation or decline. Collins reorganized the Boston Development Authority, which rebuilt vast sections of the city. One successful venture created a "walkway to the sea," consisting of architecturally distinct government structures and completely renovated buildings extending from Scollay Square to the waterfront. Other projects rebuilt the South Station and Copley Square areas. In August 1967 the city presented plans for a privately financed, $325 million capital improvement of the Back Bay section. In December the John Hancock Life Insurance Co. declared that it would construct a 60-story office tower as the project's central facility.

Considered an unusually honest administrator, Collins became involved in an antipoverty project scandal in 1965. For two days in November the Labor Department froze funds for the Neighborhood Youth Corps because of charges that a Collins aide interfered for political reasons in the distribution of Youth Corps monies. A Labor Department investigation, however, failed to prove that Collins had in any way directly participated in the affair.

Collins had long planned to seek the 1966 Democratic nomination for the U.S. Senate. The Republicans appeared likely to nominate state Attorney General Edward W. Brooke [*q.v.*], and a January 1966 poll revealed that Brooke held a commanding lead over Collins. As a result, the regular Party leadership, never enthusiastic about the independently minded Mayor, searched for another candidate. When Postmaster General Lawrence F. O'Brien [*q.v.*] declined to enter the race, most party leaders backed former Gov. Endicott Peabody. In June Peabody won the endorsement of the Party's state convention. Just prior to the September primary, Collins again cut Boston property taxes, but Peabody still defeated him in the primary with an 8% plurality.

Collins faced major racial disturbances in Boston during the summer of 1967. Rioting began in Roxbury, Boston's black ghetto, on June 2 after about 30 black mothers staged a sit-in to protest their treatment by a neighborhood city welfare office. Following their eviction by police, a major riot began. Mobs looted 25 stores and set two multiple-alarm fires. The police arrested almost 100, and 60 to 70 injuries were reported. On June 3 Collins termed the riot the "worst manifestation of disrespect for the rights of others this city has ever seen." Black leaders, however, blamed the police for inciting the lawlessness. The riots continued until June 6. The next day Collins told reporters that he would not seek a third term.

Although a Democrat, Collins chaired the Massachusetts Committee for the Reelection of the President in 1972. The former Mayor argued that the Bay State should support Richard Nixon [*q.v.*], the candidate overwhelmingly favored to win in November, if only for the sake of the state's future relations with Washington. In the general election Massachusetts was the only state carried by Sen. George McGovern (D, S.D.) [*q.v.*].

[JLB]

COLLINS, (THOMAS) LEROY

b. March 10, 1909; Tallahassee, Fla.
President, National Association of Broadcasters, January 1961-July 1964; Director, Community Relations Service, Commerce Department, July 1964-July 1965; Undersecretary of Commerce, July 1965-October 1966.

A grocer's son, Leroy Collins served in the Florida legislature for sixteen years before becoming governor in 1954. Reelected to a four-year term in 1956, Collins opposed the Supreme Court's desegregation rulings but urged moderation to Southern governors anxious to violate the Court's orders. Hailed by many commentators as "the voice of the New South," Collins chaired the 1960 Democratic National Convention. Between 1961 and 1964 he served as president of the National Association of Broadcasters and occasionally criticized the quality of television programs and advertisements. [See EISENHOWER, KENNEDY Volumes]

Upon signing the 1964 Civil Rights Act, President Johnson appointed Collins director of the Community Relations Service (CRS), established by the new rights statute primarily to coordinate and expedite the enforcement of the law's public accomodations section through negotiation with local leaders. (As governor in 1957, Collins had called upon the federal government to create such an agency.) Under the Commerce Department until April 1966, CRS lacked the legal authority to compel integration. By February 1965, however, Collins claimed that in the 19 states without public accommodations statutes prior to the 1964 act, two-thirds of the hotels, motels, chain restaurants, theaters, sports facilities, parks and libraries had been desegregated. "Whereas formerly the desegregated facility was the noticeable exception," Collins remarked in February, "it is now the segregated facility which stands out."

Collins' most notable role as CRS director came in March 1965 as the President's personal representative during the Selma, Ala., voting rights demonstrations organized by Martin Luther King [*q.v.*]. On March 7 Alabama state troopers and sheriff's deputies physically beat back 500 civil rights activists setting out from Selma for Montgomery, the state capital, to protest the denial of voting rights to blacks. Collins arrived two days later and persuaded King not to risk another bloody confrontation by renewing the march as planned on March 10. He asked the rights leader to wait until a restraining order against the police had been obtained from Federal Circuit Court Judge Frank M. Johnson. On March 10 King halted the march just short of the police line outside Selma, although some marchers criticized his acquiescence to Collins's plea. Following the expected favorable ruling from Judge Johnson, the march began again on March 21 and ended in triumph five days later. In Washington on March 25, Collins asked for a "respite" from future civil rights demonstrations in Alabama but added that the ultimate solution was "to correct the basic causes of the demonstrations" through legislation.

Collins left CRS in July 1965 to become Undersecretary of Commerce. Journeying to Los Angeles in August following the Watts riot, he arranged for the rehabilitation of the stricken areas through the release of $1.77 million of federal antipoverty funds which had been held up because of a dispute between Mayor Sam Yorty [*q.v.*] and the local Office of Economic Opportunity. As the President's emissary Collins participated in the August 1965 steel industry labor contract negotiations, although he did not play a role in the final settlement. He left the Commerce Department on Oct. 1, 1966 to resume his law practice in Tampa, Fla.

In 1968 Collins campaigned unsuccessfully for the Senate seat vacated by Sen. George Smathers (D, Fla.) [*q.v.*]. In the Democratic primary Collins's main opponent, State Attorney General Earl Faircloth, criticized "crime in the streets," a tactic Collins denounced as an appeal to racial prejudice. "We must stop crime," Collins remarked in May, "but we can't just think in terms of suppression." He defeated Faircloth in a May runoff by 4,000 votes out of about 800,000 cast. In the general election campaign, Rep. Edward J. Gurney (R, Fla.) branded Collins "Liberal Leroy." With only 44% of the vote, the former governor lost badly to Gurney, who became the first Republican senator from Florida since Reconstruction. Collins retired from politics to practice law in Tallahassee.

[JLB]

COLMER, WILLIAM M(EYERS)

b. Feb. 11, 1890; Moss Point, Miss.
Democratic Representative, Miss., 1933-73; Chairman, Rules Committee, 1967-73.

Although Colmer supported the New Deal programs of the 1930s, he subsequently became an opponent of social welfare measures, and throughout his career he was a bitter foe of bills directed against racial discrimination. In 1960 Colmer refused to support the presidential candidacy of John F. Kennedy because of the civil rights plank in the Democratic Party's national platform. [See KENNEDY Volume]

According to *Congressional Quarterly*, Colmer supported the Southern Democrat-Republican conservative coalition on key votes between 64% and 92% of the time in the years from 1964 through 1968. Like most conservatives, he backed the Administration's Vietnam policies. Favoring the prosecution of those who urged youths to evade the draft, he asserted during the spring of 1967 that "sedition, sabotage, and—yes—treason . . . are going on in the country today."

At the beginning of the Johnson Administration, Colmer was the second ranking member of the powerful House Rules Committee, through which most bills had to pass on the way from their committee of original jurisdiction to the House floor. In 1966 the Committee's chairman, Rep. Howard W. Smith (D, Va.) [*q.v.*], lost his reelection bid, and Colmer became the panel's head in January 1967.

When Colmer assumed the Committee chairmanship, the House repealed the 21-day reporting rule, adopted two years earlier, which had facilitated the efforts of liberals to circumvent the traditionally conservative Committee. Despite the repeal Colmer had less success in blocking liberal legislation than his predecessor. In the 90th Congress the liberals had a nine to six majority on the Committee, and Colmer did not possess Smith's formidable parliamentary skills. In addition, before taking his new post Colmer had agreed to hold hearings on fixed days for the purpose of expediting the movement of legislation, a procedure that had never been followed by Smith.

On occasion, however, Colmer was able to employ his chairmanship to influence the flow and content of legislation. In the spring of 1968, for example, the House Judiciary Committee reported out a gun control bill. He delayed the measure for three weeks until Rep. Emanuel Celler (D, N.Y.) [*q.v.*], chairman of the Judiciary Committee, agreed to oppose any attempts to add registration and licensing amendments on the House floor.

In 1972 Colmer announced his retirement from political life. [See NIXON Volume]

[MLL]

CONNALLY, JOHN B(OWDEN), JR.

b. Feb. 17, 1927; Floresville, Tex.
Governor, Tex. 1963-69.

Connally grew up in a poor family near San Antonio and attended the University of Texas. He was admitted to the Texas bar in 1938 and that year became an aide to freshman Democratic Texas Congressman Lyndon B. Johnson. After serving in the Navy during World War II, he managed Johnson's bitterly fought and narrowly successful campaign for the U.S. Senate in 1948.

In 1951 Connally moved to Fort Worth to become an attorney for Sid Richardson, who had made a fortune as an oil man in the 1930s and as a leading manufacturer of petrochemicals, electronic equipment and defense-related hardware after World War II. In the process of managing Richardson's empire, Connally accumulated a wide range of Texas business connections and a network of corporate directorships in Richardson-owned firms.

Meanwhile, Connally remained closely linked to the ascending political career of Sen. Johnson, who in the 1950s became one of the most powerful figures on Capitol Hill. In 1956 he played a key role in helping Johnson capture control of the dominant conservative wing of the Texas Democratic Party from Gov. Allan Shivers. Four years later Connally directed Johnson's bid for the Democratic presidential nomination. Johnson's election to the vice presidency in 1960, with Connally obtained the post of Secretary of the Navy in the Kennedy Administration.

Connally served as Navy Secretary from January to December 1961, when he resigned to enter the Democratic gubernatorial primary in Texas. He faced bitter opposition from insurgent Democratic liberals, led by Sen. Ralph Yarborough [*q.v.*], who reviled him as a pillar of the Texas business establishment. Heavily financed by many of the state's business interests and aided by his association with the Kennedy Administration, Connally edged his liberal Democratic opponent in a primary runoff election in the spring of 1962 and went on to defeat his Republican rival the following November. He was in the presidential limousine in Dallas on Nov. 22, 1963 when President Kennedy was assassinated. The Governor suffered a serious chest wound but soon recovered. [See KENNEDY Volume]

During his three two-year terms as governor, Connally successfully promoted substantially increased expenditures for education and for the mentally ill and retarded. In most other areas, however, his positions offended the intellectuals, labor unions, blacks and Mexican-Americans who formed the major elements of the state's liberal coalition. Connally favored voluntary desegregation but opposed the Kennedy-Johnson public accomodations bill as destructive of "one of our most cherished freedoms—the right to own and manage private property." He was an ardent supporter of President Johnson's Vietnam policies and denounced anti-war demonstrators as "bearded and unwashed prophets of doubt and despair."

Connally administered Great Society programs in Texas without enthusiasm, and he was the first governor to veto a War on Poverty project. He also actively defended the state's right-to-work law, which was vehemently opposed by the Texas AFL-CIO. The Governor did not challenge the state's regressive system of taxation, and during his tenure in office the sales tax doubled without corresponding increases in taxes directed at the wealthy.

The most dramatic display of Connally's conservatism occurred in 1966 when a group of striking Mexican-American farm workers marched 400 miles from the Rio Grande Valley to Austin to ask the Governor to support a minimum farm wage law. Connally drove about 30 miles out of the capital to meet them and explain his opposition to the measure. He then drove away and was not present when the marchers reached Austin. Sen. Yarborough, on the other hand, symbolically walked with the marchers for several hundred yards. Texas political observers felt that the Governor's handling of the matter had given an impression of personal arrogance and represented a serious political blunder.

Despite the opposition that he aroused, Connally's political position in Texas was strong throughout his governorship and particularly after the assassination of President Kennedy. The injury which he suffered in the presidential limousine generated a great deal of sympathy, but the most important consequence of the assassination for Connally was the accession of Lyndon B. Johnson to the presidency. Connally's association with the new President enhanced the Governor's prestige. Furthermore, Johnson wanted left-of-center support and a united Texas Democratic Party in the 1964 national election. Therefore, he attempted to alter his role in Texas politics from conservative factional leader to party conciliator. Johnson was able to bring about a truce early in 1964 by deterring the conservatives from challenging Sen. Yarborough's reelection bid. In return, the liberals did not give full-scale support to Connally's primary opponent. Two years later Connally won reelection with little difficulty. In 1968 the truce broke down because Johnson, by then a lame-duck president, had lost much of his influence, but Connally had already announced the previous fall that he would not seek reelection for a fourth term.

Connally hoped to secure a place on the national Democratic ticket in 1968, but the defeat of his chosen gubernatorial successor, Eugene Locke, in the first round of the spring Texas primary, weakened his position. Yet, as head of the 104-vote Texas delegation, he was still a powerful figure at the Democratic National Convention in August. Connally beat back a challenge to his delegation's credentials from his liberal rival, Sen. Yarborough, who supported peace candidate Sen. Eugene McCarthy (D, Minn.) [*q.v.*], and he led the fight for a Pro-Administration Vietnam plank in the Party platform. Connally also helped deter the convention's nominee, Vice President Hubert Humphrey [*q.v.*], from placating the anti-war wing of the Party through modification of his long-standing support for the Johnson Vietnam war policies.

Connally gave Humphrey only lukewarm support in the election campaign. He was angered at the Democratic candidate for permitting the Convention to drop the unit rule for delegate voting (traditionally a source of power for the Texas conservative establishment) and for refusing to even consider him as a vice presidential running mate.

In 1969 Connally returned to private practice with a leading Texas law firm. Two years later he entered the Nixon Administration as Secretary of the Treasury. In that post he played a major role in implementing President Nixon's [*q.v.*] wage and price control program. He resigned his cabinet post in May 1972.

Two months later, immediately after the Democratic National Convention had chosen Sen. George McGovern (D, S.D.) [*q.v.*] as the Party's national standard bearer, Connally denounced the nominee's economic and military policies and endorsed President Nixon's reelection bid. He switched his allegiance to the Republican Party in May 1973. Later in the month Connally became a special adviser to the President but resigned after only two months. In July 1974 the Watergate grand jury indicted Connally for bribery and perjury in connection with an increase in federal milk price supports during his tenure as Treasury Secretary. He was acquitted in April 1975. [See NIXON Volume]

[MLL]

For further information:

Ronnie Dugger, "John Connally: Nixon's New Quarterback," *The Atlantic Monthly* (July 1971), pp. 82-90.

Robert Sherrill, "A Nasty, Brutish, Fascinating Political Feud," *The New York Times Magazine*, (April 28, 1968), pp. 36-52.

CONNOR, JOHN T(HOMAS)

b. Nov. 3, 1914; Syracuse, N.Y.
Secretary of Commerce, January 1965-January 1967.

A graduate of Harvard Law School, John Connor joined the New York law firm of Cravath, de Gersdorff, Swaine & Wood in 1939. He went to Washington in 1942 to serve as general counsel for the Office of Scientific Research and Development, where he set up a program for the development and production of penicillin that involved a large number of government, university and commercial laboratories. As special assistant to Secretary of the Navy James V. Forrestal from 1945 to 1947, Connor dismantled the military penicillin program to integrate it into the private economy.

Connor joined one of the largest drug manufacturers, Merck & Company, in 1947 as general attorney and became its president in 1955. He ably defended the firm before Sen. Estes Kefauver's (D, Tenn.) investigation of the drug industry at the end of the 1950s. During his 10 years as president, Connor expanded Merck's investments in foreign plants by 450%. [See KENNEDY Volume]

A founder and cochairman of the National Independent Committee for Johnson-Humphrey in 1964, Connor was appointed Secretary of Commerce by President Johnson in January 1965. His principal activities as Commerce Secretary lay less in the shaping of Administration policy than in the selling of Johnson's programs to the business community.

Connor's chief preoccupation was the balance of payments deficit, which had averaged $3 billion annually from 1958 through 1964. A 15% tax on American investments abroad was seriously discussed within the Administration as a possible antidote. Connor argued against this measure, and his success in substituting a program of voluntary business cooperation in reversing the dollar outflow was the major achievement in his two-year tenure in office.

The voluntary approach involved Connor's asking the top management of each of the 500 largest U.S. corporations doing business abroad to improve its balance of payments position by 15% to 20% in 1965. He suggested several means: a company could increase its exports, raise capital from foreign sources, repatriate funds held abroad or postpone planned investments overseas. Connor won a significant degree of business cooperation with the program, but its effect on the balance of payments was below expectations. The deficit for 1965 was $1.3 billion, down from $2.8 billion in 1965, but in 1966 the program reduced the deficit by only $900 million (compared to the anticipated $3.4 billion reduction.

In February 1966 *Fortune* stated: "No Commerce Secretary in years has stood higher with the business community than Connor. . . . No Secretary has done a better first-year job of administration, either." Yet on the whole Connor's voice carried less weight in economic policy councils than that of Secretary of the Treasury Henry Fowler [*q.v.*] or the chairman of the Council of Economic Advisers, Gardner Ackley [*q.v.*]. "And when he wanted a businessman's point of view," *Newsweek* reported, "the President was prone to forget his own Secretary of Commerce; instead he would pick up the telephone and call someone like Henry Ford II [*q.v.*] or Frederick Kappel [*q.v.*]."

During the aluminum price rise dispute between the industry and the federal government in the fall of 1965, Connor argued within the Administration that the increase was not unjustified. He opposed the Administration's decision to make a public confrontation and to use the sale of the government's aluminum stockpiles as an economic weapon. Connor was also unenthusiastic about the Administration's 3.2% guidelines for wages and prices. He played an important role, however, in the settlements of the East Coast dock strike in February 1965 and the General Electric employes' strike in October 1966.

Connor resigned as Commerce Secretary in January 1967 to become president of the Allied Chemical Corporation.

[TO]

CONTE, SILVIO O(CTTAVIO)

b. Nov. 9, 1921; Pittsfield, Mass.
Republican Representative, Mass., 1959- .

Silvio O. Conte graduated from Pittsfield Vocational High School in 1940 and briefly worked as a machinist for General Electric. A Navy Seabee during World War II, Conte earned a law degree from Boston College in 1949. The following year he won election to the state Senate and served there for eight years.

In 1958 Conte ran for the U.S. House in Massachusetts's first district against James MacGregor Burns, a Williams College political science professor, biographer and close political associate of Sen. John F. Kennedy. The first district, located in the westernmost part of the state, included the Berkshires, the Connecticut Valley, 13 colleges and universities and medium-sized industrial centers like Pittsfield. Predominately Democratic, its second and third-generation immigrants far outnumbered the old Yankee stock. As the Democrat Burns should have enjoyed the advantage, and he did obtain national attention from the news media during the campaign. But Conte, the son of Italian immigrants and married to an Irish-American, had developed a special ethnic constituency of his own. Despite a strong statewide Democratic tide, the bitterly fought struggle ended with Conte the victor with 55% of the vote. He easily won reelection in 1960 and 1962. The Democrats did not oppose his candidacy in 1964, 1966 or 1968.

Apart from his ethnic support Conte retained his office in a Democratic region largely because of his independent-minded, liberal Republicanism. He refused to endorse his Party's conservative 1964 presidential nominee, Sen. Barry M. Goldwater (R, Ariz.) [*q.v.*], who netted only 25.9% of the vote cast for president in the first district. With other members of the liberal House GOP "Wednesday Club," Conte planned the removal of Rep. Charles A. Halleck (R, Ind.) [*q.v.*] and his replacement by Rep. Gerald Ford (R, Mich.) [*q.v.*] as minority leader following the Goldwater disaster.

In his House votes Conte steered an especially nonpartisan course. During the 89th Congress, Conte supported the Johnson Administration on 67% of all the votes for which the President had announced a position. In 1966 only one other GOP representative—Rep. Ogden R. Reid (R, N.Y.) [*q.v.*]—supported Johnson more frequently. During the 90th Congress Conte voted with the Republican leadership 44% of the time, compared to a *Congressional Quarterly* average of 70% for all House Republicans.

Conte proved especially sympathetic to the Johnson Administration's foreign aid programs. During Johnson's presidency he served on the House Appropriations Committee's Foreign Operations Subcommittee, the panel responsible for foreign aid authorizations. Although GOP members grew increasingly hostile to Administration foreign assistance requests, Conte consistently defended the need for overseas aid. In December 1963 he attempted to restore $20 million cut by the subcommittee from the Administration's request but lost in two separate votes. Later in the month only two Republican House members—Conte and Rep. John V. Lindsay (R, N.Y.) [*q.v.*]—supported the President's request for a federal guarantee for the financing of trade with Communist nations. The measure passed, 189-158.

In late 1967 Conte broke with Johnson over U.S. military assistance to undeveloped nations. In November the House agreed to a Conte-sponsored ban on the use of military aid monies for "sophisticated" offensive weapons systems to all foreign assistance countries except seven bordering the Soviet Union and China. Conte feared the possibility of a Latin American or South Asian nuclear arms race. Johnson unsuccessfully tried to block the amendment.

In August 1968 Conte served on the Massachusetts delegation to the Republican National Convention. The House sponsor of a 1965 bill to regulate mail-order gun sales, he failed to win the inclusion of a specific, gun-control plank in the Party platform. Conte supported New York Gov. Nelson A. Rockefeller [*q.v.*] for the presidential nomination. Prior to the balloting for vice president, he joined a loose coalition against the designation of Maryland Gov. Spiro T. Agnew [*q.v.*]. Unable to persuade John Lindsay to run, the Conte group backed Michigan Gov. George W. Romney [*q.v.*], whom Agnew crushed, 1,128-186.

Conte won reelection through 1974 and emerged as the third-ranking Republican on the powerful Appropriations Committee. But because of his liberalism he held little sway over Party policy, either in the House or nationwide. [See NIXON Volume]

[JLB]

CONWAY, JACK T.

b. Dec. 20, 1917; Detroit, Mich.
Executive Director, Industrial Union Department, AFL-CIO, November 1963-December, 1968; Deputy Director, Office of Economic Opportunity, October 1964-August 1965.

Conway was educated at the University of Chicago, where he received a B.A. in 1940. A youthful radical, he worked in wartime aircraft factories, served in the Army and then began to work for the United Auto Workers (UAW) in 1946. Conway soon became close to UAW President Walter Reuther [*q.v.*], under whom he served as administrative assistant until 1961. When Reuther was chosen to head the AFL-CIO's Industrial Union Department (IUD) in 1957, Conway gradually took over the administrative functions of the organization.

Founded shortly after the formation of the AFL-CIO, the IUD was intended to represent the interests of industrial workers in the labor movement. In 1963, when the IUD encompassed 60 unions with a total membership of six million, Conway became its executive director. His main concern in this position was to coordinate the demands and bargaining techniques of the separate unions active in plants of the same company or industry. In 1966 Conway introduced a system of computerized information analysis covering collective contracts and working conditions to help unions consolidate their negotiations and avoid discrepancies in the agreements they reached.

Beginning in the early 1960s Conway increasingly turned his attention to a series of public service positions. In 1961 President Kennedy appointed him deputy administrator of the federal Housing and Home Finance Agency, and in 1964 he became deputy director of the Office of Economic Opportunity (OEO). He held each position for one year, while on leave from his union duties. Conway's task in the OEO was to administer the community action program, which absorbed most of the agency's budget. He tried to ensure that poor people participated in planning the projects intended for them and also worked to minimize in-fighting among state and local agencies for control over federal poverty funds. Despite his efforts divisiveness within the program persisted, drawing considerable criticism from participants as well as from opponents of the OEO.

Conway left his union post permanently in 1968 to become president of the Center for Community Change, a private organization funded by the Ford Foundation to assist community groups in low-income areas. In 1971 he was appointed president of Common Cause by John Gardner [*q.v.*] and was subsequently part of the organization's lobby against "corrupt and undemocratic government." Conway coordinated a survey of opinion in the Senate and House on the issue of congressional reform in 1972. Later he attacked the government of New York State as the most "secretive, unresponsive and oligarchical in the nation," and initiated a lobbying effort to reform the state legislature. In February 1975 Conway left Common Cause to become executive director of the American Federation of State, County and Municipal Employes.

[SLG]

CONYERS, JOHN, JR.

b. May 16, 1929; Detroit, Mich.
Democratic Representative, Mich., 1965- .

The son of a United Auto Workers (UAW) official, Conyers served as an officer in Korea and received a law degree in 1958. He worked as Rep. John Dingell's (D, .Mich.) legislative assistant until October 1961, when he was appointed a referee for the Michigan Workmen's Compensation Department. During the early 1960s Conyers was also general counsel for the Trade Union Leadership Council (TULC), an influential organization of black unionists who pressed civil rights and minority representation demands within the UAW and other Detroit-area unions. After the Michigan legislature created a new, predominantly black congressional district in Detroit, Conyers declared his candidacy in January 1964. He was backed by a militant section of the TULC but opposed by most UAW officials, the Detroit Democratic Party organization and the formal leadership of the TULC. After mobilizing a force of 2,000 volunteers, Conyers defeated his black opponent by a narrow margin in the June 1964 primary. Easily elected in November, Conyers was one of six black congressmen seated in January 1965 and was the first black representative appointed to the House Judiciary Committee.

Conyers helped sponsor the 1965 Voting Rights Act and later demanded its vigorous enforcement. In June 1966 he organized a group of eight Northern congressmen who traveled to Mississippi to observe the June 7 primary election there. At a press conference held the next day, Conyers stated that in his opinion the Voting Rights Act was being "minimally enforced" and that it would take 15 to 25 years "to have full voting at the present rate." Conyers demanded that more federal registrars be sent to the South. During the summer of 1967 Conyers returned to Mississippi to encourage voting in four counties where black candidates were running for office.

An honorary cochairman of the American Civil Liberties Union's national advisory board, Conyers strongly opposed legislation he regarded as anti-civil libertarian. He denounced the District of Columbia Crime bill as "monstrous" in October 1966 and declared it "appropriate only in a most totalitarian society." Conyers said provisions in the bill making it easier for the police to detain suspects "returns us to a system of indiscriminatory [*sic.*] investigative arrests." He predicted that the section of the bill requiring mandatory minimum sentences would cause sympathetic juries to acquit guilty persons. Despite the objections of Conyers and other liberal Democrats, both the House and Senate passed the bill in October 1966. President Johnson pocket-vetoed the bill in November 1966.

An early opponent of the Vietnam war, Conyers was one of 16 Democratic congressmen who signed a March 16, 1965 letter to President Johnson opposing the use of biological and chemical weapons in the Southeast Asian war. On May 5, 1965 he was one of seven congressmen who voted against a supplemental Vietnam appropriation, and he continued to oppose funding of the conflict during the remaining years of American involvement in the war.

In January 1967 Conyers became the only black member of a special House committee appointed to investigate charges of misconduct brought against Rep. Adam Clayton Powell (D, N.Y.) [*q.v.*]. In an opinion appended to the committee's report, which was released Feb. 23, 1967, Conyers stated that "punishment of Mr. Powell beyond severe censure is improper." He told a news conference that "racial considerations" led to the investigation of Powell, but that "on this committee the racial aspects of this case were never used." In January 1969, after Powell had been reelected by his Harlem constituency, Conyers helped formulate a compromise resolution that refrained from censuring Powell but fined him $25,000 for misuse of funds and stripped him of his seniority in the House.

Most of the unprecedented urban violence that Detroit experienced in July 1967 took place in Conyers's district. On July 4, one day after the rioting began, Conyers mounted a parked car and urged the crowd to return to their homes. He was hooted down, and two days later his district offices were sacked. On July 30 Conyers joined other black political leaders to demand an investigation of charges of police brutality during the riot.

During the 1968 presidential campaign Conyers chaired the National Committee of Inquiry, a group of nearly 1,000 prominent black leaders formed to make recommendations to black voters. On Oct. 13 the group met and failed to endorse Hubert Humphrey's presidential candidacy. At a news conference the next day, Conyers said the group would support Humphrey only if he took an unequivocal stand against the Vietnam war and made convincing pledges to help solve the problems of black people. Conyers continued to support the civil rights and anti-war movements during the Nixon years. He also played a key role in the successful fights against the confirmation of Clement Haynsworth and G. Harrold Carswell as Supreme Court justices in 1969 and 1970. [See NIXON Volume]

[DKR]

COOK, DONALD C(LARENCE)

b. April 14, 1909; Escanaba, Mich.
President, American Electric Power Company, 1961-72.

After receiving a B.A. and an M.B.A. from the University of Michigan, Cook moved to Washington, D.C., in 1935 to accept a position with the Securities and Exchange Commission (SEC). While employed in the Public Utilities Division of the SEC, he earned a law degree from George Washington University. Cook began his relationship with Lyndon Johnson in 1943 when he became special counsel to the House Committee on Naval Affairs, of which Johnson was chairman. He practiced law for a short time after the war, served for two years with a Johnson committee, the Preparedness Subcommittee of the Senate Armed Services Committee, and was named chairman of the SEC in 1952.

In 1953 Cook left the SEC to join the American Electric Power Company (AEP) and became its president in 1961. Although it served no major city and did 25% of its business in the depressed Appalachia area, the AEP was one of the largest utilities in the country, with a growth rate consistently higher than the rest of the industry. Under Cook the company continued to prosper with low rates, aggressive marketing innovations and a highly centralized management structure.

A close adviser to Johnson and, according to *Business Week*, "the man outside Washington to whom the President listens to most on economics," Cook held views on the economy considerably more liberal than the average businessman. He accepted the argument of Keynesian economists that budget deficits were not necessarily dangerous and that the federal budget need not be balanced every year, but only over a cycle of good and bad years. Cook favored tax incentives such as the investment tax credit and liberal depreciation allowances to promote business expansion. He also opposed higher interest rates as a cure for the American balance of payments deficit, preferring direct controls on the export of capital abroad.

Johnson sought Cook's advice almost immediately upon assuming the presidency. On Nov. 24, 1963 the two men had a discussion about the $11 billion Kennedy tax cut, which the House had passed in September but to which Johnson had not yet committed himself. Providing a persuasive rebuttal to the anti-tax cut advice Johnson had just received from ex-President Eisenhower and conservative businessman Robert Anderson [*q.v.*], Cook urged Johnson to follow through on the tax cut stimulus. Like Anderson and Eisenhower, Cook recommended government spending cuts to accompany the tax reduction, a course Johnson pursued after consulting with his formal economic policymaking team. The Senate passed the proposed tax cut in February 1964. In that year Cook also helped Johnson devise a program of voluntary restraints on American investment abroad in order to reduce the balance of payments deficit.

In early 1965 Johnson offered Cook the post of Secretary of the Treasury. Cook declined, however, not wanting to leave New York or lose his lucrative pension benefits at American Electric Power Company. He also feared a Senate confirmation battle, with conservatives attacking him for his "easy-money" views and liberals rejecting him as a private power advocate. Throughout the Johnson Administration Cook continued to give the President private advice and public support for Great Society programs. In May 1967 he joined a group of 21 business leaders calling upon the House to provide full funding for Model Cities legislation. Cook became chairman of the board of the AEP in 1972.

[TO]

COOLEY, HAROLD D(UNBAR)

b. July 26, 1897; Nashville, N.C.
d. Jan. 15, 1974; Wilson, N.C.
Democratic Representative, N.C., 1934-67; Chairman, Agriculture Committee, 1949-53, 1955-67.

A graduate of the University of North Carolina and Yale Law School, Cooley practiced law until a special 1934 election sent him to Congress. He assumed the chairmanship of the House Agriculture Committee in 1949 and became the chief congressional spokesman for the Democratic Party's high price-support-policy. Cooley was not, however, considered one of the most powerful House chairmen. [See TRUMAN, KENNEDY Volumes]

Cooley was not a liberal by Northern standards—the liberal Americans for Democratic Action gave his voting record scores of 69, 16 and 12 for each of the first three years of the Johnson Administration. However, he was the most loyal supporter of the President in the North Carolina House delegation, and, as chairman of the House Agriculture Committee, he introduced the Administration's major farm bills. Cooley helped secure passage of a permanent food-stamp program in 1964 and successfully opposed conservative efforts to require states to pay half the costs. He managed the 1965 omnibus farm bill, one of the Administration's biggest legislative victories, and wrote the provisions for a new cotton program included in the farm bill. The cotton provisions included direct income-support payments to farmers and an acreage diversion program to reduce production. Cooley also favored the Administration's food distribution programs abroad. In December 1965 he anticipated Secretary of Agriculture Orville Freeman's [*q.v.*] 1966 policies when he called for "an about face" in production-control policy in order to mount "a vastly expanded attack on starvation around the world." He helped push the Administration's 1966 Food-for-Peace legislation through the House.

In the area of sugar legislation, however, Cooley did not clearly side with the Administration, since he had long been closely associated with Atlantic and Gulf Coast cane sugar refiners and the Latin American exporting countries. In 1965 proponents of Western beet sugar interests, who wanted to increase their production quotas, charged that foreign lobbyists exerted undue influence over Cooley, an accusation which he strenuously denied. Despite his difficulties with domestic producers, he arranged a compromise between them and the refiners in the Sugar Act of 1965. The measure increased the domestic quota immediately but granted the first 700,000 tons of the growth of the market above 9.7 million tons a year to foreign imports exclusively. In addition, Cooley successfully persuaded the Administration to drop its plans to impose a spceial import fee on sugar.

Early in 1966 the North Carolina legislature reapportioned the state's congressional districts, and in the November elections Cooley was upset by a youthful Republican challenger, James C. Gardner, who had stressed Cooley's advanced age during the campaign. Cooley subsequently retired to his tobacco farm.

[JCH]

COOPER, JOHN S(HERMAN)

b. Aug. 23, 1901; Somerset, Ky.
Republican Senator, Ky., 1946-49, 1952-55, 1956-73.

Cooper began his political career in Kentucky's state legislature after earning a B.A. from Yale and a law degree from Harvard. In 1930 he became a judge at the county level. For several years in the 1940s and 1950s, he served on the circuit court, gaining a reputation as the "Poor Man's Judge." During this period he also served as a U.N. delegate, as ambassador to India and Nepal and most importantly, as U.S. Senator. Cooper won special elections to fill Senate vacancies in 1946, 1952 and 1956 although he lost two regular Senate elections held during that period. Elected to his first full term in 1960, Cooper's liberal voting record led President Kennedy to call him "an outstanding Republican." [See TRUMAN, EISENHOWER, KENNEDY Volumes]

Cooper considered himself a champion of small business and agriculture. During Senate hearings on a coal mine safety bill backed by the United Mine Workers, he testified on behalf of the operators of small mines. His amendment in March 1966 to render safety laws inapplicable if found "not to contribute to the safety of small mines" was defeated. He objected to legislation in April 1965 authorizing the Federal Trade Commission to regulate cigarette advertising as an unjustified inflation of the agency's power. He was successful in attaining greater state and local control over the Volunteers in Service to America (VISTA), which were heavily concentrated in his state. However, Cooper proposed to increase federal activity in the area by expanding the Tennessee Valley Authority to several Kentucky counties, but he met with defeat on this issue in July 1966.

Cooper was one of three Republicans on the Senate Rules and Administration Committee that investigated presidential aide Bobby Baker [*q.v.*] in 1964. Cooper called the investigation "a whitewash" and opposed the Committee's decision to block further hearings. His proposal for the establishment of a Senate Select Committee on Standards and Conduct was passed in July 1964, and he was named to the committee in July 1965.

Cooper was a leading Republican critic of U.S. involvement in Vietnam. President Johnson sent him, along with Averell Harriman [*q.v.*] and Secretary of State Dean Rusk [*q.v.*], to the Philippines to meet with President Ferdinand Marcos in the Administration's widely publicized "peace drive" of January 1966. Later that month Cooper criticized the renewed bombing of North Vietnam. In August 1967 he supported Sen. Mike Mansfield's (D, Mont.) [*q.v.*] proposal to bring the matter before the U.N. and in a Senate speech called for the U.S. to make the first move toward negotiations by unconditionally ending the bombing of North Vietnam. He joined Sens. Ernest Gruening (D, Alaska) [*q.v.*] and Wayne Morse (D, Ore.) [*q.v.*], the Senate's leading doves, in protesting a capitol safety bill that prohibited orderly demonstrations on the capitol grounds. During the February 1968 hearings on the Gulf of Tonkin Resolution, Cooper stated he did not believe that the incident had been provoked by the U.S. but that the nature and scope of the attack had not been sufficient to justify the adoption of the original Resolution in 1964.

Cooper was also a major opponent of the anti-ballistic missile system. He claimed that recent intelligence reports indicated that it was unnecessary and proposed that the question be deferred until after disarmament talks with the Soviet Union. His amendment to delete the proposed system from defense appropriations was defeated in October 1968.

In 1970 Cooper and Sen. Frank Church (D, Ida.) [*q.v.*] sponsored an amendment prohibiting the use of U.S. troops in Cambodia. Cooper, at age 71, retired from the Senate in 1972. [See NIXON Volume]

[MDB]

COX, ARCHIBALD

b. May 17, 1912; Plainfield, N.J.
U.S. Solicitor General, January 1961-July 1965.

A graduate of Harvard College in 1934 and of Harvard Law School in 1937, Cox spent several years in private practice in Boston. He then held several government posts during World War II, including that of an attorney in the Solicitor General's office from 1941 to 1943 and associate solicitor in the Department of Labor from 1943 to 1945. In the latter year Cox began teaching at Harvard Law School, becoming a professor in 1946. His writings on labor law over the next 15 years established him as an expert in the field. Cox chaired two wage stabilization commissions during the Korean war, arbitrated both New England and national labor disputes during the 1950s and served as a consultant to Sen. John F. Kennedy on labor legislation. He headed a research and speech-writing team for Kennedy during the 1960 presidential campaign and was named Solicitor General by Kennedy in December 1960. [See KENNEDY Volume]

As Solicitor General, the third-ranking post in the Justice Department, Cox had charge of all U.S. government litigation in the Supreme Court and decided which cases the government should appeal. A brilliant and self-confident man, Cox was known as a tireless worker and an efficient administrator. In both briefs and oral arguments before the Supreme Court, Cox was considered thorough, precise and effective.

Cox had intervened in the case of *Baker v. Carr* in 1961, and in March 1962 the Supreme Court ruled, as he had urged, that federal courts could try legislative apportionment cases. The U.S. government again appeared as a friend of the court in suits challenging the legislative districting in six states in November and December 1963. Cox argued that in all six cases the current apportionment should be found unconstitutional. The Court agreed with him in its June 1964 ruling and went on to mandate a "one-man, one-vote" standard for apportionment. In August 1964 Sen. Everett M. Dirksen (R, Ill.) [*q.v.*] introduced a bill to stay federal court action in state legislative apportionment cases for periods of up to four years. Cox joined in the negotiations to work out a compromise measure to replace the Dirksen proposal. Although an alternative bill was developed, it was filibustered in the Senate in August and September 1964.

In October 1964 Cox argued in the Supreme Court in support of the constitutionality of the public accommodations section of the 1964 Civil Rights Act. The Court unanimously upheld the law in December 1964. Cox resigned as Solicitor General in July 1965 after arguing 67 cases in the Supreme Court, more than any other living person. He went back to teaching at Harvard Law School but returned to the Supreme Court to argue several cases as a private attorney. In January 1966 he joined Attorney General Nicholas Katzenbach [*q.v.*] in urging the Court to sustain the 1965 Voting Rights Act.

In May 1968 Cox was appointed head of a five-man commission to investigate the causes of disturbances at Columbia University that spring. The Commission held 21 days of hearings. Its October 1968 report strongly criticized the University administration for conveying an "attitude of authoritarianism" in its dealings with students. The Cox Commission also scored the

New York City police for using excessive force against students in the April demonstrations and condemned the disruptive tactics used by the students as a threat to a free university.

In later years Cox represented welfare clients in several significant Supreme Court cases involving the rights of welfare recipients. He was named special prosecutor for the Watergate case by Attorney General Elliott L. Richardson, one of his former law students, in May 1973. As part of what came to be known as the "Saturday Night Massacre," Cox was fired, under President Nixon's orders, in October 1973 during a dispute over access to tapes of White House conversations concerning the Watergate case. [See NIXON Volume]

[CAB]

COX, W(ILLIAM) HAROLD

b. June 23, 1901; Indianola, Miss.
U.S. District Judge, Southern District of Mississippi, June 1961- .

A graduate of the University of Mississippi, Cox practiced law in Jackson, Miss., from 1924 to 1961 and was active in local Democratic politics. At the urging of Sen. James Eastland (D, Miss.) [*q.v.*], who was an old and close friend of Cox's, President Kennedy appointed Cox to a district court judgeship in Mississippi in 1961. Cox quickly emerged as a strongly segregationist jurist whose rulings obstructed the activities of the Justice Department and civil rights workers in the South. [See KENNEDY Volume]

Cox did order the integration of a Jackson restaurant chain in January 1966, and in a suit for damages against the Ku Klux Klan brought by relatives of a black man murdered in 1966, the judge condemned the murder and directed a verdict for the plaintiffs.

These were exceptions, however, to Cox's usual pattern of rulings in civil rights cases. On March 6, 1964 he voted to uphold the constitutionality of Mississippi's voting laws in a Justice Department suit challenging the statutes as discriminatory. The *New York Times* reported on March 9, 1964 that Cox referred to blacks trying to register to vote in Canton, Miss., as "a bunch of niggers" and said they were "acting like a bunch of chimpanzees." The remarks prompted an unsuccessful attempt by NAACP official Aaron Henry [*q.v.*] and other Mississippi civil rights leaders to have Cox disqualified from handling any more civil rights cases.

During a suit involving voter discrimination in Clarke County, Miss., Cox wanted perjury charges pressed against two black witnesses he felt were lying. After a probe by the Federal Bureau of Investigation, the Justice Department advised Cox that there was no basis for prosecution. When Cox insisted on the prosecution, Attorney General Nicholas Katzenbach [*q.v.*] ordered the U.S. attorney in Mississippi not to sign indictments against the two blacks. Cox responded in October 1964 by holding the local U.S. attorney in contempt of court and threatening Katzenbach with the same. In January 1965 the Fifth Circuit Court overturned Cox's action. The judge dismissed a Justice Department suit to integrate a Gulf Coast beach in March 1966, asserting that the beach was privately owned, and in December he voted to hold federal school desegration guidelines unconstitutional.

Cox's most famous case grew out of the murder of Andrew Goodman, Michael Schwerner and James Chaney, three civil rights workers who were reported missing on June 21, 1964. After a massive federal investigation their bodies were uncovered six weeks later in an earthen dam near Philadelphia, Miss. In January 1965 a federal grand jury in Jackson indicted eighteen men, including the county sheriff, for the murders on charges of violating federal civil rights laws. A month later Cox dismissed most counts of the indictment, causing an outcry among civil rights activists. The U.S. Supreme Court unanimously reversed Cox's decision and reinstated the charges in March 1966. The charges were again dropped for technical reasons at the Justice Department's request, but a new indictment against 19 men was handed down in February 1967. In October an all-white jury convicted seven of the defendants. Cox sentenced them to prison terms ranging from three to ten years, but he also made all the sentences "indeterminate," thus qualifying all seven for immediate consideration for parole.

[CAB]

CRAMER, WILLIAM C(ATO)

b. Aug. 4, 1922; Denver, Colo.
Republican Representative, Fla., 1955-71.

At age three William Cato Cramer moved to St. Petersburg, Fla., with his family. After serving in the Navy during World War II, Cramer graduated from the University of North Carolina Phi Beta Kappa in 1946. He earned his law degree in two years at Harvard. Returning to St. Petersburg Cramer successfully led the revitalization of the long-dormant Pinellas County Republican Party. In 1950 he won election to the state House of Representatives and served as minority leader. Four years later the 32-year-old Cramer became the first Republican Representative elected from Florida since 1875. He easily won reelection through the 1960s. His early success and statewide partisan labors made him, journalist Neal Peirce observed, "virtually the founding father of the present-day Republican Party in Florida."

In the House Cramer almost always voted with conservatives. He opposed the 1964 Civil Rights Act and annual appropriations for the Administration's antipoverty program. Cramer also voted against such Great Society endeavors as highway beautification, food stamps, mass transit and model cities. The liberal Americans for Democratic Action gave him zero ratings for the 1965, 1966 and 1968 sessions. In an unusual move, however, Cramer supported the 1965 Voting Rights Act that prohibited the poll tax and other Southern state voting practices that discriminated against minorities. Only one other Southern Republican shared Cramer's position.

Cramer played an important role in framing the final draft of the 1968 Civil Rights Act on open housing. During the first debates on the bill in August 1966 and amidst the third consecutive summer of racial rioting in the cities, he offered an amendment making it a crime to travel in interstate commerce with the intention to incite a riot or commit an act of violence. The Cramer amendment passed by an overwhelming 389-25 margin. When the Senate failed to take action on the parent open housing measure, he presented his original amendment as a separate bill in early 1967. Cramer and his cosponsors pressured Judiciary Committee Chairman Emanuel Celler (D, N.Y.) [*q.v.*], who originally opposed the proposal, into holding hearings on the measure. The Celler panel reported favorably on the bill, which the House passed in July 1967 by a 347-70 vote. Defending his legislation, Cramer declared in July that it was "aimed at those professional agitators," traveling from city to city, who "inflame the people . . . to violence and then leave the jurisdiction before the riot begins." Again the Senate failed to act, but the final open housing law, passed in April 1968, included Cramer's provision. Cramer who had never planned to vote for an open housing bill, supported the measure because of his own part in its preparation.

Until 1970 Cramer all but dominated the Florida GOP. Beginning in 1964 he represented the state on the Republican National Committee, and its chairman, Ray C. Bliss [*q.v.*], appointed Cramer to the GOP's policymaking National Coordinating Committee. The 1966 election of a Republican governor, Claude R. Kirk, Jr. [*q.v.*], however, opened a contest for control of the state Party. In 1970 Kirk, himself a candidate for reelection, worked against Cramer's primary campaign for the senatorial nomination. Cramer won, but both he and Kirk were defeated in the November general election. [See NIXON Volume]

[JLB]

CRONKITE, WALTER (LELAND)

b. Nov. 4, 1916; St. Joseph, Mo.
CBS News Correspondent.

Cronkite attended the University of Texas in Austin for two years while simultaneously working as the state capital reporter for the Scripps-Howard Bureau in 1935 and 1936. During World War II Cronkite had a distinguished career as a correspondent for United Press International. He joined the Columbia Broadcasting System in July 1950 as a member of the network's Washington staff and soon became one of its most important correspondents, acting as anchorman for the 1952 and 1956 political conventions. Cronkite also served as moderator for such popular CBS programs of the 1950s as *You Are There* and the *Morning Show*. He remained CBS's chief anchorman during the early 1960s. On Sept. 2, 1963 President Kennedy granted Cronkite an exclusive interview in which he stated that the success of the war in Southeast Asia would ultimately be determined by Vietnamese willingness to pursue the struggle.

During the mid-1960s Cronkite's ratings dropped as a result of the popularity of NBC's Huntley-Brinkley news program, and he was removed from his customary position as anchorman for the 1964 political conventions. His eclipse was temporary, however, and by the late 1960s Cronkite was back covering major news stories.

Describing himself in an early interview for *Variety* as a liberal "not bound by doctrines or committed to a point of view in advance," Cronkite in the mid-1960s reflected network wariness about coverage of the Vietnam war that was critical of the Johnson Administration. According to Erik Barnouw in *The Image Empire* (1975), Cronkite believed that the secret of his enormous popularity during this period was his reassuring and unwaveringly neutral delivery of the news about Vietnam. However, shortly before the Tet offensive in January 1968, Cronkite visited Vietnam for the first time since 1965 and reported on television that the U.S. might have to accept a stalemate in that country. According to many observers, the defection of Cronkite especially upset President Johnson, who had regarded the newscaster as an Administration ally.

During the August 1968 Democratic National Convention held in Chicago, Cronkite angrily described on the air police attacks on demonstrators and newsmen. Subsequently, he conducted an interview with Chicago Mayor Richard Daley [*q.v.*] in which Daley stated that the riots were led by "hard-core" radicals.

Renowned for a relaxed manner and a lucid style that was especially evident during "live" events, Cronkite's evening news program was broadcast by over 200 affiliated stations and led the competition with an estimated audience of 26 million by 1973.

[FHM]

For further information:
Erik Barnouw, *The Image Empire* (New York, 1970).
Edward J. Epstein, *News from Nowhere* (New York, 1973).

CURRAN, JOSEPH E(DWIN)

b. March 1, 1906; New York, N.Y.
President, National Maritime Union, 1937-73.

At sea from the age of 16, Curran led a strike aboard the *S.S. California* in 1935. The ship's crew was eventually fired, but an East Coast seamen's strike in their support, although unsuccessful, led to the formation of the National Maritime Union (NMU). Curran was elected the first NMU president in 1937, a post he held for the next 36 years. Virtually all of the other top union posts were held by Communist Party members who had been leaders in organizing the union. Curran worked closely with them until 1946, when he began a successful purge of Communist influence from the union. In that year he allied himself with a group of NMU officials who recently had been expelled from the Communist Party in a successful effort to defeat Maritime Union officials still close to the Party. Later purges led by Curran eliminated other opposition leaders, including his earlier allies. By the mid-1950s few veterans from the early days of the union were still in office, except for Curran and Treasurer Hedley Stone. [See TRUMAN Volume]

In October 1960 Secretary of Labor James P. Mitchell, acting under provisions of the 1959 Landrum-Griffin Act, brought suit to have Curran's 1960 reelection invalidated because of election irregularities. The following year Mitchell's successor, Arthur J. Goldberg [*q.v.*], dropped the suit in return for a stipulation in which Curran admitted some charges and agreed that future elections would be held in accordance with the law. [See EISENHOWER, KENNEDY Volumes]

The deterioration of the United States' passenger and merchant fleets was one of Curran's main concerns during the Johnson Administration. Curran supported government regulations that required the preferential use of U.S. ships as one way of preventing the further decline of U.S. shipping. In February 1964 he supported a boycott by the International Longshoremen's Association (ILA) of U.S. wheat being shipped to the Soviet Union. The boycott was called after the federal government waived a requirement that 50% of the wheat be shipped in U.S. vessels. The ILA, the NMU and the Seafarers' International Union (SIU) jointly demanded that the grain firms be forced to abide by the original 50% requirement and that guarantees be given that none of the wheat would be transshipped to Cuba. The boycott was ended after nine days, when President Johnson agreed that in the future 50% of the grain shipped to the USSR would be carried in U.S. ships, although contracts already signed would not be changed.

In July 1964 President Johnson appointed Curran to a new, predominantly non-government Maritime Advisory Committee, headed by Commerce Secretary John T. Connor [*q.v.*]. A subcommittee of this group, headed by labor arbitrator Theodore W. Kheel [*q.v.*], recommended in June 1965 that the then current system of operating subsidies for U.S. merchant and passenger ships be continued and extended. On Oct. 4 another group, the all-government Interagency Maritime Task Force, established June 10 and headed by Undersecretary of Commerce Alan S. Boyd [*q.v.*], recommended the elimination of subsidies for passenger vessels, a gradual phasing out of cargo preference laws and an "application of maximum automation [to U.S. ships] at as fast a rate as technology will permit." The Task Force report was immediately and unanimously rejected by the Maritime Advisory Committee, and Curran called for the resignation of Maritime Administrator Nicholas Johnson who backed the Task Force program. Shortly thereafter, Vice President Hubert H. Humphrey [*q.v.*] declared that the Task Force report was not official Administration policy. Although on Nov. 30 the Advisory Committee accepted with few changes its subcommittee report, President Johnson did not propose any new maritime policy that year, as he had originally intended to do.

Three years later, however, the Administration did offer a new program, presented to a congressional subcommittee in May 1968 by Boyd, who was then serving as the first Secretary of Transportation. The new plan included an end to passenger ship subsidies, reform of the merchant fleet operating subsidy program to limit it to legitimate national defense needs and the transfer of the Maritime Administration to the Department of Transportation. Curran, who headed the AFL-CIO Maritime Committee, as well as the NMU condemned Boyd's proposal as "inadequate, unimaginative and unsatisfactory" and "designed to kill the United States merchant marine." Following widespread criticism of the Administration proposal, Congress took no action on it.

In February 1966 Curran, SIU President Paul Hall and ILA President Thomas W. Gleason [*q.v.*] announced that their unions would boycott foreign ships that traded with North Vietnam. In August of that year Curran backed Walter P. Reuther [*q.v.*] in opposing an AFL-CIO Executive Committee resolution commending the American Institute for Free Labor Development (AIFLD), an AFL-CIO sponsored group that worked with Latin American trade unions. Reuther's brother Victor had earlier charged that the AIFLD had close ties to the Central Intelligence Agency. The AFL-CIO Executive Committee passed the resolution by a vote of 23-2.

In June 1966 Curran was reelected to his 13th term as NMU president, running unopposed on the ballot. A strong anti-Curran ticket led by James Morrissey contested other union offices, and Morrissey himself won one-third of the vote for secretary-treasurer. The opposition group charged that there had been election irregularities and illegal restrictions on candidates. In September Morrissey was badly beaten outside of the NMU headquarters. Secretary of Labor W. Willard Wirtz [*q.v.*] brought suit in December, asking for a new election under changed rules that allowed members other than those who had served at least one full term as a salaried union official to run for national office. On April 18, 1968 federal Judge Constance Baker Motley [*q.v.*] ruled that the election procedures had violated the Landrum-Griffin Act and ordered a new election, to be supervised by the Secretary of Labor. In this election Curran, running against three opponents, was reelected by a 17,395-4,891 vote, and his full slate of supporters was victorious.

Curran retired as NMU president in March 1973. He received over $300,000 in severance pay as well as a large pension. [See NIXON Volume]

[JBF]

CURTIS, CARL T(HOMAS)

b. March 15, 1905; Kearney County, Neb.
Republican Senator, Neb., 1955- .

Curtis was elected to the U.S. Senate from Nebraska in 1954 after having served in the lower house of Congress since 1939. Representing a largely rural and consistently conservative state, Curtis was one of the Senate's most frequent opponents of social welfare programs during the 1950s and early 1960s. [See EISENHOWER, KENNEDY Volumes]

Curtis opposed almost all of the Johnson Administration's Great Society programs, and according to *Congressional Quarterly*, he never voted against the Southern Democrat-Republican conservative coalition on more than 3% of the key roll-call votes during any year of President Johnson's tenure.

While opposing domestic spending measures, Curtis did not criticize large military expenditures. In 1964 he dissented from the majority of his colleagues on the Government Operations Committee's Permanent Investigations Subcommittee, who contended that the government had been paying Western Electric excessive profits for work on missile contracts farmed out to subcontractors. Three years later, during a debate on raising the national debt ceiling, Curtis asserted that domestic civilian spending, not the military budget, was responsible for increases in the debt.

Curtis supported the Administration's Southeast Asia policies and voted in favor of supplementary funds for conducting the Vietnam war. In 1968 he successfully proposed an amendment to a National Aeronautics and Space Administration (NASA) funding bill that barred NASA, with certain exceptions, from using research and development monies at colleges where anti-war demonstrators had blocked U.S. Armed Forces recruiters from campus.

Curtis was a consistent supporter of the Nixon Administration. Even after the President, in August 1974, revealed his participation in the Watergate cover-up, Curtis refused to call for his removal. In 1975 he became chairman of the Senate Republican Conference. [See NIXON Volume]

[MLL]

CURTIS, THOMAS B(RADFORD)

b. May 14, 1911; St. Louis, Mo.
Republican Representative, Mo., 1951-69.

Thomas Curtis grew up in Webster Groves, a suburb of St. Louis. After graduating from Dartmouth College and Washington University Law School, he joined his father's law firm in 1935. He made a number of unsuccessful bids for public office before his election to Congress in 1950 as a Republican from Missouri's twelfth district, which encompassed most of suburban St. Louis County. Joining the House Ways and Means Committee in 1953, Curtis gradually established himself as a leading Republican congressional spokesman on economic policy. During the Kennedy Administration Curtis's resolute fiscal conservatism led him frequently to oppose welfare, defense and revenue measures that he believed contributed to unbalanced budgets. [See EISENHOWER, KENNEDY Volumes]

As a member of the Joint Economic Committee and as second-ranking Republican on the Ways and Means Committee, Curtis was often at odds with the Johnson Administration on economic issues. He was a vigorous opponent of the Kennedy-Johnson medicare program, which financed medical care for the aged through the Social Security system. In January 1965 Curtis sponsored the American Medical Association's (AMA) alternative "eldercare" plan. The AMA plan would have made the program voluntary for those over 65; it would have been financed by individual contributions and matching state and federal grants and administered by the states. The Ways and Means Committee rejected the AMA-Curtis proposal in favor of the Kennedy-Johnson version.

Curtis often carried his opposition to federal spending beyond that of many conservatives, who usually backed compromise appropriations bills and considered military spending inviolate. In March 1964 he voted against salary increases for federal employes and in June opposed raises for federal judges and members of Congress. He also voted against the appropriations for foreign aid and the Departments of Labor and Health, Education and Welfare. In July 1966 Curtis was one of only two congressmen to oppose a $17 billion authorization for military procurement and research.

Refusing to support higher taxes in lieu of spending cuts, Curtis was against many of President Johnson's revenue-raising requests. He opposed the "interest equalization tax," a levy on foreign securities intended to cut the balance of payments deficit by making it more expensive for foreigners to borrow in the United States. Curtis said in July 1967 that the tax "merely serves to becloud the real problem—excessive government spending abroad." Curtis also fought Johnson's proposed travel tax in 1968. The tax, which was designed to discourage private spending abroad, passed the House in modified form in April but was rejected by the Senate Finance Committee in July.

Curtis was a foe of Johnson's 10% surcharge tax in 1967 and 1968. In October 1967 he voted with the majority of the Ways and Means Committee in refusing to enact the surcharge until the Administration made significant spending cuts. In June 1968, after budgetary reductions had been made to satisfy the Committee's majority, including the ranking Republican, Rep. John Byrnes (R, Wisc.) [*q.v.*], Curtis still opposed the tax increase on the ground that the cuts had not been specified.

Curtis was a moderate supporter of the Johnson Administration's civil rights program. He voted in favor of the Civil Rights Act of 1964 and the Voting Rights Act of 1965 but opposed open housing legislation in 1968. He played a major role in the 1965 revolt of younger House Republicans against the leadership of Rep. Charles Halleck (R, Ind.) [*q.v.*]. Curtis and the other "Young Turks" voted to replace Halleck as minority leader with Rep. Gerald Ford (R, Mich.) [*q.v.*]. Curtis also introduced the amendment in March 1967 to expel Rep. Adam Clayton Powell (D, N.Y.) [*q.v.*] from the House. The measure passed, 307-116.

Curtis retired from the House to run for the Senate in 1968, but he was defeated by Missouri Attorney General Thomas Eagleton. [See NIXON Volume]

[TO]

CUSHING, RICHARD J(AMES)

b. Aug. 24, 1895; Boston, Mass.
d. Nov. 2, 1970; Boston, Mass.
Roman Catholic Archbishop of Boston, 1944-70.

Cushing, the son of an Irish immigrant blacksmith, grew up in Boston. After studying at Boston College and St. Joseph's Seminary in Brighton, Mass., he was ordained a priest in 1921. The following year Cushing was assigned to the Boston office of the Society for the Propagation of the Faith, a fund-raising agency for Catholic missions throughout the world. He soon distinguished himself as a resourceful organizer, drawing in unprecedented contributions. In 1929 Cushing became director of the Society; 10 years later he was elevated to auxiliary bishop, assisting Boston Archbishop William Cardinal O'Connell. When O'Connell died in 1944 Cushing was chosen to succeed him as head of the Boston archdiocese, the third largest in the U.S. Pope John XXIII made Cushing a cardinal in 1958. In the tradition of "brick and mortar" prelates, Cushing directed a $250 million construction program that substantially increased the number of Catholic schools, hospitals and churches in the Boston area.

The Cardinal liked to be seen as a simple man with an expansive personality, artless humor and an understanding for the problems of the poor. He was important as a supporter of the liberal currents of Catholic thought aimed at "renewal" of the Church during the 1960s. He sought frequently to foster interfaith contacts and won a rare ovation at the Second Vatican Council in 1962 for his strong defense of religious freedom. Cushing also supported modernization of the Mass in 1964 and urged a greater role for the laity in Church affairs. As the controversy over birth control developed during the mid-1960s, he encouraged discussion and the presentation of procontraceptive views, but he refrained from taking an open stand against the Vatican position.

Cushing gained political recognition during the early 1960s as a confidant and strong supporter of President John F. Kennedy. A long-standing friend of the Kennedy family, he helped raise funds for Kennedy's presidential campaign, spoke at the inauguration in 1961 and officiated at the President's funeral in 1963. Cushing's association with the Kennedy family continued through the mid-1960s; he officiated at the funeral of Sen. Robert F. Kennedy (D, N.Y.) [*q.v.*] in 1968 and braved the displeasure of the Vatican as well as of many Catholic laymen by defending the marriage of Jacqueline Kennedy to the divorced Aristotle Onassis.

In political and social matters, as in secular affairs in general, Cushing frequently took impulsive and controversial positions. A strong anti-Communist, he endorsed the John Birch Society in 1960 but later withdrew his support when he learned that the Society was critical of Presidents Kennedy and Franklin D. Roosevelt. Cushing was a strong advocate of civil rights and urged Bostonians to accept school integration in 1963 and 1964. However, he opposed a black school boycott in 1964, and some observers criticized him for not doing enough to change the attitudes of white Catholics in ethnic areas. After supporting the Vietnam war during the mid-1960s, Cushing urged an end to American involvement in 1968.

Cushing's retirement in September 1970 marked the end of a 122-year period during which Irish Catholics had dominated the Church organization in Boston. His replacement as archbishop was the Spanish-speaking Humberto Medeiros, chosen because of the growing number of Latin American immigrants in Boston's Catholic community. On Nov. 2, 1970, shortly after his retirement, Cushing died of cancer.

[SLG]

DALEY, RICHARD J(OSEPH)

b. May 15, 1902; Chicago, Ill.
d. Dec. 20, 1976; Chicago, Ill.
Mayor, Chicago, Ill., 1955-76.

Richard Daley began his political career as a precinct captain in Bridgeport, an Irish working-class neighborhood on Chicago's South Side. He rose steadily in the Cook County Democratic organization. After holding state and city offices, he became chairman of the county Democratic Central Committee in 1953 and mayor of Chicago in 1955. As party chief and mayor, Daley filled the thousands of patronage jobs at his disposal with loyal Democrats. With solid ties to both business and labor and firm control over the large black vote, Daley built a political organization that made him the nation's most powerful mayor. His contribution to John F. Kennedy's 1960 electoral victory in Illinois first established him as a nationally known "king-maker." His reputation was enhanced in 1964 when President Johnson carried Illinois by 800,000 votes. [See EISENHOWER, KENNEDY Volumes]

Chicago's housing patterns were considered among the most segregated in the

North when Martin Luther King's [*q.v.*] Southern Christian Leadership Conference announced in January 1966 a campaign to make Chicago an "open city". According to Chicago civil rights activist Arthur Brazier, King chose to begin his campaign in that city because he thought "there was one man, one source of power, who you had to deal with."

On July 13 Daley and King met to discuss the newly formed Chicago Freedom Movement's demand for city action to end racial discrimination in housing. Two days later rioting broke out on the West Side, and the National Guard was called in to restore order. Daley charged on July 15 that some of Dr. King's staff members "came in here and have been talking for the past year of violence."

After a meeting later the same day with civil rights leaders, Daley and King jointly announced a "peace plan" that featured sprinklers on fire hydrants and portable swimming pools for the West Side. In August King led a series of open-housing marches into white ethnic neighborhoods in suburban Cicero and on Chicago's Southwest Side. Mayor Daley called a "summit conference" of the city's business, religious, political and civil rights leaders on Aug. 26 to come up with a plan to end housing and job discrimination in Chicago. The conference reached an agreement on Sept. 3, but the settlement lacked effective enforcement provisions. Three months later, when the immediate crisis had passed and Dr. King had left Chicago, Alderman Thomas Keane, who led the Daley majority in the City Council, announced, "There is no summit agreement."

After the assassination of Dr. King in Memphis on April 4, 1968, rioting occurred for three days on Chicago's West Side. Daley announced at an April 15 news conference that in the future Chicago policemen were "to shoot to kill" arsonists and "shoot to maim or cripple" looters. The statement aroused a storm of controversy. At a news conference the next day, New York Mayor John V. Lindsay [*q.v.*] stated, "We are not going to shoot children in New York City." The FBI "cautioned against over-responding to disturbances," and on April 17 Attorney General Ramsey Clark [*q.v.*] characterized Daley's instructions as "a very dangerous escalation of the problems we are so intent on solving." Daley revised his order on April 17. His press aide blamed the adverse response on the press, stating, "They should have printed what he meant, not what he said."

Daley again stood at the center of national attention during the 1968 Democratic National Convention, held in Chicago from Aug. 26 to 29. The security arrangements for the convention were described by Daley biographer Mike Royko as "the most massive in the history of American politics." Daley cooperated with state and federal agencies in the establishment of a 25,000-man security force. He also ordered construction of a barbwire and chainlink fence around the International Amphitheatre, the site of the Convention. Some delegates resented having to produce identification at a series of checkpoints inside the Amphitheatre, and during the Convention at least two delegates were removed from the floor for refusing to produce credentials.

Clashes between Chicago police and anti-war demonstraters began the night before the Convention officially opened when 500 city policemen cleared 1,000 demonstrators from Lincoln Park. In his welcoming address the next evening, Mayor Daley promised that "as long as I am mayor of this city, there's going to be law and order in Chicago." Although Daley urged that Sen. Edward Kennedy (D, Mass) [*q.v.*] declare his candidacy, the Mayor's intransigent opposition to the youthful supporters of Sen. Eugene McCarthy (D, Minn.) [*q.v.*] made him a symbol of the "old politics."

On Aug. 28 the most violent confrontation of the Convention took place outside the Convention hall. Inside the hall, Sen. Abraham Ribicoff (D, Conn) [*q.v.*] obtained the floor to nominate Sen. George McGovern (D, S.D.) [*q.v.*] and denounce the "Gestapo tactics in the streets of Chicago." Ribicoff was jeered by the Daley-dominated Illinois delegation. In the *New York Times* James Reston wrote that "by the end of the night, Daley had become a symbol in the Convention of the opposition within the party to the turbulent conditions of American life."

In the immediate aftermath of the Convention, the established Democratic leadership with whom Daley was identified did little to gain the allegiance of the supporters of Sen. McCarthy or the late Sen. Robert Kennedy (D, N.Y.) [*q.v.*]. At an Aug. 29 news conference, Daley described the demonstrators as "terrorists" who had come to "assault, harass and taunt the police into reacting before the television cameras." Vice President Humphrey declared on Aug. 31 that it was time to "quit pretending that Mayor Daley did anything that was wrong." Sen. McCarthy refused to endorse Humphrey after the Convention and on Oct. 8 demanded reform of the Party to prevent "another Chicago" as a condition of his endorsement. On election day Daley failed to deliver the Illinois electoral vote to Humphrey, but his organization nevertheless survived the controversy. Daley was reelected mayor in 1971 with over 70% of the vote. [See NIXON Volume]

[DKR]

For further information:
Lewis Chester, et al., *An American Melodrama* (New York, 1969).
Mike Royko, *Boss* (New York, 1971).

DAWSON, WILLIAM L(EVI)

b. April 26, 1886; Albany, Ga.
d. Nov. 9, 1970; Chicago, Ill.
Democratic Representative, Ill., 1943-70; Chairman, Government Operations Committee, 1949-53; 1955-70.

Dawson, an attorney and Republican alderman from Chicago's South Side, followed the path taken by many of his black constituents and switched parties in 1939. He was first elected to Congress in 1942 as a Democrat. Dawson was then the only black congressman; in 1949 he became the first black to head a regular standing committee of Congress.

Representing the largest black ghetto in the country, Dawson offered his constituents low-paying patronage jobs and help with their housing, welfare and legal problems. Voters responded with overwhelming support for Dawson and his handpicked candidates. According to Mike Royko of the *Chicago Daily News*, Dawson could "deliver more Democratic votes than any one politician in Chicago" by the mid-1950s. He used his influence to secure the 1955 Democratic mayoral nomination for Richard J. Daley [*q.v.*], and the powerful Dawson machine was instrumental in Daley's subsequent reelection victories. [See EISENHOWER, KENNEDY Volumes]

As head of the Committee on Government Operations, Dawson was responsible for investigating Billie Sol Estes the Texas promoter who in 1962 was convicted of fraud in connection with Department of Agriculture grain storage and cotton allotment programs. Estes's name had been prominently linked with Vice President Lyndon B. Johnson. On Oct. 12, 1964 Dawson issued a Committee report that stated, "There is no evidence that the then Vice President participated in any way in the relationships between Billie Sol Estes and the federal government or its agencies other than routinely referring to the Department of Agriculture correspondence including complaints in which Estes was involved." Observers noted that the report was issued while Congress was not in session and only a few weeks before the presidential election. Dawson sponsored no major legislation during Johnson's years as president but generally supported Administration policies.

During his first years in Congress, Dawson had fought for a permanent committee to enforce the Fair Employment Practices Act, and he also worked to outlaw the poll tax and segregation in the armed forces. During the 1950s, however, he became increasingly withdrawn from civil rights activity. In February 1964 Dawson, along with Mayor Daley and the local chapter of the NAACP (a branch allegedly dominated by Dawson workers), denounced the successful boycott that had been organized by the Congress of Racial Equality and the Student Nonviolent Coordinating Committee to protest de facto segregation in Chicago's schools. In 1966 Dawson lent no support when Rev. Martin Luther King [*q.v.*] and the Southern Christian Leadership Conference organized marches in white neighborhoods to protest Chicago's segregated housing pattern.

Angered by Dawson's apparent indifference to the civil rights movement, young blacks challenged him during each Democratic primary in the mid-1960s. A.A. (Sammy) Rayner, an undertaker and civil rights activist, ran against Dawson in 1964 but was badly defeated. A young social worker, Fred Hubbard, who tried two years later, was shot and wounded during his campaign and had no success at the polls. Rayner tried in 1968 but was again defeated. Dawson decided not to seek reelection in 1970 and died in November of that year at the age of 84. However, his powerful machine remained intact. Ralph Metcalfe, the Congressman's designated successor, was easily elected to the Dawson seat.

[JLW]

For further information:
Chuck Stone, *Black Political Power in America* (New York, 1968).

DELLINGER, DAVID

b. Aug. 12, 1915; Wakefield, Mass.
Pacifist; Editor, *Liberation*.

In the anti-war movement of the 1960s, David Dellinger represented an older generation of radical pacifists—those who had been involved in labor and community organizing in the 1930s, who had been conscientious objectors during World War II and who had organized acts of civil disobedience and moral witness on behalf of peace and civil rights throughout the 1940s and 1950s.

Dellinger graduated from Yale in 1936 and enrolled in Union Theological Seminary in 1939. In 1940, along with seven fellow students who had been living in voluntary poverty in Harlem and Newark, he refused to register for the draft. Although registration would have exempted him from any further military obligation under the automatic exemption granted clergymen, Dellinger felt the need for a dramatic act. He was sent to federal prison in Danbury, Conn., for a year. In 1943 he was again arrested for Selective Service violations and sentenced to two years in the penitentiary at Lewisburg, Pa.

After the war Dellinger organized a cooperative community, and in 1948 he joined with A. J. Muste [*q.v.*], Dwight MacDonald [*q.v.*] and Bayard Rustin [*q.v.*] in organizing the Peacemakers, a group that called for resistance to peacetime conscription by means of civil disobedience and tax refusal. In 1956 Dellinger, Muste and Rustin founded *Liberation* magazine, which became a forum for the rising agitation against nuclear arms and racial discrimination.

During the early stages of the Vietnam conflict, Dellinger favored an immediate withdrawal rather than negotiations. He also opposed the moratorium on militant action called by peace and civil rights leaders in 1964 to ensure a Democratic victory in the presidential election. When President Johnson ordered the bombing of North Vietnam, Dellinger helped organize a coalition of peace groups, calling itself the Assembly of Unrepresented People, that sponsored a series of acts of civil disobedience in Washington in August 1965. Despite opposition to the demonstration from the NAACP and the Urban League and lukewarm support from Students for a Democratic Society, 356 people forced the police to arrest them on the Capitol mall. Coinciding with the Vietnam Day Committee's attempt to block troop trains in the San Francisco Bay area, the arrests marked the first large-scale application of civil disobedience tactics to the anti-war movement.

In November 1966 Dellinger served as cochairman of the Spring Mobilization to End the War in Vietnam. The "Mobe" chose April 15, 1967 for demonstrations in New York and San Francisco. Over the next five months it organized churches, women's groups, universities, political clubs and peace groups in an attempt to show that active opposition to the war was not limited to a handful of radicals but included vast numbers of Americans. The marches in April were the largest demonstrations against government policy in American history up to that time.

Dellinger was involved in the demonstrations in Chicago during the Democratic Party's National Convention in August 1968. The violence of these events formed the basis for a five-month court trial in 1969, at which Dellinger and seven others were charged by the federal government with conspiracy to riot.

[TLH]

For further information:
David Dellinger, *Revolutionary Nonviolence* (New York, 1970).
Thomas Powers, *The War at Home* (New York, 1973).

DeLOACH, DEKE (CARTHA) (DEKLE)

b. July 20, 1920; Claxton, Ga.
Assistant to the Director, FBI, December 1965-June 1970.

DeLoach was born and raised in Claxton, Ga., a small town west of Savannah. His family was very poor, but he managed to earn enough money to attend Stetson University. After graduating in 1942 he joined the FBI and worked as an agent in Norfolk, Toledo and Akron, where he carried out investigations of Communist Party members. Disliking the work he joined the Navy in 1944. After the war De Loach returned to the Bureau and was assigned to the home office in Washington, D.C. There he carried out routine security checks of potential employes on atomic energy projects. He subsequently coordinated FBI activities with the work of the Central Intelligence Agency and the Office of Naval Intelligence.

During the early 1950s DeLoach made a favorable impression on J. Edgar Hoover, and as a result he made rapid progress within the Bureau. In 1959 he was named assistant director for the crime records division, a post which despite its title, entailed responsibility for managing the Bureau's public and congressional relations. DeLoach was skilled at political in-fighting, had an ingratiating personality and proved adept at muting congressional criticism of the Bureau and its Director. He also had access to FBI files containing a vast amount of personal information on individual congressmen. To advance the Bureau's reputation DeLoach often supplied news stories and information to friendly columnists and reporters.

In December 1965 DeLoach was promoted to the post of assistant to the director and assumed responsibility for all the Bureau's investigative activities. In the meantime he had developed a close relationship with President Johnson. Indeed, on a variety of matters Johnson preferred to communicate with DeLoach rather than Hoover, and this strained DeLoach's relations with the Director. DeLoach was the only member of the Bureau to have a direct line to the White House in his home.

DeLoach undertook a number of special assignments for the President. In the summer of 1964 he headed a special FBI squad that ostensibly had been organized to aid the Secret Service in protecting the President at the Democratic National Convention in Atlantic City, N.J. However, according to a 1976 report by the Senate Select Committee on Intelligence Activities, the FBI agents, using electronic surveillance, "bugged" the hotel room of Rev. Martin Luther King [*q.v.*] and gathered a substantial amount of purely political information having little to do with security matters. This data was turned over to the President's aide, Walter Jenkins [*q.v.*].

DeLoach subsequently supervised an investigation of Jenkins who, in the fall of 1964, had been involved in a homosexual incident in the basement of a Washington YMCA. Johnson ordered the investigation in the belief that Jenkins had been the victim of a Republican plot. The FBI could find no such evidence, and Jenkins was forced to resign.

By 1966 President Johnson was becoming increasingly sensitive to criticism of his Vietnam war policy. In March of that year he ordered DeLoach to undertake an investigation of congressmen whose criticism of the Vietnam policy, Johnson thought, had been motivated by contacts with foreign agents. In late October 1968 Johnson ordered DeLoach to begin investigating the relationship of Anna Chenault, a Chinese-born Republican socialite, and the Republican vice presidential nominee, Spiro Agnew [*q.v.*]. The President believed that Agnew, working through Chenault, had informed the South Vietnamese government that a Republican administration would be more receptive to its interests. He also believed that the Republicans had encouraged the South Vietnamese to sabotage the Paris peace talks. The FBI was unable to document Johnson's charges despite an investigation of Agnew's phone calls and electronic surveillance of the Chenault home.

Shortly after President Nixon assumed office, DeLoach's private line to the White House was removed. He nonetheless maintained relatively cordial relations with the new administration. Attorney General John Mitchell preferred to deal with DeLoach rather than Hoover on a variety of Justice Department matters.

DeLoach had hoped to succeed Hoover as FBI director. However, when it became apparent that the Director was unwilling to retire, DeLoach accepted a lucrative offer to become an executive with Pepsico, Inc. He left the Bureau in June 1970.

[JLW]

For further information:

Sanford J. Ungar, *FBI* (Boston, 1975).

U.S. Senate, Select Committee on Intelligence Activities, *Federal Bureau of Investigation* (Washington, D.C., 1976).

DePUGH, (WILLIAM) ROBERT B(OLIVAR)

b. April 15, 1923; Independence, Mo.
National Coordinator, the Minutemen.

In 1960 DePugh moved his Biolab Corporation, a producer of veterinary medicines, from Independence to Norborne, Mo. At about this time he organized the Minutemen, whose purpose was to train Americans to fight a guerrilla war in the event of a Communist takeover by either invasion or internal subversion, both of which were regarded as imminent possibilities by the group.

Its existence first came to the attention of the general public in October 1961, when an associate of DePugh's was arrested in Shiloh, Ill., for illegal weapons possession. A *New York Times* survey one month later concluded that the organization was a very loose federation of small units with a total membership of only several hundred.

The Minutemen came to light again during the presidential campaign of 1964. The group backed the candidacy of Sen. Barry M. Goldwater (R, Ariz.) [*q.v.*] because, according to DePugh, President Lyndon B. Johnson was an "opportunist who would sell the United States out to the Communists or anyone else who would pay his price." After Goldwater's defeat DePugh asserted that Communism could no longer be stopped by political means and that only the Minutemen's secret "underground army" could save liberty. In July 1966 he organized the Patriotic Party, but he conceived of it as "the political arm of a complete patriotic resistance movement."

During the next two years persons identifying themselves as Minutemen were arrested in New York, Connecticut and other places on charges of conspiring and threatening to commit acts of violence against liberal and radical organizations and individuals. According to J. Harry Jones, Jr., author of *The Minutemen*, the organization's membership during this period was probably about a thousand or possibly somewhat more.

DePugh's role in local Minutemen activities was difficult to ascertain because of the organization's decentralized structure and DePugh's contradictory statements, but he encouraged a climate of violence. For example, each issue of *On Target*, the Minutemen's newsletter which he edited, announced under its masthead, "We guarantee that all law suits filed against this newsletter will be settled out of court."

In November 1966 DePugh was convicted for violations of the federal firearms act and the following February pleaded *nolo contendere* to another charge of violating that law. While appealing his first conviction DePugh was indicted in February 1968 for conspiring to rob banks in Seattle. Shortly before this indictment was returned, he went into hiding.

DePugh was captured by the FBI in

New Mexico in July 1969 and was jailed several days later. In February 1973 he was paroled after having served three-and-a-half years of an 11-year jail term. The Minutemen organization had virtually dissolved during his period of incarceration. DePugh did not attempt to revive the group after his release from jail. Instead, he became involved with other, smaller-scale extreme right-wing political activities.

[MLL]

For further information:
J. Harry Jones, Jr., *The Minutemen* (New York, 1968).

DIGGS, CHARLES C(OLE), JR.
b. Dec. 2, 1922; Detroit, Mich.
Democratic Representative, Mich., 1955- .

Charles C. Diggs, Jr., the first black congressman from Michigan, was the son of a wealthy Detroit undertaker who also served for many years in the Michigan state Senate. His father's popularity in the black community boosted Diggs's own political career.

Diggs attended the University of Michigan and Fiske University before entering the Army Air Force in World War II. After the war he enrolled in the Wayne University Mortuary School from which he received a mortuary license in 1946. Diggs then entered the family business—one of the state's largest black funeral establishments. He also served as a disk jockey and news commentator on the family's weekly radio show broadcast over a black station. During the 1940s the elder Diggs was sentenced to a year in prison for accepting graft; this did little to hurt his popularity with ghetto voters, who returned him to the state Senate; that body, however, refused to seat him. His son, seeking to vindicate the family name, ran for his father's seat in 1950 and won an overwhelming victory. Four years later he was elected to Congress.

Diggs represented a poor, black district in downtown Detroit. In the 1960s this area, cut up by superhighways and urban renewal projects, lost 19% of its population. The 1967 riots also contributed to the population decline, hastening the exodus of middle class blacks from the district. Diggs's success in winning reelection there depended less on his voting record (which reflected a high rate of absenteeism) than on the services he offered his constituents. His office expedited the delivery of social security checks, speeded the processing of small business administration loans and performed numerous minor legal services for voters. Diggs customarily spent half his time in Detroit and was a familiar figure at black social functions and funerals.

As a member of the House District of Columbia Committee, Diggs consistently advocated home rule for Washington. His view was opposed to that of Rep. John C. McMillan (D, S.C.) [*q.v.*], the domineering Committee chairman. The two men rarely spoke, and Diggs had almost no influence over legislation. In 1972 Diggs became Committee chairman, and a home rule bill was subsequently reported out and became law.

Diggs was not conspicuous in the civil rights movement. Nevertheless, as a senior member of Congress from a major industrial state, his presence commanded the respect of black leaders. In July 1967 Diggs, Rep. Adam Clayton Powell, Jr. (D, N.Y.) [*q.v.*] and Floyd McKissick [*q.v.*], national director of the Congress of Racial Equality, were named honorary co-chairmen of the National Conference on Black Power. The meeting, held in Newark, N.J., in the aftermath of that city's riots, brought together representatives from 197 black organizations who issued a plea for greater black independence in economic, social and political affairs.

As a member of the House Foreign Relations Committee, Diggs became an outspoken opponent of U.S. involvement in Vietnam. In April 1965 he denounced American use of gas warfare in Vietnam and in January 1966 was one of seven House Democrats who sponsored a conference on Vietnam. The meeting ended in a call for the continuation of the pause in U.S. bombing of North Vietnam and a plea for negotiations between the South Vietnamese government and the National Liberation Front.

During the Nixon years Diggs, the senior black member of Congress, was elected chairman of the congressional Black Caucus, a group that sought to develop a cohesive legislative policy for the advancement of black Americans. [See NIXON Volume]

[JLW]

DILLON, C(LARENCE) DOUGLAS

b. Aug. 21, 1909; Geneva, Switzerland. Secretary of the Treasury, January 1961-March 1965.

C. Douglas Dillon was the son of a Wall Street banker who made a fortune building Dillon, Read & Company into one of the country's largest investment firms. Dillon attended Groton and Harvard. In 1931 his father bought him a seat on the New York Stock Exchange for $185,000. After serving an apprenticeship with some smaller investment houses, he joined Dillon, Read as a vice president in 1938. He followed the company's president, James Forrestal, into the Navy Department in 1940 and saw action in the Pacific toward the end of the war.

As chairman of the board of Dillon, Read after the war, Dillon supervised the firm's far-flung domestic and foreign holdings and doubled its investment portfolio in six years. He was an active Republican, working with John Foster Dulles in the 1948 presidential campaign of Gov. Thomas E. Dewey and initiating a "draft Eisenhower" movement in New Jersey in 1951. In 1953 Eisenhower appointed Dillon ambassador to France. He remained there until 1957, when Dulles recalled him to Washington to serve as undersecretary of state for economic affairs. Dillon contributed heavily to the Republican presidential candidate, Vice President Richard M. Nixon [*q.v.*], in 1960 and was considered a natural appointment to a Nixon cabinet. [See EISENHOWER Volume]

President Kennedy's selection of Dillon as Secretary of the Treasury was a surprise to many and an indication of Kennedy's strong desire to have a "sound-money" man in the nation's top economic post. Dillon remained the most influential member of Kennedy's economic policymaking team throughout the Administration. His success in persuading the President to give priority status to the balance-of-payments deficit was crucial in shaping Kennedy's moderate fiscal course, which ruled out more activist solutions to the economy's problems. As Treasury Secretary, Dillon devoted himself to alleviating the intractable payments deficit, to devising and promoting the Kennedy tax program and to spearheading the Treasury's opposition to proposals for international monetary reform and lower interest rates emanating from the Council of Economic Advisers. [See KENNEDY Volume]

After two years of opposition Dillon became persuaded in late 1962 of the need for a massive tax cut to stimulate the economy. The House passed an $11 billion tax reduction bill in September 1963, but the Senate had not acted on the measure by the time of Kennedy's assassination in November. Dillon was instrumental in convincing President Johnson to push the tax cut in the Senate and to accompany it with significant spending cuts in order to forestall inflation and conciliate Senate conservatives. As in the Kennedy Administration he exerted a conservative pull on economic policy. The Senate passed the tax bill in February 1964.

In August 1965 Dillon declared that further tax reductions were desirable, stating that "high priority should be given to a thorough overhaul of the hodgepodge of excise taxes remaining from World War II days." "Many of these taxes," Dillon said, "no longer serve their purpose. Instead, they increase business costs, weigh unevenly on consumers and are often an unnecessary nuisance to taxpayers and government alike."

In March 1964 Dillon testified against a plan of Rep. Wright Patman (D, Tex.) [*q.v.*], chairman of the House Banking and Currency Committee, to reform the Federal Reserve System. He particularly opposed a provision placing the Secretary of the Treasury at the head of a new Federal Reserve Board. "Experience over many years and in many countries," Dillon said, "has taught us the wisdom of shielding those who make decisions on monetary policy from day-to-day pressures." He also spoke against a proposal permiting interest to be paid on checking accounts.

Because of his social background Dillon never achieved the rapport with President Johnson that he had with President Kennedy. In comparing the work of Dillon and his successor Henry Fowler [*q.v.*] on the tax cut in 1963 and 1964, Johnson remarked, "He [Fowler] was there night after night, while Doug Dillon was going to tea parties or putting on his white tie and tails."

Dillon resigned in March 1965 to return to private finance. He became president of the U.S. & Foreign Securities Corporation in February 1967. Dillon was a member of the Senior Advisory Group on Vietnam, a group of prestigious Establishment figures that advised Johnson in March 1968 to de-escalate the Vietnam war. In the same month, as head of the Advisory Committee to the U.S. Treasury on International Monetary Affairs, he urged a tax increase, warning that failure to do so would "endanger worldwide confidence in the dollar" and "risk a serious upheaval in the international monetary system." Arguing against federal spending cuts as a substitute for a tax increase, he declared, "There is no feasible substitute for tax action to curtail the inflationary excesses in domestic demand that are now spilling over into imports."

[TO]

DIRKSEN, EVERETT McKINLEY

b. Jan. 4, 1895; Pekin, Ill.
d. Sept. 7, 1969; Washington, D.C.
Republican Senator, Ill., 1951-69;
Senate Minority Leader, 1959-69.

Following service in the Army artillery during World War I, Dirksen returned to his hometown of Pekin, Ill., to practice law. He won the first of his eight terms as a House Republican in 1932, and in 1950 he moved up to the Senate by defeating Majority Leader Scott Lucas (D, Ill.). In the Senate Dirksen identified himself with the GOP's conservative Old Guard. He defended Sen. Joseph R. McCarthy (R, Wisc.) and the charges the Wisconsin Senator made concerning the presence of Communists in the federal government. After McCarthy's decline in popularity, Dirksen moved toward the more moderate Republicanism of President Dwight D. Eisenhower [*q.v.*] and won the President's endorsement in his successful campaign for reelection in 1956.

Sponsored by the Party's conservative leadership, Dirksen became Senate minority whip in January 1957 and two years later won the GOP Senate leadership post. Although the Democrats had won overwhelming majorities in both houses as a result of the 1958 elections, Dirksen frustrated the ambitious legislative program of Senate Majority Leader Lyndon B. Johnson (D, TEX.). An artful persuader, he established an unusual degree of unity among his Republican colleagues. Dirksen willingly gave up his own prestigious committee assignments to younger and more liberal members. [See TRUMAN, EISENHOWER Volumes]

In the early 1960s President Kennedy needed Senate Republican support in order to overcome the opposition to his legislative program among conservative Southern Democrats. Although the minority leader endorsed little of the President's New Frontier legislation, he demonstrated a consistent loyalty to the Administration on major foreign policy questions. Dirksen provided the necessary Republican votes for the ratification of the nuclear test ban treaty in September 1963. [See KENNEDY Volume]

Dirksen's influence over Senate Republicans proved crucial to the enactment of the 1964 Civil Rights Act. Throughout 1963 Dirksen had opposed President Kennedy's request for a federal guarantee to blacks of the right to use public accommodations. However, congressional liberals, spurred on by the increasingly active civil rights movements in 1963 and 1964, insisted upon a strong public accommodations section in the Kennedy-Johnson bill. The House passed a version of the Administration's bill in February 1964 that not only included the accommodations provision but also contained a strict "fair employment" section as well. Dirksen disapproved of both parts of the House measure.

Senate liberals needed Dirksen to persuade Republican members to end the Southern Democrats' filibuster against the bill by invoking cloture and forcing a vote. In early May 1964 Dirksen agreed to negotiate with Senate majority whip Hubert H. Humphrey (D, Minn.) [*q.v.*] and Attorney General Robert F. Kennedy [*q.v.*] on the accommodations and fair-employment sections. The three men labored over the bill, and their revised version of the measure allowed the federal government to intervene only where a "pattern" of discrimination existed; otherwise, anti-discrimination suits would be left to individuals. Local agencies, where in operation, would be given time to work out the problems.

Arguing for an "idea whose time has come," Dirksen persuaded 27 GOP Senators, including many traditional opponents of cloture, to vote to cut off debate on June 10, 1964. Nine days later the Senate passed the compromise bill by a vote of 73 to 27, with only 6 Republicans in opposition. Dirksen received nationwide praise for his role in the enactment of the civil rights law. Senate Majority Leader Mike Mansfield (D, Mont.) [*q.v.*] declared on June 19 that passage of the measure represented Dirksen's "finest hour."

The Republican leader's triumph, however, lacked the endorsement of Sen. Barry M. Goldwater (R, Ariz.) [*q.v.*], the front-runner for the 1964 Republican presidential nomination. Dirksen had pleaded with Goldwater, a personal friend, to support the civil rights bill. After Goldwater failed to do so, he condemned the Arizona Republican's opposition to the measure in a Senate speech June 19. Goldwater's stand outraged Republican leaders with a strong commitment to civil rights and in part inspired Pennsylvania Gov. William W. Scranton's [*q.v.*] last-ditch fight against Goldwater for the nomination.

Dirksen dismissed Scranton's personal plea for support on June 22 and resolved, with other Midwestern GOP leaders, that no one could now stop Goldwater. Dirksen's decision, in agreement with the majority of the Illinois delegation to the Republican National Convention, seriously weakened any lingering effort by Party moderates to halt the Goldwater bandwagon. Dirksen agreed to nominate his colleague before the Convention on July 15, and the Illinois delegation cast 56 of its 58 votes for Goldwater.

In the 1965 legislative session Johnson skillfully took advantage of his large congressional majorities to enact a wide range of Great Society legislation, most of which Dirksen unsuccessfully fought with great rhetorical vigor. Senate liberals still sought his assistance, and he worked for the passage of the Administration's 1965 Voting Rights Act. Dirksen engineered one of the President's few legislative defeats in the 1965 session by leading a filibuster in October against the repeal of Section 14(b), the "open shop" provision, of the Taft-Hartley Labor Relations Law. Johnson frequently consulted with Dirksen, however, continuing a friendly relationship that dated back to their days as rival Senate leaders. The liberal Americans for Democratic Action accused the Administration in November 1965 of being "soft" on Dirksen, whom it claimed exercised "exorbitant influence" for a leader of only 32 Senators.

Dirksen suffered two important legislative defeats in the mid-1960s. In September 1966 a Dirksen amendment to overrule the Supreme Court's recent decision against prayer in the public schools failed in the Senate for want of a two-thirds majority. Senate liberals also frustrated Dirksen's efforts in 1964, 1965 and 1966 to reverse the Court's decisions requiring state legislative apportionment on a basis of population only. After repeated defests in Congress Dirksen and Sen. Roman Hruska (R, Neb.) [*q.v.*] encouraged the formation of a "Committee for Government of the People." The Committee urged state legislatures to petition Congress to call a constitutional convention to nullify the Court's reapportionment ruling. By the spring of 1967, 32 state legislatures had drawn up petitions, but the anti-reapportionment group failed to win the approval of three-fourths of the state assemblies—the number required to force Congress to act.

Dirksen projected a colorful if conservative image for the Republican congressional leadership. He gained national news coverage for the GOP by holding weekly press conferences with House Minority Leader Gerald R. Ford (R, Mich.) [*q.v.*]. Capitalizing on his well-known grandiloquence, the Minority Leader became the first Senator to make a commercial record album in December 1966. A collection of patriotic readings, *The Gallant Men* proved popular with both radio disc jockeys and the general public and won the Senator a "Grammy" award from the record industry in February 1968.

Although a Republican partisan, Dirksen steadfastly defended Johnson's foreign policy. He denied charges by Republican vice presidential candidate William E. Miller [*q.v.*] in September 1964 that the United States had agreed not to invade Cuba following the 1962 missile crisis. When, in August 1964, President Johnson asked for congressional sanction for military action against the North Vietnamese following the Gulf of Tonkin incident, Dirksen unsuccessfully sought to waive all committee testimony and to move instead to an immediate vote in favor of the White House resolution. Dirksen also gave an unqualified endorsement to the Administration's military intervention in the Dominican Republic in April 1965.

Dirksen vehemently fought efforts by Ford and other Republican leaders to charge the Administration with having mismanaged the war. When Ford criticized Johnson's trip to the Manila Conference in the fall of 1966 as "a political gimmick," Dirksen angrily decried the House leader's comments. "You don't denounce the commander-in-chief before the whole, wide world," he remarked in October. Indeed, by late 1966 Johnson received greater support on Vietnam from Dirksen than from Majority Leader Mansfield.

Following the 1966 elections Dirksen found his control over his ranks increasingly tenuous. Younger and more liberal colleagues, many of whom wanted to make the war an issue in the 1968 election, joined the Republican Senate ranks. Although no one directly challenged Dirksen for his leadership post, Sen. Thruston B. Morton (R, Ky.) [*q.v.*] formed an unofficial coalition of moderate, anti-war Republicans that stood opposed to Dirksen's wholehearted endorsement of Johnson's foreign policy. Although Dirksen obtained sufficient votes to pass a compromise open housing bill in 1968, his prestige suffered when he supported Johnson's nomination of Abe Fortas [*q.v.*] as Chief Justice in June 1968. Freshman Sen. Robert P. Griffin (R, Mich.) [*q.v.*] led an intra-Party revolt which forced the minority leader to withdraw his endorsement in late September, effectively destroying Fortas's chances of confirmation.

Dirksen chaired the Party Platform Committee at the Republican National Convention in August 1968. Accepting the Illinois designation as favorite son candidate for the presidential nomination, Dirksen deliberately forestalled the candidacy of Sen. Charles H. Percy (R, Ill.) [*q.v.*], who had expected to receive the delegation's endorsement. Dirksen withdrew his name on the eve of the convention and voted for the winning candidate, former Vice President Richard M. Nixon [*q.v.*].

Dirksen encountered greater difficulty than expected in his 1968 reelection, winning only 53% of the vote against an unknown and under-financed opponent. He was unanimously reelected minority leader in January 1969, but Dirksen played a declining role in the Party's national leadership over the last months of his life. [See NIXON Volume]

[JLB]

For further information:
Neil MacNeil, *Dirksen: Portrait of a Public Man* (Cleveland and New York, 1970).

DIXON, PAUL RAND(ALL)

b. Sept. 29, 1913; Nashville, Tenn.
Chairman, Federal Trade Commission
February 1961-December 1969.

Paul Rand Dixon attended Vanderbilt University and received his law degree from the University of Florida in 1938. He immediately joined the staff of the Federal Trade Commission (FTC) as a trial attorney. Except for wartime naval service Dixon remained with the Commission until 1957, when he was named chief counsel and staff director of Sen. Estes Kefauver's (D, Tenn.) Antitrust and Antimonopoly Subcomittee. Under Kefauver and Dixon the subcommittee carried out a series of highly publicized investigations of big business abuses, most notably price-fixing by drug companies and identical bidding by manufacturers of heavy electrical equipment. The Justice Department followed up the latter study, obtaining convictions against 45 of the colluding executives, seven of whom received jail terms in the most spectacular business scandal of the decade. Sponsored by Kefauver, Dixon was appointed chairman of the FTC by President Kennedy in 1961.

In the Clayton Act of 1914, Congress had endowed the FTC with the general responsibility of policing the market economy. The Commission was empowered to put a stop to "unfair trade practices" by means of "cease-and-desist" orders. The Celler-Kefauver Act of 1950 authorized it to prevent mergers whose effects might "substantially lessen competition." Over the years a series of studies had accused the FTC of investigative passivity, lax enforcement and preoccupation with trivial cases. Taking office with the image of a crusading trustbuster, Dixon promised to overcome the FTC's "inertia" and increase its vigilance against unfair trade practices. [See KENNEDY Volume]

During the Kennedy years Dixon had taken the FTC beyond the defense of small business and into the area of consumer protection, especially in his attack on misleading advertising. In line with Lyndon Johnson's suggestion soon after he became President that regulatory agencies concentrate on "helping, not harassing" businessmen, Dixon began to temper his approach. In a speech to the Advertising Federation of America in February 1965, he blamed false advertising on a "few bad apples" within the industry. He conceded that the FTC "has, on occasion, been overly meticulous, that it has fought wars where wars could have been better settled by persuasion." He announced that the FTC was no longer "trying to accumulate scalps" and was returning to what Woodrow Wilson intended it to be, "a clearinghouse for the facts by which both the public mind and the managers of great business undertakings shall be guided." In August 1966 Dixon vehemently opposed the creation of a cabinet-level department of consumer affairs. To improve consumer protection he recommended increasing the FTC budget.

Following the Surgeon General's 1964 report linking cigarette smoking to cancer and other diseases, Dixon fought for restrictions on cigarette advertising and health warnings on cigarette packages. In July 1965 Congress passed the Federal Cigarette Labeling and Advertising Act, which superceded the FTC's more stringent regulations. The law required all cigarette packages to contain the warning: "Caution: Cigarette Smoking May be Hazardous to Your Health." In June 1967 the FTC submitted a report to Congress urging tighter restriction of cigarette advertising.

Congress in October 1966 passed a "truth-in-packaging" bill, which Dixon had favored since 1961. The law required manufacturers to provide consumers with specific information about a package's contents in order to guard against deceptive packaging and labeling practices. It directed the FTC and the Secretary of Health, Education and Welfare to issue regulations for that purpose.

Dixon maintained that corporate concentration was the greatest threat to free enterprise in the United States. "I'd be scared to death if we had only 20 large companies in the country," he told *Forbes* in July 1966. "We have 200 now, and our job is to see that they don't eat each other up." Nevertheless, the FTC under Dixon gradually devoted a decreasing portion of its budget to anti-merger activity. In 1959 the Commission spent approximately $1 million, or 16.9% of its budget, in this area; in 1968 it spent $1.35 million, or 8.8%. Its Bureau of Textiles and Furs, by comparison, received 9.3% of the budget in 1959 and 10.5% in 1968. The period 1960-69 saw the greatest corporate merger wave in American history. In 1960-66 there were 1,664 mergers annually; by 1967-69 an average of over 3,600 mergers took place each year, 80% of which involved conglomerates. During Dixon's chairmanship, from 1961 through 1969, the FTC issued 56 complaints against mergers.

In January 1969 a team of law students, organized by consumer advocate Ralph Nader [*q.v.*], published a 185-page study of the FTC. Harshly critical of the Commission and Dixon, it charged that "alcoholism, spectacular lassitude and office absenteeism [and] incompetence by the most modest standards" were "rampant" at high levels of the FTC staff. The team accused the Commission of inadequate protection of the consumer, "collusion with business interests," secrecy and partisan politics in the hiring of staff.

The study criticized a decline in FTC enforcement activity and the increasing emphasis by the FTC on "voluntary" compliance on the part of industry. It maintained that the Commission's powerful enforcement tools, such as its right to seek preliminary injunctions and criminal penalties, were "under-used and ill-applied." The investigators, whose forays into the Commission's headquarters during the summer of 1968 had earned them the nickname of "Nader's Raiders," blamed most of the FTC's shortcomings on Dixon and called for his resignation.

Dixon issued an eight-page rebuttal which characterized the study as "a hysterical, anti-business diatribe and a scurrilous, untruthful attack on the career personnel of the Commission." He defended the enforcement policies of the FTC as "equitable and reasonable" and denied that his hiring policy favored Democrats.

In May 1969, at President Nixon's request, an American Bar Association (ABA) panel undertook a study of the FTC. The 16-member panel, headed by Philadelphia lawyer Miles Kirkpatrick, issued a report in September whose conclusions largely paralleled those of the Nader team. The ABA report said that the effectiveness of the FTC was sapped by ineffective and divided leadership, a staff ridden by "incompetence," misallocation of funds to "trivial matters" and a failure to establish goals and priorities. The panel said its study had shown that although the FTC had been armed with a rising budget and increased staff, "both the volume and force of FTC law enforcement have declined during this decade."

President Nixon replaced Dixon as FTC chairman with Casper Weinberger, who took office in January 1970. Dixon continued to serve as an FTC commissioner throughout the Nixon Administration. Mark Silbergeld, an FTC critic, was quoted in the *Washington Monthly* in October 1972 as saying that Dixon "has been about as good [an FTC commissioner] as any consumer would wish since he left the chairmanship."

[TO]

For further information:

American Bar Association, *Report of the ABA Commission to Study the Federal Trade Commission* (New York, 1969).

E. Cox, R. Fellmeth and J. Schultz, *The Nader Report on the Federal Trade Commission* (New York, 1969).

DOAR, JOHN M(ICHAEL)

b. Dec. 3, 1921; Minneapolis, Minn.
U.S. Assistant Attorney General, 1960-65; U.S. Assistant Attorney General in charge of Civil Rights Division, 1965-67.

After graduating from Princeton and receiving his law degree from the University of California, Berkeley, Doar practiced in his home town of New Richmond, Wisc., from 1950 to 1960. A Republican, Doar entered the Justice Department in the spring of 1960 and remained there for seven years, serving under two Democratic Presidents as well as Eisenhower. As first assistant in the Civil Rights Division from 1960 to 1964, Doar traveled extensively in the South to oversee Justice Department civil rights litigation, conduct investigations and help resolve such crises as the integration of the University of Mississippi in September 1962 and of the University of Alabama in September 1963. [See KENNEDY Volume]

In December 1964 Doar was named head of the Civil Rights Division following Burke Marshall's [*q.v.*] resignation. In that position he supervised all Justice Department cases dealing with civil rights and continued to spend much of his time in the South, often turning up during critical situations.

In March 1965, when Martin Luther

King [*q.v.*] led a march from Selma to Montgomery, Ala., to protest the denial of voting rights to blacks, Doar was present throughout the march to help coordinate the federal government's activities and to see that court orders barring state authorities from interfering with the march were followed. Doar went to Bogalusa, La., in July 1965 after several months of civil rights demonstrations there had flared into racial violence. As President Johnson's personal representative Doar met with rights leaders and with local and state officials, and he initiated a legal suit against the Ku Klux Klan to prevent it from harassing civil rights workers. Doar was also in Canton, Miss., on June 23, 1966 when the local police ordered some 250 people who were part of a protest march going to Jackson, Miss., to move away from their campsite. When the marchers refused to leave, the police fired tear gas at them, and Doar made a futile effort to restrain the police as they moved in with clubs to clear the area.

Doar personally led the Justice Department's prosecution in two major cases against men charged with the murder of civil rights workers in the South. On March 25, 1965, at the end of the Selma march, Viola Liuzzo, a civil rights worker from Detroit, was shot 20 miles outside of Selma. In his first criminal case in the Justice Department, Doar prosecuted the three Klan members believed responsible for her murder under an 1870 federal law making it a crime to conspire to violate an individual's civil rights. In December 1965 an all-white jury in the federal district court in Montgomery, Ala., found the three men guilty of violating the law, and each received the maximum 10-year sentence. Doar also headed the prosecution of 18 men charged with conspiracy in the June 1964 killing of three civil rights workers near Philadelphia, Miss. Once again Doar won his case. On Oct. 20, 1967 another all-white federal jury in Meridian, Miss., convicted seven of the defendants.

Doar resigned from the Justice Department in December 1967 to become executive director of the Development and Service Corporation, a private company formed to redevelop New York's Bedford-Stuyvesant ghetto. He also served as president of the New York City Board of Education in 1968 and 1969, emerging as an advocate of decentralized control of schools. In December 1973 Doar was appointed majority counsel to the House Judiciary Committee for its inquiry into the impeachment of President Richard Nixon. [See NIXON Volume]

[CAB]

DODD, THOMAS J(OSEPH)

b. May 15, 1907; Norwich, Conn.
d. May 24, 1971; Old Lyme, Conn.
Democratic Senator, Conn., 1959-71.

Thomas Dodd graduated from Providence College in 1930 and Yale Law School three years later. He worked for two years as an FBI agent and then served in the Justice Department as a special assistant to the Attorney General. After World War II he was named executive trial counsel at the Nuremberg war crimes tribunal.

Dodd twice unsuccessfully sought the Connecticut gubernatorial nomination in the late 1940s. Elected to the U.S. House of Representatives in 1952, he lost a U.S. Senate election to incumbent Sen. Prescott Bush (R, Conn.) in 1956. He won a Senate seat in 1958, running on a strong anti-Communist platform. Named to the Judiciary and Foreign Relations Committees, Dodd supported Kennedy Administration legislation on over 60% of all major issues. He maintained a militant stand against Communism throughout his public career. [See KENNEDY Volume]

Reelected to the Senate in 1964, Dodd continued to serve on the Foreign Relations and Judiciary Committees. In March 1964 he called for efforts to turn the Vietnam war against North Vietnam and deplored "the querulous, faint-hearted chorus of those who always ask the price of victory." The next year he charged that the anti-war movement was run by Communists. In 1967 Dodd declared that the U.S. should not "abandon a right moral course [in Vietnam] simply because the cost of defending it is high."

In domestic politics Dodd was a liberal,

supporting the Johnson Administration's medicare and civil rights bills. In 1965 his Juvenile Delinquency Subcommittee conducted hearings on stricter gun control legislation, and Dodd introduced a bill to restrict importation of military surplus weapons. In May 1968 the Senate rejected a Dodd amendment to the Omnibus Crime Control and Safe Streets Act that would have barred mail-order sales of rifles and shotguns while permitting any state legislature to exempt its state from the prohibition.

On June 20, 1966 the Senate Select Committee on Standards and Conduct, chaired by Sen. John Stennis (D, Miss.) [*q.v.*], opened hearings, at Dodd's request, on charges of official misconduct against the Senator. In their newspaper columns Drew Pearson [*q.v.*] and Jack Anderson [*q.v.*] had alleged that Dodd had accepted favors from businessmen, double-billed the Senate for official and private travel, converted over $100,000 in tax-free campaign contributions to his personal use and used his influence to promote the private interests of Chicago public relations man Julius Klein. Earlier, Dodd had filed a 14-count, $5 million libel and conspiracy suit against both Anderson and Pearson.

The Stennis committee hearings carried over into 1967 and focused on Dodd's misuse of campaign funds. In March Dodd defended his financial dealings, calling himself a victim of "trial by press" and one of the poorest members of Congress. However, on April 27 the Committee unanimously recommended that the Senate censure Dodd for conduct that "is contrary to accepted morals, derogates from the public trust expected of a senator and tends to bring the Senate into dishonor and disrepute."

On June 23, 1967 the full Senate formally censured Dodd by a vote of 92-5. The censure was only the seventh in the Senate's history. Dodd retained seniority and chairmanship of the Juvenile Delinquency Subcommittee and vice chairmanship of the Internal Security Subcommittee.

Campaigning as an independent for reelection in 1970, Dodd was unseated by moderate Republican Sen. Lowell Weicker (R, Conn.). Dodd died in May 1971. [See NIXON Volume]

[FHM]

DOMINICK, PETER H(OYT)

b. July 7, 1915; Stamford, Conn.
Republican Senator, Colo., 1963-75.

Peter Dominick's father, Gayer, was a partner in the family brokerage firm of Dominick and Dominick, Inc. After receiving undergraduate and law degrees from Yale, Dominick was admitted to the New York bar in 1940. He served as a pilot in the Army Air Force during World War II and then moved to Denver, where he practiced law and became active in Republican politics. After an initial defeat in 1954, Dominick was elected two years later to the Colorado House of Representatives and reelected in 1958. In 1960 Dominick defeated incumbent Democratic Rep. Byron L. Johnson to win a U.S. congressional seat and was elected to the Senate two years later, defeating another incumbent, Democrat John A. Carroll. During the Kennedy Administration Dominick generally took conservative stands in Congress, opposing the expansion of domestic federal programs but strongly supporting the military. [See KENNEDY Volume]

At the July 1964 Republican National Convention, Dominick spoke in opposition to a platform amendment repudiating political "extremism" proposed by Michigan Gov. George Romney [*q.v.*]. The amendment was opposed by the supporters of Sen. Barry M. Goldwater (R, Ariz.) [*q.v.*] and was defeated by over a two-to-one margin. Although he supported both the Civil Rights Act of 1964 and the Voting Rights Act of 1965, on most issues before Congress, Dominick continued to take a strongly conservative position. He voted against the 1964 proposal for medical care for the elderly and tried to amend the 1965 antipoverty appropriations bill to give governors a veto over proposed community action programs, which Dominick called "the focus of infection" in antipoverty activities. His amendment was defeated by a narrow margin, and Dominick voted against the final bill, which passed the Senate, 46-22. That year Dominick was also one of only 12 senators to oppose a bill providing aid to depressed areas.

In 1966 he opposed the Model Cities program and in 1967 and 1968 introduced an amendment to transfer the preschool child development Head Start program from the Office of Economic Opportunity to the Department of Health, Education and Welfare. The amendment was defeated in 1967 but passed in 1968, although it was later eliminated by a House-Senate conference report. According to *Congressional Quarterly*, Dominick supported the conservative coalition on 79% of the votes on which it formed in the 88th Congress, 81% of such votes in the 89th Congress and 70% of such votes in the 90th Congress.

Dominick was a member of the steering committee of the anti-Communist Committee of One Million, which strongly opposed admitting the People's Republic of China to the U.N. He was against "any policy of accommodation" with mainland China. An officer in the Air Force Reserve, Dominick supported the U.S. bombing of North Vietnam and in 1967 argued that the mining of Haiphong harbor should be considered. In 1968 he successfully introduced an amendment to the Senate version of the Administration tax surcharge bill to prevent countries over 90 days in arrears on debts to the U.S. from redeeming dollars for gold. (Dollars presented would be credited to their debt.)

A strong supporter of pro-business legislation, Dominick received a 100% rating on selected votes from the National Associated Businessmen, Inc., in 1968. In 1964 he had opposed a reduction in the oil depletion allowance and was the only Senate apponent of the extension of the Renegotiation Act, which permitted the government to regain "excessive profits" made by private defense and space contractors. Dominick also successfully opposed AFL-CIO efforts in 1965 to repeal Section 14 (b) of the Taft-Hartley Act, which in effect would have outlawed state right-to-work laws. He also voted against the 1966 increase in corporate income taxes and the increase in telephone and automobile consumer taxes.

Dominick was reelected to the Senate in 1968, defeating former Colorado Gov. Stephen L.R. McNichols with 58.3% of the vote. In 1972 he served as chairman of the Republican Senatorial Campaign Committee. He was defeated for reelection in 1974 by Gary W. Hart, a liberal Democrat who had managed Sen. George McGovern's (D, S.D.) [*q.v.*] 1972 presidential campaign. [See Nixon Volume]

[JBF]

DOUGLAS, PAUL H(OWARD)

b. March 26, 1892; Salem, Mass.
d. Sept. 24, 1976; Washington, D.C.
Democratic Senator, Ill., 1949-67.
Chairman, Joint Economic Committee, 1959-67.

Douglas was raised in rural Maine and worked his way through Bowdoin College. After earning a Ph.D. in economics from Columbia University in 1921, Douglas became a leading figure in the University of Chicago's department of economics. As a labor economist he published several influential books, of which the most important were *Real Wages in the United States (1890-1926)* and *The Theory of Wages*. During the Depression Douglas served on state and federal advisory panels and helped draft the legislation that became the Social Security Act. During this period Douglas gained a national reputation as a New Deal liberal. After a short tenure in the Chicago City Council, Douglas enlisted in the Marine Corps at the age of 48 and saw action in the Pacific.

With strong backing from both Illinois liberals and Chicago's Kelly-Nash machine, Douglas won election to the Senate in 1948. During the 1950s Douglas worked closely with the Americans for Democratic Action (ADA), the NAACP and organized labor in generally unsuccessful attempts to advance civil rights legislation, close tax loopholes, increase Social Security and minimum wage coverage and modify Senate Rule XXII to end Southern filibusters by imposition of cloture. In the early 1960s Douglas stood slightly to the left of President John F. Kennedy. He helped the Administration pass a $389 million area redevelopment bill early in

1961 but voted against Kennedy's 1962 tax revision package because he considered the 7% investment tax credit a new and unnecessary concession to big business. [See TRUMAN, EISENHOWER, KENNEDY Volumes]

Although Douglas criticized the 1964 Kennedy-Johnson tax bill for what he considered its failure to contain major progressive reforms in the tax code, he voted for the measure in February 1964 after successfully organizing Senate opposition to a House provision that would have lowered the effective capital gains tax by $200 million a year.

Douglas was a leading opponent of Sen. Everett M. Dirksen's (R, Ill.) [*q.v.*] attempt to delay implementation of recent Supreme Court rulings requiring both houses of a state legislature to be apportioned on the basis of population alone. In August 1964 Dirksen and Senate Majority Leader Mike Mansfield (D, Mont.) [*q.v.*] jointly sponsored a proposal that would have delayed enforcement of the Court's rulings until Jan. 1, 1966, thus giving reapportionment opponents time to organize in support of a constitutional amendment negating the recent judicial orders. Beginning on Aug. 13 Douglas and five other liberal senators began a "mild" filibuster to stop passage of the Dirksen-Mansfield measure. (A mild filibuster allowed other Senate business to continue uninterrupted.) After a Dirksen-sponsored cloture motion failed Sept. 10, the Senate ended the impasse when Mansfield offered a non-binding "sense of the Congress" amendment Sept. 24 urging district courts to give state legislatures six months to comply with the Supreme Court's reapportionment decision. The Mansfield amendment passed the same day by a vote of 44-38.

The next year Dirksen again tried to delay court-ordered reapportionment, this time by working for passage of a constitutional amendment allowing one house of any state legislature to be apportioned on a basis other than population. Douglas again rallied liberal and urban senators and defeated Dirksen's measure on Aug. 4, 1965. With only 59 votes Dirksen's constitutional amendment fell seven short of the required two-thirds.

Another important legislative victory for Douglas was the establishment after a long fight of the Indiana Dunes National Lakeshore. Since the late 1950s Douglas had worked for the preservation of Lake Michigan's Indiana sand dunes, which were frequently visited by Chicago area residents. He met stiff opposition from Bethlehem and National Steel, which planned to establish new mills there, and from some Indiana public officials who favored a new lake port and more industrial development. Chief among his opponents were Sen. Homer Capehart (R, Ind.) and Rep. Charles Halleck (R, Ind.) [*q.v.*]. Faced with a difficult reelection campaign in 1966, Douglas asked House and Senate Democratic leaders to expedite passage of the bill. A compromise measure, which rearranged somewhat the size and shape of the proposed park, passed the House Oct. 14. The Senate followed suit Oct. 18, and President Johnson signed the law Nov. 5, 1966.

Douglas strongly supported civil rights, consumer protection and Great Society legislation during the mid-1960s. His ADA rating averaged 98% in 1964, 1965 and 1966. Douglas also backed President Johnson's war policy in Vietnam. (In 1954 he had advocated the use of American air power to aid the French garrison beseiged at Dien Bien Phu.) He voted in favor of the Tonkin Gulf Resolution in August 1964 and in each succeeding year voted for the Administration's full appropriations request.

Forty-seven year old Republican businessman Charles H. Percy [*q.v.*] defeated Douglas for reelection in 1966 after a hard fought campaign in which the incumbent's support of open housing legislation emerged as the principle issue. Douglas lost votes in Cook County's ethnic suburbs after Martin Luther King [*q.v.*] led a series of demonstration marches in favor of open housing during the summer of 1966. At the same time Douglas lost votes among affluent liberals for his continued defense of the war. Percy's candidacy was indirectly aided in September by the unsolved murder of his daughter in the family's Kenilworth, Ill., home. Douglas immediately called a two-week halt to his campaign. Most observers thought the tragedy engendered a sympathy vote for Percy.

Immediately after his election defeat, Douglas was appointed chairman of the National Commission on Urban Problems by President Johnson. The Commission report, finished in December 1968, sharply criticized the Administration and the Department of Housing and Urban Development for their failure to provide promised low cost housing. Johnson disagreed with the findings of the panel and refused to officially accept the report.

With former President Dwight D. Eisenhower [*q.v.*] and Gen. Omar Bradley, Douglas also served as the organizing chairman of a Committee for Peace and Freedom in Vietnam. The Committee was formed in 1967 to back Johnson's Vietnam policy, but after the release of the *Pentagon Papers* in 1971 Douglas reassessed his defense of the war and came to the conclusion that his vote in favor of the Tonkin Gulf Resolution in 1964 had been based on "deception" by Johnson Administration spokesmen. From 1966 to 1969 Douglas served as a professor at the New School for Social Research.

[NNL]

For further information:
Paul H. Douglas, *In the Fullness of Time* (New York, 1972).

DOUGLAS, WILLIAM O(RVILLE)
b. Oct. 16, 1898; Maine, Minn.
Associate Justice, U.S. Supreme Court, 1939-75.

Born into an impoverished family and raised in Yakima, Wash., Douglas worked his way through Columbia Law School, graduating in 1925. He became a leading expert on corporate and financial law while a professor, first at Columbia and then at Yale Law School from 1927 to 1936. He was named a member of the Securities and Exchange Commission in 1936 and its chairman the next year. Appointed to the Supreme Court in March 1939, Douglas used his expertise to write some of the Court's important opinions in cases on corporate reorganization, antitrust and patent law.

These contributions, however, were eventually overshadowed by Douglas's strong defense of individual rights and his support for a broad reading and strict enforcement of the guarantees in the Bill of Rights. He was especially solicitous of First Amendment rights, eventually taking an absolutist approach toward freedom of speech, of the press and of religion. He repeatedly dissented from cases where the majority allowed what he considered infringements of these rights. Although the Court never adopted Douglas's view of the First Amendment, many of the positions he espoused in dissent in areas such as criminal rights, reapportionment and citizenship became established doctrines of the Supreme Court. [See TRUMAN, EISENHOWER, KENNEDY Volumes]

With Justice Hugo Black [*q.v.*], Douglas insisted that the First Amendment prohibited all government regulation of allegedly obscene materials, and the two Justices reaffirmed this view in obscenity decisions in June 1964 and March 1966. Douglas also joined in concurring opinions in two 1964 cases that urged the Court to hold that there was an absolute right to criticize—even maliciously—the conduct of public officials. In May 1964 Douglas wrote the Court's five-man majority opinion overturning a federal law canceling the citizenship of naturalized Americans who returned to their native land for a three-year period. Dissenting in a 1958 decision, Douglas had expressed the view that Congress could not take away American citizenship; in a May 1967 decision the Court adopted his position that citizenship could only be relinquished voluntarily.

Douglas's majority opinion in a January 1966 ruling barred the city of Macon, Ga., from withdrawing as trustee of a local park as a device to permit the park to exclude blacks. From 1961 on Douglas concurred in decisions overturning the state convictions of civil rights demonstrators. When the Court changed course in November 1966 and upheld the trespass convictions of demonstrators who had gathered in protest outside a Florida jail, Douglas wrote the dissenting opinion and asserted that a jail could be a proper place for protest.

In favor of a broad interpretation of the Bill of Rights, Douglas joined in Warren Court decisions expanding the rights of criminal defendants. He wrote the majority opinion in an April 1965 case holding it a violation of the Fifth Amendment's privilege against self-incrimination for a state judge or district attorney to comment during a trial on a defendant's refusal to take the stand. Douglas again wrote for the Court in January 1967 when it ruled that self-incriminating statements made by public employees who had been threatened with dismissal if they invoked their Fifth Amendment rights were inadmissible at trial. Generally supporting tight restrictions on police searches, Douglas was the sole dissenter from a June 1968 decision upholding the right of police to stop and frisk persons for weapons when the action seemed necessary for the safety of the policeman and others present.

In a famed and controversial opinion for the Court in the June 1965 case of *Griswold v. Connecticut,* Douglas overturned an anticontraceptive law because it invaded a right to marital privacy, which he said was guaranteed by the Constitution. In an expansive reading of the Bill of Rights, Douglas found this right to privacy in the "penumbras, formed by emanations" from the specific guarantees of the First, Third, Fourth, Fifth and Ninth Amendments. Douglas was also a foremost exponent of using the guarantee of equal protection to guard the rights of the poor and other disadvantaged groups as well as racial minorities. His majority opinion in a March 1966 case invalidated a poll tax for state elections on the ground that it was a denial of equal protection to make affluence a qualification for voting. In May 1968 Douglas also overturned a Louisiana law that denied illegitimate children certain rights given to legitimate offspring, insisting upon equal treatment of the two groups.

From 1967 on Douglas repeatedly dissented when the Court refused to hear cases challenging the constitutionality of the Vietnam war. He adhered to his absolutist views of free speech and religion, voted to sustain the rights of debtors, welfare recipients and illegitimate children and objected to Court rulings in the 1970s that narrowed the rights of criminal defendants. A controversial justice, Douglas was applauded by liberals and radicals for his willingness to hear anti-war cases, his concern for the environment and his protection of individual rights and freedoms. Conservatives often criticized his public and private behavior, however. When he was married for a fourth time in 1966 to a 23-year-old woman, an attempt was made to impeach him for having an allegedly bad moral character. In 1970, in the wake of the Senate's rejection of two Nixon nominees for the Supreme Court, Rep. Gerald R. Ford (R, Mich.) [*q.v.*] led an impeachment effort against Douglas on grounds of alleged improprieties in his professional conduct and writings. A House Judiciary subcommittee cleared Douglas of all charges in December 1970.

Douglas often disagreed with other justices who said the Court's workload was too heavy. As a conservationist and naturalist, he spent much of his free time hiking, mountain climbing and traveling. A frequent public speaker and a prolific author, Douglas wrote numerous articles and essays on the environment, his many travels and on international affairs. He retired from the Court in November 1975 after a stroke he had suffered at the beginning of the year left him unable to participate fully in the Court's work. [See NIXON Volume]

Although criticized by some for being too doctrinaire and result-oriented, Douglas has been ranked highly by most legal analysts. His "capacity for growth," wrote Vern Countryman, along with "his remarkable ability, industry and devotion to democratic principles" made Douglas one of the Court's most influential justices. Called "a bridge from an old liberalism to a new" by legal scholar John P. Frank, Douglas won special recognition for his zealous protection of the rights of the individual against the power of government.

[CAB]

For further information:
Vern Countryman, *The Judicial Record of Justice William O. Douglas* (Cambridge, Mass., 1974).

DYLAN, BOB
b. May 24, 1941; Duluth, Minn.
Musician.

Dylan was born Robert Allan Zimmerman. He grew up in a middle-class Jewish family in Hibbing, Minn., a declining mining center. In high school he led a rock-and-roll band, and during a short stay at the University of Minnesota he began publicly performing folk music. In the winter of 1960-61 Dylan came to New York City, partially to fulfill his desire to meet the then seriously ill folksinger Woody Guthrie. In New York Dylan joined a growing circle of folk musicians performing in small Greenwich Village clubs. He first received wide attention in September 1961 when *New York Times* music critic Robert Shelton favorably reviewed one of his appearances.

By the time Dylan's first record album appeared in March 1962, he had begun to write songs at a rapid rate. Over the next 15 years he produced hundreds of songs. Many of his early ones dealt with social themes. Some, like *A Hard Rain's A-Gonna Fall*, described a fundamental corruption Dylan saw pervading U.S. society. Others chronicled specific cases of injustice, particularly violence and discrimination against blacks, or commented on the arms race, fallout shelters, the blacklist and even boxing.

In the civil rights and peace movements, and in the cultural awakening of the early 1960s, Dylan found hope that a new spirit was beginning to emerge. When the singing group Peter, Paul and Mary recorded Dylan's song *Blowin' in the Wind*, it became a best-selling record, introducing Dylan's writing to millions and turning the song itself into something of an anthem for supporters of the civil rights movement. Dylan himself performed at several civil rights rallies, including the Aug. 28, 1963 March on Washington, where he sang a song about the murder of Medger Evers [*q.v.*]. In general, however, Dylan did not become personally involved in political activity.

From the start of his career Dylan was a controversial figure. Many early press accounts of him were hostile, and in June 1963 he walked out of a scheduled appearance on the *Ed Sullivan Show* when CBS refused to allow him to sing a song parodying the John Birch Society.

Recording and performing frequently Dylan had become a major influence on millions of young Americans by 1964. For his largely white, middle class audience, Dylan articulated a growing if unformed dissatisfaction with the existing society, chronicling the plight and struggles of the poor, the abused and the victims of discrimination. His songs often had a lyricism and grace that transcended the norm of much popular music. By writing about such a wide range of subjects, Dylan helped expand the range and depth of popular music in general.

By late 1964 Dylan was turning away from explicitly political themes and, as a result, was strongly criticized by many political activists. At the Newport Folk Festival the following summer, Dylan began performing with an electrified backup band. The reaction from both audiences and critics was sharply divided, with many vehemently denouncing this departure from a supposedly "pure" folk tradition. But Dylan's popularity continued to grow.

While Dylan's writing was less explicitly political, his vision of America was if anything more scathing than ever. In *Highway 61 Revisited*, an album released in 1965, Dylan portrayed a country in which everything, including war and death, had been reduced to a commodity to be packaged and sold, while bewildered liberals responded by giving "checks to tax-deductible charity organizations."

Following several hit records and successful tours of America, Europe and Australia, Dylan was seriously injured in a motorcycle accident in upstate New York in August 1966. After a period of seclusion Dylan began releasing records again in late 1967, but he did not resume regular public performances until 1974. Although some of his music in the early 1970s was weaker than his earlier work, by the middle of the decade he had once again achieved considerable artistic and popular success.

[JBF]

EASTLAND, JAMES O(LIVER)
b. Nov. 28, 1904; Doddsville, Miss.
Democratic Senator, Miss., 1941, 1943- ; Chairman, Judiciary Committee, 1956- .

Born and raised in Mississippi, Eastland was admitted to the state bar in 1927 and served in the state House of Representatives from 1928 to 1932. He spent the next nine years practicing law and running his family's 5,400-acre cotton plantation in Sunflower County, Miss. Eastland was appointed U.S. Senator from Mississippi for 90 days in 1941 to fill a vacancy and then won election to the Senate in his own right in 1942. Eastland was reelected continuously after that and over the years developed a reputation as a protector of agricultural, especially cotton, interests and as an opponent of labor, social welfare and civil rights legislation. The Mississippi Senator became chairman of the Judiciary Committee in 1956 and used that post to forestall passage of several civil rights bills in the late 1950s. Eastland opposed the Kennedy Administration's farm bill in 1962 and its minimum wage, school aid, medicare and civil rights proposals. He did support a compromise Administration-backed drug safety bill in 1962. [See TRUMAN, EISENHOWER, KENNEDY Volumes]

Eastland refused to endorse Lyndon Johnson's reelection bid in 1964. The Republican nominee, Sen. Barry M. Goldwater (R, Ariz.) [*q.v.*], carried Mississippi in the presidential election. Eastland opposed virtually all of Johnson's antipoverty programs, his school aid bills, aid to urban mass transit, medicare and a housing and urban development bill. Although he voted against the 1965 Appalachian Regional Development Act, Eastland supported an extension of the measure in 1967 when 18 counties in northeastern Mississippi were included in the measure. Eastland also supported the 1966 Auto Safety Act and one aid-to-higher-education bill in 1968. As chairman of the Senate Immigration and Nationality Subcommittee and a long-time foe of immigration law reform, however, he voted against a 1965 act ending the national origins quota system, both in committee and on the Senate floor.

As chairman of the Judiciary Committee, which had jurisdiction over civil rights legislation, Eastland had the power to bottle up civil rights bills. As of 1964 the Judiciary Committee, under his chairmanship, had never voluntarily reported out a civil rights bill, and in 1966 Eastland claimed to have defeated 127 such bills during his Senate years. To keep Eastland from blocking the Johnson Administration's civil rights measures, the Democratic leadership won Senate approval of a motion to place the 1964 Civil Rights Act directly on the Senate calendar, bypassing the Judiciary Committee altogether. The 1965 Voting Rights Act and later civil rights bills were referred to the Judiciary Committee but with orders from the Senate to report the measures back by set deadlines. Eastland objected to both maneuvers and claimed that the time-limit provisions amounted to "legislative lynching."

Eastland also opposed the appointment of Thurgood Marshall [*q.v.*] to the Supreme Court and of Constance Baker Motley [*q.v.*] to a district court judgeship. He was a strong critic of black militants and supported federal anti-riot legislation. When the Judiciary Committee, meeting a Senate deadline, reported out a bill to protect civil rights workers from injury and intimidation in November 1967, Eastland denounced the move, claiming that the bill would give "added protection to roving fomenters of violence, such as Stokely Carmichael [*q.v.*] and H. Rap Brown [*q.v.*]." He voted to add an anti-riot provision to the 1968 Civil Rights Act.

Eastland was floor manager for the cotton title of an Administration-backed farm bill in 1964. The cotton section provided for subsidies to domestic textile mills to decrease the price they paid for domestic cotton. As Eastland explained in the Senate, cheaper imported cotton textiles and synthetic fibers were destroying the market for domestic cotton. This bill, which he successfully steered through the Senate, was designed to make domestic cotton competitive in price, thus aiding both the textile industry and cotton farmers. Eastland's own cotton plantation became a source of increasing controversy in the Johnson years. Civil rights activists criticized the fact that Eastland received over $100,000 per year in cotton price supports and diversion cash payments from the government. In July 1965 a representative of the Mississippi Freedom Labor Union denounced the working conditions of black sharecroppers on Eastland's plantation in testimony before a House Education and Labor Subcommittee. In July 1967 a team of six physicians who had investigated malnutrition in Mississippi reported to a Senate Labor and Public Welfare Subcommittee that conditions in the delta region, where Eastland's plantation was located, approached starvation. Eastland and his colleague Sen. John C. Stennis (D, Miss.) [*q.v.*] immediately denied that there was mass malnutrition in the Mississippi delta.

An outspoken anti-Communist, Eastland supported Johnson's policy in Vietnam, and as chairman of the Senate Internal Security Subcommittee, he repeatedly searched for evidence of domestic Communism. In a July 1964 Senate speech, Eastland alleged that Communists and pro-Communists were active in civil rights drives in Mississippi. He suggested that the June 21 disappearances of three rights workers, later found murdered near Philadelphia, Miss., might be a Communist-inspired "hoax." During Judiciary Committee hearings on the 1965 Voting Rights Act, Eastland claimed that the Mississippi Freedom Democratic Party was Communist-influenced. In the Committee's 1967 hearings on anti-riot bills, he contended that "all these riots follow the same pattern. They follow the tactics used by the Communist party all over the world." Eastland criticized the Supreme Court's rulings on internal security laws and in 1968 sponsored a wide-ranging internal security bill designed to circumvent many of the Court's decisions. The bill, which was not acted on by Congress that year, included provisions to extend the life of the Subversive Activities Control Board (SACB) and authorize the SACB to hold hearings to determine if organizations were Communist-action groups. It also barred members of such groups from union membership and employment in defense facilities or public schools receiving federal funds and eliminated federal court jurisdiction over the actions of congressional committees.

Eastland repeatedly denounced the Court's decisions on civil rights, criminal law and reapportionment. In 1964 he supported efforts to delay the implementation of the Court's "one-man, one-vote" ruling. A strong law-and-order advocate, Eastland complained that the Court's criminal decisions "bound and gagged the dedicated lawman in a web of tangled and twisted legalities so that he is better armed with a law book than a night-stick." He voted for the 1968 Omnibus Crime Control and Safe Streets Act and against a 1968 law banning mail-order and out-of-state sales of rifles, shotguns and ammunition. In an effort to change the Supreme Court's line of decisions, Eastland opposed the appointment of Associate Justice Abe Fortas [*q.v.*] as Chief Justice in 1968.

Eastland, who was elected to his fifth Senate term in a landslide victory in 1966, held a reputation for fairness in his role as Judiciary Committee chairman. He decentralized the Committee, which had amassed the largest budget and staff of any congressional committee by 1971, leaving subcommittee chairmen with a great deal of autonomy. With the notable exception of civil rights measures, Eastland assigned bills to subcommittees on the basis of subject matter and precedent, generally did not try to hold bills in full committee and rarely delayed legislation approved by a subcommittee even when he opposed it.

During the Nixon years Eastland supported all of Nixon's Supreme Court appointments, including the nominations of Clement F. Haynsworth and G. Harrold Carswell. He voted against the Equal Rights Amendment, home rule for the District of Columbia and fought busing for school desegregation. He remained a strong supporter of the war in Southeast Asia, voting against the Cooper-Church amendment to limit American military involvement in Cambodia in June 1970. [See NIXON Volume]

[CAB]

ECKSTEIN, OTTO

b. Aug. 1, 1927; Ulm, Germany.
Member, Council of Economic Advisers, September 1964-February 1966.

Otto Eckstein's family emigrated from Germany in 1939. He completed his elementary and secondary education in New York City, entering the Army after graduation in 1946. Eckstein received his B.A. from Princeton in 1951 and his Ph.D. in economics from Harvard in 1955, when he joined the Harvard faculty. His first two books concerned the government's role in water resource development. A skilled economic forecaster, Eckstein served as a consultant to the Rand Corporation from 1957 to 1964 and was technical director of the Joint Economic Committee of Congress in 1959. During the Kennedy Administration he served as a consultant to the Treasury Department and the Council of Economic Advisers (CEA). President Johnson appointed him to the CEA in September 1964.

Like the other CEA members during the Kennedy and Johnson Administrations, Eckstein was an exponent of the Keynesian "new economics," which held that the federal government could effectively combat inflation or recession with an alert fiscal policy. Eckstein had criticized the conservative economic policies of the Eisenhower Administration and admonished Kennedy not to let the balance of payments problem weaken a vigorous anti-recession program. During the Johnson Administration inflation, not recession, was the primary danger. In 1967 Eckstein called for a temporary tax increase to curb inflation fueled by spending on the Vietnam war and Great Society programs. He argued that relying solely on monetary policy to control inflation was crippling the housing and construction industry because of high interest rates.

Eckstein left the CEA in February 1966 and returned to Harvard. He remained a prominent liberal economist throughout the decade. In the fall of 1968 he headed a special study group on inflation for Democratic presidential candidate Hubert Humphrey [*q.v.*]. The study group acknowledged that the Administration's wage-price "guideposts" policy had failed and suggested a conference with labor and management to come up with "a set of principles of responsible wage and price behavior." Humphrey said he would accept the group's suggestion if he were elected.

[TO]

EDWARDS, DON

b. Jan. 6, 1915; San Jose, Calif.
Democratic Representative, Calif., 1963- .

Edwards attended the Stanford University Law School from 1936 to 1938 but never received a degree. From 1940 to 1941 he served as an FBI agent. After World War II he founded the Valley Title Company and became a millionaire. In 1962 Edwards won a seat in the U.S. House of Representatives from the overwhelmingly Democratic ninth district of California, which included San Jose.

Edwards compiled one of the most liberal records in Congress during the mid and late 1960s. In 1965 and 1966 he was chosen national chairman of Liberal Americans for Democratic Action. He was a consistent supporter of President Lyndon B. Johnson's Great Society programs and civil rights measures, while opposing the Administration's escalation of American military involvement in Southeast Asia. In May 1965 Edwards joined six other representatives in voting against a supplementary defense authorization bill for the Vietnam conflict. Two years later he was one of three members of the lower house who opposed a defense procurement and research authorization bill that provided funds for the war.

In 1965, 1967 and 1968 Edwards unsuccessfully introduced motions against the appropriation of funds for the House Un-American Activities Committee (HUAC). During floor debate in February 1965 he asserted that the panel's existence was unconstitutional because of "its practice of investigating with no legislative purpose but exclusively for the purpose of exposure, and . . . its practice of holding legislative trials in violation of Section 9, Title I of the

Constitution proscribing bills of attainder."

In 1971 Edwards became chairman of the Judiciary Committee's Subcommittee No. Four—also known as the Civil Rights Oversight Committee. In that post he successfully pressed for House passage of a constitutional amendment guaranteeing equal rights to women. In July 1974 he voted in favor of all of the five articles of impeachment against President Richard M. Nixon considered by the Judiciary Committee. [See NIXON Volume]

[MLL]

EISENHOWER, DWIGHT D(AVID)

b. Oct. 14, 1890; Denison, Tex.
d. March 28, 1969; Washington, D.C.
President of the United States, 1953-61.

The third of seven sons born to a farming family, Dwight D. Eisenhower grew up in Abilene, Kan. There he was nicknamed "Ike" and worked at a variety of jobs in order to support his brothers' college education. In 1915 Eisenhower graduated from West Point. He served as a tank instructor during World War I and remained in the Army after the Armistice. From 1929 to 1940 he worked under Army Chief of Staff Douglas A. MacArthur, following him to the Philippines where his superior went to reorganize the Islands' defenses.

On the eve of America's entry into World War II, Eisenhower returned from the Philippines and quickly received a series of promotions that led to his command of Allied forces in the European theater. He oversaw the Allied invasions of North Africa in 1942, Sicily and Italy in 1943 and Normandy in 1944.

Eisenhower resigned as Army Chief of Staff in February 1948 to become president of Columbia University. In 1951 he assumed command of the forces newly organized under the North Atlantic Treaty Organization (NATO). One year later Eisenhower won the Republican presidential nomination as the candidate of the GOP's "Eastern" or "internationalist" wing in a bitterly waged contest against conservative Sen. Robert A. Taft (R, Ohio). The most popular war leader since Grant, with a pleasing public personality and an easy grin, Eisenhower handily defeated his Democratic opponent, Adlai E. Stevenson [*q.v.*] in 1952 and again in 1956. [See TRUMAN Volume]

Eisenhower's eight years in office proved less notable for accomplishment than for the deliberate avoidance of foreign and domestic strife. He functioned as the board chairman presiding over a cabinet of older business leaders, men characterized more by their administrative capacity than their imagination. Despite his popularity Eisenhower, who had difficulty disguising his distaste for avid partisanship, held little sway over his party's conservative Old Guard, which often opposed his modest legislative proposals in Congress. By comparison with the social legislation passed under Democratic presidents before and after him, Eisenhower took few initiatives and achieved little domestic reform.

In foreign affairs Eisenhower ended one war and prevented outright American participation in others. In July 1953 he coerced the South Korean government into accepting an armistice, thus ending the costly American-United Nations police action. A year later he rejected counsel favoring the massive deployment of American armed forces on the side of the French in Indochina. To prevent further Communist territorial advances, his Secretary of State, John Foster Dulles, negotiated regional mutual security agreements modeled after the North Atlantic Treaty Organization (NATO) in Asia and in the Middle East.

After the 1954 Geneva Conference held to resolve the Indochina conflict, Eisenhower supported the pro-West South Vietnamese regime of Ngo Dinh Diem. He acquiesced in its decision not to permit free elections on the reunification of Vietnam, a violation of the Geneva Accords, because of fear that the Communists would win. Instead, the U.S. supplied the Diem regime with military assistance which it hoped would assure political stability. Eisenhower also ordered small contingents of U.S. military advisers to assist in the training of the South Vietnamese army.

Although a career Army man Eisenhower sought to reduce defense expenditures. His "New Look" military budgets reduced defense appropriations at the expense of conventional "limited" Army and Navy systems. In his January 1961 Farewell Address, Eisenhower warned of the dangers to a democratic society from a "military-industrial complex" consisting of "an immense military establishment and a large arms industry." During the Kennedy presidency he called for cuts in the defense budget and reduced troop commitments to NATO.

In the political arena Eisenhower's own high standing did not rejuvenate the Republican Party. Younger and independent voters who faithfully voted for the General would not extend their support to his adopted party. During his presidency the percentage of registered Republicans declined. The GOP lost control of Congress in 1954 and through the end of his presidency never regained its majority. [See EISENHOWER, KENNEDY Volumes]

To the end of his life, Eisenhower remained the most popular leader in the Republican Party. In the months preceeding the 1964 Republican National Convention, reporters and presidential aspirants repeatedly sought his views on the GOP presidential nomination. According to David Halberstam, Eisenhower personally favored the nomination of his 1952 campaign manager, Ambassador to South Vietnam Henry Cabot Lodge [*q.v.*]. But Lodge, uncertain of his old candidate's real position, declined to enter the race.

By his own, possibly calculated, indecisiveness, Eisenhower proved a casualty of the 1964 battle for control of the Republican Party. Following the June 2 California primary, the nomination of conservative Sen. Barry M. Goldwater (R, Ariz.) [*q.v.*] appeared inevitable unless a broad coalition of moderate and liberal Republicans united behind a single candidate openly backed by Eisenhower. The General urged Pennsylvania Gov. William W. Scranton [*q.v.*] to challenge Goldwater. Believing that the former President would endorse him, Scranton prepared his declaration of candidacy for the June edition of the nationally televised *Face the Nation* program.

At the last moment, however, Eisenhower's first Treasury Secretary, George Humphrey, persuaded his old chief not to act on Scranton's behalf. Humphrey argued that Goldwater, whom he supported, would likely gain the nomination regardless of Scranton's candidacy and that Eisenhower would risk his own prestige in a hopeless cause. The General called Scranton and withdrew his offer. As a consequence the Pennsylvania Governor delayed his announcement and gave a confusing performance on the TV show *Face the Nation*. Four days later, after Goldwater voted against cloture in the Senate debate over the civil rights bill, Scranton decided to run with or without the former President's help. Goldwater, however, won the nomination easily. *Time* noted in its post-convention issue that Eisenhower "has probably had his last chance at exercising a major influence over Party decisions."

Eisenhower endorsed the Vietnam policies of President Lyndon B. Johnson. In 1964 discussions with the President, Eisenhower privately urged Johnson to provide more non-military assistance to Vietnam. He doubted the wisdom of large-scale military activities in a guerrilla warfare situation. However, publicly he adhered to the principle of bipartisanship in foreign policymaking and, as a military man, resented the rising and spirited protests against American involvement in Vietnam. In March 1966 Eisenhower suggested imprisonment for draft-card burners "at least for the war's duration." In October 1967 he joined former President Harry S Truman [*q.v.*] and other political and academic leaders in the formation of the Citizen's Committee for Peace and Freedom in Vietnam, organized as a counterpart to the numerous anti-war committees established in the preceeding months. In December Eisenhower reiterated his belief in the "domino theory" that he himself had first propounded. Withdrawal from South Vietnam, he warned, meant that "it will only be a question of time before every country up to the borders of India falls under the Communist heel."

As a retired general of the Army, Eisenhower frequently answered questions over strategy in Vietnam. In September

1966 he called for "as much force as we need to win." Tactical nuclear weapons, he later confided to former presidential adviser Arthur Larson, should be employed if the Communist Chinese Army entered the war in Southeast Asia.

Ironically, opponents of American involvement in Vietnam seized upon Eisenhower's own words to buttress their arguments. Some presented his concept of a "military-industrial" complex as a cause for the tragic Asian conflict. The North Vietnamese also repeated Eisenhower's frank admissions of their popularity compared to the Diem regime during the 1950s.

Ike's popular standing remained high during the 1960s, and the reputation of his presidency actually rose among intellectuals. During the decade he ranked second only to the incumbent president among the Gallup Poll survey lists of the "most admired living Americans." In January 1968 Eisenhower actually outpolled Johnson. Previously attacked by many scholars, his presidency was praised by "revisionist" historians who were disenchanted with the "imperial presidency" and its interventionist foreign policy and more appreciative of the smiling General's unifying leadership style and success at maintaining peaceful foreign relations.

In July 1968 Eisenhower endorsed Richard M. Nixon [*q.v.*], his running mate in 1952 and 1956, for the 1968 Republican presidential nomination. He denied earlier speculation that he "never really liked or supported or really believed in Nixon." Three weeks later, on the eve of the national convention, Eisenhower suffered a severe heart attack from which he never recovered. He died less than three weeks after his former vice president finally assumed the presidency.

[JLB]

For further information:

Dwight D. Eisenhower, *The White House Years* (Garden City, 1963-65).

Murray Kempton, "The Underestimation of Dwight D. Eisenhower," *Esquire*, LXVII (September 1967), p. 108.

Herbert S. Parmet, *Eisenhower and the American Crusades* (New York, 1972).

EISENHOWER, MILTON S(TOVER)
b. Sept. 15, 1899; Abilene, Kan.
President, Johns Hopkins University, 1956-67, 1971-72; Chairman, President's Commission on the Causes and Prevention of Violence, 1968-69.

Milton Eisenhower, a younger brother of Dwight D. Eisenhower, graduated from Kansas State University in 1924 and immediately entered government service. Between 1926 and 1941 he held important posts in the Department of Agriculture. Eisenhower worked for the War Relocation Authority and the Office of War Information until 1943, when he was named president of Kansas State College of Agriculture and Applied Science. He became president of Pennsylvania State University in 1950 and of Johns Hopkins University in 1956. Meanwhile, he continued to offer his services to the government. In 1945 he helped reorganize the Department of Agriculture, and from 1946 to 1948 he was chairman of the U.S. National Commission for the United Nations Economic and Social Council.

Considered more liberal and more intellectual than Dwight Eisenhower, Milton was his brother's admired and trusted adviser during the 1950s. He worked on Dwight's presidential campaigns, served as a member of the President's Committee on Government Organization and was credited with initiating changes in Latin American policy that later developed into the Alliance for Progress. In Kennedy's first year in office, Eisenhower served on the Tractors for Freedom Committee, which unsuccessfully tried to trade agricultural tractors to Cuban leader Fidel Castro in exchange for the release of prisoners captured in the Bay of Pigs invasion. [See EISENHOWER, KENNEDY Volumes]

Eisenhower was a key member of the Republican Party's liberal "brain trust." Beginning in September 1963 he headed the Critical Issues Council of the Republican Citizens Committee. He worked with 24 Republican intellectuals and experts who produced analyses and proposed alternative to national policies to those advocated by the Kennedy and Johnson Administrations. Eisenhower was responsible for a study on

Panama that recommended construction of a new canal by conventional methods (i.e., without the use of nuclear devices), a toll increase for the existing canal and larger payments to the Panamanian government. Republican moderates hoped that the Council's recommendations would be included in the Party's 1964 platform, but the work was attacked by Party conservatives, and Sen. Barry Goldwater (R, Ariz.) [*q.v.*] tried to disband the Council. Goldwater eventually met with Eisenhower in June 1964 and said that he agreed with the findings of all the studies except those on civil rights. Eisenhower nominated moderate Pennsylvania Gov. William Scranton [*q.v.*] at the Republican National Convention. The delegates chose Goldwater and ignored the Critical Issues studies in drafting the Party's platform.

President Johnson often sought Eisenhower's advice, particularly on Latin American questions. From 1965 to 1970 Eisenhower worked on the President's Commission for an Atlantic-Pacific Interoceanic Canal Study. An early proponent of educational television, he accepted appointment to the board of directors of the Corporation for Public Broadcasting in March 1968. Eisenhower resigned this post in June when the President asked him to head the Commission on the Causes and Prevention of Violence.

President Johnson formed the Commission on Violence immediately after the assassination of Sen. Robert F. Kennedy (D, N.Y.) [*q.v.*] and a few months after the shooting of Martin Luther King [*q.v.*]. The panel spent $1.6 million and employed as many as 100 staff members to produce a comprehensive study of violence. The 13-member Commission held public hearings and created task forces to study seven major areas: individual acts of violence, group violence, assassinations and political violence, the effects of violence in the mass media, firearms, the criminal justice system and the history of violence. Scholars were recruited to conduct research studies on specific issues and subjects related to the seven major areas, which the committee promised not to edit. Released as "Reports to the Commission" and not as "Reports by the Commission," these included the controversial Walker report, which charged the Chicago police with responsibility for much of the violence at the Democratic National Convention in August 1968.

The statement on campus unrest, issued in June 1969, was the first to carry the Commission's policy seal. Eight more followed throughout the year, and the final report was presented on Dec. 12, 1969. In their papers the panel members asserted that the U.S. was the most "criminogenic" of politically stable western nations, its law enforcement and criminal justice systems ineffective and its efforts to eliminate the social causes of crime inadequate. The Commission concluded that the crime rate accelerated in the 1960s in part because of the rising expectations engendered by government social welfare programs and the mass media. Only the establishment of a police state could eliminate crime, said Eisenhower, but a national commitment of at least $20 billion annually might reverse the upward trend in the crime rate. The committee specifically recommended gun-control legislation, better police training and efforts to provide full employment, reduce narcotics addiction, improve housing and schools and restructure the urban tax base. Eisenhower's only notable disagreement with other members of the Commission was his dissent from the seven-to-six majority statement of Dec. 8, 1969 that condemned all massive civil disobedience, including nonviolent action.

Eisenhower was unhappy that President Richard M. Nixon failed to act on the Commission's recommendations, but he wrote that the panel's work educated the public and may have influenced the next generation of legislators. President emeritus of the Johns Hopkins University since 1967, Eisenhower temporarily took over active leadership of the school in 1971 and 1972. The next year he was named chairman of the President's Commission on International Radio Broadcasting.

[JCH]

For further information:

Milton S. Eisenhower, *The President Is Calling* (Garden City, 1974).

ELLENDER, ALLEN J(OSEPH)

b. Sept. 24, 1890; Montegut, La.
d. July 27, 1972; Bethesda, Md.
Democratic Senator, La., 1937-72; Chairman, Agriculture and Forestry Committee, 1951-53, 1955-71.

After a career as a farmer-lawyer and city and district attorney, Ellender was elected to the Louisiana House of Representatives where he served for twelve years, the last four as speaker. Though he entered the legislature as an opponent of Huey Long, they formed an alliance in 1929 when Ellender joined Long's defense in his impeachment trial. After Sen. Long's assassination in 1935, the Long organization slated Ellender for the Senate vacancy. In office Ellender was appointed to the Agriculture Committee and coauthored the Agricultural Adjustment Act of 1937. In January 1951 Ellender became chairman of the Agriculture and Forestry Committee and in 1955 used his position as chairman to secure new sugar import quotas more favorable to Louisiana's sugar industry. He supported the Kennedy Administration's 1961 feed grain bill, which removed price support protection from farmers who declined to participate in the government's acreage retirement program. [See TRUMAN, EISENHOWER, KENNEDY Volumes]

Ellender was a leader of the Southern opposition to the Civil Rights Act of 1964. He supervised one of the three Senate filibuster teams and warned in his final speech on the civil rights bill that "its passage will bring on more strife than one can contemplate." However, once the bill became law Ellender broadcast a statewide appeal for "calm and reason" in Louisiana and called for resistance only "within the framework of the orderly processes established by law." In 1965 Ellender continued to oppose civil rights legislation and replaced Sen. Richard Russell (D, Ga.) [*q.v.*] as the leader of the Southern resistance to the 1965 Voting Rights Act. When some Southern Senators, including his colleague Sen. Russell Long (D, La.) [*q.v.*], showed signs of wavering, Ellender vowed to speak against the bill "as long as God gives me breath."

Ellender clashed with the Johnson Administration in 1964 over the Administration's new cotton commodity program. In opposition to an Administration bill that created a new cotton price and acreage system and subsidized domestic textile mills, Ellender introduced a measure, written by the American Farm Bureau Federation, to reduce the price support from 32.47¢ to 30¢ a pound and to eliminate the cotton mill subsidy. The Administration regarded this bill as excessively hard on many of the small cotton farmers of heavily Democratic portions of the Southeast. Ellender opposed the Administration's cotton provisions in committee but supported the bill on the Senate floor, where he managed to cut the program's duration from four to two years.

Ellender was floor manager for the Administration's food stamp measures of 1964 and 1967. When the program came up for renewal in March 1967, the Administration asked for at least a three-year extension, but the House would agree to appropriate money for only one year. The bill was tied up in a House-Senate conference for three months until Ellender persuaded House conferees to compromise on a two-year extension in September. Ellender resigned the chairmanship of the Agriculture Committee in January 1971 to become chairman of the Appropriations Committee. At his death in July 1972, Ellender was also President Pro Tempore of the Senate and third in the line of presidential succession. [See NIXON Volume]

[DKR]

EPSTEIN, JASON

b. Aug. 25, 1928; Cambridge, Mass.
Founder, *The New York Review of Books*.

The son of a well-to-do Jewish family involved in the textile business, Jason Epstein graduated from Columbia University in 1949. At Columbia he was a classmate of Norman Podhoretz [*q.v.*], who was later a friend and publishing colleague. In 1951 Epstein took a job as an editor of Doubleday & Co., where he began Anchor Books, the first important line of quality paperbacks. In 1958 he left Doubleday to become a senior editor and vice president of Random House.

With a reputation as a powerful and enterprising editor committed to serious literature, Epstein built an extensive network of friends and contacts among writers and literary critics. In the early 1960s he discussed with some of these intellectuals the possibility of starting a newsprint paper for book reviews on the model of the *Times Literary Supplement* of London. A prolonged newspaper strike in New York in early 1963, which shut down the *New York Times Book Review*, freed a great deal of advertising money, readers and reviewers to help Epstein realize his project. With the aid of Robert B. Silvers, a former editor of *Harper's* and the *Paris Review*, the poet Robert Lowell [*q.v.*] and Lowell's wife, Elizabeth Hardwick, *The New York Review of Books* began publication in February 1963. Silvers and Barbara Epstein (Jason Epstein's wife) were named as the editors; Hardwick was designated as an advising editor and Epstein and Lowell as members of the journal's board.

Review contributors soon included some of the most eminent members of the American literary world: F. W. Dupee, Nathan Glazer [*q.v.*], Paul Goodman [*q.v.*], Irving Howe [*q.v.*], Alfred Kazin, Dwight Macdonald] *q.v.*], Norman Mailer [*q.v.*] and Susan Sontag [*q.v.*]. Beginning regular biweekly publication shortly after its debut, the Review characteristically ran long interpretative literary and political essays rather than straightforward book reviews. The Vietnam issue arose in its pages for the first time in 1964 with an article by I. F. Stone [*q.v.*]. This was followed in late 1965 by articles and reviews on Vietnam from Hans Morgenthau [*q.v.*], Joseph Kraft, Bernard Fall and Jean Lacouture—all expressing opposition to the escalation of the war.

During the late 1960s *The New York Review* became the country's most influential publication of America's liberal-radical intellectual community. From 1965 until the end of the decade, it devoted more space to American involvement in Southeast Asia than to any other topic, and it featured such systematic critiques of American foreign policy as Noam Chomsky's [*q.v.*] influential anti-war article, "The Responsibility of Intellectuals." In April 1966 Epstein himself contributed "The CIA and the Intellectuals," an expose of liberal anti-Communism in the 1950s and early 1960s. It followed *Ramparts* magazine's revelation that the CIA had been involved in funding the National Student Association.

The review's friendliness to the New Left in this period was symbolized for many by its Aug. 24, 1967 issue, which featured a diagram of a Molotov cocktail on the cover, an article by Andrew Kopkind criticizing Martin Luther King [*q.v.*] and a defense of the Newark ghetto riots by Tom Hayden [*q.v.*]. Liberal and social democratic intellectuals like Podhoretz and Howe denounced *The Review* as a vehicle for a kind of highbrow revolution-mongering; journalist Tom Wolfe dubbed it the "chief theoretical organ of radical chic."

The New York City teachers' strike in the fall of 1968 split the New York intellectual community, with *Commentary* and *Dissent* on the side of the teachers' union and *The Review* on the side of black proponents of community control of the schools. In a series of articles on the strike, Epstein responded to the charge made by the union and its supporters that anti-Semitism was behind much of the black community's hostility to the union. "Undoubtedly," he wrote, "there have been expressions of anti-Semitism on the part of the various black demagogues, and as the largely Jewish UFT [United Federation of Teachers] insists on pitting its strength against the black community, there will be more. Yet it seems to have become the policy of the union, whenever such slanders have been committed by blacks, to amplify them in a way that suggests that the Nuremberg rallies are about to be resumed in the Abyssinian Baptist Church."

In the fall and winter of 1969 and 1970, Epstein covered the trial of the "Chicago Eight," then under federal prosecution for their roles in the 1968 protests at the Democratic National Convention. His articles on the tumultuous courtroom events were printed in *The New York Review* and later published in rewritten form in *The Great Conspiracy Trial* (1970).

Epstein continually denied having great editorial influence over *The Review*, insisting that it was the unique product of its writers and editors. But in his history of the journal, *Intellectual Skywriting*, Philip Noble suggested that Epstein was in fact a predominate influence behind *The New York Review*. During the 1970s the *Review*'s criticism of American society became iewhat less strident, and its editors fo-ed their attention more on literature and criticism.

[TLH]

For further information:

Philip Noble, *Intellectual Skywriting: Literary Politics and the New York Review of Books* (New York, 1974).

ERVIN, SAM(UEL) J(AMES) JR.

b. Sept. 27, 1896; Morgantown, N.C.
Democratic Senator, N.C., 1954-75.

A graduate of the University of North Carolina and of Harvard Law School, Ervin practiced law in his home town of Morganton, N.C., and served three terms in the state Assembly between 1923 and 1933. He was a judge on the Burke County Criminal Court from 1935 to 1937, on the North Carolina Superior Court from 1937 to 1943 and on the state Supreme Court from 1948 to 1954. He was appointed to the U.S. Senate in June 1954 and easily won election to three full terms. With legal and constitutional issues as his main interest, Ervin established a reputation as the Senate's expert on the Constitution and built a conservative record on most domestic and foreign policy issues. [See EISENHOWER, KENNEDY Volumes]

A member of the Senate Judiciary Committee, Ervin was a leader in the fight against civil rights legislation during the 1960s. In hearings on civil rights proposals, Ervin frequently engaged Administration witnesses in lengthy debates on the constitutionality and fairness of the bills. On the Senate floor he repeatedly offered major amendments to delete or seriously weaken various titles of civil rights acts. Ervin always contended that while he opposed racial discrimination, the federal laws designed to end it were unconstitutional invasions of states rights and individual personal and property rights.

As a result of his strict interpretation of the Constitution, Ervin built a liberal record on civil liberties issues. As head of the Judiciary Committee's Constitutional Rights subcommittee after 1961, Ervin conducted hearings on the rights of mental patients, military personnel, Indians and federal employes. He successfully sponsored the 1964 District of Columbia Mental Health Act, which included a patient's bill of rights; the 1964 Criminal Justice Act, providing free legal counsel to indigent defendants in federal courts; and the 1966 Bail Reform Act, making it possible for federal criminal defendants who could not afford bail to be released pending trial. He also introduced the Military Justice Act of 1968, which reformed much of the court-martial system. In March 1968 he persuaded the Senate to agree unanimously to his amendment adding an "Indian Bill of Rights" to the 1968 Civil Rights Act.

An advocate of strict separation of church and state, Ervin spoke out against a constitutional amendment to allow prayer in public schools in September 1966. His speech was credited by some observers with defeating this proposal in the Senate. He regularly introduced bills to authorize taxpayer suits challenging federal aid to religiously affiliated schools and hospitals. The Senate passed such a bill in 1966 and again in 1967, but the House failed to act. Ervin also sponsored legislation to protect the right to privacy of federal employes. Again his proposal was adopted by the Senate in 1967 but died in the House.

However, Ervin opposed many of the Warren Court's rulings expanding the rights of criminal suspects, and he backed a section of the 1968 Omnibus Crime Control and Safe Streets Act designed to override several of those decisions. He also fought the appointment of Thurgood Marshall [*q.v.*] to the Supreme Court in 1967 and the nomination of Abe Fortas [*q.v.*] as Chief Justice in 1968 on the ground that both were judicial activists likely to support Court trends he opposed.

A supporter of the war in Vietnam and a conservative on military and defense issues, Ervin also opposed much social welfare legislation. Although he voted for the 1964 Economic Opportunity Act and aid to elementary and secondary schools in 1965, he opposed programs such as medicare, model cities, aid to mass transit, child-care and Project Headstart. He supported environmental legislation but voted against gun control, financial disclosure for members of Congress and labor legislation such as the 1966 Mine Safety Act.

In later years Ervin led the fight against the Equal Rights Amendment and against Nixon Administration anti-crime proposals authorizing preventive detention and "no-knock" policy entry. He conducted hearings on Army surveillance of civilians and on invasions of privacy caused by the use of computers and data banks. With a folksy, Bible-quoting, story-telling style, Ervin won national prominence in 1973 when he headed a seven-man Senate committee set up to investigate the Watergate affair. He retired from the Senate in January 1975. [See NIXON Volume]

[CAB]

EVANS, DANIEL J(ACKSON)

b. Oct. 1925; Seattle, Wash.
Governor, Wash. 1965-77.

After receiving his B.S. and M.S. degrees at the University of Washington, Evans worked as a civil engineer in Seattle. In 1956 he was elected to the state House of Representatives, where he served twice as the Republican minority leader. In 1964 he vacated his safe seat to wage an uphill campaign for governor. In the September primary of that year, Evans, a moderate Republican, defeated a conservative pro-Goldwater candidate, Richard Christensen, by 100,000 votes. Though not previously well-known, Evans countered the Democratic landslide of 1964 to defeat two-term incumbent Albert Rossellini in the general election. His campaign, run independently of the Goldwater presidential bid, proposed a "Blueprint for Progress," a 35-point program promising increased spending for education and welfare, coupled with inducements for industrial expansion, the reform of archaic administrative structures and the abolition of the lucrative fee-appraiser system, one of the governor's choicest patronage plums.

Governor Evans's initial problem was to establish legislative reapportionment to accord with the 1964 "one man, one vote" Supreme Court ruling. Evans induced the recalcitrant Democratic-controlled Washington state legislature to enact an acceptable reapportionment plan in 1965. He also secured the total or partial passage of 24 of his 35 blueprint proposals after his first year.

After the Republican Party's devastating defeat of 1964, Evans argued that Party resurgency could be best accomplished by gaining control of state houses and exercising strong leadership at that level. With Evans serving as the Party's chief tactician in the 1966 elections, the GOP gained control of 25 governorships, a net gain of eight over the previous year.

Evans had become a spokesman for the "new federalism" by 1967. In that year he called for state government to "reassume its rightful responsibilities" in coping with local problems and to end its reliance on centrally administered federal solutions. He stressed that the states rather than the federal government could best devise solutions to economic and social problems. His 1968 keynote address at the Republican National Convention prompted a *Time* cover story praising the "creative federalism" outlined in his speech.

Evans's first term as Washington governor saw the enactment of air and water-pollution controls, the preservation of recreation areas, the initiation of a $242 million school-building construction program and the increase of state grants to localities to restore strength to the lower levels of government. Evans won reelection in 1968 by defeating the state's Attorney General, John J. O'Connell, with 54% of the vote. He was reelected to his third term in 1972. [See NIXON Volume]

[TJC]

EVERS, (JAMES) CHARLES

b. Sept. 11, 1922; Decatur, Miss.
Field Secretary, Mississippi NAACP. 1963-69.

Evers grew up in Decatur and received a B.A. from Alcorn A & M College in 1950. He moved to Philadelphia, Miss., the next year and established several successful businesses, including a funeral parlor, hotel, cafe and taxi service, all of which catered to the local black community. Evers also worked closely with his brother Medgar, who became state field secretary for the NAACP in 1954. As a result of his civil rights work, white segregationists put such severe economic pressures on Charles Evers that he was forced to leave Mississippi in 1956. He moved to Chicago and there held a variety of jobs. As he later disclosed in his autobiography, he also ran a small policy game and a brothel.

Medgar Evers was assassinated by a sniper outside his home in Jackson, Miss., on June 12, 1963. Charles returned to the state immediately and asked the NAACP to let him succeed his brother as the organization's Mississippi field secretary. Assuming the job on June 16, Evers worked in campaigns to desegregate public accommodations and register black voters, concentrating on McComb, during 1964. He was arrested in Jackson in June 1965 for leading demonstrations to protest a special state legislative session called to rewrite Mississippi's voting and registation laws.

Following passage of the federal Voting Rights Act in August 1965, Evers moved his office to Fayette in Jefferson County, one of several predominantly black counties in southwest Mississippi. From the fall of 1965 through early 1967, he organized highly effective boycotts by the black communities in Natchez, Fayette, Port Gibson and other towns in the area. In each place black demands included the integration of schools, hospitals and public accommodations, increased employment of blacks by city agencies and private businesses, the use of courtesy titles for blacks by city employes and black representation on juries and school boards. A boycott of white merchants, mass marches and picketing continued in each town until black demands were met. At the same time Evers and NAACP state president Aaron Henry [*q.v.*] organized local NAACP chapters and took advantage of the federal voting rights law to increase dramatically voter registration among blacks. Between 1963 and 1971 the number of blacks registered in Mississippi rose from 28,000 to over 250,000.

When James Meredith [*q.v.*] was shot on June 6, 1966 while on a solitary protest march from Memphis, Tenn., to Jackson, Miss., Evers joined national civil rights leaders in continuing the march. However, Evers repudiated a strongly worded march manifesto issued June 8, declaring it "too critical of President Johnson." He also complained that the highly publicized march could "turn into another Selma, where everyone goes home with the cameramen and leaves us holding the bag." After other march leaders announced on June 11 that they would encourage black voter registration while en route to Jackson, Evers supported the march's objectives and labeled the protest a "good thing." Evers led demonstrations in Natchez in February and March 1967 to protest the murder of a local NAACP official. He also led marches in Jackson in June after police shot and killed a black delivery man during disturbances at Jackson State College.

Evers ran for Congress in a 1968 special election to fill the seat vacated by John Bell Williams [*q.v.*] after he became Mississippi governor in January. Running against six white opponents, Evers won a plurality in the Feb. 27 election but lost the runoff on March 12 by over 40,000 votes. He supported Sen. Robert F. Kennedy (D, N.Y.) [*q.v.*] in his bid for the Democratic presidential nomination in 1968, serving as state cochairman for the Kennedy campaign in Mississippi. Evers campaigned for Kennedy in California and was with the Senator when he was assassinated on June 5.

The regular Mississippi Democratic Party selected Evers in July 1968 as one of four blacks in its 68-member delegation to the August Democratic National Convention (DNC). Evers rejected the offer as "tokenism," helped organize a biracial challenge delegation, the Loyal Democrats of

Mississippi, and testified before the DNC Credentials Committee. On Aug. 20 the Committee voted overwhelmingly to unseat the regular state delegation and give all of Mississippi's Convention seats to the challengers. Following the Convention Evers was chosen the Democratic national committeeman from Mississippi.

A candid, extroverted and self-confident figure, Evers remained a shrewd businessman as well as a tireless activist and organizer in Mississippi. He repeatedly argued that economic independence, with increased black employment and black-owned businesses, was a crucial underpinning for black political advancement in the South. In 1966 Evers opened the Medgar Evers Shopping Center in Fayette, and in 1970 he added a motel with a restaurant and lounge to the complex.

Evers ran for mayor of Fayette in 1969, organizing a strong drive to get out the black vote. He won the May 13 Democratic primary, was unopposed in the June election and resigned his post as NAACP state field secretary before he was sworn in as mayor on July 7. The first black mayor of a biracial community in Mississippi since Reconstruction, Evers successfully lobbied with the federal government, foundations and businesses to secure grants and new industry for Fayette. In April 1971 he was nominated to run for governor by the Loyal Democrats, but he was defeated in the November election. [See NIXON Volume]

[CAB]

For further information:
Charles Evers, *Evers*, ed. Grace Halsell (New York, 1971).

FAIRBANK, JOHN K(ING)

b. May 24, 1907; Huron, S.D.
China specialist.

John King Fairbank attended Phillips Exeter Academy and graduated summa cum laude from Harvard in 1929. A Rhodes scholar, he studied and lectured at Tsinghua University in Peking for three years. Concentrating on the impact of Western imperialism upon China, Fairbank earned a Ph.D. at Oxford in 1936 and then returned to teach at Harvard. In *The United States and China* (1948), Fairbank wrote the first definitive account of Sino-American relations. He became a full professor at Harvard the next year. Under his leadership Harvard's interdisciplinary East Asian Institute became one of the University's most distinguished divisions.

In March 1952 Fairbank's career was briefly threatened by his record of opinions and service as a civilian adviser in China during World War II. In the national obsession to fix responsibility for the "loss" of China, two senators and the F.B.I. branded Fairbank "a conscious agent" of the Soviet Union. Unlike others similarly accused, Fairbank testified forcefully on his own behalf before a Senate committee and escaped personal disaster. [See TRUMAN Volume]

Fairbank emerged from relative academic obscurity in the mid-1960s by participating in renewed public discussions of America's China policy. China's "Cultural Revolution" and the possibility of its entry into the Vietnam war revived Americans' traditional fascination with the world's most populous nation. As a result of appearances before the Senate Foreign Relations Committee, Fairbank's views gained attention among those seeking an alteration in America's China policy.

During Committee hearings on China in March 1966, Fairbank pressed the need for a greater awareness of Chinese culture and history. Opposing widely held visions of a distinctive Communist dictatorship, Fairbank saw continuity in Chinese leadership. Chairman Mao, he claimed, "is much more the successor of the [Chinese] emperors" than of Marx or Lenin. China's self-isolation and declarations of superiority, Fairbank suggested, also dated back to the imperial epoch. China, he noted, "crav[es] for greater prestige in the world to redress the balance of the last century's humiliations." Fairbank urged that U.S. policymakers take note of this mood and begin "step-by-step" discussions with the Peking government. Emphasizing patience with the regime, he did not call for immediate diplomatic recognition or for the withdrawal of the U.S. fleet from the straits separating China from Taiwan.

Fairbank found "rather striking" similarities between America's Vietnam actions and those taken in the 19th century by European powers in Asia. "The American buildup in South Vietnam is so massive it comes very close to a colonial takeover," despite its "only temporary" intent. Terming the conflict a civil war, Fairbank favored economic rather than military assistance.

Following Fairbank's testimony the news media frequently interviewed the Harvard professor on developments in Sino-American relations. He visited mainland China for the first time in nearly 25 years during the spring of 1972.

[JLB]

FARMER, JAMES L(EONARD)

b. Jan. 12, 1920; Marshall, Tex.
National Director, Congress of Racial Equality, February 1961-March 1966.

Farmer, the grandson of a slave, received a Bachelor of Divinity degree from Howard University in 1941 but refused ordination as a Methodist minister because the church was then segregated in the South. Instead Farmer turned to a career in labor and race relations work, serving during the 1940s and 1950s as an organizer for several unions. He was race relations secretary for the Fellowship of Reconciliation and program director for the NAACP. Farmer was a founder of the Congress of Racial Equality (CORE), created in the early 1940s as an interracial organization to fight racial discrimination by means of nonviolent direct action techniques. He became national director of CORE in February 1961 and in May launched the Freedom Rides, a protest that helped desegregate interstate transportation facilities and that won for both CORE and Farmer a major place in the civil rights movement. During 1963 Farmer led anti-segregation demonstrations in several North Carolina cities and in Plaquemines, La. He also served as co-chairman of the 1963 March on Washington. [See KENNEDY Volume]

In April 1964 the Brooklyn chapter of CORE announced plans for a "stall-in" of cars on major routes leading to the New York World's Fair, set to open on April 22. The proposed demonstration, intended to protest the condition of blacks in New York City, immediately became a center of controversy. Farmer publicly opposed the idea, saying the stall-in would not be orderly or nonviolent or effective in dramatizing blacks' needs. When the Brooklyn chapter refused to drop its plans, the national CORE office suspended the branch and quickly developed its own plan for demonstrations at specific sites within the fair grounds. Only 12 cars attempted to stall-in on April 22, but several hundred people demonstrated in the fair grounds, Farmer among them.

Despite his opposition to the disruptive stall-in, Farmer refused to endorse a July 1964 statement, issued by the leaders of several other civil rights organizations, that called for a "moratorium" on mass demonstrations during the 1964 presidential campaign. Farmer asserted that "people must be allowed to protest" and said CORE would engage in "all the necessary nonviolent action" to support the challenge of the Mississippi Freedom Democratic Party (MFDP) against the seating of the regular Mississippi delegation at the Democratic National Convention in August 1964. CORE workers led a round-the-clock vigil outside the Convention hall in Atlantic City while the MFDP's challenge was being considered.

In January 1965 the all-black Voters League in Bogalusa, La., invited CORE to aid in a campaign for desegregation and increased black employment in the town. Farmer joined the highly publicized protests in April, leading mass marches to the city hall on April 9 and 20. Vice President Hubert H. Humphrey [*q.v.*] reportedly intervened in late April and convinced Farmer and CORE to accept a mediation effort and halt their demonstrations. During the Bogalusa demonstrations Farmer defended CORE's controversial association with the Deacons for Defense, a black self-defense group that often supplied protection against intimidation and assaults to civil rights workers in Louisiana. After reaffirming CORE's own commitment to nonviolence, Farmer stated that CORE had "no right to tell Negroes in Bogalusa or anywhere else that they do not have the right to defend their homes. It is a constitutional right."

At its July 1965 annual convention, CORE delegates adopted a resolution calling for the withdrawal of U.S. troops from Vietnam. Although a pacifist and opponent of the Vietnam war, Farmer objected to the resolution on the grounds that the peace and civil rights movements should remain separate. He organized a successful effort to retract the resolution before the convention's end. The same convention endorsed a continuation of the civil rights drive in Bogalusa, and the campaign there was resumed on July 7. Farmer returned to the city and led 600 people in a silent march on July 11. The demonstrations continued into early August, eventually bringing Louisiana Gov. John J. McKeithen [*q.v.*] and John Doar [*q.v.*], head of the Justice Department's Civil Rights Division, to Bogalusa to try to resolve the crisis. The Bogalusa campaign finally ended with desegregation of local restaurants and theaters, the employment of two black policemen and a beginning of school desegregation under court order.

CORE announced in December 1965 that Farmer would resign as national director on March 1, 1966. Farmer explained that he was planning to establish and head a private agency, the National Center for Community Action Education, which would oversee a nationwide program to improve literacy and job skills among unemployed minorities. Farmer had submitted a proposal for this project to the Office of Economic Opportunity (OEO) in August 1965, and he later said he had received "assurances" from OEO before he left CORE that OEO would fund the center. By July 1966 OEO had not approved a grant for the project, and Farmer announced he was abandoning his plan for lack of funding. According to historians August Meier and Elliott Rudwick, several big city mayors were wary of Farmer's center and its radical supporters. Their pressure allegedly kept the Johnson Administration from funding the project. In July 1966 Farmer was named a consultant to New Jersey's antipoverty program, and in September he joined the faculty of Lincoln University as a professor of social welfare.

Farmer was a member of the Black Independents and Democrats for Rockefeller, organized in July 1968 to support New York Gov. Nelson Rockefeller [*q.v.*] for the presidency. In the same year, Farmer ran for Congress with Republican and Liberal Party endorsements in Brooklyn's 12th district but was defeated in the November election by Democrat Shirley Chisholm. During the 1968 presidential campaign Farmer had opposed Richard Nixon, calling his civil rights record "apathetic at best and negative at worst." Despite that criticism, Farmer was appointed an assistant secretary of Health, Education and Welfare in February 1969. He served in that post until December 1970. [See NIXON Volume]

[CAB]

For further information:
August Meier and Elliott Rudwick, *CORE: A Study in the Civil Rights Movement, 1942-1968* (New York, 1973).

FAUNTROY, WALTER E(DWARD)
b. Feb. 6, 1933; Washington, D.C.
Vice Chairman, District of Columbia City Council, September 1967-March 1969.

Fauntroy attended Washington public schools and graduated from the Yale Divinity School in 1958. The following year he became pastor of Washington's New Bethel Baptist Church. In 1960 Fauntroy was made the Washington bureau director of the Southern Christian Leadership Conference (SCLC), and in that post he became a close friend of Martin Luther King [*q.v.*]. He was a coordinator of the March on Washington in 1963. Fauntroy also participated in James Meredith's first march in Mississippi in 1965 and in the 1966 Selma-to-Montgomery march. On Sept. 6, 1967 the 34-year-old Baptist minister was appointed vice chairman of the Washington city council by President Johnson.

While councilman, Fauntroy remained

active in the civil rights movement. He joined with Stokely Carmichael [*q.v.*] in January 1968 in an attempt to create a "Black United Front" of moderate and radical leaders to formulate a unified black political program. The next month Fauntroy refused to bow to the demands of Rep. William J. Scherle (R, Iowa) that he resign his council seat or cease his support of the Poor People's March planned by the SCLC for later in the spring of 1968. In the aftermath of Martin Luther King's assassination that year, Fauntroy urged Carmichael to disavow his call for insurrection. He appealed to blacks to refrain from rioting and later toured part of Washington with Sen. Robert F. Kennedy (D, N.Y.) [*q.v.*]. In February 1969 President Nixon accepted Fauntroy's resignation from the District city council.

Fauntroy served as national coordinator of the ongoing Poor People's campaign in 1969. In March 1971 he was elected as the District of Columbia's first non-voting congressional delegate. A leading advocate of Washington home rule and the election of the city's mayor, Fauntroy was returned to his seat in 1974.

[TJC]

FEATHERSTONE, RALPH

b. 1939.
d. March 10, 1970.
Program Director, Student Nonviolent Coordinating Committee, 1967-69.

During the early 1960s Featherstone worked as a speech therapist in Washington, D.C. He became active in the civil rights movement in 1964, when he helped organize the Mississippi Summer Project. The Project's aim was to register black voters in the Deep South. Featherstone headed the Project's Freedom Force, which led demonstrations and attempted to raise black consciousness by organizing courses in black history and community problems. Shortly after the Project ended Featherstone began to work for the Student Nonviolent Coordinating Committee (SNCC), one of the Project's sponsors. As a SNCC field secretary in Mississippi and Alabama, he gained the reputation of being a skilled and dedicated organizer. Much of his work for SNCC was a continuation of the Summer Project—registering voters, conducting classes and leading demonstrations.

In May 1967 Featherstone became national program director of SNCC. His close friend, H. Rap Brown [*q.v.*], was named SNCC chairman at the same time. The two leaders shared a growing impatience over civil rights progress and sought to draw a line between their organization and its white liberal supporters. In August 1967 Featherstone caused a controversy by defending an anti-Zionist article which appeared in the *SNCC Newsletter*. He denied that the SNCC was anti-Semitic, but attacked "those Jews in the little Jew shops in the ghettos." Many Jewish liberals, including Theodore Bickel and Harry Golden, withdrew their support from SNCC as a result; civil rights leaders, including Whitney Young [*q.v.*] and Bayard Rustin [*q.v.*], also criticized the SNCC stand. Featherstone again alienated liberals in 1968 by attending a cultural congress in Cuba, which he called "the only free territory in America."

Featherstone left SNCC in 1969 to help establish a farm cooperative in Mississippi and a civil rights bookstore in Washington, D.C. He died in March 1970 when a bomb exploded in a car he was driving. Some blacks suspected that the Ku Klux Klan was responsible, but police claimed that Featherstone had accidentally detonated a device he was carrying in the car. Featherstone's remains were taken to Libya for interment.

[SLG]

FINDLEY, PAUL

b. June 23, 1921; Jacksonville, Ill.
Republican Representative, Ill. 1961- .

Paul Findley, publisher of *The Pike Press*, a small county weekly, represented a prosperous farming district in west central Illinois. After entering Congress he consistently called for balanced budgets and opposed Kennedy Administration domestic programs. [See KENNEDY Volume]

During the Johnson years Findley voted

against the anti-poverty, medicare and federal aid to education bills as well as most legislation favored by organized labor. As a member of the House Agriculture Committee, he denounced government price supports, acreage allotments and market quotas. He also opposed granting Communist-bloc nations credits to purchase American grain. He expressed no objections, however, to transactions with those nations involving immediate payment.

For a conservative Midwestern Republican, Findley's opinions in foreign affairs were unorthodox. A passionate defender of NATO, Findley argued that world peace and order depended on a strong union between European democracies and the U.S. He advocated giving America's NATO allies a larger decision-making role, particularly with regard to the use of nuclear weapons.

In the spring of 1967 Findley proposed that the U.S. threaten North Vietnam with nuclear attack to force it to the negotiating table. However, by the fall he began questioning the legality of American involvement in Vietnam and helped draft a petition calling for a congressional reexamination of the Gulf of Tonkin Resolution. Findley thought American involvement in Vietnam a "fundamental mistake" but nonetheless voted for war appropriations and opposed efforts to set a rigid timetable for withdrawal of American troops from the conflict.

Throughout the 1960s the liberal Americans for Democratic Action (ADA) rated Findley among the most conservative of congressmen. During the Nixon years, however, the ADA reported that Findley was beginning to vote more frequently with congressional moderates. [See NIXON Volume]

[JLW]

FISHER, ADRIAN S(ANFORD)

b. Jan. 21, 1914; Memphis, Tenn.
Deputy Director, Arms Control and Disarmament Agency, October 1961-January 1969.

A Princeton and Harvard Law School graduate, Fisher served as law clerk to Supreme Court Justice Louis Brandeis in 1938 and Justice Felix Frankfurter in 1939. After wartime service in the Army Air Force he became assistant executive officer to the assistant secretary of war and served as technical adviser to the American judges at the Nuremberg trials. After the trials Fisher joined the Washington law firm of Covington and Burling and later became vice president and counsel of the Washington Post Company.

President Kennedy appointed Fisher deputy director of the newly formed Arms Control and Disarmament Agency in October 1961. Within the Agency he directed the gathering of basic data necessary for the presentation of a partial nuclear test ban proposal offered in Geneva in August 1962. During the July 1963 Moscow negotiations that led to the signing of a partial test ban treaty in August of that year, Fisher acted as adviser to Kennedy's personal representative, W. Averell Harriman [*q.v.*]. Later that summer he helped guide the Administration's battle for ratification, which was completed in September. [See KENNEDY Volume]

Fisher continued at his post throughout the Johnson Administration. During this period he alternated with William Foster [*q.v.*] as delegate to the 18 Nation Disarmament Conference, which was attempting to formulate agreements on a comprehensive test ban, a freeze on weapons development, a non-proliferation accord and the destruction of existing weapons. Fisher offered major statements on three of these issues. On March 17, 1964 he outlined the reasons for the U.S. rejection of the Soviet plan, known as the "Gromyko Umbrella," for the scrapping of all but a limited number of strategic missiles in the first stage of complete disarmament. He warned it would produce radical shifts in the current East-West military balance, did not provide for verification to assure that additional missiles were not retained by a party of the treaty and was linked to a demand for the dismantling of all foreign bases, including those Western bases that had become an integral part of the East-West military balance.

Two days later Fisher submitted the U.S.

proposal for a "Bomber Bonfire." Under the plan the U.S. was prepared to destroy 480 operational B-47 jet bombers if the USSR would destroy an equal number of TU-16 "Badger" bombers. The Soviet Union rejected it as an attempt to pass off the retirement of obsolete aircraft as disarmament.

Fisher presented President Johnson's proposal for a freeze on nuclear missiles and bomber forces in April 1964. Under this plan the freeze was to be applied to all long-range, ground-launched, surface-to-surface missiles, all sea-launched missiles, many large strategic bombers and long-range, air-to-surface missiles. Verification was to be assured by a variety of measures including permanent international inspection of all strategic airfields, missile launching sites and research and production centers. Worn or damaged missiles were to be replaced on an inspected one-for-one basis, but no improvement of missiles was to be permitted. The Soviet Union rejected the plan on the grounds that it would not "get rid of one missile or bomber" and would require inspection measures that would open the USSR's strategic forces to Western military espionage.

In August 1965 the United States, in conjunction with several other Western delegations, tabled a non-proliferation treaty designed to prevent the spread of nuclear weapons to non-nuclear states. This proposal faced serious opposition from both the Soviet Union and the major U.S. allies. The Russians objected to the provisions of the early drafts that would have permitted the U.S. to give nuclear weapons to its North Atlantic Treaty Organization (NATO) allies under the proposed Multilateral Nuclear Force. On the other hand, America's allies, particularly Germany, insisted that the present defense system with it assurance of American nuclear protection, be maintained. In addition, the members of the European Atomic Energy Community (Euratom) objected to the treaty provision for inspection of nuclear facilities by the International Atomic Energy Agency (IAEA), believing that inspection by an agency that contained Communist bloc personnel would be tantamount to legalized espionage. Many non-nuclear nations also opposed the treaty for fear that they would be unprotected in a nuclear age.

Over a three-year period Fisher and Foster worked out drafts acceptable to all parties. Fisher, in particular, developed those provisions necessary to obtain Euratom approval. On Jan. 18, 1968 Fisher was able to announce an agreement on a treaty. As a result of his negotiations with Euratom, a provision was made allowing each non-nuclear power to negotiate an agreement with the IAEA either individually or together with other nations on the terms of inspection. Under the treaty the NATO alliance was protected by the article reaffirming the right to individual and collective self-defense. This statement was vague enough to satisfy NATO demands and yet fulfill Soviet requirements that nuclear weapons not be given to U.S. allies, particularly West Germany. In addition, the document gave non-nuclear states assurance of protection from nuclear attack by stipulating that the nuclear powers in the U.N. Security Council would "have to act immediately in accordance with their obligations under the United Nations charter" if such an attack occurred.

In January 1969 Fisher left government service to return to private law practice and to accept the position of dean and professor of international law and international trade at Georgetown University Law Center.

[EWS]

For further information:
E(edson) L(ouis) M(illard) Burns, *A Seat at the Table* (Toronto, 1972).

FITZSIMMONS, FRANK E(DWARD)

b. April 7, 1908; Jeanette, Pa.
President, International Brotherhood of Teamsters, 1967- .

The son of a brewery worker, Fitzsimmons left school at 17 to help support his family. He worked for over 10 years as a truck driver in Detroit, where he joined International Brotherhood of Teamsters (IBT) Local 299, headed by the young Jimmy Hoffa [*q.v.*]. Fitzsimmons's organizing abilities impressed Hoffa, and he became business manager of the local in 1937. Three years later he was elected vice president of Local 299 and in 1943 became secretary-treasurer of the IBT Michigan Conference. In 1961, after Hoffa had become president of the IBT, Fitzsimmons was made an international vice president and joined the union's executive council.

Fitzsimmons built his career in the IBT as a loyal assistant to Hoffa. He supported the aggressive Teamster leader in his struggle to assert his personal authority over the union's powerful regional directors. After Hoffa was convicted of jury-tampering and misuse of union pension funds, he named Fitzsimmons his successor. In 1966 a national Teamsters convention elected Fitzsimmons general vice president of the IBT, a post newly created to fill any vacancy in the presidency. Such a vacancy occurred in March 1967, when Hoffa lost his last appeal and went to prison. Fitzsimmons immediately took over his functions as head of the two-million-member union, the largest in the U.S.

The change in command came at an awkward time for the Teamsters. Union leaders were in the midst of renegotiating the national trucking industry contract, and talks with employers were thrown into confusion by Hoffa's departure. Less than a month after taking control, Fitzsimmons had to face a national lockout by trucking employers. He proved to be a skillful negotiator, however, and achieved a settlement in April 1967 that many union officials considered better than anything Hoffa could have gained. Trucking employers agreed to a wage increase of 5% (later raised to 6%) for each of the next three years.

With the contract crisis resolved Fitzsimmons turned to internal union affairs. His quiet, unassuming style contrasted so strongly with Hoffa's flamboyance that some observers doubted the new leader's ability to withstand the pressures of union politics. Fitzsimmons did survive, but only by introducing important policy changes in the IBT. At a meeting of union officials in May 1967, he promised to abandon the tight centralization enforced by Hoffa, returning power over local affairs to the regional union heads and area joint councils. From then on such matters as strike authorization and complaints against trucking firms or union officials were decided "through channels," i.e. in area offices rather than at the national union headquarters. Much of the dissatisfaction that had troubled the IBT under Hoffa subsided as a result.

One continuing problem of the union under Fitzsimmons was the reportedly close connections between organized crime and high IBT officials. Such contacts had grown during the presidency of Hoffa and his predecessor, Dave Beck. During Fitzsimmons's tenure, according to Justice Department officials, they gravitated to the regional level of the union. In *The Fall and Rise of Jimmy Hoffa*, Walter Sheridan claimed that union funds were frequently invested in mafia-sponsored construction projects and that "shakedown" payments were required from trucking employers to preserve labor peace. Fitzsimmons denounced such reports as "slanderous," but they persisted during the late 1960s.

Desiring to counteract the bad publicity focused on the IBT, Fitzsimmons formed the Alliance for Labor Action (ALA) with the United Auto Workers in 1968. The ALA was presented as a "massive program in social and community action," including efforts to organize minority workers. But the new organization damaged relations between Fitzsimmons and the AFL-CIO, which viewed the ALA as an attempt to raid the membership of other unions. Eventually Fitzsimmons won the recognition that he sought by establishing close ties with the Nixon Administration. He endorsed the wage-price freeze of August 1971 and remained on the President's wage board even after other labor leaders had quit. In 1972 he supported Nixon for reelection.

Fitzsimmons was elected president of the IBT in his own right in July 1971; at the end of the year, Nixon released Hoffa from serving the rest of his sentence on the condition that he refrain from union activity until 1980. Hoffa soon began a campaign to regain the IBT presidency, but he disappeared mysteriously in July 1975, probably murdered by individuals opposed to his return to union office. No evidence was found to connect Fitzsimmons with Hoffa's disappearance, and he was easily reelected in 1976. [See NIXON Volume]

[SLG]

FLOWERS, RICHMOND

b. Nov. 1, 1918; Dothan, Ala.
Attorney General, Ala., 1963-67.

Flowers, the son of a well-to-do, small-town banking family, practiced law until his election to the Alabama State Senate in 1955. Serving with George Wallace [*q.v.*] as floor manager for Gov. James E. Folsom's legislative programs, he remained in the Alabama Senate until 1959.

In 1962 Flowers was elected Alabama's attorney general on a segregationist platform. George Wallace was chosen Alabama governor the same year. Flowers and Wallace soon broke ranks over integration of the Alabama schools. Flowers opposed Wallace's "segregation forever" slogan and the Governor's promise to defy a court order mandating the integration of the University of Alabama. He warned that such defiance would provoke violence. Alabama's "soul," he said in his own inaugural speech, "will soon be laid before the world. God grant that we may not be ashamed of it."

Attorney General Flowers pursued a civil rights course that made him, as Andrew Kopkind wrote in the *New Republic*, "an agent of the changes Wallace dreaded." He intervened directly in the deeply controversial 1965 trial of Thomas L. Coleman for the slaying of white civil rights worker Jonathan Daniels. Daniels, a New Hampshire seminarian, was shot upon his release from a Fort Deposit jail after an arrest during civil rights picketing. Flowers, who relieved the county prosecutor, was initially "shocked and amazed" that Coleman's grand jury indictment was for manslaughter and not first-degree murder. When the allpwhite jury acquitted Coleman, Flowers declared, ". . . now those who feel they have a license to kill . . . have been issued that license. It is our duty to do what is necessary to retrieve it."

In October 1965 another all-white jury found Ku Klux Klansmen Collie LeRoy Wilkins not guilty of the March 25, 1965 slaying of Mrs. Viola Liuzzo, another Northern while civil rights worker who was murdered following the Selma-to-Montgomery march. Flowers again relieved the county prosecutor. When this jury voted for acquittal, he termed the verdict "a complete breakdown of justice and law and order." *Life* Magazine lauded Flowers for "laying his political career on the line in the pursuit of due process."

During Flowers's four years as Alabama's attorney general, he achieved national fame as a racial moderate and enemy of Gov. George Wallace. He began a gubernatorial campaign in the fall of 1965 (against Mrs. Lurleen Wallace, running as her husband's surrogate in a state that barred consecutive reelection) but was given little chance for success. He placed his electoral hopes in the hands of the state's newly enfranchised Negroes. To win their 200,000 votes, Flowers canvassed urban slums and rural shantytowns. Appealing to the small middle-class Negro community and the militant poor, he promised significant Negro appointments to state jobs, housing aid and the removal of the Confederate flag from atop the capitol. He emphasized the need for industrial development and improved educational opportunities. Flowers freely admitted that his campaign was designed to attract black support, "Sure I solicit the Negro vote. I'm promising equal opportunity, equal education and good jobs for every citizen in this state." Flowers's candidacy marked the first time in modern Alabama history that a major candidate was not a segregationist. His campaign, though it softened the rhetoric of Alabama's racial debate, was unsuccessful. Flowers polled only 18% of the vote, while Mrs. Wallace's 52% majority forestalled a runoff.

On Aug. 2, 1968 a federal grand jury in Birmingham indicted Flowers on charges of extortion conspiracy. Flowers allegedly used his power as attorney general to facilitate the extortion. He was convicted in March 1969 and paroled in October 1973.

[TJC]

FONG, HIRAM L(EONG)
b. Oct. 1, 1907; Honolulu, Hawaii.
Republican Senator, Hawaii, 1959-77.

The son of indentured plantation workers, Fong worked his way through the University of Hawaii and Harvard Law School to become a successful lawyer and millionaire businessman. He stood out in a generation of upwardly mobile Chinese-Americans who challenged the Caucasian plantation elite's economic leadership on the islands. Fong won election to the Hawaiian Territorial Legislature in 1938 as a Republican and served as speaker of that body between 1948 and 1954. In the same period he secured a working relationship with the powerful International Longshoremen's and Warehousemen's Union (ILWU), rare for a Republican.

Fong was elected to the U.S. Senate in Hawaii's first general election as a state in July 1959. He later won designation as the state's senior senator and the longer term of office. In the Senate he was characterized as a Republican moderate. He tended to take more liberal stands on domestic issues than on foreign policy and was leading sponsor of civil rights legislation. [See KENNEDY Volume]

Despite the disastrous performance of Sen. Barry Goldwater (R, Ariz.) [*q.v.*] as the Republican presidential candidate in the November elections, Fong won reelection to the Senate by a comfortable margin.

Fong was accorded modest ratings of from 30% to 40% on his voting record by both the liberal Americans for Democratic Action and the conservative Americans for Constitutional Action. In August 1964 he sponsored gun control legislation, and throughout the Johnson Administration he fought for stringent regulations. A member of the Senate Special Committee on Aging, he was one of only a few Republicans to support Johnson's 1965 proposal to set up an Administration on Aging as part of Department of Health, Education and Welfare. In 1965 he also worked to win passage for new immigration legislation, which eliminated many of the old restrictions against Asians, and successfully sponsored an amendment to the voting rights bill, which provided for poll watchers in voting districts where provisions of the bill had become effective.

In September 1968 Fong joined two other Republicans and four Southern Democrats on the Senate Judiciary Committee in voting against Johnson's nomination of Supreme Court Justice Abe Fortas [*q.v.*] to be Chief Justice. The Fortas nomination was finally defeated by a Senate filibuster in October.

Fong endorsed the candidacy of Richard M. Nixon [*q.v.*] at the 1968 Republican National Convention, and he became highly partisan and more conservative under the new Republican Administration. Consistently voting for large defense appropriations, Fong's unstinting support of Nixon's Vietnam policy hurt his popularity in Hawaii and weakened his relationship with the ILWU. Nonetheless, the ILWU and his personal organization—the Republican Party in Hawaii had become almost totally ineffective—carried him to a narrow reelection victory in 1972. [See NIXON Volume]

[JCH]

FORD, GERALD R(UDOLPH)
b. July 14, 1913; Omaha, Neb.
Republican Representative, Mich. 1949-73; House Minority Leader, January 1965-December 1973.

Gerald R. Ford grew up in Grand Rapids, Mich. He earned his B.A. at the University of Michigan, where he played center on the varsity football team. Declining offers from professional teams, he went to Yale Law School, graduating in 1941, and served in the Navy during World War II. In 1948 Ford upset an incumbent representative in the GOP House primary and easily won election 12 times. In January 1959 he supported Rep. Charles A. Halleck (R, Ind.) [*q.v.*] in his campaign for the House minority leadership, but four years later he defeated Halleck's candidate for the chairmanship of the House Republican Conference Committee. Popular with his colleagues, Ford agreed to run for the position at the urging of the House Republican "Young Turks," led by Reps. Charles

E. Goodell (R, N.Y.) [*q.v.*] and Robert P. Griffin (R, Mich.) [*q.v.*]. He frequently supported the Kennedy Administration's foreign and defense policies but remained opposed to most New Frontier domestic legislation. [See EISENHOWER, KENNEDY Volumes]

On Nov. 29, 1963 President Johnson appointed Ford to the seven-member commission headed by Chief Justice Earl Warren [*q.v.*] to investigate the assassination of John F. Kennedy. After the panel's report became public in September 1964, Ford defended its conclusions and in 1965 coauthored *Portrait of the Assassin*, which supported the Warren Commission's contention that Lee Harvey Oswald acted alone in the President's murder.

The Republicans' disastrous showing in the 1964 elections convinced many House members that their leadership needed a new image. The "Young Turks" persuaded Ford to oppose Halleck, although both the Indiana Republican and he shared similar voting records. The conservative Americans for Constitutional Action gave Halleck an 86% rating and marked Ford 83% right on the same issues. But younger House Republicans considered Halleck inattentive to their views, and liberal members strongly condemned his unofficial coalition with Southern Democrats. Ford promised his colleagues a more open and positive leadership that would make every member "a sixty-minute player." In addition, the ruggedly handsome Ford appeared an attractive alternative to the 64-year-old, overweight Halleck, who bitterly assailed the confrontation as a "beauty contest." By a vote of 73 to 67, Ford unseated Halleck on Jan. 4, 1965. However, the Party caucus then defeated Ford's candidate for minority whip, Peter H. B. Frelinghuysen (R, N.J.) [*q.v.*] and elected Leslie Arends.

Ford worked to end the House Republicans' silent partnership with Southern Democratic committee chairmen, which prevented important legislation from reaching the House floor. Instead, the new Minority Leader wanted Johnson's Great Society proposals brought out of committee in order to permit House Republicans a chance to vote for or against the legislation. He urged his colleagues to offer positive alternatives to White House legislation. "If the Southern Democrats vote with us, fine," he wrote in January 1965, "but they will be voting for a Republican position."

The new strategy failed during the 89th Congress because the massive Democratic majority enabled the President's party either to defeat, or when necessary, to incorporate Republican amendments into Great Society legislation and then assume full credit for each bill's enactment. During the Ways and Means Committee hearings on the medicare bill, Chairman Wilbur Mills (D, Ark.) [*q.v.*] agreed to amendments covering the cost of doctors' services and drugs in the measure proposed by the Committee's ranking Republican, Rep. John W. Byrnes (R, Wisc.) [*q.v.*]. Reported out of committee with the Byrnes provisions, a narrow 70-68 majority of GOP House members voted for medicare in July 1965. Ford alone of Michigan's nine-member Republican congressional delegation voted against the law.

The Republican gain of 47 House seats in November 1966 gave Ford an opportunity to demonstrate his leadership style. Through hard work and an honest, easygoing personal style, he could usually bridge the geographic and ideological differences among House Republicans. He endorsed the policy recommendation of Reps. Goodell and Albert H. Quie (R, Minn.) [*q.v.*] to replace programmed federal assistance to localities with a "block grant" appropriation to the states. After a vigorous lobbying campaign, the Administration defeated the Republican effort to include the block grant system in the May 1967 education aid bill. However the House agreed, for the first time, to implement the block grant method in the Crime Control and Safe Streets Act in August 1967. In May 1967 Ford again expressed the need for ending the conservative coalition, "to drive Southern Democrats into the arms of the Administration—where they belong." But during the 90th Congress the coalition enjoyed a vigorous revival. According to *Congressional Quarterly*, the coalition won only 25% of the votes on selected issues in 1965 and 32% in 1966; yet in

1967, its margin of victory rose to 67%.

During the debate on the war in Vietnam, Ford established a reputation for partisanship that strained relationships both with the White House and Senate Minority Leader Everett M. Dirksen (R, Ill.) [*q.v.*]. On July 29, 1965 the Minority Leader revealed to reporters that at a White House briefing Senate Majority Leader Mike Mansfield (D, Mont.) [*q.v.*] had expressed strong reservations over the President's plan to escalate the war in Vietnam. Three days later Johnson angrily assailed Ford as a man "who broke my confidence." According to J. F. ter Horst's biography of Ford, relations between the two never recovered from Ford's breach of trust. When in April 1966 Ford accused the Administration of "shocking mismanagement" of the war, Dirksen, who strongly endorsed Johnson on Vietnam, also publicly rebuked the House leader. Ford then agreed to inform Dirksen in advance of any future criticisms he made of the war and deferred to the Illinois Senator for the presentation of the foreign affairs segment of their joint Republican "State of the Union" address in January 1967.

However Dirksen rarely reviewed Ford's prepared texts, and the House leader continued to assail Johnson's war policies as secretive and excessively cautious. A constant advocate of intensive bombing, Ford asked in an August 1967 House speech, "Why are we pulling our best punches in Vietnam?" He said that he could find "no justification for sending one more American" soldier to Vietnam until the President established a sea quarantine against North Vietnamese ports and ordered air strikes against "all known oil storage targets and military and industrial bases in North Vietnam."

Ford proved equally militant when northern cities became the scene of violent race riots. Following racial disturbances in Los Angeles, Chicago and Springfield, Mass., he called for an investigation of subversive influences within the civil rights movement. In his January 1967 GOP "State of the Union" message, Ford asked that persons crossing state lines with the intent to riot be liable to federal prosecution.

In the spring of 1968 Ford confronted the first challenge of his leadership when a group of liberal republicans led by Goodell and Quie defied Ford's opposition to the open housing bill, which had just passed the Senate with Dirksen's assistance. Goodell and Quie persuaded 77 Republican members to announce support for the measure, compelling Ford to endorse the bill just before the final vote.

Ford opposed Johnson's request in January 1967 for a 6% tax surcharge and instead advocated reductions in non-military programs. He warned that Johnson's tax increase "could be a depressant which could trigger a very serious economic recession." In June 1968, however, Ford agreed to the Administration's compromise tax package when Johnson agreed to reduce federal expenditures by $6 billion for fiscal 1969 and impose a 10% surcharge.

Ford served as permanent chairman at the August 1968 Republican National Convention. As in 1960 and 1964, he received brief consideration as the Party's vice presidential candidate. Hoping for a Republican majority that would make him Speaker of the House, Ford campaigned hard for the GOP in 1966 and 1968. He remained the minority leader during the Nixon Administration until December 1973, when he succeeded Spiro T. Agnew [*q.v.*] as vice president. Upon the resignation of President Richard M. Nixon in August 1974, Ford became the 38th President of the United States. [See Nixon Volume]

[JLB]

For further information:

J. F. terHorst, *Gerald Ford* (New York, 1974).

FORD, HENRY II

b. Sept. 4, 1917; Detroit, Mich.
Chairman and Chief Executive Officer, Ford Motor Company, 1960- .

Henry Ford II was the grandson of the legendary industrialist Henry Ford and the son of Ford Motor Co. president Edsel Ford. The young Ford attended Yale University and served in the Navy during World War II. He was released from service in August 1943 and began an apprenticeship in top management under the tutelage of his 80-year-old grandfather, who had resumed control of the company following the death of Edsel Ford that May. He was named president of Ford in 1945 at the age of 28. Unlike his conservative grandfather, an autocratic manager and a bitter foe of unionism, the younger Ford developed a more flexible policy toward the demands of the United Automobile Workers (UAW). In the immediate postwar era he began a sweeping reform of the administrative structure of the company, hiring a specially recruited "Whiz Kid" management team, which included Robert S. McNamara [*q.v.*], to modernize the firm's inefficient managerial system and production techniques. To a large extent Ford adopted the more decentralized structure of its giant rival, General Motors. [See TRUMAN, EISENHOWER, KENNEDY Volumes]

Fortune magazine reported in 1964 that on the basis of total sales Ford was the fourth-largest corporation in the nation, ranking second in the auto industry behind General Motors. Ford had its best year in 1965 and its second best in 1968, when its earnings reached $626 million. Profits were much lower in 1967 because of a UAW strike in September and October. Henry Ford II, who denounced the work stoppage as "totally unjustified" and a "bludgeon against the public interest," agreed to a wage settlement providing an estimated 91-cent-an-hour increase in wages and fringe benefits over the next three years. This package substantially exceeded the Johnson Administration's then current 3.2% wage guidelines. The settlement also included, for the first time, a guaranteed-annual-income plan under which a worker with seven years service would be entitled to 52 weeks income at 95% of take-home pay in the event of a layoff. Although the union's membership ratified the new contract on Oct. 25, local plant disputes, centering on unresolved shopfloor grievances and the pace of work, continued in 33 of 101 Ford bargaining units. Full production was not resumed until Nov. 10.

Along with the rest of the auto industry, Ford vigorously opposed the enactment of auto safety standards in 1966 and 1967. He labeled the safety campaign, sparked by consumer advocate Ralph Nader [*q.v.*], "a harassment to the automobile industry" and asserted that Nader didn't know much about rear axles. In December Ford criticized many federal motor vehicle safety regulations as "unreasonable, arbitrary and technically unfeasible" and said that enforcement could shut down some Ford plants. Nader branded Ford's remarks "industrial extortion." Between September 1966 and September 1967, Ford had to recall 531,000 cars because of safety defects. In response to critics who blamed the profusion of automobiles for environmental pollution and the declining quality of city life, Ford said in July 1966: "As far as urban transportation is concerned, what people want is clear. They have voted overwhelmingly in favor of the automobile. . . . The city's problems cannot be solved by encouraging transit at the expense of the automobile."

A lifelong Republican, Ford joined 25 other business leaders in September 1964 to form a National Independent Committee for Johnson and Humphrey. In January 1966 he urged U.S. industry to invest in combating poverty and aiding education as a form of "good business." "The poor simply are not very good customers for our products," he pointed out. During the Johnson Administration he often led business efforts in support of Great Society programs. His support (along with 21 other executives) for the Model Cities program in October 1966 was said by *Congressional Quarterly* to have been a "key factor" in the acceptance of the measure by Congress. During 1967 and 1968 Ford headed a group of 500 businessmen whose lobbying proved crucial to the passage of Johnson's 10% tax surcharge in June 1968.

Ford headed a National Alliance of Businessmen (NAB) in January 1968 to promote the federal government's Job Opportunities in the Business Sector (JOBS) program. The purpose of JOBS was to expand opportunities for the chronically unemployed by giving subsidies to businesses hiring such people. Ford reported in March 1969 that the NAB was responsible for the hiring of 145,000 persons and that 87,850 were still on the job. [See NIXON Volume]

[TO]

FORMAN, JAMES

b. Oct. 4, 1928; Chicago, Ill.
Executive Secretary, Student Nonviolent Coordinating Committee
October 1961-May 1966.

A graduate of Roosevelt University and a former schoolteacher in Chicago, Forman became executive secretary of the Student Nonviolent Coordinating Committee (SNCC) in October 1961. Described by one observer of the civil rights movement as "personable, canny" and "erudite," Forman established an administrative structure for SNCC and participated in its demonstrations against segregation in Albany, Ga., in December 1961 and in Danville, Va., in June 1963. He also helped organize voter registration drives in Greenwood, Miss., and Selma, Ala., in 1963. [See KENNEDY Volume]

Forman participated in January 1964 demonstrations to desegregate public accommodations in Atlanta, Ga. He and SNCC chairman John Lewis [*q.v.*] led a Jan. 18 protest outside a segregated restaurant in which 78 were arrested. Forman himself was arrested in demonstrations at another segregated restaurant on Jan. 27. During the next few months he helped plan the 1964 Mississippi Freedom Summer, a project to increase black voter registration and to establish freedom schools and community centers for blacks in that state. He helped train the student volunteers for the project and directed SNCC's national office which was moved from Atlanta to Greenwood, Miss., for the summer. Forman accompanied the delegates of the Mississippi Freedom Democratic Party (MFDP) to the Democratic National Convention in Atlantic City in August 1964, where they challenged the seating of Mississippi's regular Democrats. When the Party leadership offered the MFDP a compromise in which it would receive two "at-large" seats in the Convention, Forman urged the delegates to reject the proposal, which they did. Forman and SNCC also supported the MFDP's unsuccessful 1965 challenge to the seating of Mississippi's five representatives in Congress.

SNCC and the Southern Christian Leadership Conference cooperated in an intensive voter registration drive in Selma, Ala., beginning in January 1965. During the campaign Martin Luther King [*q.v.*] suggested a march from Selma to Montgomery to protest the denial of voting rights to Alabama blacks. Forman opposed the idea because he felt that mass marches "create the impression" that the people were forcing change while in fact they achieved almost nothing. The march began March 7 but was quickly routed when state troopers attacked the demonstrators at the Edmund Pettus Bridge in Selma. Forman, unwilling to let such violence successfully end the protest, joined a second attempt to begin the march, which was also turned back at the bridge on March 9. The next day Forman joined in a demonstration in Montgomery, organized by students from Tuskegee Institute to protest the police attacks in Selma, in which the protesters marched to the state capitol and staged a sit-in on its steps until 2 a.m. Forman led another march on the capitol on the 16th, but the 600 marchers were attacked en route by state and county police wielding ropes, nightsticks and electric cattle prods. That evening Martin Luther King addressed a rally in Montgomery and called for a mass march on the county courthouse the next day. Forman, King and John Lewis led a March 17 demonstration of 1,600 people. When they reached the courthouse, several of the rights leaders conferred with the local sheriff and John Doar [*q.v.*] of the Justice Department, reportedly reaching an agreement that harassment of orderly demonstrations would be ended so long as rights leaders obtained parade permits for all future marches in Montgomery. Forman and local students continued demonstrations in the city until March 21, when the final march from Selma began. Forman, whose commitment to nonviolence had been tactical rather than philosophical at the time he joined SNCC, later wrote that the Montgomery protests, especially the March 16 demonstration and the police attack, "snapped" his "ability to continue engaging in nonviolent direct action."

Forman was voted out as executive secretary of SNCC at a staff meeting in Kingston Springs, Tenn., in May 1966. According to his account in *The Making of Black Revolutionaries*, he had wanted to leave the post since the fall of 1964 to give himself more time for reading, analysis and writing and to rebuild his health. (Forman had nearly died of a bleeding ulcer in January 1963 and had recurrent health problems after that.) At the same meeting SNCC adopted a resolution introduced by Forman to stop using integrated field teams, and elected Stokely Carmichael [*q.v.*] chairman over John Lewis. Forman supported Carmichael's election on the grounds that his greater militance and his emphasis on blackness represented the direction in which SNCC should move. He also supported the black power concept expounded by Carmichael after his election.

Forman remained active in SNCC as administrator of its national office during the leadership transition and as its director of international affairs after the spring of 1967. He attended the National Conference for New Politics held in Chicago over Labor Day weekend in 1967. There he supported the organization of a black caucus at the Conference and the caucus's demands for 50% of the delegate votes and for endorsement of a statement condemning Israel as an aggressive, imperialist power. Addressing the Conference on Sept. 3, Forman argued for separate political action by blacks, asserting that blacks "have the responsibility to wage our own war of liberation as we see fit" and the "right to define the manner in which we will fight our aggressors." Forman was named minister of foreign affairs of the Black Panther Party in February 1968 when the Party and SNCC formed an alliance. The alliance fell apart in July 1968, and Forman resigned his Party post because of policy differences with the Panthers on questions of security, structure and organizational discipline.

In April 1969 Forman presented a "Black Manifesto" at a Detroit conference on black economic development called by the Interreligious Foundation for Community Organization. The Manifesto called for the establishment of a permanent National Black Economic Development Conference (NBEDC). It demanded that white churches give $500 million to the NBEDC as reparations for their past wrongs to blacks, with the money to be used for educational, cultural and industrial programs in the black community. NBEDC was set up as a permanent organization, and throughout the summer, Forman presented the demand for reparations at the headquarters or conventions of various religious denominations. NBEDC named Forman the director of its programs of community organization in 1970. [See NIXON Volume]

[CAB]

For further information:

James Forman, *Sammy Younge, Jr.: The First Black College Student to Die in the Black Liberation Movement* (New York, 1968).

The Making of Black Revolutionaries (New York, 1972).

FORTAS, ABE

b. June 19, 1920; Memphis, Tenn.
Associate Justice, U.S. Supreme Court, 1965-69.

The son of a Jewish cabinetmaker who had emigrated from England, Fortas worked his way through Southwestern College in Memphis, receiving his B.A. in 1930. Three years later he graduated from Yale Law School, where he had been editor-in-chief of the *Yale Law Journal*. He then taught at the school from 1933 to 1937. During those four years he also worked part-time for the Agricultural Adjustment Administration and the Securities and Exchange Commission (SEC). From 1937 to 1946 Fortas successively held posts in the SEC, the Public Works Administration and the Department of Interior, serving as undersecretary of the interior from 1942 to 1946.

With several other New Dealers he then formed Arnold, Fortas & Porter, which soon became one of Washington's most prestigious and prosperous law firms. With a predominantly corporate practice, Fortas was known for his effectiveness in corporate counseling, antitrust litigation and practice before administrative agencies. He and his firm also developed a reputation for handling, often without charge, some important civil liberties and individual rights cases. Fortas defended several persons accused of being security risks during the McCarthy era. In 1954, serving as court-appointed counsel, he won a landmark ruling from the District of Columbia Court of Appeals that broadened the criminal insanity rule. Again as court-appointed counsel, Fortas represented Clarence Earl Gideon before the Supreme Court in 1963 and got a unanimous Court to overturn a 1942 decision to rule that the states must supply counsel to an indigent defendant accused of a serious crime.

Fortas successfully represented Lyndon Johnson in legal proceedings following his controversial victory in the 1948 Texas Democratic primary. The incident launched a long, close friendship between the two men, and Fortas became Johnson's confidant and one of his most trusted advisers. Johnson's first phone call following John Kennedy's assassination was to Abe Fortas. He often relied heavily on Fortas's counsel during his presidential years. Fortas helped organized the Warren Commission, which investigated Kennedy's assassination, and advised Johnson on appointments, speeches, legislation and foreign policy. He also participated in strategy conferences during the 1964 presidential campaign. When Walter Jenkins [*q.v.*], a top White House aide, was arrested on a morals charge in the fall of 1964, Fortas attempted to keep the story out of the press and then advised Johnson on how to handle the situation. During the Dominican crisis in the spring of 1965, Fortas acted as an unofficial contact between the U.S. and former Dominican president Juan Bosch.

In 1964 Fortas refused an offer to be named Attorney General, preferring to keep his role as Johnson's unofficial adviser. In July 1965, when Arthur Goldberg [*q.v.*] resigned from the Supreme Court to become ambassador to the U.N., Fortas also turned down a nomination to a Court seat. On July 28, however, when Johnson told Fortas he was going to announce his appointment as Associate Justice that day, Fortas acquiesced. Fortas's nomination was well received, and the Senate confirmed his appointment on Aug. 11.

On the bench Fortas was usually in accord with the liberal, activist justices of the Warren Court. He was part of the five-man majority in the June 1966 *Miranda* decision, which placed limits on police interrogation of criminal suspects. Writing for the Court in the May 1967 case of *In re Gault*, Fortas extended to children in juvenile court proceedings many of the constitutional protections required in adult trials. He also joined the majority in two June 1968 decisions. One upheld the right of police to stop and frisk persons for weapons under certain circumstances. The other barred the exclusion of individuals from murder trial juries because of their objections to capital punishment.

Fortas voted repeatedly to sustain civil rights claims. He supported, for example, a March 1966 decision holding unconstitutional a Virginia poll tax for state elections and a June 1968 ruling that an 1866 federal law prohibited racial discrimination in the sale and rental of housing and other property. Fortas's majority opinion in a March 1966 case upheld the federal prosecution, under an 1870 civil rights law, of 17 persons accused of involvement in the murder of three civil rights workers in Mississippi in June 1964. In February 1966 his opinion for the Court overturned the breach-of-the-peace convictions of five blacks who had tried to integrate a public library in Louisiana. Fortas dissented in November 1966 and June 1967 cases in which the majority voted to sustain convictions of civil rights demonstrators.

Fortas's opinion for a unanimous Court in June 1966 reversed the contempt-of-Congress conviction of a former labor union officer who had refused to answer questions before a House Un-American Activities subcommittee. In two 1967 cases Fortas voted to invalidate a Maryland loyalty oath law for public employees and a set of New York State teacher loyalty laws as violations of the First Amendment. He dissented, however, in January 1967 when the Court extended to invasion of privacy suits the rule that erroneous statements had to be made deliberately or recklessly before the press could be held liable. Fortas also voted in favor of a March 1966 ruling that "titillating" advertising could be used to convict a publisher of obscenity, although the materials sold might not in themselves be obscene. As a former corporate attorney, Fortas tended to differ with other liberal justices when they ruled against corporate mergers or altered the judgments of federal regulatory agencies in ways opposed by business.

An extremely hard worker, Fortas developed a reputation as a brilliant jurist whose legal craftsmanship resulted in thorough, scholarly opinions. While on the Court he remained a close adviser to President Johnson, counseling him on such important and delicate issues as race, urban unrest and the Vietnam war. Reportedly, neither Johnson nor Fortas saw anything wrong in continuing their close personal relationship, but their friendship became a source of controversy when Fortas was nominated for the chief justiceship.

On June 13, 1968 Chief Justice Earl Warren [*q.v.*] sent the President a letter of resignation. Announcing Warren's retirement on June 26, Johnson nominated Fortas as Chief Justice and Homer Thornberry, a judge on the U.S. Court of Appeals for the Fifth Circuit and a longtime Johnson associate, for Fortas's seat. Eighteen Republican senators, led by Robert P. Griffin (R, Mich.) [*q.v.*], declared shortly afterwards that they would try to block confirmation of the appointments. Aside from the alleged impropriety of Fortas's advisory relationship with Johnson, opponents of the nominations objected to having a "lame-duck" president choose the new Chief Justice and charged Johnson with cronyism in making his selections. In mid-July Fortas made an unprecedented appearance at the Senate Judiciary Committee hearings on his nomination. Unfriendly questioning by several senators, including Strom Thurmond (R, S.C.) [*q.v.*], made it apparent that hostility to liberal Warren Court decisions and Fortas's own position on several controversial issues was also a factor in the opposition to his confirmation.

In September it was disclosed that Fortas had received $15,000 for teaching a nine-week course in the summer of 1968 at American University Law School. The money had been raised by one of Fortas's former law partners from five prominent businessmen, one of whom had a son involved in a federal criminal case. The Senate Judiciary Committee reported out Fortas's nomination on Sept. 17, by an 11-6 vote, but a coalition of Republicans and conservative Democrats launched a filibuster against the appointment when it came up for Senate consideration late that month. A vote for cloture failed on Oct. 1, and the next day Johnson withdrew Fortas's nomination at the Justice's request. Chief Justice Warren then agreed to stay on until the new president named his successor.

During the next Court term Fortas wrote several significant opinions expanding First Amendment and criminal rights. On May 4, 1969 *Life* magazine reported that in 1966 Fortas had accepted—and then several months later returned—a $20,000 fee from the family foundation of Louis E. Wolfson, a wealthy industrialist who had since been imprisoned for selling unregistered stocks. The article touched off heavy criticism and talk of impeachment proceedings against Fortas. On May 15 Fortas announced his resignation from the Court, making him the first justice ever to resign under the pressure of public criticism. At the same time he made public a long letter to Chief Justice Warren setting forth the details of his involvement with Wolfson and insisting that he was innocent of any wrongdoing. Fortas eventually returned to the private practice of law in Washington. [See NIXON Volume]

[CAB]

For further information:
Fred Graham, "Abe Fortas," in Leon Friedman and Fred L. Israel, eds., *The Justices of the United States Supreme Court, 1789-1969* (New York, 1969), Vol. IV.

FOSTER, WILLIAM C(HAPMAN)
b. April 27, 1897; Westfield, N.J.
Director, Arms Control and Disarmament Agency, September 1961-January 1969.

Prior to his appointment as director of the U.S. Arms Control and Disarmament Agency in September 1961, Foster had a varied career in government, serving as undersecretary of commerce, administrator of the Economic Cooperation Administration and deputy secretary of defense during the Truman Administration. He left government for private industry after Dwight D. Eisenhower's 1953 election, and from 1953 to 1961 he served as an executive for a number of large chemical corporations. In 1958 Foster headed the U.S. delegation to the abortive disarmament conference with the Soviet Union. [See TRUMAN, EISENHOWER Volumes]

As head of the U.S. Arms Control and Disarmament Agency, Foster was responsible for running an autonomous department formed to coordinate and develop disarmament and nuclear testing policy. During the Kennedy Administration he advised the President on a wide range of disarmament policy decisions. He helped draw up major arms control statements including the proposal for "General and Complete Disarmament in a Peaceful World," delivered at the U.N. in September 1961, and the partial test ban treaty tabled at Geneva in August 1962. Acting with a number of high level government officials, Foster coordinated the Administration's fight for ratification of the partial nuclear test ban treaty in September 1963. [See KENNEDY Volume]

In conjunction with his deputy and "alter ego" Adrian Fisher [*q.v.*], Foster negotiated the 1968 non-proliferation treaty, designed to prevent the spread of atomic weapons to non-nuclear powers. This proposal, first tabled at the 18 Nation Disarmament Conference in August 1965, faced serious opposition from both the Soviet Union and U.S. allies. The Russians objected to the provision that would have permitted the U.S. to give nuclear weapons to NATO under the proposed Multilateral Nuclear Force (MLF). On the other hand, members of the European Atomic Energy Community (Euratom) objected to inspection of nuclear facilities by the International Atomic Energy Agency, believing that inspection by an agency that contained Communist-bloc personnel would be tantamount to legalized espionage.

Although major Soviet objections were satisfied when the Johnson Administration abandoned the MLF proposal in December 1966, Foster spent the next year negotiating the final terms of the treaty. Because of illness, Foster was not present at the climax of the negotiations. Early on the morning of Jan. 18, 1968 the U.S. and the Soviet Union finally announced in Geneva that they had reached an agreement on a non-proliferation treaty.

Foster left government service in January 1969 and became president of Porter International Company in 1970.

[EWS]

FOWLER, HENRY H(AMILL)
b. Sept. 5, 1908; Roanoke, Va.
Secretary of the Treasury, April 1965-December 1968.

Following his graduation from Yale Law School in 1934, Henry Fowler became a counsel to the Tennessee Valley Authority, the first of many government positions he held under Democratic administrations. He served on several federal agencies and wartime boards until 1946, when he entered private law practice in Washington, D.C. He rejoined the government during the Korean war, becoming director of the Office of Defense Mobilization and a member of President Truman's National Security Council. During the Eisenhower Administration Fowler resumed his prosperous law practice and also served on the Democratic Advisory Council, an arm of the Democratic National Committee designed to outline Party positions on national issues.

During the Kennedy years Fowler served as undersecretary of the treasury, bringing to the Administration's economic policymaking team experience in administration and sophistication in Washington politics. He devoted much of his attention to winning passage of the Administration's tax program, the centerpiece of which was the $11.5 billion tax cut in 1963 and 1964. Fowler left the Treasury to return to his law practice in March 1964. [See TRUMAN, KENNEDY Volumes]

One year later, while he was representing the Automotive Manufacturers Association in the industry's campaign to repeal the auto excise tax, Fowler was chosen Secretary of the Treasury by President Johnson. Johnson's first choice for the position, utility executive Donald C. Cook [*q.v.*], had turned down the job. Fowler's nomination went through the Senate "without a ripple," *Business Week* wrote, noting his "complete acceptance by the most powerful men in Congress and his solid reputation with the nation's top-most business executives and bankers."

Fowler was not as strong or independent a Treasury Secretary as his predecessor, C. Douglas Dillon [*q.v.*], had been during the Kennedy Administration. He was completely loyal to President Johnson and faithfully represented the Administration through the twists and turns of Johnson economic policy. To the extent that he influenced economic policy, it was generally on the side of caution.

Assuming office during a period of general economic prosperity, Fowler had to face the problems of inflation and the balance of payments deficit, both of which were exacerbated by massive spending on the war in Vietnam. His immediate predecessors on the Kennedy-Johnson economic policymaking team had administered the popular Keynesian policies of tax incentives and tax cuts to spur economic growth. Fowler had to apply the bitter side of the Keynesian prescription: tax increases to slow down the economy and curb inflation.

Reluctantly, Fowler argued before Congress in October 1966 for the suspension of the 7% investment tax credit, which had been passed in 1962 to stimulate business investment in plant and equipment. "This is not offered as a revenue measure, or a tax increase measure or a tax reform measure," he said. "Its purpose is clearly and simply to suspend a stimulant to forces that are proving inflationary in the current economic situation." Congress suspended the credit in October and also temporarily ended certain methods of accelerated depreciation of commercial buildings. Only six months later, however, Fowler sought restoration of the credit because of the Administration's alarm over the abrupt slowing down of business investment.

In August 1967 Fowler began a 10-month battle to win passage of the Administration's anti-inflationary 10% tax surcharge. Declaring that costs for the Vietnam war were running in excess of $22 billion a year, Fowler strongly appealed to the House Ways and Means Committee for taxing authority "to finance a war . . . with no clear prospect of an early ending." Besides the threat of inflation, Fowler said, the surcharge was needed "to avoid the risk of excessively high interest rates and limited credit in particular sectors, such as housing." He also pleaded that Congress "join with the President in making every possible expenditure reduction—civilian and military—short of jeopardizing the nation's security and well-being."

The Administration's request, however, was held up in the Committee, which voted in October 1967 to set the bill aside until the Administration came up with a specific plan to cut spending. Fowler made another strong plea for the surcharge before the Committee in November, in the wake of the devaluation of the British pound. He stressed that the soundness of the dollar depended on Congress's prompt action to reduce the deficit and control inflation. But the Committee's powerful chairman, Rep. Wilbur Mills (D, Ark.) [*q.v.*], found the Administration's new proposal to cut the budget by only $4 billion unacceptable, and the impasse over the tax increase continued.

Fowler continued his fight for the tax surcharge in the first half of 1968, testifying before the House and the Senate repeatedly and mobilizing prominent business leaders behind the measure. Passed by the House in February and the Senate in April, the tax increase, combined with $6 billion in spending cuts, won final approval from the House-Senate conference in June. The "hero" of the lobbying effort, according to

Congressional Quarterly, was Fowler, "who literally pursued bankers and businessmen around the world to seek out their support for the measure."

Fowler's other major concern as Treasury Secretary was the balance of payments deficit. The deficit, aggravated by the expense of the Vietnam war, continued unabated throughout the Johnson years. Fowler was the leading proponent within the Administration of the "go-slow" approach to the problem, while Commerce Secretary John T. Connor [*q.v.*] advocated a more far-reaching plan. Johnson adopted Fowler's advice; for the most part the Administration's balance of payments program was limited to the interest equalization tax on foreign securities and exhortations to corporations to place voluntary restraints on their overseas investments. In 1968, after the devaluation of the pound exacerbated the dollar crisis, Fowler presented a more stringent program to Congress on behalf of the Administration. A proposal to tax U.S. citizens traveling in foreign countries proved highly unpopular, however, and Congress did not act on the plan.

By the end of his tenure, Fowler's public image had suffered a severe decline. Calling Fowler "little more than a mouthpiece for Lyndon Johnson," *Fortune* in February 1968 asserted that "the Treasury has put in a generally inept performance since Fowler took over in April 1965" and "deserves some of the blame for the dissembling, the secrecy and the last-minute improvisation in economic and fiscal matters that have become standard Johnsonian practice."

Fowler resigned as Treasury Secretary in December 1968 and joined the investment banking firm of Goldman, Sachs & Co.

[TO]

FREEMAN, ORVILLE L(OTHROP)

b. March 9, 1918; Minneapolis, Minn.
Secretary of Agriculture, January 1961-January 1969.

Following his graduation from the University of Minnesota in 1940, Freeman joined the Marine Corps. After his discharge he returned to Minnesota to earn a law degree. During the late 1940s he collaborated with Hubert H. Humphrey [*q.v.*], then mayor of Minneapolis, to make the Democratic-Farmer-Labor Party (DFL) Minnesota's dominant political force. Freeman was elected governor on the liberal DFL ticket for three two-year terms beginning in 1954. [See EISENHOWER Volume]

Initially a backer of Hubert Humphrey's 1960 presidential candidacy, Freeman turned to Sen. John F. Kennedy following Humphrey's withdrawal and offered him crucial support at the Democratic National Convention. Briefly considered by Kennedy for the vice presidency, Freeman accepted an appointment as Secretary of Agriculture after he lost a bid for a fourth gubernatorial term in November.

Agriculture was an extremely sensitive post because of the inability of previous administrations to solve the "farm problem": chronic overproduction, an average income for farmers lower than the national average and an unceasing migration of rural population to the cities. In its efforts to increase farm income through price supports and storage of surpluses, the Agriculture Department had the second highest budget of any federal department and thus became the target of sharp congressional criticism. Freeman sought to solve the dilemma by a reimposition of traditional Democratic agricultural policy on a more rigorous and comprehensive scale. Higher price supports, he argued, would temporarily raise farm income, while stringent acreage and production limitations would reduce surpluses and ultimately ensure higher prices for farm products. Freeman's policies aimed at maintaining the small farm family, historically a source of Democratic strength, or at least developing alternate non-farm job opportunities in rural areas.

Freeman was partially successful during the Kennedy years. Farm income rose while acreage limitations and food relief programs abroad reduced surpluses. However, the Secretary was unable to win full authority to impose marketing controls, and the opening of the Soviet market to U.S. wheat in late 1963 only partly offset Freeman's inability to expand the West

European market for American farm products. In addition, the number of farms and the proportion of farmers in the total population continued to decline. Few were pleased with the progress of the farm program. Urban Democrats resented its expense and charged that it mainly enriched wealthy farmers. Republicans, the advocates of free enterprise, favored the gradual elimination of controls. In addition, Southern Democrats, who were avid proponents of price supports, hesitated to add to the power of the Secretary and the federal government. [See KENNEDY Volume]

In the area of price supports, controls and surpluses, Freeman continued the Kennedy policy during the Johnson years. The most important piece of legislation and a major victory for Freeman was the Food and Agriculture Act of 1965. This omnibus farm bill established price support and production control programs for the major crops (cotton, wheat and feed grains) for a four-year period. Under the law farmers would retire a portion of their land devoted to high surplus crops and put it into soil-conserving uses. Most significantly, price-support levels were reduced in order to keep prices competitive on the international market, while the government offered direct cash payments in order to offset any large loss of income to small farmers. In addition, the Secretary now had the authority to take administrative action to increase production.

Another result of the effort to reduce farm surpluses had been the expansion of food distribution programs abroad, but by 1966 production controls had succeeded to a great degree in limiting surpluses. With the growing awareness of world food shortages and famine conditions in India, the Administration no longer viewed the Food for Peace program as a vehicle for the disposal of surpluses; under 1966 legislation it became a form of foreign aid with more precise requirements and objectives. Recipient nations were now generally expected to pay for their food purchases in dollars instead of in local currencies. In addition, their willingness and ability to carry out "self-help" programs to meet food requirements determined the amount of goods they would receive. In 1966 Freeman announced acreage allotment increases for a number of crops to meet commitments abroad, including a 30% increase for wheat.

Because of the passage of the omnibus farm bill and Johnson's considerable skill in handling Congress, Freeman was able to expand the scope of Department activities. One of the most ambitious new programs was the effort to combat hunger in the cities and impoverished rural areas as part of President Johnson's War on Poverty. Despite the budgetary pressures caused by the Vietnam war, food programs were among the fastest growing outlays in the entire U.S. budget during the Johnson Administration, rising from about $836.7 million in fiscal 1965 to a fiscal 1970 projection of $1.5 billion at the end of 1968. The authorizations managed to get through the agriculture committees, dominated by Southern Democrats, because Northern liberals, as the price for their backing of the generous price-support programs, demanded the inclusion of food programs as part of legislative farm packages. In addition, authorizing food for the hungry was far less controversial politically than other Johnson antipoverty programs.

The food stamp program, which was introduced in 1961 on an experimental basis, was made permanent in 1964 and was subsequently expanded to reach larger numbers of Americans. Under the plan people whose incomes met the Department's eligibility requirements bought stamps for less than they were worth and then redeemed them for food at full value in participating grocery stores. In many parts of the country food stamps replaced direct distribution programs, which made available only a limited number of surplus commodities free to the poor. Still, direct distribution of surpluses to institutions was expanded as were school lunch and milk programs.

As Agriculture's sphere of activity expanded, criticism from both sides of the political spectrum increased. Freeman, long the object of conservative attacks, was now confronted with pressure from liberal groups. In 1965 the U.S. Civil Rights Commission cited Department officials for discrimination against Southern Negro farmers. This led Freeman to appoint three Negroes to the committees that administered federal farm programs in their respective states. Freeman's role in opening what he called "the second front of this war," the task of feeding South Vietnam and increasing its agricultural production, earned him the enmity of anti-war activists. The dramatic rise in domestic food prices in 1966, caused in part by the Vietnam war, forced him to defend farmers against the complaints of consumers. Freeman put most of the blame for increased costs on middlemen and exonerated the farmers, who, in fact, had gained little during the inflation.

The food stamp program also came under attack. In October 1967 there were reports that thousands of Southern Negroes, once surplus commodity recipients, faced starvation because they were too poor to purchase food stamps. The National Advisory Commission on Rural Poverty report, issued in December 1967, underscored the relationship between rural poverty and urban discontent and charged that the Department and other government agencies had done too little to aid the rural poor. It recommended that the government revise the food stamp program, improve the quality and availability of services up to the level found in the cities and provide jobs and a guaranteed income. In April 1968 the Citizens' Board of Inquiry into Hunger and Malnutrition in the United States, which had been organized on the recommendation of United Auto Workers President Walter P. Reuther [*q.v.*], scored the food stamp program as a "nightmare for the hungry." Stating that the Department was interested chiefly in making crop producers richer and had "little interest in feeding people," the Board recommended that food programs be transferred either to the Office of Economic Opportunity or to the Health, Education and Welfare Department.

Freeman agreed that not enough had yet been done to eliminate hunger and put the blame for the problem on members of Congress, local officials and the Department bureaucracy, which was slow to change its old habits and sense of priorities. In testimony before the House Agriculture Committee on June 12, 1968, Freeman admitted that he had underestimated the severity and extent of hunger in the U.S. By December 1968 he was able to announce a liberalization of the food stamp program.

Although Freeman's tenure as Secretary of Agriculture witnessed a dramatic reduction in farm surpluses and a rise in prices, his farm policy failed to reverse the historic decline of the American farm family. The number of farms decreased from 3.9 million in 1960 to 3.1 million in 1967, and farmers as a percentage of the total population declined from 8.7% to 5.4%. In the process farming continued to evolve into agribusiness. The small farmers the Administration had pledged to protect lost much of their political potency.

Freeman stepped down in January 1969 with the inauguration of a Republican administration. In 1970 he became president of the Business International Corporation.

[JCH]

FRELINGHUYSEN, PETER H.B.

b. Jan. 17, 1916; New York, N.Y.
Republican Representative, N.J., 1953-75.

A member of a patrician Dutch family that produced three U.S. senators and a Secretary of State, Frelinghuysen graduated from Princeton and Yale Law School. In 1952 he won election to Congress from the most Republican district in New Jersey, a wealthy suburb of New York City. A moderate Republican, Frelinghuysen supported civil rights legislation and a large international role for the United States. He was a member of the House Foreign Affairs Committee and the Education and Labor Committee, becoming the ranking Republican on the latter in 1963. He was especially active in attempting to modify Kennedy's proposed federal aid to education program. [See KENNEDY Volume]

In 1964 Frelinghuysen persistently attacked President Johnson's proposals for an antipoverty program, arguing that the creation of an Office of Economic Opportunity (OEO) would concentrate excessive and unnecessary authority on the federal level.

He drew up an alternative Republican antipoverty bill which delegated greater authority and economic responsibility to the states, gave greater emphasis to education and training and eliminated the OEO and a federal Job Corps. In response to Democratic claims that the OEO would make existing antipoverty programs more effective, Frelinghuysen insisted that its "basic purpose was political." After the passage of the Administration bill, Frelinghuysen, as head of the Republican Task Force on Economic Opportunity in 1965, charged that the War on Poverty was an "administrative shambles" and held hearings in hopes of getting a "full-scale budgetary analysis."

In 1965 Frelinghuysen left the Education and Labor Committee for seats on the Republican Committee on Committes and the Republican Policy Committee. However, he failed to win separate contests for minority whip and chairman of the House Republican Conference despite the support of recently elected minority leader Rep. Gerald Ford (R, Mich.) [*q.v.*] and the demands of Eastern liberals and moderates for representation in the House leadership.

By 1967 Frelinghuysen sat only on the House Foreign Affairs Committee. He made numerous trips abroad and emerged as a major House Republican spokesman on foreign policy. An internationalist, he supported President Johnson on approximately 80% of key roll-call votes concerned with foreign policy. At the August 1968 Republican National Convention, Sen. Everett Dirksen (R, Ill.) [*q.v.*], the Senate minority leader, asked Frelinghuysen to draft a compromise Vietnam plan for the Senator to offer to the Convention. Presidential candidate Richard Nixon [*q.v.*] and New York Gov. Nelson Rockefeller [*q.v.*] found an early plank too critical of President Johnson for not leaving key Vietnam decisions to the military but were satisfied with Frelinghuysen's draft, which stressed Vietnamization of the military effort and defense of the South Vietnamese population rather than territorial gains. The Frelinghuysen draft was adopted as part of the Republican national platform.

Because of his unswerving support of Nixon's Vietnam policy, Frelinghuysen's popularity in his affluent home district began to erode in the early 1970s, and he decided not to seek reelection in 1974. [See NIXON Volume]

[JCH]

FRIEDAN, BETTY

b. Feb. 4, 1921; Peoria, Ill.
President, National Organization for Women October 1966-March 1970.

A graduate of Smith College, Friedan gained national attention in 1963 with the publication of *The Feminine Mystique*. An immediate best-seller, her book argued that in the years after World War II a "mystique" promoted by advertisers, educators, women's magazines and psychologists had convinced American women that fulfillment for them lay only in a life of complete domesticity. Living solely as wives and mothers, however, women abandoned any efforts at self-realization or personal achievement and submerged their own identities in that of their husbands and children. The result was not happiness but what Friedan called "the problem that has no name"—a sense of emptiness and malaise and a lack of personal identity. Controversial and influential, Friedan's study was both a portent of and a contributor to the women's liberation movement.

Friedan lectured extensively on the position of women over the next several years, and in October 1966 she founded the National Organization for Women (NOW) to press for "true equality" for women. As NOW's first president, Friedan helped build an organization that emphasized education, legislation and court action to win equal rights for women. During 1967 and 1968 NOW members picketed the *New York Times*, charging that its use of "Male" and "Female" headings in classified advertisements discriminated against women. NOW also brought a suit against the Equal Employment Opportunities Commission (EEOC) for permitting such column headings and pressured the EEOC to step up its enforcement of Title VII of the 1964 Civil Rights Act, which prohibited sex discrimination in employment. Under Friedan's direction, NOW lobbied for the repeal of anti-abortion laws in New York State and for passage of the Equal Rights Amendment in Washington. NOW also instituted court cases in various states to challenge state protective labor laws applicable only to women.

Friedan stepped down as NOW's president in 1970 but remained a prominent advocate of women's rights. She issued a call for a "Women's Strike for Equality" to be held on Aug. 26, 1970, the fiftieth anniversary of the 19th Amendment. The result was the first nationwide protest for women's rights since the suffrage movement. In July 1971 Friedan helped organize the National Women's Political Caucus to work for equal representation of women with men at all levels of the political system. [See NIXON Volum]

[CAB]

FRIEDMAN, MILTON

b. July 31, 1912; New York, N.Y.
Economist.

Economist Milton Friedman was the foremost academic apostle of free market economics and an iconoclastic critic of the Keynesian theories prevailing among government economists in the 1960s. The son of immigrant parents, Friedman grew up in Rahway, N.J., and graduated from Rutgers University in 1932. He did graduate work in economics at the University of Chicago, a citadel of classical economic theory. In the late 1930s he worked as a statistician with the National Resources Committee, a federal agency. From 1941 to 1943 Friedman was the principal tax research economist at the Treasury Department. After obtaining his Ph.D. from Columbia University in 1946, he joined the faculty at the University of Chicago, where he taught for the next three decades.

Within the academic community Friedman won prominence with his persistent and provocative advocacy of the quantity theory of money, or "monetarism" as it became known. According to this theory, the dominant factor in the economy is the amount of money in circulation, not, as the Keynesians held, the fiscal policy of the federal government. Friedman marshaled considerable empirical support for this theory in *The Monetary History of the United States* (1963), in which he correlated contractions in the money supply with the occurrence of economic recessions and depressions.

At the center of Friedman's history was a radical reinterpretation of the cause of the Depression: he blamed the economic collapse not on the instability of the private market but on the monetary authorities, who allowed the money supply to shrink when it should have been expanded. His chief policy prescription was to strip the Federal Reserve of its discretionary control over the money supply and mandate that the supply be increased at the steady rate of 4% every year.

Friedman coupled his promotion of monetary, rather than fiscal, manipulation with a vigorous attack advocating laissez-faire on virtually all government interference with the private market. He favored the elimination of most federal regulatory agencies, arguing that the best guarantee of prosperity and consumer welfare was the unfettered price system. He believed that Social Security should be abolished and called for the abandonment of minimum-wage legislation on the ground that such a wage floor increased unemployment. In place of antipoverty programs and other welfare state efforts, Friedman favored a "negative income tax," which would provide direct cash payments to people whose income fell below a certain level. He defended the negative income tax as a cheaper and more direct approach to the problem of poverty than government social programs.

During the 1964 presidential campaign Friedman served as chief economic adviser to Republican presidential candidate Sen. Barry M. Goldwater (R, Ariz.) [*q.v.*]. In an October interview Friedman declared that the Senator and he agreed on the need to reduce federal spending on non-military programs, to lessen government regulation of business activity and to reduce taxes by 5% in each of the next five years. They advocated the tax cuts in order to restrict government activity and free the private sector, not as a contra-cyclical economic device, which had been the rationale behind the Kennedy-Johnson $11.5 billion tax cut enacted in February 1964. Goldwater did not endorse all of Friedman's proposals, particularly the economist's call for a free-floating exchange rate for the dollar and the elimination of all barriers to free trade.

For most of his career Friedman operated as a conservative gadfly outside the centers of economic policymaking. By the mid-1960s, however, he began to reach a wider audience with the publication of his theory of political economy in *Capitalism and Freedom* in 1962 and of his monetary history the next year and then with the commencement of a triweekly *Newsweek* column beginning 1966. The coming to power of a Republican administration in 1969 paralleled a growing national respect for Friedman's views. The next several years saw the implementation, or attempted implementation, of several of his favorite proposals, including the all-volunteer army, the publication by the Federal Reserve of regular reports on the growth of the money supply and the Nixon Administration's Family Assistance Plan, an unsuccessful attempt to enact the negative income tax. [See NIXON Volume]

[TO]

FULBRIGHT, J(AMES) WILLIAM

b. April 9, 1905; Sumner, Mo.
Democratic Senator, Ark., 1945-75;
Chairman, Foreign Relations Committee, 1959-75.

J. William Fulbright was raised in Fayetteville, Ark., where his family was economically and socially prominent. He graduated from the University of Arkansas in 1925 and studied at Oxford under a Rhodes scholarship until 1928, when he returned to the U.S. to take a law degree at George Washington University. After serving with the Justice Department and teaching law at George Washington, the young Fulbright joined the law faculty of the University of Arkansas in 1936. From 1939 to 1941 he served as president of that university.

In 1942 Fulbright was elected to the House of Representatives, and two years later he went to the Senate, where he remained for three decades. During 1946 he sponsored a law that set up the international educational exchange program bearing his name. In 1954 Fulbright defended the program against Sen. Joseph McCarthy's (R, Wisc.) charges of Communist infiltration and cosponsored the censure resolution against the Republican Senator. Through the influence of his friend Lyndon Johnson, Fulbright became chairman of the Senate Foreign Relations Committee in 1959. [See TRUMAN, EISENHOWER Volumes]

During the early 1960s Fulbright used his position to advocate a reappraisal of the basic tenets upon which Soviet-American diplomacy had been conducted. He asked the U.S. to abandon its ideological struggle with Russia and conduct diplomacy in terms of traditional great power rivalry. Pointing out that a militant Cold War philosophy endangered America's domestic interests, Fulbright urged America to divert its energy from diplomatic confrontation to solving social problems at home. [See KENNEDY Volume]

Fulbright was an enthusiastic supporter of Lyndon Johnson after Kennedy's assassination and during the first months of 1964 backed his foreign policy, including his actions in Vietnam. While calling for a reassessment of Vietnam policy, Fulbright asserted that given the unstable political and military situation the U.S. had no choice but to support the South Vietnam government and its army "by the most effective means available." The Senator ruled out a negotiated settlement as impractical because South Vietnam's military setbacks had left it in a weak bargaining position.

At the request of President Johnson, Fulbright introduced the Tonkin Gulf Resolution in the Senate on Aug. 6, 1964. The Resolution, prompted by a reported North Vietnamese attack on American warships patrolling the Gulf of Tonkin, gave the President almost blanket authority to conduct the war as he wished. In debates on the proposal Fulbright defended the measure against critics, such as Sen. Gaylord Nelson (D, Wisc.) [*q.v.*] and Sen. Wayne Morse (D, Ore.) [*q.v.*], who feared that it would lead to a large-scale military involvement without congressional control. He refused to accept a Nelson amendment that stated, "Except when provoked to a greater response, we should continue to attempt to avoid a direct military involvement in the Southeast Asian conflict." However, Fulbright assured the Senate that the amendment was an accurate reflection of Johnson's policy. The upper house passed the Resolution with only two dissenting votes on Aug. 7.

In later years Fulbright termed his support of the Tonkin Gulf resolution the most humiliating experience of his public career. The Senator attributed his unquestioning support of the President's request to his belief that his old friend would not deceive him and to his desire to see Johnson elected president in 1964. Believing that the election of conservative Sen. Barry Goldwater (R, Ariz.) [*q.v.*] would lead to a dangerous escalation of the Cold War, Fulbright later said he had not wished to jeopardize Johnson's victory by engaging in a divisive policy debate.

During February 1968 Fulbright held closed hearings to determine if the U.S. had provoked the Tonkin Gulf incident, if North Vietnam had actually attacked U.S. ships and if the Administration had misled Congress into passing the Tonkin Gulf Resolution. The probe uncovered evidence that the commander of the U.S. operation had warned his superiors that North Vietnam considered his ships enemies. It further revealed that, because of poor weather conditions and technical problems, there had been uncertainty over whether the attack had actually occurred. Appearing on national television, Fulbright charged that the resolution was introduced under "a completely false idea of what had happened" and that his own support was "based upon information which was not true." Although he denounced the Resolution Fulbright did not attempt to have it repealed at that time because he believed that some senators who opposed the war would feel compelled to support the President on this issue. The Resolution was eventually repealed in 1970.

After Johnson had ordered systematic bombing of North Vietnam in the spring of 1965, Fulbright publicly voiced his doubts about U.S. policy in Vietnam. In a speech in March and a memorandum sent to the President in April, he questioned the Administration's belief that a defeat in Vietnam would lead to Communist Chinese expansion throughout Southeast Asia. Fulbright suggested that the conflict in Vietnam was a nationalistic movement rather than the result of Chinese aggression. Despite this critique Fulbright still expressed general approval of Johnson's Vietnam policy.

Fulbright's first major dissent from Administration foreign policy occurred in a debate over U.S. intervention in the Dominican Republic, where a civil war had broken out between leftists and a rightist military junta. Alleging the danger of a Communist takeover, the President had sent American troops to the island in April 1965. Johnson said that the move was necessary to protect American property and lives and to prevent another Cuba in the Caribbean. In a speech delivered on the Senate floor in September, Fulbright warned that Johnson's action was a throwback to the Cold War period of the 1950s. He questioned the President's credibility and warned that the indiscriminate use of force in civil wars and against national movements might actually push developing nations toward Communism. Fulbright's speech resulted in an open break between the President and the Senator. Thereafter Fulbright was pointedly denied the usual courtesies extended to important committee chairmen by the White House.

Fulbright's criticisms of the Administration's Vietnam policy grew increasingly caustic during the Foreign Relations Committee hearings in February 1966. He used the televised probe to suggest alternatives to Johnson's policies and to make the public aware of the larger issues involved in the Vietnam dispute. During the opening days of the hearings, the nation heard testimony from such respected military and diplomatic figures as James Gavin [*q.v.*] and George Kennan [*q.v.*]. These men questioned the strategic need for U.S. involvement in Southeast Asia and cautioned that continued escalation could involve the U.S. in a war with Communist China. The following week Maxwell Taylor [*q.v.*] and Dean Rusk [*q.v.*] defended the Administration. They insisted that the U.S. was fighting a limited war that was necessary to prevent Chinese expansion into Southeast Asia. Throughout the investigation Fulbright tried to introduce larger issues into the discussion, asking witnesses about the propriety of drawing a peaceful people into a struggle about which they cared little and the ethics of a technologically advanced great power systematically destroying a developing nation. The debate was inconclusive, but it served the educational function Fulbright had intended.

In a series of lectures given at Johns Hopkins University in April 1966, Fulbright delivered his most critical examination of American foreign policy. The Senator stated that America was in danger of succumbing to the "arrogance of power which has afflicted, weakened and in some cases destroyed, great nations in the past." He denounced the Administration's rhetoric, which portrayed the war in terms of a moral crusade, and questioned whether the continued American presence in Vietnam was not a result of prideful reluctance to accept a solution short of victory. He warned that the war was destroying plans for social reform, endangering relations with old allies and having a corrosive effect on the American spirit. The lectures were published in 1967 as *The Arrogance of Power*, which became a best-seller.

In his book Fulbright outlined the steps he would take to achieve peace. He suggested that the U.S. cease bombing North Vietnam and reduce military activity in the South to facilitate truce negotiations. The belligerents could then draw up plans for self-determination in South Vietnam and for an eventual referendum on the reunification of the North and South. If the proposed conferences failed to produce agreements, the Senator believed that the U.S. should consolidate its military forces in defensible areas in South Vietnam and maintain them there indefinitely.

By the end of the decade Fulbright had emerged as the preeminent symbol of congressional discontent with the war. Furthermore, he believed that the Senate had abrogated its responsibility for foreign affairs and had left policymaking in the hands of presidents who increasingly abused their power. Fulbright, therefore, led the fight in Congress to restrict presidential action in foreign affairs and attempted to make the Foreign Relations Committee a watchdog and counterbalance to the powerful executive. However, he was powerless to prevent the continued expansion of the war in the late-1960s and early-1970s. In 1974, after five full terms in the Senate, Fulbright was defeated in the Arkansas Democratic primary. Political observers attributed his defeat by Arkansas Gov. Dale Bumpers to the Senator's preoccupation with foreign affairs at the expense of his constituents' domestic interests. [See NIXON Volume]

[EWS]

GALAMISON, MILTON A(RTHUR)

b. Jan. 25, 1923; Philadelphia, Pa.
Clergyman, civil rights leader.

Son of a Philadelphia postal clerk, Galamison received a Master of Theology degree from Princeton Theological Seminary in 1949. That year he was named pastor of the Siloam Presbyterian Church in Brooklyn. Under Galamison, Siloam became an important social service center. Membership increased from 500 to 2,000, giving his church the largest Presbyterian congregation in Brooklyn.

During the 1950s, as chairman of the education committee of the Brooklyn NAACP and later as Brooklyn NAACP president, Galamison pressed the New York City Board of Education to eliminate de facto school segregation. As the civil rights movement gathered momentum in the early 1960s, Galamison founded and assumed leadership of the city-wide Coordinating Committee for Integrated Schools, which represented the NAACP, the Congress of Racial Equality (CORE), the New York Urban League and his own Parents Workshop for Equality. In December 1963

Galamison stated that the entire city school system could be desegregated within three years, beginning with the integration of the junior high schools the following September.

When the Board of Education and Superintendent of Schools Calvin Gross failed to satisfy these demands, Galamison, with the assistance of March on Washington organizer Bayard Rustin [*q.v.*], issued a call for a one-day boycott of New York City schools. On Feb. 3, 1964 nearly 45% of the city's pupils were absent while 3,500 demonstrators, including many children, marched on the Board of Education offices demanding integration and the resignation of board president James B. Donovan.

In response the Board of Education proposed to pair 20 white with 20 black elementary schools to achieve integration. This plan angered members of the white parents and taxpayers associations, who opposed sending their children to attend ghetto schools. The plan also failed to satisfy Galamison, who called for a second boycott, arguing that he would rather see the system destroyed than permit it to perpetuate racism. Most New York civil rights leaders counseled against this action because they believed that a second boycott would not be effective. Although the March 5, 1964 boycott was only half as effective as the first, it established Galamison as a civil rights leader with a following independent of established civil rights organizations.

Over the course of the next two years, Galamison came to doubt that integration could be achieved over white objections. Like many civil rights activists in urban areas, he began to argue that upgrading the quality of ghetto schools should take precedence over attempts to integrate them. Black education could be improved, he suggested, only if ghetto residents won full control of their schools, including the authority to determine who would teach in them. Galamison supported the efforts of a parent-community group to win control of an experimental intermediate school in Harlem and three primary schools located in the same district. When the plan was rejected by the Board of Education in December 1966, Galamison, as president of a "people's board of education," staged a three-day sit-in at the office of the Board of Education.

During the spring of 1968 Galamison called for a one-day school boycott in support of the efforts of the Ocean Hill-Brownsville (Brooklyn) school board and its administrator, Rhody McCoy, to force a number of white teachers and administrators out of the school district. Under Albert Shanker's [*q.v.*] leadership, the United Federation of Teachers (UFT) denounced the transfer of teachers without a hearing and called for a city-wide strike in the fall if the teachers were not reinstated. To head off a strike, Mayor John V. Lindsay [*q.v.*] in July 1968 appointed Galamison to the New York City Board of Education to negotiate a settlement between McCoy and Shanker. Galamison met regularly with the two men over the summer but failed to find a solution. In the fall the UFT called a series of city-wide strikes that eventually led to the total reorganization of the Ocean-Hill board without McCoy.

After leaving the Board of Education in 1971, Galamison devoted himself to clerical duties at the Siloam Church and withdrew from active educational politics in New York.

[JLW]

For further information:
Diane Ravitch, *The Great School Wars: New York City, 1805-1973* (New York, 1974).

GALBRAITH, JOHN KENNETH

b. Oct. 15, 1908; Iona Station, Canada. Economist.

Galbraith, the son of a farmer, grew up in rural Ontario. He studied agricultural economics at the Ontario Agricultural College, the University of Toronto and the University of California, Berkeley, where he earned his Ph.D. in 1934. After several years teaching economics at Harvard and Princeton, Galbraith entered government service in 1940 and soon rose to be deputy administrator of the Office of Price Administration (OPA). His vigorous enforcement of comprehensive price controls brought growing criticism from businessmen and congressional leaders, finally prompting Galbraith's resignation in 1943. He continued to serve in other government agencies through 1948. Galbraith also served at this time as a contributing editor to *Fortune* magazine. [See TRUMAN Volume]

In 1949 Galbraith returned to Harvard as professor of economics. He established a reputation as an iconoclastic liberal and critic of accepted economic theories during the 1950s with two important and widely read books—*American Capitalism: the Concept of Countervailing Power* (1952) and *The Affluent Society* (1958). Both works attacked the traditional view of the American economy as a free market. Galbraith claimed that the system actually depended on a balance of powerful interests: large corporations, labor unions and government agencies. The role of the small consumer, in Galbraith's view, had been eliminated by the development of sophisticated advertising techniques to manipulate consumer desires. In *American Capitalism* Galbraith was optimistic about the ability of the U.S. economy to sustain a stable growth rate. *The Affluent Society*, however, concentrated on the system's shortcomings: the growth of private consumption at the expense of public services, the persistence of poverty amid affluence and the danger of inflation resulting from the ceaseless stimulation of consumer buying. Drawing on his Keynesian economic training and wartime experience, Galbraith urged the imposition of wage and price controls and greater government assistance to low income groups as a means of regulating consumption and guiding production into more socially useful areas. [See EISENHOWER Volume]

In addition to its critique of the free market, Galbraith's analysis differed from the work of more traditional economists in its emphasis on the importance of political decisions in shaping the economic system. "Galbraith knows power and is drawn to it," commented one political scientist. This attitude appeared not only in Galbraith's writings but also in his lifelong involvement in liberal politics. In 1952 and 1956 he served on the campaign staff of Democratic presidential candidate Adlai Stevenson [*q.v.*]. During the late 1950s Galbraith shifted his support to Sen. John F. Kennedy (D, Mass.) and became an important member of the intellectual circle that later helped make policy in the Kennedy White House. After serving briefly as an economic and foreign policy adviser to the Administration, Galbraith was appointed ambassador to India in March 1961. Among his most important tasks there was supervision of U.S. aid to India during the Chinese-Indian border conflict of 1962. Galbraith also visited South Vietnam in late 1961 at President Kennedy's request and sent back a report critical of the ruling Diem regime. A diary that Galbraith kept during his two years of diplomatic service was published in 1969 as *Ambassador's Journal*. [See KENNEDY Volume]

In mid-1963 Galbraith left government service to resume his faculty position at Harvard. He devoted the next four years largely to completing his third major economic work, *The New Industrial State*. Published in 1967, Galbraith's new book sought to explain the workings of the industrial system that produced the aberrations discussed in *The Affluent Society*. Of all forms of capitalist enterprise, Galbraith claimed, only the large corporation can satisfy the massive financial and organizational demands of modern technology. The survival of such corporate giants, he pointed out, depends on careful planning at every step—the purchase of materials, production and sales. Galbraith argued that effective control of corporate planning lay in the hands of managers and skilled technicians, a group he called the technostructure. In the highly complex and integrated organizations of modern business, according to Galbraith, neither formal owners nor outside forces such as government or stockholders can exercise real power.

The model of balanced economic forces that Galbraith had proposed in *American Capitalism* thus gave way in *The New Industrial State* to a view of separate forces operating with the same purpose—the development of technology and expansion of production in directions determined by corporate planners. The flaw of this system, Galbraith argued, was its inability to meet social needs that failed to coincide with the requirements of corporate growth; among these he included a clean environment, satisfactory cultural opportunities and public services. In the absence of adequate checks on corporate power within government or labor, Galbraith turned to a third group: the "educational and scientific estate" of university teachers and students. These intellectuals, he urged in *The New Industrial State*, could re-emphasize the aspects of life submerged in the corporate drive for production. Galbraith maintained that society could not long ignore intellectual pressures, pointing out that corporations rely on universities for the educated managers of the technostructure. Eventually, he speculated, the government might be persuaded to regulate corporate power by nationalizing some of the largest corporations and introducing a system of wage and price controls.

Like Galbraith's earlier books, *The New Industrial State* gained wide public attention; by the end of 1967 it had become a national best-seller. Economist Scott Gordon observed in 1968 that "Galbraith's ideas have become important elements in the contemporary popular culture of American social thought." Observers noted the contribution of *The New Industrial State* to the debate over the limits of economic growth that began during the early 1970s.

Though he never reentered government service after the Kennedy Administration, Galbraith remained active in politics during the mid and late 1960s, especially as a critic of the Vietnam war. Testifying before the Senate Foreign Relations Committee in 1966, he rejected the view that "Vietnam is a testing place of American democracy . . . or that it is strategically or otherwise important to U.S. interests." In April 1967 Galbraith was elected president of the liberal Americans for Democratic Action. At that time he called for a bombing halt in North Vietnam and intensified efforts at negotiations, charging that the Administration was seeking a "military solution" to the conflict. During the 1968 presidential primaries Galbraith supported anti-war Sen. Eugene McCarthy (D, Minn.) [*q.v.*], for whom he gave a seconding speech at the Democratic National Convention. He also spoke out frequently on financial issues at this time, urging reform of the tax structure and a "national system of income guarantees and supplements" for poverty groups.

Galbraith remained an influential writer and liberal spokesman during the early 1970s. Testifying before the congressional Joint Economic Committee in 1972, he argued against proposals for a ceiling on taxes and federal project spending. He attributed the nation's economic difficulties to the Nixon Administration's "game plan," which in his view called for "a serious recession, or a serious inflation, or a moderate amount of both" to maintain stability. Galbraith also became a strong advocate of women's rights, pushing through a feminist statement at the 1971 convention of the American Economic Association. He remained opposed to U.S. policy in Vietnam and supported the 1972 presidential candidacy of Sen. George McGovern (D, S.D.) [*q.v.*]. Galbraith retired from his Harvard faculty position in 1975. [See NIXON Volume]

[SLG]

For further information:
Charles H. Hession, *John Kenneth Galbraith and his Critics* (New York, 1972).

GARDNER, JOHN W(ILLIAM)

b. Oct. 8, 1912; Los Angeles, Calif.
Secretary of Health, Education and Welfare, August 1965-January 1968.

John W. Gardner, a psychologist with a doctorate from the University of California, taught at Connecticut College for Women and at Mt. Holyoke College. Following service in World War II with the Office of Strategic Services, Gardner joined the Carnegie Corporation, one of the nation's leading foundations. In 1955 he became the Corporation's president. Under his direction the foundation financed James B. Conant's study of American high schools in the late 1950s and the development of the "new math" program in the early 1960s. Gardner was particularly concerned with the problem of maintaining standards of excellence during an era of mass education; many of the programs that he encouraged were directed toward that end.

During 1964 Gardner served as chairman of a presidential task force studying the problems of federal aid to primary and secondary schools. The group suggested that "an agonizing tug-of-war over the church-state issue" might be avoided if federal funds to schools were disbursed on the basis of a selective formula related to the economic condition of each area. This became the basis of the 1965 Elementary and Secondary Education Act. In late July of 1965 President Johnson named Gardner, a liberal Republican, to succeed Anthony J. Celebrezze [*q.v.*] as Secretary of the Department of Health, Education and Welfare (HEW).

Shortly after he assumed office Gardner faced charges from liberal Congressmen, the NAACP Legal Defense Fund and other civil rights groups that HEW lagged in its efforts to integrate schools and hospitals. The Southern Regional Council pointed out that only 5.2% of Negro students in 11 Southern states were attending integrated schools in 1965. In February 1966 the Civil Rights Commission criticized HEW for lax enforcement of Title VI of the 1964 Civil Rights Act, which barred racial discrimination in any federally assisted program or activity.

Gardner issued a new set of guidelines for all federally assisted schools and hospitals in March 1966. The guidelines stipulated percentage rates of desegregation expected in the South for the 1966-67 school year and mandated the closing of small, inadequate schools maintained for Negro and other minority groups. They also called for an end to discrimination in the hiring of teachers and to segregation in hospital facilities. The guidelines did not apply to de facto segregation in cities outside the South.

Southern congressmen objected vehemently to the guidelines, charging that they established a quota system in violation of the Civil Rights Act of 1964. In an effort to placate this criticism, Gardner wrote to Southern governors, members of Congress and school officials in April to assure them that HEW was not attempting to impose a specific degree of "racial balance" or to require "instantaneous desegregation." But during the remainder of the year, HEW began to cut off funds from institutions not meeting the Department's stipulations, and by early 1967 34 school districts and 54 hospitals, mostly in the Deep South, had been deprived of federal funds.

In January 1967 Gardner announced the imminent termination of federal aid to Alabama because its governor, George C. Wallace [*q.v.*], had refused to permit integration of the state's welfare and mental health programs in accordance with Title VI. A year later the U.S. Supreme Court upheld Gardner's cutoff of funds.

In May 1967 Gardner announced that the power to force compliance with Title VI was being transferred from HEW subdivision administrators, including U.S. Commissioner of Education Harold Howe [*q.v.*], to a new Office of Civil Rights. Howe was particularly disliked by Southern congressmen because he had been adamant in enforcing school desegregation. Some political observers believed that by undercutting Howe's authority, Gardner was deliberately attempting to garner support from Southern Democrats for the 1967 school assistance bill. This charge was denied by Gardner and F. Peter Libassi, the new head of the Office of Civil Rights.

As head of HEW Gardner drew up plans early in 1966 for the reorganization of the public health divisions of his agency. Gardner believed that the U.S. Public Health Service could not effectively manage federally financed health programs. He proposed that a new assistant HEW secretary for health and scientific affairs assume that responsibility along with coordination of the activities of the National Institute of Health, the National Institute of Mental Health and the National Library of Medicine. This program was implemented by Gardner's successor, Wilbur J. Cohen [*q.v.*]

After conferring with President Johnson in December 1966, Gardner announced that he was planning a major organizational reform of HEW. The eight major Department bureaus and agencies, he stated, would be organized into three sub-cabinet departments: the health, the education and the individual and family services Departments.

Testifying before a Senate subcommittee in August 1966, Gardner responded to liberal complaints that the Administration was not spending enough money on the cities by warning of an American habit "of spending a lot of money to still our anxieties." He said that a "master plan" for urban areas was more important than the expenditure of large sums of money. The Administration's Demonstration Cities program, he said, provided the beginnings of such a plan.

On Jan. 3, 1967 Gardner offered new federal standards to reduce the quantity of car-exhaust pollutants. The plan proposed a requirement that 77% of hydrocarbon and 68% of carbon monoxide emissions be eliminated in 1970 automobiles. In justifying the measure Gardner estimated that "one billion gallons of gasoline annually pollute the atmosphere" as a result of motor vehicle use. The following July he backed a Federal Trade Commission recommendation for stronger health warnings on cigarette packs. Gardner stressed that such a step was particularly necessary to inhibit young people from smoking.

As HEW Secretary, Gardner controlled federal grants to institutions of higher education. He encountered criticism from educators for opposing general institutional grants and, instead, favoring categorical aid for the initiation of innovative projects. In October 1967 one educational lobbyist commented, "the trouble with this thinking is that in many instances the federal government is the only possible source of funds. If programs aren't sustained by it they will die."

In January 1968 Gardner resigned unexpectedly amidst reports that he had clashed with President Johnson over U.S. involvement in Vietnam. Gardner denied these rumors, but they persisted. During 1968 he became chairman of the National Urban Coalition, a privately supported antipoverty organization. In July, shortly after assuming that post, he spoke before the National Governors Conference and asserted that greatly increased federal spending would be required to solve the problems of the cities. In August 1970 Gardner announced the formation of Common Cause, which he described as a non-partisan citizens' lobby. The new group, headed by Gardner, was designed to seek social and political reforms and to counter partisan and corporate influence in government. [See NIXON Volume]

[JLW]

GARRISON, JIM

b. Nov. 20, 1921; Dennison, Iowa.
District Attorney, Orleans Parish, La., 1962-74.

Garrison, a native of Iowa, won a law degree from Tulane University in 1949. That year he was admitted to the Louisiana bar and began his practice in New Orleans. He served as assistant district attorney for New Orleans from 1954 to 1958. In 1962, shortly after he became district attorney for Orleans Parish, he undertook an investigation of vice and crime in New Orleans's French Quarter. Late in the year the New Orleans Criminal District Court denied Garrison's request for additional funds for his investigation. Garrison was quoted as saying that this decision "raised interesting questions about racketeering influence" on the court. In February 1963 Garrison was convicted of defaming the judges and sentenced to four months in prison and fined $1,000. Late in the year, however, the U.S. Supreme Court overturned the conviction.

In October 1966 Garrison began an investigation of the Kennedy assassination. In February 1967 he announced that Kennedy had been murdered by a group of New Orleans conspirators. Four days later David William Ferrie, a former airline pilot and prime Garrison suspect, was found dead in his New Orleans apartment. New Orleans Coroner Dr. Nicholas Chetta stated that Ferrie had died of a ruptured blood vessel in the brain, and this was confirmed by an autopsy. Garrison questioned the results of the autopsy and suggested that Ferrie had committed suicide. "Evidence developed by our office," said Garrison, "had long since confirmed that he was involved in events culminating in the assassination of President Kennedy. Apparently we waited too long."

Garrison announced on Feb. 24 that his staff had "solved" the assassination but that he would need months or even years to "work on details of evidence" and to make arrests. "We know," he said, "what cities were involved, how it was done in the essential respects and the individuals involved. It's my personal belief that [Lee Harvey] Oswald did not kill anyone that day [Nov. 22, 1963]."

On March 1, 1967 Garrison ordered Clay L. Shaw, retired director of the New Orleans International Trade Mart, arrested for "participation in a conspiracy to murder John F. Kennedy." Garrison charged that during 1963 Shaw, alias "Clay Bertrand," Oswald and Ferrie had planned the assassination. Shaw denied that he knew Oswald or Ferrie and through legal appeals sought to prevent Garrison from bringing him to trial. While the Shaw case was making its way to the U.S. Supreme Court, Garrison attempted to develop an elaborate account of the assassination. He proposed that Oswald had been a CIA operative and implied that he had been framed by the Agency. He suggested that a number of Cuban exiles working for the CIA and "having a venomous reaction from the 1961 Bay of Pigs episode" had actually murdered the President.

Garrison's allegations received extensive coverage but were soon attacked by the news media. In June 1967 the National Broadcasting Company, in a special television broadcast, charged that Garrison was intimidating potential witnesses and had offered them bribes to secure cooperative testimony. The *New York Times* reported that two Louisiana convicts had asserted that Garrison's office had offered them their freedom if they would cooperate with the investigation.

In December 1968 the U.S. Supreme Court refused to bar Garrison from prosecuting Shaw. The trial began Jan. 21, 1969. A key prosecution witness, Perry Russo, testified that in September 1963 he had heard Ferrie, Oswald and Shaw discuss the assassination. Under cross-examination Russo confessed that he had previously been hypnotized to help strengthen his recollection of Oswald and Shaw. The case went to the jury on March 1, 1969. Within 50 minutes it had acquitted Shaw. Garrison vowed that he had "just begun to fight" and had Shaw arrested on March 3 for perjury, charging that he had lied under oath in denying having known Oswald and Ferrie. Shaw in turn sued Garrison for $5 million in damages stemming from his prosecution.

Although Garrison was widely attacked in the press as a fraud, he won reelection to another term as district attorney in November 1969. In May 1970 a federal judge ordered Garrison to cease his prosecution of Shaw. This order was upheld by the U.S. Supreme Court in 1972. Shaw's suit against Garrison was delayed for several years and remained unsettled when Shaw died in 1974.

During the early 1970s Garrison had to contend with his own legal problems. In December 1971 a federal grand jury indicted him on charges that he had taken bribes to protect New Orleans gambling and pinball machine interests. He was acquitted in September 1973. He also won acquittal in March 1974 on charges of federal income tax evasion. He attributed his prosecution in these matters to a government conspiracy to prevent him from pursuing his investigation of the Kennedy assassination.

In December 1973 Garrison was narrowly defeated for a fourth term as district attorney in the Democratic primary in New Orleans. He then returned to private legal practice.

[JLW]

GAVIN, JAMES M(AURICE)

b. March 22, 1907; New York, N.Y.
Former Army officer.

James M. Gavin graduated from West Point in 1929. An early proponent of airborne operations, Gavin personally commanded a parachute combat team, which spearheaded the Allied invasion of Sicily in July 1943. Promoted to brigadier general at age 36, he led the 82nd Airborne Division on D-Day and in the Battle of the Bulge. In 1954 Gavin became chief of research and development and deputy chief of staff. He was promoted to lieutenant general in 1955.

With Army Chief of Staff Matthew B. Ridgway [*q.v.*], Gavin dissuaded President Dwight D. Eisenhower [*q.v.*] from ordering an American expeditionary force into Northern Vietnam during the battle of Dien Bien Phu in 1954. In January 1958 Gavin resigned his commission to protest what he considered the Administration's emphasis upon a policy of massive nuclear retaliation at the expense of more limited "conventional" warfare. An adviser to John F. Kennedy in his 1960 presidential campaign, Gavin was appointed ambassador to France in February 1961. He left his diplomatic post in August 1962 to return to Arthur D. Little, Inc., a Boston management consulting firm, where he had been an office after his resignation from the Army. He became chairman of the Board of Arthur D. Little in June 1964. [See EISENHOWER, KENNEDY Volume]

During the Johnson years Gavin emerged as one of the few military figures to urge a de-escalation of America's involvement in South Vietnam. In a January 1966 magazine article he proposed that American forces refrain from all offensive military operations and instead maintain those fortified support bases and cities already held as "enclaves." These centers would become bargaining instruments in subsequent negotiations. To bring about diplomatic discussions Gavin called upon the U.S. to halt all bombing raids on North Vietnam. Continued escalation of the war, Gavin warned, risked war with China. Former Army Chief of Staff Ridgway defended Gavin's suggestion, but the Administration responded swiftly and negatively to Gavin's proposals. Gen. Maxwell D. Taylor [*q.v.*] declared in February that the enclave plan's implementation would result in a "crushing defeat of international proportions" for the U.S.

Gavin grew increasingly frustrated with the President's conduct of the war. Before the Senate Foreign Relations Committee in February 1967, he described American bombing missions over North Vietnam as "militarily as well as morally wrong." In November 1967 he urged that the U.S. permit the South Vietnamese to organize "as a political entity—be it partly neutralist, or whatever it is." In his *Crisis Now*, published in January 1968, Gavin elaborated upon the enclave theory by explaining that although the American military should conduct an essentially defensive strategy, it should also "assist the South Vietnamese in bringing their own troops up to a high standard of combat performance." Gavin also called for the inclusion of representatives of the National Liberation Front of South Vietnam in peace negotiations.

Although a Democrat, Gavin felt by the summer of 1967 that only the Republican Party could defeat Johnson in 1968 and reverse the Administration's war policies. In August 1967 he resigned from the Massachusetts Democratic Advisory Council and subsequently conferred with important Republican leaders. In early February 1968 he contemplated organizing his own write-in campaign in the March New Hampshire Republican presidential primary. But New York Gov. Nelson A. Rockefeller [*q.v.*], loyal to the candidacy of Michigan Gov. George W. Romney [*q.v.*], learned of the plan and persuaded Gavin not to launch a New Hampshire effort. Gavin's compliance effectively ended his hopes of being the Republicans' "peace candidate." Richard M. Nixon [*q.v.*] won in New Hampshire and received the Republican nomination in August 1968.

Adopting many but not all of the features of the enclave theory, the Nixon Administration's strategy of "Vietnamization" de-escalated American ground operations and placed an increasing reliance upon the South Vietnamese Army. In May 1970 Gavin warned that the U.S. might be headed for a "catastrophic" confrontation with China and advocated the withdrawal of all American forces as soon as possible. He stepped down as Arthur D. Little chairman in May 1974.

[JLB]

For further information:

James B. Gavin, *War and Peace in the Space Age* (New York, 1958).

———. *Crisis Now* (New York, 1968).

GENEEN, HAROLD S(YDNEY)
b. Jan. 22, 1910; Bournemouth, England.
Chief Executive Officer, International Telephone and Telegraph Corporation, 1959- .

Geneen spent much of his youth in a Connecticut boarding school, leaving at age 16 to become a page on the New York Stock Exchange. After acquiring a degree in accounting from New York University in 1934, he worked for an accounting firm for eight years. From 1942 to 1946 he was chief accountant for the American Can Company, from 1946 to 1950 comptroller of the Bell and Howell Company and from 1950 to 1956 vice president and comptroller of the Jones and Laughlin Steel Corp.

Geneen won his reputation as a master manager by his performance as executive vice president of Raytheon Manufacturing, which he joined in 1956. Dividing the large electronics concern into 12 semi-autonomous units, Geneen applied a system of strict financial control and constant monitoring of each division by top management. Raytheon's earnings quadrupled in three years.

Upon assuming the presidency of International Telephone and Telegraph (ITT) in 1959, Geneen reorganized the communications carrier to conform to his "I want no surprises" dictum. With his aptitude for figures and sharp business acumen, he stood at the center of a system of long-range planning and relentless monitoring of business operations, which became his managerial trademark. Having transformed the management by 1963, Geneen embarked on an aggressive program of mergers and acquisitions that radically altered the nature of ITT itself. [See KENNEDY Volume]

Fearful of nationalization and growing competition overseas, Geneen worked with the investment bankers Lazard, Freres to expand and diversify his company's American holdings. The purchase in 1965 of the Avis car rental firm for $52 million was ITT's first big acquisition. Other major purchases were the housing developer Levitt and Sons in 1966 for $92 million, Pennsylvania Glass and Sand in 1968 for $112 million, Rayonier in 1968 for $293 million and Continental Baking in 1968 for $279 million. The acquired companies, along with a wide variety of smaller units absorbed by ITT, had in common only high earnings and high growth potential. Such acquisitions boosted ITT's stock value and made it still easier for ITT to expand, since it almost always paid the stockholders of the acquired companies in ITT stock. By 1974 ITT comprised several hundred companies with annual revenues totaling $8.5 billion.

Geneen encountered his greatest setback when he attempted to acquire the American Broadcasting Company (ABC). ABC's stockholders approved ITT's $400 million offer in April 1966, and the Federal Communications Commission (FCC), after extended hearings, approved the combination one year later by a four-to-three vote of the commissioners. The Department of Justice, however, refused to permit the giant merger. Challenging the FCC's judgment in the federal courts, the Department opposed the merger, charging that ITT's international interests might prejudice ABC's news operations, while ABC as a whole could not retain its autonomy in the face of "pervasive, centralized control" by ITT. The Department found Geneen's contention that ABC needed a capital infusion from ITT dubious. On Jan. 1, 1968 Geneen canceled the planned merger.

During the Nixon Administration Geneen's attempt to take over the Hartford Fire Insurance Company produced another antitrust suit by the Justice Department. The revelation of ITT's tactics in opposing the suit, particularly the publication by columnist Jack Anderson [*q.v.*] of a memo written by an ITT lobbyist connecting the settlement of the suit with an ITT promise to contribute $400,000 toward the 1972 Republican National Convention, resulted in a scandal of major proportions for the Nixon Administration. The Corporation was also embarrassed when a congressional committee disclosed that ITT had offered funds to the Central Intelligence Agency to sabotage the election campaign of Chilean President Salvador Allende. [See NIXON Volume]

[TO]

GENOVESE, EUGENE (DOMINICK)
b. May 19, 1930; New York, N.Y.
Historian.

Born and raised in Brooklyn, Genovese received a B.A. from Brooklyn College, and M.A. and Ph.D. degrees in history from Columbia University. From 1958 to 1963 he taught at Brooklyn Polytechnical Institute and in 1963 was appointed associate professor of history at Rutgers University in New Brunswick, N.J. Active in his youth in the Communist Party, Genovese continued to be involved in radical politics after his expulsion from the Party in 1950. At Rutgers he was faculty adviser to the campus chapter of Students for a Democratic Society.

At a Rutgers University anti-war "teach-in" on April 23, 1965, Genovese declared, "Those of you who know me know that I am a Marxist and a socialist. Therefore, unlike most of my distinguished colleagues here this morning, I do not fear or regret the impending Viet Cong victory in Vietnam. I welcome it." Genovese's declaration became the major campaign issue of the 1965 New Jersey gubernatorial election. Republican candidate Wayne Dumont demanded that Rutgers, New Jersey's state university, fire Genovese. His opponent, Democratic Gov. Richard J. Hughes [*q.v.*], differed with Genovese's views, but defended his right to free speech. Hughes declared that he was "determined to preserve academic freedom in the broadest sense." Both the University Board of Examiners and a state Assembly committee found that Genovese had violated no state or university regulations, and the Examiners report, released August 6, found no ground for dismissal.

The Genovese case won national publicity in the fall of 1965. In October Sen. Robert F. Kennedy (D, N.Y.) [*q.v.*], campaigning for Hughes, said that pressure to oust Genovese "would sound the death knell of higher education in the state." That same month former Vice President Richard M. Nixon [*q.v.*], on a campaign swing for Dumont, attacked Kennedy and supported the call for Genovese's ouster. In a letter to the *New York Times* Nixon said, "Any individual employed by the state should not be allowed to use his position for the purpose of giving aid and comfort to the enemies of the state." (In the November 2 election Hughes was reelected by 350,000 votes, a record plurality for a New Jersey gubernatorial race.) After the November election former Sen. Barry M. Goldwater (R, Ariz.) [*q.v.*] said that Genovese's remarks "come closer to treason than academic freedom."

Genovese published his first book, *The Political Economy of Slavery*, in 1965. He argued that slavery in the antebellum South had created a "premodern" society ruled by a small planter class increasingly at economic, ideological and moral odds with Northern bourgeoise society. By stressing that slavery was more than "simply a system of economic compulsion," but rather the basis of a paternalist system of social, economic and psychological relations between whites and blacks, Genovese stood counterposed to most liberal historians of the 1960s who were primarily interested in describing the exploitation and resistance of blacks under slave conditions.

Genovese argued that the task of all historians, including those who identified themselves as socialists, was to objectively and accurately explain the past. During the late 1960s he was especially critical of other radical historians whom he thought moralistic and willing to sacrifice historical perspective for relevance. "The study of history," wrote Genovese, "can rarely be put to direct political use; the ideologically motivated creation of a desired past can be, but only by rulers and exploiters." Although Genovese remained a critic of the Vietnam war, he was highly critical of the New Left for what he considered its "fantasies of revolutionary apocalypse" and its undiscriminating attacks on the universities and professional societies.

After leaving Rutgers in 1967 Genovese taught at Sir George Williams University and the University of Rochester. He continued to publish new works on slavery, establishing himself as one of the leading historians of the South and one of the most widely known and respected Marxist historian in the United States.

[JBF]

GILLIGAN, JOHN J(OYCE)
b. March 22, 1921; Cincinnati, Ohio.
Democratic Representative, Ohio, 1965-67.

An undertaker's son, John J. Gilligan earned a B.A. from Notre Dame in 1943 and won a Silver Star at Okinawa during World War II. After receiving a master's degree in literature from the University of Cincinnati in 1947, Gilligan taught English at Xavier University and sold insurance. In 1953 he won election on an independent reform ticket to the Cincinnati City Council and six years later won the first of three terms to the council as its sole Democrat.

Two years after losing the Democratic nomination for congressman-at-large in May 1962, Gilligan unseated the incumbent in the first district, Rep. Carl W. Rich (R, Ohio). As past president of the Cincinnati Catholic Interracial Council, Gilligan organized a large volunteer force of civil rights and labor movement activists for his campaign. Lyndon Johnson handily won in Cincinnati, helping to carry in Gilligan, who won with 51% of the vote. Only twice before in the twentieth century had the overwhelmingly Republican first district elected a Democrat to Congress.

During the 89th Congress Gilligan consistently supported the Administration. According to *Congressional Quarterly*, he opposed Johnson on only 5% of the votes for which the White House announced a position. Gilligan voted for the Vietnam war supplemental appropriation in March 1966 but joined 77 other House Democrats in an open statement urging the President to limit military operations and to negotiate a settlement. As a member of the House Interstate and Foreign Commerce Committee during the nationwide airline strike, Gilligan voted against a bill that would have forced the airline machinists back to work in August 1966. In October the freshman Democrat helped to weaken the "truth-in-packaging" law, which standarized manufacturers' packaging and quality standards. Reportedly in deference to Procter and Gamble, a large employer in his district, Gilligan won the inclusion of an amendment that modified governmental regulations proposed by Senate sponsor Philip A. Hart (D, Mich.) [*q.v.*].

As the 1966 elections drew near, Gilligan faced two major obstacles to his reelection. First, the Republican legislature had reapportioned his district in December 1964 to increase its Republican make-up. Second, former Rep. Robert Taft, Jr. [*q.v.*], scion of the district's most famous family, opposed him for reelection. Gilligan skillfully publicized the benefits to his district from the Administration's new legislation. He also called attention to a $750 million defense contract for a local plant and federal grants for area housing and cultural programs. But in the election, which the *Washington Post* described as "an all-out, no-holds-barred battle between two able, articulate exponents of 1966 conservatism and liberalism," Taft rode a strong Republican trend in Ohio to win with 53% of the vote. Gilligan ran well, however, capturing 18% more of the district's vote than the Democratic candidate for governor.

In late 1967 the leaders of the Ohio Democratic Party and the state AFL-CIO persuaded Gilligan to challenge incumbent Sen. Frank J. Lausche (D, Ohio) [*q.v.*] in the primary. In eight general election campaigns since 1944, Lausche had only lost once, but his consistent conservatism had thoroughly antagonized the state's labor leadership. The Ohio AFL-CIO's Committee on Political Education (COPE) provided Gilligan with the money and manpower needed to overcome Lausche's traditional popularity. Both the state Party committee and COPE gave Gilligan unprecedented pre-primary endorsements. Faced with Gilligan's sophisticated use of television and opinion polls, Lausche enjoyed a last hurrah, campaigning as he always had among ethnic groups, at barber shops and before largely Republican businessmen's clubs. Gilligan easily defeated his older opponent by a margin of 10% of the vote.

Gilligan organized an attempt at the August 1968 Democratic National Convention to include a platform plank on Vietnam distinct from the Administration's position. After a July meeting with Vice President Hubert H. Humphrey [*q.v.*], whom he supported for the nomination, Gilligan determined that he and a coalition of the supporters of Sen. Eugene J. McCarthy (D, Minn.) [*q.v.*] and the late Sen. Robert F. Kennedy (D, N.Y.) [*q.v.*] could force Humphrey to free himself of the charge of being the President's captive on the volatile war issue. Gilligan felt that McCarthy held no chance for the nomination, but he reasoned that his supporters together with anti-war Humphrey and Kennedy delegates might compel the Vice President to accept a "peace plank" and greatly improve his chances for victory in November. Calling upon former Kennedy aide Kenneth P. O'Donnell [*q.v.*], Gilligan worked on a plank that called for an unconditional halt to the bombing of North Vietnam, a cease-fire and participation of Communist representatives in the South Vietnamese government. He hoped that Humphrey would privately endorse the peace plank and thus insure its acceptance. The Vice President, however, remained committed to the Administration's version; pressure from the White House and hawkish Southern delegates proved insurmountable. Defeated in the platform committee hearings after unsuccessfully seeking a compromise with the Administration, the peace plank advocates presented their position to the entire convention but lost by a vote of 1,567¾ to 1,041¼.

Gilligan's prominent role in the peace-plank debate led Ohio COPE, which strongly supported the Administration's conduct of the war, to delay its general election endorsement and withhold financial support for his Senate campaign until late September. McCarthy made a rare, post-convention appearance on Gilligan's behalf in October. State Attorney General William B. Saxbe, the Republican nominee, waged a folksy, mildly "law and order" campaign and received the full support of the state's efficient Republican organization. Gilligan lost by 100,000 votes.

Gilligan briefly retired from politics to return to his Cincinnati insurance agency. In 1970 he won election to the governorship, only to lose it four years later to former Gov. James A. Rhodes (R, Ohio) [*q.v.*]. [See NIXON Volume]

[JLB]

GILPATRIC, ROSWELL L(EAVITT)

b. Nov. 4, 1906; New York, N.Y.
Deputy Secretary of Defense, January 1961-January 1964.

After graduating from Yale Law School in 1931, Gilpatric joined the New York law firm Cravath, de Gresdorff, Swaine & Moore (later Cravath, Swaine & Moore). Gilpatric was appointed assistant secretary of the Air Force in May 1951, and in October was promoted to undersecretary. In 1953 he resigned and returned to his law firm. [See TRUMAN Volume]

Gilpatric served on two task forces on national defense established by John F. Kennedy after his presidential nomination, and following Kennedy's election he was appointed deputy secretary of defense. Gilpatric headed a task force appointed by Kennedy in April 1961 that issued a series of recommendations for a moderate increase in American involvement in Vietnam. He was also a member of Excom, Kennedy's chief advisory body during the 1962 Cuban missile crisis.

Gilpatric had originally planned to serve in his Defense post for only two years, but his involvement in the TFX controversy delayed his resignation. Testimony before the Senate Permanent Investigations Subcommittee showed that Gilpatric's former law firm had done extensive legal work for General Dynamics Corp., winner of the TFX fighter/bomber contract, both before and after Gilpatric left the firm to join the Department of Defense. Some subcommittee members charged that the firm's connections with General Dynamics made improper Gilpatric's involvement in the TFX decision. However, on Nov. 20, 1963 the subcommittee gave Gilpatric an informal 5-4 "vote of confidence," and a Justice Department investigation likewise cleared him of charges of conflict of interest. [See KENNEDY Volume]

President Johnson announced Gilpatric's resignation on Jan. 9, 1964. Gilpatric rejoined Cravath, Swaine & Moore as a senior partner and was elected to the board of directors of several major corporations and cultural institutions. On Sept. 9, 1964 Johnson appointed Gilpatric one of 16 members of a non-partisan advisory panel on national security.

Two months later Johnson appointed Gilpatric the chairman of a panel to study ways of halting the spread of nuclear weapons. The Gilpatric panel report was kept secret, but according to a July 1, 1965 article in the New York Times, the report recommended that the United States give up the proposed multilateral nuclear force if necessary to achieve an accord to halt the spread of nuclear weapons. According to the *Times*, the recommendations and the secrecy surrounding them created considerable controversy within the Administration. The State Department was reported to have been critical of the report, while the Department of Defense and the Atomic Energy Commission approved it.

In November 1965 a White House citizens committee headed by Gilpatric and Massachusetts Institute of Technology Dean Jerome Wiesner urged a three-year moratorium by the United States and the Soviet Union on the production and deployment of anti-missile missile systems to avoid a new arms race. The report was submitted to the White House Conference on International Cooperation.

After leaving the government Gilpatric wrote a number of articles on disarmament, foreign policy and military affairs. In 1968 he supported the presidential candidacy of Sen. Robert F. Kennedy (D, N.Y.) [*q.v.*] and after Kennedy's death supported New York Gov. Nelson A. Rockefeller's [*q.v.*] unsuccessful fight for the Republican nomination. During the Nixon Administration he was active in opposing plans for an anti-ballistic missile system.

[JBF]

GINSBERG, ALLEN
b. June 3, 1926; Newark, N.J.
Poet.

Ginsberg's childhood was marked by poverty and psychological trauma. His mother, Naomi Ginsberg, an emigre from Russia and a Communist in her youth, died in 1956 after many years of paranoia and long confinement in a mental hospital. Her son's painful memory of her deterioration was reflected in the poem "Kaddish for Naomi Ginsberg" (1961). Ginsberg entered Columbia in 1943 on a scholarship. While at Columbia he was part of a circle that included Jack Kerouac and William S. Burroughs. In 1953 Ginsberg moved to San Francisco, where he worked for a short time as a market research consultant before quitting to devote himself to his poetry. Ginsberg became a leading figure in the literary movement known as the San Francisco Renaissance. His 1956 poem "Howl" was one of the Beat Generation's major documents. [See EISENHOWER Volume]

In 1960 Ginsberg began experimenting with drugs under the guidance of Timothy Leary [*q.v.*]. Three years later he returned from a visit to India chanting a Hare Krishna mantra and preaching the superiority of yoga and meditation over drugs, but he continued to regard psychedelics as useful aids to personal awareness and illumination. In June 1966 he testified in support of the liberalization of the laws against non-addictive psychedelics before a Senate subcommittee on narcotics. Ginsberg informed the senators that LSD had enabled him to stop hating Lyndon Johnson as a criminal and to pray for the President instead.

As a correspondent for the *Evergreen Review*, Ginsberg visited Cuba in 1965. He was quickly deported by Fidel Castro's regime, however, after he publicly condemned the government's persecution of homosexuals. On a tour of Eastern Europe in 1965, Ginsberg was expelled by the Czechoslovak government because, according to Ginsberg, it was embarrassed by the enthusiasm with which young people in Prague received a "bearded American fairy dope poet."

Back in the U.S. Ginsberg saw his role as one of bridging the gap between political radicals and hippies. In the fall of 1965 he proposed "flower power" to anti-war demonstrators in California as a means of neutralizing harassment from the police and the Hell's Angels motorcycle gang. He was also the organizer of the first hippy "Be-In," or "The Gathering of the Tribes," held in Golden Gate Park in San Francisco in January 1967. Later in the same year he was arrested, with Dr. Benjamin Spock [*q.v.*] and others, in New York City for blocking the steps of a draft board office. During the 1968 Democratic National Convention in Chicago, he was teargassed while chanting a mantra at the Lincoln Park Yippie Life Festival.

[TLH]

For further information:
"Allen Ginsberg," *Current Biography Yearbook, 1970* (New York, 1971), pp. 151-154.

GINZBURG, RALPH

b. Oct. 28, 1929; New York, N.Y.
Publisher.

Born and raised in Brooklyn, Ralph Ginzburg graduated from the City College of New York in 1949 and held a variety of newspaper and magazine jobs before he began publication in 1962 of *Eros*, a quarterly "joyfully [devoted to] the subjects of love and sex." An energetic promoter, Ginzburg sent out brochures seeking subscriptions to the magazine on a mass basis. He claimed that recent Supreme Court rulings had liberalized the law on obscenity and that *Eros* "takes full advantage of this new freedom of expression. It is *the* magazine of sexual candor." The Post Office received some 35,000 complaints about the advertisement, reportedly the largest number in its history.

An expensive and handsome hardcover magazine, *Eros* went through four editions in 1962 before Ginzburg was indicted for violating the federal obscenity statute that prohibited sending obscene literature through the mails. The indictment focused on the fourth issue of *Eros*, which included a photo-essay depicting a nude interracial couple, and two other Ginzburg publications, an issue of *Liaison: The Biweekly Newsletter of Love* and *The Housewife's Handbook of Selective Promiscuity*, a purported journal of one woman's sexual history. Ginzburg, a self-styled crusader for human liberation, went to trial before a judge in a federal district court in Philadelphia in June 1963. He contended that the publications were not obscene under the standards established by the Supreme Court. Many commentators later evaluated the works as tame compared to publications that became generally available in the early 1970s. The judge, however, found Ginzburg guilty and sentenced him to a five-year prison term and a $42,000 fine.

A U.S. Appeals Court upheld his conviction in November 1964, and Ginzburg, with support from the American Civil Liberties Union, appealed to the Supreme Court. On March 21, 1966, in a controversial five-to-four decision, the Supreme Court also affirmed Ginzburg's conviction. Justice William Brennan's [*q.v.*] majority opinion held that "pandering" in the sale of materials and the use of "titillating" advertising that emphasized the works' sexually provocative aspects could be used to convict a publisher of obscenity even if the works themselves might not be legally obscene. The decision was widely considered a reversal of a Court trend liberalizing the definition of obscenity. Many editors and legal experts questioned the validity of determining obscenity on the basis of the promotional techniques used rather than on the merits of the work itself.

While this case was on appeal, Ginzburg became embroiled in another controversy. He had begun publishing *Fact* magazine early in 1964, and in the September-October issue for that year, Ginzburg published a lead article on the mental competency of Republican presidential candidate Barry Goldwater (R, Ariz.) [*q.v.*]. Ginzburg had sent a questionnaire to every psychiatrist in the country. The majority of the approximately 20% who responded, he reported, considered Goldwater psychologically unfit for the presidency. Many psychiatrists denounced as unprofessional those colleagues who participated in this long-distance diagnosis. In September 1965 Goldwater filed a $2 million libel suit against Ginzburg and *Fact*, charging deliberate character assassination. Following a May 1968 trial in New York City, the jury found for Goldwater and awarded him $75,000 in punitive damages.

After the March 1966 Supreme Court ruling on his obscenity conviction, Ginzburg sought to have his prison sentence vacated or suspended, but he only succeeded in getting it reduced from five to three years. He spent eight months in a federal prison in 1972 before being paroled. Ginzburg published the periodicals *Avant Garde*, beginning in 1967, and *Moneysworth*, beginning in 1971.

[CAB]

GLAZER, NATHAN
b. Feb. 25, 1923; New York, N.Y.
Sociologist.

The son of a Jewish sewing-machine operator, Glazer graduated from the City College of New York in 1944 and did advanced work in anthropology and linguistics at the University of Pennsylvania. After World War II he began a long association with *Commentary* magazine, serving as an assistant editor for a short time. In 1962 Glazer received his Ph.D. in sociology from Columbia University.

In 1948 Glazer collaborated with David Riesman and Reuel Denney on a research project in mass communications which resulted in a widely read book on social adjustment, *The Lonely Crowd: A Study of the Changing American Character* (1950). Between 1955 and 1960 Glazer was, successively, a lecturer at the University of Chicago, a staff member of the Fund for the Republic's "Communism in American Life" project for which he wrote *The Social Basis of American Communism* (1961) and a visiting professor at the University of California, Berkeley, and at Bennington and Smith Colleges. In 1963 Glazer coauthored with Daniel Patrick Moynihan [*q.v.*] *Beyond the Melting Pot: The Negroes, Puerto Ricans, Jews, Italians and Irish of New York City*, a highly influential study of the persistence of racial and ethnic identity in modern America.

As a student at City College, Glazer had been a socialist, and until the end of the 1950s, he was associated with the moderate left. Over the next few years, however, Glazer moved politically to the center. He related the evolution of his thought to two experiences of the 1960s. The first was the year he spent in Washington in 1962 and 1963 as an urban sociologist with the Housing and Home Finance Agency, where he helped initiate some of the domestic projects that became the nucleus for the federal government's antipoverty program. There, Glazer later explained, he developed a respect for bureaucracy and its ability to constructively reconcile many complex social and economic interests. The second experience was his participation in some of the events surrounding the student revolt at the Berkeley campus of the University of California, where he was a faculty member from 1963 to 1969. During the Free Speech Movement (FSM) in the fall of 1964, Glazer attempted to play a mediating role between the student rebels and the University administration in the initial stages of the confrontation. He advised the students that University President Clark Kerr [*q.v.*] could not afford to compromise with them over their principal demand for the unconditional right of political advocacy on campus.

At the Berkeley Academic Senate's decisive Dec. 8, 1964 meeting, Glazer was a leader of the minority faculty group opposed to FSM. He seconded an amendment permitting student "speech or advocacy provided it is directed to no immediate act of force or violence. . . ," which Glazer later defined as including such acts of civil disobedience as those carried out by the campus civil rights movement. His motion was defeated by a large majority, and the Berkeley faculty passed in its place a pro-FSM motion barring any University restriction on "the content of speech or advocacy." In the next several months Glazer and fellow liberal Berkeley faculty members Lewis Feuer, Seymour Martin Lipset and Paul Seabury published a series of articles in *Commentary*, the *Reporter* and the *New Leader* attacking the FSM as an attempt to destroy what they viewed as a University's legitimate democratic authority.

Throughout the 1960s Glazer intensified his criticism of student radicalism in numerous speeches and articles, most of which were republished in his book *Re-*

membering the Answers (1970). In his view campus unrest posed a threat to the very existence of the university by attempting to transform it into a vehicle for direct political ends. To the charge that the university was already deeply involved in such political activity as war-related research, Glazer replied that these were marginal functions that could be reformed away; student radicals, he said, really wanted to destroy the university as a center for unbiased and unconstrained research and teaching. He characterized campus radicals as "Luddite machine-smashers," unable to find a place in modern society.

Apart from his concern for the survival of the university, Glazer admitted that he found it progressively harder in the late 1960s to support attacks on existing institutions. Increasingly pessimistic about the possibility of social reform and deliberate government planning, Glazer broadened his criticism of the ideological left to include more pragmatic liberals and many of the liberal programs he had once favored. In the pages of *Commentary* and *The Public Interest*, he wrote disapprovingly of demands for equality in economic power and social status, and he speculated that the breakdown of traditional modes of behavior and social control threatened liberal democracy in the West. In 1969 Glazer was appointed professor of education and social structure at Harvard University.

[TLH]

For further information:
Nathan Glazer, *Remembering the Answers* (New York, 1970).

GLEASON, THOMAS W(ILLIAM)

b. Nov. 8, 1900; New York, N.Y.
President, International Longshoremen's Association, 1963- .

Gleason began working on the New York docks in 1915 and four years later joined the International Longshoremen's Association (ILA). In 1935 he was appointed business agent of New York Checkers' Local 1 and later was elected as its president. In 1953 he was appointed to the specially created post of union general organizer by newly elected ILA President William V. Bradley. He was elected president of the ILA's Atlantic Coast Division and executive vice president of the union in 1961. After serving as chief negotiator during a 1962-63 longshoremen's strike, Gleason challenged Bradley for the ILA presidency. On the eve of the July 1963 election, Bradley withdrew from the race to take a salaried position as president emeritus, and Gleason became the new head of the ILA. [See KENNEDY Volume]

In the fall of 1963 Gleason agreed to cooperate with a Kennedy Administration proposal to sell wheat to the Soviet Union after the government agreed that 50% of the grain would be transported in U.S. vessels, unless such ships were unavailable. On Feb. 12, 1964 the Maritime Administration issued a waiver to the Continental Grain Corporation permitting it to ship 62% of a million-ton Soviet wheat purchase in foreign ships on the grounds that several U.S. ships offered for Continental's use were actually "unavailable" because they were either too large for Soviet ports or otherwise unsuitable.

Gleason and Seafarers' International Union (SIU) President Paul Hall reacted to the waiver by denouncing the entire policy of grain sales to the USSR. They said that they had agreed to cooperate with the sales only because the 50% provision would provide work for U.S. sailors and longshoremen. On Feb. 17 Gleason ordered ILA members to refuse to load any Soviet-bound wheat, and both the SIU and the National Maritime Union (NMU) announced their support for the action. Following conversations between President Johnson and AFL-CIO President George Meany [*q.v.*] and negotiations between union leaders, including Gleason, and Secretary of Labor W. Williard Wirtz [*q.v.*], a new agreement was reached, and the boycott ended Feb. 25. Under the new agreement, all future wheat sales to the Soviet Union would be subject to a mandatory 50% U.S. shipping requirement, but existing contracts would be permitted to stand. A union demand that the 50% requirement be extended to other types of

U.S. trade with Communist countries was to be considered in future government-union discussions.

The settlement ending the 1962-63 Atlantic and Gulf Coast longshoremen's strike postponed the resolution of the shippers' demand for a reduction in the size of work gangs by referring it to the government for study. In July 1964 the Labor Department issued a report supporting the shippers' desire for the elimination of unnecessary hiring while also upholding the ILA's insistence on increased job security. Although there was no nationwide bargaining, the New York contracts generally helped set the pattern for other ports. The ILA and the New York Shipping Association, however, were unable to agree on a new contract, and on Oct. 1 Gleason's union struck Gulf and Atlantic ports. President Johnson immediately invoked the Taft-Hartley Act, and following the issuance of a court order, the strikers returned to work.

On Dec. 16 the ILA and the New York shippers agreed on a new four-year contract. It included a phased reduction in work gang size, an annual guaranteed minimum wage for full-time longshoremen, an increase in the size of the dues checkoff, increases in wages and benefits and an agreement to seek the elimination of registration of longshoremen by the New York Waterfront Commission. Although Gleason called the agreement "the best contract we ever had," there was considerable rank-and-file opposition to it, particularly to the provision reducing the size of work gangs. As soon as the contract terms were announced, sporadic wildcats began. On Jan. 8 New York longshoremen voted to reject the contract, and three days later 50,000 longshoremen in Gulf and Atlantic ports walked off their jobs.

After an intense campaign by Gleason and other ILA officials, the New York longshoremen reversed their stand and on Jan. 21 approved the pact by a wide margin. However, union and management in many other ports failed to reach agreements, and the strike continued under the ILA policy that if one port were closed, all ports would be closed.

In an effort to end the costly strike, President Johnson named an informal committee of Wirtz, Secretary of Commerce John T. Connor [*q.v.*] and Sen. Wayne Morse (D, Ore.) [*q.v.*] to make proposals for a settlement. The union rejected the committee recommendations but agreed on Feb. 12 to resume work in ports that had already agreed to new contracts. By Feb. 17 the strike was restricted to several Southern ports. All longshoremen were back to work by mid-March. When the new contract provisions reducing gang size actually took effect on April 1, 1966, longshoremen in New York again walked off their jobs in a series of wild cat strikes, which were ended only after court restraining orders were issued.

Gleason was a strong supporter of U.S. military activity in Vietnam. Starting in the fall of 1965, he helped the U.S. government eliminate cargo-handling problems in the ports of Saigon and Cam Ranh Bay. In February 1966 Gleason, Hall and NMU President Joseph E. Curran [*q.v.*] proposed a boycott of ships from countries trading with North Vietnam. During the Nixon Administration Gleason became publicly identified with the pro-war "hard-hat" faction of organized labor. [See NIXON Volume]

[JBF]

GLENN, JOHN H(ERSCHEL)

b. July 18, 1921, Cambridge, Ohio.
Astronaut, April 1959-January 1964.

Glenn became a naval pilot in the Marine Corps in 1943 and saw action in the Pacific, where he won several medals. He remained on active duty during the Korean war and later became a naval test pilot. In 1957 he set a speed record in the first nonstop, transcontinental supersonic flight. In 1959 Glenn was made a Marine lieutenant colonel.

Glenn was among the seven men who were chosen in April 1959 from 110 military test pilots to become the first American astronauts. He was named in November 1961 to make the first American orbital flight. On Feb. 20, 1962, Glenn made three orbits of the earth in just under five hours.

Glenn's flight allayed fears that America lagged hopelessly behind in the space race and made him a national hero. Several days after his flight Glenn addressed a joint session of Congress in support of the space program's long range goals, saying that "exploration and the pursuit of knowledge have always paid dividends in the long run." A *New York Times* writer called Glenn "the Administration's star witness on Capitol Hill." [See KENNEDY Volume]

During the last half of the 1960s Glenn became a close friend of the Kennedy family. Encouraged by Attorney General Robert F. Kennedy [*q.v.*] and national Democratic strategists, Glenn resigned from the space program on Jan. 16 and the following day announced that he would seek the Ohio Democratic nomination to the U.S. Senate. Glenn won his first political test in Columbus on Jan. 20 when the Ohio Democratic convention adjourned without endorsing incumbent Sen. Stephen M. Young (D, Ohio) [*q.v.*] who had asked for the convention's endorsement and had delivered the Keynote address. Glenn appeared the likely victor against the aged Young, but on March 30 he announced his withdrawal from the race because of a severe head injury suffered in a bathroom fall which affected his sense of balance. In explaining his decision the former astronaut said that he did not want to run just as a well-known name.

In June 1968 Glenn was appointed chairman of the newly formed Emergency Committee for Gun Control, a coalition of groups formed to try to build up public pressure for tough firearms control. Two days later he testified before the Senate Judiciary Committee's Juvenile Delinquency Subcommittee in favor of President Johnson's registration and licensing proposals.

Glenn ran unsuccessfully for the Senate in 1970. He won his third attempt and took his seat in January 1975. Glenn delivered the keynote address at the 1976 National Democratic Convention. Prior to the Convention he was considered a prime candidate for the vice presidential nomination, but former Georgia Governor Jimmy Carter chose Sen. Walter Mondale (D. Minn.) as his running mate. [See NIXON Volume]

[MDB]

GODDARD, JAMES L(EE)

b. April 24, 1923; Alliance, Ohio.
Commissioner, Food and Drug Administration, January 1966-June 1968.

James L. Goddard grew up in the small industrial cities of Alliance and Warren, Ohio. He attended three colleges before earning his M.D. degree from George Washington University in 1949. Soon after his internship Goddard gave up a small-town practice in western Ohio for public health administration. He received an M.S. in public health from Harvard in 1955. Through the 1950s Goddard worked for federal, state and county health agencies in Colorado, New York, North Carolina and Washington. In leadership positions he established a reputation for being an assertive, skilled and imaginative administrator. He became the first civil air surgeon of the Federal Aviation Agency in 1959 and assistant U.S. surgeon general and head of the U.S. Public Health Service's Communicable Disease Center at Atlanta in 1962.

In January 1966 Secretary of Health, Education and Welfare John W. Gardner [*q.v.*] made Goddard commissioner of the Food and Drug Administration (FDA) Public Service Division. First organized in 1907, the FDA watched over the product safety of food and drug manufacture and distribution. The great increase in the quantity of pharmaceutical products used by Americans and the 1962 Kefauver-Harris Act regulating the drug industry greatly added to the FDA's tasks. By 1965 the agency had proved incapable of meeting its augmented responsibilities; private companies, congressmen and consumer groups all criticized agency delays in testing new drugs. Indeed, shortly after assuming office Goddard himself termed the FDA "lax, if not grossly negligent" in certain cases.

Like several prominent regulatory agency heads during Johnson's presidency. Goddard spent his first months in office castigating industries falling within his province. At an April 1966 gathering of the Pharamaceutical Manufacturers Association (PMA), Goddard expressed dismay at the drug companies' "clear attempts to slip something by us." Goddard declared that the drug industry was more concerned with profits than product safety, and suffered from a "disease" beyond the cure of drugs, that of irresponsibility. Also in April, Goddard warned the American Association of Advertising Agents against making "false claims." In May Goddard criticized the "general carelessness about the basic principles of sanitation," which, he said, the FDA had found in many food processing plants.

Under Goddard the FDA moved quickly in response to selected problems. In April 1966 the FDA began a systematic inquiry into the possibility of harmful pesticide residue levels in foods. Goddard alleviated the backlog of Agency testing by commissioning the National Academy of Science and the National Research Council to review some 4,000 drugs marketed between 1938 and 1962. These and other steps raised the once low morale of the FDA staff.

In August 1966 Goddard lifted a FDA stipulation requiring that producers of oral contraceptives recommend a two-year limit to users. Goddard found "no adequate scientific data at this time" indicating that "the Pill" was "unsafe for human use." A special FDA investigating panel, however, called for more research into the subject.

Goddard held office at a time of widespread use of drugs by adolescents and young adults, especially on college campuses. Concern mounted when the news media reported tales of the bizarre effects of the hallucinogenic LSD. In an April 1966 letter to 2,000 university administrators, Goddard said LSD has "profound effects on the mental process" and is "dangerous in exceedingly small amounts." He told college officials to be wary of the appearance of these and other drugs on campus.

In an October 1966 address at the University of Minnesota, Goddard advocated the removal of penalties for the possession of marijuana. Brought before two congressional committees the following month, Goddard said that he did not "condone the use of marijuana" but reasserted his opposition to criminal action against marijuana smokers—as opposed to dealers.

In February 1968 Goddard testified on behalf of an Administration bill that made possession of certain illegally-obtained drugs, including LSD, a federal offense. He endorsed the measure reluctantly, declaring that "it would be unwise" to risk branding "a number of young people just entering adulthood as criminals" because they possessed "a small amount of drugs for personal use." But the President and federal law enforcement agencies, Goddard stated, wanted federal criminalization, and "their judgment on the need for this provision is one which I respect."

Goddard quit the FDA July 1, 1968. FDA Bureau of Medicine chief Herbert L. Ley, Jr., a Goddard appointee, succeeded him. Goddard went to Atlanta and worked for ETP Tech., Inc. a private medical and industrial systems analysis company. He left ETP in 1970 to advise the Ford Foundation on population problems. In 1972 he became board chairman of the Ormont Drug and Chemical Company of Englewood, N.J. The following year he founded Omega Associates, a consulting firm, in Atlanta.

[JLB]

GODWIN, MILLS E(DWIN)

b. Nov. 19, 1914;
Nansemond County, Va.
Governor, Va., 1966-70, 1974- .

Godwin served in the Virginia House of Delegates from 1947 to 1952 and then in the state Senate from 1953 to 1961. As a member of the legislature, he was a stalwart supporter of the conservative Democratic machine of U.S. Sen. Harry F. Byrd [*q.v.*]. The organization had dominated the state's one-party politics since the late 1920s, implementing policies of "pay-as-you-go" financing, frugal public spending and racial separation. When the machine unsuccessfully promoted massive resistance to school integration in the late 1950s, Godwin was its spokesman in the state Senate.

In 1961 Godwin received the machine's

endorsement for the lieutenant governorship in the Democratic primary and attacked his more moderate opponent for being soft on integration and for joining with the labor union movement in opposing the state's right-to-work law. Godwin won by an unusually small margin for a machine-backed candidate. The result reflected the post World War II expansion of the state's relatively liberal urban population. Hoping to become the state's chief executive, Godwin moved towards the political center while serving as lieutenant governor, particularly after the state Democratic convention weakened Byrd's grip on the party in 1964 by endorsing President Lyndon Johnson for reelection against the Senator's wishes.

When Godwin campaigned for governor in 1965, he abandoned his defense of segregation, asserting that the issue had long since been settled and advocated substantial expansion of public services. Capturing the support of liberals and of much of the now tottering Byrd machine, he easily won the primary. Godwin then defeated Linwood Holton, the candidate of Virginia's rejuvenated Republican Party, with 47.9% of the vote to his opponent's 37.7%.

During his tenure as governor Godwin broke with some of Byrd's long-standing policies. In 1966 he successfully pressed the state legislature to pass Virgnia's first sales tax—a step that Byrd had always opposed—as a device for financing new state programs. With the aid of revenue received from that levy, Virginia moved from last among the states in school expenditures per pupil in 1961 to a figure close to the national average a decade later. Godwin introduced a system of community colleges that increased college enrollment in the state from 64,000 in the mid-1960s to 150,000 in 1973. He also sponsored a state mental health program. He jettisoned Byrd's sacrosanct "pay-as-you-go" financing by proposing an $81 million bond issue, which was approved by the voters in 1968. During the same year Godwin lay the groundwork for the modernization of Virginia's government by appointing a blue-ribbon commission to revise the state constitution.

Godwin was constitutionally barred from seeking relection in 1969. In that year more liberal elements of the Party became dominant, alienating Godwin and many other moderates and enabling the Republican Party to capture the governorship. Switching to the Republicans, Godwin successfully ran for governor on its state ticket in 1973.

[MLL]

GOLDBERG, ARTHUR J(OSEPH)

b. Aug. 8, 1908; Chicago, Ill.
Associate Justice, U.S. Supreme Court, October 1962-July 1965; Ambassador to the United Nations, July 1965-April 1968.

Goldberg, the youngest of 11 children of Russian-Jewish parents, grew up on Chicago's West Side. After working his way through college and law school, Goldberg practiced labor law and then served with the Office of Strategic Services during World War II. In 1948 he became general counsel for the United Steelworkers of America (USW) and in 1955 played a major role in merging the Congress of Industrial Organizations and the American Federation of Labor. Goldberg was the principal author of the AFL-CIO ethical practices code and helped guide the USW negotiations during the 116-day steel strike in 1959 and 1960. [See TRUMAN, EISENHOWER Volumes]

As Kennedy's choice for Secretary of Labor, Goldberg gave the office new influence by forcefully asserting the "public interest" in labor-management disputes and on occasion intervening directly to recommend strike settlements. Goldberg encouraged USW President David J. McDonald [*q.v.*] to accept a modest steel contract in early 1962 and helped President Kennedy apply public pressure on the steel corporations when they unexpectedly raised prices in April. As Secretary of Labor he directed most of the Administration's legislative attention to ameliorating the recession and lowering the level of unemployment. During 1961 and 1962 he successfully fought for the Area Redevelopment Act to aid "depressed areas," an increase in minimum wage and social security benefits, an extension of state unemployment benefits and the passage of the $435 million Manpower Development and Training Act. [See KENNEDY Volume]

Kennedy appointed Goldberg to the Supreme Court in August 1962. Siding with Justices Hugo Black [*q.v.*] and William O. Douglas [*q.v.*], Goldberg took advanced positions on civil liberties issues during his 34 months on the bench. In an October 1963 opinion, the former Labor Secretary first raised the issue of the unconstitutionality of the death penalty on the basis of the cruel and unusual punishment and due process of law clauses. In March 1964 he voted with the Court's six to three majority in ruling that congressional districts must be composed of approximately equal populations. He voted with a majority holding state loyalty oaths invalid in June and in a separate case spoke for the Court in a decision ruling that denial of passports to members of the Communist Party was "unconstitutional on its face." In the same month Goldberg wrote the Court's landmark five to four decision in *Escobedo v. Illinois*, holding that confessions cannot be used in court if police question a suspect without letting him consult a lawyer or without warning him that his answers may be used against him.

With Justice Black, Goldberg dissented from an October 1964 Supreme Court decision rejecting Sen. Barry M. Goldwater's (R, Ariz.) [*q.v.*] demand for equal free time on radio and TV to reply to an earlier televised speech by President Johnson on the international situation. In May 1965 Goldberg joined Black and Douglas in a dissent holding unconstitutional the government's curb on travel to Cuba. The next month he joined a majority of the Court in striking down Connecticut's 1879 law forbidding the use of birth control devices.

After Adlai Stevenson's [*q.v.*] death in July 1965, President Johnson sought to fill the United Nations ambassadorship he had held with another liberal of great prestige. Upon John Kenneth Galbraith's [*q.v.*] recommendation Johnson asked Goldberg to step down from the Supreme Court and fill the vacant U.N. post. Johnson told Goldberg he would have a direct hand in shaping American foreign policy and ending the Vietnam war. Goldberg, whom some observers thought restless on the high bench, accepted Johnson's offer and resigned from the Court July 28.

On issues other than Vietnam Goldberg was able to play a significant role in developing and implementing American foreign policy at the United Nations. As part of an attempt to upgrade the world body into a forum for "negotiations" rather than "debate," Goldberg announced on Aug. 16, 1965 that the U.S. would drop its demand that General Assembly voting rights be denied to the Soviet Union, France and other states who had not paid their financial assessments for upkeep of the world organization. When the India-Pakistan war broke out in the late summer of 1965, Goldberg worked privately to secure a unanimous Security Council agreement on a cease-fire resolution demanding that both belligerents pull back to their original pre-war frontiers.

Goldberg demonstrated a degree of independence from the State Department during the October 1966 General Assembly debate over the status of Southwest Africa. He introduced a resolution, prepared by the U.S. delegation at the U.N., declaring that South Africa "forfeits all rights to continue to administer the territory." Goldberg's proposal, which was linked to formation of a new U.N. commission for Southwest Africa, was widely hailed by many of the new African and Asian states. However, the resolution put greater pressure on the South African regime than the U.S. State Department itself might have wished.

In the aftermath of the June 1967 Arab-Israeli war, Goldberg sought to avoid a U.N. condemnation of Israel apart from a general solution to the Middle East conflict. In July Goldberg helped defeat a Soviet-sponsored Security Council resolution condemning Israeli aggression. But during the fall he worked closely with Soviet U.N. Ambassador Anatoly Dobrynin on behalf of a British resolution that asserted Israel's right to exist, while at the same time calling for her withdrawal from land occupied during the Six Day War. The resolution, which served as the basic U.N. position on the Middle East conflict for the next six years, was adopted Nov. 22, 1967.

The Vietnam war dominated Goldberg's U.N. tenure, and much of his work at the world body was directed toward finding a formula that might start negotiations between the United States and North Vietnam. Goldberg was unsuccessful in this task. As the *Pentagon Papers* later showed, the progressive escalation of the air war was Johnson's chief strategy for resolving the conflict. In turn, the bombing of the North proved the main stunbling block to the start of negotiations, and Goldberg, who was not privy to the highest levels of Administration decision making, often found himself out of step with or unaware of American military and political policy in Southeast Asia.

Goldberg began his term at the U.N. by announcing that the United States would "collaborate unconditionally" with the Security Council in the search for an "acceptable formula" to restore peace in Vietnam. Hanoi rejected Goldberg's request for U.N. intercession on Aug. 2, 1965 and reiterated its own conditions for an end to the conflict: an immediate halt in U.S. air attacks on the North and withdrawal of all U.S. troops from the South. (Later North Vietnam modified its second condition to one merely calling for an end to the U.S. troop buildup). During the fall of 1965 Goldberg was involved in at least two other attempts to establish contact with the North Vietnamese, first through Communist U.N. delegations, and then in December through two Italian university professors who had recently returned from Hanoi. Both "peace feelers" collapsed.

Later in December 1965 Goldberg was part of a widely publicized Johnson Administration "peace offensive." The United States declared a halt to the bombing of North Vietnam on Dec. 24, and several high-ranking American officials, including Undersecretary of State Averell Harriman [*q.v.*], Vice President Hubert Humphrey [*q.v.*] and Goldberg were dispatched to make contact with foreign heads of state in an effort to open negotiations with Hanoi. Goldberg conferred with Pope Paul VI in Rome on Dec. 29, with Italian Premier Aldo Moro on Dec. 30 and with French President Charles de Gaulle on Dec. 31. These diplomatic moves proved fruitless, in part because of the Johnson Administration's continuing commitment to the escalation of the air war.

In the fall of 1966 Goldberg made another effort, again only partially backed by the Administration, to start negotiations through the United Nations. For the previous several months U.N. Secretary General U Thant had proposed that peace talks might begin on the basis of three points: (1) cessation of U.S. bombing of North Vietnam (2) de-escalation of the ground war in South Vietnam and (3) inclusion of the National Liberation Front (NLF) in peace talks. On Sept. 22 Goldberg delivered a major speech at the U.N. responding to the U Thant proposals. He declared that the U.S. was prepared to halt the bombing and begin de-escalation of all military activity in Vietnam "the moment we are assured, privately or otherwise," that the U.S. moves would be matched by a reduction of North Vietnam's war effort. Goldberg also declared that inclusion of the NLF in any subsequent peace talks would not prove an "insurmountable problem."

Although the Goldberg speech was couched in terms somewhat more conciliatory than previous U.S. proposals, President Johnson declined to characterize the presentation as either new or important. North Vietnamese Premier Pham Van Dong rejected the Goldberg proposal on September 25 and emphasized that a prerequisite to any negotiations was a "definite and unconditional" end to the bombing of the North. On Dec. 19 Goldberg called on U Thant to "take whatever steps you consider necessary to bring about negotiations leading to a cease-fire." But this appeal, which the *Pentagon Papers* described as "window dressing" to make up for the Administration's decision not to declare a lengthy Christmas ceasefire, was rejected by U Thant Dec. 30 when he declared that an unconditional cessation of the bombing was the "first and essential" part of any step toward negotiations.

Although Goldberg was excluded from White House decision making on Vietnam, he played an important role in the March 1968 reassessment of American policy that reversed the escalation of the war and opened the way to negotiations with the North Vietnamese and the NLF. On March 15 Goldberg sent Johnson an eight-page memorandum arguing for a complete bombing halt in order to get talks started. Goldberg asserted that the efficacy of an unconditional pause "can best be determined by what actually happens during the talks rather than by any advance verbal commitments of the kind we have been seeking." According to Townsend Hoopes [*q.v.*], then undersecretary of the Air Force, the Goldberg memo won a hostile, "volcanic response from the White House." Nevertheless, Goldberg's proposal, along with a similar suggestion from Ambassador to India Chester Bowles [*q.v.*], became an important basis for discussion by the prestigious Senior Advisory Group on Vietnam, which undertook a complete reevaluation of U.S. policy during the latter part of March. Goldberg participated in many of these discussions, at one point seriously deflating the military assertion that the recent NLF-North Vietnamese Tet offensive had been an enemy defeat. Along with former Secretary of State Dean Acheson [*q.v.*], former presidential special assistant McGeorge Bundy [*q.v.*], and Gen. Matthew Ridgway [*q.v.*], Goldberg was among those who successfully argued for a bombing halt and de-escalation of the war at the decisive meetings of the Senior Advisory Group on March 25 and 26.

Goldberg submitted his resignation as Ambassador on April 25, 1968. Johnson accepted his departure in an unusually "chilly" letter that failed to praise the former Supreme Court Justice for his U.N. service. Goldberg joined the New York law firm of Paul Weiss, Rifkind, Wharton and Garrison. Former Undersecretary of State George Ball [*q.v.*] succeeded Goldberg as chief U.S. representative at the U.N.

Goldberg became active in domestic politics after his resignation. In October 1968 he assumed command of Hubert Humphrey's presidential campaign in New York State. He joined other attorneys in appealing the conspiracy conviction of Benjamin Spock [*q.v.*], William Sloan Coffin, Jr. [*q.v.*] and three other anti-war activists in January 1969. He spoke at the Oct. 15 Moratorium Day protests against the war and in December 1969 joined with Roy Wilkins [*q.v.*] and 25 other prominent citizens in a "searching inquiry" into recent clashes between the police and members of the Black Panther Party. In 1970 Goldberg challenged Nelson Rockefeller [*q.v.*] for the New York governorship but failed to unseat the three-term incumbent. [See NIXON Volume]

[NNL]

GOLDMAN, ERIC F(REDERICK)

b. June 17, 1915; Washington, D.C.
White House special consultant, February 1964-September 1966.

Goldman received his doctorate in history from Johns Hopkins in 1938, served a brief stint as a writer for *Time* and then joined the Princeton faculty in 1943. He quickly became one of the most popular teachers at the University. His reputation as an historian of the first rank was established by *Rendezvous with Destiny*, a 1952 book that traced two distinct and often contradictory traditions within the liberal reform movement in the U.S.—one concerned with protecting the individual from big government and big business, the other with using centralized power to aid human welfare.

Acting on the suggestion of one of Goldman's former students, then serving as a White House aide, President Johnson invited Goldman to the White House for a "chat" in December 1963. Named White House special consultant on Feb. 3, 1964, Goldman was charged with, among other duties, the job of maintaining a liaison between the White House and specialists and intellectuals outside the Administration. Goldman ensured that opinions from a wide range of experts received a hearing at the White House. Some members of the press saw him as the token intellectual in the Johnson White House. Goldman described the President as a "restless, adventurous kind of man [who] assumes that talent, energy and brains can solve problems."

To dispel the lingering idea that Johnson was anti-intellectual, Goldman, in February 1965, conceived the idea of a White House Festival of the Arts, which was to be, in his words, "an outgoing, warm, colorful White House salute" to U.S. artists, writers and social critics. The Festival was also intended to show off the newly formed National Council on the Arts.

The Festival was scheduled at an unfortunate time—shortly after Johnson ordered the systematic bombing of North Vietnam and two months after U.S. military intervention in the Dominican Republic. The escalation policy subjected the Johnson Administration to attack from many members of the intellectual community. Formal plans for the Festival, to be held on June 14, 1965, were approved by Johnson on May 22. The first hint that the gala would cause a furor came with Robert Lowell's [*q.v.*] elegantly worded letter to the President, published in the *New York Times*, declining the invitation because of Johnson's recent foreign policy actions. Lowell's gesture infuriated Johnson but won the support of many intellectuals in the humanities and social sciences and touched off a debate among the participating artists over whether they should attend the White House Festival. Although Goldman denounced Johnson's Vietnam policy in his study, *The Tragedy of Lyndon B. Johnson,* he wrote that in the case of some intellectuals "the LBJ [foreign] policy was not really being considered on its merits; it was being attacked in considerable measure out of snobbery, social and intellectual."

The White House Festival on the Arts convened on June 14 in an atmosphere of considerable tension. At one point *Newsweek* book critic Saul Maloff encountered novelist Saul Bellow and asked, "How can you stand up there and read from your book after what that man has done in Vietnam?" Dwight Macdonald [*q.v.*] circulated a petition supporting Lowell's refusal to attend the Festival. President Johnson appeared at the Festival only briefly; his remarks were offhand and brusque.

After the White House Festival Goldman lost favor at the White House. Johnson had been offended, and his attitude hardened toward intellectuals who opposed his war policies. Goldman submitted his resignation on Aug. 23, 1966, but it was not made public because Johnson, fearing that Goldman would write a book about the Administration, wanted to underplay the historian's departure. On Sept. 7, 1966 Goldman's resignation was finally announced to the press. His role within the Administration was denigrated by White House Press Secretary Bill Moyers [*q.v.*], who said that "Goldman has spent most of his time working with Mrs. Johnson [*q.v.*] and Mrs. [Liz] Carpenter [*q.v.*] in the East Wing." John Roche [*q.v.*] succeeded him as "intellectual-in-residence."

In 1969 Goldman published *The Tragedy of Lyndon Johnson*, a critical assessment of Johnson's character. He described the President as a man who "entered the White House unhailed, and functioned in it unloved. Only once did warmth and a degree of affection go out to him—when he told the country he was leaving the Presidency." In explaining the causes of this reaction, Goldman cited Johnson's lack of "likability," his limited preparation for the office of the Presidency and his imperious, volatile personality. He finally summed up Johnson as "the wrong man from the wrong place at the wrong time under the wrong circumstances."

Goldman returned to his teaching duties at Princeton in 1966.

[FHM]

For further information:
Eric Goldman, *The Tragedy of Lyndon Johnson* (New York, 1969).

GOLDWATER, BARRY M(ORRIS)

b. Jan. 1, 1909; Phoenix, Ariz.
Republican Senator, Ariz., 1953-65; 1969- .

Goldwater was educated at Staunton Military Academy in Virginia and then spent a year at the University of Arizona. In 1929 he joined the family department store, Goldwater's, Inc., in Phoenix, becoming president in 1937. He served as a noncombat Army flier during World War II and shortly thereafter won election to the Phoenix City Council. In 1952 he narrowly captured the Senate seat occupied by Majority Leader Ernest W. McFarland (D, Ariz.) and easily defeated him again six years later. During his second Senate term Goldwater became the most prominent spokesman of the new, more militantly anti-Communist conservatism espoused by Southern and Western Republicans. In June 1960 he led the conservative attack upon the compromise platform agreement reached by Vice President Richard M. Nixon [*q.v.*] and Gov. Nelson A. Rockefeller (R, N.Y.) [*q.v.*], leader of the Party's liberal Eastern wing. [See EISENHOWER Volume]

By the fall of 1963 Goldwater appeared to be the leading contender for the Republican Party's 1964 presidential nomination. A quietly efficient Draft Goldwater Committee, chaired by F. Clifton White [*q.v.*], had convinced many Party strategists that the Senator, opposed to the activist civil rights stance of the Kennedy Administration, would sweep the South for the GOP. Many Goldwater enthusiasts also firmly believed that the potential but untapped conservative vote would turn out in large numbers if only the Republicans would avoid nominating a "me-too" contender who supported programs established earlier by Democratic presidential administrations. [See KENNEDY Volume]

Kennedy's assassination and the elevation of Lyndon B. Johnson to the presidency hurt Goldwater's presidential prospects. His support among Republican voters in public opinion surveys fell sharply, and Johnson's probable nomination dampened enthusiasm for a Goldwater-led "Southern strategy." Moreover, Goldwater had looked forward to an issue-oriented campaign against Kennedy. With this prospect gone the Senator lost much of his personal interest in the race, and he seriously contemplated withdrawing. However, the strength of the Goldwater movement within the Republican Party effectively quashed any self-doubts he had about running. In January 1964 Goldwater officially announced his candidacy. Opposing what he regarded as the liberal tendencies of most Democratic and Republican leaders, Goldwater insisted that he offered "a choice, not an echo."

After deciding to run Goldwater restructured his campaign hierarchy. He demoted F. Clifton White and replaced him with Arizona friends: Denison Kitchel, Richard Kleindienst and Dean Burch [*q.v.*]. Although Goldwater's new managers had known the candidate for years and enjoyed his confidence, none had experience in national politics. Goldwater's campaign directors hoped to regain their candidate's momentum, lost after the assassination, with a string of state primary victories against Rockefeller.

The first and most publicized primary, New Hampshire's, demonstrated the Senator's vulnerability as a presidential aspirant. At first open and candid with journalists accompanying him, Goldwater allowed them to quote him as giving preference to a voluntary Social Security program, a statement Rockefeller quickly attacked as destructive of the retirement system. Members of the Rockefeller staff unearthed a number of controversial Goldwater statements, including one that advocated giving nuclear weapons to the NATO commander. Goldwater's inability to clarify his positions placed him on the defensive, but Rockefeller failed to benefit from the Senator's difficulties. New Hampshire voters surprised everyone in March by writing in the name of Ambassador to South Vietnam Henry Cabot Lodge [*q.v.*]. The absent Lodge won first place with 35.5% of the total vote; Goldwater, with 23%, and then Rockefeller, with 20.6%, trailed far behind.

The consequences of his poor showing in New Hampshire appeared disastrous to Goldwater's chances for the nomination. His standing in the polls, already in decline, plummeted after New Hampshire while those of Lodge and Nixon rose markedly. Goldwater won consecutive primary victories in Illinois, Texas, Indiana and Nebraska, but only against scant opposition. He withdrew from active campaigning in the May 15 Oregon contest to concentrate on the June 2 California primary. In Oregon Rockefeller upset the favored Lodge and thus ended any likelihood of the Ambassador's nomination. The New York Governor began his California drive two weeks before the vote with a clear lead in the polls. After a well-managed effort, however, Goldwater narrowly upset Rockefeller. Besting his adversary by a 2.6% plurality, he captured all 86 of California's convention delegates. Goldwater rapidly emerged as the clear front-runner for the nomination.

More than the California victory had made Goldwater the favorite. Through the spring of 1964, in a phenomenon largely ignored by their detractors, Goldwater supporters had attended unpublicized Republican precinct and district meetings to choose delegates to the National Convention. This effort was not matched by the more passive Lodge and Rockefeller backers. F. Clifton White privately estimated that the California delegation, combined with those nonprimary seats already won, gave Goldwater about 555 first ballot votes, just 100 short of the number needed for the nomination.

The spirited "grassroots" movement on Goldwater's behalf surprised many. Some liberal analysts associated the earnestness of Goldwater's support with a recent and growing anti-Communist, anti-Negro and right-wing fanaticism. Journalist Robert Novak [*q.v.*] suggested that Goldwater's defeat of the nonideological, "problem-solving" or "pragmatic" Republicanism led by Rockefeller and other moderates could be attributed to the almost evangelical quality of Goldwater conservatism. Unlike most politicians, Goldwater gave quick, blunt answers without much regard to standard political rhetoric. Political scientist Aaron Wildavsky noted that Goldwater projected an image of apolitical morality and personal integrity. This attribute inspired many Republicans who were normally outside of the political process and generally unconcerned with whether their candidate could be elected.

Following the California primary moderate and liberal Party leaders searched frantically for someone to stop the Senator. Hoping for a deadlocked Convention and a draft, Nixon decided not to alienate the Goldwater wing by his own candidacy. Instead, he urged Michigan Gov. George W. Romney [*q.v.*] to make the race. Romney declined and the anti-Goldwater forces turned their attention to Pennsylvania Gov. William W. Scranton [*q.v.*]. At first hesitant to campaign without the endorsement of former President Dwight D. Eisenhower [*q.v.*], Scranton determined to run on June 12 following Goldwater's vote against cloture on the 1964 civil rights bill.

Goldwater's stand on civil rights added to divisions already apparent within the GOP. The Senator opposed the 1964 bill on constitutional grounds and said that the measure's public accommodations and fair employment provisions would require a federal police force "of mammoth proportions" to enforce. Only six of his Party colleagues joined Goldwater in opposition, while most GOP senators followed the lead of Minority Leader Everett M. Dirksen (R, Ill.) [*q.v.*] in voting for the measure. Although Goldwater denied the charge, many construed his vote on the bill as a bid for Southern support in the election.

Goldwater's civil rights vote had little effect on his nomination prospects. At first angry over Goldwater's decision to vote against the proposal, Dirksen rejected Scranton's pleas for neutrality and agreed on July 1 to nominate Goldwater. Four days before the Convention opened, Gov. James A. Rhodes (R, Ohio) [*q.v.*] released his 58-member delegation from its favorite-son status. The loss of Illinois and Ohio by the Scranton forces, Novak wrote, "opened the flood gates." Convention floor fights over delegate credentials and Party platform planks soon demonstrated Goldwater's overwhelming strength. With 883 votes to Scranton's 214, Goldwater won the nomination on the first ballot on July 15.

Goldwater failed to heal the deep wounds created by the bitter pre-Convention contest. The intensity of the moderate-liberals attack destroyed any consideration by Goldwater of immediate reconciliation. His managers had refused to compromise on platform amendments offered by the Scranton forces and by Gov. Romney. After the balloting Goldwater chose Dean Burch, an unknown, 36-year-old aide, to chair the Republican National Committee. He declined to consult with any Party leaders, including Eisenhower and Nixon, over the vice presidential nomination, and chose the relatively obscure Republican National Committee chairman, Rep. William E. Miller (R, N.Y.) [*q.v.*]. Goldwater's acceptance speech on July 16 gave revealing proof of his bitter mood. "Those who do not care for our cause," he declared, "we do not expect to enter our ranks in any case." In a direct challenge to Party foes who had criticized his support from right-wing groups, he asserted that "extremism in the defense of liberty is no vice . . . moderation in the pursuit of justice is no virtue." Most of the Convention cheered, but several leading members of Eastern state delegations walked out in protest.

In August the Senator attempted to reunite the Party and win support for his campaign, but a leadership conference in Hershey, Pa., ended in failure. Gov. Romney and Sen. Kenneth B. Keating (R, N.Y.) refused to endorse his candidacy and ran their own reelection efforts apart from the presidential race. Rockefeller made only one appearance on the Senator's behalf, although Eisenhower, Nixon and Scranton campaigned for the national ticket.

Because Goldwater's candidacy had become equated with dangerous, right-wing extremism, the fall campaign did not prove to be a liberal-conservative dialogue, as the candidate himself had anticipated. Johnson's campaign advertisements pictured Goldwater as the enemy of Social Security, world peace and the Northeastern section of the United States. By the contest's end Johnson portrayed himself as the true conservative. "I want to be conservative," he declared in Kansas, "without being a reactionary." Isolating his opponent as a fringe-group leader, Johnson urged voters to repudiate "that small minority which has seized the Republican party."

Goldwater sought unsuccessfully to generate support for his conservative proposals. Early in September he called for a 5% tax cut each year for the next five years. He favored the abolition of the draft through the creation of an all-volunteer Army. Repeatedly he warned voters that "a government that is big enough to give everything that you need and want is also big enough to take it all away." In a series of tactless speeches he condemned the War on Poverty program while speaking in poor areas of West Virginia, attacked medicare while addressing elderly voters in Florida and reiterated in Tennessee a proposal (first made in August 1963) that the Tennessee Valley Authority should be sold to a private company. On the eve of the election most Republican candidates, regardless of their pre-Convention position, divorced their campaigns from the Goldwater-Miller effort.

Goldwater lost decisively to Johnson on Nov. 3. The Republican nominee won 38.4% of the vote and carried only five Deep South states and Arizona. The GOP lost three Senate and 40 House seats. A number of young Party leaders were defeated in the wake of the solid Democratic landslide. In the 1965 session massive Democratic majorities in Congress passed a series of Administration social welfare proposals that Goldwater had strongly opposed.

Analyses of the 1964 election indicated that Goldwater won the votes of GOP loyalists who almost automatically voted Republican but that he failed to build significantly upon this hard core of support. A number of his statements, particularly his criticisms of Social Security and his comments indicating a casual attitude towards the use of nuclear weapons, caused a large number of moderate voters to identify him with extremist groups such as the John Birch Society. As a result he lost independent and marginal Republican backing. Only in the South, among those whites who opposed President Johnson's civil rights legislation, did Goldwater win new support for the GOP.

Having relinquished his Senate seat for the presidential race, Goldwater all but surrendered his Party leadership position in the election's immediate aftermath. He agreed to the removal of Burch as Republican National Committee chairman in January 1965. Occasionally speaking out on foreign and domestic issues, Goldwater called for an expanded American military role in Southeast Asia and condemned the Administration's Great Society programs. In October 1967 he backed Nixon for the 1968 Republican presidential nomination, declining to support the more conservative Gov. Ronald Reagan (R, Calif.) [*q.v.*].

In November 1968 and again six years

later, he won election to the U.S. Senate. Becoming a less controversial but more respected figure within the GOP hierarchy, he urged Nixon to resign from office at the height of the Watergate crisis and later attacked Reagan's insurgent candidacy for the 1976 Republican presidential nomination. [See NIXON Volume]

[JLB]

For further information:
Milton C. Cummings, Jr., ed., *The National Election of 1964* (Washington, 1966).
Leon D. Epstein and Austin Ranney, "Who Voted for Goldwater: The Wisconsin Case," *Political Science Quarterly*, LXXXI (March 1966), pp. 82-94.
Robert Novak, *The Agony of the G.O.P. 1964* (New York, 1965).
Stephen Shadegg, *What Happened to Goldwater?* (New York, 1965).
F. Clifton White, *Suite 3505* (New Rochelle, N.Y., 1967).
Aaron Wildavsky, "The Goldwater Phenomenon," *Review of Politics*, XXVII (July 1965), pp. 386-413.

GOODELL, CHARLES E(LLSWORTH)

b. March 16, 1926; Jamestown, N.Y.
Republican Representative, N.Y., 1959-68.

Goodell received a law degree from Yale in 1951 and took a masters in government there in 1952. After serving as a congressional liaison with the Justice Department in 1954 and 1955, he returned to Jamestown to practice law. Goodell won a special election for a congressional vacancy in 1959, and during his first two terms he established a moderate-to-conservative record. A backer of Rep. Gerald R. Ford, (R, Mich.) [*q.v.*], Goodell was a leader in the January 1963 Republican "Young Turks" rebellion that replacd Party Conference Chairman Charles B. Hoeven (R, Iowa) with Ford. [See KENNEDY Volume]

A second Young Turks' revolt resulted in Goodell's elevation to the upper ranks of the House Republican policymakers. In January 1965 Goodell and several other younger House members managed the election of Gerald Ford over incumbent Minority Leader Charles A. Halleck (R, Ind.) [*q.v.*]. Ford planned to open up the leadership's decision-making process and to reward Goodell in particular by designating him chairman of the GOP Policy Committee. The full GOP caucus, however, selected the more conservative Rep. John J. Rhodes (R, Ariz.) [*q.v.*] instead. Undaunted, Ford created a Planning and Research Committee in February and appointed Goodell its chairman. He came to rely heavily upon its work. In August the Goodell committee released a "white paper" on President Johnson's Vietnam policy. Although it supported American participation, the report recommended that the U.S. end the war "more speedily and at a smaller cost while safeguarding the independence and freedom of South Vietnam." Beginning in 1966 Goodell and Rep. Albert H. Quie (R, Minn.) [*q.v.*] proposed a GOP Opportunity Crusade as an alternative to the Administration's War on Poverty programs. It called for the states and private industry to assume a greater share of the antipoverty effort.

In his House votes Goodell compiled a record as a moderate Republican. Like most of his GOP House colleagues, he supported the 1964 and 1965 civil rights acts. He endorsed the Appalachian Regional Development Act once he won the inclusion of a small part of New York State in the program. However, he voted against the Economic Opportunity Act of 1964, which included many of the Administration's antipoverty proposals. He also opposed the Administration's 1965 Elementary and Secondary School Act. But he voted for medicare in July 1965. During the spring of 1968 Goddell and Quie maneuvered Ford into coming out for the civil rights measure, which he had planned to work against.

Goodell supported the moderate wing of the Republican Party. He backed Pennsylvania Gov. William Scranton's [*q.v.*] abortive campaign for president in 1964 and in 1968 supported the presidential candidacy of New York Gov. Nelson A. Rockefeller [*q.v.*]. Later Goodell took part in the effort to draft New York Mayor John V. Lindsay [*q.v.*] for vice president. Goodell campaigned for both Sen. Barry Goldwater (R, Ariz.) [*q.v.*] and Richard Nixon [*q.v.*] in their respective presidential campaigns.

In September 1968 Rockefeller named Goodell to fill the unexpired term of Sen. Robert F. Kennedy (D, N.Y.) [*q.v.*], who had been assassinated in June. Although New York State Democrats strenuously objected to the appointment of a Republican to fill a seat to which a Democrat had been previously elected, Goodell soon moved to the left to accommodate what he considered a far more liberal constituency. He became closely identified with opposition to the war in Vietnam and was an opponent of Nixon's domestic programs.

In 1970 the Republican White House repudiated Goodell in favor of his Conservative Party opponent, James L. Buckley. Goodell won only 24% of the vote in the subsequent three-way election. [See NIXON Volume]

[MDB]

GOODMAN, PAUL

b. Sept. 9, 1911; New York, N.Y.
d. Aug. 2, 1972; North Stratford, N.H.
Social critic.

Goodman grew up in the New York City slums and attended the City College of New York, where he was first attracted to the anarchist principles of Peter Kropotkin. He then studied at the University of Chicago, eventually receiving his Ph.D. in English there in 1955. During the 1940s and 1950s Goodman's wide-ranging intellect produced poetry, short stories, novels and essays on sociology, linguistics and city planning. His anarchist and pacifist ideas drew little attention until 1960, when he published *Growing Up Absurd: Problems of Youth in the Organized System*, a sweeping indictment of modern American society that attributed the growing alienation of many young people to the bureaucratic dehumanization of the system itself. [See KENNEDY Volume]

Growing Up Absurd won a large audience among college students and intellectuals, and Goodman's many essays and books in the mid-1960s were an important influence on the growing student radicalism of the period. Sociologist C. Wright Mills, and Goodman were often considered the two most important intellectual influences on the early New Left. His ideas on restructuring education had special impact. In *The Community of Scholars* (1962) and in *Compulsory Mis-Education* (1964), Goodman argued that students were the "major exploited class" in the society. He suggested a wide range of experiments in educational reform, including the radical decentralization of the school system and integration of the work experience with academic life through widespread use of apprenticeship programs. Goodman's proposal for the creation of voluntary "mini-schools" in ghetto areas attracted substantial support in the mid-1960s. The Ford Foundation sponsored several such schools in 1967 and 1968.

Goodman was a vocal critic of the Vietnam war and actively supported draft resistance and civil disobedience. He was an editor of *Liberation*, a radical pacifist magazine, and a frequent contributor to the *New York Review of Books*. By the late 1960s, however, Goodman had grown increasingly critical of the New Left. Believing that it had failed to produce a creative leadership and a coherent body of thought, he doubted that the movement could significantly change American society. Goodman's disenchantment was reflected in his *New Reformation: Notes of a Neolithic Conservative* (1970). While still sympathizing with young people who were outraged by such "gut" issues as Vietnam, he was nevertheless distressed by their disinterest in "fundamental" questions and by their anti-intellectualism and authoritarian tendencies. In the last years of his life, Goodman was also alarmed that many of his ideas had been misinterpreted. The proliferation of rural communes in the late 1960s owed much to Goodman's communitarian ideas, but Goodman asserted that his anarchist principles were not intended to promote "dropping out," which he believed could never lead to basic social or political change.

Goodman died of a heart attack in 1972.

[JCH]

GOODWIN, RICHARD N(ARADHOF)

b. Dec. 7, 1931; Boston, Mass.
Presidential special assistant, December 1964-September 1965.

The son of a Lithuanian Jewish immigrant, Goodwin graduated first in his class from both Tufts University and Harvard Law School. After clerking for Supreme Court Justice Felix Frankfurter and working for the House Interstate and Foreign Commerce Subcommittee on Legislative Oversight, he joined Sen. John F. Kennedy's (D, Mass.) speechwriting staff in 1959.

Political writer Richard Rovere said that Goodwin could "write about anything . . . because . . . he knew about everything, or knew something about everything." During Kennedy's presidential campaign Goodwin set out to learn about Latin America. He later helped design the Alliance for Progress and, during Kennedy's first year in office, was one of the leading White House advisers on Latin American policy. After his appointment as deputy assistant secretary of state for inter-American affairs in November 1961, however, his influence declined. His ambitious manner and unwillingness to observe bureaucratic etiquette were resented by State Department professionals. He was later named head of the small International Peace Corps Secretariat. At the time of President Kennedy's assassination, he was scheduled to become a special presidential adviser on the arts. [See KENNEDY Volume]

Through Bill Moyers [*q.v.*], a key Johnson aide, Goodwin was one of the first members of the Kennedy staff to establish good relations with Lyndon Johnson. Johnson called Goodwin "one of the smartest men I've ever met" and reportedly said, "He's wonderful, that boy. He can cry a little. He cries with me whenever I need to cry over something." By March 1964 Goodwin was known to be one of the President's major speechwriters. At the same time he became an architect of the Administration's domestic program. He coined the term "Great Society," which so appealed to the President that it became the slogan for the Administration, the Johnson equivalent of the New Deal and the New Frontier.

Goodwin recommended that a number of task forces be set up to formulate programs for the Great Society. By June 1964, 14 task forces, each composed of about 12 to 15 intellectuals and experts, began to meet regularly. They helped formulate much of the Administration's ambitious legislative program dealing with civil rights, poverty and conservation in the mid-1960s.

Despite his access to Johnson, Goodwin was distrusted by many of his White House colleagues. Johnson aide Jack Valenti [*q.v.*] said that Goodwin "had a larger dose of the ego disease than anyone I know," and historian Eric Goldman [*q.v.*] cited Goodwin's "chameleonlike air, the feeling that he was a good bit of an adventurer."

In December 1964 Goodwin was given the formal title of special assistant, with responsibility for urban affairs and the environment, but speechwriting continued to be his chief contribution to the Administration. His best remembered speech was Johnson's celebrated address of March 15, 1965, which climaxed an explosive week of civil rights activity that focused on the voting rights drive in Selma, Ala. In the speech Johnson adopted as his own the slogan of the civil rights movement, "We Shall Overcome." The President put the federal government on the side of civil rights activists in the Southern states and called for immediate legislation that would eliminate all "illegal barriers" to the right of Negroes to vote.

Goodwin subsequently helped publicize Great Society programs, but when Johnson turned increasingly to Vietnam and ignored domestic issues, Goodwin felt less committed to the Administration. Despite the President's protestations, Goodwin left the White House in September 1965 to accept a fellowship at the Center for Advanced Studies at Wesleyan University. The last speech he wrote for Johnson was the 1966 State of the Union message.

In April 1966 Goodwin wrote an article for the *New Yorker* attacking Administration Vietnam policy as a series of blunders. A few months later the article was expanded into a book and published as *Triumph or Tragedy: Reflections on Vietnam*. Aside from a brief period in the winter of 1966, when he worked as Jacqueline Kennedy's [*q.v.*] attorney in her efforts to block the publication of William Manchester's *Death of a President*, Goodwin devoted his time to criticizing the Administration and planning a strategy to defeat Johnson in 1968. Convinced that Johnson could be beaten, he consistently urged his friend, Sen. Robert F. Kennedy (D, N.Y.) [*q.v.*], to challenge the President in a primary election. Because Kennedy hesitated to enter the race, Goodwin, then a visiting professor of public affairs at the Massachusetts Institute of Technology, joined the anti-war campaign of Sen. Eugene McCarthy (D, Minn.) [*q.v.*] in February 1968. When Kennedy announced his candidacy a month later, Goodwin, out of personal loyalty and a belief that only Kennedy could win, switched camps. After Kennedy's assassination in June Goodwin returned to McCarthy, even though he was aware that the Senator could not win the Democratic nomination. Following this second switch reporters attacked his "flexibility," while conceding Goodwin's ability as a political strategist. There were rumors that on the day after Kennedy's death Goodwin had offered his services to New York Gov. Nelson Rockefeller [*q.v.*]. Sen. Edward Kennedy (D, Mass.) [*q.v.*], however, later defended Goodwin, arguing that "to call him a hired gun is to miss the point . . . his allegiances may have changed, but he never changed his feelings about the war."

After the 1968 election Goodwin worked as a journalist and author. In 1974 he published *The American Condition*, an ambitious work that drew heavily on economics and political theory. The book expressed Goodwin's pessimism about the future of freedom in the U.S., arguing that economic bureaucracy and the disintegration of the community had augmented the coercive nature of authority and eroded democratic institutions. Goodwin asserted that he "had come to the rejection of politics as a vehicle for social change in America."

[JCH]

GORDON, LINCOLN

b. Sept. 10, 1913; New York, N.Y.
Ambassador to Brazil, August 1961-January 1966; Assistant Secretary of State for Inter-American Affairs, January 1966-January 1967.

An economist at Harvard and Oxford prior to World War II, Gordon temporarily left his Harvard teaching post to serve as a government economist during the war. After the war he helped develop the Marshall Plan and consulted with the State Department while resuming teaching and research. In 1950 he decided to devote all of his time to public affairs. Gordon worked with the North Atlantic Treaty Organization under both Truman and Eisenhower. Between 1952 and 1955 he handled economic matters in the London embassy.

When Kennedy assumed the presidency Gordon, a liberal Democrat, became more prominent in policymaking circles. Partly because of some research experience in Brazil, Gordon was asked to join a Latin American task force organized by Kennedy only a few weeks after the November 1960 election. Chaired by Adolf A. Berle, Jr. the task force recommended a Latin American policy that found its expression in the Alliance for Progress. To a considerable degree Kennedy's subsequent Latin American policy reflected Gordon's views more than Berle's. While both men wanted to counter the appeal of Communism with open U.S. support of democracy and social change, Berle proposed giving assistance, in the style of the Soviet Union, to political parties ideologically compatible with the U.S., even if these parties were not in power. In contrast to Berle's argument for democratic "subversion," Gordon thought it simpler and more effective to pressure existing governments to democratize their countries through the promise of economic aid. Gordon remained influential in planning foreign economic policy and worked on the economic features of the Alliance for Progress, which were presented to the hemisphere at Punta del Este, Uruguay in August 1961. Later that month Gordon was appointed ambassador to Brazil. [See KENNEDY Volume]

Gordon's first three years in Brazil were chaotic. President Joao Goulart's administration faced a slowdown in the economic growth rate coupled with accelerating inflation. In the meantime the right wing in the Brazilian Congress and the military plotted against him while leftists pressured him to lead a Brazilian revolution. Although depicted as a radical in some U.S. newspapers, Goulart made some effort to cooperate with Gordon and to follow his recommendations for achieving price stability, but he was unable to carry them out. Relying on his influence in the labor unions, Goulart decided to side with the left in a power struggle with the right. On March 13, 1964 Goulart announced before a Rio crowd of 125,000 the nationalization of private oil companies and the expropriation of "underutilized" estates and promised to revise the constitution, grant suffrage to illiterates and impose rent controls.

Gordon felt that a Communist takeover was imminent. U.S. economic aid was cut off. Jerome Levinson and Juan de Onis later wrote that in March North American businessmen resident in Brazil and agents of the Central Intelligence Agency (CIA) helped organize and finance anti-Goulart civic demonstrations. Gordon assured Brazilian military conspirators that the U.S. was ready to support a new government. Recognizing the overwhelming military odds arrayed against him, Goulart left Rio de Janeiro on April 1. Both President Johnson and Secretary of State Dean Rusk [*q.v.*] sent congratulatory telegrams to the new military government. The Secretary described the coup as a "move to ensure the continuity of constitutional government." Some observers took the Administration's obvious satisfaction with the coup as representative of a new Latin American policy fashioned by Johnson's assistant secretary of state for inter-American affairs, Thomas C. Mann [*q.v.*]. The Johnson-Mann policy encouraged stable government and deemphasized issues of democracy and civil liberties.

Gordon soon became discouraged with the new Brazilian regime. The "institutional act," which allowed the chiefs of the armed forces to arrest whomever they pleased, and reports of torture were at odds with Gordon's concern for constitutional processes, which initially had led him to oppose Goulart. The U.S. embassy's political counselor persuaded Gordon not to resign, arguing that Gordon could use American influence to support the moderate wing of the Brazilian military and return the country to constitutional government. Gordon accepted the argument and soon developed what North American scholar Roger W. Fontaine called an "intimate, unprofessional relationship" with Brazilian President Humberto Castelo Branco. Eschewing the nationalism prevalent within the Brazilian right, the Castelo Branco government enthusiastically supported U.S. foreign policy. Brazil broke diplomatic relations with Cuba, sent troops into the Dominican Republic in 1965 and promised to participate in the Vietnam war if the conflict widened.

Gordon soon became a defender of the Castelo Branco government. In 1964 and again in 1966 he was able to secure for Brazil $150 million loans through the Agency for International Development (AID). At the end of 1964 the U.S. and Brazil announced a $1 billion economic aid program. The largest U.S. foreign aid recipient in the hemisphere, Brazil rewarded Gordon's faith by cutting inflation and achieving high annual growth rates. Gordon's emphasis on monetary stabilization, however, ignored the drop in real wages in Brazil to 1962 levels by 1966, the reversal of the land reform process and the curtailment of development projects in the poor regions of Brazil. Furthermore, Castelo Branco failed to heed Gordon's advice that he build a popular political base. Continued political repression belied Gordon's belief that Castelo Branco would eventually restore civil liberties.

In January 1966 Gordon replaced Jack Vaughn as assistant secretary of state for inter-American affairs. Jerome Levinson and Juan de Onis noted that "there was never any doubt that Gordon was in charge of United States Latin American policy . . . [he] made economic development the keystone of U.S. foreign policy. . . ." Because of his experience in Brazil, Gordon evolved a new conception of the possible role of the military: a military that not only opposed Communism but fostered economic development through the medium of a dedicated apolitical technocracy. Technical economic concerns and a self-proclaimed pragmatism characterized the Johnson-Gordon Latin American policy. With the exception of Brazil and a few other nations, however, Gordon was dissatisfied with the economic performance of the Latin American countries. Although he tried to maintain Alliance funds, criticism of its poor record shifted money out of Latin America into Asia and Africa.

Gordon resigned in January 1967 to become president of the Johns Hopkins University. In 1971 he resumed an academic life of teaching and research.

[JCH]

For further information:
Roger W. Fontaine, *Brazil and the United States* (Washington, 1974).
Jerome Levinson and Juan de Onis, *The Alliance that Lost its Way: A Critical Report on the Alliance for Progress* (Chicago, 1970).

GORE, ALBERT A(RNOLD)

b. Dec. 26, 1907; Granville, Tenn.
Democratic Senator, Tenn., 1953-71.

A country school teacher who studied law at the Nashville YMCA night law school, Albert Gore was elected to Congress as a New Deal supporter from Secretary of State Cordell Hull's old district in 1938. A liberal, Gore backed his populist oratory with diligent study of economic issues. He was elected to the Senate in 1952 over the aged Democratic Sen. Kenneth McKeller, representative of the state's once powerful Crump machine. There Gore matched the outspoken liberalism of his fellow Tennessean, Sen. Estes Kefauver (D, Tenn.). Gore and Kefauver were two of the three senators from the states of the Old Confederacy who, in 1956, refused to sign the Southern Manifesto protesting the Supreme Court's decision banning school segregation.

Along with Sen. Paul Douglas (D, Ill.) [*q.v.*], Gore was the most determined crusader for tax reform in the Senate. In the Finance Committee and on the Senate floor, they waged a long series of usually unsuccessful battles to close tax loopholes that benefited corporations and wealthy individuals. [See TRUMAN, EISENHOWER, KENNEDY Volumes]

Gore was the foremost liberal opponent of President Kennedy's $11 billion tax cut, which was passed by the House in September 1963. He argued in a letter to the President that tax reform should take priority over tax reduction and that such a massive tax cut would fuel a conservative movement to curb spending on social programs. Gore also criticized the economic thinking behind the tax cut, which reduced rates for corporations and the rich as well as average earners, as representative of the "trickle-down" theory of former President Herbert Hoover.

Gore continued to oppose the bill even after President Johnson made Senate passage of the tax cut the leading item on his legislative agenda in early 1964. He was the only liberal on the Finance Committee to vote against the tax bill. The Committee passed the measure, 11-5, in January. In a 23-page minority report Gore denounced the bill as one of the "most ill-considered bills ever to come before Congress for serious consideration." He said that it would create more inequity, had "no resemblance to true tax reform" and was the "embodiment of fiscal folly" because it would increase debt and cut revenues in prosperous times. Defeated in most of their attempts to add reform amendments to the bill, Gore and Douglas did succeed in deleting a House-passed provision lowering the capital gains tax. In February the Senate also adopted a Gore amendment increasing taxes on foreign earnings of Americans living abroad. The tax-cut bill, providing for a $11.5 billion annual tax cut, passed the Senate on Feb. 7 and was signed into law on Feb. 26.

Gore and Douglas consistently lost in their attempts to reduce or eliminate the 27½% oil depletion allowance, a primary target of tax reformers. "The oil and gas lobby," Gore said in April 1965, "is the most diabolical influence at work in the nation's capital. It has for years succeeded in blocking the assignment of public-spirited members to the tax-writing committees of the House and Senate, and also intervened in the election of leaders and assistant leaders of both Houses."

Characterizing the tax system as "a morass of favoritism," Gore tried to eliminate tax preferences enjoyed by philanthropic foundations and by corporation executives profiting from stock options. He also fought the 7% investment tax credit, passed in August 1962 in hopes of spurring businesses to modernize plants and equipment and create jobs. To Gore it was another expensive loophole. His March 1966 proposal to suspend the investment tax credit for two years in lieu of excise tax increases was turned down in the Senate by a 75-to-10 vote. In April 1968 Gore voted in favor of President Johnson's 10% income tax surcharge.

Gore's overall voting record, although not the most liberal in the Senate, was nevertheless unusually liberal for a Southern senator. (The liberal Americans for Democratic Action gave him an average score of 58 for the Johnson years.) Moreover, his ideological zeal and his debating fervor made him conspicuous in the Senate's liberal camp. In September 1964 Gore introduced the first medicare bill to pass either House. He backed the bulk of Johnson's Great Society social welfare programs, voted against the school prayer amendment in September 1966 and favored the gun control laws enacted in September 1968.

Gore had a mixed record on civil rights measures. Although generally a supporter of legislation to end racial discrimination, he voted against the Civil Rights Act of 1964 because of its provision for withdrawal of federal funds from programs administered in a discriminatory fashion. He called the provision a "sledgehammer" that would punish the innocent in an attempt to pressure recalcitrant state or local officials. Gore's motion in June to delete this section was rejected, 74 to 25. Reelected in 1964 Gore voted in favor of the Voting Rights Act of 1965 and the open housing Civil Rights Act of 1968, although he voted for an amendment to weaken open housing coverage in the sale of certain single-family homes.

A champion of liberal monetary policies, Gore frequently attacked "Johnson high-interest rates." He unsuccessfully appealed to the President not to reappoint conservative William McChesney Martin [*q.v.*] chairman of the Federal Reserve Board in 1965. Gore also argued against the appointment of Henry Fowler [*q.v.*] as Secretary of the Treasury.

A member of the Foreign Relations Committee, Gore was an early and consistent critic of the Vietnam war. Claiming that U.S. involvement damaged relations with Russia, he proposed a ceasefire in May 1965. In October 1967 Gore called for the U.S. to "honorably extricate" itself from "the morass in Vietnam" by accepting the neutralization of Southeast Asia. He subsequently joined Sen. J. William Fulbright (D, Ark.) [*q.v.*] in claiming that the Administration had falsely presented the Tonkin Gulf incident of 1964 as an act of North Vietnamese aggression in order to gain congressional approval for war measures.

The results of the 1968 presidential election, in which liberal Democrat Hubert Humphrey [*q.v.*] won only 28% of Tennessee's votes, foreshadowed the difficulty Gore's outspoken liberalism caused him in his 1970 reelection fight. Gore maintained his progressive stance in the first two years of the Nixon Administration, attacking the appointment of David Kennedy as Secretary of the Treasury and voting against Nixon's nomination of Southerners Clement Haynsworth and G. Harrold Carswell to the Supreme Court. One of the chief targets of the Nixon Administration in the congressional elections of 1970, Gore was unseated by conservative Rep. William E. Brock in a bitter ideological contest.

In September 1972 Gore became chairman of the Island Creek Coal Company, the nation's third largest coal producer. [See NIXON Volume]

[TO]

For further information:

Albert Gore, *Let the Glory Out: My South and its Politics* (New York, 1972).

GRAHAM, KATHERINE

b. June 16, 1917; New York, N.Y.
President, Washington Post Company, 1963- .

Katherine Meyer, the daughter of banker and *Washington Post* publisher Eugene Meyer, grew up in Washington, D.C. She was educated at the University of Chicago and began her journalism career in 1938 as a reporter for the *San Francisco News*. In 1940 she married Philip Graham, a young lawyer who took control of the *Washington Post* in 1948, after her father's retirement. Graham became head of the Washington Post Company when her husband committed suicide in 1963. By this time the company's holdings included in addition to the newspaper two television stations, one radio station and the weekly magazine *Newsweek*.

Under Graham the Washington Post Company expanded by acquiring an additional radio station, a new television station and part ownership of the *International Herald-Tribune*. Graham became best known not as an empire-builder but rather as a skilled manager who could attract and keep talent in her various enterprises. One of her most important decisions was to appoint Benjamin Bradlee managing editor of the *Post* in 1965, displacing Alfred Friendly. Bradlee himself was a practiced talent scout and brought many new faces onto the newspaper's editorial staff, which doubled in size between 1963 and 1970. Largely because of these policies, the *Post* became Washington's leading daily and a major organ of liberal opinion, rivaling the *New York Times* for influence on the East Coast. Daily circulation topped 500,000 in 1970, giving the *Post* a larger share of the Washington-area readership than the *Times* enjoyed in New York.

Graham's rule in dealing with her employees was to give them a free hand in determining editorial policy and news coverage and to support them against outside attack. Despite her friendship with high officials of the Johnson Administration, she made no objection to *Newsweek*'s critical coverage of the Vietnam war during the mid and late 1960s. When Vice President Spiro Agnew [*q.v.*] criticized the Washington Post Company in 1969 for "monopolizing" public information outlets, Graham pointed out that each of the Company's enterprises functioned "autonomously."

The Washington *Post* maintained its liberal political tradition by supporting Lyndon Johnson and Hubert Humphrey [*q.v.*] in the presidential elections of 1964 and 1968. During the early 1970s the *Post* became involved in unprecedented controversies, beginning with its publication of the *Pentagon Papers* against a court order in 1971. Graham supported this action and also seconded Bradlee in backing *Post* reporters Robert Woodward and Carl Bernstein when they uncovered the Watergate affair. For its role in reporting the scandal, the paper received a Pulitzer Prize in 1974. Graham herself was honored as the *Post*'s "leading lady" at numerous dinners and testimonials. [See NIXON Volume]

[SLG]

For further information:
"Graham, Katherine," *Current Biography Yearbook, 1971* (New York, 1972), pp. 170-172.

GRAY, JESSE

b. May 14, 1923; Tunica, La.
Harlem rent strike leader, 1963-64.

Gray was educated at Xavier College and Southern University in Louisiana but left without a degree. He worked as a tailor in New York during the early 1950s, before becoming involved in community action and civil rights activities.

Gray was an early supporter of efforts to form tenant associations among black slum-dwellers and first became known as a tenant organizer in Harlem. In 1952 he joined the Harlem Tenants Council and five years later formed his own group, the Lower Harlem Council. This was later renamed the Community Council for Housing and merged into the National Tenants Association, which elected Gray its chairman. In 1964 the Community Council for Housing claimed a membership of 2,000.

Gray participated in an unsuccessful rent strike against Harlem tenement owners in 1959. Four years later he was ready for another attempt, relying on his own organization and the pride of Harlem residents in the civil rights struggles of Southern blacks. The new rent strike began in November 1963 and soon affected 300 buildings in an 18-square-block area of lower Harlem. Other tenant associations joined in 1964, spreading the strike to the Lower East Side of Manhattan and parts of Brooklyn. Gray hoped for a city-wide rent strike but could not achieve the necessary interest and coordination; by the end of 1964 the strike movement had disintegrated. Gray did gain a favorable court ruling, however, which allowed residents of dilapidated buildings to deposit their rent in escrow with a tenant organization until necessary repairs had been made.

Gray's prominence in the rent strike enabled him to speak out on broader issues affecting the black community. He soon became identified with the growing radical wing of the civil rights movement. When Harlem residents protested police treatment of blacks in July 1964, Gray called for "100 skilled black revolutionaries who are ready to die" to correct "the police brutality situation in Harlem." In April 1964 Gray joined other black militants in a group called ACT, which demanded a more forceful strategy from the major civil rights organizations and urged less reliance on white support. Gray spoke at the 1966 convention of the Congress of Racial Equality, which adopted a "black power" philosophy justifying the limited use of force against the white "establishment."

In keeping with his conviction that real change would come only when blacks shared in political power, Gray tried repeatedly to enter New York politics. In 1961 and 1969 he ran unsuccessfully for city council in a Harlem district. In 1970 he sought the congressional seat of Rep. Adam Clayton Powell (D, N.Y.) [*q.v.*] but lost again. Gray finally won election to the New York State Assembly in 1972, representing a Harlem district. Described as "a grassroots kind of guy with a finger in every pie in Harlem," Gray remained in close touch with his constituents and continued working to improve housing conditions.

[SLG]

GREEN, EDITH S(TARRETT)

b. Jan. 17, 1910, Trent, S.D.
Democratic Representative, Ore., 1955-74.

A teacher and radio commentator before her election to Congress in 1954, Green represented most of Portland and some of its suburbs. She was assigned to the House Education and Labor Committee and chaired its Subcommittee on Special Education. Described as a "flaming liberal" in her early congressional years, Green was a consistent supporter of Kennedy Administration programs and sponsored major college aid bills in the early 1960s. [See EISENHOWER, KENNEDY Volumes]

While continuing to play an important role in education legislation, Green increasingly favored greater state and local control over federal education funds. With support from Southern Democrats she sponsored a successful amendment to a March 1967 education bill to allow states to distribute appropriations for supplemental education centers. While defending the extension of the Teacher Corps in June 1967, she led an effort to shift control of the Corps from the federal government to local school systems.

Green also sponsored a local control provision in a bill that restructured the Community Action Program (CAP). Called the "bosses and boll weevil" amendment because it appealed to rural Southern and big city Democrats, the new law required that the CAP boards be composed of one-third public officials, one-third poverty-area representatives and one-third business, labor and civic organization representatives. The measure was credited with preventing Southern Democrats from supporting Republican proposals to transfer Office of Economic Opportunity funds to other agencies.

On several occassions Green voiced her opposition to the Johnson Administration's Vietnam policies. In May 1965 she was one of seven representatives who voted against a $700 million military appropriation for the war.

Green, who grew increasingly conservative in the late 1960s and early 1970s, continued to concentrate her energies on education matters until her retirement from Congress in 1974.

[MDB]

Hope Chamberlin, *A Minority of Members: Women in the U.S. Congress* (New York, 1973).

GREENBERG, JACK

b. Dec. 22, 1924; New York, N.Y.
Director-Counsel, NAACP Legal Defense and Educational Fund, October 1961- .

After graduating from Columbia College and Law School, Greenberg joined the Legal Defense and Educational Fund of the NAACP in 1949. He argued one of the five cases involved in the Supreme Court's 1954 decision *Brown v. Board of Education*, which held racial segregation in public schools unconstitutional. Greenberg served as chief assistant to the Fund's Director-Counsel Thurgood Marshall [*q.v.*] during the 1950s and was selected the new director when Marshall resigned in October 1961. Under Greenberg's direction the Fund successfully defended thousands of civil rights demonstrators and won court orders to desegregate several major Southern universities in the early 1960s. [See KENNEDY Volume]

In December 1964, with some 3,000 sit-in prosecutions still pending in the South, Greenberg won a ruling from the Supreme Court that the 1964 Civil Rights Act barred state prosecution of peaceful sit-in demonstrators. The Legal Defense Fund also brought the first court suit under the public accommodations section of the 1964 act and secured a federal court order requiring Lester Maddox [*q.v.*] to serve black customers in his Atlanta restaurant. Over the next several years Greenberg and the Fund initiated numerous legal actions to ensure full implementation of the 1964 law, especially its equal employment opportunity provisions. Subsequent actions of the NAACP Legal Defense Fund were devoted largely to implementing the Voting Rights Act, passed by Congress in 1965.

A leading exponent of the strategy of using litigation to achieve social change, Greenberg launched new Fund campaigns in 1965 for the expansion of prisoners' rights and for the abolition of capital punishment. As part of its prison reform effort, the Fund brought suits challenging disciplinary procedures, inadequate medical care and censorship of mail in prisons. Along with the American Civil Liberties Union, the Fund appealed a series of criminal convictions where defendants had received the death penalty, arguing that the death penalty was both cruel and unusual punishment in violation of the Eighth Amendment and racially discriminatory. By 1968 the campaign had achieved what Greenberg called a temporary "de facto abolition" of capital punishment. In that year there were no executions. The Fund's effort ultimately led to a 1972 Supreme Court decision, *Furman v. Georgia*, in which the death penalty was held unconstitutional when the sentencing authority was free to decide between death and some lesser penalty. (In 1976 the Supreme Court affirmed that the death penalty per se was not unconstitutional.) Greenberg also founded the National Office for the Rights of the Indigent (NORI) in 1967 to assert the rights of the poor in court. With Greenberg as its director and with a million dollar grant from the Ford Foundation, NORI, like the Legal Defense Fund, sought cases likely to set legal precedents affecting large numbers of the poor.

Throughout the 1960s Greenberg oversaw several Supreme Court cases that successfully challenged various devices used to delay school desegregation. He repeatedly pressured the Department of Health, Education and Welfare to take stronger action to speed public school desegregation and to cut off federal aid to state welfare programs administered in a racially discriminatory manner.

In 1969 Greenberg argued the case of *Alexander v. Holmes* in which the Supreme Court ordered an end to segregated school systems "at once." During the Nixon years Greenberg publicly criticized the Administration for maintaining policies that he alleged encouraged delay in school desegregation. [See NIXON Volume]

[CAB]

GREGORY, DICK
b. 1932; St. Louis, Mo.
Comedian, social activist.

The second of six children in a fatherless family, Gregory grew up during the Depression in extreme poverty. He ran track for his St. Louis high school and attended Southern Illinois University on an athletic scholarship. After serving in the Army and drifting through several jobs, Gregory began his career as a comedian in 1958 at a black nightclub in Chicago. By 1961 he had become a nationally known comedy star, commanding salaries of $6,500 a week. His ironic treatment of social issues in his routine won Gregory a reputation as "the Negro Mort Sahl" during the early 1960s. He was the first black social satirist to appeal to both black and white audiences.

Gregory became involved in civil rights in November 1962, when he spoke at a voter registration rally in Jackson, Miss. He became friendly with Medgar Evers, leader of the Mississippi NAACP, and subsequently toured the South, speaking at civil rights rallies and demonstrations. Gregory dropped out of the nightclub circuit entirely in 1966 to devote himself to college appearances aimed at encouraging student activism. During the late 1960s he became increasingly involved in opposition to the Vietnam war. Other issues, such as environmental protection and the rights of American Indians, also drew his attention.

Always an individualist, Gregory did not identify himself with any single civil rights or peace organization. However, his celebrity status enabled him to act alone for the causes he espoused. In November 1967 he began a series of fasts, lasting from 40 to 80 days, to dramatize his stand on the war and other issues. He also led anti-war demonstrations in Chicago during the 1968 Democratic National Convention and was jailed for crossing police lines—his 20th arrest since 1962. In 1967 Gregory ran a write-in campaign against Richard Daley [*q.v.*] in the Chicago mayoral election, gaining 22,000 votes. A second write-in campaign during the Democratic presidential primaries of 1968 brought him 150,000 votes. In 1969 Gregory attended the World Assembly of Peace in East Berlin, protesting "racism as the prime cause of war."

Gregory's independent crusading drew mixed reactions from other black leaders. James Farmer [*q.v.*], former leader of the Congress of Racial Equality, praised Gregory for stimulating the political interest of many blacks. But Whitney Young [*q.v.*] of the National Urban League claimed that Gregory could do more good in the entertainment industry, opening new opportunities for black performers and writers. "There are many activists, but only one Dick Gregory," Young pointed out.

Gregory, in fact, reduced his political activism after 1969, partly for financial reasons. He resumed his nightclub performances in 1970 but left show business again in August 1973. This coincided with a change in Gregory's life style; he moved with his family from Chicago to a farm outside Boston and devoted himself to pursuing a "natural" life, including a vegetarian diet, breathing exercises and running.

Gregory published a number of books at various stages of his career, including *From the Back of the Bus* (1964), *Write Me In* (1968) and *Dick Gregory's Political Primer* (1972).

[SLG]

GRIFFIN, ROBERT P.
b. Nov. 6, 1923; Detroit, Mich.
Republican Representative, Mich., 1957-66; Republican Senator, Mich., 1966- .

The son of a factory worker, Robert Griffin graduated from the Central Michigan College of Education in 1947. He earned a law degree from the University of Michigan and then co-founded a law firm in Traverse City, situated in the less-populated, northwestern tier of the state's lower peninsula. Defeating a conservative incumbent in the 1956 Republican primary for the House of Representatives, Griffin won in November and encountered no difficulty securing reelection through 1964. A specialist in labor law, he served on the Education and Labor Committee. Griffin gained a recognition unusual for a second-term representative when he cosponsored the Landrum-Griffin labor reform law in 1959. [See EISENHOWER Volume]

In January 1963 Griffin and several other younger GOP colleagues plotted the first of two successful "Young Turks" revolts against the Party hierarchy. With Rep. Gerald R. Ford (R, Mich.) [*q.v.*] as their candidate, the younger Republicans ousted Party Conference Chairman Charles Hoeven (R, Iowa), who had the support of House Minority Leader Charles A. Halleck (R, Ind.) [*q.v.*]. Two years later the Griffin faction elected Ford over Halleck to the top GOP House post.

Griffin's House voting record resembled that of most of his fellow Republicans. In the 1965 session, according to *Congressional Quarterly*, Griffin opposed key White House-endorsed legislation on 49% of all roll-call votes, a tally that closely matched that of most other GOP representatives. Yet unlike Ford and the majority of his Party, Griffin voted for medicare in April 1965 after endorsing the unsuccessful Republican substitute.

In May 1966 Gov. George W. Romney [*q.v.*] appointed Griffin to the seat left vacant by the death of Sen. Pat V. McNamara (D, Mich.) [*q.v.*]. Griffin, who, one reporter wrote, had "the presence of a certified public accountant," faced the popular and outgoing former Gov. G. Mennan Williams in the fall elections. Strongly supported by Romney, Griffin defeated Williams by just under 300,000 votes.

As in his early House career, Sen. Griffin soon violated the tradition that new members of a legislative body should defer to their Party leadership. When President Johnson proposed to elevate Associate Justice Abe Fortas [*q.v.*] to Chief Justice in June 1968, Griffin organized conservative opposition to the nomination in defiance of Minority Leader Everett M. Dirksen (R, Ill.) [*q.v.*], who supported Fortas.

Griffin himself attacked the nomination on three counts. First, the Senator claimed in July that Johnson displayed "cronyism" by choosing Fortas, an old political friend and White House counselor. Second, Griffin argued that the President, as a "lame duck," had improperly negotiated with Chief Justice Earl Warren [*q.v.*] in an unprecedented and "obvious[ly] political maneuv[er] to *create* a vacancy." (Warren had stated that he would not retire from the Court until the Senate confirmed his successor.) Dirksen angrily denied Griffin's first two objections as "frivolous, diaphanous gossamer." In September Griffin revealed that Fortas had received $15,000 for teaching a nine-week course at American University Law School in the preceding summer. His fee, Griffin added, had been paid by five "former business associates or clients" of Fortas and his old law firm; Griffin charged that this payment represented a conflict of interest.

By September Fortas's promotion appeared doomed. The Judiciary Committee recommended his nomination, 11-6, but Griffin, who was not a Committee member, then organized a filibuster against it. In early October the Democratic leadership sought to end the debate through a cloture vote; with a 45-43 vote it failed to obtain the required two-thirds margin. By then Dirksen had surrendered to Griffin and voted against cloture. Fortas thereupon withdrew his name. For the first time since 1930, the Senate had failed to confirm a presidential Supreme Court nomination. President Richard M. Nixon named Warren's successor in May 1969. Griffin came away from the conflict with a reputation as a "giant killer" and a "mild-mannered man of steel."

Eleven months after his victory in the Fortas nomination dispute, Griffin became Senate minority whip, the second youngest in congressional history. Despite his position he occasionally opposed the Nixon Administration on major votes. His reassertion of the Senate's right to reject a Supreme Court nominee added to the Senate Democrats' determination not to approve two of Nixon's high court appointments. Griffin himself voted against the confirmation of Clement F. Haynsworth, Jr., in October 1969. Winning reelection in 1972 he remained minority whip and improved his relations with the executive branch upon Gerald Ford's succession to the presidency. [See NIXON Volume]

[JLB]

GRIFFITHS, MARTHA W(RIGHT)
b. Jan. 29, 1912; Pierce City, Mo.
Democratic Representative, Mich., 1954-74.

Griffiths graduated from the University of Missouri in 1934 and received her law degree from the University of Michigan in 1940. She served as a purchasing agent for the Defense Department during World War II. After the war she and her husband started a private law practice in Michigan with G. Mennen Williams. In 1948 Williams became governor, and Griffiths won election to the state legislature. Griffiths held the office until 1952, when she made an unsuccessful bid for a congressional seat. Two years later she was elected to Congress from Detroit's mostly middle-class 17th district. Somewhat conservative by Michigan Democratic standards and lacking the close United Auto Worker ties of other Detroit Democrats, Griffiths became quite popular in the previously Republican district and won reelection by large majorities.

Throughout her congressional career Griffiths worked for laws to prohibit sex discrimination. She fought successfully for the inclusion of an anti-sex discrimination provision in the Civil Rights Act of 1964. The original Administration bill included a section outlawing racial discrimination in employment. Hoping to ensure the section's defeat, Southern Democrats introduced an amendment to forbid job discrimination on the basis of sex as well. Griffiths and other women in the House saw the conservative ploy as an opportunity to offer legal recourse to women denied employment because of their sex. Without the amendment, Griffiths said, "white women will be last at the hiring gate." When the Johnson Administration, in its unsuccessful 1966 civil rights bill, proposed to make racial discrimination in jury selection unlawful, Griffiths added an amendment to forbid any distinction on the basis of sex. The bill won approval in the House but died in the Senate because of its controversial open housing provisions.

Griffiths was a founding member of the National Organization for Women in 1966 and helped publicize data on women's employment and earnings. Dissatisfied with the Equal Employment Opportunity Commission's enforcement of sex discrimination laws, she asked Johnson to replace its members in 1967.

Somewhat idiosyncratic in her voting, Griffiths was not among the Administration's most ardent supporters. She was, however, a leading advocate of its unsuccessful 1967 rat control bill. "If you're going to spend $75 billion to try to kill off a few Viet Cong," she told Congress, "I'd spend $40 million to kill the most devastating enemy that man has ever had." She cast the House's only dissenting vote on a 1966 Administration narcotics bill. She called it a "bribe" for addicts since it allowed them to voluntarily commit themselves to medical institutions for long-term treatment in lieu of serving a prison term. On the House Ways and Means Committee, she usually supported Chairman Wilbur Mills (D, Ark.) [*q.v.*]. However, in 1965, when the Johnson Administration proposed to reduce the 10% automobile excise tax in stages to 5% in 1967, Griffiths called for elimination of the levy altogether. Mills argued that it provided necessary revenues, but he offered a compromise, later enacted, under which the tax was reduced gradually and allowed to expire in 1969.

Although she voted for Johnson's Vietnam war appropriations, Griffiths grew critical of the war toward the end of his Administration. Asked in a 1968 interview what she would do in Johnson's place, Griffiths replied, "I'd call Ho Chi Minh and tell him I was bringing the boys home." She voted for the 1970 Cooper-Church amendment prohibiting the use of American troops in Cambodia.

Griffiths was a leading proponent of the Equal Rights Amendment, and its approval by Congress in 1972 was, according to Rep. Gerald Ford (R, Mich.) [*q.v.*], "a monument to Martha." She retired from office in 1974, but continued working for the ERA in state referenda. [See NIXON Volume]

[MDB]

For further information:
Hope Chamberlin, *A Minority of Members: Women in the U.S. Congress* (New York, 1973).

GRISWOLD, ERWIN N(ATHANIEL)
b. July 14, 1904; East Cleveland, Ohio. Member, U.S. Civil Rights Commission, April 1961-September 1967; U.S. Solicitor General, September 1967-June 1973.

A 1925 graduate of Oberlin College, Griswold received a bachelor of laws degree from Harvard Law School in 1928 and a doctor of laws degree the next year. From 1929 to 1934 he worked as an attorney in the Solicitor General's office. Griswold taught at Harvard Law School beginning in 1934 and established a reputation as an expert in federal taxation and conflict of interest laws. As dean of the law school from 1946 to 1967, Griswold was credited with improving the quality of the student body, revamping the curriculum and improving the fund-raising activities and physical plant of the school.

Griswold, a registered Republican, was named a member of the U.S. Civil Rights Commission by President Kennedy in April 1961. An investigative body established in 1957, the Commission made numerous recommendations in the early 1960s for stronger federal legislation in such areas as voting rights, school desegregation, the protection of civil rights workers and employment and housing discrimination. Many of the Commission's proposals were incorporated into the 1964 Civil Rights Act and the 1965 Voting Rights Act. Following passage of these statutes the Commission also studied their enforcement, and its reports frequently recommended greater federal action to ensure full implementation of the laws.

Griswold resigned his posts on the Commission and as dean of Harvard Law School when appointed Solicitor General by President Johnson on Sept. 30, 1967. Known for his rather taciturn and gruff manner, Griswold was in charge of all U.S. government litigation in the Supreme Court as Solicitor General. In briefs and oral argument before the Court in March and May 1968, Griswold urged the justices to reject a claim that the government must turn over transcripts of any illegal eavesdropping to a defendant and his attorney. He told the Court that if such a claim were upheld, the government might have to drop some prosecutions against alleged spies for fear that its counterespionage methods would be disclosed to foreign governments. The Supreme Court by a five-to-three vote rejected Griswold's arguments in a March 1969 decision.

In September 1968 Griswold also filed a brief in a case involving a divinity student who had turned in his draft card in protest against the Vietnam war and had then lost his deferment in accordance with an October 1967 order from the Selective Service director to local draft boards. In an unusual move Griswold presented both the Selective Service System's view that the order was legal and the Justice Department's position that the directive might violate both the draft law and the Constitution by using the draft to punish anti-war dissenters. The Supreme Court's December 1968 ruling called the local draft board's action "basically lawless" and upheld the right of an individual to challenge in court the loss of a statutory draft exemption.

Griswold was retained as Solicitor General by the Nixon Administration, and he argued several important Supreme Court cases involving school desegregation, court-ordered busing and the constitutionality of anti-abortion laws. He resigned as Solicitor General on June 26, 1973 to join a Washington law firm. [See NIXON Volume]

[CAB]

GRONOUSKI, JOHN A(USTIN)
b. Oct. 26, 1919, Dunbar, Wisc. Postmaster General, September 1963-September 1965; U.S. Ambassador to Poland, September 1965-May 1968.

Gronouski was born in a small Wisconsin hamlet and raised in Oshkosh. His mother was Irish and his father of Polish extraction. He earned a Ph.D. in economics from the University of Wisconsin in 1955 and two years later joined the faculty of Wayne State University. In 1960 the governor of Wisconsin named Gronouski state commissioner of taxation.

President John F. Kennedy named Gronouski to succeed J. Edward Day as Postmaster General in August 1963. He was the first cabinet member in history to hold a Ph.D. and the first of Polish extraction. Some political observers suggested that in appointing Gronouski Kennedy was making a gesture to those Polish-Americans whose traditional loyalty to the Democratic Party had been eroded by the Administration's civil rights program.

Gronouski partially reduced a massive Post Office deficit by cutting back on overtime, closing the philatelic agency and ordering large-volume mailers to pre-sort their mail according to ZIP code numbers. However, he accomplished little in speeding the delivery of mail.

Gronouski faced a Senate Judiciary subcommittee inquiry into questionable Post Office practices and abuses in February 1965. Under a Post Office mail surveillance program, certain letters were delivered only after Post Office officials had noted all information on the envelope. Henry B. Montague, chief postal inspector, testified that the mail of about 1,000 companies and individuals was currently under surveillance—a procedure Gronouski defended as useful in solving crimes. Subcommittee Chairman Edward V. Long (D, Mo.) [*q.v.*] charged the Post Office was denying citizens their right to privacy and won a pledge from Gronouski to "tighten and centralize" the mail surveillance program.

Sen. Long also charged that the Post Office was turning over to the Internal Revenue Service the mail of delinquent taxpayers, but Gronouski testified that he had discontinued the practice. The Senate subcommittee did not discover that the Central Intelligence Agency (CIA), rather than the Post Office, continued not only to intercept but also to open first class mail sent from the Soviet Union to American citizens. According to the report of the *Presidential Commission on CIA Activities Within The United States* (1975), CIA officials in April 1965 considered briefing Gronouski but decided against it, fearing that Gronouski's pledge to Sen. Long would put him into conflict with their agency.

In the summer of 1965 President Johnson ordered the Post Office and other federal agencies to hire youths as summer replacements for regular workers on vacation. Administration critics charged the Post Office with hiring youths recommended by members of Congress and paying them salaries above the $1.25 an hour set by the President.

Despite the controversies swirling about the Post Office, President Johnson appreciated Gronouski's skill as a political campaigner, particularly in Polish-American neighborhoods. Late in the summer of 1965, Johnson named Gronouski ambassador to Poland. Over the next two and a half years, Gronouski, in his ambassadorial capacity, held a number of discussions in Warsaw with the ambassador from Communist China. (The U.S. and China did not have formal diplomatic ties, and the Warsaw talks, dating from 1958, constituted the only regular diplomatic contact between the two countries.) The discussions concerned Vietnam, disarmament and a possible Chinese-American cultural and scientific exchange program. Carried on during a period when the U.S. was deeply involved in Vietnam and during a time of internal unrest in China, the talks were inconclusive.

In May 1968 Gronouski resigned his diplomatic post to campaign for Hubert Humphrey [*q.v.*]. In September 1969 he was named dean of the Lyndon B. Johnson School of Public Affairs at the University of Texas.

[JLW]

GROPPI, JAMES

b. 1931, Milwaukee, Wisc.
Adviser, Youth Council of the Milwaukee NAACP, 1964-68.

The son of an immigrant Italian grocer, Groppi grew up on the South Side of Milwaukee. He attended Milwaukee's St. Francis Seminary, where he was ordained as a priest in 1959. Groppi became interested in civil rights at this time, due in part to the discrimination against blacks that he witnessed in the Seminary. After serving as an assistant pastor in an Italian section of Milwaukee, he was transferred to the predominantly black St. Boniface parish in 1963. He also became adviser to the youth council of the local NAACP.

Groppi's first active involvement in civil rights came in 1964, when he participated in several voter registration marches in Mississippi. One year later he supported a school boycott by Milwaukee blacks protesting segregation in the city's educational system. On this occasion he came into conflict with his church superiors in Milwaukee, who opposed clerical participation in the boycott. Groppi was arrested several times in Milwaukee during the mid-1960s for leading or participating in civil rights demonstrations.

In 1967 Groppi and the youth council of the Milwaukee NAACP began to push vigorously for a local open-housing law. When rioting erupted in the city's black ghetto during late July and early August, Groppi blamed the outbreak on the city government's continued refusal to act against discrimination in housing and education. On Aug. 28 Groppi and the NAACP Youth Council began a series of open-housing demonstrations in Milwaukee. Lasting into late November, the protests attracted national attention as the most extensive campaign in the U.S. against housing bias. Most of the marches led by Groppi passed through the city's South Side, provoking violent counter-demonstrations by white residents. After one clash on Sept. 11, Milwaukee Mayor Henry Maier claimed that "the city verged on civil war." The largest of the marches involved 2,300 people, including civil rights workers and clergymen from seven Midwestern states.

On Sept. 13 Milwaukee Archbishop William Cousins abandoned his earlier neutrality to support Groppi's demand for a municipal open-housing law. Other religious groups, including the American Lutheran Church, also gave their support. As a result of the open-housing campaign, the Milwaukee City Council passed a measure on Dec. 13 outlawing discrimination in certain types of housing; this was later expanded into a strict open housing code.

Groppi left the Milwaukee NAACP youth council in November 1968, in order to concentrate on "militant social action involvement" within the St. Boniface parish. He remained active, however, in the city's civil rights movement. In September 1969 he led a group of students and welfare recipients which occupied the Wisconsin State Assembly chamber to protest reductions in state welfare payments. This action alienated Groppi from many of his liberal supporters, who objected to the "disruptive" tactics of the demonstrators.

Groppi was transferred from the St. Boniface parish in June 1970 to the racially mixed Milwaukee parish of St. Michael. In 1972 he entered the Antioch Law School in Washington, D.C., driving a taxi part-time to support himself. Groppi was excommunicated and banned from performing priestly functions when he married in May 1976.

[SLG]

GROSS, H(AROLD) R(OYCE)

b. June 30, 1899; Arispe, Iowa
Republican Representative, Iowa, 1949-75.

Raised on a farm in southern Iowa, H. R. Gross served overseas in World War I. After working on various newspapers from 1921 to 1935, he became a radio news commentator. Elected to Congress as a Republican in 1948 from Iowa's agricultural third district, Gross distinguished himself as an isolationist, a backer of high farm subsidies and a conservative critic of what he considered government extravagance. He waged his campaign for government frugality through Republican and Democratic administrations alike and often denounced Congress for excessive staff and committees, unnecessary travel at taxpayers' expense and too frequent recesses. [See EISENHOWER, KENNEDY Volumes]

Gross was a vigorous opponent of the liberal domestic and international programs of the Kennedy and Johnson Administrations. *Congressional Quarterly* reported that Gross voted against measures favored by the Johnson Administration more than any other Representative in 1965, 1967 and 1968. He was the only Iowan to vote against medicare in April 1965 despite the fact that Iowa was the state with the second largest percentage of citizens over 65. An opponent of foreign aid since he voted against extending the Marshall Plan in April 1949, Gross labeled the Peace Corps "a haven for draft dodgers" in 1961 and called the Arms Control and Disarmament Agency "a wanton waste of the taxpayers' money" in April 1965. He opposed a $200 million U.S. subscription to the Asian Development Bank in February 1966.

Gross was best known for his maverick forays against what he considered prodigal spending in government. In July 1964 Gross successfully proposed an amendment to the Land and Water Conservation Act to prohibit issuance of free passes to members of Congress or government officials for admission to areas covered in the bill. He voted against every congressional pay raise, and in March 1964, he managed to defeat a proposed pay increase for federal employees by demanding a roll-call vote on the measure. Congress rejected an amendment by Gross in June 1965 to delete a $35,000 appropriation for elevator operators in the House's Rayburn Building, whose elevators were automatic. He was one of only two members to vote against a military pay increase in October 1967. Gross continued to act as a budgetary watchdog through the Nixon Administration. He once criticized Secretary of the Interior Walter J. Hickel because the Secretary installed $56.25-a-yard carpeting in his office.

[TO]

GRUENING, ERNEST H(ENRY)

b. Feb. 6, 1887, New York, N.Y.
d. June 26, 1974, Washington, D.C.
Democratic Senator, Alaska, 1959-69; Chairman, Subcommittee on Foreign Aid Expenditures, 1965-69.

Gruening graduated from Harvard Medical School in 1912 but chose to become a journalist. He edited several liberal publications in the 1920s and 1930s and wrote a widely read account of the Mexican Revolution. Gruening opposed U.S. military intervention in Latin America and was an early advocate of racial equality and birth control. In 1924 he headed public relations for Sen. Robert LaFollette's Progressive Party presidential campaign.

Franklin D. Roosevelt appointed Gruening director of territories and island possessions in 1934. As Governor of Alaska between 1939 and 1952, he pressed for construction of the Alcan Highway, antidiscrimination legislation aimed at protecting Alaska's Indians, a tax system designed to weaken the influence of absentee interests and for Alaskan statehood. Elected Alaska's first senator in 1959, Gruening supported most Kennedy Administration programs. [See TRUMAN, EISENHOWER, KENNEDY Volumes]

Gruening, who had long worked for more federal aid to Alaska, was angered that victims of the March 1964 Alaskan earthquake were required to pay higher interest on federal loans than were foreign aid recipients. Through his efforts federal expenditures following the earthquake were increased and the Housing and Finance Administration was authorized to purchase Alaskan bonds. He also claimed that Alaska suffered from inadequate transportation facilities due to its exclusion from federal highway programs while a territory. As a result of his efforts, appropriations were made in May 1966 for maintenance as well as construction of Alaskan highways.

Gruening had been a strong proponent of family planning since the 1920s, when he had worked with birth control advocate Margaret Sanger. He introduced a bill in April 1965 to create Offices for Population Problems in the Departments of State and of Health, Education and Welfare. As a chairman of the Government Operations Subcommittee on Foreign Aid Expenditures, Gruening held hearings on birth control services currently provided by federal and private agencies to determine whether the proposed offices would duplicate existing services. The hearings gained wide publicity for birth control ideas and had the effect of increasing the efforts of existing agencies. Later Gruening became convinced that his bill was obsolete, and he did not report it for Senate action. Instead, he released a study in January 1966 criticizing the government for lagging behind private agencies in providing family planning services.

Gruening was one of the earliest congressional critics of American involvement in Vietnam, voicing opposition to the Johnson Administration's policies in a March 1964 Senate speech entitled "The United States Should Get Out of Vietnam." In August 1964 he and Sen. Wayne Morse (D, Ore.) [*q.v.*] cast the only votes against the Tonkin Gulf Resolution, which allowed the President to take "all necessary measures to repel further attacks. . .and to prevent further aggression." Gruening later denounced the resolution as a "blank check to the President." He and Morse consistently voted against the Administration's requests for military appropriations for Southeast Asia, often forming the only opposition to such expenditures.

Gruening stated repeatedly that the area was not essential to American security and held that the U.S. was acting in violation of the 1954 Geneva Accord and the U.S. Charter. Calling for negotiations with Hanoi, Morse and he assailed the bombing of North Vietnam in February 1965. In January 1966 he was among 16 senators who sent a letter to Johnson asking for an end to the air attacks. On March 1, 1966 Gruening was the only senator to support Morse's proposal to repeal the Tonkin Gulf Resolution. At the same time the Senate rejected, by a vote of 75 to 2, his amendment to prohibit sending draftees to Southeast Asia unless they volunteered for service there.

Gruening became one of the few senators to associate himself with the early anti-war movement. In April 1965 he addressed the first large demonstration in Washington against the war, which was sponsored by a coalition of groups including Students for a Democratic Society. He later protested a Capitol safety bill in September 1967, which did not include permission for orderly demonstrations on the Capitol grounds.

During the 1960s Gruening advocated strict congressional review of American foreign aid expenditures. He opposed most foreign military assistance, especially in Latin America, where he thought it was used for purposes at variance with those of the Alliance for Progress. Gruening's efforts to tighten congressional supervision of foreign aid proved generally unsuccessful, but in the mid-1960s he won modification of Administration foreign aid bills on occasion. Gruening thought Communist influence pervasive in Indonesia, and his September 1965 amendment to cut off all aid to that country, unless deemed "essential" by the President, won Senate approval. He successfully introduced a measure in July 1966 that required the U.S. to use its voting power to prevent loans by the World Bank and its affiliates to countries already suspended from U.S. aid because of expropriation of American property. Gruening's August 1967 amendment to bar aid to any country breaking diplomatic ties to the U.S. was also accepted by the Senate. (The proposal was directed against the Arab states, which had broken relations with the U.S. following the Arab-Israeli war in June 1967.)

Gruening, 81, lost the 1968 Democratic senatorial primary to 38-year-old Mike Gravel, a real estate broker who emphasized state rather than national issues. Gravel's victory was in large measure attributed to the widespread showing of a sophisticated documentary film advancing the young challenger's candidacy. In the November general election Gruening's name was not on the ballot, but he nevertheless received a statewide write-in vote of 15%. Gruening continued to actively oppose the Vietnam war and in 1972 campaigned for Sen. George McGovern (D, S.D.) [*q.v.*] for president.

[MDB]

GUY, WILLIAM L(EWIS)

b. Sept. 30, 1919; Devils Lake, N.D.
Governor, N.D., 1961-73.

A farmer and former teacher of agricultural economics at North Dakota State University, Guy was assistant majority floor leader in the North Dakota House of Representatives from 1958 to 1960. Despite a 16-year Republican gubernatorial dynasty and Richard M. Nixon's [*q.v.*] victory in North Dakota in 1960, Guy defeated six-term Republican Lt. Gov. C. P. Dahl, a victory that signified the resurgence of the state's coalition of the old Nonpartisan League and Democratic Party regulars. Guy was reelected to his second two-year term in 1962 and reelected in 1964 to his first four-year term.

When Guy assumed his office in 1961, North Dakota faced a declining population due primarily to its almost total dependence on agriculture. In an effort to diversify and industrialize, Guy sought to reduce the state's high electric power rates by building three cooperative power plants on the Missouri River. Despite this effort the amount of new industry in the state did not significantly increase. Guy faced the problems of limited gubernatorial powers and a consistently Republican-dominated legislature. Nevertheless, he raised the state's biennial budget from $75 million to $283 million during his tenure, modernized the state government, reformed the tax system, established area mental-health clinics, expanded nursing-home facilities, consolidated school districts, and reduced the state's penitantiary population by almost 50% through revised probation and parole techniques. Guy said that "the most significant development" of his governorship was the start of a comprehensive resource plan for the Red River and its tributaries.

In May 1966 Guy was the first governor in the nation to veto Office of Economic Opportunity (OEO) programs in his state. He defended his action saying that "during this wartime inflationary period we should not permit indiscriminate expenditures of OEO funds for programs of questionable value." In September 1967 Guy was among a group of 20 "distinguished Americans" who observed South Vietnam's election, which, Guy said, was "as moving and profound an example of the desire for self-determination as can be found anywhere." As chairman of the 1967 National Governors Conference, Guy expressed hope that the Conference would pass a Vietnam resolution "in favor of the commander-in-chief." He became a member of the 1968 Humphrey-for-President Committee and won reelection to his second four-year term in November 1968.

In 1973 Guy retired to become an insurance company executive. He was narrowly defeated by five-term incumbent Sen. Milton Young [*q.v.*] in a 1974 Senate bid.

[TJC]

HABIB, PHILIP CHARLES

b. Feb. 25, 1920; New York, N.Y. Counselor for Political Affairs, U.S. Embassy, Saigon, May 1965-July 1967; Deputy Assistant Secretary of State for Far Eastern Affairs, July 1967-April 1969.

Habib's background was very different from that of most foreign service officers of his generation. The Brooklyn-born son of a Lebanese grocer, Habib worked as a shipping clerk in Flatbush before attending the University of Idaho. After receiving his doctorate in economics from the University of California in 1952, he joined the diplomatic corp and became deeply involved in Asian affairs, serving in South Korea before being assigned to South Vietnam as chief political adviser in May 1965. He was named deputy assistant Secretary of State in July 1967.

In March 1968 Habib was asked to join Lyndon Johnson's Ad Hoc Task Force on Vietnam, which had been formed to advise the President on the military's request for over 200,000 additional ground troops following the Communist Tet offensive. At these meetings Habib recommended that the increase be denied because it would continue South Vietnamese reliance on American power and delay the development of needed South Vietnamese military independence.

At the end of the month, when the President called together his Senior Advisory Group on Vietnam to study the request, Habib was one of three government officials to brief these men. In what the *Pentagon Papers* described as "an unusually frank" report, Habib, who had accompanied Gen. Earle Wheeler [*q.v.*] on the mission to Saigon that had resulted in the troop request, told the group that the South Vietnamese government was generally weaker than had been realized as a result of the Tet offensive. He also outlined the problems that resulted from corruption and the increase in refugees. As a result of these briefings and the fear of the domestic consequences of further troop increases, the group advised a policy of de-escalation.

Hearing of the descrepancy between the Habib report and the optimistic accounts offered by presidential adviser W. W. Rostow [*q.v.*], President Johnson ordered his own briefing. According to the *Pentagon Papers*, Habib was as frank with Johnson as he had been with the Advisory group and despite "tough questions" from the President "Habib stuck to his guns." Although the writers of the *Pentagon Papers* could find no definitive connection between these briefings and policy formation, on March 31, 1968 Johnson, nevertheless, announced the gradual de-escalation of the war.

In May 1968 Habib accompanied the U.S. delegation to the Paris peace talks as adviser on Vietnamese affairs. As the highest ranking career diplomat in the delegation, Habib was "the one crucial link" between the Johnson Administration's delegation, led by W. Averell Harriman [*q.v.*] and the Nixon Administration's group, later headed by Henry Cabot Lodge [*q.v.*]. In November 1969 Habib became head of the U.S. delegation at Paris. He was appointed ambassador to South Korea in September 1970.

[EWS]

HAIDER, MICHAEL L(AWRENCE)

b. Oct. 1, 1904; Mandan, N.D.
Chairman and Chief Executive Officer, Standard Oil Company of New Jersey, February 1965-September 1969.

Haider, the son of a farmer, grew up in North Dakota and California. He studied at Stanford University, where he received a chemical engineering degree in 1927, and soon began work as an engineer for the Carter Oil Co., a Midwestern subsidiary of the Standard Oil Co. of New Jersey. Haider spent the next 20 years with various subsidiaries of Jersey Standard in Canada and the U.S., working mainly in the area of oil exploration and extraction. In 1950 he advanced to executive rank as vice president of Imperial Oil, the Canadian affiliate of Jersey Standard. Three years later he moved to corporate headquarters in New York as deputy coordinator of worldwide oil production for Jersey Standard. In 1963 Haider was named president of Jersey Standard, taking responsibility for the corporation's day-to-day operation. In 1965 he became chairman and chief executive officer, with authority over long-range planning and policy.

By the time Haider assumed leadership, Standard Oil of New Jersey was the largest oil company in the world, with 300 affiliates in 100 countries. Its expansion continued under Haider, bringing total sales from $12 billion in 1965 to $16 billion in 1968. Haider, a forceful administrator who respected the opinions of his subordinates, sought to encourage this growth with decentralization measures designed to increase the corporation's flexibility. Among his innovations was creation of a series of middle-level "management companies" to oversee Jersey Standard's foreign operations. Bearing the Jersey Standard commercial trademark, they included Esso Africa, Esso Inter-America, Esso Standard Eastern (covering Asia and the Pacific) and Esso Europe. The most important of these was the European company, which helped supply the skyrocketing market for oil and chemicals in Western Europe. A major accomplishment of Esso Europe was maintaining the flow of fuel to European industry after the closing of the Suez Canal in 1967.

Haider was optimistic about the further "globalization of American business." Nevertheless, he had to face nationalistic restrictions in most places where Jersey Standard operated. Company property was seized during the late 1960s by Libya and Peru. Another government that looked suspiciously at the corporation's rapid overseas expansion was the U.S. itself; State Department and Treasury officials complained that the massive outflow of American capital would create a lasting balance of payment deficit for the U.S. To allay these fears

Haider and other multinational corporate leaders agreed in 1966 to a "voluntary payments program," promising to funnel profits more rapidly into the U.S. and to finance more of their development through foreign banks. One result of this arrangement was the rapid expansion of the Eurodollar market, a fund of U.S. currency maintained by European bankers for the use of American firms in their overseas operations; by 1967 the amount of Eurodollars in circulation had reached $2 billion.

Haider left Jersey Standard in 1969 after reaching the mandatory retirement age of 65. He was succeeded by John K. Jamieson, a long-time associate who had served as Jersey Standard's president since 1965. Haider continued to serve on the First National City Bank's board of directors, a position he had held while working at Jersey Standard, after his retirement.

[SLG]

HALABY, NAJEEB E(LIAS)

b. Nov. 19, 1915; Dallas, Tex.
Administrator, Federal Aviation Agency, 1961-65; Vice President, Pan American World Airways, 1965-68; President, 1968-69.

Halaby, the son of an art dealer, grew up in Dallas. An early aviation enthusiast and admirer of Charles Lindbergh, he earned a student flying license at 17. Halaby studied at Stanford University and Yale, where he received an LL.B. in 1940. After two years in private law practice, he returned to aviation as a wartime test pilot for Lockheed Aircraft and the U.S. Navy. Halaby subsequently served in intelligence and foreign affairs positions at the State and Defense Departments. By 1953 he had risen to deputy assistant secretary of defense. During the mid-1950s Halaby held several jobs in private industry, working to promote the development of aviation technology. He also served on the government advisory panel that recommended the creation of the Federal Aviation Agency (FAA) to regulate air traffic.

In 1961 President John F. Kennedy appointed Halaby to head the FAA, after a previous nominee had declined the job. Halaby proved to be a dynamic and highly visible administrator, personally visiting the scene of every important air accident in the U.S. He also framed new safety regulations, promoted computerized air traffic control and sought to improve the functioning of the FAA by delegating greater authority to regional administrators. Halaby's efforts helped ensure a safe transition to commercial jet travel during the early 1960s; the airline fatality rate actually dropped by two-thirds during that period. [See KENNEDY Volume]

Halaby left the FAA in 1965 to become a corporate vice president at Pan American World Airways, the largest U.S. overseas carrier. He was persuaded to make the change by Juan Trippe, Pan Am's founder and director, who reportedly hoped that Halaby's government contacts would benefit the company. During the mid-1960s Halaby managed various aspects of Pan Am operations, including military personnel flights to Vietnam and the company's business jet division. He advanced to president in 1968 and became chairman and chief executive officer of the airline in May 1970, after Trippe's retirement.

Halaby's rise within Pan Am coincided with growing financial difficulties for the company. Beginning in 1969 Pam Am operated at an average yearly loss of $35 million. Much of the deficit resulted from circumstances beyond Halaby's control, including Trippe's overpurchase of 747 jumbo jets in 1967 and increasing competition from foreign airlines on Pan Am's lucrative North Atlantic route. Nevertheless, many Pan Am executives were angered by what they viewed as Halaby's unwillingness to take a firm grip on the company's affairs. Halaby spent much of his time after 1968 negotiating with the U.S. and foreign governments in an effort to improve his airline's route pattern. This distracted his attention from the airline's day-to-day operations, and observers criticized his unwillingness to delegate authority or draw clear lines of responsibility within the company. In the absence of firm direction, the internal economy drives frequently announced by Halaby failed to affect the company's financial situation. The dismissal of nearly one-fifth of Pan Am's 36,000-man work force during the early 1970s damaged morale among the remaining employees and caused a reduction in services in many places.

In November 1971 Halaby responded to pressure for greater delegation of authority by yielding Pan Am's presidency to William T. Seawell, a former executive at American Airlines and the Rolls Royce Corporation. Four months later the Pan Am board of directors, disturbed by the airline's continued losses, removed Halaby from the chairmanship as well. Overall direction of the company was assigned to Seawell. After his departure from Pan Am Halaby settled in Hong Kong, where he opened a venture capital company to finance investments in Southeast Asia.

[SLG]

HALL, GUS

b. Oct. 8, 1910; Iron, Minn.
General Secretary, Communist Party, U.S.A., 1959- .

Hall's parents were Finnish immigrants and charter members of the American Communist Party, which Hall joined at 17. He was a leader of the Little Steel strike in Warren, Ohio, and after serving in the Navy during World War II he became head of the Ohio Communist Party. Hall briefly served as Communist Party national secretary after Eugene Dennis was jailed in 1950, but was himself imprisoned from October 1951 to March 1957 under the Smith Act for conspiring to teach and advocate the violent overthrow of the government.

In 1959 Hall was elected general secretary of the Communist Party and took over the leadership of an organization shattered by government repression, factionalism and disillusionment. In June 1961 the Communist Party again came under legal attack when the Supreme Court ruled that under the 1950 Internal Security Act (McCarran Act) the Communist Party had to file registration documents, including a complete list of its members. Simultaneously, the Court ruled that being an active member of the Party could be a crime under the Smith Act. Hall immediately announced that the Party would not register with the government, and in December the Party was indicted for its failure to do so. In March 1962 Hall and Party National Secretary Benjamin J. Davis were indicted for failing to register the Party. [See KENNEDY Volume]

Although the Communist Party was initially convicted for its failure to register, on Dec. 18, 1963 a U.S. Appeals Court overturned the conviction in a decision later upheld by the Supreme Court, and in May 1966 the Justice Department requested dismissal of the related charges against Hall. Legal restrictions on the Communist Party were further loosened on Nov. 15, 1965, when, in an 8-0 decision, the Supreme Court ruled that the McCarran Act provision requiring individual Communist Party members to register with the federal government violated Fifth Amendment guarantees against self-incrimination. Hall called the decision "a blow against the longest political-legal vendetta in our history" and said that with the decision "it will be possible to be more openly active in all fields."

In the early 1960s the Communist Party had been cautious and defensive, but during the years after 1963 it became increasingly active politically. In June 1964 a Berkeley, Calif., youth group dominated by Communist Party members, the W.E.B. DuBois Club, expanded into a national organization. That fall the Party received considerable publicity when one of its members, Betina Aptheker, became a prominent leader of the Berkeley Free Speech Movement. Although not openly endorsing President Johnson in 1964, Hall tacitly did so by calling on Communists to "join with all democratic forces to defeat the ultra-right Goldwater coalition."

In February 1966 Hall announced the publication of a new Communist Party draft program that said peaceful coexistence between communist and capitalist countries was possible. He called for the eventual formation of a new electoral party that would include all "the forces arrayed against monopoly." The new party would work for socialism through the ballot and constitutional amendment, but until such a party could be formed, the Communist Party would continue to seek change through the two-party system. The Party generally supported liberal Democrats in the 1960s, especially in those areas of its greatest strength: New York, Illinois and California.

Hall was reelected general secretary in June 1966 at the first Communist Party convention in over six years. No longer under government orders that had long restricted his travels, he visited Europe and the Soviet Union in 1966 and attended the November 1967 Moscow celebration of the 50th anniversary of the October Revolution.

Although rarely sponsoring rallies or demonstrations in its own name, the Communist Party was active in the civil rights and anti-war movements and advocated a third-party ticket for 1968. Members of the Party participated in the August 1968 National Conference for New Politics, but the Conference failed to endorse any national slate. The August 1968 Soviet invasion of Czechoslovakia sharply divided Communist Party members in the United States. New York State Chairman Gilbert Green and the majority of the West Coast Party opposed the invasion. Hall supported it, arguing that force was necessary to avert a "counter-revolutionary takeover." His position was eventually accepted by the Party, although several prominent members resigned in the aftermath of the dispute. Hall was unanimously reelected general secretary in May 1969 and in 1972 was the Communist Party presidential candidate. [See NIXON Volume]

[JBF]

HALLECK, CHARLES A(BRAHAM)

b. Aug. 22, 1900; Demotte, Ind.
Republican Representative, Ind., 1935-69; House Minority Leader, 1959-65.

Charles A. Halleck received B.A. and LL.B. degrees from Indiana University. Following admission to the state bar in 1924, he entered Republican politics. Halleck won a special election to fill a House vacancy in 1935 and served successively until his retirement in 1969. He loyally campaigned for his fellow Republican members, rose steadily on House seniority lists and became House Majority Leader following the election of Joseph W. Martin, Jr. (R, Mass.) as Speaker in January 1947. In January 1959 Halleck unseated Martin for the GOP leadership by a secret ballot vote of 74 to 70. [See TRUMAN, EISENHOWER Volumes]

Halleck's triumph marked the end of a cooperative relationship in the House between the Republican leadership and Speaker Sam Rayburn (D, Tex.). To gain his victory Halleck promised to oppose House Democrats in a partisan manner, an easy task for the Indiana Republican who frequently characterized himself as a "gut fighter." During the early 1960s he led the powerful Republican-Southern Democratic conservative coalition, which defeated much of the Kennedy Administration's legislative program. [See KENNEDY Volume]

As a precondition for the support of many younger Republican House members against Martin, Halleck had promised to rejuvenate the House Republican Conference (Policy) Committee and give it a new and enlarged role. Some Republicans, however, continued to express dissatisfaction with the policy-making procedure, and in January 1963, Rep. Gerald R. Ford, Jr. (R, Mich.) [*q.v.*] challenged Halleck's choice for the Conference Committee chairmanship. Ford recruited enough support from younger members, both liberal and conservative, to win the position by eight votes.

Halleck abandoned his resolute partisanship to support the Kennedy-Johnson civil rights bill in 1963 and 1964. While Rep. William McCulloch (R, Ohio) [*q.v.*], ranking Republican member on the Judiciary Committee, helped draft the House version, Halleck persuaded a sufficient number of his conservative GOP colleagues to join with Northern Democrats to overcome the opposition of House Southerners to the bill. In February 1964 the House overwhelmingly passed the Administration's bill, 290 to 130, with 78% of the Republican members voting for the measure.

The House version included federal employment and public accommodations guarantees which Senate Minority Leader Everett M. Dirksen (R, Ill.) [*q.v.*] opposed. Only after three months of negotiation with the bill's proponents did the Senate Republican leader agree to support the House bill. Though Dirksen received nationwide praise for his role in the enactment of the measure, Halleck's acceptance of the accommodations and employment provisions had forced the Senator's hand. White House lobbyist Lawrence F. O'Brien [*q.v.*] later called Halleck "the unsung hero" in the passage in the 1964 Civil Rights Act.

Like Dirksen, Halleck endorsed the Presidential candidacy of Sen. Barry M. Goldwater (R, Ariz.) [*q.v.*]. The Indiana Republican seconded Goldwater's nomination at the July 1964 Republican National Convention and defended the Senator in the general election campaign. Johnson defeated Goldwater in November with 61% of the vote, and the GOP lost 38 seats in the House.

Halleck proved a belated casualty of the Goldwater debacle. In December 1964 Ford announced that he would challenge Halleck for the House GOP leadership. Both men held conservative voting records. The right-wing Americans for Constitutional Action gave Halleck an 86% rating and Ford 83% on selected issues. Yet, Halleck appeared less responsive to younger and more liberal members, many of whom opposed the Party's covert alliance with Southern Democrats. Ruggedly handsome, a graduate of Yale Law School and Halleck's junior by 13 years, Ford appeared as an attractive alternative to the stout Halleck. In a secret ballot, Ford defeated Halleck by a vote of 73 to 67. "I've been through adversity before," Halleck complained after the tally, "but I've never had to run in a beauty contest." Halleck fell into relative obscurity after January 1965 and rarely participated in House debates. He retired in 1968.

[JLB]

For further information:
Lawrence F. O'Brien, *No Final Victories* (New York, 1974).
Henry Z. Scheele, *Charlie Halleck* (New York, 1966).

HAMER, FANNIE LOU

b. Oct. 6, 1917; Ruleville, Miss.
d. March 13, 1977; Mount Bayou, Miss.
Vice Chairman, Mississippi Freedom Democratic Party, 1964-77.

The daughter of a sharecropper, Hamer grew up in rural Sunflower County, Miss. Her first contact with the civil rights movement came in 1962, when she led a group of 26 blacks attempting to register to vote in Ruleville, the county seat. Not only was the attempt unsuccessful, but Hamer was jailed and beaten, and her family was evicted from the farm land where they had worked for 18 years. After this experience Hamer joined the Student Nonviolent Coordinating Committee (SNCC), a militant civil rights organization, and worked to register black voters in Mississippi. In 1964 she helped organize Mississippi Freedom Summer, a massive voter registration drive sponsored by SNCC and other national civil rights organizations. At this time she was among the founders of the Mississippi Freedom Democratic Party (MFDP), formed to give newly registered black voters an alternative to the state's white-run regular Democratic Party.

Hamer gained national attention at the 1964 Democratic National Convention, where the MFDP attempted to unseat the regular Mississippi delegation. In hearings before the Convention's credentials committee, MFDP representatives claimed that the state Democratic organization did not support President Johnson and did not represent black voters. Described by historian Thomas R. Brooks as "a robust woman of great dignity," Hamer electrified the Convention when she told how police had repeatedly beaten her in jail after her first attempt at voter registration. Despite widespread sympathy for the MFDP, the credentials committee voted to recognize the regular Democratic delegation. At Hamer's urging the MFDP rejected a compromise offer to seat two MFDP representatives as "special delegates."

The 1964 Convention was an important

event in the growing disillusionment of many civil rights activists with their white liberal allies. When SNCC leader Stokely Carmichael [*q.v.*] called for "black power" in 1966, Hamer supported him and spoke at several rallies at which black separatist principles were promoted. Nevertheless, she worked in Mississippi to broaden the base of the MFDP through cooperation with integrationist and white liberal groups, including the NAACP and the state AFL-CIO. In 1968 the MFDP joined with these groups to form a faction called the Loyal Democrats, which again challenged the regular Mississippi Democrats for recognition at the Party's national convention—this time successfully. Appearing before the 1968 Democratic National Convention as a delegate, Hamer received a standing ovation.

Hamer continued to serve the MFDP as vice chairman after 1968, working for the registration of black voters and the election of black officeseekers. Largely as a result of these efforts, nearly 60% of all black Mississippians were registered to vote in 1973. By this time Mississippi had more black elected officials (145) than any other Southern state.

[SLG]

HANNAH, JOHN A(LFRED)

b. Oct. 9, 1902; Grand Rapids, Mich.
President, Michigan State University, 1941-69.

Hannah, the son of a poultry breeder, grew up in Grand Rapids. He graduated from Michigan State University (MSU) in 1923 and became a poultry raiser. He spent most of his professional career working for his alma mater—first as a specialist in poultry raising, then as business manager and finally (beginning in 1941) as president of the University. Hannah remained MSU president for 28 years, during which time the University grew from a small land-grant campus with 6,000 students into a giant "megaversity" with an enrollment of 42,500. Hannah proved adept at "selling" his institution to the Michigan legislature by emphasizing popular and practical courses; by the mid-1960s he had an annual budget of over $100 million. To critics who claimed that he had sacrificed academic quality for expansion, Hannah replied that his aim was "not to de-emphasize scholarship but to emphasize its application."

Under Hannah MSU funds came not only from the state but also from the federal government, which paid the University to carry on foreign aid projects in Asia, Africa and Latin America. During the mid-1960s MSU became involved in a heated debate over the role of American universities in promoting government intelligence activity and the Vietnam war effort. In April 1966 an article in *Ramparts* magazine charged that a federally financed MSU project in South Vietnam had provided cover for Central Intelligence Agency (CIA) operations between 1955 and 1959. Hannah defended the project, claiming that one of its objectives had been to improve the training of the South Vietnamese police force; for this purpose, he maintained, men with experience in "counterintelligence work" were needed. He admitted the possibility of CIA infiltration of the project but denied that the University had knowingly tolerated or encouraged this.

While president of MSU Hannah served the federal government in several advisory roles. From 1955 to 1969 he headed the U.S. Commission on Civil Rights; in this capacity he sponsored the Commission's 1965 report, which recommended the expansion of federal law enforcement powers in the South. In February 1969 President Richard M. Nixon appointed Hannah director of the Agency for International Development (AID), the main organ of the U.S. foreign aid program. Hannah initially wanted to remain president of MSU while assuming his new duties but later relinquished his University position. As AID director, Hannah advocated a more "focused" assistance program, with available funds concentrated on fewer developing countries. He served as head of AID until his retirement in 1973, after which he remained associated with the Agency as a consultant. [See NIXON Volume]

[SLG]

HARLAN, JOHN MARSHALL
b. May 20, 1899; Chicago, Ill.
d. December 29, 1971;
Washington, D.C.
Associate Justice, U.S. Supreme Court, 1955-71.

A 1920 graduate of Princeton University, Harlan was a Rhodes scholar at Oxford and received a degree from New York Law School in 1924. He joined a prestigious Wall Street law firm in 1923, becoming a partner in 1931. His practice dealt primarily with corporate and antitrust cases. Harlan also served as an assistant U.S. attorney in the Southern District of New York and as special prosecutor in a New York State investigation of municipal graft in the 1920s. During World War II, he served with the bomber command of the Army Air Force, rising by the end of the war to the post of division head in the U.S. Group Control Council for Germany From 1951 to 1953 Harlan was chief counsel for the New York Crime Commission. He resigned from his law firm when President Eisenhower named him a judge on the U.S. Second Circuit Court of Appeals in January 1954.

Grandson and namesake of Supreme Court Justice John Harlan, Harlan was himself appointed to the high court in November 1954, and his nomination was confirmed in March 1955. On the bench Harlan developed a close personal and intellectual relationship with Justice Felix Frankfurter, and following Frankfurter's retirement in August 1962, he became the leading spokesman on the Court for a philosophy of judicial restraint. Harlan's views were frequently at odds with those of the Warren Court's liberal, activist majority, and he dissented from many of its rulings on criminal rights, reapportionment and the powers of state and congressional investigating committees. [See EISENHOWER, KENNEDY Volumes]

Harlan had a deep respect for precedent and rarely voted to overturn past Court decisions. He was also strongly committed to the principles of federalism embodied in the Constitution. Insisting that the Supreme Court should play only a limited role in the governmental system, he favored giving broad recognition to the powers of the federal executive and legislature and of state and local governments. Harlan argued that state criminal proceedings, for example, only had to meet a test of "fundamental fairness" under the Constitution, and he therefore dissented in June 1964 when the majority held the Fifth Amendment's privilege against self-incrimination applicable to the states. Harlan also objected to the June 1966 *Miranda* decision, in which the Court set out rules governing police interrogation of arrested suspects. His dissenting opinion argued that the majority was departing from settled constitutional doctrine and creating unnecessary difficulties for law enforcement agencies. Harlan concurred, however, when the Court in May 1967 extended certain constitutional safeguards such as the right to counsel to juvenile court proceedings. He also joined in a December 1967 ruling requiring police to obtain a judicial warrant before using electronic eavesdropping devices.

Harlan frequently voted to sustain federal laws against claims that they violated individual rights. He dissented, for example, in June 1964 when the Court invalidated a federal law denying passports to members of the Communist Party. Although he ordinarily supported congressional power to act against domestic Communists, Harlan did join in a November 1965 decision that held it a violation of the Fifth Amendment to require Communist Party members to register with the government under the 1950 Subversive Activities Control Act.

Harlan was equally wary of invalidating state legislation on constitutional grounds. He entered a sharp dissent to a March 1966 Court decision that held a Virginia poll tax for state elections unconstitutional. He also disagreed with the majority when, in May 1968, it overturned state laws mandating different treatment for legitimate and illegitimate children. In June 1965, however, Harlan concurred when the Court overturned a Connecticut law prohibiting the use of contraceptives by married couples.

In dealing with obscenity legislation Harlan used a stricter standard when judging the constitutionality of federal rather than state laws. Since the states, he argued, had primary responsibility for protecting public morals and welfare, they should be given more leeway than the federal government in regulating expression that was allegedly obscene. As a result Harlan voted repeatedly to sustain convictions under state obscenity statutes but often favored reversal in federal obscenity cases such as the March 1966 *Ginzburg* decision.

Although Harlan opposed most of the major trends on the Warren Court, he united with his more liberal colleagues in major decisions outlawing racial segregation. He also voted to sustain the public accommodations section of the 1964 Civil Rights Act in December 1964 and major portions of the 1965 Voting Rights Act in March 1966. Harlan had voted to reverse the state convictions of civil rights demonstrators in several cases in the early 1960s, but by 1964 he had changed course and joined in opinions by Justice Hugo Black [*q.v.*] arguing to uphold such convictions. He also dissented in May 1967 when the Court voided a California constitutional amendment that had nullified earlier legislation prohibiting racial discrimination in housing.

Harlan opposed extending the Supreme Court's jurisdiction into new areas and argued that state or federal legislatures, not the courts, were the proper forums for dealing with many political and social issues. He had dissented in March 1962 when the Court overturned a 1946 precedent and held that federal courts could try cases on legislative apportionment. Harlan also objected to February and June 1964 decisions in which the majority set forth a "one-man, one-vote" standard for congresssional and state legislative apportionment. In his dissenting opinion in the latter case, *Reynolds v. Sims*, Harlan summarized his objections to much of the Warren Court's activism. He labeled "mistaken" the view "that every major social ill in this country can find its cure in some constitutional 'principle,' and that this court should 'take the lead' in promoting reform when other branches of government fail to act." The Court, he added, as a judicial body, should not "be thought of as a general haven for reform movements."

In his final years on the Court, Harlan dissented when the majority overturned state residency requirements for welfare but joined in another decision holding that welfare recipients had a right to a formal hearing with constitutional safeguards before their benefits could be terminated. His opinion for the Court in a June 1971 case held that the First Amendment protected an individual who wore a jacket inscribed with a vulgarity condemning the draft. Later the same month, however, he dissented in the Pentagon Papers case when the Court upheld the right of newspapers to public materials from a classified government study on the origins of the Vietnam war. Harlan resigned from the Court on Sept. 23, 1971 because of ill health. He died in Washington on Dec. 29, 1971. [See NIXON Volume]

Although Harlan took positions that could be classified as "liberal" in certain cases, his judicial philosophy led him to dissent from many of the liberal rulings of the Warren Court. Yet, even legal scholars who disagreed with Harlan's views had great respect for a jurist who, as Professor Alan Dershowitz said, "always brought sagacity and honesty to the deliberations of the Court." Nearly blind during his last seven years on the bench, Harlan continued to work unstintingly and to act as the "conservative conscience" on a liberal, activist Court. Many observers commented on Harlan's devotion to the Court and to the Constitution, and virtually all praised the consistently high quality of his opinions. Lucid, thoroughly reasoned, and learned, those opinions won Harlan a reputation as "the leading scholar" on the Warren Court and its best legal craftsman.

[CAB]

For further information:

Norman Dorsen, "John Marshall Harlan," in Leon Friedman and Fred L. Israel, eds., *The Justices of the United States Supreme Court, 1789-1969* (New York, 1969), Vol 4.

David L. Shapiro, ed., *The Evolution of a Judicial Philosophy: Selected Opinions and Papers of Justice John Marshall Harlan* (Cambridge, Mass., 1969).

"Mr. Justice Harlan," *Harvard Law Review*, LXXXIV (December 1971), pp. 369-391.

HARRIMAN, W(ILLIAM) AVERELL
b. Nov. 15, 1891; New York, N.Y.
Undersecretary of State for Political Affairs, March 1963-February 1965; Ambassador at Large, February 1965-March 1968; Chief U.S. Representative to the Paris Peace Talks, March 1968-January 1969.

Averell Harriman, President Johnson's representative to the Vietnam peace talks, was heir to the Union Pacific Railroad fortune amassed by his father. After graduating from Yale in 1913, he joined his father's business. By 1932 he had become chairman of the board of the Union Pacific. During his first years in business, he also embarked on a number of financial ventures, including ownership of a shipyard and establishment of an investment bank. Turning to international finance in the early 1920s, Harriman was among the first Americans to seek business concessions from the Soviet government.

Harriman entered Democratic Party politics and held a series of business advisory posts during the New Deal. In 1941 Franklin D. Roosevelt sent him to the USSR, where he remained until 1946, first as minister and then as ambassador. After service as ambassador to Great Britain in 1946, Harriman was appointed Secretary of Commerce, From 1949 to 1950 he helped administer the Marshall Plan. During the Korean War he served as Truman's national security adviser. Harriman was elected governor of New York in 1954 but was defeated for reelection by Nelson Rockefeller [*q.v.*] in 1958. His attempts to win national office also failed when he ran unsuccessfully for the Democratic presidential nomination in 1952 and 1956. [See TRUMAN, EISENHOWER Volumes]

During the Kennedy Administration Harriman served in various State Department positions as the President's chief diplomatic negotiator. In 1962 he helped formulate the Laos Accords guaranteeing the neutrality of that Southeast Asian country. One year later he went to Moscow to negotiate the partial nuclear test ban treaty. [See KENNEDY Volume]

In 1965 President Lyndon Johnson appointed Harriman ambassador-at-large with the principal duty of handling Southeast Asian affairs. During 1965 and 1966 he traveled around the world seeking support for U.S. Vietnam policy while sounding out the possibilities of a negotiated settlement of the war. When Johnson's announcement of American de-escalation in March 1968 led to the opening of preliminary peace talks two months later, Harriman went to Paris as chief U.S. negotiator.

During the opening months of the conference, talks revolved around two main issues: Hanoi's insistence on a total American bombing halt as a precondition for serious discussions and Saigon's refusal to enter negotiations in which the National Liberation Front (NLF) was represented. The U.S. refused to halt bombing completely without assurances that North Vietnam would respect the demilitarized zone, cease shelling major South Vietnamese population centers and promise a withdrawal of its troops from South Vietnam. Hanoi rejected these demands and continued to insist on a total U.S. bombing halt. However, major attacks did diminish in June and July. Harriman then recommended that the lull be regarded as a signal that North Vietnam had accepted the U.S. preconditions. He advised the U.S. to institute a full bombing halt. Despite the Ambassador's continual pleas. Johnson vetoed the proposal. After four months without progress, in September the President finally gave his approval of a halt upon the "unilateral understanding" that if America stopped bombing, North Vietnam would respect the demilitarized zone. In November the U.S. ended the bombing of North Vietnam. Johnson announced that in exchange for a bombing halt, Hanoi had agreed to the participation of the South Vietnamese government at the Paris talks, while the U.S. had approved a role for the NLF.

When discussions between the U.S. and North Vietnam on procedures for holding the enlarged conference of U.S., North Vietnamese, South Vietnamese and NLF representatives finally started in December, they bogged down in an argument over seating arrangements. South Vietnam refused to participate in any negotiations at which the NLF had equal status; thus they rejected the rectangular seating arrangement demanded by Hanoi. North Vietnam insisted on such NLF representation and would not permit the use of a round table suggested by the U.S. This arrangement would have permitted each party to interpret the status of the other representatives as it wished. The impasse continued through the end of the year and was not solved until the beginning of 1969, when all parties agreed to a round table with two rectangular tables placed at opposite ends. In January 1969 Henry Cabot Lodge [*q.v.*] succeeded Harriman as chief U.S. negotiator.

During the Nixon Administration Harriman continued to press for a complete withdrawal of Americans from Vietnam on a fixed schedule and in 1970 scored the Cambodian invasion as an unwarranted expansion of the war. In 1971 he urged Congress to use its power of the purse to end the conflict.

[EWS]

HARRINGTON, (EDWARD) MICHAEL

b. Feb. 24, 1928; St. Louis, Mo.
Chairman, Socialist Party, 1968-72.

Harrington was active in civil liberties, and showed an interest in socialism as a college student in the late 1940s. After spending a year working with the Catholic Worker movement, Harrington joined the Young People's Socialist League and eventually became a leader of the Socialist Party. In the early 1960s he became convinced that the anti-Communist, socialist movement of which he was part could be most effective by working within the Democratic Party in an effort to "realign" it in a more progressive direction.

Harrington was active in civil liberties, civil rights and peace groups throughout the 1950s and early 1960s. His 1962 book, *The Other America: Poverty in the United States*, was important in directing public attention toward the large number of people living in chronic poverty within the "affluent society." The book was read by President Kennedy in the fall of 1963, shortly before he ordered the Council of Economic Advisors (CEA) to begin planning an antipoverty program. [See KENNEDY Volume]

On President Johnson's first full day in office, CEA Chairman Walter Heller [*q.v.*], advised Johnson that four days earlier Kennedy had approved the planning of a major antipoverty program. The new President gave the project his highest priority, and on Jan. 8, 1964, in his first State of the Union address, Johnson announced an "unconditional war on poverty in America."

Later that month poverty program planners asked Harrington to Washington. With Paul Jacobs, a former union organizer and West Coast radical, and Peace Corps official Frank Mankiewicz [*q.v.*], Harrington began two weeks of meetings with high government officials to prepare proposals for the new program. In their final memo Mankiewicz, Jacobs and Harrington argued that the elimination of poverty would require major changes in the allocation of government resources and certain basic structural changes in society. Newly appointed poverty program head Sargent Shriver [*q.v.*] incorporated part of the memo in his report to Johnson, who at the time responded favorably.

As United States involvement in Vietnam escalated, Harrington became involved in the growing anti-war movement. In October 1965 he spoke in a national, telephone-linked network of college teach-ins, calling for a more open policy towards the People's Republic of China and a negotiated settlement of the war in Vietnam. Harrington, however, had little sympathy for the Vietnamese Communists, from whom he felt the anti-war movement should publicly dissociate itself, and he opposed a unilateral U.S. withdrawal. As a member of the ad hoc committee arranging the Nov. 27, 1965 anti-war march in Washington, Harrington convinced Dr. Benjamin M. Spock [*q.v.*], spokesman for the Committee for a Sane Nuclear Policy, to direct the demand for a negotiated settlement to Hanoi as well as Saigon and Washington.

His opposition to U.S. policy in Vietnam led Harrington to support Sen. Eugene McCarthy's (D, Minn.) [*q.v.*] 1968 presidential primary campaign. However, when Sen. Robert Kennedy (D, N.Y.) [*q.v.*] announced his candidacy on March 16, 1968, Harrington switched his support to Kennedy, whom he felt could attract broader support around a more far-reaching program. At Kennedy's request Harrington briefly campaigned during the May 1968 California primary fight. Following Kennedy's assassination Harrington supported the Democratic candidate, Vice President Hubert Humphrey [*q.v.*].

Harrington served on the National Executive Committee of the Socialist Party throughout the Johnson Administration and wrote two books, *The Accidental Century* in 1965 and *Towards a Democratic Left* in 1968 during this period. In 1968 he became chairman of the Socialist Party. Harrington was an outspoken critic of repression in the Soviet Union, and in January 1966 he joined an international protest against the arrest and conviction of dissident Soviet writers Andrei D. Sinyavsky and Yuli M. Daniel.

During the New York City teachers' strikes of May and September-November 1968, Harrington supported the United Federation of Teachers (UFT) fight against the community school board in the predominantly black Ocean Hill-Brownsville section of Brooklyn. Harrington argued that the city's school decentralization experiment was fundamentally an attempt by the Ford Foundation, the Urban Coalition and the New York City Board of Education to manipulate growing black power sentiment to preserve the status quo. According to Harrington, the final result would be "black control of black misery and white control of the nation's wealth." His position resulted in a bitter dispute with many of his longtime friends and allies, including Dwight MacDonald [*q.v.*], who supported the decentralization experiment and opposed the UFT.

[JBF]

For further information:

Michael Harrington, *Fragments of the Century: A Social Autobiography* (New York, 1973).

HARRIS, FRED R(OY)

b. Nov. 13, 1930; Walters, Okla.
Democratic Senator, Okla. 1965-73.

Fred Harris spent his youth on a farm in southwestern Oklahoma. After completing college and law school at the University of Oklahoma, he entered the state Senate in 1956 as its youngest member and within three years became chairman of its Democratic caucus. In the state legislature he helped to create the Oklahoma Human Rights Commission to prohibit discrimination in state employment.

Harris entered the primaries for the Democratic gubernatorial nomination in 1962 but finished a poor fifth. However, in a special election in 1964 to fill the remaining years of the term of the late Democratic Sen. Robert Kerr Harris defeated Sen. J. Howard Edmondson (who as governor had appointed himself to fill the vacant seat) in the Democratic primary. In November he edged out the Republican candidate, popular football coach Bud Wilkinson, by 20,000 votes. Harris's upset victory was attributed to the 1964 Johnson landslide, endorsement by the powerful Kerr family and strong support from Oklahoma's Indian voters. (Harris's wife, LaDonna, was of Irish and Commanche descent). In the campaign Harris endorsed Johnson's Great Society programs but, downplaying ideology, characterized his own political views as "good Oklahoma common sense."

Harris compiled a more liberal voting record than his powerful predecessor. He favored most of the Great Society programs, including antipoverty bills, rent subsidies, Model Cities and aid to education but voted against medicare. He also supported Sen. Everett Dirksen's (R, Ill.) [*q.v.*] unsuccessful attempt to circumvent the Supreme Court's "one man, one vote" ruling by a constitutional amendment. Harris supported the body of civil rights legislation enacted during the Johnson years. He also established himself as a militant advocate of Indian rights.

Harris did not oppose the Vietnam war during Johnson's tenure and voted against attempts to reduce military aid. However, in 1967 he criticized the Central Intelligence Agency (CIA) for its infiltration of university activities abroad and urged the President to forbid the Agency from using any university project as a cover for CIA activities.

In 1968 Johnson appointed Harris to serve on the President's Advisory Commission on Civil Disorders. After the Commission issued its report in March 1968 citing lack of jobs as a major cause of disorders, Harris supported a bill to appropriate $10 billion over four years to provide for 2.4 million jobs. On April 11, 1968 Harris became cochairman with Sen. Walter Mondale (D, Minn.) [*q.v.*] of the United Democrats for Humphrey. According to Theodore White, Harris was seriously considered as a possible running mate for Humphrey, but at the Democratic convention Harris placed Sen. Edmund Muskie's (D, Me.) [*q.v.*] name in nomination.

In the years following 1964 Harris moved steadily toward a more pronounced liberalism, a trend that continued during the Nixon Administration. His rating by the liberal American for Democratic Action rose from 59% in 1968 to 83% in 1969 and 100% in 1970. However, his Oklahoma constituency was becoming increasingly Republican and conservative, and Harris did not run for reelection in 1972. Instead he waged an unsuccessful campaign for the Democratic presidential nomination on a platform espousing a "new populism" to curb the power of the major corporations and equalize individual wealth and income. [See NIXON Volume]

[TO]

HARRIS, OREN

b. Dec. 20, 1903; Belton, Ark.
Democratic Representative, Ark., 1941-66; Chairman, Interstate and Foreign Commerce Committe, 1957-66.

Harris was elected district prosecuting attorney of Arkansas's 13th judicial district in 1936. Four years later he was elected to the U.S. House of Representatives after defeating the incumbent in the Democratic primary. As a member of the House Interstate and Foreign Commerce Committee, to which he was appointed in 1943, Harris sponsored a bill in 1949 exempting independent natural gas producers from the rate and service regulations of the Federal Power Commission (FPC). A similar measure was passed by Congress but vetoed by President Harry S Truman.

In 1957 Harris became chairman of the Commerce Committee. Four years later he once again introduced a bill to relax FPC controls on natural gas producers, but it died in the House. During the same year he successfully opposed a Kennedy Administration bill that he believed would increase the President's control over the Federal Communications Commission. [See EISENHOWER, KENNEDY Volumes]

The Commerce Committee had jurisdiction over legislation pertaining to federal regulatory commissions. Harris often opposed what he claimed were excessive grants of power to those agencies, and he was widely regarded as friendly to the private interests regulated by the commissions. In 1964 the Commerce Committee, under Harris's guidance, weakened a bill introduced the previous year to expand the Securities and Exchange Commission's (SEC) policing power over securities trading. The Senate had passed the bill in July 1963. But as reported out by Harris's Committee in May 1964, the measure was modified to exempt insurance companies, which had lobbied strongly against the bill, from SEC jurisdiction. The final bill, signed by President Lyndon B. Johnson in August 1964, incorporated the Commerce Committee's amendment.

In February 1964 the Committee began consideration of a bill, supported by Harris, to eliminate the Interstate Commerce Commission's powers over the rate-setting activities of railroads and water carriers for agricultural and fishery products. The measure aroused strong opposition from various interests, particularly the water carriers. They contended the railroads would cut their rates below cost on routes where rail and water transportation were in competition and make up for the resulting losses by raising rates in areas where water transport was not available as an alternative to railroads. As a result of this opposition, the bill that Harris supported did not pass.

During the first two months of 1965, Harris's Committee held hearings on the illegal distribution of barbiturates and amphetamines. The panel reported out a bill to strengthen federal control over pharmaceutical companies for the purpose of curbing the diversion of those drugs from legal channels. While businessmen generally opposed increased government supervision over their operations, the drug industry almost unanimously supported this measure.

In July 1965 President Johnson nominated Harris to be a federal district judge in Arkansas, and the Senate confirmed the nomination in August. Harris resigned from the House to assume the judgeship in February 1966.

[MLL]

HARRIS, PATRICIA R(OBERTS)

b. May 31, 1924; Mattoon, Ill.
U.S. Ambassador to Luxembourg, May 1965-August 1967.

The first black woman to be appointed a U.S. ambassador, Harris attended Howard University, where she graduated summa cum laude in 1945. An early civil rights activist, she participated as a student in the campus chapter of the NAACP and joined sit-ins at segregated restaurants in the Washington, D.C. area. After graduation Harris held a number of jobs, including assistant director of the American Council on Human Rights, before attending George Washington University Law School. Following her graduation she worked as an attorney for the Justice Department and taught law at Howard University.

In July 1963 President John F. Kennedy appointed Harris to the unpaid position of cochairman of the National Women's Committee for Civil Rights, where she worked to create support among women's groups for civil rights legislation. She also worked at this time on the District of Columbia advisory committee to the United States Commission on Civil Rights.

In keeping with his announcement that he would appoint 50 women to important government posts, Lyndon Johnson named Harris to the Commission on the Status of Puerto Rico in March 1964. One year later, in May 1965, she was selected to be ambassador to Luxembourg. Harris served at the post until August 1967, when she returned to the U.S. to resume her teaching career. In 1966 and 1967 she also served as alternate representative to the United Nations.

Following the assassination of Sen. Robert Kennedy (D, N.Y.) [*q.v.*] in June 1968, President Johnson appointed Harris a member of a commission to probe the causes of violence in the U.S. When the commission report, issued in December 1969, condemned massive civil disobedience, including nonviolent action, and stated that even nonviolent civil disobedience could lead to "nationwide disobedience of many laws and thus anarchy," Harris issued a dissenting opinion. She maintained that civil disobedience, when there was a willing acceptance of the penalty, "can represent the highest loyalty and respect for a democratic society. Such respect and self-sacrifice may well prevent, rather than cause violence."

In February 1969, while Harris was serving as dean of Howard Law School, law students occupied the school as a protest against grading policies and lack of student participation in implementing academic decisions. In reaction, Harris obtained a court injunction against the students. At the end of February she resigned, charging that the University had placed her in an untenable position by negotiating with the students without her knowledge.

A lifelong Democrat, Harris had seconded the presidential nomination of Lyndon Johnson at the 1964 Democratic National Convention and campaigned for his election. With the backing of Party regulars and labor, she was elected chairman of the credentials committee for the 1972 Democratic National Convention over the objection of reform elements. [See NIXON Volume]

[EWS]

For further information: "Patricia Harris" *Current Biography Yearbook, 1965* (New York, 1966) pp. 189-191.

HART, PHILIP A(LOYSIUS)
b. Dec. 10, 1912; Bryn Mawr, Pa.
d. Dec. 26, 1976; Washington, D.C.
Democratic Senator, Mich., 1959-76.

The son of a Pennsylvania banker, Philip Hart attended Georgetown University. After receiving his law degree from the University of Michigan in 1937, he began private practice in Detroit. Seriously wounded during World War II at the invasion of Normandy, Hart returned to law practice after the war and entered government in 1949 as Michigan's corporation and securities commissioner. In 1953 he became legal adviser to Gov. G. Mennen Williams, a former law school classmate, and was elected lieutenant governor in 1954 and 1956. With strong labor support Hart ran successfully for the Senate in 1958. In that and subsequent campaigns Hart was also aided by the inherited wealth of his wife, the former Jane Briggs, daughter of Walter Briggs, auto-parts millionaire and owner of the Detroit Tigers baseball team. [See EISENHOWER, KENNEDY Volumes]

A member of both the Judiciary and Commerce Committees, Hart compiled one of the most liberal records in the Senate. The conservative Americans for Constitutional Action, for example, gave Hart and six other senators "zero" ratings for their voting records in 1966. He was a consistent supporter of the Great Society social programs of the Johnson Administration. Not a flamboyant advocate, Hart became known as a quietly effective legislative technician with a special interest in civil rights, consumer protection and antitrust matters. A strong defender of the Civil Rights Act of 1964, Hart served as floor manager of the Voting Rights Act of 1965.

In the wake of the 1967 urban riots, Hart criticized congressional attempts to enact "anti-riot" legislation. A provision of the Civil Rights Act of 1968 making it a crime for individuals to use interstate facilities for the purpose of inciting a riot passed the Senate, 82-13, in March 1968 with Hart in the minority. Hart was the floor manager for the civil rights provisions of the same omnibus bill, which provided federal protection for persons trying to exercise their civil rights and prohibited discrimination in the sale or rental of about 80% of the nation's housing.

Hart's most notable victory in the field of consumer protection was the passage of "truth-in-packaging" legislation by Congress in October 1966. During the Kennedy years he had held extended hearings before the Judiciary Committee's Subcommittee on Antitrust and Monopoly, which investigated misleading packaging and labeling practices such as short-weighting and unsatisfactory contents designation. The purpose of the 1966 law, enacted after repeated rebuffs, was to aid consumers in making price and value comparisons of some 8,000 products sold in supermarkets and drug stores.

Hart became chairman of the antitrust subcommittee following the death of Sen. Estes Kefauver (D, Tenn.) in August 1963. The flamboyant Kefauver had conducted headline-making investigations into industrial concentration and big business abuses like price-fixing and bid-rigging. Under the more reserved, judicious Hart, the subcommittee's activities attracted less attention. Hart held frequent hearings, but the volumes of testimony produced little immediate action. Where Kefauver's investigations sometimes resembled exposes and resulted in indictments, Hart's were general studies of a more academic character.

Hart was hampered by the fact that a majority of his subcommittee did not share his enthusiasm for antitrust action. After Kefauver's highly publicized hearings on drug prices in June 1961, Sen. James Eastland (D, Miss.) [*q.v.*], chairman of the Judiciary Committee, had assigned conservatives to fill vacancies on the antitrust subcommittee. The subcommittee's practice of voting to issue subpoenas to secure information from businesses, an important investigatory tool under Kefauver, fell into disuse under Hart. Although he was disturbed by the great conglomerate merger wave of the 1960s, Hart could not get a committee majority to favor strengthened antitrust laws. Instead he often used hearings and prolonged study as a device to stall attempts to provide antitrust exemptions for certain industries.

During the 1960s Hart moved slowly away

from an identification with an anti-Communist foreign policy. As late as May 1964 he had encouraged Cuban exiles in their efforts to overthrow the Castro regime, but three years later, in August 1967, he was one of only six senators to vote in favor of a $3.5 billion cut in the defense budget. Beginning in December 1968 Hart led the battle against the Sentinel ABM (anti-ballistic missile) program.

Although Hart was not an early opponent of the Vietnam war, his wife Jane became active in the anti-war movement and was among those arrested for holding a religious service at the Pentagon in November 1969. Hart emerged as a member of the Senate's anti-war bloc during the Nixon Administration [See NIXON Volume]

[TO]

HARTKE, R(UPERT) VANCE
b. May 31, 1919; Stendal, Ind.
Democratic Senator, Ind., 1959-77.

Vance Hartke was the son of a small-town Indiana postmaster and school teacher. After receiving his law degree from Indiana University, he practiced law in Evansville. Hartke was active in local Democratic Party politics and in 1955 was elected mayor of the city. Four years later he was elected the first Democratic senator from Indiana in 20 years. Hartke was a strong supporter of Kennedy Administration domestic legislation. He served on the powerful Senate Commerce and Finance Committees but, because of his low seniority, did not play an influential role in their operations. [See KENNEDY Volume]

Hartke won reelection in 1964 with 55% of the vote, a substantial margin for a liberal running in an essentially conservative state. He supported Johnson Administration civil rights, education, medicare and anti-poverty bills. By 1966, however, Hartke began to have doubts about the Administration's Vietnam war policy. In January of that year he drafted a letter sent by 15 other senators urging President Johnson not to resume the bombing of North Vietnam. The next month Hartke delivered his first major speech opposing escalation of the conflict. Nevertheless, in March he voted for a $13 billion arms appropriations bill that included funding for the war. In 1967 he wrote *The American Crisis in Vietnam* but withheld publication for a year, fearing that it would hurt Democratic prospects in Indiana during a presidential election year.

During his 1964 campaign Hartke received large cash contributions from a Chicago-based mail order firm. A year later he requested and won appointment to the Senate Post Office Committee where he worked to forestall planned postal increases for third class mail. Hartke's opponents charged that he was guilty of conflict of interest. This, coupled with his outspoken opposition to American involvement in Vietnam led many observers to consider his reelection in 1970 problematical. Hartke managed to defeat his opponent, but the election was so close that Hartke's claim to his seat was not finally settled until the U.S. Supreme Court ordered a ballot recount 18 months after the election. [See NIXON Volume]

[JLW]

HATFIELD, MARK O(DUM)
b. July 22, 1922; Dallas, Ore.
Governor, Ore., 1959-67; Republican Senator, Ore., 1967- .

Hatfield, a graduate of Williamette University, taught political science there from 1949 to 1956. During the same period he also proved remarkably adept as a practical politician, winning election to the Oregon House of Representatives in 1950 and the state Senate in 1954. He became secretary of state in 1957 and two years later became governor, the youngest in Oregon's history.

Oregon was a state with a strong progressive tradition, and Hatfield was able to maintain his popularity while supporting the civil rights movement, backing legislation for the construction of community colleges and advocating public rather than private hydroelectric power development in the Columbia River basin. He opposed state right-to-work laws and blocked a proposed effort by the legislature to impose a state sales tax. [See KENNEDY Volume]

In 1960 Hatfield nominated Vice President Richard M. Nixon [*q.v.*] for president at the Republican National Convention; four years later Hatfield was the Convention's keynote speaker. Early in 1964 Hatfield supported New York Gov. Nelson Rockefeller [*q.v.*] for President, but he campaigned for Sen. Barry Goldwater (R, Ariz.) [*q.v.*] after the Arizona Senator won the Republican nomination that year.

During the early 1960s Hatfield emerged as a promising future candidate for the Republican presidential or vice presidential nomination. In 1964, however, he began to attack American involvement in the Vietnam war, and as a result his standing within the Republican Party declined sharply. In April 1966 Hatfield was the only one of 50 governors meeting at the Governors Conference in Los Angeles to vote against a resolution of support for American policy in Vietnam. When he ran for the Senate in 1966, Hatfield only narrowly defeated Rep. Robert Duncan (D, Ore.), a supporter of the war.

During the Johnson years, Hatfield, lacking seniority, had little influence in the Senate. He generally voted with moderate Republicans in matters of domestic policy. The liberal Americans for Democratic Action gave him a 54% rating in 1967 and 71% in 1968.

In April 1967 Hatfield and Rep. Donald Rumsfeld (R, Ill.) called for an end to the draft and its replacement by an all-volunteer Army. Hatfield argued that the draft was inherently unjust and that a volunteer Army would be a superior fighting force. The Hatfield-Rumsfeld bill failed, but it marked the beginning of an effort that culmininated in the abolition of the draft in 1973.

In 1968 Hatfield supported Nixon for president, but after the election he attacked the Administration for its Vietnam war policy. In 1971 Hatfield and Sen. George S. McGovern (D, S.D.) [*q.v.*] cosponsored a widely publicized but unsuccessful amendment setting April 30, 1971 as a cutoff date for appropriations for American combat troops in Vietnam. [See NIXON Volume]

[JLW]

HAWKINS, AUGUSTUS (FREEMAN)
b. Aug. 31, 1907; Shreveport, La.
Democratic Representative, Calif., 1963- .

Hawkins moved to California with his family in 1918. Elected to the state Assembly in 1934, he served in that body for 28 years and narrowly failed to win election as its speaker in 1959. In 1962 Hawkins won a seat in the U.S. House of Representatives.

A black representative from the predominantly black areas of south central Los Angeles, Hawkins was a New Deal Democrat who was particularly concerned with the problem of poverty in his district. On the House floor and in the Education and Labor Committee, he consistently backed President Johnson's Great Society programs and civil rights measures. After the 1965 black riots in the Watts area, which was part of his district, large amounts of federal money were spent to aid his constituents, and his influence in Congress increased proportionately. In 1965 he opposed an effort to narrow the scope of the Administration's open housing bill, and the following year he criticized an attempt to restrict community participation in antipoverty programs. A consistent liberal, Hawkins received a "correct" rating of 94 for his House voting during the 1960s from the Americans for Democratic Action.

Hawkins's views on foreign policy matters were shaped largely by his estimate of their effect upon his district. During the latter years of the Johnson Administration, he became a critic of the Vietnam war on the ground that it drained funds from domestic social welfare programs. In 1966 Hawkins voted for supplementary funds for the war, but he was among 72 representatives who signed a statement urging efforts towards a peaceful settlement.

In 1971 Hawkins and 12 other black representatives organized a black caucus in the lower chamber; he was chosen vice chairman of the group. Five years later Hawkins was the House sponsor of the Humphrey-Hawkins bill, which proposed to guarantee federally funded jobs to all unemployed persons. [See NIXON Volume]

[MLL]

HAYDEN, CARL T(RUMBULL)
b. Oct. 2, 1877; Hayden's Ferry, Ariz.
d. Jan. 25, 1972; Mesa, Ariz.
Democratic Senator, Ariz., 1927-69; Chairman, Appropriations Committee, 1955-69.

Carl Hayden was born 35 years before Arizona achieved statehood and served in Congress longer than any other member in U.S. history. After attending Stanford University, Hayden served as a councilman and county sheriff. He was elected to the U.S. House of Representatives in 1912 and then to the Senate in 1926. During his first 21 years in office, Hayden did not make many speeches on the Senate floor, yet he became known as a dogged champion of legislation to improve roads and irrigation in Arizona. [See TRUMAN, EISENHOWER Volumes]

Hayden supported Kennedy Administration legislation on nearly 70% of all major issues, according to *Congressional Quarterly*. Because of his chairmanship of the Appropriations Committee, Hayden was regarded as one of the most powerful senators. During the period between President Kennedy's assassination in November 1963 and Lyndon Johnson's inauguration in January 1965, Hayden was President Pro Tempore of the Senate and third in line for presidential succession after House Speaker John McCormack (D, Mass.) [*q.v.*].

Hayden supported President Johnson on civil rights, medicare and social security issues. Throughout the 1960s he was a leader in the fight to gain passage of legislation to provide Southwestern states with water for land reclamation and irrigation. During this period he faced strong opposition from Sen. Thomas H. Kuchel (R, Calif.) [*q.v.*] and other influential California legislators who believed such legislation would reduce the supply of water their state received from the Colorado River.

In 1967 the Senate passed the Central Arizona Project (CAP), but the House took no action on the measure. The next year Congress passed the $1.3 billion Colorado River Project, which included the Arizona project and other land reclamation legislation. The $892 million authorized for the Arizona project allocated water from the Colorado River to the arid but populous region around Phoenix and Tucson via a 400-mile series of dams and aqueducts. In addition to the water-diversion system, the bill also provided for a joint public-private thermal power plant.

The Colorado River Project was described by *Congressional Quarterly* as "the largest reclamation program ever authorized in a single piece of legislation." It was subjected to some of the most intense lobbying in Senate history. At the bill's signing on Sept. 30, 1968, President Johnson took note of the architect of the legislation and declared a "Carl Hayden day."

Hayden declined to seek reelection in 1968. He returned to Arizona, where he died in January 1972 at the age of 94.

[FHM]

HAYDEN, THOMAS (EMMETT)
b. Dec. 11, 1939; Royal Oaks, Mich.
Radical, anti-war leader.

The son of a Chrysler Corporation accountant, Hayden grew up in a suburb of Detroit. After attending parochial schools he went to the University of Michigan in 1957 on a tennis scholarship. Majoring in English, he became editor of the student paper, *The Michigan Daily*. In May 1960 Hayden attended a civil rights conference sponsored by the recently revitalized Students for a Democratic Society (SDS), and that fall he helped organize VOICE, a University of Michigan student group that affiliated with SDS and soon became its largest chapter.

After graduating from Michigan Hayden was hired in the fall of 1961 as one of two paid SDS field secretaries. Working out of Altanta, he wrote articles and a pamphlet, "Revolution in Mississippi," about the Southern civil rights movement. Hayden himself was beaten in McComb, Miss., in October 1961, and that December he was arrested with 10 others in a Student Nonviolent Coordinating Committee (SNCC) effort to desegregate Albany, Ga., transit facilities.

Hayden wrote the initial drafts of the

manifesto produced by the June 1962 SDS convention at Port Huron, Mich. "The Port Huron Statement" became the most widely known formulation of New Left ideology. At the same convention Hayden was elected to a one-year term as SDS president.

Hayden helped plan and carry out an SDS experiment in community organizing, the Economic Research and Action Project (ERAP), which began in September 1963 supported by a $5,000 donation from the United Auto Workers. The following summer Hayden himself joined an ERAP group in Newark, N.J. Attempting to apply SNCC tactics in the North, Hayden and other SDS members spent two years in a predominantly black Newark neighborhood trying to develop local organizations and community campaigns on a broad range of issues. The Newark project, the most successful and longest lasting ERAP effort, ended following the July 1967 Newark riots.

In December 1965 Hayden joined Professor Staughton Lynd [*q.v.*] and U.S. Communist Party theoretician Herbert Aptheker on a 10-day trip to North Vietnam. During a 90-minute interview, the North Vietnamese Premier, Pham Van Dong, told the Americans that in spite of President Johnson's Dec. 20 statement that the Administration would knock on all doors in the quest for peace, the United States had made no direct contact with North Vietnam. Hayden was one of 41 Americans who attended a September 1967 conference with high level representatives of the National Liberation Front of South Vietnam (NLF) in Bratislava, Czechoslovakia. At the conference the possibility of the release of American prisoners held by the NLF was discussed. After another trip to Hanoi the next month, Hayden returned to Indochina, and, in ceremonies in Phnom Penh, Cambodia, three American POWs were turned over to Hayden by a NLF representative on Nov. 11 as an indication of sympathy with the American anti-war movement and with American blacks. (Two of the three prisoners were black.)

In January 1968 Hayden attended an International Cultural Congress in Havana. In April of that year, when students at Columbia University occupied campus buildings, Hayden came to the campus to lend his support and became a leader of students in one of the five occupied buildings, Mathematics Hall.

Hayden, along with other anti-war leaders, had come to believe that it was necessary to move from protests to active resistance, and in June 1968 wrote, "What is certain is that we are moving towards power—power to stop the machine if it cannot be made to serve humane ends."

Hayden and Rennie Davis, another SDS leader, helped organize the August 1968 anti-war demonstrations at the Chicago Democratic National Convention as project directors for the National Mobilization Committee to End the War in Vietnam. Over 15,000 people attended an Aug. 28 rally at Grant Park. Police attempts to disperse the demonstrators that night and on several other occasions received worldwide publicity. According to Mobilization Committee chairman David Dellinger [*q.v.*], the use of force by police and Hayden's belief that some form of violent resistance would be necessary combined to make Hayden "ambivalent" about the agreement among demonstration organizers that the protesters should remain nonviolent even if attacked. On Aug. 29 Hayden told a Grant Park rally, "It may be that the era of organized, peaceful and orderly demonstrations is coming to an end and that other methods will be needed."

In March 1969 Hayden, Davis, Dellinger and five others were indicted for conspiracy to incite a riot and crossing state lines to incite a riot in connection with the Chicago events. Their widely-publicized trial ended with Hayden and four others convicted on one count, and the seven defendants and their two lawyers receiving prison terms for contempt of court. (The eighth defendant, Black Panther leader Bobby Seale [*q.v.*], had been severed from the trial earlier.) Both the convictions and the contempt sentences were eventually reversed. Hayden continued to be an important radical leader throughout the early 1970s and organized and led the Indochina Peace Campaign. [See Nixon Volume]

[JBF]

HAYS, WAYNE L(EVERE)
b. May 13, 1911; Bannock, Ohio.
Democratic Representative, Ohio, 1949-76.

Hays, the son of a farmer, grew up in rural southeastern Ohio. After graduating from Ohio State University in 1933, he taught high school history and public speaking for several years in Flushing, Ohio. In 1939 he was elected mayor of Flushing and served three terms. He also served one term (1941-42) in the Ohio State Senate. In 1948, after two years as a county commissioner, Hays won election to the House of Representatives from Ohio's 18th district, a semi-rural area in the southeastern part of the state dominated by dairy farming, coal mining and steel production.

Known in Congress for his abrasive personality and frequent verbal attacks on his colleagues, Hays first gained attention during the early 1950s for defending tax-exempt foundations against charges that they had Communist connections. He remained a strong opponent of the House Un-American Activities Committee, which investigated allegedly subversive groups, through the mid-1960s. Hays also became active in fostering international contacts through his membership on the House Foreign Affairs Committee. He viewed the Fulbright-Hays Act of 1961, which expanded the international educational exchange program, as his most notable legislative achievement. As chairman of the Foreign Affairs Subcommittee on State Department Organization and Foreign Operations, Hays made yearly trips to Europe during the 1960s to attend the parliamentarians' conference of the North Atlantic Treaty Organization. He was also a strong anti-Communist and vehement critic of peace advocates during the Vietnam war.

Hays sponsored relatively little substantive legislation during his long congressional career. He concentrated instead on accumulating institutional power through his seniority and committee positions. Especially important in this respect was his membership on the House Administration Committee, which determined the budgets of all other House committees (except the Appropriations) and oversaw the travel and office expenses of all congressmen. During the mid-1960s Hays rose from third in seniority to senior Democrat on the Committee. He was also chairman of the Administration Subcommittee on Contracts, which played an important part in the 1966 investigation of spending irregularities on the staff of Rep. Adam Clayton Powell (D, N.Y.) [*q.v.*]. A report issued by Hays's subcommittee in January 1967 concluded that Powell had improperly placed his wife on the congressional payroll and that Powell's staff members had charged personal travel expenses to the House Labor and Education Committee, of which Powell was chairman. The report was subsequently used by other congressmen in an effort to strip Powell of his committee chairmanship and ultimately to unseat him.

Following the Powell investigation the Administration Committee received an increased budget and was assigned primary responsibility for investigating ethics violations in the House. Hays's subcommittee was enlarged and renamed the Subcommittee on Contracts and Ethics. Hays thus played a major role in both setting congressional budgets and determining whether they were misused.

During the late 1960s Hays began to use his growing power against other House committees and individual congressmen whose actions he disliked. Opponents of the Vietnam war were likely to face funding cuts and increased scrutiny of their spending; in 1969 Hays halved the budget of a House Government Operations subcommittee that had compiled a report critical of the Johnson Administration's land-reform policy in Vietnam. Hays's power—and his unpopularity in Congress—increased when he became chairman of the Administration Committee in 1971. He gained a reputation as a "bully" who openly threatened congressmen and congressional staff members. His aggressive behavior made him feared in the House, but it also frustrated his efforts to rise further; shortly after taking control of the Administration Committee, he lost a bid to become House majority leader.

One political observer noted in 1972 that "nothing short of a major scandal would depose Hays." Such a scandal occurred in

1976 when Elizabeth Ray, a member of Hays's staff, charged that Hays had kept her on the congressional payroll solely for her sexual services. Faced with charges similar to those he had investigated against others, Hays relinquished his committee positions at the urging of the House Democratic leadership. In September 1976 he resigned from Congress. [See NIXON Volume]

[SLG]

HEARNES, WARREN E(ASTMAN)
b. July 24, 1923; Moline, Ill.
Governor, Mo., 1965-73.

A native of southwestern Missouri and a graduate of the United States Military Academy, Hearnes served in the Missouri House of Representatives from 1951 to 1961. He was that body's majority floor leader from 1957 to 1961. In 1960 he was elected Missouri's Secretary of State, and in 1964 Hearnes upset the state's old-line Democratic Party hierarchy by defeating its candidate in the gubernatorial primary. Hearnes won the general election by 303,000 votes.

As a result of his defeat of the Party's establishment, Hearnes entered office with considerable power. Between 1965 and 1968 he submitted 80 bills to the legislature. Only one, a measure designed to permit private school students to attend certain public school classes, failed to pass. Hearnes was able to increase expenditures by more than any other governor in Missouri's history, but spending remained below that of other states of roughly the same size.

His major achievement was increased aid to local schools, which rose 161% during his eight-year tenure as governor. He also instituted a network of regional clinics for the mentally retarded and increased Missouri's spending for prisons and for mental and public health facilities. Hearnes established a toll-road authority to provide a source of revenue for the construction of new highways and launched an unprecedented building program that exceeded $150 million. He authorized state welfare aid to families with unemployed fathers living at home and secured public accommodations legislation. Hearnes also created a Department of Community Affairs, an Air Conservation Commission and a state-financed council on the arts during his governorship. This expansion of state services was achieved without a state tax increase, although much of it would not have been possible without the increased levies obtained by his predecessor.

Hearnes was one of the first prominent Democrats to raise public doubts about President Lyndon B. Johnson's domestic programs. In July 1968 he responded to the assertion of John Gardner [*q.v.*], chairman of the Urban Coalition, that "a great deal more" federal spending would be needed to cure the problems of the cities. Hearnes argued that "we have jobs in my state, but you have people who won't go five miles to work, and they are the ones who are hollering loudest for welfare." At the 1968 Democratic National Convention, Hearnes presented the case for President Johnson's Vietnam plank to the platform drafting committee.

Reelected to a second term in 1968, Hearnes supported President Richard M. Nixon's revenue-sharing plan. In May 1973, after his second term expired, he was briefly considered for the position of special Watergate prosecutor.

[TJC]

HEBERT, F(ELIX) EDWARD
b. Oct. 12, 1901; New Orleans, La.
Democratic Representative, La. 1941-77,
Chairman, House Armed Services Subcommittee #3, 1962-64;
Chairman, House Armed Services Subcommittee #2, 1965-71.

A newspaperman from 1919 to 1940, Hebert helped expose corruption in the administration of Louisiana Gov. Richard W. Leche in 1939. Capitalizing on his new fame Hebert successfully ran for Congress from New Orleans' first district in 1940. In subsequent elections he faced little if any opposition. A member of the Southern Democratic bloc, Hebert opposed liberal domestic programs and supported the 1948 presidential campaign of Sen. Strom Thurmond (D, S.C.) [*q.v.*], who ran on the States' Rights Democratic ticket. As chairman of the House Armed Services Special Investigations Subcommittee, Hebert led an investigation of Defense Department procurement procedures in 1951 and in 1959 probed defense industry use of retired officers as lobbyists and salesmen. Hebert, a strong supporter of the military, opposed the Kennedy Administration's attempt to impose stronger civilian control over the Pentagon. He clashed with the Administration over its 1962 effort to reorganize and reduce the National Guard and Army Reserve. In 1963 he supported the development of the RS-70 bomber, which the Department of Defense opposed. [See TRUMAN, EISENHOWER and KENNEDY Volumes]

In January 1964 testimony before the House Armed Services Committee, Secretary of Defense Robert S. McNamara [*q.v.*] reasserted the Administration policy stressing missile systems over manned aircraft. In the 1965 defense procurement budget he requested only $5 million for the study of a new manned bomber to "follow on" the retirement of the existing fleet. However, Air Force Chief of Staff Gen. Curtis E. LeMay [*q.v.*] publicly supported the "follow on" bomber, as did presidential candidate Sen. Barry M. Goldwater (R, Ariz.) [*q.v.*], who made it a campaign issue. During the House debate in February 1964, Hebert praised LeMay and attacked McNamara for ignoring the judgment of professional military officers, saying ". . . the beardless striplings of the whiz kids are superceding the judgment of the people who have devoted and dedicated their lives to the country in uniform." In the final budget, passed March 9, 1964, $52 million was included for the manned bomber project.

In 1966 McNamara and Hebert again clashed over the need for a new bomber when Hebert's subcommittee issued a report critical of McNamara's decision to phase out the B-52 and not develop a new strategic bomber. The Secretary of Defense charged that the report, which included heavily censored testimony, was "shockingly distorted," and that it incorrectly implied that McNamara was acting against the judgment of the Joint Chiefs of Staff.

Hebert and McNamara also clashed over the reorganization of Army reserve forces. On Dec. 12, 1964 McNamara announced a plan to merge the Army Reserve into the National Guard and, at the same time, reduce their combined strength from 700,000 to 550,000. Under the plan Reserve officers would have applied for new commissions from the Guard, and high federal officials, including members of Congress, would have been barred from participation in ready reserve units. (Seventy-nine congressmen were active reservists.)

Reservists immediately protested the McNamara plan, and Hebert criticized the Secretary of Defense for not consulting with Congress or seeking new legislation before ordering the reorganization. He charged that McNamara had "defied" the law and shown "contemptuous disregard of Congress." On May 15, 1965 the two men held a joint press conference at which an agreement was announced under which McNamara would delay the reorganization to allow time for congressional review and "supporting legislation." After three days of hearings that August, Hebert's subcommittee postponed consideration of the matter until the next year, effectively blocking the merger until then.

In 1966 McNamara again sought approval of the merger plan, and again he was temporarily blocked by congressional opposition. That July Hebert introduced a far-reaching reserve reorganization bill that permanently blocked any merger. In spite of Administration opposition the bill was finally passed by Congress and signed by the President in November 1967.

A strong supporter of the war in Vietnam, Hebert was an early advocate of bombing North Vietnam. The draft lottery system, proposed by President Johnson in March 1967 to counter criticism that the draft was being used as punishment for anti-war protestors, met with Hebert's vigorous opposition. When, during May 1967 hearings on the proposed draft system, Assistant Attorney General Fred M. Vinson, Jr. [*q.v.*] stated that the First Amendment fully protected people speaking in favor of draft defiance, Hebert responded that in such cases he would "forget the First Amendment."

Hebert was an opponent of the Civil Rights Act of 1964 and the Voting Rights Act of 1965 as well as against the War on Poverty and Model Cities programs. During hearings in August 1968 on the behavior of federal troops during the 1967 Detroit riots, Hebert criticized Lt. Gen. John L. Throckmorton, commander of the federal units, for ordering Guardsmen to keep their weapons unloaded and to fire only if ordered by an officer. The next year Hebert called the report of the President's Advisory Committee on Civil Disorders "propaganda ad nauseum."

Hebert continued to advocate large military spending during the Nixon Administration and in 1971 assumed chairmanship of the full Armed Services Committee. [See NIXON Volume]

[JBF]

HEINEMAN, BEN W(ALTER)

b. Feb. 10, 1914; Wausau, Wisc.
Railroad executive; White House consultant.

A graduate of the University of Michigan and Northwestern Law School, Heineman served during World War II as assistant general counsel to the Office of Price Administration. He was Illinois special prosecuting attorney under Gov. Adlai Stevenson [*q.v.*] and organized Stevenson's unsuccessful 1956 presidential campaign. That year Heineman also assumed control of the deficit-ridden Chicago and North Western Railway Company. By 1964 he had transformed it into a profitable enterprise that became a model for the industry.

During the Johnson Administration Heineman was a member of several controversial panels formed to review and make recommendations on domestic policy. In November 1965 President Johnson named Heineman to a committee created to recommend ways of revamping the entire federal effort in housing, urban poverty and mass transportation. The panel was also assigned the task of organizing the cabinet-level Department of Housing and Urban Development, established that month.

In February 1966 Johnson selected Heineman to head the White House Conference on Civil Rights, which had been called to find ways to bring Negroes into the mainstream of American society. Following its May meeting the Conference issued a report recommending public works projects to provide employment, a national minimum for welfare assistance, equality of education throughout the country and low-cost, integrated housing to revitalize the ghettos. However, the report cautioned that federal legislation was only a partial solution to the problem, and said that educational institutions business, labor and state and local government would have to become involved in the battle to end discrimination.

In January 1967 Heineman became head of the Commission on Income Maintenance, which was formed to review the welfare system. The panel's report, issued in November 1969, challenged the assumption that work was the answer to poverty and urged implementation of an income supplement based solely on need. Questioning the view that the nation could work its way out of poverty, the group argued that the U.S. "economic and social structure virtually guaranteed poverty for millions of Americans. The simple fact is that most of the poor remain poor because access to income through work is currently beyond their reach. It is wrong that so much attention is focused on a few laggards."

In 1967 Heineman was replaced as president of the Chicago and North Western Railway. However, he continued as chairman and chief executive officer.

[TJC]

HELLER, WALTER W(OLFGANG)

b. Aug. 27, 1915; Buffalo, N.Y.
Chairman, Council of Economic Advisors January 1961-November 1964.

Holding a Ph.D. in economics from the University of Wisconsin, Heller served in the tax research division of the Treasury Department during World War II. He left the Treasury in 1946 to teach economics at the University of Minnesota, but took a leave of absence in 1947 to become chief of finance of the United States military government in Germany. Heller also supplemented his campus teaching with service as a consultant to the Treasury Department and the Minnesota Department of Taxation. From 1955 to 1960 he was an economic advisor to Minnesota Gov. Orville Freeman [*q.v.*].

Appointed chairman of President Kennedy's Council of Economic Advisors (CEA), Heller was an influential advocate of the Keynesian "new economics" which held that the federal government must engage in active fiscal stimulation of the economy in order to achieve rapid growth and full employment. Arguing that the economy was being hampered by insufficient aggregate demand caused by the "fiscal drag" of heavy taxation, Heller persuaded President Kennedy to propose a major tax cut to promote economic expansion. Kennedy's tax reform package, totalling a net reduction of $11.2 billion, passed the House in September 1963 but had not reached the Senate floor by the time of Kennedy's death in November. [See KENNEDY Volume]

The chief obstacle to the tax cut when President Johnson took office was Sen. Harry Flood Byrd (D, Va.) [*q.v.*], chairman of the Senate Finance Committee and one of the leading fiscal conservatives in the Senate. An opponent of unbalanced budgets, Byrd agreed to relax his opposition to the tax cut only after Johnson promised that he would keep the fiscal budget under $100 billion. As signed into law Feb. 26, 1964, the Revenue Act of 1964, among other provisions, reduced personal income tax rates from the existing range of 20%-91% to 14%-70% and cut the corporate income tax from 52% to 48%.

Heller left the CEA in November 1964 to resume teaching economics at the University of Minnesota. He continued to speak out on economic matters, criticizing the aluminum price rise in November 1965 as "unjustified," "inflationary" and not warranted by the industry's productivity and profit performance. The price rise was subsequently rescinded under heavy Administration pressure. In 1966 and 1967 Heller endorsed a tax increase accompanied by an easing of monetary restraints. He was also the major spokesman for a plan by which the federal government would restore a portion of income tax revenues to the states, which, unlike most federal grants-in-aid, would have "no strings attached." Heller had proposed this plan, later called "revenue-sharing" or the "Heller Plan," in June 1960 and again in 1964. President Johnson was reportedly enthusiastic about the plan but dropped it from his legislative program when news of it leaked prematurely to the press. Heller continued his unofficial advocacy of the idea throughout the Johnson and Nixon years. In October 1972 President Nixon signed into law a revenue-sharing bill appropriating $30.2 billion to the states over a five-year period.

[TO]

For further information:
Walter W. Heller, *New Dimensions of Political Economy* (New York, 1966).

HELMS, RICHARD M(cGARRAH)

b. March 30, 1913; St. Davids, Pa.
Deputy Director for Plans, Central Intelligence Agency, February 1962-April 1965; Deputy Director, April 1965-June 1966; Director, June 1966-December 1972.

Richard Helms, director of the Central Intelligence Agency (CIA) during the period of social and political unrest in the late 1960s and early 1970s, was raised in an upper-middle-class family. After receiving his secondary education in Europe, Helms entered Williams College, where he graduated in 1935. For the next seven years he worked as a correspondent for the United Press and as advertising director of the *Indianapolis Times*. Commissioned a lieutenant in the Navy in 1942, Helms was transferred to the Office of Strategic Services one year later. After his discharge in 1946 he remained in intelligence work and in 1947 helped organize the CIA.

During the 1950s and 1960s, Helms became one of the CIA's key staff officers, working on covert operations and recruiting and training top agents. Helms was involved in the Agency's illegal domestic surveillance operations, including the project to photograph and open overseas mail arriving in New York, and he took part in planning schemes to assassinate such foreign leaders as Patrice Lumumba and Fidel Castro. [See KENNEDY Volume]

From April 1965 until June 1966, Helms served as deputy director of the CIA under Adm. William Raborn [*q.v.*]. Because Raborn had little experience in intelligence operations or foreign affairs, he relied heavily on his subordinate. During Raborn's term in office relations with other departments deteriorated and morale within the CIA declined. Reacting to criticism of the Agency, President Johnson appointed Helms director in June 1966. The President hoped that the appointment of an experienced CIA executive would improve morale and would result in needed organizational and management reforms.

While Helms was director of the CIA, the Agency was involved in numerous projects designed to ensure the establishment and preservation of friendly foreign governments. A congressional investigation in 1975 and 1976 revealed that the CIA had become deeply involved in Chilean domestic politics. During that country's 1964 presidential race, the CIA underwrote slightly more than half of the cost of the Christian Democratic Party campaign and mounted a massive anti-Communist propaganda drive designed to forestall the election of the Marxist candidate, Salvador Allende. The intervention enabled the moderate Christian Democrat, Eduardo Frei, who was unaware of the CIA's action, to win a clear majority in the election instead of the expected plurality. In the five years following that election, the CIA conducted a variety of covert activities designed to strengthen Chile's moderate parties. These actions included monetary support of political and intellectual groups, establishment of leftist splinter parties to draw support away from Allende, continued propaganda and liaison activities with Chile's internal security, and intelligence services to meet any threat posed by leftists. The total cost of CIA involvement in Chile during those years was $2 million. CIA activity in Chile culminated in 1970, when President Nixon instructed Helms to attempt to prevent Allende from taking power. The Agency, therefore, supported a group of military plotters planning a coup. The plot collapsed in the fall of 1970.

During Helm's tenure the CIA was also involved in numerous domestic activities that were illegal under the Agency's charter, which forbade CIA operations in the U.S. except to protect intelligence sources. Acting at the request of President Johnson, the CIA and FBI coordinated activities in 1966 to determine whether there was any foreign influence in the social protest movements of the late 1960s. Under the program the CIA, at the request of the FBI, investigated Americans traveling abroad, expanded its mail-opening operations to include leading black activists and Vietnam war dissenters and supplied the FBI with a steady stream of unsolicited information.

Under continued White House pressure the CIA also developed its own Operation Chaos to investigate possible foreign links with domestic dissidents. Acting on the premise that to investigate foreign infiltration the Agency had to know if each person in an organization had any connection with foreigners, the CIA amassed files on 10,000 U.S. citizens and groups and indexed 300,000 names in Agency computer records. CIA officials realized that these activities were in violation of the Agency's charter, and in a February 1969 letter to Henry Kissinger [*q.v.*], Helms cautioned that Chaos reports were to be kept top secret.

The CIA established two additional projects to monitor dissident groups. In 1967 the Agency, citing the need to obtain early warning of protest demonstrations that might threaten its facilities, set up Project Merrimack to infiltrate Washington-based peace and black activist groups. That year it also established Project Resistance to obtain background intelligence information on campus radical groups. In each case the CIA collected general information on radical leadership, funding and policies, as well as data on prospective demonstrations.

Throughout the 1950s and 1960s the CIA was involved in covert funding of academic and philanthropic organizations. This action remained virtually unknown until 1967, when *Ramparts* magazine disclosed CIA funding of the National Student Association. In response to the storm of criticism that followed, President Johnson organized a committee composed of Helms, Undersecretary of State Nicholas Katzenbach [*q.v.*] and Secretary of Health, Education and Welfare John Gardner [*q.v.*] to review the relationship between the Agency and U.S. educational and voluntary groups with overseas operations. The committee report, made public on Feb. 23, 1967, was not critical of CIA action. However, the panel recommended that federal agencies stop covert financial assistance to U.S. educational or private voluntary organizations and suggested that CIA funding of U.S.-based groups end by Dec. 31, 1967. Although Johnson adopted the recommendations as policy, they were not issued as executive orders or enacted into law and so had no firm legal status.

The 1975 Senate Select Committee on Intelligence Activities reported that these recommendations had a profound effect on the CIA's clandestine operations. The Agency withdrew support from a large number of organizations, transferred some projects to other sources of funding, and financed continuing efforts by giving key projects large grants before the December 1967 deadline, thus ensuring their existence for a number of years. Although the Agency instituted a series of reforms, the Senate Committee found that these were "aimed at preventing further public disclosure which could jeopardize sensitive CIA operations. They did not represent significant rethinking of where boundaries ought to be drawn in a free society."

Although President Johnson had appointed Helms director in the hope that he could carry out needed reforms of the intelligence community, little progress was made in making the organizations more efficient or in preventing their continued expansion. Uninterested in management, Helms did not attempt to coordinate the activities of the intelligence agencies. In addition, the politically astute director realized that because he was not of cabinet rank, he lacked the power to make changes opposed by the State Department or the Pentagon.

In 1967 and 1968 Helms commissioned studies of the CIA and National Security Administration. They found that the various intelligence agencies were duplicating each other's efforts. Much of the information gathered was useless and merely served to obscure more important data, according to these reports. Helms, however, did not press for reform, fearing that to do so would risk Pentagon hostility and jeopardize funding for covert operations with which he was particularly concerned.

Shortly after the 1972 election Helms was replaced as CIA director, ostensibly because of his failure to institute the needed reforms. According to former CIA operative Victor Marchetti, another factor in his dismissal was his connections with liberal congressmen on President Nixon's "enemies list." Helms was appointed ambassador to Iran in January 1973. [See NIXON Volume]

[EWS]

For further information:

Victor Marchetti and John D. Marks, *The CIA and the Cult of Intelligence* (New York, 1974).

Commission on CIA Activities within the United States (Rockefeller Commission), *Report to the President by the Commission on CIA Activities within the United States* (Washington, 1975).

U.S. Senate, Select Committee on Intelligence Activities, *Alleged Assassination Plots Involving Foreign Leaders* (Washington, 1975).

———, *Covert Action* (Washington, 1976).

———, *Final Report* (Washington, 1976).

HENRY, AARON E(DD)

b. July 2, 1922; Coahoma County, Miss.

President, Mississippi Conference of Branches of the NAACP, 1960- ; President, Council of Federated Organizations, Miss., 1962-65.

Henry grew up in Clarksdale, Miss., and opened a drugstore there after receiving a degree in pharmacy from Xavier University in 1950. Two years later he organized and became president of the Clarksdale branch of the NAACP. In 1960 he was named president of the state Conference of NAACP Branches. Henry concentrated his efforts on securing voting rights for Mississippi blacks, especially after the Council of Federated Organizations (COFO) was established in the spring of 1962. A coalition of the NAACP and other civil rights groups in the state, COFO was set up to conduct a unified voter registration campaign in Mississippi. As COFO president, Henry helped organize voter registration projects, often in the face of repeated harassment and arrest. He ran for governor in the November 1963 "Freedom Ballot," a mock election sponsored by COFO to demonstrate the magnitude of black disfranchisement in Mississippi. Some 80,000 blacks voted in the election. [See KENNEDY Volume]

COFO organized the 1964 Mississippi Freedom Summer Project, an undertaking that brought over 1,000 volunteers into the state to set up community centers, teach in "Freedom Schools," and work on voter registration. The main vehicle for political work was the Mississippi Freedom Democratic Party (MFDP), founded at a statewide convention in April 1964 and intended as an alternative to the segregationist regular Democratic Party in the state. Henry was chosen temporary chairman of the new Party at the convention and worked during the summer on the "freedom registration," which enrolled over 60,000 people as Party members. In August Henry presided at a second MFDP state convention, which selected a 68-member delegation to send to the Democratic National Convention meeting later in the month. Henry was chairman of the group that traveled to Atlantic City to challenge the seating of Mississippi's regular delegation.

The MFDP challenge posed an explosive dilemma to Democratic Party leaders. Through Vice President Hubert Humphrey [*q.v.*] and former Pennsylvania Gov. David Lawrence [*q.v.*], President Johnson proposed to split both Mississippi delegations and divide their votes equally. The MFDP rejected this proposal and in the next three days won support from many liberal Democrats. Henry, Fannie Lou Hamer [*q.v.*] and other MFDP delegates described Mississippi conditions to the Convention Credentials Committee. A proposal offered by Rep. Edith Green (D, Ore.) [*q.v.*] to effectively oust the Mississippi regulars and replace them with the MFDP delegation was defeated when Johnson made his opposition to the proposal known.

Finally on Aug. 25 Humphrey and United Auto Workers President Walter Reuther [*q.v.*] proposed another compromise offering to seat as regular delegates Henry and the Rev. Edwin King, a white minister active in the MFDP. The rest of the delegation was to be seated as "honored guests." King and Henry favored the proposal, and the Credentials Committee quickly adopted the Humphrey-Reuther plan, but the MFDP delegation as a whole voted against accepting the compromise. Aided by sympathetic delegates from other states, MFDP members made their way into the Convention seats reserved for the Mississippi regulars. In the end the fight over the MFDP at the Convention left many civil rights activists embittered with both Democratic Party liberals and their own more moderate leaders like Henry.

In the fall of 1964 Henry was one of four candidates nominated by the MFDP to run for Congress. When the state election commission ruled that the candidates could not be included on the regular ballot, the MFDP organized an independent November election in which Henry received nearly 37,000 votes in his district. The MFDP then challenged the seating of Mississippi's five regular representatives in Congress in January 1965 and asked that its representatives be seated instead. The national NAACP favored a congressional investigation of Mississippi elections but did not endorse the MFDP's effort to seat its own members in Congress. Probably because of this, Henry was the only one of the MFDP candidates who did not join the congressional challenge. The challenge was eventually rejected by the House in September 1965, by a 228-143 vote.

In April 1965 the national office of the NAACP said it was officially withdrawing from COFO. Henry, who had been elected to the NAACP's national board of directors in January, joined in the announcement. Except for Henry's key role, the NAACP had not been heavily involved in COFO. The organization had been staffed primarily by members of the Student Nonviolent Coordinating Committee (SNCC), and the NAACP decided to end its affiliation in 1965, apparently because SNCC was becoming more radical and because policymaking differences appeared in COFO.

Henry remained active in voter registration work, however. Following passage of the federal Voting Rights Act in August 1965, the NAACP, led by Henry and state field secretary Charles Evers [*q.v.*], took advantage of the law to step up registration efforts among Mississippi blacks. While Henry repeatedly called for more federal examiners and for a stronger federal effort in the state, the NAACP's registration drive helped increase the proportion of voting-age blacks registered to vote from 6.7% in 1964 to 32.9% in 1966. Henry and Evers continually expanded their program, and in 1967 12 blacks won election to state offices in Mississippi.

After the regular state Democratic Party chose only four blacks to be part of its 68-member delegation to the 1968 Democratic National Convention, Henry again helped organize a challenge delegation, the Loyal Democrats of Mississippi. He was elected state chairman of a biracial coalition, which included the NAACP, the MFDP, the state Teachers' Association and the state AFL-CIO, among others. The Loyal Democrats delegation to the Convention won the endorsement of all the major contenders for the Democratic presidential nomination. With Henry as its chairman, the insurgent delegation presented its case to the Credentials Committee, which voted overwhelmingly to unseat the regular delegation and give all of Mississippi's Convention seats to the challengers.

In February 1969 Henry was named a member of a national party committee, headed by Sen. George S. McGovern (D, S.D.) [*q.v.*], charged with democratiz-1972 Democratic National Convention. He ran for a seat in the state legislature in 1971 but lost the election by about 400 votes. Henry was made a member of the democratic National Committee in 1972 and was state campaign manager for the Party in that year's presidential election.

[CAB]

HERSHEY, LEWIS B(LAINE)

b. Sept. 12, 1893; Steuben County, Ind.
d. May 20, 1977; Angola, Ill.
Director, United States Selective Service System, August 1941-December 1946; July 1948-February 1970.

Lewis B. Hershey, a career Army officer, served as director of the selective service under all presidents from Franklin Roosevelt to Richard Nixon. As secretary and executive officer of the Joint Army and Navy Selective Service Committee from 1936 to 1940, Hershey was responsible for planning the system under which millions of American men were inducted into the armed forces to fight in World War II, in Korea and in Vietnam.

"Outside the income tax," Hershey said frequently, "there aren't many things to make the male citizen feel much responsibility to his government any more. Selective Service is one of them." During the late 1960s Hershey was vilified by members of the anti-war movement, who charged that he encouraged local draft boards to punish students protesting American involvement in Vietnam by nullifying their deferments, thereby making them liable for immediate induction into the armed forces.

In the fall of 1965, 10 University of Michigan students convicted of trespassing in an Oct. 15 sit-in demonstration at the Ann Arbor draft board were declared delinquent by the board and reclassified 1-A. The decision was widely denounced. "The draft," said Rep. Emanuel Celler (D, N.Y.) [*q.v.*], "was never intended to be used as a vehicle of castigation." Hershey stated that protesting U.S. policy in Vietnam was not in itself a cause for reclassification but that "deliberate illegal obstruction of the administration of the [draft] law by registrants cannot be tolerated." He made this policy explicit in an Oct. 26, 1967 letter to local draft boards, urging that registrants violating draft laws be drafted as soon as possible. Before issuing the letter Hershey stated that he had consulted with the White House. On Jan. 19, 1970 the U.S. Supreme Court, in a unanimous decision, ruled that the Selective Service lacked the authority to speed up the induction of men who violated draft regulations.

In several appearances before congressional committees, Hershey defended the system that he had helped plan 30 years earlier. In June 1966 he came before the House Armed Services Committee to answer charges that the draft discriminated against those who could not be deferred because they were too poor to attend college. Hershey defended the deferment system, asserting that the U.S. "paced the world in technological advance" because thousands of men had been granted deferments to receive training as scientists and engineers. Hershey pointed out that 56% of those who entered college eventually entered military service, compared to only 46% of those who did not attend college. Hershey did, however, favor a change in the law, making it possible to draft men 26 to 34 to eliminate the temptation to stay in college to escape military duty.

Important changes were made in the way the Selective Service System operated in the late 1960s. Although Hershey had long opposed a draft lottery, because it would reduce the discretionary powers of local draft boards, he acquiesced in President Johnson's order to devise such a system in March 1967. Appearing before a congressional subcommittee that month, Hershey announced his opposition to the lottery, but stated, "When the quarterback calls the signals that is the way I play them."

In February 1968 Hershey announced another major change in the draft law. Speaking on behalf of the National Security Council, Hershey abolished all deferments for graduate students except for those in medicine and dentistry or for those who had completed two or more years of graduate study by June 1968.

Because of the growing unpopularity of the draft, Hershey became an inviting target for politicians running on an anti-war platform. Sen. Eugene McCarthy (D, Minn.) [*q.v.*], campaigning in the spring of 1968 for the Democratic presidential nomination, charged that Hershey, like FBI director J. Edgar Hoover [*q.v.*], had grown so powerful that he was beyond the reach of public control. Vice President Hubert Humphrey [*q.v.*], the Democratic presidential nominee, in the fall also declared that he would replace Hershey as head of Selective Service.

In February 1970 Hershey stepped down as director to become an adviser to President Richard M. Nixon [*q.v.*] on manpower mobilization. Secretary of Defense Melvin R. Laird [*q.v.*] announced the end of the draft three years later. Hershey, 79, a four-star general and the oldest man on active duty, retired in March 1973.

[JLW]

HESBURGH, THEODORE M(ARTIN)

b. May 25, 1917; Syracuse, N.Y.
President, University of Notre Dame, June 1952- ; Member, United States Civil Rights Commission, November 1957-November 1972.

Ordained a Roman Catholic priest in 1943, Father Hesburgh taught theology at Notre Dame before becoming the school's president in 1952. He upgraded the academic reputation of Notre Dame, long famous for its football teams, and secularized its faculty and administration. Active in national education circles, Hesburgh was appointed by President Dwight D. Eisenhower [*q.v.*] to the newly formed United States Commission on Civil Rights (CRC) in November 1957.

In the early 1960s he was one of the most vocal members of the CRC in urging the adoption of comprehensive civil rights legislation. He also furthered the Catholic Church's ecumenical movement by working with representatives of other relgious groups on an international as well as a national level. His liberalism and intellectual manner helped soften the negative image of the Church held by many American liberals. [See KENNEDY Volume]

During the Johnson Administration Hesburgh served on a large number of boards and committees beside the CRC, including the National Science Board and the President's General Advisory Committee on Foreign Assistance. He was a trustee of the Rockefeller Foundation and the Carnegie Foundation for the Advancement of Teaching. However, Hesburgh remained best known for his work on the CRC.

While the early period of government-sponsored civil rights activity concentrated on discrimination against U.S. citizens, particularly blacks, Hesburgh brought the condition of Mexican migrant workers to national attention in December 1968. Serving as acting chairman of the CRC, he issued a report asserting that Mexicans working in the lower Rio Grande valley of Texas received low wages and were forced to live under conditions of "near slavery" or "peonage." The report criticized the state police and officials of Starr County for assisting local employers in breaking migrant workers' efforts to organize. The employment of migrants also left a large number of local citizens unemployed.

Hesburgh took a "hard line" against the campus disorders of the late 1960s. At a conference on racism sponsored by the National Student Association at Notre Dame in December 1968, Hesburgh met with student leaders. The students, admitting that Hesburgh had accomplished much in fighting racism in the United States, charged that his approach was not sufficiently radical and that he had done little to deal with the problem at Notre Dame. Not only were there too few black students at the school, they claimed, but maintenance of the U.S. Army's Reserve Officer Training Corps (ROTC) on campus contributed indirectly to furthering a "racist" war in Vietnam. Hesburgh did not agree with the students' logic and insisted that ROTC would remain a part of the Notre Dame curriculum.

In February 1969 Hesburgh announced a "get-tough" policy for dealing with possible campus disorders at Notre Dame, which earned the praise of President Richard Nixon [*q.v.*]. Named chairman of the CRC in March 1969, Hesburgh later came into conflict with the President over Nixon's policy of "benign neglect" in the civil rights field. Angered by Nixon's use of busing as a campaign issue, Hesburgh resigned his post in November 1972 following the President's reelection. [See NIXON Volume]

[JCH]

HEYNS, ROGER W(ILLIAM)

b. Jan. 27, 1918; Grand Rapids, Mich.
University official.

Heyns was the son of a penologist who served as a director of the Michigan Department of Correction. Roger Heyns received his B.A. in 1940 from Calvin College, a school in Grand Rapids affiliated with the Christian Reformed Church. After his discharge from the Army Air Corps in 1946, he taught psychology at the University of Michigan and received his Ph.D. in 1949. A full professor by 1957, Heyns specialized in such areas of psychology as group dynamics, the measurement of social motives and group observation methods. He was the author of several books on these subjects.

Heyns began his career as an administrator in 1954, when he was appointed assistant dean of the college of literature, science and the arts at the University of Michigan. In 1958 he became the dean of the college, and in 1962 he advanced to the office of vice president of academic affairs. In this latter capacity Heyns was credited with the creation of the University of Michigan's residential college system.

Owing to his reputation as a skilled administrator and educational reformer, Heyns was selected by the regents of the University of California to head the turbulent Berkeley campus in July 1965. He replaced Martin Myerson, who had been named acting chancellor early in 1965 after Chancellor Edward W. Strong had resigned in the wake of the Free Speech Movement (FSM). After a year of Heyns's administration, *Time* magazine commented upon the absence of radical activity on the campus while anti-draft protests were sweeping other universities. The magazine attributed the lack of activity to "the effective peacemaking of Chancellor Roger W.

Heyns . . . who was specifically—and desperately—hired last July to calm Berkeley's combatants."

As the 1966-67 academic year began, Heyns proposed restrictions on the freedom of advocacy that radical groups had enjoyed on campus since the victory of the FSM. The move was interpreted by many as an effort to "clean house" before Governor-elect Ronald Reagan's [*q.v.*] threatened investigation of the campus could get under way. Heyns's efforts centered around abolishing the noon rallies that had become a regular feature of campus political life since 1964.

The lull at Berkeley ended abruptly in November when a student strike, engaging perhaps half of the student body, raised issues more far-reaching than those of the 1964 Free Speech fight. The strike began with a spontaneous demonstration over the administration's decision to permit a Navy recruiting table in the student union while denying the same opportunity to non-student anti-war groups. Police were called on campus to arrest some of the leaders, and the next morning the strike began. The faculty, fearing a crackdown by the new governor, gave Heyns a vote of confidence and called on the students to return to classes. Although the strike was suspended after six days, Heyns was forced to grant some concessions to the strikers, including the establishment of a grievance system for graduate students employed as teaching assistants and the stipulation that Navy recruiting tables had to be manned by students.

During virtually every year of Heyns's administration, the campus was embroiled in some form of protest activity, although Berkeley lost its reputation as a model for the student movement in the late 1960s. In 1969 black and other minority students picketed and disrupted the campus to reinforce their demand for a black studies program. Heyns eventually approved the formation of an ethnic studies department, but he refused to grant the students' demand for departmental autonomy. In the spring of 1970, when campuses across the nation exploded after the Cambodian invasion and the Kent State killings, liberal faculty at Berkeley took the lead in pressuring Heyns to call a university-wide convocation on the war and in demanding that the campus suspend "normal" activities to remain open as a base for anti-war projects.

While largely unsuccessful in his efforts to bring calm to Berkeley, Heyns achieved certain educational reforms. Responding to students' charges that the University had become an impersonal "knowledge factory," he supported a faculty committee that recommended a number of innovations. A board for educational development was created to experiment with courses that students considered meaningful. By mid-1968 the board had sponsored about three dozen student-initiated courses.

In the fall of 1970 Heyns came into conflict with the regents and Gov. Reagan, who had embarked on a budget-cutting campaign that, in Heyns's view, threatened the quality of academic programs at Berkeley. As a result he resigned early in 1971 to resume teaching at Michigan. In 1972 he again left Michigan, this time to become the president of the American Council on Education, a lobbying agency in Washington for colleges and educational associations.

[TLH]

For further information:
"Roger Heyns," *Current Biography Yearbook, 1968* (New York, 1969), pp. 187-189.

HICKENLOOPER, BOURKE B(LAKEMORE)

b. July 21, 1896; Blockton, Iowa.
d. Sept. 4, 1971; Shelter Island, N.Y.
Republican Senator, Iowa, 1945-69; Chairman, Republican Policy Committee, 1962-69.

A former state legislator and Iowa governor, Hickenlooper served in the Senate from 1945 until his retirement in 1969. While in Congress Hickenlooper compiled what the *New York Times* described as a "moderately conservative" voting record. During the 1950s and 1960s the Senator supported defense, business and military assistance bills as well as most civil rights legislation. Hickenlooper opposed many foreign aid bills and in 1962 successfully added a controversial amendment to a foreign aid measure that prohibited aid to countries that did not reimburse Americans for property they had nationalized. [See TRUMAN, EISENHOWER, KENNEDY Volumes]

Reflecting the strongly held work ethic of many of his constituents, Hickenlooper voted against such domestic welfare measures as aid to education, medicare and the Johnson Administration's antipoverty program. From 1966 to 1968 the liberal Americans for Democratic Action gave Hickenlooper a rating of zero percent.

Many conservatives strongly opposed the Soviet-American consular treaty of 1967 because they felt that the establishment of Soviet consulates would increase the possibilities of Soviet espionage and correspondingly complicate the job of the FBI in controlling such activities. Hickenlooper, the ranking minority member of the Senate Foreign Relations Committee, initially opposed the treaty but changed his position before the vote. As chairman of the Republican Policy Committee, Hickenlooper worked to maintain Republican support for the Johnson Administration's policy in Vietnam. Hickenlooper retired in 1969 and died two years later.

[EWS]

HILL, HERBERT

b. Jan. 24, 1924; New York, N.Y.
Labor Secretary, NAACP, 1951- .

Attracted by the early struggles of the labor movement, Hill left New York University in the 1940s to become a union organizer among steel workers. He began to work for the NAACP in 1948 and became the organization's labor secretary in 1951. He also served as a consultant to Rep. Adam Clayton Powell (D, N.Y.) [*q.v.*] on the House Labor and Education Committee.

Beginning in the late 1950s Hill pressed both big business and big labor to give black workers greater access to the job market, especially through training programs leading to skilled work. He demanded that the Kennedy Administration enforce fair hiring practices among defense contractors, and he pressured many of these companies into promising racial equality in employment. Hill also attacked a number of labor unions, including the International Ladies Garment Workers Union, for restricting minority membership in the higher-paying skilled locals. [See KENNEDY Volume]

As the job market continued to expand during the mid-1960s, Hill increased his efforts to gain what he viewed as a fair share of employment for minority workers. In 1964 and 1966 he led protest campaigns against promotion practices at General Motors and U.S. Steel. The entertainment industry also became a target of Hill's criticism, both for discriminating against black actors and technicians and for portraying blacks in terms of "outworn stereotypes." Hill's main conflict of this period, however, was with the labor unions, particularly those in the highly skilled and well paid construction industry.

Hill repeatedly attacked the building trades unions for restricting minority membership. With the expansion of housing construction in the 1960s, civil rights groups demanded the creation of training programs designed to qualify blacks for apprenticeships and, eventually, for full-fledged construction jobs. This clashed, however, with the desire of many union officials to limit entry into their trades, both to maintain wages and to minimize unemployment in the event of a slump. In response to this practice, civil rights leaders called for a reform of union hiring-hall practices and, failing this, public supervision of apprenticeship programs. Union leaders in turn viewed these demands as an assault on union independence, reminiscent of earlier attempts at "union-busting."

Hill used several tactics in attempting to gain concessions from union leaders. In 1963 he led a nationwide campaign of sit-ins and demonstrations at publicly funded construction projects that did not meet NAACP standards of fair employment. This campaign, continuing into the late 1960s, was sometimes marked by violence. Hill also sued to block public funds from projects that refused to change their hiring practices, and he filed complaints with the Equal Employment Opportunity Commission against a number of unions for maintaining segregated locals.

All this effort, however, did not bring proportionate results. An NAACP suit to halt state- and city-supported construction in New York failed in 1963. The same year civil rights groups in Cleveland signed an agreement with the local plumbers' union, intended to increase black membership in apprentice programs, but Hill withdrew the NAACP and Urban League from the pact in 1966, claiming that the union continued to discriminate against blacks. A "biracial screening committee," set up to encourage minority employment in the New York building trades, also collapsed after a short time. One consequence of Hill's agitation was an effort by national union leaders to increase minority membership by "voluntary" means, such as disseminating information on training programs. Both the AFL-CIO and the Alliance for Labor Action, comprising the Teamsters and United Auto Workers, endorsed this approach in the late 1960s. However, Hill dismissed such programs as ineffectual "tokenism" in the absence of "sanctions, time-tables and enforcement apparatus."

Hill's activity with the NAACP during the 1960s helped loosen the traditional alliance between civil rights groups and labor. "I have given up long ago trying to satisfy Herbie Hill," stated AFL-CIO president George Meany [*q.v.*] at the height of the labor-civil rights conflict. In response to labor criticism, Hill wrote that "you must create a crisis to get something done." Most observers thought his efforts important in making the problem of job discrimination a major civil rights issue during the Johnson years.

Hill also promoted the development of black literature in the U.S. He edited and introduced two volumes of writings by black authors: *Soon, One Morning: New Writing by American Negroes* (1963), and *Anger and Beyond: The Negro Writer in the United States* (1966).

[SLG]

HILL, LISTER

b. Dec. 29, 1894; Montgomery, Ala.
Democratic Senator, Ala., 1938-69; Chairman, Labor and Welfare Committee, 1955-69.

Hill came from a wealthy family that dominated the politics of Montgomery, Ala., where his father was a prominent surgeon. In 1923, after serving as president of the Montgomery Board of Education, Hill won a special election to fill a vacant seat in the U.S. House of Representatives. In the House Hill supported New Deal programs, particularly the Tennessee Valley Authority, which played a crucial role in promoting the economic growth of northern Alabama. He ran for a vacant Senate seat in 1937 as an ally of President Roosevelt and with urban and labor support, he defeated his right-wing opponent, who reflected the views of the Ku Klux Klan.

After World War II Hill's primary legislative interests were in the areas of medicine and mental health. His major legislative accomplishment was the Hill-Burton Act of 1946, which provided federal grants for hospital construction and which Congress extended and expanded in subsequent decades. Hill became chairman of the Senate Labor and Welfare Committee in 1955. In that post and as chairman of the Appropriations Committee's subcommittee for health and welfare agencies, he was able to substantially increase federal health expenditures. [See TRUMAN, EISENHOWER Volumes]

Hill narrowly averted an electoral defeat at the hands of a conservative Republican in 1962. From that year onwards he adjusted his voting record to conform more closely to the views of his rural and more conservative constituents by opposing social welfare measures primarily directed at the problems of urban groups. [See KENNEDY Volume]

During the Johnson years Hill supported such rurally oriented programs as the Appalachia aid bill in 1965 and a 1966 bill to provide federal planning grants for the establishment of rural community development districts. But he voted against the housing and urban development bill of

1965, a rent supplement bill for low-income families in 1966 and the 1967 Demonstration Cities bill. In addition, Hill opposed repeal of the "right-to-work" clause of the Taft-Hartley Act in 1965 and a minimum wage bill in 1966.

Hill consistently opposed the Johnson Administration's civil rights measures. In 1964 he led one of the three platoons established by Southern Democratic senators to filibuster against the President's civil rights bill. Two years later he participated in Senate debate over school desegregation guidelines issued by the Department of Health, Education and Welfare under the 1964 Civil Rights Act, stating that the guidelines established racial quotas contrary to the provisions of that law. In 1967 Hill held up the Teacher Corps bill in his Labor and Welfare Committee until the Senate killed the President's open housing bill in September.

Hill continued to press for health legislation in the mid-1960s. In 1965 he offered an amendment to a supplemental appropriations bill to provide educational funds for the deaf. The following year Hill introduced an Administration bill granting new authority to plan public health services on the state level, and he successfully offered an amendment to the measure specifying that state health services must be established and maintained for persons confined to mental institutions. In 1967, as chairman of the Appropriations Committee's Health and Welfare Subcommittee, he proposed an appropriations bill amendment increasing Public Health Service funds for the treatment of chronic diseases.

Over the years Hill was the leader of successful efforts to retain the essentially rural orientation of the Hill-Burton Act, which was designed primarily to fund the construction of hospitals in the countryside rather than the modernization of old, urban hospitals. A series of Hill-Burton amendments supported by Hill in 1964 provided greater assistance for city facilities but were criticized as insufficient by a number of health officials. In 1967 Hill agreed to meet many of the needs of urban hospitals, but no action was taken in 1967 or 1968 pending a report of the President's National Advisory Commission on Health Facilities.

In January 1968, at the age of 73, Hill announced that he would not run for reelection, and the following year he retired to Montgomery.

[MLL]

HOFF, PHILIP H(ENDERSON)

b. June 29, 1924; Greenfield, Mass.
Governor, Vt., 1963-69.

A lawyer and former Democratic precinct worker, Hoff served in the Vermont House of Representatives from 1961 to 1962. He faced no primary opposition in his 1962 gubernatorial bid. His opponent in the general election, incumbent Gov. F. Ray Keyser, Jr., was hampered in his reelection attempt by his failure to reduce the income tax and increase state funding of local schools. Despite Vermont's reputation as the nation's rock-ribbed, strong-hold of conservative Republicanism, Hoff defeated Keyser by 1,348 votes, becoming the state's first Democratic governor in 109 years. He was reelected in 1964 and again in 1966.

During his tenure as governor Hoff promoted the growth of the state's economy by attracting new electronics industry, building highways and expanding the winter ski-resort and summer-home businesses. Much of this expansion was attributable to Hoff's successful venture in importing two-million kilowatts of low-cost electrical power from Canada. Hoff termed this 1966 arrangement, in a state where power rates were the highest in the country, "New England's opportunity of the century."

In December 1966 Hoff was named by President Lyndon B. Johnson to the Public Land Law Review Commission to study the nation's public land laws, practices and problems. The Commission's report, issued after five years of study, was termed by the *New York Times* "a predictable . . . tapestry of compromise." Shortly after the March 1968 Kerner Commission report had predicted the increasing polarization of American society along racial lines, Hoff and New York City Mayor John V. Lindsay [*q.v.*] developed a New York-Vermont summer project that brought children from black and white ghettos to Vermont homes for an experiment in interracial living.

In March 1968 Hoff became the first governor to give his unequivocal support to Sen. Robert F. Kennedy's (D, N.Y.) [*q.v.*] presidential bid. Two months after the assassination of Kennedy, Hoff transferred his support to Sen. Eugene McCarthy (D, Minn.) [*q.v.*] and helped draft the minority Vietnam peace plank at the 1968 Democratic National Convention. In September 1968 Hoff announced that he would not seek reelection. Hoff won the Democratic nomination for the U.S. Senate in September 1970 but was defeated as Sen. Winston L. Prouty (R, Vt.) captured his third term by winning 59% of the vote.

[TJC]

HOFFA, JAMES R(IDDLE)

b. Feb. 14, 1913; Brazil, Ind.
d. presumed July, 1975.
President, International Brotherhood of Teamsters, Chauffeurs, Warehousemen and Helpers of America, 1957-67.

Hoffa, the son of a coal miner, left school at 15 to help support his family. He soon became involved in union activity among freight handlers in Detroit; by 1931 he had gained control of Teamsters Local 299, the largest local in the union. During the 1940s Hoffa held a series of positions in the Michigan organization of the International Brotherhood of Teamsters (IBT) and managed the Central States Drivers Council, which organized long-haul truck drivers in the Midwest. In 1952 he became an international vice president of the IBT when his ally, Dave Beck, took control of the union. With a firm power base in the South and Midwest and growing influence in the East, Hoffa soon became the strongest of the union vice presidents. When indictment for tax fraud and embezzlement forced Beck's resignation in 1957, Hoffa succeeded him as president of the 1.5 million member IBT, the nation's largest union. [See EISENHOWER Volume]

During the early and mid-1960s, Hoffa worked to increase his authority over the traditionally autonomous regional Teamsters leaders. Local officials were encouraged to "call Jimmy" for strike authorization and financial support, bypassing the union's area joint councils and regional offices. IBT conventions in 1961 and 1966 approved changes in the union's constitution that increased Hoffa's power at the expense of local as well as area leaders. [See KENNEDY Volume] Such centralization enabled Hoffa, who had helped to introduce area-wide trucking contracts in the 1940s, to press for the first national contract in the trucking industry. This agreement was signed in January 1964, bringing improved fringe benefits for Teamsters and a wage increase of about 8% over three years.

The IBT prospered under Hoffa, growing in size to over two million members in the late 1960s. But his methods provoked internal opposition to his leadership. Most of the union's vice presidents disliked Hoffa's unwillingness to delegate authority and his strict control over their own activity; several resigned in 1964. Automobile haulers in a number of Eastern cities struck in June of that year against the national trucking contract, the provisions of which they disliked. Philadelphia Teamsters were especially rebellious. A truckers' strike began there against Hoffa's resistance in June 1965, and a Philadelphia local of the IBT sued to block payment of Hoffa's personal expenses from the union treasury. Reports of dissension within the union continued during the following years despite official denials.

More important to Hoffa at this time, however, were his legal difficulties. Because of reported connections between the IBT and organized crime, Justice Department officials had been watching him closely since the early 1950s. In 1961 the Senate Permanent Investigations Subcommittee accused Hoffa of misusing union funds and helping racketeers take control of a New York Teamsters local.

The following year government efforts to convict Hoffa on charges of taking "shakedown" payments from employers ended in a mistrial in Nashville, Tenn.; but in March 1964 he was found guilty of jury-tampering in the Nashville trial. Four months later another jury convicted him of fraud and misappropriation of union funds to finance a Florida land-development project. The two verdicts resulted in sentences totaling 13 years in prison. Hoffa spent much of his time in the mid-1960s fighting these convictions. The Supreme Court rejected his last appeal in December 1966, with Chief Justice Earl Warren [*q.v.*] dissenting and condemning the government's use of an informant to gain the jury-tampering conviction.

Hoffa began serving his sentence in the Lewisburg Federal Penitentiary in March 1967, in the midst of negotiations for renewal of the national trucking contract. Control of the IBT passed to Frank Fitzsimmons [*q.v.*], a loyal assistant of Hoffa who had been chosen general vice president in 1966. Hoffa did not immediately resign the union presidency, and there was speculation that he continued to control the IBT from prison. He made several unsuccessful attempts to gain release on parole. In June 1971 Hoffa finally resigned his several Teamsters offices, allowing Fitzsimmons to be elected president one month later. The following December he was pardoned and released from prison by President Nixon, with whom Fitzsimmons had established close ties. The terms of his release, however, prevented Hoffa from engaging in union activity until the end of his sentence in 1980.

In July 1975 Hoffa disappeared, evidently a murder victim, at a time when he was planning to reenter Teamster politics. [See NIXON Volume]

[SLG]

For further information:
Walter Sheridan, *The Fall and Rise of Jimmy Hoffa* (New York, 1972).

HOFFER, ERIC

b. July 25, 1902; New York, N.Y.
Longshoreman; philosopher.

Longshoreman-philosopher Eric Hoffer was a popular thinker on current issues and a controversial celebrant of the American way of life. The son of a German immigrant cabinetmaker, Hoffer was blind from age seven to 15. He became a voracious reader after regaining his sight but had had little formal education when he left New York for California in 1920. For the next two decades Hoffer worked as a migrant farm laborer and at times as a dishwasher, lumberjack and gold prospector, reading extensively in his spare time. In 1943 he began steady work as a longshoreman on the San Francisco docks.

Hoffer won wide acclaim in 1951 with the publication of his first book, *The True Believer: Thoughts on the Nature of Mass Movements*. In this study of political fanaticism, Hoffer characterized the "true believer" as "a guilt-ridden hitchhiker who thumbs a ride on every cause from Christianity to Communism." He continued to write in his spare time, publishing in 1955 *The Passionate State of Mind*, a collection of 300 epigrams, and in 1963 *The Ordeal of Change*, a series of essays whose central theme was that drastic social change was a profoundly disturbing experience and the dominant fact of modern life.

Hoffer's writings during the 1960s were collected in another slim volume, *The Temper of Our Time* (1967). In his familiar aphoristic style he voiced opinions on a range of subjects he had covered before: the role of the juvenile mentality in the making of history, idleness and creativity and the relationship between intellectuals and the masses. Hoffer excoriated the "intellectual" for his "loathing of the common man" and hostility towards America. "Rule by intellectuals," he wrote, "unavoidably approaches a colonial regime."

The most controversial essay was "The Negro Revolution," originally published in November 1964. Hoffer's sweeping denunciation of black activism earned him a storm of criticism from Negroes and liberals. "The Negro revolution is a fraud," he declared. "It has no faith in the character and potentialities of the Negro masses. . . . It wants cheap victories and the easy way." He added, "Individual achievement cannot cure the Negro's soul. . . . That which corrodes the soul of the Negro in his monstrous inner agreement with the prevailing prejudice against him." He criticized black nationalism and emphasized that "community building" was the only means by which the Negro could attain a desirable identity.

Hoffer developed a well-publicized relationship of mutual admiration with President Johnson. Hoffer vigorously supported the Vietnam war and frequently praised Johnson, whom he predicted would be "the foremost President of the 20th century." The President invited Hoffer to the White House for a half-hour talk in October 1967. In June 1968 Johnson appointed him to the National Commission on the Causes and Prevention of Violence, where his disagreements with other members attracted widespread attention. He challenged sympathetic accounts of black rage and frustration in the ghettos and asserted that Negroes could do more to help themselves. Commission member Judge A. Leon Higginbotham attacked Hoffer's stand as being based on racism. In December 1969 Hoffer joined the Commission's seven-to-six majority that condemned all massive civil disobedience, including nonviolent action.

In May 1968 Hoffer became a sponsor of the National Citizens for Humphrey Committee.

[TO]

HOFFMAN, ABBIE

b. Nov. 30, 1936; Worcester, Mass.
Yippie leader.

Although expelled from high school at 17 for striking a teacher, Hoffman managed to complete his secondary education and to attend Brandeis University, from which he graduated in 1959. He received an M.A. in psychology from the University of California, Berkeley, in 1960 and went to work as a psychologist at a Massachusetts state hospital. Hoffman was an early adherent of the New Left, working on H. Stuart Hughes's Massachusetts senatorial peace campaign in 1962 and later with the Student Nonviolent Coordinating Committee in Georgia. He also wrote frequently for the underground press, including the *East Village Other*, the *L.A. Free Press* and *The Realist*.

By 1967 Hoffman had abandoned formal politics and had begun to present himself as a spokesman for what he viewed as a growing "counterculture" of drugs, rock bands and sexual freedom. He was particularly intrigued with the possibilities of "guerrilla theater" as a means of transforming this counterculture into a revolutionary movement. In 1967 he played a major role in orchestrating several protest performances of this genre, among them an invasion of the New York Stock Exchange, in which participants tossed money from the visitors' gallery to the brokers on the trading floor. In October 1967 Hoffman and Jerry Rubin [*q.v.*] captured the attention of the media at the anti-war march in Washington, D.C., when they led a ceremony to "levitate" the Pentagon off its foundation. Late in 1967 Hoffman joined with Rubin, Ed Sanders of a rock group called the Fugs and Paul Krassner, editor of *The Realist*, to create the Yippies, or Youth International Party. In a book entitled *Revolution for the Hell of It* published in 1968, Hoffman defined the Yippies' concept of revolution as street theater, satire, confrontation, put-ons, stealing—anything that displayed irreverence for property and the Establishment. The Yippies' immediate goal was to communicate an alternative way of life to the young. "Long hair and freaky clothes are total information," he wrote. "It is not necessary to say that we are oppoed to ——. Everybody already knows. . . .We alienate people. We tear through the streets. Kids love it. They understand it on an internal level. We are living TV ads, movies, Yippie!"

During the summer of 1968 Hoffman and his fellow Yippies planned a massive "festival of life" in Chicago to coincide and contrast with what they interpreted as the "festival of death" at the Democratic National Convention. Their purpose, according to Hoffman, was to "make some statement, especially in revolutionary-action terms, about LBJ, the Democratic Party, electoral politics and the state of the nation." They came to Chicago along with hundreds of other protestors from the National Mobilization Committee, Students for a Democratic Society and the Black Panthers. The Yippies applied for permission to use city parks for rallies and for sleeping out overnight, but Chicago city officials denied them the right to remain in the parks after 11 p.m. On Aug. 23 the Yippies opened their festival by setting up camp in Lincoln Park and nominating a pig for president in the Chicago civic center. Two days later the police drove the Yippies out of Lincoln Park after the 11 p.m. curfew, beating many in the process. The following evening, at about the same time the Democratic Convention was formally opened, an even larger confrontation took place with several injuries sustained both by demonstrators and policemen. The remaining days of the Convention were full of similar disorder, much of it caught by television cameras or by news photographers.

In March 1969 Hoffman was one of eight persons indicted by a federal grand jury in Chicago in connection with the 1968 disorders. The "Chicago Eight," as they came to be known, were the first defendants tried under the anti-riot provisions of the 1968 Civil Rights Act, which made it a federal crime to cross state lines to incite a riot. After a tumultuous trial five of the eight, including Hoffman, were convicted. In November 1972 the verdicts were overturned by an appeals court on the grounds that the judge in the case had been antagonistic and had committed legal errors.

In 1971 Hoffman wrote *Steal this Book*, a do-it-yourself manual of "rip-offs," including instructions on how to shoplift, cheat the telephone company and make bombs. In 1973 he was arrested for allegedly selling three pounds of cocaine to three New York City policemen. He went underground to avoid imprisonment.

[TLH]

HOLIFIELD, CHET (CHESTER) (EARL)

b. Dec. 3, 1903; Mayfield, Ky.
Democratic Representative, Calif., 1943-75; Chairman, Joint Committee on Atomic Energy, 1961-63, 1965-67, 1969-71.

The son of a farmer, Holifield grew up in Arkansas but ran away from home at 17 and settled near Los Angeles. He became interested in politics during the Depression and by 1938 was district chairman of the California Democratic Central Committee. Holifield won election to Congress in 1942 with nearly 60% of the vote.

During his long tenure in Congress, Holifield represented California's 19th district, a predominantly blue-collar area in Los Angeles County with a large Mexican-American community. He was one of the founders of the House's liberal Democratic Study Group and served as its chairman in 1960. Alternating as chairman of the Joint Committee on Atomic Energy with Sen. John O. Pastore (D, R.I.) [*q.v.*] in the 1960s, Holifield was a strong backer of the Kennedy Administration's fallout shelter and public power proposals. [See EISENHOWER, KENNEDY Volumes]

Holifield was a consistent supporter of the programs of President Lyndon B. Johnson. According to *Congressional Quarterly*, he never opposed Administration positions on more than 5% of key House roll call votes during any year of the Johnson presidency.

However, after 1965 Holifield came under increasing criticism from liberal House colleagues. One reason was his support of President Johnson's Southeast Asia policies. In 1966 he joined 77 other Democratic representatives in signing a statement that supported supplementary appropriations for the Vietnam war, and in succeeding years he continued to take a "hawkish" position in regard to that conflict.

Furthermore, Holifield's role on the Joint Atomic Energy Committee often pitted him against certain liberal positions. He worked closely with military and quasi-military agencies and consistently supported Pentagon appropriations requests. In 1967 he opposed the efforts of civil rights groups to bar the construction of an Atomic Energy Commission facility in Weston, Ill., on the ground that housing discrimination was practiced in the area.

In 1971 Holifield exchanged his Joint Committee position for the chairmanship of the Government Operations Committee. In February 1974 he announced that he would not seek reelection. [See NIXON Volume]

[MLL]

HOLLAND, SPESSARD L(INDSEY)
b. July 10, 1892; Bartow, Fla.
d. Nov. 6, 1971; Bartow, Fla.
Democratic Senator, Fla., 1946-70.

Spessard L. Holland, a Florida attorney, and then a judge and state legislator, served as governor of Florida from 1941 to 1945. He was appointed to the U.S. Senate to fill an unexpired term in 1946 and thereafter had little difficulty winning reelection. During the 1960s he served on the Senate Agriculture, Appropriations, and Aeronautical and Space Sciences Committees. Despite his seniority he never attained the chairmanship of a major committee. Like many Southern conservatives he generally opposed the Kennedy Administration's social welfare policies. Similarly, during the Johnson years he voted against the anti-poverty, medicare and school aid bills, while supporting the Administration's Vietnam war policy. [See KENNEDY Volume]

Holland was a vigorous opponent of Administration efforts to permit greater numbers of non-Western European immigrants into the country. "Why for the first time," he asked in 1965, "are the emerging nations of Africa to be placed on the same basis as our mother countries, Britain, Germany, the Scandinavian nations, France and other nations from which most Americans have come?" Despite these objections the Administration won congressional approval in 1965 of a liberal revision of the immigration quota system.

As chairman of the Senate Agriculture Credit and Rural Electrification Subcommittee, Holland successfully opposed Administration efforts to reduce appropriations for the Soil Conservation Service, which was of particular benefit to Southern farmers. Throughout the 1960s he also opposed efforts of Senate liberals and the Administration to dismantle the "bracero" program, which permitted low-paid Mexican and Bahamian laborers into this country to harvest citrus fruit and vegetables. This program was of distinct benefit to Florida, California and Arizona farm employers.

Although Holland opposed most civil rights legislation, he differed from many of his Southern collegues on the question of the poll tax. As a state legislator Holland had helped abolish the Florida poll tax in 1937, and in every congressional session since 1949 he had introduced a bill proposing a constitutional amendment to outlaw the tax nationwide. The poll tax had been used by many Southern states to prevent poor blacks from voting. Because of the powerful opposition of many Southern senators, Holland's bill was not reported out of the Senate Judiciary Committee until 1962. That year it won the support of the Kennedy Administration and passed both houses of Congress despite the opposition of both Southern conservatives and certain civil rights groups. These organizations, which included the NAACP, argued that the Holland bill "would provide an immutable precedent for shunting all further civil rights legislation to the amendment procedure."

By February 1964 three-quarters of the states had ratified the measure, making it the 24th Amendment to the Constitution. The fear that Congress had committed itself to the cumbersome amendment process to rectify all abuses of civil and voting rights proved unfounded. Congress passed a Civil Rights Act in 1964 and a year later, a Voting Rights Act. Holland voted against both measures.

Holland retired from the Senate in 1970 and died a year later in his hometown.

[JLW]

HOOPES, TOWNSEND (WALTER)
b. April 28, 1922; Duluth, Minn.
Deputy Assistant Secretary of Defense for International Security Affairs, January 1965-October 1967; Undersecretary of the Air Force, October 1967-February 1969.

Following his graduation from Yale in 1944, Hoopes served as a newspaper editorial writer before becoming assistant to the chairman of the House Committee on Armed Services in 1947. Eighteen months later Hoopes was appointed assistant to the Secretary of Defense.

Although engaged in private business during the Eisenhower and Kennedy Administrations, Hoopes was a frequent consultant to the White House and the State and Defense Departments. In 1957 he served as executive secretary of the Rockefeller brothers' panel that produced a report on defense policy and strategy. This study advocated the abandonment of nuclear "massive retaliation" as the nation's prime defense policy and recommended the development of "gradual deterrence and flexible military response."

In January 1965 President Johnson appointed Hoopes deputy assistant secretary of defense for international security affairs. While at this post he was primarily concerned with questions of military aid in the Near East, South Asia and those nations bordering the Communist bloc.

Although aware of the problems developing in Vietnam, Hoopes was not centrally concerned with them and, by his own admission, was "not at the center of policy, but on the near periphery." His involvement with Vietnam, although remote, reflected many of the frustrations that middle echelon advisers faced in getting their opinions heard by high ranking officials and by a President who increasingly isolated himself from the counsel of all but a few close personal friends.

By the end of 1965 Hoopes had become skeptical of the validity of the Administration's goal of a military victory through a limited war and particularly of the effectiveness of the policy of achieving this aim through the intensive bombing of North Vietnam. In December he wrote his superior, John McNaughton [*q.v.*], suggesting that the bombing had been "singularly inconclusive" and that any attempt to step up the operation would unify the Communist world and draw increasing criticism from U.S. allies. Instead of escalation, Hoopes suggested that the U.S. limit its military objectives to the holding and pacification of certain defined cities and ports that could be made secure with the current level of U.S. and South Vietnamese combat forces. McNaughton told Hoopes that he agreed with the general thrust of the message, but he remained confident that the U.S. would eventually achieve victory because of its military superiority.

One month later Hoopes sent a memorandum to Secretary of Defense Robert S. McNamara [*q.v.*] repeating his argument for a bombing halt and pointing out that the military's major argument for bombing—that it prevented the death of countless American troops—was false. McNamara did not answer the memorandum.

Hoopes was far more successful in presenting his case to Clark Clifford [*q.v.*], the incoming Secretary of Defense. In a personal letter to Clifford dated February 1968, Hoopes called military victory in Vietnam a "dangerous illusion" and suggested a bombing halt and reduction in ground troops as a prelude to a negotiated settlement. One month later Hoopes reiterated his position in a report he prepared for a task force Clifford had formed to brief him on Vietnam. These reports, along with others from such men as Paul Nitze [*q.v.*] and Paul Warnke [*q.v.*] helped convince Clifford that de-escalation was necessary. Clifford, in turn, was one of the men who eventually persuaded Johnson to announce a policy of de-escalation in March 1968.

Hoopes left government service in 1969. That year he wrote a book, *The Limits of Intervention*, that described his experiences during the Johnson Administration and traced the steps that led to de-escalation. He later became executive director of the American Association of Publishers.

[EWS]

For further information:
Townsend Hoopes, *The Limits of Intervention* (New York, 1969).

HOOVER, J(OHN) EDGAR

b. Jan. 1, 1895; Washington, D.C.
d. May 2, 1972; Washington, D.C.
Director, Federal Bureau of Investigation, 1924-72.

J. Edgar Hoover served as director of the FBI under every president from Coolidge to Nixon. During the Johnson years the

Bureau, once particularly concerned with the activities of the Communist Party, began investigating other organizations that Hoover believed might also threaten national security. These included black power, "white hate," New Left and anti-war organizations.

Hoover was raised in Washington, D.C., where his father was employed by the Coast and Geodetic Survey. After graduating at the head of his class at Central High School, he went to work for the Library of Congress. He also attended night law school at the George Washington University. After receiving his law degree in 1916, Hoover served as a clerk in the Justice Department. In 1919 he was named special assistant to Attorney General A. Mitchell Palmer who was then engaged in rounding up thousands of alleged Communists and revolutionaries for possible deportation under the provisions of the Wartime Sedition Act. As head of the newly created General Intelligence Division of the Justice Department's Bureau of Investigation, Hoover was successful in his efforts to deport two well-known anarchists, Emma Goldman and Alexander Berkman.

In 1921 Hoover was appointed assistant director of the Bureau of Investigation (the name was changed to the Federal Bureau of Investigation in 1935), and in 1924 he was named director. At the time he assumed the directorship, the Bureau had been demoralized by revelations linking it to the scandals of the Harding Administration. Hoover improved morale and recruited an honest and disciplined staff.

During the 1920s the Bureau had rather limited investigatory powers, and its agents lacked authority to make arrests or carry arms. In May 1932 Congress passed legislation giving the Bureau authority to investigate bank robberies, kidnappings and extortion cases where use of the telephone was involved. Bureau agents were also empowered to carry guns and make arrests.

During the 1930s J. Edgar Hoover became a national hero as the press recorded the exploits of Bureau agents—"G men"—who arrested "Baby Face" Nelson, John Dillinger, "Pretty Boy" Floyd and other crime figures. The FBI also solved a number of kidnappings, including the celebrated Lindbergh case. Hoover also built the Bureau into a major police resource and educational center. He established a national fingerprint file, an efficient crime laboratory and a training school for local police officers. In 1939 President Roosevelt further increased FBI authority, giving the Bureau the power to investigate espionage and sabotage. This authority was subsequently affirmed in directives issued by President Truman.

After World War II information gathered by FBI agents played an important part in the prosecution of Julius and Ethel Rosenberg and Alger Hiss. The Bureau also became increasingly involved in the investigation of the American Communist Party. By the end of the 1950s investigation of Communist subversion was popularly viewed as one of the FBI's most important responsibilities. [See TRUMAN, EISENHOWER Volumes]

By the early 1960s Hoover headed a 13,000-man agency, which absorbed about 40% of the Justice Department's budget. Hoover maintained close relations with influential congressmen, including Speaker of the House John McCormack (D, Mass.) [*q.v.*] and Rep. John J. Rooney (D, N.Y.) [*q.v.*], chairman of the House Appropriations subcommittee that was responsible for approving Justice Department budgets.

Hoover was also long accustomed to dealing directly with the White House on major policy questions. However, in the Kennedy years he was obliged to communicate first with his nominal superior, Attorney General Robert F. Kennedy [*q.v.*], and the two often clashed. Hoover thought the Attorney General exaggerated the importance of organized crime, and the FBI Director was also reluctant to comply with Kennedy's order that the Bureau hire more minority group members. Despite these differences, Kennedy approved FBI requests to wiretap an Alabama Klan leader and black protest leaders Malcolm X [*q.v.*] and Martin Luther King [*q.v.*]. [See KENNEDY Volume]

Following the assassination of President Kennedy, the FBI conducted an extensive investigation and, in December 1963, issued a five-volume report that concluded that Lee Harvey Oswald, without accomplices, had murdered the President. In September 1964 the Warren Commission upheld this finding. The Commission suggested, however, that the assassination might have been prevented had the Bureau informed the Secret Service that the FBI file on Oswald indicated that he was a potential assassin. In 1975 a Senate inquiry into domestic intelligence activities disclosed that the FBI had received a letter from Oswald threatening to blow up the Dallas police station if its agents did not stop questioning his wife about Oswald's Cuban and Soviet contacts. The FBI had withheld his letter from the Warren Commission, and there was widespread speculation that Hoover had had the letter destroyed to protect the Bureau's reputation.

Robert Kennedy resigned as Attorney General in September 1964 and was succeeded by Nicholas Katzenbach [*q.v.*]. Hoover and Katzenbach clashed over a number of issues, particularly wiretapping. In 1966, after a bitter exchange between the two, Katzenbach determined that "he could no longer effectively serve as Attorney General because of Mr. Hoover's obvious resentment toward me." Katzenbach left the Department later that year to be replaced by Ramsey Clark [*q.v.*], whose relations with Hoover were also difficult. Clark organized "regional strike forces" to bring representatives from several federal law enforcement agencies together to fight organized crime in specific target cities. Hoover, mistrustful of other agencies, refused to permit his agents to participate because he did not wish them to be responsible to anyone outside the Bureau. Clark, in turn, attempted to restrict the FBI's use of wiretapping, and between 1966 and 1968 the number of taps authorized by the Attorney General declined from 107 to 43.

In July 1966 Hoover ordered an end to the Bureau's secret mail-opening program and its practice of illegal break-ins, so-called "black-bag jobs." Since 1948 Bureau agents, without warrants, had broken into homes and offices to photograph or seize documents necessary to aid on-going investigations. Several Attorney Generals knew of FBI break-ins to plant secret listening devices, but Hoover apparently did not inform any other high-ranking government official of these break-ins or mail openings. Why Hoover ordered an end to the mail-openings and black bag jobs in the summer of 1966 was never made clear. Hoover stated in June 1970 that mail-opening was "clearly illegal." At the same time, however, the Bureau continued to receive information from a Central Intelligence Agency (CIA) mail-opening program.

During the early 1960s the FBI came under attack for its failure to protect civil rights workers in the South. Rights leaders claimed that Hoover was a segregationist at heart who had little sympathy for their movement. In 1975 congressional testimony Katzenbach admitted that much of the voting rights work that should have been done by the FBI was performed instead by young civil rights lawyers. Hoover consistently maintained that the FBI was an investigative, not a peace-keeping organization which therefore could not assist the civil rights workers. In June 1964, however, three civil rights workers were slain in Meridian, Miss. In response to the public outcry, Hoover flew to Jackson, Miss., to open a new field office. Over 150 FBI agents began an investigation, and through the aid of an informer uncovered the bodies of the murder victims. The Bureau agents eventually arrested a deputy sheriff and a Klansman who were charged with violating the civil liberties of the slain workers.

In September 1964 Hoover sent a memorandum to 17 FBI field offices directing them "to expose, disrupt and otherwise neutralize" the activities of "white-hate" organizations, including the Ku Klux Klan, the Alabama States Rights Party, the American Nazi Party and several other groups. Efforts to "neutralize" these organizations were part of COINTELPRO, the program under which the FBI had earlier attempted to disrupt the activities of the American Communist Party and the Socialist Workers' Party. Both Katzenbach and Clark later denied knowing of COINTELPRO, which in the late 1960s was predominantly directed against civil rights, black power and New Left organizations.

Hoover believed that the activities of a number of civil rights leaders should also be investigated; no one troubled him more than Martin Luther King, who was particularly critical of the Bureau's failure to protect civil rights workers. According to Katzenbach, "there was no greater crime in Mr. Hoover's eyes than public criticism of the Bureau." Hoover also regarded King as a dangerous rabble-rouser and as an associate of Communists and subversives. Since the late 1950s the FBI had been investigating King and his Southern Christian Leadership Conference. In May 1962 the Bureau placed King in section "A" of its reserve index; this meant that in a national emergency King was to be rounded up and detained. In October 1963, with the approval of Attorney General Kennedy, the FBI began tapping King's home telephone. The tap remained until April 1965, when Katzenbach ordered it removed. However the Bureau continued to plant "bugs" to monitor King's conversations.

In November 1964 in a rare press conference for women reporters, Hoover called King "the most notorious liar in the country." Later that month, shortly before King was to receive the Nobel Peace Prize, the FBI sent the black leader a note suggesting that he commit suicide, and in an effort to break up King's marriage, the Bureau sent his wife tape-recorded evidence of her husband's alleged infidelity. On Dec. 1, 1964 King and Hoover met privately to settle their differences. Thereafter, King muted his criticism of the Bureau, which nevertheless continued to leak information about his personal life to the press.

Other civil rights leaders investigated by the FBI included Stokely Carmichael [*q.v.*], H. "Rap" Brown [*q.v.*] and the Rev. Elijah Muhammed [*q.v.*]. The Bureau also attempted to disrupt the Student Nonviolent Coordinating Committee, the Congress of Racial Equality and the Nation of Islam. In response to the 1967 wave of rioting in black ghettos across the country, the Bureau initiated a campaign against those who had allegedly stirred up the trouble. Agents were directed to compile a "rabble-rouser" (later known as the "agitator") index. When the Black Panther Party came to prominence in 1968, Hoover called the group the "greatest threat to the internal security of the country." FBI offices were instructed to develop programs to cripple the group, and a particular effort was made to increase dissension between the Panthers and their rivals.

FBI efforts to disrupt New Left organizations began in May 1968. The FBI had no exact definition of the New Left, but an April 1968 memorandum suggested that it had "strong Marxist, existentialist, nihilist and anarchist" overtones. The Bureau undertook to discredit New Left leaders by having them arrested on drug charges or by sending their parents or parents' employers anonymous letters about their activities. The Bureau also engaged the Internal Revenue Service to audit the tax returns of the more troublesome leaders.

While President, Lyndon Johnson requested a number of favors of the Bureau. In the summer of 1964 a team of agents was sent to the Democratic National Convention in Atlantic City, ostensibly to guard the President, but actually to gather intelligence on potential political opponents. In March 1966 the Bureau, on orders from the President, investigated congressmen whose criticisms of the Administration's Vietnam policy Johnson thought had been motivated by contacts with foreign agents. Johnson also believed that Mrs. Claire Chennault, a Washington socialite, and Republican vice presidential nominee Spiro Agnew [*q.v.*] were attempting to sabotage the Paris Peace talks. Johnson ordered an FBI investigation of Agnew and Chennault, but the Bureau could find no evidence to substantiate these charges.

In 1964 Johnson waived mandatory retirement for Hoover; President Nixon did likewise in 1971. During the Nixon Administration officials argued that the FBI was not sufficiently aggressive in its campaign against anti-war organizations, and they consequently encouraged the CIA to infiltrate and disrupt these groups.

Hoover's reputation declined in the last years of his life following revelations of widespread illegal activities carried out by the Bureau. He died on May 2, 1972. [See Nixon Volume]

[JLW]

For further information:
Jerry J. Berman and Morton H. Halperin, eds., *The Abuses of the Intelligence Agencies* (Washington, 1975).
Sanford J. Ungar, *FBI: An Uncensored Look Behind the Walls* (Boston, 1976).
U.S. Senate, Select Committee on Intelligence Activities, *Final Report* (Washington, 1976), Books II and III.

HOWE, HAROLD II

b. Aug. 17, 1918; Hartford, Conn.
U.S. Commissioner of Education, January 1966-January 1968.

Harold Howe grew up in Hartford, Conn., attended Taft prep school and graduated from Yale in 1940. After naval service in World War II Howe received a master's degree from Columbia University in 1947. During the 1950s he served as principal of high schools in Massachusetts and Ohio. In 1960 Howe was appointed superintendent of the Scarsdale, N.Y. school system, where his innovative methods impressed Parent-Teachers Association member John W. Gardner [*q.v.*], who was later to be appointed Lyndon Johnson's Secretary of Health, Education and Welfare (HEW). In 1964 Howe was named director of the Learning Institute of North Carolina, a private organization that dealt with education problems, especially those related to poverty and desegregation.

On the recommendations of both Gardner and outgoing Education Commissioner Francis Keppel [*q.v.*], President Johnson appointed Howe commissioner of education in December 1965. Howe took office in January 1966 at a time when the power and prestige of the Office of Education (OE) had grown as a result of the passage of Johnson Administration education bills.

During his tenure as commissioner, Howe's greatest efforts were concentrated in the area of desegregation. At a March 7, 1966 news conference, he set down strict guidelines for Southern school districts to follow in order to qualify for federal funds granted under the 1965 Elementary and Secondary School Act. His action was initiated to implement Title VI of the Civil Rights Act of 1964, which prohibited racial discrimination in any program or activity receiving federal assistance.

The March HEW guidelines required that between 15% and 20% of the Negro students in a school district attend desegregated schools; that school district officials mail "free choice" notices to all pupils, who could then decide which schools they wished to attend; and that a "significant start" be made in the integration of school faculties. Howe also indicated that the Office of Education planned greater emphasis on compliance reviews, field visits and investigations. He set May 6 as the deadline for compliance.

In April Alabama Gov. George Wallace [*q.v.*] declared that his state would not submit to the OE guidelines because they violated "the historic right of school boards to handle their own affairs and . . . the historic right of academic freedom." Howe reiterated that school districts failing to meet the May 6 desegregation deadline would be subject to "deferral of [federal] funds." On May 7, 1966 the OE announced that 255 Southern school districts had failed to file pledges of compliance with the guidelines, but that 1,489 districts in 17 Southern and border states had done so.

In a June speech at Columbia University, Howe expressed his displeasure with the slow pace of desegregation and accused U.S. educators of having a "blind faith in gradualism." He declared that schools remained almost as segregated as they had been in 1954, at the time of the Supreme Court's *Brown vs. Board of Education* decision, which outlawed "separate but equal" public education. Howe called upon school administrators to consider redrawing school district boundaries and confederating with neighborhood districts "even though political boundaries may remain unchanged." He insisted that educators must be willing to sacrifice their jobs for desegregation.

Howe's militant position on desegregation angered many Southern congressmen. At a September 1966 House Rules Committee hearing, Rep. L. Mendel Rivers (D, S.C.) [*q.v.*] denounced him as an "idiot" and a man who "talks like a Communist." There was also considerable friction within the Administration over Howe's position. In April 1966 HEW Secretary John Gardner attempted to soften opposition to the guidelines by assuring Southern governors, congressmen and school officials that HEW was not ordering a specific degree of "racial balance" or requiring "instantaneous desegregation" of school faculties. At an October press conference President Johnson acknowledged that there had been "some harassment and some mistakes" in civil rights enforcement.

On Oct. 19, 1966 Congress passed a bill amending the 1965 Elementary and Secondary Education Act. The law's civil rights provision restricted Howe's authority to defer funds to school districts not complying with Title VI of the 1964 Civil Rights Act. The OE was only permitted to hold funds to schools for up to 60 days pending a hearing and for another 30 days after the hearing. The expanded elementary education act mainly benefited schools in poorer states, providing them with an estimated $343 million for fiscal 1968.

In May 1967 Secretary Gardner announced that civil rights enforcement power within HEW would be transferred to the newly created Office for Civil Rights, headed by Gardner's special assistant, F. Peter Libassi. Gardner said that he had "complete confidence" in Howe and that "nothing in this change should be taken as a reflection on his standing within the Administration." However, many observers felt the move was an attempt to round up support of Southern Democrats for the 1967 school assistance bill. The measure, authorizing $9.2 billion for fiscal 1969-70, was signed into law on Jan. 2, 1968.

Shortly before his retirement as commissioner, Howe stated that progress in the integration of public schools had been "minimal." The U.S., he said, still faced a racially divided school system with "some 85% of Negro youngsters in the South still [attending] almost fully segregated schools." In a Jan. 9, 1968 interview with Norman C. Thomas, author of *Education in National Politics*, Howe described his role at the OE as "kind of a middle-level crossroads at the top of the bureaucracy." He acknowledged that during the 1960s "much policy development in education has moved from here [Office of Education] to the White House."

On Jan. 12, 1968 Howe resigned to join the Ford Foundation as a director of educational programs in India.

[FHM]

For further information:
Norman C. Thomas, *Education in National Politics* (New York, 1975).

HOWE, IRVING

b. June 11, 1920; New York, N.Y.
Literary critic; editor, *Dissent*.

Irving Howe, the son of immigrant parents from Eastern Europe, was born and raised in the Jewish slums of the East Bronx. He graduated from the City College of New York in 1940. During the 1940s and 1950s Howe emerged as a leading American literary and social critic. A prolific writer on a broad range of subjects, he was a frequent contributor to *Partisan Review* and other "little magazines." He wrote or coauthored 11 books over a 15-year period and edited 11 more. Among his works were *The U.A.W. and Walter Reuther* (1949), *William Faulkner: A Critical Study* (1952), *Politics and the Novel* (1957) and, with Lewis Coser, *The American Communist Party: A Critical History* (1957). At the same time Howe pursued an academic career as professor of English at Brandeis University from 1953 to 1961 and at Stanford University from 1961 to 1963. In 1963 he was appointed distinguished professor of English at Hunter College of the City University of New York.

As an adolescent during the Depression, Howe had been a Trotskyite. In the 1940s he was a member of the Workers Party (later called the Independent Socialist League), a small socialist group that combined revolutionary opposition to both capitalism and Communism under the difficult circumstances created by World War

II and the East-West polarization of the postwar era. By the early 1950s, however, Howe no longer regarded this position as tenable, and he left the organization, arguing for critical support of the West in the Cold War. In 1953 Howe and several other like-minded socialists founded *Dissent*, a journal "devoted to radical ideas and the values of socialism and democracy." During the 1950s *Dissent* defended the civil liberties of American Communists and criticized the celebration of American society by many formerly radical intellectuals.

In the 1960s Howe saw *Dissent* as the organ of an informal and loosely knit group of intellectual members of the "democratic left." As editor, Howe thought American social democrats could best influence national politics by working within the Democratic Party. During the early 1960s, when the civil rights movement was growing, Howe shared with many young radicals in the New Left the hope that the Democratic Party could be "realigned" on a more liberal basis through a "new politics" coalition of black, labor, liberal and church groups.

Political differences between the democratic left and its youthful allies soon emerged over two issues. The first involved what attitude the civil rights movement should take toward the Democratic Party. Howe favored continued work with the Party, and he opposed those in the Mississippi Freedom Democratic Party (MFDP) who rejected the compromise offered to them on their credentials challenge at the 1964 Democratic Convention. (The compromise, sponsored by Hubert Humphrey [*q.v.*] and Walter Reuther [*q.v.*], would have seated two members of the MFDP but left the segregationist regular Mississippi Democrats in possession of their Convention seats.) Howe criticized those in the Student Nonviolent Coordinating Committee and the Students for a Democratic Society who sought to organize a new political movement outside of and opposed to the Democratic Party. He described these radicals as "those who, in effect, want to 'go it alone' " with "a strategy of lonely assault, which must necessarily lead to shock tactics and desperation."

The gulf between Howe and the New Left was widened further by the explosive Vietnam issue. Critical of Washington's conduct of the war in the mid-1960s, Howe favored a bombing halt and a negotiated peace but supported maintenance of an American military presence in South Vietnam in order to prevent a massacre of anti-National Liberation Front elements. He thought much of the anti-war movement "apocalyptic," and he opposed its use of civil disobedience, violence and resistance to the draft. In an important 1965 article in *Dissent* entitled "New Styles in Leftism," Howe described adherents of the New Left as "desperadoes" and "kamikaze radicals" who subordinated ideology to personal style, gave explicit or covert support to Communist regimes in the Third World, and who rejected the "intellectual heritage of the West, the tradition of liberalism at its most serious, the commitment to democracy as an indispensable part of civilized life." After the Democratic National Convention in August 1968, Howe supported the presidential candidacy of Hubert Humphrey.

With the decline of the New Left after 1970, *Dissent* turned its attention to the emergence of what Howe called a "new conservatism" among those academic intellectuals associated with *Commentary* and the *Public Interest*. With other *Dissent* authors, Howe defended economic liberalism and social egalitarianism and called for a heavier commitment of the nation's wealth to traditional welfare and education programs. Howe supported the presidential candidacy of George McGovern (D, S.D.) [*q.v.*] in 1972 and was closely associated with the left-liberal Democratic Socialist Organizing Committee chaired by Michael Harrington [*q.v.*] in the mid-1970s. A prolific author, Howe published *World of Our Fathers* in 1976, a best-selling social history of the immigrant Jewish Community in New York. [See NIXON Volume]

[TLH]

For further information:

Irving Howe, *Steady Work; Essays in the Politics of Democratic Radicalism* (New York, 1966).

———, *Beyond the New Left* (New York, 1972).

HRUSKA, ROMAN L(EE)
b. Aug. 16, 1904; David City, Neb.
Republican Senator, Neb., 1954-77.

A former county official and U.S. representative, Hruska resigned his House seat in 1954 to fill a Senate vacancy created by the death of Hugh Butler. A representative of perhaps the most Republican state in the nation, Hruska was an opponent of most foreign aid proposals and of many domestic social welfare measures such as medicare, aid to education and the Johnson Administration's antipoverty program. He did, however, favor foreign military aid and supported efforts to continue the appropriation of funds for Radio Free Europe and Radio Liberty, stations that broadcast news to Communist bloc countries. In 1968 the conservative Americans for Constitutional Action gave him a 100% rating, while the liberal Americans for Democratic Action gave him a 7% score.

Hruska was a constant supporter of business and defender of "free enterprise." As a member of the Judiciary Committee's Antitrust and Monopoly Subcommittee, he scored the 1961 subcommittee report that found price-fixing policies in the drug industry. In 1964 the Senator objected to subcommittee hearings on the increased number of mergers in the U.S. A representative of an agricultural state whose economy was dependent on cattle raising and feed grain production, Hruska consistently backed price supports and measures to limit imported meat. [See KENNEDY Volume]

Hruska was a strong opponent of gun-control legislation and in the late 1960s made several successful attempts to weaken anti-gun measures. In conjunction with Sen. James Eastland (D, Miss.) [*q.v.*], he led a 1966 filibuster in the Judiciary Committee against Sen. Thomas Dodd's (D, Conn.) [*q.v.*] strong gun-control bill. The proposal would have prohibited interstate mail-order sales of pistols and other concealable weapons to individuals and tightened restrictions on sales of shotguns and rifles. In order to get some legislation to the Senate floor, Dodd was forced to accept Hruska's bill, which restricted only the mail-order sale of pistols and revolvers. The bill was reported out of committee in 1970 but died before being considered by Congress.

In 1968 Hruska successfully fought to delete from the omnibus crime control and safe streets bill a provision prohibiting the mail-order sale of rifles and shotguns. As an alternative measure he unsuccessfully offered a proposal that would have permitted the sale of hand guns but required the purchaser to file an affidavit stating that he was eligible to own a gun. The affidavit would have been sent to the police along with a description of the weapon but not its serial number. Hruska's proposal, supported by the National Rifle Association, was rejected by the Senate. Congress passed the Omnibus Crime Control Act in June 1968.

Hruska was a supporter of the Johnson Administration's Vietnam policy but opposed the use of American combat troops in either Laos or Thailand. In 1970 he gained notoriety during the hearings on the nomination of Federal District Judge G. Harrold Carswell to the Supreme Court when he remarked that mediocre people deserved representation on the high court. [See NIXON Volume]

[EWS]

HUGHES, HAROLD E(VERETT)
b. Feb. 10, 1922; Ida Grove, Iowa.
Governor, Iowa, 1962-68.

Born and raised in rural poverty, Hughes had a troubled early life, which included a seven-year struggle with alcoholism following his service in World War II. He became a trucking association executive in the mid-1950s and decided to run for a seat on the Iowa Commerce Commission in 1958 when that body failed to investigate his complaints about lax enforcement of the state's trucking laws. Hughes won the seat and remained a member of the Commission until his election as governor in 1962. As a Democrat in a traditionally conservative Republican state, his victory was a product of the gradual transition of Iowa from a rural to a semi-urban state with urban problems. Hughes tapped the latent Iowa majority that desired a more active state government.

As governor, Hughes instituted a number of important reforms: legalization of liquor by the glass, legislative reapportionment, government reorganization, tax reform for the elderly, utility regulation, penal reform, repeal of capital punishment, creation of a vocational-technical school system and industrial safety legislation. He also led an intensive industrial promotion effort, which included "Sell Iowa" trips to major U.S. cities and countries abroad.

In 1967 Hughes was criticized for his insensitivity to black issues. During the riots in the black neighborhoods of Waterloo, the Governor called in troops and walked the streets of the community in an attempt to quiet tensions. Shocked at the physical conditions and spiritual bitterness he found there, he admitted his previous lack of concern and began a program to alleviate these conditions. Hughes expanded the state Civil Rights Commission and supported a state open-housing law. In addition, he convinced Iowa's business and religious leaders to establish a civic task force and employment programs and to raise several hundred thousand dollars to implement them.

During the early years of American involvement in Vietnam, Hughes was a backer of Johnson's policy and in 1965 organized a governors' tour of Vietnam to build support for the President. However, by 1966 he was beginning to have doubts about American foreign policy. These misgivings prompted him to support Sen. Robert F. Kennedy (D, N.Y.) [*q.v.*] as a presidential candidate in 1968. When Kennedy was assassinated the Governor backed anti-war candidate Sen. Eugene McCarthy (D, Minn.) [*q.v.*] and nominated him at the Democratic National Convention in Chicago. During the same period Hughes worked for reforms in the selection of Convention delegates.

Because Hughes spent so much of his time campaigning for McCarthy, he did not devote close attention to his own campaign for the U.S. Senate and won by fewer than 7,000 votes. His narrow victory was attributed not only to his work for McCarthy, but also to the accumulated antagonism caused by his raising taxes and increasing the state budget by 150%. In addition, Hughes insisted on running his campaign on two unpopular issues—his opposition to the Vietnam War and civil rights.

In the Senate Hughes concerned himself primarily with Vietnam and the problem of alcohol and drug abuse. He often discussed his own difficulties with alcohol and privately attempted to aid Congressmen who had similar problems. Hughes continued to work for Party reform and in 1972 was mentioned as a dark-horse candidate for the Democratic presidential nomination. He retired from the Senate in 1975 to devote his time to religious work. [See NIXON Volume]

[EWS]

HUGHES, HOWARD R(OBARD)

b. Dec. 24, 1905; Houston, Tex.
d. April 5, 1976; Aboard an Acapulco-Houston flight.

With an estimated income of $2 million per year inherited from his father's oil-well drilling equipment business, Howard Hughes turned to filmmaking in the 1920s and 1930s. In 1937 he purchased Trans World Airlines (TWA), which he developed into the first intercontinental air carrier. In 1952 Hughes assumed a reclusive, mysterious and rumor-filled existence, traveling frequently throughout the world. [See TRUMAN, EISENHOWER, KENNEDY Volume]

During the 1960s Hughes was involved in antitrust lawsuits and countersuits concerning his absentee directorship of TWA. As a result of poor management and rigid contractual obligations, TWA was controlled during the early 1960s by several prominent financial lending institutions and an independently minded board of directors. Although Hughes still owned 78% of TWA stock, his position was weakened to the extent that in May 1966 he abruptly and without public explanation sold his shares for $546.5 million in the second-largest stock transaction in U.S. history.

After the TWA fiasco Hughes began buying large amounts of land and property in Nevada. He purchased the Desert Inn complex in Las Vegas, part of which he used as a fortress-like headquarters for his business operations. He also acquired the Sands Hotel, the Frontier Hotel, Las Vegas television station KLAS-TV, Alamo Airways and numerous properties in and around the city. In 1968 Hughes tried to buy another gambling house, but when the Justice Department made preliminary investigations into possible antitrust violations, Hughes withdrew his bid.

The ease with which Hughes made his Nevada purchases, including acquisition of gambling and broadcast licenses, raised questions concerning his role in Nevada politics and business affairs. Leading politicians in the state made an effort to accommodate him. Republican Gov. Paul Laxalt called Hughes in 1968, "the greatest thing that has happened to Nevada since the Comstock Lode."

Rumors about Hughes circulated constantly to the effect that he was involved with organized crime or that he was dead and his name was being kept alive by the Hughes company. The Hughes empire in Nevada was run through an ex-FBI agent, Robert Maheu, who had never actually met Hughes. In 1973 Maheu linked Charles G. Rebozo, a close friend of President Nixon's [*q.v.*], to a $100,000 political contribution made by Hughes in 1969 and 1970. Rebozo did not turn over the money to the Republican campaign committee but, according to Rebozo, kept it in a safe deposit box and later returned it to Hughes. A 1975 Senate committee implicated Maheu in an alleged 1961 CIA plot to assassinate Cuban leader Fidel Castro.

Hughes became involved in a bitter controversy in 1968 when the Atomic Energy Commission (AEC) conducted a series of underground nuclear tests at its Nevada test site. Because of his extensive landholdings in the Southwest, Hughes appealed to the AEC on April 21 to postpone the tests, ostensibly so his own experts could conduct an "independent study" of the possible consequences. The AEC refused the request and subsequently denied a Hughes organization statement that a nuclear device detonated on Jan. 19, 1968 had triggered an earthquake near Salt Lake City, 200 miles northeast of the test site.

In May 1968 *Fortune* magazine estimated Hughes's fortune at one to one and one-half billion dollars, making him, with J. Paul Getty, one of the two wealthiest Americans. By 1970 his Nevada land-holdings alone were worth $250 million.

In 1972 Hughes was the victim of a well-publicized hoax involving publication of a fake biography based on supposedly exclusive interviews with Hughes himself. His extensive political influence was highlighted during the 1973 Senate Watergate hearings when James McCord, convicted as a participant in the Watergate conspiracy, revealed a 1972 scheme to burglarize the offices of Las Vegan *Sun* owner Hank Greenspun to obtain damaging information about an unnamed presidential candidate. The plot involved escape to Central America by the burglary team in a private plane bwned by Howard Hughes. Greenspun stated that the attempted burglary's real purpose was to obtain hundreds of memoranda pertaining to Hughes's antitrust problems with the Justice Department over his extensive landholdings in the Southwest. After years of poor health, Hughes died on a flight from Mexico to Houston in April 1976. [See NIXON Volume]

[FHM]

For further information:

Albert B. Gerber, *Bashful Billionaire* (New York, 1967).

John Keats, *Howard Hughes* (New York, 1966).

HUGHES, RICHARD J(OSEPH)
b. Aug. 10, 1909; Florence, N.J.
Governor, N.J., 1962-70.

The son of a New Jersey Democratic politician, Hughes received his law degree in 1931 and began working for the Democratic Party in strongly Republican Mercer County. After losing a congressional election in 1938, Hughes was appointed assistant U.S. attorney for New Jersey in 1939. He was appointed to a county judgeship in 1948 and promoted to the appellate division of New Jersey's Superior Court in 1957. Financial and family responsibilities forced him to resign and resume his law practice the same year. In February 1961 a conference of state Democratic Party leaders chose Hughes as the Party's gubernatorial candidate. According to Neal Peirce, author of *The Megastates*, Hughes emerged as New Jersey's greatest campaigner in modern times. A large urban turnout enabled him to upset former Secretary of Labor James P. Mitchell in the 1961 New Jersey gubernatorial race.

Hughes's 1965 reelection campaign received national attention when his GOP opponent, Wayne Dumont, demanded that Rutgers history professor Eugene Genovese [*q.v.*] be fired for stating at an April 23 teach-in, "I do not fear or regret the impending Viet Cong victory in Vietnam, I welcome it." Investigations by the University Board of Examiners and a special State Assembly committee revealed that Genovese had broken no state or University regulations. Hughes, although describing Genovese's view as "outrageous," declared that he was "determined to preserve academic freedom in the broadest sense." Campaigning for Hughes in October, Sen. Robert Kennedy (D, N.Y.) [*q.v.*] maintained that the dismissal of Genovese "would sound the death knell of higher education in the state." On election day Hughes defeated Dumont by an unprecedented 350,000-vote plurality; for the first time since 1911, the Democrats also gained control of the state Senate.

One issue that occupied Hughes during both of his terms as governor was the state's apportionment system, which dated back to 1776. In November 1964 the New Jersey Supreme Court ordered reapportionment of the state legislature on a "one-man, one-vote" basis. After a prolonged conflict with the legislature over formulation of the reapportionment plan, Hughes accepted a proposal for the calling of a state constitutional convention in March 1965. The convention eventually agreed on a formula that enlarged both houses of the state legislature and redrew New Jersey's 15 congressional districts. The reapportionment measure was enacted by Hughes in June 1966. In the elections of November 1967, Democrats lost their recently won majorities in the enlarged state House and Senate, severely restricting Hughes's freedom of action during the remainder of his second term.

Another problem that Hughes faced during the mid-1960s was reform of the state's tax structure. When Hughes first assumed office in 1962, New Jersey was the seventh wealthiest state in the U.S. but one of the last in per capita state revenue. In 1966 Hughes proposed a state income tax. Opposition from the powerful Essex and Hudson County Democratic organizations left the Governor one vote short of a legislative majority, and in April Hughes agreed with the state Assembly to a substitute 3% sales tax.

Hughes took an active and controversial role in the racial violence that affected many New Jersey towns in July 1967. After Newark Mayor Hugh Addonizio [*q.v.*] phoned Hughes on July 14 requesting state police and National Guard units, Hughes personally went into the city with the troops. Touring the affected areas he called the disturbances "criminal insurrection" and expressed shock at the "holiday atmosphere" among the rioters. On July 15 Hughes discussed the underlying problems of Newark's black community with a group of black leaders. He also met with a second group of community leaders, who presented evidence of brutality by Guardsmen and state police. Hughes and Addonizio were criticized for "inflammatory statements" that allegedly led to the formation of white vigilante groups. On July 16 Hughes contended that brutality charges were based on "hearsay" and "mostly second-hand information" but promised that "justice will be done" when the facts were made clear. Declaring on July 17 that "the restoration of order is accomplished," Hughes ordered the withdrawal of most of the Guardsmen.

Eight other New Jersey communities experienced racial violence during July 1967. The most serious incidents occurred in Plainfield, where a white patrolman was shot with his own gun and beaten to death by about 30 people on July 16. The same day 46 semiautomatic rifles and ammunition were stolen from the Plainfield Machine Co. After Hughes proclaimed "a state of disaster and emergency," 300 heavily armed National Guardsmen and state troopers conducted a house-to-house search for the weapons in selected black sections on July 19. Many blacks whose homes were searched complained of extensive property damage, and on July 21 the state's American Civil Liberties Union director denounced the action. On July 25 Hughes appointed an eight-member, cabinet-level interdepartmental panel to develop programs to ease the state's urban problems. Hughes chaired a special panel of the 1967 President's Commission on Civil Disorders which investigated the difficulties suffered by residents and businessmen in riot-prone areas who sought to obtain property and liability insurance. On Jan. 27, 1968 the group issued a report recommending that tax concessions be included in a program to ease the slum insurance crisis.

Hughes strongly supported the Johnson Administration's foreign policy. At the 1966 National Governors Conference he amended the general resolution of support for the nation's global commitments to include a specific reference to Vietnam. In September 1967 Hughes observed the South Vietnamese elections and returned to announce that he had found no evidence of fraud or wrongdoing. That same year, in June, Hughes helped in the selection of Glassboro, N.J., as the location of the first meeting between President Johnson and Soviet Premier Alexei Kosygin.

At the 1968 Democratic National Convention Hughes chaired the Credentials Committee, which was forced to resolve challenges to the seating of 15 delegations. Most of these were settled at Committee meetings, but four, involving Texas, Georgia, Alabama and North Carolina, went before the Convention. The most dramatic controversy arose over the Georgia delegation, where the liberal slate led by Julian Bond [*q.v.*] challenged the seating of the regular delegation headed by Gov. Lester Maddox [*q.v.*]. In an attempt to settle the dispute, Hughes suggested seating both delegations and splitting the state's vote. However, neither side would agree to the compromise and the Convention voted to seat the regular delegation. Hughes's committee also recommended that the entire delegate selection process be reexamined and restructured.

In *The Making of the President 1968*, Theodore White wrote that Hughes was one of the three leading contenders for the second spot on Hubert Humphrey's [*q.v.*] ticket. At the insistence of Southern delegations, who were angry at the Credentials Committee's rulings, Hughes was dropped from consideration. Returning to New Jersey as a "lame duck" governor, Hughes supported former Gov. Robert Meyner's unsuccessful comeback attempt in 1969. He returned to private law practice in 1970. In November 1973 Hughes was named chief justice of the New Jersey Supreme Court.

[DKR]

HUMPHREY, HUBERT H(ORATIO)

b. May 27, 1911; Wallace S.D.
Democratic Senator, Minn., 1949-64, 1971- ; Vice President of the United States, 1965-69.

The son of a South Dakota druggist, Humphrey was profoundly influenced by his Democratic father's reverence for William Jennings Bryan and Woodrow Wilson. He was a star debater and class valedictorian in high school but had to leave the University of Minnesota early in the Depression to help out in his father's drugstore. He became a registered pharmacist and managed the store, while his father participated actively in South Dakota politics. Humphrey returned to the University of Minnesota in 1937, earned his B.A. in 1939 and an M.A. in political science from Louisiana State University a year later. His master's thesis, entitled "The Political Philosophy of the New Deal," was a glowing tribute to Franklin D. Roosevelt's response to the Depression.

Humphrey abandoned his teaching career to plunge into Minnesota politics. He played a key role in the 1944 merger of the Farmer-Labor and Democratic Parties and won election as mayor of Minneapolis the next year. As mayor he waged an anti-vice campaign, created the first municipal fair employment practices commission in the United States, expanded the city's housing program and took an active part in settling strikes. Reelected in 1947, Humphrey helped organize the liberal, anti-Communist Americans for Democratic Action (ADA) and fought a successful battle to purge the Communist faction from the Democratic-Farmer-Labor Party. He gained national attention at the 1948 Democratic National Convention with a stirring oration in favor of a strong civil rights plank, one of the most memorable convention speeches of modern times. In November 1948 Minnesota voters elected Humphrey to the Senate over the conservative Republican incumbent.

Humphrey quickly moved into the vanguard of the Senate's liberal minority, promoting a wide variety of social welfare, civil rights, tax reform and pro-labor legislation. The first bill he introduced was a proposal to establish a medical care program for the aged, which was finally enacted as medicare in 1965. The Senate's powerful conservatives, however, disapproved of Humphrey's aggressive debating style and effusive liberalism, and their hostility reduced his effectiveness.

Gradually he eased his way into the Senate "establishment," toning down his fervid ideological approach and working closely with the Democratic leader, Sen. Lyndon Johnson, who used Humphrey as his liaison with liberals and intellectuals. Humphrey, moreover, was as anti-Communist as many conservatives. He introduced the Communist Control Act of 1954, which outlawed the Communist Party. In foreign affairs he softened his anti-Communism with Wilsonian idealism. He became a leading advocate of disarmament and the distribution of surplus food to needy nations.

Humphrey's first run for the presidency began in January 1959 and ended in May 1960 with his defeat in the West Virginia primary by Sen. John F. Kennedy. Humphrey reached the peak of his legislative influence during the Kennedy Administration. As assistant majority leader, or majority whip, he became the Administration's most aggressive ally in the Senate, working tirelessly to win passage of Kennedy programs. In the process he helped to enact several measures, such as the Peace Corps and the nuclear test ban treaty, that he himself had long promoted. [See TRUMAN, EISENHOWER, KENNEDY Volumes]

In the aftermath of President Kennedy's assassination, Humphrey helped smooth the transition to the Johnson Administration by advising the new President and serving again as his link to liberals and intellectuals, many of whom viewed Johnson with apprehension. In his last year as majority whip he labored energetically to pass the Kennedy-Johnson $11.5 billion tax cut in February 1964, an economic stimulus he had called for in 1962. Humphrey was the floor manager of the landmark Civil Rights Act of 1964, the fruition of his career-long advocacy of the cause of equal rights. He orchestrated the pro-civil rights senators, maintained flagging morale throughout the frustrating struggle, persistently cultivated Senate Minority Leader Everett M. Dirksen (R, Ill.) [*q.v.*] and engineered the compromise with the Republican leader that finally broke the 57-day Southern filibuster on June 10.

At the Democratic National Convention in August, Humphrey was at the center of another civil rights imbroglio: the battle between the all-white regular Mississippi delegation and the insurgent Mississippi Freedom Democratic Party (MFDP) over which group should represent the state's Democrats at the Convention. Humphrey arranged a compromise that allowed the MFDP two votes as a special at-large delegation. Neither of the Mississippi parties accepted the plan, but it accomplished its primary purpose, which was to head off a mass Southern walk-out or an embarrassing floor fight. Chosen by Johnson as his vice presidential running mate, Humphrey was elected in November in a Democratic landslide.

Humphrey's accession to the vice presidency marked the end of an extraordinarily prolific 15 years in the Senate, during which he had introduced nearly 1,500 bills and resolutions. In his new post he spoke to a wider audience but with diminished authority, despite the numerous outlets

President Johnson gave him for his kinetic energies. He was made chairman of the President's Council on Economic Opportunity, the Peace Corps Advisory Council, the National Aeronautics and Space Council and the President's Council on Youth Fitness. In addition, Humphrey performed his constitutional duty to preside over the Senate and was Johnson's representative at a multitude of ceremonial functions.

Nevertheless, Humphrey's primary role was to sell Administration policy to Congress and the public. Through his familiar ebullient lobbying and exhortation, he had a hand in the passage of much of the social legislation he had been identified with for years: medicare, voting rights, aid to education, housing and rent supplements and Model Cities. But his most controversial cause by far was his defense of Johnson's Vietnam policy.

At the beginning of his vice presidential tenure, he earned the President's displeasure by arguing within the National Security Council (NSC) against a hard-line policy in Vietnam. The issue before the NSC in February 1965 was what form of retaliation the U.S. should take for the Communist attack on the U.S. compound at Pleiku. In the heated discussions Humphrey was in the "dove" minority, arguing in particular against an air strike while Soviet Premier Kosygin was in Hanoi and questioning the effectiveness of trying to bomb North Vietnam to the negotiating table.

A few days later Humphrey, in a private memorandum to Johnson, outlined his doubts about the Administration's Vietnam policy. Maintaining that escalation and a military solution were the "Goldwater position" and that the public would not understand why grave risks were justified to support the "chronic instability in Saigon," he urged the President to "cut losses" and apply his famous political talents to attain a Vietnam settlement. Moreover, Humphrey said, escalation would jeopardize other policies to which the Administration had committed itself: "United Nations, arms control and socially humane and constructive policies generally."

Angered by Humphrey's dissent at the NSC meeting and alarmed at the Vice President's commitment of dovish sentiments to paper, Johnson excluded Humphrey from the foreign policy decision making councils of his Administration for a year. Humphrey returned to prominence in the foreign policy area in February 1966, when Johnson sent him on a 14-day journey to nine Asian nations, including South Vietnam. The trip was a vital turning point for Humphrey, marking the renewal of Johnson's confidence in him as foreign policy spokesman and roving ambassador. In his autobiography Humphrey said his meetings with military personnel and Asian leaders "did more than anything else to confirm—against my earlier doubts—what I suppose I now wanted to confirm: that our excursion into Vietnam, bloody and expensive as it was, was indeed a responsible thing to do in defense of the freedom of millions of people in Asia."

Beginning with his Asian trip Humphrey outdid other Administration officials in his enthusiasm for and optimism about the Vietnam war. "We are the revolutionaries not the Communists," he declared. "We are the liberators not the Communists. We are the agents of reform, not the Communists." Upon his return Humphrey said that "the tide of battle in Vietnam has turned in our favor." Humphrey also assailed critics of the war, a task he frequently assumed over the next three years. He denounced a proposal by Sen. Robert F. Kennedy (D, N.Y.) [*q.v.*] to include the National Liberation Front in a future coalition government, comparing the idea to "putting a fox in a chicken coop." The zest with which Humphrey now defended the war and attacked its critics did much to alienate many of his former allies among liberals and intellectuals.

The issue of the war haunted Humphrey during his 1968 presidential campaign. The strong showing of anti-war candidate Sen. Eugene McCarthy (D, Minn.) [*q.v.*] in the New Hampshire primary revealed the extent of the divisions over Vietnam within the Democratic Party. President Johnson's withdrawal from the race later in the month left Humphrey as the candidate of the Party center, while the assassination of Sen. Robert Kennedy in June left McCarthy with the allegiance of most of the Party's anti-war wing by the time of the Chicago Convention in August.

Backed by organized labor and Party regulars, Humphrey won the nomination in August with 1,760 delegate votes. McCarthy polled 601 and Sen. George McGovern (D, S.D.) [*q.v.*], 146. But the circumstances of his selection made it a Pyrrhic victory. The Convention was a tumultuous affair, punctuated by bitter floor fights over delegates' credentials and the content of the Vietnam plank in the platform. A majority voted to endorse Johnson's policies, but heavy-handed security by Chicago Mayor Richard Daley's [*q.v.*] personnel within the hall and clashes between police and young anti-war protestors outside intensified the emotional rifts within the Party and associated the Democrats with violence and chaos in the eyes of the public. McCarthy's refusal to endorse Humphrey until the last week in the campaign symbolized the divided condition in which the Party confronted the Republicans.

According to public opinion polls taken in September, Humphrey was far behind Republican candidate Richard Nixon [*q.v.*] and appeared headed for a crushing defeat. (A Gallup poll taken between Sept. 20 and 22 indicated that 43% of the voters favored Nixon, 28% backed Humphrey and 21% chose Alabama Gov. George C. Wallace [*q.v.*].) Plagued by constant heckling, a disorganized campaign and his identification with an unpopular war, Humphrey struggled along with little progress until he delivered a Salt Lake City speech on Sept. 30, in which he pledged to stop the bombing of North Vietnam and institute a ceasefire if elected. This moderate departure from Administration policy gave the campaign its first push forward. Humphrey took the offensive, campaigning indefatigably and attacking Nixon vigorously. Despite a massive voter registration drive on his behalf by organized labor, his effort fell short by an extremely narrow margin on election day. Nixon won with 43.4% of the popular vote compared to 42.7% for Humphrey and 13.5% for Wallace; Nixon had 301 electoral votes to Humphrey's 191 and Wallace's 46.

After teaching at the University of Minnesota and Macalester College, Humphrey returned to the Senate in 1971. He made his third unsuccessful run for the presidency in 1972, losing the nomination to Sen. McGovern. [See NIXON Volume]

[TO]

For further information:

Albert Eisele, *Almost to the Presidency: A Biography of Two American Politicians* (Blue Earth, Minn., 1972).

Hubert H. Humphrey, *The Education of a Public Man: My Life and Politics* (New York, 1976).

Robert Sherrill and Harry Ernst, *The Drugstore Liberal* (New York, 1968).

INNIS, ROY

b. June 6, 1934; St. Croix, Virgin Islands.
National Director, Congress of Racial Equality, 1968- .

Innis, the son of a policeman, spent his childhood in the Virgin Islands. He moved to New York as an adolescent and attended City College after serving in the Army. In 1963, while working as a chemistry research assistant in a New York hospital, Innis joined the Harlem chapter of the Congress of Racial Equality (CORE), a militant civil rights organization. He soon became an important leader of Harlem CORE, rising in October 1965 to chapter chairman. In July 1967 Innis was elected second vice chairman of national CORE. He became the organization's acting national director one year later, after the previous director, Floyd McKissick [*q.v.*], resigned for health reasons. The national CORE convention in September 1968 confirmed Innis as head of the organization.

Innis's rise in CORE resulted largely from his position as a leading advocate of black power, which he embraced as a result of his impatience over the progress of civil rights during the early 1960s. Innis's conception of black power stressed preservation of a distinct black culture and greater reliance on black resources in the struggle for equality. In 1966 he and other Harlem CORE members concluded that the fight for integration of New York City schools was a failure and decided to press for community control over neighborhood schools. At this time Innis proposed an amendment to the New York State constitution providing independent school boards for ghetto areas. This was the first significant instance when integration was replaced by black separation as a civil rights goal. Innis had earlier formed a "black male caucus" as the chief policymaking body of the Harlem CORE, causing white members to leave the chapter. At the CORE national convention of 1966, he fought successfully for a resolution defining the organization's goal as "racial coexistence through black power."

By 1968 Innis, who was originally regarded as a CORE extremist, belonged to the organization's moderate wing. Radicals such as Brooklyn CORE chairman Robert Carson viewed the destruction of American capitalism as a necessary part of black liberation and demanded that CORE reject funds from foundations and other "establishment" sources. Innis countered these arguments with proposals for a program of "black capitalism," translating his separatist philosophy into economic activity. Government and foundation money, he argued, should be used to finance black-controlled businesses in ghetto areas. In 1967 Innis succeeded in attracting federal funds to the Harlem Commonwealth Council, which encouraged the growth of small industries in Harlem and sought to employ jobless workers. CORE also urged Congress to pass a community self-determination act to attract private capital into the ghettos through tax incentives and matching federal funds. In general, however, the level of outside help for black enterprise remained far below the expectations of CORE.

Innis's rise to the CORE leadership in 1968 was a victory not only for political moderates but also for those who wanted to give the 180,000-member organization a tighter, more centralized structure. The 1968 CORE convention, which confirmed Innis as national director, also voted measures to give the organization's central office greater control over local chapters. A yearly assessment of $100 per chapter was levied for the central treasury. This gave Innis greater influence but also provoked the secession of many chapter heads and organizers who disagreed with his policies. The organization was further reduced in size by a new provision that barred whites from active membership.

Despite these organizational reforms, CORE lost influence within the civil rights movement during the late 1960s. Black power, with its emphasis on self-help, focused attention on smaller groups—community organizations, black student groups, black caucuses in churches and professional societies. CORE's local chapters, reduced to appendages of the central office, developed little significant activity of their own. Innis himself remained active in community affairs, especially in Harlem. He won national attention in 1973 by debating physicist William Shockley on the allegation that blacks are genetically inferior to whites in intelligence.

[SLG]

For further information see:

August Meier and Elliot Rudwick, *CORE: A Study in the Civil Rights Movement* (New York, 1973).

INOUYE, DANIEL K(EN)

b. Sept. 7, 1924; Honolulu, Hawaii.
Democratic Senator, Hawaii, 1963- .

Upon graduation from high school in 1942, Inouye enlisted in the Japanese-American 442d Infantry Regiment, which became famous in World War II for its heroism and high casualty rate. Inouye, who lost his right arm in combat in Italy, rose to the rank of captain by the time of his discharge in 1947.

After studies at the University of Hawaii and George Washington University Law School, he practiced law in Honolulu. Between 1954 and 1958 he won elections to both the territorial House of Representatives and Senate. During this time he helped John Burns [*q.v.*] build the Democratic Party into the territory's dominant political machine. When Hawaii became a state in 1959, Inouye stepped aside to allow one of Hawaii's "elder statesmen," Oren Long, to seek a U.S. Senate seat. Winning election to the U.S. House of Representatives instead, Inouye inherited the Senate post in 1962 when Long announced his retirement. As in most of his campaigns, the November 1962 contest against a Republican opponent resulted in a lopsided victory for Inouye.

Inouye's voting record received high marks from the liberal Americans for Democratic Action. He solidly supported civil rights, poverty and medicare legislation, but he occasionally voted against bills considered to be in the interests of organized labor. This reflected his friendly relations with Hawaii's sugar and pineapple growers and his differences with the powerful International Longshoremen's and Warehousemen's Union (ILWU). Although the ILWU was one of the major components of Democratic power in Hawaii, Inouye, whose tremendous popularity made him less dependent than other Democrats on ILWU support for reelection, constantly tried to prevent the union from dominating the Party. He also sought a relaxation and redefinition of antitrust laws, arguing that only monopolistic corporations could compete with other nations.

A loyal Democrat concerned with maintaining Party unity, Inouye generally supported President Johnson's Vietnam policies and delivered the keynote address at the 1968 Democratic National Convention. That November he won reelection to the Senate with 88% of the total vote. Under the new Republican administration, Inouye became more critical of the Vietnam war, and in 1970 he voted for the Cooper-Church Amendment. He came to national prominence as a member of the Senate Watergate Committee in the summer of 1973. [See NIXON Volume]

[JCH]

JACKSON, HENRY M(ARTIN)

b. May 31, 1912; Everett, Wash.
Democratic Senator, Wash., 1953- ; Chairman, Interior and Insular Affairs Committee, 1963- .

Jackson was elected to the U.S. House of Representatives in 1940, and as a member of that body he had one of the most liberal voting records in Congress. He won a seat in the U.S. Senate in 1952 by defeating the Republican incumbent. In the upper house Jackson continued to support liberal domestic legislation, but his major interest turned to military and foreign policy matters. He became best known for his vociferous insistence, as a member of the Armed Services Committee, upon the maintenance of American military superiority over the Soviet Union. Some political observers attributed Jackson's interest in military affairs and support of large defense expenditures to the presence of major defense industries in his state, the Boeing Corporation being the most prominent. [See EISENHOWER Volume]

Jackson expressed reservations concerning some of the Kennedy Administration's efforts to control the arms race with the Soviet Union. In 1961 he opposed the bill creating the Arms Control and Disarmament Agency and two years later had doubts about the nuclear test ban treaty, although he ultimately backed it. Jackson criticized the Pentagon's November 1962 decision to award General Dynamics, rather than Boeing, the contract to build the swing-wing TFX fighter/bomber, and he initiated a 1963 Senate investigation of the matter. [See KENNEDY Volume]

Jackson succeeded Sen. Clinton P. Anderson (D, N.M.) [*q.v.*] as chairman of the Interior and Insular Affairs Committee in 1963, and in that post he was able to increase his influence in the Senate. The panel had jurisdiction over bills pertaining to federal power projects, the use of public land, land reclamation, mining and other matters closely related to economic growth. As chairman of the Committee, Jackson was able to promote the rapidly expanding economy of his home state. Furthermore, the chairmanship enabled him to start or stop major resource development projects in every other state, and he used this power to win support in the Senate for his positions on bills beyond the purview of the Committee.

The Interior Committee was also responsible for introducing conservation bills, and Jackson won generally favorable comments from groups interested in promoting such measures. In 1964 he spearheaded congressional passage of the Wilderness Act, which limited entrepreneurial activity in wilderness areas. Three years later he began work on a bill to establish federal guidelines for protecting the quality of the environment, a measure that was passed as the National Environmental Policy Act in 1969.

Although Jackson criticized Johnson Administration officials who predicted imminent victory in the Vietnam war, charging that they were creating false hopes that might ultimately cause disillusionment, he was one of the most enthusiastic supporters of the President's Southeast Asia policies. In 1965 he asserted that the war represented one episode in the long post-World War II struggle against world Communism and that appeasement in Vietnam would lead to other setbacks for the West. Beginning in 1966 he stressed his belief that Communist China was America's major enemy in Vietnam and that the war was part of China's effort to dominate all of Asia. Initially confident of America's ability to win a military victory in Southeast Asia, he subsequently placed much of the blame for Vietnam reverses upon the domestic peace movement.

By 1968 Jackson's position on the war had created a wide gulf between himself and many other liberals. Highly critical of the anti-war candidacies of Sens. Robert F. Kennedy (D, N.Y.) [*q.v.*] and Eugene J. McCarthy (D, Minn.) [*q.v.*], he supported Vice President Hubert H. Humphrey's [*q.v.*] bid for the Democratic presidential nomination in 1968 and coordinated Humphrey's effort to win convention delegates in the state of Washington.

In December 1968 Jackson declined President-elect Richard M. Nixon's [*q.v.*] offer to appoint him Secretary of Defense. He backed the Nixon Administration's Southeast Asia policies and voted for construction of the Safeguard Antiballistic Missile System in 1969 and the supersonic jet transport, a Boeing project, in 1970. He also identified himself with support of Israel and the rights of Soviet Jews. In 1972 Jackson competed in the race for the Democratic presidential nomination but was eliminated after the first few primaries. He gave only nominal endorsement to the Party's ultimate choice, Sen. George S. McGovern (D, S.D.) [*q.v.*], an opponent of the Vietnam war. Four years later Jackson again entered the contest for the Democratic presidential nomination but dropped out of the race. [See NIXON Volume]

[MLL]

JACKSON, JESSE L(OUIS)

b. Oct. 8, 1941; Greenville, N.C.
National Director, Operation Breadbasket, 1966-71.

The son of a maid, Jackson grew up in the poverty of a small, semi-rural Southern black community. He attended a segregated high school in Greenville and graduated from the predominantly black Agricultural and Technical College of North Carolina at Greensboro in 1964. Jackson became active in civil rights as president of the college student body and led a campaign of sit-ins in Greensboro to desegregate public facilities in 1963. While participating in the Selma voter registration drive of 1965, he came into contact with the Southern Christian Leadership Conference (SCLC) and its leader, Martin Luther King [*q.v.*]. Jackson later described King as "my father figure, my brother figure and my teacher."

After the Selma campaign Jackson enrolled in the Chicago Theological Seminary, where he was ordained in 1968. While studying in Chicago he worked as an organizer for the SCLC, helping to increase cooperation among local civil rights and community groups. When King decided to open a civil rights drive in Chicago in early 1966, he chose Jackson to supervise the campaign's economic activities. These soon developed into Operation Breadbasket, an effort to improve the economic position of blacks through the coordinated use of black purchasing power. Working through a network of community and church groups, Jackson urged Chicago blacks to buy the products of black-owned companies and to boycott stores that refused to carry these products or practiced racial discrimination in hiring. Within five months nine Chicago companies had signed agreements promising to increase the number of black employees.

The early success of Operation Breadbasket encouraged King and Jackson to extend the program beyond Chicago. In late 1966 Jackson became the head of national Operation Breadbasket, which covered 16 cities. The program's greatest achievement came in 1968, when a 14-week black boycott of the A&P food chain forced the company to sign an agreement providing for increased hiring of blacks and the display of black-manufactured products in its stores. The pact also promised that A&P stores in black neighborhoods would use the services of black truckers, advertisers and other small businessmen.

In April 1968 Jackson was standing next to King in a Memphis motel when King was assassinated. Jackson continued to work for the SCLC after King's death. In May he went to Washington to help organize the Poor People's Campaign, a series of demonstrations and lobbying efforts aimed at increasing federal antipoverty funds. In 1969 Jackson organized a highly successful Black Expo in Chicago, which publicized achievements in business and culture. The interest generated encouraged him to make Black Expo an annual event. Conflicts eventually developed, however, between Jackson and Ralph Abernathy [*q.v.*], King's successor as SCLC leader. Jackson wanted more authority in the SCLC than Abernathy was willing to give him; Abernathy, in turn, wanted control over Operation Breadbasket funds, which Jackson used in 1971 to finance the Black Expo. In December 1971 Jackson left the SCLC, followed by most of the organization's Chicago chapter.

Jackson immediately founded a new Chicago-based organization, Operation PUSH (People United to Save Humanity), to continue his work. The program's emphasis remained on black economic self-help. In addition to sponsoring the annual Black Expo, Operation PUSH negotiated "covenants" on the hiring of black workers with several large corporations. Although active in Chicago Democratic politics, Jackson urged a reorientation of the civil rights movement from political activitism to community economic development, claiming that blacks needed greater financial resources to take advantage of the political rights won in the 1960s. [See NIXON Volume]

[SLG]

For further information:
Phillip Drotning and Wesley South, *Up from the Ghetto* (New York, 1970).

JAVITS, JACOB K(OPPEL)

b. May 18, 1904; New York, N.Y.
Republican Senator, N.Y., 1957-   .

Javits, the son of a Jewish immigrant, was raised on New York's Lower East Side. He held part-time jobs while studying law at New York University. After his admission to the bar in 1927, he and his older brother established a law firm specializing in bankruptcy and corporate reorganization.

A supporter of Fiorello La Guardia, Javits joined the Republican Party during the 1930s. In 1946 he received the Party's nomination in an Upper West Side congressional district. Javits ran on a liberal platform and was the first Republican to carry the district since 1920. In the House of Representatives Javits generally voted against the Republican majority on important bills.

Javits defeated Democrat Franklin D. Roosevelt, Jr. [*q.v.*] in a race for New York State attorney general in 1954. Two years later, he won the Republican senatorial nomination and defeated New York City Mayor Robert F. Wagner, Jr. [*q.v.*] by almost half a million votes. In the Senate Javits continued to compile a liberal voting record. He attempted to strengthen the Civil Rights Act of 1960, and in 1961 he offered an amendment to expand the number of workers covered by minimum-wage legislation. The following year he cosponsored with Sen. Clinton P. Anderson (D, N.M.) [*q.v.*] an Administration-backed Social Security medicare bill. In 1962 he won his reelection bid by almost one million votes. [See EISENHOWER, KENNEDY Volumes]

Javits, who accomplished the rare Republican feat of carrying New York City in the 1962 election, fared well in the city because of his liberal voting record and Jewish religious affiliation. His Party label also enabled him to carry easily the traditionally Republican upstate region. As a result, he was one of the most successful vote-getters in New York State's history. But in the Senate Javits's liberalism and combative style prevented him from becoming part of the upper chamber's Republican leadership. He tried to compensate for his lack of influence by serving on as many committees and subcommittees as possible and by expressing his views on a wide range of issues.

According to *Congressional Quarterly*, Javits was among the two leading Republican opponents of the Senate's conservative coalition from 1964 through 1967. He consistently supported President Lyndon B. Johnson's civil rights measures and generally backed his Great Society programs. He was sometimes more liberal than the Administration itself. In April 1966 he introduced an amendment to the President's housing legislation that expanded the Demonstration Cities program to permit the participation of more than one neighborhood in eligible cities. The following July Javits opposed appropriations for work on a proton accelerator at Weston, Ill., because of alleged housing discrimination in the area.

Javits was best known as a supporter of liberal legislation. However, in his *Order of Battle* (1964) he criticized the Democratic left for what he regarded as its inclination to look to the federal government for the solutions to all social ills. The Senator stated that he favored attacking national problems through a partnership of government and business. In April 1964 he criticized a majority report of the Labor and Public Welfare Committee's Employment and Manpower Subcommittee that advocated an increase of federal expenditures by at least $5 billion a year to increase demand in proportion to rising labor productivity. Javits, a member of the subcommittee, commented that the report's "aggressive expenditures" policy "implies a note of rigidity and planning inconsistent with a free economy." The following August Javits opposed a temporary, retroactive tax on the purchase by Americans of foreign securities, arguing that it would "erect an artificial wall to the free flow of private capital. . . ." Two years later he supported a bill providing for U.S. participation in the Asian Development Bank but said that he did not "believe that sufficient emphasis on the development of private enterprise is indicated . . . in the operation of the Bank."

In 1965 and 1966 Javits supported Administration policy in Vietnam while stressing, as he stated in February 1966, that he favored "limited objectives and limited military force." Early in the following year Javits began to express strong reservations about the war, and in October he joined 22 other senators in supporting a resolution that urged an intensified effort to find a peaceful solution to the conflict.

Javits was a strong supporter of Israel. At the end of the June 1967 Mideast war he asserted that the U.S. "must not stand by as Israel is asked to pull back from positions gained through the expenditure of so much blood and heroism . . . until it is made certain that Israel's future security is guaranteed."

During the mid-1960s Javits was a close political ally of New York Gov. Nelson A. Rockefeller [*q.v.*]. In 1964 Javits supported the Governor's effort to win the Republican presidential nomination. Later he declined to endorse conservative Sen. Barry M. Goldwater (R, Ariz.) [*q.v.*], the Party's ultimate choice. Two years later Rockefeller proposed Javits as a vice presidential nominee to run with Michigan Gov. George Romney [*q.v.*] in 1968. This suggestion gained some support within the Party, but as Romney's hopes for the nomination faded so did the Senator's chance to become the first Jew to run on a national ticket. In 1968 Javits endorsed another unsuccessful bid by Rockefeller to win the Republican presidential nomination. This time he supported the Party's eventual nominee, Richard M. Nixon [*q.v.*]. During the same year Javits won reelection to the Senate in a three-man race with a plurality of over one million votes.

In 1970 Javits backed the Cooper-Church

Amendment to bar funds for U.S. forces in Cambodia. During the same year he supported efforts to repeal the Gulf of Tonkin Resolution. Some opponents of the Indochina war, however, felt that the Senator was not sufficiently outspoken in his criticism of the conflict. During the late 1960s and early 1970s Javits was also a leading advocate of consumer protection legislation. In 1970 he and Sen. Abraham Ribicoff (D, Conn.) [*q.v.*] cosponsored a bill to establish an independent Consumer Protection Agency. In 1974 Javits was reelected with a margin of less than 400,000 votes. [See NIXON Volume]

[MLL]

For further information:
Jacob K. Javits, *Order of Battle—A Republican's Call to Reason* (New York, 1964).
Milton Viorst, "Could this Jew be President?," *Esquire* (April, 1966), pp. 100-101+.

JENKINS, WALTER W(ILSON)
b. March 23, 1918; Jolly, Texas.
White House Special Assistant,
November 1963-October 1964.

After two years at the University of Texas, Jenkins joined Rep. Lyndon B. Johnson's (D, Tex.) staff in 1939. During Johnson's Senate years Jenkins served as his general office manager, personnel chief, private secretary and administrative assistant.

After Johnson became President in 1963, Jenkins was named a White House special assistant. He occupied a unique position on the Johnson staff with a wide range of duties, including those of general manager, chief of payroll and personnel, congressional liaison and adviser on domestic policy. Jenkins sat in on all cabinet meetings and was one of the few special assistants authorized to sign the President's name to letters.

Once described as a "faceless anonymous servant," Jenkins first received national attention during the 1964 Senate Rules and Administration Committee investigations into the business affairs of former Senate Majority Secretary Robert G. "Bobby" Baker [*q.v.*]. One of Baker's associates in a life insurance business, Don B. Reynolds of South Carolina, had twice sold $100,000 life insurance policies to Lyndon Johnson. In return for this favor, Jenkins allegedly requested that Reynolds purchase advertising time on the Johnson-owned television station, KTBC-TV. In a sworn affidavit Jenkins stated that he "had no knowledge of any arrangements by which Reynolds purchased advertising on the television station." Over strong Republican opposition, the Rules and Administration Committee voted to end the Baker probe on March 25, 1964, before Jenkins could be called to testify.

On Oct. 7, 1964 Jenkins was arrested in a Washington, D.C., men's room on a charge of "indecent gestures." He resigned his post as White House special assistant on Oct. 14. News of the arrest was suppressed by major Washington newspapers at the request of Clark Clifford [*q.v.*] and Abe Fortas [*q.v.*], who appealed to the editors not to publish the story for "humanitarian" reasons. Only after Republican National Chairman Dean Burch [*q.v.*] had issued a statement that "the White House is desperately trying to suppress a major news story," did United Press International release the full details.

Coming just before a national election and on the heels of the Bobby Baker scandal, the news provoked "a wave of fear" in the White House, according to columnists Rowland Evans and Robert Novak [*q.v.*]. Because Jenkins had access to the highest classified material in the White House, Johnson ordered a probe by the FBI. The Bureau reported to the President on Oct. 22 that it could find no evidence that Jenkins had violated national security.

Emphasizing the issue of "government morality," the Republican national ticket sought to make the Jenkins incident a major campaign issue. Presidential candidate Sen. Barry Goldwater (R, Ariz.) [*q.v.*] lamented Lyndon Johnson's "curious crew," and vice presidential candidate Rep. William E. Miller (R, N.Y.) [*q.v.*] stated that U.S. security had been violated by the presence of Jenkins in the White House.

After waiting a full week to comment on

the Jenkins matter, President Johnson, on Oct. 24, 1964, called the Jenkins incident "unfortunate" and "distressing." However, the full impact of the Jenkins resignation had already been muted somewhat by the fall from power of Soviet Premier Nikita Khrushchev on Oct. 14 and the detonation of Communist China's first nuclear device on Oct. 16.

After his resignation Jenkins returned to Texas, where he took a job with the Johnson-owned radio and television stations.

[FHM]

JENNINGS, PAUL J(OSEPH)

b. March 19, 1918; New York, N.Y.
President, International Union of Electrical, Radio and Machine Workers, 1965- .

Jennings, who studied electronics at the Radio Corporation of America Institute, worked as a technician for Sperry Rand and helped organize a local of the United Electrical and Radio Workers of America (UE) there in 1939. During the 1940s he rose within his local union to become a leader of the UE's anti-Communist faction. In 1949, when the UE was expelled from the CIO for alleged Communist domination, Jennings joined former UE President James Carey in founding a CIO-chartered rival union, the International Union of Electrical, Radio and Machine Workers (IUE), with Carey as its president. In 1953 Jennings was elected executive secretary of the union's largest district, which included New York and New Jersey and claimed one-third of the IUE's national membership.

During the late 1950s and early 1960s, the IUE suffered a precipitous drop in membership as wages and working conditions deteriorated relative to those of workers in other mass production industries. The central problem for labor in the industry was the division of electrical workers among several unions which negotiated individually with a few corporate giants. This lack of unity enabled General Electric to practice "Boulwareism," a bargaining tactic named for a former GE vice president under which the company's first offer was its last. IUE President Carey provided ineffective and erratic leadership and refused to coordinate bargaining strategy with other unions. In the early 1960s rank-and-file opposition to his autocratic methods grew and crystallized around Jennings.

At the September 1964 IUE convention, Jennings won enough support to attempt the first challenge to Carey's leadership in the union's 15-year history. The first election count, taken in December, showed Carey the victor by 2,000 votes out of some 133,000 cast. Jennings demanded a Department of Labor recount. In April 1965 the Labor Department reported that he had, in fact, defeated Carey by a vote of 78,475 to 55,159.

Jennings acted quickly to revitalize the IUE. In preparation for the upcoming 1966 contract negotiations with GE he initiated "coalition bargaining" in which each AFL-CIO union negotiating team included representatives from the other unions. While 10 other unions awaited the outcome of the IUE negotiations, Jennings sought not only improved wages and benefits but also the destruction of GE's traditional negotiating policy. GE, which fought the coalition plan, eventually relented and offered a 4% wage and cost-of-living increase over the three-year contract period. The unions rejected this offer as too low and scheduled a strike for Oct. 3.

Because interruption of GE's extensive military production would have affected the conduct of the Vietnam war, President Lyndon Johnson persuaded union officials to postpone the strike. Both sides agreed to move negotiations from New York to Washington. There Secretary of Defense Robert S. McNamara [*q.v.*], Secretary of Labor Willard Wirtz [*q.v.*] and Secretary of Commerce John T. Connor [*q.v.*] participated in the continuing talks. On Oct. 14 the 11 unions and GE signed a contract providing for a 5% increase in wages and benefits, or more than 51¢ an hour over a three-year period. Although the agreement did not satisfy the unions' demands for arbitration of all contract grievances and reduction of regional wage differentials, the coalition had forced GE to raise its original offer and abandon Boulwareism as a bargaining strategy. A week later the group of unions signed an agreement with Westinghouse Electric.

Jennings became an AFL-CIO vice president in 1965 and won reelection by acclamation at the IUE's 1968 convention. In 1969 he again led the IUE into coalition bargaining with GE and directed a 102-day strike beginning that October. An active member of New York's Liberal Party, Jennings remained at the head of the IUE through the 1970s. [See NIXON Volume]

[MDB]

JOHNSON, HAROLD K(EITH)

b. Feb. 22, 1912; Bowesmont, N.D.
U.S. Army Chief of Staff, June 1964-July 1968.

In naming then Lt. Gen. Johnson as Chief of Staff, President Johnson bypassed 31 lieutenant generals and 12 four-star generals who outranked him in seniority. According to journalist David Halberstam, Gen. Johnson, of all members of the Joint Chiefs of Staff, was initially the most unwilling to see the U.S. become deeply involved in Vietnam. In February 1965 Johnson told two *New York Times* reporters that he feared U.S. involvement in Vietnam would be worse than in Korea. The enemy, he stated, would begin using sanctuaries against which the U.S. would be unable and unwilling to employ its full power.

In February 1965 Communist guerrillas attacked the American bases at Pleiku and Qui Non. In retaliation the U.S. began bombing North Vietnam. President Johnson, deeply disturbed by the course of events in Vietnam, met with Gen. Johnson in early March. Following the interview, Gen. Johnson left immediately to consider alternatives to bombing.

One of the important questions the General had to consider was whether the U.S. should commit combat troops to the war. Gen. William C. Westmoreland [*q.v.*], commander of the U.S. Military Assistance Command in Vietnam, had already urged that two battalions of combat-ready Marines be sent to help defend the air base at Da Nang. This request was approved by the President while Gen. Johnson was still in Saigon. Westmoreland, however, wanted more troops and the power to maneuver them anywhere in the South. On the other hand, U.S. Ambassador Maxwell D. Taylor [*q.v.*] feared that an initial commitment would only lead to further requests until the U.S. found itself deeply involved in a difficult Asian land war. If U.S. troops were sent, Taylor said, their role should be limited to the defense of strategic coastal bases. Gen. Johnson, in his report of March 14, sided with Westmoreland in recommending that one division of combat troops be sent to South Vietnam's central highlands. He also suggested stepped-up bombing and removal of some of the restrictions on targets in the North, proposals that were approved by the White House.

In July 1965 Gen. Johnson brought together a group of talented young officers to work on a report entitled *Pacification and Long-Term Development of South Vietnam.* Completed in March 1966, the report recommended that the U.S. revive and modify its earlier effort to win the loyalty of the South Vietnamese peasants. It noted that there had been considerable conflict among the various U.S. agencies involved in earlier rural pacification efforts and recommended that the U.S. ambassador to South Vietnam become the sole manager of all non-military U.S. activities in that country. According to the *Pentagon Papers*, many of the recommendations of this report were never implemented, but "the influence of the study was substantial" in reviving the rural pacification programs.

In August 1967 Johnson appeared before the Senate Preparedness Subcommittee to advocate heavier bombing of North Vietnam. He stated that he expected to see "very real evidence of economic and social progress" in South Vietnam and that with an addition of 45,000 more American troops and heavy bombing, the U.S. could have the war well in hand within 18 months and could begin bringing home its troops.

Gen. Johnson retired in July 1968 to become a director of Genesco, Inc. He was succeeded as Army Chief of Staff by Gen. Westmoreland.

[JLW]

JOHNSON, (CLAUDIA TAYLOR) LADY BIRD

b. Dec. 22, 1912; Karnack, Tex.
First Lady, 1963-68.

As a small child Claudia Alta Taylor was given the sobriquet Lady Bird. She was born in an ante-bellum mansion on the Texas-Louisiana border, the daughter of a wealthy Texas merchant and landowner. After taking a degree in journalism from the University of Texas in Austin, she married Lyndon Johnson in November 1934. Johnson was then executive secretary to a Texas congressman. With his wife's financial support, Johnson won a runoff election to Congress in 1937, and he and Lady Bird began a 30-year political career in Washington.

In addition to her public duties as a prominent politician's wife, Mrs. Johnson also proved to be a capable businesswoman. In 1943 she purchased a small debt-ridden radio station, KTBC in Austin, and turned it into a business enterprise that by the late 1960s was worth several million dollars.

Lady Bird Johnson came to the White House in 1963 with a background as both a business and a political professional. During the Administration she stressed her role as wife and mother, summing up her advisory duties with the phrase, "I infiltrate." But according to historian and former White House special assistant Eric Goldman [*q.v.*], "a good many important figures, in and outside the White House, were advanced, eased out, or went up or down in influence depending on the impression they left on Lady Bird Johnson."

During the 1964 political campaign Mrs. Johnson undertook a widely publicized five-day, eight-state, 1,682-mile, whistle-stop campaign trip through the South in an effort to lure potential Goldwater votes for the President despite his signing of the Civil Rights Act the previous July. Many observers credited the "Lady Bird Special" with helping the President to carry half the Southern states in the November general election.

After the election Mrs. Johnson used the White House as a public forum for bringing environmental issues to national attention. In February 1965 she created the First Lady's Committee for A More Beautiful Capital, chaired by Secretary of the Interior Stewart Udall [*q.v.*]. In October of the same year, at Mrs. Johnson's urging and under pressure from President Johnson, Congress passed the Highway Beautification Act, which the President declared "does not represent all we want, or all we need, or all the national interest requires. But it is a first step." The measure authorized use of federal funds to help states control billboards and junkyards along non-commercial sections of interstate and primary highways. In addition, $80 million was granted by the government over a two-year period to pay 75% of compensatory costs to billboard and junkyard owners. The Highway Beautification Act also gave $240 million in federal funds to the states over two years for landscaping and roadside development.

In the middle and late 1960s Mrs. Johnson ranked at or near the top of the Gallup Poll's list of "most admired" women. She accompanied the President on many overseas trips and was considered a goodwill asset. However, during the late 1960s, when the Vietnam war provoked strong reactions throughout the nation, Mrs. Johnson was occasionally the target of anti-war protests and demonstrations. In a widely publicized incident at a January 1968 White House luncheon, singer Eartha Kitt accused Mrs. Johnson of sending "the best of this country off to be shot and maimed." The next day Mrs. Johnson said she regretted that "only the shrill voice of anger and discord" had been heard at the luncheon. In March 1968 Mrs. Johnson was instrumental in helping the President make his decision not to seek reelection to the presidency.

Two years after leaving the White House, Mrs. Johnson published *A White House Diary*, an informal view of her years as First Lady. Following Lyndon Johnson's death in 1973, she involved herself in the operations of the Johnson Library in Austin and the prosperous LBJ ranch in Johnson City, Tex. She also maintained her strong interest in the environment.

[FHM]

JOHNSON, LYNDON B(AINES)
b. Aug. 27, 1908; Stonewall, Tex.
d. Jan. 22, 1973; Stonewall, Tex.
President of the United States,
November 1963-January 1969.

Lyndon Johnson, the grandson of a populist member of the Texas state legislature and the son of a cattle speculator, was born on a farm in the rugged hill country of south-central Texas, near Austin. He attended local public schools, graduated from Southwest Texas State Teachers College in 1930 and the next year became secretary to a Texas congressman. While in Washington Johnson was urged to pursue a political career by Rep. Sam Rayburn (D, Tex.) a close political confidant and later speaker of the House of Representatives. In 1934 he married Claudia Alta Taylor, known as Lady Bird [*q.v.*], who was credited with being a steadying influence on him.

In 1935 President Roosevelt appointed Johnson as Texas state administrator of the National Youth Administration. The job also provided Johnson with a wide political base for a successful congressional campaign in 1937. He ran on a strong New Deal platform rooted in a personal relationship with Roosevelt, who Johnson later declared "was like a Daddy to me." But after 1938 Johnson, like many other Southern congressmen, became more conservative. His political career was interrupted by service with the Navy in World War II. In 1948 he won a bitterly fought Democratic senatorial primary runoff election by 87 votes out of one million cast. In 1977 a former Texas voting official, Luis Salas, said that he had certified enough fictitious ballots to enable Johnson to win the election. [See TRUMAN Volume]

Befriended by powerful Sen. Richard Russell (D, Ga.) [*q.v.*], a member of the Senate "establishment," Johnson rose quickly through the Senate hierarchy, winning the post of Senate minority leader in 1953 and majority leader two years later. In 1955 he made a rapid recovery from a massive heart attack.

As majority leader, Johnson established a near-legendary reputation for his command of the legislative process and his assessment of the needs, ambitions and weaknesses of individual senators. As his own national ambitions increased, Johnson's political stance moved from conservative to moderate. He guided through Congress a number of programs that were opposed by the Republican Administration and helped gain passage for the Civil Rights Acts of 1957 and 1960, despite considerable Southern resistance.

Johnson's 1960 presidential strategy was to remain aloof from the primaries in the hope that the announced candidates, Sen. John F. Kennedy (D, Mass.) and Sen. Hubert H. Humphrey (D, Minn.) [*q.v.*], would either drop out of the race or become deadlocked before reaching the Convention. However, Kennedy soon won a series of primary victories, and big-city political machines, labor unions and black voters in the Party moved solidly behind his candidacy. Johnson formally announced his own candidacy for the Democratic presidential nomination on July 5, but eight days later Kennedy won the nomination at the Los Angeles Convention on the first ballot, with 806 delegate votes to Johnson's 409.

With the presidential nomination secured, Kennedy surprised his Northern liberal and labor backers by selecting Johnson as his running mate in order to attract Southern and Western votes in the general election. Johnson's nomination was generally considered to be a critical factor in the Kennedy-Johnson victory over Vice President Richard M. Nixon [*q.v.*] and Henry Cabot Lodge [*q.v.*] in the November election. [See EISENHOWER Volume]

As vice president, Johnson chaired the National Aeronautics and Space Council and the President's Committee on Equal Opportunity. He also visited some 34 countries on trips many observers likened to Johnson's domestic campaign swings. Despite the publicity Johnson won on these trips, his 30 months as vice president were frustrating. He later told biographer Doris Kearns that the vice presidency "is filled with trips around the world, chauffeurs, men saluting, people clapping, chairmanships of councils, but in the end, it is nothing. I detested every minute of it."

In both 1962 and 1963 there were persistent rumors, denied by President Kennedy, that Johnson would be dropped from the 1964 Democratic ticket. This possibility seemed more real when Robert G. Baker [*q.v.*], secretary to the Senate majority and a Johnson protege, was charged with having used his influential post to advance several business enterprises.

On Nov. 21, 1963 President Kennedy flew to Texas with Johnson on a precampaign swing designed to reconcile rival factions of the Texas Democratic Party. The next day Kennedy was assassinated while riding in a Dallas motorcade. At 2:39 p.m. the same day, Lyndon Johnson was sworn in aboard Air Force One as the 36th President of the United States. In a brief address to the nation that evening at Andrews Air Force Base in Washington, Johnson said, "This is a sad time for all people. We have suffered a loss that cannot be weighed. . . . I will do my best, that is all I can do. I ask for your help and God's." [See KENNEDY Volume]

Recognizing that his most important contribution during the crisis of succession would be to exercise his authority prudently and confidently, Johnson initiated a series of conferences with congressional leaders, urged anguished Kennedy staffers to stay at their posts and took the measure of several heads of state gathered for his predecessor's funeral. Acutely conscious that he was a Texan during a time of profound national anger after Dallas and that he was also the first Southern president since Woodrow Wilson, Johnson immediately sought to allay Northern fears about his presidency. On Nov. 27 he addressed a packed and tense joint session of Congress and in a moving speech urged the earliest possible passage of Kennedy's civil rights bill as a memorial to the late President. "We have talked long enough in this country about equal rights," said Johnson. "It is time now to write . . . it in the books of law." Two days later Johnson appointed a prestigious bipartisan commission, chaired by Chief Justice Earl Warren [*q.v.*], to investigate the assassination of President Kennedy.

By the end of 1963 Johnson had decided on his legislative strategy for the next year: passage at all costs of the Kennedy civil rights bill and the late President's $11 billion tax cut to stimulate the economy. In addition, Johnson decided to add a third measure to his list of "must pass" legislation: an antipoverty measure that would be the first major legislation of his own Administration. Although the new President inherited a Congress that had repeatedly frustrated Kennedy, Johnson proved adept at bending the legislature to his will. As majority leader in the 1950s and now as President, Johnson was a brilliant legislative tactician. His well-known ability to spur on his friends and persuade his enemies became known as the "Johnson treatment," a technique, according to the *New York Times*, that "consisted of a combination of cajolery, flattery, concession, arm-twisting and outright wooing, all applied by Mr. Johnson with an endless succession of phone calls."

Johnson first turned his attention to passage of the long-stalled, $11 billion tax cut. His principal opponent in the Congress was Sen. Harry Byrd (D, Va.) [*q.v.*], conservative chairman of the Senate Finance Committee. After much discussion with Johnson, Byrd agreed that if the new budget stayed below $100 billion he would allow the Finance Committee to approve the bill. Johnson submitted a $97.9 billion budget in January 1964 and publicized his commitment to economy in government by personally turning out unneeded White House lights. The Finance Committee soon approved the tax cut, and the Senate passed it in February by a vote of 77 to 21. The same month Johnson informed Senate Democratic leaders Mike Mansfield (D, Mont.) [*q.v.*] and Hubert Humphrey that he was willing to sacrifice all Senate legislation to break the prospective Southern filibuster on the equal accommodations and equal employment civil rights bill. Meanwhile, civil rights groups, labor unions, liberal organizations and church bodies lobbied furiously and effectively all through the spring of 1964. A Southern filibuster lasting 57 days was finally broken when Senate Minority Leader Everett M. Dirksen (R, Ill.) [*q.v.*] announced that he would vote for cloture. The Senate vote to end debate passed June 10, and Johnson signed the historic 1964 Civil Rights Act on July 2.

Johnson moved beyond Kennedy's legislative program with his "declaration of an unconditional War on Poverty" in his 1964 State of the Union address. He initially requested $1 billion to fund the new Office of Economic Opportunity (OEO) under the command of former Peace Corps Director Sargent Shriver [*q.v.*]. The OEO administered a wide range of services directed at making the poor employable. Many were highly controversial, especially the Community Action Program and Volunteers in Service to America, both of which soon developed politically activist orientations. Though the OEO never had a budget of more than $2 billion a year, it was the centerpiece of Johnson's Great Society domestic legislative program.

Although Johnson was widely praised for his legislative triumphs in 1964, he was fearful that the Kennedy wing of the Democratic Party had not fully accepted him as president. Robert Kennedy [*q.v.*], who still served as Attorney General in the cabinet, was ready to accept the vice presidency, but Johnson feared him as a symbol of the Kennedy power and mystique. The President therefore eliminated him as a vice presidential prospect and chose instead the equally liberal Hubert Humphrey as his running mate. The selection of Humphrey, in turn, completed the process of reconciling liberals, especially those in the civil rights movement and in labor, to Johnson's leadership of the Party.

Nominated by acclamation at the Democratic National Convention in August 1964, Johnson faced conservative Sen. Barry Goldwater (R, Ariz.) [*q.v.*] in the November election. Attacking Goldwater as political reactionary, Johnson campaigned as the candidate of a broad liberal consensus on domestic social issues. Meanwhile, Democratic Party political advertisements played skillfully upon the widely-held view that Goldwater was a "trigger-happy" militarist. In contrast, Johnson campaigned as a peace candidate and rebuffed any suggestion that he was considering an escalation of the war in Vietnam. "We are not about to send American boys nine or ten thousand miles away from home to do what Asian boys ought to be doing for themselves," he told voters. As the candidate of moderation, Johnson won the support of many independents and Republicans. Not even the October arrest of Johnson's closest aide, Walter Jenkins [*q.v.*], on a morals charge stemmed the impending Johnson landslide.

On election eve Johnson told a confidant, "It seems to me tonight . . . that I have spent my whole life getting ready for this moment." The next day he swamped Goldwater by 43 million to 27 million—the greatest vote, the greatest margin and the greatest percentage (over 61%) in American history. Johnson captured 486 electoral votes to Goldwater's 44, all of which were from the Deep South and Arizona. Equally important was the enormous gain made by the Democrats in Congress. They captured two additional Senate seats and gained 37 in the House. This gave liberal and moderate Democrats majorities in both houses of Congress for the first time since the heyday of the New Deal.

These rare majorities enabled Johnson to pass a phenomenal 69% of his legislative program during the 89th congress. Two Kennedy measures, medicare and aid to elementary and secondary education, were passed in the first half of 1965. The new Congress also liberalized the immigration law, increased antipoverty funds and added substantially to the amount of land protected by the national parks and wilderness areas. It also began enactment of consumer protection and environmental pollution laws. In 1965 combined expenditures for education, health and welfare totaled $7.6 billion or 6.9% of the federal budget. By 1970 they had grown to $29.7 billion or 15.1% of the budget.

Johnson's most dramatic moment as a legislative leader also came in 1965. After a series of tumultuous civil rights demonstrations in Selma, Ala., the President appeared before a joint session of Congress to throw the weight of the government behind the demands of the demonstrators in Alabama for a new and stringent voting rights law. Taking as his own the refrain of the popular movement anthem, "We Shall Overcome," Johnson asked for immediate passage of a federal Voting Rights Act that would end Southern discrimination against black voters. Passage of the landmark bill five months later led to the enfranchisement of some 3.5 million new black voters within the decade, but it also marked the last time in which the federal government and the increasingly militant civil rights movement were able to work in tandem. In each summer beginning with 1965, racial rioting exploded in the cities of the North and West. Some in the movement adopted the "black power" slogan, and a white backlash sentiment grew evident among many of the same lower middle class and working class whites who had stood at the center of the Johnson consensus. After a 1966 open housing measure failed to pass, the President moved cautiously in the civil rights area, appointing a series of commissions to study the causes of rioting and violence but proposing little new legislation. It was not until April 1968, in the wake of the assassination of Martin Luther King [*q.v.*], that Congress passed a strong open housing bill.

During the same years in which Johnson demonstrated his mastery of the domestic legislative process, he was becoming increasingly involved and ultimately preoccupied with foreign affairs. In January 1964 widespread rioting broke out in the Panama Canal Zone. The Panamanian government suspended diplomatic relations with the U.S. and demanded a revision of the 1903 Canal Zone treaty. Johnson, who had little experience in foreign affairs, took an unexpectedly hard line in the crisis, insisting that law and order be restored before negotiations could begin. In April 1965 Johnson faced another Latin American crisis when the Dominican Republic's ruling military junta was threatened by rebel forces. On April 27 the President announced that he had ordered the evacuation of U.S. citizens from Santo Domingo; the next day he revealed that 400 U.S. Marines had been dispatched to the city. As the number of troops there rose to 30,000, the President asserted that Communist influence in the rebellion justified U.S. military intervention. Johnson came under vigorous criticism for his policy in the Dominican Republic, and Sen. J. William Fulbright's (D, Ark.) [*q.v.*] Foreign Relations Committee conducted nine days of closed-door hearings on the crisis. Many liberals who supported the President's escalation of the war in Vietnam were nevertheless sharply critical of what they regarded as a new, hard-line foreign policy in Latin America.

Johnson's awkward handling of the Dominican crisis was soon overshadowed by the larger problem of Vietnam, but the Caribbean incident was significant because it furthered the belief, held especially among journalists and intellectuals, that the Johnson Administration suffered from a "credibility gap." Johnson's "very appearance and mannerisms," recalled White House aide Eric Goldman [*q.v.*], "suggested the riverboat gambler." The President compounded his difficulties by a penchant for secrecy and an overly sensitive mistrust of anyone who criticized his policies. "His almost desperate need for loyalty was the other half of the coin of [his] insecurity. . . ," wrote journalist David Halberstam. He was "the Texas ruffian among the perfumed darlings of the East." Johnson soon surrounded himself with loyalists from Texas like Jack Valenti [*q.v.*], Horace Busby, Joseph Califano [*q.v.*] and Harry McPherson [*q.v.*], who further isolated the President from adverse criticism. Among the most independent members of the Johnson staff was Bill Moyers [*q.v.*], but the youthful Texan left the Administration in late 1966 in a dispute over the handling of Vietnam news.

In the first several months of his presidency, Johnson's chief concern in Vietnam was to continue the policy he had inherited from President Kennedy. He retained Kennedy's top foreign policy advisers—Dean Rusk [*q.v.*], Robert McNamara [*q.v.*], W. W. Rostow [*q.v.*] and McGeorge Bundy [*q.v.*]—and relied heavily upon their advice in the conduct of the war. Johnson believed firmly in the "domino theory." Shortly after the assassination he told Ambassador to South Vietnam Henry Cabot Lodge, "I am not going to lose Vietnam. I am not going to be the President who saw

Southeast Asia go the way of China." Plans for an escalation of the war began in early 1964, when it became apparent to the White House that the South Vietnamese government could not hold its own against the National Liberation Front (NLF). In February 1964 the U.S. initiated a secret "Operation Plan 34A" by which the U.S. provided tactical air support for South Vietnamese air strikes against the North. In April Johnson named Gen. William Westmoreland [*q.v.*] commander of the 20,000-man U.S. force in South Vietnam, and in June he appointed Gen. Maxwell Taylor [*q.v.*] as ambassador to South Vietnam to replace Lodge. Both Westmoreland and Taylor favored greater use of U.S. troops in the South.

On Aug. 4, 1964 two U.S. destroyers patrolling the Gulf of Tonkin off the coast of North Vietnam reported that they were under enemy attack. Although Johnson soon received information suggesting that the reported attack might not have occurred or, if it had, had been grossly exaggerated, he withheld this information from the public and ordered retaliatory bombing of North Vietnamese coastal bases and oil depots. At Johnson's request Congress three days later passed the Tonkin Gulf Resolution, which gave the President broad authority to use military force throughout Southeast Asia "to prevent further aggression." The resolution passed both houses of Congress with only two dissenting votes.

Throughout the autumn of 1964 Johnson received reports that the NLF was tightening its hold on the South Vietnamese countryside. Taylor and Westmoreland urged the President to authorize systematic bombing of North Vietnam as a means of bolstering morale in the South and cutting infiltration from the North. Campaigning as a peace candidate in the fall, Johnson postponed action on their requests. Nevertheless, the *Pentagon Papers* later disclosed that the actual decision to undertake the bombing of the North had been made as early as October 1964. "I suddenly realized that doing nothing was more dangerous than doing something," Johnson told Doris Kearns.

In February 1965 Communist guerrillas attacked the U.S. military compounds at Pleiku and at Qui Nhon. Johnson immediately ordered retaliatory air raids on North Vietnamese military and industrial sites. By the end of the month, the bombing of the North had become continuous, though limited to targets outside the Hanoi area. Johnson also authorized the landing of two combat-ready Marine battalions to defend the large airbase at Da Nang. On April 1 Johnson agreed to Westmoreland's request that he be authorized to use the troops for offensive actions anywhere in South Vietnam. By early June there were 50,000 American ground troops in Vietnam. Over the next three years Johnson agreed to almost all of Westmoreland's troop increase requests. In 1968 there were over 500,000 American soldiers in Vietnam.

Backed by Bundy and McNamara, Johnson's escalation of the war took place in a gradual, step-by-step fashion. He chose this course for three reasons. First, Johnson and most of his civilian advisers feared that a major escalation would precipitate active Chinese or Russian intervention in the war. Second, they hoped that the relatively slow increase in the pressure on the North might force Hanoi to negotiate in order to prevent the terrible damage that large-scale bombing would inflict. Third, Johnson feared the domestic consequences of a rapid expansion of the war. In 1965 he worried that congressional conservatives would use the war as an excuse to reduce funding for Great Society programs. Later, after Johnson himself had begun to cut back on domestic social legislation, he feared that a dramatic escalation of the war would add to the growing list of liberal war critics.

During the years from 1965 to 1967, Johnson announced repeatedly that he favored negotiations with the North Vietnamese, and several bombing halts were called, ostensibly to facilitate the start of talks. Hanoi leaders did not respond to the President's numerous "peace feelers," in part because the Communists insisted upon an American commitment to an unconditional halt to the bombing of the North but also because they were convinced they were winning the war in the South. Meanwhile, the Joint Chiefs of Staff continually pressed Johnson for an expansion and intensification of the bombing, but Secretary of Defense McNamara grew increasingly skeptical over the diplomatic or military efficacy of continued air attacks. In a September 1967 speech delivered at San Antonio, Johnson promised to halt the air war indefinitely if North Vietnam agreed promptly to begin peace negotiations and not to "take advantage" of the bombing cessation to send men and material to the South. Since over 100,000 North Vietnamese troops had to be supplied in the South, Hanoi soon rejected the "San Antonio Formula."

As a result of the 1964 tax cut and the growing expenditures for the Vietnam war, the American economy under Johnson enjoyed its longest period of sustained growth in the postwar era. The Gross National Product increased by more than 7% per annum during the years 1964 to 1967. Meanwhile, both the inflation and unemployment rates remained at unusually low levels. At first Johnson tried to pay for the Vietnam war without cutting Great Society programs or increasing federal taxes, but by the end of 1965 he was forced to limit expansion of the antipoverty program because of the increasing cost of the war. As the price of the war escalated ($17 billion in 1967 alone), inflationary pressures increased throughout the economy. Johnson and his economic advisers tried to hold down wage and price increases by "jawboning" labor and management, but their appeals proved a failure by late 1966.

To stem the mounting inflation Johnson asked Congress for a 10% tax surcharge in August 1967. As Johnson had feared, congressional conservatives, led by Ways and Means Chairman Rep. Wilbur Mills (D, Ark.) [*q.v.*], demanded substantial cuts in domestic social programs before they would support the tax surcharge. After several months of stalemate, Johnson reluctantly agreed to $6 billion in non-defense reductions. The surcharge finally went into effect at the end of 1968. Partially as a result of the delay, the federal budget deficit grew from $8.7 billion in 1967 to $25.2 billion the next year. This deficit added to inflationary pressures, and the Consumer Price Index, which had increased less than 3% per year until 1967, rose by 5% in 1968 and by even more in subsequent years. Most economists have concluded that Johnson's politically motivated underfinancing of the Vietnam war was a major contributing factor leading to the economic dislocations of the early 1970s.

As the Vietnam war dragged on and its domestic consequences began to make themselves felt, Johnson encountered ever growing anti-war sentiment. The students and intellectuals who protested the war as early as 1964 were joined by an increasingly large number of congressional liberals in 1966 and 1967. Even Vietnam war "hawks" grew dissatisfied with Johnson's conduct of the war because of the restraints he imposed upon the military. By 1967 the hostility of the protest movement had virtually barred Johnson from most public appearances except those held on military bases. He denounced his critics as "nervous nellies . . . blind to experience and deaf to hope," but Johnson was personally shaken when close associates like Moyers, McNamara and Bundy shifted to a more "dovish" position. Meanwhile, the Republicans made large gains in the 1966 off-year elections. Johnson's personal approval ratio, as measured by the Gallup Poll, dropped more than 30 points during the course of the war. By November 1967, 57% of the public disapproved of his handling of the conflict.

Johnson reached the decision to begin de-escalation of the war only after the enemy's dramatic Tet offensive of February 1968 forced a reassessment of strategic thinking in the White House. Following the NLF's invasion of the South Vietnamese cities, Gen. Westmoreland asked for over 200,000 more troops, but Johnson hesitated to fulfill this request. Instead, the President appointed his new Secretary of Defense, Clark Clifford [*q.v.*], as head of a task force to study the proposal and examine its impact on the budget, public opinion and future prospects for negotiations. Although a "hawk" until then, Clifford came to the conclusion that the war had to be wound down. By repeatedly reminding Johnson that the cost of victory had risen sharply and by rigorously challenging the optimistic reports from Saigon,

Clifford helped check the momentum for increasing the war effort.

Johnson simultaneously was receiving further evidence of public disenchantment with the war. In the New Hampshire primary Sen. Eugene McCarthy (D, Minn.) [*q.v.*], a vigorous critic of the war, ran a surprisingly strong race against the President in the March 13 balloting. Three days later Robert Kennedy announced he would enter the race for the Democratic Party's nomination on an anti-war platform.

Johnson relieved Westmoreland of his command on March 22. Shortly thereafter he convened at the White House an extraordinary informal advisory group, composed of such Establishment figures as Dean Acheson [*q.v.*], George Ball [*q.v.*], Douglas Dillon [*q.v.*], Arthur Goldberg [*q.v.*], Matthew Ridgway [*q.v.*] and Henry Cabot Lodge. After listening to detailed briefings, a solid majority of the group concluded on March 26 that Johnson had to de-escalate the war and begin negotiations with the North Vietnamese.

Johnson went before a nationwide television audience on the night of March 31 to announce a unilateral halt to air and naval bombardment of North Vietnam except in the area immediately north of the demilitarized zone. He called on North Vietnam "to respond positively and favorably to this new step toward peace." At the close of his speech Johnson stunned the nation by declaring, "I shall not seek and will not accept the nomination of my Party for another term as your President." Three days later North Vietnam agreed to open negotiations in Paris, and the long-sought talks finally began in May.

Although Johnson had pledged to remain aloof from domestic politics in 1968, his influence on the campaign was considerable. He threw his still substantial influence behind the candidacy of Hubert Humphrey, thus helping the Vice President to win the Democratic presidential nomination despite a series of primary victories by his two anti-war opponents. At the Democratic National Convention Johnson vetoed a compromise Vietnam plank, which favored an immediate halt in all bombing of North Vietnam. In the fall Johnson maintained a continued pressure on Humphrey to adhere to the Administration's hard-line policy until late October, when Johnson himself announced a complete end to American bombing of North Vietnam. Many historians have speculated that if Johnson had softened his position on the war somewhat earlier, Humphrey might have won the presidential election in November.

After 37 years in Washington, Johnson retired to his Texas ranch following Richard Nixon's inauguration. In May 1971 he dedicated the $18.6 million Lyndon Baines Johnson Library complex on the Austin campus of the University of Texas. In November of that year his memoir, *The Vantage Point: Perspectives on the Presidency, 1963-1969*, was published to reviews that were generally critical of the book's blandness. During the next two years Johnson's health declined, and on Jan. 22, 1973 he died of a heart attack at his ranch.

Although most historians have applauded Lyndon Johnson's extraordinary skill in pushing through Congress the landmark civil rights and Great Society legislation of the mid-1960s, his reputation as President remained tarnished by his immense failure in Vietnam. Eric Goldman saw Johnson as a "tragic figure" whose preoccupation with Vietnam destroyed the potential of his latter-day New Deal liberalism. Arthur Schlesinger, Jr. [*q.v.*] offered a darker interpretation from the vantage point of the mid-1970s. He argued that Johnson's decision to escalate the Vietnam war without fully informing either Congress or the American people of his real intentions was a decisive step in the growth of an "imperial presidency" that Richard Nixon then sought to strengthen and institutionalize.

[FHM, NNL]

For further information:

Rowland Evans and Robert Novak, *Lyndon B. Johnson: The Exercise of Power* (New York, 1966).

Eric F. Goldman, *The Tragedy of Lyndon Johnson* (New York, 1969).

Lyndon B. Johnson, *The Vantage Point: Perspectives on the Presidency, 1963-1969* (New York, 1971.)

Doris Kearns, *Lyndon Johnson and the American Dream* (New York, 1976).

Tom Wicker, *JFK and LBJ* (New York, 1969).

JOHNSON, PAUL B(URNEY), JR.
b. Jan. 23, 1916; Hattiesburg, Miss.
Governor, Miss., 1964-68.

The son of a Mississippi congressman and governor, Johnson practiced law in Jackson and Hattiesburg after receiving his law degree from the University of Mississippi in 1940. He served as an assistant U.S. attorney in Mississippi from 1948 to 1951 and won election as lieutenant governor in 1959. In that post he joined Gov. Ross Barnett in trying to block the court-ordered enrollment of James Meredith [*q.v.*] at the University of Mississippi in September 1962. Johnson ran for governor in 1963 as an ardent segregationist, and after defeating a more moderate candidate in the August Democratic primary runoff, he was easily elected in November. [See KENNEDY Volume]

After his strong campaign statements on race, Johnson startled many observers by delivering a far more temperate address at his January 1964 inauguration. Although he pledged to fight any authority he thought morally or constitutionally wrong, Johnson also promised that "hate, or prejudice, or ignorance will not lead Mississippi while I sit in the governor's chair." While Johnson continued to oppose integration throughout his term, his inaugural signaled a shift away from the tactic of defiance adopted by his predecessor. Concerned with improving the state's national image, Johnson repeatedly urged that efforts to oppose integration be limited to the courts, and he took a strong stand against public disorder and violence. He ended Barnett's policy of awarding state grants to the segregationist Citizens Councils. Johnson also allowed the State Sovereignty Commission, established in 1956 to fight for segregation, to fall into obscurity by never calling a meeting throughout his administration.

During Johnson's first year as governor, a coalition of civil rights groups organized a Mississippi Freedom Summer Project to bring large numbers of civil rights workers into the state to conduct voter registration drives and establish freedom schools. Johnson condemned the project, at one point claiming that many project leaders had "Marxist backgrounds." However, when three rights workers disappeared near Philadelphia, Miss., on June 21, Johnson welcomed federal assistance in searching for them, promised full cooperation from the state and urged area residents to aid in the search. He also ordered a state investigation of the series of bombings and shootings that plagued the McComb area that summer, and he played a major role in ending the violence there.

Johnson denounced the 1964 Civil Rights Act and was reportedly against voluntary compliance with the public accommodations section of the law until it had been tested in court. He fought the Mississippi Freedom Democratic Party's (MFDP) challenge to the seating of the regular state delegation at the Democratic National Convention in August 1964. When the Convention adopted a compromise by which the regular delegates would be seated if they took a loyalty oath and two MFDP representatives would be seated as at-large delegates, Johnson led the regular delegation in voting against the compromise and then in walking out. By October Johnson publicly supported Sen. Barry Goldwater (R, Ariz.) [*q.v.*] for the presidency, and Goldwater carried Mississippi in the November election with 87% of the vote.

In June 1964 Johnson called a special session of the state legislature to adopt a plan of tuition grants to private schools in an effort to circumvent court-ordered school desegregation. Johnson did not physically obstruct school desegregation, however, and he sent state police into Grenada in September 1966 to protect black youths who had been attacked by a mob when they entered the city's previously all-white public schools. Early in 1965 Johnson urged the state's white leaders to testify at U.S. Civil Rights Commission hearings on complaints of discrimination in Mississippi, and he made a surprise appearance himself when the commission opened hearings in February in Jackson.

Johnson opposed the 1965 Voting Rights Act. In June, while the bill was still pending in Congress, he called a special legislative session to rewrite the state's voting and registration laws. The MFDP led demonstrations against the special session in which over 800 protesters were arrested in Jackson that month. Most of the bills and amendments Johnson introduced were passed by the legislature and ratified by the state's voters in August. The legislation liberalized Mississippi's voting and registration laws. It was an attempt, as Johnson said, to put the state "in the most advantageous position possible" with respect to the federal voting rights law.

When Martin Luther King [*q.v.*] and other civil rights leaders decided in June 1966 to continue a march from Memphis, Tenn., to Jackson, Miss., begun by James Meredith, Johnson labelled the march "a very, very foolish thing," but promised police protection for the demonstrators. He reduced the number of highway patrolmen escorting the march on June 16, however, asserting that the state did not intend "to wet-nurse a bunch of showmen all over the country." Johnson increased the police escort again after the marchers were attacked by a mob in Philadelphia on June 21. He ordered the National Guard onto the campus of all-black Alcorn A&M College in April 1966, when demonstrations there led to some violence, and into Jackson State College in May 1967, when the school's black student body clashed with police.

Gov. Johnson welcomed federal economic aid in Mississippi and generally approved grants from the federal Office of Economic Opportunity to community action programs throughout the state. In April 1966 a special presidential task force reported that Mississippi ranked second in per capita receipt of antipoverty funds. Despite such aid Mississippi still had one of the lowest per capita income levels in the nation. A team of doctors who studied hunger and poverty in six Mississippi counties told a Senate Labor and Public Welfare subcommittee in June 1967 that nutritional and medical conditions in the state were "shocking" with many children facing starvation. Johnson then sent a team of prominent Mississippi doctors into the same areas and reported in August that, while there was malnutrition in some localities, the physicians had found no conditions approaching starvation.

Barred by the state constitution from seeking a second consecutive term as governor, Johnson ran for lieutenant governor in 1967. He placed third in a field of six candidates in the Aug. 8 Democratic primary and was thus eliminated from the race.

[CAB]

JOHNSON, U(RAL) ALEXIS

b. Oct. 17, 1908; Falun, Kan.
Deputy Undersecretary of State for Political Affairs, April 1961-July 1964; September 1965-July 1966; Deputy Ambassador to South Vietnam, July 1964-September 1965; Ambassador to Japan, July 1966-January 1969.

A career diplomat, Johnson was an expert on Far Eastern affairs. Joining the State Department in 1935, he served in Japan, Korea, China and Manchuria before the war. With the exception of a wartime assignment in Brazil and a tour of duty as ambassador to Czechoslovokia from 1953 to 1958, he continued to concentrate on Far Eastern affairs throughout the postwar period. When President John F. Kennedy appointed him deputy undersecretary of State for political affairs an April 1961, Johnson became the highest-ranking career foreign service officer in the State Department. During the Kennedy and Johnson Administrations Vietnam was the central focus of Johnson's attention. He was an early advocate of military intervention to prevent a communist takeover, urging this course as early as October 1961. [See KENNEDY Volume]

Johnson was appointed deputy ambassador to Vietnam in July 1964. While at that post he advocated immediate retaliation for Communist raids and continued increases in both bombing sorties and ground troop commitments. While in Saigon he was instrumental in getting the South Vietnamese government to accept these measures but failed in his drive to strengthen local government and reform the Vietnamese Army.

In January 1965 Johnson sketched a proposal for terminating the war while achieving military victory. Under this plan South Vietnam would agree to grant either amnesty and civil rights to insurgents or give safe passage to those wishing to go to the North. In addition the U.S. would offer a progressive reduction of military personnel, restoration of trade with North Vietnam and participation of all parties in an American sponsored development program for Southeast Asia. In return, the North would stop infiltration, cease National Liberation Front (NLF) insurgency and agree to the neutrality of Laos. Negotiations were to be carried on between North and South Vietnam, but the NLF would not be recognized. This plan was never put into effect. In March 1965 Johnson was a member of the Honolulu Conference that recommended further military escalation.

Johnson was one of the officials who advocated a bombing pause in December 1965 as a possible way of getting North Vietnam to negotiate. According to the *Pentagon Papers*, this pause was also meant as "a means of clearing the way for an increase in the tempo of the air war in the absence of a satisfactory response from Hanoi."

Johnson succeeded Edwin Reischauer [*q.v.*] as ambassador to Japan in July 1966. He left that post in January 1969 to become undersecretary of State for political affairs and in 1973 was appointed chief delegate to the Strategic Arms Limitation Talks (SALT). [See NIXON Volume]

[EWS]

JONES, E(VERETT) LEROI

(Imamu Amiri Baraka)
b. Oct. 7, 1934; Newark, N.J.
Writer, black political activist.

The son of a postal supervisor and a social worker, Jones graduated two years ahead of his class at Newark's Barringer High School and received his B.A. from Howard University in 1953. After serving in the Air Force, Jones settled in New York, where he did graduate work in comparative literature at Columbia and developed a reputation as an avant-garde writer. Jones's poetry, jazz criticism and plays displayed an extraordinary sensitivity to black culture and to what he perceived as the debilitating effect of white society on black Americans. In *Dutchman*, winner of the 1964 Obie Award, Jones depicted a subway car confrontation between a sexually provocative white woman and a black intellectual whose middle class appearance conceals an explosive hostility to white people.

In April 1965 Jones left his white wife and their two children and moved to Harlem, where he founded the Black Arts Repertory Theatre, a multifaceted cultural center. A year later Jones moved the center to a dilapidated three-story building in Newark's Central Ward which he named Spirit House. In January 1968 he founded the Black Community Development and Defense Organization. *Ebony* characterized Organization in 1969 as one "dedicated to the creation of a new value system for the Afro-American community" based on Afro-Islamic cultural principles. Members of the group adopted the Kuwaida Muslim faith and Jones, whose early vocational aspiration had been the Christian ministry, became a Kuwaida religious leader and was addressed by members as Imamu Amiri Baraka, the name which he assumed publicly in the 1970s.

A 1960 trip to Cuba stimulated Jones's first political commitments. Upon returning he wrote of the contrast between the popular enthusiasm in Cuba and the "ugly void" of American life and described white Americans as an "old people" not needed by the "new peoples in Asia, Africa [and] South America." Jones exempted "the captive African," whom he described as "the only innocent in the bankruptcy of Western culture," from his indictment of American life.

After his arrest on two counts of carrying concealed weapons during the July 1967 Newark riots, Jones's political influence in Newark increased. (P.E.N., the association of writers, and the United Black Artists came to Jones's aid when the sentencing judge stated that his disagreement with sentiments expressed in one of Jones's poems contributed to the length of Jones's prison sentence. The conviction was overturned in 1968.) While on bail he taught a course at San Francisco State College and met regularly with Ron Karenga, founder of the black politico-cultural group US. Returning to Newark in January 1968, Jones helped create the Committee for a United Newark, a coalition of black and Puerto Rican community organizations that sought to secure political power for Newark's black and Puerto Rican population. In November 1969 the Committee held a convention and nominated a slate of candidates for the June 1970 municipal elections.

During the campaign incumbent Mayor Hugh Addonizio [*q.v.*] denounced Kenneth Gibson, the convention's mayoral candidate, as a "puppet" for black extremists, notably Jones, whose 1967 arrest made him a symbol of racial militancy. Gibson defeated Addonizio to become the first elected black mayor of a large East Coast city, and Jones was credited with a major role in the victory. Jones received national recognition at the 1972 National Black Political Convention which he cochaired with Mayor Richard Hatcher of Gary, Ind., and Rep. Charles C. Diggs, Jr. (D, Mich.) [*q.v.*]. [See NIXON Volume]

[DKR]

JORDAN, B(ENJAMIN) EVERETT

b. Sept. 8, 1896; Ramseur, N.C.
d. March 15, 1974; Saxapahaw, N.C.
Democratic Senator, N.C., 1958-73; Chairman, Rules and Administration Committee, 1963-73.

A wealthy North Carolina textile manufacturer and state Democratic Party fund raiser, Jordan served as chairman of the Democratic state executive committee from 1949 to 1954. During that time he moved from the liberal faction of the Party to its conservative wing. In April 1958 Gov. Luther Hodges appointed him to fill a U.S. Senate vacancy, and the following November he was elected to complete the final two years of the term.

During the early 1960s Jordan compiled a conservative voting record, opposing most social welfare and civil rights measures. He became chairman of the Senate Rules and Administration Committee in 1963. In the last days of the Kennedy Administration, the panel began an investigation of the activities of Robert G. (Bobby) Baker [*q.v.*], secretary to the Senate majority, who had been accused in a civil suit of using his influence to obtain government contracts. [See KENNEDY Volume]

The Baker probe continued into 1964. The majority report, signed by Jordan, asserted that Baker had been guilty of "gross improprieties." But it dismissed allegations that had linked Baker's activities to prominent Democrats, including President Lyndon B. Johnson, who as Senate majority leader had worked closely with Baker.

Don B. Reynolds, a former business associate of Baker, testified that Johnson had purchased life insurance policies from their firm in 1957 and 1961. He asserted that after both purchases Johnson aide Walter W. Jenkins [*q.v.*] had suggested to him that the insurance company buy advertising on a Johnson family radio-television station and that Baker had urged him to buy a hi-fi set for Johnson. Jordan, who had been a strong Johnson-for-President supporter in 1960, questioned the veracity of Reynolds's testimony and on Jan. 31, 1964 stated, "There has been a lot of reckless talk about the President's part in all this."

Jordan generally voted against Johnson's domestic programs. According to *Congressional Quarterly*, he was the fourth and tenth most frequent Democratic senatorial opponent of Administration-supported bills in 1966 and 1968, respectively.

In 1971 Jordan surprised many observers by announcing his opposition to the Vietnam war. The following year Rep. Nick Galifianakis, who had a more liberal voting record than Jordan, defeated the incumbent in the Democratic senatorial primary. Jordan died in 1974.

[MLL]

JORDAN, VERNON E(ULION)

b. Aug. 15, 1935; Atlanta, Ga.
Director, Voter Education Project, Southern Regional Council, 1964-68.

The son of a postal inspector, Jordan grew up in Atlanta. He was educated at DePauw University and the Howard University Law School, where he received an LL.B. in 1960. Jordan became involved in the civil rights movement immediately after graduation, serving as a clerk for Atlanta civil rights lawyer Donald Hollowell. In 1961, when Hollowell won a suit to desegregate the University of Georgia, Jordan gained national attention by escorting the first black student onto the University campus through a mob of angry whites. After he became field secretary for the Georgia NAACP in 1962, he expanded the organization and coordinated the activities of existing branches. In Augusta, Ga., Jordan led the South's first successful boycott of stores that refused to hire blacks.

In 1964 Jordan was named director of the Voter Education Project, an Atlanta-based effort to increase black voter registration in the South. The project was sponsored by the Southern Regional Council, a coalition of major civil rights organizations ranging from the militant Student Nonviolent Coordinating Committee to the more moderate NAACP and Southern Christian Leadership Conference. Much of Jordan's time as director was spent mediating conflicts among the various participants. The project succeeded, however, in registering between one and a half and two million Southern black voters between 1964 and 1968, fulfilling a major goal of the civil rights movement.

After leaving the Voter Education Project in 1968, Jordan worked briefly as an attorney for the Office of Economic Opportunity in Atlanta. He moved to New York in 1970 to become director of the United Negro College Fund, the financial arm of 36 black colleges in the U.S. In January 1972 Jordan was named director of the National Urban League. Under Jordan the Urban League continued to concentrate on the problems of the urban poor, including police-community relations, tenant and welfare issues and summer jobs for black students. Jordan joined other civil rights leaders such as Jesse Jackson [*q.v.*] in urging increased emphasis on black economic advancement, to take advantage of the political gains made during the 1960s.

[SLG]

JUDD, WALTER H(ENRY)

b. Sept. 25, 1898; Rising City, Neb.
Republican Representative, Minn., 1943-63.

After earning his medical degree from the University of Nebraska, Walter H. Judd left for China as a medical missionary. Except for a four-year leave of absence, Judd worked as a doctor and hospital superintendent in Fukien Province from 1925 to 1938. Six months after the Japanese Army invaded Fukien, Judd left China for Minneapolis. He won election to the House four years later and acquired a reputation, particularly among Republicans, as a congressional expert on the Far East. He strongly advocated American aid to the Nationalist Chinese government of Chiang Kai-shek, first against the Japanese and ultimately against the Chinese Communists.

After Chiang's defeat and exile from the mainland in 1949, Judd became identified with the American "China Lobby" composed of business, editorial and congressional leaders who urged American support for the Nationalist regime on Taiwan. In 1953 Judd and others organized the "Committee of One Million" against the admission of Communist China to the United Nations. The group directed a massive letter-writing campaign to Congress and the State Department in opposition to any normalization of relations with mainland China. Judd remained a prominent spokesman for Republican anti-Communism until 1962 when, following redistricting, he lost his House seat to a Democratic opponent. [See EISENHOWER, KENNEDY Volumes]

Still powerful in Minnesota politics and well-remembered by many Party officials for his anti-Communist attack on the Democrats at the 1960 Republican National Convention, Judd won designation as his state's favorite-son candidate for President in 1964. Managers for presidential candidate Sen. Barry M. Goldwater (R, Ariz.) [*q.v.*] failed to defeat the Judd delegate slate at the Minnesota Republican Convention in June 1964. Nominated at the national gathering the following month, Judd won a total of 22 votes on the first ballot.

During the general election campaign Goldwater indicated that Judd would serve as an adviser in the organization of his presidential administration. On Oct. 31 the *Chicago Tribune* reported that Goldwater planned to name Judd U.N. ambassador if elected.

In political retirement after the campaign, Judd continued to speak out on public issues. He consistently opposed both the Kennedy and Johnson medicare proposals, and in June 1965 he ran an unsuccessful campaign for the presidency of the American Medical Association. Judd continued to fight against any change in American policy toward China. He told the Senate Foreign Relations Committee in March 1966 that the Communist government "does not represent the Chinese people any more than the Quisling regime in Norway represented the Norwegian people." Judd added that American recognition of China would undermine the Nationalists and threaten the security of the Philippines. In October 1966 the State Department announced Judd's appointment to a 19-member advisory panel on East Asian and Pacific Affairs.

Judd continued his opposition to Communist China even after President Richard Nixon [*q.v.*] initiated closer ties with the mainland regime in the early 1970s. As chairman of the Committee of One Million, claiming 40,000 members in 1971, Judd decried the U.N. General Assembly's admission of mainland China as a member and its expulsion of the Nationalists in October 1971. He called the Assembly's vote "a cynical affront to human justice." He made no official statement, however, on President Nixon's visit to Peking in February 1972.

[JLB]

KAPPEL, FREDERICK R(USSELL)

b. Jan. 14, 1902; Albert Lea, Minn.
Chairman and Chief Executive, American Telephone and Telegraph Corporation, August 1961-January 1967.

Frederick Kappel joined the Northwestern Bell Telephone Company (an American Telephone and Telegraph [AT&T] subsidiary) immediately after he graduated from the University of Minnesota in 1924 with a degree in electrical engineering. An "operations" man, Kappel rose steadily through Northwestern's ranks, moving to New York as an AT&T vice president in 1949. He was chosen president of AT&T's manufacturing and supply unit, the Western Electric Company, in 1953 and became president of AT&T itself in 1956. In that year Kappel handled the final stages of negotiations with the government by which AT&T was allowed to keep Western Electric. (The Justice Department had been trying to force the corporation to divest its manufacturing subsidiary since 1949.) Kappel was elevated to chairman at AT&T in August 1961. [See KENNEDY Volume]

With assets of $35 billion in 1966, AT&T was the largest private enterprise in the world. It set an earnings record that year, when its profits exceeded $2 billion for the first time. AT&T had more stockholders, over 2 million, and employes, over 730,000, than any other company. Its $4 billion outlay for capital construction dwarfed that of every other corporation. AT&T had a very healthy earnings record during Kappel's tenure: its annual earnings growth totaled 35% over his last five years as president. Earnings growth came to only 8% in the five years following his departure, however.

When the Federal Communications Commission (FCC) announced in October 1965 a full-scale investigation of interstate telephone rates, Kappel, who had fought the investigation behind the scenes, denounced the probe as "totally unwarranted." In July 1967 the FCC ordered a cut of $120 million in annual AT&T charges for long-distance service. The FCC charged that AT&T was entitled to a 7% to 7½% return on its investment but had been earning more than 8%.

Despite this setback, Kappel enjoyed considerable influence within the Johnson Administration. *Newsweek* reported that "when he wanted a businessman's view, the President was prone to forget his own Secretary of Commerce; instead he would pick up the telephone and call someone like Henry Ford II [*q.v.*] or Frederick Kappel."

After leaving AT&T in Jaunary 1967, Kappel was appointed by President Johnson as head of a special commission to undertake an "exhaustive review" of the postal system. In July 1968 the commission issued a report recommending that the Post Office Department be converted into a non-profit government corporation.

[TO]

KASTENMEIER, ROBERT W(ILLIAM)

b. Jan. 24, 1924; Beaver Dam, Wisc.
Democratic Representative, Wisc., 1959- .

Kastenmeier, whose father was a farmer and sometime court clerk, grew up near Madison in the district he would later represent in Congress. After serving in the Philippines during World War II, he studied law at the University of Wisconsin. Admitted to the bar in 1952, Kastenmeier became active in the state's revived Democratic Party and was narrowly elected to Congress in 1958. His majorities remained unimpressive until redistricting removed an affluent Republican suburb in 1963. Thereafter Kastenmeier, a strong liberal, was returned to office by comfortable margins, which grew as the Vietnam war escalated and Madison's university community became increasingly politicized.

Kastenmeier attempted to forge an alliance between liberal congressmen and academics soon after his arrival in Washington. In 1960 he announced the formation of the "Liberal Project," a small group of congressmen who joined with scholars from various fields to develop new liberal policies. *The Liberal Papers*, published by the Project in 1962, urged a reappraisal of Cold War foreign policy and recommended, among other things, admission of Communist China to the U.N.

A consistent supporter of the Johnson Administration's Great Society programs, Kastenmeier was a member of the Judiciary Committee and worked to strengthen the civil rights legislation passed in the mid-1960s. As chairman of the Ad Hoc Advisory Committee on Voting and Civil Rights, he issued a report in January 1966 that called for more vigorous congressional action to implement the 1965 Voting Rights Act.

Kastenmeier was an early congressional opponent of the Vietnam war. Although he voted for war appropriations in 1965, in March of that year he had 15 other congressmen wrote to President Johnson criticizing American use of tear gas and defoliants in Vietnam. That summer Kastenmeier participated in an unsuccessful attempt to persuade the House Foreign Affairs Committee to hold public hearings on the war. Defeated in this effort, he then organized his own hearings on Vietnam in Madison. The meetings, at which more than 50 people spoke, resembled the campus Vietnam teach-ins of that April and May. The transcript of the hearings was published the following year as *Vietnam Hearings: Voices from the Grassroots*.

Kastenmeier joined 16 other congressmen who sent Johnson a letter in December 1965 urging him not to bomb Hanoi and Haiphong. In January 1966 Kastenmeier and seven other congressmen proposed contacts between South Vietnam and the National Liberation Front.

Maintaining a staunch liberalism in the early 1970s, Kastenmeier became a prominent advocate of prison reform legislation. During the 1974 House Judiciary Committee hearings on the possible impeachment of President Nixon he won national attention as a consistent proponent of Nixon's removal from office. [See NIXON Volume]

[MDB]

KATZENBACH, NICHOLAS deB(ELLEVILLE)

b. Jan. 17, 1922; Philadelphia, Pa.
U.S. Deputy Attorney General, 1962-64; Acting U.S. Attorney General, 1964-65; U.S. Attorney General, 1965-66; U.S. Undersecretary of State, 1966-69.

A 1945 graduate of Princeton University, Katzenbach received a degree from Yale Law School in 1947 and then was a Rhodes scholar at Oxford University for two years.

Between 1952 and 1960 he taught at Yale and the University of Chicago Law School. Appointed assistant attorney general in charge of the Justice Department's Office of Legal Counsel in January 1961, Katzenbach was named deputy attorney general, the second highest position in the Justice Department, in April 1962. He helped draft the Kennedy Administration's foreign trade program and the Communications Satellite Act of 1962. In December 1962 he helped coordinate a government effort to assemble food and medical supplies needed to secure the release of prisoners captured during the April 1961 Bay of Pigs invasion of Cuba. Katzenbach was also concerned with civil rights questions, directing Justice Department operations on the scene during the crises over desegregation of the University of Mississippi in September 1962 and of the University of Alabama in June 1963. Katzenbach also acted as a major broker in the long negotiations with Congress over the 1964 Civil Rights Act. [See KENNEDY Volume]

Katzenbach worked closely with the Warren Commission in its investigation of President Kennedy's assassination, and in September 1964 President Johnson named him to a four-member panel to advise him on execution of the Commission's recommendation. When Robert Kennedy [*q.v.*] resigned as Attorney General on Sept. 3, 1964, Katzenbach, at Kennedy's urging, was named Acting Attorney General. President Johnson appointed him Attorney General on Jan. 28, 1965.

Prior to the civil rights march from Selma to Montgomery, Ala., which began on March 21, 1965 and was led by Martin Luther King [*q.v.*], Katzenbach had the Justice Department seek a federal court order barring state officials from interfering with the demonstration. He kept in close touch with Justice Department aides in Alabama throughout the march. Working closely with congressional leaders of both parties, Katzenbach also drafted the Johnson Administration's voting rights bill, introduced in Congress in March 1965, and then worked to secure its passage. Once the bill became law in August 1965, Katzenbach oversaw its enforcement and successfully defended its constitutionality in the Supreme Court in January 1966. Both the U.S. Civil Rights Commission and rights leaders criticized the Attorney General's enforcement efforts, however, saying he should have sent more federal voting examiners into the South to increase black voter registration.

Katzenbach stepped up the Justice Department's efforts to achieve school desegregation for 1965-66. In December 1965 he issued guidelines for government agencies on cutting off funds, under provisions of the 1964 Civil Rights Act, to federally aided programs found to be practicing racial discrimination. Katzenbach played an important role in drafting the Johnson Administration's 1966 civil rights bill, which included provisions prohibiting racial discrimination in housing and in the selection of juries and providing protection for civil rights workers. Although the bill passed the House, it died in the Senate in September 1966, when its supporters were unable to end a filibuster against it.

Katzenbach helped write the Administration's anti-crime proposals of March 1965, and in the spring of that year he called for new legislation to aid in the fight against organized crime, supported curbs on interstate mail-order sales of firearms and endorsed several proposals for federal prison reform. In July 1965 Katzenbach was named head of a presidential Commission on Law Enforcement and the Administration of Justice. The Commission's February 1967 report recommended more than 200 measures to reduce the causes of crime and improve law enforcement at the local, state and federal levels.

In the period when Katzenbach served as Attorney General, the FBI, a division of the Justice Department, engaged in a number of activities that clearly violated the law and in others that were of questionable legality. These included the opening of first-class mail and the development of COINTELPRO, an effort to disrupt and discredit the Communist and Socialist Workers' parties and "white hate groups," particularly the Ku Klux Klan. In November 1975 testimony before a Senate Select Committee on Intelligence Activities, Katzenbach denied knowledge of the mail openings and COINTELPRO and held FBI Director J. Edgar Hoover [*q.v.*] directly responsible. Katzenbach did admit that he had known of Bureau efforts to disrupt the Klan in the South. He pointed out that Klan members were not "ordinary citizens seeking only to exercise their constitutional rights" but terrorists who threatened the lives of blacks and civil rights workers. He considered the FBI campaign against the Klan fully justified, even "magnificent."

Katzenbach also admitted that he had been aware that the FBI had wiretapped the home telephone of leader Martin Luther King. He ordered an end to the tap on April 1965, but the FBI tapped King's hotel bedrooms on three subsequent occasions without Katzenbach's approval. In 1966, after a bitter exchange between Katzenbach and Hoover on the question of wiretapping, Katzenbach concluded that "he could no longer effectively serve as Attorney General because of Mr. Hoover's obvious resentment of me."

Katzenbach was appointed undersecretary of state on Sept. 21, 1966. He accompanied Secretary of Defense Robert S. McNamara [*q.v.*] on fact-finding missions to South Vietnam in October 1966 and July 1967. Katzenbach headed several diplomatic missions abroad, including a 12-nation tour of Africa in May 1967, a January 1968 trip to Western Europe to explain the Administration's new measures for improvement of the U.S. balance of payments position and a July 1968 visit to India for a broad review of U.S.—Indian relations. He also toured Europe in October 1968 to demonstrate to Yugoslavia and other nations continuing American concern for European security following the August 1968 Soviet occupation of Czechoslovakia.

In February 1967, following disclosures that the CIA had secretly supplied funds for the overseas programs of the National Student Association and other private American organizations, President Johnson named Katzenbach to a three-member commission ordered to review these CIA activities. The commission, which was criticized by those who wanted full disclosure of covert CIA subsidies, reported that the Agency had acted in accord with National Security Council policies established in the 1950s. On March 29 President Johnson followed the commission's recommendation that all covert government aid to private educational, philanthropic and cultural organizations be barred.

A supporter of President Johnson's policies in Vietnam, Katzenbach aroused controversy with his testimony before the Senate Foreign Relations Committee in August 1967. He asserted that a formal declaration of war was unnecessary because the Gulf of Tonkin Resolution, passed by Congress in August 1964, authorized the President's use of armed forces in Vietnam. According to Eric Goldman [*q.v.*], Katzenbach also implied that the President could act largely as he pleased in foreign affairs without regard to Congress, and this testimony was a factor in Sen. Eugene McCarthy's (D, Minn.) [*q.v.*] decision to enter the race for the 1968 Democratic presidential nomination on an anti-war platform.

According to a *New York Times* report of Nov. 12, 1967, Katzenbach was frustrated in his effort to introduce modern management techniques to the State Department, a reform which he believed would help restore the Department's primacy among government agencies operating overseas. He did, however, work out personnel-sharing arrangements with various government agencies that were designed to broaden diplomats' experience with domestic problems and encourage a cross-fertilization of ideas between the Foreign Service and other government operations. Katzenbach resigned as undersecretary on Nov. 8, 1968, following the presidential election, but he agreed to stay on in the State Department during the transfer of power to the Nixon Administration. In 1969 he joined the International Business Machines Corp. as vice president and general counsel.

[CAB]

For further information:

Eric F. Goldman, *The Tragedy of Lyndon Johnson* (New York, 1969).

Victor S. Navasky, *Kennedy Justice* (New York, 1971).

KENNAN, GEORGE F(ROST)
b. Feb. 16, 1904; Milwaukee, Wisc.
Historian, diplomat.

Kennan graduated from Princeton University in 1925 and joined the Foreign Service the following year. For the next two decades he served in nearly a dozen posts in Eastern and Central Europe, including two tours of duty in Moscow (1933-35; 1944-46) that secured his reputation as an expert on Soviet-American relations. During his second stay he outlined what came to be known as the "containment" policy, a design to resist Soviet expansionism in the postwar period. As a result of his work in formulating the new policy, Kennan was named director of the State Department's policy planning staff in 1947. Kennan served briefly as ambassador to the Soviet Union in 1952 but was declared *persona non grata* by the Soviets because of his criticism of their treatment of Western diplomats. He formally retired from the Foreign Service in 1953 to take a post at the Institute for Advanced Study at Princeton, where he wrote several important works on Soviet-American relations. [See TRUMAN, EISENHOWER Volumes]

In February 1961 President Kennedy named Kennan ambassador to Yugoslavia. Kennan, who had long advocated policies to weaken the internal unity of the Soviet bloc, sought to strengthen Yugoslavia's ties to the West. However, the American Congress, suspicious of economic cooperation with any Communist nation, undermined Kennan's efforts by restricting trade with Yugoslavia. He resigned his ambassadorship in May 1963 and later wrote that Congress was partly responsible for Soviet-Yugoslav reconciliation in the early 1960s. [See KENNEDY Volume]

Kennan resumed his academic career in July 1963 but returned to the public spotlight in the mid-1960s as an important critic of American policy in Vietnam. In numerous articles and speeches and in testimony before several congressional committees, Kennan argued that Vietnam was not vital to American strategic or diplomatic interests. He warned that precipitous escalation of the war in Vietnam would destroy the possibility of a negotiated settlement and force a rapprochement between the Soviet and Chinese Communists.

Kennan's analysis received its widest hearing when Sen. J. William Fulbright (D, Ark.) [*q.v.*] invited him to testify before a nationally televised session of the Senate Foreign Relations Committee in February 1966. Kennan charged that because of the Administration's "preoccupation with Vietnam," Europe and the Soviet Union were not receiving proper diplomatic attention. Kennan argued that the U.S. had no binding commitment to South Vietnam and questioned whether American credibility or prestige would be seriously damaged by a withdrawal. Kennan counseled a minimal military effort to maintain a U.S. presence in Vietnam until a peaceful settlement could be reached. Always a European-oriented diplomat, Kennan "emphatically" denied the applicability of the "containment doctrine" to Southeast Asia while urging its retention in Europe. After the USSR invaded Czechoslovakia in August 1968, Kennan urged stationing 100,000 additional American troops in West Germany until the Russians left Czechoslovakia.

Kennan was a strong proponent of a professional diplomatic corps that could generally function without concern for momentary domestic political pressures. He thought highly publicized summit conferences among heads of state generally unproductive and often disruptive of long-standing diplomatic relationships. In the late 1960s Kennan was also a severe critic of the student left, which he considered moralistic and anti-intellectual.

Kennan was inducted into the American Academy of Arts and Letters in 1964 and served as the Academy's president from 1967 to 1971. He was also president of the National Institute of Arts and Letters from 1964 to 1967. During the spring of 1967 Kennan assisted Svetlana Alliluyeva, daughter of the late Soviet dictator Joseph Stalin, when she was deciding to seek residence in the U.S. Kennan read a manuscript copy of her autobiography and then met her in Switzerland after she had left the Soviet Union. Accompanying her to the U.S., he urged Americans to accept Alliluyeva on her own terms, as a "courageous, sincere and talented" human being.

[JCH]

For further information:

George F. Kennan *On Dealing with the Communist World* (New York, 1964).

———, *Memoirs, 1925-1950* (Boston, 1967).

———, *Democracy and the Student Left* (Boston, 1968).

KENNEDY, EDWARD M(OORE)

b. Feb. 22, 1932; Brookline, Mass.
Democratic Senator, Mass., 1962- .

Edward Kennedy was the younger brother of President John F. Kennedy and Sen. Robert F. Kennedy (D, N.Y.) [*q.v.*]. He attended private schools in England and America before entering Harvard in 1951. In his freshman year he was suspended for cheating, but after spending two years in the Army he returned to the University and graduated in 1956. He earned a law degree from the University of Virginia Law School three years later.

Kennedy had his first experience in practical politics when he served as manager of John Kennedy's 1958 senatorial reelection campaign. In 1960 he was put in charge of the Kennedy presidential campaign in the Mountain states. Most were carried by Vice President Richard M. Nixon [*q.v.*].

Amid Republican and liberal accusations of "nepotism" and charges that the Kennedy family was attempting to start a political dynasty, Edward Kennedy announced his candidacy for the Senate in 1962. His opponent in the Democratic primary was Edward J. McCormack, Massachusetts attorney general and nephew of House Speaker John McCormack (D, Mass.) [*q.v.*]. The voters' negative reaction to Edward McCormack's personal attacks on Kennedy's youth and inexperience contributed to an easy Kennedy victory in the Democratic primary. He went on to win the general election with 57% of the vote over the equally inexperienced George Cabot Lodge in a campaign that was billed as the "battle of the dynasties."

Unlike his older brother, who used the Senate as a stepping-stone to national office, Edward Kennedy was careful to fit smoothly into the Senate "Establishment" by courting such senior senators as James O. Eastland (D, Miss.) [*q.v.*] and Richard B. Russell (D, Ga.) [*q.v.*]. Appointed to the Judiciary and the Labor and Public Welfare Committees, he supported President Kennedy on most major issues in 1963. He was presiding over the Senate on Nov. 22 when word came that his brother had been assassinated in Dallas. [See KENNEDY Volume]

In 1965 Kennedy assumed his first important role as a senator, when he successfully managed passage of the Johnson Administration's immigration bill, which abolished national origin quotas and allowed about 300,000 immigrants into the U.S. annually. In February he proposed authorization of a National Teachers Corps to provide financial incentives for instructors who volunteered to work in poverty areas. His idea was incorporated into a portion of the 1965 Higher Education Act.

Edward Kennedy generally followed his brother Robert's cautious opposition to the Vietnam War. He recommended a complete overhaul of the Selective Service System at House Armed Services Committee hearings in 1966. He favored selection of men for the military by a national lottery, but his proposal was blocked by Sen. Richard Russell and other conservatives until late 1969.

Kennedy's greatest impact was in his effort to focus national attention on the plight of Vietnamese refugees. Through his chairmanship of the Senate Subcommittee on Refugees and Escapees, he became in his biographer Theo Lippman's phrase, "*the* American expert on the war's impact on the people of Vietnam." During the late 1960s he was a consistent critic of what he considered the Administration's inhumane handling of the refugee problem. In August 1968 he condemned the war, called for a withdrawal of all U.S. and North Vietnamese troops from South Vietnam and recommended increased political and economic aid to the South.

After Robert Kennedy's assassination during his 1968 presidential campaign, Edward

Kennedy refused to run for the Democratic nomination or to accept a draft, despite pleas from his brother's liberal supporters and Chicago Mayor Richard Daley [*q.v.*]. Many saw him as a possible 1972 presidential contender until he was involved in a July 1969 automobile accident on Chappaquiddick Island, off Martha's Vineyard, Mass., in which a young woman drowned.

In 1969 Kennedy defeated Sen. Russell Long (D, La.) [*q.v.*] for the post of majority whip, and the next year he was easily reelected to the Senate. Aided by a strong political organization in Massachusetts, a competent staff and the lingering attractions of the Kennedy mystique, he emerged as one of the most powerful members of the Senate in the early 1970s. He was particularly active in the drive to enact national health insurance legislation. [See NIXON Volume]

[FHM]

For further information:
James MacGregor Burns, *Edward Kennedy and the Camelot Legacy* (New York, 1976).
Theo Lippman, Jr., *Senator Ted Kennedy* (New York, 1976).

KENNEDY, JACQUELINE (LEE BOUVIER)

b. July 28, 1929; Southampton, N.Y.
First Lady, January 1961-November 1963

Born to wealth and social prominence, Jacqueline Bouvier briefly attended Vassar and the Sorbonne before graduating from George Washington University in Washington in 1951. First introduced to Sen. John Kennedy (D, Mass.) in 1952, the couple was married on Sept. 12, 1953, in one of the most publicized society weddings of that year.

During her husband's Administration Mrs. Kennedy made an effort to restore the White House as a period mansion of the 18th and 19th centuries. Her expertise in this area was highlighted on Feb. 14, 1962, when she conducted an hour-long televised tour of the White House. Mrs. Kennedy was also instrumental in introducing various prominent writers, artists and musicians to White House functions that had previously been restrictive and formal. A trend-setter in fashion, Mrs. Kennedy proved to be a surprising political and diplomatic asset to the President, especially during their trip to Paris in June 1961 and on a visit to India she made alone in March 1962. [See KENNEDY Volume]

Mrs. Kennedy accompanied the President to Texas in November 1963, and she was sitting beside him when he was shot to death in an open car on Nov. 22. Later the same day she witnessed the swearing-in of President Johnson aboard Air Force One. Her dignified conduct and bearing during the aftermath of the assassination earned her worldwide respect and contributed to the power of the Kennedy mystique later in the decade. Throughout the 1960s Mrs. Kennedy remained among the country's most admired women and in 1965 and 1966 led the Gallup poll in that category.

In March 1964 Mrs. Kennedy commissioned William Manchester to write a version of the events surrounding the assassination of her husband. After Manchester had finished the manuscript in December 1966, she instituted a well-publicized legal action against the author, his publishing firm of Harper and Row, Inc. and Cowles Communications (publishers of *Look* magazine) to block publication and serialization of Manchester's *Death of a President.* Mrs. Kennedy charged that the defendants had violated a previously agreed upon 11-point contract and invaded "her dignity and privacy." Mrs. Kennedy further insisted that Manchester had exploited her emotional state when he recorded her recollections of the assassination. The dispute was resolved in January 1967 when Manchester agreed to a number of deletions and modifications in the text, specifically those relating to alleged hostility between the Kennedy and Johnson factions in Dallas and one that described Mrs. Kennedy as "frantic, hysterical, ferocious" in the immediate aftermath of the assassination. Concerning the case, columnist James Reston wrote in the *New York Times* that Mrs. Kennedy had been deceived into thinking she could "make Kennedy as history conform to Kennedy as legend."

Despite the controversy over the Manchester book, Mrs. Kennedy's popularity remained undiminished until her October 1968 marriage to Greek shipping magnate Aristotle Onassis. Thereafter Mrs. Kennedy lived in France, Greece and New York.

[FHM]

KENNEDY, ROBERT F(RANCIS)

b. Nov. 20, 1925; Brookline, Mass.
d. June 6, 1968; Los Angeles, Calif.
Attorney General, January 1961-September 1964; Democratic Senator, N.Y., 1965-68.

Robert Kennedy was the seventh of nine children in a wealthy and politically ambitious Irish Catholic Massachusetts family. After naval service in World War II, he graduated from Harvard in 1948 and the University of Virginia Law School three years later. He served briefly as a Justice Department lawyer before resigning to manage his brother John F. Kennedy's successful 1952 Senate race.

In the early and mid-1950s, Kennedy served as assistant counsel and then chief Democratic counsel for the Senate Permanent Subcommittee on Investigations. In 1957 he was named chief counsel for Sen. John L. McClellan's (D, Ark.) [*q.v.*] Senate Rackets Committee, where he won national prominence for his investigations of Teamsters Union leaders James Hoffa [*q.v.*] and David Beck. He resigned in 1959 to manage his brother's presidential campaign. [See EISENHOWER Volume]

Kennedy was appointed Attorney General by the President-elect in December 1960. Although plagued through his tenure by criticism of his youth and inexperience, he attracted exceptionally competent lawyers to the Justice Department, launched a successful drive against organized crime and became increasingly committed to the support of the civil rights of Southern blacks. Because of his position as the brother of the President, he also assumed tasks well beyond his purview as Attorney General. During the 1962 Cuban missile crisis, for example, he helped secure a consensus on the decision to blockade Cuba and then negotiated with the Soviets on removal of the weapons. [See KENNEDY Volume]

Robert Kennedy was stunned by his brother's assassination in Dallas on Nov. 22, 1963 and in the next few weeks delegated many of his responsibilities at the Justice Department to subordinates. His last major action as Attorney General was to announce, in August 1964, the establishment of an Office of Criminal Justice to ensure that federal law enforcement was fair and objective, especially as it regarded the arrest system and the right of the poor to counsel.

Kennedy believed that he was a logical vice presidential candidate on a 1964 Johnson ticket. However, with Lyndon Johnson as President, a political rivalry that originated in the 1960 presidential campaign resurfaced. Johnson biographer Doris Kearns wrote: "There was between them a dislike so strong that it seemed almost as if each had been created for the purpose of exasperating the other. . . . Johnson identified Bobby as the agent of an effort to destroy his political career."

While Kennedy did have the support of many Northern liberal political leaders, Johnson clearly did not regard him as necessary to ensure a November Democratic victory, particularly since Sen. Barry M. Goldwater (R, Ariz.) [*q.v.*], the likely Republican presidential nominee, appeared to be a weak challenger. In July Johnson circumvented a direct public confrontation with Kennedy, and a possible division of the Democratic Party, by announcing that he was eliminating all members of his cabinet from vice presidential consideration.

In August Kennedy announced that he would seek the U.S. Senate seat from New York held by Sen. Kenneth B. Keating (R, N.Y.). In the initial stages of his campaign, Kennedy was widely criticized as a "carpetbagger" who merely sought the New York seat as a stepping stone to the presidency. To dispel these doubts, and the reputation he had earned as a "ruthless" politician, Kennedy waged a vigorous statewide campaign that stressed his political liberalism and the importance of having a Democratic senator to influence a Democratic presidential administration. Aided by the Johnson landslide and by Keating's ineffectiveness as a campaigner, Kennedy won the November election by 719,000 votes.

In the Senate Kennedy was assigned to the Government Operations and Labor and Public Welfare Committees. Although he compiled a consistently liberal voting record, the day-to-day legislative process bored him. "They only take about one vote a week here," he once declared, "and they never can tell you in advance what it is going to be so you can schedule other things." As a senator, Kennedy used his great popularity to focus attention on the plight of the nation's minorities. Though an opponent of the "black power" concept, he strongly backed greater government anti-poverty efforts and passage of new civil rights legislation. He further identified himself with black aspirations as a founder of the Bedford-Stuyvesant Restoration Corporation in Brooklyn's black ghetto. In March 1966 he traveled to Delano, Calif., to publicly "break bread" with farm worker leader Cesar Chavez [*q.v.*], who was ending a 25-day fast dedicated to the reaffirmation of nonviolence in his movement.

In 1965 Kennedy said that he "basically" supported the Johnson Administration's position on Vietnam. However, over the next three years he became increasingly outspoken about Administration policy. In February 1966 he recommended that the National Liberation Front (NLF) be "admitted to a share of power and responsibility in a future coalition South Vietnamese government." In March of the next year he proposed suspending U.S. bombing of North Vietnam as part of a three-point plan to help end the war, but his proposals were immediately rejected by the Administration. In November 1967 he made his strongest criticism of the war, asserting that the U.S. "moral position" in Vietnam had been undermined by the Johnson Administration. "We're killing South Vietnamese," he said, "we're killing women, we're killing innocent people because we don't want to have the war fought on American soil."

By early 1967 many liberal Democrats hoped Robert Kennedy would oppose President Johnson in the next year's Democratic primaries. They sought Kennedy's candidacy as a means of de-escalating the war and of restoring and continuing in some measure the original Administration of John F. Kennedy. As David Halberstam said in *The Unfinished Odyssey of Robert Kennedy*, "There were not just two political parties in America in the late 1960s, but really three—the Democrats headed by Johnson, the Republicans, and the Kennedys, almost a party unto themselves. It was a government in exile with its own shadow cabinet and with Robert Kennedy as the titular head."

Despite 1967 polls showing that Democrats favored him over Johnson, Kennedy repeatedly asserted that he would back the President for reelection in 1968. After Sen. Eugene J. McCarthy (D, Minn.) [*q.v.*] made a surprisingly strong showing in the March 12, 1968 New Hampshire primary, Kennedy announced that he was "reassessing" his position. On March 14, according to Theodore Sorensen, Kennedy offered to stay out of the presidential race if Johnson appointed a commission to study a revision of U.S. policy in Vietnam, an offer the President summarily turned down.

On March 16 Kennedy formally announced his candidacy for the Democratic presidential nomination, declaring, "At stake is not simply the leadership of our Party and even of our country. It is the right to the moral leadership of the planet." He also asserted that the New Hampshire results had removed the possibility of a "personal struggle" between himself and the President. Kennedy later called Johnson's March 31 decision not to seek reelection "truly magnanimous."

Kennedy was particularly anxious not to antagonize youthful voters or members of the anti-war movement, many of whom supported McCarthy. Throughout the campaign Kennedy was careful to maintain a surface cordiality, although Kennedy privately considered McCarthy vain and lazy. McCarthy openly regarded the New York Senator as arrogant and opportunistic.

His broad national constituency of

minorities, young professionals and blue-collar workers reflected Kennedy's "extraordinary capacity to stress both the principle of equal access and the role of the law in gaining social cohesion," according to columnist Max Lerner. His candidacy, particularly among the disadvantaged, often assumed an evangelical fervor rare in American politics.

He easily won the Indiana primary on May 7 and the Nebraska primary, with 52% of the vote, one week later. However, the Oregon campaign turned bitter, with McCarthy asserting there would be "further involvements like Vietnam" if Kennedy were elected. Oregon had no large Negro or ethnic groupings and few blue-collar workers, and Kennedy's early role in the rackets hearings cost him the support of the state's powerful Teamsters Union. McCarthy won the May 28 primary with 45% of the vote to 39% for Kennedy, who described his defeat as a "setback I could ill afford" and declared that he would "abide by the results" of the California primary. It was the first electoral defeat by any Kennedy in 29 contests.

Kennedy campaigned in California to the point of exhaustion, and he managed to put together a broad coalition of blacks, migrant laborers and blue-collar workers. On May 31 he and McCarthy met in an informal TV "debate" on the issues. The encounter, later termed inconclusive by the press, revealed that the two men were in agreement on many important issues. However, they did clash on housing policy, with McCarthy advocating a housing program designed to disperse ghetto dwellers from the inner cities to suburban areas and Kennedy opposing this as politically and economically impractical.

On June 4 Kennedy won the primary and its 172 delegates with 46% of the vote to McCarthy's 42%. Shortly after leaving the victory rally, he was shot and critically wounded by Sirhan B. Sirhan [*q.v.*], an Arab alien. Kennedy died of his wounds on June 6, 1968. His death marked the fourth assassination of an important American political leader within five years. President Johnson declared a national day of mourning. The train bearing Kennedy's funeral procession from New York to Washington was remimiscent of those of Lincoln and Franklin Roosevelt, with thousands lining the railroad tracks to pay their respects as it passed.

[FHM]

For further information:
Lewis Chester, Godfrey Hodgson, Bruce Page, *An American Melodrama* (New York, 1969).
David Halberstam, *The Unfinished Odyssey of Robert Kennedy* (New York, 1968).
William V. Shannon, *The Heir Apparent* (New York, 1967).
Theodore H. White, *The Making of the President 1968* (New York, 1968).

KEPPEL, FRANCIS

b. April 16, 1916, New York, N.Y.
Commissioner of Education, March 1963-September 1965; Assistant Secretary of Health, Education and Welfare, September 1965-April 1966.

Francis Keppel, son of a former dean of Columbia College, attended Groton and graduated from Harvard in 1938. After studying sculpture in Rome for a short period following his graduation, he returned to Harvard University where he served as dean of freshmen. Following the war he was assistant to the provost of the University. Keppel was named dean of the Harvard graduate school of education in 1948. Over the next 14 years he increased the size, endowment and prestige of the school.

President John F. Kennedy chose Keppel to succeed Sterling M. McMurrin as Commissioner of Education in November 1962. Throughout 1963 Keppel worked on behalf of a number of Kennedy Administration measures that were passed shortly after the President's death. These included the Higher Education Facilities Act, the Library Services Act, the Vocational Education Act and the Manpower Training and Development Act. Keppel also demonstrated a remarkable ability to mediate between the competing interests of the National Education Association (NEA), representing over a million elementary and secondary public school teachers, and the National Catholic Welfare Conference (NCWC) representing Catholic parochial schools. [See KENNEDY Volume]

Shortly after the 1964 presidential election, President Johnson suggested to Keppel that he undertake the delicate task of framing legislation, acceptable both to parochial and public school groups, authorizing federal aid to elementary and secondary schools. According to Eugene Eidenberg and Roy D. Morey in *Act of Congress: The Legislative Process And The Making of Education Policy*, Keppel was "the one man who was able to bridge the gaps that separated various factions on the [bill]. . . ." Aided by Wilbur J. Cohen [*q.v.*], assistant secretary of the Department of Health, Education and Welfare (HEW), and White House aides Douglass Cater, Jr. [*q.v.*] and Lawrence F. O'Brien [*q.v.*], Keppel arranged a crucial compromise in which the NEA agreed to permit some form of public assistance to sectarian schools while the NCWC settled for substantial but less than equal participation of parochial schools in the various aid programs.

The Administration bill stipulated that aid was to be distributed to local school districts on the basis of the number of children in each district who came from families with incomes under $2,000. It was left to state authorities to determine how much assistance should go to public, private and parochial schools. The bill specifically authorized appropriations for private and parochial schools for library books and educational materials. This was the principal means by which such schools benefited from the legislation.

The Elementary and Secondary Education Act became law in April 1965. Keppel moved quickly to reorganize his office, recruiting a number of young and innovative staffers to deal with the heavy burden of administering the new law. As head of the Office of Education, Keppel was authorized under the 1964 Civil Rights Act to withhold federal aid to racially segregated school systems. He announced in April 1965 that the nation's 27,000 school districts would be required to desegregate by September 1967. He notified the Illinois Board of Education in October 1965 that federal funds totaling $34 million were being withheld from the Chicago public school system as a result of a complaint filed by a group representing 75 civil rights organizations. Mayor Richard J. Daley of Chicago, a power in Democratic Party politics, was incensed over the cutoff of funds and personally protested to President Johnson. The President sent Wilbur Cohen to Chicago to negotiate a compromise. The Chicago Board of Education agreed to establish a committee to review the drawing of school boundaries to alleviate segregation. The federal funds were then quickly released. This compromise was generally considered a defeat for Keppel. In September 1965 he was named assistant HEW secretary, ostensibly a promotion but really an effort by the Johnson Administration to remove him from his politically sensitive post.

Keppel resigned from HEW in April 1966 to become chairman and chief executive officer of the General Learning Corporation. He also served as vice chairman of the New York City Board of Education and as a trustee of the Carnegie Corporation and the Russell Sage Foundation. In 1974 he became director of the Aspen Institute Program in Education for a Changing Society.

[JLW]

For further information:
Eugene Eidenberg and Roy D. Morey, *An Act of Congress: The Legislative Process and The Making of Education Policy* (New York, 1969).

KERNER, OTTO

b. Aug. 15, 1908; Chicago, Ill.
d. May 9, 1976; Chicago, Ill.
Governor, Ill., 1961-68.

Kerner was the son of a prominent Chicago judge who served on the U.S. Court of Appeals (7th Circuit). After receiving a law degree from Northwestern University in 1934, he practiced corporate law for many years in Chicago. In 1947 he was appointed U.S. district attorney for the northern district of Illinois. In 1954 Kerner won election as county judge for Cook

County. In 1960, with the support of Chicago Mayor Richard Daley [*q.v.*], he won the Democratic gubernatorial nomination and defeated incumbent William G. Stratton in the general election.

During his first term Kerner won legislative approval of a state fair employment practices act, a revision of consumer credit laws and the criminal code, the establishment of a state board of higher education and a program of statewide mental health clinics. [See KENNEDY Volume]

In 1964 Kerner won reelection, defeating his Republican challenger, Charles Percy, by a substantial margin. During his second term Kerner was faced with racial disturbances in Chicago and Cairo, Ill. On Aug. 14, 1965 he ordered 2,000 Illinois National Guardsmen to stand by in Chicago armories to help, if necessary, in the suppression of rioting in the largely black Lawndale neighborhood of the city's West Side. City police managed to quell the riot without the use of the Guardsmen. In July 1966 Kerner, at the request of Mayor Daley, again dispatched Guardsmen to Chicago. This time 2,000 of them entered the riot area on the West Side to halt widespread looting and arson. On July 17 the Governor toured the riot area; two days later the troops were withdrawn to the armories. Guardsmen were not needed in Chicago during 1967, but in July of that year they were sent to suppress rioting in Cairo, a racially troubled town in southern Illinois.

In July 1967 President Lyndon B. Johnson named Kerner chairman of a Special Advisory Commission on Civil Disorders to probe the causes of riots in black ghettos. New York Mayor John V. Lindsay [*q.v.*] served as vice chairman. In February 1968 the Commission issued a report, popularly known as the Kerner report, that warned that "America is moving toward two societies, one black, one white—separate and unequal." The study attributed the rioting in black neighborhoods to poverty and despair resulting from racism. It called for sweeping reforms in federal and local law enforcement, welfare, employment, housing and education and recommended massive federal appropriations to improve the quality of life in the ghettos. The report was hailed by many civil rights leaders, but President Johnson pointed out that it was unrealistic to expect multi-billion dollar appropriations for black neighborhoods at a time when Congress was only reluctantly funding existing social welfare programs. The Kerner report did not lead to the passage of major social legislation.

Gov. Kerner was vacationing in Florida when rioting again broke out in Chicago's black neighborhoods following the April 4, 1968 assassination of the Rev. Martin Luther King [*q.v.*]. After consulting with Gov. Kerner by telephone, Lt. Gov. Samuel Shapiro ordered 6,000 National Guardsmen into the city. On April 6 Johnson placed the Guardsmen under federal control while ordering 5,000 federal troops to assist them. By April 10 the riot had been quelled. The federal troops were withdrawn, and the National Guard was returned to state control.

In May 1968 Kerner resigned as Governor to become a judge on the U.S. Court of Appeals (7th Circuit), the same post his father had held. In December 1971 Kerner was indicted on charges of bribery, fraud, conspiracy and income tax evasion resulting from his purchase and sale of race track stock while governor of Illinois. During his trial a race track owner and a former Illinois state racing board chairman testified that in 1962 Kerner and his revenue director, Theodore J. Isaacs, were given the opportunity to purchase race track stock at low prices. The two men made the purchase and then sold the securities for windfall profits. In exchange for the favor, Kerner intervened with the state racing board to ensure that the race track owner would be assigned prime dates on which to hold races. Kerner was convicted, and in April 1973 he was sentenced to three years in prison and fined $50,000. He appealed his sentence on the ground that a federal judge could not be tried until first impeached. His appeal was dismissed by the U.S. Supreme Court, and in July 1974 he began serving his sentence. In March 1975 the U.S. Parole Board granted Kerner release on medical grounds. After undergoing lung surgery, he died in May 1976.

[JLW]

KERR, CLARK

b. May 17, 1911; Stony Creek, Pa.
President, University of California, 1958-67.

Kerr graduated from Swarthmore College in 1932 and then earned a Ph.D. in economics from the University of California, Berkeley. He taught at Stanford and the University of Washington in the early 1940s, acquiring at the same time a reputation as a leading private and federal mediator in labor-management disputes on the West Coast. In 1945 Kerr returned to the University of California to become the director of the Institute of Industrial Relations at Berkeley. The author of a number of books on labor economics and industrial relations sociology, including *Unions, Management and the Public* (1948) and *Industrialism and Industrial Man* (1960), he argued that strikes and other forms of conflict would decline in a fully industrialized society.

In 1952 Kerr was appointed chancellor of the Berkeley campus, and in 1958 he succeeded Robert Gordon Sproul as president of the seven-campus University of California. Kerr's tenure as president coincided with the rapid growth of California's higher education system, the nation's largest. He presided over a near doubling of the University's 50,000 student enrollment, the dramatic expansion of several campuses, and a growing consensus among scholars that the University's faculty and the quality of its research made it, perhaps, the most distinguished in the country.

With the California higher educational system considered by many as a model for the nation in the early 1960s, Kerr achieved considerable influence as an educational theorist. His book *The Uses of the University* (1963) justified the role of the "multiversity"—a term coined by Kerr—in contemporary American society. Kerr argued that a great university of necessity catered to an elite but its existence was justified in a nation dedicated to egalitarianism by its role as a "prime instrument of national purpose," a "service station" for society. He pointed to the university's many "constituencies"—government, industry, faculty, students and the general public—and described the university administrator's role as one of mediating among the demands of these groups. [See KENNEDY Volume]

Sproul, Kerr's predecessor, had maintained a virtual ban on student advocacy of political causes; even Adlai Stevenson [*q.v.*] was not allowed to speak on the Berkeley campus. Kerr, on the other hand, was regarded as a liberal when he assumed office, chiefly because of his role in fighting a special loyalty oath imposed on the faculty in 1949. As president, Kerr lifted a few of Sproul's restrictions, including a ban against Communist speakers on campus—an action that earned him the Alexander Meiklejohn award for contributing to academic freedom from the American Association of University Professors.

Kerr's liberalization of University rules was put to the test by the growth in 1963 and 1964 of civil rights groups on the Berkeley campus who antagonized local citizens and businesses with aggressive campaigns against racial discrimination in hiring that often employed civil disobedience and resulted in arrests. These groups had become accustomed to using a "free speech" area, consisting of a section of sidewalk at the south entrance to the campus, as a place for recruiting and collecting funds. In September 1964 the campus administration asserted that the area was owned by the University and not by the city of Berkeley, as had long been assumed, and barred its use for the purpose of recruiting or fund raising for off-campus political actions. In the face of the ensuing student protest, Kerr defended the ban by contending that the mounting of political action directed at the surrounding community was incompatible with the University's educational purposes.

Student activists denounced the new ruling as a denial of their constitutional rights, and several campus groups joined together to form the Free Speech Movement (FSM) with the aim of opening up the entire campus to political advocacy. On Sept. 29 students violated the ban by setting up literature tables without authorization. On Oct. 1 campus police attempted to arrest a non-student who had also broken the ban by setting up a Congress of Racial Equality table in the Sproul Plaza area in front of the campus administration building. The police were prevented from removing him from the plaza by a massive 30-hour sit-in around the police car. The next day Kerr met with a delegation from the protesters, led by Mario Savio [*q.v.*]. Informal agreements were reached that apparently resolved the students' most pressing grievances. When these understandings collapsed by late November, the FSM, charging bad faith, led a mass occupation of the administration building on Dec. 2. Ignoring Kerr's advice to "let the students sit it out," Gov. Edmund G. Brown [*q.v.*] ordered police to arrest them on Dec. 3. The outraged response on campus was such that within a week Kerr and the administration were almost completely isolated. The Berkeley Faculty voted overwhelmingly Dec. 8 to grant the essence of the FSM's demands for free political activity on campus. The controversy lingered for several weeks with attempts by the regents to amend the settlement, but it was clear the students had won.

Continuing student activism at Berkeley made Kerr's role as a mediator between the University and state government impossible. In 1967 Kerr came into conflict with the newly elected Governor, Ronald Reagan [*q.v.*], over the latter's proposals to cut the University's operating budget and to end free college education in California to impose tuition fees. Kerr's resistance to these moves led the state Board of Regents to dismiss him as University president on Jan. 20, an action that provoked widespread protest on campuses throughout the state. Afterwards a spokesman for the regents explained that Kerr's relations with the Board had been "adversely affected" by his handling of the 1964 unrest at Berkeley and that they had "deteriorated further" since then.

No longer president, Kerr retained his teaching post in the University's School of Business Administration. He was also appointed to head a Carnegie Commission study on the future structure and financing of higher education. In 1968 the Commission called for a federal civilian bill of educational rights that would guarantee a college education to any qualified student regardless of his ability to pay. In subsequent years Kerr continued to press for equality of educational opportunity. During much of the Vietnam war era Kerr was a leading figure in the National Committee for a Political Settlement in Vietnam—Negotiations Now.

[TLH]

For further information:

Hal Draper, *Berkeley: the New Student Revolt* (New York, 1965).

Seymour M. Lipset and Sheldon S. Wolin, eds., *The Berkeley Student Revolt* (Garden City, 1965).

KHEEL, THEODORE W(OODROW)

b. May 9, 1914; New York, N.Y.
Labor arbitrator.

After receiving a law degree from Cornell in 1937, Kheel, son of a Brooklyn businessman, joined the legal staff of the National Labor Relations Board. Kheel began his career as an arbitrator with the World War II National War Labor Board and in 1944 became the Board's executive director. He became the impartial arbitrator for New York City's private bus lines in 1949, assumed a similar role in 1956 for the public transit system as well. As arbitrator Kheel prevented a 1961 strike by ordering the New York City Transit Authority to delay introduction of an automated subway train. Kheel helped settle the 114-day, 1962-63 New York newspaper strike and the January 1963 East and Gulf Coast dock strike. He also served as permanent arbitrator for the National Maritime Union (NMU). A supporter of the civil rights movement, Kheel was president of the National Urban League from 1956 to 1960. [See KENNEDY Volume]

In 1964 Kheel helped resolve a 4½-year-old dispute between the railroads and five rail unions over the introduction of new work rules. On April 9, at the personal request of President Johnson, the unions agreed to postpone a nationwide rail strike for an additional 15 days after it had already been postponed by legislation for 180 days the previous year. Meanwhile the railroads agreed to delay introducing the new work rules, which would have eliminated firemen on most diesel locomotives. Kheel served on the Administration mediation team, headed by Secretary of Labor W. Willard Wirtz [*q.v.*], that met with both sides in sessions often attended by Johnson himself. On April 22, Johnson announced a settlement that provided for a pay raise for about half of the 200,000 operating employes involved but permitted job reductions awarded in previous arbitration and allowed greater latitude in the assignment of work crews. Differences in interpretation of the agreement were to be submitted to Kheel and George W. Taylor, another member of the mediation panel.

As a member of a special presidential panel in July 1964, Kheel began to try to resolve differences between the International Longshoremen's Association and East and Gulf Coast shippers over the reduction of work crews. A one-day strike in October was ended by a federal injunction, and on Dec. 16 a settlement was reached. The contract permitted a reduction in the size of work gangs, but in return the shippers guaranteed a fixed number of hours' work each year for union members and increased wages, vacation time and holidays. Scattered wildcat strikes protesting the agreement soon collapsed.

In New York City Kheel served as a mediator in 1965 contract negotiations involving newspaper employes and public school teachers that ended without strikes. When a Newspaper Guild strike against the *New York Times* for greater job protection led to a shutdown of seven New York papers, a Kheel proposal served as the basis for settling the 25-day strike. Kheel also played a central role in settling the 13-day January 1966 New York City transit strike and in conducting the December 1967 New York transit negotiations.

In his capacity as permanent NMU arbitrator, Kheel brought an end to a three-day seamen's strike in July 1968. He was also hired by the National Football League owners to conduct their 1968 negotiations with the Players Association, which was acting for the first time as a bargaining agent. In April of that year he attempted to negotiate a settlement at Columbia University between the administration and black students occupying a campus building but failed in that effort.

[JBF]

KING, CORETTA SCOTT

b. April 27, 1927; Heiberger, Ala.
Civil rights activist.

Coretta Scott, the daughter of a store owner and laborer, grew up in Heiberger. After graduating from a missionary high school in nearby Marion, she continued her education at Antioch College (where she and her older sister were the first full-time black students) and at the New England Conservatory of Music in Boston. In 1953 she gave up plans for a music career to marry Martin Luther King [*q.v.*], a philosophy graduate student whom she had met in Boston. Both Mrs. King and her husband completed their studies in 1954 and returned to Alabama, where he took a position as minister in a black Montgomery church.

Mrs. King soon became deeply involved in her husband's civil rights activities, which began with the Montgomery bus boycott of 1955 and led to the creation of the Southern Christian Leadership Conference (SCLC) in 1957. She marched beside him in demonstrations, accompanied him on tours of Europe and Asia and sang in numerous "freedom concerts" to raise money for the SCLC. At the same time she raised the couple's four children. Coretta King also made a place for herself in the peace movement of the mid-1960s, serving on the Committee for a Sane Nuclear Policy and the Mobilization to End the War in Vietnam. In 1964 the Federal Bureau of Investigation, as part of its campaign of harassment against Martin Luther King, sent her a tape recording that purported to prove her husband's unfaithfulness. Mrs. King nevertheless remained with her husband and continued to support his work.

In April 1968 Mrs. King won national admiration for the dignity and fortitude with which she responded to her husband's assassination. Her conduct and her position as Martin Luther King's widow made her an important civil rights figure. On April 11 she took her husband's place in Memphis at the head of a massive, orderly demonstration in support of the city's striking sanitation workers. Her speech following the march stressed the theme: "We must carry on." In May and June 1968 Mrs. King participated in the Poor People's Campaign in Washington, organized by the SCLC to press for larger federal antipoverty expenditures. Speaking before the Lincoln Memorial, she urged American women "to unite and form a solid block . . . to fight the three great evils of racism, poverty and war." Shortly afterwards she was named to the executive bodies of both the SCLC and the National Organization for Women, a major feminist group.

In the late 1960s and early 1970s Mrs. King participated in numerous civil rights and peace rallies. In early 1969 she made a tour of Europe and India, during which she accepted the Nehru Award for International Understanding on behalf of her husband. Using money raised on the trip and other contributions, she established the Martin Luther King Memorial Center in Atlanta for the study of nonviolent social change. This soon became a source of dispute between Mrs. King and Ralph Abernathy [*q.v.*], her husband's successor as head of the SCLC, who claimed that the funds absorbed by the Center were sorely needed by the SCLC itself.

Mrs. King took little public interest in the 1969 trial of James Earl Ray [*q.v.*], her husband's accused assassin, but expressed her belief that the assassination resulted from a conspiracy extending beyond Ray.

[SLG]

For further information:

Coretta Scott King, *My Life with Martin Luther King* (New York, 1969).

"Coretta (Scott) King," *Current Biography Yearbook, 1969* (New York, 1970), pp. 239-241.

KING, JOHN W(ILLIAM)

b. Oct. 10, 1918; Manchester, N.H.
Governor N.H., 1963-69.

John W. King, a graduate of Harvard and the Columbia Law School, practiced law for many years in Manchester, N. H. In 1956 he won election to the General Court (the New Hampshire state legislature) and served there for six years. In 1962 he ran for governor and defeated John Pillsbury, the candidate of a badly divided Republican Party. King's opponent had the support of William Loeb [*q.v.*], editor of the archconservative *Manchester Union Leader;* but this did not seriously damage the Democratic candidate, who won by a margin of over 40,000 votes. King thus became the first Democrat since the 1920s to serve as a New Hampshire governor.

In April 1963 King gained national attention when he signed into law a bill authorizing the state to conduct a sweepstakes lottery to aid New Hampshire schools. Not since 1894 had a state operated a legal lottery. King called the measure a "legitimate fiscal experiment," stressing that the expected yearly proceeds of $4 million would be used exclusively for aid to education. Later, following New Hampshire's lead, New York, New Jersey and Connecticut, all hard-pressed for new sources of revenue and unwilling to impose additional taxes, also adopted lotteries. [See KENNEDY Volume]

Early in 1968 King and Sen. Thomas McIntyre (D, N.H.) [*q.v.*] assumed responsibility for defending the Administration's Vietnam policies, then under attack by Sen. Eugene J. McCarthy (D, Minn.) [*q.v.*], who had come to New Hampshire to challenge President Johnson in the state's March presidential primary. During the primary King was widely criticised by liberals within his Party for his statement that a vote for McCarthy would "be greeted with cheers in Hanoi." In the election McCarthy won 42% of the Democratic vote and 20 of New Hampshire's 24 delegates. McCarthy's surprising showing helped induce Johnson not to seek reelection.

King was reelected governor in 1964 and 1966. In November 1968 he ran for the Senate and was defeated by Sen. Norris Cotton (R, N.H.) [*q.v.*]. With the expiration of his final term as governor, King returned to his legal practice in Manchester. He later was named to the New Hampshire Supreme Court.

[JLW]

KING, MARTIN LUTHER, JR.
b. Jan. 15, 1929; Atlanta, Ga.
d. April 4, 1968; Memphis, Tenn.
President, Southern Christian Leadership Conference, 1957-68.

King grew up in Atlanta, Ga., and was ordained in 1947 at the Ebenezer Baptist Church, which his grandfather had founded and where his father was then pastor. He received a B.A. from Morehouse College in 1948, a divinity degree from Crozer Theological Seminary in Chester, Pa., in 1951 and a Ph.D. in systematic theology from Boston University in 1955. King accepted his first pastorate in September 1954 at the Dexter Avenue Baptist Church in Montgomery, Ala. In December 1955 he was chosen to direct the black community's boycott of Montgomery's segregated buses. As leader of the year-long boycott, a protest which marked the beginning of an era of nonviolent direct action by Southern blacks, King won national prominence. He helped establish the Southern Christian Leadership Conference (SCLC) early in 1957 to coordinate direct action protests in the South and was named its first president. King participated in the May 1957 Prayer Pilgrimage to Washington, which demanded desegregation and voting rights for blacks. In January 1960 he moved to Atlanta, site of the SCLC's headquarters, to become co-pastor at his father's church. [See EISENHOWER Volume]

King encouraged the student sit-ins that began in the South in February 1960 and helped organize the Student Nonviolent Coordinating Committee (SNCC), which emerged from those demonstrations. He also supported the 1961 Freedom Rides, a protest aimed at desegregating transportation facilities, and was chosen head of a Freedom Rides Coordinating Committee organized in May. From mid-December 1961 through September 1962, King led an antisegregation campaign in Albany, Ga. The Albany Movement was plagued by disunity among its local leaders and by insufficient planning and organization. Even though intensified demonstrations in the summer of 1962 attracted national attention, the campaign did not win substantial gains for the city's black population.

From the defeat in Albany, however, King and his aides learned valuable lessons which they put to use in a desegregation drive in Birmingham, Ala. Preceded by months of careful preparation, the Birmingham campaign began on April 3, 1963. King and the SCLC led a series of daily demonstrations and marches which received nationwide publicity, especially when Birmingham's police began savage attacks on the demonstrators early in May. The campaign ended on May 10 after a desegregation agreement had been negotiated. The agreement brought only limited changes to the city, but the historic Birmingham demonstrations had a major national impact. They dramatized the problem of Southern discrimination as never before, were crucial in forcing the Kennedy Administration to call for strong civil rights legislation and made King the key leader of the civil rights movement in the eyes of the general public. Following the Birmingham campaign King helped organize the Aug. 28 March on Washington. The "I Have a Dream" speech he delivered there was one of the highlights of the day and became the best-known statement of King's vision of full equality for American blacks. [See KENNEDY Volume]

In all of these demonstrations King was guided by a philosophy of nonviolent resistance. He had first encountered the precepts of Gandhian civil disobedience while a student, and both the Montgomery boycott and a trip to India in February 1959 advanced King's understanding of and commitment to nonviolence. Throughout the 1960s King was the major proponent of nonviolent direct action within the civil rights movement. It allowed blacks, he said, to challenge segregation and discrimination but called on them to love and forgive their oppressors, to "struggle without hating." Nonviolence was a "creative force," for by remaining nonviolent in the face of white resistance and brutality, civil rights demonstrators transformed and redeemed their oppressors. To white opponents King declared, "We will match your capacity to inflict suffering with our capacity to endure suffering" and "in winning our freedom we will so appeal to your heart and conscience that we will win you in the process."

King joined in demonstrations against segregated public facilities in Atlanta in late 1963 and early 1964 that were organized primarily by SNCC. Beginning in March 1964 King and the SCLC gave their support to a desegregation drive in St. Augustine, Fla. The almost daily demonstrations and marches were repeatedly attacked by crowds of whites. The campaign was intensified in May and June. When local police failed to provide protection for the demonstrators, King called for federal intervention but to no avail. By the end of June a stalemate had developed, and when Florida's governor appointed an emergency biracial committee to "restore communications" between the races, King agreed to a temporary truce. Following passage of the Civil Rights Act in July 1964, local black leaders secured federal court orders for desegregation of public facilities in St. Augustine, and a measure of desegregation was finally won in the city.

On July 18, when a riot erupted in Harlem, New York's Mayor Robert Wagner [*q.v.*] asked King to come to the city. King was criticized by Harlem leaders for conferring with Wagner and for touring the riot area without having contacted them first. His main recommendation to Wagner—a civilian review board to investigate charges of police brutality—was rejected by the Mayor. King abhorred the violence of the Harlem riot, but he said its sources lay in the economic and social deprivation blacks suffered in Northern ghettos. He placed the blame for the rioting, as he would repeatedly in the future, on white society's failure to remedy ghetto conditions.

Later that summer King toured Mississippi, encouraging blacks to enroll in the newly organized Mississippi Freedom Democratic Party (MFDP). He also supported an MFDP delegation when it challenged the seating of the regular Mississippi delegation at the August 1964 Democratic National Convention and testified before the credentials committee on the MFDP's behalf. When the Convention refused full recognition of the group and voted for a compromise measure, however, King urged the MDFP delegates to accept it, but they overwhelmingly rejected the compromise. King also joined several other rights leaders in a July 1964 call for a moratorium on civil rights demonstrations until after the November elections, a call which the more radical SNCC and the Congress of Racial Equality (CORE) refused to endorse.

King went on a speaking tour of Europe in the fall of 1964. Shortly after his return in mid-October, it was announced that he had been chosen as the Nobel Peace Prize winner for 1964. While preparing for a trip to Oslo, to accept the prize in December, King was attacked by FBI Director J. Edgar Hoover [*q.v.*] as "the most notorious liar in the country" for allegedly having said that FBI agents would not act on civil rights complaints in the South because they were Southerners. King replied in a telegram to Hoover that the FBI was not fully effective in the South but not because of the presence of Southerners on its staff. He called Hoover's statement "inconceivable."

There were reports after King's death that the FBI had tapped his telephone for extensive periods during the 1960s. In February 1975 Justice Department officials confirmed reports that President Johnson had ordered the agency to bug King's hotel suite at the 1964 Democratic National Convention. A Senate Select Committee on Intelligence disclosed in November 1975 that prior to King's assassination, the FBI had conducted a six-year campaign aimed at discrediting the civil rights leader. Aside from numerous telephone taps and bugs in King's hotel rooms, the program of harassment included attempts to disrupt functions at which King was to appear. In late 1964 and early 1965 the agency anonymously sent King and his wife Coretta [*q.v.*] two tape recordings that supposedly revealed instances of infidelity on his part and a letter implying that King should commit suicide. In testimony before the Senate committee, FBI officials acknowledged there had been no legal basis for these actions.

Awarded the Nobel Peace Prize on Dec. 10, King returned to the United States ready to launch another major campaign, this time to pressure the federal government to act to secure voting rights for blacks. He chose to focus the campaign on Selma, Ala., a Black Belt city where only one per cent of the 15,000 blacks were then registered to vote and where SNCC organizers had been at work during the previous two years. King announced a voter registration drive in Selma on Jan. 2, 1965, and during the next two months he and other SCLC and SNCC leaders led almost daily marches to the county courthouse there. Thousands of demonstrators were arrested and many were assaulted by Sheriff James Clark [*q.v.*] and his volunteer posse. By the end of February a stalemate was developing, and King called for a mass march to Montgomery to present black grievances to Gov. George C. Wallace [*q.v.*].

Wallace announced on March 6 that the demonstration would not be permitted. When some 500 people, led by SNCC's John Lewis [*q.v.*] and the SCLC's Hosea Williams [*q.v.*], started the march the next day, they were met at the bridge leading out of Selma by Sheriff Clark, his possemen and state troopers. The demonstrators, given two minutes to disperse, were attacked with tear gas and by possemen on horseback using cattle prods and clubs. King, who was in Atlanta that day, vowed to return to Selma to lead a second march on March 9. The attack on the demonstrators received national publicity. While supporting marches were held throughout the country, other civil rights leaders and scores of Northern white clergy and sympathizers journeyed to Selma to join the next march.

A federal judge enjoined a march planned for March 9, and Administration officials pressured King and his aides to abide by the injunction. When the 1,500 demonstrators crossed the bridge on the outskirts of Selma, they were met once again by state troopers who ordered them to disperse. After briefly kneeling in prayer King turned the marchers around and told them to go back to Selma. King denied charges that he had made a prior agreement with federal officials to halt the march at the bridge.

Whatever his reasons for turning back, King's decision marked a key turning point in his relations with black militants, especially the youths in SNCC. Well before Selma many members of SNCC had criticized King for being too cautious, too ready to compromise and too closely allied to the federal government and the white establishment. By 1965 many SNCC workers were also questioning the efficacy of King's strategy of nonviolence. Before Selma King had served as a mediator between the militant and traditionalist wings of the black protest movement. After his new loss of credibility among the militants, it became far more difficult for King to play such a role.

On March 17 federal district Judge Frank M. Johnson authorized the Selma march, and it began on March 21 under the protection of a federalized Alabama National Guard and Army troops. Under the court order, only 300 people could march along the entire route, but 25,000 people came to Montgomery for the final leg of the march to the state capitol. Like Birmingham in 1963, the Selma demonstrations and march did not bring immediate improvement in the condition of local blacks. But Selma, and especially the March 7 assault on the demonstrators and the deaths of three civil rights workers during the campaign, aroused national protests that forced the federal government to act. On March 15 President Johnson addressed a joint session of Congress to decry the violence in Selma and announce that "We shall overcome." Johnson called for prompt passage of a voting rights bill to suspend the use of literacy tests and other devices that denied blacks the vote and to install federal registrars in the South and other areas where voter registration lagged. King was present on Aug. 6 when Johnson signed the bill into law.

After Selma King began to speak out against American involvement in Vietnam, calling for a negotiated settlement from July 1965 on. By 1966 he was outspoken in his opposition to the war, and in 1967 he openly identified himself with the anti-war movement. In addition to violating his precept of nonviolence, King argued that the war diverted money and attention from domestic programs to aid the black poor.

He was strongly criticized by most other civil rights leaders for attempting to link the civil rights and anti-war movements. He also alienated President Johnson; at a White House conference on civil rights in June 1966, King was virtually ignored by Administration officials and he found the federal government increasingly less receptive to appeals for aid or intervention in his campaigns.

Although King remained a resident of Atlanta, he also began giving greater attention to the problems of the black poor in Northern ghettos. Early in 1964 he called for a federal "Bill of Rights for the Disadvantaged." The Watts riot of August 1965 reinforced King's conviction that massive federal aid to improve the economic and social conditions of blacks in the Northern ghettos was needed. With an invitation from some local community groups, the SCLC began planning a drive in Chicago in the summer of 1965. On Jan. 7, 1966 King announced the beginning of the Chicago Freedom Movement to end discrimination in housing, schools and employment. King was in and out of Chicago over the next several months while his aides, led by the Rev. James Bevel [*q.v.*], did the day-to-day organizing of the campaign. King announced on May 26 that a mass march on city hall would be held one month later, to be followed by "a long hot summer of peaceful nonviolence."

These plans were delayed when King learned on June 6 that James Meredith [*q.v.*], in the course of a solitary protest march from Memphis, Tenn., to Jackson, Miss., had been shot from ambush just over the Mississippi border. King rushed to Memphis and on June 7 he, Stokely Carmichael [*q.v.*], the newly elected chairman of SNCC, and Floyd McKissick [*q.v.*] of CORE, announced they would continue the march. Despite an attack on the demonstrators by a white mob in Philadelphia, Miss., on June 21 and by police in Canton, Miss., two days later, the protesters reached Jackson and held a final rally at the state capitol on June 26.

The most notable feature of the Meredith march was the public divisions among civil rights leaders it revealed. A manifesto issued June 8 declared the march was "a massive public indictment and protest" against the failure of American society and government to fulfill blacks' rights. Roy Wilkins [*q.v.*] of the NAACP and Whitney Young [*q.v.*] of the National Urban League refused to sign the manifesto, while King signed it with reluctance. During the march Carmichael raised the cry of "black power," a slogan that reflected the rising anti-white sentiment and militance within SNCC. King deplored the slogan, which quickly captured national attention, arguing that it carried connotations of violence; he continued to speak out against black power after the march. He later softened his opposition somewhat, saying he supported the emphasis on black pride and the call for blacks to amass political and economic strength to achieve their legitimate goals. But King remained opposed to black separatism and encouragement of violence.

King returned to Chicago after the Meredith march. Following a rally attended by some 30,000 at Soldiers' Field on July 10, he led 5,000 marchers to city hall to present the movement's demands. King met with Chicago Mayor Richard Daley [*q.v.*] the next day. On July 12 a three-day riot broke out on Chicago's West Side ghetto. In late July King launched a series of marches into white ethnic neighborhoods in the city to protest housing discrimination. Continuing through most of August, the marches resulted in repeated assaults on the demonstrators by angry crowds of whites. On Aug. 21 King announced that the protesters would march the following Sunday into Cicero, an all-white suburb considered a volatile enclave of anti-black sentiment. Two days before the march negotiations between black leaders and city business and government officials resulted in a 10-point agreement, and the demonstrations were halted.

Although King hailed the agreement as a victory, most of SCLC's staff later admitted that the Chicago Movement did not really achieve its goals. King's biographer David Lewis labeled the agreement "little more than a good-will pledge from the city, business, and realtors" to act against housing discrimination. In the months after Chicago

King publicly recognized the fact that changes in black economic and social conditions would not come quickly. At the same time he became more of a political and economic radical. In the summer of 1967 King told an interviewer he had abandoned his earlier ideas of step-by-step reform of American institutions. Now, he said, "I think you've got to have a reconstruction of the entire society, a revolution of values," which would involve the rebuilding of the cities, the nationalization of some industries, a review of American foreign investments and the establishment of a guaranteed annual income. In his speeches and writings King continued to argue that nonviolent methods could bring real change, but he also displayed less optimism than in earlier years about white America.

Following the Chicago campaign King's public stature began to decline. While traditional civil rights leaders condemned his anti-war statements and activities, the militants attacked King for his adherence to nonviolence and his refusal to endorse black power. He was also losing his base of support among Northern whites. A growing number of white radicals, more sympathetic to black militants, considered King and his methods outdated. White liberals called for slowing down the pace of the civil rights movement. Contributions to the SCLC declined. Even among King's supporters there was a growing conviction that his strategy could not be successfully applied to the problems of Northern poverty and discrimination.

In June 1967 the Supreme Court upheld contempt of court convictions of King and seven other ministers resulting from the 1963 Birmingham demonstrations. While serving his five-day prison term beginning Oct. 30, King discussed with his aides a plan to assemble an interracial coalition of the poor which would pressure the federal government into enacting new antipoverty legislation. He devoted the next several months to organizing the Poor People's Campaign, an effort designed to prove the continuing viability of nonviolence in addition to seeking a massive program of federal aid for the poor. The plans for the campaign, completed in February 1968, called for a mass march on Washington by poor whites, American Indians and Mexican-Americans as well as blacks. In Washington there would be daily nonviolent protests until Congress acted to guarantee jobs to all those able to work, a viable income for those unable to work and an end to discrimination in housing and education. King's plans met strong opposition from government officials and hostility or indifference from other civil rights organizations.

In March 1968 King took time off from recruitment for the Poor People's March to aid a sanitationmen's strike in Memphis. King led a mass march in Memphis in support of the strikers on March 28. The demonstration ended in violence when some protesters broke away from the main crowd and began smashing windows and looting stores. Although the number involved in the violence was relatively small, King was troubled by the violence and angered when press reports focused on the incident, resulting in a storm of criticism from both blacks and whites. King was back in the city on April 3 to begin preparations for a second march. At about 6 p.m. the next evening, as he stood on the balcony outside his motel room in Memphis, King was shot in the head by a sniper and died almost immediately. James Earl Ray [*q.v.*], arrested in London in June 1968 and extradited to the United States in July, was charged with King's assassination and pleaded guilty to the charge in March 1969. In later years Ray attempted to change his plea and secure a new trial. This plus the 1975 disclosures of FBI harassment of King led many of his former associates and others to call for a new investigation of King's assassination.

King's unique position and leadership during much of his life were due in part, as David Lewis noted, to "forces external to himself." King lived in an era when the impulse toward social reform and black protest was rising and when many whites were willing to heed that protest. Still, King himself was a singular man, "a rare personality, endowed with an ample intelligence, great courage and convictions, and an arresting presence." Even as his influence declined in the last years of his life, King remained an unusual figure. He was seeking a solution to the problems of economic injustice for all the poor, not simply the black poor, at the time of his death. His opposition to the Vietnam war began well before the anti-war movement became respectable or popular and represented for King a broadening of his commitment to nonviolence from the national to the international level.

[CAB]

For further information:
Lerone Bennett, Jr., *What Manner of Man: A Biography of Martin Luther King, Jr.* (Chicago, 1968).
Martin Luther King, Jr., *Why We Can't Wait* (New York, 1964).
———, *Where Do We Go From Here: Chaos or Community?* (New York, 1967).
David Lewis, *King: A Critical Biography* (New York, 1970).
August Meier, "On the Role of Martin Luther King," *New Politics*, IV (Winter, 1965), 52-59.

KIRK, CLAUDE R(OY), JR.

b. Jan. 7, 1926; San Bernardino, Calif.
Governor, Fla., 1967-71.

The son of a mobile-home salesman who later manufactured vending machines, Claude R. Kirk grew up in Chicago and Montgomery, Ala. During World War II Kirk served in the Marine Corps. After the war he received his B.S. degree from Duke and LL.B. from the University of Alabama. Starting with limited capital Kirk made his fortune between 1956 and 1962 by establishing a Jacksonville life insurance agency and shrewdly exercising stock options.

Kirk soon quit the insurance business for Republican politics. He had headed Florida's Democrats for Nixon in the 1960 presidential campaign and subsequently changed his registration to Republican. In 1964 Kirk campaigned as a resolute conservative against Sen. Spessard L. Holland (D, Fla.) [*q.v.*]. With only 36 % of the vote, he ran far behind the Republican presidential and gubernatorial nominees in the state.

Two years later, however, Kirk became the first Republican governor of Florida since 1872. After a divisive primary the Democrats nominated the moderate-liberal mayor of Miami, Robert King High. Kirk branded High a captive of Northern liberals and attacked proposed open housing legislation with the slogan "Your home is your castle—protect it." Defeating High 55% to 45%, Kirk ran well throughout the state; he fared poorly only in the black wards.

Kirk stirred controversy during his first days in office. He announced that a private detective firm paid through public voluntary donations would investigate organized crime and political corruption in the state. His move immediately set off a debate over the methods and scope of the agency's proposed work. Most Democratic officials and many law enforcement leaders condemned the hiring of the firm, with some referring to it as "the Governor's Gestapo." Although Kirk rejected these attacks, he reversed himself in May 1967. At his request the legislature agreed to the creation of a special state-financed and operated law enforcement bureau.

During the debate over the state anti-crime force, Kirk scored an important political victory. In February a federal circuit court ordered a reapportionment of the Florida legislature and a special election in the redrawn districts. After a vigorous campaign Kirk and the state GOP scored impressive gains; they garnered 35% of the legislature's seats, thus making the best legislative showing of any Republican Party in the South.

The March elections reinforced Kirk's earlier desire to seek national office. Shortly after the balloting he hired public-relations consultant William Safire to boost his possible national candidacy. Aiming for a vice presidential nomination on a ticket that they then suspected would be headed by a liberal-moderate, Kirk and Safire decided to present an "ultra-conservative" image.

At the same time Kirk sought a national rather than sectional appeal. In April 1967 he criticized Gov. Lurleen Wallace (D, Ala.) [*q.v.*] for suggesting that Southern governors meet to formulate a strategy to combat federal court school desegregation orders. Kirk declared that his state "cannot join attempts to subvert or delay" the Supreme Court's edicts. He termed Wallace's proposal "divisive and unwise."

Having criticized Lurleen Wallace, the unpredictable Kirk personally greeted Black Power advocate H. Rap Brown [*q.v.*] during another summer of racial turmoil. When Brown, whom most whites associated with the spread of black rioting, came to Miami for an address before 300 blacks in August, Kirk was on hand to meet him. "You're welcome here as long as you understand we don't want any talk about guns," Kirk declared. Brown declined Kirk's proffered hand. The Governor's unusual performance gained him national attention.

Although he received still more publicity as the host governor of the August 1968 Republican National Convention in Miami, Kirk never came close to national office. His willingness to endorse liberal Gov. Nelson A. Rockefeller [*q.v.*] for president and his feud with Florida GOP Chairman William Murfin denied him any sway over the state's 34-member delegation. Ignoring Kirk, Chairman Murfin promised Florida's votes to Richard M. Nixon [*q.v.*]. Nixon, the Convention's ultimate choice, never considered Kirk for vice president.

Racial violence in Miami marred the Republican gathering. Personal appeals by Kirk and civil rights leader Ralph Abernathy [*q.v.*] could not quell the disturbances. On the riot's second day Kirk offered local officials "whatever force is needed" and subsequently sent in units of the state highway patrol and 1,000 National Guardsmen.

In November 1968 Florida voters approved a new state constitution promoted by Kirk. The Governor had called the legislature back into session three times in 1967 until it agreed to present the new constitution to the electorate. Replacing an 1885 charter, the new constitution provided limited home rule for cities and counties, consolidated state agencies and required the legislature to meet annually.

The electorate grew disenchanted with Kirk after 1968, partly because of a scandal in the appropriation of state monies and a bitter 1970 GOP gubernatorial primary. He lost his reelection bid to Democrat Reuben Askew, a Pensacola lawyer. [See NIXON Volume]

[JLB]

KIRWAN, MICHAEL J(OSEPH)

b. Dec. 2, 1886; Wilkes-Barre, Pa.
d. July 27, 1970; Bethesda, Md.
Democratic Representative, Ohio, 1937-70; Chairman, Democratic Congressional Campaign Committee, 1947-70; Chairman, Appropriations Public Works Subcommittee, 1964-70.

The son of Irish Catholic immigrants, "Big Mike" Kirwan served in the American Expeditionary Force during World War I and after a brief career in business entered Youngstown Democratic politics as a city councilman in 1932. Four years later he won the first of 16 terms in the House. With the unionization of the steel industry, the district's predominant Republicanism, which had dated back to the earliest years of the GOP, gave way to the New Deal's Democratic alliance with second-generation immigrants who worked in the area's iron and steel works. From the very start of his political career, Kirwan maintained strong ties with organized labor and consistently supported the national Party leadership. In 1947 he became chairman of the House Democratic Congressional Campaign Committee, charged with the allocation of funds for congressional elections. He further enhanced his power by acquiring the number two position on the Appropriation Committee's Public Works Subcommittee during the Kennedy years.

Upon the death of Rep. Clarence Cannon (D, Mo.) in May 1964, Kirwan succeeded to the Public Works Committee chairmanship. A blunt, strong-willed figure, Kirwan tended to approve authorizations for the districts of fellow Democrats most faithful to the official Party leadership. In his study of Congress Sen. Joseph S. Clark (D, Pa.) [*q.v.*] termed Kirwan "almost a czar" as Committee chairman. A *Cleveland Plain Dealer* reported labeled the Youngstown representative the "Prince of Pork."

Kirwan had to defend his budgets against

annual Republican attacks. He argued in July 1967 that Congress could not reduce funds for water resource development (reservoirs, canals, etc.)—a prime feature in the annual authorizations—without creating "critical water problems" for the future. At the same time, however, he successfully led the opposition to floor amendments to increase funds spent on water pollution control.

Throughout his long House career Kirwan called for the construction of an 120-mile Lake Erie-to-Ohio River canal, which would have run through his district. Nicknamed "Mike's Ditch," the proposed water route met with determined opposition. Pennsylvania officials and railroad lobbyists feared the loss of the Ohio-Pennsylvania interstate trade to the southern Mississippi Valley states. Both groups fought hard against the measure. Ohio's senior senator, Frank J. Lausche [*q.v.*], also spoke against the waterway. Acknowledging the canal's popularity in the Youngstown, Painesville, and Ashtabula areas, Lausche otherwise found "no unity of opinion in Ohio about the desirability of the canal." But Kirwan persisted. Finally, out of respect to the veteran Ohio Democrat, the House agreed in a September 1966 voice vote to a $500,000 Army Corps of Engineers feasibility study. With Lausche in dissent, the Senate voted 61-4 in October to include the Corps of Engineers study in its public works appropriations. The canal scheme expired with Kirwan's death in July 1970.

[JLB]

KISSINGER, HENRY A(LFRED)

b. May 27, 1923; Furth, Germany.
State Department adviser.

Kissinger was born into a middle-class Jewish family in Furth, Germany. Fleeing Nazi persecution, his family settled in New York City in 1938. He served in the Army in World War II and was a district administrator with the military government of occupied Germany from 1945 to 1946. After obtaining his B.A. summa cum laude from Harvard in 1950, Kissinger continued graduate studies there while working as executive director of the Harvard International Seminar. He obtained his Ph.D. in 1954, writing his dissertation on European diplomacy during the era of the Congress of Vienna. Kissinger's work focused on the efforts of Castlereagh and Metternich to restore order and stability to Europe through maintenance of a balance of power in which each country had a vested interest. He admired their skillful use of secret negotiations and their willingness to use force to maintain order. Their diplomacy "may not have fulfilled all the hopes of an idealistic generation," wrote Kissinger, "but it gave this generation something perhaps more precious: a period of stability which permitted their hopes to be realized without a major war or a permanent revolution."

In 1955 Kissinger became study director of a Council on Foreign Relations project seeking to explore alternatives to the massive retaliation policy of the Eisenhower Administration. The project report, published in 1957, accepted the view that the Soviet Union was an expansionist power seeking to undermine the stability of the West. However, it rejected Eisenhower's stress on all-out nuclear warfare to stem Soviet aggression and proposed instead a strategy based on the use of limited nuclear weapons at the onset of an international conflict. In Kissinger's view, "Limited nuclear war represents our most effective strategy against nuclear powers."

Kissinger's work at the Council on Foreign Relations brought him to the attention of Nelson A. Rockefeller [*q.v.*], who in 1956, appointed him a director of a Rockefeller Brothers Fund special project formed to study the nation's major domestic and foreign problems. The project's final foreign affairs report, published as, warned against optimism over prospects for a Russian-American detente and stressed the need for a strategy centered on tactical nuclear weapons. It called for an expansion of a nationwide civil defense system and for a major increase in defense spending to meet the expected Soviet challenge.

Kissinger returned to Harvard as a lecturer in the government department in 1957 and eventually became a professor in 1962. From 1959 to 1969 he was director of Harvard's Defense Studies Program. Kissinger also served as a consultant to the Arms Control and Disarmament Agency from 1961 to 1967 and to the State Department from 1965 to 1969. Between 1961 and 1962 he was an adviser to the National Security Council but resigned because of his disapproval of Kennedy's Multilateral Nuclear Force (MLF) proposal.

Kissinger's writings during this period focused on America's relations with Europe. In *The Troubled Partnership: A Reappraisal of the Atlantic Alliance* (1965) and *American Foreign Policy: Three Essays* (1969), he denounced American policy as arrogant in its failure to consider European interests or consult Western allies. Kissinger stressed that the U.S. could not be the sole defender of the West.

In 1965 Kissinger began an involvement with Vietnam, a trouble spot that would become his major preoccupation by the end of the decade. In July 1965 Ambassador to South Vietnam Henry Cabot Lodge [*q.v.*] asked McGeorge Bundy [*q.v.*] to appoint Kissinger as a State Department consultant to develop new ideas on the conduct of the war. Kissinger visited South Vietnam in October 1965 and, in the summer of 1966, published an article supporting American policy in that country. He believed that a victory by North Vietnam would encourage further attempts at Communist expansion and demoralize Asia. He concluded that "a demonstration of American impotence in Asia cannot fail to lessen the credibility of American pledges in other fields."

In October 1966 Kissinger returned to South Vietnam to aid a program designed to instigate high-level defections from the North. Between June and October 1967 he served as a contact in "Pennsylvania," the code name for an indirect exchange of letters between Hanoi and Washington that was designed to exchange a U.S. bombing halt for Hanoi's agreement to promptly enter productive negotiations. The attempt failed but proved a prelude to other secret negotiations begun the following year.

While pursuing his academic and diplomatic activities, Kissinger also served as foreign policy adviser and speech writer to Nelson Rockefeller in his unsuccessful 1964 and 1968 bids for the Republican presidential nomination. In 1968 Kissinger helped draw up Rockefeller's Vietnam peace plan. The proposal, presented on July 13, envisioned a restoration of peace in four phases: (1) a troop pullback on both sides and the interposition between them of a neutral, international peace-keeping force; (2) the withdrawal of North Vietnamese and most allied troops from South Vietnam; (3) free elections under international supervision; and (4) direct negotiations between North and South Vietnam on reunification. The Rockefeller plan also proposed that the U.S. reduce search and destroy missions, cut back American personnel and gradually turn the war over to the Vietnamese.

Kissinger became assistant to the President for National Security Affairs in 1969. Four years later he was appointed Secretary of State. During the Nixon Administration Kissinger played a vital role in shaping American Vietnam policy, in opening up contacts with Communist China, establishing detente with the USSR and initiating peace talks in the Middle East. [See NIXON Volume]

[EWS]

For further information:
Marvin Kalb and Bernard Kalb, *Kissinger* (New York, 1974).

KOMER, ROBERT W(ILLIAM)

b. Feb. 23, 1922; Chicago, Ill.
Presidential Assistant for Vietnamese Non-Military Affairs, March 1966-October 1968; Ambassador to Turkey, October 1968-April 1969.

Described as an ebullient, always optimistic man by journalist David Halberstam, Komer served as pacification program chief in Vietnam. Following his graduation from Harvard Business School in 1947, Komer joined the Central Intelligence Agency. During the Kennedy Administration he served as White House special assistant for non-committed nations and often advised the President on disarmament policy.

As the United States became increasingly involved in the Vietnam war, Komer became one of the Johnson Administration's chief advocates of the Vietnam pacification program. This effort, termed "the other war" by President Johnson, was defined as an attempt to provide the Vietnamese rural population with local security and to develop positive economic and social programs to win their active support. Dormant during the opening months of the Johnson Administration, it was revived in February 1966 as a result of American failures in the ground war and the need to show that the U.S. was helping to develop South Vietnam. Komer was put in charge of coordinating the effort in Washington. He played a part in allocating Agency for International Development funds in Vietnam, expanding programs designed to train local political and military leaders for South Vietnamese hamlets and attempting to define the goals of the pacification project. But, according to the *Pentagon Papers*, Komer's major contribution to the program was to raise the priority of pacification and other non-military efforts within the Administration.

Despite his continuing optimistic assessments of the pacification program, Komer soon criticized its organization and recommended that troops be committed to the effort. In May 1967 Johnson, angered at the program's failure to show visible results, ordered Gen. William Westmoreland [*q.v.*] to take it over. Komer was appointed his deputy and, in effect, ran the program. This new effort, known as Civil Operations and Revolutionary Development Support (CORDS), stressed security rather than positive social and economic proposals, which had been an important part of previous plans. Its goal became the relocation of all Vietnamese living in areas that could not be put or kept under military control. The result was the dislocation of large segments of the rural population; anti-war critics charged that two million refugees were generated by this program. To counter Communist kidnappings and murders, Komer also began a program designed to coordinate intelligence resources and "neutralize the Communist infra-structure" by using methods similar to those employed by the Communists. As a result, he came under criticism for planning political assassinations.

In October 1968 Komer was appointed ambassador to Turkey. He resigned in April 1969 to became senior social science researcher for the Rand Corporation.

[EWS]

For further information:
U.S. Department of Defense, *The Pentagon Papers*, Senator Gravel Edition (Boston, 1971), Vol. II.

KUCHEL, THOMAS H(ENRY)
b. Aug. 15, 1910; Anaheim, Calif.
Republican Senator, Calif., 1953-69.

Kuchel was born into a pioneer family that had helped found the town of Anaheim in 1859 and owned and edited the Anaheim *Gazette*. He attended the University of Southern California Law School and in 1935 opened a law practice. In the following year Kuchel won his first electoral contest running for the state Assembly from Orange County. Following a number of terms in the state Assembly and Senate and wartime service in the Navy, Kuchel was named state controller by Republican Gov. Earl Warren [*q.v.*] in February 1946 and that November won election to a full term. After Richard Nixon [*q.v.*] was elected vice president in 1952, Warren appointed Kuchel to Nixon's U.S. Senate seat.

Beginning his Senate career as a conservative, Kuchel became known as a moderate and, by the early 1960s, was a target of attacks by right-wing California Republicans. His political moderation, however, was advantageous in a state where, despite a large Democratic majority among registered voters, ticket-splitting was common. Kuchel had substantial Democratic support in winning reelection in 1956 and 1962. By the early 1960s he held the highest elected office of any California Republican. [See EISENHOWER, KENNEDY Volumes]

As the Senate Republican whip since 1959, Kuchel was responsible for getting out the Republican vote on issues on which the Party position had been determined by the Republican Policy Committee. He also sat on the Senate Appropriations Committee and the Interior and Insular Affairs Committee. Although his voting record was a mixed one as evaluated by the liberal Americans for Democratic Action (ADA), Kuchel clearly sided with the Republican liberal minority in the Senate on the most important domestic issues. In 1964, for example, he was the Republican floor manager for the civil rights bill and was one of only five Republicans to vote for medicare.

Just as in his home state, however, Senate conservatives criticized Kuchel more harshly than other liberals, partly because of his occasional expressions of contempt and irreverence for his colleagues. During Sen. Barry Goldwater's (R, Ariz.) [*q.v.*] 1964 presidential campaign, Kuchel openly mocked Goldwater's aspirations in front of other senators. According to journalist Neil McNeil, he coined his own version of the Arizonan's campaign slogan: "In your guts you know he's nuts." Kuchel's indiscretions, combined with his refusal to support Goldwater in the general election, led conservative Sens. Karl Mundt (R, S.D.) [*q.v.*] and Carl Curtis (R, Neb.) [*q.v.*] to attempt to replace him as minority whip in January 1965. However, the minority leader, Sen. Everett M. Dirksen (R, Ill.) [*q.v.*], who had helped Kuchel win his post in 1959, quashed the maneuver. Dirksen personally liked Kuchel and believed it necessary to keep a liberal in a Party leadership post.

In foreign affairs Kuchel favored international cooperation but urged a strong defense policy and energetic protection of U.S. interests. He was a firm supporter of President Johnson's Vietnam policy, although he did not join with Republican conservatives in demanding an escalation of the conflict. Extremely critical of draft resisters, he characterized them in 1965 as "vile and venomous" and charged that their demonstrations would "sow the seeds of treason." Also in 1965 Kuchel proposed a successful amendment to the foreign aid bill that barred aid to any country that extended its jurisdiction for fishing purposes over any area of the seas beyond that recognized by the U.S.

As the ranking Republican on both the Interior and Insular Affairs Committee and the Appropriations Committee's Public Works Subcommittee, Kuchel played a significant role in the passage of two important 1968 conservation measures, the Redwood National Park bill and the Colorado River basin bill. Kuchel consistently backed the Johnson Administration's plan to save the world's oldest and tallest trees in Northern California from the time the Redwood National Park bill was introduced in 1965. He helped work out a compromise satisfactory to lumber companies and California Gov. Ronald Reagan [*q.v.*], who originally opposed the park, by guaranteeing compensation to both the companies and the state of California for land appropriated for inclusion in the park. In addition, the park was enlarged and moved further south in response to pressure from conservationist groups. The Senate approved the compromise bill in 1967 and the House did likewise the following year. During debate on the Colorado River bill, Kuchel defended California's traditional claims to 4.4 million acre-feet per year of Colorado water. Although the final bill included the Central Arizona Project, a plan to divert the Colorado's waters to the arid urban centers of Arizona, California's claims were also guaranteed, even in the event of water shortages.

Since Kuchel's victory over a right-wing challenger in the 1962 Republican primary, his position in the state Party had deteriorated as conservatives gradually took over its organizational apparatus. Although many conservatives considered Kuchel a disloyal Republican for his relatively liberal views, his refusal to endorse fellow Republicans in general elections was more crucial to his decline. In 1962 he did not back Richard Nixon's gubernatorial candidacy. In 1964 Kuchel managed New York Gov. Nelson Rockefeller's [*q.v.*] unsuccessful primary campaign, but he in November refused to work for either Goldwater or George Murphy [*q.v.*], who was running for the Senate from California. In the 1966 gubernatorial primary Kuchel backed George Christopher, the former mayor of San Francisco, and when Christopher lost to Ronald Reagan, Kuchel withheld his support from Reagan. Many California Republicans planned to "punish" Kuchel when he sought reelection in 1968. However, political observers believed that Reagan and other Party professionals only wanted to "scare" Kuchel, since his Senate seniority was valuable to California. Kuchel's primary opponent was the extreme conservative Max Rafferty [*q.v.*], the state's superintendent of public instruction. Assuming that he would win easily, Kuchel conducted a desultory campaign. He lost to Rafferty in June by 70,000 votes. In 1969 Kuchel returned to private legal practice with a Beverly Hills firm.

[JCH]

KUNSTLER, WILLIAM M(OSES)

b. July 7, 1919; New York, N.Y.
Civil rights attorney.

Raised in a middle-class Jewish family in New York, Kunstler attended Yale University and took a law degree at Columbia in 1948. During the 1950s Kunstler joined his brother in a successful legal practice. He gradually became involved in civil liberties cases toward the end of the decade. His most important case in this period was that of William Worthy, a black reporter for the Baltimore *Afro-American*, to whom the State Department had denied passport renewal following his visit to mainland China. In the early 1960s Kunstler became deeply committed to the civil rights movement after he volunteered to defend freedom riders in Mississippi who had been arrested during their 1961 attempt to integrate interstate transportation facilities in the South.

In 1962 and 1963 Kunstler successfully appealed the conviction of the Rev. Fred L. Shuttlesworth [*q.v.*] and other blacks who had challenged segregated seating on buses in Birmingham, Ala. During the same years he tried unsuccessfully to win a court ruling favorable to Dewey Greene, a Negro student denied admission to the University of Mississippi. Later Kunstler served as special counsel for Martin Luther King [*q.v.*] and the Southern Christian Leadership Conference. He was a member of the legal advisory staff of the Council of Federated Organizations, the coalition that directed the massive voter registration drive in Mississippi in the summer of 1964. Kunstler also worked with the Mississippi Freedom Democratic Party and with the Student Nonviolent Coordinating Committee (SNCC).

In 1966 Kunstler defended SNCC chairman Stokley Carmichael [*q.v.*] on charges arising out of the civil rights demonstrations in Selma, Ala., the year before. During the same year Kunstler challenged the constitutionality of federal grand jury selection procedures in the Southern District of New York, arguing that the system of selection used intentionally excluded members of ethnic minority groups. Kunstler was also part of the team hired by Jack Ruby [*q.v.*], accused murderer of Lee Harvey Oswald, to participate in the trial to determine whether he was sane and therefore competent to hire and dismiss his own lawyers. Kunstler participated, without fee, in the October 1966 appeal that reversed Ruby's conviction in the Oswald murder. (Lawyers for Ruby successfully argued that undue publicity had biased the jury.) The next year Kunstler was Rep. Adam Clayton Powell's (D, N.Y.) [*q.v.*] chief defense lawyer in the Congressman's fight to prevent his expulsion from Congress. Kunstler argued that to remove the Congressman would unconstitutionally deprive his constituents of the representative of their choice. The Supreme Court eventually ruled that the House had violated the Constitution in excluding Powell from his seat. During the same year that he defended Powell, Kunstler also represented black militant H. Rap Brown [*q.v.*]. Kunstler claimed that the $25,000 bail set in Brown's arraignment on federal charges of carrying a gun across state lines while under indictment was "excessive and outrageous." He also charged that the government's attempt to place Brown, then chairman of SNCC, in solitary confinement was a "political maneuver." Kunstler's motion that the high bail violated Brown's constitutional rights was rejected by an appeals court. In May 1968 Brown was convicted of violating the Federal Firearms Act. Kunstler unsuccessfully urged suspension of Brown's five-year prison sentence and $2,000 fine because of the "horrendous gap between white and black people in this country."

By the end of the 1960s Kunstler had thoroughly committed himself to legal and political support of those in the civil rights and anti-war movements who sought radical change in American society. Kunstler thought the legal profession offered the possibility of a "dedicated life" in which the "worker-lawyer is the equivalent of the worker-priest." Kunstler received little money from his many clients in the late 1960s. Most of his income came from the Law Center for Constitutional Rights, which paid him about $100 a week plus expenses, and lecture fees that brought his annual income to approximately $20,000 a year.

Kunstler became the center of national attention in late 1969 and early 1970 when he served as counsel for the Chicago Seven, a group of anti-war activists accused of conspiracy to incite a riot during the 1968 Democratic National Convention. A Chicago jury later found none of the defendants guilty of conspiracy but five guilty of incitement to riot. Judge Julius J. Hoffman found all of the defendants, including Kunstler and his co-counsel, Leonard Weinglass, guilty of contempt of court. Kunstler was sentenced to over four years in prison for his courtroom behavior. The sentence was later suspended. [See NIXON Volume]

[NNL]

LAIRD, MELVIN R(OBERT)
b. Sept. 1, 1922; Omaha, Neb.
Republican Representative, Wisc., 1953-69.

Laird grew up in Marshfield, Wisc., where his mother's family had extensive lumber interests. After graduation from Carleton College and wartime service in the Navy, he won election to the Wisconsin Senate in 1946, filling the seat vacated by the death of his father. In 1952 Laird moved on to the House of Representatives, where he effectively represented the dairy and lumber interests which dominated his north central Wisconsin district. On national issues Laird presented himself as a "pragmatic conservative" with a strong interest in military affairs. His Book *A House Divided: America's Strategy Gap* (1962) advocated an augmented military establishment, reduced domestic spending and closer coordination between U.S. foreign policy and military strategy. Laird was chosen vice chairman of the Platform Committee at the 1960 Republican National Convention and became Committee chairman at the 1964 Convention. Although not a partisan of Sen. Barry Goldwater (R, Ariz.) [*q.v.*], he served as Goldwater's foreign policy adviser in the 1964 presidential campaign. [See KENNEDY Volume]

During the mid-1960s Laird, who was the second-ranking Republican on the Defense Subcommittee of the House Appropriations Committee, became one of the Republican Party's chief spokesmen on military affairs. Together with subcommittee member Gerald R. Ford (R, Mich.) [*q.v.*], he repeatedly criticized Administration defense budgets, which he claimed covered the rising cost of the Vietnam war by cutting into strategic weapons development. Laird urged, instead, that Great Society programs be reduced in scope. "We are entering once again a period when a choice must be made between guns and butter," he declared in 1965. In 1967 he supported an Administration proposal for a tax surcharge to finance increased military expenditures. He also opposed any negotiated settlement of the Vietnam conflict that would include Communists in the South Vietnamese government.

Laird's importance as a Republican spokesman in military affairs helped him enter the Party's congressional leadership during the mid-1960s. In 1967 he became chairman of the House Republican Conference; he also served on the Republican Policy and Congressional Campaign Committees. Hoping to reinforce his argument for a cutback in federal domestic spending, Laird became an early advocate of revenue sharing. In 1967 he introduced a bill that sought to return 5% of federal income tax receipts to the states and provide federal tax credits for state and local taxes paid. The proposal failed, but Laird continued to push revenue sharing in subsequent years. The conservative Americans for Constitutional Action gave Laird a 90% "correct" rating for the mid-1960s.

In 1968 Laird was a strong supporter of Richard M. Nixon's [*q.v.*] presidential candidacy. He served on the "key issues" committee of the Nixon campaign staff, and in January 1969 he was named Secretary of Defense in the new Administration. Laird remained at the head of the Defense Department for four years. During his tenure the military draft was suspended, the ground war in Vietnam reduced and the air war expanded. He continued his strong advocacy of strategic weapons programs, including the anti-ballistic missile system (ABM). Laird served as domestic adviser to President Nixon during the Watergate affair. After leaving the White House staff in 1974, he became senior counselor for the Readers Digest Corporation. [See NIXON Volume]

[SLG]

LANDRUM, PHIL(LIP) M(ITCHELL)

b. Sept. 10, 1907; Martin, Ga.
Democratic Representative, Ga., 1953-77.

After serving as a school superintendent and executive assistant to the governor of Georgia, Landrum won election to Congress in 1952. He represented rural northeast Georgia's ninth district, where textile manufacturing and poultry raising were important industries. Landrum achieved a brief moment of national recognition in 1959 when he coauthored with Rep. Robert Griffin (R, Mich.) [*q.v.*] the Landrum-Griffin Labor-Management and Disclosure Act. The law was bitterly opposed by organized labor and won Landrum the enmity of the AFL-CIO, which blocked for a time his move from the House Labor and Education Committee to the more powerful Ways and Means Committee. [See EISENHOWER, KENNEDY Volumes]

Although Landrum frequently voted with the Southern Democratic-Republican coalition in the 1960s, he played a decisive role in House passage of the Equal Opportunity Act of 1964. Landrum sponsored the War on Poverty legislation in the House, and he was instrumental in winning the votes of 60 of 100 Southern Democratic members for the bill. In exchange Johnson Administration forces agreed to a provision in the bill that gave state governors veto power over community action projects proposed by the new Office of Economic Opportunity. The compromise measure passed the House in August 1964 and was signed by the President in the same month.

Landrum opposed the civil rights acts of 1964 and 1965, but he voted for medicare in 1965 and supported Model Cities, urban renewal and urban rat-control programs in 1967. He took a special interest in trade legislation as head of the unofficial House Committee on Textiles, and he worked strenuously for import quotas on foreign cloth and clothing. The 1970 Trade Act, with its provisions for such import restrictions, had Landrum's backing. [See NIXON Volume]

[NNL]

LANE, MARK

b. February 24, 1927; New York, N.Y.
Author, attorney.

A graduate of Long Island University and Brooklyn Law School, Lane opened a law office in East Harlem in 1952. There he became known for his interest in civil liberties, opposition to the House Un-American Activities Committee and concern for such community problems as narcotics addiction, slum housing and police relations. Lane also participated in the civil rights movement, journeying south in June 1961 with Percy Sutton, president of the Manhattan branch of the NAACP, to assist the freedom riders.

As a founder of the East Harlem Democratic Club, Lane defeated the Tammany regular in 1960 and took his seat as representative of East Harlem/Yorkville in the state Assembly. In December 1961 he charged Assembly Speaker Joseph F. Carlino with conflict of interest in a $100-million fallout shelter program. The Assembly (which voted against Lane 143 to 1) exonerated Carlino of wrongdoing. Lane decided not to seek reelection in 1962.

Lane attained national prominence in January 1964 when he volunteered to go before the Warren Commission, then investigating the assassination of President Kennedy, to defend the interests of Lee Harvey Oswald, Kennedy's alleged assassin. Oswald had himself been murdered by night club proprietor Jack Ruby [*q.v.*] before he could stand trial. Lane feared that the Commission was disposed to pronounce Oswald guilty before hearing the defense. Oswald's mother accepted Lane's offer to defend her son's name, but the Commission rejected Lane's request to appear on Oswald's behalf.

Lane then undertook his own investigation and appeared before the Commission on March 4, 1964. He claimed that on Nov. 14, 1963, eight days before the assassination, a meeting had taken place in Ruby's night club between Ruby, Bernard Weissman, the leader of a right-wing group hostile to Kennedy, and J.D. Tippit, the Dallas policeman allegedly slain by Oswald during his getaway. Lane implied that Oswald might have been framed by these men, but he refused to disclose who had told him of the night club meeting nor was he able to prove that it had, in fact, taken place. In its final report the Warren Commission declared that Oswald, acting alone, had murdered the President.

Lane's rebuttal, *Rush to Judgment,* published in August 1966, became a best-seller. A number of reviewers suggested that while Lane had failed to prove Oswald innocent, he had argued convincingly that the Warren Commission, through a preconceived determination to uphold a single-assassin theory, had overlooked or dismissed substantial evidence to the contrary.

Lane charged that the Commission had failed to examine important witnesses in the matter of the alleged Ruby-Weissman-Tippit meeting. More importantly, he argued that ballistic evidence undermined the Commission's claim that Oswald alone could have killed President Kennedy and wounded Texas Governor John B. Connally [*q.v.*] riding in the same car. *Rush to Judgment,* along with a number of other books attacking the Warren Commission, raised doubts about the assassination that persisted throughout the next decade.

Lane became active in the anti-war movement in the late sixties. His book *Conversations With Americans,* published in the fall of 1970, attempted to demonstrate in a series of interviews with veterans and deserters that atrocities committed by American troops in Vietnam were widespread. Lane, along with lawyer William M. Kunstler [*q.v.*], also served in the successful defense of Indian activists Dennis Banks and Russell Means during their trial and appeal stemming from the occupation of Wounded Knee, S.D., in 1973.

[JLW]

For further information:
Mark Lane, *Rush to Judgment; A Critique of the Warren Commission's Inquiry into the Murders of President John F. Kennedy, Officer J.D. Tippit and Lee Harvey Oswald* (New York, 1966).

LAUSCHE, FRANK J(OHN)

b. Nov. 14, 1895; Cleveland, Ohio.
Democratic Senator, Ohio, 1957-69.

The son of Slovenian immigrants, Frank J. Lausche worked as a street-lamp lighter, court interpreter and semi-professional baseball player before receiving an LL.D. from a Cleveland law school in 1920. After nine years on the Cleveland municipal bench, Lausche won election as mayor on the Democratic ticket in 1941. Three years later he won the first of five campaigns for governor. Frugal with state funds and possessor of a cheery, nonpartisan campaign style, Lausche won support among the state's normally Republican majority. In the first of two successful campaigns for the U.S. Senate, Lausche unseated Sen. George H. Bender (R, Ohio) in November 1956. He proved nearly as conservative in Washington as in Columbus. During the early 1960s Lausche led efforts in the Senate to defeat the Administration's mass transit aid proposals. [See TRUMAN, EISENHOWER, KENNEDY Volumes]

Lausche maintained his independence from the national Democratic leadership throughout the Johnson years. In July

1964 he helped engineer the Administration's only defeat during the enactment of its War on Poverty program. Lausche amendments reduced rural poverty aid appropriations by 30% and deleted from the bill a section that would have created farm-development corporations to buy rural land at market value and then resell it in family size units. According to *Congressional Quarterly*, during the 89th Congress the conservative Ohio Democrat supported Johnson on only 46% of the roll call votes for which the White House announced a position. On votes indicating agreement with the Republican-Southern Democratic conservative coalition in 1966, Lausche held by far the highest margin of support (87%) of any Northern Democrat. Lausche voted for the 1964 and 1965 civil rights laws and for medicare. However he opposed the formation of the Housing and Urban Development Department and endorsed the campaign of Senate Minority Leader Everett M. Dirksen (R, Ill.) [*q.v.*] to modify the Supreme Court's legislative reapportionment rulings. In August 1966 Lausche and Sen. William Proxmire (D, Wisc.) [*q.v.*] voted with Senate Republicans to reduce by one-third the White House's mass transit aid bill for fiscal years 1968 and 1969. By 1967 the Ohio Democrat's record of agreement on the positions endorsed by the liberal Americans for Democratic Action fell to a career low of 8%.

As a member of the Senate Foreign Relations Committee, Lausche usually supported the foreign policies of the Johnson Administration, although he voted against the Administration's consular treaty with the Soviet Union in March 1967. Lausche castigated critics of America's intervention in Vietnam. In October 1965 he condemned the early anti-war demonstrations as "substantially" the "product of Communist leadership" and decried the "countless youth" who unknowingly "are following the flags of Reds." Attacking Sen. Robert F. Kennedy (D, N.Y.) [*q.v.*] in April 1967, Lausche complained that "the President is being plagued and hit from every side" because he had been "following out his honest judgment." In March 1968 he criticized "these vitriolic condemnations of our country" arising from the war protests. In July he spoke out in favor of a House amendment to the fiscal 1969 Labor-Health, Education and Welfare appropriation that would have denied federal aid to any student convicted of using force to disrupt a university.

Lausche began to modify his stand on Vietnam in February 1968 following the North Vietnamese Tet offensive and the opening of the Foreign Relations Committee's hearings on the August 1964 Gulf of Tonkin incident. A secret Committee report on Tonkin Gulf, Lausche admitted, "tends to prove" that Congress should not have condoned the President's aggressive response. During a March 1968 Senate debate on the war, Lausche proposed that the Senate repeal the Tonkin Gulf resolution and called upon the military to adopt the defensive "enclave" strategy of Lt. Gen. James M. Gavin [*q.v.*].

Lausche, along with Sen. Strom Thurmond (R, S.C.) [*q.v.*], led the effort to include an anti-riot amendment to the 1968 civil rights bill. As proposed, the Lausche-Thurmond amendment made it a federal offense to travel by interstate commerce or to use interstate communications systems with the intent to participate in a riot. Their provision broadly defined both a riot and "intent"; the Senate modified and adopted their proposal by an 82-13 vote.

In one of the greatest upsets in Ohio politics, Lausche lost the May 1968 Democratic primary to liberal former Rep. John J. Gilligan (D, Ohio) [*q.v.*]. Inattentive to the state's organized labor leadership, Lausche infuriated the Ohio AFL-CIO in October 1965 by opposing the repeal of the "open shop" provision of the Taft-Hartley Act. In January 1968 Gilligan received the endorsements of the state AFL-CIO and the Democratic state committee. Well financed by the AFL-CIO, Gilligan waged an aggressive media campaign as "the Real Democrat," while Lausche appeared at numerous barber shops and businessmen's clubs, most of whose members were Republicans. With 55% of the vote, Gilligan decisively defeated Lausche, who retired from public life in January 1969.

[JLB]

LEARY, TIMOTHY (FRANCIS)
b. Oct. 22, 1920; Springfield, Mass.
Psychologist, drug cult leader.

The son of an Army officer, Leary grew up in an atmosphere of devout Catholicism. After a year at Holy Cross College, a Jesuit school in Worcester, Mass., and another year at the U.S. Military Academy at West Point, he began his studies in psychology at the University of Alabama. He received a B.A. from Alabama in 1942 and a Ph.D. in 1950 from the University of California, Berkeley. From 1950 to 1955 Leary taught psychology at Berkeley, and from 1955 to 1958 he was director of psychological research at the Kaiser Foundation Hospital in Oakland. While at Kaiser Leary developed a personality test that was widely used by private and governmental agencies, including the Central Intelligence Agency, and was later administered to Leary himself during one of his many incarcerations on drug charges.

In 1959 Leary became a lecturer at Harvard University. There he began to develop a perspective that viewed social interplay and personal behavior as stylized games, a view later popularized by Dr. Eric Berne in his best-selling book *Games People Play*. At the same time Leary and several other clinical psychologists at Harvard became interested in LSD as a consciousness-altering substance that produced hallucinatory effects which seemed to resemble schizophrenia. Leary began taking exploratory "trips" along with a colleague, Richard Alpert, a number of student volunteers and occasional collaborators such as Allen Ginsberg [*q.v.*], Richard Watts, Aldous Huxley and Arthur Koestler. These experiments suggested the drug's usefulness in treating alcoholism and mental illness, but they also began to alter Leary's own preception of himself and of the world around him. He became an evangelist for LSD, claiming its users became aware of numerous levels of consciousness beyond what Leary called the everyday, ego or game-level consciousness.

Leary's notoriety embarrassed the Harvard administration. In December 1962 a Harvard dean publicly accused him of conducting dangerous experiments with unprepared undergraduates. Leary, who denied the charge, was eventually fired from the University. After a brief attempt to continue his experiments in Mexico, he moved into a 60-room mansion on an estate in Millbrook, N.Y., which was owned by William Mellon Hitchcock, a millionaire sympathizer. There Leary set up the Castalia Foundation, a legal entity under which he carried on his work with psychedelic drugs.

Leary soon lost interest in science and began to explore what he viewed as the redemptive potential of LSD. In 1965 he was formally converted to Hinduism during a trip to India. Upon his return in 1966 he founded the League for Spiritual Discovery, a quasi-religious cult that rejected the external physical world for an inner world of self-awareness. Also at this time Leary publicized his belief that psychedelic drugs and the life-style associated with them would produce a political and spiritual revolution in the U.S. by spreading spontaneously throughout the country. In 1967 he told an interviewer, "It will be an LSD country in 15 years. Our Supreme Court will be smoking marijuana. . . . There'll be less interest in warfare, in power politics." Casting his lot with the emerging hippie movement, Leary became an almost messianic figure for thousands of young people in search of spiritual experience. In January 1967 he spoke at a huge "Gathering of the Tribes" organized by Allen Ginsberg in San Francisco's Golden Gate Park. Dressed entirely in white and holding a daffodil, he told the audience of 20,000 to "turn onto the scene, tune into what's happening and drop out—of high school, college and grad school, junior executive, senior executive—and follow me, the hard way." This message was later shortened to the popular slogan: "Turn on, tune in, drop out."

In 1965 Leary and his 18-year-old daughter were seized in Laredo, Tex., for possession of several pounds of marijuana. Tried on a charge of failure to pay tax on the drug, he was convicted and sentenced to 30 years in jail. He appealed the case, and in 1969 the Supreme Court overturned the sentence on the grounds that the marijuana tax law required self-incrimination and was therefore unconstitutional. In 1970 Leary was again arrested on a marijuana charge, this time in California, and was convicted and sentenced to 10 years in jail. Denied bail pending appeal, he entered the minimum security section of the California State Prison near San Luis Obispo. On the night of Sept. 13, 1970 he escaped. The radical press reported that he had become a political revolutionary and that he had been aided in his escape by members of the Weatherman, an underground revolutionary group.

Shortly afterward Leary reappeared in Algiers, where he was granted political asylum by the Algerian government. He announced his intention to work with Eldridge Cleaver [*q.v.*], the fugitive Black Panther leader. Soon under criticism by the Panthers for his continued use of LSD, Leary also antagonized the Moslem government of Algeria. He went to Switzerland in July 1971 where he was arrested and later released on $18,000 bail to await extradition hearings at the request of U.S. authorities. Leary then fled to Afghanistan, where local officials turned him over to U.S. narcotics agents. In April 1973 he was sentenced by a California court to from six months to five years for his 1970 escape. He was released in 1976, reportedly after providing the government with information against those who helped in his escape.

[TLH]

For further information:
"Timothy Leary," *Current Biography Yearbook, 1970* (New York, 1971), pp. 244-247.

LEE, RICHARD C(HARLES)

b. March 12, 1916; New Haven, Conn.
Mayor, New Haven, Conn., 1954-70.

Richard C. Lee, a native of New Haven, worked as a reporter for a local paper after graduating from high school. He so enjoyed covering city hall that he decided to seek office himself. Running as a Democrat Lee was elected to the city's Board of Aldermen in 1939. After brief service in World War II, he worked as a public relations man for Yale University.

Lee ran unsuccessfully for mayor in 1949; he ran again two years later and lost by only two votes. Lee finally achieved victory in 1953. Shortly after the election he began laying plans for a revival of the downtown area, where merchants had been steadily losing customers to suburban shopping centers. With the aid of Edward J. Logue, a talented attorney, Lee won substantial federal assistance for his urban renewal projects. By the late 1950s whole blocks in the heart of New Haven were being razed to make way for new offices, department stores, middle-income apartments and parking garages. Lee and Logue both won national reputations as urban renewal experts. Lee served as an urban affairs adviser in John F. Kennedy's 1960 presidential campaign. In 1962 he was elected president of the U.S. Conference of Mayors. [See EISENHOWER, KENNEDY Volumes]

During the early 1960s Lee became increasingly concerned with the problems of the city's poor, particularly its black population. In 1962 his administration established Community Progress, Inc. (CPI), a private corporation that administered one of the nation's first antipoverty programs. CPI received a $2.5 million grant from the Ford Foundation and funds from the U.S. Department of Labor. In November 1964 it also became the first local antipoverty group to receive a grant from the U.S. Office of Economic Opportunity. CPI created job-training, placement and counseling programs, established pre-kindergarten (Head Start) classes and offered legal services to the poor. By March 1966 it had provided job training and placement for 4,700 persons.

In 1963 Lee established a 10-man Human Rights Committee to deal with racial discrimination. A year later this group was instrumental in securing passage of an ordinance prohibiting racial discrimination in housing and employment. Lee personally persuaded building trades unions to admit more black members.

By the mid 1960s Mayor Lee was at the height of his fame. The decline of New Haven's downtown had been reversed, and major New York City retailers began setting up branches in New Haven. On a per-capita basis, the city was receiving far more urban renewal funding than any other municipality in the nation. In January 1966 Robert C. Weaver [*q.v.*], Secretary of the Department of Housing and Urban Development, proclaimed that New Haven "came closest to our dream of a slumless city." On Aug. 19, 1967, however, a riot broke out in the predominently black Hill section of New Haven. Over the next five days blacks burned and looted local stores and threw rocks at police and firemen. Many other cities suffered riots that summer, but Lee's critics suggested that his slum clearance programs, which had uprooted hundreds of poor families, had contributed directly to racial problems in New Haven. Even the Mayor's supporters admitted that he had torn down more low-income dwellings than had been built.

Lee retired in 1970 and subsequently taught political science at Yale and the University of Connecticut.

[JLW]

For further information:
Allan R. Talbot, *The Mayor's Game: Richard Lee of New Haven and the Politics of Change* (New York, 1970).

LeMAY, CURTIS E(MERSON)

b. Nov. 15, 1906; Columbus, Ohio.
Air Force Chief of Staff, June 1961-January 1965.

Curtis E. LeMay studied engineering at Ohio State University, won a chance to study flying in the Army and rose through the ranks to become, at 37, a major general in the Army Air Corps. An innovator in the tactical use of massed bombers. LeMay played an important role in planning the B-29 raids that destroyed a large part of Tokyo in March 1945. LeMay became the commander of the U.S. Air Force in Europe in 1947, directed the Berlin airlift for several months in 1948 and later that year became commanding general of the Strategic Air Command (SAC). During the 1950s the SAC bombers, bearing nuclear weapons, were considered by defense specialists to be the country's primary deterrent against Soviet attack.

By the time LeMay succeeded Gen. Thomas D. White as Air Force Chief of Staff in 1961, he had become embroiled in a dispute with the Kennedy Administration over the question of continued production of manned bombers. Although Secretary of Defense Robert S. McNamara [*q.v.*] thought that in the missile age the bomber was becoming obsolete, LeMay argued that the U.S. needed a flexible attack system and that only bombers could "show the flag" by providing visible evidence of American striking power. LeMay had little difficulty winning congressional appropriations for research and development of the new RS-70 bomber, but McNamara diverted a substantial part of the funding to other purposes. [See KENNEDY Volume]

By 1964 LeMay admitted that Russian defense systems had rendered the RS-70 obsolete, but he insisted that the U.S. desperately needed a replacement for its aging fleet of B-52s. He also criticized the Defense Department for failure to keep pace with the Russians in the development of high-yield nuclear weapons. Testifying before the House Appropriations Defense Subcommittee in February 1964, he called for manufacture of a 100-megaton bomb.

Fearing that LeMay might become a serious political threat upon retirement, both Kennedy and Johnson repeatedly extended his tour of duty. LeMay's attacks on Administration policy were welcomed by conservatives like Sen. Barry Goldwater (R, Ariz.) [*q.v.*], who stated in 1964 that he "would rather put my faith in a man like Gen. LeMay than a man like McNamara who puts his primary reliance on computers."

When he finally retired in 1965 to join the board of Network Electronics Corporation, LeMay began attacking the Johnson Administration for its "no win" conduct of the Vietnam war. As a member of the Joint Chiefs of Staff, LeMay had long advocated massive air strikes against North Vietnam's ports, depots and supply lines. "My solution to the problem," he wrote in 1965, "would be to tell them [the North Vietnamese] frankly, that they've got to draw in their horns and stop their aggression, or we're going to bomb them back into the Stone Age. And we would shove them back into the Stone Age with air power or naval power—not with ground forces." LeMay believed that bombing could effectively destroy the enemy's ability to make war and argued that the Administration's restrictions on bomber runs were needlessly costing the lives of American fighting men.

In October 1968 Alabama Gov. George C. Wallace [*q.v.*] chose LeMay to be his vice presidential running mate on the American Independent Party ticket. During the campaign LeMay denounced President Johnson's decision to halt the bombing of North Vietnam and promised that if elected he would resume the air war against the North. LeMay stated the U.S. could win the war in Vietnam without the use of nuclear weapons but that the U.S. should "use anything that we could dream up, including nuclear weapons if it was necessary." LeMay also declared that the nation had a "phobia" about the use of such force and that "the world won't come to an end if we use a nuclear weapon." These remarks, attacked by the major party candidates, placed Wallace on the defensive and were thought to have injured his candidacy.

To liberal and radical opponents of the war in Vietnam, LeMay typified the irresponsibility and amorality of the military mind—the "cave man in a jet bomber," I.F. Stone [*q.v.*] once called him. To his supporters, however, LeMay was a lone voice promising a victorious end to a long and humiliating conflict.

[JLW]

For further information:
Curtis E. LeMay with McKinley Kantor, *Mission with LeMay: My Story* (New York, 1965).

LEMNITZER, LYMAN L.

b. Aug. 29, 1899; Honesdale, Pa.
Chairman, Joint Chiefs of Staff, October 1960-July 1962; Supreme Allied Commander, Europe, January 1963-June 1969.

After a distinguished career in a series of command positions in Europe and the Far East, Gen. Lemnitzer was appointed Army Chief of Staff in 1959 and Chairman of the Joint Chiefs of Staff in 1960. As Chairman, Lemnitzer advised President Kennedy to proceed with the Bay of Pigs invasion in April 1961 and urged the commitment of American air and naval power to the operation. He also counseled the President on the necessity of a large-scale commitment of men and weapons to win a war in Southeast Asia. [See KENNEDY Volume]

In January 1963 Lemnitzer replaced Gen. Lauris Norstad as Supreme Commander of Allied Forces, Europe. During the 1964 Cyprus crisis, Lemnitzer served as President Johnson's personal envoy to Turkey, warning that country not to land troops on Cyprus. In August Lemnitzer, in his capacity as Supreme Allied Commander, also successfully appealed to both Greece and Turkey to return troops intended for invasion forces to the North Atlantic Treaty Organization (NATO).

Like Lauris Norstad, Lemnitzer was a proponent of a Multilateral NATO Nuclear force (MLF) as well as an advocate of increasing conventional troops in the alliance. Following his predecessor's recommendation Lemnitzer also championed the development of a multinational mobile unit designed to show a potential aggressor that the allies were capable of quick, united action.

Lemnitzer's plans were directly challenged by the French decision to withdraw from NATO in 1966 to pursue an independent foreign policy and by threatened British and U.S. troop reductions made to ease those countries' foreign exchange problems. In 1967 Lemnitzer warned the allies of the implications of these moves. In the event of attack, the French withdrawal meant the earlier commitment of reserve forces and the possibility of earlier deployment of nuclear weapons. Lemnitzer scored the British and American plans as adversely affecting the "credibility" of the deterrent force. Warning that the enemy's military capabilities were very substantial and its policy increasingly aggressive, he urged the continued build up of forces in Europe. His pleas went unheeded until Russia's 1968 invasion at Czechoslovakia, after which allied commitments to NATO were substantially increased.

Lemnitzer retired from the Army and from his position as commander of NATO in June 1969.

[EWS]

LEWIS, JOHN

b. Feb. 21, 1940; Troy, Ala.
Chairman, Student Nonviolent Coordinating Committee, June 1963-May 1966.

Born and raised in rural Alabama, Lewis became a Baptist minister at age 16. He was a seminary student in Nashville when the sit-in movement began in February 1960. Lewis joined the Nashville sit-ins that month, helped found the Student Nonviolent Coordinating Committee (SNCC) in April 1960 and participated in the Freedom Ride of May 1961. Elected chairman of SNCC in June 1963, Lewis spoke at the March on Washington as the groups representative. [See KENNEDY Volume]

Lewis helped lead demonstrations in January 1964 to integrate public accommodations in Atlanta, Ga. He led over 150 black high school students in a Jan. 7 protest at the mayor's office and was arrested 11 days later in a demonstration outside a segregated restaurant. He was jailed again during anti-segregation demonstrations in Nashville in April and May of 1964 and during a July 1964 march against voter discrimination in Selma, Ala. Lewis also helped organize and raise funds for the Mississippi Freedom Summer of 1964, a project to encourage community organizing and voter registration among the state's black citizens. In July 1964 Lewis met with A. Philip Randolph [*q.v.*] and the leaders of other rights organizations at a strategy conference in New York City. The meeting resulted in a call for a "moratorium" on mass civil rights demonstrations until after the 1964 presidential election. After consulting with other members of SNCC, Lewis refused to sign the call.

Following the election, the Southern Christian Leadership Conference (SCLC), led by Martin Luther King [*q.v.*], decided to make Selma, Ala., its focal point for 1965. Beginning in January it cooperated with Lewis and SNCC, which had been active in Selma since early 1963, in an intensive voter registration drive. By March the two organizations had made little headway because of strong opposition from local whites, and King called for a march to Montgomery to protest the denial of voting rights to Alabama blacks. SNCC did not endorse the march because some members insisted that voter registration work in Selma should take precedence over mass demonstrations. Lewis supported the march, however, and independent of SNCC helped organize it. On March 7 Lewis and Hosea Williams [*q.v.*] of the SCLC led 500 marchers from the Brown Chapel in Selma to the Edmund Pettus Bridge leading out of town. There they were met by 200 state troopers and sheriff's deputies who ordered them to disperse. When the marchers failed to move, the troopers fired tear gas and attacked them with whips and nightsticks. Lewis suffered a concussion in the melee, yet he and Williams were able to lead many of the marchers back to Brown Chapel. Lewis then participated in marches in Harlem and in Montgomery to protest the violence in Selma and on March 21 was a leader of the final march that did go from Selma to Montgomery.

During the summer of 1965 Lewis led other voting rights demonstrations in Mississippi and Georgia. He also helped plan the challenge brought by the Mississippi Freedom Democratic Party to the seating of the state's five representatives in Congress, a move voted down by the House on Sept. 17. In January 1966 Lewis issued a SNCC policy statement that denounced the Vietnam war and supported those men unwilling to be drafted. He then helped found the Southern Coordinating Committee to End the War in Vietnam. Despite his opposition to Johnson's war policies, in February Lewis accepted an invitation to become a member of the President's council for the White House Conference on Civil Rights scheduled for June.

Lewis was ousted as chairman of SNCC in May 1966. During the previous year he had helped establish a SNCC policy that the organization and the civil rights movement should be led by blacks, but Lewis continued to support integration as the goal of the movement, with white participation in SNCC and nonviolence as the means of protest. By early 1966, however, many black members of SNCC were opposed to white involvement and were rejecting nonviolent tactics. Lewis was criticized for these policy differences and also for having supported the Selma march and for being on the council for the White House Conference. At an all-night SNCC meeting near Nashville on May 14 and 15, Lewis lost his chairmanship to the more militant Stokely Carmichael [*q.v.*]. At the same meeting, SNCC decided to stop using integrated field teams.

Lewis was named to a 10-member policymaking central committee in SNCC, and later that month he signed a statement in which SNCC withdrew from the White House Conference, charging that President Johnson was not serious about ensuring blacks' constitutional rights. On July 22 Lewis resigned from SNCC, by then identified with Carmichael and "black power." Publicly, Lewis refused to take issue with SNCC, but privately he was reported to be distressed by the group's turn away from integration and nonviolence.

Lewis continued his civil rights work as a staff member of the Field Foundation in 1966 and 1967 and later as director of community organization projects for the Southern Regional Council (SRC). He worked in Sen. Robert Kennedy's (D, N.Y.) [*q.v.*] 1968 presidential campaign. In March 1970 he was named director of the SRC's Voter Education Project.

[CAB]

LINDSAY, JOHN V(LIET)

b. Nov. 24, 1921; New York, N.Y.
Republican Representative, N.Y., 1959-65; Mayor, New York, N.Y., 1965-73.

The son of an investment banker, Lindsay graduated from Yale in 1943. After serving in the Naval Reserve during World War II, he received his law degree from Yale in 1948. A leader of the New York Young Republican Club and an Eisenhower partisan, Lindsay worked as executive assistant to U.S. Attorney General Herbert Brownell from 1953 to 1956. He was first elected to Congress in 1958 as the representative from Manhattan's East Side "Silk Stocking" district. His strong support for civil rights and civil liberties legislation won him a reputation as one of the most liberal Republicans in Congress. In 1964 Lindsay was one of three Republican congressmen who refused to support Sen. Barry M. Goldwater's (R, Ariz.) [*q.v.*] presidential campaign. [See KENNEDY Volume]

In New York City Lindsay's public image was untainted by ties to local political bosses and enhanced by his handsome appearance. Announcing his Republican candidacy for mayor in May 1965, he challenged the city's traditional liberal-labor Democratic Party alliance by pledging to professionalize and revitalize city government. Lindsay's chances of election advanced dramatically when he won the backing of New York's Liberal Party, which usually endorsed Democrats. He was aided further by the entry of William F. Buckley, Jr. [*q.v.*], founder and editor of *National Review*, as a third candidate on the Conservative line.

Lindsay ran as a fusion candidate and attracted diverse support. While Democratic candidate Abraham Beame appealed to the long-standing Democratic Party loyalties of New York's white ethnic groups, a *New York Times* analysis later showed that both Lindsay and Buckley cut into that territory. Lindsay, however, found particularly strong support among blacks, Puerto Ricans and reform Democrats, all of whom he courted strenuously. Backed politically and financially by Gov. Nelson A. Rockefeller [*q.v.*], Lindsay spent a record $2.5 million in his campaign. Both the *New York Times* and the *New York Post* endorsed Lindsay, while the city's Central Labor Council backed Beame. Lindsay was elected in November 1965 with a 45% plurality.

Even before he took office Lindsay was plunged into the first crisis of his Administration's stormy relationship with organized labor. The Transport Workers Union, whose contract was due to expire at midnight Dec. 31, the hour Lindsay was scheduled to take office, demanded a 30% wage increase and a shortened work-week. Union president Michael J. Quill [*q.v.*] requested that Lindsay attend or send a representative to the December contract negotiations. Lindsay at first refused, saying that it was outgoing Mayor Robert F. Wagner's [*q.v.*] responsibility to settle the dispute. Furthermore, Lindsay was determined not to work through what he termed "the power brokers," such as New York Central Labor Council President Harry Van Arsdale. However, Wagner, Lindsay and Quill later agreed to the appointment of a three-member mediation panel.

Lindsay's first counter-proposal to the union's demands, made Dec. 31, was flatly rejected by Quill, who thereupon called a subway and bus strike for the next morning. Lindsay pleaded with workers dependent on public transportation to remain at home unless their jobs were "absolutely critical," but auto traffic soon became chaotic, and New York experienced the "longest rush hour" in its history. The city's economy, particularly small business and the garment industry, was badly hurt by the walkout, and school operations were disrupted.

Considered by many observers the victim of his own idealism and inexperience, Lindsay settled the strike after 12 days when he agreed to a 15% pay increase for transit workers and conceded a $500 a year pension bonus. In reaching the settlement Lindsay did not consult his own Transit Authority, which had long opposed the special bonus. The agreement was criticized by President Johnson for violating anti-inflationary wage-price guidelines. When New York teetered on the edge of bankruptcy in 1975, many observers recalled the 1966 transit pact, and particularly its pension provisions, as a milestone on the city's slide toward fiscal insolvency.

With the strike behind him Lindsay began implementation of a program to reorganize city government. He recruited modern managers with national reputations, coordinated city functions by merging various agencies sharing similar operations into 10 "super-agencies" and tried to establish a "little city hall" in each of the five boroughs. His program encountered immediate resistance from councilmen and borough presidents, who sensed a threat to their power. His ambitious plans to rationalize and decentralize city government were only partially accomplished.

During Lindsay's first term in office, the city budget grew from $3.8 to $6.1 billion. This 60% growth in expenditure was due primarily to a doubling of the welfare roles, a rapid increase in pension benefits and a substantial rise in the number of city employes. These increased costs were met by the enactment in 1966 of a city income tax, a doubling of the subway fare and an increase in state and federal assistance. Real estate tax revenues also rose substantially as a result of an apartment house and office building boom in Manhattan.

Lindsay worked to cultivate a warm relationship with New York's black and Puerto Rican minority groups. While racial violence erupted in other cities, Lindsay's personal appearance in Harlem's streest in August 1967 was believed to have had a calming influence on New York's ghetto residents. Lindsay's conciliatory approach to racial disturbances was further highlighted in April 1968, when riots flared in Chicago and other cities after the assassination of Martin Luther King [*q.v.*]. After Chicago Mayor Richard J. Daley [*q.v.*] instructed police there to "shoot to kill" arsonists and to "shoot to maim or cripple" looters, Lindsay pointedly told a news conference the next day, "We are not going to turn disorder into chaos through the unprincipled use of armed force. . . .We are not going to shoot children in New York City."

Though free from the serious racial violence that swept other large cities in the late 1960s, New York became increasingly polarized as minority group demands clashed with the interests of other groups. Identifying himself with social change and the needs of the black and Puerto Rican communities, Lindsay was considered insensitive to organized labor and the white middle class. Despite his growing prominence as a spokesman for massive federal aid to the cities, his local popularity among traditionally liberal elements declined. His effort to form a civilian review board to consider citizen complaints against the police department was supported by civil rights groups and liberals but bitterly opposed by the Police Department and the Patrolmen's Benevolent Association. In a November 1966 referendum voters rejected the board by a two-to-one margin. Lindsay suffered another setback in February 1968 when his refusal to negotiate with the sanitation workers union led to a nine-day strike. The Mayor called on Gov. Rockefeller to use the National Guard to collect garbage, but instead Rockefeller appointed a mediation team that approved a wage increase that ended the strike on terms close to those proposed by the union.

Probably the most bitter controversy of Lindsay's first administration was the struggle over community control of city schools and the resulting teachers strikes of 1968. By 1966 non-white enrollment in the public schools had risen above the 50% level, while the city's teaching staff remained overwhelmingly white and heavily Jewish. Minority groups considered the schools unresponsive to their needs, but integration had proven an elusive goal in sprawling New York. Decentralization became an issue when Lindsay requested that the state legislature consider the city's five boroughs as separate districts in order to increase state aid. The legislature agreed, provided that Lindsay submitted a plan for decentralizing the system. While the highly centralized Board of Education was willing to implement administrative decentralization and establish local boards, parents and community activists in ghetto areas sought much greater community control of these governing boards.

In July 1967 the Board of Education established three demonstration school districts whose boards were given some of the powers previously held by the central board. The United Federation of Teachers (UFT) agreed to such decentralization but opposed removing the power to hire and fire from the central Board of Education because of a fear that local school boards in non-white areas would undermine the job security and working conditions of the mostly white unionized teachers. In May 1968 the governing board of Brooklyn's Ocean Hill-Brownsville district ordered 13 tenured teachers transferred out of the district. Community boycotts and demonstrations protested the central board's ruling that the transfers were illegal, while UFT teachers in the district struck for the duration of the school year. The state legislature, pressured by community control advocates to adopt a citywide decentralization plan, passed a compromise after heavy UFT lobbying and voted to enlarge the Board of Education, enabling Lindsay to appoint pro-decentralization members.

The first of three fall UFT strikes began on the initial day of school when the Ocean Hill-Brownsville governing board refused to reinstate 10 of the 13 teachers dismissed in May. Lindsay sided with the governing board as the conflict divided increasingly on racial lines. Tension between non-whites and New York's traditionally liberal Jewish community flared as community control supporters accused the union of racism and the UFT denounced the governing board and its supporters as anti-Semitic. The final strike ended Nov. 19 when the city agreed to reinstate the transferred teachers and turn the district over to a state trustee.

Lindsay supported Rockefeller for the Republican presidential nomination in 1968 and campaigned actively for him in the primaries. Some Party liberals considered Lindsay a potential vice presidential candidate, but he refused to allow his name to be placed in nomination and made the seconding speech for Spiro Agnew [*q.v.*] at the Republican National Convention.

In 1969 Lindsay lost the Republican mayoral primary but won reelection as a Liberal in a four-way race. In 1971 he left the Republican Party and declared himself a Democrat, and in 1972 he ran unsuccessfully in several presidential primaries. He left office in 1973. [See NIXON Volume]

[MDB]

For further information:

Nat Hentoff, *A Political Life: The Education of John V. Lindsay* (New York, 1967).

Woody Klein, *Lindsay's Promise: The Dream that Failed* (New York, 1970).

LING, JAMES J(OSEPH)
b. Dec. 31, 1922; Hugo, Okla.
Chairman, Ling-Temco-Vought, 1961-70.

Ling was the son of an Oklahoma railroad fireman. He dropped out of school in his mid-teens, took a series of odd jobs, served in the U.S. Navy during World War II and then returned to set up his own Dallas-based electrical contracting firm, Ling Electric Co. By 1955 Ling had turned the company into a million-dollar business. Within five years the corporation had returned six times its original investment of $2.25 a share.

In the late 1950s Ling began a rapid series of business acquisitions and mergers. He first purchased a struggling company that built vibration-detection devices for the aerospace industry and then merged it with his Ling Electric Co. After buying the Altec Lansing Co., a sound equipment firm, he purchased a large corporation dealing in defense contracts, the Temco Electronics and Missiles Co., in 1960. Ling's biggest acquisition was the 1961 purchase of the aerospace firm Chance Vought, Inc., whose board of directors was initially reluctant to merge with Ling. He subsequently trimmed the company's management personnel from 700 to 166.

Ling became chairman of the board and chief executive officer of Ling-Temco-Vought (LTV) in 1963. Two years later, when the Kennecott Copper Corporation was ordered to divest itself of its cable subsidiary, Okonite Co., LTV purchased Okonite and saw its earnings increase more in 1966 than they had in the previous six years combined. Such rapid growth led *Fortune* magazine in July 1966 to call Ling-Temco-Vought the fastest-growing company in the U.S. for the decade from 1955 to 1965. In 1967 LTV acquired Wilson & Co., whose $1 billion in yearly sales from meat-packing, sporting goods and pharmaceuticals further diversified Ling's holdings. The Wilson adquisition, among others, catapulted Ling-Temco-Vought from 204th among the top 500 companies in the U.S. in 1965 to 14th in 1968, with sales of $2.8 billion.

Ling's purchase of a majority interest in Jones and Laughlin Steel Corporation, the nation's sixth largest steel company, touched off a 1969 Justice Department anti-trust suit. Many observers considered the suit by the Nixon Administration politically motivated because Ling was a Democrat and a strong supporter of both Presidents John F. Kennedy and Lyndon B. Johnson. The Justice Department suit dovetailed with an economic recession that forced Ling-Temco-Vought's stock price down and prompted Ling's removal in 1970 as chairman of the board of LTV. As part of the settlement of the suit, Ling became chairman and 25% owner of Omega-Alpha, Inc., a holding company with small industrial subsidiaries. [See NIXON Volume]

[FHM]

For further information:
"James J(oseph) Ling", *Current Biography Yearbook, 1970* (New York, 1971), pp. 253-255.

LODGE, HENRY CABOT
b. July 5, 1902; Nahant, Mass.
Ambassador to Vietnam, August 1963-April 1964, July 1965-April 1967.

Henry Cabot Lodge, Lyndon Johnson's ambassador to South Vietnam, was born into a distinguished New England family that included several cabinet members and powerful congressmen. The young Lodge graduated from Harvard in 1924 and worked as a reporter and editorial writer for the *New York Herald Tribune* before entering the Massachusetts House of Representatives in 1933. He was elected to the U.S. Senate in 1936 and, with the exception of periods of Army service in World War II, remained there for the next 15 years.

In 1951 Lodge helped persuade Dwight D. Eisenhower [*q.v.*] to run for the Republican presidential nomination; he later managed the candidate's primary campaign. His work for Eisenhower forced him to ignore his own political career, and Lodge was defeated for reelection by Rep. John F. Kennedy in 1952. During the remainder of the decade, the former Senator served as ambassador to the U.N. In 1960 he was the Republican Party's vice presidential candidate on a ticket headed by Richard M. Nixon [*q.v.*]. From August 1963 until April 1964 Lodge served as ambassador to South Vietnam. [See TRUMAN, EISENHOWER, KENNEDY Volumes]

While Lodge was in Vietnam, liberal Republicans opened a Lodge for President campaign designed to prevent conservative Sen. Barry Goldwater (R, Ariz.) [*q.v.*] from capturing the 1964 Republican presidential nomination. Relying only on write-in votes, the Lodge forces won the March 1964 New Hampshire primary, and the Ambassador emerged as the Party's most popular candidate. His liberal record, public exposure as U.N. ambassador and personal appeal contributed to popular movements on his behalf in California, Colorado and Oregon. However, Lodge refused to leave his post to campaign and disavowed the efforts on his behalf.

In April 1964 Lodge resigned as ambassador because of his wife's ill health. By that time he had also become alarmed at the possibility of a Goldwater nomination and so returned to campaign for liberal Pennsylvania Gov. William Scranton [*q.v.*]. His efforts failed as did his eloquent plea for a Republican platform promising a "Marshall Plan" for U.S. cities. At the July Republican Convention the Party nominated Goldwater and adopted the Arizona Senator's conservative platform.

At the request of President Johnson, Lodge toured North Atlantic Treaty Organization countries in August and September 1964 to acquaint their leaders with American policy in Vietnam. In February he became a presidential "consultant" on Vietnam and helped shape the decisions to launch an air war on North Vietnam and to make major ground troops commitments to the struggle. Lodge supported both of these measures on the grounds that the U.S. could not abandon a country it had promised to protect and that a defeat would encourage new Communist aggression in Asia.

In July 1965 Johnson asked Lodge to serve a second tour in Vietnam. The Ambassador, who had been a popular figure in that Southeast Asian country, replaced Maxwell Taylor [*q.v.*], whose relations with the government and the opposition leaders had become increasingly strained. Even before assuming his post Lodge attempted to convince Washington to reemphasize the pacification program, which had been stressed in 1962 but had been subordinated to military considerations during the early days of the Johnson Administration. Lodge insisted that the military situation could be settled if the government secured the political support of the people. This, he believed, could be achieved only by a program designed first to provide protection and then to carry out economic and social reforms that would raise the living standards of the rural population of South Vietnam.

By late 1965 both Washington and Saigon had acceded to Lodge's request. The South Vietnamese government established the Revolutionary Development Cadres, financed by $400 million in Agency for International Development (AID) funds. Once the program had been established, the Ambassador's involvement became inconsistent and irregular, particularly after February 1966 when Johnson put William Porter [*q.v.*] in complete charge of the effort. Lodge objected to a subordinate controlling the program and refused to support his recommendations or press for further Administration backing. Despite the embassy's optimistic reports on the success of pacification, the program floundered. After Lodge left Vietnam the effort was restructured in hopes of improving its effectiveness, but rural pacification eventually proved a failure.

While Lodge's emphasis on pacification was lauded by many for its stress on development rather than military destruction, such critics as Frances Fitzgerald believed that the results bore little relation to the enormous amount of money spent. She also questioned the techniques and statistical compilations used to evaluate the program, pointing out that the standardized reports used by the pacification cadres were skewed toward registering success and ignoring failure.

Because Lodge saw himself as a presidential adviser rather than as a manager of the American civil-military effort in Vietnam, he did not try to formulate an integrated program of U.S. involvement. He respected the American generals leading the war and so did not play an active role in making military decisions. Lodge concurred with the Pentagon's claim that intensified bombing of the North would raise South Vietnamese morale, and he recommended quick resumption of bombing raids after the December 1965-January 1966 bombing pause failed to lead to peace negotiations with the North Vietnamese government.

During the spring of 1966 Lodge became involved in efforts to end the conflict between the central government, led by Premier Nguyen Cao Ky, and the Buddhist-dominated Struggle Movement led by Tri Quang. Prompted by the regime's failure to set a definite date for elections and its dismissal of the leading Buddhist general, Nyugen Chanh Thi, the Movement demanded the overthrow of Ky and the installation of a civilian government. By the end of March anti-government Buddhists and sympathetic elements of the South Vietnamese Army had gained control of Hue and Da Nang. Although Lodge supported Ky and termed the Buddhists demands "a naked grab for power," he tried to prevent a head-on collision between the two groups. When conciliatory efforts failed Lodge concurred in Ky's decision to use force. In early April the U.S. Military Assistance Command in Vietnam airlifted loyal South Vietnamese troops to Da Nang in an unsuccessful attempt to quell the disturbances.

To avoid heightening anti-American feelings, Lodge did not involve American men or equipment or use economic leverage in Ky's later attempts to end the protests. At the direction of the State Department, he maintained relations with both factions and urged moderation. When Ky again sent troops to the rebel cities against Lodge's advice, the U.S. gave no assistance and withdrew its military advisers from army units of both factions. The Movement was put down by a combination of force and negotiations in June 1966. Reacting to criticism that America should not be fighting for a country afflicted with petty political squabbles, Lodge defended American involvement, saying that the nation's strategic interest in the war lay "in avoiding World War III."

During the summer of 1966 the Ambassador opened secret negotiations with Hanoi that were designed to explore the North's reaction to a possible bombing pause. In November Lodge relayed communications from Washington suggesting that the U.S. would halt bombing North Vietnam in return for a secret commitment from Hanoi "after some adequate period" to reduce its infiltration of South Vietnam. The proposed delay in the North's reaction was designed to give the impression that its withdrawal of troops was not related to the bombing pause. In December Lodge received word that Hanoi seemed ready to negotiate on American proposals. However, during the following days the U.S. resumed heavy bombing near population centers around Hanoi. Despite Lodge's attempts to halt the air strikes, they continued and the talks collapsed. Lodge resigned his post in April 1967.

In March 1968 Johnson asked Lodge to become a member of the Senior Advisory Group on Vietnam convened to consider the military's request that over 200,000 additional troops be sent to Vietnam following the Tet offensive. During the group's meetings he was one of the men dissatisfied with current policy who were still reluctant to vote for a dramatic change. The panel recommended rejection of the troop increase request and favored adoption of a policy of de-escalation. Johnson announced this policy on March 31, 1968.

From April 1968 until January 1969 Lodge was ambassador to West Germany. He served as U.S. chief negotiator at the Paris peace talks between January 1969 and June 1970 and was then named presidential envoy to the Vatican. [See NIXON Volume]

[EWS]

For further information:

Alden Hatch, *The Lodges of Massachusetts* (New York, 1973).

Henry Cabot Lodge, *The Storm Has Many Eyes* (New York, 1973).

William J. Miller, *Henry Cabot Lodge* (New York, 1967).

LOEB, WILLIAM

b. Dec. 26, 1905 Washington, D. C.
Publisher, *Manchester Union Leader*, 1948- .

William Loeb grew up in fashionable Oyster Bay, Long Island, attended the Hotchkiss School and graduated from Williams College in 1927. He bought a share in New Hampshire's *Manchester Union Leader* in 1946 and gained full control of the newspaper two years later, using it as a forum for his conservative and often erratic views on U.S. politics.

During the 1960 New Hampshire Democratic presidential primary, Loeb supported the candidacy of an obscure Chicago ballpoint pen manufacturer, Paul C. Fisher, over Sen. John F. Kennedy (D, Mass.), whom he regarded as soft on Communism. In the 1960 presidential campaign Loeb subjected Kennedy to repeated editorial attacks and after the inauguration in January 1961 called the new President "the No. 1 liar in the United States." Loeb was involved with antitrust litigation in the early 1960s that resulted in a fine of $3 million, which he borrowed in installments from the Teamsters Union. Throughout the Kennedy years Loeb lent vigorous editorial support to Teamster president James R. Hoffa [*q.v.*] in his running legal battle with Attorney General Robert F. Kennedy [*q.v.*]

In the 1964 New Hampshire Republican primary, Loeb supported conservative Sen. Barry Goldwater (R, Ariz.) [*q.v.*]. He reserved his strongest editorial invective for New York's Gov. Nelson A. Rockefeller [*q.v.*] whom he referred to as a "wife-swapper" and for Ambassador Henry Cabot Lodge, Jr. [*q.v.*], against whom Loeb held a long-standing personal grudge. Lodge, however, who was not even on the ballot, won the primary by 13,000 votes.

Loeb devoted much of the mid-1960s to restoring the popularity of the Republican Party in New Hampshire after the disastrous Goldwater defeat in 1964. In the 1966 Senate race Loeb induced an obscure candidate named Harrison R. Thyng, a retired brigadier general, to run on the Republican ticket against Sen. Thomas McIntyre (D, N.H.) [*q.v.*]. According to biographer Kevin Cash, Thyng was portrayed by Loeb as a combination of "the Wright Brothers, Billy Mitchell, Eddie Rickenbacker, Alvin York and Rocky Marciano." McIntyre ignored Thyng during the campaign and ran exclusively against the editorial policies of William Loeb, winning the election by a comfortable 18,000-vote margin.

National interest concentrated on New Hampshire and William Loeb once again in the 1968 presidential primary. Loeb boosted Richard Nixon's [*q.v.*] candidacy on the Republican side, while referring to Sen. Eugene McCarthy (D, Minn.) [*q.v.*] as a "skunk's skunk." Loeb regarded the Minnesota Senator as merely a stalking horse for Robert Kennedy's (D, N.Y.) [*q.v.*] presidential ambitions.

Loeb again had an impact on national politics in the 1972 primary and was instrumental in damaging Sen. Edmund Muskie's (D, Me.) [*q.v.*] candidacy when a highly personal *Union Leader* attack on Muskie's wife provoked a widely publicized emotional outburst from the Senator. Loeb withdrew support from President Nixon after Nixon's trip to mainland China and in the Republican primary supported Rep. John Ashbrook (R, Ohio). [See NIXON Volume]

[FHM]

For further information:
Kevin Cash, *Who the Hell is William Loeb?* (New Hampshire, 1975).

LONG, EDWARD V(AUGHAN)

b. July 18, 1908; Whiteside, Mo.
d. Nov. 6, 1972; Clarksville, Mo.
Democratic Senator, Mo., 1961-68.

Edward Long was a descendant of Missouri settlers. Admitted to the Missouri bar in 1932, he became active in local politics and was elected to the Missouri General Assembly in 1946. After winning the lieutenant governorship in 1956, Long was appointed to the Senate seat vacated by the death of Thomas C. Hennings (D, Mo.). He defeated his Republican opponent in a November 1961 special election.

Long was a moderate liberal who supported Kennedy on over 60% of all Administration-backed bills. Elected to a full term in 1962, he was particularly active in drug reform legislation and vigorously supported the 1962 Federal Food, Drug and Cosmetic Act, which required substantial evidence of a drug's effectiveness before allowing it on the market. However, Long generally disapproved of what he regarded as excessive federal intervention in private enterprise and acted to prevent two important Senate investigations into the drug industry during 1963.

Long, who had one of the highest absenteeism records in the Senate, generally supported major Johnson Administration domestic and foreign policy legislation. Active in the fight for civil rights, he was a floor captain of the section of the 1964 civil rights bill reforming and extending the life of the Civil Rights Commission. In 1964 he sponsored two unsuccessful measures to authorize federal courts to hear suits brought by individuals against federal agencies and to make the surveillance of a citizen's mail by postal authorities a punishable act. Two years later Long sponsored the 1966 Freedom of Information Act.

In May 1967 *Life* magazine published charges that Long had used "his Senate subcommittee as an instrument for trying to keep [Teamsters president] Jimmy Hoffa [*q.v.*] out of prison." The article alleged that as chairman of the Judiciary Committee's Administrative Practice and Procedure Subcommittee, which had been conducting an investigation of wiretapping and electronic eavesdropping by federal agencies, Long had tried to get Hoffa's conviction for jury-tampering and misuse of union pension funds reversed. The article further charged that Long had received $48,000 from Morris A. Shenker, Hoffa's chief counsel, and stated that Long had been influenced to take up the investigations of federal agencies by Teamsters union leaders. According to *Life*, the hearings had hurt the effectiveness of the Justice Department's drive against organized crime by discrediting governmental investigative agencies, particularly the Internal Revenue Service. It had been a major contention of Hoffa's attorneys that evidence against Hoffa had come from illegal federal wiretapping.

Long denied the charges on May 21, 1967. He admitted that he had accepted the funds but insisted that the payments—allegedly $2,000 a month for 1963 and 1964—were for nongovernmental cases referred to Shenker's firm. Long also declared that "big money interests in the East" were behind the charges. However, *Life* later contended that the actual figure paid to Long by Shenker was well over $100,000 and that Long had not practiced law during the entire time the payments were being made.

On Oct. 25, 1967 the Senate Committee on Standards and Conduct cleared Long of charges stemming from the *Life* article. Chairman John Stennis (D, Miss.) [*q.v.*] stated that the Committee had "found no facts" to show that payments for Shenker's legal services had any connection with Long's "activities as a member of the Senate." *Life* later called the Committee's findings a "whitewash." The article's impact in Missouri was regarded as a decisive factor in Long's defeat by Thomas Eagleton in the 1968 Democratic senatorial primary. After his defeat Long returned to private business. He died on Nov. 6, 1972.

[FHM]

LONG, RUSSELL B(ILLIU)

b. November 3, 1918; Shreveport, La.
Democratic Senator, La., 1949- ;
Assistant Senate Majority Leader, 1964-69; Chairman Finance Committee, 1966- .

As the eldest son of Huey Long, the Louisiana politician who dominated the state in the 1920s and 1930s, Russell Long was marked for a political career. After law school and World War II naval service, he aided uncle Earl K. Long's successful gubernatorial campaign in 1947. The following year Russell Long was elected U.S. Senator after a barnstorming effort reminiscent of his father's campaigns.

Long sought the membership in the Senate's "inner club" that had been denied to his father. His entree was confirmed in January 1965 when Long was elected assistant Senate majority leader (majority whip). Most of his support came from

Southern Senators, but Long also won the votes of such liberals as Clinton Anderson (D, N.M.) [*q.v.*] and Paul Douglas (D, Ill.) [*q.v.*]. He was opposed by other Senate Democrats largely because of his opposition to civil rights, medicare, the nuclear test ban treaty and foreign aid legislation.

In 1965 Long reversed his position and voted for the medicare bill. But before the bill reached the Senate floor, Long offered amendments to remove any time limit on a patient's hospital care and to provide for graduated social security payments on the basis of income. Long's amendments were introduced on the last day of the Finance Committee's hearings on the bill and approved by an 8-6 vote. Certain that their adoption by the Senate would kill medicare when it reached the House-Senate Conference, the American Medical Association supported Long's amendments. President Johnson learned of the amendments only after they had been accepted by the Finance Committee, but he successfully pressured the Committee into reversing its vote. Ultimately Long worked for the bill's final passage.

Long vigorously supported the Administration's policies in South Vietnam and the Dominican Republic. He defended the "domino theory," declaring in February 1965 that if the United States withdrew from South Vietnam "there will be no place to stop until we reach our own borders." Long supported the landing of American troops in Santo Domingo, since "to stand aside" would be to "risk another Cuban-type Communist takeover." Despite his tough stance toward challenges in Latin America and Asia, Long supported the reduction of North Atlantic Treaty Organization forces in Europe.

Long's accession to the chairmanship of the Finance Committee in January 1966 provided the Democratic leadership with the rationale for appointing four assistant whips. The appointments were said to reflect the Administration's disappointment with Long's performance as majority whip. Democratic Senators were irritated at Long's unreliability and willingness to delay Senate business. In 1966 Long's Presidential Campaign Fund Act, permitting taxpayers to voluntarily allot $1 of their annual income tax payment to a campaign fund, was enacted as a rider to the Foreign Investors Tax Act. The next year Long and Sen. Albert Gore (D, Tenn.) [*q.v.*] engaged in a protracted debate over the retention of the Campaign Fund Act. The debate delayed passage of the Administration's bill to restore the 7% investment tax credit.

Senate Democratic irritation increased when, on May 18, 1967, Long announced that he would act as counsel for Sen. Thomas Dodd (D, Conn.) [*q.v.*] in his defense against a Senate motion to censure. Long charged that "half the Senate" couldn't stand a similar investigation and requested a six-week delay in calling up the censure resolution so that he might prepare a "proper defense." The Senate leadership granted a three-week delay, making clear that the postponement was granted to accommodate Dodd rather than Long. Long defended Dodd in a rambling six-hour speech on June 16 and later offered an amendment to substitute for the censure an admonishment to Dodd to avoid any conduct "which might be construed" as derogatory to the ethics of a Senator. The substitute was defeated and only four Senators (Dodd included) joined Long in voting against the motion to censure. These incidents contributed to Long's loss of his majority whip post to Sen. Edward M. Kennedy (D, Mass.) [*q.v.*] in January 1969. [See NIXON Volume]

[DKR]

LOVE, JOHN A(RTHUR)

b. Nov. 29, 1916; Gibson City, Ill.
Republican Governor, Colo., 1962-73.

A Colorado Springs attorney, Love first became active in public life in 1961, when he unsuccessfully sought a county Republican chairmanship. The following year he rose from almost total political obscurity to defeat David Hamil, a former speaker of the Colorado House of Representatives and 1948 Republican nominee for governor, in a bitter gubernatorial primary. Although the liberal incumbent, Democratic Gov. Steve McNichols, was favored to gain reelection in 1962, Love won due to the unpopularity of a regressive tax program passed under McNichols.

Love was a moderate Republican who reflected the political inclinations of the burgeoning Denver suburbs. Within 16 days of taking office in 1963, Love signed into law a personal income tax reduction of 15%. However, he so increased expenditures for education that in 1965 he was forced to ask the state legislature for a sales tax increase to balance the budget. He was a progressive on racial and social issues. In April 1966 Love signed an executive order declaring that the state would refuse to deal with any company that practiced discrimination. The most controversial action of his administration came a year later when he signed a bill giving Colorado what was then the most liberal abortion law in the country.

Although the Colorado Republican Party was becoming increasingly conservative during the 1960s, Love sided with the moderate wing of the national Republican Party. He directed the short-lived presidential campaign of Pennsylvania Gov. William Scranton [*q.v.*] in the Rocky Mountain states; although he supported Sen. Barry Goldwater (R, Ariz.) [*q.v.*] in the fall, he was among those liberal Republicans who insisted that the conservatives relinquish control of the Party following the election. In 1968 Love again broke with Colorado conservatives when he supported the presidential candidacy of New York Gov. Nelson Rockefeller [*q.v.*].

Love was chairman of the 1969 Governor's Conference and was reelected in 1970 to his third term as governor. In June 1973 he resigned the governorship to become President Richard M. Nixon's first Federal Energy Administrator.

[TJC]

LOWELL, ROBERT (TRAILL SPENCE), JR.

b. March 1, 1917; Boston, Mass.
Poet, playwright.

A member of a famous New England patrician family, Robert Lowell was the great-grandnephew of James Russell Lowell. The poet Amy Lowell was a distant cousin. Lowell began to write poetry in high school, and his subsequent search for a poetic mentor took him from Harvard to Kenyon College, where he received a B.A. in 1940. At Kenyon and later at Louisiana State University Lowell studied under the Southern poets John Crowe Ransom and Robert Penn Warren and converted to Roman Catholicism.

When the U.S. entered World War II, Lowell at first attempted to enlist (he was rejected as physically unfit); but when drafted somewhat later he refused to serve because he opposed the Allied bombing of civilians that had occurred in the interim. As a result he served six months in prison. Not long after his release in 1944 his first volume of poetry, *Land of Unlikeness*, was published. In 1947 *Lord Weary's Castle* made Lowell one of the country's most highly honored poet, with a Pulitzer prize, a Guggenheim fellowship and an appointment as poetry adviser to the Library of Congress. He subsequently lectured in poetry and creative writing at the University of Iowa, Kenyon and Boston University. His collections of poetry included *The Mills of the Kavanaughs* (1951), *Life Studies* (1959) and *For the Union Dead* (1965). In 1966 he published three one-act plays in free verse—"My Kinsman, Major Molineux," "Benito Cereno" and "Endicott and the Red Cross"—which were staged in 1964 and 1968.

In 1965 Lowell played an important role in opening the breach between the Johnson Administration and a large part of the American artistic and intellectual community. When he was invited to attend a White House Festival of the Arts in May 1965, he refused in an open letter to the President, explaining that he could "only follow our present foreign policy with the greatest dismay and distrust." The letter was reported in the *New York Times* in a front-page story on June 3. At the same time Robert Silvers, the editor of the *New York Review of Books* (of which Lowell was a founder), sent a telegram signed by 20 distinguished writers and artists to the President supporting Lowell's actions. Other guests at the Festival were thus placed in the position of having to join or repudiate Lowell. Many refused to attend as a result, and Johnson was furious. The Festival's organizer, historian Eric F. Goldman [*q.v.*], pronounced it an "unmitigated disaster" in the end.

In September 1967 Lowell was part of a group of 320 American professors, writers, ministers, and other professionals who signed a statement in support of draft resistance which appeared in the *New Republic* and the *New York Review of Books*. The statement was entitled "A Call to Resist Illegitimate Authority." In October of that year Lowell was a leading participant in the March on the Pentagon to protest the war in Southeast Asia, and he figured prominently in Norman Mailer's [*q.v.*] subsequent account of the event, *The Armies of the Night* (1968).

Lowell was an enthusiastic supporter of Sen. Eugene McCarthy's (D, Minn.) [*q.v.*] campaign for the Democratic presidential nomination in 1968. He admitted that he admired McCarthy "first for his negative qualities: lack of excessive charisma, driving ambition, machinelike drive and the too great wish to be President." In 1971 Lowell moved to England, explaining his expatriation in a 1972 interview: "I'm not here in protest against conditions in America, though here there's more leisure, less intensity, fierceness. . . .After 10 years living on the front lines in New York, I'm rather glad to dull the glare."

[TLH]

For further information:
"Robert Lowell," *Current Biography Yearbook, 1972* (New York, 1973), pp. 290-293.
Norman Mailer, *The Armies of the Night* (New York, 1968).

LOWENSTEIN, ALLARD K(ENNETH)

b. Jan. 16, 1929; Newark, N.J.
Democratic Congressman, New York, 1969-70.

Lowenstein, the son of a prominent physician and restauranteur, grew up in New York. He studied at the University of North Carolina and Yale Law School, where he received an LL.B. in 1954. A Committed liberal, Lowenstein quickly showed his talents as a political organizer. He served as president of the National Student Association during the early 1950s and directed student volunteers for Democratic presidential candidate Adlai Stevenson [*q.v.*]. He also worked as educational adviser to the American Association for the United Nations. In 1959 Lowenstein toured the U.N. trust territory of Southwest Africa; his impassioned attack on South African rule in the area, *Brutal Mandate*, was published in 1962.

After directing the successful 1960 congressional campaign of reform candidate William Fitts Ryan (D, N.Y.) [*q.v.*], Lowenstein taught political science during the early 1960s at Stanford and North Carolina State University. He was also active in the civil rights movement, organizing student volunteers for voter registration work in Mississippi and advising the Southern Christian Leadership Conference on legal matters. In 1966 and 1967 Lowenstein served as a civilian observer of elections held in the Dominican Republic and South Vietnam.

A strong opponent of American policy in Vietnam, Lowenstein became convinced in early 1967 that the war could be ended only by denying President Johnson the Democratic Party's renomination. He became a pivotal figure at this time, linking Sen. Robert Kennedy (D, N.Y.) [*q.v.*] and other liberal Democratic leaders with the growing anti-war movement. Throughout the year Lowenstein worked to fan "dump Johnson" sentiment in such liberal organizations as the Americans for Democratic Action and the California Democratic Council. He also helped organize the Conference of Concerned Democrats, which worked for the election of peace candidates pledged to de-escalate the war. Beginning in the summer of 1967, Lowenstein searched for a well-known liberal whom anti-war Democrats could support against Johnson in the 1968 party primaries.

Lowenstein first approached Sens. Robert Kennedy and George McGovern (D, S.D.) [*q.v.*], but both turned him down, believing that Johnson was unbeatable in the primaries. Later, Lowenstein unsuccessfully sought to interest such liberals as Rep. Don Edwards (D, Calif.) [*q.v.*] and Sen. Frank Church (D, Idaho) [*q.v.*]. He finally turned to Sen. Eugene McCarthy (D, Minn.) [*q.v.*], a somewhat less prominent opponent of the war. McCarthy surprised Lowenstein and other anti-war Democrats in late October by agreeing to run.

Campaigning in hundreds of cities and campuses throughout the country, Lowenstein and his followers threw their enthusiastic support behind McCarthy's candidacy. Student volunteers recruited and organized by Lowenstein played an important part in McCarthy's surprisingly strong showing in the March 1968 New Hampshire primary, which did much to persuade the President to withdraw from the race. In August 1968 Lowenstein helped form the Coalition for an Open Convention, a group that attempted unsuccessfully to block the nomination of Vice President Hubert Humphrey [*q.v.*] and to insert a peace plank into the Democratic platform during the National Convention. Though a leader of opposition delegates at the Convention, Lowenstein later alienated many anti-war Democrats by supporting Humphrey in his campaign against Republican candidate Richard M. Nixon [*q.v.*].

While organizing peace forces for the Convention, Lowenstein himself ran as a peace candidate in a Long Island congressional district. After a vigorous campaign conducted largely by student volunteers, he defeated his conservative Republican opponent in November 1968 and entered the House of Representatives. As a freshman congressman Lowenstein compiled a consistently liberal voting record. With other junior legislators he attempted to reform the rigid House seniority system and to relax committee rules to allow for more rapid movement of legislation. Lowenstein also joined a bipartisan group of congressmen, including Paul McCloskey (R, Calif.), that coordinated strategy for measures to end the Vietnam war.

Lowenstein lost his bid for reelection in 1970, after the boundaries of his congressional district had been altered by the New York State legislature. He remained active in liberal politics, however, and in May 1971 was elected president of the Americans for Democratic Action. He also cooperated with Rep. McCloskey and others in organizing a bipartisan voter registration drive aimed at newly enfranchised 18-to-21-year-olds, who were expected to increase the chances of peace candidates in coming elections. Viewed with hostility by the Nixon Administration, Lowenstein was included on the White House "enemies list" compiled in 1971. After he was narrowly defeated in a New York Democratic primary race in June 1972, Lowenstein returned to teaching at the Yale School of Urban Studies in 1970; he moved to the University of Massachusetts in 1972 and New York's New School of Social Research in 1973. [See NIXON Volume]

[SLG]

For further information:

"Allard Lowenstein," *Current Biography Yearbook, 1971* (New York, 1972), pp. 235-238.

Lewis Chester, Godfrey Hodgson, Bruce Page, *An American Melodrama, The Presidential Campaign of 1968*, (New York, 1969).

LUCE, HENRY R(OBINSON)

b. April 3, 1898; Tengchow, China.
d. Feb. 28, 1967; Phoenix, Ariz.
Editor-in-chief, *Time* and Time Inc., 1923-64; Editorial chairman, Time Inc., 1964-67.

A Presbyterian missionary's son, Henry R. Luce grew up in China and received a B.A. from Yale in 1920. Luce and Briton Hadden edited the *Yale Daily News* while in college and in 1923 founded *Time*, the weekly news magazine. Hadden died in 1929 but Luce and his publishing concern prospered with the notable additions of *Fortune* in 1930 and *Life* in 1936. By 1964 the circulation of all Time Inc. publications totaled about 13 million. Although Time had no editorial page, its influential news reportage clearly reflected the views of its editor-in-chief. "I am a Protestant, a Republican and a free-enterpriser," Luce once snapped at a critic, "which means I am biased in favor of God, Eisenhower and the stockholders of Time Inc.—and if anybody who objects doesn't know this by now, why the hell are they still spending 35 cents for the magazine?" [See TRUMAN, EISENHOWER, and KENNEDY Volumes]

Luce retired as editor-in-chief in April 1964 but retained much of his authority over the magazine as editorial chairman. As in previous presidential campaigns the Luce press attempted to influence the outcome of the 1964 contest. Defense Secretary Robert S. McNamara [*q.v.*] received highly favorable coverage in the hope that President Johnson would name him as his running mate. Early in the Republican race *Life* promoted dark-horse presidential contender Pennsylvania Gov. William W. Scranton [*q.v.*], whose brother-in-law served as president of Time Inc. When the Republicans nominated conservative Sen. Barry M. Goldwater (R, Ariz.) [*q.v.*], Luce reluctantly abandoned his tradition of Republican campaign support. Although his wife, Clare Booth Luce, seconded Goldwater's nomination at the Republican National Convention in July and *Life* ran a two-part exposé of Johnson's personal finances in August, the magazine formally endorsed Johnson in September. Luce also personally praised much of the President's domestic social program.

The Luce magazines encouraged American military intervention in South Vietnam. In an April 1964 speech Luce termed Vietnam "troublesome" but added that it represented an "entanglement in the cause of human freedom." The August 1964 Tonkin Gulf incident was covered as an unprovoked challenge to freedom of the seas in the Luce magazines, with their reports bolstered by confidential Defense Department information that seemed to justify the Administration's militant response. A 1965 issue of *Time* described American troops as "lean, laconic and looking for a fight" and told its 2.9 million subscribers that "the Viet Cong's once-cocky hunters have become the cowering hunted." *Time* made Army Gen. William C. Westmoreland [*q.v.*] its "Man of the Year" in January 1966. Only after the Communists' February 1968 Tet offensive (one year after Luce's death) did Time-Life modify its support of the Administration's Vietnam policy.

Luce retained a journalist's curiosity until his death. Despite his long association with the pro-Chiang Kai-shek "China Lobby," Luce sought a visa to travel to mainland China in 1966. Luce died of a heart attack in Phoenix, Ariz., on Feb. 28, 1967.

[JLB]

For further information:

John Kobler, *Luce* (Garden City, 1968).
W. A. Swanberg, *Luce and His Empire* (New York, 1972).

LYND, STAUGHTON (CRAIG)

b. Nov. 22, 1929; Philadelphia, Pa.
Historian, anti-war activist.

Lynd's parents were the sociologists Robert and Helen Lynd, who coauthored the classic *Middletown* and *Middletown in Transition*. A Quaker, Staughton Lynd lived for a time in the Macedonia Community in New York, which had been established by World War II conscientious objectors. He graduated from Harvard in 1951 and obtained a Ph.D. in history from Columbia in 1962. In 1966 he was appointed an assistant professor at Yale, where he became a noted historian of colonial America.

Throughout the 1960s Lynd was deeply involved in the civil rights and anti-war movements. He worked with the Students for a Democratic Society (SDS), was an editor of the radical historical journals *Liberation* and *Studies on the Left*, directed the Freedom Schools for the Mississippi Summer Project in 1964 and helped organize the nationwide teach-ins on the Vietnam war held in the spring of 1965.

Lynd was encouraged by the growing militancy and self-confidence of the anti-war movement, but he was an outspoken opponent of what he considered its reliance on the liberal wing of the American Establishment. Speaking at the Vietnam Day teach-in at Berkeley in May 1965, he attacked liberals, such as Arthur Schlesinger, Jr. [*q.v.*], who were mildly critical of the conduct of the war, insisting that for the anti-war movement to ally itself with the liberals would amount to a "coalition with the Marines." In the June-July 1965 issue of *Liberation*, Lynd criticized Bayard Rustin's [*q.v.*] proposal for a strategy of coalition within the Democratic Party. Recalling an SDS-sponsored anti-war march in Washington during April of that year, Lynd offered his own vision of nonviolent revolution: "It seemed that the great mass of people would simply flow on through and over the marble buildings, that our forward movement was irresistibly strong, that had some been shot or arrested nothing could have stopped that crowd from taking possession of its government. Perhaps next time we should keep going. . . ."

Late in 1965 Lynd accompanied student leader Tom Hayden [*q.v.*] and Communist Party theoretician Herbert Aptheker on a highly publicized visit to North Vietnam. He returned in January 1966 to report on Hanoi's peace terms and on the effects of American bombing. Federal officials insisted that Lynd had broken the law by traveling in an area banned to U.S. citizens without government permission, and the State Department suspended his passport. Later, after a trip to London where he spoke at a rally in Trafalgar Square, Lynd's passport was canceled.

Lynd was an early proponent of the resistance strategy that began to emerge in the anti-war movement in 1966. He wanted to overcome the isolation of individual acts of moral witness, and he hoped that by organizing large-scale aggressive noncooperation with the induction process the movement could communicate a spirit of refusal and defiance to the mass of draftees. In July 1966 a group of eight young men met with Lynd in New Haven and signed a statement pledging to "return our draft cards to our local boards with a notice of our refusal to cooperate until American invasions are ended." At the same time Lynd and SDS president Carl Oglesby [*q.v.*] drafted a statement containing a broad list of acts of resistance which the signer was asked to encourage: sending medical aid to the National Liberation Front, obstructing troop movements, refusing induction, refusing orders to fight in Vietnam and refusing to pay income taxes. Eventually Lynd withdrew his statement in favor of a similar one drafted by Arthur Waskow and Marc Raskin of the Institute for Policy Studies in Washington. Entitled "A Call to Resist Illegitimate Authority," it was published in the *New York Review of Books* and the *New Republic* in September 1966. It received over 2,000 signatures by the end of the following year. Lynd was an enthusiastic supporter of the Resistance, an anti-draft organization formed in the fall of 1967. With Michael Ferber, he later wrote *The Resistance* (1971), a history of the anti-draft movement.

During this time Lynd was also an active scholar. His book *Class Conflict, Slavery and the United States Constitution* was published in 1967, and it was followed in 1968 by *Intellectual Origins of American Radicalism.* In May 1967 Lynd requested a leave of absence from Yale, with the understanding that he was leaving the Ivy League school to find a teaching post in the "inner city." He was attracted to Chicago and applied at the University of Illinois and Northern Illinois University but was rejected without explanation. In the fall of 1967 he was hired by Chicago State College. When the Illinois Board of Governors of State Colleges and Universities attempted to block the appointment, Lynd threatened a breach of contract suit and forced the Board to back down. In March 1968 he helped form the New University Conference, an organization of university faculty and graduate students that set up radical caucuses in the academic disciplines.

In the 1970s Lynd devoted himself to the study of labor history and to community organizing in the Calumet area of South Chicago and northern Indiana. With his wife Alice, he wrote *Rank and File: Personal Histories of Working-Class Organizers* (1973), and with Gar Alperovitz, *Strategy and Program: Two Essays Toward a New American Socialism* (1973).

[TLH]

For further information:

Staughton Lynd and Michael Ferber, *The Resistance* (New York, 1971).

Thomas Powers, *The War at Home* (New York, 1973).

McCALL, TOM (LAWSON)
b. March 22, 1913; Egypt, Mass.
Governor, Ore., 1967-75.

McCall graduated from the University of Oregon in 1936 and worked for 25 years in Portland as a journalist and radio and television commentator. An executive assistant to Republican Gov. Douglas McKay from 1949 to 1952, he lost his initial bid for elective office in 1954 when he challenged Edith Green [*q.v.*] for a seat in the U.S. House of Representatives. In 1964 McCall won election to Oregon's second-ranking elective office, secretary of state, as an avowed liberal Republican.

In November 1966 McCall defeated Democratic State Treasurer Robert Straub in a campaign that centered largely upon the issue of environmental pollution. Succeeding Republican Mark O. Hatfield [*q.v.*] as governor in January 1967, he immediately announced plans for the preservation and improvement of Oregon's natural resources. In 1967 environmentalists termed the Willamette River, along whose valley the bulk of Oregon's population lived, a "biological cesspool." Shortly after taking office McCall appointed himself temporary chairman of the state's environmental commission and ordered statewide hearings on water quality standards. In addition, McCall instituted a series of tax credits and state bonds, which enabled industries and municipalities to install effective water treatment plants. The commission also published an enforcement plan covering every Oregon waterway. McCall appointed John D. Mosser, one of the country's toughest water pollution control officers, as permanent chairman of the control board. By 1969 the Willamette River was once again clean enough to support salmon spawning, swimming, boating and fishing. Aside from conservation and ecology, McCall expanded state subsidies to education at all levels. In order to finance this increase he adjusted income-tax rates instead of raising the state sales tax and property tax as some advocated.

In 1969 McCall called for abortion law reform, stating that anti-abortion statutes were "callous tools of shame instead of useful tools of society." He scored a major legislative victory in winning state government reorganization in 1969. This reform provided for the most thorough revamping of Oregon's state agencies in this century and gave the Governor exclusive control over almost all state agencies for the first time. McCall was reelected to a second term in 1970.

Though he remained largely unknown in the rest of the country, E. J. Kahn attributed Oregon's "bellwether" approach to the problems of energy, abortion, ecology, conservation and campaign finance to McCall's "innovative and bizarre" approach. McCall hoped to be remembered, Kahn wrote, for what he termed "the Oregon message," which was "a story of innovation and regeneration that can actually be used anywhere." [See NIXON Volume]

[TJC]

McCARTHY, EUGENE J(OSEPH)
b. March 29, 1916; Watkins, Minn.
Democratic Senator, Minn., 1959-71.

Eugene McCarthy rose to unexpected prominence in the late 1960s as the foremost critic of President Johnson's Vietnam policy. The early successes of his unorthodox campaign for the presidency in 1968 helped drive Johnson from office and brought a corps of idealistic young volunteers from the anti-war movement into the Democratic Party, where they had a significant impact on American politics.

In the 13 years following his graduation from St. John's University in Minnesota in 1935, McCarthy taught economics and sociology at Catholic high schools and colleges. He also spent nine months in a monastery as a Benedictine novice in 1942 and 1943. McCarthy was teaching sociology at St. Thomas College in St. Paul when he first entered politics as a supporter of Hubert Humphrey's [*q.v.*] fight against the Communist-led wing of Minnesota's Democratic Farmer-Labor Party (DFL). After leading a successful drive to take control of the DFL in St. Paul and Ramsey County, McCarthy won election to the

House of Representatives in 1948.

In the House McCarthy compiled a liberal, pro-labor voting record. He organized an informal caucus of liberal House Democrats—later institutionalized as the Democratic Study Group—which agitated for more ambitious legislative programs than those proposed by the Democratic leadership. He entered the Senate after defeating a Republican incumbent in 1958. With his scholarly demeanor and air of detachment, McCarthy stood apart from his colleagues in the Senate's liberal bloc. His voting record continued to favor positions endorsed by the liberal Americans for Democratic Action, but he failed to exercise the leadership he had shown in the House, and he did not use his position on the powerful Finance Committee to advance the cause of tax reform as many liberals had hoped. [See EISENHOWER, KENNEDY Volumes]

Early in the Johnson Administration McCarthy emerged from the Senate shadows when Administration figures began mentioning him as a serious vice presidential candidate. As a prospective running mate for Johnson, McCarthy's intelligence, grace and attractiveness enhanced his complementary value as a Northern liberal Catholic. Nevertheless, McCarthy's colleague Sen. Hubert Humphrey (D, Minn.), won the nomination, a blow to McCarthy, whose hopes had been encouraged by Johnson almost up to the Atlantic City Convention in August. According to his biographer, Albert Eisele, "McCarthy was humiliated by his treatment at Atlantic City. . . . He was deeply offended by Johnson's playing with him like a puppet on a string, and he never forgave Johnson for it."

Aided by the publicity resulting from his vice presidential possibilities, McCarthy won reelection easily in 1964. His assignment to the seat on the Foreign Relations Committee vacated by Humphrey gave him the long-desired opportunity to have a greater voice in the making of foreign policy. McCarthy stood out as a critic of U.S. policy in several important areas. Long an advocate of closer congressional oversight of U.S. intelligence agencies, he called for a "full and complete investigation" of the Central Intelligence Agency (CIA) in November 1965. "The role of the CIA in the Dominican Republic, Vietnam, Cuba and a number of other critical areas has raised serious questions about the relationship of the Agency to the process of making and directing foreign policy," he said, adding that there was some evidence that the CIA had gone beyond its statutory purpose of collecting and evaluating intelligence.

McCarthy was also a veteran critic of the large volume of U.S. arms sales to undeveloped nations. He charged that such sales undermined other foreign policy goals, such as peace and disarmament, exacerbated world tensions and led to the dangerous militarization of the Third World. Criticizing the Pentagon's effort to promote sales of U.S. weapons abroad, he warned in January 1967 that "we may be subsidizing weapons manufacturers to a dangerous and undesirable extent."

Through his opposition to the Vietnam war, McCarthy exerted a profound and dramatic impact on the course of American foreign policy. He was not an early dissenter, having voted for the Gulf of Tonkin Resolution in August 1964 and avoided any public criticism of Johnson's war policy until January 1966. At that time he joined 14 other senators in sending a letter to the President calling for continued suspension of air strikes against North Vietnam. The bombing, which had been halted during the holiday truce period, was resumed on Jan. 31. McCarthy maintained that the bombing had not had a "beneficial political or diplomatic effect" in the past. He suggested that the war in Vietnam called for "a national debate . . . and a real searching of the mind and the soul of America."

Whatever his private doubts about U.S. policy, McCarthy remained mild and hesitant in his dissent throughout 1966. In March he said, "I think that the kind of escalation we now have, in which we're sending in more troops, is defensible on the part of the Administration," while "bombing civilian areas in North Vietnam" is a "change of substance" and "should be challenged." McCarthy indicated in May that the U.S. should stay in South Vietnam even if a newly elected government opposed the American presence.

In early 1967 McCarthy became more vocal in his opposition. "We should hesitate to waste our strength—economic, military, and moral—in so highly questionable a course," he said on Feb. 25. Three days later he told a student audience that the war was "morally unjustifiable." In April he criticized President Johnson's use of Gen. William Westmoreland [*q.v.*] as a spokesman for his Vietnam policy as a "dangerous practice" and an "escalation of language, method and emotions." He was particularly upset by Undersecretary of State Nicholas Katzenbach's [*q.v.*] August 1967 defense of the Johnson Administration's broad interpretation of the Gulf of Tonkin Resolution and Katzenbach's dismissal of the lack of a congressional declaration of war in Vietnam as a matter of "outmoded phraseology." An angry McCarthy was quoted by a *New York Times* reporter as saying, "This is the wildest testimony I have ever heard. There is no limit to what he says the President can do. There is only one thing to do—take it to the country." In October McCarthy published *The Limits of Power*, a strong critique of U.S. foreign policy.

After persistent urging by anti-war liberals, McCarthy announced on Nov. 30 that he was running for the Democratic presidential nomination in order to further the campaign for a negotiated settlement of the war. "I am concerned," he declared, "that the Administration seems to have set no limit to the price which it's willing to pay for a military victory." He also voiced his hope that his campaign might alleviate "this sense of political helplessness and restore to many people a belief in the processes of American politics."

Dismissed by many as a futile and quixotic venture, McCarthy's New Hampshire primary campaign slowly gained momentum. The character and spirit of his race were decidedly unorthodox. Grass-roots canvassing was carried out by legions of idealistic young volunteers instead of experienced party workers, an innovation that became known as the "new politics." The style of the candidate was equally novel. McCarthy wrote many of his own speeches, which were laced with wit and literary allusions. Yet he often frustrated his supporters and risked losing audiences with his flat, unemotional delivery. Besides the evil of the war, McCarthy stressed the grave danger of the growing power of the presidency, the erosion of the role of Congress in the making of foreign policy, and the alleged mendacity and arrogance of President Johnson.

McCarthy's unexpectedly strong showing in the March 11 New Hampshire primary won him recognition as a serious presidential contender. In light of the widespread assumption that the President would score an easy victory over his obscure opponent, McCarthy's winning 42% of the popular vote (Johnson received 49%) was not only a stunning moral victory for the anti-war candidate but also a revelation of Johnson's personal vulnerability: an NBC poll taken after the primary showed that more than half of the Democrats questioned had not known where McCarthy stood on the war.

The reverberations from McCarthy's New Hampshire upset quickly transformed the 1968 presidential campaign. Sen. Robert F. Kennedy (D, N.Y.) [*q.v.*] declared his own candidacy two days after the New Hampshire results were in, and on March 31 President Johnson announced that he would not seek reelection. The President's withdrawal made McCarthy's victory over Johnson in the Wisconsin primary a few days later seem anticlimactic. On April 27 Vice President Humphrey formally entered the presidential race.

McCarthy and Kennedy were the major combatants in the remaining primaries. With their essential agreement on the key issues and their visceral dislike for one another, the focus of their contests became personal and bitter. McCarthy considered Kennedy opportunistic and ruthless, while Kennedy supporters charged that McCarthy had been a lazy senator and circulated controversial "fact sheets" accusing McCarthy of inconsistency in his voting record.

McCarthy could not match Kennedy's emotional appeal to minorities and blue-collar whites, and Kennedy won the majority of their primary contests. After Kennedy triumphs in Indiana and Nebraska, McCarthy revived his campaign with a victory in Oregon, but he lost the crucial California primary on June 5. The assassination of Kennedy on the night of the primary made McCarthy the leader of the Democratic Party left in opposition to Humphrey and the regular Party organization.

As the Convention approached, McCarthy attracted enthusiastic crowds everywhere, but he failed to seek or win the allegiance of many Kennedy delegates. The candidate himself showed a waning commitment to his cause and a fatalistic attitude about a Humphrey victory. At the Chicago Convention in late August, Humphrey won the nomination with 1,760 delegate votes to McCarthy's 601 and Sen. George Mc Govern's (D, S.D.) [*q.v.*] 146. McCarthy was alienated by the circumstances of Humphrey's victory: the packing of the convention galleries with supporters of Chicago Mayor Richard Daley [*q.v.*], the violence used by the Chicago police against young anti-war marchers, and the control of much of the delegate-selection process by the Party machine. Unconvinced that Humphrey had changed his position on the war, McCarthy refused to endorse the nominee after the Convention. He withheld his support until Oct. 29, when he offered a lukewarm endorsement, stating that Humphrey showed "a better understanding of our domestic needs and a stronger will to act" than his Republican opponent, Richard M. Nixon [*q.v.*].

McCarthy unexpectedly resigned from the Foreign Relations Committee in 1969 and retired from the Senate in 1971. He made lackluster runs for the presidency in 1972 and 1976, but he never ignited the enthusiasm he had fired in 1968, partly because of his occasional indifference and enigmatic behavior. Even while he personally was attracting little support, however, national party politics revealed the far-reaching effects of the movement he had crystalized: the reform of Democratic Party procedures, the introduction of thousands of young people as a potent factor in electoral politics, and eventually the ending of the Vietnam war. [See NIXON Volume]

[TO]

For further information:

Albert Eisele, *Almost to the Presidency: A Biography of Two American Politicians* (Blue Earth, Minn., 1972).

Eugene McCarthy, *The Year of the People* (New York, 1969).

McCARTHY, MARY (THERESE)

b. June 21, 1912; Seattle, Wash.
Novelist and critic.

Mary McCarthy was orphaned at the age of six when her parents died in the influenza epidemic of 1918. She and her three brothers were then placed in the care of their paternal Irish Catholic grandparents, who arranged to have them looked after by a great uncle she later described as harsh and repressive. After five years McCarthy went to live with her maternal Protestant grandfather and Jewish grandmother in Seattle. Her grandfather, a prosperous lawyer, saw that she received a classical education at the exclusive Forest Ridge Convent in Seattle and the Annie Wright Seminary in Tacoma. McCarthy later described this upbringing in her vivid, autobiographical *Memoirs of a Catholic Girlhood* (1957).

McCarthy attended Vassar College, and after graduating in 1933 she took up residence in New York City, where she wrote book reviews for the *Nation* and the *New Republic*. In 1937 she joined the editorial staff of *Partisan Review*, for which she wrote theater criticism until 1948. During the 1940s and 1950s McCarthy contributed to a number of magazines. The more important of these writings, including essays on such wide-ranging topics as politics, travel, women and literature, were collected in *On the Contrary: Articles of Belief: 1946-1961* (1961). In *Venice Observed* (1956) and *Stones of Florence* (1959) she combined commentary on contemporary life in these cities with history and art criticism.

McCarthy reached her largest audience through her fiction. In 1942 she wrote *The Company She Keeps*. This was followed by a short novel *The Oasis* (1949), a collection of short stories entitled *Cast a Cold Eye* (1950) and her full-length novels, *The Groves of Academe* (1952) and *A Charmed Life* (1955). *The Group* (1963), a fictional chronicle of eight Vassar girls from the class of 1933, became a best-seller and a movie (1966).

In the late 1930s McCarthy had been associated with the group of leftist intellectuals around *Partisan Review*, who had broken away from the Communist Party orthodoxy and were briefly attracted to Trotskyism before moving towards some form of liberalism or democratic socialism in the 1940s. Summarizing this experience, McCarthy observed: "For my generation, Stalinism, which had to be opposed, produced the so-called non-Communist Left, not a movement, not even a sect, but a preference, a political taste, shared by an age group resembling a veterans' organization." Although she continued to describe her political taste as "libertarian socialist," she remained for the most part uninterested in political writing during the 1940s and 1950s.

With the escalation of the Vietnam war in 1965, McCarthy began to search for a way to contribute personally and dramatically to the anti-war effort. Early in 1966 Robert Silver, the editor of the *New York Review of Books*—which had given Jean Lacouture and Bernard Fall an early opportunity to present their views on the war to an important American audience—asked her to go to South Vietnam for the magazine. Despite her lack of experience as a reporter, McCarthy went to Saigon in 1967 and Hanoi in 1968. Her reports on these trips—published serially in the *New York Review of Books* and later in pamphlet form as *Vietnam* (1967) and *Hanoi* (1968)—were unique at the time. McCarthy was the first American novelist to go to Hanoi and only the second important literary figure to go to South Vietnam, having been preceded only by John Steinbeck, who supported the war. In her reports she renounced any claim of journalistic objectivity, declaring that she went "looking for material damaging to American interests." In particular, she deplored the Americanization of South Vietnam and the moral corruption that followed. Her impressions of North Vietnam, where she was a guest of the government, were generally sympathetic.

In 1973 McCarthy attacked David Halberstam for what she said was an inappropriate stress on the personal failures of high Administration figures in explaining America's involvement in Vietnam. This article was republished, along with *Vietnam*, *Hanoi*, and a report on the trial of Capt. Ernest Medina for his role in the My Lai massacre, in *The Seventeenth Degree* (1974).

[TLH]

For further information:
Mary McCarthy, *The Seventeenth Degree* (New York, 1974).

McCLELLAN, JOHN L(ITTLE)

b. Feb. 25, 1896; Sheridan, Ark.
Democratic Senator, Ark., 1943- ;
Chairman, Government Operations Committee, 1949-53; 1955-72.

McClellan entered private law practice at the age of 17. He served as city attorney of Malvern, Ark., from 1920 to 1926 and as prosecuting attorney of the state's seventh judicial district from 1927 to 1930. In 1934 McClellan was elected to the U.S. House of Representatives, where he supported most New Deal programs. He lost the Democratic senatorial primary four years later but won a Senate seat in 1942.

During the postwar years McClellan opposed civil rights legislation and compiled a generally conservative voting record. He first received national attention when, as the ranking minority member on the Government Operations Committee and its Permanent Investigations Subcommittee, he led Democratic protests against what he charged were Committee Chairman Joseph McCarthy's (R, Wisc.) undemocratic methods. McClellan gained further attention as chairman of the Select Committee on Improper Activities in the Labor and Management Fields, an ad hoc panel that investigated corruption in labor unions from 1957 to 1960. [See TRUMAN, EISENHOWER Volumes]

By 1960 Sen. McClellan had established a reputation as a stern, effective and fair investigator, and for the next decade his senatorial career centered around his role as chairman of the House Permanent Investigations Subcommittee.

From February through November 1963 McClellan led the panel's investigation of reports of pressure and favoritism in the Defense Department's award of the multi-billion dollar TFX (Tactical Fighter Experimental) swing-wing, fighter/bomber contract to General Dynamics. In September and October of the same year, Joseph Valachi, a convicted murderer and self-described former member of a crime syndicate, testified before the subcommittee on the structure and operations of organized crime in one of the panel's most publicized probes. [See KENNEDY Volume]

In September 1964 the subcommittee issued a report on its 1963 investigation of Texas businessman Billie Sol Estes. The probe had been launched to determine why Estes's illegally acquired cotton allotments had not been canceled by the Agriculture Department until after his arrest on other charges. McClellan issued a statement of individual views that reflected the position taken by the report of the panel's Democratic majority. He said that the Department had demonstrated "timidity, vacillation and indecision" in the Estes affair but exonerated the Kennedy Administration from major responsibility by commenting that "the prevailing system had been established and the procedures developed during previous administrations and over a long time." McClellan and his fellow Democrats also asserted that they had uncovered no evidence of favoritism within the Agriculture Department. The panel's Republican minority, on the other hand, charged that the Department had given Estes special treatment.

In March 1964 the subcommittee issued a report, based on a 1962 investigation, that criticized the government's missile procurement policies. It asserted that excessive profits were being paid to companies for work that they farmed out to subcontractors and stated that money paid to other companies for subsystems "should not of itself generate profit." During the following year McClellan's panel and the House Banking and Currency Committee investigated an increase in federally insured bank failures and the "milking" of bank assets by criminal elements. As a result of these probes, legislation was introduced to tighten federal bank-regulatory procedures.

In February 1967 President Johnson proposed crime legislation to provide funds for the improvement of crime prevention and control methods at the state and local levels. The bill was sent to McClellan's Judiciary Committee's Subcommittee on Criminal Laws and Procedures. McClellan believed that a number of recent Supreme Court decisions had, through what he regarded as the unwarranted expansion of the rights of criminal defendants, seriously undermined the effectiveness of the criminal justice system. By the time the Administration bill came to the Senate floor in May 1968, the subcommittee had added to it a number of provisions overturning some of those decisions.

One of the most important of the provisions declared that confessions were admissible if the trial judge ruled that they had been voluntarily given. This stipulation was a challenge to the Supreme Court's *Miranda v. U.S.* (1966) ruling, which barred interrogation of a suspect until he was informed of his rights. In floor debate McClellan argued that if the Supreme Court decisions were not reversed "the lawbreaker will be further . . . reassured that he can continue a life of crime and depredations profitably with impunity. . . ." The subcommittee version of the crime bill also permitted wiretapping in many federal and state cases. The enactment of the Omnibus Crime Control and Safe Streets Act in June 1968 in essentially the form proposed by the subcommittee represented a major defeat for congressional liberals.

One of the factors contributing to congressional sentiment for stronger crime legislation was the rioting in black urban neighborhoods during the summer of 1967. In August 1967 the Permanent Investigations Subcommittee was selected by the Rules Committee to examine the causes of the disturbances. Some liberals opposed the choice on the ground that McClellan, because of his segregationist views and belief in vigorous law enforcement, would ignore what they felt were the underlying social causes of the riots. At the beginning of the panel's hearings the following November, McClellan added to their fears by stating that the subcommittee would examine the immediate causes of the riots. He also condemned "callous and deliberate disregard for law and order, spurred on by inflammatory speeches and proclamations of those who publicly advocate the use of violence. . . ." In 1968, as the hearings progressed, he denounced the Office of Economic Opportunity for granting funds to black street gangs.

In 1969 the subcommittee continued its probe of urban riots and also examined campus disturbances. During July McClellan introduced a bill to impose fines and jail sentences upon persons who disrupted federally assisted colleges. The following year the panel investigated terrorist bombings. In the same year McClellan proposed what became the Organized Crime Control Act of 1970, the most comprehensive law ever passed to fight organized crime.

In August 1972, after the death of Sen. Allen J. Ellender (D, La.) [*q.v.*], chairman of the Appropriations Committee, McClellan gave up his Government Operations chairmanship to become head of the Appropriations panel. [See NIXON Volume]

[MLL]

McCLOY, JOHN J(AY)

b. March 31, 1895; Philadelphia, Pa.
Presidential adviser.

John J. McCloy, one of the architects of American foreign policy in the 1940s, was an adviser to Presidents Kennedy and Johnson during the 1960s. Following his graduation from Harvard Law School in 1921, McCloy worked in several New York law firms where he specialized in international corporate law. During World War II he served as a high-ranking member of the War Department. McCloy resumed private law practice in 1946 but became head of the World Bank a year later. In 1949 he was appointed military governor and high commissioner for Germany. He left that country in 1952 and for the next nine years served as chairman of the Chase Manhattan Bank. In 1962 he returned to private law practice, where he handled international legal problems for some of America's largest oil companies. From 1953 to 1965 he was also chairman of the Ford Foundation. [See TRUMAN, EISENHOWER Volumes]

During the opening months of the Kennedy Administration, McCloy served as the President's principal disarmament adviser. Throughout the summer of 1961 he successfully negotiated terms for the resumption of East-West disarmament talks. McCloy also helped draft the legislation that led to the establishment of the U.S. Arms Control and Disarmament Agency in the fall of 1961. Following the October 1962 discovery of Russian offensive missiles in Cuba, McCloy took part in negotiations at the U.N. on the ground rules involving U.S. inspection of Soviet removal of weapons from the island.

In late 1963 Lyndon Johnson appointed McCloy to the Warren Commission, formed to probe the death of John F. Kennedy. The Commission report, issued in September 1964, concluded that Lee Harvey Oswald had acted alone in assassinating President Kennedy. During the Johnson Administration McCloy also served on government panels investigating ways of forestalling the spread of nuclear weapons and ensuring world peace.

In April 1966 McCloy was appointed a special presidential consultant on the crisis precipitated by French President Charles de Gaulle's decision to withdraw his nation's troops from the North Atlantic Treaty Organization (NATO). NATO unity was threatened again that summer when Germany announced its desire to renegotiate financial arrangements made to offset U.S. balance of payments deficit caused by the presence of American troops in Germany. Under existing agreements Bonn had purchased U.S. military goods to compensate for the drain. But Germany, facing serious budget problems because of the rising cost of its welfare programs, suggested that its other payments and services be considered as part of the compensation. The situation was inflamed still further by the British desire to withdraw some of its troops from Germany to stem its own currency drain and by a Senate resolution stating that the U.S. should take similar action.

To prevent a weakening of the alliance, Johnson proposed multilateral negotiations between Britain, West Germany and the U.S. and asked McCloy to serve as American envoy to the October 1966 talks. Under the final plan announced in April 1967, the U.S. would redeploy its troops on a rotating basis with two of three brigades and four of nine fighter bomber squadrons returned to the U.S., where they would maintain a high degree of readiness. To help offset the dollar deficit, West Germany agreed to invest $500 million in medium-term U.S. government securities and promised to continue its policy of not converting dollars into gold.

become a member of the Senior Advisory Group on Vietnam, convened to consider the military's request that over 200,000 additional troops be sent to Vietnam. During the committee's meetings McCloy was among those men, along with Henry Cabot Lodge [*q.v.*], Arthur Dean and Gen. Omar Bradley, who were dissatisfied with the existing policy but were reluctant to declare for a dramatic change. Nevertheless, the majority of the group recommended rejection of the troop buildup request and the de-escalation of the war. Johnson announced this policy on March 31, 1968.

In 1974 a Senate investigation of the petroleum industry revealed that since 1961 McCloy had been in the forefront of attempts to unite U.S. oil companies in their negotiations with the producing nations. He had also used his influence to obtain Justice Department approval for multi-company bargaining in 1971. McCloy's efforts proved fruitless because the Shah of Iran insisted that the oil companies conclude separate price arrangements with the producing states.

[EWS]

McCONE, JOHN A(LEX)

b. Jan. 4, 1902; San Francisco, Calif.
Director of Central Intelligence, November 1961-April 1965.

John McCone was born into a prosperous San Francisco family. He graduated from the University of California in 1922 and over the next 25 years amassed a fortune in the steel and shipbuilding industries. During the Truman Administration McCone held several high posts in the Defense Department, where he helped James Forrestal in the creation of the Central Intelligence Agency (CIA). From 1958 to 1961 he served as chairman of the Atomic Energy Commission. [See TRUMAN, EISENHOWER Volumes]

In an attempt to appease conservative critics of the Agency's handling of the Bay of Pigs invasion, President Kennedy appointed McCone director of the CIA in September 1961. While at the Agency McCone focused his attention on improving the quality of intelligence work and developing new technological data collection systems. He also tried to coordinate the activities of the various intelligence services under the leadership of the Director of Central Intelligence. However, his attempts were blocked by the Defense Department, which under Robert McNamara [*q.v.*] had dominated the technological intelligence field. [See KENNEDY Volume]

Despite McCone's attempts to develop new intelligence-gathering techniques, the CIA's emphasis remained on covert activities. In 1962 the Agency began a secret war in Laos and instituted counter-terrorist programs in Vietnam. It committed $3 million to the 1964 Chilean election to prevent Communist-backed Salvador Allende from winning the presidency. Throughout the decade, it also continued efforts to block the development of leftist governments in Italy and Greece. Until 1966 the CIA used private foundations to channel money to groups and projects the Agency thought helpful to its mission. According to a 1976 congressional report, at least 14% of all grants over $10,000 given by 164 American foundations (excluding the Ford, Rockefeller and Carnegie Foundations) were partially or completely funded by the CIA. Nearly one half of those in the field of international activities involved Agency funding.

Although McCone was director of the CIA, he may not have known about some of the Agency's most controversial activities. These included the illegal opening of foreign mail sent to U.S. citizens and several unsuccessful attempts to assassinate such foreign leaders as Cuban Premier Fidel Castro. In hearings before the Senate Select Committee on Intelligence in 1975, McCone testified that he had not authorized the efforts and had never even been informed of them. The Committee reported that McCone probably had not known about the mail openings. However, because the system of executive command in the Agency was purposely ambiguous (to permit "plausible denial"), McCone's role in the assassination plots remained undetermined by Committee investigators.

As Johnson's chief intelligence officer, McCone became increasingly involved in Vietnam policymaking. Although personally hawkish on the war, McCone was fair in presenting the views of more dovish experts in the Agency. McCone was reportedly one of the few high Administration officials willing to give Johnson unbiased, often pessimistic reports on the progress of the war.

During the debate on the possible introduction of combat forces in Vietnam in the spring of 1965, McCone cautioned against the move unless it was accompanied by an expansion of bombing in the North. He believed that the war could not be won in the South. The U.S. could achieve victory only by inflicting such serious injury on North Vietnam that it would be forced to negotiate. Therefore, McCone said, the number of bombing raids would have to be vastly increased and targets expanded to include airfields, power stations and military compounds. McCone's advice went unheeded. U.S. Marines began offensive operations in April. Although raids were increased during May and June, they did not reach the high levels advocated by the Director.

In April 1965 McCone resigned as director of the CIA because Johnson did not support his efforts to centralize intelligence operations. Four months later he headed an eight-member commission investigating the major riot in the Watts section of Los Angeles. The panel's report, submitted to California Gov. Edmund G. Brown (D) [*q.v.*] in December 1965, found many causes for the disturbances: long-term frustrations, "the angry exhortation of civil rights leaders" and the publicity given federal antipoverty programs that did not fulfill the expectations they raised. To prevent future riots and improve living conditions among blacks and Mexican-Americans, the committee recommended increasing educational and job-training programs and upgrading mass transit and health facilities in the slum area. It cautioned that only "a change in attitude" by both black and white communities would prevent racial violence in the future. The panel also discussed suitable tactics and strategies for dealing with racial disorders. Its report called for reliance on non-lethal deterrents and outlined rigorous procedures for riot training, which became a guide for police departments throughout the U.S.

[EWS]

For further information:

David Halberstam, *The Best and the Brightest* (New York, 1972).

U.S. Senate Select Committee on Intelligence Activities, *Alleged Assassination Plots Involving Foreign Leaders* (Washington, 1975).

———, *Foreign and Military Intelligence* (Washington, 1976).

———, *Intelligence Activities and the Rights of Americans* (Washington, 1976).

David Wise and Thomas B. Ross, *The Invisible Government* (New York, 1964).

McCORMACK, JOHN W(ILLIAM)

b. Dec. 21, 1891; Boston, Mass.
Democratic Representative, Mass., 1928-71; Speaker of the House, 1962-71.

McCormack, who grew up in the poor, tightly-knit Irish community of South Boston, left school to go to work at age 13 after his father died. He read law and passed his bar exams when he was 21. In 1917 McCormack was elected a delegate to the Massachusetts Constitutional Convention. Three years later he entered the state legislature and served there for six years. In 1926 McCormack ran unsuccessfully for the U.S. House of Representatives, but two years later he won a special election to fill a House vacancy.

In Congress McCormack was a strong supporter of New Deal programs and worked closely with the House Democratic leadership as a member of the important Ways and Means Committee. When House Majority Leader Sam Rayburn (D, Tex.) became Speaker of the House in 1940, McCormack moved into Rayburn's former post.

As majority leader, McCormack gained a reputation as an unswervingly loyal deputy of Rayburn. He made many political friendships in the House by helping obtain committee assignments for colleagues and influencing the scheduling of their bills. McCormack also became known for his sharply partisan debating style. [See TRUMAN, EISENHOWER Volumes]

McCormack almost always backed the legislative positions of President John F. Kennedy. However, he was a devout Catholic with close ties to many of the Church's high clerics, and in 1961 he favored federal aid to parochial schools, a policy opposed by the President. In January 1962, after the death of Rayburn, McCormack drew upon the political debts he had accumulated as majority leader to win election to the speakership. At age 70, he was the first Catholic and the second-oldest man to be chosen for that post. [See KENNEDY Volume]

The Speaker of the House is in a position to exert great influence upon the flow of legislation. He has the right to refuse recognition to representatives and can also refuse to entertain motions from the floor. In January 1965 the Speaker's power was enhanced when the House adopted the 21-day rule, which enabled him to call to the floor bills that were being blocked by the Rules Committee (The rule was not renewed by the House in 1967.) The most important foundation of a Speaker's power, however, is the informal influence he exercises over his colleagues.

According to the *New York Times*, McCormack, despite the numerous ties he had established with his fellow representatives over many years, "never developed, either through disinclination or inability, the same sort of elaborate network of information and rewards that enabled Mr. Rayburn to keep the House a relatively tightly run political apparatus." Many of his associates, and particularly the younger liberals of the House, believed that he was not forceful enough to be an effective leader. Some thought McCormack too old to competently exercise the functions of his position.

McCormack's age, then 71, became the subject of considerable public discussion when the assassination of President Kennedy placed the Speaker first in line to succeed President Lyndon B. Johnson under the Presidential Succession Act of 1947. Some politicians and political observers felt that because of both age and ability McCormack was not competent to serve as the nation's chief executive, but the Speaker indignantly rejected suggestions that he resign his post. In 1964 the Senate proposed a constitutional amendment to provide for filling a vacancy in the office of vice president. The House did not act on the matter because, most observers believed, its members did not wish to offend McCormack. But the following year he indicated his support of the proposed 25th Amendment, and the House adopted it.

McCormack consistently backed President Johnson's domestic programs. As a militant anti-Communist who believed the President should have a free hand in conducting foreign policy, he also supported the Administration's military involvement in Vietnam. Early in 1966, during House debate over a supplemental defense authorization for the war, he stated that in supporting the authorization "I am also voting again for the [Tonkin Gulf] Resolution. . . . Thus, we will convey to the actual and potential enemy and also the rest of the world that America is united." As opposition to the war increased during the last years of the Johnson Administration, liberal Democrats became increasingly critical of McCormack's unwavering support of the President's Indochina policies.

In a matter relating to the war, McCormack defended what he believed was the constitutionally prescribed independence of the legislature from the judiciary. During August 1966 Federal District Judge Howard F. Corcoran ordered the House Un-

American Activities Committee (HUAC) to cease its investigation of persons aiding North Vietnam or the National Liberation Front. McCormack and other House leaders decided that HUAC's investigation should proceed. The Speaker commented, "The Constitution provides for three independent branches of government. If the judicial branch can enjoin the legislative branch, it could result in judicial control of the American government. . . ." The next day a three-judge federal court lifted Corcoran's order and a month later ruled that it lacked jurisdiction to determine the constitutionality of the Committee's hearings.

In the fall of 1969 Dr. Martin Sweig, a longtime aide of McCormack, and Nathan Voloshen, a friend of the Speaker's, were accused of employing their connection with McCormack to engage in influence-peddling. Sweig and Voloshen were indicted in January 1970. In May 1970, after U.S. attorneys cleared McCormack of any involvement in the matter, he announced that he would retire at the end of the year. [See NIXON Volume]

[MLL]

McCULLOCH, WILLIAM M.

b. Nov. 24, 1901; Holmes County, Ohio.
Republican Representative, Ohio, 1947-73.

After earning a law degree from Ohio Northern University, William M. McCulloch practiced law in Piqua, Ohio. In 1932 he won the first of six terms in the Ohio House of Representatives. A Republican, McCulloch served as state house minority leader (1936-38) and speaker (1939-44). In a special election in 1947, he was elected to the U.S. House of Representatives. The ranking Republican on the Judiciary Committee by 1959, McCulloch worked closely with Committee Chairman Rep. Emanuel Celler (D, N.Y.) [*q.v.*]. After negotiations among the Ohio Republican, President Kennedy and Justice Department officials, McCulloch gave crucial aid to the Administration in drafting a comprehensive civil rights statute in the fall of 1963. The Judiciary Committee approved a bill co-authored by McCulloch in October 1963. [See KENNEDY Volume]

With the full support of President Johnson, McCulloch, House Minority Leader Charles A. Halleck (R, Ind.) [*q.v.*] and liberal Republicans joined Administration Democrats in winning full House approval for the Committee's bill. Although he represented a rural, western Ohio district with a small (3%) black constituency, McCulloch championed the new civil rights legislation. "The belief in the inherent equality of man induces me to support this legislation," he declared in January 1964. Opponents of the measure failed to amend it, and on Feb. 10 it passed the House by a vote of 290 to 130. Of the GOP membership, over three-quarters supported the measure. The Senate modified certain provisions and passed the bill in June. The most far-reaching civil rights legislation since Reconstruction, it became law in July.

Except for civil rights, McCulloch was a traditionally conservative Republican. He wrote a mild civil rights plank for the 1964 Republican Platform Committee and supported the presidential candidacy of conservative Sen. Barry M. Goldwater (R, Ariz.) [*q.v.*], who had voted against the 1964 civil rights bill. On positions preferred by the liberal Americans for Democratic Action (ADA) during the Johnson years, McCulloch received generally low marks, ranging from 4% in 1964 to 13% in 1967. Local Democrats never mounted a serious challenge against McCulloch; in 1968 they declined even to field a candidate.

In July 1965 McCulloch offered a voting rights bill that, unlike the White House version, did not provide for federal voter registration machinery. Johnson's opposition to—and Southern Democratic support for—the McCulloch substitute killed any chance of enactment. After a 215-166 defeat McCulloch endorsed the Administration bill, and a majority of the GOP membership followed his example. McCulloch also accepted an "open housing" amendment to the 1966 civil rights bill offered by liberal Rep. Charles McC. Mathias, Jr. (R, Md.) [*q.v.*]. As a result of the Mathias provision, Minority Leader Gerald R. Ford (R, Mich.) [*q.v.*] came out against the bill and assured its defeat. Despite Ford's opposition, McCulloch continued to seek a ban on discrimination in real estate transactions. In April 1968 a group of moderate Republicans led by Reps. Charles E. Goodell (R, N.Y.) [*q.v.*] and Albert H. Quie (R, Minn.) [*q.v.*] rebelled against Ford's position and forced him to back a House bill, approved by McCulloch, that provided for an open-housing regulation. In recognition of McCulloch's civil rights record, Johnson appointed the Ohio Republican to two presidential commissions: one on civil disorders, chaired by Gov. Otto Kerner [*q.v.*], and one on the causes and prevention of violence, chaired by Milton S. Eisenhower [*q.v.*].

McCulloch kept a wary eye on the Nixon Administration's enforcement of civil rights legislation and criticized the Republican President's proposed revision of the 1965 Voting Rights Act. He retired from the House in 1973.

[JLB]

McDONALD, DAVID J(OHN)

b. Nov. 22, 1902; Pittsburgh, Pa.
President, United Steelworkers of America, 1952-65.

The son of an Irish Catholic steelworker, McDonald became the personal secretary to Philip Murray, then a United Mine Workers vice president, in 1922. McDonald worked closely with Murray during the bitter coal strikes of the 1920s and the organizing drive in steel in the late 1930s. When Murray died in December 1952, McDonald moved from secretary-treasurer to president of the United Steelworkers of America (USW). Although McDonald emphasized a cooperative relationship with steel industry management, he led his union on strike for 116 days in 1959 after industry officials sought to eliminate important union work rules in the plants. McDonald strongly supported John F. Kennedy in the 1960 election and later cooperated closely with his Administration's economic policy. During the 1962 and 1963 industry-wide negotiations, McDonald agreed to keep union wage demands within the 3.2% "guidelines" Kennedy Administration economists recommended.

Growing internal opposition plagued McDonald's tenure as USW president. His candidate for union vice president was unsuccessfully opposed by a coalition of district directors in 1955. The next year a two-dollar-a-month increase in dues sparked a rank-and-file "Dues Protest Movement" whose candidate for union president against McDonald garnered 35% of the union-wide vote in 1957. McDonald failed to win another increase in dues at the USW's September 1962 international convention. [See EISENHOWER, KENNEDY Volumes]

In the fall of 1964 a new and more serious challenge to McDonald's leadership emerged when I. W. Abel, [*q.v.*], the longtime USW secretary-treasurer, announced his candidacy for the union presidency. McDonald was vulnerable to attack on several counts. By late 1964 the USW had not won an across-the-board wage increase in over three years. Moreover, a section of the union's top leadership objected to McDonald's use of a labor-management "Human Relations Committee" to negotiate secretly with steel industry management. McDonald, charged Abel, had grown distant from the rank and file while developing close social ties with important government and business figures. The insurgent candidate accused McDonald, who occasionally frequented New York and Hollywood night spots, of "tuxedo trade unionism." In contrast, Abel promised "hard-nosed, arm-length bargaining" with the steel industry.

When Abel formally opened his campaign in December, careful advance preparations had neutralized many of the natural advantages McDonald might have held as incumbent president. Abel's slate, which included the highly respected district directors Walter J. Burke and Joseph Molony, secured several hundred more local union nominations than their opponents. Abel also held the allegiance of about half the USW district directors, including Joseph Germano, powerful head of the Chicago area's District 31, the largest in the union.

In his autobiography *Union Man*, published in 1969, McDonald reported that he was "totally incredulous" that Abel, after 12 years of loyal service as secretary-treasurer, would challenge him for the top union office. the Union President first belittled the Abel candidacy, but after opinion polls showed his opponent gaining, McDonald emphasized that a vote fror the Abel-Burke-Molony slate was a vote for a strike when the current contract expired in April 1965. Abel countered that he did not propose a work stoppage, but simply wished to "restore rank-and-file control over basic policy." (The USW contract was extended for four months on March 31, and in July a new wage settlement was reached without a work stoppage.)

Despite McDonald's expenditure of about $500,000 on a well-publicized campaign, Abel held an 8,000-vote lead out of some 606,000 total votes cast when the ballots were counted following the Feb. 9 election. Abel supporters swept all union-wide offices and took firm control of the United Steel Workers executive board. Voting irregularities probably occured on both sides in the election, and McDonald first considered appealing for a recount or another vote to the Department of Labor or the courts. After his lawyers persuaded him that the attempt would be time-consuming and probably futile, McDonald vacated the union presidency on June 1, 1965. With his wife Rosemary, he retired to Palm Springs, Calif.

Abel's victory in the 1965 steelworkers election was the most important defeat for an incumbent union president since the early postwar period. It climaxed a series of elections in unions such as the American Federation of State County and Municipal Employees, the International Union of Electrical Workers and the American Federation of Teachers in which incumbents were voted out of office.

[NNL]

For further information:

John Herling, *Right to Challenge: People and Power in the Steelworkers Union* (New York, 1972).

David J. McDonald, *Union Man* (New York: 1969).

MACDONALD, DWIGHT

b. March 24, 1906; New York, N.Y.
Author and critic.

Macdonald graduated from Yale in 1928, worked as a staff writer for *Fortune* over the next seven years and then became associate editor of *Partisan Review*, a journal that then combined radical politics with an avant garde approach to the arts. In the late 1930s and 1940s Macdonald was successively a Trotskyist, anarchist and pacifist. Always a prolific and witty essayist, he published his own "little magazine," *Politics*, from 1944 to 1949.

In the early 1950s Macdonald shifted his attention from politics to social-cultural reporting, chiefly in the pages of the *New Yorker*, for which he became a staff writer in 1951. Macdonald was a caustic critic of what he considered the suffocating spread of "mass culture" in American life. Many of his critical essays on culture and society were collected in *Against the American Grain*, published in 1962.

Macdonald's long review-essay of Michael Harrington's [*q.v.*] *The Other America* in the *New Yorker* helped establish Harrington's expose of poverty amid affluence as one of the most influential books of the decade.

Spurred by the growth of the civil rights and anti-war movements, Macdonald returned to political activism in the 1960s. He attended President Johnson's White House Festival of the Arts in June 1965 and circulated an anti-war petition among the guests there. Six months later Macdonald and other intellectuals protested the Soviet imprisonment of writers Andrei D. Sinyavsky and Yuli M. Daniel for their publication of allegedly anti-Soviet works abroad.

Macdonald defended the tactic of civil disobedience used by the anti-war and student movements. In October 1967 he participated in the March on the Pentagon, where he unsuccessfully courted arrest. Observing the scene at Columbia University the next spring, when a group of student radicals marched on Low Library, Macdonald likened the action to the start of the Russian Revolution. Applauding the sense of camaraderie evinced by the student takeover of University buildings, he concluded, "I've never been in or near a revolution. I guess I like them."

In the fall of 1968 Macdonald took part in a bitter exchange of letters with social critic Michael Harrington, whom he had once praised so highly, over the New York City teachers' strike. Writing in the *New York Review of Books*, he opposed the United Federation of Teachers (UFT) strike as one against community control and accused Harrington of misrepresenting the UFT's strike demands. Macdonald later called UFT President Albert Shanker [*q.v.*] a "racist demagogue."

Describing himself as a "conservative anarchist" and described in turn by novelist Norman Mailer [*q.v.*] as "America's oldest living anti-Stalinist," Macdonald remained at the end of the 1960s one of the most prominent critics of contemporary society.

[FHM]

McGEE, GALE W(ILLIAM)

b. March 17, 1915; Lincoln, Neb.
Democratic Senator, Wyo., 1959-77.

Gale W. McGee grew up in Nebraska and graduated from Nebraska State Teachers College in 1936. He earned an M.A. from the University of Colorado three years later and a Ph.D. from the University of Chicago in 1947, writing his dissertation in American diplomatic history. McGee accepted a professorship at the University of Wyoming in 1946, and he studied Soviet foreign policy for the Council on Foreign Relations in 1952 and 1953. Endorsed by Eleanor Roosevelt, McGee made his first campaign for public office in Wyoming's 1958 Senate race. He unseated a conservative Republican incumbent with 50.8% of the vote. During the Kennedy years, McGee supported Administration programs while taking few legislative initiatives on his own. [See KENNEDY Volume]

McGee won reelection in his normally Republican state in 1964 and proved equally loyal to the Johnson Administration. He supported the 1964, 1965 and 1968 civil rights acts, medicare and the repeal of Section 14(b) of the Taft-Hartley Act. A strong proponent of non-military foreign assistance programs, McGee criticized congressional cutbacks in foreign aid in October 1968 as "a discouraging retreat from our responsibility" to aid nations "struggling to break free from the endless cycle of poverty and despair."

McGee gave consistent and vocal endorsement to American intervention in Vietnam. In a February 1966 debate over American participation in the war, McGee asked his colleagues to "look at the prize at stake" in Southeast Asia. "Three-hundred million people or more. Most of the rice in the world. Oil, tin bauxite and rubber. These would be sparkling diamonds in the resources of great powers."

In January 1968 McGee challenged a proposal by Sen. Robert F. Kennedy (D, N.Y.) [*q.v.*] that the U.S. halt the bombing of North Vietnam as an indication of American willingness to negotiate. Appearing on a television news program with Kennedy on Jan. 21, McGee branded the New York Senator's suggestion "totally irresponsible." The real issue in Vietnam, McGee declared two days later, was "stability in all Eastern Asia." As a member of the platform committee at the Democratic National Convention in August, he defended the majority plank on Vietnam, which endorsed the President on the war. The Party's anti-war faction, McGee told the delegates, must "not hobble [the next President] with restraints and particulars" that would "complicate the task of negotiators."

As a partial consequence of his stand on the war, McGee's Senate voting rating by the liberal Americans for Democratic Action fell from 90% in 1966 to 57% in 1968. Organized labor, however, continued to give the Wyoming Democrat high marks, with the AFL-CIO ranking him 90% "correct" on its key votes in 1968. Early in January 1969, antiwar Sen. Eugene J. McCarthy (D, Minn.) [*q.v.*] stepped down from his place on the Senate Foreign Relations Committee, and McGee, next in seniority, assumed McCarthy's position. At the same time, McGee became chairman of the Senate Post Office and Civil Service Committee. [See NIXON Volume]

[JLB]

McGOVERN, GEORGE S(TANLEY)
b. July 19, 1922; Avon, S.D.
Democratic Senator, S.D., 1963- .

The son of a Methodist minister, George McGovern grew up in Mitchell, S.D. He excelled at debating in high school and at Dakota Wesleyan University. After service as a bomber pilot during World War II, McGovern trained for the ministry but abandoned it to undertake graduate work in history at Northwestern University, where he began a sympathetic study of the 1913-14 Colorado Coal Strike. Northwestern awarded him his Ph.D. in 1953. He supported the third party candidacy of Henry Wallace in 1948.

From 1943 to 1953 McGovern taught history and political science at Dakota Wesleyan, leaving to become executive secretary of the state Democratic Party. He was the only full-time organizer for the feeble organization; South Dakota Democrats then held only two out of 110 seats in the state legislature. Crisscrossing the state alone in an automobile, McGovern laboriously reconstructed the Party apparatus. In the 1954 elections Democrats increased their representation in the legislature to 25 seats. Alongside the Party organization, McGovern built a personal following as well. He ran for Congress in 1956 on a liberal platform, attacking the umpopular farm policies of Republican Secretary of Agriculture Ezra Taft Benson and won an upset victory over the Republican incumbent. Reelected in 1958 McGovern ran for the Senate in 1960 against the conservative Sen. Karl E. Mundt (R, S.D.) [*q.v.*] but lost to the incumbent in a sharp ideological confrontation. Appointed by President Kennedy as director of the Food for Peace program, McGovern ran for the Senate again in 1962 and won by an extremely narrow margin. [See KENNEDY Volume]

McGovern was assigned to the Senate Agriculture and Forestry Committee and the Interior and Insular Affairs Committee. Representing an agricultural state whose chief products were wheat and beef cattle, McGovern fought for higher wheat price supports and restrictions on imported beef. He was the floor manager of the wheat title of the 1964 farm bill, which raised supports and made acreage allotment voluntary instead of mandatory as it had been in 1963. McGovern's espousal of higher wheat prices frequently brought him into conflict with Secretary of Agriculture Orville Freeman [*q.v.*], a antagonist during his Food for Peace tenure. McGovern also supported higher appropriations for Food for Peace during the Johnson Administration and argued that its utility in disposing of agricultural surpluses should not supersede its humanitarian functions. He called for the removal of restrictions on the program that prevented the U.S. from selling or giving food to Communist nations.

Unlike fellow South Dakotan Karl Mundt, McGovern was a strong supporter of the social welfare legislation of the Johnson Administration. He consistently voted for the civil rights enactments of the period and said in June 1964: "What is usually referred to as 'the race problem' is, in fact, . . . the white problem . . . white racism." He displeased organized labor, however, in October 1965 with his vote to maintain the controversial "right to work" section 14(b) of the Taft-Hartley Act. The strength of the pro-business National Right to Work Committee in South Dakota influenced his stand. He later admitted, "It was a straight political decision." Although the balance of his voting record was pro-labor, the AFL-CIO often cited this vote as an explanation for their coolness towards McGovern's subsequent presidential candidacies.

McGovern's maiden Senate speech in March 1963 was a critique of U.S. Latin American policy, and he continued throughout the decade to denounce what he considered the militaristic bent of U.S. foreign policy and the burgeoning defense budget. He regularly voted to reduce defense appropriations and opposed much of the Pentagon's expensive new weaponry, including the Air Force's advanced manned bomber and the anti-ballistic missile system. He also sought to reduce military assistance to foreign countries.

McGovern was most conspicuous as an early, outspoken foe of the Vietnam war. He first criticized U.S. involvement in September 1963, although he did vote for the Gulf of Tonkin resolution the following August. (The next day he inserted some second thoughts in the *Congressional Record*: "I do not want my vote for the resolution to be interpreted as an endorsement for our long-standing and apparently growing military involvement in Vietnam.") In January 1965 he called the war "a South Vietnamese problem . . . not basically a military problem but a political one." He proposed a negotiated solution, leading to gradual withdrawal of U.S. troops and the neutralization of Vietnam protected by a U.N. presence. He visited Vietnam in November 1965 and returned to call for a bombing halt and recognition of the National Liberation Front. In April 1967 he castigated U.S. policymakers for "distorting history to justify our intervention" and "backing a dictatorial group in Saigon against a competing group backed by a dictatorial group in the North." McGovern's attacks escalated during the Nixon Administration, culminating in the unsuccessful McGovern-Hatfield amendments of 1970-71 designed to cut off all funding for the Vietnam war.

In the fall of 1967 the liberal anti-war activist Allard K. Lowenstein [*q.v.*] tried to persuade McGovern to run in the presidential primaries against Lyndon Johnson. McGovern, who faced what he thought would be a difficult reelection contest in 1968, turned Lowenstein down, and suggested that he approach either Lee Metcalf (D, Mont.) [*q.v.*] or Eugene McCarthy (D, Minn.) [*q.v.*], two Senate "doves" who did not face election challenges the next year. To McGovern's surprise McCarthy accepted Lowenstein's offer to become the candidate of the "Dump Johnson Movement." Publicly, McGovern remained neutral during the early presidential primaries of 1968 but clearly favored Sen. Robert F. Kennedy (D, N.Y.) [*q.v.*] after the New York Senator announced his candidacy in March.

Following Kennedy's assassination in June, a number of former Kennedy supporters and staff workers urged McGovern to run for the nomination. On Aug. 10 he announced his candidacy, saying that he hoped to "serve as a rallying point for his [Kennedy's] supporters . . . ." In a 16-day campaign McGovern denounced the Vietnam war, advocated a "systematic reduction of our overgrown military-industrial complex" and the diversion of the resulting resources to the reconstruction of the cities and rural America. McGovern also criticized "empty-headed cries for law and order" for their "undertone of racism." In a climactic three-way televised appearance with McCarthy and Vice President Hubert Humphrey [*q.v.*] before the 174-member California delegation on Aug. 26, McGovern delivered a strong attack on American policy in Vietnam which many observers thought "won" the debate for his anti-war candidacy. Nevertheless, Mc Govern finished a distant third in the convention balloting with 146 votes, behind Humphrey with 1,761 and McCarthy with 601. McGovern then endorsed Humphrey and campaigned for him against Richard Nixon [*q.v.*]. In the 1972 campaign McGovern made an early start and, by slowly winning support on a platform advocating immediate withdrawal from Vietnam and sweeping tax reform, won the nomination after an unexpectedly strong performance in the primaries. He was defeated by a large margin in November. [See NIXON Volume]

[TO]

For further information:
Robert Sam Ansen, *McGovern: A Biography* (New York, 1972).

McINTIRE, CARL

b. May 17, 1906; Ypsilanti, Mich.
Anti-Communist preacher.

The son of a Presbyterian minister, Carl McIntire attended Princeton Theological Seminary where he studied under J. Gresham Machen, a strict fundamentalist. As pastor of the Presbyterian Church in Collingswood, N.J., McIntire took Machen's side when the denomination was split by modernist-fundamentalist quarrels in the 1930s. The Presbytery of New Jersey defrocked McIntire in 1935 for ecclesiastical disobedience and replaced him with a new pastor, but most of the congregation followed McIntire into his new Bible Presbyterian Church in 1936.

From this base McIntire waged a vociferous crusade in the ensuing decades against the leaders of the major Protestant denominations, whom he accused of having Communist tendencies. His chief organizational targets were the National Council of Churches and the World Council of Churches. Denouncing these bodies for their liberalism and their "apostasy," McIntire set up the American Council of Churches in 1941 and the International Council of Churches in 1948 to promote his brand of theological conservatism. He also established a college, seminary and resort hotel in New Jersey to perpetuate his fundamentalist movement.

In the 1960s McIntire expressed his views through a weekly newspaper, *The Christian Beacon,* and *The 20th Century Reformation Hour*, a radio show broadcast daily over some 600 stations. His polemics by then encompassed a broad range of political and religious institutions. He criticized civil rights demonstrations, Social Security, fair-employment legislation, the United Nations and the YMCA (for sponsoring teenage dances). He backed a constitutional amendment to permit prayer and Bible-reading in public schools and continued his defense of a literal interpretation of the Bible and his campaign against "modernism, liberalism and Roman Catholicism." He supported Israel in her 1967 war with the Arab states and was an enthusiastic advocate of escalation of the Vietnam war.

Beginning in 1964, 19 religious and civic groups petitioned the Federal Communications Commission (FCC) to deny license renewal for McIntire's radio station WXUR on the grounds that the station was a forum for anti-Catholic, anti-Semitic and anti-black propaganda. The American Civil Liberties Union defended McIntire in the suit. In July 1970 the FCC voted 6-0 to revoke the license, saying that the station management had no regular procedure for reviewing its presentations on controversial issues. [See NIXON Volume]

[TO]

McINTYRE, THOMAS J(AMES)

b. Feb. 20, 1915; Laconia, N.H.
Democratic Senator, N.H., 1963-

McIntyre, a small-town New Hampshire lawyer active in Democratic politics, won a special November 1962 election held to fill the seat of the late Sen. Styles Bridges (R) [*q.v.*]. He thereby became the first New Hampshire Democrat to be sent to the Senate since 1932. During his freshman year McIntyre generally supported the Kennedy Administration's foreign and domestic policies. [See KENNEDY Volume]

McIntyre also supported key Johnson Administration legislation, including the civil rights, antipoverty, medicare and school-aid bills. He devoted substantial time to advancing New Hampshire interests in the Senate. As a member of the House Armed Services Committee, McIntyre opposed government efforts to close the naval base at Portsmouth. He also called for higher tariffs on textiles and shoes to protect New Hampshire industries that were hard-hit by foreign competition. At the same time he campaigned for liberalized oil import quotas to permit New Englanders to purchase fuel oil at lower prices.

As a member of the Senate Banking Committee, McIntyre sponsored the Administration's truth-in-lending bill, which required banks to specify their interest rates on loans. Although most lending institutions opposed the bill, it passed both houses and became law in May 1968. McIntyre also worked to reduce fees charged by mutual funds and to allow commercial banks to sell mutual fund shares.

McIntyre ran for reelection in 1966 and faced a difficult test in predominently Republican New Hampshire. He was opposed by retired Air Force Gen. Harrison Thyng, who had the support of William Loeb [*q.v.*], the arch-conservative publisher of the only major newspaper in the state. Thyng charged that the Johnson Administration had failed to mount the aggressive military campaign he thought necessary to win the war in Vietnam. McIntyre defended the Johnson policy of gradual escalation and publicly challenged Thyng and Loeb to a debate. They declined, and his challenge, unusual for an incumbent, coupled with the fact that Republicans were badly divided, enabled McIntyre to win the election with 54% of the vote.

In February and March 1968 McIntyre was once again called upon to defend Johnson Administration war policies, this time under attack from Sen. Eugene J. McCarthy, (D, Minn.) [*q.v.*], the peace candidate who had entered the New Hampshire presidential primary. McIntyre and New Hampshire Gov. John King [*q.v.*] first ignored McCarthy's challenge to the President, but as McCarthy developed a powerful organization, they sharpened their criticism, charging that a vote for McCarthy was a vote for "weakness and indecision." On March 12, Johnson barely outpolled McCarthy, and the Minnesota Senator was widely credited with a stunning upset. On March 31 Johnson announced that he would not seek reelection.

During the Nixon years McIntyre abandoned his support of the war and advocated legislation establishing a specific date for withdrawal of American troops from Vietnam. [See NIXON Volume]

[JLW]

McKEITHEN, JOHN J(ULIAN)

b. May 28, 1918; Grayson, La.
Governor, La., 1964-72.

A lawyer, farmer and protege of the powerful Long political machine in Louisiana, McKeithen served in the state House of Representatives as Gov. Earl Long's floor leader from 1948 to 1952. In 1954 McKeithen was named to the Louisiana Public Service Commission, where he remained until 1962. In January 1964 McKeithen defeated the former mayor of New Orleans and ambassador to the Organization of American States, deLesseps S. Morrison, in a Democratic gubernatorial primary run-off. In that campaign McKeithen alleged that Morrison had made a deal with the NAACP for votes. This charge cost McKeithen the support of moderate and liberal Democrats, white and black, in the general election. The Republicans nominated Charleton H. Lyons, a Shreveport oilman and Goldwater supporter. McKeithen won the election, but his margin of victory was the smallest received by a Louisiana Democratic gubernatorial candidate in the twentieth century.

McKeithen's first objective in office was to establish a good government image in order to enhance the state's attractiveness to industry. This effort was impeded by 1967 *Life* magazine allegations that the McKeithen Administration had closed its eyes to widespread Mafia influence in Louisiana. As a further inducement to industry, the state passed a series of "right-to-profit" laws, which extended tax credits to industrial users of natural gas and provided other business incentives. Partly owing to these measures, Louisiana's industrial growth more than doubled during McKeithen's tenure.

Although his campaign had been geared towards strongly pro-segregationist voters, McKeithen was a moderate on racial matters. He made the first significant appointment of blacks to government positions in the South, including the selection of two blacks as judges. In April 1965 the Congress of Racial Equality (CORE) centered an intensive civil rights campaign on Bogalusa, La. In July McKeithen proposed a 30-day moratorium on demonstrations following months of severe racial tension and violence. His proposal, which earned him attention as a peacemaker, was rejected by Negro leaders. McKeithen termed that rejection a "tragic mistake." During the rest of his term the Governor took no further significant actions on civil rights.

In 1966 McKeithen won adoption of a state constitutional amendment permitting a governor to succeed himself. During his second term McKeithen confronted the problem of busing to achieve the racial balance mandated by the 1964 Civil Rights Act. While specifically rejecting violence as a recourse to court directives, he wrote in August 1971 that he anticipated "using police power or whatever other power I have" to stop busing. In November 1972 State Senator J. Bennett Johnson, Jr., defeated McKeithen in his bid to fill the seat of the late U.S. Sen. Allen Ellender.

[TJC]

McKELDIN, THEODORE R(OOSEVELT)

b. Nov. 20, 1900; South Baltimore, Md.
d. Aug. 10, 1974; Baltimore, Md.
Mayor, Baltimore, 1964-68.

McKeldin, the son of Scotch-Irish and German immigrants, worked at various jobs while attending the University of Maryland Law School at night. Soon after obtaining his degree in 1925 he entered politics, working for the election of William F. Broening to the Baltimore mayoralty. When Broening won in 1927, McKeldin was made his executive secretary.

McKeldin waged an unsuccessful campaign for mayor of Baltimore in 1939 and three years later for governor of Maryland. In 1943, having gained a solid black and Jewish political base as well as the support of many other Democratic voters, he was elected mayor of Baltimore. An outspoken critic of racial discrimination, McKeldin appointed Baltimore's first Negro member of the school board and placed blacks on his staff and in the city solicitor's office. He resumed a private law practice after losing his bid for governor in 1946 but returned to public life to win the gubernatorial election in 1950. He served in that position until 1959. A vigorous campaigner and orator, McKeldin nominated Dwight D. Eisenhower [*q.v.*] for president at the 1952 Republican National Convention. [See Truman, Eisenhower Volume]

McKeldin was elected to his second term as mayor of Baltimore in 1964. Two years later the city was the scene of racial clashes after the Congress of Racial Equality (CORE) announced that Baltimore would be a target city for the integration of housing and public accommodations. According to CORE representatives who met with the Mayor in May, McKeldin stated that CORE "was doing a good job" for racial progress in Baltimore and "was delighted to have them help." At the CORE national convention held in Baltimore in July 1966, McKeldin welcomed the delegates, saying that he supported them "if they can point up the facts of segregation—which I think is good for the city." Because of McKeldin's stand he was attacked as a "super-pompous, jackassie nigger-lover" at a National States Rights Party rally in Baltimore. Incited by the rally, white teenage gangs invaded the black district in East Baltimore. A full-scale riot was avoided by the arrest of the white supremacist leaders and the personal intervention of the Mayor.

McKeldin was chosen as one of the observers of the 1967 South Vietnamese election and returned declaring that the balloting had been fair. In the years that followed, however, he opposed continued involvement in Southeast Asia and demanded that the U.S. stop bombing North Vietnam and rapidly withdraw from the South. In 1968 McKeldin testified in support of the abolition of the death penalty at congressional hearings. The former Maryland executive said he was "ashamed" that during his term in office he had allowed four men to be hanged because "I yielded to public clamor and did not have the character to do what I should have done."

McKeldin retired in 1968 and died in 1974.

[EWS]

McKISSICK, FLOYD B(IXLER)

b. March 9, 1922; Asheville, N.C.
National Director, Congress of Racial Equality, 1966-67.

The son of a hotel employe, McKissick grew up in Asheville. After military service during World War II, he attended North Carolina College and studied law at the University of North Carolina; in 1952 he became the first black in the school's history to receive an LL.B. McKissick opened a law practice in Durham, N.C., and soon became senior partner in the firm McKissick and Burt.

An ambitious lawyer, McKissick resented racial discrimination in the North Carolina bar. During the 1950s he served as youth chairman of the North Carolina NAACP, and in 1960 he became legal counsel for the Congress of Racial Equality (CORE), a more militant civil rights organization. Much of McKissick's work during the early 1960s consisted of defending CORE demonstrators arrested while protesting segregation at public facilities in Southern cities. McKissick also helped expand the network of CORE chapters in North Carolina. In 1962 he left the NAACP, which had fallen into a dispute with the North Carolina CORE over the planning and leadership of desegregation marches.

Beginning in 1963 McKissick's role in CORE was determined by the growing militance developing in the civil rights movement. Black activists were proud of their earlier struggles, but many were also impatient with the pace of civil rights progress and disappointed by the continued economic misery of American blacks. This unrest gave rise to a desire for greater black self-reliance and independence from white liberal supporters of civil rights. CORE responded to this sentiment by choosing McKissick, known as "a down-home black lawyer," to be national chairman in June 1963; the unpaid position had earlier been held by whites.

McKissick himself was affected by the new currents in the civil rights movement and increasingly stressed the importance of black self-help and control over decision-making in CORE. Speaking at the 1963 CORE convention, he claimed that civil rights litigation had gone as far as possible in the courts, leaving direct action as the only avenue of black advancement. In 1965 McKissick attempted to shift the organization's funding base from middle-class whites to blacks. He also invited Black Muslims to speak for the first time at a CORE national convention in January 1966, dramatizing his commitment to separate black cultural development. The same convention elected McKissick CORE's national director after James Farmer [*q.v.*] announced his departure from the organization. At this time CORE had a national membership of 180,000 in 200 local chapters.

Under McKissick's leadership CORE remained on the militant side of the civil rights spectrum. McKissick followed civil rights leader Stokely Carmichael [*q.v.*] in adopting the rhetoric of black power, calling blacks "a nation within a nation." The greatest support for black separatism came from CORE chapters in Northern cities, and McKissick shifted the organization toward a stronger focus on urban poverty problems. He tried repeatedly to attract federal and foundation money for voter education, job training and aid to black businesses in the ghetto. In a symbolic action McKissick moved CORE's national headquarters to Harlem in August 1966. He also became one of the strongest critics among black leaders of the Vietnam war, denouncing "black men going over . . . and dying for something they don't have a right for here."

Despite McKissick's policies, many CORE members were not satisfied with his leadership. Much of the tension within the organization resulted from its growing financial difficulties. The rise of black power sentiment had alienated many white financial supporters, and McKissick could not find adequate replacement funding in the black community. To avoid bankruptcy he was forced in January 1967 to curtail a number of CORE projects. This caused resentment in local chapters whose projects were affected and increased competition for remaining funds. According to historians August Meier and Elliot Rudwick, militant CORE staffers also viewed McKissick as a follower rather than a leader of black power, and there were complaints that his Southern background prevented him from relating to blacks in the Northern ghettos. In September 1967 McKissick took a leave of absence from CORE. He resigned as national director in 1968 to be replaced by Roy Innis [*q.v.*], former head of CORE's Harlem chapter.

After leaving CORE McKissick established his own consulting firm, which dealt with poverty problems. He also planned and collected funds for a community in North Carolina called Soul City, intended to provide economic opportunities for rural blacks. McKissick supported the reelection of Richard Nixon [*q.v.*] in 1972, claiming that blacks should gain influence in the Republican Party and reform it.

[SLG]

For further information:
August Meier and Elliot Rudwick, *CORE: A Study in the Civil Rights Movement, 1942-1968* (New York, 1973).

McMILLAN, JOHN L(ANNEAU)
b. April 12, 1898; Mullins, S.C.
Democratic Representative, S.C., 1939-72; Chairman, District of Columbia Committee, 1948-72.

After a childhood spent on a farm in South Carolina's tobacco region, John McMillan served in the Navy during World War I. He graduated from the University of North Carolina and then the University of South Carolina Law School in 1923.

Elected as a Democrat to Congress from South Carolina's sixth district in 1938, McMillan assumed the chairmanship of the House District of Columbia Committee in 1948. He also served as vice chairman of the House Agriculture Committee, where he oversaw South Carolina's tobacco interests.

As chairman of the District Committee, which was controlled by conservative Southern Democrats, McMillan successfully blocked home-rule legislation through three presidential administrations. His opposition, which he said was based on constitutional principles, was often attributed by observers to a bias against black control of the city. (The District of Columbia ranked ninth in population among U.S. cities, with a 63% black majority.)

During the Kennedy Administration McMillan voted with the conservative coalition on over 75% of all major issues; in 1963 he voted with the conservatives on 100% of key issues. McMillan voted against medicare, the 1964 Civil Rights Act and the 1965 Voting Rights Act.

In 1965 President Johnson stated that "the restoration of home rule to the citizens of the District of Columbia must no longer be delayed." Over the next two years the House District Committee, in a series of highly intricate legislative maneuvers, managed repeatedly to block the Administration's home-rule bill. Debate on the issue lasted until 1967 when the President, circumventing the Committee, used the authority given him under a government reorganization act to change the city's form of government. Since 1874 Washington had been governed by Congress and a three-member board of commissioners selected by the president. Under the new plan the three commissioners were replaced by a single commissioner, a deputy commissioner and a nine-member city council. The President appointed a black, Walter E. Washington [*q.v.*], to the newly created post of commissioner in September 1967.

In 1970 columnist Jack Anderson [*q.v.*] wrote that McMillan "accepts favors from used-car dealers, parking-lot barons and liquor lobbyists," in return for "obstructing public parking, welfare payments, and home rule." His administration of the House District Committee was once described by journalist Neal Peirce as ranging from "dilatory to dictatorial."

In 1970 McMillan won a close primary reelection race. Two years later organized labor and black groups coalesced around a Democratic state legislator half McMillan's age, who defeated the 16-term Congressman. [See NIXON Volume]

[FHM]

McNAMARA, PATRICK V(INCENT)
b. Oct. 4, 1894; North Weymouth, Mass.
d. April 30, 1966; Washington, D.C.
Democratic Senator, Mich., 1955-66.

A pipe fitter by trade, McNamara served as president of Detroit Pipe Fitters Local 636 of the American Federation of Labor for 20 years. As a member of the Detroit Board of Education, the relatively unknown McNamara defeated the incumbent Republican, Homer Ferguson (R, Mich.), in 1954 on a platform calling for repeal of the Taft-Hartley Act and federal aid-to-education. Named to the special Senate committee investigating labor (the Senate Rackets Committee) in 1957, McNamara quit in April 1958 and accused the Committee of persecuting the labor movement. He criticized Senate Majority Leader Lyndon Johnson (D, Tex.) [*q.v.*] in January 1958 for holding too few Democratic caucuses.

McNamara became chairman of the Senate Public Works Committee in 1963. He was also ranking Democrat on the Labor and Welfare Committee and the Special Senate Committee on Aging. During the

Kennedy and Johnson years, he was a strong supporter of aid-to-education, wages-and-hours legislation and medical aid for the aged. He proved an important figure in the passage of much of the early Great Society legislation. In January 1964 he sponsored an Administration bill to extend minimum wage coverage and overtime provisions to 2.6 million additional workers. He was the floor manager in July for the Administration's omnibus antipoverty program, the Economic Opportunity Act of 1964. [See KENNEDY Volume]

McNamara sponsored the Older Americans Act of 1965, which created an Administration on Aging in the Department of Health, Education and Welfare. This bill was strongly backed by the AFL-CIO, as was McNamara's unsuccessful attempt in September 1965 to repeal Section 14(b) of the Taft-Hartley Act. The controversial section of the law allowed states to outlaw the "closed shop." A cloture motion to end the filibuster against repeal was defeated, 45-47, on October 11. *Congressional Quarterly* reported that McNamara's voting record was among the four highest in support of President Johnson's proposals in 1964 and 1965. He died of a stroke on April 30, 1966.

[TO]

McNAMARA, ROBERT S(TRANGE)

b. June 9, 1916; San Francisco, Calif.
Secretary of Defense, January 1961-February 1968.

McNamara graduated with honors from the University of California, Berkeley, in 1937 and the Harvard Business School in 1939. He worked briefly for a San Francisco accounting firm before returning to Harvard to accept a teaching post at the business school. In World War II he served with the Army Air Corps, where he helped develop the logistical system for mass bomber raids on Germany and Japan.

Following the war McNamara joined a group of talented young ex-Army officers, later dubbed "the whiz kids," who worked for the financially troubled Ford Motor Company. As a Ford general manager and later as a vice president, McNamara helped revive the Company with emphasis on strict cost-accounting methods. He supported the development of the Falcon, a compact economy automobile and the four-door version of the Thunderbird, a luxury car. Both were financial successes. In November 1960 McNamara was named the company president, the first man outside the Ford family to hold that position.

McNamara served in his new post only one month before President John F. Kennedy named him Secretary of Defense. During his first years in office he worked to modernize the armed forces and make the Pentagon more efficient by centralizing decision-making in his own office. He also restructured Pentagon budgetary procedures to ensure that each service would coordinate budget requests to avoid costly duplication. McNamara refused to approve the development of costly weapons systems of unproven or dubious value. During 1961 and 1962 he would not spend funds appropriated by Congress for the development of the RS-70, an experimental Air Force bomber that he considered obsolete in the missile age. McNamara also resisted pressure from the Navy to develop nuclear-powered surface ships, which he considered over-priced and of little strategic value.

When the Air Force and Navy each requested permission to develop a new aircraft, McNamara instructed them to cooperate in the construction of an aircraft adaptable for both services. In November 1962 McNamara and his aides awarded the contract for the fighter/bomber, the TFX (tactical fighter experimental), to the General Dynamics Corporation. Because military officials found the Boeing Corporation's design preferable, McNamara and his aides were called before a Senate Committee to justify their selection. The TFX hearings, lasting nine months, embarrassed McNamara because they revealed long-smoldering differences between civilians and the military in the Defense Department. McNamara's decision was upheld, but the TFX proved far more costly than Defense Department estimates and, because of various structural problems, did not perform up to expectations.

Although McNamara was a strong advocate of the 1963 nuclear test ban treaty and strategic arms limitations talks, his defense strategy called for a buildup of U.S. military power in two areas. He favored an accelerated program to replace vulnerable liquid-fuel intercontinental ballistic missiles (ICBMs) with solid-fuel missiles, which could be widely dispersed and fired from submarines and underground silos. These new weapons would give the U.S. a "second-strike" capability, i.e., the ability to absorb a nuclear attack while retaining the capacity to launch a devastating counterattack. Second-strike capability would reduce pressure on the U.S. to retaliate on the basis of ambiguous radar information that might erroneously indicate an enemy missile attack. McNamara also called for a stepped-up fallout shelter program to prevent loss of life following a nuclear attack.

The Secretary's second goal was to develop a large, highly mobile strike force to permit the U.S. to deal with guerrilla or conventional wars without nuclear weapons. The Eisenhower Administration's doctrine of "massive retaliation," he argued, had limited U.S. ability to react in crisis situations while increasing the probability of nuclear confrontation. In developing a "flexible response" capability, McNamara won approval for a 300,000-man increase in U.S. fighting strength and authorization for a vast buildup in troop airlift capacity. [See KENNEDY Volume]

From his earliest days as vice president, Lyndon B. Johnson thought McNamara the most talented member of the Kennedy cabinet. When he became President, Johnson was gratified that McNamara remained as Defense Secretary, particularly at a time when Vietnam was becoming a more troublesome problem. McNamara had first visited South Vietnam in 1962 and had declared upon his return that "every quantitative measurement shows that we are winning this war." At that time the U.S. had approximately 10,000 servicemen stationed in the area as advisers to the South Vietnamese Army. McNamara believed that the U.S. should commit itself to the defense of South Vietnam because a Communist victory there could lead to a Communist takeover of other Southeast Asian nations. He remained confident that the U.S., with its enormous military power and its newly developed counter-insurgency techniques, could defeat the National Liberation Front (NLF) and its North Vietnamese allies.

In March 1964 McNamara again visited South Vietnam. His report was pessimistic. The Communist position remained very strong; plans for the reduction in the number of U.S. advisers in South Vietnam had been dropped. Responding to congressional criticism that U.S. advisers were forced to use inferior equipment, McNamara replied that U.S. forces in Vietnam had a "blank check" on arms, manpower and funds. The statement startled some reporters who had long associated McNamara with "cost effectiveness," but President Johnson supported his Defense Secretary. (Between 1965 and 1967, when McNamara left office, defense spending for Vietnam rose from $1 billion to $20.6 billion.) By April 1964 McNamara was so closely identified with Vietnam policy that Sen. Wayne Morse (D, Ore.) [*q.v.*] dubbed the conflict "McNamara's war." "I think it is a very important war," replied McNamara, "and I am pleased to be identified with it and do whatever I can to win it."

By 1964 U.S. aircraft were aiding the South Vietnamese armed forces in carrying out covert raids on North Vietnam's coastal installations and attacks on infiltration routes in Laos and Cambodia. Despite these actions Communist forces threatened to overwhelm South Vietnam. Consequently, Pentagon strategists began drawing up plans for possible direct U.S. intervention.

An opportunity to implement those plans came on Aug. 4, 1964, when two U.S. destroyers were allegedly attacked by North Vietnamese gunboats in the Gulf of Tonkin. Adm. Ulysses S. Grant Sharp, commander-in-chief of U.S. Pacific forces, and members of the Joint Chiefs of Staff urged immediate retaliation against North Vietnam. President Johnson agreed. McNamara, however, delayed action for several hours. Evidence of the night attack, based largely on radar and sonar readings, was ambiguous; consequently, McNamara telephoned Sharp in

Honolulu advising him to "make damned sure what happened." Despite the fact that only one shell from the alleged skirmish was discovered, Sharp remained convinced of the attack. Therefore President Johnson, with the approval of McNamara, ordered air strikes against North Vietnamese shipping and coastal installations. McNamara presented evidence of the attack to Congress, which on Aug. 7 approved the Tonkin Gulf Resolution, giving the President broad power to "take all necessary measures to repel . . . further aggression" throughout Southeast Asia.

Throughout the fall of 1964 McNamara received reports of significant gains by Communist forces in South Vietnam. Gen. William Westmoreland [*q.v.*], commander of U.S. ground advisers in Vietnam, and Gen. Maxwell Taylor [*q.v.*] urged the President to permit systematic bombing of North Vietnam to destroy its will to make war. McNamara argued against such a course, suggesting that the bombing of the North might escalate the conflict and that it could in no significant way force the North to abandon its support of Communist guerrillas in the South. President Johnson deferred the bombing decision until after the 1964 presidential election.

In February 1965, following Communist attacks on U.S. bases at Pleiku and Qui Nhon in South Vietnam, McNamara joined other members of the National Security Council in approving retaliatory air strikes. By the beginning of March, the U.S. was carrying out systematic bombing of the North. At the request of Gen. Westmoreland, 3,500 Marines were also sent to help defend the airbase at Da Nang. Despite these actions South Vietnamese forces appeared unable to stay the Communist advance. In April McNamara reported that "the intensification of infiltration [by North Vietnamese troops] has grown progressively more flagrant. . . ." After another meeting with Westmoreland in July, McNamara approved the General's request that 185,000 troops be sent to Vietnam by the end of the year. Johnson granted the request but rejected, as politically unpalatable, McNamara's proposal for calling up the reserves and a tax increase to pay for the war.

By November U.S. troops were engaged in major battles against North Vietnamese regulars in the Central Highlands. That month Westmoreland recommended that up to 400,000 troops be sent to Vietnam by the end of 1966. McNamara concurred but cautioned that "deployments of the kind I have recommended will not guarantee success. U.S. killed in action can be expected to reach 1,000 a month, and the odds are even that we will be faced in early 1967 with a 'no decision' at an even higher level." What McNamara had come to realize was that North Vietnam would counter a U.S. troop buildup by sending more of its own troops South.

At McNamara's request, the U.S. initiated a halt in the bombing of North Vietnam in December 1965. The Secretary argued that the bombing halt might induce North Vietnam to enter peace negotiations with the U.S. If not, then more intensive bombing could be justified. Gen. Westmoreland and the Joint Chiefs opposed the halt because they feared the North Vietnamese would take advantage of the lull to resupply their troops. The pause proved unproductive, and the bombing was renewed on Jan. 31, 1966.

Bombing strategy was a continual source of conflict between McNamara and the military. The President, McNamara, Secretary of State Dean Rusk [*q.v.*] and McGeorge Bundy [*q.v.*] retained the right to review all proposed bombing targets in North Vietnam. McNamara and his staff charged that the Joint Chiefs too often selected targets that were of dubious military significance. The Joint Chiefs, in turn, argued that McNamara placed unnecessary restrictions on U.S. air power.

In October 1966 McNamara visited South Vietnam for the eighth time. Publicly he was optimistic, stating that military progress "exceeded our expectations." Privately he had growing doubts. The air war had not forced North Vietnam into peace negotiations; U.S. troops had prevented a Communist victory but were now stalemated; casualties were high and prospects for a quick end to the war were nil. He was becoming increasingly sensitive to anti-war opinions, particularly those of Sen. Robert F. Kennedy (D, N.Y.) [*q.v.*]. In a speech delivered in Montreal in the spring of 1966, McNamara seemed to question the wisdom of the U.S. military commitment. Referring to the government of South Vietnam, he stated, "We have no charter to rescue floundering regimes, who have brought violence on themselves by deliberately refusing to meet the legitimate expectations of their citizens."

Such statements were rare. For the most part McNamara continued to urge Americans to remain firm in their resolve to resist Communist aggression. He was, in turn, denounced by anti-war leaders, who considered his references to "body counts" and "search-and destroy missions" ruthless and cold-blooded. McNamara, who had enjoyed his student days and brief career as a college teacher, was no longer welcome on many campuses. In a November 1966 visit to Harvard University, he was challenged to debate the war and was then hooted down. Yelling above the crowd, he recalled his student days, "I was a lot tougher and a lot more courteous than you. I was tougher than you and I am tougher today."

During 1967 McNamara became openly skeptical over the effectiveness of bombing the North to prevent resupply of Communist troops in the South. Hoping to find a more effective means of preventing infiltration by North Vietnamese regulars, McNamara announced that the U.S. would construct a barrier of barbed wire, mines and electronic sensors south of the demilitarized zone. The barrier proved ineffective and was abandoned in 1969.

While concerned about the military conduct of the war, McNamara became increasingly interested in finding a way to end the conflict through a negotiated settlement. During the summer of 1967 McNamara, Paul Warnke [*q.v.*] and Paul Nitze [*q.v.*] drew up the "San Antonio Formula," a peace proposal offered privately to North Vietnam in August. The plan was a significant change in the U.S. terms for ending bombing and beginning negotiations. Prior to the communication the U.S. had offered to end the bombing if North Vietnam would stop its infiltration of the South. The San Antonio Formula modified this demand. It asked only for productive discussions in exchange for an end to the bombing. The U.S. requested no specific guarantee from Hanoi that it would end its infiltration. The only condition made was that the U.S. reserved its right to act if it concluded that the North Viewnamese were taking advantage of the bombing lull. The proposal, made public in September, was rejected by North Vietnam in October.

By the fall of 1967 McNamara was losing his influence within the Administration. His doubts about the bombing and his desire for a negotiated settlement conflicted with Johnson's hopes for a decisive military victory. Johnson, consequently, began to accede to the generals, who demanded more intensive bombing, increasing the number of available bombing targets in Vietnam. In November 1967 McNamara submitted a memorandum to the President in which he recommended that the U.S. freeze its troop levels, end the bombing of the North and turn over major responsibility for ground combat to the South Vietnamese Army. Johnson rejected the recommendations.

In November McNamara announced that he would resign in February to become the president of the World Bank. In January 1968, a few weeks before McNamara left office, Communist forces launched a major offensive against Saigon, Hue and other South Vietnamese cities. After intense fighting the Communists were driven out of the cities, but the Tet offensive seemed to confirm McNamara's pessimistic assessment of the war.

In response to the Communist offensive, the military requested more than 200,000 additional troops for the war. Johnson, concerned about the possible reaction to another increase, convened a senior advisory group on Vietnam to study the request. The panel, which included McNamara's successor, Clark Clifford [*q.v.*], recommended de-escalation. Johnson accepted their recommendations and at the end of March announced restrictions on future bombing of the North and a renewed bid for negotiations.

McNamara remained at the World Bank through the mid-1970s, where he attempted to increase loans to developing nations and channel funds to programs directly related to the daily life of the poor rather than to large civil engineering projects, which formerly had been favored by the Bank. He also campaigned for industrial nations to increase their level of development assistance. [See NIXON Volume]

[JLW]

For further information:
Henry L. Trewhitt, *McNamara: His Ordeal in the Pentagon* (New York, 1972).
U.S. Department of Defense, *The Pentagon Papers*, Senator Gravel Edition (Boston, 1971).

McNAUGHTON, JOHN T(HEODORE)

b. Nov. 21, 1921; Bicknell, Ind.
d. July 19, 1967; Hendersonville, N.C.
Assistant Secretary of Defense for International Security Affairs, July 1964-July 1967.

John T. McNaughton, a Rhodes scholar and Harvard University law professor, joined the Defense Department in the summer of 1961, where he dealt with arms control and disarmament problems. In July 1963 McNaughton served as a member of the diplomatic team that successfully negotiated a treaty with the Soviet Union barring above-ground testing of atomic weapons. [See KENNEDY Volume]

McNaughton was named assistant secretary of defense for international security affairs in June 1964. He maintained a close working and personal relationship with Secretary of Defense Robert S. McNamara [*q.v.*] and soon became McNamara's chief assistant in developing strategy in Vietnam.

In September 1964 McNaughton completed his "Plan for Action for South Vietnam," in which he advised the Administration to support the government of South Vietnam in its rural pacification programs and its naval and air warfare against North Vietnam. McNaughton argued, however, that indirect assistance might not be sufficient to forestall a Communist victory. He therefore proposed that the U.S. renew its naval patrols off the coast of North Vietnam. According to the authors of the *Pentagon Papers*, the measures proposed in the Plan "were conceived not only as [a] means to provoke North Vietnam into responses justifying U.S. punitive actions. They were also believed to make possible postponement . . . of a decision regarding . . . more serious escalation."

A North Vietnamese attack against American ships had allegedly taken place a month earlier in the Gulf of Tonkin, and McNaughton and McNamara endorsed the President's decision at that time to stage limited retaliatory air attacks against North Vietnamese military and industrial sites. If the North Vietnamese could be induced to attack again, he said, the U.S. could legitimately enter the war and begin a "crescendo of military actions" that would eventually include bombing and mining North Vietnamese harbors. Such actions, he believed, would force the North Vietnamese to enter peace negotiations. In the face of Communist aggression, he wrote, the U.S. had to demonstrate that it was "willing to keep promises [to its allies], be tough, take risks, get bloodied and hurt the enemy badly."

In November 1964 McNaughton joined the National Security Council working group, headed by Assistant Secretary of State William P. Bundy [*q.v.*], which was considering ways to deal with the deteriorating situation in South Vietnam. The panel recommended that the Administration support "graduated military moves against infiltration targets first in Laos and then in North Vietnam," coupled with attempts to open negotiations with Hanoi and Peking. Johnson accepted the committee's proposals in February 1965. These recommendations determined the course of the war until July of that year, when the Administration committed extensive ground forces to the war.

In March 1965 the U.S., in response to Communist guerrilla attacks on its South Vietnamese bases at Pleiku and Qui Nhon, began systematic bombing of the North. However, by that time it had become increasingly clear that for the U.S. to prevent a Communist victory, thousands of American combat troops would have to be sent to

Vietnam. At this juncture McNaughton attempted to define U.S. goals in Southeast Asia: "70 percent—to avoid a humiliating U.S. defeat (to our reputation as a guarantor); 20 percent—to keep SVN [South Vietnam] (and adjacent territory) from Chinese hands; 10 percent—to permit the people of SVN to enjoy a better, freer way of life; also—to emerge from crisis without unacceptable taint from methods used; not to 'help a friend' although it would be hard to stay in if asked out."

McNaughton also argued in March that the air war against North Vietnam would not force Hanoi to abandon its aggression in the South. He recommended, therefore, that three U.S. and two Korean divisions be sent to Da Nang and Pleiku. He cautioned that it might take "massive deployment" of U.S. troops to change the military situation. This memo was one of the factors that induced Johnson in early April to employ Marine units previously deployed for defensive purposes in active combat operation against Communist guerrillas. By the end of 1965 U.S. troop strength in South Vietnam stood at 184,314.

In July 1965 McNaughton and McNamara, increasingly skeptical about the advantages of bombing the North, began planning, over the objections of the Joint Chiefs of Staff, for an extended bombing halt. A halt was initiated on December 24. McNaughton believed that the North would not yet consider negotiating but that the U.S. should at the very least "create a public impression of willingness 'to try everything' before further increases in military action." There was no satisfactory response from Hanoi, and the bombing was renewed on Jan. 31, 1966.

McNaughton was one of a number of Defense Department officials who met with Secretary McNamara at weekly sessions to review a list of bombing sites in North Vietnam proposed by the Joint Chiefs of Staff. The military consistently argued that the civilian planners imposed illogical and arbitrary restrictions on the bombing. Mc Naughton countered that many of the requested military targets were of no strategic value and endangered the lives of civilians. He suggested that the bombing could be more effective if concentrated on infiltration routes south of Hanoi.

During 1966 McNaughton became increasingly pessimistic about the progress of the war, and he began to revise his thinking about what the loss of South Vietnam would mean. In November 1964 he had argued that a Communist victory in South Vietnam would endanger the sovereignty of many non-Communist states in Southeast Asia. However, in April 1966 he suggested that the loss would "not affect the present line of containment from Korea to the Philippines." McNaughton reiterated the importance of fighting "to avoid humiliation" but cautioned that this thesis might be carried too far. Fighting a futile war was also damaging the U.S. reputation abroad, he contended.

By May 1967 McNaughton became so alarmed by the growing public protest against the war that he wrote President Johnson to warn "of a feeling widely and strongly held that 'the Establishment' is out of its mind. The feeling is that we are trying to impose some U.S. image on distant people we cannot understand." He advised Johnson not to accede to a request from Gen. William Westmoreland [*q.v.*] for an additional 80,000 troops at a time when there were over 400,000 American soldiers already stationed in South Vietnam. At the same time McNaughton advised the President to press on with military, pacification and political programs in the South and "drive hard to increase the productivity of Vietnamese military forces." The U.S. had prevented a Communist victory in 1965, he said, but victory would ultimately depend on the South Vietnamese themselves.

In June 1967 McNaughton became Secretary of the Navy. On July 19, shortly before he assumed his new post, McNaughton, his wife and younger son were killed in an airplane crash in North Carolina.

McNaughton received little attention in the press during his lifetime, but with the publication of the *Pentagon Papers* in 1971, he emerged as a controversial figure. To journalist Ralph Stavins, McNaughton was a man "torn between committing 'unbridled acts' of the most egregious sort and detaching the U.S. from an untenable situation. It would seem that his reason compelled him to urge a pullout but fear of being too weak to employ massive violence and his positive desire to wield power swayed him to betray his own reason." Robert McNamara, on the other hand, called him "a voice of reason" in the Pentagon, a restraining influence on the military whose persistent and informed opposition to the bombing in the North helped pave the way for its cessation in 1968. McNamara also recalled that during the Kennedy years McNaughton had been very active in advancing policies of disarmanent and arms control.

[JLW]

For further information:
U.S. Dept. of Defense, *The Pentagon Papers*, Senator Gravel Edition (Boston, 1971), Vols. II and III.

McPHERSON, HARRY C(UMMINGS)

b. Aug. 22, 1929; Tyler, Tex.
Assistant Secretary of Defense for Education and Cultural Affairs, July 1964-August 1965; Special Assistant to the President, August 1965-February 1966; Special Counsel to the President, February 1966-January 1969.

Harry McPherson was born in the East Texas community of Tyler. After two years at Southern Methodist University, he transferred to the University of the South in Sewanee, Tenn., from which he graduated in 1949. McPherson dropped out of Columbia University—where he did graduate work in English literature—to join the Air Force in 1950. Following his discharge McPherson received a degree from the University of Texas Law School in 1956. The same year he took a job as assistant counsel to the Senate Democratic Policy Committee, chaired by Sen. Lyndon Johnson. McPherson was named general counsel to the Committee in 1961. In August 1963 he was appointed deputy undersecretary of the Army for international affairs.

After Johnson became President, Mc Pherson remained at his Pentagon post. In July 1964 he requested and was granted the post of assistant secretary for educational and cultural affairs, a job that appealed to his strong intellectual interests. In August 1965, primarily thanks to the backing of White House Press Secretary Bill Moyers [*q.v.*], McPherson was named to the temporary position of counsel to the President. In February of the next year he succeeded Lee C. White as special counsel.

McPherson was described by journalist Patrick Anderson as "one of the most attractive, cultivated, and well-intentioned men" to serve on the White House staff in years. He served as the President's personal lawyer, drafted many presidential executive orders and worked with the Justice Department on legal matters concerning civil rights cases and presidential pardons. Along with special assistants Douglass Cater [*q.v.*] and Joseph Califano [*q.v.*], Mc Pherson acted as presidential liaison with several government agencies, coordinating education, antipoverty and urban programs with the White House. Because of his intellectual credentials, he was often sent to college campuses to sound out the academic community's reaction to Great Society proposals.

In his post as special counsel, McPherson saw most major bills that crossed the President's desk and commented on each of them. Of the 1968 Safe Streets Act, McPherson wrote the President: "I recognize that you must sign this bill. But it is the worst bill you will have signed since you took office. Title III, the wiretapping-eavesdropping provision, is extremely dangerous."

McPherson's most important role in the Administration was serving as the President's top speechwriter. In a March 23, 1968 memorandum, McPherson recommended that the President, in his upcoming address on the Vietnam war, order the cessation of bombing north of the 20th parallel and announce that the U.S. would send representatives to Geneva and Rangoon to await a North Vietnamese response. McPherson believed that such an announcement would "show the American people that we are willing to do every reasonable thing to bring about talks."

McPherson's proposals were incorporated into the March 31 speech. Johnson did announce the de-escalation of the war and said that Averell Harriman [*q.v.*] and Llewellyn Thompson [*q.v.*] would be available to go to Geneva "or any other suitable place" to begin peace talks.

In his 1970 book, *The Twilight of the Presidency*, former White House press secretary George Reedy [*q.v.*] noted that in the Kennedy and Johnson Administrations special counsels Theodore Sorensen [*q.v.*] and McPherson were rarely consulted on legal matters. Rather, "it was open knowledge, not only in the White House but to the Washington community at large, that their ability to put on paper sentences that would parse grammatically was the key to their position in the hierarchy."

In 1969 McPherson entered private law practice in Washington.

[FHM]

For further information:
Harry McPherson, *A Political Education* (New York, 1972).
Charles Roberts, *L.B.J.'s Inner Circle* (New York, 1965).

MADDOX, LESTER G(ARFIELD)

b. Sept. 30, 1915; Atlanta, Ga.
Governor, Ga., 1967-71.

After holding a variety of jobs, Maddox opened a drive-in restaurant called the Pickrick in Atlanta, Ga., in 1947. The restaurant, which refused service to blacks, expanded nine times over the next 15 years. As it prospered Maddox took an increasing interest in politics. He ran as a segregationist candidate for mayor of Atlanta in 1957 and 1961 and for lieutenant governor in 1962. Although he lost all three elections, his campaign for lieutenant governor made him well-known throughout the state of Georgia.

Maddox received national attention in the summer of 1964, when he defied the provision in the newly adopted Civil Rights Act prohibiting racial segregation in public accommodations. When three black ministerial students tried to enter the Pickrick on July 3, they were chased away by Maddox, who brandished a gun, and by his white patrons, who carried ax handles. Similar incidents occurred when other blacks tried to enter Maddox's restaurant in July and August. The three ministerial students sued Maddox in federal court, and in what proved to be the first court test of the 1964 Civil Rights Act, a three-judge federal panel in Atlanta upheld the public accomodations law on July 22. The court ordered Maddox to desegregate his restaurant within 20 days. After this order was affirmed by Supreme Court Justice Hugo Black [*q.v.*] on Aug. 10, Maddox decided to close his restaurant rather than open it to blacks. Blaming President Johnson for his troubles and arguing that the civil rights law was an attack upon Americans' "right to the private enterprise system," Maddox picketed the White House and the Democratic National Convention in August. Early in 1965 he erected a monument in front of his former restaurant, opened a stand there which sold souvenir ax handles and shifted from the restaurant to the furniture business.

Maddox announced his candidacy for the Democratic nomination for governor of Georgia in October 1965. He spent most of the next year conducting a vigorous grass-roots campaign on a platform of support for segregation and opposition to alleged federal encroachment on state and individual rights. Maddox placed second in a field of five candidates in the Sept. 14, 1966 Democratic primary. He then defeated former Gov. Ellis G. Arnall in the Sept. 28 runoff even though Arnall, a racial moderate, had the support of most Georgia newspapers and the state's Democratic hierarchy. In the November election neither Maddox nor his Republican opponent, Rep. Howard H. Callaway (R, Ga.) received a majority of the popular vote. Georgia law required the state legislature to choose the governor in this situation. Even though Callaway had received about 3,000 more popular votes than Maddox, the legislature selected Maddox as governor by a vote of 182 to 66 on Jan. 10, 1967.

Sworn in as governor the same day, Maddox delivered a moderate inaugural address. He promised not to close any schools to prevent desegregation and said no "extremist organization or group" would have "any voice or influence in any state program." He urged respect for federal authority, declared there was "no necessity" for any federal-state conflict and said any disagreements should be solved "under the framework of the Constitution."

Considered a buffoon by many of his critics and a populist hero by his supporters, Maddox surprised most observers with his inaugural and with his actions during his first years in office. He quickly invited Alabama's former Gov. George C. Wallace [*q.v.*] to address the state legislature, but he also met with President Johnson early in 1967, declaring afterwards that he was "pleasantly surprised" to find Johnson "so knowledgeable." Maddox appointed blacks to local draft boards, to the Georgia Bureau of Investigation and to various special commissions and interim legislative committees. He ordered an investigation of conditions in state prisons after four escaped black prisoners surrendered to him at the governor's mansion to tell him of penal conditions.

Maddox also accepted antipoverty funds from the federal government but denounced federal guidelines on school desegregation and praised a local school board when it again segregated black and white teachers despite the potential loss of federal funds. He criticized President Johnson's formation of a federal commission to investigate the cause of urban riots in 1967, saying government officials knew that the violence was "Communist inspired and directed." Maddox also challenged the need for greater federal spending to cure the country's urban problems and said the country should instead "start instilling" in the urban poor the spirit of initiative "that made this country great."

On August 17, 1968 Maddox announced his candidacy for the Democratic presidential nomination, declaring he represented the "conservative element of American society." He labeled the major aspirants for the nomination "socialists" and, in a nationally televised address, emphasized the need for a stronger American commitment to fight world Communism and for greater law and order at home. His candidacy was generally considered inconsequential, however, and Maddox withdrew his name from consideration shortly before the balloting began at the August 1968 Democratic National Convention.

Meanwhile, in accordance with long practice in Georgia, Maddox and the state Democratic Party chairman personally selected the 107 members of Georgia's delegation to the National Convention. They chose only six blacks and a few moderate or liberal whites. As a consequence, a coalition of blacks and white liberals organized a challenge delegation headed by State Rep. Julian Bond [*q.v.*]. The Convention Credentials Committee suggested two different compromises between the regular and the challenge delegations, but Maddox rejected both and then resigned as a delegate on the ground that he was then a candidate for the presidential nomination. On Aug. 27 the Convention accepted one compromise proposal under which both delegations would be seated and the Georgia vote split between them. Most of the regular delegation walked out after the compromise was voted, and Maddox left the Convention shortly afterwards, proclaiming that the Party had been infiltrated by "socialists, beatniks, and misfits."

During the remainder of his term, Maddox denounced federal school desegregation suits and met with several other Southern governors to devise means to stop busing for school desegregation. He also urged a full American military victory in Vietnam and continued to warn against socialism and communism within the U.S. While in Washington in February 1970 to testify at Senate hearings on a voting rights bill, Maddox created a furor by passing out his souvenir ax handles at the House restaurant. The state constitution barred Maddox from a second consecutive term as governor. After he lost a court suit to overturn this provision, Maddox ran for lieutenant governor in 1970. He defeated three opponents, including the incumbent, in the September Democratic primary and then won the November election. [See NIXON Volume]

[CAB]

MAGNUSON, WARREN G(RANT)
b. April 12, 1905; Moorhead, Minn.
Democratic Senator, Wash., 1944- .

Orphaned in infancy, Magnuson was raised by an immigrant Scandinavian family. At 19 he left home and settled in Seattle, where he received his law degree from the University of Washington in 1929. Elected to the state legislature in 1932, Magnuson sponsored the nation's first unemployment compensation law. He served as county prosecutor in Seattle from 1934 until his election to Congress in 1936.

In Congress Magnuson sought to generate public work projects to revive his state's economy. Water development programs soon became his dominant interest. He won election to the Senate in 1944 and continued to promote federally operated dams and power projects in the upper house. Strongly supported by organized labor, Magnuson fought against the more restrictive provisions of the Taft-Hartley Act in 1947 and introduced a bill in 1950 that restored the maritime union hiring hall. Because his state's economy relied heavily on federal defense contracts and resource development, Magnuson's seniority on key committees and ability to deliver federal programs made him an extremely valuable legislator. In 1955 he became chairman of the powerful Senate Interstate and Foreign Commerce Committee (later renamed the Commerce Committee). He also served on the Appropriations Committee and the Aeronautics and Space Sciences Committee. In addition to liberal social legislation, Magnuson favored large defense expenditures. He and Sen. Henry Jackson (D, Wash.) [*q.v.*] were sometimes called "the Senators from Boeing." [See TRUMAN, EISENHOWER Volumes]

During the early 1960s Magnuson continued to focus on legislation designed to boost Washington's economy, particularly its aerospace, shipbuilding and extractive industries. However, his emphasis in committee began to shift to issues of broader national significance. In the Commerce Committee and later on the Senate floor, Magnuson figured prominently in the passage of the controversial public accommodations section of the Civil Rights Act of 1964. [See KENNEDY Volume]

The pace of Magnuson's activity continued to rise with the quickening legislative tempo of the mid-1960s. Magnuson was a longtime Senate ally and close friend of President Johnson, who was best man at his 1964 wedding. He introduced most of the Johnson Administration's major consumer protection bills and guided them through the Commerce Committee and onto the Senate floor where, because of the Democratic majority and Magnuson's stature, they were usually assured of passage.

In January 1965 Magnuson introduced a bill requiring a health hazard warning and statement of tar and nicotine yields on all cigarette packs as of January 1966. His bill also prohibited the imposition of any other package warning requirements by government agencies and effectively banned warning requirements on advertisements. A stronger measure, sponsored by Sen. Maurine Neuberger (D, Ore.) [*q.v.*], which would have permitted the Federal Trade Commission to retain its authority to set labeling requirements and would have required uniform label and advertisement warnings, was defeated in committee despite support from Surgeon General Luther Terry [*q.v.*]. The Magnuson bill, minus the provision for tar and nicotine yield, passed without difficulty and was signed in July. Many health and consumer organizations saw the act as a victory for the tobacco industry, which had launched a massive lobbying campaign against stiffer legislation.

Magnuson was more willing to use his influence to curb the manufacture of unsafe motor vehicles and tires. Mounting public pressure, aroused by the publication of Ralph Nader's [*q.v.*] *Unsafe at Any Speed* in 1965, propelled the Johnson Administration and Congress into action on auto safety. Nader attacked the automobile industry for placing style and sales above safety and argued that the introduction of safety features could substantially reduce traffic casualties.

In March 1966 Magnuson introduced an Administration bill authorizing the Secretary of Commerce to establish auto safety standards if, after two years, he concluded they were necessary. Responding to pressure from Nader and such senators as Robert Kennedy (D, N.Y.) [*q.v.*] and Abraham Ribicoff (D, Conn.) [*q.v.*], Magnuson later agreed to make the establishment of safety standards mandatory and to hasten the effective date for compliance. He also supported an amendment to include criminal rather than civil penalties for manufacturers found in violation of the law, but this was defeated 14-62. The House and Senate passed the bill without opposition. A tire safety bill, introduced by Magnuson in October 1965 and already approved by the Senate, was incorporated into the Auto Safety Act during the House-Senate Conference.

In accordance with the Act, a National Traffic Safety Agency (NTSA) was formed in November 1966. Its chairman issued federal safety standards later that month, but car manufacturers, who had first favored a voluntary industry safety program and later supported discretionary federal standards, complained that they would be unable to meet the federal standards in the allotted time. In January 1967 the NTSA announced a revised set of standards, less stringent than those originally established. The new set shifted the compliance deadline from September 1967 to January 1968 and temporarily withdrew some of the original standards pending further study. To evaluate the NTSA's new standards, Magnuson held Commerce Committee hearings in March 1967 during which Nader accused NTSA of having a "protective attitude" toward the automotive industry. No further action was taken. Magnuson also criticized the President for requesting only $26 million of the more than $91 million authorized for the first year of safety programs.

In addition to the cigarette labeling and auto safety laws, Magnuson introduced numerous less significant consumer protection bills requested by the Administration, most of which passed with little debate or opposition. These included the 1966 Child Protection Act authorizing labeling requirements on dangerous household items, the 1967 Flammable Fabrics Act authorizing the establishment of flammability standards and a 1967 law creating the National Commission on Product Safety. The Commission's task was to review the adequacy of existing regulations and to identify hazardous products already on the market, although it was prohibited from listing them by brand name. Magnuson's 1966 "truth-in-packaging" bill also had the Administration's backing and passed the Senate easily. However, it was diluted in the House, where manufacturers concentrated their lobbying efforts. Magnuson's original proposal, giving federal officials the authority to set standard weights and sizes for packages, was eliminated in favor of requirements for uniform labels indicating quantity. A radiation control bill and a gas pipeline safety bill, also introduced by Magnuson and passed in 1968, were similarly weakened by effective industry lobbying in the House.

Although heavily involved in consumer protection, Magnuson did not neglect his state's welfare. In 1966 he won a "sea-grant" college bill to aid oceanography research, and he was a major congressional spokesman for increased federal aid to the merchant marine. He also worked to liberalize trade with the Soviet bloc. Hoping to revive Washington's Oriental trade, he called for recognition of Communist China. Of all federal programs affecting Washington's economic health, aerospace spending remained most crucial; consequently, Magnuson continued to champion the development of Boeing's supersonic transport jet. The effectiveness of Sens. Magnuson and Jackson in promoting their state's interests was clearly demonstrated by Washington's share of public works funds, which in 1972 came to 15% of the national total.

Magnuson served as chairman of the Democratic Senatorial Campaign Committee and was known in the Senate for his willingness to remain in the background so other Democrats more in need of publicity might benefit from the exposure. He appointed himself chairman of the Commerce Committee's newly created Consumer Subcommittee in 1967, but after he won reelection in 1968 he stapped down in favor of Sen. Frank Moss (D, Utah) [*q.v.*].

Magnuson supported Johnson's policies in Vietnam but opposed the war after Richard Nixon took office. In the early 1970s he promoted a system of national health care. Despite his continued support for the supersonic transport, he championed environmental protection legislation. Magnuson was also a leading force in Congress behind the creation of Amtrak, the federal passenger rail system. [See NIXON Volume]

[MDB]

MAHON, GEORGE H(ERMAN)

b. Sept. 22, 1900; Mahon, La.
Democratic Representative, Tex., 1935- ; Chairman, Appropriations Committee, 1964- .

In 1908 George Mahon moved with his family to the Texas panhandle. After receiving his law degree from the University of Texas, Mahon entered politics and successively won election as district attorney, judge and Democratic representative from the rural 19th congressional district. A supporter of Roosevelt and Truman Administration foreign policy, defense and agriculture programs, Mahon delivered few speeches during the course of his steady rise on House seniority lists. As chairman of the Appropriations Committee's Department of Defense Subcommittee, Mahon urged greater military spending and opposed efforts by the Eisenhower Administration to trim the defense budget. During the Kennedy years he endorsed increased defense expenditures sought by the White House. [See EISENHOWER, KENNEDY Volumes]

With the death of Rep. Clarence Cannon (D, Mo.) in May 1964, Mahon assumed the chairmanship of the full Appropriations Committee and thus became one of the most influential House leaders. As head of the Committee that reviewed all budgetary requests made by the executive branch, he shared much of the authority Cannon had tended to monopolize.

Mahon proved a key congressional supporter of Johnson's Vietnam policy. Cooperating with the Administration, he defeated efforts by congressional "hawks" in October 1965 to amend a defense appropriations bill with a clause denying U.S. aid to nations trading with North Vietnam. Six months later Mahon's Committee approved the $13.1 billion supplementary budget request made by the Defense Department. "When we vote for this bill," Mahon proclaimed in March 1966, "I think we will show to the nation and to the entire world that the elected representatives of the people stand firmly together in resisting any program of appeasement."

Mahon failed to support many key measures in the President's domestic program. He opposed the 1964 Civil Rights Act, although he refused to join Southern Democratic colleagues in advocating nonenforcement of the law's provisions. In the 1965 session he declined to support the Voting Rights Act, medicare and the aid-to-Appalachia program. However, in 1965 he voted with the White House in supporting repeal of the right-to-work provision of the Taft-Hartley Act and backed extending coverage of the minimum wage law to farm workers.

In the 90th Congress Mahon's disenchantment with Great Society programs grew more apparent. In January 1967 he appointed four conservative Democrats to the Appropriations Committee's Labor, Health, Education and Welfare Subcommittee. Violence in Northern cities provoked him to condemn calls by liberal Democrats for greater spending in the ghetto areas. "A spending spree was not the answer to the riots," Mahon declared in July 1967, defending Congress's record in social legislation. Angered by the March 1968 report of the Kerner Commission, Mahon denounced its recommendations. Already engaged in the Administration's fight for a surtax, Mahon rejected any increase in social spending. "If you can't pass a surtax of 10%," he asked, "how can you expect to cover the cost of massive new programs?"

In the area of defense spending, Mahon retained the leadership role that he had played during the Kennedy Administration. He endorsed Secretary of Defense Robert S. McNamara's [*q.v.*] proposal in 1967 for a "Chinese-oriented" anti-ballistic missile defense system (ABM) at an initial cost of

$5 billion. To liberal critics of the system's expense, he replied that "those who speak of the ending of the conflict in Southeast Asia as the beginning of a time when we can have a mere skeletonized Defense Department are not thinking along realistic lines." The following month the House authorized the ABM expenditure.

During his years of service in the House, Mahon earned a reputation for personal integrity and hard work. As liberal Sen. William Proxmire (D, Wisc.) [*q.v.*] noted in 1970, Mahon did not practice "pork barrel" politics for his West Texas constituency. Proxmire reported that the Congressman's district was "not weighed down with Army bases or Air Force runways, although Texas has been the recipient of vast military and space contracts." [See NIXON Volume]

[JLB]

MAILER, NORMAN

b. Jan. 31, 1923; Long Branch, N.J.
Novelist, journalist.

Mailer grew up in Brooklyn, graduated from Harvard in 1943 with a degree in aeronautical engineering and served with the Army in World War II. Out of his experiences as an infantryman, Mailer wrote the 1948 bestselling novel, *The Naked and the Dead*. In 1951 and 1955 Mailer published two novels, *Barbary Shore* and *The Deer Park*. The first concerned Mailer's disillusionment with communism, the second, the psychopathology of sexuality and power—two of Mailer's most important themes in later years.

In the early 1960s Mailer began a monthly column for *Esquire* magazine. His most significant article was called "Superman Comes to the Supermarket," a glamorization of John F. Kennedy as an existential hero. Many of Mailer's articles and columns on Kennedy were collected in his 1963 book, *The Presidential Papers*.

Pressed for money, Mailer wrote a serialized novel in 1965 for *Esquire* called *An American Dream.* Utilizing the familiar Mailer themes of violence, sex, existential anguish, satanism and magic, the novel was considered by many critics to be an imaginative vehicle for Mailer's own variant of Reichian psychology.

With the publication of his novel *Why are We in Vietnam?* in 1967 and the Pulitzer prize-winning *Armies of the Night* in 1968, Mailer returned to radical politics. Subtitled "History as Novel, the Novel as History," *Armies of the Night* was an exercise in subjective journalism that described the Oct. 21, 1967 March on the Pentagon and Mailer's own participation in the anti-war demonstration. Combining a careful presentation of facts, first-person narration and a spectacular mix of ideology and sensation, the work provided a biting but often moving description of the anti-war movement, its leaders and the extraordinary tension that existed between the author's private ego and his public persona.

Mailer continued to mix journalism and personal narrative with another widely read 1968 book, *Miami and the Siege of Chicago.* This account of the two nominating conventions described Mailer's guarded respect for Richard Nixon [*q.v.*] and admiration for Sen. Eugene McCarthy (D, Minn.) [*q.v.*].

In the late 1960s and early 1970s Mailer also directed, edited, produced and acted in three films—*Beyond the Law, Wild 90* and *Maidstone.* "Existential" in the sense that they were unscripted and depended for their drama on the interplay among the actors, the films reinforced Mailer's self-generated image as "personage," an image nurtured by all his works since publication of *The Deer Park* in 1955.

In 1969 Mailer ran a seriocomic campaign for mayor of New York City. Columnist Jimmy Breslin ran on the same ticket for president of the city council. Advocating community control and statehood for the City, Mailer and Breslin won 5% of the vote in the Democratic primary held in June. In 1971 Mailer published *Of a Fire on the Moon,* a favorable account of the American space effort, and *Prisoner of Sex,* a searing attack on the women's liberation movement. [See NIXON Volume]

[FHM]

For further information:
Leo Brandy, ed., *Mailer: A Collection of Critical Essays* (New York, 1972).

MALCOLM X
b. May 19, 1925; Omaha, Neb.
d. Feb. 21, 1965; New York, N.Y.
Black nationalist spokesman.

Malcolm X was born Malcolm Little in Omaha, Neb., where his father was a Baptist minister and organizer for Marcus Garvey's United Negro Improvement Association. After a move to Michigan and his father's death, Little migrated to Boston to live with a half-sister. He developed a reputation in the black ghettos of Boston and New York as a "hustler" and in February 1946 received a prison sentence for burglary. In jail he discovered the teachings of Black Muslim leader, Elijah Muhammad [*q.v.*] and changed his name to Malcolm X. Released from prison in August 1952, Malcolm settled in Detroit and was appointed assistant minister of Muslim Temple No. 1. He was placed in charge of the Muslim's New York temple in 1954 and in 1963 became the Muslims's first "national minister."

A charismatic speaker and aggressive recruiter who employed his first-hand knowledge of the ghetto to build the Black Muslim organization, Malcolm emerged in the early 1960s as the Muslim's leading spokesman and heir apparent to Elijah Muhammad. He frequently described himself as "the angriest black man in America," and his call for self-defense appealed to many blacks impatient with the nonviolent integrationist strategy of the civil rights movement.

The first public indication of trouble between Elijah Muhammad and Malcolm X occurred in December 1963, when Muhammad silenced Malcolm for 90 days because Malcolm described President Kennedy's death as a case of "chickens coming home to roost." A rumor that Malcolm was suspended indefinitely from his leadership functions spread throughout the Muslim organization. On February 26, 1964 Malcolm telephoned Muhammad and asked for a clarification of his status.

Muhammad's reply did not satisfy Malcolm, and on March 8, 1964 he announced that he was leaving the Muslims to form an organization that would stress "black nationalism as a political concept and form of social action against the oppressors." A month later he embarked on a five week pilgrimage to Mecca and Africa, returning again to Africa later the same year. During his first trip abroad he wrote the well-publicized *Letter from Mecca* describing experiences with Caucasian Muslims that caused him to favorably re-evaluate the role which white people in America might play in the struggle against racism. He also adopted the Arabic name El-Hajj Malik El-Shabazz.

According to Alex Haley, Malcolm's trips abroad "sorely tested the morale of even his key members" in his newly formed Organization of Afro-American Unity. Upon returning from his second trip abroad in September 1964, Malcolm sought to solve the financial problems of both his new organization and his family by accepting numerous speaking engagements. He also sought to establish a cooperative relationship with the civil rights movement. On February 3, 1965, he visited Selma, Ala., during the voter registration drive there and, according to Martin Luther King's [*q.v.*] biographer, David Lewis, confided to Coretta King [*q.v.*] that he counted on his own militant reputation to "scare" white people to her husband's cause. In public he stopped labeling black integrationists "Uncle Toms."

The relationship between Malcolm X and the Black Muslims continued to deteriorate, and in early 1965 Malcolm reported several death threats. On February 14 Malcolm's home was firebombed. One week later, as he addressed a rally at the Audubon Ballroom in New York City, he was assassinated by men thought to be linked to the Black muslims. The posthumous publication of his *Autobiography*, which detailed his rise from ghetto hustler to militant black spokesman, contributed to his reputation as a martyred symbol of black pride and militancy.

[DKR]

For further information:

George Breitman, *The Last Year Of Malcolm X*, (New York, 1967).
Malcolm X and Alex Haley, *Autobiography of Malcolm X*, (New York, 1965).

MANKIEWICZ, FRANK
b. May 16, 1924; New York, N.Y.
Peace Corps Director for Latin America, 1964-66.

The son of author and film writer Herman Mankiewicz, Frank was educated at the University of California at Los Angeles (UCLA), Columbia and the University of California, Berkeley. He ran unsuccessfully for the California state legislature in 1950 on a Democratic ticket headed by Helen Gahagan Douglas. Mankiewicz remained involved in California politics through 1954, serving as chairman of the state Democratic committee. In 1955 he received an LL.B. from UCLA and practiced law for the next six years in California. Mankiewicz joined the Peace Corps in 1962 as director of the organization's programs in Lima, Peru. In 1964 he became regional director of the Peace Corps for Latin America, returning to Washington to coordinate programs and supervise recruitment.

Mankiewicz first met Sen. Robert Kennedy (D, N.Y.) [*q.v.*] in 1965, when he was called upon to brief the Senator for an upcoming Latin American trip. Six months later he left the Peace Corps to become Kennedy's press assistant. Mankiewicz's liberal political views sharpened during his service on the Kennedy staff. As the Vietnam war intensified in 1967, he joined other Kennedy aides and friends in urging the Senator to challenge President Lyndon Johnson for the 1968 Democratic presidential nomination. When Kennedy entered the primary race in March 1968, Mankiewicz helped project the candidate's strong appeal to students and minority groups that was largely responsible for Kennedy's impressive victory in the California primary of June 5. Like his fellow staff members, Mankiewicz was completely devoted to Kennedy and crushed by his assassination on the day of the California victory. It was Mankiewicz, as Kennedy's press secretary, who had to announce the Senator's death in the early morning of June 6.

As the Kennedy staff disbanded, Mankiewicz sought another political channel for the support that the Senator had accumulated. During the 1968 Democratic Convention he tried unsuccessfully to transfer Kennedy's delegates to Sen. George McGovern (D, S.D.) [*q.v.*], the presidential contender whom he viewed as closest to Kennedy on major issues. Mankiewicz also participated in pre-Convention meetings between anti-war leaders and Democratic regulars who wished to negotiate a compromise Vietnam plank for the Party's platform. These efforts to avoid a Convention dispute over the war were frustrated by President Johnson's refusal to accept any platform statement that did not reaffirm Administration policy on Vietnam.

Mankiewicz undertook a number of activities in the years that followed the 1968 campaign. Together with Tom Braden, he wrote a syndicated news column which soon became known in Washington for its literary style and liberal outlook. Drawing on his earlier government experience, Mankiewicz accepted a $15,000 Ford Foundation grant in 1969 to study "the effects of Peace Corps community development projects in Latin America and the Caribbean." He also served on the board of directors of the Center for Community Change, a privately funded organization that aided self-help programs in low-income areas of the U.S.

In 1971 Mankiewicz joined the McGovern staff and quickly gained a reputation as a shrewd campaigner who helped McGovern win his surprising primary victories. Mankiewicz's tactic was to saturate a small area with publicity and volunteers for a short time, then withdraw to analyze experience and prepare for the next effort. This succeeded in the primaries but not in the national election. Insufficient funds and McGovern's "radical" image prevented Democratic campaigners from breaking through to the larger electorate, resulting in the overwhelming reelection of Richard Nixon.

Following the 1972 campaign Mankiewicz returned to journalism, this time as a television writer and producer. In 1973 he published a book on the Watergate affair, *Perfectly Clear: Nixon from Whittier to Watergate*. [See NIXON Volume]

[SLG]

MANN, THOMAS (CLIFTON)
b. Nov. 11, 1912; Laredo, Tex.
Assistant Secretary of State for Inter-American Affairs, December 1963-February 1965; Undersecretary of State for Economic Affairs, February 1965-April 1966.

Mann grew up in the border town of Laredo, where he learned to speak fluent Spanish with a Mexican accent. Educated at Baylor, he worked in the family law firm from 1934 to 1942. He then joined the State Department and gained an expertise in Latin America and international economics. He became a Foreign Service officer in 1947. Except for one year in Greece, his career was concerned solely with Latin America. In 1957 he was named assistant secretary of state for inter-American affairs and with C. Douglas Dillon [*q.v.*] attempted to make U.S. policy more sensitive to Latin America's economic needs. He encouraged the Latin Americans to control the production and, thus, the prices of their major exports. At the same time he realized that the U.S. had to exercise restraint in unloading its farm surpluses in Latin America, where they could drastically disturb the balance of internal markets. Mann's sympathetic and flexible views on Latin America served as a bridge between the Eisenhower Administration and Kennedy's Alliance for Progress. He served as ambassador to Mexico under Kennedy. [See EISENHOWER, KENNEDY Volumes]

When Johnson appointed Mann assistant secretary of state in December 1963, the President also gave him two other posts. Mann succeeded Teodoro Moscoso as head of the Alliance for Progress and, as the President's special assistant, coordinated the Latin American policy of all departments. As Secretary of State Dean Rusk [*q.v.*] said, Mann was "Mr. Latin America," with an extraordinary measure of authority in all aspects of hemisphere policy.

Mann's appointment was a highly controversial one. Many New Frontier liberals thought Mann far too accommodating to North American business and unsophisticated about the Communist threat in Latin America. Many recalled that in 1962 Mann (then ambassador to Mexico) had refused Edward M. Kennedy's [*q.v.*] request to entertain Mexican Communists and leftists at the U.S. embassy. Sen. Hubert Humphrey (D, Minn.) [*q.v.*] advised against Mann's appointment and Teodoro Moscoso suggested that if Mann replaced him in the Alliance for Progress Johnson's prestige would decline with both Latin Americans and Spanish-speaking voters at home. However, Mann's appointment was very popular with the North American business community. As Alphonse de Rosso of the Standard Oil Company of New Jersey later said, "Not until Tom Mann came back . . . did the business community feel that it was 'in' again with the United States government."

The new Latin American policy was soon known as the Mann doctrine. It consisted of four basic objectives: (1) to foster economic growth and to be neutral on internal social reform; (2) to protect U.S. private investments in the hemisphere; (3) to downplay U.S. concern for the establishment of representative democratic institutions; and (4) to oppose Communism. During Mann's tenure U.S. business investments in Latin America increased substantially, and the U.S. supported military governments more frequently and less cticially than it had under the Kennedy Administration.

Despite Mann's overall control of Latin American policy, President Johnson's domestic political concerns sometimes limited his authority. In January 1964 fighting broke out in Panama between Panamanian students and young North American residents of the Canal Zone over the flying of the Panamanian flag within the Zone. When U.S. Canal Zone police killed some Panamanians during the riots, Panama broke off diplomatic relations, and Mann was dispatched as head of a peace mission to Panama. Although Mann suspected that Communists had exacerbated the conflict in the Canal Zone, he was not adverse to the Panamanian demand that the U.S. agree to "review" the 1903 treaty that established U.S. sovereignty in the Zone. However, when the Organization of American States

(OAS) worked out an agreement acceptable to Mann in March, Johnson publicly repudiated it. Johnson was conscious of the upcoming 1964 elections and did not wish to appear "weak" to Congress and the electorate. When the situation quieted in April, Johnson reestablished relations with Panama and in December agreed to renegotiate the Canal treaty.

In February 1965 Mann became undersecretary of state for economic affairs but continued to advise Johnson on Latin American policy. Although he played only a minor role in the decision to send Marines into the Dominican Republic in April 1965, he was blamed for Johnson's failure to inform the OAS of the action. Along with McGeorge Bundy [*q.v.*] and Cyrus Vance [*q.v.*], he left for Santo Domingo on May 15 to help set up a provisional government. Mann wanted to form a government acceptable to democratic groups within the Dominican Republic, but the mission ended in failure. Ellsworth Bunker [*q.v.*] and the OAS successfully completed the task in September. Although he argued that the U.S. would have worked through the OAS "had no lives been in danger," Mann was heavily criticized in the press and left the government in April 1966. After spending some time as a visiting lecturer, he became president of the Automobile Manufacturers Association in 1967.

[JCH]

MANSFIELD, MIKE (MICHAEL) (JOSEPH)

b. March 16, 1903; New York, N.Y.
Democratic Senator, Mont., 1953-77;
Senate Majority Leader, 1961-77.

After his mother died, Mansfield was sent at the age of three to live with relatives in Montana. He served successively in the Army, Navy and Marines from 1918 to 1922, and for the next eight years worked as a miner and mining engineer in Montana. Mansfield received Bachelor and Master of Arts degrees from Montana State University in 1933 and 1934. He remained there to teach Latin American and Far Eastern history.

Mansfield lost a Democratic congressional primary in 1940 but won a seat in the U.S. House of Representatives two years later. With his academic background in foreign affairs, the freshman Congressman was assigned to the Foreign Relations Committee.

In 1952 Mansfield entered the Senate by defeating an incombent Republican senator and was assigned a seat on the Senate Foreign Relations Committee the following year. In 1957 the Senate majority leader, Lyndon B. Johnson, chose Mansfield as his assistant, or whip. Johnson reportedly chose Mansfield because the latter was a political moderate and ununassertive man unlikely to challenge his authority. In January 1961 Johnson assumed the vice presidency, and the Senate Democratic Caucus chose Mansfield to succeed him. During the early 1960s observers credited Mansfield with helping to secure Senate passage of the controversial aid-to-education bill of 1961 and the mass transit and area redevelopment bills of 1963, all of which were blocked in the House. [See EISENHOWER, KENNEDY Volumes]

The position of majority leader, although unrecognized by either the Constitution or the Senate rules, gave its occupant great potential power. By tradition he had nearly total control over the scheduling of bills and considerable influence over committee appointments and policy through the chairmanship of his party's steering and policy committees and of the full party conference. Johnson, a forceful and dominant leader, used all of the powers at his disposal to shape legislation and control the votes of his Democratic colleagues. He served as floor manager for almost every major bill and as the Democrats' chief strategist, parliamentarian and whip when majority leader.

Mansfield had a different concept of the role of the majority leader. Under the Democratic Administrations of Presidents Kennedy and Johnson, the Montana Senator shared with the White House the function of directing the Senate majority. His role was especially diminished under President Johnson, who employed his Senate experience and his extensive network of Senate connections to guide Administration bills through the upper house. Furthermore, Mansfield had a mild-mannered and scholarly disposition, preferring to win votes by the use of persuasion rather than cajolery and threats, which were often Johnson's most effective techniques. Unlike Johnson, Mansfield shared his power. He left the arrangement of deals and the employment of pressure to his whips, Sens. Hubert H. Humphrey (D, Minn.) [*q.v.*] and Russell B. Long (D, La.) [*q.v.*]. He allowed committee chairmen to act as floor managers of their own bills. Mansfield also generally avoided intricate parliamentary maneuvering and long sessions to enforce his will.

A number of Democrats regarded Mansfield as an indecisive and ineffective leader. Liberal Democratic senators criticized him for working too closely with minority leader Sen. Everett M. Dirksen (R, Ill.) [*q.v.*]. One such instance occurred in May 1964 when Mansfield and Dirksen introduced modifying amendments to the Administration's civil rights bill. However, it was widely acknowledged that in this and other instances, liberal measures could not have been passed over Southern opposition without amendments to draw Republican support. His critics also cited Mansfield's opposition to the addition of an open housing amendment to a 1968 bill protecting civil rights workers on the grounds that the amendment would drag the bill down to defeat. In this case his caution seemed excessive when the measure passed both houses with the housing proviso intact.

As a member of the Foreign Relations Committee, Mansfield was a mild critic of the Administration's Indochina policies. In January 1966, after returning from a fact-finding mission to Vietnam, Mansfield took the position that a military victory in the foreseeable future was highly unlikely, and in April he called for intensified American efforts towards a negotiated settlement. Later in the year he suggested U.S.-Chinese talks and a meeting between President Johnson and French President Charles de Gaulle to discuss possible approaches to peace. In October 1967 Mansfield offered a Senate resolution urging the President to bring the matter before the U.N. Security Council. The Administration subsequently endorsed the resolution.

After the Republicans gained control of the White House, Mansfield was somewhat more assertive. In 1971 he pushed through the Democratic Policy Committee a resolution calling for an end to American military involvement in Indochina. During the early 1970s Mansfield also called upon the Senate to play a more active role in the formulation of foreign policy. In March 1976 Mansfield announced that he would not seek reelection that year. [See NIXON Volume]

[MLL]

MARCUSE, HERBERT

b. July 19, 1898; Berlin, Germany
Philosopher, social critic.

Marcuse was born into a family of prosperous, assimilated Berlin Jews. After completing his military service in World War I, he briefly became involved in politics in a soldiers' council in Berlin during the revolutionary ferment of late 1918. In 1919 he quit the Social Democratic Party, which he had joined two years earlier, in protest against its role in the suppression of the revolutionary Berlin uprising in January. Shortly afterwards he abandoned politics altogether to study philosophy at the University of Berlin and the University of Freiburg, from which he received his doctorate in 1923. When the Nazis came to power in 1933, Marcuse left Germany for Switzerland and taught at Geneva for a year. In 1934 he came to the U.S. and took a post as lecturer at Columbia University. There he was a colleague of the German neo-Marxist sociologists Max Horkheimer and Theodore W. Adorno at the Institute of Social Research, which they had moved from Frankfurt in 1933.

During World War II Marcuse served under a fellow-refugee, the sociologist Franz Neumann, as a European intelligence analyst with the Office of Strategic Services (OSS). After the war, when the OSS's interest shifted from Germany to the Soviet Union and its name was changed to the Office of Intelligence Research, Marcuse became chief of the Eastern European section. After establishing a reputation in this office as an expert on Soviet affairs, he became a research fellow at the Russian Institute at Columbia in 1951. In the following year he lectured at the Russian Research Center at Harvard. From 1954 to 1967 Marcuse taught at Brandeis University, and in 1967 he became a professor of philosophy at the University of California's San Diego campus.

Marcuse's first book in English was *Reason and Revolution* (1941), an interpretation of Hegel and Marx. Marcuse sought to refute the charge that Hegelian philosophy had helped pave the way for the rise of Nazism in Germany. He identified the fundamental antithesis in modern thought as one between Marx and Hegel, on the one hand, and the tradition of positivism on the other. In *Eros and Civilization* (1955) Marcuse attempted a synthesis of Marx and Freud. Assuming, from a Marxist standpoint, that under capitalism men were dominated and exploited not only by external oppressors but also by forms of consciousness that prevented them from liberating themselves, he turned to Freud for the social psychology he found lacking in Marxism. Marcuse argued that Freud had been correct only up to a point in his account of the history of civilization; while pre-modern history required social domination and instinctual repression in order to remove scarcity and lay the technological foundations for abundance, Marcuse insisted that advanced industrial societies now demanded more repression of sexual energies than was necessary. Human liberation required that sexuality be freed from what Marcuse called false renunciation and asceticism. In *Soviet Marxism* (1958) he applied much of this critique to the new system of authority created by Joseph Stalin and his heirs.

One-Dimensional Man (1964) was Marcuse's most influential work, and it contained his fullest critique of industrial society. In contrast to the utopianism considered possible in *Eros and Civilization*, it was permeated with a pessimistic fear that the "power of negative thinking," which Marcuse considered the sole source of creativity in social life, was threatened with oblivion. His thesis was that the technology of modern industrial societies had enabled them to eliminate conflict by assimilating the forces of dissent. Marcuse attributed this, in part, to affluence, which by satisfying human needs removed the reasons for protest and fostered identification with the established order. Ironically, in claiming that conflict had basically disappeared, Marcuse accepted the central argument of Daniel Bell and other theorists of pluralism and consensus. Like them he assumed that affluence and the institutions of the welfare state had domesticated the working classes and made the Marxist doctrine of class struggle inapplicable to industrialized societies. Despite his rejection of classical Marxism, Marcuse thought that revolutionary protest was now in the hands of "the substratum of outcasts and outsiders, the exploited and persecuted of other races and other colors, the unemployed and unemployable."

Eros and Civilization and *One-Dimensional Man* were widely read by New Leftists in the 1960s. On a lecture tour of European countries in early 1968 Marcuse met with Rudi Dutschke, the leader of a student uprising at the University of Berlin. Later in the spring of that year Dutschke's name was prominently identified with the university rebellions in Paris, Rome and New York. A rumor that Marcuse planned to bring Dutschke to San Diego as his graduate student brought a demand for his removal from a local newspaper. The University's faculty and administration came to Marcuse's defense, however, and he was retained.

The wave of international student protest in the late 1960s led Marcuse to revise his pessimistic perspective in *An Essay on Liberation* (1969). He now argued for the existence of revolutionary minorities capable of redeeming industrial civilization. These he identified as the student movement in the U.S., the black population of the American urban slums, the Chinese cultural revolution and the Castro regime in Cuba. In an earlier essay, "Repressive Tolerance" published in *A Critique of Pure Tolerance* (1967), Marcuse granted these revolutionary minorities the right to withdraw "toleration of speech and assembly from groups and movements which promote aggressive policies, armament, chauvinism, racial and religious discrimination or which oppose the extension of public services." Marcuse later said that he "would restrict expression only in the case of movements which are definitely aggressive and destructive." Despite his support for the student left, Marcuse insisted that he had "never advocated destroying the existing universities," which he said he regarded as in many cases "still enclaves of relatively critical thought and relatively free thought."

[TLH]

For further information:
Alastair MacIntyre, *Herbert Marcuse: An Exposition and a Polemic* (New York, 1970).
"Herbert Marcuse," *Current Biography Yearbook, 1969* (New York, 1970), pp. 282-284.

MARKS, LEONARD C(HARLES)

b. March 5, 1916; Pittsburgh, Pa.
Director, U.S. Information Agency, July 1965-October 1968.

Leonard C. Marks, a graduate of the University of Pittsburgh Law School, taught law there for four years. In 1942 he went to Washington to serve with the Office of Price Administration and subsequently with the Federal Communications Commission. In 1946 he established a law partnership with Marcus Cohn. The two men specialized in communication law, and among the many radio and television stations they represented were those owned by Lady Bird Johnson [*q.v.*]. In the fall of 1962 President Kennedy appointed Marks to a 13-member panel to establish and incorporate the Communications Satellite Corporation (COMSAT). He was elected to the board of directors of COMSAT in 1964.

Marks, an old friend of President Johnson's, served as the treasurer of the Johnson-for-President Committee in 1964. In July 1965 the President named him to succeed Carl T. Rowan as the director of the United States Information Agency (USIA). Rowan had resigned during a controversy over whether the Agency's radio network, Voice of America should present objective news reports and air the views of dissenters or serve as a propaganda vehicle and transmit only official viewpoints. At his confirmation hearing before the Senate Foreign Relations Committee, Marks avoided taking a position on this matter by asserting that the use of propaganda was not necessary for presenting the American way of life. Confirmed on July 21, 1965, he assumed control of a 12,000-person Agency established in 1953 "to help achieve U.S. foreign policy objectives by influencing public attitudes in other nations. . . ."

One of Marks's major objectives was the expansion of USIA activities in Southeast Asia, where American military involvement was rapidly escalating. In September 1965 he asked a group of news executives, including CBS President Frank Stanton, to go to Saigon to study the USIA program in Vietnam. The following month he requested an additional $13 million for the Agency's work in Indochina. More than half of the funds were to be used for building a powerful transmitter in Thailand, a project that Congress approved in 1967.

Meanwhile, the USIA's programs in Europe were being cut back, and the closing of the Agency's London library in December 1965 aroused considerable opposition in America. In March 1966 the United States Advisory Commission on Information, establish by law to counsel the USIA, issued a report criticizing the cutbacks. Marks promised that there would be no further library closings in Europe and pledged to try to bolster the USIA's efforts there.

Marks served as an adviser to the President and Defense Department on the Vietnam pacification programs in 1966. Early in 1967 he proposed to Secretary of State Dean Rusk [*q.v.*] an extension of the Tet suspension of the bombing of North Vietnam "in 12 or 24-hour periods" contingent upon, among other things, a halt to infiltration from the North.

In October 1968 Marks announced his resignation from the USIA to head a conference on the use of satellites for international communications. He later returned to his law practice in Washington.

[JLW]

MARSHALL, BURKE

b. Oct. 1, 1922; Plainfield, N.J.
U.S. Assistant Attorney General in charge of the Civil Rights Division, February 1961-December 1964; Chairman, National Advisory Commission on Selective Service, July 1966-March 1967.

A graduate of Yale University in 1943 and of Yale Law School in 1951, Marshall was a member of the Washington law firm of Covington and Burling in the 1950s, where he specialized in antitrust litigation. He was named assistant attorney general in charge of the Justice Department's Civil Rights Division in February 1961, and he played a key role in the development of the Kennedy Administration's civil rights policies. Marshall also significantly increased the number of voting discrimination suits brought by the Justice Department. A quiet, cool and skillful negotiator, he had a major part in the federal government's handling of racial crises such as the 1961 Freedom Rides and the spring 1963 Birmingham, Ala., demonstrations. When the Justice Department met strong criticism for not doing more to protect civil rights workers in the South, Marshall answered the charges by insisting that the Constitution did not give the federal government the authority to act against all assaults on civil rights workers. [See KENNEDY Volume]

Marshall also helped draft the Kennedy civil rights bill submitted to Congress in June 1963 and negotiated with members of Congress on a compromise measure in October 1963. He worked for passage of the measure, which was signed into law on July 4, 1964, and then oversaw the Justice Department's efforts to ensure enforcement of the statute.

Marshall resigned his post on Dec. 18, 1964, saying it "would not be wise" for the same person to have his job for more than one presidential term. He then spent several months aiding Vice President Hubert H. Humphrey [*q.v.*] in his capacity as coordinator of the federal government's policies and programs in civil rights. Although he formally returned to private law practice in January 1965, Marshall joined top Justice Department officials in March of that year to oversee the federal government's activities during the protest march from Selma to Montgomery, Ala., led by Martin Luther King [*q.v.*]. In February 1966 Marshall was appointed to a 28-member presidential council that prepared a special report and recommendations for the June 1966 White House Conference on Civil Rights.

President Johnson named Marshall chairman of a National Advisory Commission on Selective Service in July 1966. Ordered to make a broad study of the draft, the Commission issued a report on March 4, 1967 that found that the existing Selective Service system resulted in many inequities. The panel called for changes in the draft, including call-ups by an impartial and random process and the replacement of local draft boards with some 500 area centers, which would apply uniform classification standards. The report was one basis for Johnson's March 1967 proposals for reform of the Selective Service system.

In June 1965 Marshall joined the International Business Machines Corp. (IBM) as vice president and general counsel. He was named a senior vice president in 1969.

[CAB]

MARSHALL, THURGOOD

b. July 2, 1908; Baltimore, Md.
U.S. Circuit Judge, Second Circuit Court of Appeals, 1961-65; U.S. Solicitor General, 1965-67; Associate Justice, U.S. Supreme Court, 1967- .

A graduate of Lincoln University and Howard University Law School, Marshall joined the NAACP as assistant special counsel in 1936. He was named special counsel in 1938 and, in 1940, became director-counsel of the newly created NAACP Legal Defense and Educational Fund. During his 23 years as head of the NAACP's legal program, Marshall directed the series of cases against segregated education that culminated in the 1954 Supreme Court decision *Brown v. Board of Education.* He also won court victories in suits challenging segregated housing, transportation and recreational facilities and discrimination in voting and jury selection. [See TRUMAN, EISENHOWER Volumes]

Marshall was named to the U.S. Second Circuit Court of Appeals by President Kennedy in September 1961, but because of opposition from Southern Democratic senators, he was not confirmed until a year later. On the bench Marshall developed a reputation as a liberal jurist who curbed government authority when it infringed on individual liberties but gave the government broad powers in economic affairs. [See KENNEDY Volume]

President Johnson appointed Marshall U.S. Solicitor General in July 1965. The first black to serve in that post, Marshall's chief areas of concern were civil rights and eavesdropping by government agencies. He won Supreme Court approval of the 1965 Voting Rights Act, persuaded the Court to reinstate indictments in two cases against defendants charged with conspiracy to murder civil rights workers and joined in a suit that successfully overturned a California constitutional amendment prohibiting open housing legislation. Convinced that all electronic eavesdropping that involved an illegal trespass was unconstitutional, Marshall voluntarily informed the Supreme Court in two cases that the government had used electronic devices to collect information on suspects charged with violation of federal laws. He had no similar qualms about the use of government informers, however, and he successfully argued in the Supreme Court that the government's use of an informer did not invalidate the convictions of James Hoffa [*q.v.*] and three other Teamster union officials for jury tampering. Marshall argued 19 cases for the government before the Supreme Court, winning all but five.

On June 13, 1967 President Johnson nominated Marshall as an associate justice of the U.S. Supreme Court to fill the vacancy created by the retirement of Justice Tom C. Clark [*q.v.*]. Once again Marshall was the first black appointed to this position. In announcing Marshall's nomination Johnson declared that this was "the right thing to do, the right time to do it, the right man and the right place." The Senate confirmed the nomination on Aug. 30 by a 69-11 vote, with all of the opposition coming from Southern senators. Sworn in on Oct. 2, Marshall joined the Court's liberal bloc. Legal scholars rated his performance on the Court as average and noted that Marshall's best writing was in the area of his greatest expertise and concern: equal protection, due process and the First Amendment.

Marshall was not actively engaged in the civil rights movement after 1961 because of the government positions he held, but his career exemplified that segment of the movement that relied primarily on the judicial process to win political and social advancement for blacks. In a May 1969 speech at Dillard University in New Orleans, Marshall criticized those blacks who advocated violence saying, "Anarchy is anarchy, and it makes no difference who practices it, it is bad; it is punishable, and it should be punished." Younger black militants, in turn, criticized Marshall's and the NAACP's legal approach during the 1960s as ineffective "gradualism." However, Marshall remained a symbol of black achievement for his work in the NAACP and for the recognition he won in his various federal appointments. [See NIXON Volume]

[CAB]

For further information:
Randall W. Bland, *Private Pressure on Public Law: The Legal Career of Justice Thurgood Marshall* (Port Washington, 1973).

MARTIN, GRAHAM A(NDERSON)

b. Sept. 22, 1912; Mars Hill, N.C.
Ambassador to Thailand, July 1963-July 1967; Special Assistant to the Secretary of State for Refugee and Migration Affairs, July 1967-September 1969.

A newspaper reporter and aide to the administrators of several New Deal social agencies before the war, Martin joined the foreign service in 1947. During the postwar period he served in various economic missions and was deputy U.S. coordinator for the Alliance for Progress from 1962 to 1963.

President Kennedy appointed him ambassador to Thailand in July 1963.

Martin became ambassador during the period when Communist guerrilla attacks were increasing in Thailand and threatening to extend the Indochina war to that country. Convinced that the lack of adequate early American aid had led to a full-scale war in Vietnam, Martin was instrumental in securing and increasing U.S. military and civilian assistance to Thailand in 1964 and 1965. In January 1966, when armed insurgency increased, Martin convinced the Thai government to establish a counterinsurgency office and accept U.S. aid in setting up the program. Eager to start counteraction as quickly as possible, he initiated several pilot projects in separate areas in the hope that experimentation might uncover a successful method of defeating the guerrillas. People's Assistance teams, similar to those used in Vietnam, were started to improve villagers' welfare, demonstrate the government's interest and provide security. Other efforts were made to increase protection and collect intelligence.

In January 1967 Martin admitted that the U.S. was building large air bases in Thailand to supply its troops in Vietnam, a fact that had been known to many observers for over a year. Martin was replaced as ambassador to Thailand by Leonard Unger in July 1967. He returned to Washington to become special assistant to the secretary of state for refugee and migration affairs. Martin served in that post until named ambassador to Italy in September 1969. In 1973 President Nixon appointed him ambassador to South Vietnam. He remained in Saigon until April 1975. [See NIXON Volume]

[EWS]

MARTIN, WILLIAM McCHESNEY

b. Dec. 17, 1906; St. Louis, Mo.
Chairman, Board of Governors of the Federal Reserve System, 1951-70.

Martin was the son of a banker who had aided in the drafting of the Federal Reserve Act of 1913 and had become president of the Federal Reserve Bank of St. Louis, Mo. The product of a strict Presbyterian background, he graduated from Yale in 1928. Martin spent a year as a clerk at the St. Louis Federal Reserve Bank and then left to become head of the statistical department of a St. Louis brokerage firm. In 1931 he acquired a seat on the New York Stock Exchange to become his firm's Wall Street representative. Martin became president of the Exchange in 1938 at the age of 31. While in the Army during World War II, he served in an important administrative position with the Munitions Allocation Board and supervised much of the Russian Lend-Lease.

President Truman made Martin a director of the Export-Import Bank in 1945 and appointed him assistant secretary of the treasury in 1949. Two years later the President named him chairman of the Board of Governors of the Federal Reserve System. Independent of the national Administration, Martin and the Federal Reserve pursued a conservative course designed to halt the threat of inflation by keeping interest rates high. Martin eased monetary policy somewhat during the Kennedy Administration but still exerted a strong conservative pull on the course of economic policy. He generally supported Treasury Secretary C. Douglas Dillon [*q.v.*] in opposing the more liberal fiscal policies of Walter Heller [*q.v.*], chairman of the Council of Economic Advisers. In February 1963 President Kennedy appointed Martin to another four-year term as chairman of the Federal Reserve Board. [See TRUMAN, EISENHOWER, KENNEDY Volumes]

As chief custodian of the nation's money supply, Martin was a figure of great controversy throughout the 1950s and 1960s. Conservatives praised him as a symbol of financial integrity, while liberal Democrats castigated him for his "tight money" policies. During the Johnson Administration he let interest rates soar to the highest levels since the 1920s in an effort to curb the inflation fueled by a booming economy and Vietnam war spending.

In the first year of the Johnson Administration, Martin reluctantly continued a relatively expansionary monetary policy in order to avoid undoing the stimulative effect of the $11.5 billion Kennedy-Johnson tax cut of 1964. Yet he was uncomfortable with the inflationary possibilities inherent in the economic boom of the mid-1960s. In June 1965 he gave a widely publicized speech in which he warned of "disquieting similarities between our present prosperity and the fabulous 20s." Martin drew a number of unsettling analogies between the contemporary boom and the prelude to the Great Depression: large increases in private and international debt, the "uneasy" balance of payments situations in the U.S. and Great Britain and the instability of the dollar, which he equated with the British pound before its devaluation in 1931. The "stable dollar," Martin said, was "the keystone of international trade and finance" and of "economic growth and prosperity at home." Martin's speech was followed by a sharp drop in prices on the New York Stock Exchange.

In December 1965 Martin cast the deciding vote in the Federal Reserve Board's four-to-three decision to raise the discount rate from 4% to 4.5%. The rate increase was made just as the first inflationary pressures were being felt from the escalation of the Vietnam war, but while the Johnson Administration was still forcasting only a limited rise in defense spending to pay for the conflict. Hence the change in monetary policy put Martin at the center of a major controversy. In raising its rate the Federal Reserve Board stated that the increase was made in order "to dampen mounting demands on banks for still further credit extensions that might add to inflationary pressures." Led by Martin, the Federal Reserve was strongly signaling the Johnson Administration and the business community its belief that the economy needed to be slowed down. Its action marked the first time in five years that the Federal Reserve Board had openly dissented from Kennedy-Johnson economic policy.

The discount rate increase generated much protest from the White House and from the Congress. The President expressed "regret" at "any action that raises the cost of credit, particularly for homes, schools, hospitals, and factories." He "particularly" regretted that the Board's action was not coordinated with Administration policy and was taken before "the full facts" of the budget for fiscal year 1967 had been made available. Taking issue with Johnson, Chamber of Commerce President Robert Gerholz said that the business community should be grateful to Martin "for acting to check a dangerous inflationary condition."

AFL-CIO President George Meany [*q.v.*] criticized the increase as "mistaken and costly" and suggested that presidential influence should be exerted to rescind it and that representation on the Federal Reserve Board should be broadened to include labor. Martin's most persistent adversary, Rep. Wright Patman (D, Tex.) [*q.v.*], denounced the move and called for Martin's resignation "to prevent the country from being thrown into economic chaos." Questioning Martin sharply at hearings before his Joint Economic Committee, Patman predicted that the rate rise would "destroy the savings and loan industry." During 1966 $2.4 billion was drained from savings and loan associations, which were forced to cut their mortgage lending by one-third. The result was a $6 billion decline in home building. Interest rates rose to the highest level since the 1920s.

Disturbed that monetary policy was being forced to battle inflation alone, Martin, in the spring of 1966, began urging a tax increase as the "logical way" to deal with inflation. He indicated that if a tax increase were not forthcoming, the Federal Reserve might have to take further action. Martin persisted in this exhortatory campaign for the next two years. When Johnson finally recommended a 10% tax surcharge in the summer of 1967, Martin advised the Administration that a tax increase was no longer sufficient and should be combined with substantial budget cuts as well. He issued ominous public warnings of the dangers if an anti-inflationary fiscal course were not followed. "The nation is in the midst of the worst financial crisis since 1931," Martin declared in April 1968. "We are faced with an intolerable budget deficit and also an intolerable deficit in our international balance of payments. Both have to be corrected over the next few years or the United States is going to face either an uncontrollable recession or an uncontrollable inflation." In June 1968 Congress passed the 10% surtax along with a $6 billion spending reduction.

Despite their differences, Johnson appointed Martin to another four-year term as chairman of the Federal Reserve Board in March 1967. At a time when the position of the dollar was deteriorating, the Administration needed Martin, the symbol of the sound dollar, to reassure the financial community. In December 1968 President-elect Richard M. Nixon asked Martin to remain in his post until his term expired on January 31, 1970. [See NIXON Volume]

[TO]

MATHIAS, CHARLES McC(URDY)
b. July 24, 1922; Frederick, Md.
Republican Representative, Md., 1961-69.

Elected to Congress from a traditionally Democratic Maryland district that voted for conservative Republicans on the national level, Mathias emerged as one of the Republican Party's more liberal spokesmen by the end of the decade. Prior to his election to the House in 1960, Mathias had been a practicing lawyer, city attorney and member of the Maryland House of Delegates. During his early years in Congress, Mathias voted against many of President Kennedy's domestic proposals, including housing subsidies, area redevelopment and aid to education. But in the mid-1960s he supported much of the Johnson Administration's social welfare program including medicare, aid for urban redevelopment, aid to education and antipoverty programs. [See KENNEDY Volume]

While in the House Mathias was primarily concerned with District of Columbia affairs and civil rights legislation. As a member of the District of Columbia Committee, Mathias introduced legislation in 1963 to give the District a non-voting delegate in the House as a step toward full voting representation. In 1965 he was one of four congressmen to sponsor a proposal for a territorial form of government for the District with an elected assembly and a presidentially appointed governor. The bill was defeated, and a weaker measure providing for the election of a charter-drafting committee and the popular ratification of the charter was passed by the House.

As a member of the Judiciary Committee, Mathias was one of the men who shaped the Civil Rights Act of 1964 and the Voting Rights Act of 1965. In 1966 the Congressman led the fight for a civil rights bill that included a ban on racial discrimination in the sale or rental of all housing. When intense opposition to the provision threatened to defeat the entire measure, Mathias sponsored a controversial compromise that exempted the sale of individual homes or small owner-occupied multiple dwellings from the law in an effort to save the entire proposal. The House passed the amended bill, but the Senate killed it by a filibuster in September.

In 1967 Mathias sponsored several major resolutions, including a proposal to create a select committee to watch over the standards and conduct of House members. He also called for disclosure and regulation of political spending. Concerned with protecting the privacy of citizens, Mathias opposed President Johnson's 1967 wiretap bill because of its lack of safeguards against abuses. That year he and seven other liberal Republican congressmen proposed a five-stage plan to end the bombing of North Vietnam in return for de-escalation by Hanoi. By the end of the decade Mathias had accumulated a 78 "correct" rating from the liberal Americans for Democratic Action; the conservative Americans for Constitutional Action gave him a correct rating of only 15.

In 1968 Mathias challenged incumbent Daniel Brewster (D, Md.) [*q.v.*] for election to the U.S. Senate. Supported by many unions and even by several state Democratic leaders, Mathias defeated his opponent by nearly 100,000 votes in November. In the Senate he supported many of President Nixon's domestic proposals but continued his opposition to delays in ending the Vietnam war and maintained his support for congressional reform. [See NIXON Volume]

[EWS]

MEANY, GEORGE
b. Aug. 16, 1894; New York, N.Y.
President, AFL-CIO, 1955- .

Meany, the son of an Irish-Catholic plumber, grew up in New York. He entered his father's trade after high school and gained his first full-time union post at 28 as business manager of a plumbers' local in New York. Meany gradually rose within both the Plumbers Union and the American Federation of Labor (AFL), a national organization dominated by craft unions. In 1940 he was chosen secretary-treasurer of the AFL, and 12 years later he succeeded William Green as the organization's president. Meany's first important act as the head of the AFL was to negotiate a merger with the Congress of Industrial Organizations (CIO), a smaller grouping of unions organized chiefly on an industry-wide basis. The merger took place in 1955, with Meany assuming the presidency of the united AFL-CIO; Walter Reuther [*q.v.*], head of the United Auto Workers union (UAW) and former CIO president, took control of the new Federation's Industrial Union Department. [See TRUMAN, EISENHOWER Volumes]

With 12.4 million members in 130 affiliated unions, the AFL-CIO included more than 90% of the nation's trade unionists at the time of its creation. Meany himself, blunt-spoken and cigar-smoking, became the Federation's chief policymaker on issues of both domestic and foreign politics. He was already known from his work in the AFL as a firm liberal and militant anti-Communist. He endorsed the social welfare legislation of the Kennedy Administration, but criticized President Kennedy—as he had President Eisenhower—for being "overly timid" in efforts to reduce unemployment. At the same time Meany gave unqualified support to anti-Communist initiatives in U.S. foreign policy. In 1962 the AFL-CIO created the American Institute for Free Labor Development (AIFLD), which provided money and training to Latin American union leaders who agreed to oppose Communist politicians. Funded largely by U.S. government agencies, the AIFLD became an important instrument of U.S. policy in Latin America. During the mid-1960s it trained insurgent union leaders who helped overthrow anti-American regimes in British Guiana and Brazil. [See KENNEDY Volume]

Meany's role within the AFL-CIO was limited by the organization's federal structure, which prevented him from influencing the bargaining strategies or strike decisions of member unions. His own concept of union integrity and independence made Meany a strong defender of union autonomy. Although he expelled the notoriously corrupt Teamsters union from the AFL-CIO in 1957, Meany generally referred complaints of union misdeeds to individual union leaders. Meany also resisted the demands of civil rights organizations that racial quotas be introduced in union apprenticeship programs to guarantee blacks a proportionate share of skilled jobs. The AFL-CIO leadership did support the Civil Rights Act of 1964, which banned discrimination in union locals and created a Fair Employment Practices Commission to investigate charges of bias. Yet Meany remained suspicious of activist civil rights groups and helped keep them at a distance from American labor. He repeatedly came into conflict with Herbert Hill [*q.v.*], labor secretary of the NAACP, who frequently charged AFL-CIO-affiliated union locals with excluding blacks and other minority group workers from their membership.

The mid-1960s were years of unusually close cooperation between U.S. labor and government, embodied in the friendship between Meany and Johnson. Relations between the two were not cordial from the start, however. Meany had bitterly opposed the choice of Johnson as vice president in 1960; he viewed the Texan's congressional voting record on labor issues as "horrible." Only Johnson's determined advocacy of Great Society programs beginning in 1964 changed Meany's opinion. The Civil Rights Act, the $11.5 billion tax cut of 1963-64 and the medicare plan of 1965 all had enthusiastic labor support. Meany also appreciated Johnson's willingness to approve an increase in the minimum wage in 1966, despite objections from the President's Council of Economic Advisers.

Another policy area where Johnson could count on Meany's complete approval was Vietnam. The growing conflict stimulated Meany's traditional anti-Communism, and he went on record repeatedly in support of "all measures the Administration deems necessary . . . to secure a just and lasting peace." In addition to policy statements, the AFL-CIO provided equipment and training for South Vietnamese trade union leaders and also helped solve logistical problems at U.S. supply bases. Labor support on Vietnam became increasingly important for Johnson as opposition to the war grew in 1967 and 1968. Meany denounced war critics as "kooks" and "jitterbugs," accepting Johnson's assurances that the Administration's war aims could be achieved without curtailment of the Great Society program. Opposition to the war among some union officials was easily put down at AFL-CIO conventions, which Meany controlled totally.

Labor's only legislative disappointment during the mid-1960s was its failure to gain repeal of Section 14(b) of the Taft-Hartley Act. This provision permitted states to pass "right-to-work" laws barring the closed union shop. Meany viewed elimination of 14(b) as "the number one legislative issue confronting the trade union movement," and Johnson promised to work for repeal in 1965. It soon became apparent, however, that the Administration was not willing to fight hard enough to overcome conservative resistance in Congress. According to his biographer, Joseph C. Goulden, Meany rejected the alternative of making a deal with Senate conservatives, who offered to accept repeal in exchange for labor support of a bill aimed at blocking congressional reapportionment. Although Meany vowed "never to quit" in his opposition to Section 14(b), the measure remained in effect, forcing unions to fight open-shop legislation in a number of states.

Disappointment over 14(b) did not make Meany regret his support of Johnson in the 1964 presidential race or deny his support to Johnson in 1968. Meany endorsed the President for reelection as early as February 1967, praising Great Society legislation as "a record unsurpassed in any period of democratic government." When Johnson announced his unexpected decision not to seek reelection in March 1968, Meany immediately turned to Vice President Hubert Humphrey [*q.v.*], political heir to both the Great Society and the Vietnam war. The AFL-CIO vigorously supported Humphrey's candidacy in 1968 through computer-designed voter registration campaigns in 16 states and the massive distribution of literature. Noting Humphrey's rapid rise in popularity during the last part of the campaign, Meany later claimed that "if we had had another week we might have elected Hubert Humphrey."

Meany faced difficulties during the late 1960s not only in domestic politics but also on the policymaking Executive Council of the AFL-CIO. His main problem there was a growing conflict with Walter Reuther [*q.v.*], head of the UAW and of the AFL-CIO Industrial Union Department. Reuther, more eloquent and outgoing than Meany, was his chief rival for leadership of the American union movement. As former leader of the CIO, he resented Meany's domination of the AFL-CIO's Executive Council. Reuther also clashed with Meany on a number of policy issues. Although opposed to the Communist system, he disliked Meany's militant anti-Communism, criticized U.S. policy in Vietnam and favored relaxation of East-West tensions. Reuther protested in 1966 when Meany withdrew U.S. representatives from the International Labor Organization, a United Nations affiliate, after a Polish union leader had been elected president of the agency.

Another point of conflict between Reuther and Meany involved the growth of the union movement. Many observers noted during the 1960s that American labor was "resting on dead center." The membership of AFL-CIO-affiliated unions stagnated until 1964; it subsequently increased (from 12.7 million in 1964 to 15 million in 1968), but only at a rate equal to the expansion of the work force. To stimulate union growth, Reuther repeatedly urged a large-scale organizing drive concentrating on farm laborers, white-collar employes and workers in economically depressed areas. Meany, reflecting the traditions of craft unionism, showed less interest in organizing workers outside the "mainstream" of American labor; during the mid-1960s he suspended aid to the AFL-CIO-affiliated United Farm Workers Organizing Committee of Cesar Chavez [*q.v.*]. Reuther objected to this fund cutoff and continued sending separate aid to Chavez through the UAW.

Relations between Meany and Reuther moved towards an open break in November 1966, when Reuther refused to attend a special Executive Council session to reaffirm the AFL-CIO stance in foreign affairs. Describing the Federation as "the comfortable complacent custodian of the status quo," Reuther ordered UAW officials to resign their AFL-CIO positions in February 1967. In early 1968 the UAW began to withhold its dues from the AFL-CIO. Meany suspended the 1.6-million-member union from the Federation on May 16, denouncing Reuther for failing to use the "democratic forums" the AFL-CIO provided for expression of dissent. Meany also criticized Reuther in September 1968 for joining Teamsters leader Frank Fitzsimmons [*q.v.*] to form the Alliance for Labor Action (ALA). Meany viewed the new organization as an attempt to "raid" the membership of AFL-CIO unions, and he expelled the Chemical Workers Union from the Federation when it joined the ALA in 1969.

With internal opposition largely eliminated from the AFL-CIO, Meany continued to control union policy during the early 1970s. The Federation remained a strong supporter of the Vietnam war under President Richard Nixon and withheld support from anti-war Sen. George McGovern (D, S.D.) [*q.v.*] in the 1972 presidential campaign. Meany initially cooperated in the Nixon Administration's economic program but left the President's Pay Board in 1972, rejecting what he viewed as an overly restrictive wage policy. [See NIXON Volume]

[SLG]

For further information:

Joseph C. Goulden, *Meany* (New York, 1972).

J. David Greenstone, *Labor in American Politics* (New York, 1969).

MEREDITH, JAMES H(OWARD)

b. June 25, 1933; Kosciusko, Miss.
Civil rights activist.

Meredith achieved fame in September 1962 as the first black to enter the University of Mississippi at Oxford. His admission came after 15 months of litigation in federal courts, and it touched off a confrontation between the federal government and state officials who tried to prevent the court-ordered desegregation of "Ole Miss." Mississippi's Gov. Ross Barnett ended his resistance to Meredith's admission on Sept. 30, 1962, but a riot erupted on the University campus that night and National Guard and Army units had to be brought in to quell it. Meredith registered at the University on Oct. 1, 1962 and had federal protection throughout his three terms there. He graduated with a B.A. in political science on Aug. 18, 1963. [See KENNEDY Volume]

Meredith left Mississippi following his graduation but returned briefly in June 1966 for a pilgrimage from Memphis, Tenn., to Jackson, Miss. Then a second-year student at Columbia University Law School, Meredith said on May 31 that his march was intended to encourage voter registration among Mississippi's blacks and to "challenge the all-pervasive and overriding fear that dominates the day-to-day life of the Negro in the United States—especially in the South and particularly in Mississippi." He began his walk on June 5 accompanied by a few friends. The next day, about 10 miles over the Mississippi border, Meredith was shot from ambush along U.S. Highway 51. He suffered over 60 superficial wounds in the head, back and legs and was taken to a Memphis hospital for emergency surgery. On June 7 civil rights leaders Martin Luther King [*q.v.*], Floyd McKissick [*q.v.*] and Stokely Carmichael [*q.v.*] retraced Meredith's route. On their return to Memphis that evening, they vowed to carry on his march all the way to Jackson. The march was resumed on June 8. During its three-week course divisions among the leadership became increasingly apparent. While King continued to speak of interracial cooperation and nonviolence, Carmichael raised the cry of black power and urged self-defense rather than nonviolence when attacked.

Meredith himself returned to New York City on June 8 to recuperate. There he occasionally expressed some criticism of the way the march was run, but he rejoined the march on June 24 at Canton, Miss., and spoke at a final rally in Jackson on June 26. By the end of the march, however, Meredith's original protest had been overshadowed by indications of a schism among the major civil rights leaders.

Meredith, who was considered a loner and an individualist within the civil rights movement, expressed support for Carmichael and the black power concept in a television interview in August 1966. He asserted that America was "a military-minded nation" and that nonviolence was "incompatible with American ideas." In the same interview Meredith said he "fully" supported the war in Vietnam and considered it "one of the best things happening to the Negro."

After Harlem Congressman Adam Clayton Powell (D, N.Y.) [*q.v.*] was excluded from the House of Representatives on March 1, 1967, Meredith announced that he would run on the Republican ticket in a special election for Powell's seat scheduled for April. Meredith said he was acting in accordance with his "divine responsibility," but local black leaders almost unanimously opposed his candidacy. On March 13, after meeting with Floyd McKissick of the Congress of Racial Equality and Mississippi rights leader Charles Evers [*q.v.*], Meredith withdrew from the race. He went back to Mississippi on June 24, 1967 to complete the march against fear he had initiated the year before. Meredith walked from the place where he had been shot to Canton, Miss., the town where he had rejoined the 1966 march.

Following his graduation from law school, Meredith became a businessman in New York City. In July 1969 he staged a walk from Chicago to New York to "promote Negro pride and positive goals in the black community." Meredith announced in June 1971 that he was moving back to Mississippi. He said that the racial atmosphere in the South had improved greatly and that on a "day-to-day basis," it was a "more liveable place for blacks." In February 1972 he entered the race for the Republican Senate nomination in Mississippi but lost in the July primary election.

[CAB]

METCALF, LEE

b. Jan. 28, 1911; Stevensville, Mont.
Democratic Senator, Mont., 1961- .

Prior to his election to the Senate in 1960, Metcalf had served as a state legislator and associate justice of the Montana Supreme Court. From 1953 to 1961 he represented Montana in the House of Representatives, where he was a major supporter of conservation measures. In the lower house Metcalf earned a reputation as one of Congress's "young Turks," a group of liberals pushing for progressive social legislation and reform of congressional procedures. While in the Senate Metcalf supported most Kennedy and Johnson Administration domestic programs. [See EISENHOWER, KENNEDY Volumes]

During the 1960s the Senator focused his attention on three major areas: education, the regulation of power companies and conservation. In 1965 Metcalf steered the Elementary and Secondary Education Act, which gave aid to impoverished inner city and rural schools, through the Senate. A year later he led efforts to extend G.I. Bill educational benefits to recent veterans and to improve vocational training programs.

Metcalf had long been an opponent of private utility companies because he believed they used excessive profits to subsidize conservative political activity and propaganda favorable to the industry. In 1967 he published a detailed examination of the industry. In his study the Senator scored state regulation of the companies as a failure because the government did not have the resources to discipline the utilities. The following year Metcalf unsuccessfully introduced a bill to set up an office of consumers' counsel to represent the public before regulatory commissions.

In the field of conservation Metcalf unsuccessfully introduced the 1962 "save our streams" bill to protect recreational resources from destruction by federal highway development and sponsored the Senate version of the Wilderness Act, which led to the establishment of the National Wilderness Preservation System in 1964. One year later he worked for the passage of the Water Systems Act, which increased expenditures for watershed restoration.

During 1965 and 1966 Metcalf served on the Joint Committee on the Organization of Congress. The Committee report, issued in July 1966, recommended a series of steps designed to reform and modernize the legislature. These included: curtailing the power of committee chairmen; creating new committees to reflect growing public concerns; opening committee sessions to the public; and decreasing the workloads of individual senators. No action was taken on these measures in 1966.

During the late 1960s and early 1970s, Metcalf continued to be a strong supporter of conservation and consumer legislation. In addition, he campaigned for reassertion of congressional authority over spending as a way of curbing excessive presidential power. [See NIXON Volume]

[EWS]

MILLER, GEORGE P(AUL)

b. Jan. 15, 1891; San Francisco, Calif.
Democratic Representative, Calif., 1945-73; Chairman, Science and Astronautic Committee, 1961-73.

Miller represented California's eighth district, which included southern Oakland, several of the city's suburbs and part of rural Alameda county. Most of the district's voters belonged to white blue-collar families. In the 1940s, 1950s and early 1960s, he compiled a moderately liberal voting record. Interested in scientific matters, Miller was chairman of the House Merchant Marine and Fisheries Committee's Subcommittee on Oceanography in the late 1950s. In 1961 he became chairman of the House Science and Astronautics Committee. In the latter post he enthusiastically supported the Kennedy Administration's space program. [See KENNEDY Volume]

During the presidency of Lyndon B. Johnson, Miller generally backed Administration policies. According to *Congressional Quarterly,* he never opposed the Administration position on more than 5% of the key House roll call votes in any of the years of President Johnson's tenure. His support of the President's policies included approval of the conduct of the Vietnam war and of large military expenditures.

Miller continued to endorse large appropriations for the National Aeronautics and Space Administration during the Johnson Administration. In 1967 the President awarded him the Goddard Prize for his contributions in the space field. Miller was also a staunch supporter of federal grants for scientific research. He was appointed to the House Select Committee on Government Research in September 1963. Early in the following year he stated that the panel's preliminary report of February 1964 did not give sufficient recognition to the important contributions of federally supported research programs in improving the quality of American life in the areas of transportation, medicine, energy production and communications.

In the late 1960s and early 1970s, Miller's views remained substantially unchanged, when many liberals were becoming increasingly disenchanted with the Vietnam war, large military budgets, unrestricted technological growth and the space program. As a result Miller lost the 1972 Democratic primary in his district to a candidate who articulated this trend. [See NIXON Volume]

[NLL]

MILLER, JACK (RICHARD)

b. June 6, 1916; Chicago, Ill.
Republican Senator, Iowa, 1961-73.

Jack Miller and his family moved to Sioux City, Iowa in 1932. He received his A.B. from Creighton University and his LL.B. from Columbia. Miller served as an instructor in the Air Force during World War II. Returning to Iowa, Miller practiced law in Sioux City and intermittently lectured on taxation law. Although largely unknown in the state despite six years in the Iowa Senate, Miller won the 1960 GOP senatorial nomination. With just under 52% of the vote, he narrowly upset Democratic Gov. Herschel Loveless, a victim of John Kennedy's poor showing in Iowa. Miller easily won reelection in 1966, carrying every county.

In the Senate Miller was a moderate conservative, voting with the majority of his Republican Senate colleagues on almost every issue. Like them he voted for the 1963 nuclear test ban treaty and the 1964 and 1965 civil rights acts. He opposed medicare legislation in 1962, 1964 and 1965 and the 1968 Civil Rights Act. The conservative Americans for Constitutional Action gave Miller a "correct" rating of 78 for his Senate votes during the 1960s. Miller's predictability and unexciting personality led journalists David Broder and Stephen Hess to describe him as "a most anonymous Senator from Iowa."

Miller gained notoriety in the Senate for his submissions of last-minute amendments to bills without regard to the legislative strategy of the Party hierarchy. This tactic annoyed Minority Leader Everett M. Dirksen (R, Ill.) [*q.v.*], while Sen. Thruston B. Morton (R, Ky.) [*q.v.*] dubbed him "Jack-the-Amendment" Miller. Many Senate observers felt that Miller used amendments to make his position on many issues ambiguous, developing over the years "a voting record which can be used to prove almost anything." Miller himself viewed his position as "conservative in monetary and fiscal affairs" and "liberal in the areas of education and human rights." During the Senate voting on the committee investigation of former Secretary to the Senate Majority Bobby Baker [*q.v.*] in April and September 1964, Miller offered amendments (later defeated) that explicitly called for an inquiry into President Johnson's alleged involvement.

In August 1964 and June 1965 Miller introduced provisions to the annual foreign aid bill that would have denied all U.S. assistance to United Nations-member states failing to pay their U.N. dues and assessments. About 96% of the nations receiving U.S. aid, Miller claimed in July 1966, would be affected by his legislation. That month the Senate finally agreed to a version of the Miller ban giving the President the right to waive the provision in the "national interest."

A September 1965 Miller proposal would have reversed the Democratic leadership's plan to weaken the stringent 1952 McCarran Immigration Restriction Act. By voice vote the Senate rejected Miller's amendment to set a 290,000-person annual quota or entry limit. Miller eventually voted for the final, more liberal legislation, which eliminated most ethnic and racial quotas.

A member of the Armed Services Committee, Miller consistently backed a vigorous military policy in the Vietnam war. In September 1967 he told reporters that if an intensified bombing of North Vietnam "might shorten the war, even by one day, then we ought to take the risks." Later that month he and three other GOP Senate "hawks" criticized Sen. John Sherman Cooper (R, Ky.) [*q.v.*], the senior Republican on the Foreign Relations Committee, for favoring a halt to the bombing as a signal of America's willingness to negotiate. Similarly, near the end of the North Vietnamese Tet offensive in February 1968, when some Party colleagues began to back away from their earlier support of the war, Miller recommended expanded bombing of the North.

At the August 1968 Republican National Convention, Miller strongly opposed the designation of Gov. Spiro T. Agnew [*q.v.*] for vice president. Judging Agnew an obscure and weak addition to the national ticket, Miller and an unusual alliance of liberal and conservative Party figures urged New York City Mayor John V. Lindsay [*q.v.*] to run against the Maryland Governor. Lindsay refused, and the anti-Agnew coalition nominated Michigan Gov. George W. Romney [*q.v.*], who lost by a wide margin.

Between 1969 and 1972 Miller steadfastly supported the incumbent Republican administration. Up for reelection in 1972, Miller underrated his opposition, congressional aide Dick Clark, and lost, with only 43% of the vote, in a stunning upset. [See NIXON Volume] [JLB]

MILLER, WILLIAM E(DWARD)
b. March 22, 1914; Lockport, N.Y.
Republican Representative, N.Y., 1951-65; Chairman, Republican National Committee, June 1961-July 1964; Republican vice presidential candidate, 1964.

The son of a janitor, William E. Miller received a B.A. from Notre Dame in 1935 and a LL.B. with honors from Union University Law School in 1938. During World War II Miller served with Army Intelligence and in 1946 was an assistant prosecutor at the Nuremberg war crimes trials. In 1950 Miller won election to the first of seven consecutive terms in the House of Representatives. As chairman of the Republican Congressional Campaign Committee in 1960, Miller campaigned personally in 34 states. In November the GOP gained 22 seats. Miller received substantial credit for the Party's success, and in June 1961 he was elected chairman of the Republican National Committee. In the next three years, Miller gave over 500 sharply partisan speeches in 49 states. Under his leadership the National Committee eliminated a $750,000 debt and appropriated funds for "Operation Dixie," designed to make the Republicans more competitive in Southern elections. In the 1962 elections, however, the GOP gained only six seats in the House and lost four in the Senate. Republicans replaced Democratic governors in Ohio, Pennsylvania and Michigan, but losses in other states kept the number of GOP governors limited to 16. [See KENNEDY Volume]

Although the second-ranking Republican on the House Judiciary Committee, Miller played a limited role in Congress. Voting on only 33% of the roll call votes in 1964 and 41% in the 88th Congress, Miller held the lowest voting participation record of New York's 41-member delegation. A partisan congressman, Miller supported the Kennedy and Johnson Administrations on only 15% of the votes for which the White House announced a position in 1963-64. However, with the majority of his Party colleagues in the House, Miller voted for the Administration's civil rights bill in February 1964.

Miller remained neutral through the bitter struggle for the 1964 Republican presidential nomination. In January 1964 he announced that he would not seek reelection to Congress in November and would step down as Party chairman following the Republican National Convention in July. F. Clifton White [*q.v.*], a key lieutenant in the campaign of Sen. Barry M. Goldwater (R, Ariz.) [*q.v.*], claimed that Miller tended to favor the anti-Goldwater forces. Following Goldwater's victory in the June 2 California primary, however, Miller urged all Party leaders to unite behind the Arizona Senator and avoid a potentially divisive effort to deny him the nomination. Pennsylvania Gov. William W. Scranton [*q.v.*], Goldwater's tentative choice for a running mate, declined to follow Miller's advice and waged a desperate month-long campaign for the nomination. Scranton's unsuccessful effort eliminated him from consideration by Goldwater for the vice presidential nomination.

Following his nomination on July 15, Goldwater chose Miller as his vice presidential candidate, and the Republican Convention nominated the New Yorker the next day. In naming Miller, Goldwater hoped to aid his campaign in the South and among Catholic voters. Because of his advocacy of Operation Dixie while Party chairman, Miller enjoyed the support of Southern delegates. Since Miller was a Roman Catholic, Goldwater believed that Johnson would feel compelled to choose Attorney General Robert F. Kennedy [*q.v.*], a Catholic, as his running mate to prevent defections by Catholic voters to the GOP. Because of the unpopularity of Kennedy's leadership of the Justice Department among many Southerners, Goldwater thought that Kennedy's position on the ticket would increase his base of Southern support. Johnson briefly considered choosing Kennedy or Sen. Eugene J. McCarthy (D, Minn.) [*q.v.*], also a Catholic, following Miller's nomination, but when polls indicated that the President would overwhelmingly defeat the Goldwater ticket despite Miller's religion, he selected Sen.

Hubert H. Humphrey (D, Minn.) [*q.v.*] instead.

Although well-known among Party professionals, Miller never overcame his lack of national recognition. His nomination represented another opportunity lost by Goldwater to placate bitter Party liberals and moderates, for Miller held nearly as conservative a voting record as the Arizona Senator. The presidential nominee justified his selection by saying that Miller's partisanship "drives Johnson nuts." Because of his running mate's qualities as a "gut fighter," Goldwater reportedly believed he, himself could campaign on a more statesmanlike level.

Miller campaigned in 40 states and traveled over 40,000 miles for the national ticket. In August he attacked Johnson for his ownership of an Austin, Tex., radio-television station and alleged that the President had made more than $10 million as a result of favorable treatment by federal regulators when Johnson served in the Senate. The same month Miller criticized Johnson's brief military service during World War II. The Goldwater staff mildly rebuked him because of its fear that such attacks would provoke sympathy for the President. Undaunted, Miller turned his attention to Humphrey in September, describing his Senate record as "clearly one of the most radical in Congress." He denounced Humphrey's close ties with the liberal Americans for Democratic Action, which he declared "preaches a philosophy of foreign socialistic totalitarianism." When Washington police in October arrested White House aide Walter W. Jenkins [*q.v.*] on a morals charge, Miller derided the White House contention that "this type of man" did not "compromise national security."

Miller faced charges of conflict of interest in late September when columnist Drew Pearson alleged that as a congressman in 1951 or 1952 Miller had offered then Rep. Frank Smith (D, Miss.) $350 to $500 a month as a public relations consultant for Lockport Felt Company if he voted for legislation favored by that upstate New York company. Miller owned a part of Lockport Felt and received an annual retainer of $7,500 from the company. He denied any wrong-doing and accused his Democratic detractors of "Gestapo tactics" and "sleazy, unsubstantiated smears." On Oct. 1 Rep. W. Don Edwards (D, Calif.) [*q.v.*] demanded a House investigation, but the Democratic leadership declined to pursue the charge. Edwards and others also critiziced Miller for keeping one of his Buffalo, N.Y., law partners on his congressional payroll.

On Nov. 3, 1964 Goldwater and Miller polled but 38.4% of the vote and carried only five Southern states and Arizona. Two weeks after the election, Miller became a vice president of Lockport Felt. In 1968 he helped plan the campaign of Gov. Nelson A. Rockefeller (R, N.Y.) [*q.v.*] for the Republican presidential nomination, and he seconded Rockefeller's name at the August 1968 Republican National Convention. He opposed the nomination of Gov. Spiro T. Agnew (R, Md.) [*q.v.*] for vice president. In 1974 Miller emerged from near-obscurity to appear in television commercials for the American Express Credit Card Company.

[JLB]

For further information:
F. Clifton White, *Suite 3505: The Story of the Draft Goldwater Movement* (New Rochelle, 1967).
Theodore White, *The Making of the President, 1964* (New York, 1965).

MILLS, WILBUR D(AIGH)

b. May 24, 1909; Kensett, Ark.
Democratic Representative, Ark., 1939- ; Chairman, Ways and Means Committee, 1957-74.

The son of a country banker, Mills attended Arkansas public schools and Methodist-affiliated Hendrix College before entering Harvard Law School in 1930. He returned to Arkansas without receiving a degree in 1933, taking a job as a cashier in his father's bank. In 1934 he was elected county and probate judge for White County and remained in that post until his election to the House of Representatives in 1938.

Mills was reelected in every subsequent election with little or no opposition.

Joining the tax-writing Ways and Means Committee in 1934, Mills industriously applied himself to his work, becoming by the 1950s the House's foremost tax expert. He compiled a moderate voting record and joined his Southern colleagues in voting against all civil rights proposals. In late 1957 Mills became chairman of the Ways and Means Committee; he was the youngest man ever to hold that post. [See TRUMAN, EISENHOWER, KENNEDY Volumes]

The peculiar structure of the Ways and Means Committee and the Committee's prestige and unique prerogatives within the House enabled Mills to exert extraordinary influence on the writing of tax laws. In addition to its economic responsibilities, the Ways and Means Committee also functioned as the Committee on Committees, doling out committee assignments to House members. Mills was at the center of this crucial process. The fact that Ways and Means, alone among House committees, had no subcommittees further centralized its legislative responsibilities in Mills's hands. Bills emerging from the Committee, moreover, operated on the House floor under a "closed rule," meaning that no amendments were permitted; only total approval or absolute rejection was possible.

The result was almost always approval, in part because of Mills's impressive abilities. No congressman could match his vast knowledge of the tax laws. Most stood in awe of his mastery of the complex subject matter, and many owed their grasp of complicated bills to Mills's lucid explanations, which at times brought members of both parties to their feet in applause. Equally important to Mills's success on the floor of the House was his insistence on achieving a consensus in committee. He refused to report out controversial measures by narrow majorities, preferring to delay, remove or water down controversial features until he had attained unanimity or a large majority. By compromising in the Committee he managed to head off potential opposition in the House. Consistently smooth passage of measures introduced by Mills enhanced his aura of power. However, his fear that a defeat on the floor of the House would diminish that aura often led him to pursue a strategy of delay on important legislation until he felt assured of a safe majority.

Until 1965 Mills was the principal congressional obstacle to passage of the Kennedy-Johnson Administration's medicare program. Medicare, a plan to finance medical care for the aged through the Social Security system, had been bottled up in the Ways and Means Committee for almost a decade. Mills had raised doubts as to the fiscal prudence of the plan, but his basic objection was based less on principles than on practicality: he felt the measure could not pass the House. He could have pushed the bill through the Committee by a slim majority, but he resisted doing so, fearing defeat on the floor of the House and the wrath of the medical establishment if his proved the critical swing vote. The Senate finally approved medicare in September 1964 as an amendment to a Social Security increase, but Mills engineered the amendment's defeat in the House-Senate conference the next month.

Mills ended his opposition to medicare after the election of 1964 returned pro-medicare majorities to the House and the Ways and Means Committee. Faced with its inevitable passage he shifted to support of the program and became its principal legislative architect.

The compromise legislation that Mills crafted in March 1965 was a response to a tactical shift on the part of House Republicans and the American Medical Association (AMA), the most vociferous and unrelenting foe of compulsory medical insurance for the aged. In addition to its traditional denunciation of medicare as "socialized medicine," the AMA began to attack the program as inadequate because its proposed benefits covered hospital costs but not doctors' fees. Rep. John Byrnes (R, Wisc.) [*q.v.*], ranking Republican on the Ways and Means Committee, offered the Republican leadership's alternative to medicare, a bill providing federal subsidies for voluntary private health insurance policies for the aged.

In a surprise move Mills took the "voluntary" portion of the Byrnes plan and grafted it into the "compulsory" medicare program: one part paid for hospital and nursing home costs, financed by increased Social Security taxes; the second part took care of doctors' fees, financed by federal subsidies and small voluntary payments by individuals. "It took the most brilliant legislative move I'd seen in 30 years," said Assistant Secretary of Health, Education and Welfare Wilbur Cohen [*q.v.*]. "In effect, Mills had taken the AMA's ammunition, put it in the Republicans' gun, and blown both of them off the map."

On March 23 Mills's medicare package passed the Committee in a 17-8 straight party-line vote. He introduced the measure in the House on April 8. After defeating the Republicans' voluntary health plan by a 236-191 vote, the House passed the Mills proposal 313-115. Following Senate passage of a more extensive program in July, Mills eliminated most of the Senate additions in the House-Senate conference on the bill. Yet, in its final form medicare was far more comprehensive than the limited versions he had opposed for years. The increase in the Social Security tax was also double the amount that medicare's proponents had urged, one-half of one per cent instead of one-fourth, due to Mills's insistence that the program be sound actuarially.

Mills again became the center of attention in 1967 and 1968 with his opposition to the Administration's August 1967 request for a 10% tax surcharge to curb inflation. His demand that the tax increase be accompanied by $6 billion in budget cuts involved him in a 10-month confrontation with the Johnson Administration. At the Committee's hearings Mills questioned Administration representatives as to why they had consistently underestimated expenses and overestimated revenues. In October the Committee voted 20-5 to postpone action on the tax request until the Administration had made sufficient budget cuts. Secretary of the Treasury Henry Fowler [*q.v.*] and Budget Director Charles Schultze [*q.v.*] returned to the Committee in late November to pledge $4 billion in budget cuts, but Mills declared that the figure was not high enough and that his Committee needed "more, particularly more specific, information" about Administration spending plans before any increase would be enacted. The impasse continued through the first half of 1968. In June the Administration finally agreed to the $6 billion reduction. The measure passed the Ways and Means Committee, and Mills steered it through the House by a 268-150 vote.

Mills's voting record was considerably more conservative in the second half of the 1960s than the earlier part of the decade. He voted for major measures favored by the liberal Americans for Democratic Action 69% of the time in 1964, 37% in 1965, 6% in 1966, 20% in 1967 and 8% in 1968. He backed the Vietnam war and consistently voted against civil rights bills. Despite public statements in favor of a total overhaul of the tax code, no sweeping tax reform was undertaken during Mills's tenure as Ways and Means Committee chairman. His habit of extended study and insistence on consensus served, instead, to smother prospects for reform within the Committee.

In late 1974 Mills resigned as chairman after a scandal involving his relationship with an Argentine striptease dancer and his public confession of alcoholism. He left the House in January 1977. [See NIXON Volume]

[TO]

For further information:

Richard Harris, *A Sacred Trust* (New York, 1966).

John F. Manley, *The Politics of Finance: The House Ways and Means Committee* (Boston, 1970).

MINK, PATSY T(AKEMOTO)

b. Dec. 6, 1927; Paia, Hawaii.
Democratic Representative, Hawaii, 1964-77.

Born in Hawaii of Japanese ancestry, Mink graduated from the University of Hawaii in 1948 and received a law degree from the University of Chicago in 1951. The second woman of Oriental ancestry admitted to the Hawaii bar, Mink found that no law firm would hire her, and so she began teaching business law at the University of Hawaii. In the 1950s, while the state Democratic Party consolidated its near-dominance of the territory's politics, Mink was active in the Hawaii Young Democrats and became its president in 1956. She was elected to the territorial legislature in 1955 and entered the Democratic congressional primary in 1959. Unsuccessful in that attempt, Mink won election in 1964 as one of Hawaii's two representatives-at-large.

A consistent liberal, Mink was an enthusiastic supporter of President Johnson's Great Society legislation and won an Americans for Democratic Action rating of 100% in 1968. Mink usually voted in accordance with AFL-CIO preferences, which was not surprising since the International Longshoremen and Warehousemen's Union was a primary source of strength for Hawaii's Democrats. A member of the House Education and Labor Committee and the Interior and Insular Affairs Committee, Mink was particularly concerned with educational legislation. In 1965 she sponsored a successful bill for the construction of schools in the Pacific territories. Her proposal to use federal money to help maintain a 3% interest rate on private loans for college construction programs was incorporated into the 1967 Housing and Urban Development Act. Mink introduced a bill in May of 1967 to appropriate $300 million for public and private, non-profit day-care centers. Her efforts in behalf of day-care programs continued beyond the bill's defeat and culminated in the Child Development Act of 1971, a measure that cleared Congress but was vetoed by President Nixon. She also sponsored legislation favorable to residents of U.S. possessions in the Pacific.

Mink supported early military appropriations for Vietnam. However, in March 1967, despite the dependence of Hawaii's economy on federal defense expenditures, she was one of 18 House members who supported a bill that would have prohibited the use of supplemental defense funds for Vietnam.

Mink won her bids for reelection easily and in 1970 ran unopposed in the newly organized second district. She became an increasingly vocal opponent of U.S. policies in Indochina and a congressional spokeswoman for feminist issues. Mink entered the 1972 presidential primaries but withdrew before the Democratic convention. [See NIXON Volume]

[MDB]

For further information:
Hope Chamberlin, *A Minority of Members: Women in the U.S. Congress* (New York, 1973).

MITCHELL, CLARENCE M.

b. March 8, 1911; Baltimore, Md.
Director, Washington Bureau, NAACP, 1950- .

Mitchell, a black lawyer, became director of the Washington bureau of the NAACP in 1950. His major function in that post was serving as the organization's lobbyist for civil rights measures in the legislative and executive branches of the federal government.

The NAACP and other civil rights groups criticized the Administration of John F. Kennedy for its failure to introduce significant anti-discrimination bills in the early 1960s. Mitchell charged that the problem was not the absence of a strong constituency for such measures but the unwillingness of the President to press vigorously for civil rights laws. In 1962 and early 1963 he testified before congressional committees in favor of anti-bias riders to federal aid bills, but these provisos did not have Administration support and were not passed by Congress. Kennedy introduced a civil rights bill in June 1963, but Mitchell denounced the Administration's subsequent opposition to strengthening amendments added by a House Judiciary Committee subcommittee. [See KENNEDY Volume]

President Lyndon B. Johnson's strong efforts on behalf of civil rights legislation, however, were welcomed and supported by Mitchell and most other rights leaders. On Capitol Hill Mitchell lobbied intensively on behalf of the Civil Rights Act of 1964 and the Voting Rights Act of 1965. In March 1968 he worked closely with House Democratic leaders in an effort to overcome Southern Democratic and Republican resistance to the Administration's open housing bill, covering four-fifths of the nation's housing, which had already been passed by the Senate. Rep. Gerald R. Ford (R, Mich.) [*q.v.*], the minority leader, wanted a House-Senate conference committee to modify the bill, which was stalled in the House Rules Committee. But Democratic managers of the bill, after meeting with Mitchell, decided to press for the Administration version. The assassination of Martin Luther King [*q.v.*] on April 4 helped generate the additional support needed to bring the bill out of the Rules Committee and pass it on the House floor.

Mitchell was a staunch defender of the Administration's antipoverty program. Many Republicans charged that the black urban riots of the summer of 1967 demonstrated the failure of the program and sought to reduce its budget. Mitchell denounced the attacks on the program as political opportunism and, contending that the riots stemmed from injustice, urged an increase in antipoverty funds.

Although some blacks regarded President Johnson's civil rights record as inadequate, Mitchell defended it in a speech to the NAACP Southeast Regional Conference in April 1968. He praised the President's contributions to the welfare of blacks, citing the civil rights acts of 1964, 1965 and 1968, the antipoverty program and the appointment of two blacks, Robert C. Weaver [*q.v.*] and Thurgood Marshall [*q.v.*], as Secretary of Housing and Urban Development and Supreme Court Justice, respectively. President Johnson, he asserted, "has given more successful leadership on civil rights than any other President of the United States."

Mitchell, supporting the Johnson Administration and unsympathetic to the peace movement, backed Vice President Hubert H. Humphrey's [*q.v.*] bid for the Democratic presidential nomination in 1968. In December 1968 he criticized President-elect Richard M. Nixon's [*q.v.*] plan to promote black-owned businesses. Some civil rights leaders, influenced by black nationalist ideology, supported the program. But Mitchell feared it represented "a desire on the part of some to shift away the government assistance to the private enterprise approach" under which the benefits would "trickle down" from wealthy entrepreneurs to the poor.

Mitchell regarded the Nixon Administration's civil rights record as retrogressive. He opposed the President's 1969 effort to replace the Voting Rights Act of 1965 with a new bill, charging that the Administration was seeking to stem the tide of civil rights progress in order to win Southern segregationist support. Three years later he denounced the President's legislative proposals to limit busing as "the most blatant products of racism that I have seen in the federal government." [See NIXON Volume)

[MLL]

MONDALE, WALTER F(REDERICK)
b. Jan. 5, 1928; Ceylon, Minn.
Democratic Senator, Minn., 1965-76.

Walter Mondale was of Norwegian descent. He grew up in the village of Ceylon, Minn., graduated from the University of Minnesota in 1951 and served in the Army during the Korean War. He took his law degree from the University of Minnesota in 1956 and that same year began practice with the prestigious Minneapolis law firm of Larson, Loevinger, Lindquist, Freeman and Fraser. Mondale first entered politics in 1958 as campaign manager for Gov. Orville L. Freeman [*q.v.*], who had been a partner in Larson, Loevinger. After serving for two years as a special assistant to the state's attorney general, Mondale was appointed by Freeman in May 1960 to fill out Miles W. Lord's unexpired term as attorney general. He was elected to a full term in November of that year and reelected two years later. In 1963 Mondale received national attention for filing an *amicus curiae* brief with the U.S. Supreme Court in defense of Clarence Early Gideon, a Florida convict who had petitioned the Court in order to establish the right of a defendant to free counsel. Mondale also helped write the civil rights plank for the 1964 Democratic platform.

In November 1964 Gov. Karl F. Rolvaag appointed Mondale to the U.S. Senate seat vacated by Sen. Hubert H. Humphrey (D,

Minn.) [*q.v.*] shortly after Humphrey's election as vice president. Mondale was assigned to the Senate Aeronautical and Space Sciences, Banking and Currency and Agriculture and Forestry Committees. Regarded as an activist liberal with a special interest in the disadvantaged, he supported Johnson Administration policies on over 70% of all major issues.

In 1965 Mondale supported the Elementary and Secondary Education Act, the Voting Rights Act and medicare. The next year he introduced nearly 100 bills in the Senate, including an amendment to the Administration's traffic and motor vehicle safety bill to require auto makers to shoulder more responsibility for safety defects in automobiles and to require public disclosure of such defects. In November 1966 Mondale defeated his Republican opponent, Robert A. Forsythe, by 100,000 votes and won a full term in the Senate.

Mondale remained one of the Senate's strongest advocates of automobile safety. In 1967 he expressed concern that car prices in 1968 would be substantially higher than those of 1967 and joined with consumer advocate Ralph Nader [*q.v.*] to protest the increases. Mondale declared, "One begins to wonder whether safety is being used as an excuse to raise prices or whether price increases are being used to promote opposition to future vehicle safety standards—or perhaps both."

Mondale led the fight for the open housing amendment in the 1968 civil rights bill, which in its modified form prohibited discrimination in the sale or rental of about 80% of the nation's housing. The open housing amendment was passed only after Senate Republican leader Everett M. Dirksen (R, Ill.) [*q.v.*] switched from opposition to support of the measure. After adoption of the amendment Mondale stated that it was "far stronger than we believed possible."

During the Nixon Administration Mondale continued as one of the Senate's most prominent liberal spokesmen. He was reelected in 1972. In 1976 he won election as vice president. [See NIXON, CARTER Volumes]

[FHM]

MONRONEY, A(LMER) S(TILLWELL) MIKE

b. March 2, 1902; Oklahoma City, Okla.
Democratic Senator, Okla., 1951-69.

A 1924 graduate of the University of Oklahoma, Monroney was a political reporter for the *Oklahoma News* from 1924 to 1928. He then ran the family furniture business in Oklahoma City. Elected to the House of Representatives in 1938, Monroney served six terms there before winning a Senate seat in 1950. In both chambers he supported most liberal domestic legislation and became known as an advocate of congressional reorganization and of aviation interests. [See TRUMAN, EISENHOWER, KENNEDY Volumes]

Chairman of the Aviation Subcommittee of the Senate Commerce Committee, Monroney sponsored bills extending the federal aid-to-airports program, which passed Congress in 1964 and 1966. After an intensive two-year study, his subcommittee reported in January 1968 on current and anticipated problems in the national airport system and recommended new federal financing methods, including establishment of an airport trust fund. In June 1968 Monroney introduced the Administration's airport development act, but Congress took no action that year on this or other proposals to relieve the problem of airport congestion. Monroney also supported development of the controversial supersonic transport (SST) and opposed efforts to decrease federal funding of the program.

In 1965 Monroney was a co-chairman of the Joint Committee on the Organization of Congress, which conducted the first major review of congressional operations since 1946. The Committee was barred from proposing changes in House or Senate rules, and its July 1966 report also avoided the controversial question of altering the seniority system. The report did, however, recommend many reforms in committee structure, procedures and staffing, changes in Congress' work schedule and other measures to streamline legislative operations, to evaluate and review the budget and to regulate lobbyists. Monroney sponsored bills embodying most of the Committee's recommendations in 1966 and again in 1967. Passed by the Senate, they were bottled up by the House Rules Committee through the end of the 90th Congress.

Monroney became chairman of the Senate Post Office and Civil Service Committee in April 1965. He served as Senate floor manager between 1966 and 1968 for several bills raising postal rates and the salaries of federal employees and appropriating funds for the Post Office and Treasury Departments. In July 1965 he was named a member of the newly established Senate ethics committee and participated in its investigation of charges of misconduct by Sen. Thomas J. Dodd (D, Conn.) [*q.v.*]. Monroney supported the Senate's censure of Dodd for misuse of political funds in June 1967.

Monroney usually voted for the Johnson Administration's domestic and foreign policy programs, supporting civil rights and Great Society measures and U.S. policy in Vietnam. Trying for a fourth Senate term in 1968, Monroney easily defeated four opponents in the August Democratic primary, but he lost the November election by some 33,000 votes to his Republican opponent.

[CAB]

MONTOYA, JOSEPH

b. Sept. 24, 1915; Pena Blanca, N.M.
Democratic Senator, N.M., 1964-77.

Montoya, the son of a county sheriff and politician, grew up in northwestern New Mexico. He studied at Regis College in Denver and Georgetown University, where he received an LL.B. in 1938. Montoya's political career began in 1936, when he won election to the New Mexico House of Representatives. He remained in the state legislature for 10 years and subsequently served two terms as lieutenant governor. Montoya was elected to the U.S. House of Representatives in 1957; he served in the House until 1964, when he defeated a conservative Republican to become the junior senator from New Mexico.

Montoya's main problem as both a congressman and a senator was how to satisfy the diverse elements of his constituency, ranging from the liberal Spanish-Americans and Indians of northern New Mexico to the conservative whites of Albuquerque and "little Texas" in southeastern New Mexico. He survived politically by establishing himself as a moderate and paying close attention to "pork barrel" legislation that directly benefited his constituents. During the mid-1960s Montoya was a strong advocate of land reclamation projects, agricultural price supports, aid to small business and vocational training programs for unemployed and migrant workers. On these and other issues he was an ally of Sen. Robert Byrd (D, W.Va.) [*q.v.*], whose state resembled Montoya's in its chronic high unemployment and heavy dependency on federal aid. Montoya's Senate committee assignments—Agriculture and Forestry, Public Works, Small Business and Government Operations—enabled him to influence key aid legislation affecting New Mexico during the mid-1960s.

Montoya's political moderation made him a "swing" voter on many issues of national importance. The rating he received from the liberal Americans for Democratic Action ranged from 82% "correct" in 1965 to 36% "correct" in 1968. Montoya came out against U.S. involvement in Vietnam as early as 1967 and consistently supported congressional attempts to limit the war. He also worked to limit military spending despite the heavy dependence of New Mexico industry on defense contracts and military installations. Another liberal cause that Montoya favored was consumer protection; in 1969 he proposed creation of an independent agency for consumer affairs.

Montoya was reelected to the Senate in a hard-fought 1970 campaign with 52% of the vote. During the early 1970s he clashed repeatedly with the Nixon Administration over agricultural policy. Montoya gained national prominence in 1973, when he was named to the Senate committee that investigated the Watergate affair. He subsequently became a strong advocate of campaign reform legislation and worked to limit the investigatory powers of the Justice Department. [See NIXON Volume]

[SLG]

MOORE, DANIEL K(ILLIAN)
b. April 2, 1906; Asheville, N.C.
Governor, N.C., 1965-69.

An attorney and jurist, Moore was a judge on the North Carolina Superior Court from 1948 to 1958. After returning to private life as chief counsel for a paper company, Moore entered the June 1964 Democratic primary. Moore was pitted against Gov. Terry Sanford's [*q.v.*] handpicked successor, L. Richardson Preyer, and militant segregationist I. Beverly Lake. The primary provided a clear-cut battle between the state's liberals and conservatives. Preyer was the candidate of youthful progressives committed to policies in line with those of the national Democratic Party. Moore, with the backing of the state's old-line conservatives, defined his position as middle-of-the-road in matters of racial and economic policy. Moore finished second, polling 34% of the vote. Preyer took 37%.

Because no candidate had won a majority, a runoff was held. Moore campaigned as a man of common sense surrounded by racial and economic extremists. He depicted Preyer as too radical for North Carolina and as compromised by his support from "tremendous financial interests" and "other special interests including the high leadership of the AFL-CIO and the NAACP." Moore promised to enforce any law passed by Congress but viewed the 1964 civil rights bill as a "mixed bag of legalistic nonsense." He pledged to bring a "calm, moderate approach" to the civil rights problem. In the runoff Lake endorsed Moore, who won by polling an overwhelming 62% of the vote. The *New York Times* viewed Moore's victory as having potentially national implications, "for it reflected a seething resentment against the racial policies set down by Washington." Moore easily won the general election in November.

In his January 1965 inaugural address Moore promised that, like former Gov. Sanford, he would continue to make education a top priority in his administration. He was soon involved in a major controversy over freedom of speech on state college campuses. In 1963 the North Carolina legislature had passed a law banning members of the Communist Party from speaking in state-supported educational facilities. In response the Southern Association of Colleges and Schools threatened North Carolina schools with loss of accreditation. In late 1865 Moore warned that "the public controversy arising from this law is damaging to the state." Although Moore had campaigned against repeal of the ban, he now proposed amending the law to give university officials "discretion in having speakers they deem proper." Backed by Moore the State General Assembly established a study commission on the issue. In a special legislative session held in November 1965, the Assembly voted to substantially repeal the ban.

Moore also moved to curb the influence of the Ku Klux Klan in North Carolina. In August 1965 Klansmen attacked civil rights workers in Plymouth, N.C. Moore immediately dispatched 100 highway patrolmen to the scene to prevent additional Klansmen from moving into the area. He also met privately with Robert Jones, the "grand dragon" of the North Carolina Klan, to warn him that his followers should stay away from Plymouth. In early September Moore sent his administrative assistant and a civil rights aide to Plymouth, where they were instrumental in setting up a biracial committee. Demonstrations planned for early September were suspended after reports that progress was being made by the new panel. At Moore's request the state Assembly passed legislation in 1967 making the burning of crosses without permission of the affected property owner a felony. The Assembly also passed a law increasing the penalty for bombings directed against persons to 10 years minimum imprisonment.

Barred by the state constitution from seeking reelection, Moore was succeeded by Lt. Gov. Robert Scott. A member of the North Carolina delegation to the 1968 Democratic National Convention, he was nominated for President as a favorite son candidate but withdrew his name on the first ballot. In 1969 Moore was named an associate justice of the North Carolina Supreme Court.

[TJC]

MOORER, THOMAS H(INMAN)
b. Feb. 9, 1912; Mt. Willing, Ala.
Commander in Chief, Pacific Fleet, July 1964-March 1965; Supreme Allied Commander in the Atlantic, April 1965-July 1967; Chief of Naval Operations, August 1967-June 1970.

Thomas H. Moorer, a career naval officer who attained the rank of admiral in 1964, was directly involved in U.S. naval and military activity in Vietnam and the Dominican Republic.

On Aug. 2, 1964, shortly after Moorer assumed command of the U.S. Pacific fleet, the U.S. destroyer *Maddox*, patrolling the Gulf of Tonkin, exchanged fire with North Vietnamese torpedo boats. Moorer dismissed the shelling of the *Maddox* as an impulsive act of a local commander and suggested that retaliatory action was not warranted. However, he cabled his subordinate, Roy L. Johnson, commander of the Seventh Fleet, that "in view of the incident it was in the U.S. best interest to assert its right of freedom of the seas." He therefore recommended resuming Gulf of Tonkin patrols as early as possible. Moorer, with the approval of Adm. U.S. Grant Sharp [*q.v.*], commander of all U.S. forces in the Pacific, the Joint Chiefs of Staff and the Johnson Administration, ordered the destroyer *C. Turner Joy* to join the *Maddox* in the Tonkin Gulf and to patrol within eight nautical miles of the North Vietnamese coast, inside an area that some authorities suggested North Vietnam claimed as its territorial waters.

On the night of Aug. 4, North Vietnamese torpedo boats were reported to have attacked the *Maddox* and *C. Turner Joy*, although no damage was inflicted on either ship. A 1969 Senate investigation later revealed that even as Moorer was attempting to confirm the attack, President Johnson, with the support of the Joint Chiefs, was ordering retaliatory air strikes against North Vietnamese coastal installations. After the U.S. action Moorer affirmed that there had been sufficient evidence to prove that U.S. destroyers had been attacked on the high seas and that the bombing of North Vietnam was fully justified. As a result of the Tonkin Gulf incident, Congress passed the Tonkin Gulf Resolution on Aug. 7, giving the President broad military authority to combat Communist aggression in Vietnam.

In April 1965 Moorer became commander of all U.S. forces in the Atlantic. Later that month, with civil war raging in the Dominican Republic, he assumed command of the U.S. troops sent to that Caribbean nation to protect the lives and property of U.S. citizens and to prevent left-wing forces from seizing control of the Dominican government. U.S. forces remained in the Dominican Republic until September.

In August 1967 Moorer succeeded David L. McDonald as chief of naval operations. Testifying that summer before the Senate Preparedness Investigating Subcommittee, Moorer argued that only heavier bombing of North Vietnam would force it to abandon its war effort. As chief of naval operations, Moorer consistently maintained that unless the U.S. steadily acquired new ships it would fall behind the Soviet Union as a naval power. Therefore, Moorer pushed for the acquisition of a new type of fast, quiet nuclear submarine.

Moorer was named chairman of the Joint Chiefs of Staff in April 1970 and served at that post until May 1974. [See NIXON Volume]

[JLW]

MORGAN, THOMAS E(LLSWORTH)
b. Oct. 13, 1906; Ellsworth, Pa.
Democratic Representative, Pa., 1945- ; Chairman, Committee on Foreign Affairs, 1958- .

A practicing physician, "Doc" Morgan grew up in the depressed coal-mining districts of southwestern Pennsylvania, where his father was an organizer for the United Mine Workers. Following medical studies and an internship in Detroit, he became involved in Democratic politics in Fredericktown, Pa. By 1939 he had assumed leadership of the local organization. In 1944 Morgan was selected to run for Congress. Since his district was overwhelmingly Democratic, Morgan never faced serious opposition in subsequent general elections.

Characterized as an "organization man" by the *New York Times*, he consistently voted with his party and was an especially vigorous advocate of measures favorable to organized labor. In 1958 Morgan became chairman of the House Foreign Affairs Committee. Well liked by members of both parties, Morgan was a master of bipartisan politics, and he conceived of his role as that of the floor manager for Democratic foreign aid programs. [See EISENHOWER, KENNEDY Volumes]

In early 1964 Morgan initiated a dispute with his Senate counterpart, J. William Fulbright (D, Ark.) [*q.v.*], over the form in which the Administration should submit its annual foreign aid budget to their respective committees. Fulbright, preferring to use his Senate Foreign Relations Committee as a forum for the discussion of foreign policy, wanted to consider only economic assistance requests, leaving foreign military assistance to the Senate Armed Services Committee as part of the Defense Department budget. He also hoped to get four-year authorizations for development projects. Morgan, who represented a district with a high rate of unemployment, argued that military assistance helped make foreign aid packages more palatable to congressmen and voters who resented spending U.S. dollars abroad. In addition, Morgan wanted two-year authorizations at the most, warning that longer authorization periods would deprive Congress of its control over foreign policy.

In 1966 President Johnson, bowing to Fulbright's pressure, asked Congress for permission to submit foreign military assistance as part of the defense budget, but the Congress decisively rejected the Fulbright proposal. In the same year Morgan managed the Administration's aid budget more skillfully than Fulbright, whose relations with Johnson were already strained over the war in Vietnam. Morgan kept spending cuts to a minimum and won three-year authorizations for the development loan program and the Alliance for Progress. In 1967, however, Morgan could not prevent Congress, disenchanted with the conduct of the war in Vietnam and large budget deficits, from passing the lowest foreign aid authorization in history.

Morgan strongly supported President Johnson on most legislative issues and vigorously backed the Vietnam war. As a consequence, he was often compared unfavorably to Fulbright, whose committee undertook critical investigations of the war. Morgan's committee did not begin Vietnam hearings until 1971, and he did not announce his opposition to the war until 1972. [See NIXON Volume]

[JCH]

MORGENTHAU, HANS J(OACHIM)

b. Feb. 17, 1904; Coburg, Germany.
Political scientist.

Morgenthau received a Juris Utriusque Doctor (doctorate of canon and civil law) from the University of Frankfurt in 1929 and two years later was appointed assistant to its faculty of law. In 1932 he went to Switzerland to teach German public law at the University of Geneva. He came to the United States in 1937 and taught law, history and political science at Brooklyn College and the University of Kansas City before becoming a visiting professor of political science at the University of Chicago in 1943. He became a full professor at that university six years later. In 1950 Morgenthau was appointed director of the Center for the Study of American Foreign and Military Policy at the University of Chicago.

In the late 1940s and the 1950s Morgenthau, through the publication of *Politics and Nations* (1948), *In Defense of the National Interest* (1951) and other books, became known as a proponent of the "realist" approach to foreign policy. Rejecting Wilsonianism, he argued that America should not seek to transform the world according to its own political ideals but should instead concern itself with the promotion of vital national interests. Believing that popular passions often interfered with patient pursuit of the fixed designs required in diplomacy, Morgenthau felt that democratic societies like the United States found it difficult to pursue a coherent, rational foreign policy founded upon a consistent sense of the national interest.

Writing in the November 1962 issue of *Commentary*, Morgenthau advocated the employment of any necessary means, including an invasion, to remove Soviet missiles from Cuba. He wrote that since the promulgation of the Montoe Doctrine, America had claimed Latin America as a sphere of influence and stated that "if the United States is unwilling—nobody doubts its ability—to protect one of its vital interests, regarded as such for a century and a half, is it likely to protect interests elsewhere. . . ? Mr. Khrushchev, in particular, cannot help but ask himself that question."

Regarding Southeast Asia as beyond the American sphere of influence, Morgenthau criticized escalating United States intervention in Vietnam as contrary to the national interest during the mid and late 1960s. In an April 1965 *New York Times Magazine* article, he asserted that China rather than America would inevitably exert the predominant cultural and political influence on the Asian mainland. Morgenthau contended that, nevertheless, Vietnam might retain considerable independence as a Communist state of the Titoist variety because of its historical enmity towards China. He concluded that American intervention in an unwinnable war would merely force the Vietnamese Communist leaders into a closer relationship with China.

Morgenthau was a prominent participant in a number of the early university teach-ins on the Vietnam war. On May 15, 1965 he criticized Administration policy at a Washington, D.C. teach-in sponsored by the Inter-University Committee for a Public Hearing on Vietnam. His talk was transmitted via a special radio hookup to over 100 campuses. McGeorge Bundy [*q.v.*], special assistant to President Johnson on national security affairs, was scheduled to be the major defender of the Administration, but he announced that he was unable to attend because of official business. Morgenthau told the teach-in audience that the government was creating a myth of North Vietnamese subversion of South Vietnam to justify American involvement in a civil war there. Two months later he finally debated Bundy on a special CBS television broadcast. Bundy contended that escalation or complete and immediate withdrawal were the only alternatives to the President's policy. Morgenthau declined to endorse withdrawal, asserting that the Administration could find a face-saving way of extricating America from the conflict without overt surrender.

In November 1965 Morgenthau addressed a New York meeting of Clergy Concerned About Vietnam, and the following March he appeared before the Senate Foreign Relations Committee to urge abandonment of the policy of military containment of China. As the anti-war movement became increasingly radical during the late 1960s, Morgenthau's prominence as an Administration critic receded. In 1968 he served as a foreign policy adviser to anti-war presidential candidate Sen. Eugene J. McCarthy (D, Minn.) [*q.v.*].

In 1968 Morgenthau joined the faculty of the City College of New York. Concerned with the problems of Soviet Jews, he attended the Brussels Congress on Soviet Jewry in February 1971. In August 1975, as chairman of the Academic Committee on Soviet Jewry, he protested the suppression of nonpolitical Jewish publications in the USSR.

[MLL]

For further information:
Hans J. Morgenthau, *Truth and Power: Essays of a Decade, 1960-70* (New York, 1970).

MORSE, WAYNE (LYMAN)

b. Oct. 20, 1900; Madison, Wisc.
d. July 22, 1974; Portland, Ore.
Republican Senator, Ore., 1945-52;
Independent Senator, Ore., 1952-55;
Democratic Senator, Ore., 1955-69.

Morse majored in labor economics at the University of Wisconsin, graduating in 1923. In 1928 he received a law degree from the University of Minnesota. The following year Morse became an assistant professor of law at the University of Oregon, and two years later he was appointed dean of the University's law school.

During the 1930s Morse served as an arbitrator in West Coast labor disputes. In January 1942 he was selected as a public member of the National War Labor Board. Although generally sympathetic to the interests of labor, Morse resigned from the panel two years later in protest against what he regarded as excessive concessions to John L. Lewis's United Mine Workers.

Later that year Morse defeated the incumbent U.S. senator in Oregon's Republican primary and won the general election. On Capitol Hill Morse quickly established a reputation as an argumentative and individualistic liberal who frequently refused to modify strongly held views for the sake of legislative compromise. His opponents acknowledged his intelligence and legal expertise but criticized him as a rigid, humorless egotist who displayed a self-righteous and scornful attitude towards those who disagreed with him. His persistent tendency to antagonize his colleagues barred him from playing a major leadership role in the Senate, but his admirers regarded him as a fearless maverick who placed principle above expediency and who served as a watchdog against injustice.

Morse denounced the 1952 Republican national platform as "reactionary," and in October of that year he resigned from the Party to become an independent. He persistently criticized the Eisenhower Administration for showing excessive concern for the interests of big business and in April 1953 led a liberal filibuster against a bill giving the states title to offshore oil. Early in 1955 Morse joined the Democratic Party.

Morse was a strong advocate of the settlement of international disputes through multilateral cooperation and a system of world law. In 1946 he successfully pressed for American participation in the World Court. During the 1950s he criticized John Foster Dulles for bypassing the United Nations in his execution of American foreign policy. [See TRUMAN, EISENHOWER Volumes]

In 1960 Morse made a brief, unsuccessful bid for the Democratic presidential nomination. Under the Kennedy Administration Morse for the first time belonged to the same party as the President. As chairman of the Labor and Public Welfare Committee's Education Subcommittee, he promoted the Kennedy Administration's education bills. But he did not give up his role as a gadfly, and during the summer of 1963 Morse led a liberal filibuster against an Administration bill creating a privately owned communications satellite corporation. [See KENNEDY Volume]

During the mid and late 1960s Morse was best known for his opposition to President Johnson's escalation of American military involvement in Vietnam. In August 1964 he and Sen. Ernest Gruening (D, Alaska) [*q.v.*] were the only Capitol Hill opponents of the Tonkin Gulf Resolution, which authorized the President to take all necessary steps to repel North Vietnamese aggression. He questioned the Administration's account of alleged North Vietnamese attacks upon American naval vessels in the Tonkin Gulf. During Senate debate on the Resolution, Morse suggested that the vessels may have been positioned to defend South Vietnamese ships that were shelling North Vietnamese islands.

In a Texas speech delivered in May 1965, Morse denounced both the United States air raids on North Vietnam, which had begun the previous February, and the subsequent dispatch of American combat troops to South Vietnam. He asserted that the conflict in the South was a civil war rather than an invasion from the North and that the United States was intervening on behalf of a despotic South Vietnamese regime with little popular support. On the Senate floor during the same month, Morse stated that "my government stands before the world drunk with military power" and that it was laying the foundation for "intense Asiatic hatred."

In February 1966 Morse condemned the Administration for lawlessly pursuing hostilities without a congressional declaration of war and in violation of the charter of the Southeast Asia Treaty Organization, which he said provided for collective rather than unilateral action in Southeast Asia. He believed that either the U.N. or the SEATO nations should intervene to separate the Vietnamese combatants and reestablish peace.

On March 1, 1966 the Senate defeated a

Morse amendment to repeal the Tonkin Gulf Resolution, which President Johnson had repeatedly cited as the legal authorization for his Vietnam policies. Critics of the Senator contended that the amendment was an example of Morse's tendency to undercut his own cause by taking extreme positions regardless of political considerations. They noted that a number of senators who had reservations about the war but who did not want to totally repudiate the President had been forced to vote with the Administration.

Another of Morse's major concerns was the defense of the civil liberties of the individual. In August 1965, as a member of the District of Columbia Committee, he opposed a D.C. crime bill that would have permitted three hours of interrogation of criminal suspects before arraignment. The bill sought to modify the Supreme Court's ruling in *Mallory v. U.S.* (1957), which barred "unnecessary delay" in the arraignment of criminal defendants. Morse stated that the measure abridged rights guaranteed by the Fourth, Fifth, Sixth and Eighth Amendments. During the same month he sought to protect the rights of criminal defendants from the effects of prejudicial pretrial publicity without impinging upon freedom of the press by proposing restrictions on the comments of attorneys prior to trial. In May 1968 he opposed an omnibus crime bill that attempted to overturn several Supreme Court decisions broadly defining the rights of criminal defendants and that authorized wiretapping in a wide range of federal and state cases. Morse argued that the provisions overruling the Supreme Court "could start us down the road toward a government by police state procedures" and that the wiretapping provisions could permit "total invasion of our homes through spying."

Despite his differences with Johnson over Vietnam, Morse worked closely with the Administration in the field of labor legislation, on which he was considered an expert. In January 1966 Morse supported an unsuccessful effort to repeal Section 14(b)—the right-to-work clause—of the Taft-Hartley Act, which gave states the option of outlawing the union shop. But he did not believe that workers should have the right to strike if their action jeopardized the public interest. During July 1966, in the face of an airline strike, he proposed legislation to require airline workers to return to their jobs for 180 days and establish mediation procedures. The strike was settled before Congress acted. In May 1967 he introduced in the Senate an Administration plan for ending a railroad strike that provided for compulsory arbitration. The plan was enacted in July, and President Johnson appointed Morse to head a panel assigned to settle the strike. The panel devised a settlement in September, and it took effect the following month after labor and management failed to reach a voluntary agreement.

In 1968 Morse was defeated in a reelection bid by Republican challenger Robert W. Packwood, who supported the Administration's Vietnam policies. Four years later Morse won a Democratic senatorial primary but lost the election to incumbent Republican Sen. Mark O. Hatfield [*q.v.*]. In 1974 Morse again won a senatorial primary. But on July 22, in the midst of his campaign, he died of kidney failure.

[MLL]

For further information:
A. Robert Smith, "Senator Morse's Advice and Dissent," *The New York Times Magazine* (April 17, 1966), pp. 24-52.

MORTON, THRUSTON B(ALLARD)

b. Aug. 19, 1907; Louisville, Ky.
Republican Senator, Ky., 1957-69.

A seventh generation Kentuckian, Morton received a B.A. from Yale University in 1929. He won election three times to the House as a Republican beginning in 1946 and voted with the GOP's liberal, internationalist wing. Morton supported Gen. Dwight D. Eisenhower [*q.v.*] for the 1952 Republican presidential nomination, and in January 1953, Eisenhower appointed him assistant secretary of state for congressional relations. Three years later Morton unseated Sen. Earle C. Clements (D, Ky.). In 1959 he won appointment as chairman of the Republican National Committee, serving through the 1960 election. Morton opposed most of President Kennedy's domestic programs and in his 1962 senatorial campaign found himself a target of the national Democratic leadership. He won reelection with 52.8% of the vote. [See EISENHOWER, KENNEDY Volumes]

Morton sought the middle ground during the Republican Party's divisive 1964 presidential campaign. Although respected by many Party leaders, he declined to enter the presidential contest himself and in April withdrew his name as Kentucky's favorite son candidate. His move unintentionally aided Kentucky supporters of Sen. Barry M. Goldwater (R, Ariz.) [*q.v.*], who won 21 of the state delegation's 24 votes. Morton served as permanent chairman of the July National Convention, which nominated Goldwater. Following the Republican defeat in November, the Kentucky Senator refused to join moderate and liberal Party leaders demanding the ouster of National Committee Chairman Dean Burch [*q.v.*], a Goldwater appointee. "This is not the time for bloodletting," Morton remarked on the anti-Burch movement in December 1964. "Our Republican Party blood is too thin, and there is too little of it." However, in September 1965 Morton attacked the John Birch Society, which liberals had frequently associated with the Goldwater campaign, and accused the extreme right-wing group of "infiltrating" the GOP.

Morton voted against most of the Johnson Great Society programs. Although supporting the Appalachia Regional Development Act for his state, he opposed the Elementary and Secondary Education Act and efforts to repeal Section 14(b) of the Taft-Hartley Act. In both the Kennedy and Johnson Administrations, Morton fought White House proposals for federal medical insurance for the elderly. He advocated a voluntary program financed through general federal revenues granted to the states, which would then share control of the program with private insurance companies. Morton, however, was the only Republican senator to support consistently the Administration's campaign finance legislation in 1966 and 1967.

Morton voted for the 1964, 1965 and 1968 Civil rights acts and insisted that the Republican Party actively seek the support of black voters. He told an Alabama Party gathering in March 1966 that the GOP could not afford to place itself "on the right of the [Southern] Democratic position on civil rights," explaining that "there just isn't much room on their right!" When in July 1966 a national Republican leadership group criticized Johnson for the "state of anarchy" in Northern cities, Morton strongly condemned its action. Describing urban rioting as a "national tragedy" and the "worst domestic crisis since the Civil War," he denounced efforts to place violence in the cities "in the political arena." He proposed that an unrestricted $1 billion "anti-riot chest" be placed at the disposal of mayors for housing, welfare, education and antipoverty programs. No other Republican leader joined Morton in his attack on the Party leadership's report.

The 1966 elections added to the ranks of Senate Republican liberals and moderates, and Morton began the following year to challenge some of the positions taken by Senate Minority Leader Everett M. Dirksen (R, Ill.) [*q.v.*]. Morton led the campaign for the ratification of the 1967 consular treaty with the Soviet Union, even though Dirksen had announced himself against the agreement as an unwarranted hazard to domestic security. Angry over the Minority Leader's stand, Morton overcame State Department reluctance to fight Dirksen and the powerful anti-Communist "Liberty Lobby" in order to win Senate approval of the treaty in March by a 66-28 vote. Morton's success represented the first successful Republican challenge to Dirksen's Senate authority.

Following his activity on behalf of the consular treaty, Morton came out against the Administration's Vietnam policies in 1967. Morton had never been one of the Senate's more militant or "hawkish" proponents of the Vietnam war, but he had supported Johnson in his escalation of American involvement in Southeast Asia. Conscious of a decline in the public's support for the war, Morton attempted to move the GOP away from any identification with Johnson's war policies. In August Morton called for a de-escalation of military operations, adding that "we're on a bad wicket and should try something else."

One month later Morton condemned America's war effort in stronger language. Responding to a comment by presidential candidate George W. Romney [*q.v.*] that he had been "brainwashed" during a recent Vietnam tour, Morton declared on Sept. 27 that the President himself had been "brainwashed" by the "military-industrial complex" into believing that a military victory could be achieved. Morton accused Johnson of having been "mistakenly committed to a military solution in Vietnam for the past five years, with only a brief pause" during the 1964 election "to brainwash the American people" with promises not to engage American troops. Morton asked for an indefinite halt to the bombing of North Vietnam and a curtailment of American military operations in South Vietnam. Dirksen, a loyal supporter of Johnson's Vietnam actions, sternly criticized Morton's address in an October speech.

Although Morton never challenged Dirksen for the Senate Republican leadership post, he appeared a likely opponent or successor following his success on the consular treaty and his break with the Minority Leader over Vietnam. Yet, Morton denied any interest in Dirksen's position, declaring it to be "a lousy job" and himself "too lazy to do the work." He pledged never to oppose Dirksen for the minority leadership. Weary of the Senate's pace and in poor health, Morton surprised the Washington community in February 1968 by announcing that he would not run for reelection in November. Instead, Morton urged New York Gov. Nelson A. Rockefeller [*q.v.*] to seek the 1968 Republican presidential nomination. Morton later served as an adviser in the unsuccessful Rockefeller campaign of that year. He retired to Kentucky in 1969, occasionally returning to Washington to lobby for banking and horse racing interests.

[JLB]

For further information:
F. Clifton White, Suite 3505: *The Story of the Draft Goldwater Movement* (New York, 1967).

MOSES, ROBERT

b. Dec. 18, 1888; New Haven, Conn. Chairman, Triborough Bridge and Tunnel Authority, 1936-68; President, New York World's Fair Corporation, 1960-67.

Although his initial interest was in government reform and reorganization, it was as New York's "Master Builder" that Moses achieved fame. In 1924 he became head of the state park system, which he greatly extended with a series of magnificent new beaches, parks and parkways. In 1934 Moses became New York City's first citywide comissioner of parks as well, and he continued to acquire new jobs until at one point he simultaneously held twelve different state and city posts. A pioneer in the use of bond-issuing public authorities to finance and build public works, Moses achieved unprecedented power over public construction in New York City and much of the state and was virtually immune from criticism or control. However, in May 1960, partially as a result of scandals in the slum clearance program he headed, Moses resigned his city posts to assume the presidency of the New York World's Fair, planned for 1964-65. When two years later New York Gov. Nelson A. Rockefeller [*q.v.*] attempted to replace Moses as head of the New York State Council of Parks, Moses resigned his state posts as well, leaving him as head of only the World's Fair and New York's powerful Triborough Bridge and Tunnel Authority. [See TRUMAN, EISENHOWER, KENNEDY Volumes]

Even before the World's Fair opened, Moses had been involved in a controversy over charges of favoritism in the assignment of lucrative contracts and franchises. When the Bureau of International Exhibitions failed to sanction the Fair, most European governments decided not to sponsor pavilions, leaving the Fair with an unusually high proportion of corporate exhibitors.

When the Fair was opened by President Johnson on April 22, 1964, the ceremonies were marked by the presence of civil rights demonstrators, protesting the plight of New York's black population. Almost 300 demonstrators, including James Farmer

[*q.v.*] and Bayard Rustin [*q.v.*], were arrested, but a threatened "stall-in" blocking approach roads failed to materialize. Leaders of the American Jewish Congress also appeared at the Fair to picket an allegedly anti-Semitic mural displayed at the Jordanian pavilion.

Although attendance topped 27 million the first season, revenues were considerably below the projected figure and, combined with an extravagant operating budget, pushed the Fair into a serious financial crisis. Moses initially tried to conceal the situation, claiming a surplus of $12 million at the end of the first year. But in January 1965 an audit revealed that the Fair had a deficit of $17.5 million and would be unable to repay a $24 million loan from New York City. However, new bank loans were obtained, and the Fair reopened April 21, 1965.

In spite of increased ticket prices and Moses's successful attempt to attract new exhibits, the fair closed on Oct. 17, 1965 with a $10 million deficit. Bonds were repaid at one-third their face value, leaving $8.6 million for demolition and some park improvements—nowhere near enough money for the chain of parks Moses had initially envisioned as the Fair's legacy.

In January 1966, shortly after his election as mayor of New York, John V. Lindsay [*q.v.*] proposed merging New York City's money losing Transit Authority, which ran subways and buses, with the Triborough Bridge and Tunnel Authority, which was accumulating large surpluses from automobile tolls. Moses opposed the plan and was able to muster enough support to easily defeat the proposal.

However, Gov. Rockefeller, who had failed to support the Lindsay plan, the next year proposed a more extensive merger including the two agencies, the Long Island Railroad, the Penn Central commuter lines and other transportation bodies to form a new Metropolitan Transportation Authority (MTA). Moses, promised a significant role in the new agency, agreed to support it. On March 1, 1968 the MTA was formed, headed by long-time Rockefeller aide William J. Ronan. Moses, however, was offered only a consulting job with no real power. After over four decades of public life, serving under six New York governors and five mayors, Robert Moses's career effectively ended.

[JBF]

For further information:

Robert A. Caro, *The Power Broker: Robert Moses and the Fall of New York* (New York, 1974).

Robert Moses, *Public Works: A Dangerous Trade* (New York, 1970).

MOSES, ROBERT P(ARRIS)

b. Jan. 23, 1935; New York, N.Y.
Field Secretary, Mississippi Student Nonviolent Coordinating Committee, 1961-65; Director, Mississippi Council of Federated Organizations, 1962-65; Director, Mississippi Freedom Summer Project, 1964.

Born and raised in Harlem, Moses received a B.A. from Hamilton College in 1956 and an M.A. in philosophy from Harvard University in 1957. He began teaching at Horace Mann, an elite private school in New York City, the next year. In the summer of 1960 Moses went to Atlanta as a volunteer for the newly organized Student Nonviolent Coordinating Committee (SNCC). He quit his teaching job in June 1961 to become a full time SNCC worker, and in July he moved into Amite and Pike Counties in southwestern Mississippi to begin a voter registration drive.

The first member of SNCC to undertake a voter registration project, Moses quickly emerged as SNCC's most significant figure in Mississippi. He was named project director of the Council of Federated Organizations (COFO), a body set up by SNCC and other civil rights groups in Mississippi in the spring of 1962 to conduct a unified voter registration program in the state. Moses helped plan and oversee all registration work in Mississippi during 1962 and 1963 and joined directly in registration projects despite repeated arrests, jailings and beatings. Moses also directed the November 1963 Freedom Ballot, a mock election sponsored by COFO open to all blacks over 21. Intended to prove that Mississippi blacks did want the vote, the Freedom Ballot campaign brought some 80,000 blacks to its polling places. [See KENNEDY Volume]

Following the Freedom Ballot Moses urged COFO and SNCC to make a major voter registration effort in Mississippi during the summer of 1964. According to former SNCC Executive Secretary James Forman [*q.v.*], Moses argued that a concentrated civil rights drive, especially when aided by white student volunteers, would capture national attention and force the federal government to intervene in Mississippi to uphold blacks' civil and political rights. Moses also wanted to begin building viable community institutions among the state's blacks. His advocacy was in large part responsible for the organization of the 1964 Mississippi Freedom Summer Project. Moses served as director of the effort, which brought over 1,000 volunteers into the state to set up community centers, teach in "freedom schools" and work on voter registration.

Violence flared repeatedly throughout the summer. Three civil rights workers were murdered near Philadelphia, Miss., in June, and in October COFO reported that there had been at least 35 shootings, 80 beatings and assaults, over 1,000 arrests and over 60 churches and homes burned or bombed. Very few blacks were actually registered to vote, and only half of the nearly 100 freedom schools and community centers established during the project continued after the summer. Although the immediate tangible results appeared limited, the project directed national attention to the plight of Mississippi blacks and greatly diminished their isolation from the rest of the civil rights movement. "The Mississippi Summer", wrote historian Howard Zinn, "had an effect impossible to calculate on young Negroes in the state."

The summer project was also the vehicle for organizing the Mississippi Freedom Democratic Party (MFDP). Founded in the spring of 1964, the MFDP was open to all citizens and was intended as an alternative to Mississippi's segregationist regular Democratic Party. Moses helped organize the Party and the "Freedom Registration" drive, which enrolled over 60,000 people as MFDP members during the summer. In August the MFDP held county and district conventions and then a state convention in Jackson where delegates for the August Democratic National Convention were elected.

Moses accompanied the MFDP delegates to Atlantic City, where they challenged the seating of Mississippi's regular delegation at the Convention. When the Convention voted a compromise in which two MFDP members would be seated as at-large delegates and the regular Mississippi delegates would be seated if they took a Party loyalty oath, Moses counseled the MFDP against acceptance. The delegates rejected the compromise by a vote of 60 to 4, and at Moses's suggestion, they staged a sit-in on the Convention floor on the night of Aug. 25.

By the end of the summer, Moses had become uneasy about his role in the civil rights movement. As director of COFO and the 1964 Summer Project, Moses was often forced to make key decisions on policy and strategy. Always reluctant to exercise such leadership, he shared with many others in SNCC a strongly democratic, anti-leadership philosophy. SNCC, Moses once explained, was "in revolt not only against segregation but also against the type of leadership where you have had a select few to speak for the Negro people." He saw his goal as simply helping local people organize so they would be able "to speak for themselves." In addition, Moses's courage, ability and hard work had made him an extremely respected figure among many SNCC members and Mississippi blacks by 1964. Quiet and reflective, Moses feared that a cult was growing around his name. To halt this development he changed his name to Robert Parris in February 1965 and shortly afterwards left both Mississippi and SNCC. He was active in the peace movement for a time, but by 1966 Moses had dropped from public view. In August 1973 the *New York Times* reported that Moses was teaching school in Tanzania.

[CAB]

For further information:

James Forman, *The Making of Black Revolutionaries* (New York, 1972).

Howard Zinn, *SNCC: The New Abolitionists* (Boston, 1964).

MOSS, FRANK E(DWARD)

b. Sept. 23, 1911, Holladay, Utah.
Democratic Senator, Utah, 1959-77.

A devout Mormon, Moss received his law degree from George Washington University in 1937 and then worked for the Securities and Exchange Commission. In 1940 he won election as a Salt Lake City judge and served as a judge advocate in the Army Air Corp during World War II. He was Salt Lake County attorney until his election to the Senate in 1958.

A liberal with strong labor support, Moss won his Senate seat in 1958 with a plurality of 38% when a former Republican governor ran as an independent and split the state's traditionally conservative vote. An energetic representative of his state's natural resource interests, he served on the Interior and Insular Affairs Committee and was chairman of its Subcommittee on Irrigation and Reclamation. In the early 1960s Moss advocated a cabinet-level department of natural resources. President Kennedy remarked at the time that Moss "has preached the doctrine of the wise use of water with, I think, more vigor than almost any other member of the U.S. Senate." Moss also cosponsored truth-in-lending legislation and favored controls on political campaign contributions. During his first term he began to work for the ban on television cigarette advertising. This brought him increased electoral support from those Utah Mormons for whom smoking is a sin. [See KENNEDY Volume]

Although Sen. Barry M. Goldwater (R, Ariz.) [*q.v.*] ran strongly in Utah in 1964, Moss had established his reputation as an able representative of his state's interests and was reelected with 57% of the vote. During his second term he continued to press for federal action on water use, an important issue for Utah. In 1967 he wrote *The Water Crisis*, in which he argued that the competition between federal and local authorities for jurisdiction exacerbated the water shortage crisis. Charging that "no one is in charge of the federal effort," Moss called again for a federal department of natural resources and for the establishment of "effective planning agencies for all water resource regions." He also worked with great success for the enlargement of Utah's parks.

Moss continued to urge government restrictions on cigarette advertising and was also active in other health-related issues. In June 1965 he cosponsored Sen. Ernest Gruening's (D, Alaska) [*q.v.*] bill to establish offices of population problems in the Departments of State and of Health, Education and Welfare. He also called for the development of a national program of and standards for nursing homes and housing for the aged.

A liberal supporter of the Great Society's social programs, Moss was the chief Senate sponsor in 1965 of the Law Enforcement Assistance Act. In 1968 he proposed an amendment to the Safe Streets Act to grant federal aid for the improvement of local police departments. Although he voted for appropriations for the Vietnam war in 1966, Moss was one of 15 Democratic Senators who sent a letter to Johnson in February of that year urging that he continue the suspension of air attacks on North Vietnam.

Moss's opposition to U.S. involvement in Vietnam grew in the early Nixon years. As a Democrat in a Republican state, he faced a difficult election in 1970 when the Nixon Administration threw its weight behind his opponent, but he was able to win a third term with support from labor and anti-war groups. Moss remained active in the areas of resource development, consumer affairs and health. [See NIXON Volume]

[MDB]

MOSS, JOHN E(MERSON)

b. April 13, 1913, Hiawatha, Utah.
Democratic Representative, Calif., 1953- .

Moss ran an appliance retail business in Sacramento and was active in local Democratic politics before serving in the Navy during World War II. After the war he joined his brother's real estate firm and won election to the California state Assembly in 1948. Moss was first elected to Congress in 1952 from Sacramento County as a self-described "really liberal Democrat."

Moss was among the most consistent

supporters of Johnson Administration legislation, but his main interest was the reform of laws concerning public access to government information. In 1955 he became chairman of the Government Operations Committee's newly created Foreign Operations and Government Information Subcommittee. One of the subcommittee's tasks was to conduct periodic investigations of government agency information procedures. Moss soon became convinced that the 1946 Administrative Procedure Act, which governed agency information disclosure, allowed federal agencies too much latitude in forming their own information policies and enabled them to withhold important information from the public.

In February 1965 Moss introduced a freedom of information bill to require federal agencies to open their files and records to the public. Specific exceptions to the bill included defense secrets, medical and personnel files, trade secrets and similar documents. At the same time Moss's Government Information Subcommittee undertook a survey of the information policies of 105 federal agencies and discovered a wide variety of information procedures. The American Bar Association, members of the press and civil liberties groups all supported the freedom of information bill, while most government agencies and many business groups opposed it. Moss, who described the bill as "moderate," acted as its floor manager in the House. It was unanimously approved in June 1966. Although Moss later expressed "some disappointment that it has not been utilized as much as it should have," the Act facilitated the investigations of Ralph Nader [*q.v.*] and other public interest advocates.

Moss was also outspoken in 1965 congressional hearings on the use of lie detectors by the federal government in interrogation procedures. "People have been deceived by a myth that a metal box in the hands of an investigator can detect truth or falsehood," said Moss, who stated that he would "absolutely refuse to submit to a polygraph examination for any purpose." In 1966 he introduced a bill that would have prohibited the interstate shipment of eavesdropping and wiretapping devices, but no action was taken on the proposal.

As chairman of the Commerce and Finance Subcommittee of the Interstate and Foreign Commerce Committee, Moss backed legislation of interest to labor and consumer groups. He protested that the health warnings required on cigarette packs by the Cigarette Labeling Act of 1965 were insufficient. In December 1967 he called for a federal investigation of the auto insurance industry by the Department of Transportation. He voted for repeal of the Taft-Hartley Act's "right-to-work" provisions, which allowed states to ban union shops, and opposed Administration efforts to impose compulsory arbitration to force strikers in critical industries back to work.

Moss was an early supporter of the Vietnam war but later grew critical of its conduct. After an investigatory trip to Southeast Asia in 1966, Moss's Foreign Operations and Government Information Subcommittee reported that U.S. aid programs there were riddled with corruption. Moss came to oppose U.S. involvement in Indochina and voted for the 1970 Cooper-Church Amendment to limit the President's authority to continue the American military presence in Cambodia. He resigned as chairman of the Government Operations Subcommittee when the 1970 Legislative Reorganization Act required him to relinquish one of his two subcommittee chairmanships. Nevertheless, he remained active in civil liberties legislation as well as in consumer affairs. [See NIXON Volume]

[MDB]

MOTLEY, CONSTANCE BAKER

b. Sept. 14, 1921; New Haven, Conn.
Associate Counsel, NAACP Legal Defense and Educational Fund, 1961-65; Democratic State Senator, N.Y., 1964-65; President, Manhattan Borough, New York City, 1965-66; U.S. District Judge, Southern District of N.Y., 1966- .

A graduate of New York University and Columbia University Law School, Motley joined the staff of the Legal Defense and

Educational Fund of the NAACP in 1945. She was a key attorney in numerous school desegregation cases handled by the Fund, including Autherine Lucy's effort to enter the University of Alabama in 1956 and the struggle to integrate the University of Georgia in 1961. Motley was also chief counsel for James Meredith [*q.v.*] and won court orders for his admission to the University of Mississippi in September 1962. In September 1963 she directed the Fund's legal efforts to prevent Gov. George C. Wallace [*q.v.*] from blocking school desegregation in four Alabama counties. Appointed associate counsel of the Fund, its second highest position, in October 1961, Motley also aided civil rights demonstrators in the South in the early 1960s. She successfully fought the May 1963 suspension of over 1,000 black public school students in Birmingham, Ala., for participating in demonstrations there that spring. She also persuaded a federal court in November 1963 to declare unconstitutional an insurrection law carrying the death penalty under which four civil rights workers in Americus, Ga., had been convicted.

Running as a Democrat early the next year, Motley won a special Manhattan district election to become the first black woman elected to the New York State Senate. In February 1965 she was chosen Manhattan borough president by the island's city councilmen, and nine months later she won the general borough election by a large margin. As borough president Motley repeatedly pressed for city and federal funds to rehabilitate housing and increase employment in Harlem. She also endorsed proposals to increase local community involvement in New York City planning boards and to improve educational facilities in the city. Motley represented the city on the march from Selma to Montgomery, Ala., in March 1965.

At Sen. Robert F. Kennedy's (D, N.Y.) [*q.v.*] request, President Johnson nominated Motley in January 1966 for a federal district court judgeship in the Southern District of New York. The Senate confirmed her nomination in August, and Motley became the first woman appointed to the federal bench in American judicial history. In one of her first major decisions Motley issued a controversial April 1967 ruling that New York City public school students were entitled to be represented by an attorney at hearings on their possible suspension or expulsion. In April 1968 Motley invalidated the results of a 1966 election of officers in the National Maritime Union on the ground that eligibility rules for union candidates had been "unreasonably restrictive" and a violation of the Landrum-Griffin Act.

[CAB]

MOYERS, BILL(Y DON)

b. June 5, 1934; Hugo, Okla.
White House Special Assistant, November 1963-June 1965; White House Press Secretary, July 1965-December 1966.

Bill Moyers, the son of an unskilled laborer, grew up in Marshall, Tex. While a sophomore at North Texas State College he took a summer job in Sen. Lyndon B. Johnson's Washington office and then, at Johnson's urging, transferred to the University of Texas at Austin, from which he graduated in 1956. After a year abroad at the University of Edinburgh, Moyers returned to take a divinity degree from the Southwestern Baptist Theological Seminary in 1959. The same year he rejoined Lyndon Johnson's staff and quickly advanced from personal assistant to executive assistant, directing Johnson's vice presidential campaign and acting as liaison with the Kennedy political team. After the inauguration Moyers resigned from Johnson's staff to become publicity director of the Peace Corps. Moyers was successful in helping to sell the Peace Corps concept to both the Congress and the public. In January 1963 he was named deputy director.

In the aftermath of the Kennedy assassination, Moyers left his Peace Corps post to again become one of Lyndon Johnson's most important advisers. In the early months of the Johnson Administration, he acted as liaison with Kennedy Administration holdovers, as well as chief interpreter of the unique Johnson "style."

During the first year of the new Administration, Moyers and special assistant Richard Goodwin [*q.v.*] organized and supervised 14 task forces established to focus on Great Society legislative proposals. In his memorandum to the President setting up guidelines for the task forces, Moyers made it a key provision that government officials be mixed with outside experts. His plan stood in marked contrast to the 1961 Kennedy task forces, which had consisted almost entirely of non-governmental personnel and had created hostility within the federal bureaucracy.

Moyers's work on the domestic task forces was interrupted by the 1964 presidential campaign. According to Theodore White [*q.v.*], Moyers was Johnson's "chief idea channel of the campaign." At the Democratic National Convention in Atlantic City, Moyers helped write the Party platform, which included a strong civil rights plank. After the Convention Moyers created what journalist Patrick Anderson called "the most effective, most savage media campaign in political history." It was Moyers who approved the controversial one-minute "daisy girl" television advertisement that appeared only once on national television and showed first, a girl plucking daisy petals and next, a nuclear mushroom cloud. The ad was intended to leave the impression that Republican presidential candidate Sen. Barry Goldwater (R, Ariz.) [*q.v.*] would be dangerously irresponsible as president. While neither Goldwater nor the Republican Party was mentioned in the commercial, the reaction in the Goldwater camp was one of outrage.

After Walter Jenkins's [*q.v.*] resignation in October 1964, Moyers took over as President Johnson's chief of staff. Following the election he returned to his notably successful work on the task forces, which made their reports on Nov. 15, 1964. Moyers's principal impact on the project was in creating the organizational framework within which the task forces could operate. He regarded the first six months of 1965, when bill after bill came from Congress for the President's signature, as the most rewarding period of his life.

In July 1965, while still functioning as the President's chief of staff, Moyers replaced George Reedy [*q.v.*] as White House press secretary. He took over the post after the legislative euphoria of 1964 and early 1965 had worn off and the President's relations with the press had begun to erode because of mounting criticism over U.S. involvement in the Vietnam war. One of Moyers's tasks was to divert media attention from the Johnson personality and to focus it on the Administration's legislative successes. He was frequently given high marks by reporters for candor and for reducing the "credibility gap" between President Johnson and the press. However, Moyers also brought a high degree of political sophistication to his job as press secretary. In an interview in January 1966, Moyers declared that press conferences were held "to serve the convenience of the President, not the convenience of the press," and acknowledged that he had "planted" some questions at President Johnson's Aug. 29, 1965 news conference "to make sure that the news [about steel negotiations] got out that day." As press secretary, Moyers said he preferred "informal conversations" between the President and reporters to "televised extravaganzas." Moyers also criticized the press, declaring that President Johnson felt he was better served by radio and television than by newspapers. It was Moyers's belief that the press was often "poorly informed" and wrote "its opinion" rather than the facts.

During his nearly two years as press secretary, Moyers earned a reputation as one of the White House's most prominent "doves" on Vietnam. His doubts about the war were well publicized. Moyers's growing reputation as what Patrick Anderson called "the most powerful White House assistant of modern times" and his favorable press coverage led to inevitable friction with the President. (Significantly, in his 1971 memoir, *The Vantage Point,* Johnson accorded his former top aide only seven citations, two of which were footnotes.)

During 1966 Moyers was increasingly frustrated by his inability to gain access to the President and by the enormous amount of detail-work involved with the press secretary's job. Because of a lack of expertise, he was also unable to obtain foreign affairs posts that he yearned for, such as undersecretary of state or executive secretary of the National Security Council.

Moyers resigned as press secretary in December 1966 to become publisher of the Long Island newspaper *Newsday*, the nation's largest suburban daily newspaper. He immediately hired such innovative editors and fresh writers as Daniel P. Moynihan [*q.v.*] and Pete Hamill in an effort to help the paper shed its conservative image.

After *Newsday* was sold to the Times-Mirror Co., Moyers wrote *Listening to America; a Traveler Rediscovers His Country*, a best-selling 1971 book based on his travels through the nation. Moyers later joined New York City's public television station, where he was host of the highly praised *Bill Moyers's Journal*. In May 1976 Moyers accepted a position with the Columbia Broadcasting System.

[FHM]

For further information:
Patrick Anderson, *The President's Men* (New York, 1968).

MOYNIHAN, DANIEL PATRICK
b. March 16, 1927; Tulsa, Okla.
Assistant Secretary of Labor, March 1963-June 1965.

Moynihan was raised in difficult circumstances in various slum neighborhoods in Manhattan. His father, a former Tulsa newspaperman, deserted the family when Moynihan was an infant. His mother managed to support the family with income from a tavern she owned and managed. Moynihan attended Benjamin Franklin High School in Harlem. After graduating in 1943 at the head of his class, he went to work on the Hudson River railroad docks. He briefly attended City College and enlisted in the Navy in 1944. After his discharge in 1947, Moynihan won his bachelor's degree from Tufts University. He later took an M.A. from Tufts's Fletcher School of Law and Diplomacy and did post-graduate work at the London School of Economics.

During the 1950s Moynihan served as assistant secretary and later acting secretary to New York Gov. W. Averell Harriman [*q.v.*]. From 1958 to 1960 he was secretary of the public affairs committee of the New York State Democratic Party.

During the 1960 presidential campaign Moynihan wrote a number of position papers on urban affairs for John F. Kennedy. Shortly after he took office Kennedy appointed Moynihan special assistant to Secretary of Labor Arthur Goldberg [*q.v.*]. In March 1963 Moynihan was promoted to the post of assistant secretary of labor for policy planning and research. In this job he undertook an extensive study of employment problems throughout the country. During 1963 President Kennedy appointed Moynihan, Sargent Shriver [*q.v.*], James Sundquist and Adam Yarmolinsky [*q.v.*] to draft the legislation that became the 1964 Economic Opportunity Act.

In March 1965 Moynihan, Paul Barton and Ellen Broderick released a Labor Department study called *The Negro Family: The Case for National Action*. Commonly known as the "Moynihan report," this study suggested that the high rates of juvenile delinquency and illiteracy among black children could be traced to the fact that in nearly 40% of black families the father was absent.

Moynihan and his coauthors suggested that blacks stood little chance of improving their position in American society as long as their family structure was matriarchal. The report proposed that the federal government develop social welfare policies to make it possible for more black fathers to remain with their families. In June 1965 President Johnson, relying on Moynihan's report, delivered a speech at Howard University calling for a White House conference on problems in the black community. Many civil rights leaders, including Floyd McKissick [*q.v.*] and Martin Luther King [*q.v.*], were critical of the report. They suggested that by documenting the abject status of blacks, the report came close to asserting that the black way of life was inherently debilitating. Many blacks considered the report patronizing and condescending.

In June 1965 Moynihan resigned his Labor Department post to seek the Democratic nomination for president of the New York City Council. He was defeated and served for a time as an aide to New York City Comptroller Abraham D. Beame in his unsuccessful mayoralty campaign against John V. Lindsay [*q.v.*].

While active in politics Moynihan managed to maintain his standing in academic circles. In 1961 the Fletcher School at Tufts awarded him a doctorate. In 1963 Moynihan and Nathan Glazer completed *Beyond The Melting Pot*, an important study that suggested that the various immigrant groups of New York City were not being assimilated but instead retained striking individual characteristics from one generation to the next.

In October 1965 Moynihan won a fellowship to Wesleyan University, where he began work on an extensive study of the black family. In June 1966 he was named director of the Harvard-Massachusetts Institute of Technology Joint Center for Urban Studies.

In the spring of 1968 Moynihan served as an adviser to Sen. Robert F. Kennedy (D, N.Y.) [*q.v.*] in his quest for the Democratic presidential nomination; after Kennedy was assassinated Moynihan worked briefly on behalf of the candidacy of Sen. Eugene J. McCarthy (D, Minn.) [*q.v.*]. He supported Vice President Hubert Humphrey [*q.v.*] in the fall. Because Moynihan was generally associated with the liberal wing of the Democratic Party, his political and academic colleagues were surprised in December 1968 when he joined the Nixon Administration as an assistant to the President for urban affairs. Moynihan won Administration support for new legislation providing federal assistance to families with incomes below a fixed level. The assistance was intended to supplement or replace local welfare payments. But the proposed legislation met with considerable resistance from both liberals and conservatives and was defeated in 1970.

In a confidential memorandum to the President, Moynihan in February 1970 suggested that "the time may have come when the issue of race could benefit from a period of 'benign neglect.' " This statement was leaked to the press and created outrage among black leaders, who suggested that it reflected the Administration's hostility to the pursuit of black social and political equality.

In 1971 Moynihan resigned from his post as a presidential assistant and returned to academic life as a sociology professor at Harvard University. In December 1972 he was named ambassador to India. In May 1975 he was appointed U.S. ambassador to the U.N. A year later Moynihan resigned. He won a Senate seat from New York in November. [See NIXON Volume]

[JLW]

MUHAMMAD, ELIJAH

b. Oct. 7, 1897; Sandersville, Ga.
d. Feb. 25, 1975; Chicago, Ill.
Leader of the Nation of Islam "Black Muslins," 1941-75.

Muhammad was born Elijah Poole in a tiny hamlet between Macon and Augusta, Ga. His parents were ex-slaves turned sharecroppers, and his father also served as a Baptist preacher. Poole worked as a field hand from the age of nine and at 16 left home, eventually settling in Detroit, where he found work in the auto industry.

In 1931 Poole met W. D. Fard, a door-to-door salesman of silks and yard goods in Detroit's black ghetto. Fard founded the Temple of Islam, and by 1933 Poole was his most trusted lieutenant. Before mysteriously disappearing in June 1934, Fard renamed Poole Muhammad and appointed him chief minister of Islam. Other disciples disputed Muhammad's leadership claims and forced him to flee to Chicago, where he established a new headquarters. During World War II Muhammad was jailed for failure to comply with the Selective Service Act. Muhammad successfully controlled the Muslims from prison and upon his release returned to Chicago as their undisputed leader. Stressing strict personal discipline and unswerving obedience to Muhammad, the Muslims recruited actively in the nation's ghettos and prisons during the 1950s. C. Eric Lincoln, author of *The Black Mus-*

lims, estimated that by 1964 the sect had over 50,000 members.

In the early 1960s the Muslims began to receive national attention when Muhammad allowed the charismatic Malcolm X [*q.v.*] to establish himself as the organization's chief spokesman and heir apparent. The two leading Muslims officially split on Dec. 4, 1963 when Muhammad censured Malcolm for a statement made three days earlier describing President Kennedy's death as a case of "chickens coming home to roost." On March 8, 1964 Malcolm X, who reportedly was unhappy with Muhammad's condemnation of Caucasian Muslims and nonengagement policy in civil rights and political affairs, announced that he was leaving the Black Muslims to form an organization that would stress "black nationalism as a political concept and form of social action against the oppressors." Malcolm was shot to death on Feb. 21, 1965 by men thought to be linked to the Black Muslims.

Although Muhammad strenuously denied responsibility for the assassination, law enforcement officials feared that Malcolm's supporters would attempt to retaliate. Five days after Malcolm's death the Black Muslim's national convention opened as scheduled in Chicago, and Muhammad received police protection comparable to that received by the President. At the convention Muhammad denounced Malcolm X as a "hypocrite" who "got just what he preached" and warned Malcolm's followers that "we will fight to protect ourselves."

During the 1960s the Muslims accumulated extensive economic holdings as part of their program of economic self-sufficiency. Their holdings included numerous small businesses, a bank and 15,000 acres of farmland. According to C. Eric Lincoln, the "Black Mulsims were the most potent organized economic force in the black community" by 1970. Elijah Muhammad died of congestive heart failure on Feb. 25, 1975. His son Wallace succeeded him as Chief Minister of Islam.

[DKR]

For further information:

C. Eric Lincoln, *The Black Muslims* (New York, 1970).

MUNDT, KARL E(RNST)

b. June 3, 1900; Humboldt, S.D.
d. Aug. 16, 1974; Washington, D.C.
Republican Senator, S.D., 1949-72.

Karl Mundt, a former speech teacher, was first elected to Congress in 1938. There he became known as a staunch anti-Communist. In 1948 the Congressman became nationally prominent as the acting chairman of the Un-American Activities Committee, which was then investigating the Alger Hiss case. That same year Mundt, in conjunction with Rep. Richard M. Nixon (R, Calif.) [*q.v.*], sponsored the measure requiring the registration of Communist-front organizations and their officers that became part of the Internal Security Act of 1950. Mundt was elected to the Senate in 1948 and carried his anti-Communist crusade to the upper house. In 1954 he served as chairman of the committee that conducted a probe into the dispute between Sen. Joseph McCarthy (R, Wisc.) and the U.S. Army. Three years later he voted against the Senate censure of Sen. McCarthy. During the Kennedy Administration Mundt became a prominent critic of the Defense Department's conduct in awarding TFX fighter/bomber contracts and of the Agriculture Department's dealings with Billie Sol Estes. [See TRUMAN, EISENHOWER, KENNEDY Volumes]

Throughout the 1960s Mundt remained a powerful spokesman for the conservative views predominant in postwar South Dakota. He voted consistently with the conservative coalition of Southern Democrats and Republicans, supporting that group over 80% of the time during the Johnson Administration. Although conservative on most domestic issues, the Senator backed civil rights measures, farm subsidy bills and legislation for cooperation with allies.

In 1967 Mundt led Senate resistance to ratification of the U.S.-Soviet consular treaty, which detailed procedures for operating additional new consulates in the two countries. The agreement was opposed by a large number of conservatives because of its provision granting complete criminal immunity and extending diplomatic immunity to consular officials and employes. Mundt claimed that this would make the FBI's counterespionage job "more difficult" and questioned the propriety of the agreement in light of Soviet support of North Vietnam in the Indochina war.

Prior to the ratification vote the Senator offered two amendments to the treaty. One would have authorized U.S. consular officials to distribute statements of U.S. policy to the Soviet press and would have provided for the number of U.S. newsmen in the USSR to be equal to the number of Soviet newsmen in the U.S. The other sought to prevent the treaty from taking effect until U.S. combat forces were no longer needed in Vietnam or until the removal of U.S. troops from Vietnam was not being delayed by Soviet military aid to North Vietnam. The treaty was ratified without his amendments.

In January 1968 Mundt called for an investigation of the mission of the captured American spy ship *Pueblo*. In a closed session of the Foreign Relations Committee, held on Jan. 28, he reportedly told Secretary of State Dean Rusk [*q.v.*] that the Administration had "bungled very badly" in permitting the *Pueblo* to operate near the North Korean coast and, if such close-in operations were necessary, in not providing protection for them.

In 1969 Mundt suffered a debilitating stroke that prevented him from appearing on the Senate floor or at committee meetings. However, the Senator refused to resign. Two years later, in a precedent-setting decision, the Senate relieved him of his posts as ranking Republican on the Government Operations Committee and second-ranking minority member of the Foreign Relations and Appropriations Committees. Mundt died in the capital in August 1974. [See NIXON Volume]

[EWS]

MURPHY, GEORGE (LLOYD)

b. July 4, 1902; New Haven, Conn.
Republican Senator, Calif., 1964-71.

George Murphy spent his boyhood in Philadelphia, where his father coached track at the University of Pennsylvania. After briefly studying mining engineering at Yale, Murphy went into show business in New York as a dancer and Broadway performer. In the 1930s he starred in Hollywood musicals. Beginning in 1939, when he switched his party affiliation the the Republicans, politics and the entertainment industry became equally important and interconnected parts of his life. He served two terms as president of the AFL-affiliated Screen Actors Guild, battled leftists in the movie industry, was a delegate to the Republican National Conventions in 1948 and 1952 and directed entertainment for the Eisenhower inaugural festivities. He retired from films in 1952 to devote more time to work as a public relations executive for film companies and to assume a larger role in the California Republican organization, including a one-year term as state committee chairman.

In December 1963 Murphy announced that he would seek the Republican nomination for the U.S. Senate. His candidacy was seen as an act of party loyalty since he would have to run against popular incumbent Sen. Clair Engle (D, Calif.), but Engle's death in July 1964 changed the odds in the November contest. Murphy's opponent was now President Kennedy's former press secretary, Sen. Pierre Salinger (D, Calif.) [*q.v.*], who, after winning the Democratic primary, had been appointed by Gov. Edmund G. Brown [*q.v.*] to complete Engle's term. Murphy brought legal suit in August seeking to invalidate the appointment on the ground that Salinger was not a qualified California voter. Although the suit failed, the "carpetbagger" issue served Murphy well. In addition, Salinger's vocal opposition to Proposition 14, an effort to repeal an unpopular state fair housing law, proved helpful to Murphy. Derided as a "song and dance man" by the Democrats, Murphy's show business personality appealed to Californians, and he slowly chipped away at his opponent's early lead in the public opinion polls. Some political analysts saw the professional Murphy campaign as one of the first to fully exploit the political potential of television. He defeated Salinger by 215,000 votes out of more than 7 million cast. Salinger allowed Murphy to replace him on Dec. 31, 1964 so that he would have seniority over other newly elected senators.

Although Murphy described himself as a "dynamic conservative" in the Eisenhower tradition, his victory was interpreted as part of the right-wing revival in California politics, and he proved to be one of the most conservative members of the Senate. As of 1968, for example, the conservative Americans for Constitutional Action gave Murphy's cumulative voting record a score of 83. According to *Congressional Quarterly*, Murphy voted in disagreement with the Senate's conservative coalition on only 5% of key roll-call votes during 1965 and 1966. As a member of the Labor and Public Welfare Committee, Murphy often expressed the minority conservative viewpoint on Administration-sponsored antipoverty legislation, sharply attacking the "bureaucratic bungling" of the new programs. He vigorously sought to expand the role of the states in the management of federal programs and to give governors veto power over the allocation of federal funds in their respective states. In September 1965 Murphy broke his usual pattern by voting with the Labor and Public Welfare Committee majority to report a bill that would repeal state "right-to-work" laws, but in October he opposed a cloture vote to stop debate on the bill. As a member of the Labor and Public Welfare Committee's Migratory Labor Subcommittee, he sided with California's large farmers in 1966 in opposing the Labor Department's limitations on the importation of Mexican farm workers. In general, Murphy objected to the extension of national labor legislation to agriculture.

Murphy sometimes supported social welfare measures, as in April 1967, when he urged the President to take more vigorous action to combat hunger and in May 1968, when he voted to expand the Department of Agriculture's food distribution program. In September 1968 he reversed his 1967 position on the Teacher Corps by voting for fund increases, stating that he was "now satisfied that the program is doing a good job."

In the late 1960s Murphy, an extreme hawk on the Vietnam war issue, criticized President Johnson for imposing too many restraints on the U.S. Army in the field. He later became a steadfast supporter of President Nixon's prosecution of the war. Despite growing disenchantment with the conflict among California voters, it was assumed that Murphy would be reelected easily. However revelations early in 1970 that he had been on the payroll of Technicolor, Inc., since he entered the Senate badly hurt his reputation. In the November election Rep. John Tunney (D, Calif.), a moderate and an opponent of the war, defeated Murphy by nearly 600,000 votes.

[JCH]

MUSKIE, EDMUND S(IXTUS)

b. March 28, 1914; Rumford, Me.
Democratic Senator, Me., 1959- .

Muskie, the son of an immigrant Polish tailor, grew up in Rumford, Me. He studied at Bates College in Lewiston, Me., and at Cornell Law School, where he received an LL.B. in 1939. After military service during World War II, he returned to Maine and won election to the state House of Representatives, serving two terms as a Democrat. In 1951 he left the legislature to become state director for the Office of Economic Stabilization.

Muskie first gained wide political attention three years later, when he revived Maine's weak and demoralized Democratic Party by defeating the incumbent Republican governor. Although he won reelection in 1956 by a wide margin, Muskie's effectiveness as governor was limited by Republican domination of the state legislature. Rather than seek a third term in 1958, he decided to run for the U.S. Senate. Muskie defeated the Republican incumbent with 61% of the vote and became the first Democrat elected to the Senate in Maine's history. Observers attributed his victory to the state's economically depressed condition and the growing proportion of ethnic voters in the largely rural population.

Muskie began his Senate career inauspiciously, offending powerful Majority Leader Lyndon Johnson by voting for an anti-filibuster measure that Johnson opposed. As a result Muskie was denied the Foreign Affairs Committee assignment he had requested and placed instead on the Banking and Currency, Public Works and Government Operations Committees. Muskie sought to make the best of what he viewed as a bad situation by working conscientiously at his committee tasks. He soon became known in the Senate as an expert at formulating workable legislation and mobilizing support for it. Johnson himself, despite his initial hostility towards Muskie, later praised him as "one of the few liberals who's a match for the Southern legislative craftsmen." [See KENNEDY Volume]

As Muskie gained experience in the Senate, he discovered that his committee assignments were not as unfavorable as they had seemed at first. The Public Works Committee, in particular, involved him in environmental matters, which greatly concerned the voters in Maine's scenic and undeveloped areas. In 1962 he was named chairman of the Public Works Subcommittee on Air and Water Pollution. By the time pollution became a major national issue during the mid-1960s, Muskie was the leading Senate authority in the field and the sponsor of several landmark environmental measures. These included the Water Quality Acts of 1963 and 1965, the Clean Air Act of 1963 and the Clean Rivers Restoration Act of 1966. All provided federal funds for pollution control programs and mandated the Interior Department and the Department of Health, Education and Welfare to set standards for pollutant emissions. Muskie was also instrumental in establishing new agencies to coordinate and encourage work on pollution control. These included the Federal Water Pollution Control Administration and the Environmental Quality Council, created in 1969 in the Office of the President.

In addition to his liberal stand on environmental issues, Muskie was a strong and steady supporter of President Johnson's Great Society programs. The liberal Americans for Democratic Action consistently gave him "correct" ratings of 85% to 90%. Muskie won the Administration's gratitude in 1966 by successfully floor-managing the Model Cities Act, an urban development program that faced strong opposition from Senate conservatives and rural congressmen. That year he was appointed assistant Democratic whip in the Senate, and in 1967 he became chairman of the Democratic Senatorial Campaign Committee. On Vietnam policy Muskie generally followed the Administration's lead during the mid-1960s, though leaning privately towards a more "dovish" position. In January 1968 he expressed reservations about the bombing of North Vietnam in a private letter to President Johnson. At the 1968 Democratic National Convention, however, he opposed the anti-war platform proposal, which demanded an unconditional bombing halt.

Despite his growing influence in the Senate and the development of national concern over environmental issues, Muskie remained little known outside Maine and Washington during the mid-1960s. Vice President Hubert Humphrey [*q.v.*] thus gave Muskie national exposure for the first time by choosing him as his running mate in the 1968 presidential contest. Most political observers agreed that Muskie made a favorable impression during the campaign with his low-keyed approach and appeals for reasoned judgment on public issues. He was particularly effective in politely but firmly dealing with anti-war hecklers at his campaign appearances. Humphrey himself viewed Muskie as his "greatest asset" in the close race, and Democratic campaign manager Larry O'Brien [*q.v.*] called him "a co-performer with Hubert." National polls indicated that Muskie was considerably more popular than Republican vice presidential candidate Spiro T. Agnew [*q.v.*].

Muskie returned to his Senate duties after the narrow Democratic defeat in November 1968. He continued to concentrate on environmental issues and sponsored several pollution control bills during the early 1970s. His importance within the national Democratic Party was far greater than before, and he maintained a busy speaking schedule. During the 1970 congressional campaign Muskie gained wide approval with a nationally televised talk criticizing Republican claims that Democratic candidates were "soft on crime." He was an early contender for the Democratic presidential nomination in 1972 but lost to Sen. George McGovern (D, S.D.) [*q.v.*]. In 1976 Muskie, who did not make a second effort at the presidency, was given consideration as a possible running mate of Democratic nominee Jimmy Carter but was passed over in favor of Sen. Walter Mondale (D, Minn.) [*q.v.*]. [See NIXON Volume]

[SLG]

For further information:
David Nevin, *Muskie of Maine* (New York, 1972).

MUSTE, A(BRAHAM) J(OHANNES)

b. Jan. 8, 1885; Zierikzee, Netherlands.
d. Feb. 11, 1967; New York, N.Y.
Clergyman, peace activist.

Raised in Michigan, Muste was ordained as a Dutch Reformed minister in 1909. His first position brought him to New York, where he joined the Fellowship of Reconciliation, a non-denominational pacifist group, in 1916. A socialist and an opponent of World War I, Muste was drawn to labor radicalism and helped lead the 1919 Lawrence, Mass., textile strike. He directed the Brookwood Labor School in the 1920s and was an organizer of the successful Toledo Auto-Lite strike in 1934.

"Nonviolence," Muste told a group on the eve of World War II, "is not apathy or cowardice or passivity." His opposition to U.S. support of the war caused his influence to decline in the late 1930s and 1940s, but by the late 1950s his ideas were again becoming widely known, especially in the new postwar peace movement. He joined David Dellinger [*q.v.*] and Bayard Rustin [*q.v.*] in founding *Liberation* magazine in 1956 and the following year became chairman of the Committee for Nonviolent Action (CNVA). Muste's pacifism influenced Martin Luther King [*q.v.*], who joined the Fellowship of Reconciliation in the early 1950s. [See TRUMAN, EISENHOWER Volumes]

During the early 1960s Muste opposed all nuclear tests and urged unilateral disarmament. He helped organize the 1961 San Francisco-to-Moscow Walk for Peace and was co-chairman of the 1962 Hiroshima Day Committee and the United Easter Peace Demonstrations Committee in 1963. [See KENNEDY Volume]

Muste was a leading opponent of U.S. involvement in Vietnam and worked with various anti-war groups, including the War Resisters League and the Mobilization Committee to End the War. In a June 1965 meeting, which he termed frustrating, Muste presented his views to Secretary of Defense Robert McNamara [*q.v.*] while anti-war protesters distributed pamphlets in the Pentagon.

As chairman of the Committee for a Fifth Avenue Peace Parade, Muste led several marches and demonstrations in New York in 1965 and 1966. At a draft-card burning rally in November 1965, he called for an expanded program of civil disobedience. He refused to pay his federal income tax in 1966 in order not to participate in the government's "serious crimes against humanity."

Muste and five other pacifists were expelled from South Vietnam in April 1966 for attempting to hold anti-war demonstrations there. Accompanied by two other clergymen, he traveled to Hanoi in January 1967. The three conferred with Ho Chi Minh, who, they said, had invited President Johnson to Hanoi for peace talks. Although the Defense Department maintained that only military targets had been scheduled for bombings, Muste later reported having seen residential sections of the North Vietnamese capital that had been bombed on Dec. 13 and 14, 1966. The three urged an immediate, unconditional end to U.S. bombing of North Vietnam, warning that otherwise there could be no progress toward ending the war. Before his death the following month, Muste described himself as "an unrepentant unilateralist, on political as well as moral grounds."

[MDB]

For further information:
Nat Hentoff, *Peace Agitator: the Story of A. J. Muste* (New York, 1963).

NADER, RALPH
b. Feb. 27, 1934; Winsted, Conn.
Consumer activist.

The son of Lebanese immigrants, Nader grew up in a small Connecticut town where his father owned a restaurant. He attended Princeton University and Harvard Law School, where he edited the student newspaper, the *Record*. It was at Harvard that Nader became absorbed in the subject of auto safety, particularly the dangers of vehicle design. After receiving his law degree in 1958, he served a six-month stint in the Army, traveled around the world as a free-lance journalist, conducted a law practice in Hartford, Conn., and continued his campaign for stricter auto safety legislation in Massachusetts and Connecticut.

In 1964 Nader carried his crusade to Washington, D.C., as a consultant to Assistant Secretary of Labor Daniel P. Moynihan [*q.v.*], who had been working on the issue of auto safety since the mid-1950s. Nader devoted a year to producing for Moynihan a 234-page report criticizing the government's role in highway safety. Moynihan used the report, which very few people read, to buttress his own efforts to win Administration support for federal regulation of automobile manufacture. In May 1965 Nader left the Labor Department to write a book on the role of vehicle defects in automobile crashes. Simultaneously, he was associated, unofficially and without pay, with the Senate Government Operations Subcommittee on Executive Reorganization, which, under Chairman Abraham A. Ribicoff (D, Conn.) [*q.v.*], was holding hearings on traffic safety. Nader supplied the subcommittee's staff director, Jerome Sonofsky, with ideas, technical information and questions for witnesses.

Nader achieved some public recognition with the publication in November 1965 of *Unsafe at Any Speed: The Designed-in Dangers of the American Automobile*, a scathing indictment of the automobile industry for emphasizing style, speed and comfort to the detriment of safety. By focusing on the dangerous features of automotive design, he intended to refute the prevailing belief that driver deficiencies were the main cause of automobile deaths and injuries. He detailed the various hazards of the "second collision" that occurred when the car's occupant was thrown against the interior of the vehicle after a crash to injure himself on protruding knobs, rigid steering wheels and easily shattered windshields. Nader singled out for special attack the General Motors (GM) Corvair for having an unsafe rear suspension system and other dangerous defects. He castigated the Corvair design as "one of the greatest acts of industrial irresponsibility in the present century."

Nader won widespread public attention in March 1966, when he charged before Ribicoff's subcommittee that GM had initiated an investigation into his personal life in order "to obtain lurid details and grist for invidious use." More than 50 of his friends and relatives had been questioned by private investigators about his sex habits, political beliefs and attitudes towards Jews. Nader also asserted that he had been followed, had received harassing telephone calls and had had two suspicious encounters with young women who tried unsuccessfully to lure him to their apartments.

At first GM called Nader's charges "ridiculous," but a few days later the corporation acknowledged the investigation, labeling it "routine" and denying that it involved "harassment or intimidation." On March 22, in a nationally televised hearing, GM President James Roche [*q.v.*] appeared before the subcommittee and admitted that GM had initiated an investigation into Nader's private life and that there had been some harassment. He conceded that the probe was "most unworthy of American business" and publicly apologized to Nader. Roche denied that any girls had been employed as "sex lures," however. Ribicoff characterized the investigation as "an attempt to downgrade and smear a man," adding that the detectives had been unable to find "a damn thing wrong" with Nader.

In November 1966 Nader filed an invasion-of-privacy suit against GM for $26 million. He was awarded $425,000 in August 1970 in an out-of-court settlement. Nader said that he would use the money to monitor GM's activities in the safety, pollution and consumer relations areas.

The revelation of GM's harassment of Nader aroused public indignation and gave an impetus to the campaign for federal regulation of automobile manufacture. Nader continued his persistent lobbying effort and participated in the drafting of the actual legislation. In the summer of 1966 the Traffic and Motor Vehicle Safety Act passed the Senate by vote of 76 to 0 and the House by 331 to 0. The new Act was a strong law directing the Secretary of Commerce to prescribe detailed safety standards for all new cars, buses, trucks and other motor vehicles. Nader applauded the bill's passage but voiced his disappointment that it did not contain criminal penalties for manufacturers who violated its provisions.

Nader's crusade for auto safety did not end with President Johnson's signing of the measure in September 1966. He became an active and critical watchdog of the National Highway Safety Agency, which was set up to promulgate safety regulations and ensure their enforcement. Before the first set of standards was issued on Jan. 31, 1967, he charged that the Agency showed "disturbing signs of being intimidated" by the auto industry. After they were issued he denounced the new regulations as being too lenient and "considerably weakened" to meet industry objections. Nader said the Agency's leaders "did not compromise with the industry" but "surrendered to it." In March he criticized the auto manufacturers for "banding together" to claim that strict standards were impossible when in fact they were practicable and to exaggerate the costs of the safety improvements. The combination of harsh invective, a solid array of technical information and an unwillingness to compromise became hallmarks of Nader crusades.

The auto safety campaign was the first of many probes by Nader into areas where he believed citizens were being victimized. In mid-1967 he attacked the unwholesome conditions in intrastate meat-packing plants, which were not subject to federal inspection. Through publicity and congressional lobbying he contributed to the passage in December of the Wholesome Meat Act, which gave states two years to bring their inspection systems up to federal standards. Other Nader campaigns resulted in the passage of the Natural Gas Pipeline Safety Act of 1968 and the Coal Mine Health and Safety Act of 1969.

In the summer of 1968 a team of law students organized by Nader began an investigation of the Federal Trade Commission (FTC), the regulatory agency charged with the general responsibility of policing the market economy and protecting consumers. The investigators, whose invasion of the Commission's headquarters in Washington earned them the nickname "Nader's Raiders," produced a 185-page report in January 1969 harshly critical of the FTC. They accused the Commission of inadequate protection of the consumer, "collusion with business interests," secrecy and lassitude. The group's effort led to the revitalization of the FTC under the Nixon Administration.

The birth of Nader's Raiders, first institutionalized as the Center for Study of Responsive Law in 1969, signified the expansion of Nader's personal crusade into an organized network of well-educated young people working on behalf of the public interest. Inspired and guided by Nader, teams of his young followers labored to expose and correct corporate abuses and government failures in a host of new areas, including air and water pollution, antitrust enforcement, taxation, land policy in California, nursing homes, federal regulatory agencies and the U.S. Congress. They used Nader's techniques of investigation, exposure, lobbying and litigation to galvanize movements for reform in these areas.

Nader himself occupied a position unique in American political life. His spartan lifestyle and his refusal to capitalize on his fame set him apart from other figures in public life and strengthened his image as a selfless champion of the public interest. He held no elective or appointive office, but his name attached to an obscure or controversial cause could do more to arouse public awareness and disarm skepticism than that of any other individual. [See NIXON Volume]

[TO]

NEAL, JAMES F.

b. Sept. 7, 1929; Sumner County, Tenn.
Special Assistant to the Attorney General of the United States, 1961-64.

Neal was educated at the University of Wyoming and Vanderbilt University, where he received an LL.B. in 1957. He entered private practice in Tennessee and studied at Georgetown University for an LL.M., which he received in 1960.

Neal entered government service in 1961, when he joined the staff of young lawyers assembled by Attorney General Robert F. Kennedy [*q.v.*] to investigate corruption in the Teamsters union. He was assigned to investigate charges that Teamsters President Jimmy Hoffa [*q.v.*] had accepted substantial payments from a trucking employer to preserve labor peace. Working closely with Walter Sheridan, chief Justice Department investigator in Teamsters affairs, Neal accumulated enough evidence to indict Hoffa in May 1962. This was the 25th indictment against Hoffa filed during the Kennedy Administration. The trial began on Oct. 27 in Nashville, Tenn., with Neal as chief prosecutor. It ended two months later in a mistrial, with charges from the judge that associates of Hoffa had attempted to "fix" the jury.

Neal and Sheridan were able to bring Hoffa to trial again in January 1964 for jury-tampering. The government's main witness in the trial was Edward Partin, secretary-treasurer of a Teamsters local in Baton Rouge, La., who was himself accused of embezzling union funds. Partin had attached himself to Hoffa during the Nashville trial and had transmitted information to Sheridan concerning Hoffa's plan to bribe jurors. Hoffa was found guilty by a Chattanooga jury on March 5 and sentenced to eight years in prison and a $10,000 fine. Neal was again chief prosecutor in the trial, thus winning credit for the government's first conviction of the Teamster leader. Hoffa went to prison in 1967 and subsequently lost his several union offices.

After prosecuting Hoffa Neal left Washington to become U.S. attorney for the middle district of Tennessee. He returned to private practice in Nashville in 1966 and taught law at Vanderbilt University until 1974. Neal briefly resumed his public career in 1973, as a staff member of the Watergate Special Prosecution Force.

[SLG]

For further information:
Walter Sheridan, *The Fall and Rise of Jimmy Hoffa* (New York, 1972).

NELSON, GAYLORD A(NTON)

b. June 4, 1916; Clear Lake, Wisc.
Democratic Senator, Wisc., 1963-   .

Gaylord Nelson was the son of a Wisconsin country doctor who was a devoted supporter of Robert M. LaFollette's Progressive Party. After earning a law degree and serving in the Pacific during World War II, Nelson ran as a Republican in 1946 for a seat in the Wisconsin state Assembly. He lost, along with many other followers of Sen. Robert M. LaFollette Jr., but was elected to the state Senate as a Democrat in 1948. After 10 years service in the Senate, Nelson was elected in 1958 as Wisconsin's first Democratic governor since 1932. As governor, Nelson attacked industrial polluters and launched an Outdoor Resources Acquisition Program, financed by a penny tax on cigarettes. The program committed the state to a $50 million land acquisition program to preserve wild and unspoiled areas against developers. He also carried out the first major reform of the state's tax system in 50 years, introducing a state sales tax. Nelson was elected to the U.S. Senate in 1962 over the incumbent Republican, Sen. Alexander Wiley [See KENNEDY Volume]

In the Senate Nelson joined the bloc of liberal Democrats. *Congressional Quarterly* reported that in 1964 he voted against the conservative coalition of Republicans and Southern Democrats more than any other senator. Nelson supported the Great Society legislation of the Johnson Administration, taking a special interest in the Teacher Corps, which he and Sen. Edward M. Kennedy (D, Mass.) [*q.v.*] cosponsored in 1965. Created as part of the Elementary and Secondary Education Act of 1965, the Corps was designed to alleviate the shortage of teachers in poverty areas by training young volunteers and supporting them while they gained teaching experience in low-income districts. In September 1968 Nelson successfully introduced an amendment to raise the funding of the Corps from $17 million to $31 million.

An early environmentalist, Nelson introduced the first legislation to ban DDT in 1965, but he was unable to find any cosponsors for the proposal. In the same year he introduced a bill to place a tax on strip mining to finance reclamation. As a member of the Senate Interior and Insular Affairs Committee, many of his efforts were directed against industrial pollution of the Great Lakes. He was particularly concerned about the activities of the Reserve Mining Company, which was dumping tons of waste from its taconite processing plant into Lake Superior. Since 1963 Nelson had fought to get a federal enforcement conference held on the matter. He finally succeeded in January 1969 when outgoing Secretary of the Interior Stewart Udall [*q.v.*] signed the order for the Lake Superior conference. (As of 1975 prlonged litigation had failed to put an end to the dumping of taconite into the lake.) Nelson achieved recognition as the originator of "Earthweek" in April 1970. In October of that year the *New Republic* said of him, "Nelson . . . probably comes closest to being [the Senate's] resident national philosopher on ecology."

Influenced by consumer advocate Ralph Nader [*q.v.*], Nelson became active in the campaign to legislate automobile and tire safety. He introduced a bill in February 1965 to authorize the Secretary of Commerce to prescribe safety standards for all automobiles sold in the United States. The standards were to be the same as those already required by the General Services Administration for the purchase of government vehicles. In April Nelson proposed a bill to mandate tire safety standards, claiming that "tire production was dominated by the automobile industry, which has a great incentive to reduce unit costs in every possible way." This "discourages the production of really high quality tires, which many motorists should be using." A revised version of Nelson's bill was introduced by Sen. Warren Magnuson (D, Wash.) [*q.v.*] and became the Tire Safety Act of 1966.

Nelson was one of the earliest Senate opponents of the Vietnam war. In the 1964 debate on the Gulf of Tonkin Resolution, Nelson proposed an amendment to clarify the intent of the Resolution and prevent it from being used to justify later expansion of American involvement. He withdrew his amendment, however, after Sen. J. William Fulbright (D, Ark.) [*q.v.*] assured him it was superfluous, and Nelson voted for the Resolution. Unlike most anti-war senators, Nelson consistently voted against supplemental appropriations to pay for the war. From 1965 to 1968 only Wayne Morse (D, Ore.) [*q.v.*] and Ernest Gruening (D, Alaska) [*q.v.*] joined Nelson in this form of opposition.

In November 1967 Nelson secured $20 million in tax relief for the American Motors Corp. (AMC). His amendment permitted AMC's losses to be carried back five years instead of three. Nelson said that the tax break was essential to enable the company, Wisconsin's largest employer, to continue to compete with the Big Three automakers and to give it "working capital at a most critical time in its recovery."

Nelson was reelected in 1968 with 62% of the vote, an impressive showing in a year when Wisconsin gave its electoral votes to Richard Nixon and also elected a Republican governor. Following the election Nelson continued an investigation into the drug industry that he had begun in 1967 as chairman of the Subcommittee on Monopoly of the Select Small Business Committee. [See NIXON Volume]

[TO]

NEUBERGER, MAURINE (BROWN)
b. Jan. 9, 1907; Cloverdale, Ore.
Democratic Senator, Ore., 1960-66.

Maurine Neuberger taught English and physical education in Oregon's public schools before joining her husband Richard in the state legislature in 1951. As a Democratic state representative she sponsored bills on education and consumer protection. After her husband's election to the U.S. Senate in 1954, she worked as his unpaid research and public relations assistant. When he died in March 1960, Maurine Neuberger was elected first to complete his unexpired term and then to a six-year term of her own.

In the Senate she gained a reputation as a liberal and participated in a 1962 filibuster against the Kennedy Administration's communications satellite bill because the new system was privately owned and operated. Neuberger sponsored a variety of reform measures, including an anti-billboard bill and a tax amendment that allowed working women to deduct the cost of child care from their taxable income.

Neuberger wrote *Smoke Screen: Tobacco and the Public Health* in 1963. When the U.S. Surgeon General's report, linking smoking and lung cancer, was released in January 1964, she became a leading congressional spokeswoman for legislation on smoking. Neuberger wrote the bill that required cigarette labels and ads to include the warning that "smoking may be hazardous to your health." She proposed that the Federal Trade Commission establish standards for the labeling and advertising of cigarettes and that the Department of Health, Education and Welfare research the effects of smoking, study methods of reducing its hazards and conduct a national educational program on smoking. Her proposal in January 1965 that these regulations be made effective within a year was rejected unanimously by the Senate Commerce Committee in favor of a three-year grace period for cigarette companies. Neuberger was also a major supporter of an unsuccessful bill introduced in 1967 to require that warning labels for each brand of cigarettes include their tar and nicotine levels.

Along with "truth in packaging," Neuberger favored "truth in lending" and cosponsored a bill that would have required lenders to disclose the amount and rate of interest in advance. Although endorsed by President Johnson in January 1965, he did not press for the measure's passage and no action was completed on the bill.

Neuberger introduced a successful bill in 1966 to authorize the Housing and Urban Development Agency to study the scenic and economic effects of overhead powerlines. Her repeated attempts to add the Oregon Dunes National Seashore to the National Parks system were successfully opposed by Sen. Wayne Morse (D, Ore.) [*q.v.*] and local developers despite support from the President.

In January 1966 Neuberger joined 15 other senators who sent a letter to Johnson calling for continued suspension of the air strikes against North Vietnam. Near the end of her term, the Subcommittee on the Health of the Elderly, which she chaired, held hearings on detection and prevention of chronic diseases and utilization of multiphasic health screening techniques. She retired from Congress in 1966 but continued her campaign against smoking. In February 1967 Johnson appointed Neuberger to be the first woman on the Arms Control and Disarmament Agency, and in August 1967 he made her chairwoman of the Citizens Advisory Council on the Status of Women.

[MDB]

For further information:
Hope Chamberlin, *A Minority of Members: Women in the U.S. Congress* (New York, 1973).

NEWTON, HUEY P(ERCY)

b. Feb. 17, 1942; New Orleans, La.
Minister of Defense, Black Panther Party, 1966- .

The son of a sharecropper and Baptist preacher, Newton grew up in Oakland, Calif. He attended high school in Oakland and graduated from Merritt College, a two-year institution, in 1965. He also took courses at the University of San Francisco Law School. Newton's education was interrupted in 1964 by a six-month prison term, which resulted from a political argument in which he threatened an adversary with a knife. While attending Merritt Newton met Bobby Seale [*q.v.*], a fellow student who shared Newton's interest in black nationalism and the problems of the ghetto. Inspired by the ideas of Malcolm X [*q.v.*], the two founded the Black Panther Party in October 1966, with Seale as chairman and Newton as minister of defense.

Initiated as a grass-roots organization in Oakland, the Panthers sought to protect ghetto residents against what they considered police harassment and other forms of government oppression. Taking advantage of a California law that permitted bearing arms in public, Black Panthers with weapons appeared as "observers" in police-citizen encounters. The Party was generally unknown outside the Bay Area until May 2, 1967, when 30 armed Panthers marched into the California State Assembly to protest a gun-control measure then under consideration. The national attention that this action received stimulated the growth of the Panthers, who reached the apex of their membership at about 2,000 in the late 1960s, with chapters in most major cities of the North and West.

The growth of heavily armed Panther groups also drew the attention of the police and the Federal Bureau of Investigation. According to the American Civil Liberties Union, police killed or wounded at least 24 Panthers in shootouts between 1967 and 1969. During this period the Black Panthers developed from a militant "self-defense" organization into an openly revolutionary group, with an emphasis on guerrilla tactics and urban warfare. In 1968 the Panther established close contact with a number of white radical groups, joining them to form the Peace and Freedom Party.

One of the first casualties of police-Panther animosity was Newton himself; he was wounded in Oakland on Oct. 28, 1967 in a shootout that left one policeman dead and another wounded. Put on trial for first-degree murder in July 1968, Newton won the support of black and white radicals throughout the country, who considered him a political prisoner. Demonstrators crying "Free Huey" repeatedly converged on the Oakland courthouse, where the trial was held. Newton, who claimed that he was unconscious as a result of a previous gunshot wound during the gun battle, was convicted of voluntary manslaughter. He spent two years in prison before his conviction was overturned by the California Court of Appeals, which found that the judge in the first trial had "omitted instructions" to the jury concerning Newton's claim of unconsciousness.

Released from prison in August 1970, Newton found the Panthers in disarray. Membership had dropped to less than 1,000 due to police harassment and factional quarrels, both within the Panthers and between them and other militant groups. It was later revealed that some of this strife resulted from letters forged by the FBI and accusations spread by infiltrators. Newton attempted to pull the Party together by de-emphasizing violence and anti-police activity. He involved the Panthers in a number of community action programs, including free breakfasts for school children and health clinics for ghetto residents. The Panthers also supported the United Black Fund, a church organization that subsidized social services in ghettos.

Newton's turn to social action brought him into conflict with Panther Education Minister Eldridge Cleaver [*q.v.*], who had fled to Algeria in 1968 to escape imprisonment for a parole violation. Cleaver believed the Panthers should remain an openly revolutionary organization with continued emphasis on armed resistance. In 1972 he withdrew from the Party, taking much of the East Coast membership with him. Senate investigations of U.S. intelligence activities later revealed that this conflict was also exacerbated by threats and accusations planted by the FBI. Newton and Seale remained in control of the Panthers on the West Coast, where they continued their policy of community involvement.

Newton wrote *Revolutionary Suicide*, published in 1973. He also published a collection of interviews and speeches entitled *To Die for the People* (1972).

[SLG]

For further information:

Gilbert Moore, *A Special Rage* (New York, 1971).

"Huey P. Newton," *Current Biography Yearbook, 1973* (New York, 1974), pp. 307-310.

NITZE, PAUL H(ENRY)
b. Jan. 16, 1907; Amherst, Mass.
Secretary of the Navy, November 1963-June 1967; Deputy Secretary of Defense, June 1967-January 1969.

A high State Department official during the postwar years, Nitze helped prepare the congressional legislation responsible for the Marshall Plan. In his capacity as head of the Policy Planning Staff in 1950, he drafted "NSC-68," a National Security Council document proposing that America accept unilateral responsibility for the defense of the non-Communist world. [See TRUMAN Volume]

Out of office during the Eisenhower years, Nitze returned to public service in 1959 as adviser to the Senate Foreign Relations Committee and in 1960 as head of John F. Kennedy's pre-election task force on national defense problems. During the Kennedy Administration Nitze served as assistant secretary of defense for international security affairs and head of the President's task force on Berlin in 1961. As a member of the Executive Committee of the National Security Council, he urged Kennedy to use massive air strikes to prevent the buildup of Soviet missiles in Cuba in 1962, a position he later recanted. [See KENNEDY Volume]

In October 1963 Kennedy appointed Nitze Secretary of the Navy. Believing that one of the keys to a successful defense policy was the effective management of the service's extensive technological capability, the Secretary reorganized the Department of the Navy in 1966. His chief reform was creating the Office of Chief of Naval Material to direct the allocation of manpower and material resources.

In an attempt to coordinate the technological capabilities of the Air Force and Navy, Nitze was an early advocate of the multi-service TFX, the swing-wing fighter/bomber whose cost overrides and technological problems made it a controversial project during the 1960s and 1970s.

During April 1967 Nitze worked closely with Secretary of Defense Robert McNamara [*q.v.*] in the Secretary's attempts to de-escalate the bombing of North Vietnam. They proposed that the Administration cease bombing above the 20th parallel, a plan rejected by President Johnson in the absence of what he considered enemy willingness to reciprocate.

In June 1967 President Johnson appointed Nitze deputy secretary of defense. Two months later Nitze again joined McNamara in writing a conciliatory proposal modifying the Administration's previous demand for North Vietnamese de-escalation before peace negotiations could begin. The "San Antonio Formula," sent privately to Hanoi, stated, "The United States is willing immediately to stop all aerial and naval bombardment of North Vietnam when this will lead promptly to productive discussions." On Oct. 3 North Vietnam emphatically rejected the plan.

During the first days of March 1968, Nitze was a member of the Ad Hoc Task Force on Vietnam formed to study the military's request for over 200,000 additional ground troops following the Communist Tet offensive. Within this group Nitze was a strong opponent of further escalation. Arguing that the Administration should view U.S. involvement in Vietnam in the wider context of U.S. interests elsewhere in the world, he cautioned that further troop increases could lead to direct military confrontation with China or jeopardize military commitments elsewhere. Instead of continued escalation he advised a policy of strengthening the South Vietnamese Army and withdrawing American troops. After deliberation the committee rejected Nitze's recommendation and supported the request for ground troops. Most of the additional troops, however, were never sent to Vietnam. On March 31 President Johnson, on the advice of a group of senior statesmen and counselors, announced a policy of gradual de-escalation.

As deputy secretary, Nitze strongly supported the development of a limited antiballistic missile system, known as Sentinel, to protect the United States from a potential attack by Communist China. Nitze served as deputy secretary until January 1969. In November 1969 he went to Helsinki as a member of the U.S. delegation to the Strategic Arms Limitation Talks.

[EWS]

NIXON, RICHARD M(ILHOUS)
b. Jan. 9, 1913; Yorba Linda, Calif.
Republican presidential nominee, 1968.

Nixon grew up in Whittier, Calif., where he worked in the family grocery store and attended public schools and Whittier College. A competitive student, he won a scholarship to Duke University Law School. After graduation in 1937 Nixon practiced law in Whittier. He went to work for the Office of Price Administration in 1942 and seven months later joined the Navy.

In 1946 Nixon conducted an aggressive campaign for the House of Representatives in which he capitalized on anti-Communist sentiment by questioning the patriotism of his liberal opponent, Rep. Jerry Voorhis (D, Calif.). Nixon defeated Voorhis and, as a member of the House Un-American Activities Committee, gained national attention by playing the most prominent role in the early investigation of former State Department official and accused spy Alger Hiss. Nixon's part in the Hiss probe aided him in his 1950 senatorial campaign in which he defeated Rep. Helen Gahagan Douglas (D, Calif.) by a wide margin. [See TRUMAN Volume]

At the July 1952 Republican National Convention, presidential nominee Dwight D. Eisenhower [*q.v.*] selected as his running mate the 39-year-old Nixon, whose youth and conservative domestic policy record made him an attractive concession to the GOP's Old Guard. Elected in 1952 and reelected in 1956, Nixon wielded very little real power, but he received more public exposure than most vice presidents. In contrast to Eisenhower, Nixon played a partisan political role while holding national office. He campaigned more frequently than the incumbent President and established close ties with countless Party officials. At the President's initiative Nixon visited 56 nations between 1953 and 1959. An attack on Nixon and his wife by a left-wing mob in Caracas, Venezuela, in 1958 and Nixon's "kitchen debate" with Soviet Premier Nikita Khrushchev in Moscow in 1959 reinforced the Vice President's stature as a spokesman for the West. Once a political "no man's land," the vice presidency became a political stepping-stone under Nixon. [See EISENHOWER Volume]

In 1960 Nixon ran as the Republican nominee for president, but his campaign failed to find a decisive issue upon which he could distinguish himself from John F. Kennedy. On foreign policy questions Nixon was unable to outflank Kennedy on the right, since both candidates accepted the basic tenets of U.S. strategy in the Cold War and employed similar rhetoric. Domestically, Nixon made little headway in the South or among traditional Democratic voters in the North. Though he won more states than Kennedy, he lost the electoral college by 303 to 219 votes.

Nixon ran a disastrous campaign for governor of California two years later. Rated an easy victor in the early polls, he lost to Gov. Edmund G. Brown [*q.v.*] by 52% to 47%. The morning after the election Nixon offered a concession speech in which he attacked the press for biased reporting throughout his career. "You won't have Nixon to kick around any more," he told the assembled reporters, "because, gentlemen, this is my last press conference." With his political career apparently over, Nixon left California in June 1963 for a lucrative law practice in New York City. [See KENNEDY Volume]

Despite his two defeats Nixon still felt that he had a chance for the 1964 Republican presidential nomination. Immediately after Kennedy's assassination his support among Republican voters outranked all other potential candidates. Nixon decided not to actively seek the nomination; rather, he hoped for a Convention deadlock between conservative Sen. Barry Goldwater (R, Ariz.) [*q.v.*] and liberal New York Gov. Nelson A. Rockefeller [*q.v.*], both of whom campaigned in the primaries. At the National Governors Conference shortly after the June 2 California primary, Nixon tried to maneuver Michigan Gov. George W. Romney [*q.v.*] into the race as a last-minute "stop-Goldwater" candidate. Romney declined, and Nixon accepted Goldwater's candidacy as inevitable.

When Nixon returned from a trip abroad at the end of June, he held a strategy session with senior advisers at Montauk, Long

Island, that would chart the course for a successful presidential campaign four years later. Although Nixon and his aides believed that Goldwater had no chance of election, they decided that Nixon should campaign vigorously for the national ticket after the Convention to win for the former Vice President the gratitude of Goldwater's GOP constituency.

Nixon carefully followed the Montauk strategy. He appeared before the Republican National Convention and introduced Goldwater prior to the candidate's acceptance speech. Between Sept. 30 and Nov. 3 he conducted a 36-state, 150-stop speaking tour for the Republican candidate. Nixon, Goldwater recounted appreciatively in January 1965, "worked harder than any person for the [1964] ticket." Following Goldwater's defeat Nixon negotiated with the 1964 nominee to prevent a fight over the removal of former Goldwater aide Dean Burch [*q.v.*] as Republican National Committee chairman.

Nixon's law practice permitted him to make annual world tours that enhanced his image as a foreign policy specialist. *Reader's Digest*, published by political supporters of Nixon, reprinted his major foreign policy statements. A 1964 Asian visit confirmed Nixon's earlier militancy concerning Communist insurgency in Vietnam. The next year Nixon said the U.S. was "losing the war in Vietnam" and recommended an escalation of American air and naval activity in North Vietnam. In the 1966 off-year elections, Nixon campaigned hard for GOP congressional candidates. Of the 86 gubernatorial and congressional candidates whom he aided, almost 70% won.

In the race for the 1968 Republican presidential nomination, Nixon initially ran second in the polls to Gov. Romney, who enjoyed the support of Rockefeller and other liberal GOP leaders. Through 1967, however, Romney's careless, impromptu remarks reduced his credibility as a national candidate. By the end of the year, press coverage of Romney's mistakes had cost the Governor his lead over Nixon among Republicans and independents. In late February 1968, just two weeks prior to the first presidential primary in New Hampshire, Romney dropped out of the race. Three weeks later Rockefeller announced that he would not challenge Nixon.

Nixon's early 1968 campaign strategy called for a heavy emphasis upon foreign policy. Amid growing public concern over America's Vietnam policies, Nixon told a Hampton, N.H., audience on March 4 that he would end the war, but he avoided explaining how he would fulfill the promise. After President Johnson announced a halt in the bombing and the beginning of negotiations with the North Vietnamese, Nixon announced that he would no longer discuss Vietnam or his "plan" for ending the war. He argued that to do so might jeopardize Vietnam peace talks scheduled to open in May.

During the spring Nixon took important steps towards the nomination. His "loser" image had been countered somewhat by overwhelming wins in the primaries against unofficial, makeshift campaigns for Rockefeller and California Gov. Ronald Reagan [*q.v.*], Nixon's two main competitors. In June Nixon secured the endorsement of Sen. Strom Thurmond (R, S.C.) [*q.v.*], which assured him substantial support from Southern Republicans. In exchange Nixon promised to support construction of an anti-ballistic missile system and to consult the conservative Southerner in the selection of a running mate and the nomination of new Supreme Court judges acceptable to the South. Though ideologically closer to Reagan, Thurmond and Goldwater backed Nixon largely because polls clearly showed him to be the stronger candidate. In June Sen. Mark O. Hatfield (R, Ore.) [*q.v.*], the leading anti-war Republican and a liberal, endorsed Nixon. Hatfield's support gave credence to Nixon's presentation of himself as a Party "centrist" standing between the liberal Rockefeller and conservative Reagan.

With 692 delegate votes, 25 more than required, Nixon won the 1968 Republican presidential nomination on the first ballot. Nixon then surprised the convention by naming little-known Maryland Gov. Spiro T. Agnew [*q.v.*] as his vice presidential running mate. Nixon chose Agnew in part because he was acceptable to the Southern conservative wing of the Party and in part because Nixon himself did not want to share the limelight with an attractive, well-known figure like Reagan, Hatfield or New York Mayor John Lindsay [*q.v.*].

Nixon entered the fall campaign with a commanding lead in the polls. Division within the Democratic Party over Vietnam hampered its presidential nominee, Vice President Hubert Humphrey [*q.v.*], while Alabama Gov. George C. Wallace [*q.v.*], campaigning as the candidate of the American Independent Party, threatened to take Northern blue-collar votes from the Democrats. In mid-september Nixon led Humphrey and Wallace in the Gallup Poll 43%-31%-19%, respectively.

In a year of widespread protest and violence, Nixon, like Wallace, searched for the votes of those Americans least identified with the tumult. In his acceptance speech Nixon spoke of "the forgotten Americans, the non-shouters, the non-demonstrators." Aiming his campaign at this group of voters, he made crime a major issue; he assailed the Johnson Administration for allegedly favoring criminals and promised to fire Attorney General Ramsey Clark [*q.v.*]. Nixon and his trusted adviser John Mitchell [*q.v.*] shaped a $42 million campaign that they considered appropriate for a front-runner: meticulously planned, relatively unhurried, strongly based on television coverage and the avoidance of specific proposals on important issues. Nixon virtually wrote off the black vote, visiting only two black communities during the entire autumn.

Nixon's front-runner strategy was sharply challenged in early October, when Humphrey's campaign suddenly gained momentum. On Sept. 30 Humphrey broke with Administration policy on Vietnam and called for a halt to all American bombing missions over North Vietnam. A mild position compared to that of anti-war Democrats, it nevertheless became a rallying point for Party "doves" opposed to Nixon. Two days before the election a Gallup Poll reported that Nixon's lead over Humphrey had shrunk to two percentage points.

Nixon responded to the narrowing of the race by raising a new campaign issue. In an Oct. 24 speech he claimed that concentration of military spending on the Vietnam war had created the danger of a "strategic gap" in missile strength between the U.S. and USSR. Even strategic parity, he claimed, would be a "moral victory" for the Soviet Union, which had fewer economic resources for its military programs. Nixon continued to emphasize a hard line on defense during the rest of the campaign. In the last days before the election, he told a Fort Worth, Tex., audience, "I am the one that stands for a stronger U.S., and Mr. Humphrey for a weaker U.S."

Nixon's narrowing lead was further jeopardized on Oct. 31, when President Johnson announced that the U.S. would halt the bombing of North Vietnam and broaden the Paris peace talks to include the National Liberation Front and the Saigon government. Anna Chennault, a conservative Republican with ties to the South Vietnamese rulers, sought to undermine Johnson's peace initiative by inducing South Vietnamese President Nguyen Van Thieu to declare just prior to the election that he would not join the Paris discussions. Although Humphrey learned of Chennault's interference, he believed Nixon innocent of any involvement and declined to make her activity public. Observers speculated after the election that to have done so might have brought a critical sympathy vote to the Democrats.

Nixon won the election, one of the closest in U.S. history, with 43.4% of the vote to Humphrey's 42.7% and Wallace's 13.5%. He narrowly captured New Jersey, Ohio, Illinois and California, as well as most Border, Western and Middle Western states to win 302 Electoral College votes, just 42 more than necessary. Nixon's performance among blacks and Eastern suburbanites was worse in 1968 than in 1960. He replaced these losses, however, with better margins in ethnic working-class areas and in the South. Nixon's election established as Party policy Goldwater's emphasis on winning the growing "Sun Belt" states, running from the Southeast to California, and his relative indifference to the populous, industrialized states of the Northeast.

Nixon's political "resurrection" was subsequently attributed to many causes. Between 1962 and 1968 Nixon displayed a keen political acumen acquired from many years in Party leadership posts. Yet he also enjoyed spectacular good fortune. As he himself admitted, the divisive 1964 election caused the defeat of several potential rivals for the 1968 nomination. It also made the choice of a liberal or conservative contender seem a threat to Party unity.

Nixon spent his first term as President "winding down" the Vietnam war. Soon after his inauguration he de-escalated U.S. military participation in Vietnam while renewing bombing raids over the North and ordering the invasion of neutral Cambodia. Following the Cambodian "incursion," as he termed it, and the withdrawal of most American ground forces, anti-war demonstrations steadily dwindled in size, number and intensity. In January 1973 the U.S. ended its role in Vietnam through a negotiated peace, the terms of which failed to prevent South Vietnam's collapse in April 1975.

In other foreign policy initiatives, Nixon helped calm Cold War tensions between East and West. He pursued the Johnson Administration's policy of detente with the Soviet Union, and in February 1972 he visited Communist China, to the horror of many of his old, anti-Communist political allies.

Economics difficulties dominated domestic policy during Nixon's presidency. Unemployment rose with a recession that lasted from 1969 to 1971 and, contrary to economic theory, so did inflation. Reversing his previously stated positions Nixon imposed wage-price controls in 1971. This action caused a sharp deterioration in his relationship with most of the U.S. labor movement, led by AFL-CIO president George Meany [*q.v.*].

Nixon won a landslide reelection victory in November 1972, but it was marred by the revelation of a June 1972 break-in at Democratic National Headquarters in Washington by staff members of his reelection committee. Following the burglars' arrest, Nixon, his Attorney General and other aides attempted to cover-up the link between Watergate and the campaign. Nixon's role in the affair was eventually revealed when, after a long court fight, White House tape recordings became public in 1974. Shortly after the House Judiciary Committee voted articles of impeachment in late July 1974, Nixon resigned the presidency. His successor, Gerald R. Ford [*q.v.*], granted him a full pardon in September 1974. [See NIXON Volume]

[JLB]

For further information:
Kevin P. Phillips, *The Emerging Republican Majority* (New Rochelle, 1969).
Jules Witcover, *The Resurrection of Richard Nixon* (New York, 1970).

NOVAK, ROBERT D(AVID) S(ANDERS)

b. Feb. 26, 1931; Joliet, Ill.
Syndicated columnist.

Novak graduated from the University of Illinois in 1952, served in the Army during the Korean conflict and joined the Associated Press in 1954. After a stint as a political columnist for the *Wall Street Journal,* he began the syndicated column "Inside Report" with fellow journalist Rowland Evans in May 1963. While Evans was considered the "lightweight" of the team, supplying Washington contacts and dealing with publishers, Novak earned a reputation for his investigative persistence and his bluntness in expressing his views. Specializing in columns that gave inside information on domestic politics and foreign affairs, the team employed polls, questionnaires of rank-and-file voters and personal interviews to lend substance and depth to their stories. By the late 1960s Evans and Novak were syndicated by 300 newspapers and had become the most widely read political columnists in the U.S.

A close friend of Lyndon B. Johnson's before the 1964 election, Novak maintained his credentials as a "maverick" by withdrawing much of his earlier support for the President by the end of his term. This prompted Johnson to say on more than one occasion, "I never have to be told when Bob Novak's around. I can *smell* him." In 1966 Evans and Novak published *Lyndon*

B. Johnson: The Exercise of Power, an account of Johnson's business interests, rise through the Senate, vice-presidential years and his use of power in the White House. The book included a vivid description of what the two columnists called "The Johnson Treatment," which was employed whenever Johnson needed a vote or a favor: "From his [Johnson's] pockets poured clippings, memos, statistics. Mimicry, humor, and the genius of analogy made "The Treatment" an almost hypnotic experience and rendered the target stunned and helpless."

Early in the Johnson Administration Evans and Novak assailed campus unrest, the anti-war movement and radical civil rights organizations like the Student Nonviolent Coordinating Committee (SNCC). Described by *Time* magazine as the "zealots of the Center," the team repeatedly and vociferously attacked the candidacy of Sen. Eugene McCarthy (D, Minn.) [*q.v.*] during the 1968 presidential campaign. In the 1972 election they called Sen. George McGovern (D, S.D.) [*q.v.*] "the doyen of the Democratic Party's left fringe," while describing Sen. Edmund Muskie (D, Me.) [*q.v.*] as "splendid" and "tough-mineded." Their heavy reliance on Democratic Party regulars and conservative sources led to a dramatic underestimation of McGovern's strength in the 1972 presidential primaries.

[FHM]

For further reading:

Timothy Crouse, *The Boys on the Bus* (New York, 1972).

Rowland Evans and Robert Novak, *Lyndon B. Johnson: The Exercise of Power* (New York, 1969).

O'BOYLE, PATRICK A(LOYSIUS)

b. July 18, 1896; Scranton, Pa.
Roman Catholic Archbishop of Washington, 1948-73.

O'Boyle, the son of an Irish immigrant steelworker, grew up in Scranton. He was ordained in 1921 after graduating from St. Thomas College (later Scranton University) and St. Joseph's Seminary in New York. Assigned to work in several New York social service agencies, O'Boyle proved himself an able administrator; in 1947 New York Archbishop Francis Cardinal Spellman [*q.v.*] appointed him director of the city's Catholic charities. One year later O'Boyle was elevated to archbishop as leader of the New archdiocese of Washington, D.C. He became a cardinal in 1967.

O'Boyle aroused considerable controversy in the Washington area during the early 1950s as a strong advocate of civil rights. In 1951, before the Supreme Court decision barring segregation in public schools, he ordered the integration of Catholic schools and other institutions in his archdiocese. In 1963 O'Boyle organized the Interreligious Committee on Race Relations, which attempted to promote the economic advancement of Washington's inner-city blacks. He delivered an invocation at the 1963 March on Washington and pressed for a special declaration against discrimination at the Second Vatican Council in Rome. O'Boyle was also one of the few Catholic church leaders in the U.S. to create a special office in his archdiocese devoted to urban affairs. Some civil rights advocates criticized O'Boyle for not going far enough in opposing discrimination, especially in the social functions of Washington parishes. However, a 1965 *Washington Post* survey revealed great respect for the Archbishop among black leaders.

Though O'Boyle was known as a "liberal" in secular affairs, he was a conservative on matters of religious ritual and doctrine. He opposed changes in the Mass, especially the substitution of English for Latin in 1964. During the late 1960s O'Boyle became involved in a heated controversy over birth control. A five-day student strike broke out in 1967 at Washington's Catholic University, a center of liberal Catholic thought in the U.S., when O'Boyle ordered the dismissal of a theology professor for advocating the limited use of contraception. O'Boyle, who was chancellor of the University, relented after meeting with the board of trustees and allowed the professor's reinstatement.

When Pope Paul VI reaffirmed the church's traditional ban on birth control in

1968, O'Boyle strongly supported the Vatican position. This brought him into conflict with a number of priests in his archdiocese, who refused to counsel against birth control and signed a declaration recommending that Catholics use contraception "according to their consciences." O'Boyle eventually dismissed 40 dissenters from their priestly functions, an action that brought further protest and unrest in his archdiocese. In September 1968 several hundred worshippers walked out on a sermon he was delivering at Washington's St. Matthew's Cathedral. The dispute was settled only in 1971 by a Vatican decision affirming the correctness of O'Boyle's position but allowing the priests to resume their functions without recanting their views.

Excoriated by opponents as "the Mayor Daley [Chicago Mayor Richard Daley (*q.v.*)] of Catholicism" for his stand on birth control, O'Boyle spent his last years in office under a cloud of criticism and unpopularity. He offered his resignation in 1971 and retired as archbishop in March 1973.

[SLG]

O'BRIEN, LAWRENCE F(RANCIS)

b. July 7, 1917; Springfield, Mass.
Special Assistant to the President for Congressional Relations, January 1961-August 1965; Postmaster General, November 1965-April 1968.

O'Brien grew up in Springfield. His father, a real estate dealer and businessman, was active in the local Democratic Party and awakened an early fascination with politics in the young O'Brien. At 15 O'Brien was a part-time Democratic worker, and he continued his political involvement while taking night courses at Boston's Northeastern University. After graduating in 1942 and serving three years in the Army, he reentered politics to manage the congressional campaign of his friend, Foster Furcolo. Defeated in 1946, Furcolo won two years later and invited O'Brien to accompany him to Washington as his administrative assistant. O'Brien remained with Furcolo until 1950, when he began working for Rep. John F. Kennedy (D, Mass.)

As chief campaign organizer on the Kennedy staff, O'Brien managed Kennedy's successful senatorial drives of 1952 and 1958 as well as his 1960 presidential race. With great care and thoroughness O'Brien created a network composed largely of volunteers to handle everything from distribution of campaign literature to voter registration drives.

In January 1961 President Kennedy appointed O'Brien as his special assistant for congressional relations. This post was especially important for the new Administration, which faced strong opposition to its legislative program from Republicans and Southern Democrats on Capitol Hill. For the next three years O'Brien attempted to narrow the distance between Congress and the President, supervising a network of liaison offices in all federal agencies and departments that presented Administration positions to the legislators. O'Brien's efforts helped pass a number of liberal measures during the early 1960s, including an increase in the minimum wage, an omnibus housing bill and a constitutional amendment barring the state poll tax. [See KENNEDY Volume]

At President Johnson's urging O'Brien remained with the new Administration as congressional liaison after the Kennedy assassination. As he recounted in his autobiography, *No Final Victories* (1974), O'Brien continued his lobbying efforts to carry through the remainder of Kennedy's legislative program and then to take advantage of the new opportunities for liberal legislation which opened with the large Democratic congressional gains of 1964. Among the measures that he pushed strongly in 1965 were medicare, aid to education and the Voting Rights Act; at the end of the 1965 congressional session the Administration could point to a record of 87 major bills proposed and 84 passed. O'Brien also served as Johnson's "eyes and ears" on important issues, traveling frequently around the country to gauge public opinion. He sent back early warnings of growing public concern over Vietnam, an issue that he considered partly responsible for Democratic losses in the 1966 congressional elections.

In November 1965, with a large part of the Administration's legislative program either enacted or near passage, President Johnson appointed O'Brien Postmaster General. Although O'Brien continued to advise the President on legislative matters, he sought to be more than a "figurehead" in the Post Office Department and applied himself seriously to his new task. He soon became disturbed by what he viewed as antiquated postal facilities, inadequate promotion procedures and high turnover among the large number of low-level minority group postal employes. In April 1967 he proposed a postal reform plan involving replacement of the existing Post Office Department with a non-profit government corporation managed by a professional executive. O'Brien's proposal was set aside for "study" during the Johnson Administration but later enacted by President Richard Nixon.

In early 1968 O'Brien joined the growing number of Democratic leaders who warned President Johnson of increasing unrest within the Party over Vietnam. During the New Hampshire primary campaign, he wrote several memos to the President urging a bombing pause and the phased reduction of American forces. After Johnson's primary setbacks and his withdrawal from the race in late March, O'Brien resigned as Postmaster General to direct the presidential campaign of Sen. Robert F. Kennedy (D, N.Y.) [*q.v.*]. Using his tested campaign techniques, he organized the Kennedy primary drives in Indiana, Nebraska, Oregon and California. All but the Oregon contest ended successfully for Kennedy, and O'Brien was optimistic about his candidate's chances for gaining the Democratic nomination when the campaign was cut short by Kennedy's assassination on June 5.

As the Kennedy staff disbanded O'Brien shifted his support to Vice President Hubert Humphrey [*q.v.*], whose campaign he helped manage in the last weeks before the 1968 Democratic National Convention. During negotiations over the Party platform, O'Brien attempted to preserve Democratic unity by working for a compromise Vietnam plank. This effort was frustrated, however, by Johnson's refusal to accept any statement that did not affirm Administration policy. Although O'Brien had originally intended to leave the campaign after the Democratic Convention, he changed his mind at Humphrey's request and accepted appointment as chairman of the Democratic National Committee. Working to counter the Democratic disarray that followed the Convention, O'Brien quickly created a campaign organization that dramatically narrowed the initial lead of Republican candidate Richard M. Nixon [*q.v.*] during the last weeks of the contest. Inadequate campaign funds continued to hamper the Democratic effort and played a major role, according to O'Brien, in Humphrey's narrow defeat.

In January 1969 O'Brien resigned from the Democratic National Committee to take a position with McDonnell and Co., a New York investment firm. He left seven months later and was again appointed chairman of the Democratic National Committee in March 1970. O'Brien was an important Democratic spokesman during the 1970 congressional elections, attacking Republican emphasis on the crime issue as "the politics of fear." He later helped implement reforms in the selection of delegates for the 1972 Democratic Convention and presided over stormy debates at the Convention itself. During the 1972 presidential primary campaign, O'Brien became the principal target of the Republican intelligence-gathering efforts that led to the Watergate affair. Some observers speculated that the Administration was interested in information on O'Brien's possible connection with the affairs of billionaire Howard Hughes [*q.v.*], with whom he had once contracted to do public relations work. In 1973 O'Brien again resigned from his chairmanship of the Democratic National Committee, passing the office to former Committee Treasurer Robert Strauss of Texas. [See NIXON Volume]

[SLG]

For further information:
Lawrence F. O'Brien, *No Final Victories* (New York, 1974).

O'DONNELL, KENNETH P(ATRICK)
b. March 4, 1924; Worcester, Mass.
Special Assistant to the President, January 1961-January 1965.

Kenneth O'Donnell grew up in Boston, served in the Army Air Force during World War II and graduated from Harvard with a degree in politics and government. His relationship with John F. Kennedy dated from Kennedy's first race for Congress in 1946, when he served as a campaign aide.

O'Donnell served as chief political tactician in the 1960 presidential campaign. As appointments secretary during the Kennedy Administration, O'Donnell's job gave him wide but often concealed powers. He controlled access to the President, allocated White House office space, served as liaison with the FBI and Secret Service and dispensed political patronage. He also handled the logistics of all presidential trips both in the U.S. and abroad.

In November 1963 O'Donnell was in charge of the political arrangements for President Kennedy's visit to Dallas, Tex., which involved delicate negotiations with the feuding Gov. John Connally [*q.v.*] and Sen. Ralph Yarborough (D, Tex.) [*q.v.*]. In the aftermath of Kennedy's assassination, O'Donnell, despite interference from local officials, saw to it that Kennedy's body was returned immediately to Washington aboard Air Force One. [See KENNEDY Volume]

Among the most vigorous opponents of Johnson's vice presidential nomination, O'Donnell, nevertheless, remained on the Johnson staff the longest of the old Kennedy team. While acknowledging that O'Donnell's first allegiance was to the political ambitions of Robert Kennedy [*q.v.*], Johnson needed O'Donnell as a link to the big-city Democratic leaders who were virtually unknown to the new President. Shortly before the 1964 Democratic National Convention, Johnson urged O'Donnell to act as liaison with Robert Kennedy and to request Kennedy's voluntary withdrawal from consideration for the vice presidential nomination on the Johnson ticket. O'Donnell refused to take any action because of his anomalous position as an assistant to Johnson and a supporter of Robert Kennedy. On July 30, 1964 Johnson announced a decision—clearly formulated with Kennedy in mind—to bar cabinet members from the vice presidential candidacy. During the 1964 campaign O'Donnell, who was still a White House aide, was named executive director of the Democratic National Committee and given the assignment of arranging Johnson's campaign schedule.

O'Donnell resigned from Johnson's staff on Jan. 16, 1965. The next year he ran in the Democratic gubernatorial primary in Massachusetts, losing to Edward McCormack by nearly 100,000 votes. While Robert Kennedy supported O'Donnell, Sen. Edward Kennedy (D, Mass.) [*q.v.*], anxious not to alienate House Speaker John McCormack (D, Mass.) [*q.v.*], whose nephew he had defeated in the 1962 Senate race, remained neutral. The O'Donnell campaign demonstrated that the Kennedy political legacy did not necessarily carry over to the late President's subordinates.

In 1968 O'Donnell actively supported Robert Kennedy's presidential candidacy. He collaborated with former White House special assistant David Powers on *Johnny, We Hardley Knew Ye*, a 1970 memoir that was particularly vivid in its description of the Irish-Catholic milieu from which the career of John Kennedy developed.

[FHM]

For further information.
Kenneth P. O'Donnell and David F. Powers, *Johnny, We Hardly Knew Ye* (New York, 1970).

O'DWYER, (PETER) PAUL
b. June 29, 1907; Bohola, Ireland.
Member, New York City Council, 1963-65.

Arriving in New York from Ireland in 1924, O'Dwyer met for the first time his older brother William, later mayor of New York (1946-50). Following his brother's example O'Dwyer studied law at night while working in New York garment shops and on the Brooklyn docks. Later he served as legal counsel for the Transit Workers and other New York unions. An active supporter of the Zionist movement from 1946 on, an early advocate of civil rights for blacks and a one-time president of the National Lawyers Guild, O'Dwyer developed a reputation as a perennial supporter of liberal and left-wing causes.

O'Dwyer ran for Congress from Manhattan's Upper West Side in 1948 with the backing of the Democratic and American Labor Parties, but he lost in a close race to incumbent Rep. Jacob K. Javits (R, N.Y.) [*q.v.*]. In 1958 O'Dwyer, Eleanor Roosevelt, Herbert H. Lehman and other liberal Democrats founded the Committee for Democratic Voters and launched the New York Democratic reform movement. O'Dwyer sought and failed to gain the New York Democratic senatorial nomination in 1962, but he won a seat on the New York City Council the following year.

O'Dwyer went South at the request of the Congress of Racial Equality in the summer of 1964. He defended civil rights demonstrators and worked with the Mississippi Freedom Democratic Party (MFDP). That August, as a New York delegate to the Democratic National Convention, O'Dwyer supported the MFDP's bid to be seated in place of the segregationist, regular Mississippi Democratic delegation. The Credentials Committee voted to seat the regular delegation and offered two at-large voting seats to Freedom Democratic Representatives. The MFDP delegation voted to reject the compromise)

O'Dwyer began a campaign for the Democratic nomination for mayor of New York in June 1965. In the Sept. 14 primary he finished a distant fourth behind New York City Controller Abraham D. Beame [*q.v.*] and two other candidates. (Beame lost the general election to the Republican-Liberal candidate, Rep. John V. Lindsay [*q.v.*].)

In October 1966 O'Dwyer successfully defended Ernest Gallashaw, a 17-year-old black youth accused of fatally shooting an 11-year-old boy during racial violence that July in Brooklyn's East New York district. During the same year O'Dwyer also won a U.S. Supreme Court decision granting Puerto Rican citizens the right to take voting literacy tests in their native language.

A critic of United States policy in Vietnam, O'Dwyer was an early and important supporter of Sen. Eugene J. McCarthy's (D, Minn.) [*q.v.*] 1968 presidential campaign. O'Dwyer himself sought New York's senatorial nomination in a primary fight against Nassau County Executive Eugene Nickerson, a supporter of Sen. Robert F. Kennedy (D, N.Y.) [*q.v.*], and Rep. Joseph Y. Resnick (D, N.Y.), who supported Vice President Hubert H. Humphrey [*q.v.*]. O'Dwyer was given little chance of victory. He continually attacked Administration policy in Vietnam and pledged that even if McCarthy were defeated, "I would not support Humphrey. Period." O'Dwyer won a narrow victory in the June 18 primary.

O'Dwyer was a leader of the strong McCarthy group in the New York delegation to the Democratic National Convention in Chicago. During the Aug. 28 platform debate, O'Dwyer spoke in favor of the minority plank on Vietnam, which called for an unconditional bombing halt, a negotiated U.S. withdrawal and urged the South Vietnamese government to negotiate a political reconciliation with the National Liberation Front. The Administration's majority plank was passed 1,537 to 1,041. That same night O'Dwyer was involved in a melee on the Convention floor when New York delegate Alex Rosenberg refused to show security guards his credentials. O'Dwyer intervened when guards attempted to expel Rosenberg. In the resulting commotion Chicago police came onto the Convention floor, and both O'Dwyer and Rosenberg were briefly detained.

In New York O'Dwyer's senatorial campaign against Republican-Liberal incumbent Jacob K. Javits and Conservative Party candidate James L. Buckley focused on the Vietnam war. O'Dwyer called for a cease-fire and an end to the draft. He also called for community control of schools, free heroin distribution to registered addicts and an end to "hypocritical talk" about law and order. O'Dwyer's refusal to endorse the national ticket continued until Nov. 1 when, following President Johnson's announcement of a halt to the bombing of North Vietnam, he finally endorsed

Humphrey. Four days later O'Dwyer lost by over a million votes to Javits, who continued his record as New York State's leading vote-getter. O'Dwyer remained active in public life and in 1973 was elected president of the New York City Council. In 1976 he ran unsuccessfully for the Democratic Senatorial nomination. [See NIXON Volume]

[JBF]

OGLESBY, CARL

b. July 30, 1935; Akron, Ohio.
President, Students for a Democratic Society, June 1965-September 1966.

Son of an Akron, Ohio rubber worker, Oglesby attended public schools and Kent State University. He spent a year in New York's Greenwich Village and wrote three plays. In the early 1960s Oglesby—by then married and the father of three children—worked as a technical writer for the Bendix Systems Division in Ann Arbor, Mich. In the fall of 1964 Oglesby wrote an article critical of U.S. policy in the Far East, prompting local members of Students for a Democratic Society (SDS) to contact him. Oglesby soon became active in SDS anti-war activity. At the SDS National Council meeting following the group's April 1965 anti-war rally in Washington, D.C., Oglesby proposed that SDS establish a research, information and publication bureau. The proposal was accepted, and Oglesby was hired to staff the bureau.

Oglesby was elected SDS president at the organization's June 1965 convention. A member for less than a year, Oglesby was the first SDS president to come from outside the "old guard" that had revitalized the organization in the early 1960s. His election reflected the growing influx of Midwestern and Southwestern students attracted to SDS by its anti-war activities. Immediately after his election Oglesby traveled to South Vietnam and Japan to meet with anti-war groups.

During Oglesby's presidency SDS grew rapidly and established itself as the leading campus opponent of the escalating United States intervention in Vietnam. Although generally critical of national demonstrations, SDS endorsed the plans of the National Coordinating Committee to End the War for anti-war demonstrations on Oct. 15-16, 1965. On the eve of the protests, columnists Rowland Evans and Robert Novak [*q.v.*] alleged that SDS was mounting a campaign to get men to resist and evade the draft and was drawing up "a master plan" designed to "sabotage the war effort." Although Evans and Novak's claim was based on a proposal SDS had already rejected, several U.S. senators and Deputy Attorney General Nicholas B. Katzenbach [*q.v.*] joined the attack on SDS. The criticism and the demonstrations brought SDS far more publicity than it had ever previsouly received, and its chapter membership virtually doubled to an estimated 10,000 members. At a widely publicized press conference shortly after the demonstrations, Oglesby and SDS National Secretary Paul Booth announced a proposal to exempt from military service men participating in alternative "service for democracy," but SDS itself later repudiated the plan, which had not been approved by its rank-and-file membership.

SDS participated in the Nov. 27, 1965 Committee for a Sane Nuclear Policy's march in Washington. Oglesby delivered what was generally considered the day's most influential speech. He argued that the Vietnam war was a product of "American liberalism," which served as an ideological justification and defense of the "corporate state." The speech, which Oglesby later called "an attempt to describe imperialism without giving it that name," was reprinted and became one of the most popular pieces of SDS literature. In June 1966, in a change of position, Oglesby joined the new chairman of the Student Non-Violent Coordinating Committee, Stokely Carmichael [*q.v.*], in rejecting alternate service and calling for an end to the draft.

After leaving office in September 1966, Oglesby coauthored a critical study of United States foreign policy, *Containment and Change*, and in 1967 was one of three United States members of Stockholm-based International War Crimes Tribunal sponsored by Bertrand Russell. In June 1968

Oglesby again became active in SDS when he was elected to the eight-member National Interim Committee. Oglesby opposed both the Progressive Labor Party and those supporting the "Revolutionary Youth Movement" strategy, the two strongest factions in SDS. As a result he did not play a major role in SDS's split the next year. During the 1970s Oglesby wrote articles analyzing the American power structure and the role of the intelligence community in domestic politics.

[JBF]

For further information:
Carl Oglesby and Richard Schaull, *Containment and Change: Two Dissenting Views of American Society and Foreign Policy in the New Revolutionary Age* (New York, 1967).
Kirkpatrick Sale, *SDS* (New York, 1973).

OKUN, ARTHUR M(ELVIN)

b. Nov. 28, 1928; Jersey City, N.J.
Chairman, Council of Economic Advisers, January 1968-January 1969.

Arthur Okun took a leave of absence from the economics department at Yale University to serve on the staff of the Council of Economics Advisers (CEA) during 1961 and 1962. Specializing in projecting the Gross National Product (GNP), he formulated "Okun's Law," which correlated each 1% decrease in the unemployment rate, when the rate was high, with a 3.2% increase in the GNP. Okun's estimate of a generally predictable relationship between employment and economic growth provided a statistical rationale for the CEA's advocacy in 1963-64 of massive tax cuts to stimulate lagging demand.

Okun was made a member of the CEA in 1964 and appointed its chairman in January 1968. An adherent of the Keynesian "new economics," Okun, like his predecessors Walter Heller [*q.v.*] and Gardner Ackley [*q.v.*], believed that the federal government could generate rapid growth and maintain price stability through an aggressive and alert fiscal policy. As early as January 1967 Okun had argued that the economy's main problem was not sluggishness but rising prices. His major efforts as CEA chairman were directed against inflation, which had been exacerbated by the simultaneous expansion in spending for the Vietnam war and the Administration's domestic programs. Okun defended the Administration's main deterrent against inflation, the 10% tax surcharge, passed by Congress in May 1968. The measure also restored the 10% phone and the 7% automobile excise tax and mandated a $6 billion budget reduction.

Okun took a firm stand on the Johnson Administration's second line of defense against inflation, the struggle to moderate industrial wage settlements and price rises. As part of the Administration's reaction to Bethlehem Steel's announcement of a 5% across-the-board steel price rise in July 1968, followed by similar increases on the part of other major producers, Okun sent telegrams urging the steel companies to consult with the government prior to price decisions. When U.S. Steel, the largest producer, posted increases averaging 2½%, Bethlehem and the other producers reduced their own increases to that level. Okun was a major figure in the Administration's campaign of pressure and exhortation to curb auto prices following an announcement by Chrysler in September of an $89, or 2.9%, increase on its 1969 models. Chrysler lowered its increase to the government-recommended 2% level after Ford and General Motors held their 1969 increases to that amount. Okun left the CEA in January 1969 and became a senior fellow at the Brookings Institution.

[TO]

OTTINGER, RICHARD L(AWRENCE)

b. Jan. 27, 1929; New York, N.Y.
Democratic Representative, New York, 1965-70, 1974- .

Ottinger's father founded U.S. Plywood Co. and his uncle, Albert Ottinger, ran as a Republican against Franklin Roosevelt in the 1928 race for the New York governorship. Richard Ottinger, a Democrat, graduated from Cornell in 1950 and took a law degree from Harvard in 1953. Ottinger was a subregional director of the Peace Corps from 1961 until 1964, when he defeated the incumbent Republican congressman from New York's 25th district, spending over $200,000 of his family's money.

Representing the western half of Westchester County, Ottinger established a liberal voting record, which earned him an Americans for Democratic Action rating of 82% by the end of his first term. An early congressional spokesman for environmental problems, Ottinger's concern about pollution in the Hudson River led him to criticize the 1965 anti-water pollution bill as inadequate for the needs of New York State. The new appropriations authorized by the bill, he said, "will be little more than a sigh in a hurricane." When 1966 water pollution legislation required the development of interstate water basin plans, Ottinger, claiming that the other states involved would be only minimally affected, engineered a compromise that allowed New York and New Jersey the power to veto any plan for the Hudson. Ottinger testified in 1966 on the need for a federal study of the environmental effects of power lines and tried, unsuccessfully, to add 60,000 miles of gas-gathering lines to a 1967 gas pipeline safety bill. In 1968 he supported elimination of funds for the supersonic transport (SST) airliner.

Ottinger consistently supported the Johnson Administration's foreign and domestic policies during his first two terms. He urged federal research on non-punitive drug addict rehabilitation plans and in 1967 attempted, without success, to increase hospital construction funds. However, Ottinger was one of two representatives to vote against the 1967 military construction bill that appropriated funds for the Vietnam war. In June 1968 Ottinger offered an amendment to limit the President's power to increase the number of U.S. troops in South Vietnam, invade North Vietnam or other Southeast Asian countries or use nuclear weapons there.

Ottinger also opposed Johnson's plan for compulsory arbitration of the 1967 railroad strike, which Congress approved. Ottinger denounced arbitration that denied the right to strike because, he said, it "takes away from the railroads involved in the dispute any incentive to bargain collectively."

Ottinger remained in Congress until 1970, when he ran for the Senate. He came in second in a three-way race against Republican Charles Goodell [*q.v.*] and the victor, Conservative James Buckley. He returned to Congress in 1974, when he won election from Westchester's other congressional district, previously held by Ogden Reid [*q.v.*].

[MDB]

PASSMAN, OTTO E(RNEST)

b. June 27, 1900; Washington Parish, La.

Democratic Representative, La., 1947-77; Chairman, Foreign Operations Subcommittee Appropriations Committee, 1955-77.

Passman became a member of the House Appropriations Committee in 1949. Six years later Committee Chairman Rep. Clarence Cannon (D, Mo.) appointed Passman to head the panel's Foreign Operations Subcommittee, which initiated congressional consideration of foreign aid appropriations bills. Dominating the subcommittee, Passman became the most powerful foe of foreign assistance programs on Capitol Hill. With the support of Cannon he succeeded in sharply reducing Eisenhower and Kennedy Administration annual foreign aid requests. In 1963 President Kennedy's assistance proposal was cut by 33.8%, the largest reduction since the beginning of the foreign aid program. [See EISENHOWER, KENNEDY Volumes]

Cannon died in May 1964 and was replaced as Appropriations Committee chairman by Rep. George H. Mahon (D, Tex.) [*q.v.*]. President Lyndon B. Johnson had been a colleague of Mahon in the Texas congressional delegation. and the new chairman, although not a friend of foreign aid, was amenable to Administration influence. Furthermore, Mahon was determined to assert control of the Committee and decided to begin by challenging Passman's previously unquestioned authority over foreign assistance bills. In addition, President Johnson used his extensive network of connections on Capitol Hill to undermine Passman's support on the foreign operations panel.

As a result, Passman's attempt to cut $515 million from the Administration's $3.5 billion foreign aid request was rejected by the subcommittee in the spring of 1964 by a vote of seven to five. Ultimately, Congress voted to reduce the foreign aid program by only 7.6%.

The following year Mahon revamped the membership of the subcommittee to further reduce Passman's support on the panel. Again his efforts to substantially reduce foreign aid were rebuffed, and Administration requests were cut by just 6.9%.

During the last three years of the Johnson Administration, opposition to foreign aid increased as the cost of the Vietnam war placed pressure upon the remainder of the budget. In 1966 and 1967 Congress cut foreign aid requests by 13.3% and 28.8%, respectively. In 1968 the Administration's proposed figure was slashed by 39.7%, which represented a record cut.

Passman, the floor manager of the 1968 aid bill, declared, "We believe this is a bill which should satisfy those of us who have been trying to bring the annual aid appropriations . . . down to a reasonable amount."

He remained the most outspoken opponent of foreign aid in Congress and continued to have influence in that area. But Passman never regained the unchallenged power over assistance appropriations he had possessed. In January 1975 liberals in the House Democratic Caucus failed in a bid to remove Passman from his subcommitee chairmanship.

[MLL]

PASTORE, JOHN O(RLANDO)

b. March 17, 1907; Providence, R.I.
Democratic Senator, R.I., 1950-77.

John Pastore grew up in Providence, R.I. He graduated from Northeastern University Law School in 1931 and then launched a career in local politics. He was elected lieutenant governor of Rhode Island in 1944 and assumed the governorship one year later, following the resignation of J. Howard McGrath. In 1950 Pastore became the first Italian-American ever elected to the U.S. Senate.

A liberal Democrat, Pastore supported the Kennedy Administration on most major issues. As chairman of the Communications Subcommittee of the Senate Commerce Committee, he was active in the regulation of television and other broadcast media. In his post as vice chairman of the Joint Congressional Atomic Energy Committee, Pastore was a vigorous and occasionally volatile supporter of the 1963 limited nuclear test ban treaty. [See EISENHOWER, KENNEDY Volumes]

Pastore supported the Johnson Administration on over 65% of all major issues. He led the Senate fight for Title VI of the 1964 Civil Rights Act, which prohibited racial discrimination in any program or activity receiving federal assistance. He voted for the 1965 medicare bill, and he was a strong supporter of the President's Vietnam policies. In 1965 he lost a close fight for the post of majority whip to Sen. Russell Long (D, La.) [*q.v.*].

Pastore delivered the keynote address at the 1964 Democratic National Convention in Atlantic City, N.J., and set the rhetorical tone for the presidential campaign to follow. Speaking of the "prosperity, preparedness and peace" of the Kennedy years and the previous "nine miracle months" of the Johnson Administration, Pastore declared that Sen. Barry Goldwater (R, Ariz.) [*q.v.*] and the Republican Party had been "captured" by extremists. He urged the nation to keep a "safe" trigger-finger on the atomic bomb.

In 1966 Pastore introduced a resolution of support for the Administration's efforts to achieve a nuclear nonproliferation treaty. He requested that the treaty include a requirement for international inspection of nuclear facilities and recommended that Communist China be included in disarmament talks. Later that year Pastore criticized the Administration for rejecting "out of hand" a 1965 proposal by Communist China asking that both nations agree never to take the initiative in the use of nuclear weapons against each other.

Pastore was a consistent advocate of a strong national defense posture. He declared in 1967 that the U.S. "should move full-speed ahead on building an anti-ballistic missile system [ABM]" and said that if the country was able to spend $24 billion a year in Vietnam it could "certainly spend as much to insure the life and security of our American society." Later, Pastore supported the Nixon Administration's ABM program.

In 1969 Pastore's Communications Subcommittee conducted widely publicized hearings on the effects of televised violence on children. He was reelected to the Senate in 1970 by a large margin. [See NIXON Volume]

[FHM]

PATMAN, (JOHN WILLIAM) WRIGHT

b. Aug. 6, 1893; Patman's Switch, Tex.
d. March 7, 1976; Bethesda, Md.
Democratic Representative, Tex., 1929-76; Chairman, Banking and Currency Committee, 1963-75.

Wright Patman adhered for a lifetime to the anti-Wall Street populism prevalent in the turn-of-the-century rural Texas of his youth. A cotton farmer before entering the Army in World War I, he served as a member of the Texas legislature and then as Texarkana district attorney before his election to the House of Representatives from a poor northeast Texas district in 1928.

In Congress Patman quickly emerged as the figure of controversy he was to remain for over four decades, becoming the most persistent legislative opponent of the concentration of economic power in the hands of major commercial banks and Federal Reserve officials. In the early 1930s, against the wishes of Presidents Hoover and Roosevelt, Patman pushed the bonus bill to provide $2.2 billion to World War I veterans as an anti-Depression measure. Payment of the bonus did not affect the economy, and Patman blamed the Federal Reserve for simultaneously nullifying its impact by doubling bank reserve requirements, thus cutting consumer purchasing power. Patman also championed small businessmen in the Depression, helping to establish the Small Business Administration and later insisting that they share in World War II defense contracts. He favored national economic planning and backed the Employment Act of 1946, a landmark measure that declared "maximum employment, production and purchasing power" permanent objectives of national policy. By the early 1960s Patman was conspicuous chiefly for his attacks on the power of giant commercial banks and the policies of the Federal Reserve Board. His ascension to the chairmanship of the Banking and Currency Committee in January 1963 gave him a prominent forum in which to crusade for his unorthodox monetary views. [See TRUMAN, EISENHOWER, KENNEDY Volumes]

Patman repeatedly attacked the Federal Reserve for its policy of "tight money" and high interest rates. Charging that the resulting constriction of the money supply was the chief cause of high unemployment, he led the "easy money" forces in calling for low interest rates to stimulate the economy. To check inflation he advised the Federal Reserve to raise bank reserve requirements rather than interest rates.

Patman's structural criticism of the Federal Reserve System and his radical solutions were not endorsed by any administration. The major shortcoming of the Federal Reserve, Patman argued, was its domination by powerful private banking interests. The two conspired to keep interest rates artificially high, he contended, swelling bank profits but injuring small businessmen and farmers in need of cheap credit. Patman proposed a drastic restructuring of the Federal Reserve to end its "independence" from Congress and the White House and thus curb the influence of the financial community and enable the Administration to coordinate fiscal and monetary policy. "I would have the monetary system in the charge of and directed by public servants, who owe no allegiance to any group," Patman said in November 1962. On the first day of every session Patman introduced his perennially unsuccessful Federal Reserve reform bill.

Patman's chief adversary was the chairman of the Federal Reserve Board, William McChesney Martin [*q.v.*]. When the Federal Reserve raised the discount rate from 4% to 4.5% in December 1965, Patman immediately denounced the move and initiated an investigation by the Joint Economic Committee, which he chaired in alternate years. Characterizing the Federal Reserve action as "arrogant" and a "complete betrayal of the will of the people," he subjected Martin to sharp questioning and called for Martin's resignation. Patman predicted that the rate increase would "destroy the savings and loan industry" and would "create poverty" and "harm education and hospitals." Martin defended the Board's action as necessary to prevent inflation.

Another Patman foe was Comptroller of the Currency James J. Saxon [*q.v.*], whose liberalization of banking regulation was welcomed by the large national banks. As the champion of the nation's small banks and savings and loan associations, Patman excoriated Saxon's initiatives and blocked his proposal to permit national banks to establish branches where states had prohibited branch banking. In March 1965 Patman introduced a bill that would have abolished the Office of the Comptroller of the Currency and consolidated all regulatory functions in the Secretary of the Treasury.

Despite the highest interest rates in a generation during the Johnson Administration, Patman refrained from any criticism of President Johnson himself. Patman had shared a desk with Johnson's father in the Texas state legislature and for the next 40 years took a paternal interest in the younger Johnson. He generally aided in the passage of programs favored by the President. For example, Patman pushed through the Banking and Currency Committee a Johnson-backed bill allowing the federal government to "pool" certain mortgages and other loan assets held by the government and sell the paper to banks. The government thus obtained cash to reduce the visible budget deficit. Patman hurried the measure through the Committee after only a few hours of testimony.

Patman was also a strong supporter of Johnson's Vietnam policy and a backer of most Great Society social legislation, with the exception of civil rights bills. He voted against the Civil Rights Act of 1964 and the Voting Rights Act of 1965.

Patman's other major target was the tax-exempt foundation. Using his Small Business Committee as a forum, in 1961 he began the most comprehensive investigation of foundations ever undertaken. In a series of reports issued over the decade, the Committee detailed abuses and irregularities in the operations of the 534 foundations studied. In general, Patman found that many foundations were virtually unregulated and placed the pursuit of profits and tax avoidance above their philanthropic functions. In March 1968 Patman's sixth foundation report criticized the use of foundations by wealthy persons to avoid estate taxes. "As a result of the Treasury's inaction, ineptness and lethargy," he said, "the same old tax-dodging devices exist today that have been used for decades." Patman suggested that for the duration of the Vietnam war foundations contribute their gross receipts to the federal government "in support of our defense of democracy in Southeast Asia."

Patman's populist crusades made him a figure of great controversy and a maverick among committee chairmen in Congress. On the Banking and Currency Committee, some members resented and even rebelled against his attacks on the financial establishment and his autocratic style as chairman. A revolt occurred in 1965 when some Committee members met without Patman's knowledge in a darkened committee room to approve a bill liberalizing bank mergers that Patman had been blocking. The incident infuriated Patman, who overturned the action on the ground that a quorum had not been present. A compromise measure passed a few months later, with Speaker of the House John McCormack (D, Mass.) [*q.v.*] acting as a peacemaker, but bitter feelings remained on the Committee.

Patman was unseated as chairman by the

House Democratic caucus in January 1975. In January 1976 Patman announced that he would not seek reelection. He died of pneumonia on March 7, 1976. [See NIXON Volume]

[TO]

PEARSON, DREW (ANDREW) (RUSSELL)

b. Dec. 13, 1896; Evanston, Ill.
d. Sept. 1, 1969; Washington, D.C.
Syndicated columnist.

The son of a Quaker professor, Pearson grew up in Swarthmore, Pa. He graduated from Swarthmore College in 1919 and worked as a traveling free-lance journalist until 1929, when he joined the *Baltimore Sun*. In 1932 Pearson collaborated with journalist Robert Allen on a column entitled "Washington Merry-Go-Round," which specialized in exposing corruption in government. By 1942 "Washington Merry-Go-Round" was syndicated in 350 newspapers and had earned for Pearson a reputation as the nation's most prominent liberal "muckraker" and as a "minor political power around the capital."

Pearson ensured that his column remained popular by filling it with gossip on the private lives of public figures and acerbic criticism of his political opponents. He never lost sight, however, of the issues behind Washington's personalities. During the 1950s Pearson was an important backer of many liberal causes, including the fight against Sen. Joseph McCarthy (R, Wisc.). In 1958 he was the first Washington journalist to expose the influence-peddling activities of presidential assistant Sherman Adams, and his column later investigated the close relationship between President Eisenhower and powerful business interests. After an extensive interview with Soviet Premier Nikita Khrushchev in 1961, Pearson became an early advocate of East-West detente. He also criticized increasing U.S. aid to South Vietnam's Diem regime, which he blamed partly on the Catholicism of President John F. Kennedy. [See TRUMAN, EISENHOWER, KENNEDY Volumes]

Pearson's most important cause during the mid-1960s was his fight against Sen. Thomas Dodd (D, Conn.) [*q.v.*]. In more than 100 columns Pearson and his associate Jack Anderson [*q.v.*] accused Dodd of using his political influence to promote the private interests of Julius Klein, a Chicago public relations man. The columnists also charged that Dodd had diverted tax-free campaign contributions to his personal use. In May 1966 Dodd filed a $5 million libel and conspiracy suit against Pearson, but it was subsequently dropped. On June 20 the Senate Select Committee on Standards and Conduct, chaired by Sen. John Stennis (D, Miss.) [*q.v.*], opened hearings on Dodd's alleged misconduct. The Committee's lengthy investigation resulted in Dodd's formal censure in June 1967 by a Senate vote of 92 to 5. Dodd was unseated in 1970 by Republican challenger Lowell Weicker.

In 1968 Pearson collaborated with Jack Anderson on the best-selling book *The Case Against Congress*, an indictment of the corruption and abuse of power common on Capitol Hill. By 1969 Pearson's newspaper column was syndicated by more than 650 papers, making it the most widely read in the U.S. When Pearson died in September 1969, the column was taken over by Jack Anderson, who had been Pearson's associate since 1965.

[FHM]

For further information:
Oliver Pilat, *Drew Pearson* (New York, 1973).

PELL, CLAIBORNE (DEBORDA)

b. Nov. 22, 1918; New York, N.Y.
Democratic Senator, R.I., 1960- .

The scion of a patrician Newport family, Claiborne Pell graduated from Princeton in 1940 and served in the Coast Guard during World War II. Following work in the Foreign Service, a partnership in an investment banking firm and political recognition as a top state Democratic fund raiser, Pell entered the 1960 Democratic senatorial primary. A Protestant in a predominately Catholic state, Pell defeated two strong

Democratic candidates and went on to win the general election with a record 69% of the vote.

Named to the important Labor and Public Welfare Committee, Pell supported most Kennedy Administration legislative programs, but his diplomatic background had given him a particular interest in foreign affairs. In February 1963 Pell was a member of a four-man Senate study group headed by Sen. Mike Mansfield (D, Mont.) [*q.v.*] that toured Southeast Asia and issued a report questioning the high level of U.S. military and economic aid to South Vietnam. [See KENNEDY Volume]

Regarded as a liberal, Pell supported Johnson programs on over 65% of all issues in the 88th, 89th and 90th Congresses. He was named to the Senate Foreign Relations Committee in 1965. Pell was instrumental in the passage of the 1964 National Arts and Cultural Development Act, which established a National Council on the Arts and provided for federal matching grants and nonprofessional groups to promote the arts. A member of the Rules and Administration Committee, which issued two 1965 reports on the investigation of former Secretary to the Senate Majority Leader Robert G. ("Bobby") Baker [*q.v.*], Pell proposed that all senators who were lawyers should list the clients of their firms with the Comptroller General.

Pell devoted much of his first term in the Senate to dealing with the decline of railway passenger service in the Northeast. He sponsored several Senate resolutions proposing an eight-state public authority to provide high-speed intercity rail service for the busy "Northeast corridor." Many conservative senators opposed Pell's plan because they believed it would involve excessive federal intrusion in the railroad industry. Pell was a strong supporter of the 1965 High-Speed Ground Transportation Research Act, which granted $90 million for research into advanced ground transportation systems.

Reelected to the Senate in 1966, Pell was a firm but not particularly vocal opponent of U.S. involvement in Vietnam. In May 1967 he warned that indefinite escalation of the war might lead to China's intervention and "the start of a domestic clamor to use nuclear weapons. . . ."

In 1970 President Nixon appointed Pell a delegate to the U.N. General Assembly. Pell was reelected to the Senate for a third term in 1972. [See NIXON Volume]

[FHM]

PERCY, CHARLES H(ARTING)

b. Sept. 27, 1919; Pensacola, Fla.
Republican Senator, Ill., 1966- .

Percy, the son of a bank clerk and office employe, grew up in Chicago. He worked his way through the University of Chicago by operating a campus equipment agency, which eventually earned $150,000 a year. After graduating in 1941 Percy went to work for Bell and Howell, a manufacturer of cameras and photographic equipment. An innovative executive, he rose rapidly within the company and was appointed corporate secretary on his return from military service in 1946. Three years later, at 29, Percy became the youngest chief of a major American business when he succeeded William H. McNabb as Bell and Howell's president. The company prospered under Percy, nearly doubling its sales during the first three years of his leadership to become the largest camera equipment manufacturer in the U.S.

Percy's involvement in politics began during the mid-1950s, when he worked as a fund raiser for the Republican Party in Illinois. In 1959 he established and led the Party's Committee on Program and Progress, which formulated long-range policy proposals; with this experience he was chosen to head the Platform Committee at the 1960 Republican National Convention. A member of the Party's liberal wing, Percy reluctantly supported the presidential candidacy of Sen. Barry Goldwater (R, Ariz.) [*q.v.*] in 1964. At the same time he gave up direction of Bell and Howell to run for governor of Illinois. He lost to incumbent Otto Kerner [*q.v.*] by a narrow margin in the Democratic landslide of 1964.

Percy took the next opportunity to run for high office by challenging Sen. Paul Douglas (D, Ill.) [*q.v.*] in 1966. The campaign developed into a closely watched contest centering on the issues of Vietnam and open housing. Percy took a "dovish" position on the war, attacking Douglas for his uncritical support of Administration policy and urging a negotiated peace settlement. On housing questions Percy was more conservative than Douglas, who antagonized many Chicago residents by advocating a ban on racial discrimination in white neighborhoods. The vigorous campaign was interrupted in September by the unexplained murder of Percy's daughter Valerie. Resumed after one month, the race ended in a victory for Percy, who gained 55% of the vote. Some observers claimed that the intensive publicity resulting from the murder and inquest helped Percy to win, although Douglas later admitted that Percy had already pulled ahead during the summer. Percy's strongest support came from suburban areas in northern Illinois.

In the Senate Percy soon became known as an aggressive newcomer who did not let his low seniority prevent him from seeking public attention. Frequently rumored as a potential presidential or vice presidential candidate, he fed speculation by making well-publicized statements on a wide variety of issues. Percy was especially critical of the Administration's Vietnam policy. In early 1967 he urged "greater efforts" by the Administration to achieve a negotiated settlement, claiming that previous U.S. peace offers were "simply too vague to be practical." He also introduced a "sense of the Senate" resolution demanding greater participation in the war by Asian allies of the U.S. Percy's statements on Vietnam were generally far more "dovish" than the sentiments of most of his Republican colleagues. In late 1967 Percy made a trip to South Vietnam, gaining considerable publicity when he came under Communist fire in an abandoned village.

During his first term in the Senate, Percy maintained a generally liberal voting record and a reputation as a political independent. Percy's first important legislative effort was a 1967 proposal to provide federal aid for low-income homeowners through creation of a private, nonprofit mortgage loan corporation. Though overridden by Democrats on the Senate Banking and Currency Committee, the plan was later reformulated and incorporated into the Open Housing Act of 1968. In subsequent years Percy was one of the leaders in the unsuccessful fight for creation of a consumer protection agency. He also devoted considerable attention to the problems of elderly Americans as a member of the Senate Special Committee on Aging.

Percy won reelection to the Senate in 1972 with 62% of the vote. He gained seniority rapidly during the early 1970s due to the defeat or retirement of a number of older Senate Republicans. Despite persistent rumors of his own desire for higher office, Percy remained a strong supporter of New York Gov. Nelson Rockefeller's [*q.v.*] presidential aspirations. [See NIXON Volume]

[SLG]

For further information:
Robert Hartley, *Charles H. Percy: A Political Perspective* (New York, 1975).

PEREZ, LEANDER H(ENRY)

b. 1891; Plaquemines Parish, La.
d. March 19, 1969; Plaquemines Parish, La.
President, Plaquemines Parish Commission Council, Plaquemines Parish, La., 1961-67.

In 1924 Perez became district attorney of both Plaquemines Parish, located along the Mississippi River between New Orleans and the Gulf of Mexico, and of adjoining St. Bernard Parish. He held this post for the next 36 years, using it as a power base to become the almost undisputed political boss of Plaquemines and a major influence within both the Democratic state central committee and the state legislature. His biographer, James Conaway, wrote that while Louisiana politics was traditionally ruthless, Perez brought to it "a particularly aggressive style, unhampered by either subjective or purely moral considerations." He employed violence and chicanery to both repel state government encroachment upon his local power and suppress his parish opponents.

An unabashed racist, Perez helped organize the States' Rights Party in 1948 and the White Citizens Councils in 1954. By 1960 he was charging that Communists and "Zionist Jews" were behind the civil rights movement. In 1960 Perez resigned as district attorney in favor of his son, Leander, Jr. However, he continued to dominate Plaquemines's politics, assuming the presidency of the newly created Parish Commission Council in 1961. During the Kennedy Administration he successfully resisted racial integration in his parish. He was excommunicated from the Catholic Church in 1962 for his opposition to the desegregation of parochial schools. [See KENNEDY Volume]

Early in 1964 Perez denounced President Lyndon B. Johnson for his support of civil rights legislation. He led the conservative faction of the Democratic state central committee in an effort to exclude Johnson from the Louisiana ballot in favor of an independent slate of electors sympathetic to Alabama Gov. George C. Wallace [*q.v.*]. Ultimately he backed the Republican nominee, Sen. Barry M. Goldwater (R, Ariz.) [*q.v.*].

In the summer of 1964 Perez announced that he had prepared an isolated 18th-century Spanish fort on the Mississippi River for the incarceration of any civil rights workers who might enter the parish. He asserted, "We're not near ready to surrender our peaceful, beautiful parish to the Communists. And if Martin Luther King [*q.v.*] comes in, we'll guarantee his transportation across the river—part way, that is."

In 1965 Perez testified against the Johnson Administration's voting rights bill before the Senate Judiciary Committee. His charge that the measure was Communist-inspired amused many of the panel members, and Sen. Everett M. Dirksen (R, Ill.) [*q.v.*] called the claim "as stupid a statement as I've ever heard."

Shortly after the passage of the Voting Rights Act, federal registrars entered Plaquemines, where only 96 of the parish's 6,500 blacks had been registered as of February 1964. Despite harassment by Perez and his supporters, the registrars enrolled about 2,000 additional blacks. In 1966 a federal district court ordered the desegregation of the parish's public schools. Perez, unable to block integration, established a private school system, which about half of the district's white students attended.

The following year Perez resigned the presidency of the Parish Commission Council and was succeeded by his son, Chalin. In 1968 he enthusiastically backed the Wallace presidential campaign. Perez died on March 19, 1969. Shortly after his death a spokesman for the Roman Catholic Church in New Orleans announced that Perez's excommunication had been lifted a year earlier, after he had made a conciliatory speech.

[MLL]

For further information:
James Conaway, *Judge: The Life and Times of Leander Perez* (New York, 1973).

PETERSON, RUDOLPH A(RVID)

b. Dec. 6, 1904; Svenljunga, Sweden.
President, Bank of America, 1963-69.

Peterson, the son of a Swedish immigrant farmer, grew up in Hilman, Calif. After graduating from the University of California, Berkeley, in 1925, he began work as a field representative for a loan and credit company. In 1936 Peterson joined the Bank of America (BOA), one of California's leading financial institutions. His skill as a credit manager made him a protege of A. P. Giannini, BOA's founder, who built his enterprise by concentrating on loans and banking services for small customers. Peterson spent 29 years in various BOA executive positions before moving in 1955 to the Bank of Hawaii, where he became president one year later. He arrived in the islands at a time of rapid expansion of the Hawaiian economy, and he ensured that the bank kept pace with this growth by cultivating small customers and aggressively seeking new business. Peterson's success at the Bank of Hawaii (where deposits more than doubled during the five years of his leadership) prompted BOA to seek his return in 1961 as corporate vice president. He accepted and was appointed president of the bank in 1963.

By the time Peterson returned to California, BOA was the largest bank in the U.S., with 731 branches and $10.2 billion in deposits. Concerned that bigness might bring complacency and a loss of competitiveness, Peterson quickly introduced several innovations he had first tested in Hawaii. Among these were efforts to "personalize" banking by making bank employes and managers more accessible to all customers.

Peterson was also a strong advocate of automation and expanded BOA's computerized checking-account system, one of the first in the country. In his long-range planning he prepared for a time when computers would handle most transactions, reducing the use of cash and even checks. In line with this projection Peterson gave high priority to expanding BankAmericard, the pioneering BOA-operated credit card company. BankAmericard holders increased from 1.3 million in 1965 to 27.5 million in 1969. Deposits nearly doubled during the mid-1960s, and the number of overseas BOA branches increased from 44 to 96.

Peterson's success as BOA president made him an important spokesman of the banking industry in political affairs. In 1965 he began to advocate a government austerity program in response to the financial demands of the Vietnam war. Among the measures he urged at this time were deferment of some Great Society programs and a 5% surcharge on personal and corporate income taxes. BOA itself responded to the inflationary pressures of the mid-1960s by tightening its loan policy, although Peterson tried to ensure that the small customers who accounted for most of BOA's business would remain relatively unaffected by the squeeze.

A growing problem for Peterson during the late 1960s was BOA's close connection with the California food industry. Substantial BOA loan funds were invested in various agribusiness concerns, and Peterson himself served on the board of directors of the DiGiorgio Corporation, one of California's leading wine manufacturers. This made BOA a target of criticism from supporters of Cesar Chavez's [*q.v.*] United Farm Workers union, which was attempting to organize California farm workers against the resistance of agribusiness concerns, Leftist students also viewed BOA, with its size and international contacts, as an important agent of what they regarded as U.S. imperialism in developing countries. One result of this unfavorable publicity was a series of bombings and burnings directed against BOA branches in 1970; the Isla Vista branch, located near the Santa Barbara campus of the University of California, was damaged several times.

Peterson left BOA in late 1969 at the mandatory retirement age of 65. Several months later President Richard M. Nixon appointed him to lead a 16-man advisory panel investigating the U.S. foreign aid program. Among the panel's far-reaching proposals was a recommendation for the pooling of U.S. foreign aid contributions with those of other industrial nations in an international development fund. Peterson also urged an increase in U.S. contributions to the World Bank. In 1972 Peterson was named administrator of the United Nations Development Program, a technical assistance fund for developing countries. He also served on the boards of directors of several large corporations, including Standard Oil of California, Consolidated Foods and Time, Inc.

[SLG]

PIKE, JAMES A(LBERT)

b. Feb. 14, 1913; Oklahoma City, Okla.
d. September 1969; Israel.
Protestant Episcopal Bishop of California, 1958-66.

Raised in Los Angeles, Pike studied for the Roman Catholic priesthood, but he became an agnostic and subsequently began a legal career. After rediscovering his religious faith during wartime service in the Navy, he was ordained a Protestant Episcopalian priest in 1946. Dean of New York's Cathedral of St. John the Divine and a professor of religion at Columbia University in the early 1950s, Pike became well-known for his iconoclastic views through numerous books and articles and his own television show. He championed civil rights, the state of Israel and planned parenthood while vehemently attacking book and film censorship and the methods of the House Un-American Activities Committee. Pike also espoused extremely unorthodox theological ideas that prompted charges of heresy and, occasionally, Communism from his conservative colleagues. Always independent and unpredictable, Bishop Pike sided with conservative Protestants in an attack on the Supreme Court's 1962 decision banning prayer in the public schools. In 1962 and 1963 Pike also worked with anti-Castro groups in the United States. [See KENNEDY Volume]

Pike was again embroiled in controversy when he headed the California Advisory Committee to the U.S. Civil Rights Commission (CRC). His committee issued a statement in January 1966 attacking the official government investigation of the 1965 Watts riot. Pike's group charged that the prestigious commission, headed by former CIA chief John J. McCone [*q.v.*], had "whitewashed" the role played by Los Angeles Mayor Sam W. Yorty [*q.v.*] and Police Chief William H. Parker during the riot. Pike suggested that the CRC investigate "Negro complaints concerning police malpractices" and that the U.S. Housing and Urban Affairs Department "designate Los Angeles as an area for top priority attention " in its investigation of discrimination in housing. Mayor Yorty later accused Pike and his committee of turning its report into a political attack on the police.

As a result of Pike's denial of much Episcopal church doctrine—including the virgin birth, the Trinity, the incarnation and the bodily resurrection of Jesus—charges of heresy were frequently raised against the Bishop in the mid-1960s. Pike thought the church out of date theologically. In September 1966, for example, he elevated a woman to ministerial status despite a resolution by the Episcopal House of Bishops banning women from serving communion. Partly because of the resulting furor, Pike decided to resign the bishopric of California in May 1966 to join the staff of the Center for the Study of Democratic Institutions as resident theologian. In October Pike also resigned as auxiliary bishop as well.

At this time the House of Bishops refused demands for a heresy trial but issued a majority report chiding Pike for his "irresponsible" utterances and for his frequent "cheap vulgarization of great expressions of faith." Following the reprimand Pike moved further out of the mainstream of American Protestantism, meeting with mediums, for example, in efforts to contact his son, who had recently committed suicide. In September 1967 Pike published *If This Be Heresy* in defense of his beliefs.

In October 1967 Pike, as a member of the Clergy and Laymen Concerned About Vietnam, signed a statement promising "to aid and abet" American youths in resisting the military draft. He also remained active in the Southern Christian Leadership Conference and other civil rights groups.

While in Israel to gather information for a biblical study, Pike's car stalled in the desert. He died of exposure sometime during the week of Sept. 1, 1969.

[JCH]

POAGE, W(ILLIAM) R(OBERT) "BOB"

b. Dec. 28, 1899; Waco, Tex.
Democratic Representative, Tex., 1937- ; Chairman, Agriculture Committee, 1967- .

After twelve years in the state legislature, Bob Poage was elected to the House of Representatives in 1936 and appointed to the Agriculture Committee in 1941. Poage encountered little opposition in his subsequent reelection efforts. In Congress Poage aligned himself with the conservative Southern Democratic-Republican majority on the House Agriculture Committee and in the years after 1945 opposed the efforts of Secretaries of Agriculture Charles Brannan and Ezra Taft Benson to create a more flexible farm price support system.

While fighting to maintain high farm subsidies, Poage sought to hold down the cost of farm labor. In 1951 he helped establish the "bracero" program for the temporary migration of Mexican farm laborers into the U.S. He called the program "the best kind of foreign aid" for Mexican families who might otherwise starve. Poage also opposed minimum wage standards for American farm workers and in 1959 declared a minimum wage "illegal, impractical, and immoral." [See TRUMAN, EISENHOWER Volumes].

In the early 1960s Poage supported President Kennedy's efforts to require farmers to accept stiff controls over crop yields rather than acreage allotments before they could benefit from government price guarantees. Poage voted for both the original omnibus food and agriculture bill of 1962, which Congress rejected, and the compromise measure that became law on Sept. 27, 1962.

After the electoral defeat of Harold D. Cooley (D, N.C.) [*q.v.*] in November 1966, Poage became chairman of the House Agriculture Committee. There he opposed attempts in June 1967 to limit subsidy payments to large farmers because "when those large farmers cease to be part of the program and produce without limitation . . . the amount of production is going to destroy the income of these small farmers." During the October 1967 hearings on reforms in the food stamp program, Poage referred to food stamp recipients as "a bunch of drones" and suggested that "maybe we have gotten too far away from the situation of primitive man" when the "drones" were killed. Poage's reluctance to enlarge the food stamp program led to clashes with citizens groups critical of the government's food assistance programs. After the Committee on School Lunch Participation and the Citizens Board of Inquiry into Hunger and Malnutrition in the United States issued widely circulated studies on hunger in America, Poage mailed letters to all the county health officers in the nation asking if they were aware of any cases of starvation or serious malnutrition in their districts. On June 16, 1968 the House Agriculture Committee issued its own "hunger study" based upon 181 replies to Poage's inquiry. According to the Committee, the report "leads to the unmistakable conclusion that there is very little actual hunger in the United States but widespread malnutrition caused largely by ignorance as to what constitutes a balanced diet."

The Committee's report ascribed the few instances of borderline starvation and hunger to parental neglect of infants, adding that most of these cases involved mentally retarded parents. When the report was issued Poage added, "There seems to be little or no evidence that substantial hunger in this country exists as the result of the refusal of assistance agencies, public and private, to give needed aid to those who are unable to work." Poage charged in July 1969 that a proposal to establish a free food stamp program would lead to "socialism." [See NIXON Volume]

[DKR]

PODHORETZ, NORMAN

b. Jan. 16, 1930; New York, N.Y.
Editor-in-Chief, *Commentary*, 1960- .

Podhoretz, the son of immigrant Jewish parents, grew up in a poor section of Brooklyn. After majoring in English literature at Columbia University, he graduated in 1950 with a scholarship for further study in England. He received a second B.A. from Cambridge University in 1952 but gave up plans to seek a Ph.D. in favor of beginning a career as a literary critic. Returning to the U.S. Podhoretz attracted attention with book reviews published in respected journals such as *Commentary* and *Partisan Review*. After two years in the Army, he joined the editorial staff of *Commentary*, rising to associate editor by 1958. Podhoretz left *Commentary* at this time in a dispute over editorial policy. He returned to the magazine as editor in 1960, however, following the death of the previous editor, Eliot Cohen.

Founded in 1945 as a journal of liberal Jewish opinion, *Commentary* suffered during the late 1950s from what many critics regarded as a stagnant format and overly predictable viewpoint. Podhoretz worked to restore the magazine's readership and reputation by opening its pages to more radical ideas and social criticism, at the same time de-emphasizing topics of narrow concern to Jews and academics. The first success of Podhoretz's new editorial policy came with the serialization of Paul Goodman's [*q.v.*] *Growing Up Absurd*, which won wide attention among intellectuals for its criticism of American education. Podhoretz himself contributed to his journal's flow of social observation with a 1963 essay "My Negro Problem—and Ours," a controversial critique of black-white relations in the U.S. The "new" *Commentary* tripled its readership under Podhoretz, reaching 60,000 by 1966. [See KENNEDY Volume]

Podhoretz continued the critical tradition of *Commentary* in his autobiography *Making It*, published in 1968. Here he frankly discussed the importance of the drive for success in his professional life, generalizing his own experience to those of most Americans. Ambition, he claimed, had replaced sex as "the dirty little word" of contemporary life. Podhoretz did not condemn the success drive itself, but only the embarrassment and hypocrisy resulting from its concealment. "American society is a society devoted to success," he stated, "and everybody is in the act for all practical purposes." This affirmative attitude and the confessional nature of much of the book drew unfavorable responses from many critics, which helped estrange Podhoretz from a significant part of the New York literary "establishment." Among those with whom Podhoretz broke at this time was Jason Epstein [*q.v.*], formerly a close friend and a founder of the *New York Review of Books*.

Podhoretz's increasingly favorable view of American society was reflected in the political position of *Commentary*, which shifted to the right during the mid and late 1960s. One important issue prompting this change was the Vietnam war. While the *New York Review of Books* and other left-wing periodicals excoriated the Johnson Administration over the Vietnam war, *Commentary* was only mildly critical of American policy in Indochina. Only in the journal's May 1971 issue did Podhoretz and sociologist Nathan Glazer [*q.v.*] call for immediate withdrawal from Vietnam.

A strong supporter of civil rights, Podhoretz nevertheless became alarmed by the anti-Semitic overtones found in the black nationalist rhetoric of the late 1960s. At a time when radicals and many liberals celebrated Black Panther leader Bobby Seale [*q.v.*] as a victim of government persecution, *Commentary* attacked the Black Panthers as a "totalitarian organization" identified with "world Communism." The journal also gave strong support to New York City school teachers in their 1968 conflict with the Ocean Hill-Brownsville school board. For Podhoretz the central issue in the dispute was not community control of schools, as demanded by many blacks, but proposals to reduce the protection of tenure and seniority for the city's largely Jewish teaching force. Condemning white liberal tolerance of anti-Jewish feeling among blacks, Podhoretz attacked what he said was a "readiness to purchase civil peace in the United States . . . at the direct expense of the Jews."

Podhoretz remained editor of *Commentary* during the 1970s at a time when he became increasingly critical of the American New Left. Along with Nathan Glazer he announced his shift in 1970 from "mild radicalism" to "mild conservatism." Among Podhoretz's most frequently expressed views at this time were strong support of Israel, skepticism concerning government spending programs and opposition to affirmative action and quotas in universities. [See NIXON Volume]

[SLG]

For further information:
Norman Podhoretz, *Making It* (New York, 1968).

POOL, JOE (RICHARD)

b. Feb. 18, 1911; Fort Worth, Tex.
d. July 14, 1968; Houston, Tex.
Democratic Representative, Tex., 1963-68.

Pool received a law degree from Southern Methodist University in 1937 and entered private law practice. In 1952 he was elected to the Texas House of Representatives, where he served three consecutive two-year terms. During his tenure in that body, Pool drafted a bill to outlaw horror and sex comic books. In 1958 and 1960 he unsuccessfully sought election to the

U.S. House of Representatives from Dallas. Two years later he won a seat in the House as an at-large Texas congressman. Pool, who generally opposed Kennedy and Johnson Administration programs, compiled a conservative record in the House.

In January 1966 Pool, a supporter of intensified American military activity in Vietnam, introduced a bill imposing fines of up to $20,000 and prison terms of up to 20 years upon persons convicted of giving material aid to a hostile foreign power or impeding the movement of armed forces personnel or materiel. The bill was aimed at elements of the anti-war movement that were collecting funds for medical supplies for the National Liberation Front and North Vietnam and blocking troop and military supply trains.

Pool first gained national attention in August 1966 when he headed a House Un-American Activities Committee (HUAC) subcommittee investigating alleged Communist influence within the anti-war movement. On Aug. 15, as the hearings were about to begin, a federal district court judge enjoined the panel from initiating its investigation on the ground that HUAC procedures violated the rights of witnesses. A constitutional confrontation between Congress and the judiciary was avoided when a three-judge appeals court dissolved the restraining order on the following day, minutes before Pool was prepared to begin hearings in defiance of the lower court.

The subcommittee went on to conduct a stormy four-day investigation. Anti-war activists subpoenaed as witnesses expressed contempt for the panel, while their sympathizers in the audience disrupted the proceedings. Arthur Kinoy, a lawyer for one of the witnesses, was dragged from the hearing room when he refused to sit down at Pool's behest. Administration witnesses opposed the bill as unnecessary and possibly unconstitutional.

On Aug. 29 the full Committee reported favorably on an amended version of Pool's bill, and the House passed the measure by a 275-64 vote on Oct. 13. The Senate, however, did not act on the measure. HUAC reported out the bill again in May 1967, but the House did not take up the proposal.

Pool died of a heart attack on July 14, 1968.

[MLL]

PORTER, WILLIAM J(AMES)

b. Sept. 1, 1914; England.
Ambassador to Algeria, December 1962-July 1965; Deputy Ambassador to South Vietnam, September 1965-March 1967; Ambassador to South Korea, May 1967-February 1974.

A veteran foreign service officer, Porter spent much of his career at posts in the Middle East, North Africa, Greece and Turkey. Although scheduled to become ambassador to Saudi Arabia in July 1965, he was appointed deputy ambassador in Saigon in September 1965 at the request of Henry Cabot Lodge [*q.v.*], then ambassador to South Vietnam.

In February 1966, as a result of the U.S. failure to win the ground war in Vietnam, President Johnson decided to reorganize the Saigon mission and place increasing stress on the pacification program. Although its goals were never clearly outlined, pacification was designed to protect the Vietnamese rural population and provide positive social, economic and educational programs to win active support for the Saigon regime. Under this reorganization Porter was given authority to oversee operations of the American civilian agencies involved in pacification, including the Central Intelligence Agency, the Agency for International Development and the U.S. Information Agency. Although some functional coordination was achieved, particularly at higher levels, the reform was unsuccessful because of the failure of Lodge to back the decisions of his deputy, the hostility of the agencies involved and the lack of coordinated support in Washington.

As a result of this failure, President Johnson ordered Porter to reorganize the components of the program into a single Office of Civilian Operations (OCO) in October 1966. This office also failed to produce the dramatic increases in economic and social development demanded by the

President. In analyzing the reasons behind its lack of success, the authors of the *Pentagon Papers* said, "Washington had decreed OCO and had given Porter great responsibility. Unfortunately they had failed to give him the authority and stature needed to make the agencies work together."

In March 1967 Johnson put the pacification program under military control. Porter left Vietnam shortly thereafter and became ambassador to South Korea in May 1967. In February 1974 he was appointed ambassador to Canada.

[EWS]

For further information:
U.S. Department of Defense, *The Pentagon Papers*, Senator Gravel Edition (Boston, 1971), Vol. II.

POWELL, ADAM CLAYTON, JR.

b. Nov. 29, 1908; New Haven, Conn.
d. April 4, 1972; Miami, Fla.
Democratic Representative, N.Y., 1945-67, 1969; Chairman, Education and Labor Committee, 1961-67.

In 1937 Powell succeeded his father as pastor of Harlem's Abyssinian Baptist Church, whose 12,000 members constituted the largest Protestant congregation in the country. During the 1930s and 1940s the younger Powell set up soup kitchens for the needy, organized a bus boycott that compelled the Transport Workers Union to accept Negro drivers and used similar tactics to win concessions from the telephone company and Harlem merchants. In 1941 he became the first Negro elected to the New York City Council and four years later won a seat in Congress as the representative from Central Harlem. The church, throughout Powell's long tenure in Congress, served as his political machine, helping him overwhelm all challengers in his district.

As a congressman in the 1950s, Powell was best known for his efforts to bar federal appropriations to state projects that practiced racial discrimination. The so-called Powell Amendment to a 1956 school construction bill seriously divided liberal Democrats because it forced them to choose between federal aid to education and de facto support of segregated school systems. Adlai Stevenson [*q.v.*] refused to support the amendment or to meet privately with Powell to discuss civil rights matters in general. As a result Powell broke Party ranks in 1956 to support the reelection of Dwight D. Eisenhower.

Powell's attendance record, among the worst in Congress, and his penchant for congressionally financed vacations abroad, were repeatedly condemned in the press. Shortly before Powell became chairman of the House Committee on Education and Labor in 1961, the *New York Times* wrote that his "miserable record as a legislator and his extreme absenteeism all tend to disqualify him as a reasonable and effective chairman." During his first years as chairman, however, he headed a remarkably productive Committee that reported out minimum wage, education and antipoverty legislation generally favored by the Kennedy Administration. [See KENNEDY Volume]

Powell's relations with President Johnson were at first cordial. Nevertheless, Powell's conduct as chairman during 1965 and 1966 alienated liberal Democrats, organized labor, and the Johnson Administration and contributed decisively to his political demise. Powell's delay of the 1965 Elementary and Secondary Education Act threatened the passage of that legislation, angering President Johnson. In 1966 the poverty bill was delayed four months while Powell spent the summer fishing off the island of Bimini in the Bahamas. That same year Powell blocked legislation, strongly favored by organized labor, permitting "common site picketing." By September 1966 moderate and liberal members of Powell's Committee were in open revolt not only over these matters but also over his alleged "capricious" dismissals of Committee staff, his vetoes of legislation approved by subcommittee and his misuse of congressional funds.

On Sept. 22, 1966 the Education and Labor Committee adopted, by a vote of 27 to 1, new rules making it difficult for Powell to delay legislation favored by the majority. Also in September, the usually inactive House Administration's Special Subcommittee on Contracts, under the chairmanship of Rep. Wayne Hays (D, Ohio) [*q.v.*], began an investigation that culminated in a report demanding that Powell's wife, who lived in Puerto Rico, be removed from the congressional payroll.

Meanwhile, Powell was in contempt of court for his refusal to pay a $211,739 judgment (later reduced to $46,500) stemming from a defamation suit brought against him in 1960. Powell faced arrest if he returned to New York, but his influence remained strong in Harlem, and he was reelected in 1966.

In the mid-1960s Powell aligned himself with Stokely Carmichael [*q.v.*] and others in the black power movement. As early as March 1963 Powell had demanded that blacks boycott all civil rights organizations (including the NAACP) "not totally controlled by us." Powell refused to vote for the 1965 Voting Rights Act or the 1966 open housing bill, which he charged was "a phony carrot" for the Negro Middle classes.

In January 1967, at the beginning of the 90th Congress, Powell was ousted from his Committee chairmanship and barred from taking his seat pending an investigation of his fitness to hold office. With the support of House Majority Leader Carl Albert (D, Okla.) [*q.v.*], Rep. Morris Udall (D, Ariz.) [*q.v.*] moved to seat Powell pending the outcome of the investigation. The motion was defeated by an overwhelming majority, with many Northern liberals voting with Republicans and Southern Democrats against the Harlem Congressman.

On Feb. 23, 1967 a nine-member select House committee under Rep. Emanuel Celler (D, N.Y.) [*q.v.*] reported that Powell had "wrongfully and willfully appropriated" public funds and had "improperly maintained his wife" on the congressional payroll. The committee recommended that Powell be censured for "gross misconduct," fined $40,000 and stripped of his seniority.

The House rejected the committee's recommendations on March 1, 1967 and—for only the third time in American history and the first time in 46 years—voted 307 to 116 to exclude a duly elected representative. Rep. Celler saw "an element of racism in the vote . . . accompanied by the hysteria that had resulted from the climate of opinion due to Mr. Powell's antics and peculiarities and swagger and defiance."

Black leaders from around the country denounced the expulsion. Floyd McKissick [*q.v.*], national director of the Congress of Racial Equality, called it "a slap in the face of every black in the country," while A. Philip Randolph [*q.v.*] of the Brotherhood of Sleeping Car Porters said it was "a mockery of democracy without precedent." However, *Congressional Quarterly* reported that "the most notable aspect of the lobby action in the Powell affair was the lack of concerted effort in Powell's behalf by the organized civil rights lobby." Roy Wilkins [*q.v.*], chairman of the NAACP, explained that "Powell never called on [the] civil rights movement . . . never invited [its] help."

In April 1967 a special election was held to fill Powell's seat; he was reelected by a margin of 7 to 1. The seat remained vacant for two years. In January 1969, after paying a $25,000 fine, Powell was permitted to return to the House, but he was stripped of all seniority. In June the Supreme Court ruled that Powell's expulsion had been unconstitutional. He was stricken with cancer that year, and before he could decide to retire from politics lost his seat to Charles B. Rangel, who narrowly defeated him in a June 1970 primary. Powell died two years later.

Powell was among the most controversial politicians of his time. To journalist Theodore White he was "the most egregious and frightening" exception to the general excellence of black elected officials. To Chuck Stone, Powell's chief congressional assistant, he was "a mercurial personality who wavered erratically between tub-thumping militancy and cowardly silence"—a man so driven by "hedonistic compulsions" that he undermined his role as a black leader. However, Julius Lester, a black author, remembered him as the man who once "gave blacks a national voice" when other were quietly submissive and deferential.

[JLW]

PRICE, CECIL R(AY)
b. 1938(?)
Chief Deputy Sheriff, Neshoba County, Miss., 1964-68.

Price became chief deputy sheriff of Neshoba County, Miss., in January 1964. The following June three civil rights workers—Andrew Goodman and Michael H. Schwerner, whites from New York, and James E. Chaney, a black from Meridian, Miss.—entered the county to investigate the recent burning of a Negro church, which was to have been used as a Freedom School in the Mississippi Summer Project. The three civil rights workers disappeared, and their bodies were discovered in August in a dam near Philadelphia, Miss., the county seat.

Although these events produced a national outcry, Mississippi authorities never brought any charges in connection with the case. In December 1964 FBI agents arrested Price, County Sheriff Lawrence A. Rainey and 19 others. The Justice Department asserted that a plan to kill the three had been arranged by the White Knights of the Ku Klux Klan. Price was accused of detaining the victims in Philadelphia, recapturing them on a highway and then turning them over to a lynch mob of which he was a member.

Price and the others were indicted under an 1870 statute for conspiring to injure citizens in the free exercise of federal rights. The indictment was struck down by Federal District Judge W. Harold Cox [*q.v.*] in February 1965, but his decision was overturned by a unanimous ruling of the U.S. Supreme Court in March 1966. New indictments were issued a year later, and in October 1967 Price and six other defendants were found guilty in what was believed to be the first conviction in a civil rights slaying in Mississippi. Price received a prison term of six years.

The U.S. Supreme Court upheld the conviction in February 1970, and Price went to jail shortly thereafter. In July 1973 the U.S. Parole Board refused to grant the seven men a pardon and stated that they would have to complete their terms.

[MLL]

PROXMIRE, (EDWARD) WILLIAM
b. Nov. 11, 1915; Lake Forest, Ill.
Democratic Senator, Wisc. 1957- .

Voted the "most energetic" and "biggest grind" by his high school classmates, Proxmire earned a B.A. from Yale and an M.B.A. from Harvard. He moved to Wisconsin in 1948 and was elected the following year to the state Assembly. Proxmire became known during the 1950s as an effective Democrat in a Republican-dominated legislature, a foe of Sen. Joseph McCarthy (R, Wisc.) and a perennial loser in gubernatorial elections. In a special election held in 1957 to fill the seat left vacant by the death of Sen. McCarthy, Proxmire won an upset victory over Republican Walter J. Kohler, a former governor. In the Senate he alienated Majority Leader Lyndon Johnson (D, Tex.) [*q.v.*] when, in February 1958, he criticized Johnson's "unwholesome and arbitrary power" and demanded more frequent Party caucuses. During the Kennedy years Proxmire earned a reputation as a maverick liberal by combining an active opposition to the oil industry with fervid efforts to reduce government spending and balance the budget. [See KENNEDY Volume]

During the Johnson Administration Proxmire was a member of the Senate Banking Committee, the Appropriations Committee and the Joint Economic Committee. He was a leader in the 1964 battle waged by Senate liberals against Sen. Everett M. Dirksen's (R, Ill.) [*q.v.*] proposed constitutional amendment to supersede the Supreme Court's "one-man, one-vote" decision. Proxmire orchestrated the liberal filibuster, which delayed Dirksen's bill and gave civil rights and labor groups time to build outside pressure against it. He continued a successful strategy of delay until the proposed amendment died with Dirksen in 1969. Proxmire was also the chief sponsor of a "truth in lending" law signed in May 1968, which required most lenders to disclose the actual amount of interest charged borrowers.

Proxmire supported the war in Vietnam in the mid 1960s and served as a member of the steering committee of the Committee of

One Million Against Admission of Communist China to the United Nations in 1965. On Jan. 6, 1965 he stated that "it's a mistake to negotiate when losing." He criticized the Johnson Administration in February 1967 for estimating the cost of the war for fiscal 1967 as $10 billion when it was actually costing double that amount. This error, he said, "destroyed all our economic plolicies." Proxmire opposed a tax increase to finance the war and urged instead that the budget be balanced by spending cuts, especially in the space and public works programs and by withdrawing four of the six U.S. divisions in Europe. He also asked Congress to restore the investment tax credit, which he had originally opposed in 1962.

Although a supporter of most Great Society programs, Proxmire's persistent advocacy of a balanced budget set him apart from other Senate liberals. In August 1964 he unsuccessfully tried to reduce appropriations for the Civil Aeronautics Board, the Federal Aviation Agency and the National Aeronautics and Space Administration. He tried and failed to reduce NASA's funds in each succeeding year. His amendment to reduce the oil depletion allowance in April 1967 was also rejected. In July he urged the abolition of the Subversive Activities Control Board, calling it a "ridiculous extravagance."

Proxmire's greatest success came in his eight-year struggle to kill the supersonic transport plane (SST). In November 1963 he was one of six senators to vote against the initial appropriation of $20 million for research and development. Proxmire was joined by 18 senators in his April 1967 attempt to delete funds for the SST from the Department of Transportation's budget. After the defeat of his amendment, Proxmire was the only senator to vote against the entire Transportation Department appropriation bill because it included the SST expenditure, which he called a "wasteful blunder." He temporarily grounded the project in March 1971, aided by Russell Train, Chairman of the President's Council and Environmental Quality, who testified before Proxmire's subcommittee that the SST could deplete the atmosphere's ozone layer that shields the earth from dangerous ultraviolet radiation.

Proxmire achieved prominence by calling attention to waste and mismanagement in the Pentagon's budget from his position as chairman of the Joint Economic Committee's Subcommittee on Economy in Government. His main target was the C-5A cargo plane, whose cost history Proxmire investigated in November 1968. He helped disclose a $2 billion cost overrun since the project's inception in 1965. His amendment to delete $533 million from the Defense Department's budget for 23 additional planes was defeated 64-23 in September 1969, but the Pentagon announced in November that it would reduce its original objective from 120 planes to 81. [See NIXON Volume]

[TO]

For further information:

Jay G. Sykes, *Proxmire* (Washington, 1972).

QUIE, ALBERT H(AROLD)

b. Sept. 18, 1923; Dennison, Minn.
Republican Representative, Minn., 1958- .

Albert H. Quie grew up on his family's dairy farm. A Navy pilot during World War II, Quie received his B.A. from St. Olaf College in 1950. Four years later he won election to the state Senate and served there until a successful special U.S. House campaign in February 1958. Quie never encountered serious opposition in his reelection contests after 1958.

A Party regular from a rural area of the Middle West, Quie generally voted with the GOP leadership. In February 1964 he joined a majority of his GOP colleagues in support of the House version of the civil rights bill. In April Quie led the opposition to the bill permanently establishing the food stamp program, one of the President's 30 "priority" measures of the 1964 session. Yet, rather than reject the Democrats' idea altogether, Quie proposed that the states pay for 50% of the costs. The House rejected his amendment.

In 1965 Quie participated in the "Young Turks" revolt that toppled the leadership of Rep. Charles Halleck (R, Ind.) [*q.v.*] and ended in the selection of Gerald R. Ford (R, Mich.) [*q.v.*] as House minority leader. Once elected Ford shared the leadership's policy functions. Beginning in 1966 Quie and Charles E. Goodell (R, N.Y.) [*q.v.*] helped formulate and campaign for a comprehensive Republican alternative to the Administration's War on Poverty programs. The two Representatives accused the President of engaging the nation in an antipoverty war without a fully developed strategy. The Quie-Goodell proposal transferred many of the Office of Economic Opportunity's (OEO) programs to other, existing cabient agencies. Another Quie measure required that at least one-third of OEO local community action board members be representative of, and chosen by, the poor, a provision aimed at limiting the OEO's patronage powers. Quie and Goodell also called for an increased state role in the programs and the "massive involvement of private enterprise." With the exception of the community board proposal, approved in September 1966, no action was taken on their ideas during the final years of the Johnson presidency.

Quie's own leadership role first became widely known in the debate over the 1967 federal aid-to-education bill. Through an amendment submitted in May, he sought to alter fundamentally the federal government's distribution of assistance funds. Quie's proposed measure provided for federal "block grants" to states rather than to impacted localities; its proponents argued that bureaucratic "red tape" would be restricted by entrusting fund allocations to existing state authorities. Most Republicans and Southern Democrats backed the Quie amendment. However, the Administration strongly opposed the provision and rallied religious, civil rights and educational organizations to its side. In late May White House forces defeated the proposal by a 168-197 vote. Although not original to Quie, the "revenue sharing" concept became a constant demand of the GOP House leadership during debates over the Administration's Great Society legislation.

In the spring of 1968 Quie and Goodell pressured Ford into supporting an open housing bill. Their move represented the first—and one of the few—challenges to Ford's House leadership. Ford gave up his opposition to the bill just before the vote, after Quie and Goodell had announced endorsement of the bill by 77 GOP House members.

During the Nixon presidency Quie's influence in the House grew. Loyal to Presidents Richard M. Nixon and Gerald Ford on foreign policy matters, Quie was more liberal than the two Republican presidents on several domestic questions. [See NIXON Volume]

[JLB]

For further information:
Melvin R. Laird, ed., *Republican Papers* (New York, 1968).

QUILL, MICHAEL J(OSEPH)

b. Sept. 18, 1905; Gourtloughera, Ireland
d. Jan. 28, 1966; New York, N.Y.
President, Transport Workers Union (TWU), 1935-66.

Quill came to New York in 1926, after having been active in his youth in the Irish Republican Army. He worked at a variety of jobs on New York's subways and was among a small group of Irish workers and Communist Party organizers who founded the Transport Workers Union (TWU) in 1934. Quill was elected union president the next year. Between 1937 and 1949 he served three terms on the New York City Council, twice representing the American Labor Party and once serving as an independent. Quill broke with the Communist Party in March 1948 and, after a bitter, year-long struggle, won control of the union. Quill led several New York bus strikes, and in January 1963 directed a 20-day strike against the Philadelphia transit system. In New York, however, in spite of frequent strike threats, the TWU did not strike the subway system in the early 1960s. Although in increasingly poor health Quill was reelected president of the TWU in 1961 and 1965. [See TRUMAN, KENNEDY Volumes]

Worried about the effect of automation on the transit industry during the 1963 TWU negotiations with the New York City Transit Authority, Quill demanded, in addition to a 15% wage hike, a four-day, 32-hour workweek and six weeks vacation after one year of service. Quill suggested that New York eliminate the bus and subway fare and provide free transportation as a public service, financed by taxes on the "big real estate interests." A new contract was signed only after Quill dropped the demand for a shorter workweek just before the twice-postponed Jan. 1, 1964 strike deadline. Although the pact was approved by TWU members by a four-to-one margin, over 1,000 workers picketed the union headquarters, calling the contract a sellout.

Quill was an outspoken critic of the war in Vietnam and likened the insurgents there to the insurgents in Ireland, whom he had long supported. In New York municipal elections Quill generally supported the Democrats and in 1965 backed Abraham D. Beame in his unsuccessful race for mayor against Rep. John V. Lindsay [*q.v.*].

Two days after the election, on Nov. 4, Quill announced that the TWU would once again seek a four-day, 32-hour workweek and six weeks vacation, in addition to a 30% wage hike. Since the TWU contract expired at the same time Lindsay took office, midnight Dec. 31, Quill requested that Lindsay attend or send a representative to the contract negotiations. However, Lindsay avoided any direct role, saying it was up to the outgoing Mayor Robert F. Wagner [*q.v.*] to settle the dispute. Tensions with Lindsay, whom Quill contemptuously called "strictly Silk Stocking [New York City's wealthy east side district] and Yale," increased. On Dec. 2 Quill responded to Lindsay's charge that he was not bargaining in "good faith" by calling off all talks and setting a Dec. 15 strike deadline. A week later, when Wagner, Lindsay and Quill agreed to the appointment of a three-member mediation panel including long-time transit arbitrator Theodore W. Kheel [*q.v.*], the deadline was returned to 5 a.m. Jan. 1.

It was not until Dec. 31 that Lindsay personally attended a bargaining session, where he was called a "juvenile," a "pipsqueak" and an "ass" by Quill. At 11:45 that night Lindsay and the Transportation Authority presented their first counterproposal to the union, a $25 million package immediately rejected by Quill. The strike was scheduled for the morning as Quill declared, "The only way to stop it is to shoot the workers down." Thirty-three thousand TWU members and 1,800 members of the Amalgamated Transit Union left their jobs, stopping all service on public buses and subways and on five of the city's six private bus lines. According to the *New York Times*, some six million riders were affected. In spite of Lindsay's pleas that workers remain at home unless their jobs were "absolutely crucial," New York experienced mammoth traffic jams and disruption of its economy and school system.

Both the Transit Authority and the TWU made new offers on Jan. 2, but they remained too far apart for a settlement. On Jan. 4 Quill and eight other strike leaders were jailed for violating an anti-strike injunction. At the Civil Jail Quill, who had a history of heart disease, collapsed from congestive heart failure and was rushed to Bellevue Hospital. Union Vice President Douglas L. MacMahon replaced Quill as chief negotiator. On Jan. 6, at Lindsay's request, President Johnson sent Secretary of Labor W. Willard Wirtz [*q.v.*] to New York to aid settlement efforts, but Wirtz returned to Washington the next day, having made no progress.

On Jan. 13 both sides accepted a mediation panel proposal ending the 12-day-old strike. The new two-year contract called for a 15% wage increase spread over 18 months but did not include the shorter workweek or the six weeks vacation originally demanded by the union. The same day President Johnson denounced the settlement as violating the Administration's anti-inflationary wage guideposts.

Quill was released from Bellevue on the day of the settlement and entered a private hospital. He left the hospital on Jan. 24 and held a press conference the following day. On Jan. 28 he died of heart failure.

[JBF]

RABORN, WILLIAM F(RANCIS)
b. June 8, 1905; Decatur, Tex.
Director of Central Intelligence, April 1965-June 1966.

William F. Raborn, a career naval officer who attained the rank of vice admiral, specialized after World War II in the development of guided missile systems. In 1955 he became head of the Navy's $10-billion Polaris submarine missile program and assumed responsibility for the construction of the first Polaris submarine base at Charleston, S.C. In January 1962 Raborn was named deputy chief of naval operations in charge of weapons development. He retired from the Navy a year later to join the Aerojet General Corporation.

In April 1965 Raborn succeeded John McCone [*q.v.*] as director of the Central Intelligence Agency (CIA). Shortly afterwards, President Johnson asked Raborn for his opinion on U.S. strategy in the war in Vietnam. He favored increased bombing of North Vietnam but also suggested that the U.S. keep in mind the possibility of a bombing pause to bring the North Vietnamese to the negotiating table and "to exploit any differences on their side." The Johnson Administration, over the strenuous objections of Joint Chiefs of Staff, did halt the bombing in May 1965 and for 37 days in December 1965 and January 1966, but these temporary pauses did not induce the North Vietnamese to negotiate.

According to Victor Marchetti and John D. Marks, authors of *The CIA And The Cult of Intelligence*, Raborn was an "ineffective" CIA director who, after 14 months, resigned "to the relief of all members of the intelligence community." Raborn later defended his tenure at the CIA on the grounds that he had introduced modern planning and management procedures at the Agency and developed an efficient worldwide system of communications among its operatives. He contended that within a year of assuming his post he had achieved his goals for the Agency and could, in good conscience, return to Aerojet General. Raborn was succeeded by Deputy CIA Director Richard Helms [*q.v.*].

[JLW]

RAFFERTY, MAX(WELL) (LEWIS), JR.
b. May 7, 1917; New Orleans, La.
Superintendent of Public Instruction, California, 1963-71.

Max Rafferty grew up in New Orleans and Soux City, Iowa, and in 1931 moved to Los Angeles where his father found work in an auto plant. An excellent student, Rafferty entered the University of California at Los Angeles (UCLA) two years later and became a member of the UCLA Americans, a right-wing campus group composed primarily of athletes and fraternity men. He returned to UCLA after graduation to study at the School of Education, where he came to oppose the progressive education doctrines of John Dewey that were taught there. Beginning his teaching career in 1940, Rafferty rose through the ranks of the state education system, becoming superintendent of the Needles Unified School District in 1955 and earning an Ed.D. at the University of Southern California in 1956. He turned Needles into one of the best school districts in the country, raising teachers' salaries to reduce turnover, initiating new programs for the gifted and for athletes and making scholarships available to minority students. In 1961 Rafferty became superintendent of schools in La Canada, a suburb of Los Angeles.

Rafferty's political career began in the summer of 1961, when he delivered a speech called "The Passing of the Patriot" to a La Canada school board meeting. Rafferty blamed the education system for producing a generation of youth, the worst of whom were "leather-jacketed slobs" while the best were without "positive standards, with everything in doubt." He called for putting patriotism back into education in order to make "our young people informed and disciplined and alert—militant for freedom, clear-eyed to the filthy menace of Communist corruption. . .happy in their love of country." The speech elicited strong reactions, and reprints made Rafferty a celebrity among right-wingers, some of whom urged him to run for the nonpartisan office of state superintendent of public instruction. Rafferty came in second in a field of nine in the 1962 primaries. With the backing of wealthy conservatives, he won the runoff election by 200,000 votes over a liberal opponent who had the almost unanimous support of the California educational establishment.

Despite his campaign oratory, Rafferty could do little to change the state's elementary and secondary education during his tenure. His power was limited by the liberal California Board of Education. Furthermore, as critics pointed out, Rafferty's programs did not differ greatly in substance from those of his "progressive" predecessors. His most significant changes were the adoption of grammar texts in the elementary schools and the introduction of compensatory education in fundamentals for potential dropouts. Liberals were pleased that Rafferty brought Negroes and Mexican-Americans into his department. The best-publicized aspect of Rafferty's first years in office was his unsuccessful battle with the Board of Education to impose a "little censorship" over the books placed in California high school libraries.

As one of the most prominent figures in the California right-wing revival, Rafferty became one of the best-known educators in the country. His reputation grew with a *Reader's Digest* reprint of the 1961 speech, a syndicated newspaper column begun in 1964 and the publication of his books, *Suffer, Little Children* (1962) and *What They are Doing to Your Children* (1964). His arguments for greater discipline and patriotism in education won the approval of many Americans disturbed by the social changes of the 1960s. Many liberals agreed that the reintroduction of the phonics system and the substitution of classic literature for Dick and Jane stories might reverse the downward trend in elementary reading scores.

Despite the nonpartisan nature of his office, Rafferty endorsed the gubernatorial candidacy of conservative Republican Ronald Reagan [*q.v.*] in 1966. Rafferty blamed Democratic Gov. Edmund G. Brown [*q.v.*] and other liberals for the "weakness" that had made the University of California, Berkeley, "look more like a skid row than an institution of higher learning." Both Rafferty and Reagan successfully used Berkeley student unrest as a major campaign issue. Rafferty was reelected by a landslide of almost 3,000,000 votes. Following the election Rafferty, as an *ex officio* member of the University of California's Board of Regents, backed Reagan's attacks on student radicals and his removal of Clark Kerr [*q.v.*] as president of the University.

In February 1968 Rafferty took a long-predicted step by declaring his candidacy for the U.S. Senate. He hoped to unseat the only liberal California Republican still in high office, Sen. Thomas Kuchel [*q.v.*], who, in Rafferty's opinion, was not in the Party's "mainstream." Gov. Reagan decided not to choose sides in the primary contest, but Rafferty found many wealthy supporters to help him win a 70,000-vote victory. In the regular election against Democrat Alan Cranston, Rafferty campaigned as an enemy of the "four deadly sins" of violence, pornography, drugs and lawlessness. But the defection of Kuchel followers to Cranston and revelations that Rafferty had avoided military service in World War II on a claim of physical disability ensured his defeat. Cranston won by over 350,000 votes.

Rafferty lost his 1970 reelection bid to Wilson Riles, a Negro he had appointed deputy superintendent of public instruction. In 1971 he became dean of the School of Education at Troy State University in Alabama.

[JCH]

RANDOLPH, A(SA) PHILIP

b. April 15, 1889; Crescent City, Fla.
President, Brotherhood of Sleeping Car Porters, 1929-68.

As a Southern migrant to Harlem, Randolph joined the pre-World War I Socialist Party and in 1917 co-founded the radical black journal *The Messenger*. In the late 1920s Randolph threw his energy into the organization of the Brotherhood of Sleeping Car Porters, which won recognition from the Pullman company after an epic 12-year struggle. By this time the cool and dignified Randolph was perhaps the most important black leader of his time. His threat of a march on Washington in June 1941 generated the first mass movement among blacks since Marcus Garvey and wrestled from a reluctant Roosevelt Administration an executive order banning racial discrimination in federal employment and in new defense industries. Randolph's postwar protest campaign against segregation in the armed services helped pressure President Truman into issuing another executive order, in July 1948, ending segregation in the military. [See TRUMAN Volume]

In the late 1950s and early 1960s Randolph urged that the AFL-CIO make greater efforts to end discrimination within affiliated unions. He strongly supported the new civil rights movement of that period and, with Bayard Rusin [*q.v.*], provided the initial impetus for a new March on Washington, which drew over 200,000 people to the capital in August 1963. [See EISENHOWER, KENNEDY Volumes]

As the civil rights movement began to break into factions in the years after the March, Randolph cast his prestige with those advocating legal tactics and integrationist goals. Reconciled by 1964 to what he considered a slow but steady AFL-CIO anti-discrimination effort, Randolph dropped his ties with the increasingly militant Negro American Labor Council (NALC) and gave his blessing to the formation of the A. Philip Randolph Institute. (The NALC soon withered away without Randolph.) Under Bayard Rustin's direction, the Institute worked closely with the AFL-CIO to advance unionism among blacks and build a liberal-labor-black coalition within the Democratic Party, which Rustin and Randolph by then saw as the key to racial and economic progress. Fearful that the series of riots and demonstrations in the summer of 1964 would harm Lyndon Johnson's chances for election, Randolph joined with civil rights leaders Roy Wilkins [*q.v.*], Martin Luther King [*q.v.*] and Whitney Young [*q.v.*] on July 29 to announce a "broad curtailment if not total moratorium" on mass demonstrations. Although not all in the movement accepted the moratorium, few protest demonstrations took place during the presidential campaign itself.

After the Student Non-Violent Coordinating Committee (SNCC) raised the "black power" slogan in June 1966, Randolph criticized the idea as a divisive and racist. He attacked SNCC for sponsoring a picket line at Luci Johnson's August 1966 wedding and in October 1966 joined with seven other moderate black leaders to "repudiate any strategies of violence, reprisal or vigilantism" and to "condemn both rioting and the demagoguery that feeds it . . . ." He again denounced riots in the summer of 1967 and in August joined with Bayard Rustin to reject SNCC's public defense of the Arabs in their June war with Israel. In the fall of 1968 Randolph supported the New York City United Federation of Teachers strike against the Ocean Hill-Brownsville Community School Board, although many in the black community supported the board as an experiment in greater local control of the schools.

Randolph was one of the strongest supporters of Rep. Adam Clayton Powell (D, N.Y.) [*q.v.*] when the House sought to expel the Harlem congressman in early 1967. Randolph valued Powell for the power he wielded as chairman of the House Education and Labor Committee and organized two important meetings in his defense, the first in December 1966 at the Brotherhood's Harlem headquarters and the second in January 1967 in Washington. The January meeting, called a "Negro Summit Conference," was canceled at the last moment because its organizers claimed "demand for attendance and participation was too great for meaningful and creative discussion."

As part of his general social program, Randolph favored a larger federal role in economic affairs. In the fall of 1966 Randolph helped sponsor proposals for a $186-billion "Freedom Budget" designed to eliminate poverty in the United States in ten years. Written by a team of economists headed by Leon Keyserling, ex-chairman of the Council of Economic Advisers under President Truman, the budget called for a guaranteed annual income, full employment and greater federal funding of health, housing, welfare and education programs. The budget was to be paid for by the "fiscal dividend" generated by a projected five percent annual rise in the Gross National Product. These budget proposals proved incompatible with the economic demands of the Vietnam war. In December 1966 Randolph attacked cutbacks in President Johnson's antipoverty program as a strategy designed to put the burden of the war on the white and black poor.

In September 1968 Randolph, aged 79 and ailing, resigned as president of the Brotherhood of Sleeping Car Porters, a union reduced by that year to a mere 2,000 members due to the postwar collapse of the railroad passenger industry.

[NNL]

For further information:
Jervis Anderson, *A. Philip Randolph* (New York, 1972).

RANDOLPH, JENNINGS

b. March 8, 1902; Salem, W. Va.
Democratic Senator, W. Va., 1958- ;
Chairman, Public Works Committee, 1966- .

After working as a journalist and as head of the department of public speaking and journalism at Davis and Elkins College in Elkins, W. Va., Randolph was elected to the U.S. House of Representatives in 1932. In the House he was a strong supporter of New Deal domestic programs and a promoter of legislation for the development of civilian aviation. Randolph was defeated in the 1946 Republican electoral sweep. During the next decade he was an assistant to the president and director of public relations for Capitol Airlines. In 1958 Randolph was elected to fill a vacant Senate seat; two years later he won a full term.

During the early 1960s Randolph supported most Kennedy Administration social welfare legislation. However, he devoted particular attention to measures that dealt with the economic problems of West Virginia. The state produced about 30% of the nation's coal, but mechanization of the mines after World War II created considerable unemployment. Randolph spoke in favor of area redevelopment bills in 1961 and 1963 and supported a manpower retraining bill in 1961. [See KENNEDY Volume]

In 1964 and 1965 Randolph, as the second-ranking member of the Public Works Committee, was the Senate floor manager of the Administration's Appalachian development bill for reviving the region's economy. In January 1965, responding to charges that the measure gave preferential treatment to one area of the country, he asserted that Appalachia had 8.5% of the nation's population but received less than 5% of public expenditures.

With the death of Sen. Pat McNamara (D, Mich.) [*q.v.*] in April 1966, Randolph became chairman of the Public Works Committee, a powerful post that gave him significant influence over the distribution of pork barrel legislation. He used his position to promote federal highway programs in West Virginia, a mountainous state with a backward country road system. Randolph regarded a modern highway system as crucial to the state's economic growth.

The Public Works panel handled most air and water pollution legislation, and Randolph was accused by some observers of acting in collusion with coal operators and United Mine Workers officials in opposing strong anti-pollution laws. During testimony before the Committee in 1967 on an air quality bill, Randolph challenged the Public Health Service's (PHS) recommendation that emissions of sulphur dioxide, a coal by-product, be strictly controlled. He contended that a PHS report on the effects of sulphur dioxide pollution was based on "vague" and "incomplete" evidence and successfully proposed an amendment that authorized the states, rather than the federal government, to establish emission standards for specific pollutants.

Randolph was also charged with backing a weak coal-mine health and safety bill in 1969. The operators' National Coal Association acknowledged that it had suggested many of the bill's provisions. Initially cool towards legislation for coal miners' "black lung" compensation introduced in 1970, Randolph subsequently took a more sympathetic position after miners staged wildcat strikes and demonstrations in support of such proposals. [See NIXON Volume]

[MLL]

RANKIN, J(AMES) LEE
b. July 8, 1907; Hartington, Neb.
General Counsel, President's Commission to Investigate the Assassination of President Kennedy (Warren Commission), December 1963-September 1964; New York City Corporation Counsel, January, 1966-June 1972.

Rankin received a law degree in 1930 from the University of Nebraska and then joined a law firm in Lincoln, Neb., becoming a partner in 1935. A Republican, he managed Thomas E. Dewey's presidential campaign in Nebraska in 1948 and headed a state committee for Eisenhower in 1952. From 1953 to 1956 Rankin served as assistant attorney general in charge of the Justice Department's Office of Legal Counsel. He was named solicitor general in August 1956 and over the next few years argued important cases before the Supreme Court involving membership in the Communist Party and school desegregation in Little Rock, Ark. When a Democratic administration took over in January 1961, Rankin entered private practice in New York City. [See EISENHOWER Volume]

In December 1963 Rankin was unanimously selected by members of the Warren Commission, investigating the assassination of John F. Kennedy, as its general counsel. Sworn in on Dec. 16, Rankin supervised the investigation and the writing of the Commission's final report. He assembled much of the panel's staff, examined and acted as the liaison between the Commission and other government agencies and between Commission members and the staff. The Warren Commission's report, made public on Sept. 27, 1964, concluded that Lee Harvey Oswald, acting alone, had killed President Kennedy. The report was well received at the time, although many of the Commission's findings were disputed over the next decade by a series of new assassination theories. Until the mid-1970s the government made no move to reopen the investigation. Then, in the wake of disclosures that the Central Intelligence Agency (CIA) and FBI had kept certain information from the Commission, particularly knowledge of CIA plots to assassinate Cuban Premier Fidel Castro, several senators began restudying the Kennedy assassination, and there were calls for a new investigation.

On Dec. 2, 1965 Mayor-elect John V. Lindsay [*q.v.*] named Rankin New York City corporation counsel; he took office on Jan. 1, 1966. With more than 300 attorneys working under him, Rankin was responsible for all litigation the city had to prosecute or defend, for giving legal opinions when necessary on the validity of actions taken by city departments and for supervising legislation for submission to the city council and the state legislature. In December 1966 Lindsay also appointed Rankin head of a 17-member task force to draft a New York City program for the upcoming state constitutional convention. The task force's May 1967 report to the convention urged greatly expanded home rule powers for all cities and countries in the state. Rankin resigned as corporation counsel in June 1972 to enter private law practice with his son.

[CAB]

RAUH, JOSEPH L(OUIS)
b. Jan. 3, 1911; Cincinnati, Ohio.
Lawyer; Vice Chairman, Americans for Democratic Action, 1952-55, 1957- .

Rauh, the son of an immigrant German businessman, grew up in Cincinnati. After graduating in 1935 from the Harvard Law School, he served as legal assistant to Supreme Court Justices Benjamin N. Cardozo and Felix Frankfurter. Rauh was an enforcement official for the Wage and Price Administration and worked on the staff of the Army's Pacific Command during World War II. Returning to private law practice after the war, Rauh became an important defender of civil liberties and other liberal causes; among his clients were the United Auto Workers union, the Brotherhood of Sleeping Car Porters and a number of Americans accused of Communist affiliations. In 1948 Rauh was one of the founders of the Americans for Democratic Action (ADA), a liberal anti-Communist group that opposed what it regarded as the conservative orientation of both major political parties. He was subsequently chief public spokesman of the ADA and served the organization in several executive positions, including chairman and national vice chairman. He also worked for the Democratic Party as a member—later chairman—of the Party's District of Columbia committee.

Rauh was a close friend and strong supporter of Sen. Hubert Humphrey (D, Minn.) [*q.v.*], whom the ADA favored for president in 1960. After the election of John F. Kennedy, Rauh and the ADA frequently criticized the new Administration for failing to provide "dynamic, crusading leadership" in civil rights and other reform causes. Among the specific Administration actions that Rauh attacked were proposals for the legalization of wiretapping in some cases and creation of a private corporation to operate the planned communications satellite system. Rauh also charged that federal funds continued to flow into racially segregated housing, despite Administration promises to stop this practice. [See KENNEDY Volume]

As the pace of reform accelerated during the mid-1960s, Rauh became increasingly associated with the growing civil rights movement. In 1964 he began serving as general counsel of the Leadership Conference on Civil Rights, a coalition of national civil rights groups that lobbied in Washington for anti-discrimination measures. During the next several years Rauh played an important part in formulating and gaining passage of several landmark bills, including the Civil Rights Act of 1964, the Voting Rights Act of 1965 and the Fair Housing Act of 1968. In early 1964 Rauh became counsel for the Council of Federated Organizations (COFO), another civil rights coalition working to increase black voter registration in the South. He also served as adviser to the Mississippi Freedom Democratic Party (MFDP), a COFO offshoot which encouraged blacks to run for office in an attempt to break the power of the all-white regular Democratic organization in Mississippi.

In the summer of 1964 the MFDP chose a group of civil rights workers to challenge the seating of Mississippi's regular Democartic delegation at the 1964 Democratic National Convention. Rauh accompanied the MFDP group to the Convention and argued its case before the Credentials Committee. Emphasizing the refusal of the regular Mississippi Democrats to accept the political participation of blacks or to endorse President Johnson for reelection, he argued that the MFDP was an open party firmly committed to the President. A stream of witnesses called by Rauh, including civil rights worker Fannie Lou Hamer [*q.v.*], testified before the Convention on police brutality and the victimization of blacks in Mississippi.

Rauh's presentation won widespread sympathy for the MFDP but failed to unseat the regular Mississippi delegation. Johnson, eager to avoid a split among Southern Democrats, offered the MFDP two at-large Convention seats plus assurances that the regular Mississippi delegates would be required to take a loyalty oath to the Democratic ticket and that future Party conventions would prohibit discrimination in the selection of delegates. These terms were conveyed to the MFDP by supporters of Hubert Humphrey. According to historians Steven F. Lawson and Mark Gelfand, Rauh was informed that rejection of the compromise might jeopardize Humphrey's chance of being chosen as Johnson's running mate. Under these circumstances Rauh accepted the proposal, although he could not persuade most MFDP delegates to endorse what some of them called a "back-of-the-bus" arrangement. Despite their disappointment, two MFDP members did join the Convention as at-large delegates.

In addition to his civil rights activities, Rauh was an energetic proponent of other liberal causes during the mid-1960s. In 1965 and 1966 he proposed and lobbied for legislation providing home rule for Washington, D.C., including an elected mayor and city council. Rauh was also one of the first liberal leaders to oppose the Vietnam war. In April 1965 he met with President Johnson and protested strongly against American bombing in Vietnam. Two years later he helped found Negotiations Now, a national anti-war group which circulated petitions calling for an immediate ceasefire and halt to U.S. bombing. Rauh's stand symbolized the division between "new" and "old" liberals over the war issue. Humphrey, whom Rauh in 1965 had called "the finest man in American public life," gradually distanced himself from his former friend by his continued support of U.S. Vietnam policy.

Rauh's political influence and his opposition to the war made him an important figure in the planning of anti-war strategy during the 1968 presidential campaign. Although initially doubtful that any peace candidate could defeat President Johnson, Rauh put himself firmly behind Sen. Eugene McCarthy (D, Minn.) [*q.v.*] after he entered the race in October 1967. Besides gaining the ADA's endorsement of McCarthy, Rauh initiated negotiations between anti-war leaders and Democratic regulars over a compromise statement on Vietnam for the Party's 1968 platform. After these efforts failed he directed McCarthy forces at the Democratic National Convention in challenging the seating of all-white (and pro-Vietnam war) delegations from several Southern states. Among those successfully challenged were the Georgia and Mississippi groups, which had not reformed their selection procedures since 1964. Humphrey's nomination at the 1968 Convention failed to bring Rauh back to his former loyalty; although the ADA favored Humphrey over Republican candidate Richard M. Nixon [*q.v.*], Rauh took no notable part in the national campaign.

Rauh continued to work for liberal causes after the 1968 election, opposing the Nixon Administration on many issues. In 1969 and 1970 he played an important part in arousing opposition to Nixon Supreme Court nominees Clement Haynesworth and G. Harrold Carswell. He also criticized the vice presidential appointment of Rep. Gerald Ford (R, Mich.) [*q.v.*] in 1973, claiming that Ford had consistently worked against civil rights and social welfare legislation. In 1969 Rauh began serving as counsel for dissident members of the United Mine Workers union (UMW), who accused union leader Tony Boyle [*q.v.*] of corruption and laxity in defending members' interests. Rauh's efforts helped reform candidate Arnold Miller win the UMW presidency in 1972 and spurred investigations that resulted in the conviction of Boyle and other UMW leaders for the 1969 murder of dissident leader Jock Yablonsky. [See NIXON Volume]

[SLG]

For further information:

Lewis Chester, Godfrey Hodgson and Bruce Page, *An American Melodrama* (New York, 1969).

Simon Lazarus, *The Genteel Populists* (New York, 1974).

RAY, JAMES EARL

b. March 10, 1928; Alton, Ill.
Convicted assassin of Martin Luther King, Jr.

James Earl Ray, one of eight children, was raised in St. Louis and Ewing, Mo. His father, an unemployed laborer, was frequently away from home; his mother was an alcoholic. Ray left school in the eighth grade. At 16 he went to work in a tannery in Hartford, Ill. Two years later he enlisted in the Army. He served with the military police in Germany but was given a general discharge in December 1948 because of "ineptness and lack of adaptability to military service."

Over the next decade Ray drifted back and forth between Chicago and the West Coast. He was arrested several times and charged with vagrancy, burglary and armed robbery. In 1955 he was found guilty of forging a Post Office money order and served three years in Leavenworth federal penitentiary. In October 1959 he was arrested for armed robbery in connection with a St. Louis supermarket holdup and was sentenced to 20 years at the Missouri State Penitentiary at Jefferson City. In April 1967 he concealed himself in a large breadbox being sent from the prison bakery and made a successful escape.

According to the FBI, on April 4, 1968, Ray, alias "John Willard," registered at a rooming house across from the Lorraine Motel in Memphis, Tenn., where Martin

Luther King [*q.v.*] was staying. Around 6:00 p.m. Ray shot the civil rights leader, as King was leaning over the second floor balcony railing of his motel room. King was rushed to the hospital and pronounced dead at 7:05. It was later reported that Ray fled the murder scene in a white Mustang. On April 20 Ray was placed on the FBIs 10 most wanted list.

On April 8 Ray had entered Canada, and on the 24th he obtained a Canadian passport. He flew from Toronto to London on May 6 and then, a day later, on to Lisbon. He returned to London May 17. On June 8 Scotland Yard detectives seized Ray at Heathrow Airport in London. In July he was extradited and returned to Memphis, where he was charged with murder.

In August Ray's attorney, Arthur J. Hanes, asked the court to dismiss charges because widespread publicity had made it impossible for his client to receive a fair trial. Judge W. Preston Battle rejected the request. In November Ray dismissed Hanes and hired Percy Foreman, a celebrated trial lawyer, to represent him.

On March 10, 1969 Ray pleaded guilty to murdering King and was sentenced to serve 99 years in prison. Within 24 hours, however, Ray attempted to reverse his plea. Ray stated that he had sold the rights to his life story to journalist William Bradford Huie to raise money for his legal defense. He charged that Huie, Hanes and Foreman had all pressured him to plead guilty. According to Ray, Huie had told him that a book about a man who did not kill King would not sell. Ray also stated that Foreman had promised that he would be pardoned after John Jay Hooker, Jr., son of a Foreman law associate, was elected governor of Tennessee. Ray later told one reporter that he had been "browbeaten, badgered and bribed into pleading guilty."

Foreman denied that Ray had been coerced into pleading guilty. He also suggested that Ray, a racial bigot, had slain Dr. King because "he wanted recognition and praise from his old inmates back at Jefferson City [site of the Missouri State Penitentiary]." Ray dismissed Foreman, but his new defense team was unable to win a new trial on appeal.

The Ray case was in many respects puzzling and controversial. His motives for killing King were unclear. His first attorney, Hanes, stated that he never heard Ray express hate or resentment in discussions about race or politics. James L. Bevel [*q.v.*], a Southern Christian Leadership Conference official and a longtime associate of King, was convinced that Ray was innocent, and Mrs. Coretta King [*q.v.*], suggested that the murder of her husband was the result of a conspiracy.

Some commentators suggested that Ray might have been given financial and other aid to help him flee the country. Ray himself protested that he was innocent. He claimed that in the summer of 1967 he had become involved with a mysterious French-Canadian named Raoul who in April 1968 sent him to Memphis to aid in a gun-smuggling operation. Ray stated that he knew nothing of the assassination, that Raoul was responsible and that Raoul had framed him. The FBI and Attorney General Ramsay Clark [*q.v.*], however, concluded that Ray alone had murdered King. In the absence of sufficient evidence to reopen the case, Ray remained confined to a maximum security prison near Petros, Tenn.

[JLW]

REAGAN, RONALD (WILSON)

b. Feb. 6, 1911; Tampico, Ill.
Governor, Calif., 1967-75.

Reagan's father was an Irish-Catholic shoe salesman and his mother an English-Scottish Protestant with a lively interest in the theater. In High School Reagan excelled in athletics and dramatics and served as student body president. He attended Eureka College, where he was again school president and was noted for his leadership of a successful student strike. Following graduation Reagan realized a childhood ambition by becoming a radio sportscaster in Iowa. He soon acquired a national reputation. In 1937, while covering the Chicago Cubs spring training on the West Coast, he received a film contract from Warner Brothers. Reagan subsequently appeared in over 50 movies, often playing the all-

American "good guy" who fails to "get the girl."

After three years Army service in World War II, Reagan returned to his film career and played an active role in liberal Democratic politics. In 1947 he was elected to the first of five consecutive terms as president of the Screen Actors Guild. However, Reagan's political views gradually shifted to the right. In 1949 he cooperated with motion picture industry efforts to purge actors alleged to have Communist associations. In 1952 he married for the second time. His wife, actress Nancy Davis, strengthened his conservative inclinations and encouraged his political activities. Reagan made few films in the late 1950s and 1960s, appearing in only one after 1957. From 1954 to 1962 he worked for the General Electric Company, hosting the company's weekly television series. He toured its plants and gave lectures to workers on the evils of big government and the advantages of the free-enterprise system. Though still a registered Democrat, Reagan campaigned for Republican presidential candidates in 1952, 1956 and 1960.

When Reagan became a Republican in 1962, he was already a popular figure among California's ultra-conservatives. He campaigned for John Birch Society member John Rousselot [*q.v.*] in the 1962 congressional elections. In 1964 he backed the senatorial candidacy of his Screen Actors Guild colleague George Murphy [*q.v.*], strongly supported an ultimately successful proposition to repeal a state open housing law and served as co-chairman of California Republicans for Goldwater. According to the *New York Times*, Reagan's television speech on behalf of Sen. Barry Goldwater (R, Ariz.) [*q.v.*], "drew more contributions than any other single speech in political history."

Reagan's Goldwater speech convinced many wealthy conservatives that he was a prime political prospect. Murphy's successful 1964 campaign showed that being an actor was not a political handicap and, in the age of television and image politics, might, in fact, be an asset. In 1965 a group of California businessmen hired the public relations firm of Spencer-Roberts and Associates to "package" a Reagan gubernatorial candidacy for 1966. Reagan toured the state, making a favorable impression on Republican voters, and in January 1966 he announced his candidacy. He easily won the June primary against a former San Francisco mayor, George Christopher.

Public opinion polls showed Reagan far in front of the incumbent Democratic governor, Edmund G. "Pat" Brown [*q.v.*], and the 1966 general election was bitter and sharply contested. The Democrats repeatedly emphasized Reagan's lack of experience in public office and his associations with "ultra-conservatives" and derided his show business background. The Reagan camp downplayed their candidate's relationship with the far right, and Reagan turned the other criticisms into advantages. He was far more self-assured and handsome on the television screen and in fielding questions before live audiences than was Brown, and he prided himself on being a "citizen politician." Throughout the campaign Reagan delivered essentially one basic speech—political writers called it "The Speech"—in which he blamed the professional politicians, specifically Brown, for the ills of modern society. His chief targets were high taxes and wasteful government, racial and student unrest, rising crime rates and rampant immorality. Citing student unrest on the University of California's Berkeley campus and the Watts racial disturbances, Reagan charged that Brown was "soft" on militants and criminals. He attacked the waste in President Johnson's Great Society programs and offered, instead, a "creative society" in which an efficient and unobtrusive government would call upon individuals to contribute their special talents for the good of all. The professional Reagan campaign was a huge success; he defeated Brown by almost a million votes out of the approximately 5.4 million cast. Suddenly elevated to the governorship of the nation's largest state, Reagan immediately became a potential Republican presidential candidate.

Reagan and his staff, many of them businessmen, were hampered in their first year in power by their lack of experience. Yet, Reagan was able to retain his political image as an economizer despite an inability to keep all his campaign pledges. Although he presented the legislature with a $5-billion budget—the largest in the state's history—and the biggest tax increases since 1959, he was able to blame the necessary taxes on the Brown Administration, which had preferred not to impose them in the election year of 1966. Working in cooperation with Democratic Speaker of the Assembly Jesse Unruh [*q.v.*], Reagan made the increased taxes more palatable by shifting the burden from local property taxes to sales and income taxes and levies on banks and corporations. In addition, Reagan ordered freezes on hiring and the purchase of new state equipment and made well publicized cuts in the state's mental hygiene and higher education programs. Among his conservative supporters only the most extreme turned against Reagan because of his new budget.

Liberals remained hostile to Reagan. Besides dissatisfaction with the budget cuts, they were angered by his plan to impose tuition at the University of California. They also opposed the Board of Regents' dismissal, at Reagan's urging, of University President Clark Kerr [*q.v.*]. The Governor's proposals for escalating the Vietnam war and punishing war dissenters further alienated liberals. His remarks on the unimportance of redwood trees and the desirability of turning federally protected land over to individuals irritated conservationists. The Governor also attacked welfare "cheats" and sided with California agribusiness growers in their opposition to farm workers' organizing activities.

Some of Reagan's measures, however, surprised many of his liberal critics. Though often charged with racism, he appointed a record number of minority citizens to top posts in his administration. In June 1967 the Governor signed a liberalized abortion law and in August approved a gun-control bill that prohibited the carrying of loaded firearms in public. Despite his anti-conservationist views, Reagan was persuaded to agree to a federal plan to set up a Redwoods National Park in 1967. In addition, the Governor strongly supported an automobile smog-control bill that made California's air pollution laws the strictest in the world.

In 1968 Reagan enthusiasts encouraged the Governor to enter the race for the Republican presidential nomination, but he preferred to maintain non-candidacy status and planned to lead the California delegation to the National Convention as a favorite-son candidate. Still, in the months before the August Convention, Reagan issued position papers and toured the country as a Party fund raiser, becoming the Republicans' biggest speaking attraction. He was particularly effective in the South. Despite his popularity among rank-and-file Republicans, his unwillingness to wage a campaign and Richard Nixon's [*q.v.*] string of unopposed primary victories reduced Reagan's chances of winning the nomination at the Convention. He finally declared his candidacy on Aug. 5 but could not get the support of prominent conservatives already pledged to Nixon. Following Nixon's nomination Reagan promised his complete support of the ticket and campaigned vigorously for his Party's candidate. Political writer Lou Cannon noted that during the campaign Nixon borrowed heavily from those Reagan speeches that stressed the virtues of the American pioneer spirit and the need to reduce the role of government in the individual's daily life.

Reagan was easily reelected governor in 1970, but a few months later his popularity suffered a decline when it was revealed that he paid no state income taxes in 1970. Nonetheless, when he left office in January 1975, he remained one of the most popular Republicans on the national scene. Many observers agreed that few politicians knew how to use television as effectively as Reagan. In 1976 he opposed Gerald Ford [*q.v.*] for the Republican presidential nomination but lost on the first ballot at the Kansas City Convention. [See NIXON Volume]

[JCH]

For further information:

Bill Boyarsky, *The Rise of Ronald Reagan* (New York, 1968).

Lou Cannon, *Ronnie and Jesse: A Political Odyssey* (Garden City, 1969).

Ronald Reagan, *Where's the Rest of Me?* (New York, 1965).

REEDY, GEORGE E(DWARD)

b. Aug. 5, 1917; East Chicago, Ind.
White House Press Secretary, March 1964-July 1965.

A congressional correspondent for United Press (UP) after his graduation from the University of Chicago in 1938, Reedy served in the Army Air Force during World War II before returning to the Washington bureau of UP in 1946. In 1951 Reedy met Sen. Lyndon B. Johnson. Under Johnson's guidance he served as staff counsel to the Senate Armed Services Preparedness Subcommittee and staff director of both the minority and majority policy committees. When Johnson became vice president in 1961, Reedy was named his special assistant to coordinate speechwriting and press relations.

In March 1964 Reedy replaced Pierre Salinger [*q.v.*] as White House press secretary. When White House polls commissioned after Johnson's 1964 election landslide indicated that the President was not viewed with warmth by large segments of the general public, Johnson eased Reedy out in favor of Bill D. Moyers [*q.v.*]. This July 1965 action came as no surprise to many observers, including columnists Rowland Evans and Robert Novak [*q.v.*], who felt that, because of his easy-going nature, Reedy was being made a scapegoat for Johnson's "image" problems. In a July 9, 1965 article in the *New York Times*, columnist Tom Wicker wrote: "Mr. Johnson never gave George Reedy the free reins, the full range of information, the power to make decisions, the full authority of an official voice." The advent of Moyers as White House press secretary effectively ended ready press accessibility to Lyndon Johnson. Moyers not only governed presidential relations with the media, but as Johnson's chief of staff he also influenced policymaking.

Reedy returned to the White House briefly as a special assistant in late 1965. He resigned in April 1966 to enter private business. In July 1966 President Johnson appointed him to the National Advisory Commission on Selective Service, a committee that recommended changes in the draft laws, including the establishment of a lottery system. Later Reedy wrote for various magazines and lectured on college campuses. In 1972 he was named Nieman Professor at Marquette University's College of Journalism.

In 1970 Reedy published *The Twilight of the Presidency,* a well-received book which lamented the increasing isolation of modern presidents. Describing the presidency as an "American Monarchy" and the White House as "a structure designed for one purpose and one purpose only—to serve the material needs and desires of a single man," Reedy likened life at the White House to that of a "barnyard," where below the President there was a distinct pecking order and a "mass of intrigue, posturing, cringing, strutting and pious 'commitment' to irrelevant windbaggery."

[FHM]

For further reading:
George E. Reedy, *The Twilight of the Presidency* (New York, 1970).

REID, OGDEN R(OGERS)

b. June 24, 1925, New York, N.Y.
Republican representative, New York, N.Y.
1963-72; Democratic Representative, 1972-75.

An heir to the *New York Herald Tribune* fortune, Reid graduated from Yale in 1949 after serving as an Army captain during World War II. He worked on the historically Republican *Tribune* until 1959 when President Eisenhower appointed him ambassador to Israel. Two years later New York Gov. Nelson A. Rockefeller [*q.v.*] named Reid chairman of the New York State Commission for Human Rights.

Reid first won election to Congress in 1962 from a district encompassing the eastern two-thirds of Westchester County. Known for its wealthy suburbs, the area also included middle class as well as impoverished sections. Since 1945 the district had experienced an industrial boom. Reid served on the Government Operations and Education and Labor Committees and soon established his political independence, voting against his party more often than not. Despite his liberal voting record, he backed Sen. Barry M. Goldwater's (R, Ariz.) [*q.v.*] presidential candidacy in 1964 but ran well ahead of Goldwater's tally in the traditionally Republican district.

A strong supporter of Johnson Administration social legislation, Reid frequently sided with the Democrats on the Education and Labor Committee. He advocated large federal expenditures for education and was one of two Republicans on the Committee in 1965 to favor repeal of Section 14(b) of the Taft-Hartley Act. Repeal would have made state "right-to-work" laws barring union shops illegal, but the attempt was defeated by a filibuster. Reid also proposed at this time to amend the 1964 civil rights bill to strengthen the powers of the Equal Employment Opportunity Commission in dealing with discrimination by labor unions. He also proposed to repeal the loyalty oath required for recipients of National Defense Education Act funds, but the effort died in committee.

Reid was a vigorous supporter of civil rights legislation and was one of a group of five Republicans to oppose the seating of the Mississippi congressional delegation in 1965. After Congress seated the delegation, the group issued a statement that the result "effectively condoned the disenfranchisement of more than 400,000 American citizens in Mississippi and missed an opportunity to rectify the wrong." Reid was among a group of Northern congressmen who observed the 1966 primary elections in Mississippi. They subsequently reported that the 1965 Voting Rights Act was being "minimally enforced."

Reid voted for the 1966 Vietnam war appropriations bill but questioned the Johnson Administration's analysis of the situation there. In August 1967 he traveled to South Vietnam with a subcommittee of the Government Operations Committee. On its return the group warned that unless the government there made "substantive" economic reforms, "the advisability of continued U.S. involvement is questionable." A letter to Secretary of State Dean Rusk [*q.v.*] signed by Reid and subcommittee Chairman John E. Moss (D, Calif.) [*q.v.*] urged a "firmer stand" on reform of the Vietnamese government and was very critical of the role of the Agency for International Development, whose officials, the letter said, "have too often attempted to avoid 'rocking the boat' rather than pressing for necessary reforms."

Reid's liberalism, though popular at general election time, created problems for him in his own party. He drew criticism from Republicans in 1968 when he accepted the designation of New York's Liberal Party in addition to the Republican nomination for reelection. In 1972 Reid followed the example of New York City Mayor John V. Lindsay [*q.v.*] when he left the Republicans to join the Democratic Party. Reid backed McGovern for president in 1972 and was reelected as a Democrat despite the efforts of former ally Nelson Rockefeller [*q.v.*], who financed his opponent's campaign. Reid forfeited his congressional seat in 1974 when he declined to run, seeking instead the Democratic gubernatorial nomination. Democrats of longer standing within the Party dominated the race, and Reid soon withdrew his candidacy. He was appointed as New York State's commissioner of environmental conservation in 1975 by Gov. Hugh Carey [*q.v.*]. He resigned that post in April 1976. [See NIXON Volume]

[MDB]

REISCHAUER, EDWIN O(LDFATHER)

b. October 15, 1910: Tokyo, Japan.
Ambassador to Japan, April 1961-July 1966.

Born in Tokyo of American missionary parents, Edwin Reischauer spent his formative years in Japan, coming to the United States to attend Oberlin College. In the United States Reischauer devoted himself to Far Eastern affairs, as a graduate student in Far Eastern languages at Harvard, as a Harvard instructor (1938-1942) and then as a senior research analyst for the State and War Departments (1941-42) and the Army (1942-45). After the war he became the chairman of the State Department's Japan-Korea secretariat and special assistant to the director of the Office of Far Eastern Affairs before resuming his Harvard career. Appointed associate professor of Far Eastern languages in 1946, he became professor of Japanese history in 1950 and director of the Harvard-Yenching Institute in 1956. While at Harvard he wrote several monographs on Asian history and collaborated with historian John K. Fairbank [*q.v.*] in producing a widely respected textbook, *East Asia: The Great Tradition* (1960). In his writings and public statements. Reischauer was critical of U.S. policy toward Japan, particularly American conduct of the occupation, restrictions on Japanese trade and tacit approval of the sometimes undemocratic methods that the Japanese government used to pass the unpopular Japanese-American Mutual Security Treaty of 1960.

Between April 1961 and July 1966 Reischauer served as U.S. ambassador to Japan. There his enormous personal popularity, based on his affinity for Japanese culture, served to strengthen ties between the two countries. In 1966 he resigned his post to return to Harvard. [See KENNEDY Volume]

During the Johnson era Reischauer became a leading academic critic of Asian policy. In January 1967 he appeared before the Senate Foreign Relations Committee to denounce the bombing of North Vietnam and call for a rethinking of the U.S. position in the Far East. Although Reischauer was a supporter of the Administration's objectives in Vietnam, he called the bombing of the North a "psychological blunder" made in the mistaken belief that it would force Hanoi to negotiate. Reischauer advocated "prudent de-escalation of bombing" and suggested that it be replaced with a massive border blockade to prevent North Vietnamese expansion into the South. For a long-range Asian policy he proposed action guided by four goals: (1) minimize military involvement; (2) avoid formal alliances; (3) shun sponsorship of political, social or economic change because such sponsorship leads to "responsibility for the existence or nature of the regime;" and (4) not attempt to play the role of "the leader" in Asia. He also stressed the need for reconciliation between Communist China and the U.S.

In December 1967 Reischauer, along with 13 other scholars, issued a report that asserted a need to "deter, restrain and counter-balance" Communist China's power in Asia to prevent a major war. But along with "a firm and explicit set of deterrents to extremism," the scholars urged the establishment of "inducements to moderation." The report also recommended that limited experimental steps be taken to de-escalate the Vietnam war as an indication that "there is no inevitable progression upward." In January 1968 Reischauer signed a statement by Harvard's Ad Hoc Commitee on Vietnam, which called on President Johnson to refrain from further escalation and to make "serious and sustained efforts, including de-escalation," to reach a negotiated settlement.

Throughout the 1960s and 1970s Reischauer continued to publish textbooks and foreign policy studies including: *Beyond Vietnam: The United States in Asia* (1967); *Japan, the Story of a Nation* (1970); *East Asia: Tradition and Transformation* (1973); and *Toward the 21st Century: Education for a Changing World* (1973).

[EWS]

RESOR, STANLEY R(OGERS)

b. Dec. 5, 1917; New York, N.Y.
Secretary of the Army, July 1965-June 1971.

Stanley R. Resor, born into a wealthy New York family, attended Groton, Yale and the Yale Law School. In 1955 he became a partner of the prominent New York law firm of Debevoise, Plimpton, Lyons and Gates. Resor left this firm in February 1965 to become undersecretary of the Army. In June of that year, President Johnson named him to succeed Stephen Ailes as Secretary of the Army.

In his reorganization of the Pentagon, Secretary of Defense Robert S. McNamara [*q.v.*] had stripped the secretaries of the Army, Navy and Air Force of much of their planning and budgetary authority. Therefore, Resor was concerned more with administrative than with policymaking decisions.

On several occasions between 1965 and 1967 Resor testified before congressional committees on behalf of a plan proposed by McNamara to merge the Army National Guard with Army Reserve units. This plan, bitterly opposed by the Reserve Officers Association, met such extreme opposition on Capitol Hill that Congress passed a bill in 1967 formally prohibiting the Defense Department from implementing the merger.

Resor served as civilian head of the Army during the critical period when the U.S. began committing ground troops to the Vietnam war. Draft quotas were vastly increased to meet the demands of the war; the number of men serving in the Army rose from 961,000 in January 1966 to 1.5 million by June 1968. During this period several servicemen attempted to use court orders to enjoin Resor and McNamara from sending them to Vietnam to take part in what these soldiers argued was an illegal and immoral conflict. In November 1967 the U.S. Supreme Court in a six to two decision refused to intervene on behalf of these soldiers on the ground that it lacked jurisdiction in a case where the issues were primarily political and military.

On the evening of July 24, 1967 Resor, McNamara, Gen. Harold K. Johnson [*q.v.*] and FBI director J. Edgar Hoover [*q.v.*] met with President Johnson and agreed that federal paratroops should be sent to Detroit because city police and National Guardsmen had been unable to halt rioting in the city's black ghetto. The paratroops succeeded in bring the situation under control, but the National Guard was widely criticised for its lack of discipline in dealing with the rioters. In response to this criticism, Resor testified before the Senate Armed Services Committee in February 1968 that the National Guard was being given special training and equipment to handle future civil disturbances.

Resor, a Republican and one of the few Johnson appointees retained by President Richard M. Nixon [*q.v.*], continued as Secretary of the Army until the spring of 1971. During this period he faced congressional probes concerning the draft, atrocities in Vietnam, corruption in the management of officers' clubs and charges that the Army spied on American citizens. [See NIXON Volume]

[JLW]

REUSS, HENRY S(CHOELLKOPF)

b. Feb. 12, 1912, Milwaukee, Wisc.
Democratic Representative, Wisc., 1955- .

The grandson of a Wisconsin bank president who had emigrated from Germany in 1848, Henry Reuss grew up in Milwaukee, where he practiced law after earning an LL.B. from Harvard in 1936. After wartime service with the Office of Price Administration and the Army, Reuss resumed his law practice and served on the board of directors of several companies, including the Marshall and Ilsley Bank at Milwaukee. A Republican until 1950, Reuss switched to the Democratic Party in that year because he considered Sen. Joseph McCarthy (R, Wisc.) "a disgrace to Wisconsin." He helped to organize an anti-McCarthy movement in the state and ran unsuccessfully for the offices of state attorney-general in 1950 and U.S. senator in 1952. Reuss won election to the House of Representatives from Milwaukee's fifth district in 1954 against a pro-McCarthy Republican incumbent, Rep. Charles J. Kersten.

Reuss proved himself to be a staunch liberal and, in the Kennedy years, a reliable supporter of the President's legislative program. A member of the House Banking and Currency Committee and the Joint Economic Committee, Reuss became a House expert in the subjects of trade and finance and a sponsor of measures to protect the environment. [See KENNEDY Volume]

As chairman of the International Finance Subcommittee of the Banking and Currency Committee, Reuss became an active supporter of mechanisms to channel financial assistance to developing nations in the mid-1960s. In May 1964 Reuss was the floor manager for a bill to authorize a $312-million increase in the U.S. contribution to the International Development Association, which could provide credit on easier terms than its parent body, the

World Bank. Reuss favored the multilateral approach to foreign aid partly because, he argued, it deflected bilateral diplomatic pressures away from the U.S. He was also a consistent supporter of increasing U.S. contributions to the Inter-American Development Bank, which made "soft loans" to high priority development projects in Latin America.

Although a faithful backer of Great Society social legislation, Reuss came to oppose the Johnson Administration on the issues of the Vietnam War and the burgeoning defense budget. In January 1966 he suggested a continuation of the Christmas bombing pause and urged the President to seek negotiations with and recognize the National Liberation Front as the chief enemy belligerent. Reuss was one of only seven congressmen in October 1968 to vote against the entire defense budget, which contained an appropriation of $25.5 billion for the war in Vietnam.

Reuss was an early opponent of the supersonic transport plane (SST). In March 1964 he made an unsuccessful attempt to eliminate $24.7 million earmarked for research on the project. He continued to criticize the plane throughout the decade, arguing in July 1966 that "the convenience of a few VIPs in getting to their destinations a few minutes earlier is less a national priority" than the continuation of federal programs to aid the cities and combat water pollution. In August 1967 Reuss called upon the federal government to bring about a ten-fold expansion of the nation's supply of low and moderate income housing.

Reuss responded to the breakdown in 1966 of the Administration's 3.2% guideposts for annual wage increases by proposing that the Joint Economic Committee of Congress came up with its own guidelines after consulting with labor and management. He emerged during the Nixon years as one of the strongest advocates of wage-price controls. [See NIXON Volume]

[TO]

For further information:
Henry S. Reuss, *Critical Decade: An Economic Policy for America and the Free World* (New York, 1964).

REUTHER, WALTER P(HILIP)
b. Sept. 1, 1907; Wheeling, W. Va.
d. May 9, 1970,; Pellston, Mich.
President, United Automobile Workers (UAW), 1946-70.

Reuther was raised as a socialist in a family of German immigrants. After completing high school in Wheeling, Reuther moved to Detroit in 1926 and became a skilled tool and die worker at Ford. Discharged for union activity in 1931, Reuther attended classes at Wayne University and campaigned actively for Norman Thomas's 1932 presidential candidacy. After a three-year world tour Reuther returned to Detroit and, with his brothers Victor and Roy, plunged into organizational work for the fledgling United Auto Workers (UAW). Walter Reuther was first elected to the UAW executive board in 1936 but only achieved real power in the union after he helped organize 30,000 auto workers on Detroit's West Side early the next year.

Over the next decade the Reuther brothers organized and led their own caucus, which fought for control of the UAW. In 1945 Reuther led the union in an aggressive 113-day postwar work-stoppage against General Motors (GM). His articulate leadership of the GM strike won for Reuther the support of the Union's restive membership, a national reputation as a leader of the non-Communist left and the presidency of the million-member UAW in March 1946.

In the next few years Reuther consolidated his control of the UAW, helped found the liberal Americans for Democratic Action and served as president of the Congress of Industrial Organizations from 1952 until its merger with the American Federation of Labor in 1955. Reuther also negotiated for the UAW a series of pacesetting collective bargaining agreements, which won for the union's membership substantially improved fringe benefits and higher real wages. The recession of 1958 cut the UAW from 1.5 to 1.1 million members and ended the era of important contract gains. As working conditions deteriorated in the auto industry in the late 1950s and early 1960s, Reuther faced recurrent local wildcat strikes following negotiation of each company-wide contract. [See TRUMAN, EISENHOWER and KENNEDY Volumes]

In September and October 1964 Reuther negotiated new collective bargaining agreements substantially exceeding the Johnson Administration's 3.2% wage guideposts. Reuther first directed his union's pressure against Chrysler because he knew that the weakest of the big three auto makers, then enjoying its first significant profits in several years, would be reluctant to endure a strike. The Chrysler agreement, reached Sept. 9, was later copied by Ford on Sept. 18 and by GM on Oct. 5. The new contracts increased retirement and insurance benefits, raised wages and added 12 minutes a day relief-time and two more paid holidays. The final settlements totaled about 60 cents an hour and averaged 4.9% of the industry's labor costs. The White House, anxious for labor's support in an election year, called the contracts "reasonably close" to its wage guidelines.

Although Ford and GM had quickly agreed to the economic package Reuther negotiated at Chrysler, contract talks between the UAW and the two larger auto companies broke down over resolution of local plant disputes involving grievance procedures and working conditions. Ford and GM sought to absorb much of the new contract's increased labor costs through greater productivity, but local union negotiators resisted what they considered company "speed-ups." To head off a wildcat strike movement, Reuther authorized local strikes; he called GM working conditions below "the minimum standards of human decency." Ford was shut down for 20 days and GM for 31, but few important grievances were permanently resolved. "The 1964 auto walkouts", concluded labor historian Thomas R. Brooks, "reflected membership dissatisfaction with the union's lack of power to solve in-plant job problems." Such disputes plagued the UAW's top leadership throughout the 1960s. In February 1967 a wildcat strike by a GM local in Mansfield, Ohio stopped much of the corporation's production, idling 174,000 men in over 57 other plants. Reuther declared the strike illegal, called the local's leadership to Detroit and ordered a return to work. When the strike continued in March, Reuther asked for a UAW executive board "seizure" of the local and ordered a resumption of work.

Another internal union problem faced by Reuther in the mid-1960s was the demand by skilled tool, die and maintenance workers for wage parity with non-UAW craft unionists. At the auto union's May 1966 convention, leaders of the skilled trades were Reuther's most vocal opponents. To meet their criticism the UAW amended its constitution to give the skilled trades department, which contained less than 20% of the UAW's members, veto power over all national contracts. After a seven-week strike against Ford in September and October 1967 the union won a special 30-cents-an-hour wage increase for skilled workers. In return for this concession and other wage and benefit increases averaging six percent a year, the union agreed to a three-year ceiling of 18 cents an hour on automatic cost-of-living boosts. After Reuther made an unusual televised appeal, about 90% of the production workers and 70% of the skilled workers voted to approve the pact. Most of the contract provisions of the Ford settlement were later agreed to by Chrysler, GM and American Motors.

As president of the politically active UAW Reuther served as a symbol of and spokesman for the liberal wing of the Democratic Party during much of the 1960s. His union lobbied heavily for the Johnson Administration's Great Society and civil rights legislation and contributed to Democratic electoral campaigns throughout the decade. At the 1964 Democratic National Convention Reuther played an important and controversial role as Hubert Humphrey's [*q.v.*] agent in the fight over seating the Mississippi Freedom Democratic Party (MFDP). Reuther urged members of the MFDP to accept a Humphrey-Johnson proposal that would seat the regular segregationist Mississippi delegation, give observer status to the MFDP and seat two of its members as "delegates-at-large."

The MFDP rejected the proposal and Joseph Rauh [*q.v.*], then acting as counsel for the Mississippi civil rights group, sought delay in the implementation of the plan so that he could take the issue to the Convention floor. Reuther refused and virtually demanded that Rauh accept the Humphrey-Johnson plan regardless of MFDP opposition. The MFDP itself felt betrayed by Reuther and other liberals and later staged a sit-in on the Convention floor. Rauh, who had long worked closely with the UAW, throught Reuther used too much "muscle" in the conflict, but Humphrey later praised the union leader as a "practical liberal" in the emotional dispute. In 1968 the UAW hierarchy solidly backed Humphrey for president, both before and after the Democratic Convention in Chicago.

Reuther worked to advance liberal and labor causes in arenas outside of the Democratic Party as well. The UAW was primarily responsible for formation of a private Citizen's Crusade Against Poverty in November 1965. Chaired by Reuther, the group directed over a million dollars in funds to a variety of civil rights and antipoverty organizations and to several urban organizing projects of the Students for a Democratic Society, (SDS). Reuther participated in the Selma to Montgomery voting rights march in early 1965 and in December flew to Delano, Calif., to pledge a UAW contribution of $5,000 a month to the National Farm Workers Association led by Cesar Chavez [*q.v.*]. Reuther also contributed $50,000 in UAW funds to the Memphis, Tenn., sanitationmen's strike in April 1968 shortly after Martin Luther King's [*q.v.*] assassination in the strife-torn city. Following the July 1967 Detroit riots, Reuther joined Henry Ford II [*q.v.*] and other prominent business and civic leaders in formation of a New Detroit Committee to help rebuild the city and improve minority employment and housing conditions.

During the mid-1960s Reuther clashed repeatedly with AFL-CIO President George Meany [*q.v.*] over what Reuther considered the labor organization's "complacency" at home and rigid anti-Communism abroad. Reuther supported President Johnson's conduct of the Vietnam war in its early phases but favored greater efforts toward negotiations and a bombing halt in 1966 and 1967. Relations between Reuther and Meany deteriorated following a well-publicized attack by Victor Reuther on the AFL-CIO's American Institute for Free Labor Development. Using the UAW's May 1966 Long Beach convention for a platform, Reuther's brother charged that the Institute's Latin American operations were largely funded by the CIA and supervised in a conspiratorial fashion by Meany's foreign affairs aide Jay Lovestone. (The *Saturday Evening Post* later disclosed that both Reuther brothers had accepted CIA funds in 1951 for distribution to West German trade unions.)

When in June 1966 Meany withdrew American representatives from the International Labor Organization (ILO) after a Polish Communist had been elected ILO president, Walter Reuther protested that the AFL-CIO president should have consulted his executive council before taking such unilateral action. Two months later Reuther characterized recent AFL-CIO statements on the Vietnam war and domestic dissent as "intemperate, hysterical and jingoistic." Reuther demanded a special meeting of the AFL-CIO Executive Council to review union foreign policy, but the UAW leader unexpectedly failed to attend the session when it convened in November 1966. Reuther may have known that he faced "overwhelming defeat", wrote historian Ronald Radosh, "and he did not wish to suffer personal embarrassment."

The UAW began to loosen its ties with the national AFL-CIO in December 1966 when Reuther announced that the auto union would "speak out on fundamental issues" if and when it found itself in disagreement with the parent labor organization. Reuther and other UAW officals resigned from their AFL-CIO posts in February 1967, and in April a UAW convention authorized the union executive board to formally withdraw from the AFL-CIO if it thought such action necessary. At the same time Reuther called on the national organization to launch an $87 million "national crusade" to organize white-collar employes and migratory and other poorly paid workers.

When the AFL-CIO took no action on Reuther's proposals in 1967, the UAW began to withhold its dues. The AFL-CIO formally suspended the 1.6-million member UAW in May 1968 and later issued a "white paper" denouncing Reuther for failing to use "democratic forums [within the AFL-CIO] to press his views. . . . " In July 1968 the UAW and the International Brotherhood of Teamsters formed an Alliance for Labor Action which Reuther hoped would "revitalize" the labor movement. However, the Alliance disintegrated in the early 1970s after the Teamsters raided the fledgling farmworkers union in California and endorsed President Richard Nixon for reelection in 1972.

Reuther, his wife and four others were killed near Pellston, Mich., on May 9, 1970 when their chartered jet crashed on landing. [See NIXON Volume]

[NNL]

For further information:
Frank Cormier and William J. Eaton, *Reuther* (Englewood Cliffs, 1970).

RHODES, JAMES A(LLEN)

b. Sept. 13, 1909; Jackson, Ohio.
Governor, Ohio, 1963-71.

James A. Rhodes quit Ohio State University after one semester to help support his family. Deciding upon a political career, he served in several minor city positions in Columbus until 1943, when he won election as mayor. In 1952 Rhodes successfully ran for state auditor, serving in that position for a decade. In his only general election defeat, he failed to unseat then incumbent Gov. Frank J. Lausche [*q.v.*] in 1954.

Rhodes's impressive reelection campaign for auditor in 1960, in which he won by just under 700,000 votes, set the stage for a second gubernatorial campaign. In 1962 he defeated incumbent Gov. Michael V. DiSalle, a liberal Democrat who had angered many voters by raising taxes in 1959. Republicans captured every other state office and retained control of both houses of the legislature.

Once elected, Rhodes proved faithful to the one pledge he had made to Ohio voters: not to raise taxes. To keep that promise and to eliminate a massive deficit inherited from DiSalle, he removed several thousand workers from the state payroll and reduced state expenses (exclusive of education) by 9.1%. The Governor consistently presented a balanced budget to the legislature during his tenure in office. Upon their elections in 1966 conservative Republican Govs. Ronald Reagan (Calif.) [*q.v.*] and Claude R. Kirk, Jr. (Fla.) [*q.v.*] sought out Rhodes's counsel when they prepared their first state budgets.

To fund extensive and popular highway and state university construction programs, Rhodes campaigned energetically, and usually with success, for state bond issues. Voters approved bond referendums in 1963 and 1965. In May 1967, however, the electorate rejected the Governor's proposed Ohio Bond Commission, which would have transferred the right to issue state notes from the voters to a special state agency.

Rhodes devoted much energy to promoting tourism and bringing new industries to Ohio. As the state's salesman, he traveled throughout the nation and most of the non-Communist world. In full-page ads in the *Wall Street Journal,* the Rhodes Administration proclaimed, "Profit is *Not* a Dirty Word in Ohio." His efforts proved successful. In 1966 Ohio attracted an unprecedented $2.1 billion in new industry. Aided by the mid-1960s economic boom, the number of new companies relocating in Ohio increased five times between 1962 and 1966. "I don't say we invented industrial development," Rhodes remarked, "but we perfected it." To create a tourist industry for the state, Rhodes fostered an impressive advertising campaign, which hailed "The Wonderful World of Ohio," and oversaw the rehabilitation of the state fair and parks system. His Ohio Development Department established a model for other state administrations to follow.

In the eyes of some observers, however, Rhodes's frugality starved state services. When measured against its capacity to pay in the late 1960s, Ohio ranked 48th among the states in educational support, 43rd in health care and 38th in welfare expenditures. Running for reelection in 1966, Rhodes argued that his emphasis upon creating jobs had reduced the need for greater public welfare spending and had increased state revenues. His little-known Democratic opponent attacked the state's record in welfare programs but lost badly to the incumbent, who won 62.2% of the total vote. Rhodes refrained from a "no taxes" pledge during his 1966 campaign. As expected, he asked for, and received, a 1% increase in the state sales tax in 1967. The state remained, however, one of the largest in the nation without a personal income tax.

Republican Party leaders came to regard Rhodes as unpredictable, if not untrustworthy. At the June 1964 National Governors Conference in Cleveland, Rhodes approved a campaign to prevent the nomination of conservative Sen. Barry Goldwater (R, Ariz.) [*q.v.*]. However, the Governor all but ended the presidential drive of Pennsylvania Gov. William W. Scranton [*q.v.*] at the eve of the July Convention by releasing the 58-member Ohio delegation to Goldwater. By then Rhodes recognized Goldwater's clear lead and determined not to weaken further the Senator's fall campaign by aiding the desperate Scranton effort. His move came as a surprise to State Chairman Ray Bliss [*q.v.*] and to Rep. Robert Taft, Jr. (R, Ohio) [*q.v.*], who was running for the Senate. Rhodes publicly predicted that Goldwater's vote against the 1964 civil rights bill would win powerful voter "backlash" support and that the Senator would carry Ohio. In fact, Goldwater lost the state by a million votes and carried Taft to defeat with him.

Perhaps because of the 1964 debacle, Rhodes privately fought hard for the nomination of a liberal-moderate presidential candidate in 1968. He wanted New York Gov. Nelson A. Rockefeller [*q.v.*] to win the nomination and urged Gov. Reagan to enter the campaign in the hope that he would split the forces allied to former Vice President Richard M. Nixon [*q.v.*]. At the August 1968 Party gathering, he kept the Ohio delegation pledged to his "favorite son" candidacy on the first ballot. Despite his efforts, Nixon won the nomination on the first ballot.

Scandal, tragedy and political defeat marred the last two years of Rhodes's second term. *Life* magazine published an April 1969 article connecting some of the Governor's activities with Ohio mobsters. Professing his innocence, Rhodes ran against Rep. Taft for the 1970 Republican senatorial nomination in the Ohio GOP's most bitter intraparty fight in a generation. Shortly before the primary, Rhodes ordered the Ohio National Guard onto the campus of Kent State University, scene of demonstrations protesting President Nixon's decision to order American troops into Cambodia. Guardsmen shot into a crowd of protesters on May 4, killing four and wounding eleven. The following day Taft narrowly defeated Rhodes for the nomination.

At age 65 Rhodes enjoyed an unanticipated comeback. He upset incumbent Democratic Gov. John J. Gilligan [*q.v.*] in November 1974 and returned to the governor's mansion after four years in retirement. [See NIXON Volume]

[JLB]

RHODES, JOHN J(ACOB)

b. Sept. 18, 1916; Council Grove, Kan.
Republican Representative, Ariz., 1953- ; Chairman, Republican Policy Committee, 1965-73.

In 1952 Rhodes was elected to the U.S. House of Representatives from Arizona's first district, which included Phoenix and its suburbs. The population of Phoenix increased more than five-fold between 1950 and 1970, largely as a result of an influx of conservative Midwesterners and Southerners. Rhodes's voting record in Congress paralleled the views of these constituents. During the early 1960s he generally opposed the domestic social welfare programs of the Kennedy Administration. [See KENNEDY Volume]

In the mid-1960s Rhodes continued to compile a conservative voting record. According to *Congressional Quarterly*, he supported the House's conservative coalition on at least three-quarters of roll call votes in each year of the Johnson Administration.

Rhodes had a mixed record in the area of anti-discrimination legislation, opposing the Civil Rights Act of 1964 while backing the Voting Rights Act of 1965. But he voted against the large majority of President Johnson's Great Society programs and in 1967 supported an amendment to eliminate the Model Cities program and sharply reduce urban renewal funds.

Taking a hard-line anti-Communist position in foreign policy, Rhodes voted in 1964 against allowing surplus farm goods to be sent to Communist countries. He supported each step of President Johnson's escalation of the Vietnam war and consistently backed large defense appropriations.

As ranking minority member of the Public Works Subcommittee of the House Appropriations Committee, Rhodes played a key role in Congress's passage in 1968 of a compromise bill establishing the Central Arizona Project to provide for the diversion of water from the Colorado River to arid areas around Phoenix and Tuscon. The compromise included concessions that resolved many of the objections of California and the Northwestern states, which had opposed the project for over two decades. Rhodes and Rep. Morris K. Udall (D, Ariz.) [*q.v.*] established their own House whip systems to organize support for the bill.

In 1965 Rhodes became a member of the House Republican leadership group when he joined Rep. Gerald R. Ford (R. Mich.) [*q.v.*] and other relatively young Republican representatives in a rebellion against minority leader Charles A. Halleck (R, Ind.) [*q.v.*]. The rebels did not oppose the conservative views of Halleck but felt that he was not providing forceful leadership. The House Republican Conference chose Ford to replace Halleck in January 1965, and later in the month Rhodes was chosen to replace Rep. John W. Byrnes (R, Wisc.) [*q.v.*] as chairman of the House Republican Policy Committee. The function of the Committee was to recommend and attempt to enforce Party positions on issues before the House.

Rhodes was a staunch supporter of the Nixon Administration in the late 1960s and early 1970s. When Rep. Ford became vice president in 1973, Rhodes succeeded him as House minority leader. [See NIXON Volume]

[MLL]

RIBICOFF, ABRAHAM A(LEXANDER)

b. April 9, 1910; New Britain, Conn.
Democratic Senator, Conn., January 1963-

Ribicoff, the son of an immigrant Jewish factory worker, grew up in New Britain. He worked his way through New York University and the University of Chicago Law School as sales representative of a buckle and zipper factory. After receiving his LL.B. in 1933, he returned to Connecticut and opened a law practice. Ribicoff's political career began in 1938, when he won election to the Connecticut General Assembly. He served two terms in the state legislature, followed by five years as a police court judge. Ribicoff ran successfully for the House of Representatives in 1948; he remained in Congress until 1952, when he lost a close race for the Senate. Two years later he was elected governor of Connecticut. Ribicoff won wide attention in the state house for his vigorous traffic safety program and his efforts to increase the efficiency of state government. He was reelected governor by a wide margin in 1958. [See EISENHOWER Volume]

While serving in the House, Ribicoff had become close friends with Rep. John F. Kennedy (D, Mass). He was one of Kennedy's earliest supporters in national politics, working for both his vice presidential bid in 1956 and his presidential candidacy in 1960. Kennedy rewarded Ribicoff after the 1960 election by appointing him Secretary of Health, Education and Welfare (HEW), a position Ribicoff himself chose in preference to other, more prominent cabinet posts. Ribicoff remained in the cabinet for two years, spending much of his time in unsuccessful efforts to gain legislative approval for Administration medicare and aid-to-education proposals. His experience in HEW convinced him that the Department's bureaucracy was too complex and unwieldy to handle the nation's social problems. Ribicoff resigned from the Administration in 1962 and returned to Connecticut to run successfully for the Senate. [See KENNEDY Volume]

As a senator, Ribicoff remained interested in many of the problems that had confronted him as governor of Connecticut and Secretary of HEW. He soon became known as a "cautious crusader," giving strong support to liberal causes but ready to compromise or defer action when necessary. In 1964 and 1965 he endorsed the Johnson Administration's medicare program, even though he objected to provisions that limited the length of coverage for specific medical problems. As chairman of the Senate Government Operations Subcommittee on Executive Reorganization, Ribicoff held a series of hearings on traffic safety in 1965 and 1966. These hearings became a forum for the widely publicized conflict between U.S. auto company executives and consumer advocate Ralph Nader [*q.v.*], who claimed that auto firms intentionally manufactured vehicles with important safety defects. Ribicoff generally supported Nader's position and used information collected in the hearings to push for a National Traffic and Motor Vehicle Safety Act. As passed in March 1966, the measure required the Departments of Commerce and Transportation to establish federal safety regulations for all new domestic and imported cars.

Ribicoff again gained national attention in 1966, when the Subcommittee on Executive Reorganization conducted hearings on the problems of U.S. cities. Leaders of business, government, civil rights organizations and labor unions appeared before the panel to discuss approaches to urban renewal. Ribicoff originally wanted to determine the impact of federal agencies and programs on inner-city areas; as the hearings progressed, however, he became increasingly interested in the possible role of private enterprise and community groups in reversing urban decay. After the conclusion of the subcommittee hearings, Ribicoff urged the upper chamber to initiate a major program of urban renewal. In January 1967 he introduced 13 bills in this area, including a $40 billion provision for inner-city housing renovation and a program of government loans and tax credits to attract industry into cities. The Administration was reluctant to sponsor new domestic programs at this time, however, and Congress did not act on Ribicoff's proposals.

Ribicoff came out in mid-1968 in opposition to the Vietnam war, which he blamed for the Administration's unwillingness to undertake new domestic spending. He supported the presidential candidacy of antiwar Sen. George McGovern (D, S.D.) [*q.v.*] at the 1968 Democratic National Convention. Ribicoff further alienated Democratic Party leaders by denouncing, from the Convention podium, the alleged "Gestapo tactics" used by Chicago Mayor Richard Daley [*q.v.*] in handling demonstrators during the Convention. Because the Connecticut Democratic Committee strongly supported the candidacyof Hubert Humphrey [*q.v.*], it gave Ribicoff relatively little support in his 1968 campaign for reelection to the Senate. He was nevertheless popular enough to win the election with 54% of the vote.

Ribicoff continued to champion liberal causes during the early 1970s. As a member of the powerful Senate Finance Committee, he fought unsuccessfully for welfare reform, including federalization of the welfare system and introduction of a guaranteed annual income. He also advocated several tax reform measures and urged creation of a Consumer Protection Agency; most of these proposals also failed to gain Senate approval or were frustrated by Nixon Administration inaction. In 1972 Ribicoff again supported the presidential candidacy of George McGovern. He was offered the vice presidential spot on McGovern's ticket but declined, preferring to continue his activity in the Seante. [See NIXON Volume]

[SLG]

RICKOVER, HYMAN G(EORGE)

b. Jan. 27, 1900; Makow, Russia.
Director of Naval Research, Atomic Energy Commission; Director of Nuclear Propulsion Navy Bureau of Ships, 1953- .

A Russian immigrant raised in Chicago, Hyman Rickover was credited with the development of the world's first atomic submarine. Upon graduation from Annapolis in 1922, Rickover served in routine assignments before being sent to work on an atomic submarine project for the Atomic Energy Commission in 1946. As a result of this experience he pressed for the development of a nuclear submarine in the late 1940s. In the face of naval opposition, Rickover managed to get congressional approval for the building of the *Nautilus* in 1952. When it appeared to many important officers that the Navy had refused to promote Rickover from captain to vice-admiral in 1951 and 1952 because of his abrasive advocacy of the nuclear ship, Congress organized an investigation which resulted in his promotion in 1953.

During the 1950s Rickover campaigned for the development of a nuclear navy while continuing to supervise both civilian and military nuclear projects. As a result of his experience in recruiting men for his staff and dealing with what he regarded as the poor workmanship of civilian contractors, Rickover became a leading critic of American education, maintaining that it failed to teach Americans to use their minds fully and to instill in them the desire for excellence required by an advanced technological society. In the Kennedy years he continued to advocate a nuclear navy, particularly the building of a second nuclear aircraft carrier, and to campaign for reforms in American education. [See EISENHOWER, KENNEDY Volumes]

Although scheduled to retire in 1964 at the mandatory age of 64, Rickover was retained in his position by presidential order. During the Johnson years Rickover denounced the close connection between business and the military which he said was one of the major reasons for the Navy's acceptance of inferior materials. In testimony given before the Joint Congressional Atomic Energy Committee on Jan. 9, 1965, Rickover maintained that the sinking of the atomic submarine *Thresher* in 1963 proved that the Navy had "to change its way of doing business to meet the requirements of modern technology." He stated that 14 months before the *Thresher* sank he had complained of poor workmanship in the yard where the ship was built. He also denounced the failure of the Navy to consider the safety of its personnel in "casually" sending atomic submarines down to great depths.

In March 1965 Rickover asked the Joint Congressional Atomic Energy Committee for authorization to build a "seed blanket" reactor. This reactor, conceived by the Admiral, was designed to produce more fuel than it consumed. At the end of 1965 the proposal was dropped because of unexpected technical problems.

[EWS]

RIDGWAY, MATHEW B(UNKER)

b. March 3, 1895; Fort Monroe, Va.
Retired Army Officer.

Gen. Matthew B. Ridgway commanded the 82nd Airborne Division in World War II and the 8th Army in Korea. In 1951 he succeeded Gen. Douglas MacArthur as United Nations commander in Korea. Ridgway subsequently served as supreme commander in Europe and Army Chief of Staff. He retired from the Army in June 1955 to become director of Colt Industries. [See TRUMAN, EISENHOWER Volumes]

During the Johnson years Ridgway was one of a number of military men, including Gen. James M. Gavin [*q.v.*] and U.S. Marine Corps Commandant David M. Shoup [*q.v.*], who attempted to persuade the Administration to limit U.S. involvement in Vietnam. In an article published in *Look* magazine in April 1966, Ridgway proposed that the U.S. maintain a middle course between unilateral withdrawal from Vietnam and "all-out war." He believed that the U.S. should press for a negotiated settlement that would guarantee South Vietnamese security. Ridgway feared that increasing U.S. military involvement would lead to direct Chinese intervention. He opposed the suggestion of Air Force Gen. Curtis E. LeMay [*q.v.*] that the U.S. bomb North Vietnam "back into the Stone Age." Ridgway wrote that "there must be some moral limit to the means we use to achieve victory." The use of nuclear weapons against North Vietnam, he said, would be "the ultimate in immorality." Instead of a dramatic expansion of the war, he supported Gavin's plan for a permanent halt in air strikes against North Vietnam and the limitation of U.S. troop operations to coastal enclaves in the South.

In March 1968 President Johnson invited Ridgway and a number of prominent former government officials and military men to the White House to advise him on Vietnam strategy. The panel, known as the Senior Advisory Group, argued that the U.S. could not achieve victory in Vietnam even with increased troop strength and stepped-up bombing of the North. The group advised the Administration to seek a negotiated settlement with North Vietnam. Johnson heeded this advice. At the end of March he announced his decision to de-escalate the conflict and begin negotiations.

[JLW]

RIVERS, L(UCIUS) MENDEL

b. Sept. 28, 1905; Gumville, S.C.
d. Dec. 29, 1970; Bethesda, Md.
Democratic Representative, S.C., 1941-70; Chairman, House Armed Services Committee, 1965-70.

After brief tenures as state representative and special attorney for the U.S. Department of Justice, Mendel Rivers was elected to the House of Representatives in 1940, where he was assigned to the Naval Affairs Committee (later merged into the Armed Services Committee). Rivers associated himself with the conservative Southern Democratic bloc in Congress. He supported Strom Thurmond's (D, S.C.) [*q.v.*] 1948 presidential campaign and backed Republican Dwight D. Eisenhower [*q.v.*] in 1952 and 1956. During this period Rivers consistently opposed anti-poll tax and civil rights legislation in Congress. He encountered little electoral opposition in his district; by 1960 he had served his Charleston area constituency longer than any other congressman in the district's history.

During his term in Congress Rivers frequently used his seniority on the Armed Services Committee to promote the construction of military installations in his district. In the early 1950s Rivers succeeded in reopening two installations closed after World War II and during the next 13 years secured a Marine Corps air station, three Air Force installations and a Polaris submarine base for his district. By the late 1960s military bases and defense-related industry accounted for 35% of the payroll in the Charleston area. Rep. Robert Sikes (D, Fla.) [*q.v.*] once quipped that if Rivers put anything else in his district, "the whole place will sink completely from sight from the sheer weight of military installations."

Upon the retirement of Representative Carl Vinson (D, Ga.) [*q.v.*], Rivers became chairman of the Armed Services Committee in January 1965. Rivers viewed the Committee as "the only official important voice the military has in the House of Representatives." Unlike his predecessor, Chairman Rivers met regularly with the Committee's seven senior members, known on Capitol Hill as "the Junta."

As chairman, Rivers first clashed with the Johnson Administration over what he termed Secretary of Defense Robert McNamara's [*q.v.*] "unilateral" decision to close unnecessary military bases. To counter McNamara's plan, Rivers added a provision to the 1965 Military Construction Authorization Act that subjected any base-closure plans to a veto by either chamber of Congress. President Johnson vetoed the measure, and Congress passed a new bill that included a provision giving the legislature 30 days to review base-closing plans submitted by the Secretary. During the floor debate on this bill, Rivers stated that the executive branch was now convinced that Congress "must be a partner" in military affairs.

Rivers again differed with the Administration in July 1965 by supporting the third major raise in military pay in three years, a 10% increase that doubled the Defense Department's request. During the House debate Rivers opposed an amendment submitted by Rep. Richard Kastenmeier (D. Wisc.) [*q.v.*] to alter the pay-increase scale in favor of junior officers and enlistees with two or three years of service. Rivers described the amendment as an abandonment of the "longevity principle" and dismissed as "fallacious" the argument that the pay increases in Kastenmeier's amendment might constitute a first step towards elimination of the draft. In 1967 Rivers supported another increase of 4.5% and successfully obtained a provision for automatic raises in military pay comparable to the upward adjustments in civilian federal employes' salaries.

Rivers vigorously defended the draft and the military's conduct of the war in Vietnam. In a Hartford, Conn., speech on Aug. 11, 1965, Rivers called for turning "the conduct of the war over to those trained in war—the professional military men." He warned that unless the United States was willing to employ nuclear weapons against mainland China, an American victory in South Vietnam was "merely postponing the final victory of Red China." After North Korea seized the *U.S.S. Pueblo* in January 1968, Rivers asserted that the U.S. should do anything "including declaring war if necessary" to recover the ship. Rivers also advocated that strong measures be taken against opponents of the war and the draft. He described war protesters as "traitors" in May 1967 and maintained that anti-war protests "undoubtedly. . .mislead the enemy and prolong the war." Rivers continued as chairman of the House Armed Services Committee until his death in December 1970. [See NIXON Volume]

[DKR]

ROBERTSON, A. WILLIS

b. May 27, 1887; Martinsburg, W. Va.
d. Nov. 1, 1971; Lexington, Va.
Democratic Senator, Va., 1946-66;
Chairman, Banking and Currency Committee, 1959-66.

Robertson served in the Virginia Senate from 1916 to 1922. For the next six years he was the commonwealth's attorney for Rockbridge County. In 1932 he won election to the U.S. House of Representatives, where he served until chosen to fill the unexpired U.S. Senate term of Carter Glass in 1946. Robertson was reelected for full terms in 1948, 1954 and 1960.

According to Virginia historian J. Harvie Wilkinson, Robertson "personified Spartan discipline, pioneer individualism [and] Calvinist morality." He was as conservative as his fellow-senator, Harry F. Byrd [*q.v.*], whose Democratic machine dominated Virginia's politics from the late 1920s to the mid-1960s. Like Byrd, Robertson opposed extension of federal power, social welfare programs and racial integration. But he was not on close terms with Byrd or the other organization leaders. It was the strength of his own extensive, informal network of supporters and friends that forced the machine to back him in 1946. [See TRUMAN, EISENHOWER, KENNEDY Volumes]

In 1959 Robertson became one of the leading spokesmen for Capitol Hill's Southern Democrat-Republican coalition when he obtained the chairmanship of the Senate Banking and Currency Committee. At the beginning of the Johnson Administration he was also the sixth-ranking member of the Senate Appropriations Committee. Unlike Byrd, he gave nominal endorsement to Johnson's candidacy in 1964 as an act of Party loyalty, but he persistently opposed Administration programs in Congress. In 1964, 1965 and 1966 he was, according to *Congressional Quarterly*, among the seven Senate Democrats who most often voted against Johnson-supported bills.

Robertson was especially opposed to the Administration's Great Society social welfare programs. In September 1964 he denounced the Appalachian development bill, asserting it would set a bad precedent because "every part of the country will want to have a piece of the pie." He argued that the best way to combat poverty was to reduce dependence on public welfare programs. During 1965 Johnson's public housing bill came before the Banking and Currency Committee, and in June Robertson attacked it as a measure that would "breed and foster reliance on the government and discourage private initiative." However, the Committee reported the bill out favorably and it ultimately became law.

During the Johnson years Robertson was best known for the bank-related measures he was concerned with as chairman of the Banking and Currency Committee. In 1964 the Committee failed, as it had during the early 1960s, to report out a "truth-in-lending" bill, which would have required lenders to disclose in advance the actual amount of a borrower's commitment and the actual annual rate of interest. Sen. Paul Douglas (D, Ill.) [*q.v.*], a member of the Banking and Currency Committee and the sponsor of the bill, criticized Robertson for not permitting the Committee to consider the measure.

The most controversial banking legislation handled by Robertson during President Johnson's tenure was a measure to revise the Bank Merger Act of 1960. In the spring of 1965 Robertson introduced a bill to prohibit the Justice Department from bringing antitrust action against banks involved in mergers approved by the appropriate federal regulatory agency. After objections were raised by small banks, the Banking and Currency Committee adopted an amendment offered by Sen. William Proxmire (D, Wisc.) [*q.v.*] which gave the Justice Department 30 days to challenge approved mergers. But the bill, which was eventually reported to the floor and which Robertson supported, exempted from antitrust action all of the six proposed mergers then being contested by the Department. House Banking and Currency Chairman Wright Patman (D, Tex.) [*q.v.*] regarded the bill as too favorable to large banks, and the measure did not become law until February 1966. The final version exempted only three of the proposed mergers from antitrust suits.

In 1966 William B. Spong, Jr., a moderate state senator, challenged Robertson in the Democratic primary. Spong charged that Robertson was a pawn of big banks and cited the incumbent's favorable attitude towards bank mergers. The accusation gained credence when the challenger was able to show that Virginia's banks were contributing heavily to Robertson's campaign. Robertson's prospects were also diminished by the growing number of urban and black voters, who were pushing the state's electorate towards the political center. Spong won the primary by 611 votes out of over 433,000 cast. After his loss Robertson resigned from the Senate and became a consultant to the International Bank for Reconstruction and Development. He died on Nov. 1, 1971.

[MLL]

ROCHE, JAMES M(ICHAEL)

b. Dec. 16, 1906; Elgin, Ill.
President, General Motors Corporation, 1965-67; Chairman of the Board, 1967-72.

James Roche joined the Cadillac division of General Motors (GM) as a statistical clerk in 1927. He stayed at Cadillac for the next 33 years, rising through all of the division's operations. He was made a vice president in charge of General Motors's international operations in 1962. This division represented 13% of the company's net earnings in 1964 and was becoming increasingly important as a key to future growth, since the company felt greater penetration of the domestic auto market would be met with government antitrust action. Roche became president of GM in June 1965 and chairman of the board in November 1967. In 1968 he earned $794,000, which made him the highest salaried individual in the U.S.

In the 1960s GM had the highest annual sales of any corporation in the world. Its net income was over $2.1 billion, the largest profit every made by an American company up until that time. From 1952 to 1968 GM earned an average return of over 20% after taxes on stockholders' equity. In 1968 GM employed 738,000 people and captured 53.3% of the U.S. car market. Many observers believed that GM refrained from aggressive price competition against its smaller rivals, Ford, Chrysler and the American Motors Corp., for fear of driving them out of business and making GM a monopoly vulnerable to government antitrust attack.

As president of GM, Roche became involved in a highly publicized involving Ralph Nader [*q.v.*], the auto industry critic and consumer advocate. In 1965 the 32-year-old lawyer wrote *Unsafe at Any Speed: the Designed-In Dangers of the American Automobile,* which charged that the industry had concentrated on style changes and horsepower instead of safety features. Much of his attack was directed against the GM Corvair, which Nader argued had an unsafe rear suspension system and other dangerous defects.

Before a Senate Commerce subcommittee hearing in March 1966 Nader charged that GM had initiated an investigation into his personal life in order "to obtain lurid details and grist for invidious use." More than fifty of his friends and relatives had been questioned by private investigators about Nader's sex habits, political beliefs and attitudes toward Jews. Nader also claimed that he was followed, had received harassing telephone calls and had had two suspicious encounters with young women who unsuccessfully tried to entice him to their apartments.

GM first called the charges "ridiculous" but on March 9 acknowledged the investigation and labeled it "routine." The corporation denied that it involved "harassment or intimidation." On March 22 Roche appeared before the subcommittee accompanied by GM's counsel Theodore C. Sorensen and accepted responsibility for GM's actions. He formally apologized to Nader and conceded that the probe was "most unworthy of American business." Roche admitted that the company had investigated Nader's personal affairs and that there was some harassment, but he maintained that the investigation had been initiated, conducted and completed without his knowledge. In November 1966 Nader filed an invasion-of-privacy suit against GM. He was awarded $425,000 in August 1970 in an out-of-court settlement; Nader said he would use the money to monitor GM's activities in the safety, pollution and consumer relations areas.

The Nader incident proved an embarrassment to GM and its campaign to forestall enactment of federal safety standards for motor vehicles. Roche had argued against such requirements, including mandatory exhaust controls, in July 1965. He presented the industry's case that traffic deaths were not the manufacturers' fault but were due to "road, driver and vehicle maintenance deficiencies." (The major auto manufacturers disclosed in May 1966 that since 1959 they had recalled 8,700,000 cars to repair defects.)

Roche maintained that state and local governments had primary responsibility for traffic safety. The industry's opposition to any federal standards gave way during 1966 to an endorsement of a voluntary industry approach, then a combined industry-state approach and then discretionary federal standards. The National Traffic and Motor Vehicle Safety Act and the Highway Safety Act, which mandated comprehensive government-enforced standards, passed Congress in the summer of 1966 by unanimous votes.

GM aroused the opposition of the Johnson Administration in December 1967, when Roche privately informed Gardner Ackley [*q.v.*], chairman of the Council of Economic Advisers, that GM was raising its 1968 car prices by an average of $61. This was the second increase in the 1968 model year, following upon a $120 price rise announced in September. Ackley told Roche that the second increase was inflationary and might drive the Administration into a public confrontation with GM. "I believe I shook him up a little," Ackley wrote later in a memo to President Johnson. GM lowered the increase to $23, a level which it said reflected the added cost of the safety shoulder harnesses made mandatory by law. Roche retired from GM in December 1971 at age 65. [See NIXON Volume]

[TO]

ROCHE, JOHN P.

b. May 7, 1923; New York, N.Y.
White House special consultant, September 1966-September 1968.

After graduating from Hofstra College in 1943, Roche served in the Army Air Force during World War II. He received his doctorate from Cornell University in 1949 and the same year began teaching political science at Haverford College near Philadelphia. In 1956 Roche moved to Brandeis as professor of politics, later serving as the University's dean of the faculty of arts and sciences. While on the Brandeis faculty he wrote several political studies, including *Courts and Rights* (1961), *The Quest for the Dream: Civil Liberties in Modern America* (1963) and *Shadow and Substance: Studies in the Theory and Structure of Politics* (1964).

In addition to his scholarly work, Roche served as chairman of the liberal Americans for Democratic Action (ADA) from 1962 to 1965. His period of leadership was one of growing dissatisfaction within the organization over U.S. involvement in Vietnam, culminating in an April 1966 ADA declaration deploring "the continuing intensification" of the war. Roche, a strong supporter of Administration policy, opposed this trend. After a meeting of top ADA officials with President Lyndon Johnson in April 1965, Roche split openly with ADA vice chairman and long-time spokesman Joseph Rauh [*q.v.*], who opposed American bombing of North Vietnam. According to journalist David Halberstam, the incident convinced Johnson that liberal sentiment on the war was divided and that opposition could be easily neutralized. Roche resigned from the ADA in February 1968, when the organization endorsed Sen. Eugene McCarthy (D, Minn.) [*q.v.*] in his campaign against President Johnson.

Roche's academic background and his strong support of Administration foreign policy made him an attractive candidate for the position of White House "intellectual in residence," vacated by historian Eric Goldman [*q.v.*] in 1965. Johnson, always sensitive to his standing among intellectuals, was angered by growing criticism of the Vietnam war among writers and academics; he blamed Goldman for the failure of the July 1965 White House Festival of the Arts, at which some participants openly attacked American involvement in Vietnam. Roche took over Goldman's post in September 1966 but had no greater success than his predecessor in restoring ties between the Administration and the intellectual community. Faced with vehement opposition to Administration policy in the *New York Review of Books* and other influential periodicals, Roche attacked the "alienated intellectuals" of the "New York artsy-crafty set" as an isolated group of critics out of touch with American society. Many intellectuals, for their part, agreed with literary critic Irving Howe [*q.v.*] in viewing Roche's appointment as a sign of "official contempt" towards the academic community. Frustrated in his contacts with intellectuals, Roche spent most of his time at the White House as a speech writer for the President.

Roche left his White House position in September 1968, returning to his teaching duties at Brandeis. He also wrote a nationally syndicated news column. In 1973 he accepted an appointment as Henry R. Luce professor of civilization and foreign affairs at the Fletcher School of Law and Diplomacy. Roche's memoirs of his White House service, entitled *Sentenced to Life,* were published in 1974.

[FHM]

ROCKEFELLER, DAVID

b. June 12, 1915; New York, N.Y.
President, Chase Manhattan Bank, 1960-69.

Born into one of the wealthiest families in the U.S., David Rockefeller graduated from Harvard in 1936, briefly attended the London School of Economics and took his doctorate in economics from the University of Chicago in 1940. After service with the U.S. Army during World War II, he joined the Rockefeller-controlled Chase National (later Chase Manhattan) Bank in 1946 as an assistant manager in the foreign department. He worked his way quickly up through the ranks, until by 1960 he was president and chairman of the executive committee and one of the chief spokesmen for American business. During the early 1960s Rockefeller expanded the overseas operations of Chase Manhattan, particularly in Latin America. He supported many of the Kennedy Administration tax programs, including the President's call for a $10 billion tax cut in 1963.

With assets of $13 billion, 28 foreign branches of its own and a globe-encircling string of 50,000 correspondent banking offices, the Chase Manhattan was the second-largest bank in the U.S., smaller only than the California-based Bank of America. It exerted direct minority control over more than 50 U.S. companies and, through a system of interlocking directorates, influenced the decision-making policies of many more.

Rockefeller generally supported President Johnson's foreign and domestic policies. He was one of a bipartisan group of leading businessmen, including Henry Ford II

[*q.v.*], who endorsed the 1966 Model Cities bill, which provided a plan to rebuild large urban areas through a coordinated federal program. He supported Johnson's September 1966 plan to suspend business tax benefits and on Nov. 29, 1966 urged a tax increase of up to $10 billion "to stem the tide of inflation." Rockefeller also supported Johnson's Vietnam policy. In an April 25, 1968 *New York Times* article, he stated that the war cost Chase Manhattan some $1.5 billion a year in foreign exchange, but that the bank "must be prepared to shoulder this kind of financial burden in the defense of freedom."

Under Rockefeller's leadership the assets of the Chase Manhattan Bank grew from $13 billion to $23 billion between 1960 and 1969. During this period Rockefeller served as a director and trustee of many companies, including several philanthropic organizations, and increased his influence within the business community.

Along with his brother, New York Gov. Nelson Rockefeller [*q.v.*], he was active in New York city urban renewal and, in his capacity as chairman of the Downtown Lower Manhattan Association, instrumental in planning the 110-story World Trade Center. Because the Chase Manhattan bank was one of the principal bondholders of the Triborough Bridge and Tunnel Authority, David Rockefeller also played a central role with his brother in the 1968 formation of the Metropolitan Transportation Authority. The new agency was a merger of the Triborough Authority, the money-losing New York City Transit Authority and two bankrupt commuter rail lines.

On Oct. 30, 1968 Rockefeller succeeded George Champion as chairman of the board of Chase Manhattan and thereafter took a less direct role in day-to-day operations of the bank. During the late 1960s the First National City Bank of New York replaced Chase as the nation's second largest commercial bank. The Chase Manhattan's growth was smaller than that of its major competitors and in the 1970s it suffered substantial loses as a result of high-risk loans to domestic real estate investment trusts.

[FHM]

ROCKEFELLER, NELSON A(LDRICH)

b. July 8, 1908; Bar Harbor, Me.
Governor, N.Y., 1959-73.

Nelson Rockefeller was the grandson of John D. Rockefeller, the founder of the Standard Oil Company of New Jersey and one of the wealthiest men in the world. Nelson's father, John D. Rockefeller, Jr., was a strict Baptist who devoted most of his public activity to the family's philanthropies. Nelson, his five brothers and his sister were taught thrift, self-reliance and a sense of social responsibility in their early years.

Nelson graduated from Dartmouth College in 1930. He subsequently worked in his family's Chase National Bank and leased space in the new Rockefeller Center in Manhattan. From 1935 to 1940 he was a director of the Creole Petroleum Corporation, a Standard Oil affiliate with large holdings in Venezuela. While in that post he concluded that a massive economic assistance program for Latin American was needed to alleviate poverty and improve the political climate for investment by North American corporations.

Because of Rockefeller's interest in Latin America, President Franklin D. Roosevelt appointed him to head the Office of the Coordinator of Inter-American Affairs in 1940. After four years in that post, he became assistant secretary of state in charge of Latin American relations. After World War II Rockefeller established private organizations to promote Latin American economic development by providing technological aid and encouraging corporate investment. From 1950 to 1951 he was an adviser to President Harry S Truman on the implementation of the Point Four program.

During the Eisenhower presidency Rockefeller served as undersecretary of health, education and welfare from 1953 to 1954 and as a special assistant to the President from 1954 to 1955. Many members of the Administration regarded him as too liberal, while Rockefeller was critical of what he regarded as the short-range, stopgap aspects of the President's policies. Rockefeller left Washington at the end of 1955.

Having concluded that appointive office did not bestow substantial influence upon its occupant, Rockefeller decided in 1956 to seek the governorship of New York. For the next two years he cultivated Republican political contacts in his capacity as chairman of New York's Committee on the Preparation of the State Constitutional Convention. Some prominent Republicans believed that the Rockefeller name would prevent him from winning the election. The negative impact of Rockefeller's wealth upon his 1958 campaign, however, was reduced by the fact that the Democratic incumbent, Gov. W. Averell Harriman [*q.v.*], like the Republican nominee, was a multimillionaire. Furthermore, Rockefeller's dynamic, self-confident and quick-witted campaign style stood him in good stead against the uncharismatic Harriman. Outspending his rival by $1.8 million to $1.1 million and employing an exceptionally able staff, Rockefeller won the election by over a half-million votes. [See EISENHOWER Volume]

Extremely sanguine about the problem-solving ability of government, Rockefeller introduced or expanded a broad array of civil rights, labor and social welfare programs during the first five years of his governorship. He successfully pressed for civil rights legislation that barred discrimination in the areas of housing, lending and public accommodations. Rockefeller established the state's first uniform minimum wage at $1.00 an hour in 1960 and increased it to $1.15 in 1962. State aid to education rose from $600 million to $1 billion. The state's middle-income housing program increased by more than tenfold. A vast program to enlarge the state university was begun. A school-to-employment program (STEP) to deter juvenile delinquency and a youth employment service (YES) were also created.

The high cost of many of these programs necessitated great increases in state expenditures. Since the state constitution mandated a balanced budget, Rockefeller asked for substantial tax hikes in 1959 and 1963. The 1963 request created considerable resentment among the voters because, during his reelection campaign of the previous year against Democrat Robert Morgenthau, the Governor had pledged not to increase taxes.

From the time Rockefeller became governor, he demonstrated an active interest in the presidency. In 1959 he sent out political feelers to ascertain his chances for heading the 1960 Republican national ticket. Finding that Vice President Richard M. Nixon [*q.v.*] had overwhelming support, Rockefeller announced on Dec. 26, 1959 that he was withdrawing his name from consideration for his Party's presidential nomination. In July 1960 he earned the enmity of the Party's conservatives by pressuring Nixon into endorsing a number of proposed liberal planks for the Party's national platform.

Immediately after Nixon's defeat Rockefeller began planning a 1964 presidential campaign. He had established himself as the leader of the Party's Eastern, liberal wing, and for most of the Kennedy presidency he was the front-running candidate for the Republican nomination. But in May 1963, after the recently divorced Governor married Margaretta "Happy" Fitler Murphy, also recently divorced and almost 20 years his junior, he fell behind conservative Sen. Barry M. Goldwater (R, Ariz.) [*q.v.*] as the favorite presidential candidate of Republican voters. In July 1963 Rockefeller attempted to halt his decline in popularity among Republicans by issuing a stinging attack upon the extreme right-wing elements in the Party. He officially announced his candidacy on Nov. 6, 1963. [See KENNEDY Volume]

Even after Kennedy's assassination, when Goldwater's Southern-based strategy appeared threatened by the accession to the presidency of Texan Lyndon B. Johnson, Rockefeller's standing in the polls did not improve. He hoped to revive his prospects by a victory in the New Hampshire primary in March 1964 but finished third behind write-in candidate Henry Cabot Lodge [*q.v.*] and Goldwater.

During the spring Rockefeller denounced Goldwater's opposition to civil rights and social welfare legislation as "the height of extremist folly" while concentrating his efforts on the May primary contest in liberal Oregon. He won an upset victory in that state over Lodge, thereby destroying the latter's moderate candidacy. The one remaining primary was a winner-take-all contest in California. Even with a victory there Rockefeller's nomination appeared unlikely, because Goldwater had done extremely well in nonprimary states. But the Governor campaigned vigorously, charging that Goldwater's conservatism was outside of the Party's "mainstream." On June 2 Goldwater defeated Rockefeller by 59,000 votes out of 1.1 million cast. Some observers attributed Rockefeller's narrow defeat to a revival of the remarriage issue that resulted when his wife gave birth to a boy on the Sunday before the primary.

The Governor withdrew from the contest on June 15 and threw his support to Pennsylvania Gov. William Scranton [*q.v.*], who had entered the race three days earlier as the last hope of Republican moderates and liberals. At the July Republican National Convention, Rockefeller was loudly booed by Goldwater supporters in the galleries as he spoke on behalf of the Scranton forces' platform proposals supporting civil rights legislation and criticizing extremist groups. Goldwater easily won the presidential nomination on the first ballot.

During the mid-1960s Rockefeller continued to press for liberal programs in New York State. In 1965 the State Commission on Human Rights was granted authority to bring complaints on its own initiative against any alleged discrimination in employment, education, housing or public accommodations. The minimum wage was increased to $1.60 in 1968. Rockefeller's vast network of social welfare programs was extended. In 1966 the state's medicaid plan, the most ambitious of its kind in the nation, was launched. It provided free medical care for any family of four or more with an after-tax income of less than $6,000 a year. Almost a third of the state's 18 million residents were eligible for the program. In 1968 the maximum income for eligibility was reduced to $5,300. A Narcotics Addiction Control Commission was established in 1966 to provide treatment for addicts. It possessed authority to commit addicts for treatment regardless of their wishes. State aid for all levels of education amounted to $2.4 billion of the 1968-69 budget, a larger sum than the entire New York budget at the beginning of Rockefeller's governorship.

The Albany Mall project, a huge highway construction program and the creation of such planning agencies as the Metropolitan Transit Authority (established in 1968) entailed enormous expenditures, and the state budget increased from $1.7 billion in 1958-59 to $5.4 billion for 1968-69. At the beginning of his governorship, Rockefeller employed pay-as-you-go financing to meet the constitution's balanced-budget requirement. But tax revenues, even after they were enlarged by the creation of a state sales tax in 1965 and a hike in the state income tax in 1968, were insufficient to meet the cost of his programs. Therefore, the Governor ultimately turned to bond issues for funds.

The constitution required voter approval for the sale of bonds backed by the credit of the state. In 1965 the electorate sanctioned a $1 billion bond issue to assist municipalities in eliminating water pollution, and two years later it endorsed a $2.5 billion transportation bond issue to build highways, airports and mass transit facilities. The voters, however, did not always back bond proposals: in 1964 and 1965 public housing referenda were defeated at the polls.

To circumvent the risk of voter rejection of bond issues, Rockefeller's aides devised a plan to create quasi-independent agencies that would issue so-called moral obligation bonds. These institutions were responsible for redeeming the bonds, while the state assumed a moral, but not legally binding, commitment as their ultimate guarantor. The first such agency was the State University Construction Fund, established in 1962. A number of others were created in the mid-1960s, including the Urban Development Corporation, established in 1968 to promote the building of low-income housing. Some observers, including Democratic State Comptroller Arthur Levitt, contended that this method of financing state projects was anti-democratic, of dubious constitutionality and more expensive than voter-approved bonds.

The resentment created by the tax increases necessitated by Rockefeller's programs proved a significant problem in the Governor's 1966 reelection bid. Polls taken early in the campaign showed him trailing Frank O'Connor, his Democratic opponent, by 26 points. The Rockefeller campaign organization reacted with a massive television advertizing blitz. Between 3,000 and 4,000 television spots were shown on 27 commercial stations throughout the state. New York newspapers estimated that between $5 and $6 million were spent on the campaign, eight times the amount spent by the O'Connor forces and a new national record for any state election. Much of the money reportedly came from Rockefeller and his family. Rockefeller defeated O'Connor by approximately 400,000 votes in a four-candidate race.

In May 1966, as Rockefeller was launching his gubernatorial campaign, he stated that he was "completely and forever, without reservation" removing himself from contention for the 1968 Republican presidential nomination. He proposed a liberal slate consisting of Michigan Gov. George Romney [*q.v.*] for president and Sen. Jacob Javits (R, N.Y.) [*q.v.*] for vice president. But Romney's following dwindled after a series of campaign blunders in 1967, and he withdrew from the race in February 1968, two weeks before the first primary. Despite pressure to enter the campaign, Rockefeller reiterated his noncandidacy on March 21, 1968.

However, President Johnson's announcement at the end of the month that he would not seek reelection made a Republican victory in November seem more likely, and a number of Party leaders began expressing a preference for Rockefeller as the most attractive candidate the Republicans could offer. On April 30 the Governor reversed his position and offered himself as an alternative to Nixon, by that time the front-running candidate.

Rockefeller did not enter the Republican primaries. His strategy was to demonstrate through extensive personal and media campaigning that he was the most popular Republican among the general electorate. In May, June and July he visited 45 states, addressing rallies and negotiating with uncommitted delegates and Party leaders. Beginning in June he conducted a television and newspaper campaign that cost at least $3 million.

Against the advice of his campaign managers, who urged him to move towards the ideological center of the Party, Rockefeller presented himself as a liberal Republican. He advocated a "universal compulsory national health insurance" plan, urged a vast program to "save and rebuild" the nation's cities and eschewed use of the crime issue, asserting that "to keep law and order, there must be justice and opportunity." Unlike Nixon, Rockefeller presented in July the details of a Vietnam peace plan. It called for a gradual withdrawal of troops by both sides, free elections and direct negotiations between North and South Vietnam that were to include the National Liberation Front "if it renounces force." Rockefeller's platform earned him considerable support from independent voters and liberals of both parties.

The Republican Party was somewhat chastened by the overwhelming Goldwater defeat of 1964. However, most Republicans, while prepared to nominate a more pragmatic conservative like Nixon in 1968, were unwilling to back the liberal Rockefeller, even though he fared better than Nixon in the presidential preference polls.

Rockefeller's negative image within the Republican Party was strengthened by his actions during a New York City sanitationmen's strike early in 1968. He rejected a request of John V. Lindsay [*q.v.*], mayor of the city and a fellow Republican, to send in the National Guard to collect garbage. Instead, the Governor promoted a settlement of the dispute favorable to the union. Lindsay brought the matter to national attention and highlighted Rockefeller's close relationship with organized labor in New York State when he denounced the Governor for "capitulation to extortionist demands . . . giving in to blackmail."

The final blow to Rockefeller's nomination hopes was a Gallup Poll taken on the eve of the August Republican National Convention. The July 29 survey showed Nixon, for the first time, running better than Rockefeller against Vice President Hubert Humphrey [*q.v.*], the anticipated Democratic nominee. For Republicans who did not wish to endorse the Governor in any case, the poll conveniently served to eliminate his only claim to the nomination. Nixon won a first ballot victory with 692 votes to Rockefeller's 277 and conservative California Gov. Ronald Reagan's [*q.v.*] 182.

In 1970 Rockefeller won reelection to a fourth gubernatorial campaign by defeating former Supreme Court Justice Arthur Goldberg [*q.v.*] with a 700,000 vote margin. The cost of the Rockefeller campaign was estimated at between $12 and $15 million, while the Goldberg forces reported spending $1.7 million.

During the early 1970s the Governor moved sharply to the right. In his January 1971 message to the legislature, he said that the state was approaching fiscal bankruptcy and could no longer either finance new programs or maintain old ones at former levels. The legislature immediately proceeded to cut medicaid, welfare and many other programs. During the next two years Rockefeller publicly "recanted" his views on government spending programs, denounced "welfare chiselers" and successfully advocated mandatory life sentences for certain categories of narcotics offenders. In 1971 he refused to negotiate personally with rebelling Attica state prison inmates and sent state troopers to quell the uprising.

Many observers regarded Rockefeller's change of views as representing a new presidential strategy aimed at winning conservative Republican support. When he resigned the governorship in 1973 to set up a study group called the Commission for Critical Choices, many believed that the new organization was intended to serve as a Rockefeller springboard to the presidency.

In August 1974 President Gerald Ford nominated Rockefeller for the vice presidency. At Rockefeller's confirmation hearings he stated that his personal wealth and that of his wife and children totaled about $230 million. A family spokesman placed the wealth of all the Rockefellers at well over $1 billion. Some observers estimated it to be about $5 billion. His nomination was confirmed in December 1974. In November 1975 Rockefeller announced that he did not wish to be renominated for the vice presidency in 1976. [See NIXON Volume]

[MLL]

For further information:

Robert H. Connery and Gerald Benjamin, eds., *Governing New York State: The Rockefeller Years* (New York, 1974).

Myer Kutz, *Rockefeller Power* (New York, 1974).

ROCKEFELLER, WINTHROP

b. May 12, 1912; New York, N.Y.
d. Feb. 22, 1973; Palm Springs, Calif.
Governor, Ark., 1967-71.

Winthrop Rockefeller, grandson of John D. Rockefeller, was born into one of America's wealthiest families. He dropped out of Yale after three years, worked as a roustabout in the Texas oil fields and in January 1941 joined the Army as a private. After his discharge in 1946 as a lieutenant colonel, he worked as an employe-specialist with Socony-Vacuum. In 1953 he moved to Arkansas and bought a tract of land, which he later expanded into a 50,000-acre model cattle farm.

In addition to cattle raising, Rockefeller aided cultural, health, civic and educational undertakings. In 1955 Gov. Orval Faubus appointed him chairman of the Arkansas Industrial Development Commission, where he helped bring much new industry to the state. During the 1957 Little Rock crisis Rockefeller publicly objected when Gov. Faubus placed National Guardsmen at Little Rock's Central High School to prevent nine black students from integrating classes.

Rockefeller unsuccessfully challenged Faubus for the governorship in 1964. Two years later he faced arch-segregationist Jim Johnson in a second try for the state house. In a fiercely contested election Johnson's image as an intemperate segregationist drove thousands of independent and moderate Democrats and a majority of the black vote into Rockefeller's column. With 54% of the total vote, Rockefeller became the first Republican elected Arkansas governor since 1873.

As governor, Rockefeller's major objectives were to increase the state's financial commitment to education and to launch a major expansion of other social services. During his administration the state enacted its first general minimum wage statute and in 1969 substantially liberalized its abortion law. Rockefeller proposed to increase the state budget by 50% and place a heavier tax burden on the wealthy, but the Democratic-controlled legislature repeatedly rejected his tax-reform proposals by large margins.

Shortly after Rockefeller became governor, an investigation of the Arkansas prison system found "barbaric conditions" in existence at some state institutions. In February 1967 Rockefeller fired the superintendent and three wardens at the Tucker Prison Farm. In early 1968, after three human skeletons were found buried in crude wooden coffins at another prison farm, Rockefeller asked the state legislature to establish a Department of Corrections to carry out a thorough reform of the state prison system. A special session of the Arkansas legislature approved his proposals in February 1968.

Rockefeller won reelection to a second two-year term in 1968, but Dale Bumpers, a Democratic moderate, overwhelmingly defeated him when he ran again in 1970. Rockefeller died of cancer in February 1973.

[TJC]

ROCKWELL, GEORGE L(INCOLN)

b. March 9, 1918; Bloomington, Ill.
d. Aug. 25, 1967; Arlington, Va.
Commander, American Nazi Party.

The son of George "Doc" Rockwell, a well-known vaudeville comedian of the 1920s and 1930s, Rockwell spent much of his youth on the road with his parents until their divorce. He entered Brown University in the late 1930s and did art work for the college's humor magazine. A psychiatrist later described his drawings of that period as indicating a preoccupation with "the recurrent themes of death, cannibalism, blood and bombing." Rockwell contended that he had merely been imitating cartoonist Charles Addams.

Rockwell left Brown to join the Navy in 1940. After the war he established a successful advertising agency but left after arguing with his partners. When the Korean conflict began he was recalled into the Navy, eventually attaining the rank of commander. Until then Rockwell had been largely apolitical, but during the early 1950s he became interested in racist and anti-Semitic literature. After reading *Mein Kampf* he regarded himself as a desciple of Adolf Hitler. In 1958, while still in the Navy, he organized a fascist group which by 1960 called itself the American Nazi Party. The Navy discharged him that year for his efforts to propagate Nazism.

Believing that Communism was a Jewish-inspired movement, Rockwell at different times advocated either the sterilization or extermination of American Jews. He also asserted the superiority of the "white race" and favored the deportation of blacks to Africa.

Rockwell frequently staged grotesque and provocative demonstrations. In one case he provided his supporters with gorilla suits and pro-civil rights placards. Often donning stormtrooper uniforms with swastika armbands, the Nazis received a hostile reception from even racist and extreme right-wing organizations. Throughout the period of Rockwell's leadership, the Party's membership was generally estimated at below 100.

After New York City's parks commissioner had denied Rockwell a speaking permit on the grounds that the preaching of hatred might produce rioting, the U.S. Supreme Court upheld his right to speak in November 1961. [See KENNEDY Volume]

Whatever his constitutional rights, Rockwell often had difficulty in finding a forum for expressing his views. In October 1966 the Brown University student union withdrew an invitation to Rockwell after the University's president objected to the Nazi's appearance. In March 1967 the Idaho Board of Education vetoed an invitation from students at Idaho State University.

But Rockwell gained publicity by appearing at many major liberal and leftist political rallies, usually for the purpose of organizing counter-protests. His presence often produced violence and arrests. In January 1965 he was arrested for disturbing the peace outside a church in Selma, Ala., where a civil rights meeting was being held. The following November he and other Nazis scuffled with persons carrying the National Liberation Front flag at an anti-Vietnam war demonstration in Washington.

In April 1965 Rockwell announced he would run for president in 1972. Later in the year he entered the Virginia gubernatorial contest, polling only a few votes.

Rockwell scored his greatest success in Chicago during open housing demonstrations led by Rev. Martin Luther King [*q.v.*] in the summer of 1966. Many whites reacted violently to the demonstrations and a large number of youths carried swastikas distributed by Rockwell and other Nazis. Apparently trying to follow up on his Chicago effort, he announced in December 1966 that his Party would change its name to the National Socialist White People's Party and would replace its "sieg heil" slogan with "white power." But the Nazis made few converts in their attempt to identify themselves more closely with the "backlash" against the civil rights movement.

On Aug. 25, 1967 Rockwell was shot and killed in Alexandria, Va., by John Patler, a former Nazi who had been expelled from the Party the previous spring because, according to one account, he had denounced his more Nordic-looking colleagues as "blue-eyed devils." Matt Koehl succeeded Rockwell as party leader.

[MLL]

For further information:
Fred C. Shapiro, "The Last Word (We Hope) on George Lincoln Rockwell," *Esquire* (February 1967), pp. 101-105.

RODINO, PETER W(ALLACE)

b. June 7, 1909; Newark, N.J.
Democratic Representative, N.J., 1948- .

Rodino grew up in the large Italian-American section of Newark, N.J. He graduated from the New Jersey School of Law (later Rutgers) in 1938 and opened a private law practice in Newark. After military service during World War II, Rodino tried unsuccessfully in 1946 to unseat conservative Congressman Fred Hartley (R, N.J.). Hartley's retirement two years later opened the way for Rodino to win election to the House of Representatives from a district that included most of Newark and several surrounding communities. The Essex County Democratic machine was powerful in Rodino's ethnically and racially mixed constituency, and Rodino was careful to repay favors and maintain contacts with local politicians. His district returned him to Congress by large margins in subsequent elections.

Rodino served in the House on the Judiciary Committee, where he gradually accumulated seniority and gained the favor of powerful Committee Chairman Emanuel Celler (D, N.Y.) [*q.v.*]. By the mid-1960s Rodino was the fourth-ranking Democrat on the Judiciary Committee and the third-ranking Democrat on Judiciary Subcommittee Number 1, which considered immigration and naturalization matters. During 1965 he played an important part in securing House passage of an Administration bill that eliminated the nationality quota system of immigration control. Rodino also manifested his interest in immigration matters, which affected many ethnic families in his district, by serving as an American delegate on the Inter-governmental Committee for European Migration and by traveling overseas to inspect the operations of the United Nations High Commission for Refugees.

Rodino's position on the Judiciary Committee also gave him the opportunity to act on civil rights legislation, which he firmly supported. In 1966 he was floor sponsor for the open housing provision of the Administration's proposed civil rights act; he praised open housing at this time as a means of "breaking the last link in the chain of racial discrimination which exists today." Rodino continued his support of civil rights despite the Newark riots of 1967 and 1968, which heightened racial tensions in his district and produced a white backlash. He voted more conservatively, however, on other matters coming before the Judiciary Committee. This was especially true of strong anti-crime legislation, which he generally supported. The liberal Americans for Democratic Action gave Rodino an 85% "correct" rating for the mid and late 1960.s

Rodino's influence in the Judiciary Committee continued to increase during the early 1970s, as a number of senior Democrats retired or were defeated. In 1971 he became chairman of Subcommittee Number 1, and in 1973 he succeeded Celler (who had been defeated for reelection) as chairman of the full Judiciary Committee. Rodino gained national attention in 1974, when he led the Committee in its deliberations on the impeachment of President Nixon. He voted for four articles of impeachment. Rodino also implemented a series of reforms that changed the number and jurisdiction of judiciary subcommittees. [See NIXON Volume]

[SLG]

ROMNEY, GEORGE W(ILCKEN)
b. July 8, 1907; Chihuahua, Mex.
Governor, Mich., 1963-69.

Born to an American Mormon family living in Mexico, George W. Romney grew up in Texas and Idaho and attended the University of Utah and George Washington University. After working as a lobbyist for the aluminum and automobile industry, Romney accepted an appointment as special assistant to the chairman of the board of Nash-Kelvinator in 1948. Six years later he became president and board chairman of its successor firm, American Motors. His advocacy of the compact car over what he called "the dinosaur in your driveway" helped the company overcome severe financial problems.

In June 1959 Romney led in the formation of "Citizens for Michigan," which successfully sponsored a new state constitution. He ended 14 years of Democratic rule in Michigan by winning election as governor in November 1962. Even before his election Romney had been considered a prospect for the 1964 Republican presidential nomination. Despite rank-and-file support within the GOP, Romney limited his political activities to Michigan. He maintained a strong civil rights record and opposed right-wing elements within the Michigan Republican Party. Romney suffered a major political setback in November 1963, when the state legislature rejected his call for a state income tax on individuals and corporations. [See KENNEDY Volume]

Following the California presidential primary on June 2, 1964, it appeared that the victorious conservative Sen. Barry M. Goldwater (R, Ariz.) [*q.v.*] would capture the Republican presidential nomination. At the National Governors Conference in Cleveland the following weekend, former Vice President Richard M. Nixon [*q.v.*] urged Romney to run against Goldwater. Govs. Nelson A. Rockefeller (R, N.Y.) [*q.v.*], William W. Scranton (R, Pa.) [*q.v.*] and James A. Rhodes (R, Ohio) [*q.v.*] all promised to back the Michigan Republican's candidacy at the Republican National Convention in July. However Romney had pledged to run for reelection, and Detroit's two major newspapers strongly opposed a Romney presidential campaign. The Governor decided not to oppose Goldwater, although he declared that the Senator's nomination would "commence the suicidal destruction of the Republican Party." Romney refused to support Scranton's last-minute candidacy. He also refused to back Scranton-Rockefeller platform amendments on civil rights, nuclear arms policy and right-wing extremism in the Party. Instead, Romney presented his own amendments denouncing extremism without mentioning specific right-wing organizations supporting Goldwater and calling for the enforcement of the 1964 Civil Rights Act, which Goldwater had opposed. Although some Goldwater supporters privately urged endorsement of Romney's proposals as a friendly gesture to the Party's liberal-moderate wing, the Arizona Senator's high command refused to allow its delegates to vote for the Romney amendments. Michigan's delegation supported Romney as its favorite son, and the Governor recieved 41 votes on the first ballot.

Following the Convention Romney declined to endorse Goldwater and criticized the candidate's civil rights record and his campaign's alleged appeal to racist "white backlash" votes. In November Romney was the only Republican to win state-wide in Michigan, defeating his Democratic opponent by almost 400,000 votes, while Johnson carried the state by a million-vote margin. Soon after the election Romney renewed his criticism of the Goldwater campaign and in December demanded the resignation of Republican National Committee Chairman Dean Burch [*q.v.*], a Goldwater appointee. Romney's victory enhanced his chances for the 1968 presidential nomination, but his unwillingness to endorse Goldwater and his failure to carry any other GOP candidates with him in 1964 damaged his standing among Party conservatives and loyalists.

Between 1963 and 1966, Romney broke the decade-old stalemate between previous Democratic governors and their Republican legislators. Under his leadership Michigan acquired its first minimum-wage and construction-safety legislation, increased state aid to education and avoided a fiscal crisis engendered by the need for comprehensive tax reform. The strength of Michigan's economy during Romney's tenure increased state revenues while reducing unemployment.

In his 1962 and 1964 campaigns, Romney had appealed for votes in a nonpartisan manner similar to his efforts as leader of Citizens for Michigan. In 1966, however, Romney ran as a partisan Republican and overwhelmed his opponent with 60.5% of the vote. His landslide helped elect Sen. Robert P. Griffin (R, Mich.) [*q.v.*] and five new Republican representatives. In demonstrating his capacity for electing Republicans in a Democratic state, Romney emerged in November 1966 as the clear front-runner for the 1968 presidential nomination.

In the winter and spring of 1967 Romney stumbled in his role as the leading Republican contender for president. In February reporters quoted the Governor, without his permission, as referring to newly elected Sen. Charles H. Percy (R, Ill.) [*q.v.*] as an "opportunist." The press also pointed out inconsistencies in Romney's position on the war in Vietnam. Attempting to clarify his views in a major foreign policy address in April, the Governor descirbed U. S. withdrawal from Vietnam as "unthinkable" but declared that "the failure to induce negotiations at this time should not result in massive escalations." Although he criticized the Administration for the use of American troops in the war, he attacked the President so mildly that Johnson immediately wired a note of appreciation. Romney's popularity in the polls declined in the late spring of 1967, and a long but successful fight in May and June for a state income tax forced him to remain in Michigan.

On July 23, 1967 racial rioting erupted in Detroit. On the following day Romney and Mayor James P. Cavanagh [*q.v.*] asked President Johnson to send federal troops to assist local police and the Michigan National Guard in quelling the disturbance. Romney claimed on July 31 that "quibbling" over the phrasing of his request had unnecessarily delayed the troops' arrival, and he accused Johnson of having "played politics in a period of tragedy and riot." White House staff members admitted that the relationship between the President and his most likely GOP opponent in 1968 had not been wholly cooperative. Twenty hours after Romney's original call for troops, Johnson agreed to send Army paratroops into Detroit, but in a televised announcement he publicly regretted the action, finding it necessary "only because of the clear, unmistakable, and undisputed evidence that Governor Romney of Michigan and local officials in Detroit have been unable to bring the situation under control." Throughout his address, Johnson repeated his reference to Romney without mentioning Cavanagh, a Democrat. The Detroit riot proved the worst of the 1960s, with 43 persons killed and 7,231 arrested.

In the aftermath of the riot, Romney decried the militancy of black power activists and declared that those who "preach revolution and preach the use of guns should be charged with treason." However, Romney did not shift to the right after the riots. In September he said that "the seeds of revolution have been sown in America more by our own failures and shortcomings than by any outside subversive ideology." Romney and state labor and automotive industry leaders unsuccessfully recommended to the state legislature a fair housing law and an emergency school aid appropriation for Detroit.

Romney's hopes for the presidency collapsed in the early fall of 1967. The Governor had been moving away from a militant "hawkish" stand on Vietnam. In an Aug. 31 Detroit interview, he defended his new stance by asserting that during a 1965 Vietnam tour, "I just had the greatest brainwashing that anybody can get" from American officials on the scene. Supporters of the President's policies immediately attacked Romney's remark, while other governors on the 1965 trip with Romney refused to confirm his allegation of indoctrination by government officials. Although a few Republican leaders defended Romney, most found his remark indicative of an inability to deal with Vietnam or other foreign policy issues. On Sept. 9 the *Detroit News* urged that Romney withdraw from the race and that Gov. Rockefeller enter as his replacement. Richard Nixon, Romney's major opponent for the nomination, increased his standing among Republicans in the Gallup Poll from 35% to 40%, while Romney's fell from 24% to 10%.

Romney fought hard to restore his lead and in November 1967 announced his formal candidacy. However, he never overcame the effects of his "brainwashing" statement. "Watching George Romney run for the presidency," Gov. James Rhodes (R, Ohio) remarked, "was like watching a duck try to make love to a football." Romney's campaign called for the restoration of old virtues and employed the slogan "George Romney Fights Moral Decay." He tried to capitalize on his controversial "brainwashing" remark by moving toward a distinctly anti-war position. On Jan. 15, 1968 the Governor proposed that the U. S. guarantee the neutralization of South Vietnam through a settlement between the Saigon government and the Communist insurgents. His anti-war strategy failed to generate support among Republican voters, and his own polls showed that despite an active campaign he would be overwhelmingly defeated by Nixon in New Hampshire's March primary. In February Rockefeller indicated for the first time, after reasserting his enthusiasm for Romney, that he would accept a "draft" for the nomination. Hurt by the growing sentiment for Rockefeller and his own poor showing in the polls, Romney withdrew his candidacy on Feb. 28, 1968, less than two weeks before the first primary. At the Republican National Convention in August, Romney received Michigan's votes as its favorite son candidate on the first ballot.

Following Nixon's nomination at the Convention, a group of Party leaders opposed to Nixon's selection of Gov. Spiro T. Agnew (R, Md.) [*q.v.*] for vice president persuaded Romney to allow them to nominate him as the anti-Agnew candidate. The abortive move against Agnew failed when most of the large state delegations supported Nixon's nominee. Romney received 178 votes to Agnew's 1128. He served as Secretary of Housing and Urban Development in the first Nixon Administration. [See NIXON Volume]

[JLB]

For further information:
Clark R. Mollenhoff, *George Romney* (New York, 1968).

ROOSEVELT, FRANKLIN D(ELANO), JR.

b. Aug. 17, 1914; Campobello Island, Canada.
Undersecretary of Commerce, March 1963-May 1965; Chairman, Equal Employment Opportunity Commission, May 1965-May 1966.

The third son of Franklin Delano and Eleanor Roosevelt, Franklin D. Roosevelt, Jr., attended Harvard and the University of Virginia Law School. While in the Navy during World War II, he earned a Silver Star. Roosevelt helped to found the liberal Americans for Democratic Action in 1947 and won election to Congress from New York City in May 1949 as the candidate of the Liberal Party. After losing the Democratic gubernatorial nomination at the 1954 state convention to W. Averell Harriman [*q.v.*], Roosevelt agreed to run for state attorney general. Unexpectedly, he lost to Rep. Jacob K. Javits (R, N.Y.) [*q.v.*]. He resumed his New York law practice and alienated many liberal allies in 1956 by accepting a $150,000 legal retainer from Rafael Trujillo, the dictator of the Dominican Republic.

Early in 1960 Roosevelt campaigned for John F. Kennedy's presidential nomination. In the crucial West Virginia primary in May, he attacked Sen. Hubert H. Humphrey (D, Minn.) [*q.v.*] for not having served in the armed forces during World War II. In March 1963 he accepted appointment as undersecretary of commerce. [See EISENHOWER, KENNEDY Volumes]

Roosevelt continued in a variety of roles cast for him by Kennedy as commerce undersecretary. A negotiator in the sale of $250 million worth of American wheat to the Soviet Union in the fall of 1963, Roosevelt lobbied against efforts by Senate conservatives in late November 1963 that would have denied credit to Communist buyers. As chairman of the federal-state Appalachian Regional Commission, he led in the planning of the area's economic revitalization; his group's work foreshadowed the President's more ambitious rural War on Poverty in 1964 and 1965. He also contributed to the settlement of a long labor dispute involving the nuclear-powered ship *Savannah*. Yet to Roosevelt's dismay, Johnson passed over him in naming a successor to Commerce Secretary Luther D. Hodges in December 1964.

Instead, Johnson named Roosevelt to the politically sensitive chairmanship of the Equal Employment Opportunity Commission (EEOC) in March 1965. Created by the 1964 Civil Rights Act and empowered to present "cease and desist" orders, enforceable in court, EEOC forbade employers and unions from discriminating against prospective employees or members on the basis of race, color, religion, national origin or sex. Roosevelt approached his new task with enthusiasm. In August EEOC prohibited job listings in newspapers that required specific racial, religious or ethnic backgrounds, although it put off a final determination on employment notices requesting a male or female only. On Dec. 12 the Roosevelt panel filed 12 job discrimination complaints, including one against a union. Six days later one of the violators, Crown Zellerbach Corp., agreed to Commission guidelines and ended its more flagrant abuses in promotion procedures.

Roosevelt resigned from EEOC in May 1966 to run for the New York Democratic gubernatorial nomination. His hopes for the nomination depended upon a preconvention endorsement from Sen. Robert F. Kennedy (D, N.Y.) [*q.v.*], the state's most popular Democrat. Kennedy refused to support any candidate openly, however, and Party leaders preferred New York City Council President Frank D. O'Connor, who had withdrawn from the 1965 mayoralty race in return for private pledges of assistance in the securing of the gubernatorial nomination. With no chance of defeating O'Connor at the upcoming state gathering, Roosevelt released in August a memorandum proving that a deal had been made between O'Connor and Party chieftains in 1965. Calling the convention a "boss-controlled masquerade," he withdrew from the race on Aug. 25. O'Connor received the Democratic nomination two weeks later.

An angry Roosevelt agreed to run as the Liberal Party's candidate for governor in early September. The Liberal Party, the state's largest third party since World War II, had been Roosevelt's original base of support in his 1949 congressional race. But it had suffered recent setbacks in the making of Democratic Party policy and in voter support. The state's new Conservative Party out-polled the Liberals in the 1964 senatorial and 1965 New York City mayoral elections. Denying the Democratic gubernatorial nominee its usual endorsement, Liberal Party leaders gambled that the once magical Roosevelt name would enable the Party to recapture third place in the balloting.

Roosevelt himself hoped to poll between one million and two million votes and to reassert his name in state politics, laying claim to a more likely statewide victory on the Democratic line in 1968 or 1970. The Roosevelt campaign cost about $250,000, and the candidate appeared throughout the state. In November, however, Conservative nominee Paul Adams, an unknown Rochester college president whose committee spent about $40,000, narrowly out-polled Roosevelt, 510,023 to 507,234 votes. O'Connor had run a lackluster campaign, never escaping from Roosevelt's charge of "bossism," and lost to incumbent Gov. Nelson A. Rockefeller (R, N.Y.) [*q.v.*]. Roosevelt's political career, once bright, then frustrated, had finally ended. He retired from active politics.

[JLB]

For further information:
Mitchell Levitas, "Rise, Fall and —— of F.D.R. Jr.," *The New York Times Magazine* (Oct. 23, 1966), p. 27+.

ROOSEVELT, JAMES.

b. Oct. 15, 1898; Warsaw, Poland.
d. Dec. 28, 1976; New York, N.Y.
President, United Hatters, Cap and Millinery Workers International Union, 1950-76; Vice Chairman, Liberal Party, 1944-76.

The eldest son of President Franklin D. Roosevelt, James Roosevelt, like his father, attended Groton and Harvard. At age 24 he managed his father's first presidential campaign in Massachusetts. In January 1937 he became an administrative assistant to the President. He resigned in November 1938 to work in the California film and radio industries. He was a Marine officer during World War II.

After the war Roosevelt began a 20-year career in California Democratic politics. His challenge to Republican Gov. Earl Warren [*q.v.*] in 1950 failed by one million votes. Four years later, however, Roosevelt won election to the House from a traditionally Democratic Los Angeles district. In Congress Roosevelt fought for liberal causes such as the elimination of racial segregation and the abolition of the House Un-American Activities Committee.

In 1964 and again in 1965 Roosevelt sought higher office in California. At the February 1964 meeting of the liberal, influential California Democratic Council, Roosevelt campaigned for the gathering's endorsement in the June senatorial primary. He lost to State Comptroller Alan Cranston and withdrew from contention. In the non-partisan April 1965 Los Angeles mayoral election, conservative Democrat Sam Yorty [*q.v.*] netted 60% of the total vote despite competition from Roosevelt and six other Democrats.

In the 1965 House session Roosevelt figured in two legislative battles of importance to organized labor. On behalf of the AFL-CIO and ahead of the White House's legislative agenda, Roosevelt and Rep. Phillip Burton (D, Calif.) [*q.v.*] introduced legislation repealing Section 14(b) of the Taft-Hartley Act. Their measure would have abolished that provision of the labor law that gave states the right to forbid closed shop contracts. The House repealed 14(b) in July, but the Roosevelt-Burton proposal failed in the Senate that fall due to a filibuster. Similarly, the House enacted in June a bill, for which Roosevelt served as floor manager, that extended the 1952 Mine Safety Act's provisions to smaller mines. The Senate did not take action on the measure.

In September 1965 Roosevelt resigned from Congress to become U.S. representative to the United Nations Economic and Social Council. He left that position the following January and returned to private life.

[JLB]

ROSE, ALEX

b. Oct. 15, 1898; Warsaw, Poland.
President, United Hatters, Cap and Millinery Workers International Union, 1950- ; Vice Chairman, Liberal Party, 1944- .

The son of a well-to-do tanner, Rose came to the U.S. hoping to study medicine but became a millinery operator instead. He had been active in the Labor Zionist Organization and joined the "Jewish Legion" of the British Army in 1918, serving in the Middle East for two years. Returning to the U.S. in 1924, he defeated a Communist-backed opponent and became the secretary-treasurer of his local in the Cloth Hat, Cap and Millinery Workers Union. By 1927 he had become a vice president, a position he retained when the union subsequently merged with the United Hatters of North America to form the United Hatters, Cap and Millinery Workers International Union in 1934.

In 1950 Rose was appointed president by the union's executive board and was subsequently elected to the post. "The class struggle is a thing of the past in my union and in many others," he said. During the 1950s the union loaned large sums to faltering hat manufacturers, purchased real estate in New York's millinery district and became the largest stockholder in the Merrimac Hat Corporation, preventing its liquidation.

With International Ladies Garment Workers Union (ILGWU) President David Dubinsky and others, Rose assisted in the forming of form the American Labor Party in 1936, offering New Yorkers the opportunity to support the New Deal without voting the Democratic, and therefore Tammany, line. The Communists won control of the Party in 1944, and Rose, who had served as state secretary until then, withdrew and helped form the Liberal Party. Dubinsky and Rose continued to support Democrats in most major elections. Although the Liberal Party ran an occasional congressional candidate, its major influence was in its impact on the Democrats. The Party was active in urban renewal, reapportionment and civil rights and sponsored rent control legislation. [See TRUMAN, EISENHOWER Volumes]

In 1961 Rose and the Liberal Party helped incumbent Mayor Robert Wagner [*q.v.*], who had repudiated his former Tammany supporters, win the backing of reform Democrats and thus gain reelection. The Liberals endorsed the Democratic slate in the 1962 state elections, in which Nelson A. Rockefeller [*q.v.*] won his second term as governor and Sen. Jacob K. Javits (R, N.Y.) [*q.v.*] was reelected. [See KENNEDY Volume]

In the mid-1960s the Party had a state enrollment of about 90,000, of which 50,000 were registered in New York City. In general elections the Party often drew 400,000 votes on its ballot line. About one-third of its financing and much of its manpower came from the ILGWU. Only a few districts maintained year-round clubs, however, and young activists found domination of the Party by Rose and Dubinsky unattractive. "The [Democratic] Reform movement siphoned off the cream of the young people," a Liberal spokesman told the *New York Times*. "It's just more exciting. Nobody fights in Liberal meetings."

The Party supported Robert F. Kennedy's [*q.v.*] successful bid for the Senate in 1964 and also endorsed the national Democratic ticket. Following Wagner's announcement that he would not run for mayor in 1965, the Liberal Party turned to independent Republican Rep. John V. Lindsay [*q.v.*]. With Liberal backing Lindsay's fusion campaign attracted sufficient Democratic support to help him defeat Democratic Controller Abraham Beame.

Charging "bossism" among Democrats, Rose refused to support the 1966 Democratic candidate for governor, Frank O'Connor. With some dissension the Liberals nominated their own choice, Franklin D. Roosevelt, Jr. [*q.v.*], instead. Democrats contended that Rose's move was motivated by a desire to retain "Line C," the third line on the state ballot. But the Liberals were replaced as the state's third largest party by the new Conservative Party, whose gubernatorial candidate outpolled Roosevelt.

In 1968 an ILGWU faction in the Liberal Party, charging that the organization was not democratically run, defied the Party policy committee's endorsement of Javits for reelection and entered an opponent against the Senator in the Liberal primary. Javits, however, easily won the contest. The Liberals also supported Sen. Hubert Humphrey's (D, Minn.) [*q.v.*] presidential candidacy in September.

Rose continued to dominate the Party, which again played an independent role in 1969. Mayor Lindsay, who lost the Republican primary, nevertheless won reelection as a Liberal with 45% of the vote. [See NIXON Volume]

[MDB]

For further information:
Nat Hentoff, *A Political Life: The Education of John V. Lindsay* (New York, 1967)

ROSTOW, EUGENE V(ICTOR)
b. Aug. 25, 1913; New York, N.Y.
Undersecretary of State for Political Affairs, October 1966-January 1969.

Rostow grew up in New Haven and studied at Yale University, where he received an LL.B. in 1937. His younger brother was Walt Whitman Rostow [*q.v.*], who gained prominence as an economist and foreign affairs adviser to President Lyndon Johnson. After a brief period in private law practice, Eugene joined the Yale Law School faculty in 1938. He served during World War II as a legal adviser in the State Department, where he worked for Assistant Secretary of State Dean Acheson. Returning to Yale after the war, Rostow soon became known as a liberal legal scholar. An article he wrote for the *Yale Law Journal* in 1945 helped persuade the federal government to restore the property and citizenship of Japanese-Americans confined to detention camps during the war. Rostow's book *A National Policy for the Oil Industry*, published in 1949, aroused considerable controversy by calling for reorganization and increased government regulation of oil companies.

In 1955 Rostow was appointed dean of the Yale Law School, a post he held for 10 years. During this time he supervised the development of an innovative curriculum, which gave Yale one of the most liberal law programs in the U.S. Rostow's goal was a "humane and broadly based" legal education relating law to history, economics and other social sciences. Despite initial resistance from conservative alumni, the new program was eventually considered a great success.

Rostow's academic career did not prevent him from maintaining the contacts he had developed in Washington during the war. Along with his brother Walt, he was an important link between the academic community and the federal government. In 1961 Rostow served on the Peace Corps Advisory Council and subsequently held a position as consultant to the State Department. He gave strong support to the foreign policy of the Johnson Administration, defending American involvement in Vietnam and the 1965 invasion of the Dominican Republic.

Rostow began full-time government work in October 1966, when President Johnson appointed him undersecretary of state for political affairs. Three months later he was named an alternate governor of the International Monetary Fund and the World Bank. During his two years in these posts. Rostow concerned himself largely with international financial matters. In January 1967 he visited India and other countries to confer on U.S. food assistance. He urged a "concerntrated international effort in the war against hunger." In February 1968 he participated in a United Nations conference that recommended a system of preferential tariffs to encourage the growth of industry in developing countries. Rostow also represented the U.S. in May 1968 in important negotiations over the financing of U.S. troops in West Germany; as a result of the talks the West German government agreed to reimburse the U.S. in 1969 for a large part of the cost of maintaining the troops. Rostow, meanwhile, continued to defend the Vietnam war, criticizing opponents of American involvement for stimulating a new isolationist spirit in the U.S.

In January 1969 Rostow left government service and returned to Yale as Sterling Professor of Law and Public Affairs. His defense of postwar American diplomacy, *Peace in the Balance: the Future of U.S. Foreign Policy*, was published in 1972. In this work he argued for continued attention to the international balance of power as "the key to any system of law . . . that seeks to assure liberty in peace."

[SLG]

ROSTOW, WALT W(HITMAN)
b. Oct. 7, 1916; New York, N.Y.
Chairman, State Department Policy Planning Council, December 1961-April 1966; Special Assistant to the President for National Security Affairs, April 1966-January 1969.

Rostow was one of three sons of a Russian-Jewish immigrant family. He attended Yale as an undergraduate and, following two years as a Rhodes Scholar at Oxford, received his Ph.D. from Yale in 1940. Following wartime service in the Office of Strategic Services, he worked briefly in the State Department and then spent two years as assistant to the executive secretary of the Economic Commission for Europe. He returned to academic life in 1950, when he received a teaching appointment at the Massachusetts Institute of Technology (MIT). From 1951 to 1960 he was associated with MIT's Central Intelligence Agency (CIA)-backed Center for International Studies.

Rostow wrote extensively on foreign policy and international developments and on economic history. His best-known book, *The Stages of Economic Growth: A Non-Communist Manifesto*, published in 1960, argued that economic growth was a multi-staged process, stimulated by a widespread desire for the improvement of life as well as the search for profits. This "modernization" process, Rostow said, was characterized by a crucial "takeoff" period of rapid growth stimulated by the expansion of a few key economic sectors. Rostow counterposed his model to that of Marx and used it as the ideological underpinning for his policy approach towards the developing countries of Asia, Africa and Latin America.

Rostow began advising Sen. John F. Kennedy (D, Mass.) on foreign policy in 1958 and was active in Kennedy's 1960 presidential campaign. Kennedy appointed Rostow deputy special assistant to the President for foreign security affairs in the incoming Administration. Rostow was a participant throughout 1961 in the formulation of U.S. policy towards Laos and Vietnam, generally advocating a strong U.S. diplomatic and military role in fighting Communist insurgencies.

As part of a general November 1961 shuffle of foreign policy officials, Rostow was moved to the State Department as counselor and chairman of the Policy Planning Council. In his new post he was in charge of long-range analysis and planning in a broad range of foreign policy areas, but was no longer centrally involved in the White House decision-making process. [See KENNEDY Volume]

In May 1964 President Johnson appointed Rostow to the additional post of U.S. representative to the Inter-American Committee on the Alliance for Progress (CIAP). Created in November 1963, CIAP was a special committee of the Organization of American States intended to provide Latin American countries with a greater say in the direction of the Alliance for Progress.

Although at this time Rostow did not directly participate in making high-level decisions on Southeast Asia, he exerted continued influence through State Department memoranda and—starting in June 1964—through direct access to the President. His most important contribution in this period was a presentation of his general perspective on Vietnam-like situations, which came to be called the "Rostow thesis." It was prepared in December 1963 but was not widely circulated until the following summer. Rostow restated his long-standing belief that externally-supported insurgencies could be stopped only by military action against the source of external support. A series of escalating military measures, designed to impart the maximum possible psychological blow, would, he argued, make it clear that continued support of insurgency would result in heavy costs. This in turn would lead to a cessation of the support.

This policy approach flowed from Rostow's belief that modernization created certain dislocations and discontents, which although transitional, could be used by Communists to gain support. It was therefore necessary to hold off any Communist challenge until full modernization was achieved, eliminating the problems that fed insurgency.

Consistent with this general framework, Rostow argued in February and April 1964 that it was crucial that the U.S. take action to force North Vietnam to abide by the provisions of the 1958 and 1962 Geneva Accords forbidding foreign troops in Laos or South Vietnam. In June he advocated increased military pressure against North Vietnam combined with a strong public stance against their support for rebel forces in Laos and South Vietnam.

In August 1964 the "Rostow thesis" was

widely circulated inside the Administration. A detailed critique was prepared by the Defense Department. It concluded that serious difficulties were involved in attacks on North Vietnam and questioned whether domestic and international support could be rallied for such a program. Therefore, the report argued, acceptance or even public dissemination of the Rostow position was probably unwise. But, according to the authors of the *Pentagon Papers:* "These reservations notwithstanding, the outlook embodied in the 'Rostow thesis' came to dominate a good deal of Administration thinking on the question of pressures against the North in the months ahead."

As a National Security Agency working group was again reexamining the future direction of U.S. policy in Vietnam, Rostow contended in November 1964 that the U.S. had to convince the North Vietnamese of American determination to apply limited but sustained military pressure upon them until they ceased support of the National Liberation Front in South Vietnam. He urged the movement of a large retaliatory force to the Pacific area, the introduction of some U.S. ground troops in Laos and South Vietnam and the initiation of a naval blockade and bombing against North Vietnam. (Although all of these steps were eventually taken, the immediate White House decision favored more limited military action.)

Rostow became increasingly and publicly identified with the Administration's Vietnam policy in 1965. On arriving in Tokyo in April for a series of speaking engagements, he was met by 1,000 anti-American demonstrators. During this period of rising campus opposition to the war, Rostow defended the Administration's position at a May 15-16 national teach-in on Vietnam, broadcast to over 100 colleges.

On March 31, 1966 President Johnson appointed Rostow special assistant to the President for national security affairs, succeeding McGeorge Bundy [*q.v.*], who had resigned to become president of the Ford Foundation. In this post Rostow worked closely with Johnson for the remainder of the Administration on virtually all foreign policy issues. He selected the information to be presented to him, accompanied him on his foreign travels and sat in on meetings with foreign leaders. Rostow genuinely admired the President, and as criticism of U.S. policy in Vietnam grew, Rostow's continued optimism about the war and his willingness to defend it publicly led to an increasingly close relationship with President Johnson. (In September 1966 Johnson appointed Rostow's older brother, Eugene V. Rostow [*q.v.*], undersecretary of state for political affairs.)

Although sustained U.S. bombing of North Vietnam began in March 1965, the targets were limited in nature. In September 1965 the Joint Chiefs of Staff began urging the bombing of more "lucrative" targets, including petroleum and oil facilities. A debate over the expansion of bombing targets went on for several months. In May 1966 Rostow came out in strong support of "systematic and sustained bombing" aimed at destroying the petroleum and petroleum-product facilities of North Vietnam. Rostow argued that a similar program—on which he had worked—had been effective against the Germans in World War II and would be equally effective against North Vietnam. Others, including the CIA, disagreed. After a period of hesitation in late May, Johnson approved the new air strikes, which included targets in the Hanoi-Haiphong area. In spite of initial reports of success, however, the program failed to limit the ability of the North Vietnamese to support the war in the South.

Throughout 1967 there was renewed conflict within the Administration over the bombing campaign against North Vietnam. Most military leaders urged an extension of bombing and the elimination of existing restrictions. Many civilian officials, particularly Assistant Secretary of Defense for International Security Affairs John T. McNaughton [*q.v.*] and Secretary of Defense Robert S. McNamara [*q.v.*], urged limiting the bombing to the southern panhandle of North Vietnam. In May Rostow, who attended the regular Tuesday meetings at which the President chose specific bombing targets, wrote an important memorandum indicating basic support for the McNamara-McNaughton position, although he argued that the option of future strikes in the Hanoi-Haiphong area had to be kept open. The President took a middle course and in July ordered a continuation of the "Rolling Thunder" bombing program along essentially existing lines, with only sporadic raids in the Hanoi-Haiphong area.

In June 1967 Rostow accompanied the President at the Glassboro, N.J., meeting with Soviet Premier Aleksei N. Kosygin. The following month he worked closely with Johnson during the Arab-Israeli war. He also served on a special group headed by Bundy that Johnson established to work on both the immediate crisis and long-range solutions to the Middle East situation.

On Nov. 1, 1967 an increasingly skeptical McNamara prepared a memo to the President in which he called for "stabilizing" the U.S. war effort in Vietnam, reexamining the ground fighting to try to reduce U.S. casualties and shift a greater burden of fighting to the South Vietnamese Army and instituting a bombing halt before the end of the year. Johnson gave the memo to Rostow and other senior advisers for comment. Rostow supported the first two proposals but opposed an unconditional bombing halt. His position was similar to that Johnson himself soon took.

Following the Tet offensive in late January and early February 1968, Johnson established a new group under incoming Secretary of Defense Clark Clifford [*q.v.*] to thoroughly reexamine Vietnam policy. Rostow drafted the directive to the group and participated in its deliberations. He apparently continued to oppose any new restriction on the bombing of North Vietnam. (By the end of March, however, Johnson decided on a partial bombing halt as a step towards negotiations.)

In the final months of Johnson's term of office, overtures were reportedly made in Rostow's behalf to MIT and several other leading universities to secure for him a teaching position after the Administration's end. These feelers were apparently rebuffed, partially due to Rostow's role in the planning and conduct of the war in Vietnam. Rostow eventually accepted a position as professor of economics and history at the University of Texas at Austin, where a Lyndon B. Johnson School of Public Affairs was planned. In the final hours of his presidency, Johnson awarded Rostow and 19 others the Medal of Freedom, the country's highest civilian honor.

In Texas Rostow resumed teaching and writing and helped Johnson organize his foreign policy papers for inclusion in his presidential library. Rostow continued to defend U.S. military involvement in Vietnam. Rostow published *The Diffusion of Power, 1957-1972,* an account of the U.S. role in world affairs which included some material on his own activities in the period covered.

[JBF]

For further information:

W.W. Rostow, *The Diffusion of Power, 1957-1972* (New York, 1972).

U.S. Department of Defense, *The Pentagon Papers,* Senator Gravel edition (Boston, 1971), Vols. III and IV.

ROUSSELOT, JOHN H(ARBIN)

b. Nov. 1, 1927; Los Angeles, Calif.
Western District Governor, John Birch Society, 1963-64; National Director of Public Relations, John Birch Society, 1964-67.

Rousselot operated a public relations consulting firm from 1954 to 1958. He served as director of public information for the Federal Housing Administration in Washington, D.C., from 1958 to 1960. In the latter year he was elected to Congress from a conservative suburban area of Los Angeles County. In April 1961 Rousselot acknowledged his membership in the ultra-right wing John Birch Society. He went on to compile an extremely conservative voting record in the House during 1961 and 1962. His bid for reelection in 1962 was unsuccessful. [See KENNEDY Volume]

Early in 1963 Rousselot became the Western district governor of the Birch Society. In the summer of 1964 he was appointed national public relations director of the organization. While holding this post he was generally regarded as being second-in-command to Robert H.W. Welch, Jr. [*q.v.*], the group's leader. In his new position he used his congenial personality and public relations experience to attempt to modify the society's image as an irresponsible, extremist organization.

In the 1950s Welch had written that President Dwight D. Eisenhower [*q.v.*] was an agent of a world Communist conspiracy. Rousselot stressed that this assertion represented Welch's personal view and not the official position of the Society. Rousselot also played down some of the membership's more bizarre views, such as their fear of a Communist plot to confine patriotic Americans to mental asylums. In addition, he created a professional and efficient public relations department, which placed Sunday supplements in major newspapers across the country and which sent Society members and their sympathizers to speak before a wide range of civic groups.

According to John Birch Society critics Benjamin R. Epstein and Arnold Forster, the Society's membership grew from less than 40,000 to 80,000 between 1964 to 1966, in large measure as a result of Rousselot's efforts. But Rousselot did not succeed in fundamentally altering the organization's image because even those views of the Society that he accepted and stressed were regarded by many Americans as extremist. In August 1964 he charged that 59 major leaders of the NAACP belonged to 450 "identifiable Communist fronts." Rousselot declared in July of the following year that the United Nations was created and controlled by Communists. He also believed that Chief Justice Earl Warren [*q.v.*] should be impeached for his allegedly pro-Communist Supreme Court decisions.

In January 1967 Rousselot announced that he would soon resign his post to return to private business but that he would continue to work for the Society as a volunteer. In 1970 he was again elected to the House of Representatives from the Los Angeles suburbs and was reelected in 1972 and 1974.

[MLL]

For further information:

Benjamin R. Epstein and Arnold Forster, *The Radical Right: Report on the John Birch Society and its Allies* (New York, 1967).

RUBIN, JERRY

b. July 14, 1938; Cincinnati, Ohio
Political activist.

Son of a bakery truck driver who became an official in his Teamsters Union local, Jerry Rubin grew up in a middle-class Jewish neighborhood in Cincinnati. He attended Oberlin College briefly but quit school when he was offered a job as a sports reporter for the *Cincinnati Post*. Later he became the *Post's* youth editor and started taking courses at the University of Cincinnati. He received a B.A. in 1961. Restless and uncertain about what to do with his life, Rubin left Cincinnati shortly after finishing college and drifted for several years throughout Europe, India and Israel. Early in 1964 he arrived in Berkeley and attended the University of California for six weeks before dropping out of school permanently.

In Berkeley Rubin quickly gravitated towards the radical movement. In the spring of 1964 he joined the local chapter of the Congress of Racial Equality and participated in a number of "shop-ins" at a Berkeley grocery store that allegedly refused to hire blacks. That summer he traveled with a group to Cuba in defiance of a State Department ban. During the fall he was active in the Free Speech Movement on the Berkeley campus.

In the spring of 1965 Rubin was a leading figure in the organization of a two-day teach-in held in late May. Over a continuous 36-hour period some 12,000 students and faculty heard a series of speakers, including Norman Mailer [*q.v.*], Dr. Benjamin Spock [*q.v.*], Norman Thomas [*q.v.*] and Isaac Deutcher, denounce the war. Out of the teach-in came the Vietnam Day Committee (VDC), one of the largest and most active anti-war organizations in the country. As a leader of the VDC and its most prominent public spokesman, Rubin acquired a reputation as a skilled organizer with a flair for winning the attention of the media. In August 1965 the VDC staged several unsuccessful, but well publicized, attempts to stop troop trains carrying Vietnam-bound soldiers as they passed through Berkeley. In October the VDC organized two large marches from Berkeley to the nearby Oakland Army Terminal. Both of the marches were halted and turned back by police at the Oakland city line. Rubin also served briefly during the fall of 1965 as *Ramparts* magazine editor Robert Scheer's [*q.v.*] campaign manager in his attempt to gain the Democratic nomination for the House of Representatives from California's seventh district.

After disputes with Scheer over campaign tactics, Rubin became increasingly concerned with developing and projecting a radical, self-expressive style of protest. In August 1966, when he was subpoenaed to appear before the House Un-American Activities Committee in Washington, he decided to use his appearance as an exercise in what he called "guerrilla theater." Rubin walked into the televised hearings wearing a Revolutionary War uniform. Despite his protests, the startled Committee refused him permission to testify.

During the spring of 1967 Rubin entered the race for mayor of Berkeley and received 22% of the vote on a platform advocating legalization of marijuana and community control of the police. Following the election he moved to New York, where he became friends with a drug-oriented circle that included Timothy Leary [*q.v.*], who pronounced him "Merry Jerry, the Lysergic Lenin, the grass Guevara, the mescaline Marx." Rubin also befriended Abbie Hoffman [*q.v.*]. Together they were prominent organizers of the March on the Pentagon that October.

Rubin declared the march of several thousand a victory. "We had symbolically destroyed the Pentagon . . . by throwing blood on it, pissing on it, dancing on it, painting 'Che lives' on it." Rubin was convinced that the anti-war movement was at root a generational conflict of youth in search of fun and excitement against their elders. In January 1968 Rubin, Hoffman and Paul Krassner, editor of *The Realist*, formed the Yippies, or Youth International Party, a politically oriented countercultural group.

During that summer Rubin and his fellow Yippies planned a massive "festival of life" in Chicago to coincide and contrast with what they interpreted as a "festival of death" at the Democratic National Convention. The Yippies applied for permission to use city parks for rallies and for sleeping out overnight, but Chicago city officials denied them the right to remain in the parks after 11 p.m. On Aug. 23 the Yippies opened their festival by setting up camp in Lincoln Park and nominating a pig for president in the Chicago civic center. Two days later, after the 11 p.m. curfew, the police drove the Yippies out of Lincoln Park. The following evening, at about the same time the Democratic Convention was formally opened, an even larger confrontation took place, and a number of injuries were sustained both by demonstrators and policemen. The remaining days of the Convention were full of similar disorder, much of it caught by television cameras and by news photographers.

Rubin and seven others were later indicted by a federal grand jury in Chicago in connection with the 1968 disorders. The "Chicago Eight," as they came to be known, were the first defendants tried under the anti-riot provisions of the 1968 Civil Rights Act, which made it a federal crime to cross state lines to incite a riot. Rubin said that he welcomed the indictment, calling it "the greatest honor of my life" and the "Academy Award of Protest." Following the tumultuous trial five of the eight, including Rubin, were convicted. In November 1972 the verdicts were overturned by an appeals court on the grounds that the judge in the case had been antagonistic and had committed legal errors. In 1976 Rubin published *Growing Up (at 37);* he asserted that both he and Hoffman had in fact gone to Chicago to disrupt the Convention and the normal life of the city. The government's case in the Chicago Eight's trial, wrote Rubin, was "right in theory, wrong in specifics." After the trial Rubin turned his interests from politics to introspection and various forms of group therapy.

[TLH]

For further information:

Jerry Rubin, *Do It* (New York, 1968).

———, *Growing Up (at 37)* (New York, 1976).

RUBY, JACK
b. March 25, 1911?; Chicago, Ill.
d. Jan. 3, 1967; Dallas, Tex.
Assassin of Lee Harvey Oswald.

Jack Ruby, born Jacob Rubenstein, was raised in a troubled home in Chicago. Beginning in 1922 Ruby, his two younger brothers and a sister had to be placed, from time to time, in foster homes. Ruby quit school at 16 and worked as a ticket scalper, a hawker of race-track tip sheets and as an organizer for the Scrap Iron and Junk Handlers Union. In the early 1940s he established the Spartan Novelty Company in Chicago. After service in the armed forces, Ruby went to Dallas in 1947 to help his sister open a nightclub. He remained in Dallas, where he owned and managed various clubs for the next 16 years.

On the morning of Nov. 24, 1963 Ruby made his way to the basement of the Dallas Police and Courts Building where Lee Harvey Oswald, the alleged assassin of President John F. Kennedy was being held. At 11:20 Oswald, surrounded by police, reporters and cameramen, was being escorted to the car which was to take him to the county jail. Ruby approached, drew his Colt .38 and fired one shot into Oswald's abdomen. The shooting was witnessed by millions on live television. Oswald died within two hours.

Ruby said he had killed Oswald in a temporary fit of depression and rage over the death of the President. He denied that he had ever known Oswald or had been connected in any way with a plot to assassinate the President.

Ruby's defense team, headed by the flamboyant San Francisco attorney Melvin Belli, contended that the defendant could not get a fair trial in Dallas, but requests to move the proceedings were denied by Judge Joseph Brantley Brown.

In February 1964 after two weeks of difficult questioning in which the defense exhausted all its peremptory challenges, a jury was selected. All but two of the jurors had seen the shooting on television. During the trial, which began March 4, the defense pleaded that Ruby, suffering from psychomotor epilepsy, was not guilty by reason of insanity. Psychologists and neurologists for the prosecution contended the evidence, including electroencephalograms, introduced by the defense was insufficient to support the plea. On March 14 the jury found Ruby guilty and directed that he be sentenced to death. Belli called the proceedings a kangaroo court and charged that the Dallas "oligarchy wanted to send Ruby to the public abattoir. . .to cleanse this city of its shame."

In June 1966 a state court jury in Dallas ruled that Ruby was sane and competent to dismiss his lawyers. A new defense team that included New York attorney William Kuntsler [*q.v.*] took the case to the Texas Court of Appeals. In October 1966 that court's three judges—in separate opinions—agreed that Ruby's conviction should be reversed. The holding of Ruby's trial in Dallas had been in error, said the court, and it ordered that he be retried outside Dallas County.

Before he could be tried again, Ruby, who was suffering from cancer, died of a blood clot in the lungs on Jan. 3, 1967.

Although Ruby consistently denied that he knew Oswald, a contention upheld by the Warren Commission investigating the Kennedy assassination, rumors persisted that Ruby had in some way been involved with Oswald and possibly in a conspiracy to assassinate the President. In the fall of 1975 a congressional committee investigated these rumors.

[JLW]

For further information:
William Manchester, *The Death of a President* (New York, 1966).
President's Commission on the Assassination of President John F. Kennedy (Warren Commission), *Report* (Washington, 1964).

RUDD, MARK (WILLIAM)
b. June 2, 1947; Irvington, N.J.
Student leader.

Rudd grew up in an upper-middle-class Jewish family in suburban New Jersey. His father was in the real estate business and a lieutenant colonel in the Army Reserve.

During his freshman year at Columbia, 1965-66, Rudd became active in a campus anti-war group, the Independent Committee on Vietnam. In the fall of 1966 he joined the newly formed Columbia chapter of Students for a Democratic Society (SDS). Rudd was among 46 people arrested at a large demonstration protesting Secretary of State Dean Rusk's [*q.v.*] appearance at the New York Hilton Hotel in November 1967.

Throughout 1967 Columbia SDS was led by members of the so-called "praxis axis," who stressed research, education and propaganda, avoiding confrontations in hopes of building a broad base of student support. Rudd and others, labeled the "action faction," advocated more militant tactics. After returning from a three-week SDS trip to Cuba in February 1968, Rudd was elected chairman of Columbia SDS. A week later, on March 20, members of the "action faction" threw a pie in the face of a Selective Service official speaking at Columbia, in spite of a previous SDS vote against any disruption. Rudd later said that this was the turning point in winning SDS over to more aggressive tactics.

SDS had long opposed Columbia's participation in the Institute for Defense Analysis (IDA), a 12-university consortium conducting weapons evaluation and research for the Department of Defense. The radical organization had more recently joined the opposition to Columbia's proposed new gym, to be built in city-owned Moringside Park. Plans for the gym included limited facilities for use by local residents. It rapidly became a symbol for many at Columbia and in the adjacent Harlem community of the University's alleged indifference to its poor, non-white neighbors.

On March 27 Rudd led a noisy demonstration inside Columbia's main administration building, Low Library, demanding severance of all University ties with IDA. The protest violated a recent University ban on indoor demonstrations, and on April 22 Rudd and five others, the "IDA six," were placed on disciplinary probation after their request for an open hearing had been denied. That day, in an open letter to Columbia President Grayson Kirk, Rudd wrote: "We, the young people, whom you so rightly fear, say that the society is sick and you and your capitalism are the sickness. You call for order and respect for authority, we call for justice, freedom and socialism."

The next afternoon, following speeches by Student Afro-American Society (SAS) and SDS leaders, several hundred students marched to Low Library to demand an open hearing for the six students. Finding Low locked, part of the crowd went to the site of the gym. There, in a scuffle with police, one person was arrested. Returning to the campus, the students went to Hamilton Hall, where they vowed to stay and block the exit of a Columbia dean until the University cut all ties with IDA, canceled the gym project and agreed to take no disciplinary action against the "IDA six."

Late that night, at the request of SAS leaders, the white students in Hamilton Hall left the building and occupied Low Library. Other students took over three more buildings during the next two days. Throughout the week-long occupation, Rudd was a key leader and chief spokesman for the white protestors. (The black students in Hamilton acted independently.) The Columbia administration refused to agree to the demands, and faculty-initiated negotiations failed. At 2:30 a.m. on April 30, 1,000 New York City police, at Columbia's request, cleared the occupied buildings. Over 700 persons, 80% of them students, were arrested and 148 injured. Rudd himself avoided arrest.

Activists called a highly effective student strike and on May 1 formed an enlarged Strike Steering Committee, co-chaired by Rudd. Rudd and other SDS leaders wanted a continued focus on the original demands, but the faculty and the more moderate students among the 4,000 strikers were equally interested in restructuring the University. On May 17 Rudd was among 117 people arrested when community activists took over a Columbia-owned tenement from which tenants were being evicted.

Initially, disciplinary proceedings for the April protests were begun only against Rudd and three others from the original "IDA six." On May 21 several hundred students marched to Hamilton Hall, where parents and lawyers of the four met with a college dean. When it was announced that the four were suspended for refusing to attend the meeting, the demonstrators decided to remain in Hamilton Hall until amnesty was granted to the participants in all of the recent protests. Police were again called, and at the building and in a later sweep of the campus, 68 persons were injured and 178, including Rudd, arrested. Rudd and 72 others were suspended from school, and Rudd's draft board was immediately notified that he was no longer eligible for a deferment. (He was later rejected by the Army.)

Rudd ran for the SDS National Interim Committee in June but was elected only as an alternate. That fall, still suspended by Columbia, to which he never returned, Rudd went on several national speaking and fund-raising tours for SDS. At a December 1968 SDS conference Rudd supported a "Revolutionary Youth Movement" proposal that committed SDS to organizing working-class youth as well as students. Rudd was one of eleven coauthors of the "Weatherman" statement presented to the June 1969 SDS convention. When the organization split Rudd became a leader of the faction supporting and named for the statement. Rudd was a leader of the Weatherman "Days of Rage" demonstrations in Chicago in October 1969, and was later indicted for his role, but the FBI failed to apprehend him.

[JBF]

For further information:
Jerry L. Avon, *Up Against the Ivy Wall* (New York, 1968).

RUSK, DEAN

b. Feb. 9, 1909; Cherokee County, Ga.
Secretary of State, January 1961-January 1969.

Dean Rusk, the son of a poor Presbyterian minister, worked his way through Davidson College in North Carolina. He studied at Oxford on a Rhodes Scholarship and in 1934 joined the political science department of Mills College in California. Rusk became dean of the faculty in 1938.

While in the Army during World War II, Rusk became a protege of Gen. George Marshall. At Marshall's behest Rusk joined the State Department in 1946 as assistant chief of the division of international security affairs. In 1950 he was appointed assistant secretary of state for Far Eastern affairs, where he helped formulate policy on Korea and China.

Rusk left the State Department to become president of the Rockefeller Foundation in 1952. During his tenure he helped expand Foundation projects in Asia, Africa and Latin America. President Kennedy appointed him Secretary of State in 1961. As Secretary, Rusk advised the President on major crises in Berlin, Cuba, Laos and the Congo. However, because Kennedy wanted to be his own Secretary of State and because he relied on close personal aides rather than on his cabinet for advice, Rusk had little impact on foreign policy formation during these years. [See KENNEDY Volume]

When Rusk took office he inherited an unwieldy bureaucracy whose creativity and effectiveness has been crippled by the anti-Communist crusades of the late 1940s and early 1950s, which had driven many capable men from the Department. At Kennedy's urging new men were brought to State and permitted to explore new policies in Asia, Africa and Latin America. G. Mennen Williams, for example, was allowed to foster closer ties between the U.S. and leftist regimes in Africa. Roger Hilsman was permitted to work for a less belligerent policy toward Communist China. However, after Lyndon Johnson assumed the presidency, backing for these departures diminished, and Rusk reverted to more traditional policies.

Rusk's influence increased during the last half of the decade. According to Presidential Assistant W.W. Rostow [*q.v.*], Johnson built his advisory system around Rusk, Secretary of Defense Robert McNamara [*q.v.*] and Presidential Assistant McGeorge Bundy [*q.v.*], with Rusk as the central figure. He counseled the President on all important foreign policy matters, including the 1965 decision to send Marines to the Dominican Republic to evacuate Americans and keep peace between feuding factions in that nation's civil war.

In late May and early June 1967, following Egypt's deployment of troops on Israeli borders and its closing of the Gulf of Aqaba to Israeli shipping, Rusk worked closely with Johnson in an attempt to prevent a Middle East war. Fearing congressional disapproval of American unilateral action, Rusk counseled Johnson against an attempt to use American troops to force open the canal and attempted to gain support for allied action to pressure Egypt into changing its policy. His efforts failed; war broke out in the Middle East on June 6.

Rusk became one of the President's chief advisers on the Vietnam war. He helped Johnson make important decisions on the escalation of the conflict and, just as importantly, reinforced the President's own commitment to the American effort there. Rusk saw the conflict in Southeast Asia as an attempt by a militant Chinese government, prompted by the Marxist theory of world revolution, to expand its influence throughout Asia by means of "wars of liberation." Consequently, he argued, the U.S. was not in Vietnam simply because of its treaty commitments but because of the need to show that such expansion was doomed to failure. Although asserting that a victory in Vietnam was necessary for American security, Rusk did not define the war primarily as a battle for a strategic area but rather emphasized that it was a "psychological struggle for the conquest of minds and souls." The loss of Vietnam would mean "a drastic loss of confidence in the will and capacity of the free world to oppose aggression" and would bring the world considerably closer to a great power conflict, according to Rusk.

Because of his belief in the need for a military victory in Vietnam, Rusk consistently supported the Administration's escalation of the war. In August 1964 he backed Johnson's decision to stage retaliatory raids against North Vietnam for that nation's alleged attacks upon U.S. ships in the Gulf of Tonkin. He also supported systematic bombing of the North, begun in March 1965, as a means of forcing Hanoi to end infiltration of the South.

During 1964 and 1965 Rusk opposed attempts to negotiate a settlement. With the National Liberation Front controlling more than half of South Vietnam and the Saigon government crumbling, the U.S. could not bargain from a position of strength. Until military pressure on Hanoi tilted the balance of power toward the South, Rusk asserted, the North would have little incentive to negotiate and that whatever talks could be started would have little value. Rusk opposed the bombing halt of December 1965-January 1966 for the same reasons. Believing that a pause could be effectively employed only once, he recommended that the halt be postponed until the bombing had escalated to the point where North Vietnam could no longer tolerate the damage and would be forced to accept a settlement favorable to the U.S.

During the Johnson years Rusk emerged as the chief public defender of the Administration's position. In February 1966 he appeared at televised hearings of the Senate Foreign Relations Committee, chaired by Sen. William Fulbright (D, Ark.) [*q.v.*], to explain Administration policy. Rusk sought to refute Fulbright's charge that the conflict was a civil war in which the U.S. had no strategic interest by describing what he believed to be a long-term pattern of Communist Chinese aggression. One year later, in an October 1967 press conference, he justified the U.S. presence as necessary to protect the region from the future threat of "a billion Chinese on the mainland, armed with nuclear weapons." Rusk often used the analogy of Munich to explain the American war effort in Vietnam. In a January 1967 letter to 100 student leaders, he maintained that the failure of the world community to stop aggression in Ethiopia, Manchuria and Central Europe during the 1930s had resulted in World War II. "In short," he wrote, "we are involved in Vietnam because we knew from painful experience that the minimum condition for order on our planet is that aggression must not be permitted to succeed. For when it does succeed, the consequence is not peace, it is the further expansion of aggression. And those who have borne responsibility in our country since 1945 have not for one moment forgotten that a third world war would be a nuclear war."

According to journalist David Halberstam, as Secretary of Defense Robert McNamara [*q.v.*] began to question U.S. policy during 1967, Rusk felt it his duty to be more steadfast in his support of the President's actions. In Halberstam's words, Rusk "became a rock, unflinching and unchanging and absorbing, as deliberately as he could, as much of the reaction to the war as possible."

Following the Communists' Tet offensive of February 1968, the military requested over 200,000 additional troops for the war. Rusk recommended that the President approve the increase. However, a bipartisan panel of statesmen specially convened to advise Johnson on the proposal opposed a further increase because of the detrimental effects it could have on the U.S. economy and society. Johnson accepted the panel's advice and on March 31 announced a policy of de-escalation. He hoped that the step would prompt Hanoi to enter negotiations. Hanoi quickly accepted the offer with the provision that initial meetings deal only with conditions for a total bombing halt. According to Undersecretary of the Air Force Townsend Hoopes [*q.v.*], Rusk "tried to slow down, and if possible avoid altogether" the initial talks. He emphasized the limited purpose of the discussions and denigrated the possibility of a complete bombing halt. Preliminary peace talks began in Paris in May 1968. Rusk played little part in them; the American delegation was headed by W. Averell Harriman [*q.v.*].

Rusk left office in January 1969. After a few months in semi-retirement, he became professor of international law at the University of Georgia.

[EWS]

For further information:
David Halberstam, *The Best and the Brightest* (New York, 1972).
Townsend Hoopes, *The Limits of Intervention* (New York, 1969).
U.S. Department of Defense, *The Pentagon Papers*, Senator Gravel Edition (Boston, 1971), Vols. III and IV.

RUSSELL, RICHARD B(REVARD)

b. Nov. 2, 1897; Winder, Ga.
d. Jan. 21, 1971; Washington, D.C.
Democratic Senator, Ga., 1933-71; Chairman, Armed Services Committee, 1951-53, 1955-69.

Elected to the Georgia Assembly in 1921, Russell became its speaker six years later. In 1930 he won a two-year term as governor of the state and in 1932 was elected to fill a vacant U.S. Senate seat. During his early years in the Senate, he generally supported New Deal programs, but after World War II he became an opponent of most social welfare measures.

Throughout his career Russell was an unrelenting foe of civil rights measures, and by the late 1940s he was the solidly established leader of the Southern bloc in the upper house of Congress. At the 1948 Democratic National Convention, he was put forward as his region's candidate for the Party's presidential nomination, but he did not join the Dixiecrat bolt from the national ticket after the nomination of President Harry S Truman.

Despite Russell's identification with the dissident Southern wing of the Democratic Party, he was highly regarded by almost all senators. A member of a patrician family, he was known for his dignified bearing and courteous manner as well as for his formidable intelligence. Aided by this reputation and a single-minded dedication to his work, an intimate knowledge of parliamentary procedure and his leadership of the powerful Southern senatorial caucus, Russell became one of the most influential members of Congress in the 1940s and 1950s.

Russell reached the peak of his prestige in 1951, when he chaired an investigation of President Truman's removal of Gen. Douglas MacArthur from his Korean command. He was credited with defusing a potentially explosive situation by his tactful handling of the matter. The following year Russell made a serious bid for the Democratic presidential nomination but was hampered by his sectional identification and received only 294 out of 1,200 votes at the Party's convention. Somewhat embittered by the loss, he declined an opportunity to become Senate minority leader in 1953, preferring to serve as a spokesman for the South. Instead, he successfully promoted Sen. Lyndon B. Johnson (D, Tex.) for the post of majority leader.

Russell became chairman of the Senate Armed Services Committee in 1951 and in that position played a major role in the area of military affairs in the 1950s and early 1960s. An advocate of a strong national defense, Russell criticized the Eisenhower and Kennedy Administrations for depending too heavily upon nuclear deterrence as their prime military strategy, and he succeeded in increasing appropriations for Air Force bombers during the Kennedy presidency. In that period he also led Southern resistance to the Civil Rights Acts of 1957 and 1960 and directed a successful filibuster against a bill barring discriminatory use of literacy tests by voting registrars. In 1963 he declared his vehement opposition to the public accommodations bill proposed by President Kennedy in June. [See TRUMAN, EISENHOWER, KENNEDY Volumes]

Russell's power declined in the 1960s as the Southern delegation in Congress became less ideologically conservative with the election of younger and more moderate men. However, he remained an influential figure during those years. In addition to his Armed Services Committee chairmanship and second-ranking position on the Appropriations and Aeronautical and Space Sciences Committees, he was a member of the Democratic Policy Committee and led the conservative majority on the Democratic Steering Committee, which distributed committee assignments. Early in 1965 liberal Democratic senators attempted to reform the Steering Committee, but Russell succeeded in preserving a slender conservative edge on the panel. Writing in *The Reporter* in May 1964, Meg Greenfield stated that "he is the unofficial chairman of what amounts to an interlocking directorate of Southern committee and subcommittee chairmen without whose cooperation it is not possible to run the Senate."

In 1964 Congress considered the public accommodations bill originally proposed by President Kennedy; it was the most far-reaching anti-discrimination measure since Reconstruction. When the bill was received by the Senate in February after House passage, Russell directed the Southern forces in a debate that involved some of the most complex parliamentary maneuvering in the history of the Senate. His goal was to delay passage of the bill until the summer, believing that the Administration would then drop it to avoid the spectacle of an intra-party dispute during the Democratic National Convention.

However, President Johnson indicated to the Senate leadership that he was prepared to sacrifice all other legislation rather than abandon the bill in the face of a Southern filibuster. Meanwhile, public sentiment in favor of legislation promoting racial equality was steadily mounting. On June 10 the Senate voted to close off debate on an anti-civil rights filibuster for the first time in its history. Angry over his defeat Russell shouted on the Senate floor, "We're confronted here not only with the spirit of the mob but of the lynch mob." Some observers believed that Russell had made a strategic error by his refusal to accept a compromise bill.

Russell was hospitalized for emphysema in 1965 and could not lead the fight against the voting rights bill. In the remaining years of the Johnson Administration, he suffered additional defeats in the area of civil rights. Despite these setbacks and the growing size of the black electorate in Georgia, he refused to modify his views.

Although Russell voted for President Johnson's mass transit and Appalachia aid bills, he generally opposed Great Society programs. In 1964 he refused to campaign for Johnson or even to endorse him by name. But the two men had developed a close friendship during their years in the Senate, and the President discussed political strategy with Russell even concerning matters on which they disagreed.

Russell supported swift and decisive military actions, such as the invasion of the Dominican Republic in 1965, but he was wary of involvement in protracted foreign wars. He had opposed American assistance to the French in Indochina and felt strong misgivings about the escalation of the conflict in Vietnam during the mid-1960s. Russell believed, however, that the American commitment in Southeast Asia, once made, had to be honored. In 1964 he and the three other ranking members of the Senate Armed Services and Foreign Relations Committees introduced the Gulf of Tonkin Resolution in the upper house. Two years later he opposed an amendment by Sen. Wayne Morse (D, Ore.) [*q.v.*] to repeal the Tonkin Resolution and urged its rejection as a "reaffirmation of the President's power." In 1966 Russell and Sen. Leverett Saltonstall (R, Mass.) [*q.v.*] cosponsored an amendment granting the President new authority to mobilize substantial numbers of reservists to meet manpower requirements for the Vietnam war.

However, during the same year Russell warned that the war was unpopular and that Americans would not indefinitely support a policy that did not promise foreseeable victory. Ultimately, he said, political pressure would compel a change in policy. In April 1966 Russell indicated his own view of the direction in which change should occur, asserting that he hoped that "our bombing operations will be intensified to take in all of the military targets in Vietnam. . . . I think we should use our full strength to push this war to a conclusion."

After the National Liberation Front's Tet offensive early in 1968, Russell, believing that the time for a change in policy had come, declared that he would not support the sending of additional ground troops to Indochina unless there was a drastic escalation of the air war. He said that the initial American entry into the war was a mistake but that the United States could not abandon South Vietnam to the Communists.

Russell's personal influence in defense matters was largely responsible for the Senate's 1967 decision to drop Administration-requested funds for a fleet of fast ships designed to give the United States a rapid transport capability in future brushfire wars. Fearing that such ships might encourage further entanglements like Vietnam, he commented, "If it is easy for us to go anywhere and do anything, we will always be going somehwere and doing something."

Although Russell wanted to avoid future American entry into similar wars and opposed the funding of military projects that would facilitate such involvement, he was a leading congressional advocate of defensive missile installations. In 1966 he played a key role in securing Senate approval of funds for production of the Nike-X, an extensive antiballistic missile system, which the Defense Department regarded as ineffective. The Administration did not build the Nike-X system, but in 1967 it supported a more modest Sentinel antiballistic missile (ABM) system for defense against a Chinese nuclear attack. Russell, still favoring the larger program, did not regard the threat of a Chinese attack as a serious possibility and ridiculed the proposal. But the following year, when the Sentinel ABM was presented as a defense against Soviet as well as Chinese missiles, Russell supported it as "the first step in a defense system against atomic attack from the Soviet Union," and the Senate appropriated construction funds.

In 1969 Russell stepped down as chairman of the Armed Services Committee to head the Appropriations Committee. During the same year he became President Pro Tempore of the Senate. In 1970 a United Press International poll found that Russell was one of three Democratic senators supporting President Nixon's decision to send U.S. troops into Cambodia. On Jan. 21, 1971, while still a senator, he died of respiratory insufficiency after six weeks of hospitalization. [See NIXON Volume]

[MLL]

For further information:
Meg Greenfield, "The Man Who Leads the Southern Senators," *The Reporter* (May 21, 1964), pp. 17-21.
Don Oberdorfer, "The Filibuster's Best Friend," *Saturday Evening Post* (March 13, 1965), pp. 90-92.

RUSTIN, BAYARD
b. March 17, 1910; West Chester, Pa.
Civil rights leader.

An illegitimate child, Rustin was raised by his grandparents in West Chester, Pa. His grandmother belonged to the Society of Friends, and he was influenced by the

Quakers' pacifist principles. Rustin later recalled that when traveling with his high school football team he was physically ejected from a restaurant because of his race and decided at that point never to accept segregation.

Rustin joined the Young Communist League (YCL) in 1936 because he believed that it was committed to peace and equal rights for blacks. He came to New York City as an organizer for the League in 1938 and attended the City College of New York at night. Rustin left the YCL in 1941 when, after the Nazi invasion of the Soviet Union, the Communists abandoned their opposition to World War II.

Upon leaving the YCL Rustin became a socialist and joined the Fellowship of Reconciliation (FOR), a pacifist nondenominational religious group opposed to the war and racial injustice. In 1941 he worked with A. Philip Randolph [*q.v.*], president of the Brotherhood of Sleeping Car Porters, in planning a march on Washington to demand fair employment practices in the nation's rapidly growing defense industries. In 1947 he helped organize and participated in the Congress of Racial Equality's first Freedom Ride into the South. At about the same time, Rustin became director of Randolph's Committee Against Discrimination in the Armed Forces.

During World War II Rustin was a conscientious objector and served more than two years in jail. He became executive secretary of the War Resisters League in 1953 and in 1958 went to England to assist the Campaign for Nuclear Disarmament in organizing the first of its Aldermaston-to-London peace marches.

During the 1950s Rustin became one of the leading strategists of the civil rights movement. In 1955 he played a key role in organizing the Montgomery, Ala., bus boycott led by Martin Luther King [*q.v.*], and he subsequently drafted the plan for what became the Southern Christian Leadership Conference. In the late 1950s he served as an adviser to King. [See EISENHOWER Volume]

In 1960 Rustin, acting on behalf of King and Randolph, organized civil rights demonstrations at the Democratic and Republican National Conventions. When Rep. Adam Clayton Powell (D, N.Y.) [*q.v.*] threatened to publicly denounce Rustin for his radical background and alleged homosexuality, Rustin left the project and for the next two years was isolated from much of the civil rights movement.

During the winter of 1962-63, however, Randolph asked Rustin to draw up plans for a mass march on Washington. Rustin believed that blacks could overcome their second-class citizenship only if they went beyond demands for integration and stressed the need for fundamental economic and social reforms. The original plans for the march, which emphasized demands for federal action in the areas of jobs, housing and education, reflected Rustin's views. But during the two months preceding the August 1963 demonstration, the march's leaders shifted its emphasis towards traditional civil rights objectives in order to win the support of black moderates. The well-ordered, peaceful demonstration, of which Rustin was the chief organizer, drew 200,000 to 250,000 persons to Washington on Aug. 25, 1963. [See KENNEDY Volume]

During the mid-1960s Rustin elaborated upon the strategy he had proposed during the early planning phase of the March on Washington. His program was presented most comprehensively in "From Protest to Politics: The Future of the Civil Rights Movement," an influential article that appeared in the February 1965 issue of *Commentary*. Rustin contended that the legal basis of American racism had been destroyed during the decade between the Supreme Court's school desegregation decision of 1954 and the Civil Rights Act of 1964 but that the desegregation of public accommodations was "relatively peripheral . . . to the fundamental conditions of life of the Negro people."

To effect basic change in the lives of blacks, Rustin continued, the civil rights movement had to extend its concern beyond race relations to fundamental economic problems. The private sector of the economy, he argued, could not fulfill the aspirations of blacks because it was not producing enough jobs. Furthermore, Rustin wrote, technology was eliminating unskilled jobs while creating positions that required professional training. The result, he said, was that the individual no longer could work his way up from the bottom of the economic ladder on personal initiative alone. He concluded that it was essential for blacks to promote federal programs for full employment, the abolition of slums and the reconstruction of the educational system. To win such programs, Rustin said, blacks should place less stress upon protest demonstrations and devote more attention to electoral politics.

Rustin argued that the great majority of blacks had more in common with white workers than with Negro businessmen and that his proposals for federal action represented a program around which a majority coalition could be formed within the Democratic Party. The organized labor movement, Rustin asserted, was the major natural ally of the mass of poor blacks. He urged black organizations to work with the established AFL-CIO leadership to create such a coalition. Black separatism, he argued in a September 1966 *Commentary* article, was not a viable alternative because it would merely solidify the black bourgeoise's control of Negro communities, isolate blacks politically and foster anti-black sentiments.

In the mid-1960s Rustin, who had previously devoted most of his attention to behind-the-scenes organizing of civil rights protests, began to appear frequently before black, union and liberal organizations to promote his political perspective. A tall, grey-haired figure with the appearance of both urbanity and athletic prowess, Rustin, who had cultivated a British accent in the radical, anti-American days of his youth, was an imposing figure and a forceful speaker. Late in 1964 he became executive director of the newly created A. Philip Randolph Institute, an AFL-CIO-supported organization which attempted to place young blacks in union apprenticeship training programs and promote political proposals for the labor-liberal-black coalition, which Rustin thought Lyndon Johnson's landslide 1964 election victory had inaugurated.

Though Rustin generally supported the policies of President Johnson, he frequently criticized the Administration's antipoverty program as inadequate. With other civil rights leaders and liberal economists, Rustin advocated a 10-year, $185 billion "freedom budget" by which the federal government could put all employable persons to work rebuilding ghettoes, constructing hospitals and schools and aiding other socially useful projects.

In 1968 Rustin strongly endorsed the presidential candidacy of Vice President Hubert H. Humphrey [*q.v.*]. Noting the seating of Julian Bond [*q.v.*] and of the integrated Mississippi delegation at the Democratic National Convention, Rustin wrote in the Sept. 21 New York *Amsterdam News* that "the Negro-labor-liberal forces are clearly on top in the Democratic Party." He praised Humphrey as having an outstanding record in the area of civil rights and on matters pertaining to the welfare of workers. Rustin noted "the divisions among the progressive forces over Vietnam," but he attempted to minimize that issue, stating that the progressive coalition should not allow itself to become divided over the war because it "will end before long, but our problems at home will haunt us for generations if we do not act now."

Rustin's close relationship with the AFL-CIO, his support of coalition politics and his allegiance to integration increasingly isolated him within the ranks of black leadership in the late 1960s. In February 1964 he had organized a one-day New York City school boycott for integration led by Rev. Milton A. Galamison [*q.v.*], a strike that was supported by most black leaders. But by 1968 many blacks had lost hope in the possibility of integration and were supporting the decentralization of the New York school system and black control of local school boards. During that year the United Federation of Teachers (UFT) went on strike when the black-controlled governing board of the Ocean Hill-Brownsville demonstration school district ordered 13 tenured teachers transferred out of the district. Rustin, who still staunchly supported integration and a black-trade union alliance, was one of the few prominent blacks who backed the UFT. A large number of blacks felt that the UFT and its president, Albert Shanker [*q.v.*], were hostile to their aspirations, and Rustin was widely denounced within the Negro community for his support of the union.

During the late 1960s and early 1970s, Rustin continued to oppose separatist tendencies. In 1969 he denounced college officials for capitulating to black student demands for "soul courses," contending that black studies programs would not provide Negroes with economically usable skills. Philosophies of racial solidarity, Rustin argued in the January 1970 *Harper's* magazine, had the unintended effect of strengthening the political position of segregationists and conservatives. In 1972 Rustin became a co-chairman of the Socialist Party-Democratic Socialist Federation (later known as Social Democrats, USA) a group dominated by trade union leaders and others who favored the type of black-labor union coalition that he advocated.

Rustin regarded President Richard M. Nixon [*q.v.*] as an opponent of blacks and workers. In 1970 he joined other blacks in denouncing a memo by Daniel P. Moynihan [*q.v.*], a domestic adviser to President Nixon, that urged "benign neglect" of the race issue. In a May 1971 article for *Harper's* he criticized the President's Philadelphia Plan, ostensibly designed to increase the number of construction industry jobs for blacks, as an anti-union device to increase the number of workers in the industry and place deflationary pressure on wages. [See NIXON Volume]

[MLL]

For further information:

Thomas R. Brooks, "A Strategist Without a Movement," *The New York Times Magazine* (Feb. 16, 1969), pp. 24+.

Bayard Rustin, *Down the Line: The Collected Writings of Bayard Rustin* (Chicago, 1971).

RYAN, WILLIAM FITTS

b. June 28, 1922; Albion, N.Y.
d. Sept. 17, 1972; New York, N.Y.
Democratic Representative, N.Y., 1961-72.

After seven years as an assistant Manhattan district attorney, Ryan helped found an anti-Tammany Democratic club in 1957 and was elected Manhattan's only district leader opposed to the Party leadership. In September 1960 Ryan won a major victory for the newly organized Democratic reform movement, headed by Herbert H. Lehman, Eleanor Roosevelt and Thomas K. Finletter, when he defeated the organization candidate, Rep. Ludwig Teller (D, N.Y.), in a primary fight in Manhattan's Upper West Side 20th congressional district. He won the November general election by 25,000 votes.

In Congress Ryan joined a handful of other representatives in opposing appropriations for the House Un-American Activities Committee (HUAC) and voting against legislation aimed at allegedly subversive elements. Ryan was a strong supporter of civil rights and introduced several measures banning discrimination in federally funded schools, hospitals and housing programs. When his district was eliminated by reapportionment in 1962, Ryan ran in the primary in a newly expanded adjacent district against the regular organization candidate, incumbent Rep. Herbert Zelenko. Ryan defeated Zelenko by 8,000 votes and won the general election by 60,000. [See KENNEDY Volume]

Ryan's strongly liberal views matched those of his constituency, and in 1964 he was reelected with 82.5% of the vote. On the opening day of the 89th Congress, Jan. 4, 1965, Ryan led 22 representatives in challenging the seating of the five-man Mississippi delegation. Ryan, acting on behalf of the Mississippi Freedom Democratic Party (MFDP), contended that blacks had been systematically excluded from voting in Mississippi. The challenge was defeated in a key procedural vote, 276-149, and the Mississippi representitives were belatedly sworn in. Ryan called the large opposition vote an "historic achievement" and "a real warning to Mississippi for the future." The MFDP filed a new challenge on May 16, requesting that three of its members—elected in a MFDP-conducted "freedom vote"—be seated instead of the regular Mississippi delegation. The renewed challenge was bottled up by House Clerk Ralph Roberts and then by the House Administration Committee until mid-September, when a group of 31 House members led by Ryan finally forced hearings on the issue. The Administration Committee recommended that the challenge be rejected, primarily on the ground that those initiating it had not been candidates in the contested election. The full House concurred on Sept. 17 by a vote of 228-143.

President Johnson requested his first supplementary appropriation specifically for funds to fight the Vietnam war on May 4, 1965. Within 53 hours both houses had approved Johnson's request, with Ryan one of only seven representatives to oppose the measure. Throughout the remainder of the Johnson Administration, Ryan was among a small minority of congressmen voting against all funds for the Vietnam war. "So long as the Congress continues to rubber-stamp the war through the appropriations process," Ryan argued, "it is abdicating its responsibility for decision making and rational appraisal of executive policy. . . [and] the Administration will continue to rely on the possibility of military victory."

Ryan ran in a four-way Democratic primary for the 1965 New York City mayoral nomination, finishing third with about one-third of victor Abraham D. Beame's 327,934 votes. (Beame lost the general election to Republican-Liberal candidate Rep. John V. Lindsay [*q.v.*].) However, the next year Ryan was easily reelected to the House.

Ryan was a strong civil libertarian and continued to be a leader of the annual congressional fight to end appropriations for HUAC. Between 1961 and 1969 outright opposition to the Committee grew from six to 123 votes. Ryan opposed a House measure, introduced after the April 1968 demonstrations at Columbia University, that denied federal aid to any student who willfully disobeyed a lawful college or university regulation. A modified Senate version of the measure was eventually adopted by the House.

Although best known for his opposition to American intervention in Vietnam, Ryan was also a consistent supporter of Israel. In 1965 he introduced an amendment that was incorporated into the Food-for-Peace appropriation that banned the sale of food to the United Arab Republic unless the President determined that it was in the national interest. During the June 1967 Middle East war, Ryan was critical of the United States's declaration of neutrality. The next year he opposed giving foreign aid to Jordan. Ryan served in the House until his death in September 1972. [See NIXON Volume]

[JBF]

SALINGER, PIERRE E(MIL GEORGE)

b. June 14, 1925; San Francisco, Calif.
White House Press Secretary,
January 1961-March 1964;
Democratic Senator, Calif., June 1964-December 1964.

Salinger served in the Navy during World War II and graduated from the University of San Francisco in 1947. After jobs with the *San Francisco Chronicle* and *Collier's* magazine, he was hired by Robert F. Kennedy [*q.v.*] as an investigator for the Senate Rackets Committee in 1957. Sen. John F. Kennedy served on this Committee and during the 1960 presidential campaign made Salinger his press secretary. On Nov. 10, 1960 Salinger, at 35, was appointed press secretary. At that time he was the youngest man in history to hold the office. Characterized as efficient and easygoing, Salinger exerted no influence on either foreign or domestic policy. Early in the Kennedy Administration he recommended that the President employ "live" television and radio broadcasts of press conferences, an innovative idea at the time.

After Kennedy's assassination President Johnson told Salinger, "I want you to stay with me as long as you can." Salinger became one of the few Kennedy staffers to remain on good terms with Johnson. In March 1964 Salinger decided to challenge Alan Cranston for the Senate seat in California vacated by the resignation of Republican Clair Engle. The campaign's major issue centered on Cranston's charge that Salinger was a "carpetbagger" who voted and resided in Virginia. Salinger's right to contest the Senate seat was upheld by the California Supreme Court on March 25, 1964, and he went on to win the

Democratic primary in June by a plurality of 174,000 votes.

Salinger served in the Senate for 148 days, during which he fought for an amendment to the Social Security Act and coauthored, with Sen. Thomas Kuchel (R, Calif.) [*q.v.*], a regional water plan for the Pacific Southwest. In the November 1964 senatorial campaign Salinger was defeated by Republican George Murphy [*q.v.*]. He attributed his decisive loss in that election to his opponent's superior use of television and to Murphy's support of California's controversial Proposition 14, which permitted racial discrimination in the sale of single family housing. Salinger felt that Proposition 14 was racially discriminatory and that its enactment would effectively nullify the state's fair housing law. The proposition carried by a two to one vote in California, and Salinger lost to Murphy by 216,000 votes.

After the election Salinger turned to private business. He became vice president of National General Corporation in 1965 and served from 1965 to 1968 as vice president for international affairs at Continental Airlines.

During the presidential campaign of 1968, Salinger became a press aide to Sen. Robert Kennedy (D, N.Y.). Following Kennedy's death in June 1968 he shifted his allegiance to Sen. George McGovern's (D, S.D.) [*q.v.*] unsuccessful bid for the Democratic presidential nomination at the Chicago convention. After McGovern's defeat Salinger once again returned to private business. He later moved to Paris, where he made frequent guest appearances on French television commenting on American developments.

[FHM]

For further information:
Pierre Salinger, *With Kennedy* (New York, 1966).

SALISBURY, HARRISON E(VANS)

b. Nov. 14, 1908; Minneapolis, Minn.
Assistant Managing Editor, *New York Times*, 1964-72.

After editing the student newspaper at the University of Minnesota, Salisbury worked for United Press from 1930 to 1948, first as a correspondent in Chicago, Washington and New York and then during World War II in London and Moscow. From 1944 to 1948 he was the wire service's foreign news editor. He joined the *New York Times* in 1949 and spent the next five years in Moscow as bureau chief, winning the 1955 Pulitzer Prize for international reporting for a series on the Soviet Union. In 1964 he became assistant managing editor of the *Times*. Salisbury wrote a number of books about the Soviet Union, including a novel, during his years as a reporter.

In the mid-1960s Salisbury made repeated efforts to travel to North Vietnam, where few American reporters had visited since the escalation of United States military activity in Southeast Asia. During the summer of 1966 he traveled to several Asian nations in an unsuccessful effort to obtain a visa to enter either North Vietnam or China.

Although the United States had been carrying out a sustained bombing campaign against North Vietnam since February 1965, through 1966 attacks on the Hanoi area were still relatively rare. On Dec. 2, 1966 a new series of raids on Hanoi began, culminating in heavy bombing attacks on Dec. 13 and 14. The North Vietnamese government charged that American planes had bombed non-military targets and inflicted heavy civilian casualties. On Dec. 15 Salisbury received a cable from Hanoi granting him a visa, and he immediately left for North Vietnam.

On Dec. 25 the *New York Times* printed Salisbury's first dispatch. "Contrary to the impression given by United States communiques," Salisbury reported, "on-the-spot inspection indicates that American bombing has been inflicting considerable civilian casualties in Hanoi and its environs for some time past. . . ." The following day, in response to Salisbury's report, officials in Washington said that although U.S. policy was to attack only military targets, American pilots had in fact accidentally struck civilian areas. On Dec. 27 Salisbury reported that Nam Dinh, 50 miles southeast of Hanoi, had been repeatedly bombed since June 28, resulting in a large number of civilian casualties. "Whatever the explanation," he wrote, "one can see that United States planes are dropping an enormous weight of explosives on purely civilian targets." Salisbury's dispatches indicated that in spite of the intensive bombing, the North Vietnamese population seemed energetic and purposeful and the country's leadership appeared willing to fight a prolonged war if necessary.

The *Times* reports began an intense debate over the bombing. President Johnson was forced to say at a Dec. 31 press conference that he regretted "every single casualty" in both North and South Vietnam and to reassert that the raids were aimed solely at military targets, with all efforts taken to avoid civilian casualties. Salisbury's dispatches were attacked by both government officials and other newspapers for failing to specify the sources of information on casualties and damage. *Newsweek* said of Salisbury's report of heavy civilian casualties in Hanoi, "To American eyes, it read like the line from Tass or Hsinsha." The *Washington Post* reported that the casualty figures Salisbury cited for Nam Dinh were similar to those appearing in a North Vietnamese pamphlet. Clifton Daniel, managing editor of the *Times*, responded that this was not surprising since "they both came from the same source—the North Vietnamese government."

Before leaving Hanoi Salisbury interviewed a leading official of the National Liberation Front of South Vietnam and North Vietnamese Premier Pham Van Dong, who insisted that there could be no settlement unless "the United States put, unconditionally and for good, an end to the bombing and all hostile activity against the North."

For his reporting from North Vietnam, Salisbury received the George Polk Award for foreign reporting, a Sidney Hillman Award and the Asia Magazine Award. The Pulitzer Prize journalism jury recommended that Salisbury be given the international reporting prize, but the advisory board voted 5-4 to reject the jury recommendation, a decision that was widely criticized.

[JBF]

SALTONSTALL, LEVERETT

b. Sept. 1, 1892; Chestnut Hill, Mass.
Republican Senator, Mass., 1944-67.

Leverett Saltonstall was a member of one of Massachusetts's oldest and most politically prominent families. After his graduation from Harvard in 1914 and Harvard Law School three years later, Saltonstall served in the Army during World War I. While practicing law in Boston after the war, Saltonstall entered state politics at the local level. He rose quickly through the Yankee-dominated Republican hierarchy to attain the governorship in 1938 and a Senate seat in 1944. In the 1950s Saltonstall was chairman of the Armed Services Committee for two years and later Republican whip and assistant Republican Senate leader. During the Kennedy Administration Saltonstall maintained a moderately liberal voting record. Although he was ranking Republican on the Armed Services Committee and chairman of the GOP conference, he exerted little influence within the Senate. [See TRUMAN, EISENHOWER, KENNEDY Volumes]

Saltonstall voted for the Johnson Administration's civil rights bill in 1964. In January 1965 he introduced an alternative to the Administration's Social Security-financed medicare bill. The Saltonstall measure called for a voluntary medicare program for persons over 65 with incomes under $3,000 a year. Benefits were to vary according to the individual's choice of one of three plans. The program was to be administered by the states and financed by federal-state funds and graduated contributions by participants. Although his measure failed to pass, in July the Senate adopted a Saltonstall amendment to the medicare bill making basic home-nursing benefits available to persons over 65 regardless of whether they had been hospitalized.

In February 1965 Saltonstall supported Senate Minority Leader Everett Dirksen's (R, Ill.) [*q.v.*] charge that senators advocating a negotiated settlement of the Vietnam war were "run[ning] up the white flag" of defeat. In June of the next year, Saltonstall asserted that, in widening the air war to include the bombing of Hanoi-Haiphong oil installations, President Johnson had acted "in the best interest of accomplishing our objective in Vietnam." He also declared that the air raids were worth the risk of Chinese intervention.

Pressure from the Massachusetts Republican Party, which supported the growing political aspirations of Massachusetts Attorney General Edward Brooke [*q.v.*], led Saltonstall to announce his retirement from the Senate in December 1965. The next year Brooke won election to Saltonstall's old seat to become the first black to serve in the Senate since Reconstruction.

[FHM]

SAMUELSON, PAUL A(NTHONY)

b. May 15, 1915; Gary, Ind.
Economist.

Paul Samuelson was the author of an immensely popular economics textbook and a prolific disseminator of Keynesian economic thought in both popular and professional journals. He earned his Ph.D. in economics at Harvard during the 1930s under the tutelage of Alvin Hansen, the most prominent exponent of Keynesian theory in America. The British economist John Maynard Keynes had argued that cycles of boom and depression were not inevitable but could be moderated by government fiscal action. He urged deficit spending to combat economic slowdowns and heavy unemployment and a budget surplus when inflation was the primary threat. Adjusting such monetary mechanisms as interest rates was another Keynesian tool to maintain economic stability.

Samuelson promoted these modern concepts in his textbook, *Economics: An Introductory Analysis*, first published in 1948 and destined to become the most widely read economics textbook in America. He taught economics at the Massachusetts Institute of Technology, wrote often on current issues and served as a frequent consultant to government agencies. He exerted a strong impact on economic policy during the Kennedy Administration. Described as "Kennedy's favorite economist," Samuelson, at the outset of the Administration, headed a task force on economic policy whose recommendations foreshadowed the basic outlines of policy during the Kennedy years. Throughout his tenure in office Kennedy sought and often followed Samuelson's advice. [See KENNEDY Volume]

Samuelson was further from the center of power during the Johnson years, but he continued to be a leading shaper of public opinion on current economic issues through his column in *Newsweek*. He was an enthusiastic advocate of the massive tax cut proposed during the Kennedy Administration and signed by President Johnson in February 1964. Samuelson praised the tax cut for its stimulative effect on the economy and foresaw a "long period of continuous growth, with rising living standards." He felt there would never be a recurrence of a great depression like that of the 1930s as long as there existed a government ready to intervene with the appropriate fiscal and monetary remedies.

In his column Samuelson offered the Johnson Administration a steady stream of advice on how to meet the threat of inflation without bringing on a recession. Early in 1966 he urged a tax increase in order to forestall "demand-pull" inflation, that is inflation caused by an excess of dollars in the hands of consumers. The Administration did not raise taxes, however, and a year later, amid calls from a diverse array of economists for a tax increase, Samuelson changed his position and argued against raising taxes. In "An Open Letter to LBJ" in January 1967, Samuelson maintained that the time to raise taxes had passed and that to do so would bring "loss of momentum in this greatest of all peacetime economic expansions." "Too often in the past," he said, "governments have brought prosperity to and end by a misguided concern for budget-balance ideology."

Late in 1967 Samuelson returned to advocacy of a tax increase. He argued that the threat of demand-pull inflation was paramount and could not be checked by the Federal Reserve's tight money policy alone. Nevertheless, Samuelson exhorted the government not to sacrifice its antipoverty and social welfare programs to fight inflation. "I favor a tax increase," he said in November 1967. "Let me make it clear that I do not favor it at any price. If its costs were a legislative deal to cripple important welfare programs, I would have to point out that a degree of open inflation is not the greatest evil." In June 1968 Congress passed a 10% tax surcharge accompanied by $6 billion in budget cuts.

Samuelson continued to promote his mainstream liberal economic thinking throughout the Nixon Administration. By 1970 he had earned approximately $2.5 million in royalties from his textbook. In that year he was awarded the 1970 Nobel Prize for doing "more than any other contemporary economist to raise the level of scientific analysis in economic theory." [See NIXON Volume]

[TO]

For further information:
Paul Samuelson, *The Samuelson Sampler* (Glen Ridge, N. J., 1973).

SANDERS, CARL E(DWARD)

b. May 15, 1925; Augusta, Ga.
Governor, Ga., 1963-67.

Sanders received his legal degree from the University of Georgia in 1947 and joined an Augusta law firm the following year. Elected to the state Assembly in 1954 and to the state Senate in 1956, he became president pro tempore of the latter body in 1960. Sanders became known as a racial moderate for the key role he played in the Senate's passage of "open school" bills, which barred the closing of the state's public schools as a device for avoiding integration.

In 1962 Sanders entered the Democratic gubernatorial primary against former Gov. Marvin Griffin, a white supremacist who vowed undying opposition to integration. Sanders's greatest strength was in the urban centers of the state, which were less inclined than the rural areas to resist federal pressure against segregation. Aided by a federal court decision in the spring of 1962 voiding the state's county unit voting system which had favored rural areas, Sanders defeated Griffin by 462,000 to 305,000 votes. Sanders subsequently ran unopposed in the general election. [See KENNEDY Volume]

As governor, Sanders did not support integration. In July 1963 he opposed the Kennedy Administration's civil rights bill, calling it unconstitutional. When Lyndon Johnson assumed the presidency the following November and announced his intention to pursue Kennedy's programs, Sanders pledged his support in all areas but that of civil rights. At the Democratic National Convention of 1964, Sanders urged the Platform Committee to respect the local traditions of the South when considering racial matters.

Sanders's primary concern, however, was to promote the economic growth of Georgia. During his first year in office, he pursued this goal by successfully promoting bills to expand educational opportunities and to streamline the state's administrative apparatus. Believing that racial peace was essential to progress, he continued to oppose resistance to legally mandated integration and sought to compromise with civil rights groups. When civil rights demonstrations in Americus led to violence during the summer of 1965, Sanders urged the unyielding local administration to submit to mediation. In January 1966 the Georgia House of Representatives voted not to admit Julian Bond [*q.v.*], a leader of the Student Nonviolent Coordinating Committee (SNCC), to his elected seat because he had opposed the Vietnam war and backed avoidance of the draft. Sanders, who was a supporter of Administration war policy, opposed the exclusion of Bond, saying that it would make him a martyr and provoke SNCC demonstrations.

Barred by the state's constitution from running for reelection in 1966, Sanders considered challenging Sen. Richard Russell [*q.v.*] in the Democratic primary of that year. But political trends were running against racial moderates in Georgia, and Sanders decided not to undertake the effort. In 1970 he entered the Democratic gubernatorial primary but was defeated by Jimmy Carter.

[MLL]

SANFORD, (JAMES) TERRY
b. Aug. 20, 1917; Laurinburg, N.C.
Governor, N.C., 1961-65.

The son of a North Carolina hardware merchant, Sanford attended the University of North Carolina and, following wartime service in the Army, returned there to earn a law degree in 1946. During the 1950s he practiced law while becoming active in state politics. In 1960 Sanford won the governorship by attracting the support of city dwellers, organized labor, businessmen and blacks. His tenure was marked by broad educational reform as well as increases in social services and attempts to end racial discrimination. [See KENNEDY Volume]

Constitutionally barred from seeking another term, Sanford returned to the practice of law in 1965. During the remainder of the decade, he continued his interest in education, which he considered a "vital tool" for economic development, the elimination of poverty and prejudice and "the cultivation of all human capacities." At their July 1965 conference, U.S governors adopted Sanford's "Compact on Education," which stressed the need for states to join the federal government in studying ways to improve education. That same month he was appointed to the National Advisory Commission on Education of Disadvantaged Children. He was also a member of the Carnegie Commission on Educational Television whose report, issued in January 1967, proposed the creation of a noncommercial educational television network funded by a federal tax on new televisions.

Sanford's other major concern during the decade was the strengthening of the states in the federal-state relationship. In November 1964 he urged a greater role for the states in supplying leadership and initiative to carry out federally sponsored programs. In April 1965 Sanford became director of a two-year study funded by the Ford Foundation and the Carnegie Corporation to determine ways of increasing the role of the states in educational reform. The Commission's first report, in 1966, recommended the creation of an educational commission for the states, which would strive to unite the efforts of educators and politicians for the benefit of education at all levels.

In October 1967 Sanford completed the Ford Foundation study and outlined his program for the reform and revitalization of the states as a means of defending the nation's federal system against the "possible abuses of centralized power" and meeting "the challenge of the urban areas." He suggested a reform of state tax structures and recommended the use of state power as the only means of ordering urban growth and avoiding the "unordered piling up of problems upon problems."

In June 1968 Sanford was elected president of Urban America, Inc., a private, nonprofit city improvement group that rendered financial assistance and technical advise to sponsors of nonprofit housing developments. One month later he also became director of Esquire, Inc., a producer of educational films and books.

Sanford seconded the nomination of Hubert H. Humphrey [*q.v.*] for president at the July 1968 Democratic National Convention and served as the national chairman of the Citizens for Humphrey-Muskie committee. He was named president of Duke University in December 1969. Sanford was the chairman of the 1972 Democratic Charter Commission and was an unsuccessful Democratic presidential aspirant before supporting Sen. George McGovern's (D, S.D.) [*q.v.*] effort. He withdrew as a candidate for the 1976 Democratic presidential nomination in January 1976 to return to Duke University. [See NIXON Volume]

[TJC]

SAUNDERS, STUART T(HOMAS)
b. July 16, 1909; McDowall, W. Va.
Chairman and Chief Executive, Pennsylvania Railroad Company, October 1963-January 1968; Chairman and Chief Executive, Penn Central Transportation Company, January 1968-June 1970.

Stuart Saunders attended Roanoke College in Virginia and Harvard Law School, from which he received his degree in 1934.

After practicing law in Washington, D.C. for five years, he joined the legal department of the Norfolk & Western Railroad Company (N&W) in 1939. He moved up through the N&W's legal ranks and advanced to the company presidency in 1958. Under Saunders the N & W, a consistently profitable coal hauler, continued to perform well; in 1962 it realized a profit of over $65 million after taxes on a gross revenue of roughly $250 million. Saunders arranged the N&W's absorption of the Virginian Railway, the first railroad merger approved by the Interstate Commerce Commission in the twentieth century. In October 1963 Saunders became chairman of the board of the Pennsylvania Railroad Company, the nation's largest railroad.

Saunders worked to enlarge the Pennsylvania's income by expanding and diversifying its holdings. He supplemented the railroad's sizeable land holdings with extensive real estate investments in Florida, California and the Southwest. Saunders concluded the Pennsylvania's purchase of the Buckeye Pipe Line Company, an 8,000-mile petroleum pipeline, and also bought a 57% interest in Executive Jet Aviation, a young company providing charter service to businessmen.

The Pennsylvania gained the capital for these acquisitions partially through the sale of its own assets, such as its 98% interest in the Wabash Railroad and 25% in the N&W. In 1966 it sold the deficit-ridden Long Island Railroad to New York State for $65 million. Saunders built good stockholder relations with his policy of paying out high dividends; such payments increased in his first three years at the Pennsylvania from $6.8 million to $32 million.

Saunder's major task in the mid-1960s was the arrangement of the merger of the Pennsylvania with its largest rival, the New York Central. The proposed merger faced strong opposition from labor unions, the Department of Justice, small railroads and Pennsylvania businessman Milton J. Shapp. On Oct. 1, 1963, the day Saunders took over the Pennsylvania, Assistant U.S. Attorney General William Orrick declared that the government would oppose the merger because "the combination would eliminate a vast amount of beneficial rail competition" and endanger "the continued existence of several smaller railroads." The railway brotherhoods feared that workers would lose their jobs because of the merger. Shapp charged in May 1966 that the merger was "a legalized multibillion-dollar swindle that would put the old robber barons to shame."

Saunders worked for four years to overcome the opposition to the merger. He argued that the merger was vital for the railroads' survival and would result in savings of $80 million due to greater efficiency. He won over the railway unions by promising to rehire all workers with five years seniority who had been furloughed between the spring of 1964 and the time of the merger. This agreement cost $38 million in the two years after the merger. The Justice Department dropped its opposition in November 1967, after Saunders had promised that the merged railroads would also take over the bankrupt New Haven Railroad.

The government's shift was also the result of Saunders's assiduous cultivation of the Johnson Administration. Saunders was an active supporter of Administration policies within the business community. As co-chairman with Henry Ford II [*q.v.*] of the Business Committee for Tax Reduction he helped to rally support behind the Kennedy-Johnson $11.5 billion, tax-reduction bill in 1964-64. During the Johnson Administration he served as chairman of the National Alliance of Businessmen in the Philadelphia area, an Administration-inspired program to provide jobs for the unemployed. Saunders also served on the President's Advisory Committee on Labor-Management Policy and was chairman of the Department of Commerce Advisory Committee on Foreign Direct Investments. "I could not have gotten the merger through without help from members of the Administration," Saunders said in January 1968. "They got the Justice Department to change its thinking."

The merger creating the Penn Central Transportation Company in February 1968 was the greatest combination in American history. The Penn Central had assets of

$6.3 billion and annual revenues of almost $2 billion and was both the nation's biggest railroad and its largest landlord. *Saturday Review* named Saunders "Businessman of the Year" for 1968.

On June 8, 1970 the Penn Central's board of directors fired Saunders. Two weeks later the Penn Central filed for bankruptcy, the largest corporate bankruptcy in American history. Among the reasons cited for its collapse were poor execution of the merger, bad management, expensive labor contracts, losses in the real estate market and jet subsidiaries and the unprofitability of its commuter railroad divisions.

Under Saunders the Penn Central management had employed what *Fortune* magazine called "virtuoso bookkeeping" to conceal the company's losses from its shareholders, directors and the financial community. By reporting sales of assets as normal income, counting uncollectable freight bills as earnings, listing operating expenditures as capital expenses and by using other such devices, the Penn Central had inflated its profits by millions of dollars when it was actually losing money. Despite its cash shortage the company paid out $100 million in dividends in its first two years of operations.

In September 1975 Saunders and more than 50 other directors and officers of the bankrupt railroad agreed to pay $12.6 million to its shareholders, debenture holders and trustees who had sued them for dereliction of duty in issuing false financial statements. [See NIXON Volume]

[TO]

For further information:
Joseph R. Daughen and Peter Binzen, *The Wreck of the Penn Central* (New York, 1971).

SAVIO, MARIO

b. Dec. 8, 1942; New York, N.Y.
Leader, Berkeley Free Speech Movement.

Savio was the son of a religious, working-class Italian-American couple. After graduation from high school he entered Manhattan College, a school run by the Christian Brothers, but he found it "too parochial" and transferred to Queens College. At Queens he was president of the Fraternity of Christian Doctrine, and he spent the summer of 1963 in the Taxco area of Mexico, helping to build a laundry there to prevent cholera infection. In the fall of 1963 he transferred again, this time to the University of California, Berkeley, where he majored in philosophy.

At Berkeley Savio was dismayed by what he viewed as the depersonalized, regimented quality of the University's operations, and he was attracted to the flourishing student political activity on and around the campus. Briefly associated with the Young People's Socialist League, he read Marx and was particularly impressed with his concept of alienation as a human response to bureaucratic institutions. In the summer of 1964 Savio taught at one of the Mississippi Freedom Schools and worked as a voter registrar with the Student Nonviolent Coordinating Committee (SNCC). When Savio returned to Berkeley in the fall of 1964, he was elected chairman of the University Friends of SNCC. Thus, it was as a leader of one of the several civil rights groups on campus that he took part in the free speech fight that fall.

The conflict arose initially over the University administration's refusal to allow the right of students to collect money and recruit members for off-campus causes on a narrow strip of sidewalk at the south entrance to the campus. Savio and a number of others formed a committee to resist the ban. At first the coalition represented a wide spectrum of student groups from socialists to Goldwater supporters. After conducting an unsuccessful legal protest, the United Front, as it was called, took direct action by setting up tables in violation of the ban. As a result, on Oct. 1 Savio and seven other students were suspended from the University. That same afternoon Jack Weinberg, a non-student member of the campus chapter of the Congress of Racial Equality (CORE), was arrested for sitting at a table in front of the administration building. Students immediately sat down around the police car to prevent his removal. The sit-in was joined by thousands, and Savio, speaking from the top of the police car, quickly emerged as the leading spokesman of the growing protest. The next day Savio led a delegation to University President Clark Kerr [*q.v.*], who agreed to negotiate the free speech issue, drop charges against Weinberg and submit the case of the suspended students to a faculty committee, which would determine whether or not the suspensions should stand.

Preparing for a meeting of the University's Board of Regents that was to consider new political regulations and the case of the suspended students, the political groups broadened their base to include hundreds of young people unaffiliated with the University. The new organization called itself the Free Speech Movement (FSM), and Savio was elected to its steering committee. The Regents' meeting of Nov. 20 disappointed student expectations, however, by stipulating that on-campus advocacy of "illegal" off-campus action—i.e., civil rights sit-ins—would make their advocates liable to University discipline. The FSM contended that this would subject students to double jeopardy, that is, to punishment by both the courts and the campus administration. The students were further aroused at the end of November when the administration, on the advice of the faculty committee, brought charges against Savio and three other FSM leaders for actions committed during the Oct. 1-2 events. Interpreting this move as a hardening of the administration's position, the FSM called a mass rally on Dec. 2. There Savio declared to a crowd of 6,000 that "there is a time when the operation of the machine becomes so odious, makes you so sick at heart, that you can't take part. . .you've got to put your bodies upon the wheels and upon the gears, upon the levers. . .and you've got to make it stop." With that, some 2,000 students occupied Sproul Hall, the administration building. Eight hundred, including Savio, elected to stay the night, and early in the morning they were evicted and arrested by several hundred state, city and county police.

On Dec. 3 a campus strike began. It lasted five days and enlisted the support of a majority of the student body of 27,000. As a result, Kerr agreed to a liberalization of political regulations. The FSM leaders, however, charged that the administration's promises were vague and unreliable and insisted on faculty intervention to guarantee both amnesty and free political advocacy. On Dec. 7 the Kerr proposals were presented to 18,000 students and faculty at an outdoor amphitheater. When Savio approached the microphone to attempt to speak, he was grabbed by campus police and hustled off the stage. Although Savio was eventually allowed to speak, the incident angered the audience. At an FSM rally later that day, leading members of the faculty stood with Savio and other student leaders on the steps of Sproul Hall and told thousands of assembled students that "power is in your hands." At the Academic Senate meeting on Dec. 8, the faculty, ignoring the Kerr proposals, passed a resolution ending restrictions on the content of advocacy and demanding that disciplinary authority be taken away from the administration and given to the faculty. Their resolution endorsed most key points in the FSM platform.

The Regents of the University of California, meeting on Dec. 18, refused to grant disciplinary authority to the faculty but acknowledged the primacy of the First and 14th Amendments in future University regulations. They also appointed a new chancellor for the Berkeley campus, who eased a number of restrictions covering student political activity.

Despite the initial success of the FSM, the Berkeley campus administration regained the initiative in the spring of 1965 during the "filthy speech movement," when a group of students and non-students demanded the right to publicly display signs bearing obscene words. By this time the FSM had become dormant, existing only as a committee of the 700 sit-in defendants whose cases were still before the courts. Moreover, there was little student interest in defending the "dirty word" group when its members were disciplined in April. Savio at first called for a protest, then unexpectedly announced that he was withdrawing from campus activity, saying that he did not wish to dominate the movement.

In June 1965 Savio was one of 155 students convicted on charges arising out of the Dec. 2 sit-in. He received the most severe sentence of those convicted—120 days in jail. Forced to leave school for a time, Savio was denied readmission in November 1966 on the ground that he had violated rules prohibiting non-students from distributing leaflets on the campus. He participated nevertheless in a sit-in on Nov. 30 protesting the administration's refusal to allow non-students to set up an anti-war table next to an authorized Navy recruiting table in the student union. The police were called, and Savio and four other non-students were arrested. A large but unsuccessful student strike was launched on the following day. In January 1967 Savio was convicted with four others of creating a public nuisance and sentenced to 90 days in jail. After this Savio remained in the Berkeley community for several years but withdrew from all but sporadic political activity.

[TLH]

For further information;
Hal Draper, *Berkeley; The New Student Revolt* (New York, 1965).

SAXON, JAMES J(OSEPH)

b. April 13, 1914; Toledo, Ohio.
Comptroller of the Currency, November 1961-January 1967.

During the 1960s James Saxon upset the banking status quo more than any federal regulatory official in a generation. He entered the Treasury Department in 1937 as a securities statistician in the Office of the Comptroller of the Currency. During World War II he served as a Treasury Department troubleshooter overseas, handling a variety of financial problems from the Philippines to North Africa. Following the war Saxon became special assistant to Treasury Secretary John Snyder, leaving in 1952 to work for the Democratic National Committee. After that year's election Saxon joined the staff of the American Bankers Association as assistant general counsel in the Washington office. (He had received his law degree from Georgetown University in 1950.) Saxon left in 1956 to become an attorney for the First National Bank of Chicago, where he remained until President Kennedy appointed him comptroller of the currency in November 1961. [See KENNEDY Volume]

The job of the comptroller was to supervise the 4,500 nationally chartered banks in the country. Believing that banking was an over-regulated industry, Saxon came to his position determined to liberalize the rules governing banking and open it up to more vigorous competition. He initiated an aggressive new policy of freely granting new bank charters and allowing established banks to open new branches. In his first three years he approved 434 new charters, compared to the 227 his predecessors had chartered in the previous 10 years. Saxon expanded the lending capacity of banks in a number of ways and permitted them to enter an unprecedented variety of businesses: direct leasing of equipment, selling insurance, underwriting revenue bonds, issuing credit cards and acting as travel agencies.

The national banking community, for the most part, welcomed Saxon's initiatives, while state bankers excoriated him for threatening the "dual banking" system of state and nationally chartered banks. The state banks' champion in Congress, Rep. Wright Patman (D, Tex.) [*q.v.*], managed to block almost all of Saxon's proposed reforms, the most controversial of which would have allowed national banks to establish branches even where they were prohibited by state law. Saxon accomplished his innovations, therefore, by administrative rulings. His bold policy changes combined with his combative disposition and brusque style brought him into conflict with the rest of Washington's banking regulatory apparatus: the Federal Reserve, the Federal Deposit Insurance Corporation, the Justice Department and the Securities and Exchange Commission.

Saxon's relations with other agencies came under fire in a 1965 investigation of bank failures undertaken by the Permanent Investigations Subcommittee of the Senate Government Operations Committee. The probe centered upon the infiltration of criminal elements into the operations of the San Francisco National Bank, the Brighton (Colo.) National Bank and the First National Bank of Marlin, Tex. According to *Fortune*, "Saxon and his staff people never came up with an adequate defense of their indulgence toward both the San Francisco National and the Brighton National, new banks that failed after elaborate hanky-panky by some of their leading officers." In both cases Saxon permitted the banks to do business after serious violations of the law were discovered by bank examiners. The subcommittee's report criticized him for his "failure" to notify other federal agencies that the San Francisco bank was in "dire straits" until after he closed it in January 1965.

Saxon returned to private law practice after his term as comptroller ended in January 1967.

[TO]

For further information:
Irwin Ross, "Scrappy, Happy James J. Saxon," *Fortune* (April 1966), pp. 162+.

SCHEER, ROBERT
b. April 14, 1936; New York, N.Y.
Writer, anti-war activist.

Scheer, the son of garment workers, was born in the Bronx. He graduated from the City College of New York in 1958 and went to Syracuse University to study economics and public administration. In 1961 he moved to Berkeley, where he was a fellow at the Center for Chinese Studies of the University of California.

In 1960 Scheer had visited Cuba. Impressed by the achievements of Fidel Castro's regime, he coauthored with Maurice Zeitlin *Cuba: Tragedy in Our Hemisphere* (1963), a defense of the Cuban revolution based on printed sources as well as his own impressions. By this time Scheer had left school to become a free-lance writer. In 1965 he wrote *How the U.S. Got Involved in Vietnam* under a grant from the Center for the Study of Democratic Institutions. The book was a critical study of American intervention which focused on counterinsurgency programs in South Vietnam and on the role of New York's Francis Cardinal Spellman [*q.v.*] in winning American support for Ngo Dinh Diem. In 1965 Scheer also became an editor of *Ramparts* magazine where, the next year, he helped write an expose of the relationship between the Central Intelligence Agency and Michigan State University's police training activities in Vietnam.

As an authority on Southeast Asia with an anti-Administration point of view, Scheer was chosen in August 1965 by anti-war groups in California's seventh congressional district (Berkeley-Oakland) to challenge Rep. Jeffrey Cohelan (D, Calif.) in the Democratic Party primary the following June. Cohelan, then nearing the end of his fourth term in Congress, was a liberal with a 95% rating from the liberal Americans for Democratic Action. He had strong support from organized labor and consistently backed President Johnson's Vietnam policy.

Launching his campaign under the slogan "Withdraw the Troops—End Poverty," Scheer received the support of many of Cohelan's disgruntled former backers, including an endorsement from the California Democratic Council, a statewide volunteer organization of liberal Democrats. Although many of Berkeley's anti-war activists were opposed to Scheer's decision to run in the Democratic primary rather than as an independent in the fall, the Scheer campaign drew hundreds of enthusiastic precinct workers from the campus and the surrounding liberal community.

The Scheer campaign attracted national attention and the concern of the Johnson Administration. In April Postmaster General Lawrence O'Brien [*q.v.*] helped organize a testimonial dinner for Cohelan, at which he received the endorsement of Sens. Robert F. Kennedy (D, N.Y.) [*q.v.*] and J. William Fulbright (D, Ark.) [*q.v.*]. On the night of the primary, Johnson's press secretary, Bill Moyers [*q.v.*] called election officials in the district three times to see how Cohelan was doing. Scheer lost the nomination, but he drew an impressive 45% of the vote, a higher percentage than any other radical peace candidate in 1966. Cohelan admitted that he had won in spite of his position on the war rather than because of it.

An outgrowth of the Scheer campaign was the formation of the Community for New Politics (CNP) in Berkeley and the growth of a larger New Politics movement nationally. The Berkeley CNP was soon split over the issue of independent political action. A minority wanted the immediate creation of a third radical party, while Scheer and other CNP leaders favored continuation of work within the left wing of the Democratic Party. By January 1968, however, after the minority had succeeded in re-registering 100,000 California Democrats into a new Peace and Freedom Party, Scheer himself became an active participant in the new party. In 1970 he was the Peace and Freedom candidate for senator in California.

After 1968 Scheer continued to be a prolific writer, reporting on his travels in North and South Vietnam, North Korea, the Middle East and China. He edited a collection of essays by Eldridge Cleaver [*q.v.*] in 1969 and published *America after Nixon: The Age of the Multinationals* in 1974.

[TLH]

For further information:
Thomas Powers, *The War at Home* (New York, 1973).

SCHLESINGER, ARTHUR M(EIER) JR.

b. Oct. 15, 1917; Columbus, Ohio.
Historian.

Following a brilliant academic career at Harvard and Oxford, Schlesinger joined his father in the Harvard history department in 1946. A leading spokesman for American liberalism in the postwar era, Schlesinger also wrote award-winning biographies of Andrew Jackson and Franklin D. Roosevelt, which cast both presidents as pragmatic and successful proponents of progressive social change. [See TRUMAN, EISENHOWER Volumes]

After backing Adlai Stevenson [*q.v.*] in 1952 and 1956, Schlesinger switched his allegiance to John F. Kennedy in 1959 and helped recruit a liberal "brain trust" for the new President's administration. Kennedy appointed Schlesinger a special assistant in January 1961 and assigned him, among other tasks to work on Latin American affairs. Schlesinger toured South America with Food for Peace Director George McGovern [*q.v.*] early in the year and argued for the Alliance for Progress as a means both to promote progressive democracy in the hemisphere and to counter the influence of Cuban-backed Communist movements. Although he opposed the Bay of Pigs invasion of Cuba as unwise, Schlesinger helped develop U.S. efforts to economically and politically isolate Fidel Castro's regime from other Western Hemisphere governments. [See KENNEDY Volume]

Two months after Kennedy's assassination Schlesinger resigned his post as a White House special assistant and began work on a history of the Administration. His best-selling book, *A Thousand Days: John F. Kennedy in the White House,* was published in 1965 and won the Pulitzer Prize for biography the next year. The work celebrated the youth and vigor of the late President, his unsentimental liberalism and the sophistication of Administration policymakers. In 1966 Schlesinger was appointed Albert Schweitzer Professor of Humanities at the City University of New York.

When the growing escalation of the war in Vietnam aroused debate in the American intellectual and academic community, Schlesinger first defended, albeit critically, the Johnson Administration's conduct of the war. At a May 15, 1965 Washington "teach-in" sponsored by opponents of the war, Schlesinger represented the Administration in a debate with University of Chicago Professor Hans J. Morgenthau [*q.v.*]. Schlesinger argued that the bombing of North Vietnam was counterproductive and advocated a negotiated settlement, but he nevertheless favored sending more troops to Southeast Asia. "If we took the Marines now in the Dominican Republic and sent them to South Vietnam we would be a good deal better off in both countries."

Schlesinger's guarded defense of the war

turned to a measured opposition by the middle of 1966. Late in the year he published *The Bitter Heritage: Vietnam and American Democracy,* which argued that the war must be stopped because of its "ugly side-effects" at home: "inflation, frustration, indignation, protest, panic, angry divisions within the national community, premonitions of McCarthyism." Schlesinger now favored a gradual de-escalation of the war, with an immediate halt to the bombing. In April 1967 he joined with liberals Joseph Rauh [*q.v.*] and John Kenneth Galbraith [*q.v.*] to form Negotiations Now, a group seeking a million signatures on a stop-the-bombing petition.

Although aligning himself with the growing movement against the war, Schlesinger was careful not to lend his prestige to those in the New Left who attacked the entire thrust of the United States postwar foreign policy. Schlesinger argued that American involvement in Vietnam resulted not from an inherently expansionary American foreign policy but out of a series of mistakes leading to a military-political quagmire. Writing in the journal *Foreign Affairs* in October 1967, Schlesinger attacked the revisionist historians and argued that because of the character of the Soviet state, the "most rational of American policies could hardly have averted the Cold War."

In 1967 Schlesinger first advised Sen. Robert F. Kennedy (D, N.Y.) [*q.v.*] to avoid a primary battle with President Johnson, instead urging that he throw his weight behind a peace plank at the Democratic National Convention. However, the historian-adviser reversed his position in November after Sen. Eugene McCarthy (D, Minn.) [*q.v.*] announced his candidacy for the Democratic presidential nomination. Schlesinger strongly supported Kennedy when he began his campaign in March. After Kennedy's assassination three months later, Schlesinger was among those former Kennedy aides who threw their support to Sen. George McGovern's (D, S.D.) [*q.v.*] short-lived bid for the Democratic nomination.

During the early 1970s Schlesinger was a leading academic critic of the Nixon Administration. His influential 1973 work, *The Imperial Presidency,* attacked the growing centralization of power in the executive branch and cast into a somewhat darker light the increasing power exercised by such liberal presidents as Roosevelt, Kennedy and Johnson.

[NNL]

For further information:

———, "Origins of the Cold War" *Foreign Affairs* XLVI (October 1967), pp. 22-52.

Arthur Schlesinger Jr., *A Thousand Days: John F. Kennedy in the White House* (New York, 1965).

———, *The Bitter Heritage: Vietnam and American Democracy* (New York, 1966).

———, *The Imperial Presidency* (New York, 1973).

SCHULTZE, CHARLES L(OUIS)

b. Dec. 12, 1924; Alexandria, Va.
Director of the Bureau of the Budget, June 1965-January 1968.

Charles Schultze grew up in Alexandria, leaving in 1942 to attend Fordham University in New York City. He entered the Army in 1943 and served in combat in Europe. After the war he enrolled at Georgetown University in Washington, D.C. and earned his B.A. in 1948. Studying part-time over the next 12 years, Schultze earned his M.A. in economics from Georgetown in 1950 and his Ph.D. from the University of Maryland in 1960. Over the same period he alternated between college teaching and government service. From 1949 to 1951 he taught economics at the College of St. Thomas in Minnesota, returning to Washington for a year as an economist with the Office of Price Stabilization. For the next six years he was a staff economist on the Council of Economic Advisers. After teaching at Indiana University and the University of Maryland and writing two studies analyzing inflationary trends of the previous decade, Schultze joined the Bureau of the Budget as an assistant director in September 1962. He was named head of the Bureau by President Johnson in June 1965.

Schultze applied to the Bureau the systems analysis procedures that Secretary of

Defense Robert McNamara [*q.v.*] had built into the operations of the Pentagon. Schultze employed the new management techniques to take the Bureau beyond its traditional function of calculating government revenues and expenses and allocating resources among the various departments. He installed program evaluation experts in all government agencies to measure the performance as well as the cost of programs and suggest alternatives and improvements in the execution of particular jobs. The new method, known as the "planning-programing-budgeting system," was first used in the preparation of the fiscal 1968 budget. It gave the Budget Bureau a far more active role in the workings of the federal government. *Forbes* magazine praised the new budget as "the first attempt of the U.S. government to figure out in detail what it really is spending the tax dollar for."

As budget director, Schultze was a member of the economic policy "troika", including Secretary of the Treasury Henry Fowler [*q.v.*] and Council of Economic Advisers Chairman Gardner Ackley [*q.v.*], that met regularly with President Johnson. Like Ackley, Schultze was a proponent of the Keynesian "new economics," which held that an active fiscal policy on the part of the federal government was the key to economic growth and stability. During Schultze's tenure the main goal of Johnson's economic advisers was to curb the inflation growing out of spending on the Vietnam war and Great Society social programs.

In the second half of 1967, Schultze played a leading role in the Administration's attempt to persuade Congress to pass an anti-inflationary 10% tax surcharge. In August 1967 he presented the Administration's case for a tax increase before the House Ways and Means Committee. Schultze defended the surcharge as "temporary" and necessary to forestall a possible budget deficit of $25-$35 billion, part of which was due to inaccurate budgetary estimates made earlier in the year. He said that "failure to act responsibly" would result in inflation, record-high interest rates and a worsening of the country's balance of payments difficulties. Schultze also defended the Administration's refusal to specify spending cuts until Congress had passed the tax increase.

The Ways and Means Committee rejected the tax rise without budget cuts by a 20-5 vote in October. In November Schultze returned to the Committee with the Administration's pledge to make $4 billion in budget cuts, but the Committee's chairman, Rep. Wilbur Mills (D, Ark.) [*q.v.*], rejected the new proposal as insufficient and not specific enough. The matter stood at an impasse when Schultze retired from the Budget Bureau in January 1968. The 10% tax surcharge combined with $6 billion in spending cuts finally passed Congress in June 1968.

Schultze served as a member of Vice President Hubert Humphrey's [*q.v.*] economic task force during the Vice President's 1968 campaign for the presidency. After leaving the government Schultze became a senior fellow at the Brookings Institution and wrote lengthy analyses of the federal budget during the Nixon Administration. Acknowledging that as budget director he had failed to scrutinize closely enough spending by the Pentagon, Schultze became more critical of defense spending and military policy during the 1970s.

[TO]

SCOTT, HUGH D(OGGETT)

b. Nov. 11, 1900; Fredericksburg, Va.
Republican Senator, Pa., 1959-77.

After receiving a law degree from the University of Virginia in 1922, Scott opened a law practice in Philadelphia. Between 1926 and 1941 he was assistant district attorney of that city. Elected to the House of Representatives in 1940 and 1942, he served in the Naval Reserve during World War II and returned to Congress again in 1946. In 1948 and 1949 Scott chaired the Republican National Committee, and in 1952 he joined Dwight Eisenhower's personal staff, serving as chairman of the headquarters committee during the presidential campaign. General counsel to the National Committee from 1955 to 1960, Scott was first elected to the Senate in

1958. [See TRUMAN, EISENHOWER Volumes]

Scott, who considered himself a moderate Republican, successfully challenged the Old Guard leadership of the Republican Party in Pennsylvania. In 1962 he helped sponsor the young Rep. William Scranton (R, Pa.) [*q.v.*] as the Republican candidate for governor in a successful attempt to appeal to the state's relatively liberal electorate. [See KENNEDY Volume]

In 1964 Scott was disturbed by the success of conservative Sen. Barry Goldwater's (R, Ariz.) [*q.v.*] campaign for the Republican presidential nomination. Up for reelection, he feared that a Goldwater candidacy would lead to a big Democratic victory in November in which the Arizona Senator would drag other Republicans down to defeat. Scott helped form a "stop-Goldwater" drive, and in June 1964, after the collapse of New York Gov. Nelson A. Rockefeller's [*q.v.*] campaign effort, he successfully urged Gov. Scranton to oppose Goldwater for the nomination. In July Scott agreed to serve as Scranton's Convention manager. As part of an attempt to weaken the Goldwater forces, Scott sought to add an amendment to the Party platform repudiating "irresponsible" extremist groups, such as the John Birch Society, which was specifically named in the amendment. After a bitter Convention floor fight, the measure was rejected. Scott, in turn, refused to campaign for the national ticket following Goldwater's nomination. In Pennsylvania, where President Lyndon B. Johnson won a large majority, Scott narrowly defeated his liberal Democratic opponent, Genevieve Blatt. After the elections Scott urged replacement of the entire Party leadership. For the next four years Scott worked to get the Republican National Committee to adopt "moderate" positions and, in particular, his 1964 proposal condemning extremism.

In the Senate Scott was careful to vote along the moderately liberal lines that he thought best reflected his constituency. Scott's colleague, Sen. Joseph Clark (D, Pa.) [*q.v.*], remarked, "His ear is closer to the ground than the ear of any other politician I know. . . ." Although Scott often voted with a small group of Senate Republican moderates, most of whom represented urban Northeastern states, he also tried to keep close ties with the Republican majority. Therefore, he was able to play a more influential role in national Republican politics than such men as Sens. Jacob Javits (R, N.Y.) [*q.v.*] and Clifford Case (R, N.J.) [*q.v.*]. Scott's centrism was reflected in his 1968 voting record, for which the liberal Americans for Democratic Action (ADA) and the conservative Americans for Constitutional Action (ACA) accorded him ratings of 57 and 52, respectively. He also maintained his influence in the Republican Party by occasionally taking up highly partisan issues. As a member of the Senate Judiciary Committee, Scott led Republican forces in 1964 in seeking to expand the investigation of former Johnson aide Robert "Bobby" Baker [*q.v.*].

Scott was especially conscious of his black constitutency. In June 1964 he voted for cloture on discussion of Johnson's omnibus civil rights bill and supported the bill itself. In this case, unlike many times in the past, he was joined by a majority of Senate Republicans. In July 1965 Scott was one of only seven Republicans to vote for the Administration's omnibus housing bill, which because it offered federal subsidies to low-income families, was condemed as "socialistic" by many Republicans. In 1968 he enthusiastically supported the open housing bill.

Scott also stood apart from the Republican majority in opposing Johnson's Vietnam policies. In May 1967 the Senate Republican Policy Committee issued a white paper on Vietnam that expressed reservations about war aims but affirmed Republican solidarity with the President. However, Scott and two Republican colleagues, Sens. Jacob Javits and Charles Percy (R. Ill.) [*q.v.*], offered a stronger statement calling for a "greater effort" toward negotiations and warning against initiating actions likely to bring Communist China into the war. Still, Scott voted for the 1966 Vietnam war funds appropriations and never advocated unilateral U.S. withdrawal. He consistently supported defense spending and, conscious of his Jewish constituency in Philadelphia, attacked the State Department for failing to take a clearly pro-Israeli position in the 1967 Middle East crisis.

Although Scott originally backed Nelson Rockefeller for the 1968 Republican presidential nomination, he later worked hard for Richard Nixon [*q.v.*]. In September 1969 Scott was elected Senate minority leader. As chief Senate spokesman for the Nixon Administration his voting record and policy positions became increasingly conservative. In 1970 he was again narrowly reelected to the Senate. Compromised by his unquestioning defense of Nixon during the 1973-74 Watergate Investigations and by the 1975 disclosure that he had been receiving an annual fee from the Gulf Oil Corp., Scott announced in December 1975 that he would not seek another term in 1976. [See NIXON Volume]

[JCH]

SCRANTON, WILLIAM W(ARREN)

b. July 19, 1917; Madison, Conn.
Governor, Pa., 1963-67.

Scion of a family of Pennsylvania steelmakers, William W. Scranton attended the Hotchkiss School and graduated from Yale and Yale Law School. After Army service during World War II, Scranton worked to stem the economic decline of his hometown, Scranton, Pa., and served as president of a cable television company. As an aide to the Secretary of State from 1959 to 1960, Scranton represented the United States at NATO conferences. Local Republican leaders persuaded Scranton to run for Congress in 1960 in the 10th district, and he handily defeated his incumbent Democratic opponent. In 1962 a unanimous state Republican leadership urged Scranton to run for governor. Winning election with 55.4% of the vote, he immediately emerged as a dark-horse contender for the 1964 Republican presidential nomination. [See KENNEDY Volume]

During the spring of 1964 moderate Republicans turned to Scranton as a potential nominee as conservative Sen. Barry Goldwater's (R, Ariz.) [*q.v.*] strength increased and other liberal or middle-of-the-road GOP candidates faltered. Michigan Gov. George W. Romney [*q.v.*], another prominent dark-horse possibility, declined to make the race. Ambassador to South Vietnam Henry Cabot Lodge [*q.v.*] won the March 10 New Hampshire primary in an upset write-in campaign, but despite his subsequent triumphs in New Jersey and Massachusetts, he refused to return from Saigon to run personally for the nomination. New York Gov. Nelson A. Rockefeller [*q.v.*] defeated Lodge in the May 15 Oregon primary only to lose narrowly to Goldwater in the important June 2 California contest.

Goldwater's nomination now appeared highly probable. But the prospect of his selection by the Republican National Convention alarmed many liberal and moderate GOP leaders, frightened by the Senator's accommodation to the Party's extreme right wing, his opposition to the 1964 Civil Rights bill and his advocacy of the use of tactical nuclear weapons in limited warfare situations. The youthful Scranton appeared the only candidate capable of rallying Party moderates to halt the Goldwater nomination drive. Through the spring of 1964, however, Scranton had declared himself unavailable for the nomination. He had actively discouraged primary write-in efforts on his behalf and fared poorly in preference polls of Republican voters.

In the week following the California primary, Scranton determined to seek the nomination, buoyed in part by what he thought was the endorsement of former President Dwight D. Eisenhower [*q.v.*] offered in a June 6 meeting at the General's Gettysburg, Pa., farm. With national newspaper headlines announcing Eisenhower's support, the Pennsylvania Governor prepared to make his candidacy official on the nationally televised *Face the Nation* program the next day. A few hours before the telecast, Eisenhower phoned Scranton and informed him that he could not be part of any "cabal" to stop Goldwater. In the ensuing confusion Scranton declined to announce his official candidacy. The telecast was, in the words of his own staff, "a complete and utter bomb." Four days later Scranton declared his candidacy, following Goldwater's vote against cloture in the Senate debate on the 1964 civil rights bill and a more encouraging telephone call from Eisenhower.

Despite his apparent irresolution Scranton's strength among Republican voters rose dramatically with his official entry in the campaign. His standing in Gallup polls of GOP members rose from 4% in May to 18% in late June. Paired directly against Goldwater with no other candidates listed, Scranton led his rival 55% to 34%. The Governor criticized Goldwater's "recklessness" and "philosophy of shoot-from-the-hip rather than think-from-from-the-head." Scranton strongly endorsed the 1964 Civil Rights Act, which Goldwater voted against. Although the Pennsylvania Governor won endorsements from Rockefeller, Lodge and much of the Eastern Republican Establishment and spent over $800,000 in a month-long search for Convention support, he captured few of the more than 600 delegates already pledged to Goldwater. Scranton had hoped that key Midwestern leaders would keep their delegations pledged to favorite-son candidates, but Ohio Gov. James A. Rhodes's [*q.v.*] release of his delegation to Goldwater on July 9 effectively ended the Pennsylvanian's dim prospects.

When the Republican Convention met in San Francisco on July 13, Scranton's staff composed a highly controversial open letter to Goldwater demanding a public debate between the two candidates. The letter, which accused the Arizona Senator's managers of regarding the delegates as "little more than a flock of chickens whose necks will be wrung at will," merely increased Goldwater's ranks. On July 15 Goldwater won the nomination on the first ballot with 883 votes to Scranton's 214.

Although Scranton immediately endorsed and later campaigned for Goldwater, the bitterness of the pre-Convention clash weakened the Party's campaign effort. As late as June Goldwater had sought Scranton as his vice presidential running mate, but at the Convention the Republican presidential candidate instead chose the little-known conservative Rep. William E. Miller (R, N.Y.) [*q.v.*]. During the fall President Johnson attacked Goldwater on many of the same grounds that the Republican moderates had used in the spring. "Rockefeller and Scranton had drawn up the indictment," wrote Theodore H. White in *The Making of the President 1964*, "Lyndon Johnson was the prosecutor."

After Goldwater's disastrous showing in November, Scranton called for the exclusion of right-wing and racial extremists from the GOP. In August 1965 Scranton warned that "there is a radical fringe which should never find a spiritual home in either of America's two great political parties, and the Republican Party ought to stop the hopeless task of trying to accommodate them." Barred by state law from a second gubernatorial term, Scranton told reporters in June 1966 that he would not run "ever again for any public office under any circumstances." Scranton's unqualified renunciation removed him from speculation over the 1968 Republican ticket. Instead, in August 1967 he announced his support of George Romney for the presidential nomination.

Scranton visited the Middle East for President-elect Richard Nixon in December 1968. At the Jordan River he told reporters that the U.S. should follow a "more evenhanded" policy toward Israel and its Arab antagonists. His remark set off a protest by Israeli leaders, some of whom feared that the new Administration would limit America's commitment to Israel. A Nixon aide denied that Scranton spoke for the incoming Administration, yet the ex-Governor refused to retract his comment and insisted that the new Administration correct "the impression in the Middle East" that the U.S. "is only interested in Israel." President Gerald Ford named Scranton ambassador to the U.N. in 1976. [See NIXON Volume]

[JLB]

For further information:

Robert D. Novak, *The Agony of the G.O.P. 1964* (New York, 1965).

Theodore H. White, *The Making of the President 1964* (New York, 1965).

Neal R. Peirce, *The Megastates of America* (New York, 1972).

SEABORG, GLENN T(HEODORE)
b. April 19, 1912, Ishpeming, Mich.
Chemist; Chairman, U.S. Atomic Energy Commission, January 1961-August 1971.

After completing his doctorate in nuclear chemistry at the University of California, Berkeley, Seaborg joined the faculty there. In 1940 he discovered the element plutonium, the heaviest known at the time, which was a source of fissionable material for nuclear energy. He joined the Manhattan Project's work on the atomic bomb in 1941 and served on the Atomic Energy Commission's (AEC) general advisory board from 1946 to 1950. Returning to Berkeley after the war, his research uncovered several more transuranium elements. Seaborg won the 1951 Nobel Prize for chemistry and the AEC's 1959 Enrico Fermi Award.

President Kennedy appointed Seaborg to head the AEC in 1961, and he was soon involved in a controversy over the possible separation of the Commission's operational and regulatory functions. Seaborg held that separation was possible within the agency at the management level, a position which the Joint Congressional Committee on Atomic Energy later approved. Following the resumption of nuclear tests by the Soviet Union in September 1961 he advocated resumption of U.S. atmospheric tests, but he testified in favor of the nuclear test ban treaty when Senate hearings were held in August 1963. [See KENNEDY Volume]

The responsibilities of the AEC, whose annual appropriations approached $2.5 billion, expanded greatly in the 1960s. In March 1965 Seaborg urged a subcommittee of the Joint Congressional Committee to approve a 15-year program for developing more powerful atom smashers at a proposed cost of $6 billion. The AEC announced its selection in December 1966 of Weston, Ill. as the site for a 200 bev (billion electron volt) atom smasher to be built over the next eight years. He also told the committee in March 1965 that the AEC and the state of California had agreed to develop a prototype "seed-blanket" reactor, which might also include an experimental plant for desalination.

In January 1965 Seaborg told the Joint Congressional Committee that the U.S. should support Plowshare, an international program for developing peaceful uses of atomic energy. Warning of the dangers of nuclear proliferation in July 1965, Seaborg urged an agreement "to stop the spread of nuclear weapons to additional countries beyond the five that have them." The AEC withdrew authorization for private research into the gas-centrifuge method of obtaining enriched uranium in March 1967. This was viewed as part of the Commission's effort to prevent non-nuclear nations from obtaining information on the techniques for producing fissionable atomic material. The U.S. would supply other nations' atomic fuel needs, Seaborg asserted. In June the AEC signed a contract to this effect with a private nuclear power plant in Sweden. The AEC agreed to process and supply enriched uranium for the plant, and it was hoped that other nations might be dissuaded from building their own uranium plants.

In the late 1960s critics of the AEC raised questions about the health and safety of atomic workers and residents of areas near atomic plants. Hearings held by the Department of Labor indicated that uranium miners were suffering from a "cancer epidemic," and a near-disaster occurred in October 1966 at a Lagoona Beach, Mich., plant. A nuclear reactor there overheated and began leaking radiation, leading some scientists to doubt the effectiveness of existing safeguards. Another issue which aroused great public concern was the disposal of potentially dangerous radioactive waste. A 1966 national Academy of Sciences review condemned the AEC's disposal practices, but the AEC did not release this report to the public until 1970. An AEC spokesman explained that the document had been withheld because it "went beyond its purpose" and "commented at length on operational activities."

Seaborg remained chairman of the AEC until 1971, when he returned to the University of California. James Schlesinger succeeded him as AEC chairman. [See NIXON Volume]

[MDB]

SEALE, BOBBY
b. Oct. 22, 1937; Dallas, Tex.
Chairman, Black Panther Party, 1966- .

The son of a laborer, Seale grew up in Dallas and Oakland, Calif. He dropped out of high school to enlist in the Air Force but was given a dishonorable discharge after becoming involved in a fight with an officer. Returning to Oakland, Seale finished high school at night and enrolled in Merritt College, a two-year institution. There he met Huey Newton [*q.v.*], another black student deeply interested, like Seale, in black problems. The two studied the ideas of Malcolm X [*q.v.*] and other angry black authors and in October 1966 founded the Black Panther Party. Seale was chairman and Newton was minister of defense of the new organization.

The primary stated concern of the heavily armed Panthers was to protect ghetto residents from police violence, which Newton and Seale viewed as the most obvious form of external control over the black community. In May 1967 Seale led a demonstration of armed Panthers in the California State Assembly, which was considering gun control legislation opposed by the Panthers. The incident won the Panthers national attention and helped increase their membership to about 2,000 during the late 1960s. Though an all-black organization, the Panthers welcomed cooperation with white radicals. Seale was official leader of the Party but at first had less to do with internal Panther affairs than Newton. Instead, he sought to establish contacts with other radicals in the peace and black movements. In 1968 the Panthers joined several white radical groups to form the Peace and Freedom Party.

Seale went to Chicago in August 1968 to participate in demonstrations at the Democratic National Convention; he later became one of the famous "Chicago Eight" who were indicted for violating the anti-riot provision of the new Civil Rights Act. The trial, which began in March 1969, became a radical cause celebre. For his repeated outbursts against the judge, Seale was at one point ordered gagged and bound to his chair. On Nov. 5 Seale was sentenced to four years in prison for contempt of court, and his case was severed from that of the others. The government later requested, however, that the charges against him be dropped.

With Newton in jail from 1968 to 1970 for the shooting of a policeman, Seale took a greater part in internal Panther affairs. In early 1969 he announced a drive to rid the Panthers of "provocateur agents, kooks and avaricious fools" seeking to use the organization for their own purposes. (It was later revealed that the Federal Bureau of Investigation had, in fact, placed agents in the Panthers in an attempt to disrupt the organization.) In 1971 Seale went on trial in New Haven, Conn., on charges of ordering the 1969 execution of a Panther member suspected of being a government informer. The trial began in March and again aroused the anger of many radicals, who accused the government of trying to "get Bobby." When the jury failed to reach a verdict in May, the judge dismissed the charges against Seale, claiming that "massive publicity" made a new trial impossible.

Free from legal entanglements, Seale returned to Oakland and leadership of the Panthers. He cooperated with Newton in reorienting the Party from "armed defense" to community action projects, such as health clinics for ghetto residents and a free breakfast program for school children. In 1973 Seale ran for mayor of Oakland as a Democrat, finishing second among nine candidates with 43,710 votes. Although he lost the race, Seale's surprisingly strong showing indicated to some observers that the "new" Panthers had shifted their strategy to organizing ghetto residents, with the aim of gaining political power and community self-control.

In 1970, while he was at the height of his political celebrity, Seale published a book, *Seize the Time: The Story of the Black Panther Party and Huey P. Newton*. [See NIXON Volume]

[SLG]

For further information:
Gene Marine, *Black Panthers* (New York, 1969).

SHAFER, RAYMOND P(HILIP)

b. March 5, 1917, New Castle, Pa.
Governor, Pa., 1967-71.

After a successful business career in cable television, Shafer served two terms in the Pennsylvania Senate before running for the lieutenant governorship with Republican gubernatorial candidate William W. Scranton [*q.v.*] in 1962. Scranton, limited by law to one term, backed Shafer as his successor in the 1966 election. Shafer, who also enjoyed the support of Sen. Hugh Scott (R, Pa.) [*q.v.*] and the powerful Mellon family, Shafer pledged to "Keep the Good Things Happening in Pennsylvania." Running on a platform that backed open housing legislation and opposed right-to-work laws, he defeated wealthy Democrat Milton Shapp with 53% of the vote.

Shafer's first major project was to revise the state's antiquated 93-year-old constitution. Because of six previous rejections of constitutional reform (the last in 1963), he was given little chance for success. However, in a May 1967 referendum Pennsylvania voters approved the convocation of a two-month constitutional convention. This success strengthened Shafer's leadership in the resurgent Pennsylvania Republican Party.

Shafer expanded the state's commitment to higher education. Seeing education as the key to ending Pennsylvania's economic stagnation, he continued the Scranton precedent of heavily subsidizing state-supported universities and technical schools. As a highly industrialized state, Pennsylvania was exceptionally vulnerable to environmental pollution. To combat this problem, Shafer created a new state Department of Environmental Resources and established a strike force of attorneys to stop pollution immediate by the liberal use of injunctions rather than time-consuming criminal prosecutions and fines. In January 1969 Shafer announced his proposal for a state income tax, which his fellow Republicans viewed as damaging to the prospects for continued Republican control of the state house. This measure was subsequently enacted into law by his Democratic successor, Milton Shapp.

At the Republican National Convention in 1968, Shafer urged the Platform Committee to draft a Vietnam war plank calling for a "de-Americanization of foreign involvements wherever our influence has become a way of life." At the Convention Shafer nominated New York Gov. Nelson Rockefeller [*q.v.*] for president.

Shafer returned to private life in 1971. In 1972 President Nixon appointed him chairman of the National Commission on Marijuana and Drug Abuse. The Commission's final report urged that the issue of marijuana be deemphasized, since it did not present "a major threat to public health." In 1975 Shafer became counselor to Vice President Rockefeller.

[TJC]

SHANKER, ALBERT

b. Sept. 18, 1928; New York, N.Y.
Secretary, United Federation of Teachers, 1960-64; President, United Federation of Teachers, 1964- ; Vice President, American Federation of Teachers, 1959-74.

Shanker was born on New York's Lower East Side and grew up in Queens. His parents were unionists and strong supporters of the New Deal. Shanker chaired the Campus Socialist Club at the University of Illinois in Urbana when he was an undergraduate there. While still a graduate student in philosophy and mathematics at Columbia University, Shanker began working in 1952 as a substitute teacher in the New York City school system. He soon abandoned his studies, took a permanent teaching position and became active in the Teachers Guild, the New York affiliate of the American Federation of Teachers (AFT).

Shanker worked closely with AFT organizer David Selden to enlarge and strengthen the small union and was hired as a full-time AFT organizer in 1959. In March 1960 he helped merge a militant high school teachers group with the Guild to form the United Federation of Teachers (UFT). A one-day strike by 5,000 UFT members in November 1960 forced the New York City school board to hold a union recognition election the next year. The UFT decisively won the election and, against the advice of Shanker and other leaders, successfully struck for higher wages in April 1962. These early strikes attracted 53,000 new members to the AFT, over half in New York City.

In May 1964 Shanker was elected UFT president. He negotiated in September of the next year a contract settlement that gave teachers an average annual increase of $800 in wages and benefits. Although wages were also involved in the negotiations for a new contract in 1967, it was primarily the inability to agree on non-economic issues that led to a 14-day strike that September. The Board of Education sought to reduce teacher preparation time in elementary schools, change sick-leave provisions and gain greater control over teacher assignments, while the UFT wanted an expansion of the More Effective Schools (MES) program for elementary school compensatory education, smaller teaching loads and classes and authority for teachers to remove disruptive students from their classrooms.

UFT teachers voted Sept. 10 to reject a mediation panel contract proposal that the Board of Education had adopted. The next day, opening day of the school year, 46,000 of the city's 58,000 teachers went out on strike. The strike was settled on Sept. 28 when the teachers accepted a 26-month contract, establishing a salary range slightly higher than the mediation panel proposal. The Board of Education agreed to set aside $10 million for the development of new programs for elementary schools but did not commit itself specifically to an extension of the MES program. On Oct. 4 the UFT was fined $150,000 for violating New York State's recently passed Taylor Law prohibiting strikes by public employes. Shanker was convicted of contempt of court for violating an injunction barring the strike, and on Dec. 20, he began serving a 15-day sentence.

The 1967 strike, the first extended strike by New York's regular teachers, was followed within a year by a series of four strikes over issues related to school decentralization. In July 1967 the Board of Education, under pressure from parents and community leaders in Harlem and elsewhere, had established three demonstration school districts in which local school boards were given some of the power previously exercised by the central board. The districts were all in predominantly poor, non-white neighborhoods, but they were widely viewed as a test for a possible future city-wide school decentralization plan. One such plan was proposed in November 1967 by a panel headed by Ford Foundation President McGeorge Bundy [*q.v.*]. The Bundy proposal would have given local school boards the power to hire new teachers and make future tenure decisions. Various government agencies and other private groups proposed other decentralization plans as well during that winter and spring, encouraged by Mayor John V. Lindsay [*q.v.*], who actively supported decentralization.

The UFT initially cooperated with decentralization planning, but it opposed any plan that eliminated central Board of Education control over the hiring and firing of teachers. The union feared that teachers' working conditions and job security would be threatened by powerful local school boards, especially in ghetto areas where dissatisfied minority-group parents would be running districts where, as elsewhere, the teaching force was overwhelmingly white. In the existing experimental districts relations between the UFT and the local boards had seriously deteriorated during the 1967 strike.

In May 1968 the governing board of the largest of the three demonstration districts, Ocean Hill-Brownsville in Brooklyn, ordered 13 tenured teachers and six supervisors transferred out of the district. District administrator, Rhody McCoy, charged that the 19 were trying to "sabotage" the decentralization experiment. The Board of Education said the transfers were illegal, but when it tried to overrule the local board, a series of community boycotts and demonstrations began. The UFT claimed that the transfers violated a contractual right to "due process," and 350 teachers in the district struck for the last five weeks of the school year, demanding that the transfers be rescinded. In late May, in the middle of the Ocean Hill-Brownsville controversy, Shanker led a massive UFT lobbying effort in Albany that successfully defeated an attempt to pass a strong city wide decentralization bill, and a much weaker compromise measure was passed.

Beginning on Sept. 9 the UFT called a series of three citywide strikes to protest the transfer of the Ocean Hill-Brownsville teachers and to seek changes in the Board of Education's interim decentralization plan. On the eve of the strikes Shanker said, "Decentralization is fine but not at the expense of the rights we have won and not with the smashing of the union." The final and longest of the strikes ended on Nov. 19 with an agreement by the city to reinstate the transferred teachers and give authority over Ocean Hill-Brownsville to a state trustee.

Shanker was convicted of contempt of court in February 1969 for defying court orders during the 1968 strikes. He appealed his case to the Supreme Court on the ground that he had been denied a jury trial. The Court upheld the conviction, and Shanker began serving a 15-day sentence on May 15, 1970.

The 1968 strikes resulted in a dramatic increase in racial tension in the New York area. Shanker made a major issue out of alleged black anti-Semitism when he had the UFT reproduce and widely circulate anti-Semitic material originally distributed in the Ocean Hill-Brownsville area. Teacher-parent relations deteriorated when many parents, often with the help of non-striking teachers, set up their own schools, sometimes crossing UFT picket lines or breaking into locked schools to do so. New York's liberal and intellectual communities were split over the strike. In her history of the 1968 strike, *Pickets, Parents and Power,* Barbara Carter concluded, "Like an evil vortex it drew in almost everyone—city agencies, labor groups, Jewish Communities—not only pitting them against each other but splintering them within, wheels within wheels, spinning sparks long after the strike was over."

Although Shanker emerged from the strike a controversial figure, the majority of the UFT membership strongly backed his leadership, and opposition groups within the union were isolated and ineffective. In addition to heading the UFT, Shanker was the most powerful figure in the UFT 's parent union, the AFT, since he both headed the largest local in the union and led the dominant Progessive Caucus. Although Shanker supported David Selden's successful candidacy for the AFT presidency in 1968, the two men later broke, and in 1974 Shanker easily defeated Selden to become president of the union. In 1973, while still only an AFT vice president, Shanker was appointed a vice president and member of the executive council of the AFL-CIO. [See Nixon Volume]

[JBF]

For further information:

Maurice R. Berube and Marilyn Gittell, eds., *Confrontation at Ocean Hill-Brownsville: The New York School Strikes of 1968* (New York, 1969).

Robert J. Braun, *Teachers and Power: The Story of the American Federation of Teachers* (New York, 1972).

Barbara Carter, *Pickets, Parents and Power: The Story Behind the New York City Teachers' Strike* (New York, 1971).

Stephen Cole, *The Unionization of Teachers: A Case Study of the UFT* (New York, 1969).

SHARP, ULYSSES S. GRANT

b. April 2, 1906; Chinook, Mont.
Commander of U.S. Armed Forces in the Pacific, August 1964-July 1968.

A 1927 graduate of Annapolis, Sharp commanded destroyers during World War II. He advanced through the ranks and in 1963 was named admiral and commander in chief of the U.S. Pacific fleet. In July 1964 he was designated commander of all U.S. military operations in the Pacific.

On Aug. 2 and 4, 1964, shortly after Sharp assumed command, two North Vietnamese torpedo boats were reported to have attacked two American destroyers in the Gulf of Tonkin off the coast of North Vietnam. According to documents later reprinted in the *Pentagon Papers,* Secretary of Defense Robert S. McNamara [*q.v.*] called Sharp in Honolulu advising him to check carefully to ascertain whether an attack had actually taken place. Initial reports from Capt. John J. Herrick, commander of the destroyer task force patrolling the waters off North Vietnam had been vague. On Aug. 4 Sharp called the Joint Chiefs of Staff, claiming that on the basis of "additional information" he could state positively that an attack had taken place. On that day Navy planes retaliated, bombing North Vietnamese coastal bases and oil installations. In response to the Tonkin Gulf incident, Congress overwhelmingly passed a resolution on Aug. 7 granting the President broad authority to deal with the deteriorating situation in Vietnam. However, in 1968 an investigation by the Senate Foreign Relations Committee convinced many senators and congressmen that the U.S. had either over-reacted or actually provoked the attack by the North Vietnamese in the Tonkin Gulf. Sharp was not called before the Senate Committee, but he continued to maintain that the bombing of North Vietnam was the appropriate response to an entirely unprovoked attack against U.S. warships on the high seas.

In December 1964 the Joint Chiefs of Staff ordered Sharp to begin making plans for future air strikes in the event that North Vietnam again attempted to attack U.S. forces. South Vietnamese Communist guerrillas attacked a U.S. military installation at Pleiku on Feb. 7, 1965 and three days later shelled the American installation at Qui Nhon. American bombers once again attacked the North; these raids were a response not to North Vietnamese aggression, but to that of their Communist allies in the South. Significantly, the raids were linked not to any particular incident but to "the larger pattern of aggression of North Vietnam." In a memorandum dated Feb. 17, 1965, Adm. Sharp argued that the raids should be conceived of not as reprisals but as "pressure . . . to convince Hanoi and Peiking of the prohibitive cost of their program of subversion, insurgency, and aggression in Southeast Asia." In February air raids over the North were sporadic, but by mid-March they had become routine. Operation Rolling Thunder, the air war against North Vietnam, had begun.

On March 21 Sharp recommended that bombing be undertaken not simply to demoralize the North Vietnamese but to cut their strategic supply lines to the South. This proposal also won the approval of the Pentagon and strategic bombing began in April 1965.

During 1965 Sharp, along with his subordinate Gen. William Westmoreland [*q.v.*], commander of U.S. troops in Vietnam, greatly expanded the American involvement in the ground war. On Feb. 24, 1965 Sharp urged the Joint Chiefs to immediately deploy two Marine battalions and one fighter squadron to South Vietnam to prevent the "tragedy" of a catastrophic Communist attack at Da Nang. This request was opposed by U.S. Ambassador to South Vietnam Maxwell D. Taylor [q.v.], who argued that the deployment of combat troops would only lead to requests for more troops, and that two battalions would not significantly alter the military situation. Nevertheless, on March 8, 3,500 U.S. Marines landed at Da Nang. In subsequent months Sharp supported requests by Westmoreland that troops be sent to various strategic bases along the Vietnamese coast and into the central highlands. Sharp requested another 75 battalions in December, and by 1966 there were 367,000 American soldiers in Vietnam. Supported by Sharp, Westmoreland won the power to deploy these men anywhere in the country.

Throughout 1966 and 1967 Sharp demanded that the Johnson Administration permit American pilots to bomb a wider range of targets in North Vietnam—oil refineries, electric power stations, industrial plants and the harbor at Haiphong. Gradually, the number of targets was increased. However, within the Defense Department, McNamara and other civilians doubted that bombing could effectively destroy the ability of the North to make war or send men and material to the South. In the summer of 1966 McNamara proposed that a series of electric sensors and land mines be constructed near the Demilitarized Zone as a barrier to prevent infiltration of enemy troops from the North. Adm. Sharp denounced the idea as "impractical" and thought its implementation would be used to justify reduction or elimination of the air war.

Sharp consistently maintained that the North Vietnamese would negotiate only if they were incapable of waging war. Believing that bomber attacks could force them into submission, Sharp opposed all the bombing halts called by the Johnson Administration during the course of the war.

Sharp retired in the summer of 1968 to become a consultant to the president of Teledyne Ryan Aeronautics Company of San Diego, California. He also worked on a book on the air war in Vietnam. "The war was lost in Washington," he later said, "not on the battlefield."

[JLW]

For further information:
U. S. Department of Defense, *The Pentagon Papers*, Senator Gravel Edition (Boston, 1971), Vol. III and IV.

SHELTON, ROBERT M(ARVIN), JR.

b. June 12, 1929; Tuscaloosa, Ala.
Imperial Wizard, United Klans of America, Inc., Knights of the Ku Klux Klan.

During the 1950s Shelton worked in a tire manufacturing plant and as a tire salesman while serving as an Alabama officer of the United Klans of America. In 1961 he was elected the national leader, Imperial Wizard, of the organization.

When Shelton assumed command of the group it was small and fragmented, but the Klan grew in the mid-1960s, after the passage of the Civil Rights Act of 1964 and the Voting Rights Act of 1965 and the abandonment of massive resistance to desegregation by Southern state and local governments. In the fall of 1967 the B'nai Brith Anti-Defamation League estimated that the total membership of about twelve Klan organizations had increased to 55,000 from about 20,000 early in 1964. The United Klans, according to the League, was the largest and best organized of the groups.

Shelton stated that the fundamental purpose of the Klan was to preserve white civilization by resisting integration. He denied, however, that the Klan espoused violence, contending that the group pursued its goals by educating its members, supporting political candidates and promoting white voter registration. Shelton tried to improve the image of the Klan by opening its meetings to outsiders and seeking middle class recruits.

However, members of the various Klan groups were implicated in a number of acts of violence against civil rights workers in the mid-1960s. In March 1965 Mrs. Viola Liuzzo, a civil rights worker, was shot and killed in a car during the Selma to Montgomery march. Four members of the United Klans were arrested in connection with the murder. Shelton asserted that she would not have been killed if she had stayed at home instead of "sitting on the front seat with a young buck nigra."

President Johnson responded to the slaying and arrests by denouncing the Klan as a "hooded society of bigots," and the House Un-American Activities Committee (HUAC) began an investigation of the Klan in October 1965.

Shelton was the first witness called before the Committee. He appeared but refused its request to produce Klan records. In January 1966 the Committee cited him for contempt of Congress. The House supported the contempt citation the next month by a vote of 344 to 28, with most of the opposition coming from liberal congressmen who had sought HUAC's abolition. In October 1966 Shelton was convicted in federal court and sentenced to one year in jail and a $10,000 fine. The following September, while Shelton was appealing the verdict, he was reelected Imperial Wizard at a national "Klanvocation" of the United Klans.

The U.S. Supreme Court upheld Shelton's conviction in January 1969, and he began serving his prison sentence the following month. By the time Shelton was released from jail in November 1970, the United Klans' membership had declined substantially from its peak in 1967. But the Imperial Wizard declared that he would continue his Klan activities because the nation was chained to an "infested black carcass that is dragging us down to low morals."

[MLL]

For further information:
Margaret Long, "The Imperial Wizard Explains the Klan," *The New York Times Magazine* (July 5, 1964), p. 8+.

SHOUP, DAVID M(ONROE)

b. Dec. 30, 1904; Battle Ground, Ind.
Commandant, Marine Corps, January 1960-December 1963.

A Medal of Honor winner in World War II, Shoup served in command positions in the Pacific and at the Pentagon during the post-war period. After the drowning of six Marines on a disciplinary night march at the Parris Island, S.C., boot camp, he was named to the newly created post of inspector-general of recruit training in May 1956. In 1959 President Dwight D. Eisenhower, passing over 10 generals with more seniority, nominated him as commandant of the Marine Corps for the four-year term mandated by law.

During the opening days of the Kennedy Administration in January 1961, Shoup counseled that the proposed invasion of Cuba was militarily unfeasible. In December 1961 he became a central figure in the Senate Preparedness Subcommittee's investigation of military and civilian indoctrination programs and of State Department censorship of the military. Shoup testified that he approved of such censorship as necessary in an era of sensitive diplomatic situations. He said that his major role was in training combat-ready troops and that he had no part to play in the indoctrination of either his Marines or civilians against the "menace of Communism." In August 1963 Shoup testified that he could support the limited nuclear test ban treaty if the U.S. maintained facilities for monitoring violations and resuming atomic tests. At the end of 1963 he retired as commandant and became director of the United States Life Insurance Company [See KENNEDY Volume]

During the Johnson era the former commandant became a vocal critic of the Vietnam war and a symbol to some of the depth of American dissatisfaction with the handling of the conflict. In an interview with Rep. William F. Ryan (D, N.Y.) [*q.v.*] over an New York radio station, Shoup called the idea that a military presence in Vietnam was necessary for American defense "sheer poppycock." He described the war as a civil conflict between "those crooks in Saigon" and Vietnamese nationals striving for a better life. In December 1967 Shoup urged President Johnson to announce that American military operations would cease when peace talks started and to ask North Vietnamese President Ho Chi Minh to set the time and place for negotiations. He cautioned that the U.S. could achieve a military victory over North Vietnam but only by committing "genocide on that poor little country." The war, Shoup believed, had to be won through peace talks.

Increasingly, Shoup became critical of what he believed to be growing military interference in civilian policymaking decisions. In 1969 he warned that the military leadership of the U.S. was turning the country into a "militaristic and aggressive nation." He asserted that many of the policies of the Vietnam war were due to the military's desire for glory and that the lack of credibility in reporting the war could be traced to the "hocus pocus" of the armed forces.

[EWS]

SHRIVER, R(OBERT) SARGENT, JR.

b. Nov. 9, 1915; Westminster, Md.
Director, Office of Economic Opportunity, February 1964-February 1968; Ambassador to France, February 1968-March 1970.

Born into a wealthy and socially prominent Maryland family, Shriver was educated at Yale, where he received an LL.B. in 1941. After serving in the Navy during World War II, he worked for Joseph P. Kennedy as assistant manager of the Chicago Merchandise Mart. Shriver married Kennedy's daughter Eunice in 1953 and served on the Chicago Board of Education from 1955 to 1960. During that period he became active in Midwestern Democratic politics; when his brother-in-law, Sen. John F. Kennedy, ran for president in 1960, Shriver served as a liaison between various offices of the campaign staff. In return he was assigned to develop plans for the Peace Corps after Kennedy's inauguration, and he became the agency's first director when it was established in 1961. [See KENNEDY Volume]

Shriver remained at the head of the Peace Corps until 1966. He assumed new responsibilities in 1964, however, in connection with President Johnson's War on Poverty. Eager to dramatize his commitment to improving the circumstances of the nation's poor, Johnson decided to create a new federal agency devoted entirely to poverty problems. Shriver, whose work with the Peace Corps had given him experience in setting up this type of innovative agency, was chosen by the President to establish the new organization. On Feb. 1, 1964 Johnson named Shriver director of the Office of Economic Opportunity (OEO).

Shriver not only had to launch the organization but also had to define its role. Existing federal programs aimed at assisting the poor included manpower training grants from the Department of Labor, rural development grants from the Department of Agriculture and public health projects in the Department of Health, Education and Welfare. Shriver, backed by Johnson, argued that the antipoverty effort could not succeed simply by increasing the levels of such assistance; new approaches were needed to mobilize public support and especially to stimulate the poor themselves. Shriver also recognized the necessity of pacifying the many congressmen and state and local officials who feared that the OEO would develop into a huge, centrally directed "poverty bureaucracy."

These considerations were among those leading to the creation of OEO's Community Action Program (CAP), an effort to encourage participation by local leaders and poor people in the planning and execution of antipoverty projects. CAP supervisor Jack Conway [*q.v.*], appointed Shriver's deputy in October 1964, channeled OEO funds into a number of community-based activities, ranging from job training and preschool education to health clinics and legal-aid services. Some of these projects were directed by local officials, others by community groups; most were experimental, and many failed to achieve their objectives. Nevertheless, Shriver preferred community action to centrally administered forms of assistance, because the former involved a maximum number of politicians and civic leaders in the work of OEO.

At the height of antipoverty spending under the Johnson Administration, community action projects absorbed over half of OEO's $2 billion budget. Other programs sponsored by OEO included the Job Corps, which provided work and training for unemployed teenagers, and VISTA (Volunteers in Service to America), which enlisted young people to work in projects helping Indians, migrant farm workers, the Appalachian poor and other minority groups.

OEO began its work in 1964 amidst great official optimism; some of the agency's enthusiasts predicted that the War on Poverty would be won by 1976. Problems soon arose, however, that opened the program to attack from both within and without. Increased military spending in Vietnam after 1965 meant that the amount of funds available to poverty projects stagnated or declined. The OEO budget for 1967, originally set at $4 billion, was cut by Congress to $1.75 billion. According to political scientist Robert J. Lampman, the bewildering variety of OEO projects and the lack of a clearly defined overall goal convinced many voters that no amount of spending would improve the agency's performance. Sen. Everett Dirksen (R, Ill.) [*q.v.*], a leading Republican spokesman, denounced the antipoverty program as "the very acme of waste and extravagance and unorganization and disorganization."

In addition to such external criticism, OEO had to cope with internal bureaucratic conflicts that developed among agencies competing for the same antipoverty funds. The large number of politicians and community leaders whom Shriver had involved in the OEO became a liability when the time came to apportion the agency's limited budget. OEO itself, moreover, was constantly in conflict with the established federal and state bureaucracies that had administered assistance programs before the War on Poverty. Shriver was not adept in handling such clashes. According to Washington journalists Rowland Evans and Robert Novak [*q.v.*] the OEO leader inspired great devotion among his subordinates but lacked the aggressiveness of a bureaucratic "empire-builder." Furthermore, the struggles in which Shriver had to engage took time and effort and inevitably dampened the initial enthusiasm of the antipoverty campaign.

Among those most disillusioned with the War on Poverty were the poor themselves, especially those who had helped to organize community action projects. Encouraged by Johnson and Shriver to expect the rapid elimination of poverty problems, representatives of the poor were enraged to find these problems not only remaining but in some cases worsening. Many community workers blamed the shortcomings of the antipoverty program—including budget cuts and inadequate funding—on OEO and Shriver. At a conference of community action groups held in Washington in April 1966, delegates accused Shriver of "lying" and "pussyfooting" on poverty issues. Shriver said he was "not a bit ashamed of what has been done by the War on Poverty," but shouts from the audience soon caused him to walk out of the meeting.

In February 1968 Shriver left the OEO to accept an appointment as ambassador to France. He served in that position until March 1970, when he took up private law practice in Washington and New York. In 1972 Shriver ran for vice president on the Democratic ticket with Sen. George McGovern (D, S.D.) [*q.v.*]. He made an unsuccessful bid for the Democratic presidential nomination in 1976. [See NIXON Volume]

[SLG]

For further information:
Eli Ginzberg and Robert M. Solow, eds. *The Great Society: Lessons for the Future* (New York, 1974).

SHUMAN, CHARLES B(AKER)

b. April 27, 1907; Sullivan, Ill.
President, American Farm Bureau Federation, 1954-70.

Shuman spent his boyhood on his family's Illinois farm and then went to the University of Illinois to study agriculture. He was active in farm organizations in the 1930s and became a director of the American Farm Bureau Federation in 1945 and its elected president in 1954. An outspoken defender of the free enterprise system, Shuman helped reverse Farm Bureau enthusiasm for the price supports and production controls of the New Deal. The Bureau subsequently took the position that farmers would fare better in a free market than under the government-subsidized agriculture fostered by Democratic administrations. [See EISENHOWER, KENNEDY Volumes]

The Farm Bureau, with a membership of 1.8 million farm families in 1968, was a far larger and more rapidly growing organization than its rivals, the National Farmers Union (NFU) and the National Grange. Although Shuman stated that the Farm Bureau's membership was representative of the American farming community, observers noted that it included many whose wealth and large landholdings inclined them to oppose government controls. In contrast, members of the NFU and the Grange tended to own small and medium-sized farms.

Shuman was a severe critic of President Johnson's Secretary of Agriculture, Orville Freeman [*q.v.*], who had also served under President Kennedy. Controls and price supports continued to constitute the central area of disagreement between Shuman and Freeman, who usually had the support of the NFU and the Grange. When Johnson and Freeman proposed in February 1968 to make price-support programs permanent in order to protect farmers with small holdings, Shuman charged that "the Administration wants to continue to drive down farm prices and make farmers dependent on government subsidies for a large share of their net income."

Shuman also applied his free enterprise

test to other areas of government agricultural policy. In December 1965 he criticized the Administration's program of providing technological farm aid to underdeveloped countries. He said that a condition for such aid should be the willingness of recipient nations to "replace government management with a market price system." He added that "too often our foreign aid programs have been tied to social reform when the critical need was for economic reform."

In the feverish political atmosphere of the mid-1960s, Shuman spoke out on issues not usually associated with traditional farm policy. At the Farm Bureau's national convention in December 1968, Shuman successfully urged the delegates to pass a resolution condemning the national boycott of California table grapes initiated by Cesar Chavez's [*q.v.*] United Farm Workers Organizing Committee. In addition, he suggested that Farm Bureau members not patronize stores agreeing to union boycott demands. The convention then voted to "strongly oppose extension of the National Labor Relations Act to agriculture." The convention also took a conservative position on student anti-war activists, advocating the expulsion from college of students who engaged "in lawlessness" and of faculty members who supported such activity and recommended re-enactment of the loyalty oath requirement for recipients of federal scholarships.

As on previous occasions, charges that the Farm Bureau was a tool of big business surfaced in June and July 1967, when Rep. Joseph Y. Resnick (D, N.Y.), chairman of the House Agriculture Committee's Rural Development Subcommittee, sought to undertake an investigation of the organization. Resnick charged that the Farm Bureau, "the fifth largest lobby in Washington," had a substantial nonfarm membership and that it was, in fact, a "gigantic interlocking, nationwide combine of insurance companies with total assets of over $1 billion." Resnick pointed out that Shuman was also president of the American Agricultural Mutual Insurance Co. and Farm Bureau Mutual Funds, Inc. In an official response the Farm Bureau's secretary-treasurer, Roger Fleming, argued that the insurance companies were developed to serve the needs of members. Fleming also stated that while Shuman acatually headed six other organizations not cited by Resnick, he drew compensation only from his position with the Farm Bureau. Though unsupported by his subcommittee, Resnick conducted his own hearings in August in Chicago, Omaha and Washington but with little result.

Shuman retired from the presidency of the American Farm Bureau Federation in 1970, but he remained active on the boards of a number of agencies and companies, including the Export-Import Bank, the Economic Development Administration, the Illinois Power Company and the Chicago Mercantile Exchange.

[JCH]

SHUTTLESWORTH, FRED L(EE)

b. March 18, 1922; Mugler, Ala.
Secretary, Southern Christian Leadership Conference 1957-70; President, Alabama Christian Movement for Human Rights, 1956-70.

Raised and educated in Alabama, Shuttlesworth was a Baptist minister in Birmingham during the 1950s. He organized the Alabama Christian Movement for Human Rights (ACMHR) in 1956 and, as its president, led efforts to integrate Birmingham's schools, buses and recreational facilities in the late 1950s. Shuttlesworth was also a founder of the Southern Christian Leadership Conference (SCLC) and was elected its first secretary in 1957. Although he became pastor of a Baptist church in Cincinnati in 1960, Shuttlesworth remained president of the ACMHR, the leader of Birmingham's integration movement and a top aide to SCLC President Martin Luther King [*q.v.*]. In May 1962 Shuttlesworth suggested that the SCLC join with ACMHR in an anti-segregation campaign in Birmingham. His proposal led to the climatic Birmingham demonstrations in the spring of 1963, in which Shuttlesworth played a key role. [See KENNEDY Volume]

Charging that Birmingham's white leaders had not lived up to the desegregation agreement reached in 1963, Shuttlesworth led more demonstrations in the city during the spring of 1964. He joined in an SCLC integration campaign in St. Augustine, Fla. that summer and was arrested in demonstrations at a segregated motel on June 18. Shuttlesworth helped organize the march from Selma to Montgomery, Ala., in March 1965 to protest voting discrimination in the state. He also led demonstrations against voting discrimination in Birmingham in January 1966.

In August 1965 a dispute over Shuttlesworth's leadership developed within the congregation at his Cincinnati church. When Shuttlesworth's opponents accused him of being dictatorial and misusing church funds, he denied the charges and alleged that the opposition to him was part of an effort to discredit him within the civil rights movement. The controversy ended in January 1966 when several hundred of his supporters formed a new church in Cincinnati, and Shuttlesworth accepted their invitation to become its pastor. During riots in Cincinnati in June 1967, Shuttlesworth met with city officials in an effort to reach an agreement on black demands and prevent further violence.

Between 1958 and 1969 Shuttlesworth was a party in 10 Supreme Court cases involving civil rights. Altogether the Court overturned six of Shuttlesworth's convictions resulting from his role in the 1961 Freedom Rides and in various Birmingham demonstrations. In *New York Times v. Sullivan*, decided in March 1964, the Supreme Court also reversed a $500,000 libel judgment against Shuttlesworth, three other black ministers and the *New York Times*. The suit had resulted from a March 1960 advertisement in the *Times* that criticized Alabama officials and sought to raise funds for civil rights causes. However, in June 1967 the Court upheld contempt-of-court convictions stemming from the 1963 Birmingham demonstrations against Shuttlesworth and King. Shuttlesworth served a five-day sentence in Alabama in October 1967.

[CAB]

SIEMILLER, PAUL L(EROY)
b. Sept. 4, 1904; Gothenberg, Neb.
President, International Association of Machinists and Aerospace Workers, 1965-69.

Siemiller traveled widely in the U.S. as a young man, working at odd jobs and, after World War I, was a machinist. He became an officer of the International Association of Machinists (IAM) during the Depression and later served as an organizer and general union representative. In 1948 Siemiller was elected vice president of the IAM, and during the Korean War, he served as director of manpower in the Defense Transport Administration. In July 1965, when Siemiller was four years short of the mandatory retirement age of 65, he was elected president of the renamed International Association of Machinists and Aerospace Workers.

Representing workers with wide-ranging skills in a variety of industries, the 75-year-old IAM was considered a cross between an industrial and a craft union. It had remained in the American Federation of Labor following the formation of the Congress of Industrial Organizations in 1935 and was among the largest unions in the merged AFL-CIO. However, the IAM's ranks were decimated in the late 1950s and early 1960s when automation eliminated the jobs of many members.

After his unopposed election as union president, Siemiller, who also became an AFL-CIO vice president and Executive Council member in 1965, began a successful expansion drive, which soon brought IAM membership to 900,000, its 1957 level. A Democrat, Siemiller advocated a larger political role for labor and was among the most outspoken of AFL-CIO leaders in his criticism of President Johnson's labor policies.

In the summer of 1966 a 42-day IAM strike against five major airlines shattered the Johnson Administration's 3.2% anti-inflationary wage guideposts. After months of unsuccessful mediation during the early part of the year, the union had rejected the National Mediation Board's offer of compulsory arbitration and called for a strike on April 24. However, Siemiller agreed not to call the strike when, on April 21, President Johnson created an emergency board. Following hearings, the board's recommendation for a 3.5% wage and benefit increase was submitted to the President on June 5. The IAM rejected the proposed settlement because the union felt that the airlines could easily afford to meet the union's demands for a 5% raise. Negotiations were halted on July 7, and a strike was set for the following day.

Beginning on July 8 a strike by 35,400 IAM members shut down the operations of Eastern, National, Northwest, United and Trans World Airlines. Normally the five airlines handled 60% of the nation's passengers and 70% of its air mail. Although acting Secretary of Defense Cyrus Vance [*q.v.*] said that essential travel by servicemen and civilian workers would not be disrupted, the strike took place at the height of the vacation season and cost the five struck airlines an estimated $350 million, more than any previous airline strike.

The IAM walkout represented the first time President Johnson failed to settle a major nationwide strike through personal intervention. On July 19 Johnson and Siemiller both urged acceptance of another proposed contract. However, IAM members rejected it by a 17,251 to 6,587 vote. Their chief objection to the proposal was that it would defer all benefits until the following year. Abandoning his original conciliatory position to adopt the militancy of the IAM rank and file, Siemiller declared, "We're on strike and we're going to stay that way until we come up with something the membership is satisfied with."

Following the union's repudiation of the proposal, Congress began to debate whether it or the President should order the strikers back to work. A compromise bill, introduced by Morse, passed the Senate on Aug. 4. The measure, strongly favored by the airlines but bitterly opposed by organized labor, required strikers to return to work for a limited period and authorized the President to extend the back-to-work order further if necessary. The bill was under consideration the House when Siemiller announced a new and larger contract offer, later ratified by a 2-to-1 membership vote on Aug. 19. The agreement, which Siemiller said "destroyed" the guidepost principle, provided three 5% increases in wages and benefits over the three-year contract period. In addition, it included a cost-of-living escalator clause tied to the consumer price index, which Siemiller claimed would force the Administration to reverse its opposition to such escalators.

In July 1967 the IAM struck the nation's railroads. The strike ended after two days when Congress approved an Administration mediation proposal that provided for a compulsory settlement if no voluntary agreement could be reached. Johnson charged that the strike threatened national security and, referring to Siemiller and the IAM, said, "No man and no institution can stand above the American people and our men in uniform." On July 17 Congress approved the government plan, and Morse was again appointed to head a mediation panel. However, the panel was unable to achieve a voluntary settlement, and compulsory implementation of its recommendations took effect Oct. 15.

Siemiller retired from all union positions when his term as president expired in 1969.

[MDB]

SIKES, ROBERT L.F.

b. June 3, 1906; Isabella, Ga.
Democratic Representative, Fla., 1941-44; 1945- .

Robert Sikes was a newspaper publisher and a state legislator before his election to the House from Florida's first district in 1940. His district covered the western panhandle in northern Florida and bore a closer resemblance, socially and politically, to neighboring Alabama and Georgia than to much of Florida. Sikes's moderate voting record in Congress gradually grew more conservative during the Truman and Eisenhower Administrations. Strategically positioned on the Appropriations Committee's subcommittees on defense and military construction, the representative managed to gain for the first district one of the heaviest concentrations of military installations in the nation. [See KENNEDY Volume]

Sikes's conservatism reached its peak during the Johnson Administration. The Americans for Democratic Action (ADA) reported that he voted favorably on liberal measures 31% of the time in 1964 but zero percent in 1965, 1966 and 1967. Sikes was a vigorous opponent of civil rights bills and a champion of high defense budgets and the Vietnam war. A major general in the Army Reserve, he was the leading congressional spokesman for the funding of chemical, biological and radiological warfare programs when they came under attack in the 1960s. Sikes also introduced legislation in November 1966 to make it a federal offense to desecrate the flag.

Sikes was a member of the National Rifle Association and an active foe of gun control laws. He helped to engineer the defeat of proposals for federal registration of guns and licensing of gun owners in July 1968. He introduced an amendment permitting the National Board for the Promotion of Rifle Practice to mail guns and ammunition from the Army to NRA clubs. The amendment passed, 225-198, although it was opposed by acting Secretary of the Army David E. McGiffert. Despite his refusal to endorse the national Democratic ticket in 1968, Sikes lost neither his seniority on the Appropriations Committee nor his chairmanship of the military construction subcommittee. In July 1976 Sikes was reprimanded by the House for investing in a bank on a Navy base in his district and voting for projects in which he had a financial interest. [See NIXON Volume]

[TO]

SIMKIN, WILLIAM E(DWARD)

b. Jan. 13, 1907; Merrifield, N.Y.
Director, Federal Mediation and Conciliation Service, 1961-69.

Simkin attended Earlham College and Columbia University. While teaching at the University of Pennsylvania's Wharton School of Finance during the late 1930s he became an associate of Professor George W. Taylor, the well-known labor arbitrator. Simkin shortly thereafter commenced a lengthy career in the field of labor mediation, including service on the National War Labor Board and, later, an extensive private practice.

On Feb. 2, 1961 President Kennedy appointed Simkin director of the Federal Mediation and Conciliation Service (FMCS). An independent agency within the executive branch, the FMCS was created by the Labor-Management Relations (Taft-Hartley) Act of 1947. The FMCS was notified of pending contract changes in collective bargaining agreements that affected interstate commerce. It was empowered to enter any case that developed negotiating problems, whether or not it was invited to by the concerned parties. However, the FMCS did not have authority to enforce settlements—its only instruments were persuasion and the prestige of the federal government. Though primarily an administrator, Simkin personally intervened in a number of the more crucial labor negotiations that took place during the Kennedy Administration and was usually successful in bringing both sides to agreement. [See KENNEDY Volume]

FMCS activity increased following President Johnson's settlement of the 1964 railroad strike. The FMCS was expected to spare the Labor Department direct participation in arbitration. The service sought to keep settlements within the bounds of the Administration's wage-price guidelines and, because of the Vietnam conflict, prevent strikes in industries essential to war production. In August 1966 Simkin estimated that his agency, with a staff of over 400 and a budget of $1 million, helped bring about 7,836 labor-management agreements in the fiscal year 1966.

Simkin believed that the mid-1960s marked a critical juncture in the history of labor arbitration. Contemporary labor disputes were, in his opinion, the most difficult since World War II. He felt that strikes were becoming obsolete—and even "useless" in some automated industries—making it imperative to develop new collective bargaining techniques. Simkin noted that, in order to avoid strikes and the pressure of "deadline bargaining," negotiators were finding it "wiser . . . to try out new bargaining procedures to maintain a continuing or longer-term dialogue." Concerned that his agency stay in the forefront of changes in collective bargaining techniques, Simkin developed a comprehensive training program for the FMCS staff. He also revived the practice, discontinued by the Eisenhower Administration, of employing a panel composed of management and labor leaders to assist in the settlement of strikes.

Simkin participated in many important contract talks during the Johnson Administration. The intervention of Simkin and Labor Secretary W. Willard Wirtz [*q.v.*] in November 1965 sent striking McDonnell Aircraft workers at Cape Kennedy back to work in order to ensure that Gemini space shots planned for December would go off as scheduled. In April 1967 Simkin successfully mediated a nationwide dispute between the International Brotherhood of Teamsters and the trucking industry, and in July of the same year he helped end a three-month strike in the rubber industry. In April 1965 Simkin's intervention led to a temporary postponement of a strike deadline in the steel industry, but the White House was forced to intervene five months later when negotiations failed to produce a final settlement. The pact that was eventually agreed upon exceeded the Administration's 3.2% wage-price guidelines. When 1966 negotiations in the electrical appliance industry, another important producer of war materiel, followed the same pattern, a large segment of the press and many congressmen demanded the enactment of legislation to ban strikes in industries vital to national security. Despite his own difficulties in these negotiations, however, Simkin repeatedly warned against compulsory arbitration and the forced settlement of strikes.

Simkin left the FMCS in 1969 to join the faculty of the Harvard School of Business Administration. Beginning in 1970 he was chairman of the Federal Reserve System's labor relations panel, and in the following year he became chairman of the State Department's Foreign Service Grievance Board.

[JCH]

SIRHAN, SIRHAN B(ISHARA)
b. March 19, 1944; Jerusalem, Palestine.
Convicted assassin of Robert F. Kennedy.

Sirhan B. Sirhan was born and raised in Jerusalem. His father, once the senior Arab officer in charge of the city waterworks, was a violent man who often beat his children. Sirhan's mother, a Greek Orthodox, was a religious zealot. The family moved to the U.S. in 1957, although Sirhan's father soon returned to Jordan.

Sirhan attended high school in Pasadena, Calif., and was subsequently admitted to Pasadena City College. He left the college in 1966. Sirhan hoped to become a jockey, and to gain experience he took a job as an exercise boy at the Hollywood Park Race Track. In September 1966 he was thrown from a horse and suffered head and back injuries that, according to his mother, caused some personality change. A physician who treated Sirhan thought him "a fairly explosive" type. Sirhan directed his rage against Zionists and Jews. He particularly detested Sen. Robert F. Kennedy (D, N.Y.) [*q.v.*] for his support of Israel.

In May 1968, as Kennedy campaigned in the California presidential primary, Sirhan considered assassinating him. On May 18 he wrote in his diary that "my determination to eliminate R.F.K. is becoming more of an unshakeable obsession . . . R.F.K. must die . . . Robert F. Kennedy must be assassinated before 5 June." (June 5 was the anniversary of the 1967 Arab-Israeli war.)

On June 4 Sirhan went to the Ambassador Hotel in Los Angeles, the Kennedy headquarters during the California campaign. Late in the evening, when it became clear that he had won the primary, Kennedy left his suite and made his way to the hotel ballroom to address his cheering campaign workers. After speaking briefly Kennedy headed for the press room, taking a shortcut through the hotel kitchen. Kennedy was shaking hands with the kitchen workers when Sirhan approached him. At 12:16 a.m., June 5, Shirhan opened fire with a .22 caliber pistol. Kennedy, shot in the head and armpit, fell to the ground.

Five others were also wounded, though none fatally. Roosevelt Grier, a 287-pound defensive tackle for the Los Angeles Rams and a Kennedy associate, wrested the gun from Sirhan and carried him from the room to protect him from the enraged spectators.

Early in the morning of June 6, 25 hours after the shooting, Kennedy died in Good Samaritan Hospital in Los Angeles. Sirhan was charged with first-degree murder. At his trial, which began Jan. 7, 1969, defense attorneys argued that Sirhan had shot Kennedy in a blind rage and had acted without "malice aforethought" and therefore was not guilty of first degree murder. However, the admission into evidence of Sirhan's diaries with statements concerning the planned assassination damaged the defense case. On April 17 the jury found Sirhan guilty of murder. In California the jury in capital cases could also determine the sentence, and on the 23rd it sentenced him to death in the gas chamber.

Robert Kennedy's brother, Sen. Edward Kennedy (D, Mass.) [*q.v.*], requested that the death penalty be set aside, but Judge Herbert Walker, who had the power to reduce the sentence to life imprisonment, refused to do so. No date of execution was set for Sirhan pending the outcome of a Supreme Court decision concerning the constitutionality of capital punishment. In June 1972 the Supreme Court suspended all executions until state legislatures drastically revised their capital punishment statutes. This ruling ensured that for an indefinite period Sirhan would be spared. He remained confined to death row at the San Quentin, Calif., prison.

[JLW]

SMATHERS, GEORGE A(RMISTEAD)

b. Nov. 14, 1913; Atlantic City, N.J.
Democratic Senator, Fla., 1951-69

George Smathers, the influential Senator from Florida and close friend of President Johnson, was raised in Miami, Fla. Following his graduation from the University of Florida Law School in 1938, he entered private law practice. Through the influence of Sen. Claude Pepper (D, Fla.), Smathers was appointed assistant U.S. district attorney for Dade County in 1940. After service in World War II, he was made special assistant to the U.S. Attorney General. In 1946 he was elected to the House of Representatives, where he earned a reputation as a liberal.

In 1950 Smathers, backed by business interests opposed to Pepper's liberal stand on taxes and labor legislation, won the Democratic senatorial nomination over Pepper. During what was called one of the dirtiest campaigns of the postwar period, Smathers dropped his liberal stand on social issues and accused Pepper of being a Communist sympathizer. In November Smathers won the general election. [See TRUMAN Volume]

While in the upper house Smathers became a powerful member of what was known as the "Senate establishment," the small group of senators who made committee assignments and could often decide the fate of legislation. The Senator's power was based on his close friendship with Senate Majority Leader Lyndon B. Johnson (D, Tex.), who appointed him head of the Senate Democratic Elections Committee in 1956. For the next two years Smathers used his position to distribute funds to conservatives while building important political connections among powerful Southern senators. His position was enhanced still further when he was named acting majority leader in Johnson's absence. During the Eisenhower and Kennedy Administrations, Smathers, according to political writer Robert Sherrill, used his influence on Capitol Hill to aid his political backers and law clients. Smathers opposed most civil rights bills and domestic social legislation. [See EISENHOWER, KENNEDY Volumes]

Smathers's friendship with Johnson continued after the Texan had become President. During the Johnson Administration he frequently advised the President on important legislative issues, such as the 1966 decision to suspend the 7% investment tax credit. Following the 1964 enfranchisement of 300,000 Florida blacks, Smathers became more liberal on many domestic issues and in 1965 supported the Voting Rights Act.

He opposed the addition of the medicare provision to the Social Security amendments bill in 1964, a vote supported by the American Medical Association. But when the bill with the medicare amendment attached came to the floor, Smathers voted for the measure.

During the Senate's 1964 investigation of Bobby Baker [*q.v.*], Smathers was the only Senator cited as having business connections with the former senate majority secretary, who was then under FBI investigation for fraud. Although Senate Rules Committee Chairman Everett Jordan (D, N.C.) [*q.v.*] issued a statement exonerating Smathers of any impropriety in the matter, Smathers's handling of the incident caused many to question his business dealings. The Senator announced that he had only a casual acquaintance with Baker, although both he and Baker had worked closely with Lyndon Johnson during the 1950s. He also issued conflicting statements on the profits he had made and confessed that he had lost his income tax returns for the year that could have provided him with the necessary information.

During the last part of the decade, the press continued to question Smathers about his financial affairs. These investigations revealed banking and real estate transactions that, while not illegal, opened the Senator to charges that he had used his influence to further his own business interests. In 1968 Smathers, coming under increased criticism for his business affairs and finding that his power base in Florida had eroded with the growth of the black vote, announced that for reasons of health he would not seek another Senate term.

[EWS]

SMITH, HOWARD W(ORTH)

b. Feb. 2, 1883; Broad Run, Va.
Democratic Representative, Va., 1931-67; Chairman, Rules Committee, 1955-67.

Smith first entered public life as commonwealth's attorney of Alexandria in 1918. Four years later he became judge of the corporation court of that city and in 1928 was appointed judge of the state's 16th Circuit Court. In 1930 he won election to Congress and served there for 35 consecutive years. Smith had an unprepossessing personality but was gifted with extraordinary political skills, and by the 1950s he had become one of the chief lieutenants of Sen. Harry F. Byrd's [*g.v.*] powerful and conservative Democratic political machine in Virginia.

As a congressman, Smith voiced his own and the Byrd organization's opposition to extension of federal power, social welfare spending and civil rights legislation. In 1955 he became chairman of the powerful House Rules Committee, which, since the late 1930s, had been dominated by a conservative coalition of Southern Democrats and Republicans. Most bills passing from their original committee to the House floor stopped at the Rules Committee, which determined the length and manner of floor debate. As one of its members, and particularly as its chairman, Smith played a major role in blocking liberal legislation, for the panel could prevent a bill from reaching the floor and, if the bill was released, determine if it would be subject to amendment before the full House. [See EISENHOWER Volume]

During the first month of John Kennedy's presidency, the Administration succeeded in reducing the power of the conservatives on the Rules Committee, one of the first goals of the new President. On Jan. 31, 1961 the House voted to accept a proposal offered by Speaker Sam Rayburn to increase the Committee's membership from 12 to 15. Two of the new members were moderate to liberal, giving liberals an eight-to-seven majority on the panel. In January 1963 the House voted to make the expansion permanent. However, the liberals' edge was tenuous and did not prevail on all issues. Furthermore, as chairman, Smith had considerable independent power to determine the pace at which bills were considered, and he was often able to bury Administration-sponsored measures. [See KENNEDY Volume]

During the Johnson Administration Smith had less success obstructing liberal bills.

President Johnson, relying upon a large network of friendships established during his years on Capitol Hill, was more effective than his predecessor in securing congressional support for his programs. During the first months of his presidency, he gained bi-partisan backing for the civil rights bill which had been introduced by Kennedy. Smith denounced the bill as "unmatched in harshness and brutality. . . since the tragic days of Reconstruction." But because the measure was supported by the leadership of both parties, he felt compelled to allow the Rules Committee to clear the bill for floor consideration in January 1964. During July of the same year, after an initial delay, he permitted the Administration's antipoverty bill to go to the floor.

At the beginning of 1965 Smith's ability to block Administration bills was further eroded. After the Democratic sweep in the November 1964 elections, the Party's House caucus voted to back a 21-day rule. This proviso stipulated that if the Rules Committee did not send a bill to the floor within 21 days of its approval by the committee of original jurisdiction, the Speaker could permit the House to consider the measure. The House adopted the new rule in January 1965. President Johnson, who had strongly backed the measure, commented, "It could be better, but not this side of Heaven."

The 21-day rule was rarely invoked, but the mere threat of its employment proved effective in producing the release of a number of bills from the Rules Committee, and in 1965 Smith was not able to bury a single major Administration proposal. The Committee, for example, succeeded in delaying consideration of President Johnson's voting rights bill for five weeks. But when proceedings were initiated to apply the 21-day rule, the Committee released the bill. The following year, when Smith was unyielding on a civil rights housing bill, the rule was employed to bring the measure to the floor.

While Smith was losing power in Congress, his political base in Virginia was also being undermined. A 1964 Supreme Court decision required the apportionment of legislative districts on the basis of population in order to give urban areas greater representation. In complying with this ruling, the Virginia General Assembly added a segment of the politically moderate Washington suburbs to Smith's district. In addition, the size of the black vote in Virginia increased because of the ratification by the states of the poll tax amendment to the U.S. Constitution in 1964 and the passage of the Voting Rights Act of 1965. As a result, Smith was narrowly defeated in the 1966 Democratic primary by a liberal opponent, who received 50.6% of the vote to the incumbent's 49.4%.

[MLL]

SMITH, MARGARET CHASE
b. Dec. 14, 1897; Skowhegan, Me.
Republican Senator, Me., 1949-73.

After a varied business career in Maine, Smith served as her husband's secretary when he was a congressman in the late 1930s. She was herself elected to the House of Representatives in 1940 following his death. In 1948 Smith became the first woman ever elected to the U.S. Senate. On June 1, 1950, in her first major Senate address, she offered a "declaration of conscience," denouncing Sen. Joseph McCarthy (R, Wisc.) and his tactics of "hate and character assassination." Reelected to the Senate in 1954 and 1960, Smith became known as a political independent, and she often supported liberal Democratic legislation. She took a special interest in military and defense matters and favored a policy of strong national defense. [See Truman, Eisenhower, Kennedy Volumes.]

On Jan. 27, 1964 Smith announced she would enter the race for the Republican presidential nomination to offer her Party's voters a moderate candidate and to open the way for women in presidential politics. Insisting that her Senate duties remained her first responsibility, she spent little time campaigning and limited her spending to personal and travel expenses, which she paid herself. Smith ran a poor fifth in the first primary held in New Hampshire in March. She received nearly 26% of the vote in Illinois's April primary but again ran fifth in Oregon in May. She received 27 votes on the first ballot at the Republican National Convention in San Francisco.

In the Senate Smith retained her independent stance. In *Congressional Quarterly* surveys from 1964 to 1967, she was ranked as one of the top three Republican supporters of the President's legislative program. Smith voted, for example, for civil rights, medicare, aid to elementary and secondary schools and several antipoverty programs. However, she opposed an urban mass transportation bill in 1964, voted to cut the appropriations for the War on Poverty in 1965 and opposed increased funding for other Great Society programs. She also voted against measures in 1967 and 1968 designed to increase financial disclosure by members of Congress. Although she later voted for the Equal Rights Amendment, Smith did not identify herself with the women's movement that gained strength in the late 1960s. In 1972 she wrote that if there is any one thing I have attempted to avoid it is being a feminist."

A member of the Appropriations Committee and the Aeronautical and Space Sciences Committee, Smith also headed the Senate Republican Conference from 1967 to 1972 and became the ranking Republican on the Armed Services Committee in 1967. She consistently supported spending for the Vietnam war. In March 1967, when a U.S.-USSR consular treaty was under consideration, Smith unsuccessfully proposed adding an "understanding" that it was the Senate's "hope" that no consulates would be opened until the war had ended. She explained that this was intended to be a Senate expression of disapproval of Soviet aid to North Vietnam. Smith usually supported Defense Department programs and appropriation requests, but she opposed the Safeguard anti-ballistic missile system in 1968 and 1969 on the grounds that it was ineffective, unnecessary and a waste of resources.

Smith was unopposed for renomination to the Senate in the 1966 Republican primary in Maine, and she won the general election in November with 59% of the vote. Smith joined in Senate debate only infrequently and followed a policy of never announcing in advance how she planned to vote on an issue. Between June 1955 and July 1968 she set a Senate record for not missing any roll-call votes.

Although the conservative Americans for Constitutional Action rated Smith "correct" on about 70% of her votes during President Nixon's first term, she voted against the President's nominations of Clement Haynsworth and G. Harrold Carswell to the Supreme Court. Smith also opposed the Supersonic Transport and the anti-ballistic missile system, both strongly backed by the Republican Administration. In a surprising upset, Smith was defeated in her bid for reelection to the Senate in November 1972. [See NIXON Volume.]

[CAB]

For further information:
Margaret Chase Smith, *Declaration of Conscience* (New York, 1972).

SMYLIE, ROBERT E.

b. Oct. 31, 1914; Marcus, Idaho.
Governor, Idaho, 1955-67.

Robert E. Smylie, a graduate of the College of Idaho and the George Washington University School of Law, served in the Coast Guard during World War II. He returned to Idaho after the war and became active in Republican politics while practicing law in Boise and Caldwell. He served as state attorney general from 1947 to 1954. Smylie, a Republican, was elected governor in 1954 on a platform that urged private rather than federal development of the hydroelectric power facilities in the Hell's Canyon area of the Snake River. [See EISENHOWER, KENNEDY Volumes]

Smylie was generally associated with the moderate wing of his Party, which sought to prevent conservatives led by Sen. Barry M. Goldwater (R, Ariz.) [*q.v.*] from dominating the GOP. When Goldwater won the 1964 Republican presidential nomination, Smylie supported him with reluctance. Goldwater, nonetheless, promised that if elected he would appoint Smylie to the post of Secretary of the Interior.

Following Goldwater's devastating defeat Smylie sought to remove Dean Burch [*q.v.*], a Goldwater supporter, as head of the Republican National Committee. Burch resigned the post in January 1965 and was replaced by Ray C. Bliss [*q.v.*]. In a letter to Bliss, Smylie urged the Republican National Committee to denounce the right-wing John Birch Society and to disavow the extreme conservatism that had proved disastrous to Republican candidates. The National Committee did adopt a resolution denouncing "extremist organizations" but failed specifically to mention the Birch Society.

As governor, Smylie earned a reputation as a skillful but not particularly innovative administrator. By 1965, however, he had embarked on a more activist program. He revamped the state tax structure, won increased state support for local schools and initiated a broad park and recreation program. By 1966 Smylie had thoroughly alienated conservative Idaho Republicans, who supported Don Samuelson for the Republican gubernatorial nomination. Samuelson routed Smylie in the primary. At the expiration of his term, Smylie renewed his legal practice in Boise.

[JLW]

SONTAG, SUSAN

b. Jan. 28, 1933; New York, N.Y.
Writer.

A champion of the "new sensibility" in the arts, Susan Sontag was the most celebrated younger critic of the 1960s. Through her erudite explications of "Camp," underground films, pornography, "pop art" and other manifestations of the new chic "counter-culture," Sontag did much to transform accepted standards of aesthetic judgment and to justify the educated public's eagerness to respond to "style" and "experience" as aesthetic values in their own right.

The daughter of middle-class Jewish parents, Sontag grew up in Tucson, Ariz., and Los Angeles, Calif. She entered the University of California, Berkeley, when she was 15 years old, and after a year there she transferred to the University of Chicago, receiving her B.A. in philosophy in 1951. She pursued graduate studies at Harvard and the University of Paris and, after a brief stint as an editor of *Commentary* magazine in 1959, taught philosophy at the City College of New York, Sarah Lawrence College and Columbia University.

In 1962 Sontag began to publish criticism in literary journals and magazines, including *Partisan Review*, the *New York Review of Books*, *Evergreen Review* and *Film Quarterly*, much of which was collected in *Against Interpretation* (1966). In this book's title essay she called for an end to the reductive analysis, or "interpretation," which she felt reduced the subject work of art to a mere example of the critic's preferred world view. "Interpretation," she insisted, "takes the sensory experience of the work of art for granted and proceeds from there. This cannot be taken for granted, now. . . . Ours is a culture based on excess, on overproduction; the result is a steady loss in sharpness in our sensory experience. . . . The function of criticism should be to show how [the work of art] is what it is, even that it is what it is, rather than to show what it means. In place of a hermeneutics we need an erotics of art."

This argument led Sontag to champion such new "art" forms, as the "happening," which attracted her because it "shuns rational discourse," and "camp" art because of its disengaged and depoliticized sensibility. A later collection of her essays, *Styles of Radical Will* (1969), contained a defense of pornography against its literary opponents, whom she described as weighted down by 19th century preconceptions of what fiction ought to be. According to social historian William O'Neill, Susan Sontag's abandonment of the old aesthetics helped legitimatize the breakdown in the distinction between high and low culture that was occurring in the 1960s. Although fiercely intellectual herself, Sontag's perspective welcomed the anti-intellectualism and drive for sensual immediacy that characterized the counterculture and much of the New Left.

Sontag was a prominent opponent of the

war in Vietnam. She signed the radical and widely circulated "Call to Resist Illegitimate Authority" in September 1967 and the next year publicly supported acts of draft resistance. During the same year she made a two-week visit to North Vietnam, later recorded in her essay "Trip to Hanoi." The account charted the changes in the consciousness of its highly cultured, ironic heroine, unwilling to think in terms of moral categories, yet learning finally to respond to what she viewed as the moral simplicity of the Vietnamese. Sontag was one of the few American leftist intellectuals visiting Hanoi to observe that North Vietnam was far from a model society, but on the whole she felt obliged to make allowances for the years of war and suffering endured by the Vietnamese people. Impressed by the nationalism of an embattled culture, she concluded her essay with a call on Americans to reinvent the radical patriotism of the Founding Fathers.

In the 1970s Sontag spent much of her time in Europe. She produced a series of feminist films in Sweden and took a new critical interest in photography criticism.

[TLH]

For further information:

Suan Sontag, *Styles of Radical Will* (New York, 1969).

"Susan Sontag," *Current Biography Yearbook, 1969* (New York, 1970), pp. 413-15.

SPARKMAN, JOHN J(ACKSON)

b. Dec. 20, 1899; Morgan Co., Ala.
Democratic Senator, Ala., 1946- ; Chairman, Select Small Business Committee, 1950-53, 1955-67; Chairman, Housing Subcommittee of the Banking and Currency Committee, 1955- ; Chairman, Banking and Currency Committee, 1967-75.

Sparkman opened a law practice in Huntsville, Ala., in 1925. Eleven years later he was elected to the U.S. House of Representatives, where he was a supporter of New Deal programs. In 1946 he won a special election to fill a vacant Senate seat. Sparkman was a consistent opponent of civil rights legislation, but, unlike most Southerners on Capitol Hill, he continued to support many liberal domestic programs in the postwar era. As a member of the Joint Committee on Housing and as chairman of the Banking and Currency Committee's Housing Subcommittee, he played a key role in the passage of almost all housing legislation in the late 1940s, the 1950s and the early 1960s. Because of his relatively liberal voting record, Sparkman was chosen as Adlai E. Stevenson's [*q.v.*] vice presidential running mate in 1952.

Although opposed to medicare, Sparkman backed most of the Kennedy Administration's other domestic programs. In 1961 he was the Senate sponsor of President Kennedy's omnibus housing bill. As chairman of the Select Small Business Committee, Sparkman backed increased funding for the Small Business Administration in 1962 and 1963. [See TRUMAN, EISENHOWER, KENNEDY Volumes]

Partly because of the growing influence of Gov. George C. Wallace [*q.v.*] in Alabama politics during the mid and late 1960s, Sparkman voted against liberal domestic programs more frequently than in previous years. According to *Congressional Quarterly*, he never opposed the Senate's conservative coalition on more than 23% of key roll-call votes from 1964 through 1968. However, he continued to endorse most Administration housing bills. In 1964 he backed a bill to expand urban renewal and low-rent housing programs. The following year Sparkman introduced the most extensive housing and urban development bill since the Housing Act of 1949. The measure authorized the expenditure of over $7 billion and included a new and controversial rent supplement program to provide adequate living accommodations for the poor in private housing. Congress passed the bill in July.

In 1966 Sparkman, expecting stiff conservative opposition in both the Democratic primary and the general election, declined to sponsor the Administration's hotly debated Demonstration Cities bill. He won both contests easily. In 1967 he succeeded former Sen. A. Willis Robertson (D, Va.) [*q.v.*] as chairman of the Banking and Currency Committee. In that position he opposed efforts to restrict the President's rent supplement program of 1967. The following year Sparkman backed President Johnson's bill for erecting and rehabilitating over 1.7 million housing units for low-income families. In May Sparkman asserted, during floor debate on the measure, that existing programs "have not reached down far enough to help those who need housing the most."

Sparkman's assumption of the Banking and Currency chairmanship influenced the fate of the Administration's "truth-in-lending" measure, which Robertson had stalled in the Committee for a number of years. Sparkman's support of the bill, which required lenders to provide full information about the cost of credit, facilitated its passage in 1967.

Sparkman endorsed Administration foreign aid programs, and in 1965 and 1967 he opposed the efforts of Sen. Wayne Morse (D, Ore.) [*q.v.*] to slash drastically President Johnson's assistance requests. Sparkman also backed the Administration's Vietnam war policies. In March 1968 he defended Congress's 1964 passage of the Tonkin Gulf Resolution, which the President frequently cited as justification for American military involvement in Southeast Asia.

In 1972 the increasingly conservative Sparkman narrowly avoided a primary runoff against an opponent who accused him of being too close to big banking interests. Three years later he left his Banking and Currency post to succeed former Sen. J. William Fulbright (D, Ark.) [*q.v.*] as chairman of the Foreign Relations Committee. [See NIXON Volume]

[MLL]

SPELLMAN, FRANCIS J(OSEPH)

b. May 4, 1889; Whitman, Mass.
d. Dec. 2, 1967; New York, N.Y.
Roman Catholic Archbishop of New York, 1939-67.

Ordained a Roman Catholic priest in 1916, named archbishop of New York in 1939 and a cardinal in 1946, Spellman was one of the most powerful and conservative American clergymen. His influence increased in the postwar era as Catholics moved increasingly into the middle class and took a more prominent role in national politics. Cardinal Spellman was an extremely able administrator and fund-raiser, who not only built schools and hospitals in his own diocese but also financed missionary activities abroad.

Since 1939 the military vicar general of the U.S. armed forces, Spellman visited American troops around the world and became an outspoken ally of the military. He identified Catholic interests with a vigorous prosecution of the Cold War, and he publicly defended Sen. Joseph McCarthy's (R, Wisc.) anti-Communist congressional investigations in 1953. With the assistance of his old friend Joseph Kennedy, Sr., Spellman successfully urged the Eisenhower Administration in 1955 to give full support to the South Vietnamese regime of Ngo Dinh Diem, marking the beginning of a concerted American anti-Communist counteroffensive in Southeast Asia. [See TRUMAN, EISENHOWER Volumes]

With the election of a Catholic president in 1960, the minority-consciousness of American Catholics began to dissipate. Spellman in turn was increasingly challenged as an official spokesman for U.S. Catholicism after liberal Catholics began to disagree publicly with his opinions. Although he had long supported civil rights and interdenominational cooperation, Spellman was slow to adapt to social change and to some of the innovations introduced by Pope John XXIII and the Vatican Council. [See KENNEDY Volume]

During the mid-1960s Spellman was most notable for his unconditional support of the war in Vietnam. Using language that was more extreme than any employed by the Administration, he defended the conflict as "a war for civilization" and as "Christ's war against the Viet Cong and the people of North Vietnam." Early criticism of his position came from within the American Catholic community. In December 1965 Catholic college students picketed Spellman's New York office, demanding the end of "power politics in the Church." The students protested Spellman's alleged suppression of three anti-war Jesuits, including Father Daniel Berrigan [*q.v.*], who had recently been transferred from New York to Cuernavaca, Mexico.

By 1966 Spellman's militant defense of the war had alienated him from large segments of the American religious community. By clearly contradicting the peace initiatives of Pope Paul VI, Spellman undermined his own authority in the U.S. In December the Vatican felt it necessary to state that the Cardinal "did not speak for the pope or the church" on the war issue. Despite their disagreements, Pope Paul refused Spellman's October 1966 offer to resign as archbishop because of his age.

The intensity of Catholic anti-war demonstrations, often aimed at Spellman, increased in 1967. Cardinal Spellman died of a stroke in New York City on Dec. 2, 1967.

[JCH]

SPOCK, BENJAMIN (McLAINE)

b. May 2, 1903; New Haven, Conn.
Co-Chairman, Committee for a Sane Nuclear Policy, 1963-67; Co-Chairman, National Conference for New Politics, 1967-68.

Spock's father was a successful corporation lawyer, while his mother ran a home Spock later characterized as "plain, repressed and strict." After attending private schools and Yale, Spock studied medicine at Yale and Columbia and completed residencies in pediatrics and psychiatry. In 1933 he started a private practice that he continued until entering the Navy as a psychiatrist during World War II. Spock's *The Common Sense Book of Baby and Child Care* was published in 1946 and was an immediate success. By 1969 it had sold 22 million copies, making it the all-time best-selling book by an American author. After four years at the Mayo Clinic in Rochester, Minn. and another four years at the University of Pittsburgh Medical School, Spock taught at Western Reserve University in Cleveland until his retirement in 1967. In addition to several books, Spock wrote a regular column in *Ladies Home Journal* and later *Redbook*.

Until 1960 Spock had taken public positions only on medical issues, but that year he endorsed John F. Kennedy's presidential candidacy. After Kennedy's announcement in March 1962 that the United States was resuming nuclear testing, Spock accepted a previously rejected offer to become a national sponsor of the Committee for a Sane Nuclear Policy (SANE). The next year he was elected national co-chairman of the organization.

Spock campaigned for President Johnson in 1964 and in January 1965 became a member of the National Advisory Council to the Office of Economic Opportunity. However, Spock became increasingly critical of the Administration when Johnson resumed the escalation of U.S. military activity in Vietnam shortly after his reelection. He first sent private letters to various Administration leaders. Then on June 8, 1965 he spoke at a SANE-sponsored anti-war rally in New York's Madison Square Garden. Spock was a principal speaker at the Nov. 27 march in Washington initiated by SANE, where he called on both the United States and North Vietnam to seek a negotiated settlement.

In 1966 SANE concentrated on generally unsuccessful campaigns to elect peace candidates, and Spock was a frequent campaigner. He was also one of the main speakers at a SANE demonstration held in Washington on May 15, 1966 in support of these candidates. Within SANE there was an often bitter debate over the extent to which the organization should cooperate with more radical elements in the anti-war movement. Spock favored a broadly inclusive and militant movement. Although SANE declined to work with the newly formed Spring Mobilization to End the War in Vietnam, Spock accepted co-chairmanship of the coalition's planned April 15, 1967 march. In a letter to A.J. Muste [*q.v.*] he wrote: "I now believe in leaning in the direction of recruiting more militant people into the peace movement rather than worrying over scaring off the timid ones. . . .I believe in solidarity." On April 15, Spock, the Rev. Martin Luther King [*q.v.*] and Harry Belafonte led an estimated 300,000 marchers from New

York's Central Park to the United Nations in the largest anti-war demonstration to date.

Spock was an early leader of the National Conference for New Politics (NCNP), founded in June 1966. At the August 1967 NCNP convention Spock was elected a co-chairman of the group and shortly thereafter resigned his co-chairmanship of SANE. The NCNP convention was marked by numerous disagreements and voted not to run a national third-party slate in the 1968 elections. The NCNP itself dissolved within a year.

In the fall of 1967 Spock, recently retired from teaching, was increasingly active in opposition to the war. He was one of the original signers of "A Call to Resist Illegitimate Authority," published in September 1967, which supported draft resistance and the refusal of servicemen to obey "illegal and immoral orders." He was part of a group that visited the Justice Department on Oct. 20 and handed over several hundred draft cards turned in by draft resisters. The next day he spoke at the anti-war rally that preceded a march on the Pentagon. On Dec. 5 he was arrested with 263 others at the New York City Whitehall Induction Center in a civil disobedience action during "Stop the Draft Week."

Spock, Marcus Raskin, co-director of the Institute for Policy Studies, the Rev. William Sloane Coffin, Jr. [*q.v.*], Yale University chaplain, writer Mitchell Goodman and Harvard graduate student Michael Ferber were indicted on Jan. 5, 1968 for conspiring to "counsel, aid and abet" young men to "refuse and evade service in the armed services. . . ." In pre-trial motions, Spock's lawyer, Leonard Boudin, argued that the war in Vietnam was illegal. Therefore, under the precedents established at the post-World War II Nuremberg trials, Boudin contended, the defendants had committed no crime in advising potential draftees to refuse to participate in the war and in the war crimes committed as part of it. Judge Francis J.W. Ford ruled that the legality of the war or the draft was not relevant to the case. The trial, therefore, took place over the narrower legal issue of whether or not a conspiracy had existed. All of the defendants except Raskin were convicted on June 14, 1968 of one conspiracy count; they were sentenced the next month to fines and two-year prison sentences. However, on July 11, 1969 the First U.S. Court of Appeals set aside the verdicts, citing prejudicial error in Judge Ford's charge to the jury. Charges against Spock and Ferber were dismissed. Although Goodman and Coffin were ordered retried, charges against them were eventually dropped as well. Spock was undeterred, continuing to lead demonstrations and running for president in 1972 as the People's Party candidate. [See NIXON Volume]

[JBF]

For further information:

Lynn Z. Bloom, *Doctor Spock: Biography of a Conservative Radical* (Indianapolis, 1972).

Jessica Mitford, *The Trial of Dr. Spock* (New York, 1969).

STAGGERS, HARLEY

b. Aug. 3, 1907; Keyser, W.Va.
U.S. Representative, W.Va., 1948- ;
Chairman, Interstate and Foreign Commerce Committee, 1966- .

Staggers was born in the rural, mountainous, coal-mining West Virginia district he later represented in Congress. He graduated from a small Methodist college in 1931 and held a variety of jobs, including county sheriff, before serving with the U.S. Naval Air Corps during World War II. Staggers first won election to Congress in 1948 and was assigned to the Interstate and Foreign Commerce Committee in 1951. A liberal who voted consistently with his Party's leadership, he became assistant Democratic whip four years later.

Staggers, who once described himself as a "Johnson man," assumed the chairmanship of the powerful Commerce Committee in 1966 and sponsored important Administration legislation, most notably a series of health bills. Introduced by Staggers in March 1966, the Comprehensive Health Planning Act authorized coordination of public health services on a state and regional basis; it was signed in November, as were bills he introduced to appropriate funds for health training programs and hospital modernization. In March 1967 Staggers introduced the Administration's major health legislation for that year, the "Partnership for Health" bill, which extended and expanded the Comprehensive Health Planning Act. It was signed in December.

Staggers also played a crucial role in the passage of the Johnson Administration's 1966 Traffic Safety Act, which required the establishment of federal safety standards for vehicles that were intended for public highway use. Staggers, whose committee handled the bill, favored civil penalties for manufacturers who failed to notify owners and dealers of safety defects or who were found, during on-site inspections, to be in violation of portions of the act. However, Staggers considered criminal penalties unenforceable and opposed Rep. Thomas P. O'Neill's (D, Mass.) amendment to add such penalties for violations by industry officials. Without criminal penalties, O'Neill said, the bill would repeat "the wishy-washy regulatory performance that has caused so much public disillusionment with the process of government." Staggers argued that "you cannot put a corporation in jail," and that viewpoint prevailed when O'Neill's proposal was defeated by voice vote in August. Enacted later in 1966, the Traffic Safety Act went beyond the Administration's original plan and won praise from consumer advocate Ralph Nader [*q.v.*], who was considered the most important force behind the act's passage. However, Nader also criticized the absence of criminal penalties.

Although Staggers opposed compulsory arbitration of labor disputes, he introduced the Administration's bill to prevent a nationwide railroad strike in May 1967. The bill called for a 90-day strike delay during which a settlement would be sought—and if necessary imposed—by a mediation panel. Although the Senate approved the bill, Staggers joined a majority in the House in rejecting the imposition of a binding settlement. On June 15 the railroad unions agreed not to strike while a House-Senate Conference Committee headed by Staggers attempted to reconcile the conflicting versions of the bill. However, on July 13 the unions notified the committee that their no-strike pledge would be rescinded on July 15. Members of the International Association of Machinists struck July 16. The next day the conferees agreed unanimously that they could not reach an agreement, and the Senate then reaffirmed its commitment to the original plan. By a vote of 244 to 148, the House overturned its earlier decision and gave its approval to the Senate version of the President's plan. Staggers maintained his opposition to the measure and said that "compulsory labor is foreign to America . . . it is a road America should never take." The strike ended on July 18 when Johnson appointed a five-man mediation board headed by Sen. Wayne Morse (D, Ore.) [*q.v.*]. Attempts to reach a voluntary settlement failed, and the board's recommendations went into effect into October.

In the early 1960s Staggers had begun to work on a bill to protect consumers from deceptive packaging in supermarket and drugstore products. His bill was enacted as the Truth-in-Packaging Act in November 1966. Staggers was also concerned with the Federal Communications Commission's "role as a guardian of the public interest" and during the 1968 presidential campaign held hearings on the application of the "fairness doctrine" to televised political debates. He supported a bill that would have suspended the "equal time" provision of the 1934 Communications Act for the 1968 presidential election, but the measure did not pass.

Staggers, who was a supporter of the Vietnam policies of the Johnson and Nixon Administrations, remained in Congress into the 1970s. His voting record became increasingly conservative. [See Nixon Volume]

[MDB]

For further information:
Ralph Nader Congress Project, *The Commerce Committees: A Study of the House and Senate Commerce Committees*, David Price, director (New York, 1975).

STENNIS, JOHN C(ORNELIUS)
b. Aug. 3, 1901; Kemper County, Miss.
Democratic Senator, Miss., 1947- ;
Chairman, Select Committee on Standards and Conduct, 1965-75.

The son of a farmer and merchant in Kemper County, Miss., Stennis received a degree from the University of Virginia Law School in 1928. During the same year he won a seat in the Mississippi House of Representatives. Three years later Stennis was elected prosecutor for the state's 16th judicial district, and in 1937 he became a circuit court judge.

In 1947 Stennis won a special election for a vacant U.S. Senate seat. Avoiding the race issue during the campaign, he received the support of the state's liberals and Negro community leaders, but in the Senate he was a staunch segregationist. From the late 1940s through the early 1960s, Stennis's views were consistently conservative. He favored a strongly anti-Communist foreign policy and opposed the great bulk of social welfare legislation.

In the Senate Stennis, a courtly and dignified man who was regarded as a personification of Southern gentility, acquired a reputation for fairness and personal integrity that transcended his political outlook. He won public esteem in 1954 when he served on the committee inquiring into the conduct of Sen. Joseph R. McCarthy (R, Wisc.) Believing that the maintenance of high standards of behavior in the Senate should supercede political partisanship, Stennis denounced what he considered McCarthy's vituperative and reckless allegations of Communist influence in American institutions. In November 1954 he became the first Democrat to call on the Senate floor for McCarthy's censure.

Eight years later, as chairman of the Senate Armed Services Committee's Preparedness Investigating Subcommittee, he headed an investigation into what Maj. Gen. Edwin A. Walker, a John Birch Society member, and Sen. Strom Thurmond (D, S.C.) [*q.v.*] alleged was State Department and Pentagon "muzzling" of military officers. Many of Stennis's colleagues believed that his judicious handling of the probe prevented the matter from exploding into an emotional issue reminiscent of the McCarthy era. [See TRUMAN, EISENHOWER, KENNEDY Volumes]

As a by-product of the Senate's investigation of the Bobby Baker [*q.v.*] scandal, in July 1964 the upper house established a Select Committee on Standards and Ethics to examine complaints of unethical conduct by senators and employes of the chamber. Because of his reputation for integrity, Stennis was chosen by the panel as its first chairman in October 1965. During the next two years the Committee investigated the case of Sen. Thomas Dodd (D, Conn.) [*q.v.*], who was accused of improperly aiding a registered foreign agent, using campaign funds to pay personal bills and billing trips both to the Senate and to private organizations. In April 1967 the Committee, with Stennis's concurrence, recommended the censure of Dodd on the two latter charges. Two months later the Senate voted for censure on the campaign funds accusation while dropping the other charges.

A consistent opponent of President Lyndon B. Johnson's civil rights and Great Society legislation, Stennis was among the four leading Senate Democratic opponents of Administration programs during each year from 1964 through 1968. He was a supporter of the President's military appropriations requests and, after initial doubts about the wisdom of American involvement in Southeast Asia, of the Administration's war effort in Vietnam. In a speech made early in 1966, Stennis expressed his political outlook when he stated, "Great Society programs with the billions they are gulping down should be relegated to the rear. . . . They should be secondary to the war." Favoring a prompt military victory, he asserted that North Vietnam and the National Liberation Front should be attacked "as often and whenever necessary" in order to avoid "a long, drawn-out and bloody war of possibly 10-15 years." Stennis favored maximum use of air power, and in June 1968 he spoke against Sen. William Proxmire's (D, Wisc.) [*q.v.*] amendment to reduce appropriations for a buildup in B-52 bomber operations in Vietnam.

As chairman of the Preparedness Investigating Subcommittee, Stennis expressed concern about the possible consequences of the Indochinese conflict for the overall military strength of the United States. In August 1965, after the panel had completed a one-year study of the combat readiness of the Army, he contended that the war was rapidly draining the armed forces' stock of supplies. During subcommittee hearings in August 1966, he voiced the fear that the Vietnam war might establish a precedent for American entry into future conflicts without congressional approval and for the conduct of such conflicts with minimal legislative involvement.

In June 1967 a Senate subcommittee heard a group of doctors testify that many Mississippians were suffering from malnutrition approaching stavation. On July 11 Stennis called this claim "a libel." But despite his denial and his opposition to social welfare programs, in July Stennis introduced a bill authorizing $10 million for emergency food and medical services.

In 1969 Stennis succeeded Sen. Richard B. Russell (D, Ga.) [*q.v.*] as chairman of the Armed Services Committee. At about the same time that Stennis became head of the panel, vocal liberal opposition to large military budgets began to emerge on the previously quiescent Committee. However Stennis, who sometimes supported military appropriations cuts but rarely had serious differences with the Pentagon, was generally able to prevail over Committee opponents of high defense expenditures. In January 1973 Stennis was shot and seriously wounded during a robbery attempt in front of his home in Washington, D.C., but he recovered rapidly. [See NIXON Volume]

[MLL]

STEVENSON, ADLAI E(WING)

b. Feb. 5, 1900; Los Angeles, Calif.
d. July 14, 1965; London, England.
Ambassador to the United Nations, January 1961-July 1965.

Stevenson was the son of a newspaper executive whose family had long been prominent in national politics. He was educated at Princeton, Harvard Law School and Northwestern University, where he received an LL.B. in 1926. After several years of private law practice in Chicago, Stevenson entered government service in 1933 and became legal assistant to the Secretary of the Navy during World War II. In 1945 he helped plan the conference that organized the United Nations, and he subsequently served as an adviser on the staff of the U.S. delegation to the U.N. Returning to Chicago in 1947, Stevenson ran for governor as a reform candidate, defeating his Republican opponent by a wide margin. Despite a Republican-dominated legislature, he compiled an impressive record of progressive legislation and administrative reform during his one term as Illinois governor. [See TRUMAN Volume]

By the early 1950s Stevenson had become a national figure in the Democratic Party. In 1952 and 1956 he ran as the Democratic candidate for president, but was defeated by the overwhelmingly popular Republican candidate, Dwight D. Eisenhower. After the failure of a draft-Stevenson movement at the 1960 Democratic National Convention, the former candidate played an important part in reconciling his Party's liberal wing with the Democratic nominee, John F. Kennedy. Although he had hoped to be named Secretary of State after Kennedy's election, Kennedy instead appointed Stevenson U.S. ambassador to the United Nations, a position that carried little policymaking responsibility. Lack of personal rapport between Stevenson and the new President, as well as the White House view that Stevenson was "soft" on foreign policy issues, prevented him from gaining much influence in the Kennedy Administration. Stevenson was not consulted before the 1961 Bay of Pigs invasion, and his advice was ignored during the Cuban missile crisis of 1962. [See EISENHOWER, KENNEDY Volumes]

Shortly after Kennedy's assassination, Stevenson met at the White House with President Lyndon Johnson, who urgently requested the Ambassador to remain at his post. Stevenson agreed and initially developed a good working relationship with the new President. Both men were approximately the same age, admired each other's political skills and had shared a covert resentment of the younger John Kennedy. Yet Johnson's penchant for secrecy and his demand for greater centralization of foreign policy decisions during the Vietnam war prevented Stevenson from exercising any influence in foreign affairs. Stevenson again became little more than an Administration spokesman, reading speeches prepared by the State Department and approved in advance by Johnson. He defended U.S. policy before the United Nations on such important occasions as the Panama Canal Zone riots of January 1964, the first U.S. bombing raids on North Vietnam in early 1965 and the U.S. troop landings in the Dominican Republic in May 1965.

As the Vietnam war escalated in 1965, Stevenson continued his public support of Administration foreign policy. Friends and associates, however, reported that he had strong private doubts on U.S. actions in Southeast Asia. In September 1964 and January 1965 Stevenson cooperated with U.N. Secretary General U Thant in attempting to arrange exploratory talks with the North Vietnamese government in Burma; but this "peace feeler" was later rejected by the Administration. Speaking before the American Newspaper Publishers Association in April 1965, Stevenson urged a "subtle shift" in U.S. diplomacy towards greater reliance on mediation through international organizations. In June 1965 writers Paul Goodman [*q.v.*], Dwight Macdonald [*q.v.*] and Harvey Swados visited Stevenson to urge him to repudiate American policy in Vietnam and join the growing anti-war movement. Stevenson refused, claiming that he was "on the [Administration] team." Friends later reported, however, that Stevenson had tentatively made the decision to resign from his U.N. post.

In late June relations between Stevenson and the President deteriorated sharply when Johnson refused to read a speech prepared by Stevenson for celebrations marking the 20th anniversary of the signing of the U.N. Charter. The speech had been inadvertently leaked to the press, and Johnson ordered a new version prepared without consulting Stevenson. Friends indicated that Stevenson took the incident as a personal affront, confirming his decision to leave the U.N. Before he could do this, however, Stevenson died of a heart attack during a London visit in July 1965.

[FHM]

For further information:
Kenneth S. Davis, *The Politics of Honor* (New York, 1967).

STEWART, POTTER
b. Jan. 23, 1915; Jackson, Mich.
Associate Justice, U.S. Supreme Court, 1958- .

Stewart grew up in Cincinnati and graduated from Yale University in 1937 and Yale Law School in 1941. After several years with a New York City law firm, Stewart joined a leading Cincinnati firm in 1947 and held several local offices there before his appointment to the Sixth Circuit Court of Appeals in 1954. A Republican, he was then named to the U.S. Supreme Court by Eisenhower in 1958. In his early years on the bench, Stewart cast the deciding vote in several important cases and was considered a "swing" justice between the Court's liberal and conservative wings.

As a solid liberal majority emerged on the Warren Court in the 1960s, Stewart's position became less decisive, although he was still viewed as a moderate and independent jurist. He frequently voted to uphold government security legislation against First Amendment challenges but also insisted that the government meet strict procedural standards. The lone dissenter in cases holding prayer and Bible reading in public schools unconstitutional, Stewart joined in several decisions expanding the rights of criminal defendants in the early 1960s. [See EISENHOWER, KENNEDY Volumes]

In a May 1964 ruling Stewart's majority opinion held that incriminating statements deliberately elicited by the police after indictment and in the absence of counsel were inadmissible in federal courts since the defendant's right to counsel had been violated. The next month, however, he dissented when the Court extended the right to counsel to a suspect under police investigation but not yet formally indicted or arraigned. He also objected to the Court's ruling that the First Amendment's protection against self-incrimination applied to state cases. In a series of cases expanding criminal rights over the next few years, Stewart repeatedly dissented, arguing that the rights of defendants should be balanced against the society's interests. He objected, for example, to the Court's June 1966 *Miranda* ruling, which placed limits on police interrogation of suspects. Stewart also dissented from a May 1967 ruling applying the procedural rights of the Fifth and Sixth Amendments to juvenile court proceedings. Writing the opinion of the Court in a December 1967 case, however, Stewart overturned a 39-year-old precedent to hold that electronic surveillance was subject to the Fourth Amendment's guarantee against unreasonable searches and seizures and to require police to obtain judicial warrants before using electronic eavesdropping devices.

Stewart continued to support government security legislation, dissenting when the Court overturned a federal law prohibiting Communist Party members from serving as labor union officials in June 1965 and when it invalidated a set of New York State teacher loyalty laws in January 1967. In obscenity cases, however, Stewart took positions that expanded the scope of free speech. In his concurring opinion in a June 1964 case, for example, Stewart defined obscene material as "hard core pornography," a definition narrower in effect than the one supported by some of the Court's more liberal members. But Stewart aroused much hilarity and criticism by adding that while he could not define hard core pornography, "I know it when I see it."

Stewart repeatedly dissented from Court rulings that legislative districts must be apportioned on an equal population basis. He objected in a February 1964 case to the application of this "one-man, one-vote" standard to congressional districting and argued that the Constitution had no provision determining the manner of apportionment such districts. In a series of cases involving state legislative reapportionment beginning in June 1964, Stewart insisted that such state plans be rational and that they not frustrate the will of the majority of the electorate. But aside from this, Stewart thought districts could be drawn to reflect economic, geographic and other interests in addition to population.

Justice Stewart also dissented in March 1966 when the majority voided a Virginia poll tax for state elections and in June 1966 when it upheld a provision in the 1965 Voting Rights Act designed to guarantee the right to vote to Spanish-speaking citizens. In December 1964 and February and November of 1966, he voted to uphold state court convictions of civil rights protesters. His majority opinion in a June 1967 case sustained the contempt-of-court convictions of Martin Luther King [*q.v.*] and seven other black leaders resulting from the 1963 Birmingham demonstrations. However, Stewart also wrote the majority opinion in a June 1968 case which held that an 1866 federal law prohibited racial discrimination in the sale or rental of property and sustained the law's constitutionality under the 13th Amendment.

When Earl Warren [*q.v.*] retired from the Court in 1969, President Nixon considered appointing Stewart to the chief justiceship. Stewart reportedly refused the post because he felt the new chief justice should be chosen from outside the Court. On the Burger Court Stewart was once again labeled a "swing" justice between the new, more conservative members and the other liberal justices. Stewart's opinions, usually brief, lucid and well-reasoned, have been highly regarded, and he has been evaluated as a capable and temperate legal craftsman. [See NIXON Volume]

[CAB]

For further information:

Helaine M. Barnett and Kenneth Levine, "Mr. Justice Potter Stewart," *New York University Law Review*, XL (May 1965), pp. 526-562.

Jerold H. Israel, "Potter Stewart," in Leon Friedman and Fred L. Israel, eds. *The Justices of the United States Supreme Court, 1789-1969* (New York, 1969), Vol. IV.

STOKES, CARL B(URTON)

b. June 21, 1927; Cleveland, Ohio.
Mayor, Cleveland, Ohio, 1967-71.

Left fatherless at age two, Carl B. Stokes and his brother Louis helped to support their mother by carrying newspapers and clerking in neighborhood stores. Carl dropped out of high school at age 16 and served in the Army during the Allied occupation of Germany. Later Stokes finished his secondary education and worked his way through four different colleges, earning a B.S. from the University of Minnesota in 1954. He received his LL.B. degree from Cleveland Marshall Law School in 1956. During the 1950s Stokes served as a liquor inspector and assistant city law director under Mayor Anthony J. Celebrezze [*q.v.*]. Active in Democratic politics and local civil rights organizations, Stokes served on the executive committees of the Cleveland NAACP and the county Democratic organization. In November 1962 he won election as the first Negro Democrat to the Ohio House of Representatives. He was reelected in 1964 and 1966.

In the mid-1960s Cleveland ranked 11th in size among American cities. As in other large northern cities, the minority population had grown dramatically. The black share of the city's population had risen from about 10% in 1940 to about 37% in 1965. The heavily polluted Cuyahoga River divided the city racially: blacks dominated the city's East Side neighborhoods while whites, primarily second and third generation immigrants from eastern and southern Europe, lived in the western half.

Although blacks had increased their share of the total population, Cleveland's political officeholders remained overwhelmingly white. In 1963 civil rights groups began a protest over the de facto segregation of city schools. In April of the following year, 85% of the system's black school children boycotted classes. The success of the 1964 student boycott demonstrated the black community's capacity for unity.

Stokes decided to run for mayor in 1965. He declined to oppose incumbent Democratic Mayor Ralph S. Locher in the primary and instead ran in the general election as an independent. Two other candidates—both white—entered the 1965 race. Locher received the endorsement of the regular Democratic organization and both the city's major newspapers. Although Stokes won 97% of the black city vote, he lost the general election to Locher by 1%.

Little occurring after Locher's close 1965 victory suggested an easier campaign for him two years later. Rioting in the Hough section of Cleveland in July 1966 created serious doubts about the white Mayor's ability to deal with a turbulent racial crisis. The Locher Administration's urban renewal program fell so far behind its original projections that the federal government reduced Cleveland's share of federal antipoverty funds. By early 1967 both of the city's dailies—the *Press* and the *Plain Dealer*—attacked the Mayor and demanded new leadership.

In June 1967 Stokes announced that he would oppose Locher again. This time he entered the Democratic primary, reportedly because White House officials promised Stokes full support only if he ran as a Democrat. A third candidate, former Lakewood Mayor Frank P. Celeste, a white, joined in the October primary. Locher easily won the endorsement of the city's Democratic machine. Celeste and Stokes joined in a series of debates throughout the city, thus assuring Stokes of needed exposure in white neighborhoods. In recognition of its candidate's telegenic appeal, the Stokes primary campaign spent an unusually large amount for television spots. The Cleveland chapter of the Congress of Racial Equality lent crucial assistance to the Stokes's campaign by utilizing part of a $175,000 Ford Foundation grant to register blacks for the primary. The turnout in black neighborhoods averaged 15% higher on primary day than in white precincts. Stokes defeated Locher and Celeste with 52.7% of the total primary vote. He captured 96% of the black Democratic vote and between 12% and 15% of the Party's white electorate.

In the month between the primary and general election, Stokes engaged in a bitter contest with Republican nominee Seth C. Taft, grandson of President William Howard Taft and cousin of Rep. Robert Taft, Jr. (R, Ohio) [*q.v.*]. An admirer of New York Mayor John V. Lindsay [*q.v.*], Taft sought to overcome his party's weak showing in previous mayoral elections and his family's political conservatism by emphasizing his own liberal Republicanism. Stokes, however, enjoyed the endorsement of both major dailies and greater financial support. In November he improved on his share of the White Democratic vote and defeated Taft by a thin margin. With the simultaneous election of Richard Hatcher [*q.v.*] as mayor of Gary, Ind., liberal observers hailed the black politicians' triumph as the harbinger of a rising generation of high-level black officeholders.

Stokes enjoyed a series of personal triumphs as mayor in the spring of 1968. In the days following the assassination of Dr. Martin Luther King [*q.v.*], he successfully staved off the racial troubles which plagued most other urban centers. On May 1 he announced an ambitious new plan for the reconstruction of Cleveland. With the full support of the city's business and press establishments, Stokes's "Cleveland: NOW!" project planned to attack a wide range of city problems over the next 10 years at an estimated cost of $1.25 billion. Less than a week later, Louis Stokes, the Mayor's brother, won the Democratic nomination in the city's newly apportioned "black" congressional district; Democratic Party endorsement assured his election in November.

Stokes's popularity proved short-lived, however. In July 1968 reports reached Cleveland police that a local book store operator, Fred (Ahmed) Evans, and his "Black Nationalists of New Libya" had gathered an arsenal of semiautomatic weapons with the intention of inciting the black community to riot. For reasons which remain unclear, shooting broke out on the night of July 23 between the Evans nationalists and police in the Glenville section. Subsequent looting took place throughout much of the East Side. Within hours, seven men—three militants, three police officers and one black who had attempted to aid the police—lay dead. After consultation with local black leaders, Stokes decided upon an "all-black" strategy in which white policemen and National Guardsmen would be withdrawn from the riot zone. Only black patrolmen would be stationed in the Glenville area. Few incidents followed the implementation of the Mayor's plan.

Although Stokes had played the leading role in ending the Glenville riots, he faced a wave of criticism over the incident. The city council and local Fraternal Order of Police strongly condemned the Mayor's exclusive use of black police officers in the resolution of the riot. The most devastating blow to the Mayor's prestige, however, came with the revelation that Evans's New Nationalists had received $10,000 in "Cleveland: NOW!" funds. (Evans was found guilty on seven counts of first-degree murder in May 1969.)

Stokes never again enjoyed the near-unanimous popularity of April and May 1968. Several embarrassing appointments and adverse economic conditions beyond his control severely hampered Stokes's effectiveness. He remained a black leader, but the city continued to be racially segregated by the Cuyahoga. Stokes narrowly defeated a white Republican opponent in November 1969 but declined to seek a third term in 1971. In March 1972 Stokes announced that he had accepted a newscasting job with WNBC in New York City. He then withdrew his name as a delegate to the 1972 Democratic National Convention from Ohio. [See NIXON Volume]

[JLB]

For further information:

National Commission on the Causes and Prevention of Violence, *Shoot-Out in Cleveland* (Washington, 1969).

Estelle Zannes, *Checkmate in Cleveland* (Cleveland, 1972).

STONE, I(SIDOR) F(EINSTEIN)

b. Dec. 24, 1907; Philadelphia, Pa.
Editor, *I.F. Stone's Weekly*, 1953-67 (*Biweekly*, 1967-71).

Stone was raised in Haddonfield, N.J. He left the University of Pennsylvania in 1927 during his junior year. A member of the Socialist Party, he worked for Norman Thomas's [*q.v.*] presidential campaign in

1928. From 1933 to 1952 he was employed by a number of liberal and left-wing publications, including the *New York Post*, the *Nation* and *PM*. From 1945 to 1950 Stone, who was sympathetic to the Zionist movement, spent much of his time in Palestine reporting the events surrounding the creation of Israel. An opponent of American policies in the Cold War, he supported the Progressive Party presidential candidacy of Henry Wallace in 1948. Four years later Stone wrote *The Hidden History of the Korean War*, which suggested that South Korea, in collaboration with the United States, had instigated that conflict.

After *PM*, the last newspaper that he worked for, folded in 1952, Stone was unable to find a job because of his controversial views. The following year he began publishing *I.F. Stone's Weekly*, an independent newsletter. Among the *Weekly's* first targets were Sen. Joseph R. McCarthy (R, Wisc.), the House Un-American Activities Committee and the practice of blacklisting Communists and alleged Communists. In the early 1960s he criticized President John F. Kennedy's counterinsurgency program, warning that Communism could be stopped only by responding to the needs of the world's poor nations. Stone also cautioned that counterinsurgency would be implemented by secret organizations such as the Central Intelligence Agency, which might ultimately turn their attention to suppressing domestic dissenters. By 1963 his *Weekly* had a circulation of over 20,000. [See TRUMAN, EISENHOWER, KENNEDY Volumes]

Describing himself as a democratic socialist, Stone was an independent radical who shunned affiliation with organized political groups and spoke only for himself. In his role as a journalist he was also independent. His newsletter did not accept advertising, and Stone did all his own research, reportorial and editorial work, while his wife handled the newsletter's business affairs.

Stone's reputation was built upon his iconoclastic skill in exposing the inconsistencies, mistakes and hypocrisy of public officials and his ability to detect the early signals of changes in government policy. Although he was based in Washington D.C., his information did not come from personal contacts with highly placed sources, of which he had few, or from official briefings, from which he was often excluded. Stone's journalistic method was the diligent sifting and comparison of government publications that were available to everyone but generally went unread.

During the mid and late 1960s Stone's attention focused on the Vietnam war, which he had opposed from the first American involvement during the Kennedy presidency. Rejecting the U.S. contention that the National Liberation Front (NLF) was an arm of North Vietnamese aggression, Stone wrote in February 1964, "The biggest obstacle to a settlement is the myth that the South Vietnamese war is an invasion, not a rebellion."

In August 1964 Stone questioned the Administration's version of the events surrounding alleged North Vietnamese attacks upon American military vessels in the Tonkin Gulf. He noted Sen. Wayne Morse's (D, Ore.) [*q.v.*] contention that the vessels were on patrol near South Vietnamese ships that were shelling two North Vietnamese islands and were in a position to protect those ships. Stone also pointed out that during Senate debate on the Tonkin Gulf Resolution, which authorized the President to take all necessary steps to repel North Vietnamese aggression, neither Sen. J. William Fulbright (D, Ark.) [*q.v.*] nor Sen. Richard B. Russell (D, Ga.) [*q.v.*], the chairmen of the congressional committees that were briefed by the Administration on the Tonkin incident, denied any of Morse's facts.

In March 1965 Stone analyzed a State Department White Paper on alleged North Vietnamese aggression issued in defense of the escalating American intervention in Vietnam. He compared the number of Communist-made weapons captured from South Vietnamese guerrillas listed in an appendix to the White Paper with what he learned from the Pentagon press office were the much larger quantities of American weapons seized by the rebels. Stone concluded that the Communist world supplied the rebels with only a tiny fraction of their munitions. Stone also wrote that although the White Paper contended that about 75% of the NLF guerrillas who infiltrated South Vietnam from North Vietnam in the first eight months of 1964 were natives of the North, most of the guerrillas whose case histories were presented in the text and the appendices were from the South.

Next to Vietnam, the condition of American blacks was Stone's primary concern during the years of the Johnson presidency. In August 1966 he stated that the most urgent need of blacks was jobs and asserted that the growing nationalist sentiment among Negroes did not offer a realistic program to meet that need. But Stone thought that black nationalism enabled the Negro to overcome self-contempt and concluded that "his racism, answering ours, is a necessary step toward our ultimate reconciliation."

As opposition to the war in Vietnam mounted, Stone's *Weekly* became increasingly popular, and by 1968 it had a circulation of 38,000. But he incurred criticism when, after the Mideast war of 1967, he urged Israel to take a more conciliatory position towards the Arabs, particularly on the issue of resettlement of the Palestinian refugees. He argued that if Israel were not magnanimous in the wake of its overwhelming victory in that conflict, an Arab desire for revenge would spark future wars.

In December 1971 Stone announced that he would cease publication of his newsletter. At the same time he became a contributing editor to the *New York Review of Books*, for which he had been writing occasionally since 1964.

[MLL]

SULLIVAN, LEONOR K(RETZER)

b. Aug. 21, 1904; St. Louis, Mo.
Democratic Representative, Mo. 1953- ; Chairman, Banking and Currency Subcommittee on Consumer Affairs, 1963- .

After a career in business education, Leonor Kretzer married Rep. John B. Sullivan (D, Mo.) in 1941 and served as her husband's administrative assistant until his death in January 1951. Assuming that a woman could not be elected, the St. Louis Democratic Committee refused to slate her for her late husband's seat, and she sat out the special election. However, in the May 1952 primary election, she defeated seven Democratic rivals and in November defeated the Republican incumbent by a 2-to-1 margin.

In Congress Sullivan soon gained a reputation as a strong liberal on social issues. She and 23 other House members urged the formation of a permanent House committee to study consumer protection in 1953. In 1957 Sullivan guided the bill that became the Poultry Products Inspection Act through the House. In 1959 she successfully included a food stamp plan in the Administration's agriculture program, but Secretary of Agriculture Ezra Taft Benson withheld operation funds. A letter from Rep. Sullivan to President Kennedy, recalling his past support for her food stamp plan and reminding him that now he had "a chance to prove he meant it," reached the White House the day after Kennedy's inauguration. Kennedy set up a pilot food stamp program, and in 1964 Sullivan sponsored the bill that established the permanent food stamp system.

When the food stamp program came up for renewal in 1967, opponents of the program supported a proposal to assess the states 20% of the program's cost. According to *Congressional Quarterly*, Sullivan believed this amendment was designed to scuttle the entire program, and she successfully opposed the measure on the House floor. When the bill reached the House Senate conference, Agriculture Committee conservatives refused to compromise and kept the renewal measure in conference for more than two months. In retaliation, Sullivan led a coalition of Northern Democrats who successfully defeated a peanut acreage bill favored by Committee conservatives on Aug. 21, 1967. A month later the conferees reported a compromise bill acceptable to Sullivan, and the peanut acreage bill was allowed to pass.

An early supporter of "truth-in-lending" legislation, Rep. Sullivan introduced a House bill on July 20, 1967 which wa stronger than either the Administration's bill or the bill Sen. William Proxmire (D, Wisc.) [*q.v.*] had guided through the Senate earlier that month. Sullivan's bill, which went beyond simple disclosure of finance charges to include comprehensive credit protection for the consumer, became law in May 1968. Sullivan fought especially hard for the application of the rate disclosure principle to revolving charge accounts and opposed wage garnishment, which she termed "a successor to debtor's prison." When he signed the Consumer Credit Protection Act, President Johnson praised her fight "for a strong and effective bill when others would have settled for less." During the Nixon Administration Rep. Sullivan co-sponsored a 1969 bill establishing a permanent office of consumer protection and sought unsuccessfully to liberalize the federal housing law. [See NIXON Volume]

[DKR]

SULLIVAN, WILLIAM C(ORNELIUS)

b. May 25, 1912; Bolton, Mass.
Assistant Director in charge of the Domestic Intelligence Division, FBI, 1961-70.

Sullivan was raised on a farm outside Bolton, Mass. He earned a B.A. from the American University in 1936 and went to work for the Internal Revenue Service in Boston. He joined the FBI in 1941 and after service in various cities was sent to Spain to track down German espionage agents. After the war Sullivan moved up steadily through the ranks of the Bureau. During the 1950s he earned a reputation as a popular and entertaining speaker who lectured frequently on the menace of Communism in the U.S. In 1961 he was named assistant FBI director in charge of the Domestic Intelligence Division.

In response to rumors that the Communist Party was encouraging its members to join the Aug. 28, 1963 March on Washington, Sullivan's department undertook an investigation of Communist influence in the civil rights movement. But on Aug. 23 Sullivan reported that the Communist Party had "obviously" failed to win control of civil rights organizations. According to a 1976 Senate Select Committee report, this conclusion so outraged FBI Director J. Edgar Hoover [*q.v.*], who believed the Party's influence on those groups was great, that Sullivan and members of his division feared that they would be transferred or even fired. Sullivan indirectly apologized to Hoover and a few weeks later wrote a memorandum suggesting that there was "an urgent need for imaginative and aggressive tactics to be utilized through our counterintelligence program . . . to neutralize or disrupt the Communist Party's activities in the Negro field." To further placate Hoover, Sullivan stated that he agreed with the Director's opinion that Martin Luther King, [*q.v.*] was coming under Communist influence and that he was one of the most dangerous black leaders in the nation.

In October 1963 Attorney General Robert F. Kennedy [*q.v.*] granted the FBI permission to wiretap King's home telephone. Sullivan then assumed control of a wide-ranging effort, utilizing wiretaps and "bugging," to gather information about King's private life. This information was subsequently leaked to select government officials. In an attempt to destroy King's marriage, the Bureau sent his wife information concerning his extramarital affairs. According to the 1976 report of the Senate Select Committee on Intelligence Activities, in January 1964 Sullivan proposed that once King had been publicly disgraced, the Bureau should promote its own black candidate to lead the civil rights movement. In November the Bureau sent King a letter suggesting that he commit suicide.

Beginning in 1967 Sullivan's Domestic Intelligence Division also attempted to discredit Elijah Muhammed [*q.v.*], H. Rap Brown [*q.v.*] and Stokely Carmichael [*q.v.*] and to disrupt the activities of the Southern Christian Leadership Conference, the Student Nonviolent Coordinating Committee, the Congress of Racial Equality and other black groups it considered dangerous.

Sullivan was not exclusively concerned with the subversion of the civil rights movement by Communists or the activities of what the Bureau called ghetto "rabble rousers." According to journalist Sanford Ungar, by the fall of 1964 he had won permission from Hoover to "expose . . . and neutralize" the Ku Klux Klan and other "white hate groups." It was also reportedly on Sullivan's urging that in May 1968 New Left organizations became targets of the Bureau's COINTELPRO campaign. Bureau agents faked documents to create dissension within various anti-war groups and sent intimidating letters to their leaders; the Bureau also requested that the Internal Revenue Service audit the tax returns of key members of the anti-war movement.

Appearing before a Senate Select Committee in November 1975, Sullivan was asked whether members of the Bureau ever questioned the fairness of COINTELPRO tactics. "We never gave any thought to this realm of reasoning," he said, "because we were just naturally pragmatists. As far as legality is concerned, morals or ethics [the problem] was never raised by myself or anybody else."

During the early Nixon years Sullivan maintained close relations with the Administration. At the request of the President and Henry Kissinger [*q.v.*], then national security adviser, Sullivan's office managed wiretaps that had been placed on the phones of government officials and newsmen to determine how secret information was being leaked to the press.

In June 1970 Hoover promoted Sullivan to the post of assistant director in charge of all investigative activities. By the fall of 1970, however, relations between the two men had begun to deteriorate. At one point Sullivan suggested that the Bureau was in decline because the Director had surrounded himself with "cringing, frightened sycophants." Hoover then requested that Sullivan retire. Before doing so in October 1971, Sullivan turned over to the White House wiretap logs that Hoover could have used to blackmail the Administration. [See NIXON Volume]

After leaving the Bureau Sullivan worked for the Insurance Crime Prevention Institute and briefly for the Office of National Narcotics Intelligence. By the mid-1970s he had retired to his home in New Hampshire.

[JLW]

For further information:

U.S. Senate Secret Committtee on Intelligence Activities, *Final Report* (Washington, 1976), Books II and III.

Sanford J. Ungar, *FBI: An Uncensored Look Behind The Walls* (Boston, 1976).

SULLIVAN, WILLIAM H(EALY)

b. Oct. 12, 1922; Cranston, R.I.
Special Assistant to the Undersecretary of State for Political Affairs, March 1963-December 1964; Ambassador to Laos, December 1964-March 1969.

A career foreign service officer, William Sullivan specialized in Far Eastern affairs. Shortly after World War II he served in Bangkok, Calcutta and Tokyo. In 1952 he was sent to Rome and in 1955 to The Hague before resuming his Far Eastern assignments as officer-in-charge of Burma affairs for the Department of State in 1958. In 1960 Sullivan was appointed U.N. adviser for the Bureau of Far Eastern Affairs.

During the Kennedy Administration Sullivan served as a member of the U.S. delegation to the 1961 Geneva conference called to guarantee the neutrality of Laos. At the conference he was appointed deputy to Ambassador W. Averell Harriman [*q.v.*], who led the delegation. In December Sullivan became acting head when the Ambassador left to assume the position of assistant secretary of state for Far Eastern affairs. During the spring of 1962 Sullivan worked with Harriman in a series of negotiations with Laotian leaders designed to gain acceptance of a neutralist coalition government in that country. [See KENNEDY Volume]

On Feb. 24, 1964 President Lyndon B. Johnson appointed Sullivan chairman of the Vietnam Working Group, a body formed to plan the possible escalation of the war and to coordinate policy decisions and statements between the Defense Department the Central Intelligence Agency (CIA) and the U.S. Information Agency.

In May, after a visit to Vietnam, Sullivan

reported that the South Vietnamese did not have the will to fight because of a "lack of purpose on the part of the government." He therefore proposed the introduction of U.S. personnel into all levels of Vietnamese government to promote the war effort. His idea was discarded at the Honolulu Conference held in early June 1964.

When Maxwell Taylor [*q.v.*] assumed the post of ambassador to South Vietnam in July 1964, Sullivan became executive secretary of Mission Council, the group of high-level American leaders in Saigon who met regularly to coordinate the U.S. effort there. It was his job to prepare the agenda for meetings and to monitor the decisions that were made.

Sullivan opposed the demands of American military leaders for intensive bombing of North Vietnam after the August 1964 Gulf of Tonkin incident. Working with Michael Forrestal, he developed a plan of limited action in which bombing targets were to be fewer and further from population centers than those demanded by the armed forces. As Sullivan defined it, his goal was not to crush North Vietnam but to bring it to the negotiating table. The Administration rejected the Forrestal-Sullivan proposal in the fall of 1964.

In December 1964 Sullivan was appointed ambassador to Laos. There he controlled the secret war carried on by the U.S. to prevent North Vietnam from using Laos as a supply route to the South. Because Sullivan had worked closely with and was trusted by high officials in Washington, he was able to centralize the effort under his command. As ambassador, Sullivan, rather than the military, chose the bombing targets and the types of aircraft used. His control was so complete that Assistant Secretary of State William Bundy [*q.v.*] said, "There wasn't a bag of rice dropped in Laos that he didn't know about."

During his tenure Sullivan tried to impose two crucial conditions on American actions in Laos. He urged that the war be carried out in relative secrecy to avoid embarrassing either the neutralist leader Souvanna Phouma or the Russians. He also insisted that no regular U.S. ground combat troops be allowed into Laos. Despite continued pressure from Gen. William Westmoreland [*q.v.*], Sullivan managed to keep American troops out of Laos, although he was forced to accept a smaller, CIA-controlled force in the country.

In April 1968, when the North Vietnamese first gave indications that they were willing to come to the negotiating table, the message was transmitted by private American citizens to Sullivan. Until the site for the peace talks was agreed upon in May, formal communications between Hanoi and Washington on the problem were channeled through Sullivan in Laos.

Sullivan was appointed deputy assistant secretary of state for East Asia in 1969.

[EWS]

For Further Information:
Charles A. Stevenson, *The End of Nowhere: American Policy Towards Laos Since 1954* (Boston, 1972).

SYLVESTER, ARTHUR

b. Oct. 21, 1901; Montclair, N.J.
Assistant Secretary of Defense for Public Affairs, January 1961-January 1967.

Prior to becoming assistant secretary of defense for public affairs in January 1961, Arthur Sylvester had been the Washington reporter and bureau chief for the *Newark Evening News.*

As the Defense Department's chief press officer, Sylvester was credited with opening up the Pentagon to a wider flow of information and forcing officials who once would not be interviewed to answer questions. Yet Sylvester became a central figure in both the Kennedy and Johnson Administrations not as an advocate of press freedom but as a man who continually clashed with the press and advanced the belief that the government had the right to manage the news in certain critical situations. Following the Cuban missile crisis of 1962, Sylvester, in an informal interview on Oct. 30, allegedly maintained that "the generation of news by the government" was "one weapon" to be used in a crisis situation. In a Dec. 6 statement he argued, "It's inherent in government's right. . .to lie to save itself when it's going up into nuclear war." [see KENNEDY Volume]

During the next Administration Sylvester continued to defend these ideas, causing congressional critics to attribute the growing "credibility gap" in reporting the Vietnam war to the Johnson Administration's acceptance of the Press Secretary's news philosophy. A climax in Sylvester's clash with the press occurred during an interview in Saigon on July 17, 1965. According to newsmen present at the meeting, Sylvester had maintained that "the American correspondents had a patriotic duty to disseminate only information that made the United States look good" and that the press should be the "handmaiden" of the government. In response to complaints about the lack of credibility of American officials, the news secretary replied, "Look, if you think any American official is going to tell you the truth, then you're stupid. Did you hear that?—stupid." As a result of continued complaints about the Administration's credibility gap, the Senate Foreign Relations Committee held hearings on the subject in September 1966 at which Sylvester testified.

In January 1967 Sylvester resigned his post for personal reasons.

[EWS]

SYMINGTON, (WILLIAM) STUART

b. June 26, 1901; Amherst, Mass.
Democratic Senator, Mo., 1953-77.

A descendent of a distinguished Southern family, Symington attended Yale University after serving in World War I. Following his graduation in 1923, he began a successful business career that earned him the reputation of being a "doctor of ailing corporations" because of his ability to revive foundering enterprises and deal with labor problems.

During the Truman Administration Symington held important appointed posts in several federal agencies and from 1946 to 1950 served as Secretary of the Air Force. Believing that the U.S. had to act from a position of military superiority against the expansionist policies of the Soviet Union, Symington became a leading proponent of increased defense spending. Symington particularly advocated the development of a large nuclear-equipped Air Force as the cornerstone of a modern defense system. In 1950, shortly before the Korean War, the Secretary resigned to protest a series of economy-minded armament reductions. [See TRUMAN Volume]

During the Kennedy years Symington backed the Defense Department in the "muzzling" probe of 1962 and supported the development of the controversial TFX multi-service fighter/bomber in 1963. That same year he chaired hearings on stockpiling abuses during the Eisenhower Administration. [See KENNEDY Volume]

Although he had initially supported the war in Vietnam, Symington came out against U.S. involvement in that country in 1967. His change in position was influenced both by his experience on the Senate Foreign Relations Committee, to which he had been assigned in 1961, and by his sympathy for the Air Force and its personnel. Symington maintained that his tenure on the Foreign Relations Committee and his work with Senators J. William Fulbright (D, Ark) [*q.v.*] and Mike Mansfield (D, Mont.) [*q.v.*] had taught him to think in terms of America's global commitments and total foreign policy requirements. Viewing Vietnam in this light Symington became convinced that the war was not vital for U.S. security and that it was endangering the American economy. As a result of several trips to Vietnam, he had also learned of the growing discontent among American pilots who felt constricted by the Administration's target limits and believed that the government was willing to sacrifice American lives to prevent North Vietnamese civilian casualities. Symington maintained that if pilots were going to be forced to fight a limited war, it would be better to pull out of Vietnam than to sacrifice their lives. In October 1967 he therefore urged a unilateral ceasefire aimed at initiating peace negotiations. His position on both the Foreign Relations Committee and the Armed Services Committee made him a powerful advocate of de-escalation and withdrawal in Congress.

Throughout his career Symington had

voted in favor of most foreign aid bills, but after 1967 he opposed those measures because of his belief that the U.S. was economically and militarily overcommitted throughout the world. He also voted against new weapons development projects because of the frequency with which they were changed or canceled.

During the Nixon Administration Symington spoke out against extension of the war in Cambodia and Laos and demanded American troop withdrawals from Europe. Pointing out that many major military commitments of the 1960s and 1970s had been made through executive agreements without the knowledge or consent of Congress, Symington campaigned for the reassertion of congressional authority in foreign policy matters during the 1970s. He did not run for reelection in 1976. [See NIXON Volume]

[EWS]

TAFT, ROBERT, JR.

b. Feb. 26, 1917; Cincinnati, Ohio.
Republican Representative, Ohio, 1963-65; 1967-71.

The grandson of a president and the son of the late Sen. Robert A. Taft (R, Ohio), Robert Taft, Jr., graduated from Yale in 1939 and received a LL.B. degree from Harvard in 1942. After naval duty in the Pacific during World War II, Taft became a corporation lawyer in his father's Cincinnati law firm. "Young Bob" declined to run for his father's Senate seat following the elder Taft's death in July 1953 despite pleas from Ohio Republican leaders and friends. Instead, Taft won the first of four terms to the Ohio House of Representatives in 1954 and served as majority floor leader in 1961 and 1962. Richard M. Nixon chose Taft, whose name was revered by many Old Guard Republicans, to second his presidential nomination at the July 1960 Republican National Convention.

In November 1962 Taft defeated an obscure Democratic foe by 620,000 votes in the race for Ohio's congressman-at-large. He voted for the Civil Rights Act in February 1964 but opposed the Johnson Administration's antipoverty program in July. Taft unsuccessfully sought to place the Office of Economic Opportunity (OEO) within the Labor Department.

Taft ran for the U.S. Senate in 1964 as a strong favorite to win over 74-year-old Sen. Stephen M. Young (D, Ohio) [*q.v.*]. With a strong labor record, however, Young received substantial support from the Ohio AFL-CIO, and his campaign skillfully tied his reelection to President Johnson's race against Sen. Barry M. Goldwater (R, Ariz.) [*q.v.*]. Although Taft disagreed with the Republican presidential nominee on nuclear arms policy, civil rights, housing and aid-to-education, he loyally appeared with Goldwater in Ohio. In November Goldwater lost Ohio by just over a million votes. This disastrous showing in a traditionally Republican state deprived Taft of his expected victory; Young defeated him by 16,000 votes.

In 1965 Republican National Committee Chairman Ray C. Bliss [*q.v.*] reportedly persuaded Taft to run against Rep. John J. Gilligan (D, Ohio) [*q.v.*] the following year. Gilligan had narrowly upset a Republican incumbent in 1964, and the Administration boosted the Democrat's reelection prospects with defense contracts and housing and cultural appropriations for his Cincinnati-area district. The Republican-controlled Ohio legislature, however, had redrawn Gilligan's district in December 1964 to include more Republican voters.

In 1966 Taft and Gilligan fought a bitter and expensive race which attracted national attention. Sen. Robert F. Kennedy (D, N.Y.) [*q.v.*] and Vice President Hubert H. Humphrey [*q.v.*] appeared on Gilligan's behalf, but Taft ran with the advantage of a strong Republican resurgence in Ohio. With 53% of the vote Taft defeated Gilligan in the November balloting.

Returning to the House after two years, Taft occasionally strayed from Old Guard conservatism. He opposed a $225 million cut in the Model Cities program in May 1967 but supported a $460 million reduction in the antipoverty program in November. He supported the 1967 and 1968 House civil rights bills and in May 1968 sought to increase by 71% the appropriation for the Equal Employment Opportunity Commission. The liberal Americans for Democratic Action gave Taft a 33% rating for selected issues in the 1968 session, while the conservative Americans for Constitutional Action gave Taft a mark of 60%. Before the Republican National Convention's Platform Committee hearings in July 1968, Taft said that the GOP "must convince people that we do care, that we have dreams and answers and that we will do the job."

Declining to challenge Sen. Frank J. Lausche (D, Ohio) [*q.v.*] in January 1968, Taft easily won reelection to the House in November. Waiting two more years, he captured Young's Senate seat in November 1970. [See NIXON Volume]

[JLB]

TALBOT, PHILLIPS

b. June 7, 1915; Pittsburgh, Pa.
Assistant Secretary of State for Near Eastern and South Asian Affairs, April 1961-July 1965; Ambassador to Greece, July 1965-January 1969.

Phillips Talbot, U.S. ambassador to Greece during the Johnson Administration, had been a journalist and Asian scholar before joining the State Department. Talbot earned his B.A. in journalism from the University of Illinois in 1936 and for the next two years studied Asian affairs in London and India. He eventually received his Ph.D. from the University of Chicago in 1954. Between 1936 and 1950 Talbot worked as a journalist specializing in Indian and Pakistani affairs and taught at the University of Chicago. From 1951 to 1961 he was the executive director of the American Universities Field Staff.

Talbot was appointed assistant secretary of state for Near Eastern and South Asian affairs in 1961. During the Kennedy Administration much of his attention was focused on India and Pakistan. In October and November of 1962, Talbot helped coordinate American aid to India in its border war with Communist China and carried on diplomatic negotiations designed to prevent Pakistan from entering the conflict. The following year he unsuccessfully tried to convince Pakistan and India to accept mediation of their border dispute over Jammu and Kashmir. Talbot's handling of these problems, and particularly his failure to be forceful in his dealings with Pakistan, earned him the criticism of John Kenneth Galbraith [*q.v.*], the influential ambassador to India, who termed him "soft," "uncommitted and capable of being controlled."

In July 1965 President Lyndon Johnson appointed Talbot ambassador to Greece, a major diplomatic post because of that country's strategic importance to the North Atlantic Treaty Organization (NATO). Because the U.S. desired to maintain a strong pro-Western government in Greece, the Central Intelligence Agency (CIA), the State Department and the U.S. military played highly influential roles in Greek domestic politics. The general U.S. strategy was to support a conservative regime that backed a strong Greek military, but the efforts of the Americans were not coordinated, and the CIA, in particular, often acted without the knowledge of other U.S. agencies.

When Talbot took office in October 1965, a rightist regime loyal to the King was in power. However, public opinion polls indicated that elections scheduled for May 1967 would give a parliamentary majority to the center-left Center Union Party led by George Papandreou and his son Andreas. Fearful of a turn to the left, Greek generals, with the support of the King, were plotting a coup and the establishment of a dictatorship.

In talking to Greek political leaders, Talbot expressed his dislike of both a dictatorship and of the Papandreous and suggested that the King establish a coalition government composed of center and rightist elements. Such a government was organized in 1967 but proved unpopular; polls showed that it would be defeated in the May elections. Unwilling to accept a leftist drift, the generals planned a coup for four days before the election. Talbot, while willing to approve a suspension of the constitution "only for a few months" if this would prevent the establishment of a leftist government, hoped that there would be no military takeover. Realistically, however, he saw little hope for avoiding such a coup, which, according to some reports, was surreptitously encouraged by American intelligence operatives.

Unknown to the embassy a group of colonels, led by George Papadopoulos, were also plotting to counter the leftists by establishing a military dictatorship. On April 21, 1967 the colonels overthrew the civilian government. The move took Talbot by surprise. In his first telegram to the State Department following the takeover, he characterized it as "a violation of Greek democracy" and recommended a very strong statement denouncing the junta. The U.S. government took no action, and ties between the U.S. and the colonels remained strong, particularly after the June Middle East war, when Greece opened its military bases in Crete to Israeli military aircraft.

In December 1967 Talbot was informed of a proposed countercoup by King Constantine, but neither the U.S. military mission nor the American embassy took part in the plan. (However, some writers have questioned whether the CIA may have been involved.) The Dec. 14 coup was crushed immediately, and the King was forced to flee. With the King in exile, the U.S. maintained that the junta had lost its claim to legitimacy and suspended formal recognition of the regime. However, normal contacts were resumed in January 1968.

Talbot resigned his post in January 1969 and a year later became president of the Asia Society.

[EWS]

For further information:

John A. Katris, *Eyewitness in Greece: The Colonels Come to Power* (St. Louis, 1971).
Peter Schwab and George D. Frangos, eds., *Greece Under the Junta* (New York, 1970).

TALMADGE, HERMAN E(UGENE)

b. Aug. 9, 1913; McRae, Ga.
Democratic Senator, Ga., 1957-   .

Herman Talmadge was the son of Eugene Talmadge, a fiery white supremacist and anti-New Deal orator who was elected governor of Georgia four times in the 1930s and 1940s by appealing to the poor white farmers of the predominantly rural state. In a special 1948 election Herman was chosen to complete the last term of his father, who had died shortly after winning the gubernatorial race in 1946. Herman Talmadge was reelected for a full four-year term in 1950.

Although less flamboyant than his father, the younger Talmadge also played strongly upon the racial fears of rural whites. But unlike his father he made a serious effort to improve education and to attract industry to the state. In 1956 Talmadge won a seat in the U.S. Senate. Although his family name was associated with political demagoguery, Talmadge quickly gained a reputation among his fellow-senators as an intelligent and well-informed legislator. In the early 1960s he compiled a conservative record, opposing both civil rights and social welfare legislation while supporting measures favorable to private enterprise. [See EISENHOWER, KENNEDY Volumes]

During the mid-1960s Talmadge continued to vote against liberal domestic legislation. According to *Congressional Quarterly,* he never opposed the Senate's conservative coalition on more than 12% of roll call votes in any of the years of the Johnson Administration.

In April 1965 Talmadge attacked President Johnson's voting rights bill as "grossly unjust and vindictive in nature." In 1968 the Administration offered an open housing bill, which included a provision protecting persons attempting to exercise their civil rights from injury, intimidation or interference. Talmadge successfully offered an amendment to extend this protection to store owners or operators during civil disorders but voted against the final bill.

During the Johnson Administration, Talmadge became less vociferous in his opposition to racial equality as the number of black voters in his state increased. In 1966, speaking before a predominantly black Atlanta organization, he stated that there would be no more "race-baiting" campaigns in Georgia.

During the early years of the Johnson presidency, Talmadge strongly supported the Vietnam war. In 1965 he denounced student opponents of the conflict as guilty of "treason and anarchy." The following year, speaking as a member of Congress's Joint Economic Committee, Talmadge urged restraint in domestic spending so that military needs in Indochina could be met. But in 1967 Talmadge stated that foreign aid and military spending were responsible for America's unfavorable balance of payments. The following year, citing graft and corruption in Vietnam, he expressed doubts about the worth of the Administration's request for $480 million in aid to that country.

During the Nixon Administration Talmadge became an opponent of the Indochina conflict. In 1969 he questioned the purpose of fighting a war that the government, in his view, was not attempting to win. Two years later he favored the withdrawal of American troops from Indochina.

In the face of an enlarged and increasingly articulate black and urban electorate in Georgia, Talmadge became somewhat more disposed to support social welfare programs in the late 1960s and early 1970s. In 1971 he became chairman of the Senate Agriculture and Forestry Committee and two years later was appointed to the Senate Select Committee to Investigate Presidental Campaign Activities, popularly known as the Watergate Committee. [See NIXON Volume]

[MLL]

TATE, JAMES H(UGH) J(OSEPH)
b. April 10, 1910; Philadelphia, Pa.
Mayor, Philadelphia, Pa., 1962-72.

Born into an Irish-American family of modest means, Tate worked his way through school and received a law degree from Temple University in 1938. He soon joined the Democratic Party in Philadelphia, advancing through the ranks as committeeman, ward leader, state assemblyman and city councilman. When Mayor Richardson Dilworth resigned to run for governor in January 1962, Tate, as city council president, was automatically sworn in as mayor.

Unlike his Democratic predecessors, reformers Dilworth and Joseph Clark [*q.v.*], Tate did not move easily in the social circles of the Main Line elite. He was known as an "organization man," but he failed to get the backing of the city's Democratic organization, headed by Francis Smith, when he ran for a full term in 1963. Support from Clark-Dilworth reformers and President Kennedy helped Tate to win in both the primary and the general election.

Racial tension marked Tate's first full term as mayor, with widespread riots breaking out in the North Philadelphia ghetto in August 1964. Although some militant black leaders charged the mayor with racism, Tate generally retained a liberal image and the support of the black community. His administration passed strong anti-discrimination statutes and insisted on the hiring of minorities in city-financed construction.

Many Philadelphia whites felt that Tate had yielded too easily to black demands, and by the end of his first term the Mayor had modified his political stance. Although he continued previously enacted programs and policies, such as urban renewal, and was a spokesman for the cities through the National League of Cities, of which he was elected vice president in December 1966, Tate brought the pace of reform to a standstill in the mid-1960s. In opposing reforms and minority-oriented programs for the Philadelphia public school system, he came into conflict with Dilworth, whom Tate had appointed school board president.

By the 1967 mayoral campaign Tate had lost much of his liberal backing while failing to settle his differences with the regular organization. He compensated for these political problems by making substantial concessions to the wage demands of municipal unions and winning the almost unanimous support of organized labor. He also cultivated the colorful and conservative Deputy Police Commissioner Frank Rizzo, whom he elevated to commissioner in 1967. By identifying himself with Rizzo's "law and order" image, Tate satisfied those voters who had viewed him as too lenient with anti-war activists and black militants.

Although characterized by the *New York*

Times as a "colorless career politician" and "not . . . a strong personal party leader," Tate defeated the Philadelphia Democratic organization in the May primary and then outpolled the young and attractive Arlen Specter in November. Tate then ousted Francis Smith as Democratic Party leader in December and emerged as the "most powerful political leader in Philadelphia in many years."

Tate's new power enabled him to deliver a large Philadelphia vote to Hubert Humphrey [*q.v.*] in the 1968 presidential elections, thereby giving the plurality of the statewide vote to the Democratic nominee. During his second term Tate became more closely identified with Rizzo and the police. When Tate picked Rizzo to succeed him, it was clear that the reform era in Philadelphia had ended and that Democratic electoral strength in city elections was now based on white ethnic leadership and support. Tate left office on Jan. 1, 1972. He remained active in local politics and became affiliated with Common Cause, a nationally organized reform group. When Rizzo repudiated the Democratic organization and Tate's leadership, Tate became a leading critic of his administration and opposed Rizzo's reelection in 1975.

[JCH]

For further information:
Conrad Weiler, *Philadelphia: Neighborhood, Authority, and the Urban Crisis* (New York, 1974).

TAYLOR, MAXWELL D(AVENPORT)

b. Aug. 26, 1901; Keytesville, Mo.
Chairman of the Joint Chiefs of Staff, October 1962-June 1964; Ambassador to South Vietnam, June 1964-July 1965.

Taylor graduated fourth in the West Point class of 1922. During World War II he was artillery commander of the 82nd Airborne Division in the Sicilian and Italian campaigns and commander of the 101st Airborne in the Normandy invasion. From 1945 to 1949 he was superintendent of West Point.

During the next six years Taylor served in a number of command and staff positions before being named Army Chief of Staff in 1955. In that post he criticized the Eisenhower Administration's emphasis on massive nuclear retaliation and argued for strong ground forces capable of fighting conventional wars. Taylor presented his views to the public in *The Uncertain Trumpet*, published in 1959 after his retirement from the Army. [See EISENHOWER Volume]

After the Bay of Pigs failure, President Kennedy appointed Taylor to head an investigation of the Central Intelligence Agency's role in the unsuccessful Cuban invasion. In June 1961 he became a military representative of the President, and in October of that year he headed a mission to South Vietnam following a series of National Liberation Front (NLF) victories. To the surprise of many, upon his return he advocated the commitment of 8,000 American combat troops to the conflict. Taylor's recommendation was not carried out, but Kennedy did increase military aid and made contingency plans for the dispatch of combat troops.

In July 1962 Kennedy nominated Taylor for Chairman of the Joint Chiefs of Staff. A consistent supporter of Administration policies, he provided crucial backing for the nuclear test ban treaty in congressional testimony during August 1963. Two months later Taylor and Secretary of Defense Robert S. McNamara [*q.v.*] went on a mission to South Vietnam. Taylor concluded that the undemocratic nature of President Ngo Dinh Diem's regime would not hamper the war effort. [See KENNEDY Volume]

In June 1964 President Johnson selected Taylor to replace Henry Cabot Lodge [*q.v.*] as ambassador to South Vietnam. Previously unconcerned about the political situation there, Taylor concluded, shortly after arriving in Saigon, that the repressiveness of the South Vietnamese government was a serious impediment to the successful prosecution of the war. He pressed Maj. Gen. Nguyen Khanh, who had replaced Diem as national leader following a November 1963 military coup, to arrange for the creation of a civilian-drawn constitutional charter. A provisional, civilian High National Council was established in September 1964, but in December it was overthrown by dissident military officers, led by, among others, Air Commodore Nguyen Cao Ky and Gen. Nguyen Van Thieu. Shortly afterwards Taylor called a meeting of the officers and said, "I told you all clearly . . . we Americans were tired of coups. Apparently I wasted my words . . . .Now you have made a real mess." Despite Taylor's exhortations the officers refused to reestablish civilian rule.

Taylor supported the sustained American bombing of North Vietnam that began in March 1965. But when the bombing failed to alter North Vietnam's policies, he tried to resist the ensuing pressure from the U.S. military for the sending of large numbers of American combat troops to South Vietnam. In late March Taylor returned to Washington for a series of major strategy conferences. The Joint Chiefs of Staff and General William Westmoreland [*q.v.*] favored the deployment of at least two American divisions on search-and-destroy missions in the South Vietnamese interior. Taylor argued for the dispatch of a much smaller number of troops to guard enclaves around U.S. bases. He maintained that the arrival of American combat forces would encourage the South Vietnamese Army to slacken its efforts, arouse anti-Americanism and lead to ever-increasing U.S. military involvement.

Taylor's point of view was accepted by the Administration in early April. But at another high-level strategy conference held in Honolulu on April 19-20 an additional 40,000 American troops were committed to the war effort, although the enclave strategy was not altered. In June Westmoreland argued that the deteriorating military situation in South Vietnam necessitated the introduction of combat troops. In a dispatch to Washington Taylor agreed that circumstances were grave. David Halberstam, in *The Best and the Brightest*, stated that the Ambassador's concurrence with Westmoreland's pessimistic assessment of the direction of the war "removed the last restraint" against the use of American soldiers as combat troops.

In July 1965 Taylor was replaced as ambassador to South Vietnam by the returning Lodge. Later in the year President Johnson appointed him a special presidential consultant, but in that post Taylor no longer had a major influence on policymaking decisions.

Taylor consistently took a hawkish position on the Vietnam war during the remaining years of the Johnson Administration. In March 1968, when Administration sentiment turned against further escalation of American involvement, Taylor, as a member of the Senior Advisory Group on Vietnam, unsuccessfully supported Westmoreland's request for over 200,000 additional troops.

[MLL]

TERRY, LUTHER L(EONIDAS)

b. Sept. 15, 1911; Red Level, Ala.
Surgeon General, April 1961-September 1965.

Dr. Luther L. Terry, a medical specialist in hypertension, was named U.S. Surgeon General in the spring of 1961. As head of the Public Health Service, a division of the Department of Health, Education and Welfare, Terry was responsible for a variety of public health programs including the monitoring of the levels of radioactive fallout from Soviet and American aboveground nuclear explosions and the testing and distribution of polio and measles vaccines. [See KENNEDY Volume]

Terry won national prominence in January 1964 when he released a controversial study of the effect of smoking on health. He had commissioned the study 14 months earlier following a report by the Royal College of Physicians of London that cigarette smoking caused cancer and bronchitis.

The Surgeon General's report, which Terry issued Jan. 11, 1964, suggested that there was a definite correlation between cigarette smoking and lung cancer. It also suggested that the incidence of heart, respiratory and circulatory diseases among smokers exceeded that of non-smokers and concluded that "cigarette smoking is a health hazard of sufficient importance in the United States to warrant appropriate remedial action."

Following the release of the report, the value of tobacco stocks plummeted. Cigarette sales also declined but subsequently rose to levels only slightly below those of the previous year. Meanwhile Paul Rand Dixon [*q.v.*], chairman of the Federal Trade Commission (FTC), announced that the FTC would require all cigarette packages and advertising to state: "Smoking is dangerous to health and may cause death from cancer and other diseases." Dixon's announcement was bitterly denounced by cigarette manufacturers and by many congressmen from tobacco-growing states, who contended that the Surgeon General's report was allegedly inaccurate and misleading because it was based on limited research. In August 1964 Dixon agreed to delay implementing his order pending congressional action.

In appearances before congressional committees in June 1964 and March 1965, Terry argued that HEW could more effectively enforce cigarette labeling provisions than the FTC. He asserted that HEW should be granted broad authority by Congress to determine the content of the smoking hazard warning. Congress, which was under great pressure from the tobacco lobby, passed legislation in July 1965 requiring the following printed warning on cigarette packages and cartons: "Caution: Cigarette Smoking May Be Hazardous To Your Health," a statement which superseded the more ominous FTC warning. The new legislation prohibited any government agency from imposing an additional warning and postponed the warning requirement for cigarette advertisements until July 1969. The new legislation was considered a victory for the tobacco industry and a defeat for Terry and the Public Health Service.

In the fall of 1965 Terry resigned as Surgeon General to become vice president for medical affairs of the University of Pennsylvania.

[JLW]

For further information:

A. L. Fritschler, *Smoking and Politics: Policymaking and the Federal Bureaucracy* (New York, 1969).

THOMAS, NORMAN (MATTOON)

b. Nov. 20, 1884; Marion, Ohio.
d. Dec. 19, 1968; Huntington, N.Y.
Spokesman, Socialist Party.

Thomas studied at the Union Theological Seminary, where he was attracted to the social gospel movement. In 1911 he received a bachelor of divinity degree and entered the ministry. Five years later Thomas joined the Fellowship of Reconciliation, a religious pacifist group. He opposed American involvement in World War I.

Thomas joined the Socialist Party in 1918 and, in the same year, abandoned his religious activities. During the 1920s he succeeded Eugene V. Debs as the leader of the Party, and he headed its national ticket in every presidential election from 1928 through 1948. He garnered his greatest support in 1932, receiving 844,000 votes. In 1950 Thomas urged the Party to abandon its increasingly ineffectual electoral efforts He supported Democrat Adlai E. Stevenson [*q.v.*] rather than the Socialists' national tickets in 1952 and 1956. [See TRUMAN Volume]

While believing in the moral superiority of the West over the Communist bloc, in the 1950s Thomas asserted that peaceful coexistence on the military level was necessary to avoid thermonuclear annihilation. In 1957 he was a founder of the Committee for a Sane Nuclear Policy (SANE). In 1962 Thomas helped found Turn Toward Peace, a league of peace and civic organizations. During the early 1960s he supported the activities of the civil rights movement and urged government action to ensure jobs for unskilled blacks in an age of increasing automation. [See EISENHOWER, KENNEDY Volumes]

By the 1960s Thomas was held in high esteem by most liberals and even some conservatives. Part of the reason was the good-humored, democratic character of his socialism. He had always favored the development of a "cooperative commonwealth" within the framework of constitutionalism, opposed violent revolution and rejected the doctrines of class conflict and the dictatorship of the proletariat. But the great regard in which Thomas was held also derived from a belief in his personal integrity. Furthermore, the compassion for the weak and the moral concern that formed the foundation of his views earned him wide admiration if not agreement with his ideas. But since Thomas's concerns were moral rather than organizational, he was not an effective party leader. Bernard K. Johnpoll, one of his biographers, wrote, "Thomas's failure as a politician was merely a reflection of his success as a human being."

Thomas had given up his party posts by the 1960s but remained the unofficial spokesman for the organization. However, the Party no longer had any significant political influence, and Thomas's activities during the last years of his life centered around his individual advocacy of various liberal causes.

In 1964 Thomas campaigned actively for President Lyndon B. Johnson, praising his record on civil rights and poverty while denouncing the Republican candidate, Sen. Barry M. Goldwater (R, Ariz.) [*q.v.*], as "the greatest evil" in American politics. But Thomas was one of the earliest critics of the President's escalation of the American military involvement in Vietnam. In January 1965 Thomas warned against intervention in what he regarded as a civil war in Southeast Asia. The following June he contended that American efforts to act as the world's policeman would unify an increasingly polycentric Communist bloc. Thomas assisted in the organization of a November 1965 anti-war rally in the District of Columbia at which he denounced the Indochina conflict as "cruelly immoral and politically stupid." However, Thomas opposed an abrupt unilateral withdrawal from Vietnam because of his fear of a massacre of Vietnamese opponents of the National Liberation Front. He praised the young people who opposed the war but expressed concern over what he felt were the violent and irrational tendencies within the New Left. In 1968 Thomas backed the peace candidacy of Sen. Eugene J. McCarthy (D, Minn.) [*q.v.*].

A supporter of the right of Soviet Jews to emigrate freely, Thomas joined civil rights leader Bayard Rustin [*q.v.*], John C. Bennett [*q.v.*], president of Union Theological Seminary, and others in March 1966 to hold public hearings as the Ad Hoc Committee on the Rights of Soviet Jews. At the conclusion of its investigation in December, the Committee urged the Soviet Union to permit Soviet Jews to settle in Israel or any other country.

As chairman of the Institute for International Labor Research, created in 1957 to train democratic leaders in Latin America, Thomas denounced American intervention in the Dominican Republic in April 1965 during a rebellion against that country's military junta. In June of the following year, Thomas and other observers went to the Dominican Republic to ensure that a scheduled presidential election would be conducted fairly. Although the country's leading democratic political figure, Juan Bosch, was defeated, Thomas and his colleagues were satisfied that the election was fair.

In February 1967 it was revealed that the Institute had been receiving Central Intelligence Agency (CIA) funds. Thomas denied any knowledge of the CIA financing and expressed surprise that the Agency had supported an organization promoting liberal democracy.

During the fall of 1967 Thomas suffered a stroke. He died in a nursing home on Dec. 19, 1968.

[MLL]

For further information:

Harry Fleischman, *Norman Thomas—A Biography: 1884-1968* (New York, 1969).

Bernard K. Johnpoll, *Pacifist's Progress: Norman Thomas and the Decline of American Socialism* (Chicago, 1970).

THOMPSON, FRANK, JR.

b. July 16, 1918; Trenton, N.J.
Democratic Representative, N.J.
1955- .

The son of a newspaperman and nephew of former New Jersey Democratic leader Crawford Jamieson, Thompson was elected to the state Assembly in 1949, the year after his admission to the bar. He won a

House seat as a self-styled "New Deal-Fair Deal Democrat of the Adlai Stevenson school" in 1954. Assigned to the Education and Labor Committee, Thompson was a principal sponsor of several major education acts, including controversial proposals in 1959 and 1961 to provide federal grants to increase teachers' salaries. In 1959 Thompson co-founded the Democratic Study Group, which sought to develop a liberal legislative program and reform such "antiquated and obstructive" House procedures as the seniority system. [See KENNEDY Volume]

Thompson's efforts to fund the arts and humanities bore fruit in September 1965 when the President signed a bill, sponsored by Thompson, establishing a national foundation on the arts and humanities. During the House debate Thompson described the United States as "the last civilized nation on the earth to realize that the arts and humanities have a place in our national life."

Thompson, who was once a member of the United Auto Workers union, voted in agreement with the AFL-CIO's Committee On Political Education's (COPE) recommendation on every issue COPE considered important during the Johnson years. In 1966 he was floor manager of the labor-endorsed bill permitting "common-site" picketing on construction jobs. The bill never came to a vote because Education and Labor Chairman Adam Clayton Powell, Jr. (D, N.Y.) [*q.v.*] succeeded May 4 in having House Speaker John McCormack (D, Mass.) [*q.v.*] remove the bill from the House calendar.

Powell's action angered Committee members. According to *Congressional Quarterly,* Thompson "became one of the chief architects of the Committee revolt against Powell." Thompson claimed credit for drawing up the new committee rules to reduce the chairman's authority. The adoption of the new rules in September 1966 brought to the surface widespread congressional opposition to Powell on other issues. This hostility, combined with revelations of misuse of government funds on Powell's staff, resulted in the March 1, 1967 vote to exclude him from the 90th Congress.

During the Nixon years Thompson was regarded as a highly articulate liberal Democrat. He continued to work for congressional reform and supported Rep. Morris Udall's (D, Ariz.) [*q.v.*] unsuccessful attempt to unseat Speaker McCormack in 1969 and his equally unsuccessful candidacy for House majority leader in 1971. [See NIXON Volume]

[DKR]

For further information:
Augusta E. Wilson, *Liberal Leader in the House* (Washington, 1968).

THOMPSON, LLEWELLYN E.

b. Aug. 24, 1904; Las Animas, Colo.
d. Feb. 2, 1972; Bethesda, Md.
Ambassador at Large and Special Adviser on Soviet Affairs to the Secretary of State, August 1962-October 1966; Ambassador to the Soviet Union, January 1967-January 1969.

Following his graduation from the University of Colorado, Thompson entered the foreign service in 1929. After initial assignments in Ceylon and Geneva, he specialized in Soviet affairs, serving first as consul in Moscow from 1940 to 1944 and then as chief of the State Department's Division of Eastern European Affairs. He was appointed deputy assistant secretary of state for European affairs in 1949. In 1952 Thompson became U.S. high commissioner and ambassador for Austria. In that post he helped to negotiate the Italian-Yugoslav Trieste settlement and to formulate the treaty restoring Austria's full independence. In April 1957 President Dwight D. Eisenhower selected Thompson to succeed Charles E. Bohlen [*q.v.*] as U.S. ambassador to Moscow. There he became a trusted acquaintance of many of the men in the Soviet hierarchy, who respected him not only for his knowledge of the Russian language and culture but also because he had shared their suffering during the siege of Moscow in World War II. [See TRUMAN, EISENHOWER Volumes]

Thompson remained in Moscow during the first two years of the Kennedy Administration before being appointed ambassador at large and special adviser to the State Department on Soviet affairs in August 1962. During these years he not only performed the daily functions of an ambassador but became one of the President's most respected foreign policy advisers on issues such as Berlin, disarmament and, particularly, the Cuban missile crisis. [See KENNEDY Volume]

Thompson continued at his post during the early years of the Johnson Administration. As special adviser to the Secretary of State, he attended all high-level Soviet-American talks, including those held in December 1964 between Secretary of State Dean Rusk [*q.v.*] and Soviet Foreign Minister Andrei Gromyko. He also conducted congressional briefings on major Soviet developments, including the ouster of Premier Nikita S. Khrushchev from power in October 1964.

Thompson's own standing with Russian leaders was so high that after an American RB-66 was shot down over East Germany in March 1964, President Johnson asked his adviser to denounce personally Soviet charges that the plane was on a spy mission. As Johnson had hoped, foreign officials were inclined to believe his statement because they felt that the U.S. government would not wish to jeopardize Thompson's prestige and reputation among foreign leaders by having him make a false denial.

In January 1967 President Johnson asked Thompson to return as ambassador to Moscow to try to repair relations that were being increasingly strained by the Vietnam war and to attempt to interest the Soviet Union in promoting Vietnam peace negotiations. Thompson never achieved this goal and, indeed, never had a single serious talk with Communist Party First Secretary Leonid I. Brezhnev. He did, however, help lay the groundwork for the inconclusive but cordial summit conference between Premier Aleksei N. Kosygin and President Johnson that took place in Glassboro, N.J., in June 1967.

Following his resignation as ambassador in January 1969, Thompson served as a foreign affairs consultant until his death on Feb. 2, 1972.

[EWS]

THROCKMORTON, JOHN L(ATHROP)

b. Feb. 28, 1913; Kansas City, Mo.
Deputy Commanding General, U.S. Military Assistance Command to South Vietnam, August 1964-November 1965; Commanding General, U.S. Third Army, August 1967-April 1969.

Throckmorton, a 1935 West Point graduate, saw action in Europe during World War II. In the Korean war he commanded the 5th Regiment Combat Team and subsequently served as a senior aide to the Joint Chiefs of Staff. From 1962 to 1964 Throckmorton was commander of the 82nd Airborne Division at Fort Bragg, N.C. He was named lieutenant general in August 1964 and that month joined Gen. William Westmoreland's [*q.v.*] staff in Vietnam. Throckmorton subsequently became involved in the decision to commit U.S. combat troops to Vietnam.

On Feb. 22, 1965 Westmoreland dispatched Throckmorton to the coastal base at Da Nang, a probable target of Communist guerrillas. Throckmorton toured the scene and recommended that two battalions of U.S. Marines be sent to Da Nang to bolster its defenses. Westmoreland accepted this judgment, Washington agreed, and on March 8, 3,500 Marines landed at Da Nang.

President Johnson suggested to Westmoreland in April 1965 that he consider strengthening the South Vietnamese Army by putting some units under control of American officers, and Throckmorton was ordered to consider the matter. In his report of April 18, he rejected a large-scale program of "encadrement" on the grounds that the language barrier between the Americans and their South Vietnamese allies would prevent effective communications between officers and men. "Encadrement," moreover, would prove demoralizing to the Vietnamese soldiers, he added. The idea was dropped.

In November 1965 Throckmorton was routinely transferred from Vietnam to head the Office of Army Reserve Components. In testimony before a Senate Preparedness subcommittee, reported in May 1966,

Throckmorton stated that supplies for Army reserve units had been seriously depleted by the American war effort in South Vietnam. His testimony tended to support the contention of the subcommittee's chairman, Sen. John C. Stennis (D, Miss.) [*q.v.*], who argued that the armed forces outside Vietnam were generally under-supplied and unprepared to fight.

During 1966 Throckmorton served as director of the office of special studies under the Army Chief of Staff and as U.S. Army representative to the military staff of the United Nations.

In the last week of July 1967, Throckmorton found himself in command of federal troops who, for the first time in 24 years, were charged with quelling a local civil insurrection. On July 23 large-scale rioting began in Detroit, and on July 24 Gov. George W. Romney [*q.v.*] requested that federal troops be sent to put down the riot. Throckmorton took charge of the 4,700 federal paratroops who were airlifted that day to Selfridge Air Force Base, 25 miles northwest of Detroit. On the afternoon of the 24th, Throckmorton and President Johnson's personal representative, former Deputy Secretary of Defense Cyrus Vance [*q.v.*], toured the city. About 30 fires were still burning but seemed to be under control; half of Michigan's National Guard had not yet been committed to patrol duty. Throckmorton and Vance agreed that federal troops were not yet needed. With nightfall, however, sniper fire increased, and new fires and looting broke out. By 11 p.m. the National Guard and the city police were fully committed and the situation seemed unmanageable. At 11:20 p.m. President Johnson nationalized the Michigan National Guard and authorized the use of the federal paratroops in Detroit. Throckmorton now assumed command of all the forces in the city. He ordered the paratroops into the area west of 12th street; to the east, the National Guard remained in control.

One of Throckmorton's principal tasks was to bring discipline to the ranks of the National Guardsmen, who were inadequately trained for riot duty. He ordered both the paratroops and the Guard to unload their weapons and fire only if ordered to do so by an officer. The paratroops obeyed, but the order was widely ignored by the guardsmen. The paratroops, 20% of whom were blacks, quickly restored order in the western sector and began street cleaning and garbage collection, but to the east the guardsmen, overwhelmingly white, continued to exchange fire with snipers. Not until July 27 did Throckmorton bring the Guard under control and return order to the city. Forty-three persons were dead, 1,500 were injured and many blocks were in ruins.

Throckmorton, generally praised for his handling of the riot, was attacked by some congressmen for "casting aspersions" on the National Guard. Rep. Porter Hardy (D, Va.) called his order to unload weapons "preposterous," and F. Edward Hebert (D, La.) [*q.v.*], chairman of the House Armed Services Committee, said he could not see how the Guard could be expected "to take cover if fired upon and await the arrival of an officer."

In May 1969 Throckmorton was promoted to the rank of four-star general and was named commander in chief of the U.S. Strike Command. He retired from the Army in January 1973.

[JLW]

THURMOND, STROM

b. Dec. 5, 1902; Edgefield, S.C.
Democratic Senator, S.C., 1954-56, 1956-64;
Republican Senator, S.C., 1964- .

Thurmond, the son of a South Carolina politician, was elected governor in 1946 after having served as a state senator and circuit court judge. In 1948, after the Democratic National Convention adopted a civil rights plank for its platform, the breakaway States Rights Party selected Thurmond as its presidential candidate. Denying that he was a white supremacist, Thurmond contended that the goal of the Party was to prevent unconstitutional federal interference in the affairs of the states. He carried five states in the Deep South and received a total of 39 electoral votes. In 1950 Thurmond lost a race for a U.S. Senate seat, but he made a successful effort four years later as a write-in candidate.

Thurmond was one of the leading opponents of antidiscrimination measures on Capitol Hill. However, he stood somewhat apart from his Southern colleagues because many of them regarded his displays of flamboyance as self-serving and harmful to the anti-civil rights clause. Furthermore, while Thurmond and most other Southern congressmen opposed social welfare legislation and favored a militantly anti-Communist foreign policy and large defense appropriations, the South Carolina Senator was one of the few to associate himself with the causes of ideological right-wing groups like the John Birch Society and the Young Americans for Freedom in the early 1960s. [See TRUMAN, EISENHOWER, KENNEDY Volumes]

Thurmond transferred his allegiance from the Democratic to the Republican Party in September 1964 so that he could work openly for the presidential candidacy of conservative Sen. Barry M. Goldwater (R, Ariz.) [*q.v.*]. During each of the remaining four years of the Johnson presidency, Thurmond was among the five leading Republican supporters of the Senate's conservative coalition.

A foe of all of the Johnson Administration's civil rights proposals, he asserted that the voting rights bill of 1965 would usurp the constitutional authority of the states to establish voter qualifications and would create a "totalitarian" federal government. He denounced a 1967 measure to protect civil rights workers from harassment, stating that it would give "added protection to roving fomenters of violence, such as Stokely Carmichael [*q.v.*] and H. Rap Brown [*q.v.*]." Equally opposed to most Great Society programs, Thurmond attacked such measures as the 1965 housing bill and the 1967 elementary school aid bill as promoting dangerous expansion of federal power.

A hard-line opponent of what he regarded as unrelenting Communist expansionism, Turmond favored the unrestrained use of military force in Vietnam. He charged in August 1966 that the Administration was following a "no-win" policy in Southeast Asia. The following April he criticized an East-West treaty governing the peaceful exploration and use of outer space as "another step in the artificial and unrealistic atmosphere of detente with Communism. . . ."

In 1968 Thurmond backed Richard M. Nixon [*q.v.*] for the Republican presidential nomination and was credited with convincing most Southern Republican delegates to the Party's National Convention to vote for Nixon instead of right-wing Gov. Ronald Reagan [*q.v.*] of California. Many observers believed that the formulation of Nixon's "Southern strategy" originally was based on an agreement between the candidate and the South Carolinian in which Nixon, in exchange for Thurmond's support, pledged to oppose school busing, appoint "strict constructionists" to the Supreme Court, reduce federal spending and promote a strong military establishment.

Thurmond wielded considerable influence in the White House during the Nixon Administration. Harry Dent, his former aide, was a political adviser to the President, and about 20 other friends and associates of the Senator received significant administrative jobs.

In the early 1970s Thurmond continued to vote against social welfare programs, but he began to make serious attempts to secure federal housing and welfare funds for South Carolina. A major reason for his efforts was the Senator's desire to win the votes of the growing black electorate in the state. [See NIXON Volume]

[MLL]

TOWER, JOHN G(OODWIN)

b. September 29, 1925; Houston, Tex.
Republican Senator, Tex., 1961- .

During the 1950s Tower served on the Texas Republican Party's executive committee in the 23rd senatorial district, and in 1956 he was a delegate to the Republican National Convention. In 1960 Tower lost a bid for a U.S. Senate seat to incumbent Lyndon B. Johnson but received 41% of the vote, a high figure for the perennially unsuccessful state Republican Party.

In 1961 Tower narrowly defeated Democrat William Blakley in a special election to fill Johnson's vacated seat. Excluding presidential elections, this represented the first statewide electoral success for Texas Republicans since Reconstruction. Contrary to Republican expectations, however, the Tower victory did not lead to the development of a competitive two-party system in the state. The Texas Republican Party was solidly conservative, and since liberal Democrats, led by Sen. Ralph Yarborough [*q.v.*], failed in their efforts to capture their state Party's machinery during the 1960s, right-of-center voters had little reason to transfer their allegiance to the Republicans.

Although Tower's election did not substantially alter political alignments in Texas, he gained national attention from his articulate exposition of conservative views and his close political relationship on Capitol Hill with Sen. Barry Goldwater (R, Ariz.) [*q.v.*]. Like Goldwater, he favored a militantly anti-Communist foreign policy and believed that President Kennedy was too conciliatory towards the Soviet Union. During the Kennedy years the two senators, as members of the Senate Labor and Public Welfare Committee, often issued joint minority reports expressing opposition to Administration-sponsored social welfare proposals. [See KENNEDY Volume]

In 1964 Tower was chairman of the unanimously pro-Goldwater Texas delegation to the Republican National Convention. On the eve of the Convention, he declared that the Republicans had an excellent chance of capturing the White House if they nominated Goldwater. However, the selection of the Arizona Senator proved to be a disaster for Texas Republicans. The Johnson sweep in Texas defeated the Party's two U.S. representatives and of most of its 10 members in the state legislature.

Tower won reelection in 1966 with 56% of the ballots. During the election many liberal Democrats abstained or voted for Tower in protest against the conservative views of his opponent, state Attorney General Waggoner Carr. Again, however, Tower's victory did not result in a significant improvement in the state Party's fortunes.

Tower continued to compile a consistently conservative record on Capitol Hill during the Johnson Administration. In 1964 he unsuccessfully opposed the granting of agricultural credits to Communist nations. Tower was an adamant supporter of America's Vietnam war effort. In March 1967 Senate Majority Leader Mike Mansfield (D, Mont.) [*q.v.*] offered an amendment to a war appropriations bill urging international negotiations as a means of resolving the Vietnam conflict. Tower denounced the proposal, asserting that "if there is any way to strengthen the will of our opponents, it is to attach to an authorization of an appropriation to take care of our forces in the field another plaintive plea for peace."

In domestic policy Tower remained a foe of social welfare measures. He joined Sen. Goldwater in the summer of 1964 to denounce a bill for extending a defense education act as representing "the slow but relentless advent of federal regulation of education carried out on the installment plan and seeking to remain undetected under the protective cloak of 'national defense.' " The following year he opposed the Johnson Administration's housing and medicare bills, and in 1966 he voted against Demonstration Cities and mass transit measures. In 1968 the liberal Americans for Democratic Action gave Tower's voting record a zero percent rating, while the Americans for Constitutional Action, a conservative group, supported 94% of his key votes.

Tower was the favorite son choice of the Texas delegation to the 1968 Republican National Convention, but in June he offered his endorsement to Richard Nixon [*q.v.*] and released the delegates. He was reelected to the Senate in 1972. [See NIXON Volume]

[MLL]

TOWNSEND, LYNN A(LFRED)

b. May 12, 1919; Flint, Mich.
President, Chrysler Corp., 1961-66; Chairman and chief executive officer, 1966-75.

Townsend spent his boyhood in Los Angeles, where his father ran an auto repair shop. His mother, a school teacher, wanted her son to be an actor, and for years he took elocution lessons at the Hollywood Conservatory of Music and Arts. After receiving degrees in business administration from the University of Michigan, Townsend joined the accounting office of the Detroit firm Ernst and Ernst in 1941. He left in 1947 to become a partner and supervising accountant of Touche, Niven, Bailey & Smart, where he audited the books of the Chrysler Corp., the firm's major client. He became so expert in the automaker's financial condition that Chrysler hired him as its controller in 1957. A rapid series of promotions followed, culminating in Townsend's appointment as president in 1961. He was elected chairman of the board in 1966.

When Townsend took over in 1961, Chrysler was the weakest of the auto industry's Big Three; its sales were declining and it held a diminishing share of the market. Company morale was low because of the resignation of Townsend's predecessor as a result of a conflict-of-interest scandal. Townsend's reversal of this downward spiral was one of the most dramatic corporate successes of the decade. Between 1961 and 1968 Chrysler's sales tripled to $7 billion while profits grew to $300 million. Equally important, its share of the auto market, which had fallen to 9.6% in 1962, climbed to 16.6% by 1968. Among Townsend's innovations were the reorganization of the firm's management and dealership system, a $1.7 billion expansion program, a reduction in the number of annual style changes and the institution of an unprecedented 5-year, 50,000-mile guarantee for Chrysler buyers. He also extended the company's foreign operations, buying into Rootes Motors of Great Britain and purchasing 25% of Simca of France.

Townsend joined other auto industry executives in opposing the enactment of mandatory federal safety standards in 1966. Their efforts, however, did not prevent the passage of the National Traffic and Motor Vehicle Safety Act and the Highway Safety Act in the summer of that year. Townsend declared that the acts' requirements would "pose very serious problems for Chrysler." In November 1967 he argued against using any money from the Highway Trust Fund to finance mass transit facilities. In September 1968 Chrysler announced a 2.9% price increase on its 1969 models, but it later lowered the increase to 2% in response to Administration pressure. In March 1969 President Richard Nixon [*q.v.*] appointed Townsend vice chairman of the National Alliance of Businessmen, a non-partisan group organized during the Johnson Administration to find jobs for poor youths. [See NIXON Volume]

[TO]

TRUMAN, HARRY S

b. May 8, 1884; Lamar, Mo.
d. Dec. 26, 1972; Kansas City, Mo.
President of the United States, April 1945-January 1953.

Except for service in France as an artillery captain during World War I, Harry Truman spent his first 50 years in Missouri. He grew up in Independence, managed a farm near Grandview from 1906 to 1917 and after the war started a haberdashery business in Kansas City, which failed in the depression of 1922. Backed by the powerful Pendergast Democratic machine, Truman was elected judge of the Jackson County Court in 1922 and presiding judge in 1926. He was elected to the U.S. Senate in 1934 on a platform endorsing the New Deal. Truman first came to national attention during World War II, when he chaired the "Truman Committee" investigating abuses in the defense program. In 1944 Truman was chosen at the Democratic Convention to replace Vice President Henry A. Wallace as President Franklin D. Roosevelt's running mate. Elected in November, Truman became President upon Roosevelt's death in April 1945.

A vigorous anti-Communist, Truman initiated the postwar containment policy designed to halt Communist advances. On the domestic front Truman fought to extend the New Deal with his own social welfare program. Despite some advances in Social Security, civil rights and housing, most of his Fair Deal was stymied by conservative congresses. A feisty campaigner, Truman won an upset reelection victory in 1948 against New York Gov. Thomas E. Dewey.

Despite a sweeping "loyalty" program designed to root out Communists from the government, Truman spent much of his second term defending himself against charges by Sen. Joseph R. McCarthy (R, Wisc.) and other Republicans that his Administration was infiltrated by subversives. His popularity diminished by these attacks and the stalemated Korean war, Truman declined to run for reelection in 1952.

Following his return to Independence in 1953, Truman issued numerous public statements throughout the decade, usually attacking the Eisenhower Administration, defending his own record or supporting Democratic candidates. He backed Gov. Averell Harriman's [*q.v.*] unsuccessful candidacy for the Democratic presidential nomination in 1956. After endorsing Sen. Stuart Symington's (D, Mo.) [*q.v.*] effort in 1960, Truman campaigned for the Kennedy-Johnson ticket. His dislike of the Kennedy family was outweighed by his party loyalty and his loathing for the Republican candidate, Vice President Richard M. Nixon [*q.v.*]. [See TRUMAN, EISENHOWER, KENNEDY Volumes]

Truman was a strong backer of the Johnson-Humphrey ticket in 1964 and expressed general support for the Great Society legislative program. President Johnson flew to Independence in July 1965 to sign the law creating medicare at a ceremony honoring Truman, who in 1945 had been the first president to propose federal health insurance financed through the Social Security system. He endorsed the civil rights enactments of the Johnson Administration, although he spoke critically of civil rights agitation itself. In April 1964 Truman attacked civil rights demonstrators engaging in stalling and sit-in tactics at New York World's Fair. He called the March 1965 civil rights march in Selma, Alabama a "silly" bid to attract attention, and the next month he characterized Dr. Martin Luther King [*q.v.*] as a "troublemaker."

Truman was a consistent supporter of Johnson's Vietnam policy. In February 1965 he stated that U.S. troops were in South Vietnam "to help keep the peace and to keep ambitious aggressors from helping themselves to the easy prey of certain newly formed independent nations." Truman derided "irresponsible critics" and "sideline hecklers" of Johnson's policies. In October 1967 he joined the Citizens Committee for Peace with Freedom in Vietnam, a pro-war group opposing "surrender, however camouflaged" and advocating continued resistance to "naked aggression." Truman served as honorary chairman of the Humphrey-for-President committee in April 1968. He died on Dec. 26, 1972 at the age of 88.

[TO]

TURNER, DONALD F(RANK)

b. March 19, 1921; Chippewa Falls, Wisc.

Assistant Attorney General, Antitrust Division, April 1965-May 1968.

Donald Turner obtained a Ph.D. in economics from Harvard in 1947. From 1947 to 1950 he was an instructor in economics at Harvard and simultaneously a student at Yale University Law School, where he was editor-in-chief of the *Yale Law Review* in his final year. Upon receiving his degree in 1950, Turner worked for a year as law clerk to Supreme Court Justice Tom C. Clark [*q.v.*]. He practiced in Washington, D.C., until 1954, when he returned to Harvard to teach law.

In collaboration with Harvard economist Carl Kaysen, Turner published *Antitrust Policy: An Economic and Legal Analysis* in 1959. *Antitrust Policy* became a standard text and, along with an array of important articles in professional journals, established Turner's reputation as the leading academic expert in the field of antitrust. At the recommendation of Attorney General Nicholas Katzenbach [*q.v.*], who had attented Yale Law School with Turner, President Johnson appointed Turner assistant attorney general in charge of the Antitrust Division in April 1965.

Katzenbach and Turner shared a less aggressive attitude toward antitrust enforcement than Turner's Kennedy-appointed predecessors, Lee Loevinger and William Orrick, Jr. In light of recent Supreme Court decisions that had greatly expanded the Justice Department's power to stop mergers, Katzenbach asserted in May 1965 that the Department might have "more power than is necessary" and "may be able to block more mergers than it makes economic sense to block." He felt a "breathing spell" for business was needed. Turner had frequently argued before his appointment that antitrust law, a mass of legal precedents, was inconsistent, vague and lacking in any guiding philosophy.

Resolving to "rationalize antitrust," Turner upgraded the Division's Policy Planning and Evaluation Section, whose function was to review all cases sent up by the trial staff with the aim of formulating a unified Division policy. Turner's application of greater manpower and meticulous care in the preparation of cases was generally credited with the improved quality of the Division's briefs. In fiscal 1967, for example, 47 civil and nine criminal cases were terminated without any being lost in the courts. But another result was a significant decline in the Division's productivity; the average annual number of cases filed fell from 65 under the three previous antitrust chiefs to a total of 49 during Turner's three years.

Turner also sought to rationalize enforcement with the promulgation of "Merger Guidelines," released on May 28, 1968, Turner's last day in office. In an effort to clarify antitrust law for the benefit of corporations, the guidelines detailed those market percentages below which mergers were permissible. In general, corporate lawyers welcomed the greater predictability of antitrust policy. Some antitrust advocates criticized the new guidelines, insisting that an effective antitrust law should not be too precise, or it would eliminate that uncertainty which in their belief forestalled many contemplated mergers.

Turner's single most significant antitrust victory came in blocking a proposed merger between the International Telephone and Telegraph Corp. (ITT) and the American Broadcasting Companies, Inc. (ABC). The Federal Communications Commission approved the merger in June 1967, but Turner refused to drop the Justice Department's suit. The Department opposed the merger on several grounds: ITT's international interests might affect ABC's news operations, the incentive for ITT to develop competing technologies like CATV (community antenna TV) would be inhibited and the companies' rationale that ABC needed ITT's resources to improve its position against the other networks was dubious. ITT canceled the planned merger in January 1968.

Despite this suit and another filed in 1966 against the merger of the First National City Bank of New York and Carte Blanche, Turner exhibited a notable tolerance toward conglomerate mergers. He believed that bigness per se was not harmful and that the increase in the percentage of industrial assets controlled by the top firms was not necessarily dangerous. The *Wall Street Journal* reported in February 1967, "Chances are better than they've been in years that the government's antitrusters will not try to block a corporate marriage."

The greatest wave of corporate mergers in American history occurred during Turner's tenure. During the first six years of the decade an average of 1,664 mergers took place annually; from 1967 through 1969 the annual average increased to 3,605 mergers, 80% of which were conglomerates. Turner approved a series of major mergers within the energy industry: Pure Oil Co. and Union Oil Co., Atlantic Co. and Richfield Co. and the Continental Oil Co. and the Consolidation Coal Co.

Turner followed an erratic course against the nation's two largest corporate giants, General Motors (GM) and the American Telephone and Telegraph Co. (AT&T). He personally negotiated a settlement in the decade-old GM bus case in November 1965. The agreement permitted GM to retain its 85% monopoly of the intercity bus market, with a provision requiring compulsory licensing of new firms entering the market. Turner dropped a court case pending against GM's monopoly of the locomotive market, an action which earned criticism from Loevinger, who had initiated the suit. Turner maintained that GM's monopoly was due simply to greater efficiency. He also declined to bring a criminal action suit against the automobile manufacturers for conspiracy to suppress the development of pollution control devices. A Los Angeles grand jury had been prepared to indict in the case, and Turner reportedly admitted he could have obtained a conviction from a jury. Regarding AT&T, Turner sent a proposed complaint against its 1956 acquisition of Western Electric Co. to Katzenbach's desk in July 1966. The complaint charged monopolization of telephone equipment since 1956, but no action was taken.

Turner investigated the possibility of testing the limits of the Sherman Act with suits against "shared monopolies," or oligopolies. He had in mind industries like automobile production—dominated by GM, Ford and Chrysler—and soap marketing, in which Procter and Gamble, Lever Brothers and Colgate predominated. In June 1966 Turner broached the possibility of suing against excessive advertising on the grounds that it raised entry barriers to new competitors and preserved oligopolies. No shared monopoly or excessive advertising cases were filed during Turner's tenure, however. Robert Wright, first assistant to Loevinger and Orrick, later declared, "Don Turner talked innovation but just never filed innovative suits." Turner resigned in June 1968 and returned to teaching at Harvard. In July, as a consultant to his successor Edwin Zimmerman, Turner proposed a suit to break up GM and Ford.

[TO]

For further information:
Mark Green, et. al., *The Closed Enterprise System* (Washington, 1972).

TYDINGS, JOSEPH D(AVIES)

b. May 4, 1928; Asheville, N.C.
Democratic Senator, Md., 1964-70.

Tydings, the adopted son of former Sen. Millard E. Tydings (D, Md.), grew up in Maryland. After receiving an LL.B. from the University of Maryland in 1953, he entered private law practice in Baltimore. Tydings was elected to the Maryland Chamber of Deputies in 1955 and became known for his efforts to reform state insurance laws following a savings and loan scandal. In 1961 he was appointed U.S. attorney for Maryland by President John F. Kennedy, a close friend of the Tydings family. Three years later Tydings won election to the U.S. Senate, defeating incumbent Republican J. Glenn Beall with 64% of the vote. A strong voter registration campaign undertaken by civil rights organizations helped Tydings overwhelm his opponent in Baltimore and in liberal, suburban Montgomery County.

In the Senate Tydings was assigned to the Judiciary, District of Columbia and Public Works Committees. The first two committee assignments led him to concentrate his attention on legal and judicial affairs. In 1967 Tydings sponsored a Senate bill that banned discrimination in the selection of federal juries. Tydings was a strong advocate of gun control legislation, which he unsuccessfully supported on the Judiciary Committee in 1966 and 1968. He also played a significant part in the debate over the District of Columbia crime bills of 1966 and 1970 and the omnibus crime bill of 1968. All three measures sought to restrict the rights of defendants and bolster the investigatory powers of police. Tydings generally took a liberal position in favor of defendants' rights, opposing provisions of the 1966 and 1968 bills that would have eased restrictions on the use of confessions and increased the difficulty of entering a plea of insanity. Tydings broke with Senate liberals, however, when he supported the wiretapping section of the 1968 bill and the controversial "no-knock" provision of the 1970 bill, which allowed police to enter a home or office surreptitiously.

In other matters before the Judiciary Committee, Tydings opposed the Supreme Court nominations of Clement Haynsworth in 1969 and G. Harrold Carswell in 1970. A steadfast liberal on most issues, Tydings was absent from the Senate floor during a number of important votes, including several concerning congressional powers in foreign affairs. As a result, his "correct" rating from the liberal Americans for Democratic Action dropped from 94% in 1965 to 63% in 1970.

Facing reelection in 1970, Tydings found himself in grave political difficulty among

Maryland voters. Observers noted that his advocacy of gun control legislation had alienated conservatives, while his approval of the "no-knock" provision estranged liberals. These problems were compounded in August 1970, when *Life* magazine accused Tydings of improperly influencing a government agency to help a company in which he owned stock. Though later exonerated by the Justice Department, Tydings suffered from the charge during the campaign. Strongly opposed by the anti-gun control lobby, he lost a close race to J. Glenn Beall, Jr., the son of the Republican whom Tydings had defeated in 1964. Tyding's share of the vote was 48%.

After his political defeat Tydings joined a law firm in Washington, D.C. He remained a private lawyer during the early and mid-1970s, serving also as special counsel to the United Nations Fund for Population Activities. Tydings lost a political comeback attempt in 1976, when he ran unsuccessfully for senator in the Maryland Democratic primary.

[SLG]

UDALL, MORRIS K(ING)

b. June 15, 1922; St. Johns, Ariz.
Democratic Representative., Ariz., 1961- .

Morris Udall was the grandson of a Mormon missionary. He served in the Army Air Force during World War II, played briefly with the National Basketball League's Denver Nuggets and then took his law degree from the University of Arizona in 1949. That same year Udall entered law practice with his brother Stewart [*q.v.*].

During the 1950s Udall participated in local Democratic politics. He served first as chief deputy attorney for Pima County and then as county attorney. In 1956 he was chairman of the Arizona Volunteers for Stevenson.

After Stewart Udall gave up his seat from Arizona's second congressional district to become Secretary of the Interior in President Kennedy's cabinet, Morris Udall won a special election in May 1961 to fill the vacany. He was assigned to the Post Office and Civil Service and the Interior and Insular Affairs Committees. As chairman of the former panel's Compensation Subcommittee, he sponsored the House version of the 1965 federal pay raise bill.

According to *Congressional Quarterly*, Udall backed the Johnson Administration on over 80% of key House roll-call votes during four of the five years of the Johnson presidency. But, in an October 1967 speech delivered in Tucson, Ariz., he declared that the U.S. was on "a mistaken and dangerous road" in Vietnam and should stop further escalation and "start bringing American boys home and start turning this war back to the Vietnamese." Udall said that his previous support of Administration Vietnam policies had been a "mistake."

In 1968 Udall played a vital role in gaining passage of the $1.3 billion Colorado River Project, which was the culmination of a legislative battle fought for half a century over allocation of the waters of the Colorado River. Udall earlier had clashed with the California-based Sierra Club over a proposal, initially made in 1963, for construction of the Bridge Canyon and Marble Canyon hydroelectric dams in a section of the Grand Canyon in northern Arizona. He later said of the Sierra Club's successful effort to block the dams' construction, "I can't think of any group in this country that has had more power in the last eight years."

The final Colorado River bill was a compromise facilitated by a series of skillful legislative maneuvers, in which Udall was a crucial figure. He set up his own whip system in the House and contacted congressmen in order to establish their voting preference on the measure. Success for the strategy depended upon preventing congressmen from Northwestern states, who generally opposed the project, from forcing a roll-call vote on a recommittal motion. According to *Congressional Quarterly*, "the whip system was so highly organized that at a signal from him [Udall] on the House floor, 180 phone calls could be made to colleagues' offices within six or seven minutes." Principally as a consequence of Udall's efforts, the Colorado River Project passed Congress on Sept. 12, 1968 and was signed into law by President Johnson on Sept. 30.

In December 1968 Udall announced his candidacy for speaker of the House, a post held by Rep. John McCormack (D, Mass.) [*q.v.*]. In a letter to all House Democrats, Udall expressed "genuine respect and affection" for McCormack but stated that there was an overriding need for new leadership. In January Udall lost his bid for the speakership by a vote of 178 to 58.

Udall was reelected in 1970, 1972 and 1974. He ran an unsuccessful campaign for the Democratic presidential nomination in 1976. [See NIXON Volume]

[FHM]

UDALL, STEWART L(EE)

b. Jan. 31, 1920; St. Johns, Ariz.
Secretary of the Interior, January 1961-January 1969.

Udall belonged to a politically prominent Arizona family descended from Mormon pioneers. He served in the Army Air Force during World War II and in 1948 earned an LL.B. from the University of Arizona. Udall was elected to the U.S. House of Representatives in 1954, and, despite the strength of conservative Republicanism in Arizona, he won three successive reelection contests easily. In the House Udall was one of the Interior and Insular Affairs Committee's most vigorous proponents of conservation, reclamation and national park improvement legislation. He helped sponsor "seminars" for freshman representatives and was a member of the liberal Democratic Study Group.

An early supporter of Sen. John F. Kennedy's presidential aspirations, Udall was named Kennedy's Secretary of the Interior in December 1960. In his first three years in the cabinet, Udall strongly favored public over private power in his efforts to meet the nation's rapidly expanding water and energy needs. He sought to retain public lands and develop large areas for recreational purposes. In his book *The Quiet Crisis* (1963), he called for greater public efforts to control pollution and preserve unspoiled wilderness areas. [See KENNEDY Volume]

During Udall's tenure as Secretary of the Interior, 2.4 million acres were added to the National Park Service, compared to only 30,000 acres added in the entire decade before 1960. Four entirely new national parks were created. Seven of the 11 National Recreation Areas were established in the three years after 1965 alone.

In his efforts to add new land to the park system, Udall often found himself attacked by conservationists, on the one hand, and timber, mining and cattle interests, on the other. Final establishment of the Redwood National Park in 1968 culminated a four-year dispute involving lumber companies, the state of California, the Agriculture Department's Forest Service and conservationist groups. Environmentalists, led by the Sierra Club, succeeded in getting a park that was larger and located farther south than Udall's original Administration proposal. Meanwhile, California Gov. Ronald Reagan [*q.v.*] ensured that the park affected four lumber companies equally, instead of damaging only one, and that the state received compensation for its lands lost to the park.

Two other important conservation-recreation measures, both passed in 1968, were the National Trails System, the result of a three-year study supervised by Udall, and the Wild and Scenic Rivers System. The National Trails System established national scenic trails in wilderness areas for hiking and camping and national recreation trails near urban areas for jogging, bicycling and similar activities. The rivers system prohibited incompatible water resource development, pollution or commercialization of certain stretches of rivers. In some cases land around the rivers was to be set aside for limited recreational uses.

In 1967 Udall recommended federal measures to regulate surface mining operations and reclaim lands already damaged by harmful mining techniques. President Johnson proposed a surface mining reclamation bill in 1968, but Congress did not act on it. In 1967 Udall also offered a program to tap the immense oil shale deposits of the Green River Formation in the Rocky Mountains. The deposits, 80% of which were government-owned, were estimated to contain enough shale to produce two trillion barrels of oil. Udall's proposal to lease government land to individuals, corporations and municipalities for research and production was attacked by congressional liberals led by Sen. William Proxmire (D, Wisc.) [*q.v.*]. They believed that development should be turned over to a quasi-public corporation or a government agency. Former Sen. Paul Douglas (D, Ill.) [*q.v.*] announced the formation of a public oil shale watchdog committee to ensure that the government was not excessively generous to corporate claims. In 1968 Congress took no action on bills aimed at providing "the orderly leasing of publicly owned oil shale."

The drought that afflicted the Northeast from 1961 to 1965 bolstered Udall's view that the government ought to take steps to ensure that water supply and quality would keep pace with the nation's increasing needs. The Water Resources Planning Act of 1965, which furthered federal-state cooperation in developing water resources, also established a Federal Water Resources Council. As council chairman, Udall directed a survey of Northeast drought conditions in August 1965. In his report the Secretary was extremely critical of New York City, which, he said, had the reputation "of having one of the leakiest and most loosely managed water systems." In contrast, he praised Philadelphia's metered water system, telling the Senate Interior Committee that Congress "had every right to insist that U.S. cities do what Philadelphia is doing" to qualify for drought assistance. Congress voted emergency funds to increase the storage capacities of Northeastern reservoirs. In addition, following Udall's survey, New York City and Philadelphia made an agreement for establishing a "strategic water bank" of 200 million gallons to be utilized in emergencies.

Although the drought ended soon after Udall's study, the Secretary believed that its lesson for the public and legislators was clear. He persistently urged the creation of a National Water Commission to develop long-range plans on water resources. Congress finally established the commission in 1968. Udall also supported continuation and expansion of the government's desalination program. In 1967 Congress authorized the Interior Department to participate in construction of a nuclear-powered desalting plant in Southern California. Probably the most important piece of water legislation was the Water Quality Act of 1965, which set purity standards for all interstate waters, making it easier for government authorities to take action against polluters. A 1966 bill made funds available to states and communities to enforce the standards.

Although reclamation projects did not figure as prominently in the Johnson-Udall programs as they had under President Kennedy, few public works bills aroused as much controversy as the Colorado River Basin Project of 1968. At a cost of $1.3 billion, it was the largest reclamation program ever authorized in a single piece of legislation. Designed to divert the Colorado's waters to south-central Arizona, the plan had been long delayed because of disagreement among the Southwestern states over the allocation of Colorado River water. Meanwhile, rapid population growth in the arid Southwest threatened the region's water supply. In 1963 Udall proposed the Southwest Water Plan, a regional development scheme that included two dams on the Colorado River. By 1966 all seven Colorado River basin states had finally agreed to implement the plan. However, the Sierra Club and other environmental organizations undertook an intensive lobbying effort against the proposal, directing most of their campaign against Udall's proposal to build two hydroelectric dams on a section of the Colorado that ran through the Grand Canyon. Because of the Sierra Club's pressure, Udall dropped both dams and suggested, instead, that the government buy an interest in a joint public-private thermal power plant. This plan was incorporated into the Administration's Colorado River Basin Project bill.

Udall's association with the Johnson Administration sometimes made it difficult for him to maintain his liberal credentials. In October 1967, for example, Udall unsuccessfully made a well publicized effort to prevent his brother, Rep. Morris Udall (D, Ariz.) [*q.v.*], from declaring his opposition to the Administration's Vietnam policy. Liberals sharply criticized two Interior Department agencies, the Bureau of Indian Affairs and the Bureau of Mines. In each case, however, Udall admitted the agency's inadequacies. In April 1966 he agreed that the Indian Affairs Bureau had been "lethargic" and "rigid" in coping with Indian economic problems and promised a reorganization of the Bureau, a greater emphasis on Indian education, a larger voice for Indians in their own affairs and greater access to modern business techniques. In June 1968 Udall accepted safety critic Ralph Nader's [*q.v.*] assertion that the Bureau of Mines had been lax in protecting the health of coal miners. In September of the same year President Johnson proposed a Federal Coal Mine Safety and Health Act, and in December Udall formed a national Conference to Make Coal Mining Safe.

Near the end of the Johnson Administration, Udall tried to convince the President to add over 7.5 million acres to the National Park System under the provisions of the Antiquities Act of 1906. The President, however, yielded to the demands of Rep. Wayne Aspinall (D, Colo.) [*q.v.*], chairman of the House Interior Committee and a foe of conservationists, in adding only 384,500 acres to the park system. Johnson defended the proclamation, his last act as President, arguing that to add more than 7 million acres "would strain the Antiquities Act beyond its intent."

In 1969 Udall became board chairman of the Overview Corporation, an environmental consulting firm. In 1970 he began to write a syndicated column on the environment. In addition, Udall published a number of books, including *America's National Treasures* (1971) and *The National Parks* (1972). His *1976: Agenda for Tomorrow* (1968) outlined a proposal to rebuild the nation's cities and carry out other domestic reforms necessary for entering "the era of greatness that has eluded us too long."

[JCH]

For further information:
Stewart Udall, *1976: Agenda for Tomorrow* (New York, 1968)

UNRUH, JESSE M(ARVIN)
b. Sept. 30, 1922; Newton, Kan.
State Assemblyman, Calif., 1955-71;
Speaker, California State Assembly, 1961-69.

The son of an illiterate sharecropper who migrated to Texas during the Dust Bowl years, Jess Unruh was the only member of his family to graduate from high school. After undertaking a program of self-education during wartime service in the Naval Air Corps, Unruh attended the University of Southern California under the GI Bill. At the University the campus Communists appealed to his idealism and class consciousness, but his wife helped direct his political interests into the Democratic Party. He worked for the Democrats in 1948 and ran unsuccessfully for the State Assembly in 1950 and 1952. In 1954, a big Democratic year, Unruh was elected as the assemblyman from Inglewood in Los Angeles County.

Despite his lack of seniority, Unruh quickly became one of the most powerful members of the Assembly. He accepted both campaign contributions and direction from Sacramento lobbyists, and he rationalized his actions by using his new resources to sponsor liberal legislation and advance the candidacies of liberal Democrats. Unruh argued that, since a politician could not survive without the lobbyists, at least a united bloc of liberal legislators could put their money to good use and minimize their corrupting influence.

By 1961 Unruh was speaker of the Assembly and the Kennedy Administration's chief ally in California, even though the governor, Edmund G. Brown [*q.v.*], was a Democrat. Political analysts considered Unruh to be the most powerful state legislator in the country. Unruh, who said that the only "difference between a dictatorship and a democracy . . . is an independent legislature," professionalized the Assembly and improved the size and quality of its staff in an effort to make it equal in power to the executive branch. In July 1963, at the height of his power, he suffered a great loss of prestige by keeping Republican assemblymen sequestered inside the Assembly chamber until they agreed to vote on the state budget. The adverse public and press reaction to "The Lockup" eventually led Unruh to alter his "boss" image and trim his enormous waistline, which had earned him the nickname "Big Daddy." [See KENNEDY Volume]

Although less inclined and less able to exercise blatantly his power in the mid-1960s, Unruh continued his factional fight with Gov. Brown. Unruh developed Assembly programs in ways that Brown thought challenged the executive's prerogatives. Sensing a conservative trend in the California electorate, Unruh became less inclined than Brown to aggressively back liberal legislation. He refused to support consistently the interests of organized labor and sought to reduce the influence of the liberal California Democratic Council (CDC) within the state Democratic Party. Both the unions and the CDC remained loyal to Brown while attacking Unruh's leadership.

In 1964 California Democrats began to vie for the U.S. Senate seat of the ailing Sen. Clair Engle (D, Calif.). Brown supported the CDC's founding president, State Controller Alan Cranston [*q.v.*], and Unruh tacitly backed Pierre Salinger [*q.v.*], formerly President John F. Kennedy's press secretary and a native Californian. Salinger won the primary, and Brown reluctantly appointed him to take over Engle's Senate seat following the latter's death. Salinger proved to be a poor candidate. His November 1964 loss to Republican George Murphy [*q.v.*] further damaged Unruh's position in state and national Democratic circles. Even Murphy agreed with political analysts that he would have been defeated by Cranston.

In 1965 relations between Unruh and Brown deteriorated even further. When Gov. Brown announced his intention to run for a third term in 1966, Unruh, who believed Brown had made a commitment to give him a chance for the governorship, hesitated before endorsing Brown. He made a point of spending the month before the November 1966 elections abroad, only returning to California after the victory of Republican Ronald Reagan [*q.v.*].

During Gov. Reagan's first term Unruh transformed his public image from that of an aggressive, insensitive political boss into that of a statesman and master of political strategy. However, his efforts to oppose Reagan on issues involving the University of California were generally unsuccessful. He failed to stop Reagan from persuading a majority of the University's Board of Regents to dismiss Clark Kerr [*q.v.*] as president of the University in January 1967. In August of the same year he again opposed Reagan when the Governor sought to impose tuition in the state university system. Reagan succeeded in doubling the University's fee schedule without employing the unpopular term "tuition." Although he attacked campus radicalism as forcefully as Reagan, Unruh won the praise of many of California's teachers, students and liberals by demanding that the University's high standards be maintained while liberalizing its admissions policies.

In March 1968 Unruh became one of the first Democrats of national stature to support the presidential candidacy of Sen. Robert F. Kennedy (D, N.Y.) [*q.v.*], and he quickly adopted Kennedy's criticism of President Johnson's Vietnam policies. The Unruh staff played a key role in Kennedy's campaign in the crucial California primary in June, but on the evening of his victory Kennedy was assassinated in a Los Angeles hotel. Following Kennedy's death Unruh appeared to move sharply to the left. Though leader of the California delegation to the Democratic National Convention, Unruh decided not to impose a unit-voting regulation on his delegates and opened all state caucus meetings at the Convention to the press. He cast his own delegate vote for anti-war candidate Sen. Eugene McCarthy (D, Minn.) [*q.v.*] after his efforts to initiate a draft in favor of Sen. Edward M. Kennedy (D, Mass.) [*q.v.*] had failed. Unruh was widely praised for the democratic manner in which he led his delegation and for his effective leadership of dissident elements within the national Party. Now recognized as an exponent of the "new politics," with a reliance on the support of the poor, minorities and the young, Unruh was able to reestablish friendly relations with

California liberals and the CDC. He gave wholehearted support to the senatorial candidacy of his old enemy, Alan Cranston, but did not announce his endorsement of the Humphrey-Muskie ticket until late in September.

Since the Democrats lost their majority in the Assembly in the 1968 elections, Unruh was forced to step down as speaker in January 1969. In 1970 he relinquished his Assembly seat to run against Ronald Reagan in the gubernatorial contest. Following his loss to Reagan, Unruh devoted himself to college teaching and became a popular figure on the lecture circuit. In 1974 he was elected California state treasurer.

[JCH]

For further information see:
Lou Cannon, *Ronnie and Jesse: A Political Odyssey* (Garden City, 1969).

VALENTI, JACK J(OSEPH)

b. Sept. 5, 1921; Houston, Tex.
White House Special Assistant, November 1963-May 1966.

Jack Valenti grew up in Houston, flew 51 missions in the Army Air Force during World War II and, after graduation from the University of Houston, took an MBA degree at Harvard Business School in 1948. In 1952 Valenti opened a Houston-based advertising and public relaitons firm. He was named Houston's Outstanding Young Man of the Year in 1956.

In 1957 Valenti formed a friendship with Sen. Lyndon Johnson (D, Tex.), who later selected Valenti's firm to handle Democratic Party advertising throughout Texas during the 1960 presidential campaign.

Valenti was in Dallas on business when he heard the news of President Kennedy's assassination. After riding back to Washington aboard Air Force One, Valenti became an indispensable special assistant to President Johnson. During the first few weeks of the new Administration, Johnson commissioned Valenti and aide Horace Busby to prepare position papers on civil rights, urban affairs and foreign policy.

Valenti's duties as a White House special assistant subsequently included speechwriting, appointments scheduling and a variety of other tasks, but his governmental position was subordinate to his role as personal aide to the President. Described by columnist Tom Wicker as "at once the most enigmatic and the most omnipresent of the Johnson men," Valenti was the staff member most often seen in Johnson's company during the early days of his Administration. Because of his unabashed worshipfulness of the President and perhaps because of his personal closeness to him, Valenti became an object of condescension among the Washington press corps. He was described as a "glorified valet" and "the President's personal whipping boy."

The attitude of the press was sharpened by a notorious speech Valenti made on July 3, 1965 before the Advertising Federation of America. Using a rhetorical style that made him the object of considerable mockery, Valenti stated, "The President, thank the good Lord, has extra glands . . . that give him energy that ordinary men simply don't have . . . . I sleep each night a little better, a little more confidently, because Lyndon Johnson is my President."

In May 1966 Valenti resigned from the White House staff to accept a highly paid position as president of the Motion Picture Association of America, Inc.

[FHM]

For further reading:
Patrick Anderson, *The President's Men* (New York, 1968).
Jack Valenti, *A Very Human President* (New York, 1976).

VANCE, CYRUS R(OBERTS)

b. March 27, 1917; Clarksburg, W. Va.
Secretary of the Army, July 1962-January 1964; Deputy Secretary of Defense, January 1964-June 1967; Deputy Delegate to the Paris Peace Talks, May 1968-February 1969.

After receiving his law degree from Yale in 1942, Vance served in the Navy. Following the war he entered private law practice in New York. From 1957 to 1960, while still a practicing attorney, he became special counsel to the Senate committees investigating the satellite and missile programs. An associate special counsel for the Senate Committee on Aeronautical and Space Science, he became a protege of Committee Chairman Lyndon Johnson, who recommended him for a high position in the Kennedy Administration. Vance was appointed general counsel for the Department of Defense in January 1961.

At the Defense Department Vance developed a close working relationship with Secretary of Defense Robert S. McNamara [*q.v.*], who asked Vance to aid him in the reorganization of the Pentagon bureaucracy and in the modernization of the Army. Vance became Secretary of the Army in July 1962. As Secretary, he advised President Kennedy to send federal troops to the South during the violence that followed the October 1962 attempt to integrate the University of Mississippi and the May 1963 riots in Birmingham, Ala. [See KENNEDY Volume]

Vance succeeded Roswell Gilpatric [*q.v.*] as deputy secretary of defense in January 1964; he served at that post until June 1967, when ill-health forced him to retire from government. Vance was one of Johnson's closest aides and throughout the Administration acted as "presidential troubleshooter" in many important foreign crises. In January 1964 Johnson sent him to Panama in an unsuccessful attempt to negotiate the restoration of diplomatic relations, which Panama had severed after American troops fired on rioters protesting the U.S. presence in the Canal Zone. A month after intervention by American marines in April 1965, Vance was part of a team sent to the Dominican Republic to try to establish a coalition government satisfactory to both sides in that nation's civil war. The mission failed, but peace was finally restored in August as a result of the diplomatic efforts of Ellsworth Bunker [*q.v.*] and the Organization of American States. Two years later Vance worked with representatives of the North Atlantic Treaty Organization (NATO) and the U.N. to establish a temporary truce in the civil war in Cyprus. Following North Korean raids on Seoul and the seizure of the *U.S.S. Pueblo*, Vance went to South Korea in February 1968 to assure the government of continuing American support and to explain that the U.S. would not increase military aid in light of its commitment in Vietnam.

In July 1967, shortly after Vance's resignation from the Pentagon, Johnson asked him to be his on-the-scene representative during the Detroit riots. In consultation with Gov. George Romney [*q.v.*] and Mayor Jerome Cavanagh [*q.v.*], Vance recommended that the President call in federal troops on the night of July 25, when local authorities failed to contain the growing violence. Several months after the incident, in September 1967, Vance wrote a report on his mission known as the "Detroit Book." This document became the source of a series of recommendations designed to minimize the danger of shooting civilians when dealing with urban riots. His report called for the use of "overwhelming law enforcement manpower" coupled with military and police restraint and the heavy use of tear gas instead of gunfire.

While involved in these troubleshooting missions, Vance also advised the President on Vietnam policy. According to the *Pentagon Papers*, he was "overwhelmingly in favor of prosecuting the war vigorously with more men and material, with intensified bombing of North Vietnam and with increased efforts to create a viable government in the South." He was one of the men who recommended bombing North Vietnam following the Tonkin Gulf incident of Aug. 4, 1964. In October of that year, when the decision was made to resume the small-scale attacks staged by South Vietnam against Northern coastal installations, Vance and McGeorge Bundy [*q.v.*] coordinated the selection of these targets. After the Communists carried out a major attack on American helicopter installations and the U.S. Army advisers' barracks in Pleiku in February 1965, Vance urged that retaliatory air strikes be undertaken immediately.

In June 1967 Vance slightly modified his position on the conduct of the war. Along with McNamara he recommended a change in bombing policy from an emphasis on heavy bombing of North Vietnam to one that would stress attacking infiltration routes south of the 20th parallel.

After leaving the Defense Department Vance continued to advise the President on Vietnam. Following the military's February 1968 request for over 200,000 additional troops, Vance became a member of the Senior Advisory Group on Vietnam, formed to study the proposal. In meetings held on March 25 and 26, Vance, along with Dean Acheson [*q.v.*], George Ball [*q.v.*] and Clark Clifford [*q.v.*], advocated de-escalation of the war, fearing that the political, social and economic life of the U.S. would be torn apart by continued escalation. Johnson announced a policy of de-escalation on March 31, 1968.

When the Paris peace talks between the U.S. and North Vietnam began in May 1968, Vance was appointed deputy delegate. In that role he handled the organizational meetings associated with the talks, including those dealing with delegation size, languages to be used and seating arrangements. In December, when discussions for holding the enlarged conference between the U.S., North Vietnam, South Vietnam and the National Liberation Front (NLF) bogged down over seating arrangements, Vance negotiated the compromise settlement. Instead of the rectangular table demanded by Hanoi, (which would have implied that the NLF was of equal status with the other members), or the round table suggested by the U.S., (which would have left the status of the NLF ambiguous) the conference agreed to a round table with two rectangular tables placed flanking it.

Vance resigned his post in February 1969 to resume law practice in New York.

[EWS]

VANIK, CHARLES A(LBERT)

b. April 7, 1913; Cleveland, Ohio.
Democratic Representative, Ohio, 1955- .

Charles A. Vanik received both bachelor's and law degrees from Western Reserve University and served in the Navy during World War II. Entering politics at the war's end, he won a state Senate seat and a municipal judgeship before unseating a 19-term House incumbent in 1954. Of Czech heritage, Vanik represented an overwhelmingly Democratic district of blacks and second-generation Eastern European immigrants.

In January 1965 House leaders transferred Vanik, considered an Administration loyalist, from the Banking and Currency Committee to Ways and Means. The leadership moved Vanik to the powerful taxation panel because of his strong support for medicare, long opposed by Ways and Means Chairman Wilbur D. Mills (D, Ark.) [*q.v.*]. With the Committee majority against him, Mills agreed to a compromise federal medicare plan later in the year. In October 1967 Vanik stood with four other Democratic Committee members in favor of the President's tax surcharge against a Mills-led majority (20-5), which voted to postpone the request.

Vanik voted with the President on 89% of all issues during the 89th Congress and 83% of the time during the 90th Congress. Initially he warmly endorsed the Administration's Vietnam policy, writing in December 1965 that "America has not turned its back on the plea for democracy and freedom on the Asiatic mainland." But in the early spring of 1968, he came out against American involvement; in May he won election as a delegate supporting Sen. Eugene J. McCarthy (D, Minn.) [*q.v.*] for president at the Democratic National Convention. Together with five other Democratic colleagues in October, he voted against the Defense Department appropriation bill for fiscal 1969, which passed 213 to 6.

In 1968 Vanik ran for reelection in a new Cleveland district. A year earlier the Republican state legislature had redrawn Cleveland's four congressional districts. In the process it had created an overwhelmingly black district from Vanik's old one. Declaring that his district should now have a black representative (in this instance Louis B. Stokes, the brother of Mayor Carl B. Stokes [*q.v.*]), Vanik filed in the adjacent district of 82-year-old Rep. Frances P. Bolton (R, Ohio) [*q.v.*]. In a hotly contested election, Vanik charged that his wealthy opponent possessed "the provincial views of the hunt-club set." With 55% of the total vote, Vanik defeated Bolton.

Vanik easily won reelection in 1970, 1972 and 1974. During the Nixon presidency he supported major tax and welfare reforms. A foe of the seniority system, Vanik joined in a successful January 1975 coalition that stripped Mills of his chairmanship. [See NIXON Volume]

[JLB]

VAUGHN, JACK H(OOD)

b. Aug. 18, 1920; Columbus, Mont.
Ambassador to Panama, April 1964-March 1965; Secretary of State for Inter-American Affairs and Coordinator of the Alliance for Progress, March 1965-January 1966; Peace Corps Director, January 1966-March 1969.

Vaughn grew up in Mexico and Montana, where his father worked as a ranch hand. After military service during World War II, he studied at the University of Michigan, receiving an M.A. in Latin American studies in 1947. Vaughn entered government service one year later as program director for the United States Information Agency (USIA) in La Paz, Bolivia. He spent four years with the USIA in Bolivia and Costa Rica before joining the International Cooperation Administration (ICA), a planning agency for U.S. foreign aid projects. Vaughn worked for the ICA in Latin America, western Africa and in the agency's Washington headquarters. In 1961 he became director of Latin American projects for the newly formed Peace Corps.

Vaughn remained at the Washington headquarters of the Peace Corps until April 1964, when President Lyndon Johnson appointed him ambassador to Panama. This post had been vacant for seven months following violent demonstrations by Panamanians against U.S. control of the Panama Canal. Hoping to improve U.S.-Panamanian relations, Vaughn toured the countryside extensively, acquiring a reputation as "the peasant ambassador." He urged Panamanians to concentrate on rural development, rather than the canal, as their main source of economic growth. At the same time he conducted negotiations for revision of the Panama Canal treaty, expressing U.S. willingness "in principle" to recognize Panamanian sovereignty over the canal and to cooperate with Panama in managing the waterway. The negotiations Vaughn began eventually led to a tentative Canal Zone agreement, which Panama nevertheless rejected because it allowed the U.S. to retain a predominant role in operating the canal.

In 1965 Vaughn left Panama to become an assistant secretary of state and U.S. coordinator of the Alliance for Progress. He served in these posts largely as a roving envoy to Latin America, attempting to reassure heads of state who feared that U.S. interest in the region had declined during the Johnson Administration. The Alliance for Progress, Vaughn claimed, remained as vigorous during the mid-1960s as at the time of its creation in 1961. Back in Washington, however, he urged the Administration to pay closer attention to specific Alliance programs; he especially favored community development projects of the kind undertaken by the Peace Corps.

Vaughn's enthusiasm for the Peace Corps, which had never wavered since the early 1960s, was rewarded when he became the agency's director in early 1966. He replaced Sargent Shriver [*q.v.*], who had resigned to devote full time to the Administration's poverty program. Vaughn served for three years as Peace Corps director, for the most part administering and developing existing programs. He aroused controversy in 1967 by demanding that 92 Peace Corps volunteers in Latin America disassociate themselves from a statement opposing the Vietnam war. One year later, however, he endorsed the right of volunteers to oppose U.S. foreign policy while serving overseas.

Vaughn's forthrightness on controversial issues made him important enemies in Congress. Rep. Otto Passman (D, La.) [*q.v.*] demanded his resignation for supporting dissent within the Peace Corps, while Sen. Wayne Morse (D, Ore.) [*q.v.*] accused him of favoring authoritarian governments in Latin America. Vaughn resigned from the Peace Corps in March 1969. Two months later he was appointed ambassador to Colombia by President Richard Nixon; but he left this post after one year, reportedly disappointed by the lack of attention he received from the Administration.

During the early 1970s Vaughn served as president of the National Urban Coalition, a research and funding agency for community development projects, and as dean of international studies at Florida International University. Later he became director of foreign development for the Children's Television Workshop, a communications firm.

[SLG]

VINSON, CARL

b. Nov. 18, 1883; Baldwin County, Ga.
Democratic Representative, Ga., 1914 - 65; Chairman, Armed Services Committee, 1949-53, 1955-65.

Vinson won a race for a vacant seat in the U.S. House of Representatives in 1914. He succeeded to the chairmanship of the Naval Affairs Committee in 1931, and in 1949 he became chairman of the Armed Services Committee. The Georgia Congressman believed that peace depended upon a strong military posture, and in 1950 he attacked reductions in defense expenditures proposed by Secretary of Defense Louis Johnson. Vinson opposed the Eisenhower Administration's "massive retaliation" doctrine and emphasized the need to maintain a military force capable of dealing with less than total war. During the early 1960s he criticized the Kennedy Administration's plans to begin phasing out manned bombers in favor of missiles. He also opposed Secretary of Defense Robert S. McNamara's [*q.v.*] policy of transferring power from the individual military services to the Department of Defense. [See TRUMAN, EISENHOWER, KENNEDY Volumes]

As chairman of the Armed Services panel, Vinson established himself as a crucial force in the shaping of military-related legislation. He exercised firm control over the Committee by centralizing its power in his hands. Rather than establishing regular subcommittees with defined jurisdictions, he divided the panel into three equal groups and decided which would receive each bill. He was an extremely skillful floor manager, and almost all bills cleared by the Committee were approved by the House.

In 1964 Vinson continued to advocate, over Defense Department opposition, the appropriation of funds for manned bombers. In February his Committee added to Administration defense authorization requests $92 million for the development of strategic aircraft to replace the B-52 and B-58 bomber fleets. During floor debate he asserted that if those planes were retired "we will be in the position of depending entirely on missiles, a thing none of us wants to do." The final bill, passed by both houses, appropriated $52 million for developing new manned bombers.

In April 1964 Vinson opposed a legislative stipulation, first established in 1962, requiring that at least 35% of all funds for naval ship repair be assigned to private rather than Navy shipyards. Noting that the Defense Department planned to close a number of Navy shipyards by the end of the year, he urged a return to the earlier practice of assigning at least 75% of repair funds to the Navy yards in order to preserve their existence. The formula, however, was not altered.

Early in 1964 Vinson announced that he would not seek reelection that year. On March 20 President Lyndon B. Johnson, in a tribute to Vinson, stated, "No man in the history of this republic knows more about the posture of our defense, and no man has done more to improve it. . . ." On Nov. 14, 1964 Vinson became the first representative to serve in the House for 50 years.

[MLL]

VOLPE, JOHN (ANTHONY)

b. Dec. 8, 1908; Wakefield, Mass.
Governor, Mass., 1961-63, 1965-69.

Rising from hod-carrier to millionaire building contractor, Volpe entered Massachusetts politics in 1948. He became deputy chairman of the Republican State Committee in 1950 and was appointed commissioner of public works by Massachusetts Gov. Christian Herter in 1953. During three years in that office, he undertook one of the largest highway construction programs in the state's history. In late 1956 President Eisenhower named Volpe interim federal highway administrator, a position he filled for four months. In 1960 Volpe became the first Italian and Catholic in Massachusetts's history to be nominated for governor.

The prinicipal campaign issue in the 1960 Massachusetts campaign was maladministration and scandal in highway building and other state programs. In November 1960 Volpe's appeal to "Vote the Man: Vote Volpe" won him the necessary support from independent voters and disgruntled Democrats to make him the only Republican survivor of the 1960 Kennedy landslide in Massachusetts.

At the start of his 2-year term in January 1961, Volpe proposed a reform program including reduction of the tax burden of cities and towns without recourse to new taxes, elimination of unnecessary political offices, revision of the Massachusetts constitution to provide a four-year term for the governor and other elective state offices and a code of ethics for public officials. In the wake of widespread public corruption in the state, Volpe established a state crime commission that reported, "Corruption permeates the state from town governments to the State House and involves politicians, lawyers and ordinary citizens." In his 1962 annual message to the legislature, he stressed as his principal objective the reaffirmation of "the moral fiber and moral consciousness" of the state.

In 1962 Volpe was challenged and narrowly defeated for reelection by Endicott Peabody. After two years of Peabody rule, Volpe recaptured the governorship in 1964 by defeating Lt. Gov. Francis Bellotti. The Democratic primary was embittered by ethnic animosities. On May 10, 1965 Volpe signed a bill repealing an 87-year-old Massachusetts ban on the dissemination of contraceptives and birth control information. (Massachusetts was the last state in the nation to repeal such a law.) In August 1965 Volpe signed a measure making racial imbalance illegal in Massachusetts's public schools. This statute, the first to outlaw racial imbalance or de facto segregation in public schools, provided for the withholding of state funds from any school committee that refused to take speedy and effective steps to eliminate such discrimination.

Volpe sought a third term in a 1966 election campaign that aroused white backlash and involved allegations that Volpe's construction company was involved in a conflict of interest. He defeated Edward J. McCormack, the nephew of House Speaker John W. McCormack [*q.v.*], with 63% of the vote and won the state's first four-year gubernatorial term. In his 1967 inaugural address Volpe noted that the extended term presented the opportunity for "an atmosphere unfettered by consideration of partisan politics." In the same speech Volpe asked for a comprehensive study of the state's tax structure in an effort to develop a "master tax plan" for the next 10 years.

Volpe resigned the governorship in 1969 to become the nation's second Secretary of Transportation. In 1973 he was appointed ambassador to Italy by President Nixon. [See NIXON Volume]

[TJC]

WAGNER, ROBERT F(ERDINAND) (JR.)

b. April 20, 1910; New York, N.Y.
Mayor, New York, N.Y., 1954-65.

Robert F. Wagner, the mayor of New York City for 12 years, was the son of a former U.S. senator from New York who was the author of the famed Wagner (National Labor Relations) Act. The elder Wagner's popularity helped greatly to advance his son's political career.

Wagner attended the Taft School and Yale University. He received a law degree from Yale in 1937 and that year was elected to the New York State Assembly. Following Pearl Harbor he resigned his seat to serve in the Army Air Corps in Europe. After the war Wagner, with the support of the regular Manhattan Democratic organization

(Tammany Hall), moved rapidly up the political ladder. He served successively as tax commissioner, commissioner of housing and buildings and chairman of the city planning commission. In 1949 he was elected Manhattan borough president. He lost his bid for the Democratic senatorial nomination in 1952 but a year later defeated Vincent Impelliteri, the incumbent, for the mayoral nomination. In the November general election Wagner swept to an easy victory.

During Wagner's three terms as mayor, thousands of poor Puerto Ricans and Southern blacks moved into the city while middle-class whites left for the suburbs. The period was marked by a rising crime rate, a drug problem and the deterioration of housing. Nevertheless, the Wagner years on the surface seemed to be a period of relative prosperity for the city. A boom in the construction of luxury apartments and office buildings in Manhattan enlarged the city's property tax base and permitted it to finance a larger police force, higher salaries for teachers and the swelling welfare rolls.

In his first two terms Wagner won passage from the city council of legislation barring racial discrimination in the sale or rental of private housing, and by executive order he gave civil servants (with the exception of the police) the right to organize unions and engage in collective bargaining with the city. In 1960 New York City thoroughly revised its zoning ordinances for the first time in 44 years. [See EISENHOWER Volume]

Wagner was probably at the height of his power at the beginning of his third term. To retain the support of an increasingly powerful Manhattan reform movement, he broke with the regular Democratic leadership in 1961, defeated his Tammany opponent in the September primary and easily won reelection. He subsequently dominated the Tammany organization. Voters that year approved a new charter that increased the mayor's power relative to that of the borough presidents and the Board of Estimate. Wagner maintained close relations with New York City labor leaders and was instrumental in settling a number of major labor disputes, notably the 114-day 1962-63 newspaper strike. [See KENNEDY Volume]

During Wagner's last two years in office, the city was beset by increasing racial tension. On July 16, 1964 an off-duty white police officer, Lt. Thomas Gilligan, shot and killed 15-year-old James Powell, a black schoolboy who had allegedly threatened him with a knife. This incident aggravated already troubled relations between the police and the black community. Rioting broke out in Harlem on July 18 and later spread to the predominantly black Bedford-Stuyvesant section of Brooklyn. In four consecutive nights of rioting, hundreds of store windows were smashed and debris was often hurled at the police. One black was shot to death, five others were wounded, and 81 civilians and 35 policemen were injured. Wagner, who had been vacationing in Europe, flew home and in a July 22 televised address appealed for calm. He declared that "law and order are the Negro's best friend—make no mistake about that. The opposite of law and order is mob rule, the way of the Ku Klux Klan and the lynch mob."

In the aftermath of the rioting, Wagner met with Martin Luther King [*q.v.*] to discuss ways of ending violence in the black community. The Mayor subsequently proposed to create 1,500 new city jobs for unemployed black youths and to recruit more black policemen. Black leaders, including King, were disappointed by Wagner's refusal to support creation of a board independent of the police department to review cases of alleged police brutality.

The 1964 Harlem riots were particularly disheartening to the Mayor because his administration had taken the initiative in financing special programs to aid young people in slum neighborhoods. In 1961 the city, federal government and Ford Foundation had pooled funds to support Mobilization for Youth (MFY), an organization that provided job counseling and retraining to hundreds of young people on the lower East Side. MFY became the prototype for the "community action" antipoverty programs later funded by the Johnson Administration's Office of Economic Opportunity and by cities throughout the country.

In June 1964 Mayor Wagner announced that the city would provide $3.4 million in addition to the federal government's $1 million contribution for the establishment of a major antipoverty program in Harlem to be administered by Harlem Youth Opportunities Unlimited and Associated Community Teams. (The two groups merged in 1964 to form HARYOU-ACT.)

The New York City antipoverty programs soon came under impassioned attack from politicians of both the left and right. Conservative critics cited an August 1964 FBI report that charged that 30 of MFY's 300 employes had previous links to the Communist Party or Communist-front organizations. The Wagner Administration's own Antipoverty Operations Board reported in November that the MFY had hired 20 persons with subversive connections and that the organization was badly managed. Some liberals and black militants, including Harlem's Rep. Adam Clayton Powell (D, N.Y.) [*q.v.*], argued that the Wagner Administration's failure to give neighborhoods control over their antipoverty organizations violated Title II of the 1964 Economic Opportunity Act. In April 1965 Powell asked the federal government to withhold antipoverty funds from New York until the program was reorganized. The Mayor denied Powell's charges but, in response to increasing community and federal pressure, replaced his Antipoverty Operations Board with a new 17-member agency consisting of 11 mayoral appointees and six members from local antipoverty groups. Daniel P. Moynihan [*q.v.*], who served as an assistant secretary of labor under Presidents Kennedy and Johnson, later suggested that Wagner's decision not to seek a fourth term as mayor resulted partly from the "savage criticism" he had received while administering the antipoverty programs.

In June 1965 Wagner submitted a record $3.8 billion expense budget that contained a $250-million deficit. Wagner proposed to cover some of the deficit through the sale of "revenue anticipation notes" (RANS). The city had issued these notes for many years to pay its bills prior to the collection of taxes and receipt of federal and state aid, but New York's ability to issue these notes was limited by state law to the amount of money actually collected the previous year. To permit the city to borrow at unprecedented levels, the state legislature in June 1965 nullified the restrictive legislation and permitted the city to issue RANS on the basis of *estimated* anticipated revenues. The new legislation also permitted the city to borrow against taxes and fees that, though owed, were not scheduled for repayment during the upcoming fiscal year. A 1975 *Fortune* magazine analysis of the New York City fiscal crisis suggested that this legislation had been of monumental importance because it permitted the city to engage in the heavy deficit financing that, in the course of the next decade, brought it close to bankruptcy.

Early in December 1965, less than a month before his departure from office, Wagner appointed a three-man panel to negotiate a settlement between the Transport Workers Union and the New York City Transit Authority. Wagner did not play a direct role in the talks nor did Mayor-elect John V. Lindsay [*q.v.*], who was reluctant to become directly involved in the negotiations until he was sworn into office. On Dec. 31, 1965 Wagner, in a surprise move, flew to Acapulco for a vacation. On Jan. 1, 1966, Lindsay's first day in office, 33,000 transit workers struck, shutting down New York's subways and buses.

After leaving office Wagner began a private law practice but remained a familiar figure in Democratic Party circles.

[JLW]

WALLACE, GEORGE C(ORLEY)

b. Aug. 25, 1919; Clio, Ala.
Governor, Ala., 1963-67, 1970- ; Independent candidate for President, 1968.

Wallace received a law degree from the University of Alabama in 1942, served as an assistant state attorney general in 1946 and built a quasi-liberal record as a state representative from 1947 to 1952. He then won election as judge of Alabama's Third Judicial Circuit in 1952 and entered the Democratic primary for governor in 1958. He was defeated in the June runoff primary by a candidate who took an ardent segregationist stance, making Wallace appear the more moderate contender. His term as circuit judge ended in January 1959, and Wallace spent the next three years preparing for the 1962 gubernatorial primary.

Running on a militantly segregationist platform this time, Wallace was the front-runner in the May 1 Democratic primary and won the May 29 runoff with the largest popular vote of any gubernatorial candidate in Alabama history. Promising "segregation now—segregation tomorrow—and segregation forever" in his January 1963 inaugural address, Wallace repeatedly defied federal court orders for school integration in his first year in office. In June 1963 he personally blocked the entry of two black students to the University of Alabama at Tuscaloosa and stepped aside only after President Kennedy had federalized the Alabama National Guard and ordered several units onto the campus. In September 1963 Wallace forestalled court-ordered desegregation of elementary and secondary schools in four Alabama cities for eight days, and again Kennedy had to intervene to end Wallace's defiance. The Governor's actions brought him extensive national publicity and made him a symbol of Southern resistance to racial integration. [See KENNEDY Volume]

Contending that the leadership of both national parties had strayed from "the principles on which this country was founded," Wallace launched a campaign for the presidency in the spring of 1964. Repeatedly denying charges that he was a racist, Wallace campaigned against big government and the federal bureaucracy. He declared that the "federal government in Washington is reaching into every facet of society and encroaching on the rightful powers of the state." He denounced the pending civil rights act as yet another usurpation of individual liberty and local government authority and condemned the federal courts as a "judicial oligarchy," manipulating the American people "as cogs in a gigantic socialist pattern."

Wallace entered three Democratic primaries in April and May, capturing 34.1% of the vote in Wisconsin, 29.9% in Indiana and 42.8% in Maryland. The size and source of the Wallace vote thoroughly impressed political observers. He scored heavily in working-class neighborhoods in Milwaukee and Baltimore and carried every white precinct in the mill town of Gary, Ind. Wallace withdrew from the race on July 19, four days after the Republicans nominated Sen. Barry M. Goldwater (R, Ariz.) [*q.v.*], declaring that his "mission" of helping "conservatize" the national parties was accomplished.

Wallace continued his segregationist policy as governor over the next two years. Early in 1965 Martin Luther King [*q.v.*] made Selma the site of a major voter registration drive among blacks. On Feb. 2 King announced plans for a march from Selma to Montgomery to protest the denial of voting rights to Alabama's blacks. Wallace asserted on March 6 that "such a march cannot and will not be tolerated," and the next day state troopers, acting under his orders, broke up the march as it left Selma. A second march attempt was also turned back by state troopers on March 9.

On March 17 a federal district court gave its approval to the march, enjoined Wallace from interfering with the demonstrators and ordered the Governor to provide police protection for the marchers. Wallace denounced the ruling but said he would "obey, even though it be galling." He notified President Johnson, however, that Alabama could not afford the cost of mobilizing the National Guard to protect the marchers. Johnson federalized the Guard on March 20, and the marchers were protected on their five-day trek to Montgomery. Wallace refused to meet a delegation from the march when it arrived at the state capitol on March 25, but he did meet with the delegation five days later. In April 1966 Wallace ordered the resegregation of state mental hospitals, which had been integrated in March by the State Hospitals Board. In the same month he announced that Alabama would not comply with the school desegregation guidelines recently issued by the federal Office of Education, and in September Wallace won passage of a law declaring those federal guidelines "null and void" in Alabama.

During his term as governor Wallace increased state education appropriations, inaugurated a large school construction program and expanded the state's free textbook system. He improved the state's mental health facilities, sponsored a clean water act and started the largest road building project in the state's history. These measures were generally applauded, but Wallace's critics noted that his tax program was regressive, that old age pensions, unemployment compensation and welfare payments remained well below the national average during his administration and that Alabama had no minimum wage statute and weak child labor laws. There were charges, noted by the authors of *An American Melodrama*, that Wallace's campaign organization received kickbacks from highway contractors and liquor suppliers doing business with the state.

Because the Alabama constitution barred a governor from serving two consecutive terms, Wallace announced in September 1965 that he would seek a constitutional amendment to change this provision. He called a special session of the state legislature; while the House rapidly passed the succession bill, the Senate voted it down on Oct. 22. Wallace circumvented his possible political eclipse by running his wife, Lurleen Wallace [*q.v.*], for governor in 1966. Announcing her candidacy on Feb. 24, Wallace said that if his wife were elected, he would be "by her side" as governor and would "make the policies and decisions affecting the next administration." Lurleen Wallace won 52% of the vote in the May 1966 Democratic primary, defeating nine other candidates, and won the November election by a two-to-one margin. When his wife was sworn in as governor in January 1967, Wallace became her special assistant and did in fact serve as de facto governor, continuing the policies of his own administration, until she died of cancer on May 7, 1968.

Throughout 1966 Wallace indicated he would run again for the presidency in 1968. He began organizing a new campaign in the spring of 1967 and formally announced his third party candidacy on Feb. 8, 1968. In this campaign, Wallace struck many of the same themes he had in 1964. Alleging that "there's not a dime's worth of difference" between national Democratic and Republican leaders, Wallace said the central issue of his campaign was whether the federal government "can take over and destroy the authority of the states." He denounced the growing federal bureaucracy and said the average man—"the steel worker, the paper worker, the rubber worker, the small businessman, the cab driver"—was "sick and tired of theoreticians in both national parties and in some of our colleges and some of our courts telling us how to go to bed at night and get up in the morning." Portraying himself as the defender of the workingman, Wallace promised to end the trend "toward the solution of all problems with more federal force and more takeover of individual liberty and freedom." Wallace again said he was not a racist, but he attacked federal civil rights laws as a denial of property rights and an infringement on states rights and personal liberty. He attacked the national news media and, as a strong "law and order" advocate, blamed the federal courts for an increase in crime. "If you are knocked in the head on a street in a city today," he complained, "the man who knocked you in the head is out of jail before you get to the hospital" because the courts had "made it impossible to convict a criminal."

Wallace's campaign had a major impact on the 1968 elections. His supporters succeeded in getting his name on the ballot, usually as the candidate of the American Independent Party, in all 50 states. Until the mid-summer of 1968 pollsters gave Wallace 10% of the national vote at best, but June polls showed him with 16%, and both Gallup and Harris polls gave Wallace 21% of the vote in late September. At that point many believed that Wallace might well be able to carry enough states to deny either major party candidate an electoral vote majority, throwing the election into the House of Representatives, where Wallace could influence the choice of a president.

Wallace's prospects began to decline in October. Vice President Hubert H. Humphrey [*q.v.*], the Democratic candidate, launched a strong attack on Wallace as a racist and anti-unionist, and organized labor undertook a vigorous campaign attacking Wallace's record on labor issues while governor. Wallace's image was also tarnished by the disorders and protests accompanying many of his campaign appearances. On Oct. 3 Wallace announced he was choosing former Air Force Gen. Curtis E. LeMay [*q.v.*] as his running mate for the vice presidency. LeMay quickly aroused enormous controversy by saying that the U.S. should "bomb the North Vietnamese back to the Stone Age". The General also said he would advocate the use of nuclear weapons in Vietnam if necessary. Wallace won 13.6% of the national vote in November and carried five states—Arkansas, Louisiana, Mississippi, Alabama and Georgia. Over four million of Wallace's 9.9 million votes came from Northern and Western states, and many analysts believed that only last-minute vote changes kept Wallace from amassing a much larger vote. According to Kevin Phillips, who studied the 1968 election in detail in *The Emerging Republican Majority*, Wallace's candidacy hurt Republican Richard M. Nixon [*q.v.*] more than it did Humphrey. Wallace drew off many conservative votes that would have gone to Nixon in a straight Nixon-Humphrey race. Wallace came close to defeating Nixon in South Carolina and Tennessee, and in Texas he diverted enough votes from Nixon to give Humphrey a plurality. Wallace supplied his own assessment of the election on Nov. 6. Claiming victory in defeat, he contended that he had been "the bellwether for the two national parties" on campaign issues. He asserted his movement was still alive since President-elect Nixon had said "almost identically" the same things in his campaign that Wallace had.

Following the election Wallace became an outspoken critic of the Nixon Administration, charging that its economic and tax policies hurt the "little man" and that Nixon was not doing enough to end busing for school desegregation. Wallace won reelection as Alabama governor in 1970, defeating incumbent Gov. Albert P. Brewer in a close Democratic runoff primary on May 5. He announced his candidacy for the Democratic presidential nomination on Jan. 13, 1972. Between March and May he won the Democratic presidential primaries in Florida, Tennessee, North Carolina, Michigan and Maryland and placed second in primary elections in Wisconsin, Pennsylvania, Indiana, West Virginia and Oregon. Wallace was shot and seriously wounded on May 15, 1972 while campaigning in Maryland; the attack left him paraplegic. He remained a contender for the Democratic nomination despite his injuries and placed third in the balloting in the July Democratic National Convention. Saying his doctors advised against it, Wallace did not run a third-party candidacy in 1972 but made another unsuccessful presidential bid in 1976. [See NIXON Volume]

[CAB]

For further information:
Marshall Frady, *Wallace* (New York, 1968).

WALLACE, LURLEEN B(URNS)
b. Sept. 19, 1926; Tuscaloosa, Ala.
d. May 7, 1968; Montgomery, Ala.
Governor, Ala., 1967-68.

After graduating from high school and completing a short business school course, Lurleen Burns worked as a clerk at a variety store in Tuscaloosa, Ala. On May 22, 1943, at the age of 16, she married George C. Wallace [*q.v.*], and for the next 23 years, she remained inconspicuously at her husband's side while he worked his way upward in Alabama politics. Elected governor in 1962 on a militant segregationist platform, George Wallace became a symbol of Southern resistance to racial integration by repeatedly trying to block court-ordered desegregation in his state.

The Alabama constitution barred a governor from serving two consecutive terms. When Wallace failed to get legislative approval of a bill to change this provision in October 1965, he decided to enter his wife as a stand-in candidate in the 1966 gubernatorial race. Announcing his wife's candidacy on Feb. 24, George Wallace asserted that if she were elected, "we are frank and honest to say that I shall be by her side and shall make the policies and decisions affecting the next administration." Lurleen Wallace added that her election "would enable my husband to carry on his programs for the people of Alabama," and throughout her campaign she pledged to continue her husband's policies. She won a majority in the May 3 Democratic primary, defeating nine other candidates, and easily defeated her Republican opponent in the November election.

Inaugurated as Alabama's first woman governor in January 1967, Lurleen Wallace denounced "federal bureaucrats" and their interference with local schools in a tone much like her husband's. George Wallace became her dollar-a-year special assistant, and the staff he had assembled as governor was carried over intact into his wife's administration. Although Lurleen Wallace was credited with acting on her own initiative at times, for example in seeking increased appropriations for state mental hospitals, George Wallace was generally considered the state's de facto governor. He formulated the major programs of his wife's administration and dealt with lobbyists and legislators. All of his policies were continued by his wife, including his opposition to school desegregation. When a federal court in March 1967 ordered the start of desegregation in all of the state's public schools by the fall, Lurleen Wallace denounced the order and asked the state legislature to issue a "cease and desist" order to the court advising it that its actions infringed upon Alabama's police power. The following September she made the passage of a teacher-choice and a tuition-grant law, designed to inhibit school desegregation, the prerequisite for her approval of state funds for Tuskegee Institute, the famous black college in Alabama.

Shortly before she entered the race for governor, Lurleen Wallace underwent surgery for cancer. She insisted her health was excellent following the operation, but in July 1967 she was again operated on for the removal of a malignant tumor. After two more operations in February and March 1968, Lurleen Wallace died of cancer on May 7, 1968 and was succeeded in office by Lt. Gov. Albert P. Brewer.

[CAB]

WARNKE, PAUL C(ULLITON)

b. Jan. 31, 1920; Webster, Mass.
Defense Department General Counsel, August 1966-June 1967; Assistant Secretary of Defense for Internal Security Affairs, June 1967-February 1969.

Following his graduation from Yale in 1941, Warnke joined the U.S. Coast Guard Reserve, serving until 1946. Two years later he received his law degree from Columbia and joined the prestigious Washington law firm of Covington and Burling, where he spent the next 18 years, first as an associate and then as a partner. From 1962 until 1966 he served as a member of the Maryland and Washington D.C. committees advising the U.S. Commission on Civil Rights.

Warnke left Covington and Burling to become general counsel for the Defense Department in August 1966. At the Pentagon he developed a close working relationship with Secretary of Defense Robert S. McNamara [*q.v.*] and assisted him on several legal and technical problems, particularly those that dealt with the TFX fighter/bomber.

In June 1967 Warnke was appointed assistant secretary of defense for internal security affairs. Two months later he helped McNamara write the "San Antonio Formula," a conciliatory proposal designed to modify the Administration's previous demand for North Vietnamese restraint before peace negotiations could begin. The proposal, sent privately to Hanoi, stated that the U.S. was "willing immediately to stop all aerial and naval bombardment of North Vietnam when that led promptly to productive discussions." On Oct. 3 North Vietnam emphatically rejected the plan as "sheer deception."

During the first months of 1968 Warnke stepped up his efforts to reduce the level of U.S. military activity in Vietnam. Following the Tet offensive of January and February, he served as a member of a special committee, headed by the incoming Secretary of Defense, Clark Clifford [*q.v.*], that had been called together by the President to examine the military's request for over 200,000 more troops. In meetings held at the beginning of March, Warnke opposed a troop increase and questioned the military's interpretation of the Communist offensive as an act of desperation or an attempt to precipitate a popular uprising against the government of South Vietnam. He thought that the offensive was designed to show American citizens that the U.S. was not winning the war and could not without undermining its foreign and domestic interests. In his opinion the U.S. should not attempt to win a military victory but should use only the degree of force necessary to achieve a compromise political settlement. Warnke, therefore, objected to further troop increases and suggested instead a strategy designed to protect population centers rather than extend areas of control. The committee rejected Warnke's recommendation and backed the military's request.

On March 12 Warnke wrote a memorandum to Clifford suggesting that Hanoi had recently given indications that it now accepted the provisions of the "San Antonio Formula." In light of this, he recommended that the U.S. begin a policy of de-escalation as a sign of good faith. Warnke's advice in the committee meetings and in his correspondence with Clifford had an important influence on the Secretary of Defense, who in turn played a large role in convincing President Johnson of the need for de-escalation. Johnson announced this policy on March 31.

Warnke resigned his defense post in February 1969 to become a partner in a Washington law firm. In 1977 Warnke became head of the U.S. delegation to the Strategic Arms Limitation Talks (SALT). [See CARTER Volume]

[EWS]

For further information:

David Halberstam, *The Best and the Brightest* (New York, 1972).

Townsend Hoopes, *The Limits of Intervention* (New York, 1969).

WARREN, EARL

b. March 19, 1891; Los Angeles, Calif.
d. July 9, 1974; Washington, D.C.
Chief Justice of the United States, 1953-69.

Warren grew up in Bakersfield, Calif., and worked his way through college and law school at the University of California, receiving his law degree in 1914. Beginning in 1919 he held posts as city attorney in Oakland, deputy district attorney of Alameda County, Calif., and, from 1925 to 1938, county district attorney. In the latter year he successfully ran for state attorney general and four years later for governor of California. A highly popular politician, Warren was the state's first three-term governor. In that office he established a largely progressive record, although earlier in his career he had taken many conservative and anti-civil libertarian positions. The Republican vice presidential candidate in 1948, Warren tried for the Party's presidential nomination in 1952. He lost that bid, but at a crucial point in the Republican National Convention, Warren swung the California delegation to Dwight Eisenhower. In September 1953 Eisenhower appointed Warren Chief Justice of the United States.

In his earliest years on the bench, Warren was generally the cautious, moderate jurist most observers had expected him to be when he was named to the Court. The major exception came in May 1954, when he handed down the Court's unanimous opinion in *Brown* v. *Board of Education*, which held racial segregation in public schools unconstitutional. The decision was a catalyst for the civil rights revolution of the 1960s, served as the base from which the Court went on to outlaw all public discrimination and proved a better indication of Warren's future course than his other early opinions.

By the late 1950s he had clearly aligned himself with the Court's more liberal, activist members. After a solid liberal majority emerged in the early 1960s, Warren led a Court that applied new constitutional doctrines to many aspects of the law. In addition to rewriting the law on race relations, the Warren Court ordered congressional and state legislative reapportionment on a "one-man, one-vote" basis, extended most of the Bill of Rights to the states and gave a new, expansive interpretation to the rights of criminal defendants. The Court also restricted the power of government to act against individuals because of their beliefs and associations, or to suppress allegedly obscene materials. It prohibited prayer in public schools and significantly enhanced freedom of speech and of the press, restricting the government's right to suppress allegedly obscene materials. There "is not much exaggeration," Anthony Lewis declared, in labeling the record of this Court a "revolution made by judges." [See TRUMAN, EISENHOWER, KENNEDY Volumes]

Although the Court had made significant strides toward these ends prior to 1964, many of them were not fully achieved until the Johnson Administration. In March 1962 a majority had ruled that federal courts could try legislative apportionment cases. In a February 1964 decision the Court laid down a "one-man, one-vote" standard for congressional apportionment. Warren's majority opinion in six June 1964 cases held that the equal protection clause required the same standard for state legislative districting. These decisions resulted in reapportionment in virtually every state. In April 1968 the Court extended the one-man, one-vote principle to local units of government.

Similarly, in the mid-1960s the Court moved from occasional to consistent restriction of government action against members of the Communist Party. Warren himself wrote the opinion in an important June 1965 case that overturned a federal law barring Party members from serving as labor union officials. He again spoke for the majority in a December 1967 decision that nullified a federal statute making it a crime for Communists to work at defense facilities. The law was voided on the grounds that it was too broad and that it was a violation of the right of free association. In addition to limiting federal anti-subversive legislation, the Court knocked down numerous state loyalty oath laws between 1964 and 1968. Although he generally favored individual liberty over a claim of government security interests, Warren did sustain the Secretary of State's authority to refuse a citizen a passport valid for travel to Cuba in May 1965.

In December 1964 the Court unanimously sustained the public accommodations section of the 1964 Civil Rights Act. The Chief Justice also wrote the majority opinion in a March 1966 case upholding seven major parts of the 1965 Voting Rights Act. Warren spoke for the Court in an April 1965 decision that invalidated a Virginia law substituting a special registration procedure for the poll tax outlawed by the 24th Amendment. In June 1967 Warren, speaking for a unanimous Court, found unconstitutional state anti-miscegenation laws, one of the last bastions of legalized segregation. In June of the next year the Court upheld an 1866 federal statute that prohibited racial discrimination in the sale or rental of housing and other property. The Court consistently overturned state convictions of civil rights demonstrators on a variety of legal grounds up until 1966. However, in November of that year a five-man majority upheld the trespass convictions of protesters who had gathered outside a Florida jail. Warren dissented from this judgment and from a similar Court ruling in June 1967.

Throughout its history the Warren Court aroused great controversy. Its decisions on school desegregation and prayer in public schools, for example, brought the justices much criticism. By the late 1960s opposition to the Court centered on those rulings that had expanded the rights of criminal defendants. During the Johnson years the Court continued the process of extending the Bill of Rights to the states and held that the Fifth Amendment's privilege against self-incrimination and the Sixth Amendment's right to confront witnesses and to a speedy trial applied to state as well as federal courts. A series of decisions on the admissibility of confessions culminated in the June 1966 *Miranda* ruling, probably the Court's most controversial criminal justice decision. Speaking for a five-man majority, Chief Justice Warren laid down a set of protections for a criminal suspect immediately following his arrest. These included requirements that he be informed of his right to remain silent and his right to counsel and that he be supplied with an attorney if unable to afford one.

The landmark ruling was denounced by many who felt it would hinder law enforcement agencies. Republican presidential candidate Richard M. Nixon [*q.v.*] made *Miranda* and other Court rulings on criminal rights a major issue in his 1968 campaign. However, other observers noted that although the Court enhanced the rights of the accused, it also upheld the right of police to use informants and made it clear that both wiretapping and eavesdropping would be approved if properly authorized by judicial warrants. An opinion written by Warren in June 1968 also upheld police authority to stop and frisk dangerous looking persons for weapons.

In December 1966 Warren spoke for a unanimous Court in ruling that the Georgia House of Representatives had violated Julian Bond's [*q.v.*] right of free speech when it excluded him from his seat in the legislature because of his opposition to the draft and the Vietnam war. Although he normally favored expanding the right to free expression, the Chief Justice proved to be less tolerant in the realm of obscenity. He dissented from several Court decisions that restricted government suppression of allegedly obscene materials and that resulted in much greater freedom of expression in this area. In May 1968 Warren, speaking for a seven-man majority, upheld a provision in the Selective Service Act that made it a criminal offense to burn one's draft card and rejected the argument that this type of conduct was a form of symbolic speech protected by the First Amendment.

In addition to his work on the Court, Warren, at the urging of President Johnson, reluctantly accepted in November 1963 the chairmanship of a commission to investigate the assassination of John F. Kennedy. After 10 months of work, which Warren later called "the unhappiest time of my life," the Commission produced a unanimous report, concluding that Lee Harvey Oswald, acting alone, had killed Kennedy. The Warren Commission report was later disputed by other researchers who insisted that Kennedy's assassination was the result of a conspiracy. However, their arguments never led Warren to doubt the Commission's findings.

On June 13, 1968 Warren submitted his resignation to President Johnson, who accepted it pending confirmation of a new chief justice. Johnson nominated Associate Justice Abe Fortas [*q.v.*] to the post, but withdrew the nomination in October 1968 after a coalition of Republicans and conservative Democrats effectively blocked Senate confirmation of the appointment. Warren then announced that he would retire at the end of the Court's term in June 1969. In his last opinion for the Court on June 16, 1969, Warren reversed an appeals court decision written by Warren Burger, his successor as chief justice, and held that the House of Representatives had acted unconstitutionally in excluding Adam Clayton Powell [*q.v.*] from membership in March 1967.

A thoughtful man with a friendly, affable manner, Warren devoted a part of his retirement years to public speaking and to the fishing, hunting and spectator sports he so enjoyed. He died in Washington on July 9, 1974.

During his years on the bench, Earl Warren served as a symbol for the entire Court to both its admirers and its critics. Denunciations of the Court's rulings often turned into attacks on Warren personally, and he was often picketed and heckled when he delivered public speeches. His actual role in making the Warren Court the activist, liberal body it became has been widely debated. While some observers contended that he played no greater part than his fellow liberal justices, a larger number have argued that his leadership and his political and administrative skills were essential for establishing cohesion and direction on the Court. With the single exception of obscenity, Warren supported every major change in constitutional doctrine made by the Court, and thus placed the weight of his reputation behind the Court's innovative trends. Although not considered a great legal scholar or judicial philosopher, Warren has been ranked as one of America's greatest chief justices, perhaps second only to John Marshall.

Legal scholars directed their strongest criticism of both Warren and his Court at the style rather than the substance of their decisions. The Court's liberal jurists, many argued, were so oriented toward achieving desirable results that they too easily discarded precedents, failed to explain or justify their rulings with any solid legal reasoning and left themselves open to the charge that they interpreted the Constitution solely on the basis of their political preferences. Warren's own opinions were criticized for being unanalytical and more ethical than legal. His opinion in *Miranda*, setting forth a detailed code of conduct for the police, was considered a prime example of the Court's tendency to act more like a legislative than a judicial body.

No observer denied that the Warren Court had a significant impact on American society. Motivated by ideals of equality and fairness and careful to safeguard individual freedoms, the Court, as Archibald Cox [*q.v.*] remarked, "spearheaded the progress in civil rights, administration of criminal justice, protection of individual liberty and the strengthening and extension of political democracy." Most commentators have agreed with Cox that the Warren Court's rulings "brought the law more nearly in accord with the best and the truest aspirations of the American people."

[CAB]

For further information:
Alexander M. Bickel, *The Supreme Court and the Idea of Progress* (New York, 1970).
Archibald Cox, *The Warren Court* (Cambridge, Mass., 1968).
Arthur J. Goldberg, *Equal Justice: The Warren Era of the Supreme Court* (Cambridge, Mass., 1968).
Philip Kurland, *Politics, the Constitution and the Warren Court* (Chicago, 1970).
Anthony Lewis, "Earl Warren," in Leon Friedman and Fred L. Israel, eds., *The Justices of the United States Supreme Court, 1789-1969* (New York, 1969), Vol. IV.
Richard H. Sayler, et al., eds., *The Warren Court: A Critical Analysis* (New York, 1969).
Bill Severn, *Mister Chief Justice: Earl Warren* (New York, 1968).

WASHINGTON, WALTER (EDWARD)

b. Aug. 15, 1915; Dawson, Ga.
Executive Director, National Capital Housing Authority, 1961-67; Director, New York Housing Authority, 1966-67; Mayor-Commissioner, Washington D.C., September 1967- .

Washington was born in Georgia and raised in Jamestown, N.Y., but from 1934, when he became an undergraduate at Howard University, he was a resident of the District of Columbia. After graduating from Howard with a major in sociology and public administration, Washington joined the National Capital Housing Authority in 1941. As a member of an agency charged with the construction and management of low-rent housing, Washington served in a variety of capacities until named Executive Director in 1961. He remained in that post until November 1966, when New York Mayor John V. Lindsay [*q.v.*] named him to head the New York Housing Authority. In September 1967 Washington left that position to become the first mayor of Washington, D.C., which had previously had a commission form of government.

Washington's appointment came in the aftermath of a summer marked by convulsive racial turmoil in many U.S. cities, including the capital. His appointment was welcomed by the *Washington Post* as "an effective bridge between the Capital City and the Other City," and by *Ebony*, which wrote that his selection signaled "a new mood of hope and expectation in the nation's capital". The District of Columbia was beset with the highest infant mortality rate in the country, poor schools, dismal housing and a high rate of unemployment.

Accepting a $6,000-a-year cut in salary, Washington became the first black chief executive of a major American city. He was charged with the responsibility of bringing what Lyndon Johnson called the capital's "wagon-wheel government into the jet age." Washington was credited with "soothing the city's riot jitters," integrating its police department and making his office responsive to the people's needs. Shrugging off militant charges that he was an "Uncle

Tom" as well as accusations of executive mismanagement, Washington described himself as an "administrator" who worked for the good of all the people. Though street crime continued to plague the District, the Mayor's moderate stance resulted in his reappointment by the Nixon Administration in December 1968.

After Washington had served seven years as appointed executive, Congress granted the District "home rule," and in its first mayoral election in a century, Washington was elected mayor in 1974.

[TJC]

WATSON, ALBERT W(ILLIAM)

b. Aug. 30, 1922; Sumter, S.C.
Democratic Representative, S.C. 1963-65; Republican Representative, S.C., 1965-70.

Albert Watson grew up in South Carolina. He served in the Air Force during World War II, received a law degree from the University of South Carolina and was admitted to the state's bar in 1950. After five years in private law practice, Watson was elected to the South Carolina General Assembly, where he served until his election to the U.S. House of Representatives from South Carolina's second congressional district in 1962.

Watson was assigned to the Post Office and Civil Service Committee. According to *Congressional Quarterly*, he voted with the conservative coalition of Republicans and Southern Democrats on about 90% of all major issues during the Johnson Administration. He was a militant segregationist.

In 1964 Watson publicly supported the presidential candidacy of Sen. Barry Goldwater (R, Ariz.) [*q.v.*]. A House Democratic caucus met on Jan. 2, 1965 and by a vote of 157 to 115 deprived Watson and Rep. John Bell Williams (D, Miss.) [*q.v.*] of their seniority rights. The disciplinary action was more important to Williams, an 18-year veteran, than it was to Watson, who had been in the House for only two years and ranked low in seniority.

On Jan. 12 Watson announced that he would resign from Congress to run for reelection as a Republican. In the June special election to fill his own vacated seat, Watson defeated Democrat Preston H. Callison by a two-to-one margin.

As a Republican, Watson was assigned to the Interstate and Foreign Commerce Committee. In 1967 he offered an amendment directed against civil rights workers, (later incorporated into the 1968 Civil Rights Act) that provided that nothing in the measure be interpreted as conferring special privileges or immunities with respect to any person or class of persons.

In 1970 moderate Democrat John C. West defeated Watson in the South Carolina gubernatorial election with 53% of the vote in what was regarded as a stinging defeat for the Nixon Administration's "Southern strategy." Both Vice President Spiro T. Agnew [*q.v.*] and David Eisenhowever, Nixon's son-in-law, had campaigned vigorously for Watson. During the campaign Watson exhorted the citizens of Lamar, S.C., to use "*every* meas at your disposal" to block school integration. Shortly after Watson's statement 200 white men and women attacked buses carrying Negro children to a previously all-white school in Lamar. The incident was widely regarded as a major factor in Watson's defeat. [See NIXON Volume]

[FHM]

WATSON, WILLIAM M(ARVIN)

b. June 6, 1924; Oakhurst, Tex.
White House special assistant, January 1965-March 1968; Postmaster General, April 1968-January 1969.

Marvin Watson left Baylor University in 1941 to serve with the Marines in the Pacific. Returning to Baylor with the aid of the G.I. bill, he received a master's degree in business administration in 1950 and subsequently became executive assistant to E. B. Germany the conservative president of the Lone Star Steel Company. Named a member of the Texas State Democratic Committee in 1958, Watson established one of the first Johnson-for-President clubs in Texas in 1960. At the 1964 Democratic National Convention in Atlantic City, N.J.,

Johnson asked Watson to act as his convention coordinator.

Watson was named a White House special assistant in January 1965. Described as a "hard-nosed, hard-shell, no-nonsense Baptist," he served as White House appointments secretary and as liaison with Democratic governors, the Democratic National Committee, big-city mayors and the Federal Bureau of Investigation. As appointments secretary, he was characterized by Robert Sherrill in the *Accidental President* as the "White House's No. 1 Hatchet Man." Watson not only required that all incoming phone calls be logged and the name of the party on each end recorded, but he demanded that White House chauffeurs make a full report on the destination of any White House staffer using official transportation. After the resignation of Bill D. Moyers [*q.v.*] on Dec. 14, 1966, Watson assumed many of Moyers's duties as White House chief of staff; anyone wishing to see the President had to receive Watson's permission first. A principal link to the Democratic National Committee and to the Party's wealthy supporters, Watson was one of the four or five presidential aides who, in March 1968, helped Johnson make his decision not to seek reelection.

In April 1968 President Johnson, urging reform of the Post Office, appointed Watson Postmaster General to replace Lawrence F. O'Brien [*q.v.*], who resigned to manage the presidential campaign of Sen. Robert Kennedy (D, N.Y.) [*q.v.*]. In June 1968, following the assassinations of Martin Luther King [*q.v.*] and Kennedy, Watson announced new requirements governing the mailing of firearms. These included clear identification of the package's contents and police notification prior to delivery.

Watson retired as Postmaster General on Jan. 22, 1969 and was replaced by Winton M. Blount.

[FHM]

For further information:

Eric Goldman, *The Tragedy of Lyndon Johnson* (New York, 1969).

Robert Sherrill, *The Accidental President* (New York, 1968).

WEAVER, ROBERT C(LIFTON)

b. Dec. 29, 1907; Washington, D.C. Administrator, Housing and Home Finance Agency, February 1961-January 1966; Secretary, Department of Housing and Urban Development, January 1966-January 1969.

The first black ever appointed to a cabinet post, Weaver grew up in a middle-class suburb of Washington and attended Harvard University, where he received a B.A. in 1929 and a Ph.D. in economics in 1934. During the New Deal years he served as an adviser on minority problems in various federal departments and agencies, working to ensure black participation in government programs. Active in race relations work in Chicago in the mid-1940s, Weaver taught at Northwestern University and then at Columbia and New York Universities between 1947 and 1951. From 1949 to 1955 he headed the opportunity fellowships program of the John Hay Whitney Foundation.

Weaver served as New York State's rent commissioner in the late 1950s and as vice chairman of the New York City Housing and Redevelopment Board in 1960. An expert on black labor and urban renewal problems as well as housing. Weaver was chosen as administrator of the Housing and Home Finance Agency (HHFA) by President-elect John F. Kennedy in December 1960. In that post he oversaw the main housing, home finance and community development functions of the federal government and the operations of five subordinate agencies, including the Urban Renewal Administration and the Federal Housing Administration. Weaver helped draft the Kennedy Administration's June 1961 omnibus housing bill and lobbied for the 1962 Senior Citizens Housing Act. [See KENNEDY Volume]

Continuing to serve as HHFA administrator in the Johnson Administration, Weaver helped write all of President Johnson's housing and urban renewal programs, many of which were part of the Administration's larger antipoverty effort. In the summer of 1964 he lobbied for the president's housing act. Passed in August it provided $1.1 billion to augment urban renewal grants, federal assistance for improvement of slum properties, housing loans for the handicapped and elderly and other programs. Weaver also worked in 1965 for the $7.8 billion omnibus housing bill, which greatly expanded public housing and rent supplement programs for low-income families. He defended the bill's controversial rent supplement provisions, which sought to guarantee that individuals below the poverty level would not pay more than 25% of their incomes in rent. Despite strong resistance from Republicans and Southern Democrats in Congress, the bill was passed in August 1965.

Both Presidents Kennedy and Johnson repeatedly urged congressional authorization of a cabinet-level department of housing and urban affairs. The proposal made no headway during the Kennedy Administration, in part because Southern Democrats opposed the President's announced intention to name Weaver head of the new department. President Johnson gave no advance indication of his choice for such a post, and in September 1965 a law was finally adopted creating a Department of Housing and Urban Development (HUD). On Jan. 13, 1966, Johnson named Weaver the first Secretary of HUD. With Senate confirmation of his appointment four days later, Weaver assumed the highest governmental office held by a black to that time. HUD subsumed the HHFA; thus Weaver's responsibilities initially remained largely unchanged in his new position.

As Secretary of HUD, Weaver helped promote the Administration-backed Demonstration Cities and Metropolitan Development Act in November 1966 and then implemented the Model Cities program which it created. Administered by HUD, the program was designed to demonstrate in selected poor neighborhoods how various federal and local programs could be coordinated and concentrated to eliminate urban blight and restructure the total environment of the neighborhoods' residents.

In July 1967 Weaver spoke out against a plan advanced by Sen. Charles Percy (R, Ill.) [*q.v.*] to promote home ownership among the poor. Weaver contended that many poor families had incomes that were too low or too irregular to meet the mortgage payments and maintenance costs of home ownership, and he called for better funding of existing housing programs. However, the Administration's Housing and Urban Development Act of 1968 did include a program to help the poor buy their own homes, although the methods used differed from those outlined in Percy's proposal. Weaver lobbied for the 1968 bill, which became law on Aug. 1. The Act also authorized a three-year program to supply new and rehabilitated housing for low-income families, federal underwriting of the insurance industry against losses due to riots and other new urban renewal programs.

In August 1966 Weaver encountered criticism of federal urban renewal efforts when he testified before a Senate government operations subcommittee investigating the problems of the cities. Subcommittee chairman Sen. Abraham A. Ribicoff (D, Conn.) [*q.v.*] and Sen. Robert F. Kennedy (D, N.Y.) [*q.v.*] both asserted that urban redevelopment was not being achieved under existing federal programs. The many programs inaugurated during the Johnson Administration and directed in part by Weaver expanded both the size and scope of federal housing and urban renewal activities and often redirected their focus along lines favored by urban planning experts. Nonetheless most commentators agreed that although individual projects were successful, federal programs in the 1960s failed to check the spread of urban decay.

During his tenure Weaver also strongly backed the Administration's open housing bill, arguing that it would "fill a void" in the nation's policy against discrimination. On May 14, 1968 he announced that he would leave government following the presidential election. He submitted his resignation in November, effective Jan. 1, 1969. From 1969 to 1971 Weaver served as president of Bernard Baruch College, a branch of the City University of New York. In 1971 he became professor of urban affairs at Hunter College in New York City.

[CAB]

WEBB, JAMES E(DWIN)
b. Oct. 7, 1906; Tally Ho, N.C.
Director, National Aeronautics and Space Administration, February 1961-October 1968.

Before his appointment as director of the National Aeronautics and Space Administration (NASA) in 1961, Webb's career centered around aviation and administration. He learned to fly as a Marine Corps reservist in 1930 and served actively in the early 1930s and during World War II. Webb was appointed director of the Bureau of the Budget in 1946 and served as Secretary of the Treasury from 1949 to 1952. [See TRUMAN Volume]

Webb was an executive for the Sperry Gyroscope Corporation, a military contractor, during World War II. He became Sen. Robert Kerr's (D, Okla.) assistant and a director of Kerr-McGee Oil Industries in 1952. During this period he was also a director of the McDonnell Aircraft Corporation and the Oak Ridge Center for Nuclear Studies.

When Kerr succeeded Sen. Lyndon B. Johnson as chairman of the Senate Aeronautical and Space Sciences Committee following the 1960 presidential election, he and Johnson recommended Webb for the top NASA position. Webb assumed the post in February 1961 and encouraged Kennedy to accelerate the space program. Supported by Secretary of Defense Robert McNamara [*q.v.*], Webb told Kennedy, who remained skeptical about the costs, that rockets developed for the space program could launch missiles as well as spacecraft.

In April 1961 the Soviets launched the first manned space flight. American prestige declined further when the Bay of Pigs invasion failed soon after. Webb and McNamara urged Kennedy to demonstrate American strength with manned flights in space. In May 1961 Kennedy announced his commitment to land a man on the moon by 1970.

Congress, anxious to surpass Soviet accomplishments in space, almost doubled NASA's budget in 1961, and over the next five years NASA spent nearly $5 billion annually. North American Aviation won the prime Project Apollo contract in November 1961. By then, NASA and the Air Force had decided to develop separate rockets. Webb announced in 1962 that NASA would use a lunar module or "bug" to land men on the moon and that it would descend to the moon from a lunar orbit, rather than from an earth orbit or by direct ascent from earth, eliminating the need for huge rocket boosters. [See KENNEDY Volume]

During 1964 and 1965 several American and Soviet lunar probes landed on the moon. In 1965 the U.S. launched two successful Gemini craft, each with two astronauts aboard. Five more Gemini flights followed in 1966, most of them successfully completing their mission to rendezvous and dock in space.

In January 1967 a flash fire in the Apollo spaceship killed three astronauts in a rehearsal for that program's first scheduled launching. Webb, the opening witness in the subsequent House hearings, maintained that NASA's capability "demonstrated in Project Mercury and in Project Gemini. . .has not all been consumed in one Apollo fire. . . .Whatever our faults, we are an able-bodied team." However, Maj. Gen. Samuel C. Phillips, NASA's Apollo program director, testified that he had put forth a different view in a report he had presented to North American Aviation President Leland Atwood in December 1965. Rep. William F. Ryan (D, N.Y.) [*q.v.*] obtained a copy of the "Phillips report" and asserted that it indicated "incredible mismanagement" of the Apollo program. The report, Ryan said, showed unsatisfactory equipment, ineffective planning and program control, and an inability to meet schedules. The report also showed that NASA had found "a large number of discrepancies" that had escaped North American Aviation inspectors.

Webb told the Senate Aeronautical and Space Sciences Committee on April 17 that North American Aviation had been the first choice of the evaluation board that awarded the Apollo contracts. On May 9, however, he said that the Martin Marietta Corporation had been its first choice on the basis of technical superiority. Webb said that he and three other senior officials had given the contract to North American Aviation "because their proposal was lowest in cost and. . .because they had the most experience." The next day he told the House Science and Astronautics Subcommittee on NASA Oversight that he had overruled the evaluation board's decision because the board "had not done a full and complete job." According to one history of Project Apollo, Kerr, then chairman of the Senate's space committee, had pressured Webb to award the contract to North American aviation.

NASA established its own review board to investigate the fire. The review board's report was released in March 1967 and showed among the conditions that contributed to the fire: a sealed cabin with pressurized oxygen, combustible materials in the cabin, vulnerable electrical wiring and plumbing and inadequate provisions for escape, rescue and medical assistance. The report made no mention of the Phillips document and did not allocate responsibility for the fire. "Our object," Webb said, "was to get ready to fly again."

In June 1967 NASA contracted with the Boeing Company to help manage the Apollo program, and in July the Martin Marietta Company was chosen as engineering and scientific coordinator for space projects to follow the lunar landing. In addition, several top-level administrators were replaced.

A Soviet cosmonaut was killed in a test of a new space ship in April 1967, and Webb suggested that U.S.-Soviet cooperation might prevent future space accidents. However, when Congress reduced NASA's budget in 1967 and 1968, Webb warned that the Soviets would surpass the U.S. in space.

Webb cited financial restraints on NASA when he resigned as its director in September 1968. At that time he expressed doubts that the U.S. would reach the moon by 1970. "The chances of it are less than they were a year ago because we have, of course, less base from which to work." Webb added that the Soviets "are proceeding without let up."

Webb's effective resignation came in October, but he remained a consultant to the program. Nine months later the U.S. fulfilled the goal set by President Kennedy in 1961 when an Apollo lunar module landed on the Sea of Tranquility on July 19, 1969.

[MDB]

For further information:
Hugo Young, Bryan Silcock and Peter Dunn, *Journey to Tranquility: the Long Competitive Struggle to Reach the Moon* (Garden City, 1969).

WELCH, ROBERT H(ENRY) W(INBORNE), JR.

b. Dec. 1, 1899; Chowan County, N.C.
Founder, John Birch Society, 1958- .

Welch graduated from the University of North Carolina in 1916. Several years later he entered his family's candy business and became a successful sales manager. In 1957 Welch left the vice presidency of the candy company to devote his efforts to anti-Communist work. In December 1958 he founded the John Birch Society (named after an American intelligence officer killed by the Chinese Communists in August 1945). The major premise of the organization was that the Communist threat was represented not by Soviet military might but by the presence of Communists and Communist sympathizers in America.

The Society was publicly denounced in 1961 when Sen. Milton R. Young (R, N.D.) [*q.v.*] revealed that in the 1950s Welch had written and circulated a privately printed book (published in 1963 as *The Politician)* which charged that President Dwight D. Eisenhower [*q.v.*] was a Communist agent. This and similar charges directed at other widely respected Americans such as Supreme Court Chief Justice Earl C. Warren [*q.v.*] brought criticism of the Society from both left and right. [See KENNEDY Volume]

In 1964 Welch appointed John H. Rousselot [*q.v.*], a former congressman with experience as a public relations consultant, to serve as the Society's national director of public relations. Rousselot attempted, with some degree of success, to play down the Society's more extreme positions, and the group's membership reached a peak of about 95,000 during the mid-1960's.

In July 1966 national council member Revilo P. Oliver, a professor of classics at the University of Illinois whose academic credentials were prized by Welch, made anti-Semitic remarks at a Birch Society rally. Oliver resigned later in the month, and Welch denounced anti-Semitism, but the incident damaged the organization. During the same year another national council member, Dr. S.M. Draskovich, whom Welch had praised as "one of the five best-informed anti-Communists in the world," resigned from the Society, charging that it did little more than sell anti-Communist books. These events, and the resignation of Rousselot in 1967, helped thwart further membership growth.

In the late 1960s and early 1970s Welch advanced increasingly obscure conspiracy theories. One centered around a group of 18th century Bavarian monks known as the Society of the Illuminati. Another theory contended that a group of international bankers were conspiring with the Communists to dominate the world.

[MLL]

For further information:
James Phelan, "Mutiny in the Birch Society," *The Saturday Evening Post* (April 28, 1967), pp. 21-25.

WESTMORELAND, WILLIAM C(HILDS)

b. March 26, 1914; Spartanberg County, S.C.
Commander, U.S. Military Assistance Command in South Vietnam, June 1964-June 1968; Army Chief of Staff, June 1968-June 1972.

Westmoreland, son of a Spartanberg County textile plant manager, attended The Citadel, a South Carolina military college, before winning appointment to West Point. Following his graduation in 1936, he was commissioned a second lieutenant in the artillery. During World War II he fought in North Africa and Sicily. As a colonel and chief of staff of the Ninth Infantry, he led his troops in the Normandy landing and in the assault on Germany. Following the war Westmoreland took paratroop and glider training at Fort Benning, Ga., and later served as commander of a regimental combat team in Korea. He was named commander of the elite 101st Airborne Division in 1958. Two years later President Eisenhower appointed him superintendent of West Point, where he won approval to increase the size of its student body from 2,400 to 4,000 to give it parity with the U.S. Naval Academy.

In January 1964 Westmoreland was appointed an aide to Gen. Paul D. Harkins, head of the U.S. Military Assistance Command in South Vietnam. In June he succeeded Harkins. At the time U.S. troops in South Vietnam were serving as advisers to the South Vietnamese armed forces. Westmoreland soon realized, however, that the South Vietnamese could not defeat the National Liberation Front and their North Vietnamese allies without direct U.S. intervention. During 1965 Westmoreland requested that U.S. troops participate in combat missions. In February he won permission to utilize two Marine batallions to defend the Da Nang airfield from Communist attack. In July President Johnson approved his request for an additional 44 battalions to be used at Westmoreland's discretion to fight the Communists anywhere in the country. That summer Westmoreland outlined how he thought the war could be won: in "phase one" U.S. troops would halt "the losing trend" by the end of 1965; in "phase two," during the first half of 1966, U.S. and South Vietnamese troops would take the offensive against the enemy. He did not specify how long it would take to defeat the Communist forces.

Westmoreland proposed that South Vietnamese forces assume responsibility for protecting major population centers, while the U.S. attacked the Communists in the countryside. This strategy went counter to the advice of Gen. Maxwell D. Taylor [*q.v.*], U.S. ambassador to South Vietnam, and Gen. James M. Gavin [*q.v.*], who proposed that the U.S. forces limit their activities to the defense of coastal enclaves. Taylor and Gavin suggested that Westmoreland's "search-and-destroy" strategy would require a massive increase in U.S. troop strength and result in many casualties. Westmoreland argued that the U.S. had to carry the war to the enemy, and his view prevailed. By November 1965 U.S. forces were engaged in large-scale operations against the Communist troops in the central highlands of South Vietnam. Gen. Westmoreland's strategy was widely credited with preventing the Communists from overrunning South Vietnam during 1965 and 1966.

Moving to counter the U.S. troops buildup, North Vietnam had little difficulty infiltrating thousands of troops into South Vietnam via Cambodia and Laos and across the Demilitarized Zone. This, in turn, forced Westmoreland to make repeated requests for additional U.S. troops. By the end of 1965 there were 184,000 U.S. servicemen in South Vietnam; Westmoreland, however, requested that within the coming year U.S. fighting strength be increased to 443,000. By the summer of 1966 he urged a buildup to 542,000. The Johnson Administration did not immediately comply with these requests, but by June 1968 there were more than half a million U.S. troops on South Vietnam.

As U.S. casualties began to mount during 1966, Westmoreland's search-and-destroy tactics came under increasing criticism. Gavin and others charged that Westmoreland's troops became easy targets for enemy ambush when they were sent into the jungles. During 1967 and 1968 Westmoreland was also criticized for his decision to defend U.S. base camps at Con Thien and Khe Sanh in Quang Tri province. Many liberals suggested that Westmoreland was wasting men and materiel in defending bases of little strategic importance. Westmoreland replied that these bases were necessary to the defense of Quang Tri province.

Throughout the course of the war, Westmoreland issued optimistic progress reports, and he became a symbol of American determination in Southeast Asia. Amidst growing concern about the war, President Johnson brought him home in April 1967 to address a joint session of Congress. "Backed at home by resolve, confidence, patience and determination," he said, "we will prevail over the Communist aggressor." Senators and representatives stood and applauded. In November Westmoreland assured newsmen that "we have reached a point when the end begins to come into view."

On Jan. 30, 1968, at the start of the traditional Tet holiday season in Vietnam, Communist forces launched a major assault on Saigon, Hue and other South Vietnamese cities. Over the course of several weeks, U.S. and South Vietnamese forces drove the Communists out of the cities. Westmoreland suggested that the Tet offensive, which he termed a desperate act by a demoralized enemy, had been a complete failure because the Communists had sustained devastating losses. Critics of U.S. war policy charged, however, that the Tet offensive actually demonstrated that after more than three years of heavy fighting, the U.S. could not guarantee the safety of South Vietnamese cities. Efforts to "pacify" the countryside, moreover, had failed completely.

Following the Tet offensive Johnson Administration officials began considering a Westmoreland request for over 200,000 additional troops. Because such a troop increase would have required the call up of the national reserve and the imposition of another tax increase and because some officials believed it would lead to social disruption at home, the request became the basis of a complete review of U.S. policy toward South Vietnam. In March 1968 Secretary of Defense Clark Clifford [*q.v.*] and a bipartisan group of counselors called to advise the President urged Johnson not to accede to any major troops increase. The President also agreed to halt the bombing of North Vietnam and seek peace negotiations. This decision undermined Westmoreland's hardline position, and in March it was announced that he would return from South Vietnam to succeed Gen. Earle Wheeler [*q.v.*] as chairman of the Joint Chiefs of Staff. Gen. Creighton Abrams [*q.v.*] became the new commander of U.S. troops in South Vietnam.

As chairman of the Joint Chiefs of Staff, Westmoreland spoke widely at military bases and civic functions to increase public support for the war. He also organized the investigation of the My Lai massacre in which Lt. William L. Calley and other Army officers were charged with the murder of over 100 South Vietnamese civilians. Westmoreland retired from the Army in June 1972. In July 1974 he was defeated in a bid for the South Carolina Republican gubernatorial nomination.

In retirement Westmoreland openly attacked the Johnson Administration's management of the war. He bitterly denounced former Secretary of Defense Robert S. McNamara [*q.v.*] and his civilian aides who had refused to permit the Air Force to carry out the sustained and intensive bombing that he maintained could have brought the defeat of North Vietnam. He criticized these same officials for refusing to permit him to destroy Communist forces in their Cambodian sanctuaries. "What special audacity," he asked, "prompted civilian bureaucrats to deem they know better how to run a military campaign than did military professionals?" The great majority of Americans, he insisted, remained firm in their resolve to fight. Vietnam was lost in the end, he asserted, because officials in Washington refused to carry on. [See NIXON Volume]

[JLW]

For further information:
U.S. Department of Defense, *The Pentagon Papers*, Senator Gravel Edition (Boston, 1971), Vols. II, III and IV.
William C. Westmoreland, *A Soldier Reports* (New York, 1976).

WHEELER, EARLE G(ILMORE)

b. Jan. 13, 1908; Washington, D.C.
d. Dec. 18, 1975; Frederick, Md.
Army Chief of Staff, October 1962-July 1964; Chairman, Joint Chiefs of Staff, July 1964-July 1970.

Serving in combat for only a few months of World War II, Earle Wheeler rose to prominence in the Army chiefly as a result of his reputation as an administrator and as a man who understood the difference between military demand and political possibility. A protege of Gen. Maxwell Taylor [*q.v.*], Wheeler was assigned to the office of the Joint Chiefs of Staff as staff director in 1960. In that post he briefed presidential candidate John F. Kennedy on military affairs. Impressed with Wheeler's performance, Kennedy appointed him Army Chief of Staff in October 1962 when the incumbent, Gen. George H. Decker, retired.

As Army Chief, Wheeler won the favor of Secretary of Defense Robert S. McNamara [*q.v.*] for his implementation of the Secretary's program of expansion and modernization of the Army and for his articulate public defense of the nuclear test ban treaty in 1963.

President Johnson appointed Wheeler chairman of the Joint Chiefs of Staff in July 1964. During the new Administration Wheeler became increasingly involved in the Vietnam war both as a close adviser to the President and as a liaison between the Joint Chiefs and civilian decision-makers. Echoing the policies of the Joint Chiefs, Wheeler advocated an extensive military commitment in Vietnam. He told President Johnson in the spring of 1965 that the U.S. would have to engage a force of 850,000 men over a seven-year period to drive the Communists from that country. Consequently, he consistently supported the military's demands for more troops and weapons. At a conference held in Honolulu in August 1965, he advised the President to gradually increase ground troops because it was evident that primary reliance on bombing North Vietnam to prevent further Communist infiltration of the South had failed. To provide support for those troops Wheeler championed the continued use of massive bombing raids against the North and in 1967 advocated the mining of Haiphong harbor.

Throughout the early years of the war, military leaders in Vietnam had relayed demands for troop increases through Defense Secretary McNamara, who in turn negotiated with the field command to reduce the size of their requests before sending it on to the President. In early 1968 McNamara was preparing to resign; the job of dealing with the field commanders after the Communist Tet offensive was given to Wheeler, who made little attempt to lessen the military demands. On Feb. 26, 1968 Wheeler, in close consultation with Gen. William Westmoreland [*q.v.*], cabled a request for a 40% increase in the 510,000 ground troops already in the battle area. This request, which came as a shock to Pentagon civilians, served as a catalyst for a reappraisal of American policy and the eventual de-escalation of the war.

During the discussions of the high-level ad hoc task force set up to study the proposal, Wheeler continued to champion Westmoreland's demands. He was opposed by several of the President's civilian advisers, such as Paul Nitze [*q.v.*] and Nicholas Katzenbach [*q.v.*]. Despite the resistance of these men, the task force report, issued on March 7, endorsed Wheeler's proposals. President Johnson, who initially approved of the recommendations, never put them into effect. Instead, on the advice of a specially convened senior advisory group on Vietnam, which feared the domestic consequences of further build-ups, Johnson turned to a policy of de-escalation at the end of March.

As liaison between the President and the military leaders in the Pentagon and in Saigon, Wheeler faced the delicate task of inducing the generals to accept compromises on troop build-ups necessary after the President's March decision. His most difficult job was convincing Westmoreland that his February 1968 request for over 200,000 more men was politically unfeasible. Despite his own belief in the need for large manpower increases, Wheeler was able to persuade the commander in Vietnam that he could achieve his goals with only 15,000 of the men originally requested. Gen. Wheeler's skill in this type of negotiations won the admiration of both critics and supporters of the war, who credited him with preventing several high-level resignations during the conflict.

Throughout the conflict Wheeler strongly criticized those who protested the war at home. He thought that the single most important factor in prolonging the conflict was Hanoi's perception of America's weakness of purpose. Although Wheeler steadfastly believed that the United States could win the war in Vietnam, his definition of victory changed over the years. In 1965 he thought that it was possible to drive the Communists out of South Vietnam; by 1967 he echoed the Administration's position that the U.S. goal was to bring Hanoi to the conference table under conditions favorable to the U.S.

Wheeler retired from the Army and from his position as chairman of the Joint Chiefs of Staff in July 1970 and became a director of the Monsanto Corporation. In 1973 newspapers revealed that Wheeler had covered up President Richard M. Nixon's [*q.v.*] role in ordering the 1969 and 1970 secret bombing raids against Cambodia [See NIXON Volume]. Wheeler died in December 1975.

[EWS]

WHITE, BYRON R(AYMOND)

b. June 8, 1917; Fort Collins, Colo.
Associate Justice, U.S. Supreme Court, 1962- .

White grew up in Wellington, a small town in the sugar beet-growing area of Colorado. He graduated in 1938 from the University of Colorado, where he was valedictorian of his class and an All-American in football. "Whizzer" White played professional football for the Pittsburgh Steelers in 1938 and the Detroit Lions in 1940 and 1941; he was named to the National Football Hall of Fame in 1954. A Rhodes Scholar at Oxford University in 1939, White graduated from Yale Law School in November 1946 and served as law clerk to Supreme Court Chief Justice Fred Vinson during the 1946-47 term. At this time he became friendly with Rep. John F. Kennedy (D, Mass.), whom he had earlier known in England and as a naval officer in the Pacific during World War II. In 1947 White joined a prestigious Denver law firm, eventually becoming a partner and working primarily on corporate cases.

An early supporter of John Kennedy's bid for the 1960 Democratic presidential nomination, White marshaled the Kennedy forces in Colorado prior to the Democratic

National Convention and headed a nationwide Citizens for Kennedy-Johnson organization during the 1960 campaign. Named deputy attorney general in the Kennedy Administration, White helped recruit attorneys for the Justice Department, evaluated candidates for federal judicial appointments and oversaw much of the day-to-day administration of the Department. He was nominated as an associate justice of the Supreme Court in March 1962 and took his oath of office in April. [See KENNEDY Volume]

On the bench White aligned himself with the Court's conservative wing in criminal rights cases. He dissented, for example, in two 1964 decisions where the majority extended the right to counsel to include preliminary police investigation of a suspect and held the Fifth Amendment's privilege against self-incrimination applicable to the states. White also dissented from the 1966 *Miranda* ruling, in which the majority placed restrictions on police interrogation of arrested suspects. White accused the Court of making "new law and new public policy" and warned that the decision would result in the return of "a killer, a rapist, or other criminal to the streets. . .to repeat his crime."

White also voted consistently to sustain federal laws regarding citizenship and Communists. He dissented in May 1964 when the Court nullified a law canceling the citizenship of naturalized Americans who returned to their native lands for three years and when it overturned a provision in the 1950 Internal Security Act denying passports to members of the Communist Party. He was again with the minority in June 1965 when the Court overturned a provision in the Landrum-Griffin Act that barred Communist Party members from serving as labor union officials. Justice White also dissented in January 1967 when the majority held unconstitutional three New York State laws requiring public school and state college teachers to sign oaths disavowing membership in the Communist Party and ordering the removal of teachers for treasonous or seditious acts or statements.

White voted to uphold the public accommodations section of the 1964 Civil Rights Act in December 1964, but he dissented when the Court ruled that the law barred state prosecution of peaceful demonstrators who had tried to desegregate the places covered by the act prior to the law's passage. In May 1966 White wrote the majority opinion in *Reitman v. Mulkey*, overturning a California state constitutional amendment that had nullified earlier legislation prohibiting racial discrimination in the sale or rental of housing.

Justice White spoke for the majority in a 1967 decision holding that a routine municipal housing inspection of a private dwelling, conducted without a warrant, was an unreasonable search in violation of the Fourth Amendment. White wrote for a six-member majority in June 1968 upholding a New York State law that required public school districts to loan textbooks to private and parochial schools. From 1964 through 1968 White consistently voted in favor of the Court's "one-man, one-vote" rule for reapportionment of legislative districts. In an April 1968 decision, White's majority opinion extended the reapportionment rulings to local elections where representatives were elected on a district basis.

Although White has been judged a conservative in criminal justice cases by virtually all observers, his votes on other issues have led a few commentators, such as legal scholar Henry J. Abraham, to rate White overall as an independent, non-doctrinaire justice whose stance defies easy categorization. During the Nixon Administration, as the activist and liberal Warren Court gave way to the more conservative Burger Court, White occupied a centrist position on the high bench and was often a "swing" justice, providing the deciding vote in cases dividing the Court's liberal and conservative blocs. [See NIXON Volume]

[CAB]

For further information:

Fred L. Israel, "Byron R. White," in Leon Friedman and Fred L. Israel, eds., *The Justices of the United States Supreme Court, 1789-1969* (New York, 1969), Vol. IV.

Victor S. Navasky, *Kennedy Justice* (New York, 1971).

WHITE, F(REDERICK) CLIFTON
b. June 13, 1918; Leonardsville, N.Y.
Political consultant.

F. Clifton White grew up in the suburbs of New York City. During World War II he rose to the rank of captain in Army Air Corps and led bomber missions over Germany. Torn between an academic career and politics, White quit graduate study in political science at Cornell to make an unsuccessful primary bid for an upstate New York Republican House seat. After failing in his one try for elective office, White worked his way into the state GOP organization of Gov. Thomas E. Dewey, then the acknowledged leader of the Republican Party's Eastern wing. White served in Dewey's 1948 presidential campaign and headed the New York Young Republicans. Four years later he worked for Dwight D. Eisenhower's presidential campaign organization.

A public relations counselor between 1955 and 1960, White remained active in state and national politics. He managed the 1958 gubernatorial campaign of state Senate leader Walter Mahoney, who lost the GOP nomination to Nelson A. Rockefeller [*q.v.*]. Estranged from the Party organization following Rockefeller's takeover, White moved to the national arena. The national coordinator of the Citizens for Nixon-Lodge Committee in the 1960 presidential election, White was embittered by the narrow defeat of Richard M. Nixon [*q.v.*]. Like many conservative Party strategists, White believed that Nixon had all but given the election away by agreeing with his Democratic opponent on far too many issues.

Not long after Nixon's 1960 defeat, White and other like-minded Republicans began to organize a conservative delegate-gathering apparatus for the 1964 Republican National Convention. Moving to the right, White abhorred the prospect—considered likely by most observers in 1961—of Rockefeller's presidential nomination. Only by organizing early, White reasoned, could conservatives deny Rockefeller the GOP's first prize. In October 1961, White, Rep. John Ashbrook (R, Ohio) [*q.v.*] and 20 conservative journalists and minor Party officials from across the nation founded an as yet untitled nomination committee. Through 1962 and early 1963, the group, chaired by White, made contact with Party members, mapped out a delegate-search strategy and raised funds.

Sen. Barry M. Goldwater (R, Ariz.) [*q.v.*], the Party's most prominent conservative, easily ranked as the White committee's first choice. In April 1963 the group went public as the "National Draft Goldwater for President Committee" with White as director. Hesitant over his presidential prospects and up for reelection in 1964, Goldwater waited until mid-1963, when he had finally decided to run, before demonstrating any interest in the Committee's work. Because the Senator wanted to entrust his campaign to close friends from Arizona (none of whom had any experience in national politics), Goldwater demoted White upon announcing his candidacy in January 1964. Through the spring of 1964 White worked with Arizona attorney Richard Kleindienst as co-director of the individual delegate-gathering arm of the Goldwater committee.

By then White had already plotted out what proved the most important element in the Goldwater nomination. White called for the massive deployment of Goldwater partisans into precinct, municipal, county and district Party delegate selection meetings throughout the country. White wrote later that this work took place "long before it was even noticed on the state and national planes." His plan worked. While the news media and Republican leaders watched Goldwater lose the March New Hampshire primary, the Goldwater forces slowly and quietly amassed 400 delegates in other states. Not until early May did the anti-Goldwater Republicans begin to comprehend what had occurred. Goldwater's victory in California and subsequent endorsement by the heads of the large Illinois and Ohio delegations assured his nomination. He won on the first ballot with 882 votes.

Goldwater designated White as national director of the Citizens for Goldwater-Miller Committee. Designed to lure independent and Democratic voters to the Goldwater camp, the group did not play a major role in the general election. Instead, Goldwater ran his campaign through the Republican National Committee.

One month prior to the election, White became involved in a controversy over a Goldwater campaign film. A subcommittee of the Citizens Committee, "Mothers for a Moral America," had produced a 30-minute program, entitled "Choice," for national television. "Choice" dealt with the alleged moral decline of the nation; it highlighted racial rioting, street prostitution, and a brief sequence of an unidentified Texan—apparently intended to be identified as President Johnson—driving a Lincoln Continental at high speed while tossing beer cans out the window. When columnist Drew Pearson [*q.v.*] previewed the film, he termed it "racist." Democratic partisans took up the charge, and Goldwater personally forbade White from releasing the feature.

Goldwater's overwhelming defeat in November did little to steer White away from conservative Republicanism. Returning to his New York City public relations office, White waited until 1967 before beginning Gov. Ronald Reagan's (R, Calif.) [*q.v.*] campaign for the presidential nomination the following year. Following White's counsel, Reagan avoided the spring primaries and instead sought to win Southern and Western delegates uncommitted or leaning towards Richard Nixon. By the time of the August 1968 Convention, however, Nixon appeared so close to a first-ballot victory that White privately cooperated with leaders of the Rockefeller campaign. Their alliance failed. Most Southern delegates held fast to Nixon, and the former Vice President won on the first ballot.

Following the Convention, White managed the U.S. senatorial campaign of New York Conservative Party nominee James L. Buckley, brother of conservative writer William F. Buckley, Jr. [*q.v.*]. Although Buckley lost to liberal Sen. Jacob K. Javits (R, N.Y.) [*q.v.*], he amassed an impressive 1.1. million votes. His 1968 margin aided him in his successful campaign for the Senate, also managed by White, two years later.

In private life White prospered as a political consultant. In 1976 he advised the President Gerald R. Ford committee. He also directed Buckley's 1976 reelection campaign.

[JLB]

For further information:
F. Clifton White, *Suite 3505; The Story of the Draft Goldwater Movement* (New Rochelle, 1967).

WHITE, KEVIN H(AGAN)

b. Sept. 25, 1929; Boston, Mass.
Secretary of State of Massachusetts, 1960-68; Mayor, Boston, Mass., 1968- .

White, the offspring of a politically active Catholic family, grew up in the then-affluent West Roxbury section of Boston. He studied at Williams College and Boston College, earning an LL.B. in 1955. Beginning in 1960 White served three terms as Massachusetts secretary of state, a post that gave him considerable publicity while earning him few political enemies.

White's greatest political challenge came in 1967, when he ran for mayor of Boston. The city was then strongly polarized along racial lines over issues of crime and school integration. White's opponent, board of education member Louise Day Hicks, sought to exploit the "backlash" of Boston's large white ethnic community against desegregation and growing job competition from blacks. White argued in his campaign that all of Boston's residents suffered from "alienation" and a "breakdown of morale," which he promised to correct as mayor. Supported by blacks, Kennedy liberals and prosperous whites in outlying areas, he narrowly defeated Hicks in November by 12,000 votes.

In office White instituted a series of summer youth programs, named blacks to top-level municipal posts, launched scatter-housing projects for low-income groups and named a woman who was on relief to sit on the public welfare board. He also succeeded in persuading Boston banks and loan companies to provide $50 million for low-income housing. As racial unrest declined in Boston during the late 1960s,

White gained the confidence of many ethnic whites who had earlier supported Hicks. In the mayoral election of 1971, White surprised many observers by defeating Hicks by a 42,000-vote margin.

White gained increasing exposure in national politics during the early 1970s. In 1970 he joined New York Mayor John Lindsay [*q.v.*] and eight other big-city mayors to lobby in Washington for "congressional and state action to meet city needs." Among the programs favored by the group were federal revenue sharing, welfare reform, mass transit subsidies and crime-control measures. White also ran for governor of Massachusetts in 1970 but lost to incumbent Francis W. Sargent. During the mid-1970s he was frequently mentioned as a possible Democratic vice presidential candidate. White was reelected mayor of Boston in 1975, at a time when the city was again suffering racial violence resulting from court-ordered school busing. [See NIXON Volume]

[TJC]

WHITTEN, JAMIE L(LOYD)

b. April 18, 1910; Cascilla, Miss.
Democratic Representative, Miss., 1941- .

The son of a Mississippi farmer, Whitten served as a state legislator and county district attorney before winning a special election to Congress in November 1941. Representing a predominantly rural district with a sizeable black population in the northernmost part of Mississippi, Whitten became chairman in 1947 of the agriculture subcommittee of the House Appropriations Committee, which had jurisdiction over the budget for the Department of Agriculture and related agencies.

Once called the "permanent secretary of agriculture," Whitten often used his powerful position to advance programs he supported and block those he opposed. In 1966, for example, he successfully restored to the agriculture appropriations bill expenditures for certain programs which the Administration had wanted to cut. In the same year he strongly opposed the Administration's Community Development District Act, which would have set up central planning districts in rural areas to chart future growth. Early in the year Whitten had successfully led an effort to reduce drastically the funding for the Rural Community Development Service, which would have administered the new program. His opposition to the development bill was reported to be a primary reason for the House Democratic leadership's decision not to bring it up for a vote.

A defender of farm interests, Whitten regularly voted for farm subsidies and in 1966 published *That We May Live*, a book defending the use of pesticides by farmers. After congressional and private investigations in 1967 and 1968 had reported the existence of widespread hunger and malnutrition among the poor, Whitten asserted in December 1968 that the charges were "completely misleading," at least for Mississippi. At the same time he confirmed reports that FBI agents on loan to his subcommittee had questioned persons involved in protests against hunger and in studies of malnutrition among the poor. He denied, however, that the investigation was an attempt to discredit those studies and said it was simply an effort to establish the accuracy of their findings.

In October 1967 Whitten joined an effort by other Southern Democrats and conservative Republicans to cut the level of federal spending. When a continuing appropriations bill, ordinarily a routine measure, came before the House on Oct. 18, Whitten successfully introduced a substitute bill that required federal agencies, with only a few exceptions, to hold their fiscal 1968 spending to fiscal 1967 levels. The Senate Appropriations Committee, however, rejected the Whitten bill, and eventually Congress passed an Administration-suggested compromise measure.

An opponent of civil rights legislation, Whitten attempted to weaken school desegregation enforcement by the Department of Health, Education and Welfare (HEW). In June 1968 he induced the House Appropriations Committee to include in a Labor-HEW appropriations bill provisions to bar HEW from cutting off federal funds to school districts in order to force busing or the abandonment of "freedom-of-choice" school desegregation plans. The House passed the measure in June, but Whitten's language was greatly modified in the Senate. In 1969 and 1970 Whitten sponsored similar amendments to Labor-HEW appropriations bills.

A supporter of the war in Vietnam and of measures to aid industry as well as agriculture, Whitten generally voted with the conservative coalition in Congress and opposed most social welfare legislation. He voted, for example, against antipoverty legislation, medicare, federal aid to elementary and secondary schools, the Model Cities program and rent subsidies for low-income families. Reported to have one of the safest congressional districts in the country—in part because he maintained close personal contact with his constituents—Whitten faced Republican opposition in only two elections between 1941 and 1970. [See NIXON Volume]

[CAB]

WIGGINS, J(AMES) R(USSELL)

b. Dec. 4, 1903; Luverne, Minn.
Editor; Ambassador to the United Nations, September 1968-January 1969.

For 21 years the editor of the *Washington Post*, Wiggins served as U.S. ambassador to the United Nations during the last four months of the Johnson Administration. Unlike most of the editors of major U.S. newspapers, Wiggins never went to college. Instead, after graduating from high school in 1922, he worked on various small Midwestern newspapers. From 1946 to 1947 he served as assistant to the publisher of the *New York Times* and in May 1947 became managing editor of the *Washington Post*. From 1961 until his appointment as ambassador, Wiggins was editor and then executive vice president of that paper.

While editor Wiggins was credited with helping to build the *Post* from a small capital daily to a major national paper. A strong supporter of "the people's right to know," Wiggins fought against "national security" policies inimical to freedom of the press and opposed efforts to limit news coverage of crimes and trials.

During the Johnson Administration Wiggins's editorials supported both the domestic Great Society program and the Americanization of the war in Vietnam. Wiggins maintained that military intervention was justifiable if it "encouraged other small countries around the world to retain their independence in the face of aggression." The editor was opposed to the pessimism of many liberals that characterized the later years of the Johnson Administration and asserted that the right to be a conformist is as important as the right to be a dissenter in a democracy.

When George Ball [*q.v.*] resigned as ambassador to the United Nations in September 1968, President Johnson chose Wiggins to succeed him. While at the U.N. Wiggins maintained a middle-of-the-road, conciliatory position. He condemned what he considered both Arab and Israeli aggression, asserted that Soviet expressions of its desire for peace were made in good faith and deplored the efforts of Afro-Asian delegations to strip South Africa of its vote. No nation, he thought, should be deprived of a voice in the international body.

In January 1969 Wiggins resigned. Afterwards he moved to Maine where he lived in semi-retirement and edited the Ellsworth *American*.

[EWS]

For further information:
"James R. Wiggins," *Current Biography Yearbook, 1969* (New York, 1970), pp. 447-448.

WILKINS, ROY

b. Aug. 30, 1901; St. Louis, Mo.
Executive Secretary, NAACP, 1955-64; Executive Director, 1965-76.

The son of a black minister and laborer, Wilkins grew up with an aunt and uncle in St. Paul, Minn. He became associated with the NAACP while studying at the University of Minnesota in Minneapolis, where he served as secretary of the local NAACP chapter. After graduating in 1923. Wilkins went to work for the Kansas City (Mo.) *Call*, a black weekly newspaper. He first experienced segregation in Kansas City. As a result, he campaigned vigorously in 1930 against the reelection of a segregationist senator from Kansas. This activity brought Wilkins to the attention of the national NAACP leadership in New York. In 1931 he was named assistant executive secretary in the organization's central office. When Executive Secretary Walter White died in 1955, Wilkins became leader of the 400,000-member NAACP, the largest and oldest civil rights organization in the U.S. [See EISENHOWER Volume]

Under Wilkins, the NAACP maintained its traditional emphasis on legal and legislative action to achieve integration and racial equality. As the tempo of civil rights activity increased during the early 1960s, Wilkins pressed the Democratic Administration to act on earlier promises to introduce sweeping legislation against racial discrimination. This pressure helped bring about several important civil rights measures: an executive order in 1962 barring discrimination in federally financed housing; the Civil Rights Act of 1964 outlawing segregation of public facilities and extending the anti-discrimination rule to employment in federally financed projects; and the Voting Rights Act of 1965 ending the use of literacy tests in voter registration. In 1966 Congress defeated another NAACP-supported bill that would have provided for open housing on the private market and racial balance in public schools and juries. [See KENNEDY Volume]

As the volume of civil rights legislation increased, Wilkins and the NAACP gave more attention to fully implementing existing legal rights. In January 1965 Wilkins announced plans for creation of a national network of "citizenship clinics," intended to acquaint blacks with the provisions of new laws and educate them for "the assumption of full citizenship responsibilities." The NAACP subsequently sponsored voter registration drives in a number of Northern ghettos. Wilkins also participated in several civil rights marches in Mississippi and Alabama during the mid-1960s. The NAACP was not the leader, however, in the direct action movement of this period.

Developments of the mid and late 1960s put the NAACP in the midst of a growing controversy within the civil rights movement. A veteran in the struggle for racial equality, Wilkins was less impatient and frustrated than many blacks over the progress of legislative reform. He therefore reacted strongly against the call for "black power," first raised by civil rights leader Stokely Carmichael [*q.v.*] in June 1966. An NAACP convention in July 1966 attacked Carmichael's advocacy of racial separatism and his justification of the use of violence by blacks in self-defense. Wilkins joined other moderate black leaders, including Martin Luther King [*q.v.*] and Whitney Young [*q.v.*], in condemning the outbreak of rioting in many Northern ghettos during the summer of 1967; NAACP chapters were put on "red alert" on June 16 and urged to prevent unrest. Wilkins also resisted the growing opposition of many civil rights activists to the Vietnam war, claiming that civil rights and peace issues should be kept separate.

Wilkins's consistently moderate stand drew considerable criticism within the civil rights movement. More militant black leaders identified him with the white establishment and derided the NAACP's reformist strategy as "outmoded." The militant Student Nonviolent Coordinating Committee and the Congress of Racial Equality refused to join the NAACP in supporting the civil rights bill of 1966, which they viewed as a "sham." In 1967 Wilkins was the target of an abortive assassination plot by the Revolutionary Action Movement, a small black terrorist group.

Within the NAACP a group of militants known as the Young Turks sought to reduce Wilkins's influence and change what they viewed as the organization's "middle-class" image. Strongest in the Northern and Western chapters of the NAACP, the Young Turks favored closer ties to the peace movement and a more positive attitude towards black power. They attempted to gain control of the NAACP Board of Directors in 1967 and one year later demanded the right to function as an autonomous group within the organization. Wilkins defeated both challenges to his leadership but at the price of several resignations from the NAACP, including the organization's entire legal staff.

Due to internal unrest and competition from more militant civil rights groups, the NAACP grew slowly during the mid-1960s. Wilkins himself blamed this stagnation on "the uncertainty induced by violence, the punitive mood of Congress, the confusing and provocative statements of a wide variety of individuals and organizations and the frustrations induced by the overwhelming problems of the central cities."

During the early 1970s the NAACP continued to work for government action in housing, school desegregation and job opportunities for blacks. The Nixon Administration was less responsive than its predecessors, however, and NAACP officials took the unusual step of denouncing it as "anti-Negro" in 1970. Wilkins remained aloof from other civil rights leaders who espoused black power, but he continued to provide financial and legal support for community action programs in Northern ghettos. He announced that he would retire as NAACP executive director on Jan. 1, 1977. [See NIXON Volume]

[SLG]

WILLIAMS, HARRISON A(RLINGTON), JR.

b. Dec. 10, 1919; Plainfield, N.J.
Democratic Senator, N.J., 1959- ;
Chairman, Labor and Public Welfare Subcommittee on Migratory Labor, 1959-69.

Born and raised in Plainfield, N.J., Williams received his B.A. from Oberlin and his law degree from Columbia. After serving as a "sacrificial lamb" in state and municipal races in Republican-dominated districts in 1951 and 1952, Williams announced his candidacy for Congress when Rep. Clifford Case (R, N.J.) [*q.v.*] resigned in August 1953. Williams borrowed the money to finance his campaign and in November 1953 defeated a conservative Republican to become the first Democratic congressman in the sixth district's 21-year history. Williams was defeated in 1956, but two years later New Jersey Gov. Robert Meyner helped him secure the Democratic senatorial nomination. His victory in November made Williams New Jersey's first Democratic senator since 1936.

In August 1959 Williams was named chairman of the Senate Labor and Public Welfare Committee's newly formed Subcommittee on Migratory Labor. Williams introduced a series of bills in February 1961 designed to upgrade the quality of migrant life, but the only proposal enacted during the 87th Congress was a bill passed in September 1962 appropriating $3 million per year for migrant health programs. [See EISENHOWER, KENNEDY Volumes]

In 1964 several programs based on Williams's earlier proposals were incorporated into President Johnson's Great Society legislative program. The Administration's Economic Opportunity Act of 1964 authorized $15 million in fiscal 1965 for housing, education, child day-care and sanitation services for farm workers. The 1964 omnibus housing bill included a $10 million grant program to pay up to two-thirds of the development cost for low-rent housing for domestic farm workers. In addition, Williams's bill requiring annual registration of farm labor contractors passed separately and was signed into law on Sept. 7, 1964.

Williams' more far-reaching proposals for the establishment of a federal minimum wage for agricultural workers, a federal farm recruiting and placement service, farm-worker coverage under collective bargaining and other labor laws were not acted upon by Congress. In 1968 Williams was unable to get his bill permitting strikes by agricultural workers out of committee, and he announced plans to attach the measure to the Administration's farm program bill. Williams withdrew his amendment on July 20, 1968 after intense lobbying against it by the American Farm Bureau Federation and other grower organizations.

Williams was a Democratic Party loyalist. *Congressional Quarterly* credited Williams with the highest "Party unity" score among all Democratic senators in 1968. Although he was one of 15 senators who signed a Jan. 27, 1966 letter to the President calling for continued suspension of air strikes against North Vietnam, Williams voted for the 1967 and 1968 Vietnam war appropriations. Not until 1969, when he voted against the anti-ballistic missile program and for barring American ground troops from Laos and Thailand, did his voting record reflect a "dovish" perspective.

According to journalist Franklin Pierce, Williams "undercut his own effectiveness for years by heavy drinking and partying until he finally went on the wagon around the end of 1968." Just before the start of his 1970 reelection campaign, Williams publicly acknowledged that he once "drank too much." He was reelected in November by a quarter-million-vote margin. With Sen. Ralph Yarborough's (D, Tex.) [*q.v.*] primary defeat in the spring, Williams moved to the chairmanship of the Senate Labor and Public Welfare Committee in January 1971. [See NIXON Volume]

[DKR]

WILLIAMS, HOSEA

b. Jan. 5, 1926; Attapulgus, Ga.
Project Director, Southern Christian Leadership Conference, 1963-70.

Williams, the son of a black sharecropper, grew up in Attapulgus. He worked as a fruit picker in Florida and served in the Army before studying at Morris Brown College in Atlanta, where he graduated in 1951. After working briefly as a high school teacher, Williams became a research chemist in the Savannah office of the U.S. Department of Agriculture. He also did volunteer work in Savannah for two civil rights organizations, the NAACP and the Southern Christian Leadership Conference (SCLC). In 1963 he left the Department of Agriculture to become a full-time project director for SCLC.

Williams's skill in grass-roots organization soon made him one of the top assistants of SCLC leader Martin Luther King [*q.v.*]. In 1963 he led anti-segregation drives in Savannah and St. Augustine, Fla. He subsequently helped organize other important SCLC projects, including 1965 voter registration campaigns in Selma, Ala., and Americus, Ga. Williams also served as a liaison between the SCLC and leaders of the Student Nonviolent Coordinating Committee (SNCC), a militant civil rights group that joined the SCLC in many demonstrations. As a result of his activities during the mid-1960s, Williams was jailed over 40 times; on one such occasion in 1966 he initiated a suit that resulted in a court order desegregating Alabama prisons.

Williams remained with the SCLC after King's assassination in April 1968. In May he supervised Resurrection City, an encampment of 3,000 poor people and poverty workers brought to Washington by the SCLC to demonstrate for greater federal antipoverty spending. Williams became a regional vice president of the SCLC in 1970 and national program director in 1971. At this time he emerged as the leader of a radical faction within the SCLC. In 1970 he rejected integration as a civil rights goal and espoused "black power," a concept King had criticized. Williams claimed, however, that black power meant self-respect and not violence.

Williams attempted to enter Georgia politics during the late 1960s, running unsuccessfully for state assemblyman and later for president of the Atlanta City Council. In 1974 he gained election to the state Assembly.

[SLG]

WILLIAMS, JOHN B(ELL)

b. Dec. 4, 1918; Raymond, Miss.
Democratic Representative, Miss., 1947-68; Governor, Miss., 1968-73.

Consistently reelected to the U.S. House of Representatives with little or no opposition in the 1950s and 1960s, Williams was known as one of the leading opponents of civil rights measures on Capitol Hill. He refused to support either Adlai E. Stevenson [*q.v.*] for president in 1956 or John F. Kennedy in 1960 because of the civil rights planks in the national Democratic Party's platforms. [See KENNEDY Volume]

Williams not only opposed bills directed

against racial discrimination but also was a consistent foe of the entire range of liberal social legislation. According to the *Congressional Quarterly*, Williams supported the Southern Democrat-Republican conservative coalition on all key House votes from 1964 through 1967, with the exception of 2% of the roll calls in 1965.

In October 1964 Williams declared his support for the Republican presidential candidacy of conservative Sen. Barry M. Goldwater (R, Ariz.) [*q.v.*]. During the following January the House Democratic Caucus retaliated against Williams and Rep. Albert W. Watson (D, S.C.) [*q.v.*], the two Democratic Representatives who had supported Goldwater, by censuring them and stripping them of their seniority. Williams thereby lost his second-ranking position on the Interstate and Foreign Commerce Committee and his fifth-ranking post on the District of Columbia Committee. In the same month the predominantly black Mississippi Freedom Democratic Party challenged the seating of all five of the state's representatives on the grounds that blacks had been excluded from participation in the previous year's election. The House rejected the challenge in September 1965 by a vote of 228 to 143.

Two years later Williams entered the Mississippi gubernatorial race. As a result of the federal Voting Rights Act of 1965 and a series of registration drives, the number of black voters in the state had increased from 30,000 in 1963 to nearly 200,000 out of a total voter enrollment of about 800,000 in 1967. For this reason, and because it was becoming increasingly apparent that Mississippi could not successfully resist federally mandated integration, Williams and other candidates avoided the overt racial appeals to whites that had been traditional in the state's political contests.

In the Democratic primary campaign Williams stressed his belief in constitutional government and states' rights rather than directly confronting the race issue. However, he remained a supporter of segregation and defeated his more moderate opponent, state Treasurer William Winter, in the August runoff. Winter's loss was attributed to the failure of blacks to support him in sufficient numbers, particularly in the Delta region. Williams went on to easily defeat his Republican opponent in November.

In his inaugural address the following January, Williams declared that he would seek funds for federal education, poverty and welfare programs, which he had opposed in Congress. The Governor asserted, "For right or wrong, whether we like it or not, federal programs have become a way of life in America." He subsequently established a federal-state programs office to seek such aid.

Although Williams, in the same address, denounced the perpetrators of violence against blacks, as governor he continued to support traditional Southern race relations. During July 1968 he denounced Hubert Humphrey [*q.v.*] for asserting that blacks could not freely participate in Mississippi Democratic Party proceedings. At the National Democratic Convention the following month, Humphrey supported a successful black challenge to the regular Mississippi delegation, which was led by Williams. In September the Governor endorsed the third party presidential candidacy of George C. Wallace [*q.v.*].

After Hurricane Camille struck Mississippi in August 1969, Williams appointed an all-white emergency council to coordinate federal and state relief. Responding to black protests, the federal government refused to provide assistance until the Governor added blacks to the council. In 1970 Williams defended the Jackson police after two blacks were killed and 12 others were wounded during a student demonstration at all-black Jackson State College in May. [See NIXON Volume]

[MLL]

WILLIAMS, JOHN J(AMES)

b. May 17, 1904; Frankford, Del.
Republican Senator, Del., 1947-71.

The owner of a chicken-feed business before entering national politics, Williams ran for the Senate in 1946 on a platform advocating a reduction of government control over the economy. While in the Senate he compiled a conservative record as an opponent of most social welfare legislation and foreign aid measures. Williams was also a constant opponent of measures that increased the powers of the executive branch. He was one of the most consistent supporters of the conservative coalition of Southern Democrats and Republicans in the Senates, and he voted with that group on key issues about 90% of the time in the 1960s.

Throughout his career Williams carried on private probes designed to uncover official corruption. In 1951 he discovered evidence of fraud in tax collections, which led to a congressional investigation of the Internal Revenue Service. A few years later he pushed for the investigation of presidential adviser Sherman Adams. During the Kennedy Administration Williams opposed the ambassadorial appointments of several businessmen because of their involvement in questionable business dealings and scored Rep. Adam Clayton Powell (D, N.Y.) [*q.v.*] for using public funds for private expenses. [See TRUMAN, EISENHOWER, KENNEDY Volumes]

In 1963 Williams, spurred by press reports of Senate majority secretary Bobby Baker's [*q.v.*] involvement in questionable business activities, began a private investigation of Baker's affairs. His probe, uncovering information on possible tax frauds and influence-peddling in the awarding of government contracts, provided much of the information for the subsequent Senate Rules Committee hearings. Although not a member of the Committee, the Senator was invited to sit in on its sessions during the 16-month investigation. His insistence on a thorough probe of all those involved in Baker's activities, including senators, often brought him into conflict with the Committee and its staff. In reaction to a Committee ruling that limited its examination to Senate staff members, excluding senators, Williams introduced a resolution to expand the scope of the probe. After angry debate the resolution was killed.

In 1967 Williams moved to repeal the 1966 Presidential Election Campaign Fund Act that established a tax checkoff system to finance presidential campaigns. Williams opposed the measure because it had been passed without any attempt to reform campaign finance practices. The Senator's proposal that the checkoff system be suspended until Congress adopted guidelines governing the distribution of money was accepted by the Senate. The system was eventually approved by Congress in 1971.

In 1971 Williams retired after 24 years on Capitol Hill.

[EWS]

WILLIAMS, WILLIAM A(PPLEMAN)

b. June 12, 1921; Atlantic, Iowa.
Historian.

Williams grew up in Iowa and graduated from the U.S. Naval Academy in 1944. After wartime service in the Navy, he studied at the University of Leeds in England and at the University of Wisconsin, where he earned his doctorate in history in 1950. Seven years later Williams joined the history faculty of the University of Wisconsin, becoming a full professor in 1960.

In scholarly circles Williams soon became well-known for his "revisionist" interpretation of U.S. diplomatic history. In contrast to historians like George Kennan [*q.v.*] and Dexter Perkins, who held that America had acquired her commanding influence in world affairs through a series of unforeseen and often unwanted events, Williams argued that American policymakers of the late 19th and 20th centuries consciously shaped the U.S. as an imperial power to protect its growing commercial interests. This thesis, inspired by a Marxist interpretation of American history, was the central theme of Williams's first three books: *American-Russian Relations, 1784-1947* (1950), *The Tragedy of American Diplomacy* (1960) and *The Contours of American History* (1961).

U.S. presidents and their advisers, Williams claimed in these early works, traditionally sought to avoid social tensions resulting from capitalism by encouraging rapid economic expansion, first on the frontier and later overseas. To prevent European powers from monopolizing foreign markets, the U.S. enunciated the "Open Door Policy," applied first in China and then throughout the world. This claim to equal access for American business became, in Williams's view, the primary tool of American economic expansion during the 20th century. Discounting the generally accepted view of the Cold War as a product of Soviet aggression, Williams claimed that Soviet-American hostility resulted from the "sustained, ever-increasing overseas expansion" of U.S. interests.

During the early and mid 1960s Williams applied the ideas he had developed in his historical writings to current problems. His book *The United States, Cuba and Castro*, published in 1962, attributed the crisis in U.S.-Cuban relations to problems resulting from North American economic domination of the island. Williams later attacked American involvement in Vietnam and participated in an early teach-in against the war at the University of Wisconsin. Marx's analysis of capitalism, he claimed at this time, was more applicable to contemporary America than was generally acknowledged. "It becomes increasingly clear," Williams wrote in 1967, "that many of the policies and activities of the New and Fair Deals, and of the upper-class Daniel Boones of the New Frontier, are producing something less than happiness and security." His own solution, proposed in *The Great Evasion* (1964), was a system of "democratic socialism" that would place primary authority on the local and regional levels to encourage individual autonomy.

Coming at a time of intellectual ferment among liberals and radicals, Williams's ideas aroused great controversy. Writing in 1966, historian Arthur Schlesinger, Jr., [*q.v.*] a critic of Williams, attacked "the current outburst of revisionism regarding the origins of the Cold War" for its allegedly anti-American bias. Williams contributed frequent articles to *Studies on the Left*, the *New York Review of Books* and other leftist journals. A group of Williams's former students and followers at the University of Wisconsin, including Walter LaFeber, Richard W. Van Alystyn, Lloyd Gardner and Ronald Radosh, formed the "Wisconsin school" of diplomatic history during the mid-1960s. Other prominent revisionist historians, including Gabriel Kolko, also acknowledged Williams's influence. A survey undertaken in 1971 by the Organization of American Historians indicated that Williams had far greater influence than any other scholar in spreading ideas "sharply critical of U.S. foreign policy."

During the late 1960s and early 1970s, Williams resumed his analysis of American expansionism with three books: *The Roots of the Modern American Empire* (1969), *The Shaping of American Diplomacy* (1970) and *Some Presidents: From Wilson to Nixon* (1972). In these works he traced the traditional American association of "freedom and prosperity" with expansion into foreign markets, stressing that this was a tenet of popular culture as well as a goal of policymakers. The reform efforts of the Kennedy and Johnson Administrations, in Williams's view, were the latest in a series of efforts to ease social tensions in the U.S. by accumulating a greater share of the world's wealth. Williams denied, however, that such a policy could be sustained in the long run; the end of the Great Society program, he claimed, signaled the failure of "the orthodoxy which [Johnson] had been taught." In 1973 Williams, who had moved to the University of Oregon, collaborated with other historians of the Wisconsin school in producing a survey of U.S. diplomatic history entitled *From Colony to Empire*.

[SLG]

For further information:
Robert Maddox, *New Left Historians and the Cold War* (New York, 1972).

WILLIS, EDWIN E(DWARD)

b. Oct. 2, 1904; Arnaudville, La.
d. Oct. 24, 1972; St. Martinville, La.
Democratic Representative, La., 1949-69.

A lawyer in New Orleans and then in St. Martinville, La., Willis served briefly in the state Senate before winning election to Congress in 1948 from Louisiana's third district. He was appointed to the House Un-American Activities Committee (HUAC) in 1955 and became its chairman in June 1963. Willis led widely publicized HUAC investigations of unauthorized travel to Cuba by American youths in September 1963 and of the Illinois Communist Party in May 1965. In October 1966 he announced plans for a committee study of urban rioting, and a year later HUAC held seven days of hearings on the possible contribution of subversive elements to the riots. A May 1968 committee report charged that pro-Peking Communist splinter groups had aligned with extremist black nationalist organizations to create riots and named Students for a Democratic Society, the Revolutionary Action Movement and the Progressive Labor Party, among others, as participants in the alignment.

HUAC also initiated a major investigation of the Ku Klux Klan on March 30, 1965. After a six-month preliminary study, a five-man subcommittee headed by Willis opened hearings in October. The probe focused on Klan finances, the extent to which the Klan engaged in organized violence and connections between the Klan and local law enforcement agencies. The 36 days of hearings lasted into February 1966 and uncovered evidence of Klan involvement in intimidation and violence directed against blacks and civil rights workers. Willis, who once declared Klanism "incompatible with Americanism," was burned in effigy at Klan rallies in the South during the investigation, but Attorney General Nicholas Katzenbach [*q.v.*] commended the subcommittee for its "careful and illuminating" study of the Klan. The hearings eventually led to the conviction and imprisonment of Robert M. Shelton, Jr. [*q.v.*], "imperial wizard" of the United Klans of America, for contempt of Congress.

In August 1967 Willis introduced a bill to redefine the functions and procedures of the Subversive Activities Control Board (SACB), which had little to do by then because of Supreme Court rulings holding many of its powers and procedures unconstitutional. Passed by Congress late in 1967 and signed into law on Jan. 2, 1968, the SACB proposal was only the sixth HUAC-reported bill ever to become law.

A reserved and soft-spoken man, Willis was reportedly considered by his House colleagues to have a good legal mind and a keen awareness of the rights of witnesses and to have conducted hearings with fairness. Nonetheless, HUAC remained a target of criticism during the 1960s for many liberals and civil liberties organizations on the grounds that it frequently abused witnesses, held hearings aimed at exposure rather than at producing legislation and often exceeded its jurisdiction.

Also a member of the House Judiciary Committee, Willis opposed all civil rights bills and led the Southern Democratic effort to defeat or dilute the 1964 Civil Rights Act on the House floor. A supporter of U.S. policy in Vietnam, Willis had a relatively conservative record on domestic issues. He did, however, vote for some Great Society legislation, such as the Economic Opportunity Act of 1964, elementary and secondary school aid bills and the Housing and Urban Development Act of 1968. Willis also headed a special Judiciary subcommittee that completed in 1965 a six-year study of the problem of state taxation of interstate business activity, but the subcommittee's recommendations were not enacted into law.

Willis was defeated for renomination in a Democratic runoff primary in September 1968. He died in St. Martinville, La., on Oct. 24, 1972.

[CAB]

WILSON, BOB (ROBERT)

b. April 5, 1916; Calexico, Calif.
Republican Representative, Calif., 1953- ; Chairman, National Republican Congressional Committee, 1961-73.

As a U.S. representative from San Diego, the U.S. Navy's West Coast headquarters and a major center for aerospace defense contractors, Wilson reflected the conservative and pro-military sentiments of his constituency. Appointed to the House Armed Services Committee during his freshman term, he was able to channel many military installations and defense contracts into San Diego. Wilson was a close political colleague of Richard M. Nixon [*q.v.*]. He managed Nixon's vice presidential reelection campaign in 1956 and served as the scheduling director for his 1960 presidential bid.

In June 1961 Wilson became chairman of the National Republican Congressional Committee, whose role was aiding Republican candidates for the House of Representatives. During the early 1960s he began to expand the previously small-scale activities of the Committee. [See KENNEDY Volume]

Wilson generally opposed the policies of the Johnson Administration. According to *Congressional Quarterly*, he voted with the House's Southern Democrat-Republican conservative coalition on at least 67% of key floor votes in each year of the Johnson presidency. His "hawkish" position on the Vietnam war, however, coincided with the Administration's Southeast Asia policies.

Wilson succeeded in increasing the flow of contributions to the Republican Congressional Committee. His most important fund-raising innovation was the creation of the $1,000-per-member Boosters Club in 1965. By the end of the decade the Committee was giving Republican House candidates an average of $4,000, compared to $1,000 at the beginning of Wilson's tenure as chairman. Furthermore, under Wilson's leadership the Committee began to provide candidates with a wide variety of services, such as cameramen, taping facilities, news release preparation, speech editing and art work.

In 1966 Wilson employed his chairmanship to assist his long-time political friend, Richard Nixon. Wilson arranged for the Committee to pay the former Vice President's expenses in a nationwide tour on behalf of Republican congressional candidates, a tour that marked a major turning point in Nixon's recovery from his 1960 presidential and 1962 California gubernatorial election defeats.

Wilson was a consistent supporter of the Nixon Administration's domestic and foreign policies. He continued to defend the country's efforts in Vietnam during the late 1960s and early 1970s, asserting as late as 1971 that the United States was "on the verge of victory." In 1972 Wilson was implicated in the events which allegedly linked International Telephone and Telegraph's out-of-court settlement of an anti-trust suit with a financial contribution to the Republican National Convention in San Diego. In March 1973 Wilson resigned as chairman of the National Republican Congressional Committee at the request of the Administration after he had criticized the White House for monopolizing 1972 Republican campaign funds. [See NIXON Volume]

[MLL]

WINGATE, LIVINGSTON L(EROY)

b. Sept. 2, 1915; Timmonsville, S.C. Executive Director, Harlem Youth Opportunities Unlimited-Associated Community Teams, November 1964-November 1966.

Wingate, raised in Harlem, attended St. John's University at night while working as a skycap at New York's LaGuardia Airport. He earned a law degree from St. John's in 1949, practiced briefly in Harlem and in 1956 became a partner in the firm of Weaver, Evans, Wingate and Wright. In 1961 he was named counsel to the House Committee on Labor and Education. A year later he became a special assistant to the Committee's chairman, Adam Clayton Powell (D, N.Y.) [*q.v.*], the representative from Harlem.

In November 1964 the directors of Harlem Youth Opportunities Unlimited-Associated Community Teams (HARYOU-ACT), the leading antipoverty agency in Harlem, elected Wingate executive director of the agency. The decision was controversial. Dr. Kenneth B. Clark [*q.v.*], a psychology professor at City College who had helped found HARYOU, argued that Wingate would use the agency to advance Rep. Powell's interest at the expense of the community.

At the time Wingate assumed his new post, HARYOU-ACT had already been allocated $5 million in federal and city funds; another $118 million had been requested to cover a three-year period. Its programs included art and culture workshops, after-school remedial study centers, on-the-job training projects and a center for helping destitute families. In his two years as executive director of the agency, Wingate found himself on the defensive, criticised for fiscal mismanagement, political influence peddling and outright corruption. His management of HARYOU was used by critics of the Office of Economic Opportunity (OEO) as a prime example of the alleged incompetence in the direction of anti-poverty programs.

On Oct. 1, 1965 the Manhattan district attorney's office subpoenaed HARYOU records. Nine days later the OEO reported finding "deficiencies in record-keeping and overall management." A spokesman for Rep. Powell's office admitted that the books of the agency were in a "mess." Some $400,000 was missing and unaccounted for.

Wingate explained that during the previous summer the agency, hard-pressed to prevent rioting in Harlem, had hired more youths for summer-work programs than it could afford to pay. The situation had become so desperate he said, that he "reached in and took money from whatever accounts were available." Harlem, he pointed out, had been spared "a long, hot summer" of violence. Auditors failed to find any evidence of "financial malfeasance." In a speech before the National Urban League later in October, Wingate warned that militant Harlem youths were "prepared to die" in racial strife if the HARYOU agency were scuttled.

In December 1965 the HARYOU board of directors suspended Wingate to permit him to compile a report on how funds had been spent over the course of the year. He was reinstated on May 10, 1966. Ten days later, however, it was reported that HARYOU had failed to deduct withholding taxes from its employees' wages and owed the federal government $290,000 in back taxes. The employees themselves eventually agreed to pay what was owed.

In June 1966 the OEO offered HARYOU a $2.5 million grant if the agency improved accounting procedures and curbed Wingate's power. Wingate began to lose support from some board members and resigned in November 1966. He became an associate director of the Citizens Crusade Against Poverty, a private agency funded by the United Automobile Workers.

[JLW]

WIRTZ, W(ILLIAM) WILLARD
b. March 14, 1912; DeKalb, Ill.
Secretary of Labor, September 1962-January 1969.

A 1937 graduate of the Harvard Law School, Wirtz earned a reputation as an able labor mediator while serving as a member of the War Labor Board from 1942 to 1945. Wirtz later taught labor law at Northwestern University. In the early 1950s he became a trusted aide to Adlai Stevenson [*q.v.*], who as governor of Illinois appointed Wirtz a state liquor control commissioner. The two men became law partners in Chicago in 1955. Wirtz served as a key aide in Stevenson's 1956 presidential campaign. Wirtz was named undersecretary of labor in January 1961 and 20 months later succeeded Arthur Goldberg [*q.v.*] as head of the Department.

As Labor Secretary, Wirtz was involved directly or indirectly in efforts to settle major strikes involving rail, airline and dock workers during the early 1960s. He also appeared frequently before congressional committees to speak in favor of key domestic legislation favored by the Kennedy Administration and organized labor. In 1963 he won approval of amendments to the Manpower Training and Development Act that gave to the Secretary of Labor the authority to establish job training programs for high school dropouts. [See KENNEDY Volume]

Wirtz was a major White House speech writer and a close adviser to President Johnson. As in the early 1960s Wirtz was involved in many efforts to settle major labor disputes, including threatened walkouts of rail workers in 1964 and a 42-day strike of airline mechanics in 1966. In the rail dispute, which centered on wages and train-crew sizes, President Johnson announced in April 1964 that a settlement had been reached between management and labor. The settlement was considered a personal triumph for the President, and Wirtz admitted that Johnson rather than his office had played the key role. In 1967, however, neither Johnson nor Wirtz was able to negotiate a settlement and a two-day walkout tied up the nation's railroads. The strike was ended when Congress, at Johnson's request, passed a bill mandating compulsory arbitration of the dispute.

During the 1960s Wirtz worked for the enactment of the Johnson Administration's major social programs, including the federal aid to education, medicare, antipoverty and civil rights measures. He also helped win enactment in 1966 of a Johnson-supported minimum wage bill, which increased by stages the existing $1.25 nonfarm wage floor to $1.60 and extended minimum wage coverage to an estimated 9.1 million new employes. However, Wirtz and other members of the Administration failed to win approval of two measures strongly favored by organized labor: a bill to repeal section 14(b) of the Taft-Hartley Act, which permitted states to pass "right-to-work" laws banning the union shop, and a bill to permit an individual building trades union having a dispute with a single subcontractor to picket an entire construction site and thereby shut it down.

Wirtz was a strong advocate of Administration antipoverty programs, but he and Secretary of Health, Education and Welfare Anthony J. Celebrezze [*q.v.*] argued in 1965 that their departments were capable of managing antipoverty programs without the creation of a separate Office of Economic Opportunity. However, President Johnson favored the creation of such an office under the direction of former Peace Corps head R. Sargent Shriver [*q.v.*], and the Administration's 1964 antipoverty legislation reflected the President's wishes.

A strong proponent of Administration efforts to reduce unemployment through job-training programs, Wirtz in July 1967 called for the funding of Labor Department programs for the training of between 100,000 and 150,000 persons. He was cool to the suggestion of Sen. Robert F. Kennedy (D, N.Y.) [*q.v.*] that government provide tax incentives to businesses for establishing plants and jobs in ghettoes. "The most immediate problem," said Wirtz, "is a training problem not job development. . . ."

An advocate of liberalized immigration laws, Wirtz argued that an end of the national origins quota system with a consequent increase in immigration would not seriously affect employment opportunities for American workers. (Such a measure passed in 1965.) He did argue, however, that the importation of Mexicans to work in the fields at harvest time undercut the wage scale of American laborers. In 1965 Wirtz ended the "bracero" farm labor program, thereby cutting the number of such workers in this country from 200,000 to 50,000. This move was bitterly denounced by senators and congressmen from Southern and Western agricultural states, particularly Florida and California. In September 1965 Vice President Hubert H. Humphrey [*q.v.*] broke a tie vote and prevented the Senate from stripping Wirtz of his power over agricultural workers. Florida and California farmers soon learned, however, to rely on "greencard workers" (temporary immigrants) and Mexicans who entered the country illegally.

Although Wirtz supported legislation favored by organized labor, his relations with union officials were not entirely cordial. AFL-CIO President George Meany [*q.v.*] referred to Wirtz as that "blasted egghead" and complained of the Secretary's "damned superior" attitude. During 1964-65 Wirtz attempted to remove John Henning from his post as undersecretary of labor. Henning, the top-ranking labor official in government, had been appointed to his position at the request of Meany. Henning argued that teenagers in the poverty program should be paid the minimum wage. Wirtz was opposed because he felt that the poverty program's role should be primarily to provide job training for private employment. He asked for Henning's removal but President Johnson, under pressure from Meany, retained Henning in the Labor Department.

Meany also charged that Wirtz and the Administration had failed to make sufficient effort to win repeal of 14(b). Moreover, in January 1965 Meany promised Wirtz that, while organized labor opposed the Administration's official wage price guidelines, "if the President is going to hold prices in line we have got to do our part" on wages. Meany later charged, however, that the Administration had not kept its bargain and had permitted prices to soar.

Despite his increasing opposition to American involvement in Vietnam, Wirtz remained in the Johnson cabinet until the inauguration of Richard Nixon. Thereafter, he practiced law in Washington.

[JLW]

WURF, JERRY (JEROME)
b. April 18, 1919; New York, N.Y.
President, American Federation of State, County and Municipal Employees, 1964- .

In 1940 Wurf left New York University, where he was active in the Young People's Socialist League, and worked as a busboy and cashier in a New York cafeteria. He helped organize a local of the Hotel and Restaurant Employes Union there and served briefly as the local's welfare fund administrator. In 1947 Wurf was hired as an organizer by American Federation of State, County and Municipal Employees (AFSCME) President Arnold Zander. He was assigned to the union's New York District Council 37 in 1949 and was elected district president in 1959.

In the 1950s public employment increased rapidly and AFSCME membership rose as well. The union doubled its membership between 1953 and 1960, when it numbered 182,000. Striving to close the gap in wages paid by public and private employers, AFSCME began to abandon its traditional reliance on political lobbying and adopted more typical labor tactics. Citywide collective bargaining was established in Philadelphia, and District Council 37 made a major breakthrough in 1954 when New York's Mayor Robert Wagner [*q.v.*] signed an executive order requiring municipal departments to bargain with unions that had established majority representation. Meanwhile, rank-and-file pressure for more aggressive tactics increased as did members' impatience with Zander, the union's president since its birth in 1937. In 1962 Wurf, until then a spokesman for Zander, mounted an unsuccessful challenge against him. Two years later Wurf tried again and this time defeated Zander by a 21-vote margin at the union's Denver convention.

Upon taking office Wurf discovered that Zander had involved the union in Central Intelligence Agency (CIA) activities abroad. In 1967 Zander admitted that between 1958 and 1964 he had accepted more than $100,000 annually from the CIA for anti-Communist activities, including the support of strikes that helped topple Cheddi Jagan's left-wing government in British Guiana. Following his election in 1964 Wurf was contacted by government officials who asked him to continue the arrangement. Wurf, however, said that a trade union shouldn't be involved in this kind of work and public employes' union particularly." When, in 1967, several unions were revealed to have accepted CIA funding, Wurf was found to be the only labor leader who had extracted his union from such international activity.

AFSCME continued to grow rapidly during Wurf's early years as president, reaching 400,000 members in 1968, about two-thirds of them blue-collar workers. Although Wurf believed that firemen and law enforcement officers "should not and cannot strike," he opposed legal prohibitions against strikes by other public employees. Anti-strike laws "are not simply ineffectual," said Wurf. "They warp this vital process. They bring employees to the bargaining table, but as inferiors."

The New York area, an AFSCME stronghold, became a testing ground for public employees' strikes. Inspired in part by the success of strikes by New York City teachers, 8,000 members of AFSCME and the Social Service Employees Union struck the New York City Welfare Department in January 1965 in defiance of the state's Condon-Wadlin Act. Over 5,400 workers were dismissed for violating the act, and Wurf charged that Wagner used the law's provisions to break the strike. However, the dismissals were delayed, and the following year the state legislature exempted the strikers from the penalties required by the Act. In 1967 Wurf and other leaders of public employee unions vehemently opposed the Taylor Law, New York Gov. Nelson Rockefeller's [*q.v.*] replacement for Condon-Wadlin. Although the new law guaranteed organizing and collective bargaining rights for public workers, it also included heavy fines and penalties for striking unions and their members. AFSCME defied the act in November 1968, when 3,000 non-professional workers struck New York State mental hospitals. Although strike leaders were jailed under the Taylor Law, the strike forced Rockefeller to accede to the union's demands. The general effect of the New York strikes was to stimulate strikes by public employees in other areas of the country.

A strike by black sanitation workers in Memphis drew national attention to AFSCME and to Wurf's leadership in 1968. Blacks comprised 30% of AFSCME's national membership, and racial issues were at the heart of the Memphis dispute. The strike began on Jan. 31 when 22 blacks were sent home unpaid because of rain while whites remained on the job. Seeking union recognition, a grievance procedure, promotions "without regard to race" and a 15¢ raise over the $1.60 hourly minimum, the AFSCME local called a strike on Feb. 12. The black community in Memphis quickly rallied behind the strike. Wurf brought in the union's top leadership and, with local church groups, organized protests and daily marches through downtown Memphis. Wurf was among those arrested at a city hall sit-in. Following the April 4 assassination of Martin Luther King [*q.v.*], who had come to Memphis to support the strikers, Wurf helped lead marches and protests that continued for two more weeks. On April 16 the city signed a contract with AFSCME in which it recognized the union and agreed to a dues checkoff, promotions based on seniority, a two step 15¢-an-hour raise and a "no-strike" clause. Wurf called it "a good settlement that couldn't have been achieved without the coalescence of the union and the Negro community."

Wurf, who became an AFL-CIO vice president and a member of the federation's Executive Countil in 1969, dissented from the council's endorsements of the Nixon Administration's Vietnam policy. Although the union's strike activity declined in the 1970s, AFSCME claimed 700,000 members in 1976 and was the fifth largest union in the AFL-CIO. [See NIXON Volume]

[MDB]

YARBOROUGH, RALPH W(EBSTER)

b. June 8, 1903; Chandler, Tex.
Democratic Senator, Tex., 1957-71.

During the 1950s Yarborough emerged as the leader of the insurgent liberal minority within the Texas Democratic Party. The liberal faction was a coalition of intellectuals, labor unions, blacks, Mexican-Americans and East Texas farmer-populists. It was antagonistic to the state's powerful business establishment, opposed racial discrimination and Texas's extremely restrictive labor laws and supported social welfare measures to aid the poor.

Yarborough lost the Democratic gubernatorial primaries of 1952, 1954 and 1956 to candidates of the dominant conservative faction, but in each successive race he narrowed the margin of defeat. His increasing electoral strength reflected the growing power of the liberals after World War II. Control of the national Democratic Party by liberal elements, the U.S. Supreme Court's 1944 ruling against the white primary and increased political activity by Mexican-Americans were major causes of this trend. In April 1957 Yarborough won a special election to fill a vacated U.S. Senate seat, and the following year he was elected to a full term in the Senate. [See EISENHOWER Volume]

The liberals failed in their efforts to capture control of the state Party. In 1962 Don Yarborough (no relation to the Senator), their choice for governor, lost a bitterly fought primary campaign against John B. Connally [*q.v.*], who received large campaign contributions from many of the state's business interests. Connally was a close associate of Vice President Lyndon Johnson, who had been the leader of the conservative Texas Democrats since the mid-1950s. The race left in its wake an acrimonious relationship between Connally and Sen. Yarborough. During the November 1963 trip to Texas that ended with his assassination, President Kennedy had hoped to mend the factional division between the state's liberals and conservatives. [See KENNEDY Volume]

Because President Johnson wanted left-of-center support and a unified Texas

Democratic Party in the 1964 national election, he attempted to alter his role in Texas politics from factional leader to party conciliator. Early in 1964 he dissuaded major conservative aspirants to Yarborough's Senate seat from entering the Democratic senatorial primary. In return the liberals refrained from mounting a full-scale effort against Connally's reelection bid. As a result of the truce, both Yarborough and Connally won easy primary and general election victories in 1964.

In the Senate Yarborough continued to back major Administration-supported civil rights and social welfare measures. From 1965 through 1968 he was, according to the *Congressional Quarterly*, the most consistent Southern senatorial opponent of the Southern Democrat-Republican conservative coalition. He voted for the Civil Rights Act of 1964 and was one of only five Southern Democratic senators to vote for the 1965 Voting Rights Act. During the latter year Yarborough injected Texas politics into a Senate debate over a bill to extend President Johnson's antipoverty program of the previous year. A supporter of the War on Poverty, Yarborough argued in August that the power of governors to veto some of the antipoverty projects should be eliminated and charged Gov. Connally with attempting to "defeat and destroy" the program in Texas. The following month Congress adopted a bill that modified the veto power without eliminating it.

In 1968, with Johnson a lame-duck President and the nation sharply divided over the Vietnam war, the truce between liberal and conservative Democrats in Texas disintegrated. When Connally announced that he would not run for a fourth term as governor, Yarborough was inclined to enter the gubernatorial primary. He was dissuaded from doing so by his supporters in organized labor, who wanted him to remain in Washington. Instead, Don Yarborough again represented the liberals. Once more he was defeated by a conservative in a hard fought primary runoff.

Meanwhile, in the race for the Democratic presidential nomination, Yarborough supported anti-war candidate Sen. Eugene McCarthy (D, Minn.) [*q.v.*], and Connally endorsed Vice President Hubert H. Humphrey [*q.v.*]. At the August Democratic National Convention in Chicago a delegation led by Yarborough challenged the credentials of Connally's regular Texas delegation, but the challenge was rejected. Yarborough endorsed Humphrey after the Convention selected the Vice President as the party's standard bearer.

Lloyd Bentsen, Jr., one of the conservatives whom President Johnson had deterred from entering the 1964 senatorial primary, challenged Yarborough in the 1970 race. Armed with a substantial campaign treasury, Bentsen appealed to "law and order" sentiment and accused the liberal Texas Senator of being insufficiently firm in his opposition to school busing. Yarborough lost the primary by 90,000 votes out of some one and a half million cast.

[MLL]

For further information:
O. Douglas Weeks, "Texas: Land of Conservative Expansiveness," in William C. Havard, ed., *The Changing Politics of the South* (Baton Rouge, 1972).

YARMOLINSKY, ADAM

b. Nov. 17, 1922; New York, N.Y.
Special Assistant to the Secretary of Defense, January 1961-September 1965; Deputy Assistant Secretary of Defense for International Security Affairs, October 1965-August 1966.

Yarmolinsky, a graduate of Harvard and the Yale Law School, served during the 1950s as a consultant to private foundations and lectured at the American University and Yale Law Schools.

Shortly after John F. Kennedy was elected President in 1960, Yarmolinsky joined the staff of Sargent Shriver [*q.v.*], Kennedy's brother-in-law, to screen candidates for new posts in the Administration. In January 1961 he was named special assistant to Secretary of Defense Robert S. McNamara [*q.v.*]. While in the Defense Department Yarmolinsky served as temporary head of the national fallout shelter program and worked on a White House study that recommended that the Defense Department ban off-base discrimination against black servicemen. [See KENNEDY Volume]

Early in 1964 Yarmolinsky took a leave from the Defense Department to join a task force under Shriver which framed legislation for the Johnson Administration's antipoverty programs. Yarmolinsky, with the support of McNamara, proposed that abandoned Army camps be used as centers for educating semi-literate school dropouts. The idea won the support of Shriver but was bitterly denounced by Secretary of Labor Willard Wirtz [*q.v.*], Secretary of Agriculture Orville Freeman [*q.v.*] and Anthony Celebrezze [*q.v.*], Secretary of the Department of Health, Education and Welfare. They argued that the use of military bases for educational purposes would give the poverty program an unhealthy military cast. President Johnson agreed, and the program was dropped. Wirtz, Freeman and Celebreeze also argued that their respective departments could better manage the various poverty programs than the new Office of Economic Opportunity (OEO) proposed by Shriver and Yarmolinsky. Johnson, however, believed that the OEO should control most antipoverty programs, and the legislation that the Administration presented to Congress reflected that belief.

Journalists Rowland Evans and Robert Novak [*q.v.*] called Yarmolinsky "the administrative dynamo behind Shriver;" and Yarmolinsky believed that he would soon be named deputy director of OEO. However, in August 1964, eight Southern congressmen informed the White House that they would vote for the Johnson antipoverty program only if the Administration promised not to appoint Yarmolinsky to OEO. This opposition to Yarmolinsky was attributed to his role in desegregating military bases in Southern towns, his abrasive manner in dealing with Congress on military issues and a general mistrust of his liberal and intellectual background. After President Johnson made the promise, the antipoverty bill became law; however, it would have passed even without the votes of Yarmolinsky's opponents. When questioned about Yarmolinsky in August 1964, Johnson denied even considering him for an appointment in the antipoverty program.

In the fall of 1964 Yarmolinsky returned to the Defense Department, but, possibly because of his difficulties with Congress, his relations with McNamara were not as close as they had once been. Yarmolinsky worked for a time on defense problems relating to the Panama Canal and later served on a task force studying economic problems in the Dominican Republic. In October 1965 he was appointed deputy assistant secretary of defense for international security affairs, but this was a junior appointment which did not require congressional approval, and a disappointment to him.

Yarmolinsky left the Defense Department in September 1966 to teach at the Harvard Law School and the John F. Kennedy School of Government at Harvard.

In 1971 Yarmolinsky completed a book, sponsored by the Twentieth Century Fund, in which he documented the extraordinary impact of the military establishment on American life. He argued that a large military establishment was unavoidable in this country but feared that neither Congress nor the President had exercised proper control over it. He questioned whether the military should always have the primary claim to scarce economic and social resources and deplored the tendency of state and local government to rely on federal troops to put down domestic disorders.

[JLW]

For further information:
Adam Yarmolinsky, *The Military Establishment: Its Impact on American Society* (New York, 1971).

YORTY, SAM(UEL WILLIAM)

b. Oct. 1, 1909; Lincoln, Neb.
Mayor, Los Angeles, Calif., 1961-73.

Raised in the tradition of Midwestern Democratic populism, Sam Yorty came to Los Angeles after finishing high school. Initially involved in a number of the quixotic political movements which flourished in California in the early years of the Depression, Yorty was elected to the state Assembly as a Democrat in 1936. In the Assembly he sponsored both liberal legislation and the law that created the nation's first un-American activities committee.

After Yorty lost the 1940 U.S. senatorial contest to isolationist Sen. Hiram Johnson (R, Calif.), he entered private law practice. He returned to the state Assembly in 1949 and in 1950 and 1952 won election to the U.S. House of Representatives, where he championed California's oil and water claims and the interests of the Air Force. He again tried unsuccessfully to become a U.S. senator in 1954 and 1956.

Already estranged from leading figures in the Democratic state organization because of his shift to the political right, Yorty further distanced himself from the Party in 1960 when he endorsed Republican Richard Nixon [*q.v.*] over John F. Kennedy in the presidential contest. Yorty's maverick reputation helped him win an upset victory in the May 1961 Los Angeles mayoral campaign. As a Midwestern populist turned conservative, Yorty was attuned to the ideas of many of the city's conservative Democratic electorate. Yorty pioneered in the use of television as a campaign medium to overcome the disadvantages of the city's tremendous physical expanse and decentralization.

In his first term as mayor, Yorty lowered property taxes, presided over Los Angeles's share of the economic boom in Southern California and undertook the renewal of the city's dreary downtown area. Yorty kept his name before the California public through frequent appearances on popular television shows and a series of worldwide tours as a representative of the city. With greater support from the city's press and business community than he enjoyed in 1961, Yorty defeated Rep. James Roosevelt (D, Calif.) [*q.v.*]—in Los Angeles elections candidates were not listed by party—and six other candidates in the May 1965 mayoral contest. Yorty won 60% of the vote and, most importantly, helped carry his political allies to seats on the city council.

In August 1965 a riot, the first major racial disturbance of the 1960s, broke out in Watts, Los Angeles's black ghetto, resulting in 34 deaths, thousands of injuries and extensive property damage. Soon after the week of violence was over, Yorty traded public attacks with state and federal officials. The Mayor criticized Gov. Edmund Brown's [*q.v.*] lieutenant governor, Glenn M. Anderson—Brown was vacationing out of the state during the riot—for not responding quickly enough to a call for National Guard help. Yorty defended his police chief, William H. Parker, and the city force from charges of brutality, claiming that state police exacerbated the riot in its early stages.

When federal officials charged that Yorty had failed to cooperate with them to prevent such disturbances, he replied that the antipoverty program and the liberal Brown Administration had raised poor people's expectations beyond what the authorities were able to fulfill. A few months before the riot Yorty had criticized the federal Office of Economic Opportunity (OEO) for excluding city officials from direction of OEO's antipoverty projects. He now charged that the OEO's withholding of funds from Los Angeles until the city met OEO criteria contributed to riot conditions.

In January 1966 the California Advisory Committee to the U.S. Civil Rights Commission, headed by Episcopal Bishop James A. Pike [q.v.], praised Lt. Gov. Anderson, but singled out Yorty for "gross negligence" and "attitudes and actions" that contributed to riot conditions. Yorty saw the report as a personal "political attack" based on the "false charge that the police caused the rioting."

In August 1966 hearings before a subcommittee of the Senate Government Operations Committee, Sen. Abraham Ribicoff (D, Conn.) [*q.v.*] and Sen. Robert F. Kennedy (D, N.Y.) [*q.v.*] repeated the charge that Yorty had done little to improve conditions in Watts. Noting the restrictions in the Los Angeles city charter that he had long sought to revise, Yorty claimed that he lacked authority in areas such as education, health and housing that were essential to effecting the changes the senators desired. Later, Yorty asserted that Kennedy was merely using the subcommittee hearings to further his political campaign against President Johnson. He added, "Bobby is an upstart who is trying to ride on his brother's fame and his father's fortune to take over the country."

Yorty's political battle with Gov. Brown continued through the mid-1960s. In the June 1964 primaries he had unsuccessfully opposed Brown's slate of pro-Johnson delegates to the Democratic National Convention with his own slate also pledged to the President. Hoping to capitalize on the popularity his role in the Watts riot earned him among many California whites, Yorty challenged Brown for the gubernatorial nomination in 1966. The Mayor lost the June primary by about 40,000 votes.

Yorty finished second in the mayoral primary of 1969 and qualified for a runoff election against Thomas Bradley, a black attorney and former police lieutenant. Yorty won the contest in a bitter campaign in which his supporters sought to identify Bradley with black militants and other radicals. In 1973 Bradley defeated Yorty when the Mayor ran for a fourth term. [See NIXON Volume]

[JCH]

For further information see:
Ed Ainsworth, *Maverick Mayor: A Biography of Sam Yorty of Los Angeles* (Garden City 1966).

YOUNG, MILTON R(UBEN)
b. Dec. 6, 1897; Berlin, N.D.
Republican Senator, N.D., 1945- .

A farmer and former state legislator, Young was appointed to the Senate in 1945 to fill the vacancy left by the death of John Moses. Despite his long tenure, his position as ranking Republican member of the House Appropriations Committee from 1967 and his service as secretary of the Senate Republican Conference Committee from 1946 to 1971, Young was virtually unknown except on Capitol Hill and in his home state. Although supporting many civil rights measures, the Senator maintained a basically conservative position by voting against labor legislation, most foreign aid bills and public works projects except those that benefited North Dakota. In 1971 the conservative Americans for Constitutional Action gave him a cumulative rating of 66, while the liberal Americans for Democratic Action calculated his Senate voting record as "correct" only 15% at the time. [See KENNEDY Volume]

Young's conservatism was reflected in his opposition to medicare and antipoverty programs and his support of cuts in labor and health, education and welfare spending. Although he voted for the Civil Rights Act of 1964, he opposed the Voting Rights Act of 1965 and voted against the use of federal funds to achieve integration through busing. However, Young favored manpower training programs and voted against deleting $900 million from the Model Cities program in 1966.

During the 1960s Young consistently supported legislation to aid farmers, including measures to extend crop insurance and improve marketing conditions for farm products. During the last half of the decade, the Senator, concerned by North Dakota's loss of population and low per-capita income, was instrumental in obtaining lucrative military projects for his state, including the construction of antiballistic missile bases.

As early as 1954 Young spoke out against American intervention in Asia and throughout the 1960s continued to express opposition to the war in Vietnam on the ground that the area was "militarily untenable." Despite his opposition to use of American troops in Asia, Young consistently voted in favor of appropriating funds for the war. He justified his stand by saying that he intended "to support the President of the United States when we are in war whether he [the President] agrees with my views or not."

Young was returned to the Senate in 1968 and 1974. [See NIXON Volume]

[EWS]

YOUNG, STEPHEN M(ARVIN)
b. May 4, 1890; Norwalk, Ohio.
Democratic Senator, Ohio, 1959-71.

The son of a county judge, Stephen M. Young took his law degree at Western Reserve University and saw action in the 1916 Mexican campaign and both World Wars.

Young first ran for public office as a Democrat in 1912, the same year Woodrow Wilson captured the presidency. He twice won election to the state Assembly, and he served four terms as Ohio's U.S. representative-at-large, proving a strong supporter of liberal Democratic programs and organized labor. When out of office, Young practiced criminal law in Cleveland. In 1958 he scored a major political upset by defeating Sen. John W. Bricker (R, Ohio), the state GOP's top vote-getter and 1944 Republican vice presidential candidate. A freshman senator in his seventies, Young usually followed the Democratic Party leadership. [See EISENHOWER, KENNEDY Volumes]

Young survived two difficult challenges to his Senate seat in 1964. In January John H. Glenn [*q.v.*], the first American to orbit the Earth, announced his candidacy for Young's seat in the May Democratic primary. National Party strategists, concerned that the 73-year-old incumbent would lose in November, encouraged Glenn to make the race against Young. The Senator received a major setback in January when the state Democratic convention, in a thinly veiled move on Glenn's behalf, declined to endorse him for reelection. The astronaut's victory appeared certain until an ear injury compelled him to withdraw from the race in late March. Young easily won the primary on May 5.

Young's good fortune continued through the general election. His Republican opponent in the senatorial race, Rep. Robert Taft, Jr. (R, Ohio) [*q.v.*], possessed a famous name in Ohio politics and was 27 years Young's junior. But the Republican presidential campaign of Sen. Barry M. Goldwater (R, Ariz.) [*q.v.*] fared badly in Ohio, and by closely associating his campaign with that of President Johnson, Young defeated Taft in November by four-tenths of one percent of the vote. Young ran almost 575,000 votes behind Johnson's showing in Ohio.

Young voted for every major piece of Great Society legislation while pursuing his own battles against certain domestic and military spending programs. As in the Kennedy years, Young attacked civil defense appropriations, but lost in annual efforts taken to reduce the program's funding between 1964 and 1968. A member of the Senate Armed Services Committee, Young opposed the development of the Sentinel antiballistic missile system (ABM). In June 1968 he described the Administration's request as "an utter waster of taxpayers' money . . . the deployment of antiballistic missile systems ringing some cities of our nation have been fruitless and wasteful." Two of Young's colleagues joined him in voting against the $227.3 million Sentinel ABM appropriation, which passed 78-3 in June 1968.

Although his state's economy benefited from increased military production, Young became identified with the anti-war group of Democratic senators early in the debate over American participation in Vietnam. Vice President Hubert H. Humphrey [*q.v.*] and McGeorge Bundy [*q.v.*], the President's special assistant for national security affairs, met with Young and four other Senate liberals in February 1965 to dissuade them from vocal opposition to the President's escalation of the war. The Humphrey-Bundy mission failed, and Young remained a steadfast opponent of the Vietnam war for the balance of his term. In March 1965 he joined four other Democratic senators in voting against an additional $4.8 billion military appropriation for the war. In February 1966 he demanded that Johnson replace Secretary of State Dean Rusk [*q.v.*], complaining that he could not sleep well with Rusk running the State Department. In June 1968 Young and Sen. Lee Metcalf [*q.v.*] voted against a bill to enable the President to retain Gen. Earle G. Wheeler [*q.v.*] as chairman of the Joint Chiefs of Staff. On the Senate floor in September 1968, Young defended anti-war protesters in a debate over the disturbances outside the August 1968 Democratic National Convention. "Democracy was clubbed to death," Young cried, "by Mayor [Richard J.] Daley's [*q.v.*] police."

Young declined to seek reelection in 1970, and his 1964 campaign manager, Howard Metzenbaum, lost to Rep. Taft in November.

[JLB]

YOUNG, WHITNEY M(OORE) JR.
b. July 31, 1921; Lincoln Ridge, Ky.
d. March 11, 1971; Lagos, Nigeria.
Executive Director, National Urban League, 1961-71.

After receiving an M.A. in social work from the University of Minnesota, Young worked for the St. Paul Urban League from 1947 to 1950 and then became executive secretary of the Omaha Urban League. He was named dean of Atlanta University's School of Social Work in 1954 and served there until his appointment as executive director of the National Urban League in August 1961. Then a social work agency for urban blacks, the League remained relatively conservative during the 1960s, but Young broadened its programs and approach and gave it more aggressive and outspoken leadership. Urbane and articulate, Young presented a controversial proposal for a "domestic Marshall Plan" in June 1963. His plan called for a massive, wide-ranging aid program to close the social, economic and educational gap between the races. [See KENNEDY Volume]

One of the first civil rights leaders to be consulted by President Johnson in December 1963, Young cooperated closely with the Johnson Administration in the planning and passage of its War on Poverty legislation. Testifying in support of the program at congressional hearings in April 1964, Young asserted, "Negroes today are wary lest they find themselves with a mouthful of civil rights and an empty stomach." Following the passage of the Economic Opportunity Act in August 1964, Young organized a Community Action Assembly in Washington in December. Over 350 black leaders gathered to hear League officials explain in detail the provisions of the 1964 civil rights and antipoverty laws and ways in which local black organizations could implement the legislation and secure antipoverty funds. The League sponsored a series of similar workshops throughout 1965. With its own $8 million contract from the Labor Department, the League developed a major job training program for unemployed blacks.

Young supported Johnson in the 1964 presidential election and called the Republicans' nomination of Sen. Barry Goldwater (R, Ariz.) [*q.v.*] "an attempt to appeal to all of the fearful, the insecure, prejudiced people in our society." With three other civil rights leaders, Young signed a July 1964 statement urging a "moratorium" on mass civil rights demonstrations during the 1964 campaign.

Young participated in the march from Selma to Montgomery, Ala., organized by Martin Luther King [*q.v.*] in March 1965. When James Meredith [*q.v.*] was shot in June 1966 while on a solitary protest march in Mississippi, Young favored continuation of his march by other civil rights leaders. However, Young refused at first to sign a march "manifesto" containing a strong indictment of American society and government. He frowned on the cry of "black power" raised by Stokely Carmichael [*q.v.*] during the Meredith march. At an Urban League convention in July, Young deprecated black power as meaning "all things to all men." With six other black leaders he signed an October 1966 advertisement in the *New York Times* which repudiated the black power concept and reaffirmed his commitment to nonviolence, integration and the "democratic process" as the major tenets of the civil rights movement. In July 1967 Young also joined in a statement appealing for an end to riots in Northern ghettos. At an Urban League convention the next month, he added that the choice blacks faced was not one of "moderation vs. militancy" but of "militancy vs. extremism."

Young's emphasis on "responsible militancy" presaged a shift in his views on black power. Speaking at the July 1968 convention of the Congress of Racial Equality, Young endorsed a black power concept that emphasized "control of one's destiny and community affairs." He supported "as legitimate and historically consistent a minority's mobilization of its economic and political power to reward its friends and punish its enemies." At an Urban League convention the same month, Young launched a "New Thrust" program of community action in black ghettos. Labeling the program a "constructive black power" effort, Young explained that the League would now provide "technical assistance to the ghetto to help it organize, document its needs, select its own leadership and arrange for creative confrontations with appropriate officials." The "New Thrust" program signaled a major shift for the League from social service work to grass-roots organizing in the ghetto to build black economic, social and political power. Over the next several years, Young directed a major League rehabilitation program among the black poor which spent an average of $25 million per year.

Throughout the Johnson years Young was frequently called to the White House for consultation, and he served on seven presidential commissions including a national advisory council for the antipoverty program. Young went to South Vietnam in July 1966 to investigate the condition of black servicemen. When Martin Luther King made a strong statement in opposition to the Vietnam war in April 1967, Young opposed King's linking of the anti-war and civil rights movements, stating that the "limited resources and personnel" of the civil rights movement "should not be diverted into other channels." Young also joined a delegation of 22 prominent Americans who went to South Vietnam to observe the September 1967 elections there. He later said he was "terribly impressed" with the elections. In 1969, however, Young came out strongly against the Vietnam war, arguing that it divided the nation and used funds which could best be spent in the nation's cities.

During the Nixon years Young criticized the Administration for permitting what he called a "massive national withdrawal" from urban and racial problems. He also opposed an Administration proposal for pre-trial detention of "dangerous" criminals. Young endorsed bills for a national health insurance program and continued to call for greater aid to the poor. In March 1971 Young drowned while swimming in Lagos, Nigeria. [See Nixon Volume]

[CAB]

For further information:
Guichard Parris and Lester Brooks, *Blacks in the City: A History of the National Urban League* (Boston, 1971).

ZABLOCKI, CLEMENT J(OHN)
b. Nov. 18, 1912; Milwaukee, Wisc.
Democratic Representative, Wisc., 1948- .

Clement J. Zablocki, a native of Milwaukee, attended parochial schools and later studied at Marquette University, where he received a B.A. in 1936. He taught high school in Milwaukee during the late 1930s and served in the Wisconsin Senate from 1942 and 1948. He was elected to Congress in 1948 and for many years had little difficulty winning reelection.

Zablocki's district included a large white working-class area in Milwaukee's South Side and some nearby suburbs. His voting record generally reflected the views of organized labor, which gave him heavy support. In domestic affairs he usually voted for the Johnson Administration's social welfare legislation, including antipoverty, medicare and education bills. The Pentagon could also rely on Zablocki to support its requests for increased arms appropriations; as the second-ranking member of the House Foreign Affairs Committee, he consistently backed the Administration's Vietnam war policy. The American Security Council, a defense lobbying group, gave him a "correct rating of 90% in the late 1960s.

Zablocki supported civil rights legislation, but in August 1966 he came into conflict with the Negro Youth Council of the NAACP, headed by Father James E. Groppi [*q.v.*], when it demanded that Zablocki and other politicians resign from the Fraternal Order of Eagles, a national fraternity that excluded blacks. On Sept. 22, 1966, 45 demonstrators from Groppi's group picketed the Zablocki home in Milwaukee to protest his membership. Zablocki refused to resign, arguing that he preferred to try to reform the organization from within.

In 1968 Zablocki headed President Johnson's Wisconsin primary campaign. On March 31 Johnson announced that he would not seek reelection. Zablocki nevertheless urged Democrats to vote for Johnson as a statement of confidence in the Administration. On April 2 the President was defeated in Wisconsin by Sen. Eugene J. McCarthy (D, Minn.) [*q.v.*] by 150,000 votes.

During the Nixon years Zablocki remained a staunch supporter of the Administration's Vietnam war policy.

[JLW]

ZINN, HOWARD

b. Aug. 24, 1922; New York, N.Y.
Civil rights and anti-war activist.

Zinn was educated at New York University and Columbia, where he received a Ph.D. in 1958. He began teaching history in 1956 at Spelman College, a small black women's school in Atlanta; by 1963 he was professor and chairman of the department of social sciences. In 1964 Zinn took a position at Boston University, where he became professor of government in 1966.

Described by friends as an "action-oriented academic," Zinn combined political conviction and social activism with his scholarly work. He became involved in the civil rights movement while teaching at Spelman and worked closely with the Student Nonviolent Coordinating Committee (SNCC), a militant civil rights group. In 1962 he participated in an unsuccessful desegregation drive in Albany, Ga., and subsequently wrote a SNCC report that attacked the federal government for "abandoning its responsbility" to protect black demonstrators against white violence. Zinn's experience in the civil rights movement stimulated him to write *SNCC: The New Abolitionists*, published in 1964. The book's enthusiastic description of SNCC activities in the Deep South helped popularize the organization among white liberals; observers noted that Zinn's influence brought many student volunteers and organizers into civil rights projects.

During the mid-1960s Zinn joined the growing peace movement, participating in the American Mobilization Committee against the Vietnam War. His book, *Vietnam: the Logic of Withdrawal* appeared in 1967. Zinn was also known for his continuing activism. In February 1968 he flew to Hanoi with the Rev. Daniel Berrigan [*q.v.*], another member of the Mobilization Committee, to receive three U.S. prisoners of war released by the North Vietnamese government. One year later Zinn participated in a conference of anti-war scientists and scholars at the Massachusetts Institute of Technology, where he urged researchers to stop work on federally funded projects as a means of resisting "the lawlessness of government." This was the start of a series of "work stoppages" at major American universities.

Zinn's efforts to stimulate campus activism during the 1960s made him increasingly impatient with the traditional "ivory tower" detachment of academics. He argued in numerous articles that the separation of knowledge from action is "immoral"; scholars make a political statement in their choice of subject matter, he claimed, for by ignoring controversial issues they play into the hands of reactionary forces. This point of view was stressed in Zinn's book *The Politics of History*, published in 1970.

Zinn continued teaching at Boston University during the early 1970s. He remained interested in current political issues, which he discussed in *Post-War America*, published in 1973.

[SLG]

Appendix

CHRONOLOGY: THE JOHNSON YEARS

1963

NOV. 22—Kennedy is assassinated in Dallas, Tex., by Lee Harvey Oswald. Lyndon Johnson is sworn in as the 36th president.

NOV. 24—Jack Ruby kills Oswald in Dallas. The incident is seen live on TV.

NOV. 26—In a railroad work-rules dispute a government arbitration board calls for the elimination of 40,000 jobs.

NOV. 27—Johnson addresses a joint session of Congress and pledges continued support of Kennedy's programs. He asks Congress for the "earliest possible passage" of a civil rights program.

NOV. 29—The Warren Commission is set up to investigate Kennedy's assassination.

DEC. 17—The Senate ratifies the El Chamizal Treaty settling a long-standing boundary dispute with Mexico over land near the Rio Grande River.

1964

JAN. 3—Arizona Sen. Barry Goldwater announces his candidacy for the Republican presidential nomination.

JAN. 3—Johnson establishes the President's Committee on Consumer Interests and appoints Esther Peterson its chairman.

JAN. 8—Johnson delivers his first State of the Union message and calls for a War on Poverty.

JAN. 9-12—U.S. troops fire on anti-American rioters in the Panama Canal Zone.

JAN. 10—Panama breaks diplomatic ties with the U.S.

JAN. 11—U.S. Surgeon General Luther Terry's committee reports the use of cigarettes "contributes substantially to mortality."

JAN. 23—The 24th Amendment barring the use of a poll tax in federal elections is ratified.

JAN. 25—Echo II, the first U.S.-USSR cooperative space venture, is launched.

FEB. 7—Johnson orders the withdrawal of American dependents from South Vietnam.

FEB. 17—The Supreme Court rules that congressional districts must be apportioned on a "one-man, one-vote" basis.

FEB. 26—Johnson signs a $11.5 billion tax cut bill.

MARCH 4—James Hoffa is found guilty of jury tampering.

MARCH 10—Henry Cabot Lodge wins the New Hampshire Republican presidential primary on a write-in vote.

MARCH 14—Jack Ruby is found guilty of the murder of Lee Harvey Oswald.

APRIL 4—The U.S. and Panama resume diplomatic ties and pledge negotiations on the Canal Zone treaty.

APRIL 7—Alabama Gov. George Wallace receives 34.1% of the Democratic vote in the Wisconsin presidential primary.

APRIL 9—Railroad workers agree to postpone a scheduled nationwide railroad strike over work-rules changes after a personal plea from Johnson.

APRIL 11—Johnson signs a farm bill providing for major changes in federal wheat and cotton price subsidies.

MAY 15—New York Gov. Nelson A. Rockefeller wins an upset victory over Lodge and Goldwater in the Oregon Republican presidential primary.

MAY 19—Wallace polls 42.8% of the vote in the Maryland Democratic presidential primary.

JUNE 2—Goldwater defeats Rockefeller by 59,000 votes in the California Republican presidential primary.

JUNE 10—The Senate invokes cloture on the civil rights bill by a vote of 71-29, marking the first time the Senate ever voted to cut off debate on civil rights legislation.

JUNE 14—The United Steelworkers of America and 11 steel companies agree not to practice racial discrimination in the industry.

JUNE 15—The Supreme Court rules that state legislatures must be apportioned according to population.

JUNE 21—Three civil rights workers, participants in the Mississippi Freedom Summer Project, are murdered in Neshoba County, Miss.

JULY 2—Johnson signs a civil rights bill providing for the integration of public accommodations and closing voting-rights loopholes in earlier civil rights legislation.

JULY 8—The Senate Rules Committee finds Bobby Baker guilty of "many gross improprieties" while secretary to the Democratic majority.

JULY 9—Johnson signs the urban mass transportation bill providing $375 million to help public and private transit companies provide and improve urban mass transportation.

JULY 15—Barry Goldwater is nominated as the Republican candidate for president on the first ballot at the Republican National Convention. William Miller is chosen as the vice-presidential candidate at the following session.

JULY 18—Racial violence breaks out in Harlem and Brownsville, two predominately black sections of New York City. During the summer riots break out in Rochester, N.Y., suburban Chicago, Jersey City, Elizabeth and Paterson, N.J., and Philadelphia, as well.

AUG. 3—Johnson instructs the Navy to take retaliatory action against North Vietnam for its alleged attack on the U.S. destroyer *Maddox* in the Gulf of Tonkin.

AUG. 7—Congress passes the Tonkin Gulf Resolution authorizing Johnson to take "all necessary measures" to "repel any armed attack" against U.S. forces in Southeast Asia and approves in advance "all necessary steps, including the use of armed force," that the President might take to aid U.S. allies in the region.

AUG. 20—Johnson signs the economic opportunity bill of 1964, authorizing 10 separate programs, under the supervision of the director of the Office of Economic Opportunity, designed to make a coordinated attack on the causes of poverty—illiteracy, unemployment and lack of public services.

AUG. 20—Johnson signs a bill providing free legal counsel for indigents accused of federal crimes.

AUG. 26—Johnson is nominated as the Democratic candidate for president on the first ballot at the Democratic National Convention. Minnesota Sen. Hubert Humphrey is chosen vice-presidential candidate at the following session.

AUG. 31—Johnson signs a bill establishing the federal food stamp program on a permanent basis.

SEPT. 2—Johnson signs a housing bill providing for urban and rural renewal programs to alleviate blight.

SEPT. 3—Johnson signs a bill establishing a permanent national wilderness system.

SEPT. 3—Johnson signs a bill creating a National Council on the Arts.

SEPT. 24—The Warren Commission issues its report concluding that Lee Harvey Oswald "acted alone" in assassinating Kennedy.

OCT. 14—Martin Luther King is awarded the Nobel Prize for Peace.

OCT. 14—Presidential aide Walter Jenkins resigns following his arrest on a morals charge.

NOV. 3—Johnson wins reelection by a record plurality of 15,975,924 votes and captures 486 electoral votes from 44 states. Democrats win 17 governorships and increase their majorities in Congress.

NOV. 25—U.S. planes airlift Belgian paratroopers into Stanleyville to rescue white hostages held by Congolese rebels.

NOV. 28—Mariner 4 is launched to transmit close-up pictures of Mars.

DEC. 14—The Supreme Court unanimously upholds the constitutionality of the public accommodations section of the 1964 Civil Rights Act.

1965

JAN. 4—The House, 224-202, adopts a 21-day rule weakening the power of the Rules Committee to block legislation.

JAN. 11—The International Longshoremen's Association begins a strike paralyzing Atlantic and Gulf Coast shipping operations until March 5.

FEB. 7—Communist forces attack the U.S. air base at Pleiku.

MARCH 2—The U.S. begins Operation Rolling Thunder, the sustained bombing of North Vietnam.

MARCH 4—The U.S. Information Agency closes its facilities in Indonesia because of harassment. The Peace Corps withdraws the following month.

MARCH 7—About 500 blacks, beginning a protest march from Selma to Montgomery, Ala., are attacked by sheriff's deputies and state troopers.

MARCH 8-9—The first American combat troops land in Vietnam.

MARCH 9—Johnson signs an Appalachia aid bill.

MARCH 15—Johnson addresses a joint session of Congress and calls for swift passage of voting rights legislation.

MARCH 21—The civil rights march from Selma to Montgomery, Ala., begins under the protection of federal troops.

MARCH 23—The first manned Gemini flight is launched.

MARCH 24—Ranger 9 transmits pictures of the moon's surface to earth.

APRIL 6—Early Bird, the world's first commercial satellite, is launched.

APRIL 11—Johnson signs the elementary and secondary education bill, granting aid to schools with large concentrations of children from low-income families and providing funds for educational materials and the creation of educational centers.

APRIL 26—Secretary of Defense Robert McNamara states that the Vietnam war effort costs the U.S. about $1.5 billion a year.

APRIL 28—U.S. Marines land in the Dominican Republic allegedly to protect American lives during the civil war.

APRIL 29—U.S. Commissioner of Education Francis Keppel announces that public school districts will be required to desegregate schools by the autumn of 1967.

MAY 2—At a news conference Johnson states that Marines were sent to the Dominican Republic to prevent a Communist takeover as well as to protect American lives.

MAY 16—A four-man U.S. fact-finding team arrives in Santo Domingo in an unsuccessful attempt to help form a coalition government.

JUNE 3—Maj. Edward White takes the first U.S. "space walk."

JUNE 7—The Supreme Court voids a Connecticut law prohibiting the use of birth control devices.

JUNE 8—The State Department reports that Johnson has authorized the use of U.S. troops in direct combat if the South Vietnamese Army requests assistance.

JUNE 15—Three unions stage a 75-day maritime strike idling more than 100 ships in Atlantic and Gulf ports.

JUNE 17—B-52s stage the first mass bombing raid in South Vietnam.

JUNE 30—The Senate Rules Committee recommends indicting Bobby Baker for violation of conflict-of-interest laws.

JULY 27—The 18-nation disarmament conference resumes talks in Geneva.

JULY 27—Johnson signs a bill requiring health warnings on cigarette packages.

JULY 30—Johnson signs the medicare bill, providing medical care for the aged financed through the Social Security system.

AUG. 4—A proposed constitutional amendment to modify the Supreme Court's "one-man, one-vote" decision fails to receive a two-thirds majority in the Senate.

AUG. 6—Johnson signs the voting rights bill suspending the use of literacy and other voter qualification tests.

AUG. 10—Johnson signs the housing and urban development bill, providing $30 million in rent subsidies for low income families.

AUG. 11—Rioting breaks out in the black Watts section of Los Angeles. In a five-day period over 30 people are killed in the U.S.'s most destructive outbreak of racial violence in decades.

SEPT. 3—A three-year steel pact is signed immediately before a nationwide strike is scheduled to begin.

SEPT. 4—The U.S. recognizes a provisional government established in the Dominican Republic with the support of both junta and rebel representatives.

SEPT. 7—The U.S. suspends military aid to India and Pakistan as a result of the two countries' border clash.

SEPT. 9—Johnson signs a bill creating the Department of Housing and Urban Development.

OCT. 3—Johnson signs an immigration bill eliminating the 1924 national origins quota system.

OCT. 11—An Administration effort to repeal Section 14(b) of the Taft-Hartley Act fails when the Senate rejects a motion to invoke cloture against a filibuster.

OCT. 15-16—Nationwide demonstrations

against U.S. policy in Vietnam are held in about 40 cities.

OCT. 22—Johnson signs a highway beautification bill.

NOV.—Ralph Nader's indictment of the auto industry, *Unsafe at Any Speed*, is published.

NOV. 8—Johnson signs a higher education bill providing a three-year $23 billion program of college scholarships and college building construction grants.

NOV. 15—The Supreme Court holds unconstitutional a provision of a 1950 law requiring members of the Communist Party to register with the federal government.

NOV. 27—In a demonstration initiated by the National Committee for a Sane Nuclear Policy (SANE), over 15,000 marchers converge on the White House to protest U.S. involvement in Vietnam.

DEC. 5—The Federal Reserve Board raises the discount rate from 4% to 4½%.

DEC. 15—Gemini 6 and Gemini 7 achieve man's first rendezvous in space.

DEC. 24-JAN. 31—The U.S. halts the bombing of North Vietnam in efforts to get Hanoi to the negotiating table.

DEC. 31—U.S. forces in Vietnam total 184,314.

1966

JAN. 1—New York City transit workers begin a 13 day strike.

JAN. 7—Martin Luther King announces the beginning of an "open city" campaign in Chicago to attack the problems of Northern ghetto residents.

JAN. 13—Johnson appoints Robert C. Weaver Secretary of Housing and Urban Development, making Weaver the first black ever to serve in a cabinet post.

JAN. 17—Four nuclear devices are released in a B-52 collision over Spain. All are recovered by April 7.

JAN. 19—Johnson asks Congress for an additional $12.8 billion for the war in Vietnam.

FEB. 4—The Senate Foreign Relations Committee begins televised hearings on American policy in Vietnam.

FEB. 6-8—At the Honolulu Conference Johnson announces renewed emphasis on "The Other War," the attempt to provide the Vietnamese rural population with local security and develop positive economic and social programs to win their active support.

MARCH 1—The Senate rejects an amendment repealing the Tonkin Gulf Resolution.

MARCH 7—The Supreme Court upholds the constitutionality of seven major provisions of the 1965 Voting Rights Act.

MARCH 16—Gemini 8 achieves the first successful space docking.

MARCH 21—In three decisions the Supreme Court upholds the obscenity convictions of Ralph Ginzburg and another New York publisher but rules the 18th century novel *Fanny Hill* is not obscene.

MARCH 25—The Supreme Court voids the use of poll taxes for state elections.

APRIL 13—B-52 bombers are used for the first time against targets in North Vietnam.

APRIL 21—Senate Foreign Relations Committee Chairman J. William Fulbright warns that the U.S. is "succumbing to the arrogance of power."

APRIL 24—The Newspaper Guild begins a strike against New York's World-Journal-Tribune Inc., which lasts until Sept. 11. It is the longest newspaper strike in a major city.

APRIL 27—The Interstate Commerce Commission authorizes a merger between the Pennsylvania and New York Central railroads, the biggest corporate merger in U.S. history.

MAY 1—The U.S. shells Communist targets in Cambodia.

MAY 21—Johnson sends additional troops to Thailand to prevent Communist infiltration.

JUNE 1—The White House Conference on Civil Rights opens.

JUNE 2—Surveyor I lands on the moon.

JUNE 3-13—One of the largest battles of the Vietnam war is fought in the Central Highlands province of Kontum.

JUNE 6—James Meredith is shot during a solitary protest march in Mississippi.

JUNE 7—Stokely Carmichael, the newly elected chairman of the Student Nonviolent Coordinating Committee, raises the cry of "Black Power."

JUNE 13—The Supreme Court lays down guidelines for police interrogation of arrested suspects in *Miranda* v. *Arizona*.

JUNE 28—Johnson removes the last American troops from the Dominican Republic.

JUNE 29—Johnson orders the bombing of oil installations at Haiphong and Hanoi.

JULY 12—Racial violence breaks out in Chicago. During the summer of 1966 over 20 cities, including New York, Los Angeles, Atlanta, Omaha and Detroit, experience riots or serious disturbances.

AUG. 26—Civil rights leaders and Chicago officials agree on a program to end housing discrimination in Chicago.

SEPT. 8—The National Farm Workers Union, led by Cesar Chavez, starts a strike against California grape growers.

SEPT. 18-24—The U.S. records 970 casualties in Vietnam for the week.

SEPT. 19—An Administration civil rights bill, including a controversial open housing provision, fails when the Senate refuses to invoke cloture against a filibuster.

SEPT. 23—The U.S. military command in Vietnam announces that it is using defoliants to destroy Communist cover.

OCT.—The Black Panther Party is formed by Huey P. Newton and Bobby Seale in Oakland, Calif.

OCT. 10—At Administration request Congress suspends the 7% investment tax credit in order to reduce inflationary pressures.

OCT. 15—Johnson signs the bill creating the Department of Transportation.

OCT. 26—Johnson visits U.S. troops in Vietnam, which number 400,000.

NOV. 3—Johnson signs an omnibus urban assistance and housing bill establishing a Demonstration Cities program.

NOV. 4—Johnson signs a bill increasing the minimum wage to $1.40 an hour and extending coverage to 8-million additional workers.

NOV. 8—The Republicans gain three Senate seats, 47 House seats and eight governorships in the mid-term elections. Edward W. Brooke is elected U.S. Senator from Massachusetts, becoming the first black in the Senate in 85 years.

NOV. 14—By a vote of 5 to 4, the Supreme Court for the first time sustains the state convictions of nonviolent civil rights demonstrators.

NOV. 29—Johnson announces that $5.3 billion in federal programs are being canceled or postponed to save money.

DEC. 2-4—Johnson escalates the fighting in Vietnam by ordering heavy air strikes on the Hanoi area.

1967

JAN. 10—The House repeals the 21-day rule, adopted in January 1965.

JAN. 27—Astronauts Virgil I. Grissom, Edward H. White and Roger B. Chaffee are killed by a fire in their Apollo I capsule during ground tests at Cape Kennedy.

JAN. 27—The U.S. signs a 63-nation treaty prohibiting the orbiting of nuclear weapons and forbidding territorial claims on celestial bodies.

JAN. 29—Bobby Baker is convicted of income tax evasion, theft and conspiracy to defraud the government.

FEB. 11—The 25th Amendment to the Constitution, dealing with presidential disability and providing for the filling of a vice-presidential vacancy, is ratified.

FEB. 13—The National Student Association admits that it received funds from the Central Intelligence Agency between 1952 and 1966 for projects overseas.

MARCH 1—The House of Representatives votes 307-116 to deny Adam Clayton Powell his seat in Congress for improper use of government funds and other misconduct.

MARCH 6—Svetlana Alliluyeva, Stalin's only child, asks asylum at the U.S. embassy in New Delhi.

MARCH 9—Congress restores the investment tax credit 10 months sooner than originally planned.

APRIL 4—The military announces the loss of the 500th plane since Vietnam bombing raids began in 1964.

APRIL 15—One hundred thousand in New York City and 20,000 in San Francisco march to protest U.S. policy in Vietnam.

MAY 15—The Supreme Court extends to children in juvenile court proceedings the right to counsel and other procedural safeguards afforded in adult trials.

MAY 17—Sixteen senators critical of Administration policy in Vietnam warn Hanoi, in a letter drafted by Sen. Frank Church, that they are opposed to unilateral American withdrawal.

MAY 19—U.S. planes bomb a power plant in Hanoi in the first strike at the heart of North Vietnam's capital.

MAY 28—The Office of Civil Operations and Revolutionary Development Support (CORDS) is formed, placing the Vietnam pacification program under military control.

JUNE 5—War breaks out in the Middle East between Israel and Egypt, Jordan and Syria.

JUNE 7—Johnson praises a U.N. Security Council resolution calling for a cease-fire in the Mideast War.

JUNE 19—U.S. District Court Judge J. Skelly Wright orders an end to de facto segregation in Washington, D.C. public schools by the opening of the autumn term.

JUNE 23—The Senate votes 92-5 to censure Connecticut Sen. Thomas Dodd for improper use of campaign funds.

JUNE 23-25—Johnson and Soviet Premier Alexei Kosygin hold a Summit Conference at Glassboro State College in New Jersey.

JULY 7—U.S. and Communist forces suffer heavy casualties in fighting near Con Thien.

JULY 7—Congress's Joint Economic Committee issues a report stating that the Vietnam war created "havoc" in the U.S. economy during 1966 and predicting that the war will cost $4 to $6 billion more in 1967 than the $20.3 billion requested by Johnson.

JULY 12—Rioting breaks out in Newark, N.J. During the "long, hot summer" of 1967, racial violence disrupts 50 American cities.

JULY 17—Congress enacts an Administration bill ending a two-day national railroad strike and providing for a compulsory settlement by a presidentially-appointed panel if no voluntary agreement is reached within 90 days.

JULY 23—In a plebiscite Puerto Rico chooses to remain a commonwealth of the U.S.

JULY 23—The worst race riot in U.S. history breaks out in Detroit, Mich., resulting in 43 dead and 5000 homeless.

JULY 25—The National Guard enters Detroit to help curb disorders.

JULY 27—Johnson appoints a special advisory committee on civil disorders to probe urban race riots.

AUG. 3—Johnson asks Congress to enact a 10% income tax surcharge to combat inflation.

SEPT. 29—In a speech at San Antonio, Tex., Johnson modifies the U.S. position on Vietnam negotiations, saying that the U.S. is willing to stop all bombing if it will promptly lead to negotiations.

OCT. 2—Thurgood Marshall is sworn in as the first black Supreme Court justice.

OCT. 13—Johnson issues an executive order barring sex discrimination in government jobs.

OCT. 18—The House Ways and Means Committee votes 20-5 to postpone action on the 10% surcharge recommended by Johnson and demands budget cuts as well.

OCT. 21—An estimated 35,000 persons participate in a march to the Pentagon to protest U.S. policy in Vietnam.

NOV. 7—Black mayors are elected in two Northern cities, Carl B. Stokes in Cleveland and Richard G. Hatcher in Gary, Ind.

NOV. 22—In one of the bloodiest battles of the Vietnam war, U.S. forces capture Hill 875 near Dak To.

NOV. 23-28—U.S., U.N. and NATO representatives meet with Turkish and Greek leaders in an effort to avert a war over Cyprus. An agreement is reached Dec. 1.

DEC. 18—The Supreme Court holds electronic surveillance subject to the Fourth Amendment and rules judicial warrants necessary to authorize bugging.

DEC. 20—U.S. forces in South Vietnam reach 474,300.

1968

JAN. 3—Minnesota Sen. Eugene McCarthy announces his candidacy for the Democratic presidential nomination.

JAN. 23—North Korea captures the U.S. spy ship *Pueblo*.

JAN. 30—During the Tet holiday the Communists mount major offensives in three-fourths of the 44 provincial capitals of South Vietnam.

FEB. 1—Richard M. Nixon formally announces his candidacy for the Republican presidential nomination.

FEB. 8—Former Alabama Gov. George Wallace announces he will enter the presidential race as a third-party candidate.

FEB. 20—The Senate Foreign Relations Committee begins hearings on the events leading to the passage of the Tonkin Gulf Resolution.

FEB. 27—U.S. military leaders request 206,000 additional troops for Vietnam.

MARCH 2—The National Advisory Commission on Civil Disorders (Kerner Commission) issues its final report, asserting that "white racism" is chiefly responsible for black riots and warning that the U.S. is "moving toward two societies, one black, one white—separate and unequal."

MARCH 11-12—Secretary of State Dean Rusk testifies before the Senate Foreign Relations Committee on American policy in Vietnam.

MARCH 12—In the New Hampshire Democratic primary, Eugene McCarthy wins a surprising 42% of the vote against Johnson's 48%.

MARCH 16—New York Sen. Robert Kennedy announces his candidacy for the Democratic presidential nomination.

MARCH 17—Representatives of the U.S. and the London Gold Pool work out a two-price system for gold.

MARCH 22—Johnson announces that Gen. William Westmoreland will leave his post as commander of U.S. forces in Vietnam to become Army chief of staff. The move signals a turn from the goal of total victory in Vietnam.

MARCH 25-26—The Senior Advisory Group on Vietnam meets to discuss proposed troop increases and recommends against further escalation.

MARCH 31—In a televised speech Johnson announces that he has ordered a halt to the bombing of 90% of North Vietnam. He also announces that he will not run for reelection.

APRIL 1—The Supreme Court extends the "one man, one vote" standard of apportionment to local units of government which elect representatives on a district basis.

APRIL 4—Martin Luther King is assassinated in Memphis, Tenn. The killing leads to riots in Washington, Chicago and numerous other cities.

APRIL 11—24,000 military reservists are called to active duty.

APRIL 11—Johnson signs a civil rights bill barring discrimination in the sale or rental of about 80% of the nation's housing. The bill also contains anti-riot and gun control provisions.

APRIL 23—Students for a Democratic Society (SDS) at Columbia University leads a violent demonstration to protest proposed construction of a gymnasium by the University on a Harlem park site.

APRIL 26—Two hundred thousand people

participate in an anti-war rally in New York City.

APRIL 27—Vice President Hubert Humphrey announces that he will seek the Democratic presidential nomination.

APRIL 30—New York Gov. Nelson Rockefeller announces that he will seek the Republican presidential nomination.

MAY 2—The Poor People's March on Washington begins. Later in the month 3000 marchers camp near the Washington Monument on a site dubbed "Resurrection City."

MAY 3—Johnson announces that the U.S. and North Vietnam have agreed to begin formal peace talks in Paris.

MAY 6—Norman Mailer's *Armies of the Night* is published.

MAY 12—Vietnam peace talks begin in Paris.

MAY 29—Eugene McCarthy wins the Oregon Democratic presidential primary with 45% of the vote.

MAY 29—Johnson signs a truth-in-lending bill.

JUNE 4—Robert F. Kennedy wins the California Democratic presidential primary with 46% of the vote.

JUNE 5—Sirhan Bishara Sirhan assassinates Robert F. Kennedy in Los Angeles.

JUNE 13—The Senate ratifies the U.S.-USSR consular treaty.

JUNE 13—Chief Justice Earl Warren submits his resignation effective upon the approval of a successor. Johnson nominates Justice Abe Fortas as Warren's replacement.

JUNE 18—The Supreme Court rules that an 1866 civil rights law prohibits racial discrimination in the sale and rental of housing and other property.

JUNE 20—Johnson signs an omnibus crime control and safe streets bill.

JUNE 24—The police clear Resurrection City after the protesters' permit expires.

JUNE 28—Johnson signs the income tax surcharge bill, which Congress had tied to a $6 billion budget cut.

JULY 1—Johnson signs the Nuclear Non-Proliferation Treaty.

AUG. 1—Johnson signs a housing and urban development bill encouraging home ownership for low-income families.

AUG. 8—The National Republican Convention nominates Richard M. Nixon for president on the first ballot. Maryland Gov. Spiro T. Agnew is chosen vice-presidential candidate at the following session.

AUG. 10—Sen. George McGovern declares his candidacy for the Democratic presidential nomination.

AUG. 20—The Credentials Committee of the Democratic National Convention votes to unseat the regular Mississippi delegation and seat instead a liberal, biracial challenge delegation.

AUG. 21—Soviet troops enter Czechoslovakia.

AUG. 28—Anti-war protestors clash with police outside the Democratic National Convention. Police tactics are denounced from the rostrum and floor of the Convention.

AUG. 29—Hubert Humphrey wins the Democratic nomination for president. Maine Sen. Edmund Muskie is chosen as his running mate the following day.

SEPT. 23—Agnew apologizes for having used the terms "Fat Jap" and "Polack" earlier in the month.

OCT. 2—Abe Fortas asks Johnson to withdraw his name from consideration as Chief Justice following a filibuster by senators objecting to his advisory services to Johnson.

OCT. 31—Johnson announces a halt to all bombing of North Vietnam as prelude to expanded peace talks.

NOV. 5—Richard Nixon wins the presidential race with 43.4% of the popular vote and 302 out of 538 electoral votes.

NOV. 6—San Francisco State College students strike for reforms, particularly in the area of black studies programs.

DEC. 1—The National Committee on the Causes and Prevention of Violence issues its report warning against a national tendency toward violence.

DEC. 22—North Korea releases the 82 crew members of the *Pueblo*.

DEC. 27—Apollo 8 completes a mission that included circling the moon 10 times.

DEC. 31—The total number of Americans killed in Vietnam in 1968 reaches 14,592.

CONGRESS
1963-1968

SENATE

Alabama

Lister Hill (D) 1939-69
John J. Sparkman (D) 1946- .

Alaska

E. L. Bartlett (D) 1959-69
Ernest Gruening (D) 1959-69

Arizona

Carl Hayden (D) 1927-69
Paul J. Fannin (R) 1965- .
Barry M. Goldwater (R) 1953-65; 1969- .

Arkansas

J. William Fulbright (D) 1945-75
John L. McClellan (D) 1943- .

California

Clair Engle (D) 1959-64
Pierre Salinger (D) 1964
Thomas H. Kuchel (R) 1953-69
George Murphy (R) 1964-71

Colorado

Gordon Allott (R) 1955-73
Peter H. Dominick (R) 1963-75

Connecticut

Thomas J. Dodd (D) 1959-71
Abraham A. Ribicoff (D) 1963- .

Delaware

J. Caleb Boggs (R) 1961-73
John J. Williams (R) 1947-71

Florida

Spessard L. Holland (D) 1946-71
George A. Smathers (D) 1951-69

Georgia

Richard B. Russell (D) 1933-71
Herman E. Talmadge (D) 1957- .

Hawaii

Daniel K. Inouye (D) 1963- .
Hiram L. Fong (R) 1959-77

Idaho

Frank Church (D) 1957- .
Len B. Jordan (R) 1962-73

Illinois

Paul H. Douglas (D) 1949-67
Everett McKinley Dirksen (R) 1951-69

Indiana

Birch Bayh (D) 1963- .
Vance Hartke (D) 1959-77

Iowa

Bourke B. Hickenlooper (R) 1945-69
Jack Miller (R) 1961-73

Kansas

Frank Carlson (R) 1951-69
James B. Pearson (R) 1962- .

Kentucky

John Sherman Cooper (R) 1946-49; 1952-55; 1956-73
Thruston B. Morton (R) 1957-69

Louisiana

Allen J. Ellender (D) 1937-72
Russell B. Long (D) 1948- .

Maine

Edmund S. Muskie (D) 1959- .
Margaret Chase Smith (R) 1949-73

Maryland

Daniel B. Brewster (D) 1963-69
Joseph D. Tydings (D) 1965-71
J. Glenn Beall (R) 1953-65

Massachusetts

Edward M. Kennedy (D) 1962- .
Edward W. Brooke (R) 1967- .
Leverett Saltonstall (R) 1945-67

Michigan

Philip A. Hart (D) 1959-76
Pat McNamara (D) 1955-66
Robert P. Griffin (R) 1966- .

Minnesota

Hubert H. Humphrey (D) 1949-64; 1971-
Eugene J. McCarthy (D) 1959-71
Walter F. Mondale (D) 1964- .

Mississippi

James O. Eastland (D) 1941; 1943- .
John G. Stennis (D) 1947- .

Missouri

Edward V. Long (D) 1960-69
Stuart Symington (D) 1953-77.

Montana

Mike Mansfield (D) 1953- .
Lee Metcalf (D) 1961- .

Nebraska

Carl T. Curtis (R) 1955- .
Roman L. Hruska (R) 1954-77.

Nevada

Alan Bible (D) 1954-75
Howard W. Cannon (D) 1959- .

New Hampshire

Thomas J. McIntyre (D) 1962- .
Norris Cotton (R) 1954-75

New Jersey

Harrison J. Williams (D) 1959- .
Clifford P. Case (R) 1955- .

New Mexico

Clinton P. Anderson (D) 1949-73
Joseph M. Montoya (D) 1964- .
Edwin L. Mechem (R) 1962-64

New York

Robert F. Kennedy (D) 1965-68
Charles E. Goodell (R) 1968-71
Jacob K. Javits (R) 1957- .
Kenneth B. Keating (R) 1959-65

North Carolina

Sam J. Ervin, Jr. (D) 1954-75
B. Everett Jordan (D) 1958-73

North Dakota

Quentin N. Burdick (D) 1960- .
Milton R. Young (R) 1945- .

Ohio

Frank J. Lausche (D) 1957-69
Stephen M. Young (D) 1959-71

Oklahoma

J. Howard Edmondson (D) 1963-64
Fred R. Harris (D) 1964-73
A. S. Mike Monroney (D) 1951-69

Oregon

Maurine B. Neuberger (D) 1960-67
Mark O. Hatfield (R) 1967- .
Wayne Morse (R) 1945-52; (Ind.) 1952-55; (D) 1955-69

Pennsylvania

Joseph S. Clark (D) 1957-69
Hugh Scott (R) 1959- .

Rhode Island

John O. Pastore (D) 1950-77.
Claiborne Pell (D) 1961- .

South Carolina

Ernest F. Hollings (D) 1966- .
Olin D. Johnston (D) 1945-65
Donald S. Russell (D) 1965-66
Strom Thurmond (D) 1954-56, 56-64; (R) 1964- .

South Dakota

George McGovern (D) 1963- .
Karl E. Mundt (R) 1948-73

Tennessee

Ross Bass (D) 1964-67
Albert Gore (D) 1953-71
Herbert S. Walters (D) 1963-64
Howard H. Baker, Jr. (R) 1964-67

Texas

Ralph W. Yarborough (D) 1957-71
John G. Tower (R) 1961- .

Utah

Frank Moss (D) 1959- .
Wallace F. Bennett (R) 1951-75

Vermont

George D. Aiken (R) 1941-75
Winston L. Prouty (R) 1959-71

Virginia

Harry Flood Byrd, Sr. (D) 1933-65
Harry Flood Byrd, Jr. (D) 1965- .
A. Willis Robertson (D) 1946-66
William B. Spong, Jr. (D) 1966-73

Washington

Henry M. Jackson (D) 1953- .
Warren G. Magnuson (D) 1944- .

West Virginia

Robert C. Byrd (D) 1959- .
Jennings Randolph (D) 1958- .

Wisconsin

Gaylord Nelson (D) 1963- .
William Proxmire (D) 1957- .

Wyoming

Gale W. McGee (D) 1959-77.
Clifford P. Hansen (R) 1967- .
Milward L. Simpson (R) 1962-67

HOUSE OF REPRESENTATIVES

Alabama

George W. Andrews (D) 1944-71
Tom Bevill (D) 1967- .
Carl Elliot (D) 1949-65
George M. Grant (D) 1938-65
George Huddleston, Jr. (D) 1955-65
Robert E. Jones (D) 1947- .
William Nichols (D) 1967- .
Albert Rains (D) 1945-65
Kenneth A. Roberts (D) 1951-65
Armistead I. Selden, Jr. (D) 1953-69
Glenn Andrews (R) 1965-67
John H. Buchanan (R) 1965- .
William L. Dickinson (R) 1965- .
Jack Edwards (R) 1965- .
James D. Martin (R) 1965-67

Alaska

Ralph J. Rivers (D) 1959-67
Howard W. Pollack (R) 1967-71

Arizona

George F. Senner, Jr. (D) 1963-67
Morris K. Udall (D) 1961- .

John J. Rhodes (R) 1953- .
Sam Steiger (R) 1967- .

Arkansas

E. C. Gathings (D) 1939-69
Oren Harris (D) 1941-66
Wilbur D. Mills (D) 1939- .
David Pryor (D) 1966-73
James W. Trimble (D) 1945-67
John Paul Hammerschmidt (R) 1967- .

California

George E. Brown, Jr. (D) 1963-71; 1973- .
Everett G. Burkhalter (D) 1963-65
Philip Burton (D) 1964- .
Ronald B. Cameron (D) 1963-67
Jeffery Cohelan (D) 1959-71
James C. Corman (D) 1961- .
Ken W. Dyal (D) 1965-67
Don Edwards (D) 1963- .
Harlan Hagen (D) 1953-67
Richard T. Hanna (D) 1963-75
Augustus F. Hawkins (D) 1963- .
Chet Holifield (D) 1943-75
Harold T. Johnson (D) 1959- .
Cecil R. King (D) 1942-69
Robert L. Lettett (D) 1963- .
John J. McFall (D) 1957- .
George P. Miller (D) 1945-73
John E. Moss (D) 1953- .
Thomas M. Rees (D) 1966- .
James Roosevelt (D) 1955-65
Edward R. Roybal (D) 1963- .
Harry R. Sheppard (D) 1937-65
B. J. Sisk (D) 1955- .
John V. Tunney (D) 1965-71
Lionel Van Deerlin (D) 1963- .
Jerome R. Waldie (D) 1966-75
Charles H. Wilson (D) 1963- .
John F. Baldwin (R) 1955-66
Alphonso Bell (R) 1961- .
Don H. Clausen (R) 1963- .
Del Clawson (R) 1963- .
Charles S. Gubser (R) 1953-75
Craig Hosmer (R) 1953-75
Glenard P. Lipscomb (R) 1953-70
Paul N. McCloskey, Jr. (R) 1967- .
William S. Mailliard (R) 1953-74
Pat M. Martin (R) 1963-65
Robert B. Mathias (R) 1967-75
Jerry L. Pettis (R) 1967-75
Edwin Reinecke (R) 1965-69
H. Allen Smith (R) 1957-73
Burt L. Talcott (R) 1963- .
Charles M. Teague (R) 1955-74
James B. Utt (R) 1953-70
Charles E. Wiggins (R) 1967- .
Bob Wilson (R) 1953- .
J. Arthur Younger (R) 1953-67

Colorado

Wayne N. Aspinall (D) 1949-73
Frank E. Evans (D) 1965- .
Roy H. McVicker (D) 1965-67
Byron G. Rogers (D) 1951-71
Donald G. Brotzman (R) 1963-65
J. Edgar Chenoweth (R) 1941-49; 1951-65

Connecticut

Emilio Q. Daddario (D) 1959-71
Robert N. Giaimo (D) 1959- .
Bernard F. Grabowski (D) 1963-67
Donald J. Irwin (D) 1959-61; 1965-69
John S. Monagan (D) 1959-73
William L. St. Onge (D) 1963-70
Thomas J. Meskill (R) 1967-71
Abner W. Sibal (R) 1961-65

Delaware

Harris B. McDowell, Jr. (D) 1955-57; 1959-57
William V. Roth, Jr. (R) 1967-71

Florida

Charles E. Bennett (D) 1949- .
Dante B. Fascell (D) 1955- .
Don Fugua (D) 1963- .
Sam M. Gibbons (D) 1963- .
James A. Haley (D) 1953- .
A. Sydney Herlong, Jr. (D) 1949-69
D. R. Matthews (D) 1953-67
Claude Pepper (D) 1963- .
Paul G. Rogers (D) 1955- .
Robert L. F. Sikes (D) 1941-44; 1945-.
J. Herbert Burke (R) 1967- .
William C. Cramer (R) 1955-71
Edward J. Gurney (R) 1963-69

Georgia

Jack Brinkley (D) 1967- .
John W. Davis (D) 1961-65
John J. Flynt, Jr. (D) 1954- .
E. L. Forrester (D) 1951-65
G. Elliot Hagan (D) 1961-73
Phil M. Landrum (D) 1953- .
James A. Mackay (D) 1965-67
Maston E. O'Neal, Jr. (D) 1965-71

J. L. Pilcher (D) 1953-65
Robert G. Stephens, Jr. (D) 1961- .
W. S. Stuckey, Jr. (D) 1967- .
J. Russel Tuten (D) 1963-67
Carl Vinson (D) 1914-65
Charles L. Weltner (D) 1963-67
Benjamin B. Blackburn (R) 1967-75
Howard H. Callaway (R) 1965-67
Fletcher Thompson (R) 1967-73

Hawaii

Thomas P. Gill (D) 1963-65
Spark M. Matsunaga (D) 1963- .
Patsy T. Mink (D) 1965- .

Idaho

Ralph R. Harding (D) 1961-65
Compton J. White, Jr. (D) 1963-67
George V. Hansen (R) 1965-69; 1975- .
James A. McClure (R) 1967-73

Illinois

Frank Annunzio (D) 1965- .
William L. Dawson (D) 1943-70
Edward R. Finnegan (D) 1961-65
Kenneth J. Gray (D) 1955-75
John C. Kluczynski (D) 1951-75
Roland V. Libonati (D) 1957-65
William T. Murphy (D) 1959-71
Barratt O'Hara (D) 1949-51; 1953-69
Melvin Price (D) 1945- .
Roman C. Pucinski (D) 1959-73
Daniel J. Ronan (D) 1965-69
Dan Rostenkowski (D) 1959- .
Gale Schisler (D) 1965-67
George E. Shipley (D) 1959- .
Sidney R. Yates (D) 1949-63; 1965- .
John B. Anderson (R) 1961- .
Leslie C. Arends (R) 1935-75
Harold R. Collier (R) 1957-75
Edward J. Derwinski (R) 1959- .
John N. Erlenborn (R) 1965- .
Paul Findley (R) 1961- .
Elmer J. Hoffman (R) 1959-65
Robert McClory (R) 1963- .
Robert T. McLoskey (R) 1963-65
Robert H. Michel (R) 1957- .
Tom Railsback (R) 1967- .
Charlotte T. Reid (R) 1963-71
Donald Rumsfeld (R) 1963-69
William L. Springer (R) 1951-73

Indiana

John Brademas (D) 1959- .
Winfield K. Denton (D) 1949-53; 1955-67
Lee H. Hamilton (D) 1965- .
Andrew Jacobs, Jr. (D) 1965-73; 1975- .
Ray J. Madden (D) 1943-77
J. Edward Roush (D) 1959-69; 1971-77
E. Ross Adair (R) 1951-71
William G. Bray (R) 1951-75
Donald C. Bruce (R) 1961-65
Charles A. Halleck (R) 1935-69
Ralph Harvey (R) 1947-59; 1961-66
John T. Myers (R) 1967- .
Richard L. Roudebush (R) 1961-71
Earl Wilson (R) 1941-59; 1961-65
Roger H. Zion (R) 1967-75

Iowa

Bert Bandstra (D) 1965-67
John C. Culver (D) 1965-75
Stanley L. Greigg (D) 1965-67
John R. Hansen (D) 1965-67
John R. Schmidhauser (D) 1965-67
Neal Smith (D) 1959- .
James E. Bromwell (R) 1961-65
H. R. Gross (R) 1949-75
Charles B. Hoeven (R) 1943-65
Ben F. Jensen (R) 1939-65
John H. Kyl (R) 1959-65; 1967-73
Wiley Mayne (R) 1967-75
William J. Scherle (R) 1967-75
Fred Schwengel (R) 1955-65; 1967-73

Kansas

William H. Avery (R) 1955-65
Robert Dole (R) 1961-69
Robert F. Ellsworth (R) 1961-67
Chester L. Mize (R) 1965-71
Garner E. Shriver (R) 1961- .
Joe Skubitz (R) 1963- .
Larry Winn, Jr. (R) 1967- .

Kentucky

Frank Chelf (D) 1945-67
Charles P. Farnsley (D) 1965-67
William H. Natcher (D) 1953- .
Carl D. Perkins (D) 1949- .
Frank A. Stubblefield (D) 1959-75
John C. Watts (D) 1951-71
Tim L. Carter (R) 1965- .
William O. Cowger (R) 1967-71
Eugene Siler (R) 1955-65
M. G. Snyder (R) 1963-65; 1967- .

Louisiana

Hale Boggs (D) 1941-43; 1947-73
Edwin W. Edwards (D) 1965-72
F. Edward Hebert (D) 1941- .
Gillis W. Long (D) 1963-65; 1973- .
Speedy O. Long (D) 1965-73
James H. Morrison (D) 1943-67
Otto E. Passman (D) 1947- .
John R. Rarick (D) 1967-75
T. Ashton Thompson (D) 1953-65
Joe D. Waggoner, Jr. (D) 1961- .
Edwin E. Willis (D) 1949-69

Maine

William D. Hathaway (D) 1965-73
Peter N. Kyros (D) 1967-75
Clifford D. McIntire (R) 1952-65
Stanley R. Tupper (R) 1961-67

Maryland

George H. Fallon (D) 1945-71
Samuel N. Friedel (D) 1953-71
Edward A. Garmatz (D) 1947-73
Richard E. Lankford (D) 1955-65
Clarence D. Long (D) 1963- .
Harvey G. Machen (D) 1965-69
Carlton R. Sickles (D) 1963-67
Gilbert Gude (R) 1967- .
Charles McC. Mathias, Jr. (R) 1961-69
Rogers C. B. Morton (R) 1963-71

Massachusetts

Edward P. Boland (D) 1953- .
James A. Burke (D) 1959- .
Harold D. Donahue (D) 1947-75
John W. McCormack (D) 1928-71
Torbert H. MacDonald (D) 1955- .
Thomas P. O'Neill, Jr. (D) 1953- .
Philip J. Philbin (D) 1943-71
William H. Bates (R) 1950-69
Silvio O. Conte (R) 1959- .
Margaret M. Heckler (R) 1967- .
Hastings Keith (R) 1959-73
Joseph W. Martin, Jr. (R) 1925-67
F. Bradford Morse (R) 1961-72

Michigan

Raymond F. Clevenger (D) 1965-67
John Conyers, Jr. (D) 1965- .
Charles C. Diggs, Jr. (D) 1955- .
John D. Dingell, Jr. (D) 1955- .
Billie S. Farnum (D) 1965-67
William D. Ford (D) 1965- .
Martha W. Griffiths (D) 1955-75
John Lesinski, Jr. (D) 1951-65
John C. Mackie (D) 1965-67
Lucien N. Nedzi (D) 1961- .
James G. O'Hara (D) 1959-77.
Harold M. Ryan (D) 1962-65
Neil Staebler (D) 1963-65
Paul H. Todd, Jr. (D) 1965-67
Weston E. Vivian (D) 1965-67
William S. Broomfield (R) 1957- .
Garry E. Brown (R) 1967- .
Elford A. Cederberg (R) 1953- .
Charles E. Chamberlain (R) 1957-75
Marvin L. Esch (R) 1967- .
Gerald R. Ford (R) 1949-73
Robert P. Griffin (R) 1957-66
James Harvey (R) 1961-74
Edward Hutchinson (R) 1963- .
August E. Johansen (R) 1955-65
Victor A. Knox (R) 1953-65
Jack McDonald (R) 1969-73
George Meader (R) 1951-65
Donald W. Riegle, Jr. (R) 1967-73; (D) 1973- .
Philip E. Ruppe (R) 1967- .
Guy Vander Jagt (R) 1966- .

Minnesota

John A. Blatnik (D) 1947-75
Donald M. Fraser (D) 1963- .
Joseph E. Karth (D) 1959-77.
Alec G. Olson (D) 1963-67
Odin Langen (R) 1959-71
Clark MacGregor (R) 1961-71
Ancher Nelson (R) 1959-75
Albert H. Quie (R) 1958- .
John M. Zwach (R) 1967-75

Mississippi

Thomas G. Abernethy (D) 1943-73
William M. Colmer (D) 1933-73
Charles H. Griffin (D) 1968-73
G. V. Montgomery (D) 1967- .
Jamie L. Whitten (D) 1941- .
John B. Williams (D) 1947-68
Arthur Winstead (D) 1943-65
Prentiss Walker (R) 1965-67

Missouri

Richard Bolling (D) 1949- .
W. R. Hull, Jr. (D) 1955-73

William L. Hungate (D) 1965- .
Richard H. Ichord (D) 1961- .
Paul C. Jones (D) 1948-69.
Frank M. Karsten (D) 1947-69.
William J. Randall (D) 1959-77.
Leonor K. Sullivan (D) 1953-77.
Thomas B. Curtis (R) 1951-69.
Durward G. Hall (R) 1961-73.

Montana

Arnold Olson (D) 1961-71
James F. Battin (R) 1961-69

Nebraska

Clair Callan (D) 1965-67
Ralph J. Beermann (R) 1961-65
Glenn Cunningham (R) 1957-71
Robert V. Denney (R) 1967-71
Dave Martin (R) 1961-75

Nevada

Walter S. Baring (D) 1949-53; 1957-73

New Hampshire

J. Oliva Huot (D) 1965-67
James C. Cleveland (R) 1963- .
Louis C. Wyman (R) 1963-65; 1967-75

New Jersey

Dominick V. Daniels (D) 1959-77.
Cornelius E. Gallagher (D) 1959-73
Henry Helstoski (D) 1965- .
James J. Howard (D) 1965- .
Charles S. Joelson (D) 1961-69
Paul J. Krebs (D) 1965-67
Thomas C. McGrath (D) 1965-67
Joseph G. Minish (D) 1963- .
Edward J. Patten (D) 1963- .
Peter W. Rodino, Jr. (D) 1949- .
Frank Thompson, Jr. (D) 1955- .
James C. Auchincloss (R) 1943-65
William T. Cahill (R) 1959-70
Florence P. Dwyer (R) 1957-73
Peter H. B. Frelinghuysen (R) 1953-75
Milton W. Glenn (R) 1957-65
John E. Hunt (R) 1967-75
Frank C. Osmers, Jr. (R) 1939-43; 1951-65
Charles W. Sandman, Jr. (R) 1967-75
George M. Wallhauser (R) 1959-65
William B. Widnall (R) 1950-75

New Mexico

Joseph M. Montoya (D) 1957-64
Thomas G. Morris (D) 1959-69
E. S. Johnny Walker (D) 1965-69

New York

Joseph P. Addabbo (D) 1961- .
Jonathan B. Bingham (D) 1965- .
Frank J. Brasco (D) 1967-75
Charles A. Buckley (D) 1935-65
Hugh L. Carey (D) 1961-75
Emanuel Celler (D) 1923-73
James J. Delaney (D) 1945-47; 1949- .
John G. Dow (D) 1965-69; 1971-73
Thaddeus J. Dulski (D) 1959-75
Leonard Farbstein (D) 1957-71
Jacob H. Gilbert (D) 1960-71
James M. Hanley (D) 1965- .
James C. Healey (D) 1956-65
Edna F. Kelly (D) 1949-69
Eugene J. Keogh (D) 1937-67
Richard D. McCarthy (D) 1965-71
Abraham J. Multer (D) 1947-67
John M. Murphy (D) 1963- .
Leo W. O'Brien (D) 1952-67
Richard L. Ottinger (D) 1965-71; 1975- .
Otis G. Pike (D) 1961- .
Bertram L. Podell (D) 1968-75
Adam C. Powell (D) 1945-67; 1969-71
Joseph Y. Resnick (D) 1965-69
John J. Rooney (D) 1944-75
Benjamin S. Rosenthal (D) 1962- .
William F. Ryan (D) 1961-72
James H. Scheuer (D) 1965-73; 1975- .
Samuel S. Stratton (D) 1959- .
Herbert Tenzer (D) 1965-69
Lester L. Wolff (D) 1965- .
Robert R. Barry (R) 1959-65
Frank J. Becker (R) 1953-65
Daniel E. Button (R) 1967-71
Barber B. Conable, Jr. (R) 1965- .
Steven B. Derounian (R) 1953-65
Paul A. Fino (R) 1953-69
Charles E. Goodell (R) 1959-68
James R. Grover, Jr. (R) 1963-75
Seymour Halpern (R) 1959-73
Frank J. Horton (R) 1963- .
Clarence E. Kilburn (R) 1940-65
Carleton J. King (R) 1961-75
Theodore R. Kupferman (R) 1966-69
John V. Lindsay (R) 1959-65
Robert C. McEwen (R) 1965- .
William E. Miller (R) 1951-65
Harold C. Ostertag (R) 1951-65
John R. Pillion (R) 1953-65

Alexander Pirnie (R) 1959-73
Ogden R. Reid (R) 1963-72; (D) 1972-75
R. Walter Riehlman (R) 1947-65
Howard W. Robison (R) 1958-75
Katherine St. George (R) 1947-65
Henry P. Smith III (R) 1965-75
J. Ernest Wharton (R) 1951-65
John W. Wydler (R) 1963- .

North Carolina

Herbert C. Bonner (D) 1940-65
Harold D. Cooley (D) 1934-67
L. H. Fountain (D) 1953- .
Nick Galifianakis (D) 1967-73
David N. Henderson (D) 1961- .
Walter B. Jones (D) 1966- .
Horace R. Kornegay (D) 1961-69
Alton Lennon (D) 1957-73
Ralph J. Scott (D) 1957-67
Roy A. Taylor (D) 1960- .
Basil L. Whitener (D) 1957-69
James T. Broyhill (R) 1963- .
James C. Gardner (R) 1967-69
Charles R. Jonas (R) 1953-73

North Dakota

Rolland Redlin (D) 1965-67
Mark Andrews (R) 1963- .
Thomas S. Kleppe (R) 1967-71
Don L. Short (R) 1959-65

Ohio

Thomas L. Ashley (D) 1955- .
Michael A. Feighan (D) 1943-71
John J. Gilligan (D) 1965-67
Wayne L. Hays (D) 1949-76.
Michael J. Kirwan (D) 1937-71
Rodney M. Love (D) 1965-67
Walter H. Moeller (D) 1959-63; 1965-67
Robert T. Secrest (D) 1933-42; 1949-54; 1963-66
Robert E. Sweeney (D) 1965-67
Charles A. Vanik (D) 1955- .
Homer E. Abele (R) 1963-65
John M. Ashbrook (R) 1961- .
William H. Ayres (R) 1951-71
Jackson E. Betts (R) 1951-73
Frances P. Bolton (R) 1940-69
Oliver P. Bolton (R) 1953-57; 1963-65
Frank T. Bow (R) 1951-72
Clarence J. Brown (R) 1939-65
Clarence J. Brown, Jr. (R) 1966- .
Donald D. Clancy (R) 1961- .
Samuel L. Devine (R) 1959- .
William H. Harsha (R) 1961- .
Delbert L. Latta (R) 1959- .
Donald E. Lukens (R) 1967-71
William M. McCulloch (R) 1947-73
Clarence E. Miller (R) 1967- .
William E. Minshall (R) 1955-75
Charles A. Mosher (R) 1961- .
Carl W. Rich (R) 1963-65
Paul F. Schenck (R) 1951-65
J. William Stanton (R) 1965- .
Robert Taft, Jr. (R) 1963-65; 1967-71
Charles W. Whalen, Jr. (R) 1967- .
Chalmers P. Wylie (R) 1967- .

Oklahoma

Carl Albert (D) 1947-77.
Ed Edmondson (D) 1953-73
John Jarman (D) 1951-75; (R) 1975-77.
Jed Johnson, Jr. (D) 1965-67
Tom Steed (D) 1949- .
Victor Wickersham (D) 1941-47; 1949-57; 1961-65
Page Belcher (R) 1951-73
James V. Smith (R) 1967-69

Oregon

Robert B. Duncan (D) 1963-67; 1975- .
Edith Green (D) 1965-75
Al Ullman (D) 1957- .
John R. Dellenback (R) 1967-75
Wendell Wyatt (R) 1965-75

Pennsylvania

William A. Barrett (D) 1945-47; 1949-76.
James A. Byrne (D) 1953-73
Frank M. Clark (D) 1955-75
N. Neiman Craley, Jr. (D) 1965-67
John H. Dent (D) 1958- .
Joshua Eilberg (D) 1967- .
Daniel J. Flood (D) 1945-47; 1949-53; 1955- .
William J. Green III (D) 1964- .
Elmer J. Holland (D) 1942-43; 1956-68
William S. Moorhead (D) 1959- .
Thomas E. Morgan (D) 1945-77.
Robert N. C. Nix (D) 1958- .
George M. Rhodes (D) 1949-69
Fred B. Rooney (D) 1963- .
Herman Toll (D) 1959-67
Joseph P. Vigorito (D) 1965- .
Edward G. Buster, Jr. (R) 1967- .
Robert J. Corbett (R) 1939-41; 1945-71
Willard S. Curtin (R) 1957-67
Paul B. Dague (R) 1947-67

Edwin D. Eshleman (R) 1967- .
James G. Fulton (R) 1945-71
George A. Goodling (R) 1961-65; 1967- .
Albert W. Johnson (R) 1963- .
John C. Kunkel (R) 1939-41; 1961-66
Joseph M. McDade (R) 1963- .
William H. Milliken, Jr. (R) 1959-65
John P. Saylor (R) 1949-73
Herman T. Schneebeli (R) 1960-77.
Richard S. Schweiker (R) 1961-69
G. Robert Watkins (R) 1965-70
James D. Weaver (R) 1963-65
J. Irving Whalley (R) 1961-73
Lawrence G. Williams (R) 1967-75

Rhode Island

John E. Fogarty (D) 1941-44; 1945-67.
Fernand J. St. Germain (D) 1961- .
Robert O. Tiernan (D) 1967-75.

South Carolina

Robert T. Ashmore (D) 1953-69
W. J. Bryan Dorn (D) 1947-49; 1951-75
Tom S. Gettys (D) 1965-75
John L. McMillan (D) 1939-73
L. Mendel Rivers (D) 1941-70
Albert W. Watson (D) 1963-65; (R) 1965-71

South Dakota

E. Y. Berry (R) 1951-71
Ben Reifel (R) 1961-71

Tennessee

William R. Anderson (D) 1965-73
Ross Bass (D) 1955-65
Ray Blanton (D) 1967-73
Clifford Davis (D) 1940-65
Robert A. Everett (D) 1958-69
Joe L. Evans (D) 1947-77.
Richard Fulton (D) 1963-75
George W. Grider (D) 1965-67
Tom Murray (D) 1943-67.
Irene B. Baker (R) 1964-65
William E. Brock III (R) 1963-71
John J. Duncan (R) 1965- .
Dan Kuykendall (R) 1967-75
James H. Quillen (R) 1963- .

Texas

Lindley Beckworth (D) 1939-53; 1957-67
Jack Brooks (D) 1953- .
Omar Burleson (D) 1947- .
Earle Cabell (D) 1965-73
Bob Casey (D) 1959- .
Eligio de la Garza (D) 1965- .
John Dowdy (D) 1952-73
Bob Eckhardt (D) 1967- .
O. C. Fisher (D) 1943-75
Henry B. Gonzalez (D) 1961- .
Abraham Kazen, Jr. (D) 1967- .
Joe M. Kilgore (D) 1955-65
George H. Mahon (D) 1935- .
Wright Patman (D) 1929- .
J. J. Pickle (D) 1963- .
W. R. Poage (D) 1937- .
Joe R. Pool (D) 1963-68
Graham Purcell (D) 1962-73
Ray Roberts (D) 1962- .
Walter Rogers (D) 1951-67
Olin E. Teague (D) 1946- .
Albert Thomas (D) 1937-66
Lera M. Thomas (D) 1966-67
Clark W. Thompson (D) 1933-35; 1947-66
Richard C. White (D) 1965- .
Jim Wright (D) 1955- .
John Young (D) 1957- .
Bruce Alger (R) 1955-65
George Bush (R) 1967-71
James M. Collins (R) 1968- .
Ed Foreman (R) 1963-65; 1969-71 (New Mexico)
Robert D. Price (R) 1967-75

Utah

David S. King (D) 1959-63; 1965-67
Laurence J. Burton (R) 1963-71
Sherman P. Lloyd (R) 1963-65; 1967-73

Vermont

Robert T. Stafford (R) 1961-71

Virginia

Walkins M. Abbitt (D) 1948-73
Thomas N. Downing (D) 1959-77.
J. Vaughan Gary (D) 1945-65.
Porter Hardy, (D) 1947-69.
W. Pat Jennings (D) 1955-67
John O. Marsh, Jr. (D) 1963-71
David E. Satterfield III (D) 1965- .
Howard W. Smith (D) 1931-67
William M. Tuck (D) 1953-69
Joel T. Broyhill (R) 1953-75
Richard H. Poff (R) 1953-72
William L. Scott (R) 1967-73
William C. Wampler (R) 1953-55; 1967- .

Washington

Brock Adams (D) 1965- .
Thomas S. Foley (D) 1965- .
Julia B. Hansen (D) 1960-75
Floyd V. Hicks (D) 1965- .
Lloyd Meeds (D) 1965- .
Walt Horan (R) 1943-65
Catherine May (R) 1959-71
Thomas M. Pelly (R) 1953-73
K. William Stinson (R) 1963-65
Thor C. Tollefson (R) 1947-65
Jack Westland (R) 1953-65

West Virginia

Ken Hechler (D) 1959-77.
James Kee (D) 1965-73.
M. Elizabeth Kei (D) 1957-65.
John M. Slack, Jr. (D) 1959-
Harley O. Staggers (D) 1949-
Arch A. Moore, Jr. (R) 1957-69

Wisconsin

Lester R. Johnson (D) 1953-65
Robert W. Kastenmeier (D) 1959- .
John A. Race (D) 1965-67
Henry S. Reuss (D) 1955- .
Lynn E. Stalbaum (D) 1965-67
Clement J. Zablocki (D) 1949- .
John W. Byrnes (R) 1945-73
Glenn R. Davis (R) 1947-57; 1965-75
Melvin R. Laird (R) 1953-69
Alvin E. O'Konski (R) 1943-73
Henry C. Schadeberg (R) 1961-65; 1967-71
William A. Steiger (R) 1967- .
Vernon W. Thomson (R) 1961-75
William K. Van Pelt (R) 1951-65

Wyoming

Teno Roncalip (D) 1965-67; 1971- .
William H. Harrison (R) 1951-55; 1961-65; 1967-69

SUPREME COURT

Earl Warren, Chief Justice 1953-69
Hugo L. Black 1937-71
William J. Brennan 1956.
Tom C. Clark 1949-67
William O. Douglas 1939-75
Abe Fortas 1965-69
Arthur J. Goldberg 1962-65
John Marshall Harlan 1955-71
Potter Stewart 1958- .
Byron R. White 1962- .

EXECUTIVE DEPARTMENTS

Department of Agriculture

Secretary of Agriculture
Orville L. Freeman, 1961-69

Undersecretary
Charles S. Murphy, 1961-65
John A. Schnittker, 1965-69

Deputy Undersecretary
James L. Sundquist, 1963-65

Assistant Secretary—Rural Development and Conservation
John A. Baker, 1962-69

Assistant Secretary—Marketing and Consumer Services
George L. Mehren, 1963-68
Ted J. Davis, 1968-69

Assistant Secretary—International Affairs
Roland R. Renne, 1963-65
Dorothy H. Jacobson, 1964-69

Assistant Secretary for Department Admin-

istration
Joseph M. Robertson, 1961-71

Department of Commerce

Secretary of Commerce
Luther H. Hodges, 1961-64
John T. Connor, 1965-67
Alexander B. Trowbridge, 1967-68
Howard J. Samuels, (acting) 1968
Cyrus R. Smith, 1968-69

Undersecretary
Franklin D. Roosevelt, Jr., 1963-65
LeRoy Collins, 1965-66
J. Herbert Holloman, (acting) 1967
Howard J. Samuels, 1967-68
Joseph W. Bartlett, 1968-69

Undersecretary for Transportation
Clarence D. Martin, Jr., 1961-65
Alan S. Boyd, 1965-67
Reorganized under Department of Transportation, 1966

Deputy Undersecretary for Transportation
Frank L. Barton, 1961-64
E. Grosvenor Plowman, 1963-64
Lowell K. Bridwell, 1964-67
Reorganized under Department of Transportation, 1966

Assistant Secretary for Administration
Herbert W. Klotz, 1962-65
David R. Baldwin, 1965-69

Assistant Secretary for Domestic and International Business
Jack N. Behrman, 1962-64
Thomas G. Wyman, 1964-65
Alexander B. Trowbridge, 1965-67
Lawrence C. McQuade, 1967-69

Assistant Secretary for Science and Technology
J. Herbert Holloman, 1962-67
John F. Kincaid, 1967-69

Assistant Secretary for Economic Affairs
Richard H. Holton, 1963-65
Andrew F. Brimmer, 1965-66
William H. Shaw, 1966-68
William H. Chartener, 1968-70

Assistant Secretary for Economic Development
Eugene P. Foley, 1965-66
Ross D. Davis, 1966-69

Defense Department

Secretary of Defense
Robert S. McNamara, 1961-68
Clark M. Clifford, 1968-69

Deputy Secretary of Defense
Roswell L. Gilpatric, 1961-64
Cyrus R. Vance, 1964-67
Paul H. Nitze, 1967-69

Secretary of the Air Force
Eugene M. Zuckert, 1961-65
Harold Brown, 1965-69

Secretary of the Army
Cyrus R. Vance, 1962-64
Stephen Ailes, 1964-65
Stanley R. Resor, 1965-71

Secretary of the Navy
Paul H. Nitze, 1963-67
John T. McNaughton, 1967
Paul R. Ignatius, 1967-69

Assistant Secretary (Comptroller)
Charles J. Hitch, 1961-65
Robert N. Anthony, 1965-68
Robert C. Moot, 1968-73

Assistant Secretary (Installations and Logistics)
Thomas D. Morris, 1961-64
Paul R. Ignatius, 1965-67
Thomas D. Morris, 1967-69

Assistant Secretary (International Security Affairs)
William P. Bundy, 1963-64
John T. McNaughton, 1964-67
Paul C. Warnke, 1967-69

Assistant Secretary (Manpower)
Norman S. Paul, 1962-65
Thomas D. Morris, 1965-67
Alfred B. Fitt, 1967-69

Assistant Secretary (Public Affairs)
Arthur Sylvester, 1961-66
Phil G. Goulding, 1967-69

Assistant Secretary (Civil Defense)
Steuart L. Pittman, 1961-64

Assistant Secretary (Administration)
Solis Horwitz, 1964-69

Assistant Secretary (Systems Analysis)
Alain C. Enthoven, 1965-69

Director of Defense Research and Engineering
Harold Brown, 1961-65
John S. Foster, Jr., 1965-73

Joint Chiefs of Staff

Chairman
Gen. Maxwell D. Taylor, U.S. Army, 1962-64
Gen. Earle G. Wheeler, U.S. Army, 1964-70

Chief of Staff, U.S. Army
Gen. Earle G. Wheeler, 1962-64
Gen. Harold K. Johnson, 1964-68
Gen. William C. Westmoreland, 1968-72

Chief of Naval Operations
Adm. David L. McDonald, 1963-67
Adm. Thomas H. Moorer, 1967-70

Chief of Staff, U.S. Air Force
Gen. Curtis E. LeMay, 1961-65
Gen. John P. McConnell, 1965-69

Commandant of the Marine Corps
Gen. Wallace M. Greene, Jr., 1964-68
Gen. Leonard F. Chapman, Jr., 1968-72

Department of Health, Education and Welfare

Secretary of Health, Education and Welfare
Anthony J. Celebrezze, 1962-65
John W. Gardner, 1965-68
Wilbur J. Cohen, 1968-69

Undersecretary
Ivan A. Nestingen, 1961-65
Wilbur J. Cohen, 1965-68
James H. McCrocklin, 1968-69

Assistant Secretary
James M. Quigley, 1961-66

Administrative Assistant Secretary
Rufus E. Miles, Jr., 1961-65
Donald F. Simpson, 1966-69

Assistant Secretary (Education)
Francis Keppel, 1965-66
Paul A. Miller, 1966-68
Lynn M. Bartlett, 1968-69

Assistant Secretary (Health and Scientific Affairs)
Philip R. Lee, 1965-69

Assistant Secretary (Individual and Family Service)
Lisle C. Carter, Jr., 1966-68

Assistant Secretary (Comptroller)
James F. Kelly, 1966-70

Assistant Secretary (Program Coordination)
William Gorham, 1965-68
Reorganized as Planning and Evaluation 1968

Assistant Secretary (Planning and Education)
Alice M. Rivlin, 1968-69

Assistant Secretary (Community and Field Services)
Edward C. Sylvester, Jr., 1968-69

Department of Housing and Urban Development*

Secretary
Robert C. Weaver, 1966-68
Robert C. Wood, 1969.

Undersecretary
Robert C. Wood, 1966-68

Deputy Undersecretary for Policy Analysis and Program Evaluation
William B. Ross, 1966-69

Assistant Secretary for Mortgage Credit and Federal Housing Commissioner
Philip N. Brownstein, 1966-69

Assistant Secretary for Metropolitan Development
Charles M. Haar, 1966-69

Assistant Secretary for Renewal and Housing Assistance
Don Hummel, 1966-69

Assistant Secretary for Demonstrations and Intergovernmental Relations
H. Ralph Taylor, 1966-69

Assistant Secretary for Administration
Dwight A. Ink, 1966-68

Assistant Secretary for Equal Opportunity
Walter B. Lewis, 1968-69

*Established by law, September 9, 1965

Department of the Interior

Secretary of the Interior
Stewart L. Udall, 1961-69

Undersecretary
James K. Carr, 1961-64
John A. Carver, Jr., 1965-66
Charles F. Luce, 1966-67
David S. Black, 1967-69

Assistant Secretary—Fish and Wildlife
Frank P. Briggs, 1961-65
Reorganized as Fish and Wildlife and Parks, 1965
Stanley A. Cain, 1965-68
Clarence F. Pautzke, 1968-69

Assistant Secretary—Mineral Resources
John M. Kelly, 1961-65
J. Cordell Moore, 1965-69

Assistant Secretary—Public Land Management
John A. Carver, Jr., 1961-64
Harry R. Anderson, 1965-69

Assistant Secretary—Water and Power Development
Kenneth Holum, 1961-69

Assistant Secretary—Water Pollution Control
Frank C. DiLuzio, 1966-67
Max N. Edwards, 1968-69

Administrative Assistant Secretary
D. Otis Beasly, 1952-65
Robert C. McConnell, 1967-69

Department of Justice

Attorney General
Robert F. Kennedy, 1961-64
Nicholas deB. Katzenbach, 1965-66
Ramsey Clark, 1967-69

Deputy Attorney General
Nicholas deB. Katzenbach, 1962-64
Ramsey Clark, 1965-67
Warren M. Christopher, 1967-69

Solicitor General
Archibald Cox, 1961-65
Thurgood Marshall, 1965-67
Erwin N. Griswold, 1967-73

Assistant Attorney General/Antitrust Division
William H. Orrick, Jr., 1963-65
Donald F. Turner, 1965-68
Edwin M. Zimmerman, 1968-69

Assistant Attorney General/Civil Division
John W. Douglas, 1963-66
Harold B. Sanders, Jr., 1966-67
Carl Eardley, (acting) 1967
Edwin L. Weisl, 1967-69

Assistant Attorney General/Criminal Division
Herbert J. Miller, Jr., 1961-65
Fred M. Vinson, Jr., 1965-69

Assistant Attorney General/Internal Security Division
J. Walter Yeagley, 1959-70

Assistant Attorney General/Lands Division
Ramsey Clark, 1961-65
Edwin L. Weisl, 1965-67
Clyde O. Martz, 1967-69

Assistant Attorney General/Tax Division
Louis F. Oberdorfer, 1961-65
Mitchell Rogovin, 1966-69

Assistant Attorney General/Civil Rights Division
Burke Marshall, 1961-65
John Doar, 1965-67
Stephen J. Pollak, 1967-69

Assistant Attorney General/Office of Legal Counsel
Norbert A. Schlei, 1962-66
Frank Wozencraft, 1966-69

Assistant Attorney General/Administration
Ernest C. Friesen, Jr., 1966-67
Leo Pellerzi, 1968-73

Department of Labor

Secretary of Labor
W. Willard Wirtz, 1962-69

Undersecretary
John F. Henning, 1962-67
James J. Reynolds, 1967-68

Deputy Undersecretary
Millard Cass, 1955-71

Assistant Secretary for Labor-Management Relations
James J. Reynolds, 1961-67
Thomas R. Donahue, 1967-69

Assistant Secretary for International Labor Affairs
George L. P. Weaver, 1961-69

Assistant Secretary for Labor Standards
Esther Peterson, 1961-69

Assistant Secretary for Policy Planning and Research
Daniel P. Moynihan, 1963-65

Assistant Secretary for Manpower
Stanley H. Ruttenberg, 1966-69

Post Office Department

Post Master General
John A. Gronouski, 1963-65
Lawrence F. O'Brien, 1965-68
W. Marvin Watson, 1968-69

Deputy Post Master General
Sidney W. Bishop, 1963-64
Frederick C. Belen, 1964-69

Assistant Post Master General/Bureau of Operations
Frederick C. Belen, 1961-64
William M. McMillan, 1964-69

Assistant Post Master General/Bureau of Transportation
William J. Hartigan, 1963-68
Frederick E. Batrus, 1968-69

Assistant Post Master General/Bureau of Finance
Ralph W. Nicholson, 1961-69

Assistant Post Master General/Bureau of Facilities
Amos J. Coffman, (acting) 1963-64
Tyler Abell, 1964-67
John L. O'Marra, 1967-69

Assistant Post Master General/Bureau of Personnel
Richard J. Murphy, 1961-69

Assistant Post Master General/Research and Engineering
Leo S. Packer, 1966-69

Assistant Post Master General/General Counsel
Timothy J. May, 1966-69

State Department

Secretary of State
Dean Rusk, 1961-69

Undersecretary
George W. Ball, 1961-66
Nicholas deB. Katzenbach, 1966-69

Undersecretary for Economic Affairs
Thomas C. Mann, 1965-66

Undersecretary for Political Affairs
W. Averell Harriman, 1963-65
Eugene V. Rostow, 1966-69

Deputy Undersecretary for Administration
William J. Crockett, 1963-67
Idar Rimestad, 1967-69

Deputy Undersecretary for Political Affairs
U. Alexis Johnson, 1961-64
Llewellyn E. Thompson (acting), 1964-65
U. Alexis Johnson, 1965-66
Foy D. Kohler, 1966-67
Charles E. Bohlen, 1967-69

Assistant Secretary for Public Affairs
Robert J. Manning, 1962-64
James L. Greenfield, 1964-66
Dixon Donnelley, 1966-69

Assistant Secretary for Congressional Relations
Frederick G. Dutton, 1961-64
Douglas MacArthur II, 1965-67
William B. Macomber, Jr., 1967-69

Assistant Secretary for Inter-American Affairs
Thomas C. Mann, 1963-65
Jack H. Vaughn, 1965-66
Lincoln Gordon, 1966-67
Covey T. Oliver, 1967-69

Assistant Secretary for European Affairs
William R. Tyler, 1962-65
John M. Leddy, 1965-69

Assistant Secretary for Far Eastern Affairs
Roger Hilsman, Jr., 1963-64
William P. Bundy, 1964-69

Assistant Secretary for Near Eastern and South Asian Affairs
Phillips Talbot, 1961-65
Raymond A. Hare, 1965-66
William J. Handley, (acting) 1966-67
Lucius D. Battle, 1967-68
Parker T. Hart, 1968-69

Assistant Secretary for African Affairs
G. Mennen Williams, 1961-66
Joseph Palmer II, 1966-69

Assistant Secretary for International Organization Affairs
Harlan Cleveland, 1961-65
Joseph J. Sisco, 1965-69

Assistant Secretary for Administration
Dwight J. Porter, 1963-65

Assistant Secretary for Educational and Cultural Affairs
Lucius D. Battle, 1962-64
Harry C. McPherson, Jr., 1964-65
Charles Frankel, 1965-67
Edward D. Re, 1968-69

Assistant Secretary for Economic Affairs
G. Griffith Johnson, Jr., 1962-65
Anthony M. Solomon, 1965-69

Department of Transportation*

Secretary
Alan S. Boyd, 1967-69

Undersecretary
Everett Hutchinson, 1967-68
John E. Robson, 1968-69

Deputy Undersecretary
Paul L. Sitton, 1967-68

Assistant Secretary for Policy Development
Maurice Cecil Mackay, Jr., 1967-69

Assistant Secretary for Public Affairs
John L. Sweeney, 1967-69

Assistant Secretary for International Affairs
Donald G. Agger, 1967-69

Assistant Secretary for Administration
Alan L. Dean, 1967-71

Assistant Secretary for Research and Technology
Frank W. Lehan, 1967-69

*Established by law, October 15, 1966

Department of the Treasury

Secretary of the Treasury
Douglas Dillon, 1961-65
Henry H. Fowler, 1965-68
Joseph W. Barr, 1968-69

Undersecretary
Henry H. Fowler, 1961-64
Joseph W. Barr, 1965-68

Undersecretary for Monetary Affairs
Robert V. Roosa, 1961-64
Frederick L. Deming, 1965-69

Deputy Undersecretary for Monetary Affairs
Paul A. Volcker, 1963-65
Peter D. Sternlight, 1965-67
Frank W. Schiff, 1968-71

Assistant Secretaries
Stanley S. Surrey, 1961-69
James A. Reed, 1961-65
John C. Bullitt, 1963-64
Robert A. Wallace, 1963-69
Merlyn N. Trued, (acting) 1964-65; 1965-66
William T. Davis, Jr., 1965-68
Winthrop Knowlton, 1966-68
Joseph M. Bowman, Jr., 1968-69
John R. Petty, 1968-72

REGULATORY COMMISSIONS AND INDEPENDENT AGENCIES

Atomic Energy Commission

Mary I. Bunting, 1964-65
Francesco Costagliola, 1968-69
Wilfrid E. Johnson, 1966-72
Samuel M. Nabrit, 1966-67
John G. Palfrey, 1962-66
James T. Ramey, 1962-73
Glenn T. Seaborg, 1961-71; Chairman, 1961-71
Gerald F. Tape, 1963-69
Robert E. Wilson, 1960-64

Civil Aeronautics Board

John G. Adams, 1965-71
Alan S. Boyd, 1959-65; Chairman, 1961-65
John H. Crooker, Jr., 1968-69; Chairman, 1968-69
Whitney Gillilland, 1959- .
Chan Gurney, 1951-65; Chairman, 1954
G. Joseph Minetti, 1956-74
Charles S. Murphy, 1965-68; Chairman, 1965-68
Robert T. Murphy, 1961- .

Federal Communications Commission

Robert T. Bartley, 1952-72
Kenneth A. Cox, 1963-70
Frederick W. Ford, 1957-65; Chairman, 1960-61
E. William Henry, 1962-66; Chairman, 1963-66
Rosel H. Hyde, 1946-69; Chairman, 1953-54, 1966-69
Nicholas Johnson, 1966- .
H. Rex Lee, 1968- .
Robert E. Lee, 1953- .
Lee Loevinger, 1963-68
James J. Wadsworth, 1965-69

Federal Power Commission

Carl E. Bagge, 1965-70
David S. Black, 1963-66
Albert B. Brooke, Jr., 1968- .
John A. Carver, Jr., 1966-72
Lawrence J. O'Connor, Jr., 1962-71
Charles R. Ross, 1961-68
Joseph C. Swidler, 1961-65; Chairman, 1961-65
Lee C. White, 1966-69; Chairman, 1966-69
Harold C. Woodward, 1962-64

Federal Reserve Board

C. Canby Balderston, 1954-66
Andrew F. Brimmer, 1966- .
J. Dewey, Daane, 1963- .
Sherman J. Maisel, 1965-72
William McC. Martin, Jr., 1951-70; Chairman, 1951-70
A. L. Mills, Jr., 1952-65

George W. Mitchell, 1961- .
James L. Robertson, 1952-73
Charles N. Shepardson, 1955-67
William W. Sherrill, 1967-71

Federal Trade Commission

Sigurd Anderson, 1955-64
Paul R. Dixon, 1961- ; Chairman, 1961- .
Philip Elman, 1961-70
A. Leon Higginbotham, 1962-64
Mary G. Jones, 1964-73
A. Everette MacIntyre, 1961-73
James M. Nicholson, 1967-69
John R. Reilly, 1964-67

Securities and Exchange Commission

Hamer H. Budge, 1964-70; Chairman, 1969-70
William L. Cary, 1961-64
Manuel F. Cohen, 1961-69; Chairman, 1964-69
Hugh F. Owens, 1964-73; Acting Chairman, 1971
Richard B. Smith, 1967-71
Francis M. Wheat, 1964-69
Jack M. Whitney II, 1961-64
Byron D. Woodside, 1960-67

GOVERNORS

Alabama

George C. Wallace (D) 1963-67
Lurleen B. Wallace (D) 1967-68
Albert P. Brewer (D) 1968-71

Alaska

William A. Egan (D) 1959-67
Walter J. Hickel (R) 1967-69

Arizona

Paul Fannin (R) 1959-65
Samuel P. Goddard, Jr. (D) 1965-67
John R. Williams (R) 1967-74

Arkansas

Orval E. Faubus (D) 1955-67
Winthrop Rockefeller (R) 1967-71

California

Edmund G. Brown (D) 1959-67
Ronald Reagan (R) 1967-75

Colorado

John A. Love (R) 1961-71

Connecticut

John N. Dempsey (D) 1961-71

Delaware

Elbert N. Carvel (D) 1961-65
Charles L. Terry, Jr. (D) 1965-69

Florida

Farris Bryant (D) 1961-65
Haydon Burns (D) 1965-67
Claude R. Kirk, Jr. (R) 1967-71

Georgia

Carl E. Sanders (D) 1963-67
Lester G. Maddox (D) 1967-71

Hawaii

John A. Burns (D) 1963-75

Idaho

Robert E. Smylie (R) 1955-67
Don Samuelson (R) 1967-71

Illinois

Otto J. Kerner (D) 1961-68
Samuel H. Shapiro (D) 1968-69

Indiana

Matthew E. Welsh (D) 1961-65
Roger D. Branigin (D) 1965-69

Iowa

Harold E. Hughes (D) 1963-69

Kansas

John Anderson, Jr. (R) 1961-65
William H. Avery (R) 1965-67
Robert B. Docking (D) 1967-75

Kentucky

Edward T. Breathitt (D) 1963-67
Louie B. Nunn (R) 1967-72

Louisiana

Jimmie H. Davis (D) 1960-64
John J. McKeithen (D) 1964-72

Maine

John H. Reed (R) 1960-67
Kenneth M. Curtis (D) 1967-75

Maryland

J. Millard Tawes (D) 1959-67
Spiro T. Agnew (R) 1967-69

Massachusetts

John A. Volpe (R) 1961-63; 1965-69
Endicott Peabody (D) 1963-65

Michigan

George W. Romney (R) 1963-69

Minnesota

Karl F. Rolvaag (D) 1963-67
Harold E. LeVander (R) 1967-71

Mississippi

Ross R. Barnett (D) 1960-64
Paul B. Johnson (D) 1964-68
John Bell Williams (D) 1968-72

Missouri

John M. Dacton (D) 1961-65
Warren E. Hearnes (D) 1965-73

Montana

Tim M. Babcock (R) 1962-69

Nebraska

Frank B. Morrison (D) 1961-67
Norbert T. Tiemann (R) 1967-71

Nevada

Grant Sawyer (D) 1959-67
Paul Laxalt (R) 1967-71

New Hampshire

John W. King (D) 1963-69

New Jersey

Richard J. Hughes (D) 1962-70

New Mexico

Jack M. Campbell (D) 1963-67
David F. Cargo (R) 1967-71

New York

Nelson A. Rockefeller (R) 1959-73

North Carolina

Terry Sanford (D) 1961-65
Daniel K. Moore (D) 1965-69

North Dakota

William L. Guy (D) 1961-73

Ohio

James A. Rhodes (R) 1963-71

Oklahoma

Henry Bellmon (R) 1963-67
Dewey F. Bartlett (R) 1967-71

Oregon

Mark O. Hatfield (R) 1959-67
Thomas McCall (R) 1967-75

Pennsylvania

William W. Scranton (R) 1963-67
Raymond P. Shafer (R) 1967-71

Rhode Island

John H. Chaffee (R) 1963-69

South Carolina

Donald S. Russell (D) 1963-65
Robert E. McNair (D) 1965-71

Tennessee

Frank G. Clement (D) 1963-67
Buford Ellington (D) 1967-71

Texas

John B. Connally, Jr. (D) 1963-69

Utah

George Dewey Clyde (R) 1957-65
Calvin L. Rampton (D) 1965- .

Vermont

Philip H. Hoff (D) 1963-69

Virginia

Albertis S. Harrison, Jr. (D) 1962-66
Mills E. Godwin, Jr. (D) 1966-70

Washington

Albert D. Rosellini (D) 1957-65
Daniel J. Evans (R) 1965- .

West Virginia

William W. Barron (D) 1961-65
Hulett C. Smith (D) 1965-69

Wisconsin

John W. Reynolds (D) 1963-65
Warren P. Knowles (R) 1965-71

Wyoming

Clifford P. Hansen (R) 1963-67
Stanley K. Hathaway (R) 1967-75

BIBLIOGRAPHY

THE JOHNSON ERA

The controversy, excitement and sense of change that characterized the 1960s have already drawn American historians to a study of the era. Several important surveys of the decade, most focusing upon the late 1960s, have already appeared. Among the most scholarly and thoughtful are Jim F. Heath, *Decade of Disillusionment: The Kennedy-Johnson Years* (Bloomington, 1975) and David Burner, Robert Marcus and Thomas West, *A Giant's Strength: America in the 1960s* (New York, 1971). William O'Neill, *Coming Apart: An Informal History of America in the 1960s* (New York, 1971) is a lively and iconoclastic book-length essay. Three good anthologies are Ronald Lora, ed., *America in the '60s, Cultural Authorities in Transition* (New York, 1974), Edward Quinn and Paul J. Dolan, eds., *The Sense of the Sixties* (New York, 1968), and Jerome H. Solnick and Elliott Currie, eds., *Crisis in American Institutions* (Boston, 1970). See also the amusing Peter Joseph, *Good Times: An Oral History of America in the Nineteen Sixties* (New York, 1973). Two recent surveys of the postwar era devote full chapters to the Johnson era. Robert A. Divine, *Since 1945: Politics and Diplomacy in Recent American History* (New York, 1975) offers a conventional interpretation of the period. Lawrence S. Wittner, *Cold War America: From Hiroshima to Watergate* (New York, 1975) provides a left-wing critique. The Facts on File *Yearbooks* contain a wealth of information indexed for easy reference.

THE PRESIDENCY AND THE ADMINISTRATION

No full-scale biography has yet been written of Lyndon Johnson. Among the better journalistic efforts are Robert Sherrill, *The Accidental President* (New York, 1967); Rowland Evans and Robert Novak, *Lyndon B. Johnson: The Exercise of Power* (New York, 1966); and Hugh Sidney, *A Very Personal Presidency* (New York, 1968). Two memoirs of Johnson's presidency by White House participants are Eric Goldman, *The Tragedy of Lyndon Johnson* (New York, 1969) and Johnson's own rather bland *The Vantage Point* (New York, 1971). George Reedy, *The Twilight of the Presidency* (New York, 1971) and Harry McPherson, *A Political Education* (New York, 1972) are insightful accounts by two of Johnson's former aides. Two brief but provocative accounts of Johnson as president are by historians William Appleman Williams, *Some Presidents: Wilson to Nixon* (New York, 1972) and T. Harry Williams, "Huey, Lyndon and Southern Radicalism," *Journal of American History* (September, 1973). Doris Kearns offers an ambitious psychohistory in her *Lyndon Johnson and the American Dream* (New York, 1976), but Arthur Schlesinger, Jr.'s, *The Imperial Presidency* (New York, 1973) provides a more satisfying account of Johnson's acquisition of great power in his office.

Electorial politics were complex and exciting in the 1960s. The election of 1964 is recounted by Theodore White, *The Making of the President, 1964* (New York, 1965) and by John Barlow Marin, "The Election of 1964" in Arthur Schlesinger, Jr., ed., *History of American Presidential Elections, 1789-1968* (New York, 1971), Vol. IV. A participant's history of the Goldwater candidacy is F. Clifton White, *Suite 3505: The Story of the Draft Goldwater Movement* (New York, 1967). See also Stephen Shadegg, *What Happened to Goldwater?* (New York, 1965). Theodore White, *The Making of the President 1968* (New York, 1969) suffers in comparison to his earlier election volumes. A more sophisticated if somewhat partisan study by three English journalists is Lewis Chester, Godfrey Hodgson and Bruce Page, *An American Melodrama: The Presidential Campaign of 1968* (New York, 1969). David S. Broder "The Election of 1968" in Schlesinger, ed., *History of Presidential Elections* is a good survey. On Nixon's strategy see Kevin Phillips, *The Emerging Republican Majority* (New York, 1970) and the highly critical Joe McGinniss, *The Selling of the President* (New York, 1969). Gary Wills, *Nixon Agonistes* (New York, 1970) is a psychological portrait of Nixon in the 1960s. The best biography of George Wallace is Marshall Frady, *Wallace* (New York, 1968).

Other Works

Agee, Philip, *Inside the Company: CIA Diary* (New York, 1975).

Alsop, Stewart, *The Center* (New York, 1968).

Anderson, Patrick, *The President's Men* (New York, 1968).

Berkman, Richard L., and W. Kip Viscus II, eds., *Damming the West* (New York, 1973).

Berman, Jerry J., and Morton H. Halperin, eds., *The Abuses of the Intelligence Agencies* (Washington, 1975).

Buncher, Judith F., ed., *The CIA and the Security Debate: 1971-1975* (New York, 1976).

Cochen, Bert, *Adlai Stevenson* (New York, 1969).

Cook, Fred, *The FBI Nobody Knows* (New York, 1972).

Harris, Richard, *Justice: The Crisis of Law, Order and Freedom in America* (New York, 1970).

Jeffers, H. Paul, *The CIA: A Close Look at the Central Intelligence Agency* (New York, 1971).

Kim, Young H., *Central Intelligence Agency: Problems of Secrecy in a Democracy* (Lexington, 1968).

Kirkpatrick, Lyman B., *The Real CIA* (New York, 1968).

Lubell, Samuel, *The Future of American Politics* (New York, 1965).

McGarvey, Patrick J., *CIA: The Myth and the Madness* (New York, 1973).

Marchetti, Victor, and John D. Marks, *The CIA and the Cult of Intelligence* (New York, 1974).

Mazo, Earl, and Stephen Hess, *Nixon: A Political Portrait* (New York, 1968).

Miles, Rufus, *The Department of Health, Education and Welfare* (New York, 1974).

Novak, Robert D., *The Agony of the GOP, 1964* (New York, 1965).

O'Brien, Lawrence F., *No Final Victories* (New York, 1968).

Parmet, Herbert S., *The Democrats, the Years after FDR* (New York, 1976).

Perkus, Cathy, ed., *COINTELPRO: The FBI's Secret War on Political Freedom* (New York, 1975).

Ransom, Harry H., *Intelligence Establishment* (Cambridge, Mass., 1970).

Rowe, Robert, *The Bobby Baker Story* (New York, 1967).

Shriver, R. Sargent, *Sargent Shriver: a Candid Portrait* (New York, 1964).

Thomas, Norman C., *Education in National Politics* (New York, 1975).

Turner, William W., *Hoover's FBI: The Man and the Myth* (Los Angeles, 1970).

Ungar, Sanford J., *FBI: An Uncensored Look Behind the Walls* (Boston, 1976).

U.S. Commission on CIA Activities within the United States (Rockefeller Commission), *Report to the President* (Washington, 1975).

U.S. Senate, Select Committee on Intelligence Activities, *Foreign and Military Intelligence* (Washington, 1976).

———, *Intelligence Activities and the Rights of Americans* (Washington, 1976).

Watters, Pat, and Stephen Gillers, eds., *Investigating the FBI (New York,* 1973).

Whitehead, Don, *Attack on Terror: The FBI Against the Ku Klux Klan in Mississippi* (New York, 1970).

Wicker, Tom, *JFK and LBJ: The Influence of Personality Upon Politics* (Baltimore, 1968).

THE GREAT SOCIETY

The Johnson Administration programs in the areas of unemployment, welfare, health care, housing and education are examined in Eli Ginzberg and Robert M. Solow, eds., *The Great Society* (New York, 1974), a collection of essays. The War on Poverty component of the Great Society is examined from political and sociological perspectives in Chaim Isaac Waxman, ed., *Poverty: Power and Politics* (New York, 1968). Daniel P. Moynihan offered the most publicized critique of the War on Poverty in *Maximum Feasible Misunderstanding* (New York, 1969), charging that the program was implemented in a way that minimized the kind of social change desired and maximized the opposition to such change. Marvin E. Gettleman and David Mermelstein, eds., *The Great Society Reader* (New York, 1967) and Jeremy Larner and Irving Howe, eds., *Poverty: Views from the Left* (New York, 1969) present critical evaluations of Johnson's social welfare programs from a socialist perspective.

Other Works

Bailey, Stephen K., and Edith K. Mosher, *The Office of Education Administers a Law* (Syracuse, 1968).

Clark, Kenneth B., and Jeanette Hopkins, *A Relevant War against Poverty: A Study of Community Action Programs and Observable Social Change* (New York, 1969).

Donovan, John C., *The Politics of Poverty* (New York, 1973).

Elman, Richard M., *The Poorhouse State* (New York, 1968).

Harris, Richard, *A Sacred Trust* (New York, 1966). Medicare.

Hunter, David R., *The Slums: Challenge and Response* (New York, 1964).

Kershaw, Joseph, *Government Agency Poverty* (Washington, 1970).

Kramer, Ralph M., *Participation of the Poor: Comparative Community Case Studies in the War on Poverty* (Englewood Cliffs, 1969).

Lekachman, Robert, "Death of a Slogan—The Great Society, 1967," *Commentary* (January, 1967).

Leuchtenburg, William, "The Genesis of the Great Society," *The Reporter* (April 21, 1966).

Levitan, Sar A., *The Great Society's Poor Law: A New Approach to Poverty* (Baltimore, 1969).

Marmor, Theodore R., *The Politics of Medicare* (Chicago, 1973).

Matusow, Allen J., "Reform in the Great Society: The Case of Medicare," *Rice University Studies* (Fall, 1972).

Meranto, Philip, *The Politics of Federal Aid to Education in 1965: A Study in Political Innovation* (Syracuse, 1967).

Miles, Rufus, *The Department of Health, Education and Welfare* (New York, 1974).

Payne, James S., et al, *Head Start* (New York, 1973).

Seligman, Ben B., *Permanent Poverty: American Syndrome* (Chicago, 1968).

——— ed., *Poverty as a Public Issue* (Chicago, 1965).

Sundquist, James L., *Politics and Policy* (Washington, 1968).

Thomas, Norman C., *Education in National Politics* (New York, 1975).

Wicker, Tom, *JFK and LBJ: The Influence of Personality Upon Politics* (New York, 1969).

CONGRESS

The annual *Congressional Quarterly Almanac* (Washington, 1945) is an essential tool for examining the operation of Congress on a year-by-year basis. It describes the content of major bills and traces their legislative history in both chambers. Important committee investigations are also examined. Roll call votes, studies of voting patterns and membership lists of committees and subcommittees are among its other features.

Scholarly works on the organization of Congress that are pertinent to the Johnson years include John D. Lees, *Committee System of the United States Congress* (New York, 1967) and Randolph B. Ripley, *Majority Party Leadership in Congress* (Boston, 1969) and *Party Leaders in the House of Representatives* (Washington, 1967). The structure and procedures of Congress in the mid-1960s are criticized as undemocratic and inefficient in Rep. Richard W. Bolling, *House Out of Order* (New York, 1966) and Sen. Joseph S. Clark, *Congress: The Sapless Branch* (New York, 1967). *The Case Against Congress* (New York, 1968), by Drew Pearson and Jack Anderson, is in the muckraking genre. For the relationship between Johnson and Congress see James L. Sundquist, *Politics and Policy: The Eisenhower, Kennedy and Johnson Years* (Washington, 1968) and Tom Wicker's insightful *JFK and LBJ: The Influence of Politics on Personality* (New York, 1968). See also, Abraham Holtzman, *Legislative Liaison: Executive Leadership in Congress* (Chicago, 1970).

Other Works

Anderson, Clinton P., with Milton Viorst, *Outsider in the Senate: Senator Clinton Anderson's Memoirs* (New York, 1970).

Anson, Robert Sam, *McGovern: A Biography* (New York, 1972).

Burns, James MacGregor, *Edward Kennedy and the Camelot Legacy* (New York, 1976).

Chamberlain, Hope, *A Minority of Members: Women in the U.S. Congress* (New York, 1973).

Douglas, Paul H., *In the Fullness of Time* (New York, 1972).

Eisele, Albert, *Almost to the Presidency* (Blue Earth, Minn., 1972). Sens. Hubert H. Humphrey and Eugene J. McCarthy.

Esposito, John C., *Vanishing Air* (New York, 1970).

Gore, Albert, *Let the Glory Out* (New York, 1972).

Greenfield, Meg, "The Man Who Leads the Southern Senators," *The Reporter* (May 21, 1964). Sen. Richard B. Russell.

Gruening, Ernest H., *Many Battles* (New York, 1973).

Hersh, Burton, *The Education of Edward Kennedy: A Family Biography* (New York, 1972).

Johnson, Haynes, and Bernard M. Gwertzman, *Fulbright: The Dissenter* (Garden City, 1968).

Kay, Hubert, "The Warrior from Patman's Switch," *Fortune* (April, 1965). Rep. Wright Patman.

Kimball, Penn, *Bobby Kennedy and the New Politics* (Englewood Cliffs, 1968).

Levin, Murray B., *Kennedy Campaigning: The System and Style as Practiced by Senator Edward Kennedy* (Boston, 1966).

Lippman, Theo, Jr., *Senator Ted Kennedy* (New York, 1976).

McCloskey, Michael, "Wilderness Movement at the Crossroads," *Pacific Historical Review*, XLI (1972).

McNeil, Neil, *Dirksen: Portrait of a Public Man* (New York, 1970).

Manley, John F., "Wilbur D. Mills: A Study in Congressional Influence," *American Political Science Review* (June, 1969).

Nevin, David, *Muskie of Maine* (New York, 1972).

Newfield, Jack, *Robert Kennedy: A Memoir* (New York, 1969).

Ognibene, Peter J., *Scoop: The Life and Politics of Henry M. Jackson* (New York, 1975).

Powell, Adam Clayton, *Adam by Adam* (New York, 1971).

Scheele, Henry Z., *Charlie Halleck* (New York, 1966).

Shannon, William V., *The Heir Apparent: Robert Kennedy and the Struggle for Power* (New York, 1967).

Smith, Margaret Chase, *Declaration of Conscience* (New York, 1972).

Stein, Jean, *American Journey: The Times of Robert Kennedy* (New York, 1970).

Sykes, Jay G., *Proxmire* (Washington, 1972).

terHorst, J. F., *Gerald Ford* (New York, 1974).

Timmisch, Nick, and William Johnson, *Robert Kennedy at 40* (New York, 1965).

Vanden Heuvel, William, and Milton Gwirtzman, *On His Own: Robert F. Kennedy, 1964-1968* (Garden City, 1970).

Viorst, Milton, "Could this Jew be President?," *Esquire* (April 1966). Sen. Jacob Javits.

Wilkinson, J. Harvie III, *Harry Byrd and the Changing Face of Virginia Politics, 1945-1966* (Charlottesville, 1968).

Wilson, Augusta E., *Liberal Leader in the House: Frank Thompson, Jr.* (Washington, 1968).

Zwick, David, and Marcy Benstock, eds., *Water Wasteland* (New York, 1971).

Committee Studies

Ralph Nader Congress Project, *The Commerce Committees: A Study of the House and Senate Commerce Committees*, David Price, director (New York, 1975).

———, *The Environment Committees: A Study of the House and Senate Interior, Agriculture, and Science Committees* (New York, 1975).

———, *The Judiciary Committees: A Study of the House and Senate Judiciary Committees*, Peter Schuck, director (New York, 1975).

———, *The Money Committees: A Study of the House Banking and Currency Committee and the Senate Banking, Housing and Urban Affairs Committee*, Lester Salamon director (New York, 1975).

———, *The Revenue Committees: A Study of the House Ways and Means and Senate Finance Committees and the House and Senate Appropriations Committees*, Richard Spohn and Charles McCollum, directors (New York, 1975).

———, *Ruling Congress: A Study of How the House and Senate Rules Govern the Legislative Process*, Ted Siff and Alan Weil, directors (New York, 1975).

STATE AND LOCAL GOVERNMENT

The most thorough and recent state political studies have been made by Neal R. Peirce. Writing in the tradition of John Gunther, he produced *The Megastates* (New York, 1972) and followed it up with five regional surveys covering a majority of the American states. (See below.) Other good regional studies include William C. Havard, ed., *Politics of the Contemporary South* (Baton Rouge, 1972) and John H. Fenton, *Midwest Politics* (New York, 1966). Kevin P. Phillips, *The Emerging Republican Majority* (Garden City, 1969) contains good studies of state voting behavior in the 1960s.

One of the most important urban studies of the 1960s is Jane Jacobs, *The Death and Life of Great American Cities* (New York, 1969), an attack on massive urban renewal and superhighway projects that destroyed old city neighborhoods. Edward C. Banfield, *The Unheavenly City: The Nature and Future of Our Urban Crisis* (Boston, 1970), questions the ability of liberal programs to solve the problems of the cities.

Important studies of urban politics in the 1960s include Robert Caro, *The Power Broker: Robert Moses and the Fall of New York* (New York, 1974); Robert Conot, *American Odyssey* (New York, 1974), on Detroit; Mike Royko, *Boss: Richard J. Daley of Chicago* (New York, 1971); and Allan R. Talbot, *The Mayor's Game: Richard Lee of New Haven and the Politics of Change* (New York, 1967).

Other Works

Ainsworth, Ed, *Maverick Mayor: A Biography of Sam Yorty of Los Angeles* (Garden City, 1966).

Bartley, Numan V., *From Thurmond to Wallace: Political Tendencies in Georgia, 1948-1968* (Baltimore, 1968).

Bartley, Numan V., and Hugh D. Graham, *Southern Politics and the Second Reconstruction* (Baltimore, 1975).

Bollens, John C., and Grant B. Geyer, *Yorty: Politics of a Constant Candidate* (Pacific Palisades, 1973).

Cannon, Lou, *Ronnie and Jesse: A Political Odyssey* (Garden City, 1969).

Cash, Kevin, *Who the Hell is William Loeb?* (Manchester, 1975).

Clark, Thomas D., *Kentucky: Land of Contrast* (New York, 1968).

Coffman, Tom, *Catch a Wave: A Case Study of Hawaii's New Politics* (Honolulu, 1973).

Conaway, James, *The Life and Times of Leander Perez* (New York, 1973).

Connery, Robert H., and Gerald Benjamin, eds., *Governing New York State: The Rockefeller Years* (New York, 1974).

Cooke, Edward F., and Edward G. Janosik, *Pennsylvania Politics* (New York, 1965).

Costikyan, Edward N., *Behind Closed Doors: Politics in the Public Interest* (New York, 1966).

Crouch, Winston W., et al., *California Government and Politics* (Englewood Cliffs, 1967).

Davidson, Chandler, *Biracial Politics: Conflict and Coalition in the Metropolitan South* (Baton Rouge, 1972).

Delmatier, Royce D., and C. McIntosh, eds., *The Rumble of California Politics, 1848-1970* (New York, 1970).

Douglas, Marjory Stoneman, *Florida, The Long Frontier* (New York, 1967).

Ershkowitz, Miriam, and Joseph Zikmund II, *Black Politics in Philadelphia* (New York, 1973).

Fellmeth, Robert C., *Politics of Land* (New York, 1973).

Frady, Marshall, *Wallace* (New York, 1969).

Gray, Francine du Plessix, *Hawaii: The Sugar-Coated Fortress* (New York, 1972).

Greenstone, J. David, *Labor in American Politics* (Chicago, 1969).

Havard, William C., ed., *Politics of the Contemporary South* (Baton Rouge, 1972).

Heard, Alexander, ed., *State Legislatures in American Politics* (Englewood Cliffs, 1966).

Hill, Gladwin, *Dancing Bear: An Inside Look at California Politics* (Cleveland, 1968).

Hollingsworth, Harold M., ed., *Essays on Recent Southern Politics* (Austin, 1970).

Holmes, Jack E., *Politics in New Mexico* (Albuquerque, 1967).

Howard, Perry H., *Political Tendencies in Louisiana* (Baton Rouge, 1971).

Hulse, James W., *The Nevada Adventure: A History* (Reno, 1972).

Jacobs, Jane, *The Economy of Cities* (New York, 1969).

Jonas, Frank H., ed., *Politics in the American West* (Salt Lake City, 1969).

Kutz, Myer, *Rockefeller Power* (New York, 1974).

Litt, Edgar, *The Political Cultures of Massachusetts* (Cambridge, Mass., 1965).

Lowe, Jeanne, *Cities in a Race with Time: Progress and Poverty in America's Growing Cities* (New York, 1967).

McWilliams, Carey, ed., *The California Revolution* (New York, 1968).

Mitau, G. Theodore, *Politics in Minnesota* (Minneapolis, 1970).

Moscow, Warren, *What Have You Done for Me Lately? The Ins and Outs of New York City Politics* (Englewood Cliffs, 1967).

Moses, Robert, *Public Works: A Dangerous Trade* (New York, 1970).

Peirce, Neal R., *The Border South States* (New York, 1975).

———, *The Deep South States* (New York, 1974).

———, *The Great Plains States* (New York, 1973).

———, *The Mountain States* (New York, 1972).

———, *The Pacific States* (New York, 1974).

Petshak, Kirk, *The Challenge of Urban Reform: Policies and Programs in Philadelphia* (Philadelphia, 1973).

Phelan, James, and Robert Pozen, *The*

Company State: Ralph Nader's Study Group Report on DuPont in Delaware (New York, 1973).

Phillips, Herbert L., *Big Wayward Girl: An Informal Political History of California* (Garden City, 1968).

Putnam, Jackson K., *Old-Age Politics in California: From Richardson to Reagan* (Stanford, 1970).

Ravitch, Diane, *The Great School Wars, New York City, 1805-1973: A History of the Public Schools as Battlefield of Social Change* (New York, 1974).

Sayre, Wallace, and Robert Kauffman, *Governing New York City* (New York, 1965).

Sherrill, Robert, *Gothic Politics in the Deep South* (New York, 1968).

———, "A Nasty, Brutish Fascinating Political Feud," *The New York Times Magazine* (April 28, 1968).

Tindall, George Brown, *The Disruption of the Solid South* (Athens, Ga., 1972).

Turner, Wallace, *The Mormon Establishment* (Boston, 1966).

Watters, Pat, and Reese Cleghorn, *Climbing Jacob's Ladder: The Arrival of Negroes in Southern Politics* (New York, 1967).

Whittemore, L. H., *The Man Who Ran the Subways* (New York, 1968). Mike Quill.

Widick, B. J., Jr., *Detroit: City of Race and Class Violence* (Chicago, 1972).

Wilkinson, J. Harvie III, *Harry Byrd and the Changing Face of Virginia Politics, 1945-1966* (Charlottesville, 1968).

Zannes, Estelle, *Checkmate in Cleveland: The Rhetoric of Confrontation during the Stokes Years* (Cleveland, 1972).

SUPREME COURT

Leon Friedman and Fred L. Israel, eds., *The Justices of the United States Supreme Court, 1789-1969* (New York, 1969) contains biographical articles and representative opinions for each justice. Two excellent studies of the Warren Court are Alexander M. Bickel, *The Supreme Court and the Idea of Progress* (New York, 1970) and Archibald Cox, *The Warren Court* (Cambridge, Mass., 1968). Richard Sayler et al. eds., *The Warren Court* (Cambridge, Mass., 1969) and Philip B. Kurland, *Politics, the Constitution and the Warren Court* (Chicago, 1970) also provide very good analyses. Annual issues of *The Supreme Court Review* (Chicago, 1960-), ed. Philip B. Kurland, include many useful and informative essays on contemporary constitutional issues and major Warren Court decisions.

Other Works

Abraham, Henry J., *Justices and Presidents* (New York, 1974).

Black, Hugo, *A Constitutional Faith* (New York, 1968).

Bland, Randall W., *Private Pressure on Public Law: The Legal Career of Justice Thurgood Marshall* (Port Washington, 1973).

Countryman, Vern, *The Judicial Record of Justice William O. Douglas* (Cambridge, Mass., 1974).

Friedman, Stephen J., ed., *An Affair with Freedom: William J. Brennan Jr.* (New York, 1967).

Goldberg, Arthur J., *Equal Justice: The Warren Era of the Supreme Court* (Evanston, 1971).

Katcher, Leo, *Earl Warren: A Political Biography* (New York, 1967).

Murphy, Paul L., *The Constitution in Crisis Times, 1918-1969* (New York, 1972). Includes several chapters on the Warren Court.

Shapiro, David L., ed., *The Evolution of a Judicial Philosophy: Selected Opinions and Papers of Justice John Marshall Harlan* (Cambridge, Mass., 1969).

Strickland, Stephen P., ed., *Hugo Black*

and the Supreme Court (New York, 1967).

Weaver, John D., *Warren: The Man, the Court, the Era* (London, 1968).

FOREIGN AFFAIRS

Among the vast number of works that deal with Johnson's foreign policy, Walt W. Rostow, *The Diffusion of Power: An Essay in Recent History* (New York, 1972) gives an excellent overview of the period. The study, written by one of the more controversial members of the White House staff, is a favorable analysis of Johnson's policy that has come under attack by revisionist historians. Lyndon Johnson's memoir, *The Vantage Point* (New York, 1971) is a bland but extremely valuable account of the inner workings of policy formation. For an analysis of foreign policy during Johnson's first years in the White House see Philip Geyelin, *Lyndon B. Johnson and the World* (New York, 1966).

The Vietnam war dominated foreign policy decision-making during the Johnson Administration. The most valuable study of the conflict is *The Pentagon Papers,* commissioned by the Department of Defense. The *Papers,* which trace American involvement in Southeast Asia from the 1950s through the 1960s, are comprehensive but are often difficult to use because of their poor organization and use of Defense Department jargon. For a readable account of the war based on *The Papers* see Ralph Stavins et al., *Washington Plans an Aggressive War* (New York, 1971), which is highly critical of American leadership. Also critical of policymakers, particularly those who were holdovers from the Kennedy staff, is David Halberstam, *The Best and the Brightest* (New York, 1972), which focuses on the influence that Cold War attitudes and overconfidence had on the leaders' perceptions of the conflict. John Galloway, *The Gulf of Tonkin Resolution* (Rutherford, N.J., 1970) is an excellent study of the events that surrounded the passage of the 1964 Tonkin Gulf Resolution, which gave Johnson almost unlimited power to escalate the war without congressional approval. Townsend Hoopes, *The Limits of Intervention* (New York, 1969) is a first rate description of events leading to Johnson's decision to de-escalate the war in March 1968. Also important is "Viet Nam Reappraisal," *Foreign Affairs* XLVII (July, 1969) by Clark M. Clifford, a close friend and adviser of the President who was extremely influential in persuading Johnson to change his policy. For an excellent chronology of the war see Lester Sobel, ed., *South Vietnam: U.S.-Communist Confrontation in Southeast Asia* (New York, 1966-1974), Vols. I-IV.

Johnson's second important foreign crisis was his decision to send troops to the Dominican Republic in April 1965. The best account of the day-to-day events of this period is *Dominican Diary* (New York, 1965) by Tad Szulc, who was an on-the-scene correspondent in Santo Domingo. Jerome Slater, *Intervention and Negotiation: The United States and the Dominican Intervention* (New York, 1970) is essential reading as is *Overtaken by Events: The Dominican Crisis from the Fall of Trujillo to the Civil War* (New York, 1966) by John Barlow Martin, ambassador to the Dominican Republic at that time.

General Works

Allison, Graham, Ernest May and Adam Yarmolinsky, "Limits to Intervention," *Foreign Affairs* (January, 1970).

Barnet, Richard J., *Intervention and Revolution* (New York, 1968).

Bohlen, Charles E., *The Transformation of American Foreign Policy* (New York, 1969).

Brown, Seyom, *The Faces of Power: Consistency and Change in United States Foreign Policy from Truman to Johnson* (New York, 1968).

Copeland, Miles, *The Game of Nations: The Amorality of Power Politics* (New York, 1969).

Davis, Kenneth Sydney, *The Politics of Honor* (New York, 1967). Adlai Stevenson.

Draper, Theodore, *Abuse of Power* (New York, 1967).

Fulbright, J. William, *The Arrogance of Power* (New York, 1967).

Galbraith, John Kenneth, "The Plain Lessons of a Bad Decade," *Foreign Policy* (Winter, 1970-1971).

Hodgson, Godfrey, "The Establishment," *Foreign Policy* (Spring, 1973).

Horowitz, David, *Free World Colossus: A Critique of American Foreign Policy in the Cold War* (New York, 1971).

Johnson, Haynes, and Bernard M. Gwertzman, *Fulbright: The Dissenter* (Garden City, 1968).

Johnson, Richard A., *The Administration of United States Foreign Policy* (Austin, 1971).

Kolko, Gabriel, *Roots of American Foreign Policy* (Boston, 1969).

Radosh, Ronald, *American Labor and United States Foreign Policy* (New York, 1970).

Sellen, Robert W., "Old Assumptions Versus New Realities: Lyndon Johnson and Foreign Policy," *International Journal* (Spring, 1973).

Spanier, John W., *American Foreign Policy Since World War II* (New York, 1971).

Steel, Ronald, *Pax Americana* (New York, 1967).

Walton, Richard J., *The Remnants of Power: The Tragic Last Years of Adlai Stevenson* (New York, 1968).

Europe and the Cold War

Burns, Eedson L. M., *A Seat at the Table* (Toronto, 1972). Nuclear test ban discussions.

Harriman, W. Averell, *America and Russia in a Changing World* (Garden City, 1971).

Katris, John A., *Eyewitness in Greece: The Colonels Come to Power* (St. Louis, 1971).

LaFeber, Walter, *America, Russia, and the Cold War, 1945-1971* (New York, 1971).

Moulton, Harland B., *From Superiority to Parity: The United States and the Strategic Arms Race, 1961-1971* (Westport, 1972).

Neustadt, Richard E., *Alliance Politics* (New York, 1970).

Newhouse, John, *De Gaulle and the Anglo-Saxons* (New York, 1970).

Planck, Charles R., *The Changing Status of German Reunification in Western Diplomacy, 1955-1966* (Baltimore, 1967).

Tatu, Michel, *Power in the Kremlin: From Khrushchev to Kosygin* (New York, 1969).

Terchek, Ronald J., *The Making of the Test Ban Treaty* (The Hague, 1970).

Turner, Arthur Campbell, *The Unique Partnership: Britain and the United States* (New York, 1971).

Latin America

Burr, Robert N., *Our Troubled Hemisphere: Perspectives on United States-Latin American Relations* (Washington, 1967).

Craig, Richard B., *The Bracero Program: Interest Groups and Foreign Policy* (Austin, 1971).

Draper, Theodore, "The Dominican Intervention Reconsidered," *Political Science Quarterly*, LXXXVI (March, 1971).

———, *The Dominican Revolt: A Case Study in American Policy* (New York, 1968).

Kurzman, Dan, *Revolt of the Damned* (New York, 1965). The Dominican Republic.

Levinson, Jerome, and Juan de Onis, *The Alliance that Lost its Way: A Critical Report on the Alliance for Progress* (Chicago, 1970).

Lowenthal, Abraham F., "Alliance Rhetoric Versus Latin America Reality," *Foreign Affairs* (April, 1970).

———, *The Dominican Intervention* (Cambridge, Mass., 1972).

Rogers, William D., *The Twilight Struggle: The Alliance for Progress and the Politics of Development in Latin America* (New York, 1967).

Wagner, Harrison R., *United States Policy Toward Latin America: A Study in Domestic and International Politics* (Stanford, 1970).

Walton, Richard J., *Beyond Diplomacy: A Background Book on American Military Intervention* (New York, 1970). Contains a chapter on the 1965 Dominican crisis.

———, *The United States and Latin America* (New York, 1972).

Wells, Henry, *The Modernization of Puerto Rico: A Political Study of Changing Values and Institutions* (Cambridge, Mass., 1969).

Africa, Asia and the Middle East

Arsenault, Raymond, "White on Chrome: Southern Congressmen and Rhodesia 1962-1971," *Issue*, II (Winter, 1972).

Attwood, William, *The Reds and the Blacks* (New York, 1967). Guinea.

Dulles, Foster Rhea, *American Policy Toward Communist China, 1949-1969* (New York, 1972).

Emerson, Rupert, *Africa and United States Policy* (Englewood Cliffs, 1967).

Hance, William A., ed., *Southern Africa and the United States* (New York, 1968).

Heikal, Mohamed Hassanein, *The Cairo Documents* (New York, 1973).

Polk, William R., *The United States and the Arab World* (Cambridge, Mass., 1969).

Reischauer, Edwin O., *The United States and Japan* (Cambridge, Mass., 1965).

Silverberg, Robert, *If I Forget Thee O Jerusalem: American Jews and the State of Israel* (New York, 1970).

Williams, G. Mennen, *Africa for the Africans* (Grand Rapids, 1969).

Young, Kenneth T., *Negotiating with the Chinese Communists: The United States Experience, 1953-1967* (New York, 1968).

Southeast Asia

Adams, N., and A. McCoy, *Laos: War and Revolution* (New York, 1970).

Austin, Anthony, *The President's War* (Philadelphia, 1971).

Ball, George W., "Top Secret: The Prophecy the President Rejected," *Atlantic Monthly* (July, 1972).

Barnet, Richard J., *Roots of War* (New York, 1972).

Bator, Victor, *Vietnam, A Diplomatic Tragedy: The Origins of the United States Involvement* (Dobbs Ferry, 1965).

Black, Eugene R., *Alternative in Southeast Asia* (New York, 1969).

Bodard, Lucien, *The Quicksand War* (Boston, 1967).

Brandon, Henry, *Anatomy of Error: The Inside Story of the Asian War on the Potomac, 1954-1969* (Boston, 1969).

Central Office of Information, London, *Vietnam, Laos and Cambodia: Chronology of Events 1945-1968* (London, 1968).

Chandler, David P., "Cambodia's Strategy of Survival," *Current History*, LVIII (December, 1969).

Chomsky, Noam, *American Power and the New Mandarins* (New York, 1967).

———, *At War with Asia* (New York, 1970).

Cooper, Chester L., *The Lost Crusade: America in Vietnam* (New York, 1970).

Critchfield, Richard, *The Long Charade: Political Subversion in the Vietnam War* (New York, 1968).

Darling, Frank C., *Thailand and the United States* (Washington, 1965).

Dommen, Arthur J., *Conflict in Laos* (New York, 1971).

Draper, Theodore, *Abuse of Power* (New York, 1967).

Fall, Bernard B., *Viet-Nam Witness 1953-1966* (New York, 1966).

Fitzgerald, Frances, *Fire in the Lake: The Vietnamese and the Americans in Vietnam* (Boston, 1972).

Gettleman, Marvin E. and Susan, and Kaplan, Lawrence and Carol, *Conflict in Indochina* (New York, 1970).

Goldstein, Martin, *American Policy Toward Laos* (Rutherford, 1973).

Graff, Henry F., *The Tuesday Cabinet: Deliberation and Decision on Peace and War under Lyndon Johnson* (Englewood Cliffs, 1970).

Hatch, Alden, *The Lodges of Massachusetts* (New York, 1973).

Hickey, Gerald C., *Accommodation and Coalition in South Vietnam* (Santa

Monica, 1970).

Kahin, George M., and John W. Lewis, *The United States in Vietnam* (New York, 1967).

Kail, F. M., *What Washington Said: Administration Rhetoric and the Vietnam War, 1949-1969* (New York, 1973).

Kalb, Marvin, and Elie Abel, *Roots of Involvement: The U.S. in Asia 1884-1971* (New York, 1971).

Kirk, Donald, *Wider War: The Struggle for Cambodia, Thailand and Laos* (New York, 1971).

Komer, Robert W., "The Other War in Vietnam—A Progress Report," *Department of State Bulletin* (Oct. 10, 1966).

Kraslow, David, and Stuart H. Loory, *The Secret Search for Peace in Vietnam* (New York, 1968).

Lacouture, Jean, *Vietnam: Between Two Truces* (New York, 1966).

Lansdale, Edward G., *In the Midst of Wars: An American's Mission to Southeast Asia* (New York, 1972).

Leifer, Michael, *Cambodia: The Search for Security* (New York, 1967).

Lodge, Henry Cabot, *The Storm Has Many Eyes* (New York, 1973).

Lomax, Louis E., *Thailand: The War That Is, the War That Will Be* (New York, 1967).

McAlister, John T., Jr., *Vietnam: The Origins of Revolution* (New York, 1969).

Mecklin, John, *Mission in Torment: An Intimate Account of the U.S. Role in Vietnam* (Garden City, 1965).

Miller, William, *Henry Cabot Lodge* (New York, 1967).

Moore, John Norton, *Law and the Indochina War* (Princeton, 1972).

Neuchterlein, Donald E., *Thailand and the Struggle for Southeast Asia* (Ithaca, 1965).

Nighswonger, William A., *Rural Pacification in Vietnam* (New York, 1966).

Pike, Douglas, *War, Peace and the Viet Cong* (Cambridge, Mass., 1969).

Porter, Gareth, *A Peace Denied: The United States, Vietnam, and the Paris Agreement* (Bloomington, 1975).

Schlesinger, Arthur M., Jr., *The Bitter Heritage: Vietnam and American Democracy, 1941-1966* (Boston, 1967).

Shaplen, Robert, *The Lost Revolution: The U.S. in Vietnam, 1946-1966* (New York, 1966).

———, *The Road from War: Vietnam 1965-1970* (New York, 1970).

———, *Time out of Hand: Revolution and Reaction in Southeast Asia* (New York, 1969).

Shurman, Franz, Peter Dale Scott and Reginald Zelnik, *The Politics of Escalation in Vietnam* (New York, 1966).

Starobin, Joseph R., *Eyewitness in Indochina* (New York, 1968).

Stevenson, Charles A., *The End of Nowhere: American Policy Toward Laos Since 1954* (Boston, 1972).

Taylor, Maxwell, *Swords and Plowshares* (New York, 1972).

Taylor, Telford, *Nuremberg and Vietnam: An American Tragedy* (New York, 1971).

Toye, Hugh, *Laos: Buffer State or Battle Ground* (New York, 1968).

U.S. Senate, Committee on Foreign Relations, *The Vietnam Hearings 1966* (New York, 1966).

Wilson, David A., *The United States and the Future of Thailand* (New York, 1970).

Windchy, Eugene, *Tonkin Gulf* (Garden City, 1971).

Wit, Daniel, *Thailand: Another Vietnam?* (New York, 1968).

DEFENSE

During the Johnson Administration the Pentagon was primarily concerned with the conduct of the Vietnam war. The best source for the study of the conflict is *The Pentagon Papers*, a comprehensive history of the growing American commitment commissioned by Secretary of Defense Robert S. McNamara. For an excellent, highly critical account of policymaking based on *The Pentagon Papers* see Ralph Stavins, et al, *Washington Plans An Aggressive War* (New York, 1971). In a similar vein, see David Halberstam, *The Best and the Brightest* (New York, 1972). Halberstam, a correspondent in Vietnam during the early war years, describes how decision makers' Cold War attitudes contributed to escalation of the conflict. For a study tracing McNamara's evolution from "hawk" to "dove" see Henry Trewhitt, *McNamara: His Ordeal in the Pentagon* (New York, 1971). John Galloway, *The Gulf of Tonkin Resolution* (Rutherford, 1970) analyzes events surrounding the passage of the Resolution that gave Johnson advance approval of any military actions he might take in Vietnam. Townsend Hoopes, *The Limits of Intervention* (New York, 1969) details events leading to the March 1968 decision not to escalate American involvement further. Lester Sobel, ed., *South Vietnam: U.S. Confrontation in Southeast Asia* (New York, 1966-74), Vols I-IV contains an excellent chronology of the war.

Other Works

Borklund, C. W., *The Department of Defense* (New York, 1968).

———, *Men of the Pentagon: From Forrestal to McNamara* (New York, 1966).

Davis, Vincent, *The Admirals Lobby* (Chapel Hill, 1967).

Enthoven, Alain C., and K. Wayne Smith, *How Much Is Enough?* (New York, 1971).

Glines, Carroll V., Jr., *The Compact History of the United States Air Force* (New York, 1973).

McNamara, Robert S., *The Essence of Security* (New York, 1968).

Moulton, Harland B., *From Superiority to Parity: The United States and the Strategic Arms Race, 1961-71* (Westport, 1973).

Schwarz, Urs, *American Strategy: A New Perspective* (Garden City, 1966).

Schwiebert, Ernest G., *A History of Air Force Ballistic Missiles* (New York, 1965).

Smith, Bruce L. R., *The Rand Corporation: Case Study of A Nonprofit Advisory Agency* (Cambridge, Mass., 1966).

Twining, Nathan F., *Neither Liberty nor Safety: A Hard Look at U.S. Military Policy and Strategy* (New York, 1966).

Weigley, Russell F., *History of the United States Army* (New York, 1967).

Yarmolinsky, Adam, *The Military Establishment: Its Impact on American Society* (New York, 1971).

Southeast Asia

Austin, Anthony, *The President's War* (Philadelphia, 1971).

Boyle, Richard, *The Flower of the Dragon: The Breakdown of the U.S. Army in Vietnam* (San Francisco, 1972).

Brandon, Henry, *Anatomy of Error: The Inside Story of the Asian War on the Potomac, 1954-1969* (Boston, 1969).

Broughton, Jack, *Thud Ridge* (Philadelphia, 1969).

Cooper, Chester L., *The Lost Crusade: America in Vietnam* (New York, 1970).

Draper, Theodore, *Abuse of Power* (New York, 1967).

Fall, Bernard B., *Hell in a Very Small Place: The Siege of Dien Bien Phu* (Philadelphia, 1967).

Fitzgerald, Frances, *Fire in the Lake: The Vietnamese and the Americans in Vietnam* (Boston, 1972).

Graff, Henry F., *The Tuesday Cabinet: Deliberation and Decision on Peace and War under Lyndon Johnson* (Englewood Cliffs, 1970).

Hooper, Edwin Bickford, *Mobility, Support, Endurance: A Story of Naval Operational Logistics in the Vietnam War 1965-1968* (Washington, 1972).

Kahin, George M., and John W. Lewis, *The United States in Vietnam* (New York, 1967).

Kail, F. M., *What Washington Said: Administration Rhetoric and the Vietnam War, 1949-1969* (New York, 1973).

Kalb, Marvin, and Elie Abel, *Roots of In-*

volvement: The U.S. in Asia 1784-1971 (New York, 1971).
Lansdale, Edward G., *In the Midst of Wars: An American's Mission to Southeast Asia* (New York, 1972).
Littauer, Raphael, and Norman Uphoff, eds., *The Air War in Indochina* (Boston, 1972).
Marshall, S. L. A., *Ambush* (New York, 1969).
———, *Battles in the Monsoon: Campaigning in the Central Highlands of Vietnam, Summer 1966* (New York, 1967).
———, *The Fields of Bamboo* (New York, 1971).
Mulligan, Hugh A., *No Place to Die: The Agony of Viet Nam* (New York, 1967).
Oberdorfer, Don, *Tet!* (Garden City, 1971).
Taylor, Maxwell G., *Swords and Plowshares* (New York, 1972).
Westmoreland, William C., *Report on the War in Vietnam* (Washington, 1969).
———, *A Soldier Reports* (New York, 1976).
Windchy, Eugene, *Tonkin Gulf* (Garden City, 1971).

BUSINESS, LABOR AND ECONOMIC POLICY

Most of the literature on national economic policy deals primarily with the early part of the decade. Hobart Rowen, *The Free Enterprisers: Kennedy, Johnson and the Business Community* concentrates on the Kennedy years and treats only the first six months of the Johnson Administration. *Economics on a New Frontier* (Belmont, 1968) by E. Ray Canterbery is a valuable study of Democratic economic policy of the 1960s by an economist, but it too places far greater emphasis on the Kennedy period. *American Fiscal and Monetary Policy* (Chicago, 1970), edited by Harold Wolozin, provides a cross-section of economic opinion from the leading commentators on economic affairs. In the absence of any detailed historical study of the economics of the Johnson years one can benefit from *Congressional Quarterly's* lucid explanations of current economic issues and their political contexts. Rowland Evans and Robert Novak in *Lyndon B. Johnson: The Exercise of Power* (New York, 1966) give a lively account of President Johnson's decision to back the Kennedy tax cut. Jim F. Heath's *Decade of Disillusionment: The Kennedy-Johnson Years* contains a perceptive overview of the economic developments of the decade. No political decision had a greater impact on the economy of the 1960s and 1970s than the escalation of the Vietnam war, the effects of which are appraised by Robert Warren Stevens in *Vain Hopes, Grim Realities: The Economic Consequences of the Vietnam War* (New York, 1976).

No general history of labor in the postwar era exists, but Thomas R. Brooks, *Toil and Trouble* (New York, 1971) contains several chapters on labor and the labor movement after 1960. Among the best journalistic studies of labor leadership in the 1960s are Joseph C. Goulden, *Meany* (New York, 1972) and John Herling, *Right to Challenge People* (New York, 1972) and *Power in the Steelworkers Union* (New York, 1972).

Other Works

Blough, Roger, *The Washington Embrace of Business* (New York, 1976).
Cary, William L., *Politics and the Regulatory Agencies* (New York, 1967).
Cormier, Frank, and William J. Eaton, *Reuther* (Englewood Cliffs, 1970).
Deakin, James, *The Lobbyists* (Washington, 1966).
Flash, Edward S., Jr., *Economic Advice and Presidential Leadership* (New York, 1965).
Galbraith, John Kenneth, *The New Industrial State* (New York, 1967).
Gerber, Albert B., *Bashful Billionaire* (New

York, 1967). Howard Hughes.
Green, Mark J., ed., *The Monopoly Makers* (New York, 1973).
Hall, Burton H., ed., *Autocracy and Insurgency in Organized Labor* (New Brunswick, 1972).
James, Ralph C., and Estelle James, *James Hoffa and the Teamsters: A Study of Union Power* (Princeton, 1965).
Kutz, Meyer, *Rockefeller Power* (New York, 1974).
Larrowe, Charles P., *Harry Bridges, The Rise and Fall of Radical Labor in the United States* (New York, 1972).
McConnell, Grant, *Private Power and American Democracy* (New York, 1966).
McDonald, David J., *Union Man* (New York, 1969).
Mattiessen, Peter, *Sal Si Puedes: Cesar Chavez and the New American Revolution* (New York, 1969).
Melman, Seymour, *Pentagon Capitalism: The Political Economy of War* (New York, 1970).
Sampson, Anthony, *The Sovereign State of ITT* (New York, 1973).
Sobel, Robert, *The Age of Giant Corporations* (New York, 1972).
Taylor, Ronald, *Chavez and the Farm Workers* (Boston, 1975).
Whittemore, L. H., *The Man Who Ran the Subways: The Story of Mike Quill* (New York, 1968).
White, Lawrence J., *The Automobile Industry since 1945* (Cambridge, Mass., 1971).

CIVIL RIGHTS

James M. McPherson, et al., *Blacks in America* (Garden City, 1971) includes bibliographic essays on various phases of the civil rights revolution from 1954-1970. Another useful, topically arranged bibliography is Elizabeth W. Miller, *The Negro in America* (Cambridge, Mass., 1970). Benjamin Muse, *The American Negro Revolution* (Bloomington, 1968) surveys developments in civil rights from 1963-1967. David Lewis, *King: A Critical Biography* (New York, 1970) is the best biography of Martin Luther King, Jr. August Meier and Elliott Rudwick, *CORE: A Study in the Civil Rights Movement, 1942-1968* (New York, 1973) traces the history of one of the major protest organizations and supplies many useful insights into changes in the civil rights movement. Howard Zinn, *SNCC: The New Abolitionists* (Boston, 1965) covers the period from 1960-1964. One of the first and most important statements of black power can be found in Stokely Carmichael and Charles V. Hamilton, *Black Power: The Politics of Liberation in America* (New York, 1967). The *Report* (New York, 1968) of the National Advisory Commission on Civil Disorders provides a thorough analysis of the race riots of the 1960's.

Other Works

Belfrage, Sally, *Freedom Summer* (New York, 1965). A good history of the Mississippi Freedom Summer project by a participant, a member of SNCC.
Bickel, Alexander M., *The Supreme Court and the Idea of Progress* (New York, 1970).
Black, Earl, *Southern Governors and Civil Rights* (Cambridge, Mass., 1976).
Brooks, Thomas R., *Walls Come Tumbling Down: A History of the Civil Rights Movement, 1940-1970* (Englewood Cliffs, 1974).
Brown, H. Rap, *Die Nigger Die!* (New York, 1969).
Cleaver, Eldridge, *Soul on Ice* (New York, 1968).
Draper, Theodore, *The Rediscovery of Black Nationalism* (New York, 1970).
Farmer, James, *Freedom—When?* (New York, 1966).
Forman, James, *The Making of Black Revo-*

lutionaries (New York, 1972).
Hayden, Tom, *Rebellion in Newark* (New York, 1967).
King, Coretta Scott, *My Life with Martin Luther King, Jr.* (New York, 1969).
King, Martin Luther, Jr., *Where Do We Go From Here: Chaos or Community?* (New York, 1967).
———, *Why We Can't Wait* (New York, 1964). Includes King's famed "Letter from a Birmingham Jail."
Lester, Julius, *Look Out Whitey! Black Power's Gon' Get Your Mama!* (New York, 1968).
Lewis, Anthony, *Gideon's Trumpet* (New York, 1964). A study of *Gideon v. Wainwright*, the 1963 landmark Supreme Court decision extending the right to counsel.
Meier, August, "On the Role of Martin Luther King," *New Politics*, IV (Winter, 1965).
National Advisory Commission on Civil Disorders (Kerner Commission), *Supplemental Studies* (Washington, 1968).
Parris, Guichard, and Lester Brooks, *Blacks in the City: A History of the National Urban League* (Boston, 1971).
Parsons, Talcott, and Kenneth B. Clark, eds., *The Negro American* (Boston, 1966).
Rustin, Bayard, *Down the Line* (New York, 1971).
Seale, Bobby, *Seize the Time* (New York, 1970).
Wolk, Allan, *The Presidency and Black Civil Rights: Eisenhower to Nixon* (Rutherford, 1971).

THE NEW LEFT, THE ANTI-WAR MOVEMENT, DISSENT

In the late 1960s the protest against the war and domestic social injustice generated an immense contemporary literature, but historians have only recently begun to offer a more systematic appraisal. Two solid surveys are Irwin Unger, *The Movement: A History of the American New Left* (New York, 1974) and Thomas Powers, *The War at Home: Vietnam and the American People* (New York, 1973). Two books that deal critically with the prominent role played by American intellectuals in the protest movement are Ronald Berman's excellent analysis, *America in the Sixties: An Intellectual History* (New York, 1968) and Sandy Vogelsang, *The Long Dark Night of the Soul: The American Intellectual Left and the Vietnam War* (New York, 1974). The history of one of the most important New Left organizations is exhaustively recorded in Kirkpatrick Sale's *SDS* (New York, 1973). Among the best books on the campus protests of the 1960s are Hal Draper, *Berkeley: The New Student Revolt* (New York, 1965) and Jerry L. Alvorn, et al., *Up Against the Ivy Wall: A History of the Columbia Crisis* (New York, 1968). Two good anthologies of the student left are Michael Cohen and Dennis Hale, eds., *The New Student Left* (Boston, 1967) and Massimo Teodori, ed., *The New Left: A Documentary History* (New York, 1969). In his *Agony of the American Left* (New York, 1969) Christopher Lasch offers a penetrating, yet sympathetic analysis of the new radicalism. Irving Howe's *Beyond the New Left* (New York, 1970) is far more critical. The best known reports on the counter culture are Theodore Rosak, *The Making of a Counter Culture* (New York, 1969) and Charles Reich's complacent, *The Greening of America* (New York, 1970). Both should be read with sociologist Philip Slater's thoughtful *The Pursuit of Loneliness* (New York, 1970). William O'Neill, *Coming Apart: An Informal History of America in the 1960s* (New York, 1971) pays special attention to the problems and foibles of the Left.

Other Works

Annunziata, Frank A., "The Attack on the Welfare State: Patterns of Anti-Statism from the New Deal to the New Left," unpublished doctoral dissertation, Ohio State University, 1968.

Aron, Raymond, *The Elusive Revolution: Anatomy of a Student Revolt* (New York, 1969).

Bacciocco, Edward, *The New Left in America: Reform to Revolution, 1956-1970* (Stanford, 1974).

Berrigan, Daniel, *The Dark Night of Resistance* (New York, 1971).

———, *Night Flight to Hanoi* (New York, 1968).

Boskin, Joseph, and Robert A. Rosenstone, "Protest in the Sixties," *Annals of the American Academy of Political and Social Science*, 382 (1969).

Bottomore, T. B., *Critics of Society: Radical Thought in North America* (New York, 1968).

Brown, Michael, ed., *The Politics and Anti-Politics of the Young* (Beverly Hills, 1969).

Buckman, Peter, *The Limits of Protest* (Indianapolis, 1970).

Chomsky, Noam, *American Power and the New Mandarins* (New York, 1969).

———, *At War with Asia* (New York, 1970).

———, *For Reasons of State* (New York, 1970).

Clecak, Peter, *Radical Paradoxes: Dilemmas of the American Left, 1945-1970* (New York, 1973).

Connery, Robert H., ed., "Urban Riots: Violence and Social Change," *Proceedings of the Academy of Political Science*, XXIX (1968).

Cox, Archibald, et al, *Crisis at Columbia: Report of the Fact-Finding Commission Appointed to Investigate Disturbances at Columbia University in April and May 1968* (New York, 1968).

Cranston, Maurice, ed., *The New Left: Six Critical Essays* (London, 1970).

Cruse, Harold, *The Crisis of the Negro Intellectual* (New York, 1967).

Deleon, David, "The American as Anarchist: Social Criticism in the 1960s," *American Quarterly* XXV (1973).

Dellinger, David, *Revolutionary Nonviolence* (Garden City, 1971).

Diggins, John P., *The American Left in the Twentieth Century* (New York, 1973).

———, *Up from Communism: Conservative Odysseys in American Intellectual History* (New York, 1975).

Eckman, Fern M., *The Furious Passage of James Baldwin* (New York, 1966).

Farber, Jerry, *The Student as Nigger* (New York, 1970).

Gerberding, William P., and Duane E. Smith, eds., *The Radical Left: The Abuse of Discontent* (Boston, 1970).

Gerzon, Mark, *The Whole World is Watching: A Young Man Looks at Youth's Dissent* (New York, 1969).

Goodman, Paul, *The New Reformation* (New York, 1970).

———, ed., *Seeds of Liberation* (New York, 1965).

Harrington, Michael, *Fragments of the Century: A Social Autobiography* (New York, 1973).

———, *Toward a Democratic Left: A Radical Program for a New Majority* (New York, 1968).

Hays, Samuel P., "Right Face, Left Face: The Columbia Strike," *Political Science Quarterly*, LXXXIV (1969).

Heirich, Max, *The Spiral of Conflict: Berkeley, 1964* (New York, 1971).

Hentoff, Nat, ed., *The Essays of A. J. Muste* (New York, 1967).

Hoffman, Abbie, *Revolution for the Hell of It* (New York, 1970).

Hofstadter, Richard, *The Paranoid Style in American Politics and Other Essays* (New York, 1965).

Horowitz, Irving L., *The Struggle is the Message: The Organization and Ideology of the Anti-War Movement* (Berkeley, 1970).

Howe, Irving, *Steady Work: Essays in the Politics of Democratic Radicalism* (New York, 1966).

Jacobs, Paul, and Saul Landau, *The New Radicals: A Report with Documents* (New York, 1966).

Kaufman, Arnold S., *The Radical Liberal: New Man in American Politics* (New York, 1968).

Kelman, Steven, *Push Comes to Shove: The Escalation of Student Protest* (Boston, 1970).

Kempton, Murray, ed., *Trials of the Resistance* (New York, 1970).

Keniston, Kenneth, *The Uncommitted: Alienated Youth in American Society* (New York, 1965).

———, *Young Radicals: Notes on Committed Youth* (New York, 1968).

———, *Youth and Dissent* (New York, 1971).

Kennan, George F., *Democracy and the Student Left* (Boston, 1968).

Kopkind, Andrew, and James Ridgeway, eds., *Decade of Crisis: America in the '60's* (New York, 1972).

Kunen, James S., *The Strawberry Statement: Notes of a College Revolutionary* (New York, 1969).

Laing, R. D., *The Politics of Experience* (New York, 1967).

Lipset, Seymour M., and Philip G. Altbach, *Students in Revolt* (Boston, 1969).

Lipset, Seymour M. and Simon Wolin, eds., *The Berkeley Student Revolt* (New York, 1965).

Long, Priscilla, ed., *The New Left: A Collection of Essays* (Boston, 1969).

Lothstein, Arthur, ed., *"All We Are Saying . . ."—the Philosophy of the New Left* (New York, 1970).

Lowi, Theodore J., *The End of Liberalism: Ideology, Policy and the Crisis of Public Authority* (New York, 1969).

———, *The Politics of Disorder* (New York, 1971).

Lusky, Louis, and Mary R. Lusky, "Columbia 1968: The Wound Unhealed," *Political Science Quarterly*, CXXXIV (1969).

McCarthy, Eugene J., *The Year of the People* (Garden City, 1969).

McGovern, George, *A Time of War—A Time of Peace* (New York, 1968).

Mailer, Norman, *The Armies of the Night* (New York, 1968).

———, *Miami and the Siege of Chicago* (New York, 1968).

Menashe, Louis, and Ronald Radosh, eds., *Teach-ins, U.S.A.: Reports, Opinions, Documents* (New York, 1967).

Mitford, Jessica, *The Trial of Dr. Spock* (New York, 1969).

Morgenthau, Hans J., *Truth and Power: Essays of a Decade, 1960-70* (New York, 1970).

Newfield, Jack, *The New Left: A Prophetic Minority* (New York, 1966).

Nobile, Philip, *Intellectual Skywriting* (New York, 1974).

O'Brien, James Putnam, "The Development of a New Left in the United States, 1960-1965," unpublished doctoral dissertation, University of Wisconsin, 1971.

Podhoretz, Norman, ed., *The Commentary Reader* (New York, 1966).

———, *Making It* (New York, 1968).

Raskin, Marcus, *Being and Doing* (New York, 1971).

Rosenberg, Milton J., Sidney Verba, and Philip E. Converse, *Vietnam and the Silent Majority: The Dove's Guide* (New York, 1970).

Rubinstein, Richard E., *Rebels in Eden: Mass Political Violence in the United States* (Boston, 1970).

Schlesinger, Arthur M., Jr. *The Crisis of Confidence: Ideas, Power and Violence in America* (Boston, 1969).

Scimecca, Joseph and Roland Damiano, *Crisis at St. John's: Strike and Revolution on the Catholic Campus* (New York, 1967).

Stone, I. F., *In a Time of Torment* (New York, 1967).

———, *Polemics and Prophecies, 1967-70* (New York, 1970).

Thayer, George, *The Farther Shores of Politics* (New York, 1967).

Wakefield, Dan, *Supernation at Peace and War* (Boston, 1968).

Walker, Daniel, *Rights in Conflict: Convention Week in Chicago, August 25-29, 1968: A Report* (New York, 1968).

Zinn, Howard, *The Politics of History* (Boston, 1970).

CAREER INDEX

The following is a list of individuals profiled in the *Johnson Years* according to their most important public activity. In some cases names appear under two or more categories.

House of Representatives

Albert, Carl B. (D, Okla.)
Arends, Leslie C. (R, Ill.)
Ashbrook, John M. (R, Ohio)
Ashley, Thomas (D, Ohio)
Aspinall, Wayne (D, Colo.)
Blatnik, John A. (D, Minn.)
Boggs, Hale (D, La.)
Bolling, Richard W. (D, Mo.)
Bolton, Francis (R, Ohio)
Brademas, John (D, Ind.)
Burton, Phillip (D, Calif.)
Byrnes, John W. (R, Wisc.)
Carey, Hugh (D, N.Y.)
Celler, Emanuel (D, N.Y.)
Colmer, William M. (D, Miss.)
Conte, Silvio O. (R, Mass.)
Conyers, John J., Jr., (D, Mich.)
Cooley, Harold D. (D, N.C.)
Cramer, William C. (R, Fla.)
Curtis, Thomas B. (R, Mo.)
Dawson, William L. (D, Ill.)
Diggs, Charles C., Jr., (D, Mich.)
Edwards, W. Don (D, Calif.)
Findley, Paul (R, Ill.)
Ford, Gerald R., Jr., (R, Mich.)
Frelinghuysen, Peter, Jr., (R, N.J.)
Gilligan, John J. (D, Ohio)
Goodell, Charles E. (R, N.Y.)
Green, Edith S. (D, Ore.)
Griffiths, Martha (D, Mich.)
Gross, H. R. (R, Iowa)
Halleck, Charles A. (R, Ind.)
Harris, Oren (D, Ark.)
Hawkins, Augustus F. (D, Calif.)
Hays, Wayne L. (D, Ohio)
Hebert, F. Edward (D, La.)
Holifield, Chet (D, Calif.)
Judd, Walter H. (R, Minn.)
Kastenmeier, Robert W. (D, Wisc.)
Kirwan, Michael S. (D, Ohio)
Laird, Melvin R. (R, Wisc.)
Landrum, Phillip M. (D, Ga.)
McCormack, John (D, Mass.)
McCulloch, William M. (R, Ohio)
McMillan, John C. (D, S.C.)
Mahon, George D. (D, Tex.)
Miller, George P. (D, Calif.)
Miller, William E. (R, N.Y.)
Mills, Wilbur D. (D, Ark.)
Mink, Patsy T. (R, N.Y.)
Morgan, Thomas E. (D, Pa.)
Moss, John (D, Calif.)
Ottinger, Richard (D, N.Y.)
Passman, Otto E. (D, La.)
Patman, Wright (D, Tex.)
Poage, W. R. (D, Tex.)
Pool, Joe (D, Tex.)
Powell, Adam Clayton, Jr., (D, N.Y.)
Quie, Albert H. (R, Minn.)
Reid, Ogden R. (R, N.Y.)
Reuss, Henry S. (D, Wisc.)
Rhodes, John J. (R, Ariz.)
Rivers, L. Mendel (D, S.C.)
Rodino, Peter W. (D, N.J.)
Roosevelt, James (D, Calif.)
Rousselot, John H. (R, Calif.)
Ryan, William Fitts (D, N.Y.)
Sikes, Robert L. F. (D, Fla.)
Smith, Howard W. (D, Va.)
Staggers, Harley (D, W. Va.)
Sullivan, Leonard (D, Mo.)
Taft, Robert A., Jr., (R, Ohio)
Thompson, J. Frank (D, N.J.)
Udall, Morris (R, Ariz.)
Vanik, Charles A. (D, Ohio)
Vinson, Carl (D, Ga.)
Watson, Albert W. (D, S.C.)
Whitten, Jamie L. (D, Miss.)
Williams, John B. (D, Miss.)
Willis, Edwin E. (D, La.)
Wilson, Robert C. (R, Calif.)
Zablocki, Clement J. (D, Wisc.)

Senate

Aiken, George D. (R, Vt.)
Allott, Gordon L. (R, Colo.)
Anderson, Clinton P. (D, N.M.)
Baker, Howard, Jr. (R, Tenn.)
Bartlett, Edward L. (D, Alaska)
Bayh, Birch E. (D, Ind.)
Bennett, Wallace F. (R, Utah)
Bible, Alan (D, Nev.)

Brewster, Daniel B. (D, Md.)
Brooke, Edward W. (R, Mass.)
Burdick, Quentin (D, N.D.)
Byrd, Harry F., Sr. (D, Va.)
Byrd, Harry F., Jr. (D, Va.)
Byrd, Robert C. (D, W. Va.)
Cannon, Howard W. (D, Nev.)
Carlson, Frank (R, Kan.)
Case, Clifford P., Jr. (R, N.J.)
Church, Frank (D, Ida.)
Clark, Joseph S., Jr. (D, Ill.)
Cooper, John Sherman (R, Ky.)
Curtis, Carl T. (R, Neb.)
Dirksen, Everett M. (R, Ill.)
Dodd, Thomas J. (D, Conn.)
Dominick, Peter H. (R, Colo.)
Douglas, Paul H. (D, Ill.)
Eastland, James O. (D, Miss.)
Ellender, Allen (D, Ala.)
Ervin, Sam J., Jr. (D, N.C.)
Fong, Hiram (R, Hawaii)
Fulbright, J. William (D, Ark.)
Goldwater, Barry (R, Ariz.)
Gore, Albert (D, Tenn.)
Griffin, Robert P. (R, Mich.)
Gruening, Ernest (D, Alaska)
Harris, Fred B. (D, Okla.)
Hart, Philip (D, Mich.)
Hartke, R. Vance (D, Ind.)
Hatfield, Mark (R, Ore.)
Hayden, Carl T. (D, Ariz.)
Hickenlooper, Bourke (R, Iowa)
Hill, Lister (D, Ala.)
Holland, Spessard L. (D, Fla.)
Hruska, Roman L. (R, Neb.)
Inouye, Daniel (D, Hawaii)
Jackson, Henry M. (D, Wash.)
Javits, Jacob K. (R, N.Y.)
Jordan, B. Everett (D, N.C.)
Kennedy, Edward M. (D, Mass.)
Kennedy, Robert F. (D, N.Y.)
Kuchel, Thomas H. (R, Calif.)
Lausche, Frank J. (D, Ohio)
Long, Edward V. (D, Mo.)
Long, Russell B. (D. La.)
McCarthy, Eugene (D, Minn.)
McClellan, John L. (D, Ark.)
McGee, Gale W. (D, Wyo.)
McGovern, George S. (D, S.D.)
McIntyre, Thomas B. (D, N.H.)
McNamara, Pat (D, Mich.)
Magnuson, Warren G. (D, Wash.)
Mansfield, Michael J. (D, Mont.)
Mathias, Charles (R, Md.)
Metcalf, Lee (D, Mont.)
Miller, Jack R. (R, Iowa)
Mondale, Walter (D, Minn.)
Monroney, A. S. (D, Okla.)
Montoya, Joseph (D, N.M.)
Morse, Wayne L. (D, Ore.)
Morton, Thruston B. (R, Ky.)
Moss, Frank E. (D, Utah)
Mundt, Karl E. (R, S.D.)
Murphy, George (R, Calif.)
Muskie, Edmund S. (D, Me.)
Nelson, Gaylord (D, Wisc.)
Neuberger, Maurine (D, Ore.)
Pastore, John (D, R.I.)
Pell, Claiborne (D, R.I.)
Percy, Charles H. (R, Ill.)
Proxmire, William (D, Wisc.)
Randolph, Jennings (D, W. Va.)
Ribicoff, Abraham A. (D, Conn.)
Robertson, A. Willis (D, Va.)
Russell, Richard B. (D, Ga.)
Saltonstall, Leverett (R, Mass.)
Scott, Hugh D., Jr. (R, Pa.)
Smathers, George A. (D, Fla.)
Smith, Margaret Chase (R, Me.)
Sparkman, John J. (D, Ala.)
Stennis, John (D, Miss.)
Symington, Stuart III, (D, Mo.)
Talmadge, Herman E. (D, Ga.)
Thurmond, Strom (D, Ga.)
Tower, John G. (D, Tex.)
Tydings, Joseph D. (D, Md.)
Williams, Harrison A., Jr. (D, N.J.)
Williams, John J. (R, Del.)
Yarborough, Ralph W. (D, Tex.)
Young, Milton R. (D, N.D.)
Young, Stephen M. (D, Ohio)

State and Local

Addonizio, Hugh J.
Agnew, Spiro T.
Alioto, Joseph
Allen, Ivan, Jr.
Allen, James E., Jr.
Baker, Wilson
Bellmon, Henry L.
Breathitt, Edwin T., Jr.
Brown, Edmund G.
Burns, John A.
Cavanagh, Jerome P.
Chaffe, John H.
Clark, James G.
Clement, Frank G.
Collins, John
Connally, John B., Jr.
Daley, Richard J.
Evans, Daniel J.
Flowers, Richmond S.
Garrison, James C.

Judiciary

White House and Executive Branch

Foreign Affairs

CIA

Defense Department & Military

Treasury, Economic Policy, Regulatory Commissions

Business and Labor

Civil Rights

Political Dissent & Social Protest

Journalists, Academics, Churchman

National Party Politics, Organizations & Issues

Index

A

C

D

G

K

N

Q

R

T

U

Y

Z